THE ALMANAC OF AMER YERS 2018

The Only Guide to America's Hottest, Fastest-Growing Major Corporations

Jack W. Plunkett

Published by:
Plunkett Research®, Ltd., Houston, Texas
www.plunkettresearch.com

THE ALMANAC OF AMERICAN EMPLOYERS
2018

Editor and Publisher:
Jack W. Plunkett

Executive Editor and Database Manager:
Martha Burgher Plunkett

Senior Editor and Researchers:
Isaac Snider
Shuang Zhou

Editors, Researchers and Assistants:
Ashley Bass
John Brucato
Michael Cappelli
Gina Sprenkel
Suzanne Zarosky

Information Technology Manager:
Seifelnaser Hamed

Digital Production:
Uriel Rios
Special Thanks to:
U.S. Department of Labor
Bureau of Labor Statistics
U.S. Department of Commerce
*Bureau of Economic Analysis, National Technical
Information Service*

Plunkett Research®, Ltd.
P. O. Drawer 541737, Houston, Texas 77254 USA
Phone: 713.932.0000   Fax: 713.932.7080
www.plunkettresearch.com

Plunkett Research®, Ltd.
P. O. Drawer 541737
Houston, Texas 77254-1737
Phone: 713.932.0000, Fax: 713.932.7080 www.plunkettresearch.com

ISBN13 # 978-1-62831-454-0 (eBook Edition # 978-1-62831-794-7)

Limited Warranty and Terms of Use:

THE ALMANAC OF AMERICAN EMPLOYERS 2018

CONTENTS

Continued on the next page

Continued from the previous page

INTRODUCTION

THE ALMANAC OF AMERICAN EMPLOYERS is an easy-to-use solution to what would otherwise be a complicated problem: How can you tell, among America's giant companies, which firms are most likely to be hiring? Among those firms, which are the best to work for? No other source provides this book's easy-to-understand comparisons of growth, treatment of employees, salaries, benefits, pension plans, profit sharing and many other items of great importance to job seekers.

Especially helpful is the way in which THE ALMANAC OF AMERICAN EMPLOYERS enables readers with no business background to readily compare the growth potential and benefit plans of large employers. You'll see the mid-term financial record of each firm, along with the impact of earnings, sales and growth plans on each company's potential to provide employment opportunities.

Information is presented in a way that addresses the differing interests of individual employees. You'll find separate listings for dozens of categories of data that you may want to consider. While this book is aimed primarily at job seekers, it will also be of tremendous value to researchers, marketing executives and personnel professionals. THE ALMANAC OF AMERICAN EMPLOYERS is the premier guide to the most successful employers in the nation, their policies and their performance.

THE ALMANAC OF AMERICAN EMPLOYERS is your opportunity to gain valuable knowledge in a matter of minutes. Five hundred of the biggest, most successful corporate employers in America are analyzed in this book. Tens of thousands of pieces of information, gathered from a wide variety of sources, have been researched for these corporations and are presented here in a form that can be easily understood by job seekers of all types.

Thanks to THE ALMANAC OF AMERICAN EMPLOYERS' exclusive data system, potentially confusing considerations have been reduced to simple groups of focused data. By scanning the data groups and the long list of unique indexes, you can find the right employers to fit your personal needs.

The AMERICAN EMPLOYERS 500 are among the best major growth companies to work for in America. Which companies offer the best benefits, are the biggest employers or earn the most profits? Where are these companies operating? All of these things and more are made easy for the reader to determine.

Thousands of observations are made that will be of great interest to prospective employees. For many of the firms, you'll find comments about such items as plans for growth, increases or decreases in the number of employees and charitable programs. You'll also find notes about corporate culture and special programs for the convenience of employees, such as health and recreation facilities, on-site child care, job training or career paths. Finally, you'll find basic information on each company, including the home office address and telephone number; regional, national and international locations; a description of the business; and a list of selected subsidiaries and trade names. In addition, you will find fax numbers and Internet addresses.

Whether you are currently employed by one of these corporate giants or are considering applying for a job with one, you will be able to see how each company compares with the others, even if you don't have the slightest understanding of accounting, finance or employee benefits.

Whatever your purpose for researching corporate employers, you'll find this book to be an indispensable guide. Nonetheless, as is true with all resources, this volume has limitations that the reader should be aware of:

- Financial data and other corporate information can change quickly. A book of this type can be no more current than the data that was available as of the time of editing. Consequently, the financial picture, management and ownership of the firm(s) you are studying may have changed since the date of this book. For example, this almanac includes the most up-to-date sales figures and profits available to the editors as of mid-2017. This means that we have typically used corporate financial data as of the end of 2016.

- Corporate mergers, changes in corporate financial ratings or stability, acquisitions and downsizing are occurring at a very rapid rate. Such events may have created significant change, subsequent to the publishing of this book, within a company you are studying.

- Some of the companies in THE AMERICAN EMPLOYERS 500 are so large in scope and in variety of business endeavors conducted within a parent organization that we have been unable to completely list all subsidiaries, affiliations, divisions and activities within a firm's corporate structure.

- This volume is intended to be a general guide to major employers in numerous industries. That

means that researchers should look to this book for an overview and, when conducting in-depth research, should contact the specific corporations and related industry associations in question for the very latest changes and data. Where possible, we have listed contact information, telephone numbers and Internet addresses for pertinent companies, government agencies and industry associations so that the reader may get further details without unnecessary delay.

- We have used exhaustive efforts to locate and fairly present accurate and complete data. However, when using this book or any other source for business and industry information, the reader should use caution and due diligence by conducting further research where it seems appropriate. We wish you success in your endeavors, and we trust that your experience with this book will be both satisfactory and productive.

- To obtain the best results and to best understand the fields in the company profiles, you should first read the chapter titled "How to Use This Book."

Good luck in your job search. Be patient, do your research and use this book as an important start in the right direction.

Jack W. Plunkett
Houston, Texas
August 2017

HOW TO USE THIS BOOK

Dozens of excellent books already exist to help you choose a career, write a resume, apply for a job and so on. That is not the purpose of THE ALMANAC OF AMERICAN EMPLOYERS. Instead, this book's job is to help you sort through America's giant corporate employers to determine which may be the best for you, or to see how your current employer compares to others. Whether you are entering the job market and looking for your first position, or you are thinking about switching companies in mid-career to find more promising vistas, this book will be a valuable guide.

The two primary sections of the book are devoted first to general information for job seekers (trends analysis and advice on conducting employer research, along with resources, statistics and contacts), followed by the "Individual Data Listings" for THE AMERICAN EMPLOYERS 500. If time permits, you should begin your research in the front chapters of this book. Also, you will find lengthy indexes in Chapter 5 and in the back of the book.

GENERAL INFORMATION FOR JOB SEEKERS

Chapter 1: Major Trends Affecting Job Seekers. This chapter presents an encapsulated view of the major trends in business and the economy that are creating rapid changes in the employment picture at large corporations.

Chapter 2: Statistics. This chapter presents in-depth statistics on employment by education level, sex and race, along with unemployment rates, the fastest-growing occupations and more.

Chapter 3: Research—7 Keys for Job Seekers. This chapter provides a definitive list of items that job seekers should look for when conducting research into major corporate employers.

Chapter 4: Important Contacts for Job Seekers. This chapter covers contacts for important government agencies, professional societies, industry associations, job banks, reference sources and more. Included are Internet sites and contact addresses for a wide variety of job search uses.

THE AMERICAN EMPLOYERS 500

Chapter 5: THE AMERICAN EMPLOYERS 500: Who They Are and How They Were Chosen.
The companies compared in this book were chosen from nearly all industries, on a nationwide basis. They were individually chosen from the largest U.S. employers, based on selected types of business and industry sectors. For a complete description, see Chapter 5.

Individual Data Listings:

Look at one of the companies in THE AMERICAN EMPLOYERS 500's Individual Data Listings. You'll find the following information fields:

Company Name:

The company profiles are in alphabetical order by company name. If you don't find the company you are seeking, it may be a subsidiary or division of one of the firms covered in this book. Try looking it up in the Index by Subsidiaries, Brand Names and Selected Affiliations in the back of the book.

Industry Code:

Industry Group Code: An NAIC code used to group companies within like segments.

Types of Business:

A listing of the primary types of business specialties conducted by the firm.

Brands/Divisions/Affiliations:

Major brand names, operating divisions or subsidiaries of the firm, as well as major corporate affiliations—such as another firm that owns a significant portion of the company's stock. A complete Index by Subsidiaries, Brand Names and Selected Affiliations is in the back of the book.

Contacts:

The names and titles up to 27 top officers of the company are listed, including human resources contacts.

Growth Plans/ Special Features:

Listed here are observations regarding the firm's strategy, hiring plans, plans for growth and product development, along with general information regarding a company's business and prospects.

Financial Data:

Revenue (2016 or the latest fiscal year available to the editors, plus up to five previous years): This figure represents consolidated worldwide sales from all operations. These numbers may be estimates.

R&D Expense (2016 or the latest fiscal year available to the editors, plus up to five previous years): This figure represents expenses associated with the research and development of a company's goods or services. These numbers may be estimates.

Operating Income (2016 or the latest fiscal year available to the editors, plus up to five previous years): This figure represents the amount of profit realized from annual operations after deducting operating expenses including costs of goods sold, wages and depreciation. These numbers may be estimates.

Operating Margin % (2016 or the latest fiscal year available to the editors, plus up to five previous

years): This figure is a ratio derived by dividing operating income by net revenues. It is a measurement of a firm's pricing strategy and operating efficiency. These numbers may be estimates.

SGA Expense (2016 or the latest fiscal year available to the editors, plus up to five previous years): This figure represents the sum of selling, general and administrative expenses of a company, including costs such as warranty, advertising, interest, personnel, utilities, office space rent, etc. These numbers may be estimates.

Net Income (2016 or the latest fiscal year available to the editors, plus up to five previous years): This figure represents consolidated, after-tax net profit from all operations. These numbers may be estimates.

Operating Cash Flow (2016 or the latest fiscal year available to the editors, plus up to five previous years): This figure is a measure of the amount of cash generated by a firm's normal business operations. It is calculated as net income before depreciation and after income taxes, adjusted for working capital. It is a prime indicator of a company's ability to generate enough cash to pay its bills. These numbers may be estimates.

Capital Expenditure (2016 or the latest fiscal year available to the editors, plus up to five previous years): This figure represents funds used for investment in or improvement of physical assets such as offices, equipment or factories and the purchase or creation of new facilities and/or equipment. These numbers may be estimates.

EBITDA (2016 or the latest fiscal year available to the editors, plus up to five previous years): This figure is an acronym for earnings before interest, taxes, depreciation and amortization. It represents a company's financial performance calculated as revenue minus expenses (excluding taxes, depreciation and interest), and is a prime indicator of profitability. These numbers may be estimates.

Return on Assets % (2016 or the latest fiscal year available to the editors, plus up to five previous years): This figure is an indicator of the profitability of a company relative to its total assets. It is calculated by dividing annual net earnings by total assets. These numbers may be estimates.

Return on Equity % (2016 or the latest fiscal year available to the editors, plus up to five previous years): This figure is a measurement of net income as a percentage of shareholders' equity. It is also called the rate of return on the ownership interest. It is a vital indicator of the quality of a company's operations. These numbers may be estimates.

Debt to Equity (2016 or the latest fiscal year available to the editors, plus up to five previous years): A ratio of the company's long-term debt to its shareholders' equity. This is an indicator of the overall financial leverage of the firm. These numbers may be estimates.

Address:

The firm's full headquarters address, the headquarters telephone, plus toll-free and fax numbers where available. Also provided is the World Wide Web site address.

Stock Ticker, Exchange: When available, the unique stock market symbol used to identify this firm's common stock for trading and tracking purposes is indicated. Where appropriate, this field may contain "private" or "subsidiary" rather than a ticker symbol. If the firm is a publicly-held company headquartered outside of the U.S., its international ticker and exchange are given.

Total Number of Employees: The approximate total number of employees, worldwide, as of the end of 2016 (or the latest data available to the editors).

Parent Company: If the firm is a subsidiary, its parent company is listed.

Salaries/Bonuses:

(The following descriptions generally apply to U.S. employers only.)

Highest Executive Salary: The highest executive salary paid, typically a 2016 amount (or the latest year available to the editors) and typically paid to the Chief Executive Officer.

Highest Executive Bonus: The apparent bonus, if any, paid to the above person.

Second Highest Executive Salary: The next-highest executive salary paid, typically a 2016 amount (or the latest year available to the editors) and typically paid to the President or Chief Operating Officer.

Second Highest Executive Bonus: The apparent bonus, if any, paid to the above person.

Other Thoughts:

Estimated Female Officers or Directors: It is difficult to obtain this information on an exact basis, and employers generally do not disclose the data in a public way. However, we have indicated what our best efforts reveal to be the apparent number of women who either are in the posts of corporate officers or sit on the board of directors. There is a wide variance from company to company.

Hot Spot for Advancement for Women/Minorities: A "Y" in appropriate fields indicates "Yes." These are firms that appear either to have posted a substantial number of women and/or minorities to high posts or that appear to have a good record of going out of their way to recruit, train, promote and retain women or minorities. (See the Index of Hot Spots For Women and Minorities in the back of the book.) This information may change frequently and can be difficult to obtain and verify. Consequently, the reader should use caution and conduct further investigation where appropriate.

Chapter 1

MAJOR TRENDS AFFECTING JOB SEEKERS

Major trends sweeping through business and the economy that affect job seekers of all types:

1) U.S. Job Market Overview
2) Cost Control Remains a Major Concern at Employers/Consolidation Through Mergers Continues
3) Unemployment Is Down Substantially Compared to the Recent Past
4) Consumers Spend Less, Save More Than During the Last Boom, Affecting a Wide Variety of Companies
5) Technology Continues to Create Sweeping Changes in the Workplace
6) Continued Growth in Outsourcing, Including Supply Chain and Logistics Services
7) Millions Working as Temps
8) Offshoring, Reshoring and the Rebound in American Manufacturing
9) Older Americans Will Delay Retirement and Work Longer/Many Employers Find Older Employees Desirable
10) Employment Sectors that Will Offer an Above-Average Number of Job Opportunities:

Employment Sectors that Will Offer an Above-Average Number of Job Opportunities:

- Automobile Manufacturing and Retailing
- Biotechnology
- Child Care/Children's Products
- Consulting, including Technology Consulting
- Consumer Products
- Cosmetics
- Elder Care, Home Health Care, Nursing Homes and Assisted Living Communities
- Electronic Games, Games for Cell Phones
- Energy Conservation Products and Services
- Health Care Services
- Health Care Products
- Health Care Technology, Including Computerized Patient Records
- Health Foods, Organic Foods, Enhanced Foods
- Home Building
- Hotels
- Insurance
- Internet Services, Server Hosting, Cloud Computing
- Internet of Things: Connected Devices, Remote Wireless Sensors and their Networks, Machine to Machine Communications
- Online Search Services & Social Media, with Advertising Revenues
- Online-based Business and Consumer Sales and Services, including E-Commerce
- Outsourcing, Including Outsourced Business and Computer Services
- Pets: Services and Products
- Pharmaceuticals—Generics
- Restaurants
- Retailing—Basic, Including Drugstores and Supermarkets
- Retailing—Discount and Warehouse Clubs
- Robotics and Factory Automation
- Software—Artificial Intelligence
- Software—Corporate, including Development Tools and Cybersecurity
- Software—Data Analytics and Consumer Scoring
- Software—Mobile Apps
- Software as a Service
- Solar Energy Cells Installation & Maintenance
- Supply Chain Services That Create Cost-Savings
- Water Filtration and Conservation Equipment
- Wireless and Cellular Communications

1) U.S. Job Market Overview

Job seekers in 2018 should see reasonably strong hiring and rising wages, if the low unemployment rates seen in late 2017 continue, and if confidence is reasonably high for both consumers and business leaders. Nonetheless, total growth of the U.S. economy has been disappointing for several years, and this relatively slow growth has a negative effect on hiring and wages.

Job seekers who want good positions with good pay must be extremely well prepared for the process of seeking a job. A large part of the preparation requires meaningful research into prospective employers and the industries in which they operate. The fact remains that several million Americans consider themselves underemployed, and many of them will be looking for better jobs. Competition for highly desirable positions will remain fierce. Many companies receive hundreds or even thousands of resumes for every job opening. Simply sending in a resume and hoping for the best is nowhere near enough for a successful job search.

The good news is that a select set of employers and growth companies will offer superb job opportunities. Sectors such as cloud computing and health care will continue to grow and hire. A few companies with exciting new technologies or cost-saving services will see terrific growth. Salesforce.com, a highly innovative provider of online business services, has been a good example.

Solid companies that do a terrific job of providing the day-to-day needs of consumers and business will continue to hire—Costco, Amazon.com and Southwest Airlines are good examples. Other industry sectors that fall into this category include insurance firms, such as USAA and The Progressive Corporation, along with online services and apps that provide efficient or new ways for consumers and businesses to make purchases, gather data or view entertainment and news.

Growing numbers of consumers prefer to buy from firms that sell goods and services online, offering savings of time, money and car travel. This boosts companies like Amazon.com that offer low prices combined with deep selections and great customer service. Virtually all major retailers, including giants like Wal-Mart and Home Depot, are working hard to provide better online services and choices to their customers. Meanwhile, traditional department stores and many other types of traditional store-front retailers are in a long, painful period of decline.

The travel industry has been enjoying tremendous growth in revenues over the past few years. Airlines are in much better financial shape than they were in the recent past. Many have shed debt through bankruptcy and successfully reorganized as more financially stable companies. Hotels are enjoying high occupancy rates. Meanwhile, travel has become one of the most successful sectors at selling products and services via the internet, creating vast numbers of new job opportunities.

The automobile sector is booming as well. New cars have been selling very well, and hiring has been strong at car dealers and manufacturers alike.

Americans who find themselves in the market for a job will need to understand the changes surging through the economy in order to determine which companies to pursue and which to avoid. The U.S. employment market has evolved dramatically, and job seekers must be both knowledgeable and nimble in order to position themselves to find promising careers.

America's job market is looking better than it has in recent years, and job seekers, including new college grads, should see a reasonable level of job openings. There will be good opportunities for those who are diligent in seeking top employers in most business sectors.

Economic Factors Affecting the Job Market

Business Productivity: Productivity growth has been positive in recent years, but the increases have been very modest. That is, business can be produced—whether it is goods or services—by utilizing fewer workers than before. This will be extremely beneficial to the U.S. economy in the long run. Productivity is boosted by new technologies, improved management methods and other factors, sometimes as simple as reorganizing the staff and redesigning the workflow to increase output. (It can also receive a quick boost from restrained corporate hiring.) If rising productivity occurs along with rapidly rising sales and profits, then the job market will improve.

Corporate Revenues: A trend of rising revenues encourages hiring.

Corporate Profits: When profits increase sharply, companies are inclined to increase both investment and hiring. Hiring is strongest when corporate revenues, and accompanying profits, show significant growth, encouraging executives to forecast an extended period of increased demand for their products and services.

It is vital for the job seeker to use the best reference tools possible in order to seek out employers that offer a reasonable balance of financial stability, opportunities for advancement and good pay. Excellent job opportunities always exist if you know where to look.

Thousands of companies will need significant numbers of new hires. In particular, companies that offer products or services that save time and/or money will prosper—for example, many types of companies that offer services that help businesses operate more efficiently, will be hiring. Meanwhile, large companies that are not increasing their overall numbers of employees will nonetheless be hiring on a regular basis due to normal attrition—that is, the loss of employees due to retirement, relocation or other personal circumstances. Massive companies like Walgreen's or Kroger typically need to hire tens of thousands of workers yearly due to normal attrition.

2) Cost Control Remains a Concern at Employers/Consolidation Through Mergers Continues

For most firms, executives have been focusing on cost control as a means to boost profits and financial stability. Employee costs have been targeted as well, as employers seek to boost the overall productivity of their work forces. Often, companies merge with others in order to seek operating efficiencies or gain access to needed capital. Financing is readily available for large corporate mergers and acquisitions, and the number of mergers has been high. A consolidation of companies via a merger may enable the firms to combine customer bases, administrative staff, sales offices and production facilities, while cutting employees who hold duplicated jobs, in hopes of thereby creating more efficient, more profitable firms. Mergers may be spurred by economic difficulties and falling profits, or they may involve large firms seeking to acquire companies that bring advantages that may boost growth and accelerate profits. For example, online leaders Amazon, Facebook and Google have acquired numerous firms in order to bring in new technologies.

Because they face tough, global competition, manufacturing firms are frequently involved in such mergers. Good jobs in the U.S. manufacturing sector can be found, despite intense competition from manufacturers in China and other offshore markets. Overall, U.S. factories are running with fewer people per unit of output, thanks to immense investments in factory automation and robotics.

A small, but significant, number of firms are "reshoring" some of their manufacturing, by making products at American plants that were previously manufactured in overseas facilities. Even the American textile industry, which was hit hard by layoffs and bankruptcies during the late 1900s, is enjoying a modest rebound. This is positive, but it is not leading to large numbers of job openings.

Some of the statistical loss in manufacturing employment has been exaggerated by the fact that firms now outsource a good deal of their non-manufacturing operations to services companies. For example, many computer departments, company cafeterias, distribution centers and engineering needs are now outsourced to companies that specialize in such work, thus dramatically reducing the number of in-house jobs at manufacturing firms. This is the long term trend of outsourcing in action.

Also, companies in both manufacturing and service sectors have caught on to management by teams, vastly enhanced supply chain technology (such as the use of the internet for ordering and tracking components), along with networked management, distribution and manufacturing systems, which all add up to the fact that fewer mid-management, white-collar types are needed to communicate with the people doing the day-to-day work. Production workers have been encouraged to communicate among themselves. In many cases, workers are taking on unprecedented responsibilities, setting their own goals and

schedules, tracking costs and output, thereby boosting profits. Historically, these were the tasks of middle managers. Today, vast numbers of those management jobs have been eliminated. Businesses without factories are also undergoing re-engineering and leaps in productivity, often through the streamlining of processes through the use of better computers and software.

3) Unemployment Is Down Substantially Compared to the Recent Past

By the end of June 2017, the unemployment rate in America was 4.4%, down from 4.9% one year earlier. This low unemployment rate is encouraging some people to re-enter the workforce who had previously become discouraged and stopped looking for work.

Today's job market is a vast improvement over that of the dark days of 2008-10, and jobs are now very plentiful in some regions. (The U.S. unemployment rate in August 2007 was down to 4.6%. By the end of 2009, unemployment had soared to 10%, and 8 million jobs were eliminated during the Great Recession.) Many job seekers will be able to find satisfying jobs if they apply themselves to the job hunt, make sure their resumes and self-marketing skills are in superb shape, network effectively and do thorough research. The number of people applying for each job opening is often high. Consequently, it is vital for a job seeker to understand how to best apply for a job online, how to conduct research that will help him or her to shine during an interview and how to create an effective list of prospective employers.

It is also important for job seekers to face the fact that locale has a lot to do with the unemployment rate. There is wide variance in the unemployment rate from state to state and city to city.

> *Internet Research Tip:*
> The latest rankings of states by unemployment rate can be found at the Bureau of Labor Statistics, www.bls.gov.

4) Consumers Spend Less, Save More Than During the Last Boom, Affecting a Wide Variety of Companies

After piling on debt, running up their credit cards, signing mountains of mortgages and buying new cars at a soaring rate from 2002 through 2007, consumers have completely reversed course. Personal savings rates are much higher than they were during the last boom. Some categories of consumer debt have declined dramatically, to much lower, healthier levels. Welcome to a new era of increased frugality and worried consumers. Nonetheless, consumer spending has been reasonably strong, with automobile sales and online retailing doing extremely well. Consumers will remain cautious about using credit card debt.

The most successful companies will be those that offer products and services with lasting value, low prices, good customer service, cost-saving strategies or innovative technologies. Excellent examples are Wal-Mart (low prices), Costco (good service and low prices), Amazon (innovative use of online technology to provide convenience and cost-savings), travel firms like Southwest Airlines and Carnival Cruise Lines (good service, low prices, high value) and car makers like Kia and Hyundai (lasting value, low prices).

5) Technology Continues to Create Sweeping Changes in the Workplace

Technology has introduced vast changes throughout industries of all types, greatly boosting productivity and reallocating (or eliminating) workers. A major cause of change for employees, and therefore job seekers, is the tidal wave of new technologies that continues to revolutionize the workplace at all levels. Prospering companies are using new ways to communicate with customers, automate back-office tasks and factory operations, and push ahead with research and development. There is a never-ending stream of technological innovation. For example, employers long ago harnessed the power of networked desktop computers. Today, they are rapidly adopting the use of mobile computing devices such as tablets, internet-based telephone systems (VOIP and unified communication systems), voice-recognition software, cloud computing and video conferencing technologies.

The trend of using new practices and technologies while cutting layers of management is largely about communication. This is true whether it is communication between the top offices and the factory floor, communication with customers, communication between the computers in one corporate office with those in another, or communication from the sales department to the warehouse and the supply chain.

These new technologies mean continuous retraining for much of the workforce. Job seekers who want the best posts must have the training and skills that will let them utilize new technologies effectively. Hundreds of thousands of jobs are remaining unfilled at many companies because of a shortage of technically qualified people. Workforce training is a critical need nationwide.

Jobs in America are shifting to new categories of work based on technologies that didn't exist a few decades ago. For example, the job title "social media manager" emerged in recent years. Services firms, as well as manufacturers, are placing more and more employees in recently created technical and service positions, while many of the tasks once performed in-house are now provided by outsourced services providers. In the telecommunications industry, digital technology has completely changed the list of job titles while enabling phone service providers to reduce the ratio of employees to customers. In the meantime, hundreds of thousands of jobs have been created at cellular telephone companies. Now, internet-based telephony, competition from cable providers, fiber to the premises and wireless networks such as Wi-Fi and LTE continue to force telecommunications firms to evolve.

Another excellent example: Retailing, shipping and warehousing are undergoing a technology revolution due to the introduction of Radio Frequency Identification Tags (RFID). This breakthrough in inventory management is based on the placement of digitized product data within product packaging, combined with the use of special sensors in stores and warehouses that can automatically read that data. These sensors can alert a central inventory management system of product movement and the need to restock inventory. From loading docks to shelves to cash registers to parking lots, RFID sensors will eventually track the movement of each pallet or individual item. Many bar codes will eventually be replaced by RFIDs. RFID can even eliminate the need to scan each item at checkout in a retail store. Checkout stations will be equipped with sensors that read RFID-based data such as product code and price, and then automatically calculate purchase totals. Benefits can include less shoplifting and few inventory errors. Another benefit is that firms will be able to reduce overall inventory thanks to better tracking.

As online ordering, tracking and inventory management continue to become more sophisticated and cost-effective, purchasing executives at firms of all types and sizes will accelerate the use of internet-based systems for management of their supply chains. There are significant opportunities here for e-commerce services and software companies. Likewise, there is great promise for third-party logistics (3PL) companies that combine the power of internet-based information with strategically located warehouses to fulfill the inventory needs of manufacturers. Robots are being used to a rapidly growing extent in picking inventory within warehouses prior to shipment. Amazon.com is a leader in this regard.

Manufacturing is undergoing its own technology revolution. This is often referred to as factory automation. Advanced technology used with great success on the factory floor includes computer-driven machine tools that require highly skilled operators, along with robotic assemblers that are capable of working nonstop, 24/7 to create and assemble parts into finished goods.

6) Continued Growth in Outsourcing, Including Supply Chain and Logistics Services

Part of the re-engineering process at employers has been a boom in "outsourcing," or the use of outside specialty firms to do chores that firms formerly performed through in-house departments. One of the largest fields of outsourcing growth has long been in computer departments. IBM and Accenture are among the global leaders in this area. Cloud computing (the use of outsourced, remote servers to run computer functions) is the latest major trend in this regard.

However, many other business functions are commonly outsourced. ServiceMaster takes over janitorial tasks, building management and maintenance functions for giant corporate office campuses and industrial facilities. Another company outsources all of the food warehousing and distribution for nationwide restaurant chains. Why? Because it can run trucks and warehouses more efficiently while its clients concentrate on running restaurants.

While the 1960s, '70s and '80s saw many firms frantically trying to do all tasks in-house, recent trends are quite different. As a period noted for rising productivity and efficiency, the 1990s and 2000s combined were an era of specialization and focus. Companies may do a better job by focusing on their core tasks, while allowing outside firms to provide support and maintenance needs. That trend will continue to be powerful over the long term. Outsourcing, which rapidly gained popularity, will persist in leading the way to higher efficiency and profits. Many outsourced services companies continue to grow, and they will create (and displace) large numbers of jobs.

One of the fastest-growing fields in outsourcing has been supply chain and logistics management. Companies offering services in this field include giant transportation companies like UPS. "Supply chain" refers to the entire set of providers of supplies and services that are involved in creating and delivering a component or end product. For example, for an automobile manufacturer like Ford, the supply chain includes companies that make tires, batteries, interior components and engine parts, as well as the trucks and trains that ship these parts and the warehouses that hold them. This supply chain supports Ford's own manufacturing and assembly plants. At the end of Ford's business chain lie the automobile dealers that receive completed cars and deliver them to the end customers. Another example: For a clothing store chain like The Gap, the supply chain includes clothing designers, clothing manufacturers and the warehouses and transportation systems that deliver completed clothes to the stores. The Gap's supply chain is located across dozens of nations.

Logistics is the art of moving goods through the supply chain. Supply chains are so complex and so critical to a company's operations that there are countless ways to automate, improve efficiencies and cut costs. Many manufacturers and retailers are outsourcing all or part of their logistics needs to firms that specialize in creating efficiencies and saving costs. Logistics and supply chain companies have been growing rapidly over the past several years, and creating large numbers of jobs. A concept you should be familiar with is Third Party Logistics ("3PL"), a system whereby a specialist firm in logistics provides a variety of transportation, warehousing and logistics-related services to its clients. These tasks were previously performed in-house by the client. When 3PL services are provided within the client's own facilities, it can also be referred to as "Insourcing." In other words, you might find yourself working for UPS at a site within a distribution company that has no other ties to UPS.

7) Millions Working as Temps

Many major firms, both large and small, are using temporary workers to fill short-term needs, thereby cutting overall employment costs, since temps usually do not receive extensive benefits, bonuses or training. In addition to employees who are placed in temporary jobs by agencies, there are millions of people employed as "independent contractors" and "contract workers." A major development boosting this trend is the "gig economy" or "sharing economy," including companies like the ride service Uber. It now has hundreds of thousands of contract workers. (However, some of these workers are asking the courts to consider whether they are technically employees instead, and a small number of gig economy employers are now treating all of their people as employees, not contractors.)

The largest temporary help agencies tend to have vast global operations. Adecco is a Swiss staffing firm with extensive operations in the U.S., Europe and elsewhere, employing hundreds of thousands of people. Manpower, based in the U.S., does a major part of its business in dozens of nations worldwide. Kelly Services places massive numbers of people in jobs each year on a worldwide basis.

Demand for temporary workers slows dramatically during economic downturns. The use of temps enables employers to increase the workforce quickly when orders from customers increase, and reduce the workforce rapidly when sales decrease. Temporary workers are also an extremely efficient way to meet needs for one-time projects, fill the slots of permanent employees who are on leave and screen potential candidates for full-time positions by first hiring them on a temporary basis.

In addition, some Americans prefer to work as temporary employees, feeling that this gives them more flexibility in their working lives. Unfortunately, however, many people who end up working in temporary positions would greatly prefer to be employed full-time. Many of these workers have significant experience as well as college degrees. A large percentage of temps work in professional specialties, such as law, finance, engineering or accounting. Also, the number of information technology temps has increased dramatically in the past several years.

Internet Research Tip:
For data on the temporary staffing industry and the temporary workforce in the U.S., see the American Staffing Association (www.americanstaffing.net).

---

8) Offshoring, Reshoring and the Rebound in American Manufacturing

Competition from workers in such nations as Mexico, Indonesia, Thailand and, in particular, China, has been fierce. For several decades, America's manufacturing employment was declining while a vast amount of manufacturing has been sent overseas by U.S. firms.

Today, however, some U.S. industries are experiencing reshoring, or the practice of moving formerly offshored tasks back to America. As wages rise in countries such as China and India, a number of manufacturers are rethinking offshoring, taking into account higher productivity rates among American workers and higher instances of using cost-effective robotics in manufacturing.

Another factor fueling reshoring is energy costs, which continue to be lower in the U.S. than in many other countries. Savings in energy costs are being augmented by increased manufacturing efficiency. This is due to the growing adoption of robotics. 3-D printing (additive manufacturing) is another technology that is significantly lowering prototyping and product design costs.

While lower employee wages have been a factor in some offshoring, proximity to growing foreign markets is another. Giant multinational companies ranging from Apple to Kraft to General Motors find that a vast portion of their business now lies overseas, often in the rapidly-growing, emerging nations. Many of the world's largest companies find that they need to have local operations throughout the world.

Globalization has a profound effect on Americans—consumer prices become lower, while the U.S. job market changes considerably. Consumer goods are quite inexpensive due to the vast variety of items the U.S. imports from other nations, and prices for many categories of these goods have declined dramatically. Americans can purchase consumer electronics like DVD players and color televisions at extremely low prices, and the price of many types of apparel is much lower thanks to globalization. For example, over 90% of the shoes sold in America are manufactured in low cost nations, especially China.

More than ever before, the world is one vast marketplace. Globalization of business supply chains is a strong trend today and will grow even stronger in the future. Consider the rapid globalization of the automobile industry. The entire global automobile sector is dominated by only a handful of companies, including Toyota, GM, Ford, Daimler, Honda, Volkswagen and Nissan, as well as the increasingly successful Korean automakers Kia and Hyundai. Car manufacturers in China are becoming more dominant as well. Car manufacturers commonly have engineering teams collaborating from offices in multiple nations, while parts and components may be imported from a wide variety of suppliers in various countries to undergo final assembly at home.

American companies in many industry sectors have been merging and consolidating on a global basis at a rapid clip. That consolidation will continue. One benefit is that U.S. firms can enter into foreign markets through international acquisitions.

U.S. firms hold leadership positions in several key product and service sectors vital to the rest of the world, including health technology, computers, e-commerce, software and entertainment of all types. The message is clear: global trade and export markets are extremely vital to the health of American business and industry.

A growing middle class in India, China and other emerging nations has been creating demand for goods exported from the U.S., including consumer products bearing desirable brands, as well as luxury automobiles.

Also, U.S.-based firms have been enjoying great success in franchising and licensing their methods to startup businesses in China, India and elsewhere, in everything from hotels to fast food to services. American brands such as Nike and Buick are big sellers in China.

Meanwhile, the U.S. is also exporting its expertise in the booming superstore and discount retailing sectors. For instance, hundreds of Wal-Mart's stores are in foreign locations such as Argentina, Brazil, Canada, China, Korea, Mexico, and the U.K. Eventually, Wal-Mart may bring its brand of retailing to virtually all of the world's major markets.

9) Older Americans Will Delay Retirement and Work Longer/Many Employers Find Older Employees Desirable

Certain large employers, particularly national retail chains, have discovered that older workers provide a terrific pool of potential employees. This may be positive for older workers, but to younger job seekers it means more competition for work.

Many members of the immense Baby Boom generation are not planning to retire any time soon. This trend is accelerated by the fact that today's senior citizens will enjoy much longer life spans than earlier generations. Many will continue to work simply because they want to remain active, contributing members of society.

The phrase "Baby Boomer" generally refers to the 78 million Americans born from 1946 to 1964. The term evolved to describe the children of soldiers and war industry workers who were involved in World War II. When those veterans and workers returned to civilian life, they started or added to families in large numbers. As a result, this generation is one of the largest demographic segments in the U.S. Baby Boomers make more than 20% of the U.S. population.

Recently, 2011 marked the year when millions began turning traditional retirement age (65). As Baby Boomers continue to age, America will be experiencing extremely rapid growth in the senior portion of the population. Many Baby Boomers will leave their traditional, long-term jobs and turn to part-time work. Others will continue in their full-time jobs as long as possible.

By the early 2000s, many employers were already developing human resources strategies aimed at hiring or retaining older workers. On the lower end of the pay scale, retailers like Home Depot, a firm that has been known to need tens of thousands of new hires each year, have found older people to be ideal employees. They have knowledge that is extremely useful for providing advice and service to shoppers. They are experienced workers who understand the need to show up on time.

On the higher end of the employment scale, older workers with long-term experience in scientific and engineering tasks will be vital in keeping the gears of business and industry turning. During the 2000s boom, when the airline industry saw good growth, rules were altered in the U.S. to enable commercial airline pilots to keep flying until age 65, instead of facing forced retirement at age 60 as they had in the past.

Industrial firms are dealing with this challenge along two lines: First, how to document and pass along the immense treasure of work-related knowledge that these employees have, and second, how to keep these employees interested in working later into their lives. BASF, a firm with a massive employee base scattered around the world, estimates that by 2020, 50% or more of its employees will be 50 to 65 years old. It has implemented measures ranging from making the workplace more comfortable and safe for older workers, to an intense knowledge transfer program where older workers mentor younger staff members.

10) Employment Sectors that Will Offer an Above-Average Number of Job Opportunities

Job seekers should remain aware of the fact that certain industries will have above-average likelihood to offer job openings. This is due to a number of circumstances, including shifts in consumer tastes and requirements, normal employee turnover and attrition, structural changes within industries, global economic conditions and national policies and priorities.

Below is a list of industries particularly recommended to job seekers.

Employment Sectors that Will Offer an Above-Average Number of Job Opportunities:

- Automobile Manufacturing and Retailing
- Biotechnology
- Child Care/Children's Products
- Consulting, including Technology Consulting
- Consumer Products
- Cosmetics
- Elder Care, Home Health Care, Nursing Homes and Assisted Living Communities
- Electronic Games, Games for Cell Phones
- Energy Conservation Products and Services
- Health Care Services
- Health Care Products
- Health Care Technology, Including Computerized Patient Records
- Health Foods, Organic Foods, Enhanced Foods
- Home Building
- Hotels
- Insurance
- Internet Services, Server Hosting, Cloud Computing
- Internet of Things: Connected Devices, Remote Wireless Sensors and their Networks, Machine to Machine Communications
- Online Search Services & Social Media, with Advertising Revenues
- Online-based Business and Consumer Sales and Services, including E-Commerce

---

- Outsourcing, Including Outsourced Business and Computer Services
- Pets: Services and Products
- Pharmaceuticals—Generics
- Restaurants
- Retailing—Basic, Including Drugstores and Supermarkets
- Retailing—Discount and Warehouse Clubs
- Robotics and Factory Automation
- Software—Artificial Intelligence
- Software—Corporate, including Development Tools & Cybersecurity
- Software—Data Analytics and Consumer Scoring
- Software—Mobile Apps
- Software as a Service
- Solar Energy Cells Installation & Maintenance
- Supply Chain Services That Create Cost-Savings
- Water Filtration and Conservation Equipment
- Wireless and Cellular Communications

Chapter 2

STATISTICS

Contents:

U.S. Employment Statistics Overview: 2016-2017

(Labor Counts In Thousands; Seasonally Adjusted)

	Jun-16	Apr-17	May-17	Jun-17
Civilian Labor Force, Total	158,889	160,213	159,784	160,145
Employed	151,090	153,156	152,923	153,168
Unemployed	7,799	7,056	6,861	6,977
Persons 16 Years of Age and Over, Not in Labor Force	94,508	94,375	94,983	94,813
Unemployment Rate, All Workers	4.9%	4.4%	4.3%	4.4%
Adult Men (20 years and over)	4.5%	4.0%	3.8%	4.0%
Adult Women (20 years and over)	4.5%	4.1%	4.0%	4.0%
Teenagers (16 to 19 years)	15.9%	14.7%	14.3%	13.3%
White	4.4%	3.8%	3.7%	3.8%
Black or African American	8.6%	7.9%	7.5%	7.1%
Asian	3.5%	3.2%	3.6%	3.6%
Hispanic or Latino	5.8%	5.2%	5.2%	4.8%
Average Hourly Earnings, Private Industry	$25.62	$26.18	$26.21	$26.25
Weekly Earnings, Private Industry	$881.33	$903.21	$901.62	$905.63
Average Work Week, Private Industry (Hours)	34.4	34.5	34.4	34.5
Nonfarm Employment	144,166	146,030	146,182	146,404
Goods-Producing	19,705	19,969	19,982	20,007
Construction	6,690	6,871	6,880	6,896
Manufacturing	12,347	12,397	12,395	12,396
Private Service-Providing	102,246	103,736	103,882	104,044
Retail Trade	15,825	15,844	15,837	15,845
Transportation & Warehousing	4,971	5,054	5,065	5,068
Professional & Business Services	20,081	20,614	20,670	20,705
Education & Health Services	22,603	23,017	23,052	23,097
Leisure & Hospitality	15,610	15,863	15,888	15,924
Government	22,215	22,325	22,318	22,353

Source: U.S. Bureau of Labor Statistics

Plunkett Research, ® Ltd.

www.plunkettresearch.com

U.S. Civilian Labor Force:
1997-June 2017

(Persons 16 & Older; In Thousands)

Year	Civilian Workforce Level
1997	136,297
1998	137,673
1999	139,368
2000	142,583
2001	143,734
2002	144,863
2003	146,510
2004	147,401
2005	149,320
2006	151,428
2007	153,124
2008	154,287
2009	154,142
2010	153,889
2011	153,617
2012	154,975
2013	155,389
2014	155,922
2015	157,130
2016	159,187
Jun-17	160,145

Note: The civilian labor force consists of employed and unemployed people actively seeking work, but it does not include any Armed Forces personnel.

Source: U.S. Bureau of Labor Statistics

Plunkett Research, ® Ltd.

www.plunkettresearch.com

Employment by Major Industry Sector: 2004, 2014 & Projected 2024

Industry Sector	Employment (in Thousands)			Change (in Thousands)		Percent Distribution			Compound Annual Rate of Change	
	2004	2014	2024	2004-14	2014-24	2004	2014	2024	2004-14	2014-24
Total[1]	144,047.0	150,539.9	160,328.8	6,492.9	9,788.9	100.0	100.0	100.0	0.4	0.6
Nonagriculture wage & salary[2]	132,462.2	139,811.5	149,131.6	7,349.3	9,320.1	92.0	92.9	93.0	0.5	0.6
Goods-producing, excluding agriculture	21,815.3	19,170.5	19,227.0	-2,644.8	56.5	15.1	12.7	12.0	-1.3	0.0
Mining	523.2	843.8	924.0	320.6	80.2	0.4	0.6	0.6	4.9	0.9
Construction	6,976.2	6,138.4	6,928.8	-837.8	790.4	4.8	4.1	4.3	-1.3	1.2
Manufacturing	14,315.9	12,188.3	11,374.2	-2,127.6	-814.1	9.9	8.1	7.1	-1.6	-0.7
Services-providing	110,646.9	120,641.0	129,904.6	9,994.1	9,263.6	76.8	80.1	81.0	0.9	0.7
Utilities	563.8	553.0	505.1	-10.8	-47.9	0.4	0.4	0.3	-0.2	-0.9
Wholesale trade	5,663.0	5,826.0	6,151.4	163.0	325.4	3.9	3.9	3.8	0.3	0.5
Retail trade	15,058.2	15,364.5	16,129.1	306.3	764.6	10.5	10.2	10.1	0.2	0.5
Transportation & warehousing	4,248.6	4,640.3	4,776.9	391.7	136.6	2.9	3.1	3.0	0.9	0.3
Information	3,118.3	2,739.7	2,712.6	-378.6	-27.1	2.2	1.8	1.7	-1.3	-0.1
Financial activities	8,105.1	7,979.5	8,486.7	-125.6	507.2	5.6	5.3	5.3	-0.2	0.6
Professional & business services	16,394.9	19,096.2	20,985.5	2,701.3	1,889.3	11.4	12.7	13.1	1.5	0.9
Educational services	2,762.5	3,417.4	3,756.1	654.9	338.7	1.9	2.3	2.3	2.2	0.9
Health care & social assistance	14,429.8	18,057.4	21,852.2	3,627.6	3,794.8	10.0	12.0	13.6	2.3	1.9
Leisure & hospitality	12,493.1	14,710.0	15,651.2	2,216.9	941.2	8.7	9.8	9.8	1.6	0.6
Other services	6,188.3	6,394.0	6,662.0	205.7	268.0	4.3	4.2	4.2	0.3	0.4
Federal government	2,730.0	2,729.0	2,345.6	-1.0	-383.4	1.9	1.8	1.5	0.0	-1.5
State & local government	18,891.3	19,134.0	19,890.1	242.7	756.1	13.1	12.7	12.4	0.1	0.4
Agriculture, forestry, fishing & hunting[3]	2,111.3	2,138.3	2,027.7	26.9	-110.5	1.5	1.4	1.3	0.1	-0.5
Agriculture wage & salary	1,149.0	1,384.0	1,307.3	235.0	-76.7	0.8	0.9	0.8	1.9	-0.6
Agriculture self-employed & unpaid family workers	962.3	754.3	720.4	-208.1	-33.8	0.7	0.5	0.4	-2.4	-0.5
Nonagriculture self-employed & unpaid family workers	9,473.6	8,590.2	9,169.5	-883.4	579.3	6.6	5.7	5.7	-1.0	0.7

[1] Employment data for wage and salary workers are from the BLS Current Employment Statistics survey, which counts jobs, whereas self-employed, unpaid family workers, and agriculture, forestry, fishing, and hunting are from the Current Population Survey (household survey), which counts workers.

[2] Includes wage and salary data from the Current Employment Statistics survey, except private households, which is from the Current Population Survey. Logging workers are excluded.

[3] Includes agriculture, forestry, fishing, and hunting data from the Current Population Survey, except logging, which is from Current Employment Statistics survey. Government wage and salary workers are excluded.

Source: U.S. Bureau of Labor Statistics

Plunkett Research, ® Ltd.

www.plunkettresearch.com

Number of People Employed and Unemployed, U.S.: June 2016 vs. June 2017

(Persons 16 & Older; Numbers In Thousands; Not Seasonally Adjusted)

Occupation	Employed		Unemployed		Unemp. Rates (%)	
	Dec-15	Dec-16	Dec-15	Dec-16	Dec-15	Dec-16
Total*	**151,990**	**154,086**	**8,144**	**7,250**	**5.1**	**4.5**
Management, professional and related	59,181	60,705	1,712	1,440	2.8	2.3
Management, business and financial operations	25,354	25,328	646	504	2.5	1.9
Professional and related	33,827	35,377	1,067	936	3.1	2.6
Service	27,618	27,387	1,658	1,540	5.7	5.3
Sales and office	33,391	33,531	1,550	1,503	4.4	4.3
Sales and related	16,040	15,808	820	797	4.9	4.8
Office and administrative support	17,351	17,723	730	706	4.0	3.8
Natural resources, construction and maintenance	14,277	14,426	832	747	5.5	4.9
Farming, fishing and forestry	1,254	1,264	151	95	10.8	7.0
Construction and extraction	8,240	8,282	462	459	5.3	5.3
Installation, maintenance and repair	4,783	4,880	218	192	4.4	3.8
Production, transportation and material moving	17,524	18,038	1,091	1,027	5.9	5.4
Production	8,470	8,702	439	466	4.9	5.1
Transportation and material moving	9,054	9,336	652	560	6.7	5.7

* Persons with no previous work experience and persons whose last job was in the Armed Forces are included in the unemployed total.

Note: Updated population controls are introduced annually with the release of January data.

Source: U.S. Bureau of Labor Statistics
Plunkett Research,® Ltd.
www.plunkettresearch.com

U.S. Labor Force Ages 16 to 24 Years Old by School Enrollment, Educational Attainment, Sex, Race & Ethnicity: October 2016

(Numbers in Thousands, Latest Year Available)	Civilian non-institutional population	Total in Labor Force	Percent of Populace	Employed		Unemployed		Not in Labor Force
				Total	Percent of Populace	Number	Rate (%)	
Total, 16 to 24 years	38,367	20,951	54.6	18,820	49.1	2,130	10.2	17,417
Educational Attainment								
Enrolled in school	22,058	7,947	36.0	7,276	33.0	671	8.4	14,111
Enrolled in high school[1]	9,521	1,971	20.7	1,650	17.3	321	16.3	7,550
Men	4,962	900	18.1	731	14.7	169	18.8	4,061
Women	4,560	1,071	23.5	919	20.2	152	14.2	3,489
White	6,847	1,546	22.6	1,329	19.4	217	14.0	5,301
Black or African American	1,557	196	12.6	127	8.2	69	35.2	1,362
Asian	504	75	14.9	60	11.9	15	20.1	429
Hispanic or Latino ethnicity	2,179	384	17.6	307	14.1	76	19.9	1,796
Enrolled in college	12,536	5,976	47.7	5,626	44.9	350	5.9	6,561
Enrolled in 2-year college	3,070	1,792	58.4	1,656	53.9	136	7.6	1,278
Enrolled in 4-year college	9,466	4,184	44.2	3,970	41.9	214	5.1	5,282
Full-time students	10,887	4,601	42.3	4,320	39.7	281	6.1	6,286
Part-time students	1,649	1,374	83.3	1,306	79.2	68	5.0	275
Men	5,876	2,761	47.0	2,538	43.2	223	8.1	3,116
Women	6,660	3,215	48.3	3,088	46.4	127	3.9	3,445
White	9,259	4,611	49.8	4,348	47.0	263	5.7	4,648
Black or African American	1,674	753	45.0	696	41.6	57	7.6	921
Asian	1,017	318	31.2	295	29.0	23	7.1	699
Hispanic or Latino ethnicity	2,647	1,258	47.5	1,145	43.3	113	9.0	1,389
Not enrolled in school	16,309	13,004	79.7	11,544	70.8	1,460	11.2	3,306
16 to 19 years	3,120	2,102	67.4	1,674	53.7	428	20.3	1,018
20 to 24 years	13,189	10,902	82.7	9,870	74.8	1,032	9.5	2,287
Sex								
Men	8,500	7,110	83.7	6,217	73.1	894	12.6	1,389
Less than a high school diploma	1,371	954	69.6	725	52.9	229	24.0	417
High school graduates, no college[3]	4,144	3,455	83.4	3,000	72.4	455	13.2	689
Some college or associate degree	1,904	1,697	89.1	1,571	82.5	126	7.4	207
Bachelor's degree and higher[4]	1,081	1,004	92.9	921	85.2	83	8.3	77
Women	7,810	5,893	75.5	5,327	68.2	566	9.6	1,916
Less than a high school diploma	964	457	47.4	362	37.6	95	20.7	507
High school graduates, no college[3]	3,182	2,249	70.7	1,982	62.3	267	11.9	933
Some college or associate degree	2,099	1,750	83.4	1,618	77.1	132	7.5	349
Bachelor's degree and higher[4]	1,565	1,438	91.9	1,365	87.2	73	5.1	127
Race								
White	12,118	9,709	80.1	8,793	72.6	915	9.4	2,409
Black or African American	2,592	2,068	79.8	1,646	63.5	422	20.4	524
Asian	706	533	75.5	492	69.7	41	7.7	173
Hispanic or Latino ethnicity	3,686	2,844	77.2	2,545	69.1	298	10.5	842

Note: The civilian labor force consists of employed and unemployed people actively seeking work, but it does not include any Armed Forces personnel. Detail for the above race groups do not sum to totals because data are not presented for all races. Persons whose ethnicity is identified as Hispanic or Latino may be of any race. Because of rounding, sums of individual items may not equal totals.

[1] Includes a small number of persons who are in grades below high school. [2] Data not shown where base is less than 75,000.   [3] Includes persons with a high school diploma or equivalent. [4] Includes persons with bachelor's, master's, professional, and doctoral degrees.

Source: U.S. Bureau of Labor Statistics
Plunkett Research,® Ltd.
www.plunkettresearch.com

Medical Care Benefits in the U.S.: Access, Participation and Take-Up Rates, March 2017

(All workers = 100 percent)

Characteristics	Private Industry			State/Local Government		
	Access	Particip-ation	Take-up Rate[1]	Access	Particip-ation	Take-up Rate[1]
All workers	67%	49%	72%	89%	71%	80%
Worker Characteristics						
Management, professional and related	86%	65%	75%	92%	72%	79%
Service	39%	23%	61%	80%	65%	81%
Sales and office	66%	47%	71%	89%	73%	83%
Natural resources, construction and maintenance	72%	57%	79%	95%	78%	82%
Production, transportation and material moving	75%	55%	74%	85%	69%	82%
Full time	85%	63%	73%	99%	80%	80%
Part time	19%	11%	60%	27%	19%	70%
Union	93%	79%	84%	95%	73%	77%
Nonunion	65%	46%	71%	83%	69%	83%
Wage percentiles[2]						
Lowest 25 percent	33%	20%	60%	72%	58%	80%
Lowest 10 percent	22%	12%	55%	59%	46%	78%
Second 25 percent	71%	49%	69%	93%	76%	81%
Third 25 percent	85%	64%	76%	97%	78%	81%
Highest 25 percent	92%	72%	78%	95%	74%	78%
Highest 10 percent	94%	73%	78%	93%	74%	80%
Establishment Characteristics						
1 to 99 workers	55%	39%	70%	85%	68%	80%
1 to 49 workers	51%	36%	70%	82%	67%	82%
50 to 99 workers	67%	47%	71%	89%	69%	78%
100 workers or more	82%	61%	74%	90%	72%	80%
100 to 499 workers	78%	57%	73%	86%	69%	80%
500 workers or more	89%	67%	76%	92%	73%	80%

Note: For this table, a worker with access to medical care benefits is defined as having an employer-provided medical plan available for use, regardless of the worker's decision to enroll or participate in the plan. Farm and private household workers, the self-employed and Federal government workers are excluded from the survey.

[1] The take-up rate is a rounded estimate of the percentage of workers with access to a plan who participate in the plan.
[2] Surveyed occupations are classified into wage categories based on the average wage for the occupation, which may include workers with earnings both above and below the threshold. The categories were formed using percentile estimates generated using wage data for March 2017.

Source: U.S. Bureau of Labor Statistics
Plunkett Research,® Ltd.
www.plunkettresearch.com

Retirement Benefits in the U.S.: Access, Participation and Take-Up Rates, March 2017

(All workers = 100 percent)

Characteristics	Private Industry			State/Local Government		
	Access	Particip-ation	Take-up Rate[1]	Access	Particip-ation	Take-up Rate[1]
All workers	66%	50%	75%	91%	80%	88%
Worker Characteristics						
Management, professional and related	82%	70%	86%	94%	81%	86%
Service	42%	22%	54%	84%	76%	90%
Sales and office	70%	51%	72%	91%	80%	88%
Natural resources, construction and maintenance	63%	48%	77%	97%	89%	91%
Production, transportation and material moving	71%	53%	75%	90%	80%	89%
Full time	77%	60%	78%	99%	87%	88%
Part time	38%	21%	56%	46%	39%	84%
Union	92%	82%	90%	97%	83%	86%
Nonunion	64%	47%	73%	86%	77%	89%
Wage percentiles[2]						
Lowest 25 percent	42%	21%	51%	78%	68%	87%
Lowest 10 percent	33%	14%	41%	67%	58%	87%
Second 25 percent	66%	46%	70%	94%	83%	88%
Third 25 percent	78%	64%	81%	98%	86%	88%
Highest 25 percent	88%	77%	88%	97%	84%	87%
Highest 10 percent	89%	81%	90%	96%	82%	85%
Establishment Characteristics						
1 to 99 workers	53%	37%	71%	87%	79%	90%
1 to 49 workers	49%	34%	71%	85%	78%	91%
50 to 99 workers	65%	46%	70%	90%	80%	89%
100 workers or more	83%	65%	78%	93%	80%	87%
100 to 499 workers	79%	58%	73%	91%	81%	90%
500 workers or more	89%	76%	85%	93%	80%	86%

Note: Benefits may include defined benefit pension plans as well as defined contribution retirement plans. Workers are considered as having access or as participating if they have access to or participate in at least one of these plan types. Farm and private household workers, the self-employed and Federal government workers are excluded from the survey.

[1] The take-up rate is a rounded estimate of the percentage of workers with access to a plan who participate in the plan.

[2] Surveyed occupations are classified into wage categories based on the average wage for the occupation, which may include workers with earnings both above and below the threshold. The categories were formed using percentile estimates generated using wage data for March 2017.

Source: U.S. Bureau of Labor Statistics

Plunkett Research, ® Ltd.

www.plunkettresearch.com

Top 30 U.S. Occupations by Numerical Change in Job Growth: 2014-2024

(By Thousands of Employees)

Occupation	Employment		Change, 2014-24		Median annual wage, 2016
	2014	2024	Number	Percent	
Total, all occupations	150,539.9	160,328.8	9,788.9	6.5	$37,040
Personal care aides	1,768.4	2,226.5	458.1	25.9	$21,920
Registered nurses	2,751.0	3,190.3	439.3	16.0	$68,450
Home health aides	913.5	1,261.9	348.4	38.1	$22,600
Combined food preparation and serving workers, including fast food	3,159.7	3,503.2	343.5	10.9	$19,440
Retail salespersons	4,624.9	4,939.1	314.2	6.8	$22,680
Nursing assistants	1,492.1	1,754.1	262.0	17.6	$26,590
Customer service representatives	2,581.8	2,834.8	252.9	9.8	$32,300
Cooks, restaurant	1,109.7	1,268.7	158.9	14.3	$24,140
General and operations managers	2,124.1	2,275.2	151.1	7.1	$99,310
Construction laborers	1,159.1	1,306.5	147.4	12.7	$33,430
Accountants and auditors	1,332.7	1,475.1	142.4	10.7	$68,150
Medical assistants	591.3	730.2	138.9	23.5	$31,540
Janitors and cleaners, except maids and housekeeping cleaners	2,360.6	2,496.9	136.3	5.8	$24,190
Software developers, applications	718.4	853.7	135.3	18.8	$100,080
Laborers and freight, stock, and material movers, hand	2,441.3	2,566.4	125.1	5.1	$25,980
First-line supervisors of office and administrative support workers	1,466.1	1,587.3	121.2	8.3	$54,340
Computer systems analysts	567.8	686.3	118.6	20.9	$87,220
Licensed practical and licensed vocational nurses	719.9	837.2	117.3	16.3	$44,090
Maids and housekeeping cleaners	1,457.7	1,569.4	111.7	7.7	$21,820
Medical secretaries	527.6	635.8	108.2	20.5	$33,730
Management analysts	758.0	861.4	103.4	13.6	$81,330
Heavy and tractor-trailer truck drivers	1,797.7	1,896.4	98.8	5.5	$41,340
Receptionists and information clerks	1,028.6	1,126.3	97.8	9.5	$27,920
Office clerks, general	3,062.5	3,158.2	95.8	3.1	$30,580
Sales representatives, wholesale and manufacturing, except technical and scientific products	1,453.1	1,546.5	93.4	6.4	$57,140
Stock clerks and order fillers	1,878.1	1,971.1	92.9	4.9	$23,840
Market research analysts and marketing specialists	495.5	587.8	92.3	18.6	$62,560
First-line supervisors of food preparation and serving workers	890.1	978.6	88.5	9.9	$31,480
Electricians	628.8	714.7	85.9	13.7	$52,720
Maintenance and repair workers, general	1,374.7	1,458.1	83.5	6.1	$36,940

Source: U.S. Bureau of Labor Statistics
Plunkett Research, ® Ltd.
www.plunkettresearch.com

Top 30 U.S. Occupations by Percent Change in Job Growth: 2014-2024

(Employment in Thousands)

Occupation	Employment		Change, 2014-24		Median annual wage, 2016
	2014	2024	Number	Percent	
Total, all occupations	150,539.9	160,328.8	9,788.9	6.5	$37,040
Wind turbine service technicians	4.4	9.2	4.8	108.0	$52,260
Occupational therapy assistants	33.0	47.1	14.1	42.7	$59,010
Physical therapist assistants	78.7	110.7	31.9	40.6	$56,610
Physical therapist aides	50.0	69.5	19.5	39.0	$25,680
Home health aides	913.5	1,261.9	348.4	38.1	$22,600
Commercial divers	4.4	6.0	1.6	36.9	$49,090
Nurse practitioners	126.9	171.7	44.7	35.2	$100,910
Physical therapists	210.9	282.7	71.8	34.0	$85,400
Statisticians	30.0	40.1	10.1	33.8	$80,500
Ambulance drivers and attendants, except emergency medical technicians	19.6	26.1	6.5	33.0	$23,850
Occupational therapy aides	8.8	11.6	2.7	30.6	$28,330
Physician assistants	94.4	123.2	28.7	30.4	$101,480
Operations research analysts	91.3	118.9	27.6	30.2	$79,200
Personal financial advisors	249.4	323.2	73.9	29.6	$90,530
Cartographers and photogrammetrists	12.3	15.9	3.6	29.3	$62,750
Genetic counselors	2.4	3.1	0.7	28.8	$74,120
Interpreters and translators	61.0	78.5	17.5	28.7	$46,120
Audiologists	13.2	16.9	3.8	28.6	$75,980
Hearing aid specialists	5.9	7.5	1.6	27.2	$50,250
Optometrists	40.6	51.6	11.0	27.0	$106,140
Forensic science technicians	14.4	18.2	3.8	26.6	$56,750
Web developers	148.5	188.0	39.5	26.6	$66,130
Occupational therapists	114.6	145.1	30.4	26.5	$81,910
Diagnostic medical sonographers	60.7	76.7	16.0	26.4	$69,650
Personal care aides	1,768.4	2,226.5	458.1	25.9	$21,920
Phlebotomists	112.7	140.8	28.1	24.9	$32,710
Ophthalmic medical technicians	37.0	46.1	9.1	24.7	$35,530
Nurse midwives	5.3	6.6	1.3	24.6	$99,770
Solar photovoltaic installers	5.9	7.4	1.4	24.3	$39,240
Emergency medical technicians and paramedics	241.2	299.6	58.5	24.2	$32,670

Source: U.S. Bureau of Labor Statistics

Plunkett Research, ® Ltd.

www.plunkettresearch.com

Occupations with the Largest Expected Employment Increases, U.S.: 2014-2024

(By Increase in Number Employed, in Thousands)

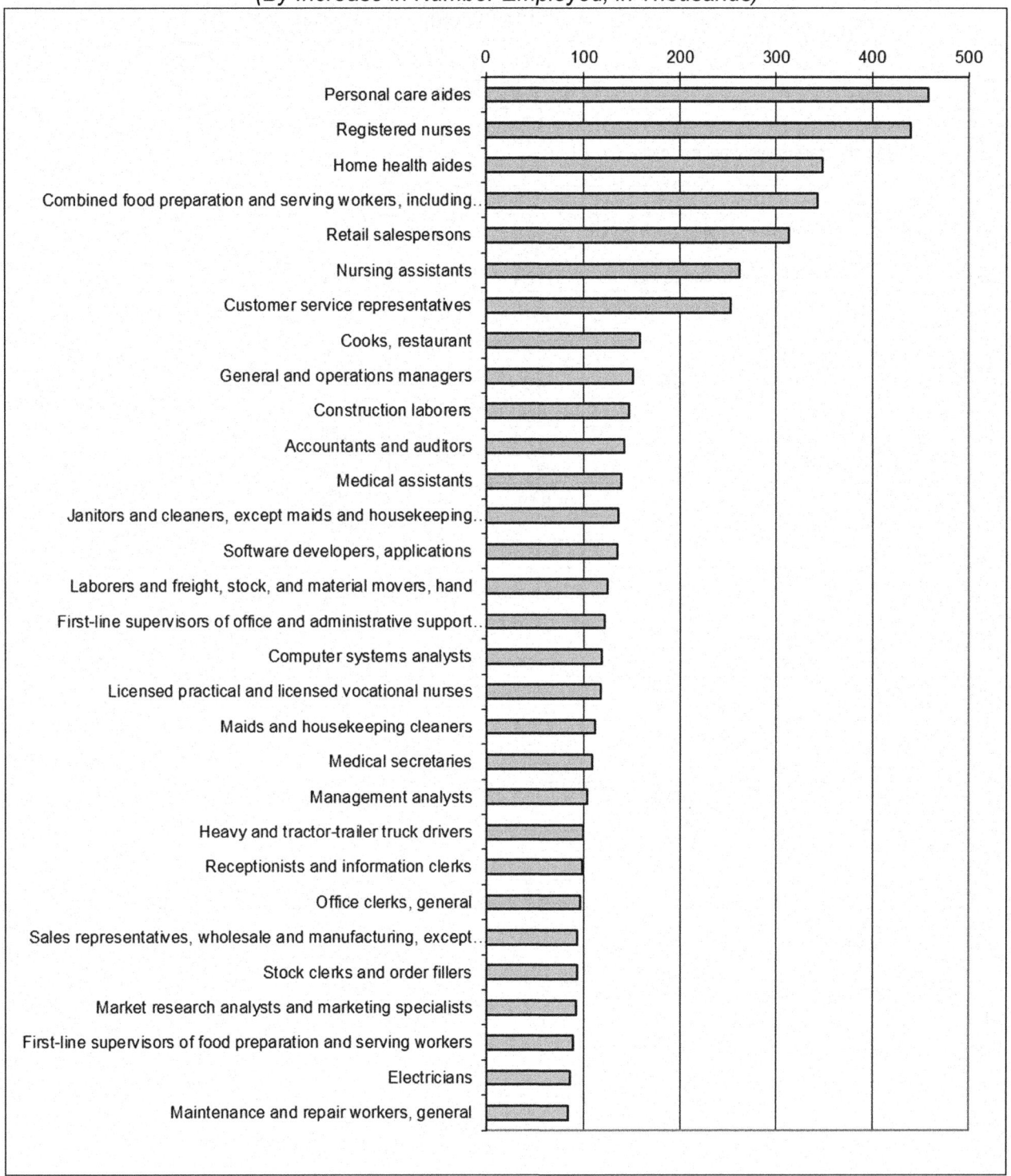

Source: U.S. Bureau of Labor Statistics
Plunkett Research, ® Ltd.
www.plunkettresearch.com

Occupations with the Fastest Expected Decline, U.S.: 2014-2024

(In Thousands)

Occupation	Employment		Change, 2014-24		Median Annual Wage, 2016
	2014	2024	Number	Percent	
Total, all occupations	150,539.9	160,328.8	9,788.9	6.5	37,040.0
Locomotive firers	1.7	0.5	-1.2	-69.9	58,230.0
Electronic equipment installers and repairers, motor vehicles	11.5	5.8	-5.8	-50.0	32,220.0
Telephone operators	13.1	7.5	-5.5	-42.4	37,000.0
Postal service mail sorters, processors, and processing machine operators	117.6	78.0	-39.7	-33.7	56,220.0
Switchboard operators, including answering service	112.4	75.4	-37.0	-32.9	28,030.0
Photographic process workers and processing machine operators	28.8	19.4	-9.5	-32.9	26,470.0
Shoe machine operators and tenders	3.5	2.5	-1.1	-30.5	26,150.0
Manufactured building and mobile home installers	4.0	2.8	-1.2	-30.0	29,810.0
Foundry mold and coremakers	12.0	8.7	-3.3	-27.7	34,790.0
Sewing machine operators	153.9	112.2	-41.7	-27.1	23,670.0
Pourers and casters, metal	9.8	7.2	-2.6	-26.6	36,180.0
Postal service clerks	69.6	51.3	-18.3	-26.2	56,790.0
Postmasters and mail superintendents	17.3	12.8	-4.6	-26.2	71,670.0
Postal service mail carriers	297.4	219.4	-78.1	-26.2	58,110.0
Textile knitting and weaving machine setters, operators, and tenders	27.9	20.6	-7.3	-26.2	27,470.0
Fabric and apparel patternmakers	5.4	4.0	-1.4	-26.0	39,650.0
Textile cutting machine setters, operators, and tenders	14.3	10.6	-3.7	-25.7	26,090.0
Watch repairers	2.7	2.0	-0.7	-25.7	36,740.0
Molding, coremaking, and casting machine setters, operators, and tenders, metal and plastic	129.5	97.2	-32.3	-25.0	30,480.0
Prepress technicians and workers	36.5	27.5	-9.0	-24.6	38,930.0
Extruding and drawing machine setters, operators, and tenders, metal and plastic	73.4	55.5	-17.9	-24.4	33,870.0
Textile bleaching and dyeing machine operators and tenders	11.7	8.9	-2.8	-23.9	27,270.0
Patternmakers, metal and plastic	3.8	2.9	-0.9	-23.4	44,210.0
Grinding, lapping, polishing, and buffing machine tool setters, operators, and tenders, metal and plastic	71.4	55.8	-15.7	-21.9	32,890.0
Textile winding, twisting, and drawing out machine setters, operators, and tenders	26.0	20.3	-5.6	-21.7	27,500.0
Model makers, metal and plastic	6.2	4.9	-1.3	-21.5	48,550.0
Forging machine setters, operators, and tenders, metal and plastic	21.6	17.0	-4.6	-21.5	36,930.0
Desktop publishers	14.8	11.7	-3.1	-21.0	41,090.0
Parking enforcement workers	9.4	7.4	-2.0	-20.8	37,950.0
Milling and planing machine setters, operators, and tenders, metal and plastic	22.4	17.8	-4.6	-20.6	39,840.0

Source: U.S. Bureau of Labor Statistics

Plunkett Research,® Ltd.

www.plunkettresearch.com

Chapter 3

RESEARCH: 7 KEYS FOR JOB SEEKERS

How to use your library, college placement office, the internet and other resources
to become well-informed about a company and its industry
<u>before</u> you ask for an interview

Research is the key to finding appropriate job openings, targeting the best possible employers and performing well when you go to job interviews. Learn what's unique about a company compared to other firms in its industry. Learn why it's prospering–or why it isn't. Where is this company going? Is it favored by stock investors? Is it privately-owned by a family, or has it been acquired by private equity investors who plan to resell it over the mid-term? What are its hottest-selling products and services? Is it investing in research and new facilities so that it may prosper in the future? Also, as many people who have been laid off from failing firms have learned the hard way, determining a company's level of financial stability can be one of the most important factors in making a career decision.

The more you're willing to dig deep at the library or your college's career planning office, and the more adept you are at using the internet for research, the better your chances of success in a job search. If you are willing to ask questions of knowledgeable businesspeople and of employees who currently work for your target employers, you will enhance your job search even further. The two secrets to successful job research are tenacity and focus. Know what to look for and where to find it.

Once you've landed an interview, you should research both the prospective employer and its industry even further. In this manner, you'll know what questions to ask before you agree to take the job, and you'll present yourself as a knowledgeable potential hire who is truly interested in the company and its business.

Here are the seven keys for research that can lead you to a great employer:

1) Financial Stability
Check bond ratings, credit ratings, debt level, growth in sales and growth in profits, along with the views of stock analysts and business journalists.

2) Growth Plans
Look for new plants, stores or offices to be opened; new technologies, products or divisions to be launched; or plans for strategic acquisitions. (See 3, 4 and 5 below.) Is the employer's growth strategy focused primarily on offshoring work to overseas locations or outsourcing work to outside services providers? Or, does it have a balanced growth strategy that will create good opportunities in its American operations?

3) Research and Development Programs
If the company is a major manufacturer or a technology-based firm, then you should investigate how it invests in R&D (research and development). Is its research and development budget growing? For many types of companies, research is a vital investment in the future.

4) Product Launch and Production
Does the company have the ability to successfully launch new products and services (see 5 below) or to invest in and utilize cutting-edge technologies needed to maintain a competitive edge?

5) Marketing and Distribution Methods
Does the firm utilize an in-house sales force? Does it work through outside dealers and distribution partners? What are its advertising methods? Is it increasing its market share, or are competitors taking customers away? Is the company growing its international sales? Is it adept at using the internet as a powerful sales tool? Is it successful at selling into vital international markets?

6) Employee Benefits

Are wealth-building benefit plans offered? Will the company match all or part of your deposits to a 401(k) savings plan? Check for tuition reimbursement, pension plans, profit sharing, stock ownership plans, discount stock purchase plans, stock options or performance-based bonuses.

7) Quality-of-Work Factors

Does the company offer continual training, wellness programs, child care, elder care support, promote-from-within policies, flexible work schedules, performance reviews, product discounts or on-site health clubs? Is it a corporate culture that fits your lifestyle?

As a serious job seeker, you should conduct in-depth research and make detailed notes about these key factors for each firm you are considering. Then compare each company's finances, plans and programs to others in the same industry. You'll begin to see what makes some firms outstanding and why those outstanding companies are the best places to make a career investment. For example, if you compare two discount store giants, Wal-Mart and Costco, you will find that Wal-Mart is by far the larger firm, but Costco has an outstanding record of providing superior employee pay and benefits.

Your research goal should be twofold: First, determine whether this is a firm you want to work for. Are the salaries and benefits appealing? Are layoffs likely? Is it planning to expand its workforce in lower-cost nations like India and then lay off U.S. employees? Is the firm growing steadily? A growing company will offer opportunities for you to advance when it launches new locations, services, technologies or product lines. Second, develop a personal understanding of both the company and its industry so you can better sell yourself as a potential employee.

Other Considerations:

Women and Minorities:

Certain industries have a greater tendency to offer advancement opportunities for women or minorities. Historically, the banking and insurance segments have tended to promote both women and minorities, as have retailing, electric utilities, apparel, consumer goods, packaged food and beverages, education, publishing and telephone companies.

Some technology companies have been terrific places for women who want to advance, and many tech companies, such as Hewlett-Packard, IBM, Yahoo, Xerox and eBay, have been known to post women to CEO spots.

Black Enterprise magazine publishes an annual list of the "Most Powerful African Americans in Corporate America," (see www.blackenterprise.com). Meanwhile, the Executive Leadership Council, www.elcinfo.com, a Washington, D.C.-based nonprofit group that conducts programs aimed at filling more executive posts with African Americans, has a unique statistic to report. Its membership is composed of senior-level black executives who have jobs that are no more than three levels below the CEO spot at Fortune 500 companies. When the group was founded in 1986, it had only a handful of members. Today, its membership is about 500 people employed in high-level executive jobs at major corporations (one-third of them are women).

The Hispanic Association on Corporate Responsibility (www.hacr.org) promotes Hispanic advancement in the areas of employment, procurement, philanthropy and governance. Another nonprofit agency, National Hispanic Corporate Achievers (hispanicachievers.org), provides an educational forum for Hispanics working for *Fortune 1000* companies.

Tips on Using Business Magazines, Newspapers and Trade Journals to Find Job Leads and Do Employer Research

Many job seekers overlook the tremendous advantages offered by industry magazines (called "trade journals") and other publications when conducting research.

Industry-specific trade journals frequently have classified ads in the back that list job openings. An example of a great magazine to study is *American Banker,* which can be found at major libraries. Additional information is available at www.americanbanker.com.

Journalists at trade journals and business newspapers continuously interview industry-leading executives regarding their companies' growth plans. New projects and company expansion plans described in these articles provide terrific job leads.

You can also get great contact information from these publications. Read the latest business stories about companies and industries that interest you and you will learn vital information. Best of all, you can glean from stories and interviews the names and titles of executives who lead projects, divisions and subsidiaries.

There are literally hundreds of these trade journals—at least one for each industry sector and sometimes dozens covering the largest industries.

Other great resources include business newspapers such as the *Dallas/Ft. Worth Business Journal*, *The Wall Street Journal*, the business pages of major newspapers like *The New York Times* and publications written for major investors like *Investor's Business Daily*. At www.bizjournals.com, you can gain access to news stories from business journals from all over the U.S.

Quality-of-Life Benefits:

Many companies offer benefits that help employees balance their personal and professional lives. The concept is that employees who are healthy and comfortable with their personal and family lives make better, more productive employees. To that end, many companies include fitness programs and family services such as extended maternity leaves and child care or elder care, whether on-site or off-site in the form of referral services. Other popular family-friendly benefits include flextime, flexible benefits spending accounts, adoption assistance and telecommuting. In many cases, benefits are listed on employers' web sites.

Work-Life has become a popular phrase for family-friendly benefits and programs among major employers such as Intel, Abbott Laboratories, Baxter International and Aramark. For additional information, you can study such organizations at WorldatWork (formerly the Alliance for Work-Life Progress) site at www.worldatwork.org.

Growth Potential and Job Stability:

A firm's growth potential should be among your top priorities. Companies are always trying to maintain or increase productivity, or the ratio of revenues per employee. If a company's sales are sliding, or if it is running out of cash, the job picture starts to collapse. A little extra research into a company's finances and true potential for growth might save you from a future layoff.

Of course, employers sometimes have to resort to layoffs due to conditions outside of their control. The devastating economic recession that officially ran from late 2007 through early 2009 led to millions of layoffs in America.

As a job seeker, you're forced to look out for your own best interests while you sort through thousands of potential employers in dozens of industries. This means that good research is vital. For example, if you put salary at the top of your list, you may have the wrong priorities. From time to time, some of the highest-paying firms have been among those cutting the largest numbers of employees. If you are looking for job stability, your biggest challenge is to pick companies that are more likely to hire now and less likely to have layoffs in the future. That's why a firm's growth outlook should be one of your guiding lights.

However, the goal is *internal* growth caused by expanding sales. Generally less appealing are firms that post a quick spike in growth through big mergers. (In many cases, merged companies lay off people who suddenly find themselves filling jobs duplicated in newly consolidated offices. Also, companies that grow excessively through acquisitions may be taking on loads of debt that can become hard to handle later. However, there are occasional exceptions to this rule, where firms are enjoying soaring demand for products or services and find it difficult to hire quickly enough to keep up.) Companies that are growing rapidly through internal expansion include those opening new stores, distribution centers or offices, developing exciting new products, moving into new markets (including international markets) and creating hot new technologies, retail formats or services. Those types of expansion frequently mean great career

opportunities, including the chance for rapid job promotion.

If you're tenacious, you can find opportunities where others will find only rejection. Identifying real prospects for growth takes more than a quick glance.

Here's an extremely important point for you to remember: You should also look for opportunities in growing divisions that serve special niches, even when the company as a whole is cutting jobs. For example, a firm's online division may be growing, even while its traditional business units are shrinking.

Additional key factors for strong corporate growth, and thereby the best job prospects, include:

1) Companies or divisions with a growing share of a promising market.

Management's ability to anticipate or create change in the marketplace makes for a growing company with great prospects. For example, Sam Walton revolutionized the department store business by realizing that consumers want everyday low prices on name-brand merchandise. He created Wal-Mart, while competitor Sears suffered by maintaining an old-fashioned policy of special sales events on private-label goods. Wal-Mart rapidly became one of the largest creators of new jobs in the private sector. Sears was forced to close multiple stores and slash its employee ranks.

Microsoft made its way to the top with unique products serving a soaring market when it developed highly functional software for personal computers. The software giant created thousands of millionaire employees through the immense increase in the value of its stock plans. HEB, an innovative grocer in Texas, has evolved continually over the decades, constantly introducing improvements to store layouts, and even creating an exciting new HEB Marketplace concept that is a retail industry leader. HEB has large numbers of job openings of many types on a continuous basis.

The point to these stories is that you shouldn't invest your career in a company with mediocre prospects. With perseverance, you can target your own list of employers that are posting growth due to competitive advantages or growing market demand. Your best bets are companies taking reasonable risks in order to move ahead. Those risks may include investments in advertising, research and development, new technology, improved techniques on the manufacturing floor, testing of new products and the opening of new retail store formats. For example, Chico's FAS stores scored a hit by filling a niche in the women's apparel market, and Genentech became a leader in the biotechnology field by risking vast amounts on research. Also, don't overlook the potential of the export market—many American firms find much of their growth by creating products and services that enjoy demand overseas as well as in the U.S.

2) Sales and profits: past and present.

The companies most likely to move along at a good clip are those with an exciting mid-term history. Firms with an average annual growth in sales of 10% to 15% or more over the past several years are generally very promising. Companies that managed to get through the recent recession with only minor drops in revenues may be remarkably stable. Many small and mid-size firms grow at much faster rates and find themselves hiring continuously.

3) Beware of fads.

Unfortunately, a few companies post meteoric growth in businesses that turn out to be mere fads. The restaurant industry suffers from this problem on a regular basis. In recent years, companies selling bagels, frozen yogurt, rotisserie chicken and the like enjoyed impressive, nationwide growth only to collapse like a house of cards a couple of years later.

How to Find and Use Expert Opinions:

Superior sources used by sophisticated job researchers include reports written by: 1) analysts; 2) professional researchers and executives; and 3) journalists at business magazines and industry-specific web sites. Many major libraries have large collections of industry-specific "trade magazines" that can give you vital clues that competing job seekers will overlook. Virtually every industry is covered by one or two major websites and trade magazines that will give you leads to growing companies. Many articles in these resources contain the names of executives you may want to contact. Also, some trade magazines publish help-wanted ads in the back. It's easy to do an online search for trade magazines and industry-specific websites, and many of them are filled with extremely useful information. For example, a recent search on Google for "pet industry trade magazine" quickly turned up leads to the top magazines for that sector.

Next, move on to reports from experts. Marketing and investment professionals are looking for some of the same clues you should use as a job seeker, and reports written by full-time analysts who cover specific companies or industries can help you find firms that are growing and hiring. Search the internet for white papers, industry reports and studies that cover your industry of interest.

Professionally written market research can be found at Marketresearch.com, www.marketresearch.com. This market research broker charges varying fees for access to the reports. However, many of the reports are reasonably priced, and the insight you gain into industries, markets and leading companies can be extremely helpful. Web sites such as this offer the ability to search for reports by a wide variety of criteria, including company name and industry.

Internet Research Tip:

Be sure to create Google "Alerts" to follow your targeted employers and profession. Google will email results to you daily.

By going to the "more" link at the top of the Google home page, and then selecting "even more" from the drop-down list, you can access Google's "Alerts" tool. Here you can arrange to receive email updates on topics of your choice. For example, you can set a general alert about an industry or locale: sales jobs in California, for example. Or something like: opportunities in the American wireless industry. Or even: sales jobs at automobile dealers.

You can use alerts to track specific jobs or employers. For example: openings at Intel. Or: regional sales manager opening Los Angeles. Finally, don't forget that you may want to put a search phrase within quotes to get an exact match to part of your phrase. For example: "loan officer" wanted.

Other Basic Resources:

Annual Reports/10-Ks/S-1s: Companies that sell their stocks to the public, including most of the firms covered in this book, publish annual reports that contain a wealth of information. Annual reports and 10-Ks cover yearly results, financial statements, management practices and other vital information for publicly held firms. S-1s provide the same type of information on companies that are selling stock to the public for the first time. You can find copies of these reports at large libraries. Online, the best place to acquire this information is at typically at the "Investors" tab on the website of the company you are researching. Alternately, try the site of the U.S. Securities and Exchange Commission. They have a user-friendly service that enables you to search for companies and access their financial reports at www.sec.gov. (Look for the "Filings & Forms" section, and then see "Search for Company Filings.") Look especially at the five-year "summary financial statement" in the back of these reports. Also, look for growth in sales and earnings. If these are falling, dig deeper to find out why. Faltering sales or profits can lead to layoffs or to a merger with another firm (which could result in deep job cuts).

Also, you can find a wealth of financial information on publicly-traded firms at Yahoo! Finance, http://finance.yahoo.com.

See Chapter 4, "Important Contacts for Job Seekers," for additional places to get basic corporate data.

Tips on Utilizing Financial Documents Filed by Publicly Held Firms

(Access these documents at the Securities Exchange Commission, www.sec.gov.)

10-K (also called Annual Report on Form 10-K): This is an annual filing required by federal law. It follows a standard format. Information includes a complete description of the business, risk factors, historical financial data and much more. It is vital reading for job seekers. You will find that these documents are written in dry, legal language, but they contain a wealth of information.

DEF 14A Proxy Statement: This is an annual document that gives shareholders certain options to consider at their annual meeting. It names the firm's board of directors and top management. It also gives the dollar value and description of salaries, bonuses, pension plans, stock options and other benefits enjoyed by the company's five highest-paid officers. Job seekers can learn a great deal about a firm's management, pay and benefits from this document. Included is a list of the people or organizations that own more than 5% of the company's stock.

S-1: This is a new registration document for companies that are going public for the first time. In other words, they are creating an IPO (initial public offering). The information includes all of the data found in the 10-K and proxy statement filed annually by companies that have been public for more than one year.

10-Q: This is a quarterly report detailing a company's latest sales, profits and balance sheet.

Press Releases: Most mid-size to large companies issue a continual stream of press releases about new products, technologies and locations; new executive appointments; community activities and a wide variety of other company developments. The best place to find these is online, at the "News" tab on the company's own web site. You can also search popular business press release services such as www.prnewswire.com and www.businesswire.com.

More Ways to Research an Employer's Financial Stability and Growth Plans:

1) Check out its bond rating.

There's no sense in trying to become a financial analyst on your own. Use internet searches to look for the bond ratings of potential employers. These ratings are based on a company's ability to pay principal and interest when due. If you're considering a major corporation with a bond rating of less than BB (an indicator that a company's debt is riskier than "investment grade"), you should do a lot more investigating before you continue chasing a job at that company.

2) Talk to vendors and current employees.

Talk to employees who work for the employer, or talk to people who do business with it. No one knows what's really going on better than people who are on the scene. If there are problems that are not yet known by the media, or if there are exciting new developments that have not yet been announced, you may find out a lot just by asking around. While you're at it, ask about corporate culture—how well are employees treated?

Popular Job-Search Internet Sites

CareerBuilder	www.careerbuilder.com
Monster	www.monster.com

Tips on Finding Information on Privately Held Employers

Our subscription service, Plunkett Research Online, and our printed Plunkett's industry almanacs, are among the world's most highly regarded sources of profiles of privately-held companies. Check with your library to see if you have access to these tools.

Study back-issue indexes and archives to major newspapers to see what journalists are reporting about a prospective private employer. Many libraries have recent issues of *The Wall Street Journal, The New York Times* and other important business newspapers. At major public and university libraries, you may be able to access online databases like ProQuest. These databases have excellent search engines that lead you into online archives of the best publications, including *The Wall Street Journal*, as well as many trade magazines and local business journals.

For smaller firms, go online and try American Journalism Review at www.newslink.org, where you'll be able to search news sites including hometown newspapers across the nation. Likewise, search local business newspapers at www.bizjournals.com, where you'll find links to dozens of major business weeklies like the *Houston Business Journal*.

Finally, consider investing in a credit report. If you really want reassurance, go to Experian SmartBusinessReports, www.smartbusinessreports.com. You can use its links to order a credit report on the employer. These reports are reasonably priced, and they can help you determine whether the company is paying its bills on time or has other problems. This could be vital in helping you determine whether to accept a job at a privately-held firm.

---

3) Use Internet search engines.

Look up your firm and industry in an internet search engine such as Google. (You may need to click on "News" instead of relying on a general web search.) There, you may find unusual articles that were recently written about a company's product breakthroughs, treatment of women or minorities, human interest stories, training programs or stories written from other unique slants.

4) Study other business books and guides.

Search at a library or at an online bookseller like Amazon.com for recent books regarding major companies. For example, if you want to apply to biotech leader Genentech for a job, don't fail to read *The Billion Dollar Molecule: One Company's Quest for the Perfect Drug.* With a little research, you can turn up many other excellent books about specific companies, from banks like Bank of America to publishers like Gannett.

Great Places for Industry Research

Plunkett Research, www.plunkettresearch.com. Go to the specific industry of your choice to see an overview of trends and statistics. At our subscription service, www.plunkettresearchonline.com, subscribers have access to thousands of pages of industry analysis, statistics, contacts and company profiles, along with multiple search and export tools.

Wetfeet.com, www.wetfeet.com. Publishes snapshots of hundreds of employers.

Vault.com, www.vault.com. This site publishes insights about careers with hundreds of leading firms.

---

5) Explore industry-specific web sites.

In particular, study the leading industry associations for the sector in which you want to work. You will find listings of hundreds of the most important organizations, professional societies and resources, personally selected by our editors, in the almanacs published by Plunkett Research, Ltd., and in the contacts databases at Plunkett Research Online.

6) Research benefits and pension plans.

For additional information about corporate pension plans, start with the government agency charged with protecting and regulating pensions: the Pension Benefit Guaranty Corporation, 1200 K St. NW, Washington, D.C. 20005-4026, 202-326-4000, www.pbgc.gov. They can answer certain questions over the telephone.

The U.S. Department of Labor publishes a useful book titled "Protect your Pension." They can be contacted at: U.S. Department of Labor, Employee Benefits Security Administration, 200 Constitution Ave. NW, Room N5635, Washington, D.C. 20210, 866-444-3272 or 202-219-8776, www.dol.gov/ebsa/publications/main.html.

The Social Security Administration, 800-772-1213, www.ssa.gov, can provide you with information regarding your potential Social Security benefits.

NOTE: Generally, employees covered by wealth-building benefit plans do not fully own ("vest in") funds contributed on their behalf by the employer until as many as five years of service with that employer have passed. All pension plans are voluntary—that is, employers are not obligated to offer pensions.

Pension Plans: The type and generosity of these plans vary widely from firm to firm. Caution: Some employers refer to plans as "pension" or "retirement" plans when they are actually 401(k) savings plans that require a contribution by the employee.

Defined Benefit Pension Plans: Pension plans that do not require a contribution from the employee are infrequently offered. However, a few companies, particularly larger employers in high-profit-margin industries, offer defined benefit pension plans where the employee is guaranteed to receive a set pension benefit upon retirement. The amount of the benefit is determined by the years of service with the company and the employee's salary during the later years of employment. The longer a person works for the employer, the higher the retirement benefit. These defined benefit plans are funded entirely by the employer. The benefits, up to a reasonable limit, are guaranteed by the Federal Government's Pension Benefit Guaranty Corporation. These plans are not portable—if you leave the company, you cannot transfer your benefits into a different plan. Instead, upon retirement you will receive the benefits that vested during your service with the company. If your employer offers a pension plan, it must give you a "summary plan description" within 90 days of the date you join the plan. You can also request a "summary annual report" of the plan, and once every 12 months you may request an "individual benefit statement" accounting of your interest in the plan.

Defined Contribution Plans: These are quite different. They do not guarantee a certain amount of pension benefit. Instead, they set out circumstances under which the employer will make a contribution to a plan on your behalf. The most common example is the 401(k) savings plan. Pension benefits are not guaranteed under these plans.

Cash Balance Pension Plans: These plans were recently invented. They are hybrid plans—part defined benefit and part defined contribution. Many employers have converted their older defined benefit plans into cash balance plans. The employer makes deposits (or credits a given amount of money) on the employee's behalf, usually based on a percentage of pay. Employee accounts grow based on a predetermined interest benchmark, such as the interest rate on Treasury Bonds. There are some advantages to these plans, particularly for younger workers: a) The benefits, up to a reasonable limit, are guaranteed by the Pension Benefit Guaranty Corporation. b) Benefits are portable—they can be moved to another plan when the employee changes companies. c) Younger workers and those who spend a shorter number of years with an employer may receive higher benefits than they would under a traditional defined benefit plan.

ESOP Stock Plan (Employees' Stock Ownership Plan): This type of plan is becoming rare, but it can be of great value to employees. Typically, the plan borrows money from a bank and uses those funds to purchase a large block of the corporation's stock. The corporation makes contributions to the plan over a period of time, and the stock purchase loan is eventually paid off. The value of the plan grows significantly as long as the market price of the stock holds up. Qualified employees are allocated a share of the plan based on their length of service and their level of salary. Under federal regulations, participants in ESOPs are allowed to diversify their account holdings in set percentages that rise as the employee ages and gains years of service with the company. In this manner, not all of the employee's assets are tied up in the employer's stock.

Savings Plan, 401(k): Under this type of plan, employees make a tax-deferred deposit into an account. In the best plans, the company makes annual matching donations to the employees' accounts, typically in some proportion to deposits made by the employees themselves. A good plan will match one-half of employee deposits of up to 6% of wages. For example, an employee earning $30,000 yearly might deposit $1,800 (6%) into the plan. The company will match one-half of the employee's deposit, or $900. The plan grows on a tax-deferred basis, similar to an IRA. A very generous plan will match 100% of employee deposits. However, some plans do not call for the employer to make a matching deposit at all. Other plans call for a matching contribution to be made at the discretion of the firm's board of directors. Actual terms of these plans vary widely from firm to firm. Generally, these savings plans allow employees to deposit as much as 15% of salary into the plan on a tax-deferred basis. However, the portion that the company uses to calculate its matching deposit is generally limited to a maximum of 6%. Employees should take care to diversify the holdings in their 401(k) accounts, and most people should seek professional guidance or investment management for their accounts. (Note: when profits are down, many employers exercise their right to suspend their contributions to 401(k)s. Employees may continue to make contributions, but they will not be matched by the employer in these cases.)

Stock Purchase Plan: Qualified employees may purchase the company's common stock at a price below its market value under a specific plan. Typically, the employee is limited to investing a small percentage of wages in this plan. The discount may range from 5% to 15%. Some of these plans allow for deposits to be made through regular monthly payroll deductions. However, new accounting rules for corporations, along with other factors, are leading many companies to curtail these plans—dropping the discount allowed, cutting the maximum yearly stock purchase or otherwise making the plans less generous or appealing.

Profit Sharing: Qualified employees are awarded an annual amount equal to some portion of a company's profits. In a very generous plan, the pool of money awarded to employees would be 15% of profits. Typically, this money is deposited into a long-term retirement account. Caution: Some employers refer to plans as "profit sharing" when they are actually 401(k) savings plans. True profit sharing plans are rarely offered.

Plunkett Research Online and Plunkett's Industry Reference Books:

1) Internet-Based Services: Plunkett Research Online is a reference service that is subscribed to by the nation's leading university placement offices, libraries and information offices. You can use it to filter prospective employers by location, industry, size and more. You can then export contact information for those companies into spreadsheets or text files. In addition, you can use the site to research the latest editions of our industry analysis. Many additional tools for job seekers are included. For an extensive online tour, see www.plunkettresearch.com.

2) Plunkett's Industry Almanacs: Plunkett Research also publishes industry-specific almanacs for the world's most vital industries. They are available in both printed and eBook editions. These are top-notch resources for job seekers.

Industry-Specific Books from Plunkett Research:

- Plunkett's Advertising & Branding Industry Almanac
- Plunkett's Aerospace, Aircraft, Satellites & Drones Industry Almanac
- Plunkett's Airline, Hotel & Travel Industry Almanac
- Plunkett's Almanac of Middle Market Companies
- Plunkett's Apparel & Textiles Industry Almanac
- Plunkett's Automobile Industry Almanac
- Plunkett's Banking, Mortgages & Credit Industry Almanac
- Plunkett's Biotech & Genetics Industry Almanac
- Plunkett's Chemicals, Coatings & Plastics Industry Almanac
- Plunkett's Consulting Industry Almanac
- Plunkett's Consumer Products, Cosmetics, Hair & Personal Services Industry Almanac
- Plunkett's E-Commerce & Internet Business Almanac
- Plunkett's Education, EdTech and MOOCs Industry Almanac
- Plunkett's Energy Industry Almanac
- Plunkett's Engineering & Research Industry Almanac
- Plunkett's Entertainment & Media Industry Almanac
- Plunkett's Food Industry Almanac
- Plunkett's Games, Apps & Social Media Industry Almanac
- Plunkett's Green Technology Industry Almanac
- Plunkett's Health Care Industry Almanac
- Plunkett's Insurance Industry Almanac

- Plunkett's InfoTech Industry Almanac
- Plunkett's Investment & Securities Industry Almanac
- Plunkett's Manufacturing & Robotics Industry Almanac
- Plunkett's Outsourcing & Offshoring Industry Almanac
- Plunkett's Real Estate & Construction Industry Almanac
- Plunkett's Renewable, Alternative & Hydrogen Energy Industry Almanac
- Plunkett's Restaurant & Hospitality Industry Almanac
- Plunkett's Retail Industry Almanac
- Plunkett's Sharing & Gig Economy, Freelance Workers & On-Demand Delivery Almanac
- Plunkett's Sports Industry Almanac
- Plunkett's Telecommunications Industry Almanac
- Plunkett's Transportation, Supply Chain & Logistics Industry Almanac
- Plunkett's Wireless & Cellular Telephone Industry Almanac

Publications from Plunkett Research Written Especially for Job Seekers:

- The Almanac of American Employers
- Plunkett's Companion to the Almanac of American Employers

Our books will give you in-depth coverage of specific industries and the leading firms in those industries, along with trends and developments in technology and services. You will find these books in public and academic libraries, college placement offices, human resources offices, corporate libraries and government agency libraries. For sample chapters and additional details, you can preview as well as purchase these books at www.plunkettresearch.com.

The Almanac of American Employers provides profiles and detailed listings of 500 hand-picked, U.S. employers of 2,500 employees or more in size

Plunkett's Companion to The Almanac of American Employers is our book that provides profiles on 500 additional, rapidly growing corporate employers. This companion book covers smaller firms than those in the main volume of *The Almanac of American Employers*.

Chapter 4

IMPORTANT CONTACTS FOR JOB SEEKERS

Contents:

1) Accountants & CPAs Associations
2) Advertising/Marketing Associations
3) Aerospace & Defense Industry Associations
4) Airline & Air Cargo Industry Associations
5) Alternative Energy-Ethanol
6) Alternative Energy-Solar
7) Alternative Energy-Wind
8) Banking Industry Associations
9) Biotechnology & Biological Industry Associations
10) Booksellers Associations
11) Broadcasting, Cable, Radio & TV Associations
12) Careers-Airlines/Flying
13) Careers-Apparel
14) Careers-Banking
15) Careers-Biotech
16) Careers-Coatings
17) Careers-Computers/Technology
18) Careers-Contract & Freelance
19) Careers-First Time Jobs/New Grads
20) Careers-General Job Listings
21) Careers-Health Care
22) Careers-Job Listings for Seniors
23) Careers-Job Listings Hong Kong, China, Singapore, Asia
24) Careers-Job Reference Tools
25) Careers-Restaurants
26) Careers-Science

27) Careers-Sports
28) Careers-Video Games Industry
29) Chemicals Industry Associations
30) Communications Professional Associations
31) Computer & Electronics Industry Associations
32) Consulting Industry Associations
33) Consulting Industry Resources
34) Corporate Information Resources
35) Disabling Conditions
36) Electronic Health Records/Continuity of Care Records
37) Energy Associations-Electric Power
38) Energy Associations-Natural Gas
39) Energy Associations-Other
40) Energy Associations-Petroleum, Exploration, Production, etc.
41) Engineering Industry Associations
42) Engineering, Research & Scientific Associations
43) Entertainment & Amusement Associations-General
44) Film & Theater Associations
45) Fitness Industry Associations
46) Food Industry Associations, General
47) Food Industry Resources, General

48) Food Processor Industry Associations
49) Food Service Industry Associations
50) Games Industry Associations
51) Grocery Industry Associations
52) Health & Nutrition Associations
53) Health Care Business & Professional Associations
54) Health Insurance Industry Associations
55) Hearing & Speech
56) Hotel/Lodging Associations
57) Human Resources Industry Associations
58) Industry Research/Market Research
59) Insurance Industry Associations
60) Insurance Industry Associations-Agents & Brokers
61) Magazines, Business & Financial
62) MBA Resources
63) Online Recruiting & Employment ASPs & Solutions
64) Outsourcing Industry Associations
65) Pensions, Benefits & 401(k) Associations
66) Pensions, Benefits & 401(k) Resources
67) Pharmaceutical Industry Associations (Drug Industry)
68) Pilots Associations
69) Printers & Publishers Associations

70) Real Estate Industry Associations
71) Recording & Music Associations
72) Satellite-Related Professional Organizations
73) Securities Industry Associations
74) Software Industry Associations
75) Stocks & Financial Markets Data
76) Telecommunications Industry Associations
77) Temporary Staffing Firms
78) Testing Resources
79) Textile & Fabric Associations
80) Travel Business & Professional Associations
81) Travel Industry Associations
82) U.S. Government Agencies
83) Water Technologies & Resources
84) Wireless & Cellular Industry Associations
85) Writers, Photographers & Editors Associations

1) Accountants & CPA Associations

American Institute of CPAs (AICPA)
1211 Ave. of the Americas
New York, NY 10036-8775 US
Phone: 212-596-6200
Fax: 800-362-5066
Toll Free: 888-777-7077
E-mail Address: *service@aicpa.org*
Web Address: www.aicpa.org
American Institute of CPAs (AICPA) represents nearly 370,000 members in 128 countries involved in the accounting profession. Its web site provides information and news for CPAs, news from the organization and a search for accounting firms.

Council of Petroleum Accountants Societies, Inc. (COPAS)
445 Union Blvd., Ste. 207
Lakewood, CO 80228 USA
Phone: 303-300-1131
Toll Free: 877-992-6727
Web Address: www.copas.org
The Council of Petroleum Accountants Societies, Inc. (COPAS) provides a forum for discussing and solving the variety of problems related to accounting for oil and gas. COPAS also provides valuable educational materials related to oil and gas accounting.

International Accounting Standards Board (IASB)
30 Cannon St.
London, EC4M 6XH UK
Phone: 44-20-7246-6410
Fax: 44-20-7246-6411
E-mail Address: info@ifrs.org
Web Address: www.ifrs.org
The International Accounting Standards Board (IASB) website hosts an electronic subscription service to the International Financial Reporting (IFRS) Standards as well access to IFRS summaries.

2) Advertising/Marketing Associations

4A's (American Association of Advertising Agencies)
1065 Ave. of the Americas, Fl. 16
New York, NY 10018 USA
Phone: 212-682-2500
Web Address: www.aaaa.org
The 4A's (American Association of Advertising Agencies) is the national trade association representing the advertising agency industry in the U.S.

Advertising Women of New York (AWNY)
28 W. 44th St., Ste. 912
New York, NY 10036 USA
Phone: 212-221-7969
E-mail Address: lynn.branigan@awny.org
Web Address: www.awny.org
Advertising Women of New York (AWNY) provides a forum for personal and professional growth, serves as a catalyst for the advancement of women in the communications field and promotes and supports philanthropic endeavors through the AWNY Foundation. The web site also provides content from Women Executives in Public Relations (WERP), such as its a dynamic job board.

American Institute of Graphic Arts (AIGA)
233 Broadway, Fl. 17
New York, NY 10279 USA
Phone: 212-807-1990
Web Address: www.aiga.org
The American Institute of Graphic Arts (AIGA) strives to further excellence in communication design, both as a strategic tool for business and as a cultural force.

American Marketing Association (AMA)
130 E. Randolph St., Fl. 22
Chicago, IL 60601 USA
Phone: 312-542-9000
Fax: 312-542-9001
Toll Free: 800-262-1150

Web Address: www.ama.org
The American Marketing Association (AMA) serves marketing professionals in both business and education and serves all levels of marketing practitioners, educators and students.

Cable & Telecommunications Association for Marketing (CTAM)
120 Waterfront St., Ste. 200
National Harbor, MD 20745 USA
Phone: 301-485-8900
Fax: 301-560-4964
E-mail Address: info@ctam.com
Web Address: www.ctam.com
The Cable & Telecommunications Association for Marketing (CTAM) is dedicated to the discipline and development of consumer marketing excellence in cable television, new media and telecommunications services.

Direct Marketing Association (DMA)
1120 Ave. of the Americas
New York, NY 10036-6700 USA
Phone: 212-768-7277
Web Address: thedma.org
The Direct Marketing Association (DMA) is the oldest and largest trade association for users and suppliers in the direct, database and interactive marketing fields.

3) Aerospace & Defense Industry Associations

American Institute of Aeronautics and Astronautics (AIAA)
12700 Sunrise Valley Dr., Ste. 200
Reston, VA 20191-5807 USA
Phone: 703-264-7500
Fax: 703-264-7551
Toll Free: 800-639-2422
E-mail Address: custserv@aiaa.org
Web Address: www.aiaa.org
The American Institute of Aeronautics and Astronautics (AIAA) is a nonprofit society aimed at advancing the arts, sciences and technology of aeronautics and astronautics. The institute represents the U.S. in the International Astronautical Federation and the International Council on the Aeronautical Sciences.

4) Airline & Air Cargo Industry Associations

International Air Transport Association (IATA)
800 Place Victoria
P.O. Box 113
Montreal, QC H4Z 1M1 Canada
Phone: 514-874-0202
Web Address: www.iata.org

The International Air Transport Association (IATA) represents about 260 airlines in order to offer the highest standards of passenger and cargo service.

5) Alternative Energy-Ethanol

Renewable Fuels Association (RFA)
425 3rd St. SW, Ste. 1150
Washington, DC 20024 USA
Phone: 202-289-3835
Fax: 202-289-7519
Web Address: www.ethanolrfa.org
The Renewable Fuels Association (RFA) is a trade organization representing the ethanol industry. It publishes a wealth of useful information, including a listing of biorefineries and monthly U.S. fuel ethanol production and demand.

6) Alternative Energy-Solar

Solar Energy Industries Association (SEIA)
600 14th St. NW, Ste. 400
Washington, DC 20005 USA
Phone: 202-682-0556
E-mail Address: info@seia.org
Web Address: www.seia.org
Established in 1974, the Solar Energy Industries Association is the American trade association of the solar energy industry. Among its operations is a web site that provides news for the solar energy industry, links to related products and companies and solar energy statistics.

7) Alternative Energy-Wind

American Wind Energy Association (AWEA)
1501 M St. NW, Ste. 1000
Washington, DC 20005 USA
Phone: 202-383-2500
Fax: 202-383-2505
Web Address: www.awea.org
The American Wind Energy Association (AWEA) promotes wind energy as a clean source of electricity worldwide. Its website provides excellent resources for research, including an online library, discussions of legislation, and descriptions of wind technologies.

8) Banking Industry Associations

American Bankers Association (ABA)
1120 Connecticut Ave. NW
Washington, DC 20036 USA
Toll Free: 800-226-5377

E-mail Address: custserv@aba.com
Web Address: www.aba.com
The American Bankers Association (ABA) represents banks of all sizes on issues of national importance for financial institutions and their customers. The site offers financial information and solutions, financial news and member access to further advice and content.

9) Biotechnology & Biological Industry Associations

Biotechnology Industry Organization (BIO)
1201 Maryland Ave. SW, Ste. 900
Washington, DC 20024 USA
Phone: 202-962-9200
Fax: 202-488-6301
E-mail Address: info@bio.org
Web Address: www.bio.org
The Biotechnology Industry Organization (BIO) represents members involved in the research and development of health care, agricultural, industrial and environmental biotechnology products. BIO has both small and large member organizations.

10) Booksellers Associations

American Booksellers Association, Inc.
333 Westchester Ave., Ste. S202
White Plains, NY 10604 USA
Phone: 914-406-7500
Fax: 914-417-4013
Toll Free: 800-637-0037
E-mail Address: info@bookweb.org
Web Address: www.bookweb.org
The American Booksellers Association is a nonprofit association representing independent bookstores in the United States.

11) Broadcasting, Cable, Radio & TV Associations

Academy of Television Arts and Sciences
5220 Lankershim Blvd.
North Hollywood, CA 91601-3109 USA
Phone: 818-754-2800
Web Address: www.emmys.tv
The Academy of Television Arts and Sciences is a nonprofit corporation devoted to the advancement of telecommunications arts and sciences and to fostering creative leadership in the telecommunications industry. It is one of three organizations that administer the Emmy Awards. It is responsible for prime time Emmys.

Alliance for Women in Media
1760 Old Meadow Rd., Ste. 500
McLean, VA 22102 USA
Phone: 703-506-3290
Fax: 703-506-3266
E-mail Address: info@allwomeninmedia.org
Web Address: www.allwomeninmedia.org/
The Alliance for Women in Media, formerly the American Women in Radio and Television (AWRT), founded in 1951, is a national nonprofit organization dedicated to advancing the role of women in electronic media and related fields.

Association of America's Public Television Stations (APTS)
2100 Crystal Dr., Ste. 700
Arlington, VA 22202 USA
Phone: 202-654-4200
Fax: 202-654-4236
E-mail Address: skarp@apts.org
Web Address: www.apts.org
The Association of America's Public Television Stations (APTS) is a nonprofit membership organization formed to support the continued growth and development of strong and financially sound noncommercial television service for the American public.

Broadcast Education Association (BEA)
1771 N St. NW
Washington, DC 20036-2891 USA
Phone: 202-429-3935
Fax: 202-775-2981
E-mail Address: tbailey@nab.org
Web Address: www.beaweb.org
The Broadcast Education Association (BEA) is the professional association for professors, industry professionals and graduate students interested in teaching and research related to electronic media and multimedia enterprises.

National Academy of Television Arts and Sciences
1697 Broadway, Ste. 404
New York, NY 10019 USA
Phone: 212-586-8424
Fax: 212-246-8129
E-mail Address: ppillitteri@emmyonline.tv
Web Address: www.emmyonline.org
The National Academy of Television Arts and Sciences is dedicated to the advancement of the arts and sciences of television and the promotion of creative leadership for artistic, educational and technical achievements within the television industry. It is responsible for awarding the Emmy Awards.

National Association of Broadcasters (NAB)
1771 N St. NW
Washington, DC 20036 USA
Phone: 202-429-5300
Toll Free: 800-622-3976
E-mail Address: nab@nab.org
Web Address: www.nab.org
The National Association of Broadcasters (NAB) represents broadcasters for radio and television. The organization also provides benefits to employees of member companies and to individuals and companies that provide products and services to the electronic media industries.

National Association of Television Program Executives (NATPE)
5757 Wilshire Blvd., Penthouse 10
Los Angeles, CA 90036-3681 USA
Phone: 310-857-1601
E-mail Address: jpbommel@natpe.org
Web Address: www.natpe.org
The National Association of Television Program Executives (NATPE) is the leading association for content professionals in the global television industry. It is dedicated to the growth of video content development, creations, production, financing and distribution across various platforms by providing education and networking opportunities to its members.

National Cable and Telecommunications Association (NCTA)
25 Massachusetts Ave. NW, Ste. 100
Washington, DC 20001-1413 USA
Phone: 202-222-2300
Fax: 202-222-2514
E-mail Address: info@ncta.com
Web Address: www.ncta.com
The National Cable and Telecommunications Association (NCTA) is the principal trade association of the cable television industry in the United States. It represents cable operators as well as over 200 cable program networks that produce TV shows.

Radio Television Digital News Association (RTDNA)
529 14th St. NW, Ste. 1240
Washington, DC 20045 USA
Fax: 202-223-4007
E-mail Address: mikec@rtdna.org
Web Address: www.rtdna.org
The Radio Television Digital News Association (RTDNA), formerly the Radio-Television News Directors Association (RTNDA), is the world's largest professional organization exclusively committed to professionals in electronic journalism.

Screen Actor's Guild, American Federation of Television and Radio Artists (SAG-AFTRA)
5757 Wilshire Blvd., Fl. 7
Los Angeles, CA 90036-3600 USA
Phone: 323-634-8100
Fax: 323-549-6792
Toll Free: 855-724-2387
E-mail Address: sagaftrainfo@sagaftra.org
Web Address: www.sagaftra.org
The Screen Actors Guild, American Federation of Television and Radio Artists (SAG-AFTRA), a product of the merger of the Screen Actors Guild (SAG) and the American Federation of Television and Radio Artists (AFTRA), is a national labor union representing actors and other professional performers and broadcasters in television, radio, sound recordings, non-broadcast/industrial programming and new technologies such as interactive programming and CD-ROMs.

Screen Actors Guild-American Federation of Television and Radio Artists (SAG-AFTRA)
5757 Wilshire Blvd., Fl. 7
Los Angeles, CA 90036-3600 USA
Phone: 323-634-8100
Fax: 323-549-6792
Toll Free: 855-724-2387
E-mail Address: sagaftrainfo@sagaftra.org
Web Address: www.sagaftra.org
The Screen Actors Guild-American Federation of Television and Radio Artists (SAG-AFTRA), a product of the merger of the Screen Actors Guild (SAG) and the American Federation of Television and Radio Artists (AFTRA), is a national labor union representing actors and other professional performers and broadcasters in television, radio, sound recordings, non-broadcast/industrial programming and new technologies such as interactive programming and CD-ROMs.

Women in Cable & Telecommunications (WICT)
14555 Avion Pkwy., Ste. 250
Chantilly, VA 20151 USA
Phone: 703-234-9810
Fax: 703-817-1595
E-mail Address: tgibson@wict.org
Web Address: www.wict.org
Women in Cable & Telecommunications (WICT) exists to advance the position and influence of women in media through leadership programs and services at both the national and local level.

12) Careers-Airlines/Flying

Aviation/Aerospace/Defense Jobs Page
920 Morgan St., Ste. T
Des Moines, IA 50309 USA
Fax: 515-243-5384
Toll Free: 800-292-7731
E-mail Address: customerservice@nationjob.com
Web Address: www.nationjob.com/aviation
The Aviation/Aerospace Jobs Page, a division of NationJob, Inc., features detailed aviation and aerospace job listings and company profiles.

AviationJobSearch.com
7955 NW 12th St., Ste. 401
Miami, 33126 USA
Phone: 786-433-7120 ext. 203
Fax: 305-716-4064
E-mail Address: info@aviationjobsearch.com
Web Address: www.aviationjobsearch.com
AviationJobSearch.com lists jobs related to the airline industry.

Avjobs, Inc.
9609 S. University Blvd., Unit 630830
Littleton, CO 80163-3032 USA
Phone: 303-683-2322
Fax: 303-683-5239
E-mail Address: info@avjobs.com
Web Address: www.avjobs.com
Avjobs, Inc. is a group of employers dedicated to helping individuals obtain aviation, airline, aerospace and airport careers.

Flightdeck Recruitment Ltd.
15 High St., W. Mersea
Colchester, Essex CO5 8QA UK
E-mail Address: contact@flightdeckrecruitment.com
Web Address: www.flightdeckrecruitment.com
Flightdeck Recruitment Ltd. provides a link between aviation recruiters who are looking for flight deck crew and pilots or flight engineers who are seeking employment.

13) Careers-Apparel

24 Seven Fashion Recruitment
120 Wooster St., Fl. 4
New York, NY 10012 USA
Phone: 212-966-4426
Fax: 212-966-2313
E-mail Address: newyork@24seventalent.com
Web Address: www.24seventalent.com

24 Seven Fashion Recruitment is an employment agency serving the fashion, beauty, entertainment, advertising, marketing and retail industries.

Fashion Career Center
950 Tower Ln., Fl. 6
Foster City, CA 94404 USA
Web Address:
www.fashioncareercenter.com
The Fashion Career Center site provides employees and employers with a place to meet and access information about employment in the fashion industry. The FashionCareerCenter.com web site offers links to fashion jobs and fashion schools, as well as offering fashion career advice.

14) Careers-Banking

National Banking & Financial Service Network (NBFSN)
3075 Brickhouse Ct.
Virginia Beach, VA 23452-6860 USA
Phone: 757-463-5766
Fax: 757-340-0826
E-mail Address: smurrell@nbn-jobs.com
Web Address: www.nbn-jobs.com/
The National Banking & Financial Service Network (NBFSN) is made up of recruiting firms in the banking and financial services marketplace. The web site provides job listings.

15) Careers-Biotech

BiotechEmployment.com
E-mail Address:
jobs@Biotechemployment.com
Web Address:
www.biotechemployment.com
BiotechEmployment.com is an online resource for job seekers in biotechnology. The site's features include resume posting, job search agents and employer profiles. It is part of the eJobstores.com, Inc., which includes the Health Care Job Store sites.

Chase Group (The)
10975 Grandview Dr., Ste. 100
Overland Park, KS 66210 USA
Phone: 913-663-3100
Fax: 913-663-3131
E-mail Address: chase@chasegroup.com
Web Address: www.chasegroup.com
The Chase Group is an executive search firm specializing in biomedical and pharmaceutical placement.

16) Careers-Coatings

CoatingsJobs.com
Web Address: www.coatingsjobs.com

CoatingsJobs.com connects coatings industry job seekers and employers. The web site offers job postings, resume postings, information for job seekers and an employment newsletter.

17) Careers-Computers/Technology

ComputerJobs.com, Inc.
1995 N. Park Pl., Ste. 375
Atlanta, GA 30339 USA
Toll Free: 800-850-0045
Web Address: www.computerjobs.com
ComputerJobs.com, Inc. is an employment web site that offers users a links to computer-related job opportunities organized by skill and market.

Dice.com
12150 Meredith Dr.
Urbandale, IA 50323 USA
Phone: 515-280-1144
Fax: 515-280-1452
Toll Free: 888-321-3423
E-mail Address: techsupport@dice.com
Web Address: www.dice.com
Dice.com provides free employment services for IT jobs. The site includes advanced job searches by geographic location and category, availability announcements and resume postings, as well as employer profiles, a recruiter's page and career links. It is maintained by Dice Holdings, Inc., a publicly traded company.

Institute for Electrical and Electronics Engineers (IEEE) Job Site
445 Hoes Ln.
Piscataway, NJ 08855-1331 USA
Phone: 732-981-0060
Toll Free: 800-678-4333
E-mail Address:
candidatejobsite@ieee.org
Web Address: careers.ieee.org
The Institute for Electrical and Electronics Engineers (IEEE) Job Site provides a host of employment services for technical professionals, employers and recruiters. The site offers job listings by geographic area, a resume bank and links to employment services.

Pencom Systems, Inc.
152 Remsen St.
Brooklyn, NY 11201 USA
Phone: 718-923-1111
Fax: 718-923-6065
E-mail Address: tom@pencom.com
Web Address: www.pencom.com
Pencom Systems, Inc., an open system recruiting company, hosts a career web

site geared toward high-technology and scientific professionals, featuring an interactive salary survey, career advisor, job listings and technology resources. Its focus is the financial services industry within the New York City area.

18) Careers-Contract & Freelance

Guru.com
5001 Baum Blvd., Ste. 760
Pittsburgh, PA 15213 USA
Toll Free: 888-678-0136
Web Address: www.guru.com
Guru.com provides contract job access for freelancers and contract workers, in fields ranging from interior design to architecture, marketing and web design, among others. Employers can post projects, and freelancers can offer bids on prospective jobs. Many tools are provided to enable freelancers to be completely informed about the scope of the work needed.

19) Careers-First Time Jobs/New Grads

Alumni-Network Recruitment Corporation
Alumni-Network Recruitment Corporation
Oakville, ON Canada
Phone: 905-465-2547
E-mail Address: karen@alumni-network.com
Web Address: www.alumni-network.com
Alumni-Network Recruitment Corporation is a professional search and recruiting firm, specializing in ERP, E-Commerce and Engineering.

CollegeGrad.com, Inc.
950 Tower Ln., Fl. 6
Foster City, CA 94404 USA
E-mail Address: info@quinstreet.com
Web Address: www.collegegrad.com
CollegeGrad.com, Inc. offers in-depth resources for college students and recent grads seeking entry-level jobs.

MonsterCollege
444 N. Michigan Ave., Ste. 600
Chicago, IL 60611 USA
E-mail Address:
info@college.monster.com
Web Address: www.college.monster.com
MonsterCollege provides information about internships and entry-level jobs, as well as career advice and resume tips, to recent college graduates.

National Association of Colleges and Employers (NACE)
62 Highland Ave.
Bethlehem, PA 18017-9085 USA
Phone: 610-868-1421
E-mail Address:
customer_service@naceweb.org
Web Address: www.naceweb.org
The National Association of Colleges and Employers (NACE) is a premier U.S. organization representing college placement offices and corporate recruiters who focus on hiring new grads.

20) Careers-General Job Listings

6FigureJobs
25 3rd St., Ste. 230
Stamford, CT 06905 USA
Phone: 203-326-8777
Toll Free: 800-605-5154
E-mail Address: info@6figurejobs.com
Web Address: www.6figurejobs.com
6FigureJobs offers executives a database of high-level positions. Membership is free for qualified individuals.

CareerBuilder, Inc.
200 N La Salle St., Ste. 1100
Chicago, IL 60601 USA
Phone: 773-527-3600
Fax: 773-353-2452
Toll Free: 800-891-8880
Web Address: www.careerbuilder.com
CareerBuilder, Inc. focuses on the needs of companies and also provides a database of job openings. The site has over 1 million jobs posted by 300,000 employers, and receives an average 23 million unique visitors monthly. The company also operates online career centers for 140 newspapers and 9,000 online partners. Resumes are sent directly to the company, and applicants can set up a special e-mail account for job-seeking purposes. CareerBuilder is primarily a joint venture between three newspaper giants: The McClatchy Company, Gannett Co., Inc. and Tribune Company.

CareerOneStop
Toll Free: 877-872-5627
E-mail Address: info@careeronestop.org
Web Address: www.careeronestop.org
CareerOneStop is operated by the employment commissions of various state agencies. It contains job listings in both the private and government sectors, as well as a wide variety of useful career resources and workforce information. CareerOneStop is sponsored by the U.S. Department of Labor.

Careers Organization (The)
4300 Horton St.
Emeryville, CA 94608 USA
Phone: 510-761-5805
Web Address: www.careers.org
The Career Organization is an online career resource center with links to jobs and other career-related web sites, as well as information regarding colleges and online degree programs.

CollegeRecruiter.com
3109 W. 50 St., Ste. 121
Minneapolis, MN 55410-2102 USA
Phone: 952-848-2211
Web Address: www.collegerecruiter.com
CollegeRecruiter.com provides college students with internship, part-time and summer job listings. Recent graduates can search for career opportunities by category and location.

ContractJobHunter
C. E. Publications, Inc.
P.O. Box 3006
Bothell, WA 98041-3006 USA
Phone: 425-806-5200
Fax: 425-806-5585
E-mail Address: staff@cjhunter.com
Web Address: cjhunter.com
ContractJobHunter is a web-based version of the magazine Contract Employment Weekly Online. It posts job listings and links to contract firms in the engineering, IT and technical fields. Libraries for reference materials and resume writing guidelines are also offered. The site is a service of C. E. Publications, Inc.

eFinancialCareers
1040 Ave. of the Americas, Ste. 16B
New York, NY 10018 USA
Phone: 212-370-8502
Web Address:
www.efinancialcareers.com
eFinancialCareers.com provides employment listings in the finance industry, as well as job tools such as salary surveys, resume writing assistance and industry news. It is owned DHI Group, Inc.

EmploymentGuide
4460 Corporation Ln., Ste. 317
Virginia Beach, VA 23462 USA
Toll Free: 877-876-4039
Web Address:
www.employmentguide.com
EmploymentGuide offers general career resources along with lists of position openings, company profiles and a resume database. It also circulates a free print publication.

EscapeArtist International
300 Caye Financial Center, Coconut Dr.
P.O. Box 11
San Pedro, Belize
Web Address: www.escapeartist.com
EscapeArtist.com provides job searches for overseas positions, as well as international working condition resources and immigration information. It's an online resource offering information, analysis and insights for international expat community in areas of business opportunities, employment, asset protection, investments and international real estate.

ExecuNet, Inc.
295 Westport Ave.
Norwalk, CT 06851 USA
Toll Free: 800-637-3126
E-mail Address:
member.services@execunet.com
Web Address: www.execunet.com
ExecuNet, Inc. is an executive career management information and contact service. It's a private career network for executives at the senior level offering career advancement, recruitment, coaching and advisory and peer networking opportunities.

HigherEdJobs.com
328 Innovation Blvd., Ste. 300
State College, PA 16803 USA
Phone: 814-861-3080
Fax: 814-861-3082
E-mail Address:
sales@HigherEdJobs.com
Web Address: www.higheredjobs.com
HigherEdJobs.com lists job vacancies in colleges and universities.

IMDiversity, Inc.
201 St. Charles Ave., Ste. 2502
New Orleans, LA 70170 USA
Phone: 281-265-2472
Fax: 281-265-2476
E-mail Address: admin@indiversity.com
Web Address: www.imdiversity.com
IMDiversity, Inc. provides job listings and career development information for minorities in the U.S., with a particular focus on African Americans, Asian Americans and Pacific Islanders, Latino/Hispanic Americans, Native Americans and women.

Indeed.com
6433 Champion Grandview Way, Bldg. 1
Austin, TX 78750 USA
Web Address: www.indeed.com
Indeed.com provides extensive lists of jobs of all types, with links directly to the employers. It covers over 60 countries,

including the U.S., Canada, India, Mexico.

Job Search USA
E-mail Address: contactjsu@jobsearchusa.org
Web Address: www.jobsearchusa.org
Job Search USA is a major job posting site that contains job opportunities classified by a variety of keywords.

Jobs in Logistics
Toll Free: 877-562-7678
Web Address: www.jobsinlogistics.com
Jobs in Logistics is an online job board, which provides contacts for job seekers in the transportation, manufacturing, freight forwarding, warehousing, purchasing, inventory management and logistics fields.

JobSearchUSA.org
Web Address: www.jobsearchusa.org
Founded in 2006, Job Search USA is an all-purpose job search web site offering job listings from various organizations including not for profits, small businesses, corporations and educational institutions. Job Search USA was developed from the concept of integrating the best features, design practices and privacy principles of the leading US job search websites.

LaborMarketInfo (LMI)
Employment Development Dept.
P.O. Box 826880, MIC 57
Sacramento, CA 94280-0001 USA
Phone: 916-262-2162
Fax: 916-262-2352
Web Address: www.labormarketinfo.edd.ca.gov
LaborMarketInfo (LMI) provides job seekers and employers a wide range of resources, namely the ability to find, access and use labor market information and services. It provides statistics for employment demographics on both a local and regional level, as well as career searching tools for California residents. The web site is sponsored by California's Employment Development Office.

MediaBistro.com
825 Eighth Ave., Fl. 29
New York, NY 10019 USA
E-mail Address: support@mediabistro.com
Web Address: www.mediabistro.com
MediaBistro.com provides news and information on current events relating to the media industry. It also offers an array of employment resources, including job listings within the industry.

Monster Worldwide, Inc.
622 Third Ave., Fl. 39
New York, NY 10017 USA
Phone: 212-351-7000
Fax: 646-658-0540
E-mail Address: ir@monster.com
Web Address: www.monster.com
Monster Worldwide, Inc., parent company of Monster.com, provides online career and personnel services. The firm operates in over 40 countries.

MyResumeAgent.com
24 Railroad St.
Kennedy Information, LLC
Keene, NH 03431 USA
Phone: 603-357-8104
Toll Free: 800-531-0007
E-mail Address: customerservice@kennedyinfo.com
Web Address: www.myresumeagent.com
MyResumeAgent.com allows senior-level professionals to have their resumes sent to executive placement firms for a fee. The site is owned by Kennedy Information, Inc.

NationJob, Inc.
920 Morgan St., Ste. T
Des Moines, IA 50309 USA
Fax: 515-243-5384
Toll Free: 888-292-7731
E-mail Address: customerservice@nationjob.com
Web Address: www.nationjob.com
NationJob.com is an online job search portal. The web site allows users to search through listings or develop a profile of the ideal job based on the criterion of location, industry, salary; and, if they provide an e-mail address, wait for appropriate listings to be sent to them through the firm's PJScout feature.

NETSHARE, Inc.
359 Bel Marin Keys, Ste. 24
Novato, CA 94949 USA
Toll Free: 800-241-5642
E-mail Address: netshare@netshare.com
Web Address: www.netshare.com
Netshare provides access to exclusive listings of executive jobs that pay $100,000 and up.

Net-Temps, Inc.
55 Middlesex St., Ste. 220
North Chelmsford, MA 01863 USA
Fax: 978-251-7250
Toll Free: 800-307-0062
E-mail Address: service@net-temps.com
Web Address: www.net-temps.com
Net-Temps, Inc. offers a web site, operated by professional career consultants, that features job listings and job seeking tips.

Recruiters Online Network
E-mail Address: rossi.tony@comcast.net
Web Address: www.recruitersonline.com
The Recruiters Online Network provides job postings from thousands of recruiters, Careers Online Magazine, a resume database, as well as other career resources.

USAJOBS
USAJOBS Program Office
1900 E St. NW, Ste. 6500
Washington, DC 20415-0001 USA
Phone: 818-934-6600
Web Address: www.usajobs.gov
USAJOBS, a program of the U.S. Office of Personnel Management, is the official job site for the U.S. Federal Government. It provides a comprehensive list of U.S. government jobs, allowing users to search for employment by location; agency; type of work; or by senior executive positions. It also has special employment sections for individuals with disabilities, veterans and recent college graduates; an information center, offering resume and interview tips and other information; and allows users to create a profile and post a resume.

21) Careers-Health Care

Health Care Source
100 Sylvan Rd., Ste. 100
Woburn, MA 01801 USA
Phone: 781-368-1033
Fax: 800-829-6600
Toll Free: 800-869-5200
E-mail Address: solutions@healthcaresource.com
Web Address: www.healthcaresource.com
Health Care Source is a leading provider of talent management, recruitment and employment services for healthcare providers. It offers a comprehensive suite of solutions, which includes features, such as applicant tracking and onboarding, recruitment optimization, reference checking, behavioral assessments, merit planning, employee performance and eLearning courseware among others.

MedicalWorkers.com
Web Address: www.medicalworkers.com
MedicalWorkers.com is an employment site for medical and health care professionals.

MedJump.com
E-mail Address: info@medjump.com
Web Address: www.medjump.com
MedJump.com is dedicated to empowering health care and medical-

related professionals with the necessary tools to market their abilities and skills.

Medzilla, Inc.
P.O. Box 1710
Marysville, WA 98270 USA
Phone: 360-657-5681
Fax: 425-279-5427
E-mail Address: info@medzilla.com
Web Address: www.medzilla.com
Medzilla, Inc.'s web site offers job searches, salary surveys, a search agent and information on employment in the biotech, pharmaceuticals, healthcare and science sectors.

Monster Career Advice-Healthcare
133 Boston Post Rd.
Weston, MA 02493 USA
Phone: 978-461-8000
Fax: 978-461-8100
Toll Free: 800-666-7837
Web Address: career-advice.monster.com/Healthcare/job-category-3975.aspx
Monster Career Advice-Healthcare, a service of Monster Worldwide, Inc., provides industry-related articles, job listings, job searches and search agents for the medical field.

NationJob Network-Medical and Health Care Jobs Page
920 Morgan St., Ste. T
Des Moines, IA 50309 USA
Fax: 515-243-5384
Toll Free: 800-292-7731
E-mail Address: customerservice@nationjob.com
Web Address: www.nationjob.com/medical
The NationJob Network-Medical and Health Care Jobs Page offers information and listings for health care employment.

Nurse-Recruiter.com
15500 SW Jay St., Ste. 26760
Beaverton, OR 97006-6018 USA
Toll Free: 877-562-7966
Web Address: www.nurse-recruiter.com
Nurse-Recruiter.com is an online job portal devoted to bringing health care employers and the nursing community together.

PracticeLink
415 2nd Ave.
Hinton, WV 25951 USA
Toll Free: 800-776-8383
E-mail Address: helpdesk@practicelink.com
Web Address: www.practicelink.com
PracticeLink, one of the largest physician employment web sites, is a free service with over 1.7 million page views each

month. There are more than 5,000 hospitals, medical groups, private practices and health systems, posting over 20,000 physician job opportunities on the web site.

RPh on the Go USA, Inc.
8001 N. Lincoln Ave., Ste. 800
Skokie, IL 60077 USA
Phone: 847-588-7170
Fax: 847-588-7060
Toll Free: 800-553-7359
Web Address: www.rphonthego.com
RPh on the Go USA, Inc. places temporary and permanent qualified professionals in the pharmacy community. This pharmacy staffing firm offers access to more than 160,000 pharmacy professionals and matches the right pharmacy personnel to help meet clients' needs.

22) Careers-Job Listings for Seniors

Dinosaur Exchange
Sutherland House, 1759, London Rd.
Leigh-on-Sea, Essex SS9 @RZ UK
Phone: 44-1702--470531
E-mail Address: CustomerSupport@dinosaur-exchange.com
Web Address: www.dinosaur-exchange.com
Dinosaur Exchange, opened in 2003, is a job forum for the elderly, which allows seniors to post resumes and be contacted by employers. Dino-X Ltd. owns and operates the web site.

Employment Network for Retired Government Experts (ENRGE)
Zavala, Inc.
P.O. Box 1532
N. Falmouth, MA 02556 USA
Phone: 508-564-4140
Web Address: www.enrge.us
The Employment Network for Retired Government Experts (ENRGE) helps government employees to remain active in their professions after retirement. ENERGE is the business name of Zavala, Inc.

Senior Job Bank
NHC Group, Inc.
P.O. Box 508
Marlborough, MA 01752 USA
Toll Free: 866-562-2627
E-mail Address: publisher@seniorjobbank.org
Web Address: www.seniorjobbank.org
The Senior Job Bank web site offers an easy, effective and free method for senior

citizens to find occasional, part-time, flexible, temporary or full-time jobs. The site is owned and managed by NHC Group, Inc.

Seniors4Hire.org
7071 Warner Ave. F466
Huntington Beach, CA 92647 USA
Phone: 714-848-0996
Fax: 714-848-5445
Toll Free: 800-906-7107
E-mail Address: info@seniors4hire.org
Web Address: www.seniors4hire.org
Seniors4Hire.org is an online career center with job postings, employment resources and information on community service employment programs for older workers, retirees and senior citizens. The site is owned and operated by The Forward Group.

YourEncore
20 N. Meridian St., Ste. 800
Indianapolis, IN 46204 USA
Phone: 317-226-9301
Fax: 317-226-9312
E-mail Address: info@yourencore.com
Web Address: www.yourencore.com
YourEncore is a program that seeks to employ retirees by matching them with member companies. The web site utilizes retirees mainly in the areas of engineering, science and product development.

23) Careers-Job Listings Hong Kong, China, Singapore, Asia

CareerJet
Web Address: www.careerjet.hk
CareerJet provides excellent search tools leading to job listings in Hong Kong, China and throughout Asia.

Careers@Gov
Web Address: www.careers.gov.sg
Careers@Gov is the government-sponsored job search site within Singapore.

CT Good Jobs
Web Address: www.ctgoodjobs.hk
CT Good Jobs provides easy to use job listings. It also offers online communities in such areas as retail, human resources and finance.

HeadHunt
Web Address: www.headhunt.com.sg/
HeadHunt bills itself as an executive job search site for Singapore.

JobMarket
Web Address: www.jobmarket.com.hk
JobMarket features a very detailed
advanced search option.

JobsCentral Singapore
Web Address: http://jobscentral.com.sg/
JobsCentral Singapore is maintained by
CareerBuilder.

jobsDB
Web Address: http://hk.jobsdb.com/hk
jobsDB provides well organized job
listings in Hong Kong, Indonesia,
Malaysia, Philippines, Singapore,
Thailand and China.

JobStreetWeb Address: www.jobstreet.sg
JobStreet is an extensive job search site
focused in positions within Singapore.

Monster Hong Kong
Web Address: www.monster.com.hk/
Monster Hong Kong provides easy online
access to thousands of jobs in Hong Kong,
Macau, Mainland China and Taiwan.

Monster Singapore
Web Address: www.monster.com.sg/
Monster Singapore is specific to the
Singapore area.

Recruit
Web Address: www.recruit.com.hk
Recruit provides job news, job tips
employer new and job listings in the Hong
Kong area.

Singapore Jobs Online
Web Address:
www.singaporejobsonline.com/
Singapore Jobs Online enables job
searches within Singapore for a wide
variety of job categories.

STJobs
Web Address: www.stjobs.sg/site/index
STJobs is an extensive web site offering
job search within Singapore and the
surrounding area.

24) Careers-Job Reference Tools

CareerXroads (CXR)
7 Clark Ct.
Kendall Park, NJ 08824-1810 USA
Phone: 732-821-6652
E-mail Address: mmc@careerxroads.com
Web Address: www.careerxroads.com
CareerXroads (CXR) publishes an annual
guide on job and resume web sites. It was
cofounded by Gerry Crispin and Mark
Mehler.

Job-Hunt.org
186 Main St.
NETability, Inc.
Marlborough, MA 01752 USA
Phone: 508-624-6261
E-mail Address: info@job-hunt.org
Web Address: www.job-hunt.org
Job-Hunt.org, rather than collecting
resumes or posting job vacancies, offers a
vast list of job listing web sites and links
to helpful job search tools. It is owned by
NETability, Inc.

jobipedia.org
E-mail Address: info@jobipedia.org
Web Address: www.jobipedia.org
jobipedia.org is a public service provided
by the HR Policy Association to help new
entrants into the workforce find jobs.
Every answer you read on jobipedia was
written by someone from a large employer
who actually hires employees for a living.

MBA Career Services Council (CSC)
P.O. Box 47478
Tampa, FL 33646-7478 USA
Phone: 813-220-3191
Fax: 813-319-4952
E-mail Address:
execdirector@mbacsc.org
Web Address: www.mbacsc.org
The MBA Career Services Council (CSC)
is a global professional association for
individuals in the field of MBA career
services and those that recruit directly
from graduate management programs.

Quintessential Careers (QC)
EmpoweringSites.com
DeLand, FL 32720 USA
Phone: 386-740-8872
Fax: 386-740-9764
E-mail Address:
randall@quintcareers.com
Web Address: www.quintcareers.com
Quintessential Careers (QC) provides a
large collection of data and links for job
seekers, including advice, tools and job
postings; it also offers a guide to
researching companies. QC is a subsidiary
of EmpoweringSites.com.

Vault.com, Inc.
132 W. 31st St., Fl. 17
New York, NY 10001 USA
Fax: 212-366-6117
Toll Free: 800-535-2074
E-mail Address:
customerservice@vault.com
Web Address: www.vault.com
Vault.com, Inc. is a comprehensive career
web site for employers and employees,
with job postings and valuable
information on a wide variety of
industries. Its features and content are

largely geared toward MBA degree
holders.

WetFeet.com
254 W 31st St., Fl. 12
New York, NY 10001 USA
Phone: 917-793-0337
Web Address: www.wetfeet.com
WetFeet.com provides an excellent
combination of links and resources for job
seekers. The site is owned by Universum.

What Color is Your Parachute?
E-mail Address:
rnbolles@jobhuntersbible.com
Web Address: www.jobhuntersbible.com
The What Color is Your Parachute?
official web site, JobHuntersBible.com, is
based on the Job-Hunting on the Internet
chapter of Richard (Dick) Bolle's best-
selling book. Designed to aid job hunters
and career changers who want to use the
Internet as part of their job search, the site
provides links to job listing, resume,
career counseling, contacts and research
sites.

25) Careers-Restaurants

FoodService.com
24 W. Camelback Rd., Ste. 104
Phoenix, AZ 85013 USA
Phone: 602-381-3663
Web Address: www.foodservice.com
FoodService.com, managed and run by
Food Service Interactive, LLC, offers web
site design and job search services for the
food service industry.

Resources in Food, Inc. (RIF)
417 S Lincolnway, Ste. B
North Aurora, IL 60542 USA
Phone: 630-801-0469
Fax: 630-357-7548
Toll Free: 877-743-1100
E-mail Address: jgrimm@rifood.com
Web Address: www.rifood.com
Resources in Food (RIF) provides
professional management placement for
the hospitality, food manufacturing, food
services, restaurants and wholesale
grocery industry.

26) Careers-Science

Chem Jobs
730 E. Cypress Ave.
Monrovia, CA 91016 USA
Phone: 626-930-0808
Fax: 626-930-0102
E-mail Address: info@chemindustry.com
Web Address: www.chemjobs.net
Chem Jobs is a leading Internet site for
job seekers in chemistry and related

fields, with a particular focus on chemists, biochemists, pharmaceutical scientists and chemical engineers. The web site is powered by Chemindustry.com.

New Scientist Jobs
Quadrant House, Sutton
Surrey, SM2 5AS UK
Phone: 781-734-8770
E-mail Address:
nssales@newscientist.com
Web Address: jobs.newscientist.com
New Scientist Jobs is a web site produced by the publishers of New Scientist Magazine that connects jobseekers and employers in the bioscience fields. The site includes a job search engine and a free-of-charge e-mail job alert service.

Science Careers
Phone: 202-312-6375
Web Address: jobs.sciencecareers.org
Science Careers is a web site that contains many useful categories of links, including employment newsgroups, scientific journals, hob postings and placement agencies. It also links to sites containing information regarding internship and fellowship opportunities for high school students, undergrads, graduates, doctoral and post-doctoral students.

27) Careers-Sports

Jobs in Sports
106 Calendar Ave., Ste. 184
LaGrange, IL 60525 USA
Web Address: www.jobsinsports.com
Jobs in Sports is an employment web site that provides job listings in areas including sports marketing, sports media, sales, health and fitness, computers and administration, as well as other job resources.

Sports Careers
Web Address: www.sportscareers.com
Sports Careers offers a range of services to help individuals and employers in the sports industry, including job listings, a resume bank, industry contacts and salary information.

Sports Job Board
Web Address: www.sportsjobboard.com
The Sports Job Board is an employment web site for the sports industry.

WomenSportsJobs.com
Women's Sport Services, LLC
P.O. Box 11
Huntington Beach, CA 92648 USA
Phone: 714-848-1201
Fax: 714-848-5111

E-mail Address:
Feedback@WSServices.com
Web Address:
www.womensportsjobs.com
WomenSportsJobs.com is an employment web site specializing in jobs for women in the sports industry. The site is managed by Women's Sport Services, LLC.

Work in Sports LLC
7335 E. Chauncey Ln., Ste. 115
Phoenix, AZ 85054 USA
Phone: 480-905-7221
Fax: 480-905-7231
Web Address: www.workinsports.com
Work in Sports LLC is an online employment resource for the sports industry that posts hundreds of jobs on its web site.

28) Careers-Video Games Industry

GameJobs
Web Address: www.gamejobs.com
GameJobs.com is independently owned and operated by the Crest Group, LLC, the managers of the Entertainment Consumers Association (ECA), a non-profit membership association. It offers both employers and job seekers in the interactive entertainment industry access to online tools and resources, such as post resume and job openings to accomplish their respective goals.

Video Game Jobs-About.com Career Planning
Web Address:
http://careerplanning.about.com/od/occupations/a/videogamecareer.htm
A useful page on About.com that contains advice and links for people interested in working in the video games industry.

29) Chemicals Industry Associations

American Chemical Society (ACS)
1155 16th St. NW
Washington, DC 20036 USA
Phone: 202-872-4600
Toll Free: 800-227-5558
E-mail Address: help@acs.org
Web Address: www.acs.org
The American Chemical Society (ACS) is a nonprofit organization aimed at promoting the understanding of chemistry and chemical sciences. It represents a wide range of disciplines including chemistry, chemical engineering and other technical fields.

30) Communications Professional Associations

Association for Women In Communications (AWC)
1717 E Republic Rd., Ste. A
Springfield, MO 65804 USA
Phone: 417-886-8606
Fax: 417-886-3685
E-mail Address: members@womcom.org
Web Address: www.womcom.org
The Association for Women In Communications (AWC) is a professional organization that works for the advancement of women across all communications disciplines by recognizing excellence, promoting leadership and positioning its members at the forefront of the communications industry.

Health and Science Communications Association (HeSCA)
P.O. Box 31323
Omaha, NE 68132 USA
Phone: 402-915-5373
E-mail Address: hesca@hesca.org
Web Address: hesca.net
The Health and Science Communications Association (HeSCA) is an organization of communications professionals committed to sharing knowledge and resources in the health sciences arena.

Health Industry Business Communications Council (HIBCC)
2525 E. Arizona Biltmore Cir., Ste. 127
Phoenix, AZ 85016 USA
Phone: 602-381-1091
Fax: 602-381-1093
E-mail Address: info@hibcc.org
Web Address: www.hibcc.org
The Health Industry Business Communications Council (HIBCC) seeks to facilitate electronic communications by developing appropriate standards for information exchange among all health care trading partners.

International Association of Business Communicators (IABC)
155 Montgomery St., Ste. 1210
San Francisco, CA 94111 USA
Phone: 415-544-4700
Fax: 415-544-4747
Toll Free: 800-776-4222
Web Address: www.iabc.com
The International Association of Business Communicators (IABC) is the leading resource for effective business communication practices.

31) Computer & Electronics Industry Associations

Electronics Technicians Association international (ETA International)
5 Depot St.
Greencastle, IN 46135 USA
Phone: 765-653-8262
Fax: 765-653-4287
Toll Free: 800-288-3824
E-mail Address: eta@eta-i.org
Web Address: www.eta-i.org
The Electronics Technicians Association International (ETA International) is a nonprofit professional association for electronics technicians worldwide. The organization provides recognized professional credentials for electronics technicians.

Semiconductor Industry Association (SIA)
1101 K St. NW, Ste. 450
Washington, DC 20005 USA
Phone: 202-446-1700
Fax: 202-216-9745
Toll Free: 866-756-0715
Web Address: www.semiconductors.org
The Semiconductor Industry Association (SIA) is a trade association representing the semiconductor industry in the U.S. Through its coalition of more than 60 companies, SIA members represent roughly 80% of semiconductor production in the U.S. The coalition aims to advance the competitiveness of the chip industry and shape public policy on issues particular to the industry.

32) Consulting Industry Associations

Association of Internal Management Consultants (AIMC)
720 North Collier Blvd., Ste. 201
Marco Island, FL 34145 USA
Phone: 239-642-0580
Web Address: www.aimc.org
The Association of Internal Management Consultants (AIMC) is a professional association representing in-house management consultants. Members work in for-profit corporations, government agencies, educational institutions and nonprofit organizations.

Association of Management Consulting Firms (AMCF)
370 Lexington Ave., Ste. 2209
New York, NY 10017 USA
Phone: 212-262-3055
Fax: 212-262-3054
E-mail Address: info@amcf.org

Web Address: www.amcf.org
The Association of Management Consulting Firms (AMCF) is a recognized leader in promoting the management consulting industry. AMCF represents a diverse list of international members, from large, multinational companies to small, regional firms.

Institute of Management Consultants USA (IMC)
631 U.S. Highway One, Ste. 400
North Palm Beach, FL 33408 USA
Phone: 561-472-0833
Toll Free: 800-837-7321
Web Address: www.imcusa.org
The Institute of Management Consultants USA (IMC) certifies management consultants in accordance with the strict international standards of the International Council of Management Consulting Institutes.

Investment Management Consultant Association (IMCA)
5619 DTC Pkwy., Ste. 500
Greenwood Village, CO 80111 USA
Phone: 303-770-3377
Fax: 303-770-1812
E-mail Address: imca@imca.org
Web Address: www.imca.org
The Investment Management Consultant Association (IMCA) provides information and communication for investment management consultants.

33) Consulting Industry Resources

Consulting Magazine
120 Broadway, Fl.5
New York, NY 10271 USA
Phone: 877-256-2472
Web Address: www.consultingmag.com
Consulting Magazine is a leading online publication for the consulting industry, and features information on consulting careers, thought leadership and corporate strategies. The web site is owned and operated by ALM Media, LLC.

34) Corporate Information Resources

bizjournals.com
120 W. Morehead St., Ste. 400
Charlotte, NC 28202 USA
Toll Free: 866-853-3661
E-mail Address:
gmurchison@bizjournals.com
Web Address: www.bizjournals.com
Bizjournals.com is the online media division of American City Business

Journals, the publisher of dozens of leading city business journals nationwide. It provides access to research into the latest news regarding companies both small and large. The organization maintains 42 websites and 64 print publications and sponsors over 700 annual industry events.

Business Wire
101 California St., Fl. 20
San Francisco, CA 94111 USA
Phone: 415-986-4422
Fax: 415-788-5335
Toll Free: 800-227-0845
E-mail Address: info@businesswire.com
Web Address: www.businesswire.com
Business Wire offers news releases, industry- and company-specific news, top headlines, conference calls, IPOs on the Internet, media services and access to tradeshownews.com and BW Connect On-line through its informative and continuously updated web site.

Edgar Online, Inc.
11200 Rockville Pike, Ste. 310
Rockville, MD 20852 USA
Phone: 301-287-0300
Fax: 301-287-0390
Toll Free: 888-870-2316
Web Address: www.edgar-online.com
Edgar Online, Inc. is a gateway and search tool for viewing corporate documents, such as annual reports on Form 10-K, filed with the U.S. Securities and Exchange Commission.

PR Newswire Association LLC
350 Hudson St., Ste. 300
New York, NY 10014-4504 USA
Fax: 800-793-9313
Toll Free: 800-776-8090
E-mail Address:
MediaInquiries@prnewswire.com
Web Address: www.prnewswire.com
PR Newswire Association LLC provides comprehensive communications services for public relations and investor relations professionals, ranging from information distribution and market intelligence to the creation of online multimedia content and investor relations web sites. Users can also view recent corporate press releases from companies across the globe. The Association is owned by United Business Media plc.

Silicon Investor
E-mail Address:
si.admin@siliconinvestor.com
Web Address: www.siliconinvestor.com
Silicon Investor is focused on providing information about technology companies. Its web site serves as a financial

discussion forum and offers quotes, profiles and charts.

35) Disabling Conditions

Job Accommodation Network (JAN)
P.O. Box 6080
Morgantown, WV 26506-6080 USA
Phone: 304-293-7186
Fax: 304-293-5407
Toll Free: 800-526-7234
E-mail Address: jan@askjan.org
Web Address: askjan.org
The Job Accommodation Network (JAN) is a free consulting service that provides guidance and information about job accommodations, the Americans with Disabilities Act and the employability of people with disabilities.

36) Electronic Health Records/Continuity of Care Records

American Health Information Management Association (AHIMA)
233 N. Michigan Ave., Fl. 21
Chicago, IL 60601-5809 USA
Phone: 312-233-1100
Fax: 312-233-1090
Toll Free: 800-335-5535
Web Address: www.ahima.org
The American Health Information Management Association (AHIMA) is a professional association that consists health information management professionals who work throughout the health care industry.

American Medical Informatics Association (AMIA)
4720 Montgomery Ln., Ste. 500
Bethesda, MD 20814 USA
Phone: 301-657-1291
Fax: 301-657-1296
Web Address: www.amia.org
The American Medical Informatics Association (AMIA) is a membership organization of individuals, institutions and corporations dedicated to developing and using information technologies to improve health care.

College of Healthcare Information Management Executives (CHIME)
710 Avis Dr., Ste. 200
Ann Arbor, MI 48108 USA
Phone: 734-665-0000
Fax: 734-665-4922
E-mail Address: staff@cio-chime.org
Web Address: www.cio-chime.org
College of Healthcare Information Management Executives (CHIME) was

formed with the dual objective of serving the professional development needs of health care CIOs and advocating the more effective use of information management within health care.

Healthcare Information and Management Systems Society (HIMSS)
33 W Monroe St., Ste. 1700
Chicago, IL 60603-5616 USA
Phone: 312-664-4467
Fax: 312-664-6143
Web Address: www.himss.org
The Healthcare Information and Management Systems Society (HIMSS) provides leadership in the optimal use of technology, information and management systems for the betterment of health care.

37) Energy Associations-Electric Power

American Public Power Association (APPA)
2451 Crystal Dr., Ste. 1000
Arlington, VA 22202-4804 USA
Phone: 202-467-2900
E-mail Address: info@PublicPower.org
Web Address: www.publicpower.org
The American Public Power Association (APPA) is a nonprofit service organization for the country's community-owned electric utilities, dedicated to advancing the public policy interests of its members and their consumers.

Edison Electric Institute (EEI)
701 Pennsylvania Ave. NW
Washington, DC 20004-2696 USA
Phone: 202-508-5000
E-mail Address: feedback@eei.org
Web Address: www.eei.org
The Edison Electric Institute (EEI) is an association of U.S. shareholder-owned electric companies as well as worldwide affiliates and industry associates. Its web site provides energy news and a link to Electric Perspectives magazine.

Women's International Network of Utility Professionals (WINUP)
P.O. Box 64
Grove City, OH 43123-0064 USA
Phone: 614-738-0603
E-mail Address: winup@att.net
Web Address: www.winup.org
The Women's International Network of Utility Professionals (WINUP) provides networking and support for women in the utility industry.

38) Energy Associations-Natural Gas

American Gas Association (AGA)
400 N. Capitol St. NW, Ste. 450
Washington, DC 20001 USA
Phone: 202-824-7000
Web Address: www.aga.org
The American Gas Association (AGA) represents a large number of natural gas providers, advocating for these companies and providing a broad range of programs and services for members.

39) Energy Associations-Other

American Association of Blacks in Energy
1625 K St. NW, Ste. 450
Washington, DC 20006 USA
Phone: 202-371-9530
Fax: 202-371-9218
E-mail Address: info@aabe.org
Web Address: www.aabe.org
The American Association of Blacks in Energy is dedicated to ensuring the input of African Americans and other minorities in discussions and developments of energy policies, regulations, research and development technologies and environmental issues.

40) Energy Associations-Petroleum, Exploration, Production, etc.

American Association of Professional Landmen (AAPL)
800 Fournier St.
Fort Worth, TX 76102 USA
Phone: 817-847-7700
Fax: 817-847-7704
E-mail Address: aapl@landman.org
Web Address: www.landman.org
The American Association of Professional Landmen (AAPL) promotes the highest standards of performance for all land professionals and seeks to advance their stature and to encourage sound stewardship of energy and mineral resources.

American Petroleum Institute (API)
1220 L St. NW
Washington, DC 20005-4070 USA
Phone: 202-682-8000
Web Address: www.api.org
American Petroleum Institute (API) represents U.S. oil and gas industries and its web site includes in-depth sections for energy consumers and energy professionals.

Independent Petroleum Association of America (IPAA)
1201 15th St. NW, Ste. 300
Washington, DC 20005 USA
Phone: 202-857-4722
Fax: 202-857-4799
E-mail Address: nkirby@ipaa.org
Web Address: www.ipaa.org
The Independent Petroleum Association of America (IPAA) provides a forum for the exploration and production segment of the independent oil and natural gas business. It also provides information on the domestic exploration and production industry.

International Association of Drilling Contractors (IADC)
10370 Richmond Ave., Ste. 760
Houston, TX 77042 USA
Phone: 713-292-1945
Fax: 713-292-1946
E-mail Address: info@iadc.org
Web Address: www.iadc.org
The International Association of Drilling Contractors (IADC) represents the worldwide oil and gas drilling industry and promotes commitment to safety, preservation of the environment and advances in drilling technology.

41) Engineering Industry Associations

National Society of Professional Engineers (NSPE)
1420 King St.
Alexandria, VA 22314-2794 USA
Fax: 703-836-4875
Toll Free: 888-285-6773
Web Address: www.nspe.org
The National Society of Professional Engineers (NSPE) represents individual engineering professionals and licensed engineers across all disciplines. NSPE serves approximately 45,000 members and has more than 500 chapters.

42) Engineering, Research & Scientific Associations

American Association of Petroleum Geologists (AAPG)
1444 S. Boulder Ave.
Tulsa, OK 74119 USA
Phone: 918-584-2555
Fax: 918-560-2665
Toll Free: 800-364-2274
Web Address: www.aapg.org
The American Association of Petroleum Geologists (AAPG) is an international geological organization that supports

educational and scientific programs and projects related to geosciences.

American Institute of Chemical Engineers (AIChE)
120 Wall St., Fl. 23
New York, NY 10005-4020 USA
Phone: 203-702-7660
Fax: 203-775-5177
Toll Free: 800-242-4363
Web Address: www.aiche.org
The American Institute of Chemical Engineers (AIChE) provides leadership in advancing the chemical engineering profession. The organization, which is comprised of more than 50,000 members from over 100 countries, provides informational resources to chemical engineers.

American Society for Healthcare Engineering (ASHE)
155 N. Wacker Dr., Ste. 400
Chicago, IL 60606 USA
Phone: 312-422-3800
Fax: 312-422-4571
E-mail Address: ashe@aha.org
Web Address: www.ashe.org
The American Society for Healthcare Engineering (ASHE) is the advocate and resource for continuous improvement in the health care engineering and facilities management professions. It is devoted to professionals who design, build, maintain and operate hospitals and other healthcare facilities.

American Society of Agricultural and Biological Engineers (ASABE)
2950 Niles Rd.
St. Joseph, MI 49085 USA
Phone: 269-429-0300
Fax: 269-429-3852
Toll Free: 800-371-2723
E-mail Address: hq@asabe.org
Web Address: www.asabe.org
The American Society of Agricultural and Biological Engineers (ASABE) is a nonprofit professional and technical organization interested in engineering knowledge and technology for food and agriculture and associated industries.

American Society of Civil Engineers (ASCE)
1801 Alexander Bell Dr.
Reston, VA 20191-4400 USA
Phone: 703-295-6300
Toll Free: 800-548-2723
Web Address: www.asce.org
The American Society of Civil Engineers (ASCE) is a leading professional organization serving civil engineers. It ensures safer buildings, water systems and

other civil engineering works by developing technical codes and standards.

American Society of Safety Engineers (ASSE)
520 N. Northwest Hwy
Park Ridge, IL 60068 USA
Phone: 847-699-2929
E-mail Address: customerservice@asse.org
Web Address: www.asse.org
The American Society of Safety Engineers (ASSE) is the world's oldest and largest professional safety organization. It manages, supervises and consults on safety, health and environmental issues in industry, insurance, government and education.

Association of Federal Communications Consulting Engineers (AFCCE)
P.O. Box 19333
Washington, DC 20036 USA
Web Address: www.afcce.org
The Association of Federal Communications Consulting Engineers (AFCCE) is a professional organization of individuals who regularly assist clients on technical issues before the Federal Communications Commission (FCC).

Institute of Industrial Engineers (IIE)
3577 Parkway Ln., Ste. 200
Norcross, GA 30092 USA
Phone: 770-449-0460
Fax: 770-441-3295
Toll Free: 800-494-0460
E-mail Address: cs@iienet.org
Web Address: www.iienet2.org
The Institute of Industrial Engineers (IIE) is an international, non-profit association dedicated to the education, development, training and research in the field of industrial engineering.

Society of Automotive Engineers (SAE)
755 W. Big Beaver, Ste. 1600
Troy, MA 48084 USA
Phone: 248-273-2455
Fax: 248-273-2494
Toll Free: 877-606-7323
E-mail Address: automotive_hq@sae.org
Web Address: www.sae.org
The Society of Automotive Engineers (SAE) is a resource for technical information and expertise used in designing, building, maintaining and operating self-propelled vehicles for use on land, sea, air or space.

Society of Broadcast Engineers, Inc. (SBE)
9102 N. Meridian St., Ste. 150
Indianapolis, IN 46260 USA
Phone: 317-846-9000

E-mail Address: jporay@sbe.org
Web Address: www.sbe.org
The Society of Broadcast Engineers
(SBE) exists to increase knowledge of
broadcast engineering and promote its
interests, as well as to continue the
education of professionals in the industry.

**Society of Cable Telecommunications
Engineers (SCTE)**
140 Philips Rd.
Exton, PA 19341-1318 USA
Fax: 610-884-7237
Toll Free: 800-542-5040
E-mail Address: scte@scte.org
Web Address: www.scte.org
The Society of Cable
Telecommunications Engineers (SCTE) is
a nonprofit professional association
dedicated to advancing the careers and
serving the industry of
telecommunications professionals by
providing technical training, certification
and information resources.

**Society of Hispanic Professional
Engineers (SHPE)**
13181 Crossroads Pkwy. N., Ste. 450
City of Industry, CA 91746 USA
Phone: 323-725-3970
Fax: 323-725-0316
E-mail Address: shpenational@shpe.org
Web Address: oneshpe.shpe.org
The Society of Hispanic Professional
Engineers (SHPE) is a national nonprofit
organization that promotes Hispanics in
science, engineering and math.

**Society of Manufacturing Engineers
(SME)**
One SME Dr.
Dearborn, MI 48121 USA
Phone: 313-425-3000
Fax: 313-425-3400
Toll Free: 800-733-4763
E-mail Address:
communications@sme.org
Web Address: www.sme.org
The Society of Manufacturing Engineers
(SME) is a leading professional
organization serving engineers in the
manufacturing industries.

**Society of Motion Picture and
Television Engineers (SMPTE)**
3 Barker Ave., Fl. 5
White Plains, NY 10601 USA
Phone: 914-761-1100
Fax: 914-761-3115
E-mail Address: marketing@smpte.org
Web Address: www.smpte.org
The Society of Motion Picture and
Television Engineers (SMPTE) is the
leading technical society for the motion
imaging industry. The firm publishes

recommended practice and engineering
guidelines, as well the SMPTE Journal.

Society of Women Engineers (SWE)
230 N La Salle St., Ste. 1675
Chicago, IL 60601 USA
Toll Free: 877-793-4636
E-mail Address: hq@swe.org
Web Address:
societyofwomenengineers.swe.org
The Society of Women Engineers (SWE)
is a nonprofit educational and service
organization of female engineers.

SPIE
1000 20th St.
Bellingham, WA 98225-6705 USA
Phone: 360-676-3290
Fax: 360-647-1445
Toll Free: 888-504-8171
E-mail Address:
customerservice@spie.org
Web Address: www.spie.org
SPIE is a nonprofit technical society
aimed at the advancement and
dissemination of knowledge in optics,
photonics and imaging.

43) Entertainment &
Amusement
Associations-General

**International Association of
Amusement Parks and Attractions
(IAAPA)**
1448 Duke St.
Alexandria, VA 22314 USA
Phone: 703-836-4800
Fax: 703-836-4801
E-mail Address: iaapa@iaapa.org
Web Address: www.iaapa.org
The International Association of
Amusement Parks and Attractions
(IAAPA) is dedicated to the preservation
and prosperity of the amusement industry.

**International Special Events Society
(ISES)**
330 N. Wabash Ave., Ste. 2000
Chicago, IL 60611-4267 USA
Phone: 312-321-6853
Fax: 312-673-6953
Toll Free: 800-688-4737
E-mail Address: info@ises.com
Web Address: www.ises.com
The International Special Events Society
(ISES) is comprised of over 7,200
professionals in over 38 countries
representing special event planners and
producers (from festivals to trade shows),
caterers, decorators, florists, destination
management companies, rental
companies, special effects experts, tent
suppliers, audio-visual technicians, event

and convention coordinators, balloon
artists, educators, journalists, hotel sales
managers, specialty entertainers,
convention center managers, and many
more professional disciplines.

44) Film & Theater
Associations

**Academy of Motion Picture Arts and
Sciences (AMPAS)**
8949 Wilshire Blvd.
Beverly Hills, CA 90211-1972 USA
Phone: 310-247-3000
Fax: 310-859-9619
Web Address: www.oscars.org
The Academy of Motion Picture Arts and
Sciences (AMPAS) is a professional
honorary organization, founded to
advance the arts and sciences of motion
pictures. Besides hosting the Academy
Awards and selecting the winners of the
Oscars, AMPAS organizes smaller events
highlighting the art of filmmaking,
including lectures and seminars, and is
currently building the Academy Museum
of Motion Pictures.

**Alliance of Motion Picture and
Television Producers (AMPTP)**
15301 Ventura Blvd., Bldg. E
Sherman Oaks, CA 91403 USA
Phone: 818-995-3600
Web Address: www.amptp.org
The Alliance of Motion Picture and
Television Producers (AMPTP) is the
primary trade association with respect to
labor issues in the motion picture and
television industry.

American Cinema Editors, Inc. (ACE)
100 Universal City Plz.
Verna Fields Bldg. 2282, Rm. 190
Universal City, CA 91608 USA
Phone: 818-777-2900
E-mail Address:
amercinema@earthlink.net
Web Address: www.ace-filmeditors.org
American Cinema Editors (ACE) is an
honorary society of motion picture editors
that seeks to advance the art and science
of the editing profession.

**American Society of Cinematographers
(ASC)**
1782 N. Orange Dr.
Hollywood, CA 90028 USA
Phone: 323-969-4333
Fax: 323-882-6391
Toll Free: 800-448-0145
E-mail Address: office@theasc.com
Web Address: www.theasc.com
The American Society of
Cinematographers (ASC) is a trade

association for cinematographers in the motion picture industry.

Art Directors Guild (ADG)
11969 Ventura Blvd., Fl. 2
Studio City, CA 91604 USA
Phone: 818-762-9995
Fax: 818-760-4847
E-mail Address: nick@artdirectors.org
Web Address: www.artdirectors.org
The Art Directors Guild (ADG) represents the creative talents that conceive and manage the background and settings for most films and television projects.

Association of Cinema and Video Laboratories (ACVL)
Phone: 805-427-2620
E-mail Address: peterbulcke@hotmail.com
Web Address: www.acvl.org
The Association of Cinema and Video Laboratories (ACVL) is an international organization whose members are pledged to the highest possible standards of service to the film and video industries.

Independent Film & Television Alliance (IFTA)
10850 Wilshire Blvd., Fl. 9
Los Angeles, CA 90024-4311 USA
Phone: 310-446-1000
Fax: 310-446-1600
E-mail Address: info@ifta-online.org
Web Address: www.ifta-online.org
The Independent Film & Television Alliance (IFTA), formerly the American Film Marketing Association (AFMA), is a trade association whose mission is to provide the independent film and television industry with high-quality, market-oriented services and worldwide representation.

International Alliance of Theatrical Stage Employees (IATSE)
207 W. 25th St., Fl. 4
New York, NY 10001 USA
Phone: 212-730-1770
Fax: 212-730-7809
E-mail Address: webmaster@iatse-intl.org
Web Address: www.iatse-intl.org
The International Alliance of Theatrical Stage Employees (IATSE) is the labor union representing technicians, artisans and crafts workers in the entertainment industry, including live theater, film and television production and trade shows.

International Animated Film Society (ASIFA-Hollywood)
2114 W. Burbank Blvd.
Burbank, CA 91506 USA
Phone: 818-842-8330

E-mail Address: info@asifa-hollywood.org
Web Address: www.asifa-hollywood.org
International Animated Film Society (ASIFA-Hollywood) is a nonprofit organization dedicated to the advancement of the art of animation.

International Documentary Association (IDA)
3470 Wilshire Blvd., Ste. 980
Los Angeles, CA 90010 USA
Phone: 213-232-1660
Fax: 213-232-1669
E-mail Address: michael@documentary.org
Web Address: www.documentary.org
The International Documentary Association (IDA) is a nonprofit member service organization, providing publications, benefits and a public forum to its members for issues regarding nonfiction film, video and multimedia.

Motion Picture Association of America (MPAA)
15301 Ventura Blvd., Bldg. E
Sherman Oaks, CA 91403 USA
Phone: 818-995-6600
Fax: 818-285-4403
E-mail Address: ContactUs@mpaa.org
Web Address: www.mpaa.org
The Motion Picture Association of America (MPAA) serves as the voice and advocate of the U.S. motion picture, home video and television industries.

Motion Picture Editors Guild (MPEG)
7715 Sunset Blvd., Ste. 200
Hollywood, CA 90046 USA
Phone: 323-876-4770
Fax: 323-876-0861
Toll Free: 800-705-8700
E-mail Address: social@editorsguild.com
Web Address: www.editorsguild.com
The Motion Picture Editors Guild's (MPEG) web site provides an online directory of editors, a discussion forum and links to related magazines and other organizations that serve the motion picture industry.

Producers Guild of America, Inc. (PGA)
8530 Wilshire Blvd., Ste. 400
Beverly Hills, CA 90211 USA
Phone: 310-358-9020
Fax: 310-358-9520
E-mail Address: info@producersguild.org
Web Address: www.producersguild.org
The Producers Guild of America, Inc. (PGA) is a nonprofit organization for career professionals who initiate, create, coordinate, supervise and control all

aspects of the motion picture and television production processes.

SAG-AFTRA
5757 Wilshire Blvd., Fl. 7
Los Angeles, CA 90036-3600 USA
Phone: 323-954-1600
Toll Free: 800-724-2387
Web Address: www.sagaftra.org
The SAG-AFTRA, representing a union of the Screen Actors Guild the American Federation of Television and Radio Artists, represents its members through negotiation and enforcement of collective bargaining agreements that establish equitable levels of compensation, benefits and working conditions for performers. The guild represents 160,000 actors worldwide.

Women In Film (WIF)
6100 Wilshire Blvd., Ste. 710
Los Angeles, CA 90048 USA
Phone: 323-935-2211
Fax: 323-935-2212
E-mail Address: info@wif.org
Web Address: www.wif.org
Women In Film (WIF) strives to empower, promote and mentor women in the entertainment, communication and media industries through a network of contacts, educational programs and events.

45) Fitness Industry Associations

American Fitness Professionals and Associates (AFPA)
1601 Long Beach Blvd.
P.O. Box 214
Ship Bottom, NJ 08008 USA
Phone: 609-978-7583
Fax: 609-978-7582
Toll Free: 800-494-7782
E-mail Address: afpa@afpafitness.com
Web Address: www.afpafitness.com
American Fitness Professionals and Associates (AFPA) offers health and fitness professionals certification programs, continuing education courses, home correspondence courses and regional conventions.

46) Food Industry Associations, General

Institute of Food Technologies (IFT)
525 W. Van Buren, Ste. 1000
Chicago, IL 60607 USA
Phone: 312-782-8424
Fax: 312-782-8348
Toll Free: 800-438-3663

E-mail Address: info@ift.org
Web Address: www.ift.org
The Institute of Food Technologies (IFT) is devoted to the advancement of the science and technology of food through the exchange of knowledge. The site also provides information and resources for job seekers in the food industry. Members work in food science, food technology and related professions in industry, academia and government.

47) Food Industry Resources, General

Food Manufacturing
199 E. Badger Rd., Ste. 101
Madison, WI 53713 USA
Phone: 973-920-7761
E-mail Address:
abmprogrequests@advantagemedia.com
Web Address:
www.foodmanufacturing.com
Food Manufacturing is a trade magazine for companies and employees in the food manufacturing industry. It is published by Advantage Business Media.

48) Food Processor Industry Associations

Grocery Manufacturers Association (GMA)
1350 I St. NW, Ste. 300
Washington, DC 20005 USA
Phone: 202-639-5900
Fax: 202-639-5932
E-mail Address: info@gmaonline.org
Web Address: www.gmaonline.org
The Grocery Manufacturers Association (GMA), formerly the National Food Products Association (NFPA), is the voice of the food, beverage and consumer products industry on scientific and public policy issues involving food safety, food security, nutrition, technical and regulatory matters and consumer affairs.

National Frozen and Refrigerated Foods Association (NFRA)
4755 Linglestown Rd., Ste. 300
Harrisburg, PA 17112 USA
Phone: 717-657-8601
Fax: 717-657-9862
E-mail Address: info@nfraweb.org
Web Address: www.nfraweb.org
The National Frozen and Refrigerated Foods Association (NFRA) promotes the sales and consumption of refrigerated and frozen foods through education, research, training, sales planning and menu development, providing a forum for industry dialogue. It represents

manufacturers, sales agents, suppliers, local associations, retailers, wholesalers, distributors and logistic providers involved in the frozen and refrigerated food industry.

49) Food Service Industry Associations

International Flight Services Association (IFSA)
1100 Fry Rd., Ste. 300
Atlanta, GA 30342 USA
Phone: 404-303-2969
E-mail Address:
ifsa@kellencompany.com
Web Address: www.ifsanet.com
The International Flight Services Association (IFSA), formerly the International Inflight Food Service Association, informs the public with respect to educational and career opportunities within the multi-billion-dollar inflight and railway food service industry. IFSA is managed by the Kellen Company.

50) Games Industry Associations

Entertainment Software Association (ESA)
575 7th St. NW, Ste. 300
Washington, DC 20004 USA
Phone: 202-223-2400
E-mail Address: esa@theesa.com
Web Address: www.theesa.com
The Entertainment Software Association (ESA) is a U.S. trade association for companies that publish video and computer games for consoles, personal computers and the Internet. The ESA owns the E3 Media & Business Summit, a major invitation-only annual trade show for the video game industry.

Fantasy Sports Trade Association (FSTA)
600 N. Lake Shore Dr.
Chicago, IL 60611 U.S.A.
Phone: 312-771-7019
E-mail Address: megan@fsta.org
Web Address: www.fsta.org
The Fantasy Sports Trade Association (FSTA) was founded in 1997 to provide a forum for interaction between companies in a unique and growing fantasy sports industry. FSTA represents more than 300 member companies.

Game Manufacturers Association (GAMA)
240 N. Fifth St., Ste. 340

Columbus, OH 43215 USA
Phone: 614-255-4500
Fax: 614-255-4499
E-mail Address: ed@gama.org
Web Address: www.gama.org
The Game Manufacturers Association (GAMA) is an international non-profit trade association serving the hobby games industry. It hosts two annual events, the GAMA Trade Show and Origins Game Fair, and publishes a quarterly information newsletter, GAMATimes.

International Game Developers Association (IGDA)
19 Mantua Rd.
Mt. Royal, NJ 08061 USA
Phone: 856-423-2990
Web Address: www.igda.org
The International Game Developers Association (IGDA) represents members involved in the video game production industry. The firm aims to promote professional development within the gaming industry and advocates for issues that affect the game developer community, including anti-censorship issues.

51) Grocery Industry Associations

National Grocers Association (NGA)
1005 N. Glebe Rd., Ste. 250
Arlington, VA 22201-5758 USA
Phone: 703-516-0700
Fax: 703-516-0115
E-mail Address:
feedback@nationalgrocers.org
Web Address: www.nationalgrocers.org
The National Grocers Association (NGA) is a national trade association representing retail and wholesale grocers that comprise the independent sector of the food distribution industry.

52) Health & Nutrition Associations

Academy of Nutrition and Dietetics
120 S. Riverside Plz., Ste. 2190
Chicago, IL 60606-6995 USA
Phone: 312-899-0040
Toll Free: 800-877-1600
E-mail Address: foundation@eatright.org
Web Address: www.eatright.org
The Academy of Nutrition and Dietetics, formerly known as the American Dietetic Association (ADA) is the world's largest organization of food and nutrition professionals, with nearly 65,000 members. In addition to services for its professional members, this organization's

web site offers consumers a respected source for food and nutrition information.

---

53) Health Care Business & Professional Associations

Advanced Medical Technology Association (AdvaMed)
701 Pennsylvania Ave. NW, Ste. 800
Washington, DC 20004-2654 USA
Phone: 202-783-8700
Fax: 202-783-8750
E-mail Address: info@advamed.org
Web Address: www.advamed.org
The Advanced Medical Technology Association (AdvaMed) strives to be the advocate for a legal, regulatory and economic climate that advances global health care by assuring worldwide access to the benefits of medical technology.

American Academy of Nursing (AAN)
1000 Vermont Ave., Ste. 910
Washington, DC 20005 USA
Phone: 202-777-1170
E-mail Address: info@aannet.org
Web Address: www.aannet.org
The American Academy of Nursing (AAN) works to enhance nursing profession by advancing health policy and practice and generate, synthesize and disseminate nursing knowledge.

American Association of Medical Assistants (AAMA)
20 N. Wacker Dr., Ste. 1575
Chicago, IL 60606 USA
Phone: 312-899-1500
Fax: 312-899-1259
Toll Free: 800-228-2262
Web Address: www.aama-ntl.org
The American Association of Medical Assistants (AAMA) seeks to promote the professional identity and stature of its members and the medical assisting profession through education and credentialing.

American College of Health Care Administrators (ACHCA)
1101 Connecticut Ave. NW, Ste. 450
Washington, DC 20036 USA
Phone: 202-536-5120
Fax: 866-874-1585
E-mail Address: wodonnell@achca.org
Web Address: www.achca.org
The American College of Health Care Administrators (ACHCA) offers educational programming, professional certification and career development opportunities for health care administrators.

American College of Healthcare Executives (ACHE)
1 N. Franklin St., Ste. 1700
Chicago, IL 60606-3529 USA
Phone: 312-424-2800
Fax: 312-424-0023
E-mail Address: contact@ache.org
Web Address: www.ache.org
The American College of Healthcare Executives (ACHE) is an international professional society of health care executives that offers certification and educational programs.

American Dental Association (ADA)
211 E. Chicago Ave.
Chicago, IL 60611-2678 USA
Phone: 312-440-2500
Web Address: www.ada.org
The American Dental Association (ADA) is a nonprofit professional association of dentists committed to enhancing public's oral health with a focus on ethics, science and professional advancement.

American Medical Technologists (AMT)
10700 W. Higgins Rd., Ste. 150
Rosemont, IL 60018 USA
Phone: 847-823-5169
Fax: 847-823-0458
E-mail Address: mail@americanmedtech.org
Web Address: www.americanmedtech.org
American Medical Technologists (AMT) is a nationally and internationally recognized nonprofit certification agency and professional membership association representing allied health professionals. Its members include laboratory health professionals, as well as medical and dental office professionals.

American Medical Women's Association (AMWA)
12100 Sunset Hills Rd., Ste. 130
Reston, VA 20190 USA
Phone: 703-234-4069
Fax: 703-435-4390
Toll Free: 866-564-2483
E-mail Address: associatedirector@amwa-doc.org
Web Address: www.amwa-doc.org
The American Medical Women's Association (AMWA) is an organization of women physicians and medical students dedicated to serving as the unique voice for women's health and the advancement of women in medicine.

American Occupational Therapy Association, Inc. (AOTA)
4720 Montgomery Ln., Ste. 200
Bethesda, MD 20814-3449 USA
Phone: 301-652-6611

Fax: 301-652-7711
Toll Free: 800-377-8555
Web Address: www.aota.org
The American Occupational Therapy Association, Inc. (AOTA) advances the quality, availability, use and support of occupational therapy through standard-setting, advocacy, education and research on behalf of its members and the public.

American Organization of Nurse Executives (AONE)
800 10th St. NW
Two City Center, Ste. 400
Washington, DC 20001 USA
Phone: 312-422-2800
E-mail Address: aone@aha.org
Web Address: www.aone.org
The American Organization of Nurse Executives (AONE) is a national organization focused on advancing nursing practice and patient care through leadership, professional development, advocacy and research.

American Public Health Association (APHA)
800 I St. NW
Washington, DC 20001-3710 USA
Phone: 202-777-2742
Fax: 202-777-2534
Web Address: www.apha.org
The American Public Health Association (APHA) is an association of individuals and organizations working to improve the public's health and to achieve equity in health status for all.

American School Health Association (ASHA)
7918 Jones Branch Dr., Ste. 300
McLean, VA 22102 USA
Phone: 703-506-7675
Fax: 703-506-3266
E-mail Address: info@ashaweb.org
Web Address: www.ashaweb.org
The American School Health Association (ASHA) advocates high-quality school health instruction, health services and a healthy school environment.

Dental Trade Alliance (DTA)
4350 N. Fairfax Dr., Ste. 220
Arlington, VA 22203 USA
Phone: 703-379-7755
Fax: 703-931-9429
Web Address: www.dentaltradealliance.org
The Dental Trade Alliance (DTA) represents dental manufacturers, dental dealers and dental laboratories.

Health Industry Distributors Association (HIDA)
310 Montgomery St.

Alexandria, VA 22314-1516 USA
Phone: 703-549-4432
Fax: 703-549-6495
E-mail Address: rowan@hida.org
Web Address: www.hida.org
The Health Industry Distributors
Association (HIDA) is the international
trade association representing medical
products distributors.

Healthcare Financial Management Association (HFMA)

3 Westbrook Corp. Ctr., Ste. 600
Westchester, IL 60154 USA
Phone: 708-531-9600
Fax: 708-531-0032
Toll Free: 800-252-4362
E-mail Address:
memberservices@hfma.org
Web Address: www.hfma.org
The Healthcare Financial Management
Association (HFMA) is one of the nation's
leading personal membership
organizations for health care financial
management executives and leaders.

Medical Device Manufacturers Association (MDMA)

1333 H St., Ste. 400 W.
Washington, DC 20005 USA
Phone: 202-354-7171
Web Address: www.medicaldevices.org
The Medical Device Manufacturers
Association (MDMA) is a national trade
association that represents independent
manufacturers of medical devices,
diagnostic products and health care
information systems.

Medical Group Management Association (MGMA)

104 Inverness Terrace E.
Englewood, CO 80112-5306 USA
Phone: 303-799-1111
Toll Free: 877-275-6462
E-mail Address: support@mgma.com
Web Address: www.mgma.com
Medical Group Management Association
(MGMA) is one of the nation's principal
voices for medical group practice. It
represents over 33,000 administrators and
executives in 18,000 healthcare
organizations in which 385,000
physicians practice.

National Association of Health Services Executives (NAHSE)

1050 Connecticut Ave. NW, Fl. 5
Washington, DC 20036 USA
Phone: 202-772-1030
Fax: 202-772-1072
Web Address: www.nahse.org
The National Association of Health
Services Executives (NAHSE) is a
nonprofit association of black health care

executives who promote the advancement
and development of black health care
leaders and elevate the quality of health
care services rendered to minority and
underserved communities.

Regulatory Affairs Professionals Society (RAPS)

5635 Fishers Ln., Ste. 550
Rockville, MD 20852 USA
Phone: 301-770-2920
Fax: 301-841-7956
E-mail Address: raps@raps.org
Web Address: www.raps.org
The Regulatory Affairs Professionals
Society (RAPS) is an international
professional society representing the
health care regulatory affairs profession
and individual professionals worldwide.

54) Health Insurance Industry Associations

America's Health Insurance Plans (AHIP)

601 Pennsylvania Ave. NW,
S. Bldg., Ste. 500
Washington, DC 20004 USA
Phone: 202-778-3200
Fax: 202-331-7487
E-mail Address: ahip@ahip.org
Web Address: www.ahip.org
America's Health Insurance Plans (AHIP)
is a prominent trade association
representing the health care insurance
community. Its members offer health and
supplemental benefits through employer-
sponsored coverage, the individual
insurance market, and public programs
such as Medicare and Medicaid.

55) Hearing & Speech

Hearing Industries Association (HIA)

1444 I St. NW, Ste. 700
Washington, DC 20005 USA
Phone: 202-449-1090
Fax: 202-216-9646
E-mail Address: mjones@bostrom.com
Web Address: www.hearing.org
The Hearing Industries Association (HIA)
represents and unifies the many aspects of
the hearing industry.

56) Hotel/Lodging Associations

American Hotel and Lodging Association

1250 I St., NW, Ste. 1100
Washington, DC 20005-3931 USA
Phone: 202-289-3100
Fax: 202-289-3199

E-mail Address:
informationcenter@ahla.com
Web Address: www.ahla.com
The American Hotel and Lodging
Association is a federation of state
lodging associations throughout the U.S.

57) Human Resources Industry Associations

HR Policy Association

1100 13th St., Ste. 850
Washington, DC 20005 USA
Phone: 202-789-8670
Fax: 202-789-0064
E-mail Address: info@hrpolicy.org
Web Address: www.hrpolicy.org
HR Policy Association is a public policy
organization of chief human resource
officers from major employers. The
association brings together HR
professionals at the highest level of
corporations to discuss changes in public
policy, and to lay out a vision and
advocate for competitive workplace
initiatives that promote job growth and
employment security.

Society for Human Resource Management (SHRM)

1800 Duke St.
Alexandria, VA 22314 USA
Phone: 703-548-3440
Fax: 703-535-6490
Toll Free: 800-283-7476
E-mail Address: shrm@shrm.org
Web Address: www.shrm.org
The Society for Human Resource
Management (SHRM) addresses the
interests and needs of HR professionals
through advocacy, publications, research
and other resource materials. The
organization has 575 affiliate chapters,
both in the U.S. and internationally,
serving over 5,000 members in
approximately 160 countries.

The Association for Talent Development (ATD)

1640 King St.
Alexandria, VA 22313-1443 USA
Phone: 703-683-8100
Fax: 703-299-8723
Toll Free: 800-628-2783
E-mail Address: customercare@td.org
Web Address: www.td.org
The Association for Talent Development
(ATD), formerly American Society for
Training & Development (ASTD) is
dedicated to those professionals in the
fields of training and development. It
provides resources such as research,
analysis, benchmarking, online
information, books and other publications

to training and development professional, educators and students. Additionally, the association brings professional together in conferences, workshops and online, while also offering professional development opportunities, certificate programs and Certified Professional in Learning and Performance (CPLP) credential.

58) Industry Research/ Market Research

Forrester Research
60 Acorn Park Dr.
Cambridge, MA 02140 USA
Phone: 617-613-5730
Toll Free: 866-367-7378
E-mail Address: press@forrester.com
Web Address: www.forrester.com
Forrester Research is a publicly traded company that identifies and analyzes emerging trends in technology and their impact on business. Among the firm's specialties are the financial services, retail, health care, entertainment, automotive and information technology industries.

MarketResearch.com
11200 Rockville Pike, Ste. 504
Rockville, MD 20852 USA
Phone: 240-747-3093
Fax: 240-747-3004
Toll Free: 800-298-5699
E-mail Address: customerservice@marketresearch.com
Web Address: www.marketresearch.com
MarketResearch.com is a leading broker for professional market research and industry analysis. Users are able to search the company's database of research publications including data on global industries, companies, products and trends.

Plunkett Research, Ltd.
P.O. Drawer 541737
Houston, TX 77254-1737 USA
Phone: 713-932-0000
Fax: 713-932-7080
E-mail Address: customersupport@plunkettresearch.com
Web Address: www.plunkettresearch.com
Plunkett Research, Ltd. is a leading provider of market research, industry trends analysis and business statistics. Since 1985, it has served clients worldwide, including corporations, universities, libraries, consultants and government agencies. At the firm's web site, visitors can view product information and pricing and access a large amount of basic market information on industries

such as financial services, InfoTech, e-commerce, health care and biotech.

59) Insurance Industry Associations

American Insurance Association (AIA)
2101 L St. NW, Ste.400
Washington, DC 20037 USA
Phone: 202-828-7100
Fax: 202-293-1219
E-mail Address: jbrodt@aiadc.org
Web Address: www.aiadc.org
The American Insurance Association (AIA) is a leading property and casualty insurance trade organization, representing companies that offer all types of property and casualty insurance.

60) Insurance Industry Associations-Agents & Brokers

Council of Insurance Agents & Brokers (CIAB)
701 Pennsylvania Ave. NW, Ste. 750
Washington, DC 20004 USA
Phone: 202-783-4400
Fax: 202-783-4410
E-mail Address: ciab@ciab.com
Web Address: www.ciab.com
The Council of Insurance Agents & Brokers (CIAB) is an association for commercial insurance and employee benefits intermediaries in the U.S. and abroad.

Independent Insurance Agents & Brokers of America, Inc. (IIABA)
127 S. Peyton St.
Alexandria, VA 22314 USA
Fax: 703-683-7556
Toll Free: 800-221-7917
E-mail Address: info@iiaba.org
Web Address: www.independentagent.com
Independent Insurance Agents & Brokers of America (IIABA) represents its over 300,000 members who are independent insurance agents and brokers.

Professional Insurance Agents (PIA)
25 Chamberlain St., P.O. Box 997
Glenmont, NY 12077-0997 USA
Fax: 888-225-6935
Toll Free: 800-424-4244
E-mail Address: pia@pia.org
Web Address: www.piaonline.org
Professional Insurance Agents (PIA) is a group of voluntary, membership-based trade associations representing professional, independent property and casualty insurance agents.

61) Magazines, Business & Financial

Bloomberg Businessweek Online
731 Lexington Ave.
New York, NY 10022 USA
Phone: 212-318-2000
Fax: 917-369-5000
Web Address: www.businessweek.com
Business Week Online offers an investor service, global business advice, technology news, small business guides, career information, business school advice, daily news briefs and more.

Forbes Online
60 5th Ave.
New York, NY 10011 USA
Phone: 212-620-2200
E-mail Address: customerservice@forbes.com
Web Address: www.forbes.com
Forbes Online offers varied stock information, news and commentary on business, technology and personal finance, as well as financial calculators and advice.

Fortune
1271 Ave. of the Americas
Rockefeller Ctr.
New York, NY 10020-1393 USA
Phone: 212-522-8528
Web Address: http://fortune.com/
Fortune, one of the world's premiere business magazines, contains news, business profiles and information on investing, careers, small business, technology and other details of U.S. and international business. Fortune is a publication of Cable News Network (CNN), a Time Warner company.

Investor's Business Daily (IBD)
12655 Beatrice St.
Los Angeles, CA 90066 USA
Phone: 310-448-6000
Toll Free: 800-831-2525
Web Address: www.investors.com
Investor's Business Daily (IBD) offers subscribers information and articles on the stock market, educational resources, advice from analyst William O'Neil, personal portfolios and updates on events and workshops.

Wall Street Journal Online (The)
1211 Ave. of the Americas
New York, NY 10036 USA
Phone: 609-514-0870
Toll Free: 800-568-7625
E-mail Address: support@wsj.com
Web Address: www.wsj.com

The outstanding resources of The Wall Street Journal are available online for a nominal fee.

62) MBA Resources

MBA Depot
Web Address: www.mbadepot.com
MBA Depot is an online community and information portal for MBAs, potential MBA program applicants and business professionals.

63) Online Recruiting & Employment ASPs & Solutions

Hrsoft
2200 Lucien Way, Ste. 201
Maitland, FL 32751 USA
Phone: 407-475-5500
Fax: 407-475-5502
Toll Free: 866-953-8800
E-mail Address:
Michael.Noland@HRsoft.com
Web Address: www.hrsoft.com
HRsoft, formerly Workstream, Inc., creates workforce management solutions through a combination of technology and services designed to integrate an organization.

Insala
2005 NE Green Oaks Blvd., Ste. 110
Arlington, TX 76006 USA
Phone: 817-355-0939
Fax: 817-355-0746
E-mail Address: info@insala.com
Web Address: www.insala.com
Insala provides job search software solutions for the outplacement industry.

Kenexa
650 E. Swedesford Rd., Fl. 2
Wayne, PA 19087 USA
Phone: 877-971-9171
Fax: 610-971-9181
Toll Free: 800-391-9557
E-mail Address: contactus@kenexa.com
Web Address: www.kenexa.com
Kenexa is a back-end recruiting and job-posting service that is used by many companies in building a workforce. Products and services include recruitment software solutions, talent consulting and recruitment process management.

64) Outsourcing Industry Associations

International Association of Outsourcing Professionals (IAOP)
2600 South Rd., Ste. 44-240

Poughkeepsie, NY 12601 USA
Phone: 845-452-0600
Fax: 845-452-6988
E-mail Address:
memberservices@iaop.org
Web Address: www.iaop.org
The International Association of Outsourcing Professionals (IAOP) represents outsourcing leaders and experts from companies of all sizes and industries around the world.

65) Pensions, Benefits & 401(k) Associations

Plan Sponsor Council of America (PSCA)
20 N. Wacker Dr., Ste. 3164
Chicago, IL 60606 USA
Phone: 312-419-1863
Fax: 312-419-1864
E-mail Address: psca@psca.org
Web Address: www.psca.org
The Plan Sponsor Council of America (PSCA), formerly the Profit Sharing/401(k) Council of America (PSCA). is a national nonprofit association of 1,200 companies and their 6 million employees. The group expresses its members' interests to federal policymakers and offers practical, cost-effective assistance with profit sharing and 401(k) plan design, administration, investment, compliance and communication. Its web site offers a thorough glossary, statistics and educational material.

66) Pensions, Benefits & 401(k) Resources

Employee Benefits Security Administration (EBSA)
200 Constitution Ave. NW
Washington, DC 20210 USA
Toll Free: 866-444-3272
Web Address: www.dol.gov/ebsa
The Employee Benefits Security Administration (EBSA) is a division of the U.S. Department of Labor, whose web site features a wealth of benefits information for both employers and employees. Included are the answers to such questions as to how a company's bankruptcy will affect its employees and what one should know about pension rights.

Pension Benefit Guarantee Corporation (PBGC)
1200 K St. NW, Ste. 9429
Washington, DC 20005-4026 USA
Phone: 202-326-4000

Fax: 202-326-4047
Toll Free: 800-400-7242
E-mail Address: webmaster@pbgc.gov
Web Address: www.pbgc.gov
The Pension Benefit Guarantee Corporation (PBGC) is a U.S. Government agency that guarantees a portion of the retirement incomes of about 41 million American workers in about 24,000 private defined benefit pension plans. Its web site contains information regarding this guarantee, along with information on retirement planning and links to several related organizations.

67) Pharmaceutical Industry Associations (Drug Industry)

American Pharmacists Association (AphA)
2215 Constitution Ave. NW
Washington, DC 20037 USA
Phone: 202-628-4410
Fax: 202-783-2351
Toll Free: 800-237-4410
E-mail Address: infocenter@aphanet.org
Web Address: www.pharmacist.com
American Pharmaceutical Association (APhA), formerly American Pharmaceutical Association is a national professional society that provides news and information to pharmacists. Its membership includes over 62,000 practicing pharmacists, pharmaceutical scientists, student pharmacists and pharmacy technicians.

Pharmaceutical Research and Manufacturers of America (PhRMA)
950 F St. NW, Ste. 300
Washington, DC 20004 USA
Phone: 202-835-3400
Web Address: www.phrma.org
Pharmaceutical Research and Manufacturers of America (PhRMA) represents the nation's leading research-based pharmaceutical and biotechnology companies.

68) Pilots Associations

Airline Pilots Association (ALPA)
1625 Massachusetts Ave NW
Washington, DC 20036 USA
Phone: 703-689-2270
E-mail Address: media@alpa.org
Web Address: www.alpa.org
The Airline Pilots Association (ALPA) is an association for professional airline pilots in the United States, in Canada and internationally. ALPA provides airline safety, security, pilot assistance,

representation and advocacy to its members.

69) Printers & Publishers Associations

Epicomm
1800 Diagonal Rd., Ste. 320
Alexandria, VA 22314-2862 USA
Phone: 703-836-9200
Web Address: http://epicomm.org
Epicomm is a non-profit business management association formed in 2014, through the merger of the National Association of Printers & Lithographers (NAPL), National Association of Quick Printers (NAQP) and the Association of Marketing Service Providers (AMSP). It represents the interests of graphic communications industry in the U.S.

In-Plant Printing and Mailing Association (IPMA)
105 S. Jefferson, Ste. B-4
Kearney, MO 64060 USA
Phone: 816-903-4762
Fax: 816-902-4766
E-mail Address: ipmainfo@ipma.org
Web Address: www.ipma.org
The In-Plant Printing and Mailing Association (IPMA), formerly the International Publishing Management Association, is an exclusive not-for-profit organization dedicated to assisting in-house corporate publishing and distribution professionals.

MPA-The Association of Magazine Media
810 7th Ave., Fl. 24
New York, NY 10019 USA
Phone: 212-872-3700
E-mail Address: mpa@magazine.org
Web Address: www.magazine.org
MPA-The Association of Magazine Media (formerly the Magazine Publishers of America, Inc.) is the industry association for consumer magazines in all formats, including printed, mobile and online.

Newspaper Association of America (NAA)
4401 Wilson Blvd., Ste. 900
Arlington, VA 22203-1867 USA
Phone: 571-366-1000
Fax: 571-366-1195
E-mail Address: membsvc@naa.org
Web Address: www.naa.org
The Newspaper Association of America (NAA) is a nonprofit organization representing the newspaper industry.

70) Real Estate Industry Associations

Institute of Real Estate Management (IREM)
430 N. Michigan Ave.
Chicago, IL 60611 USA
Fax: 800-338-4736
Toll Free: 800-837-0706
E-mail Address: getinfo@irem.org
Web Address: www.irem.org
The Institute of Real Estate Management (IREM) seeks to educate real estate managers, certify their competence and professionalism, serve as an advocate on issues affecting the real estate management industry and enhance its members' professional competence so they can better identify and meet the needs of those who use their services.

NAREC
6348 N. Milwaukee Ave., Ste. 103
Chicago, IL 60606 USA
Phone: 773-283-6362
E-mail Address: info@narec.org
Web Address: narec.org
NAREC, formerly PeerSpan and, prior to that, the National Association of Real Estate Companies, is composed of representatives of publicly and privately owned real estate companies, significant subsidiaries of publicly owned companies and public accounting firms.

National Association of Real Estate Brokers (NAREB)
9831 Greenbelt Rd., Ste. 309
Lanham, MD 20706 USA
Phone: 301-552-9340
Fax: 301-552-9216
E-mail Address: info@nareb.com
Web Address: www.nareb.com
The National Association of Real Estate Brokers (NAREB) is a national trade organization dedicated to bringing together the nation's minority professionals in the real estate industry.

National Association of Realtors (NAR)
430 N. Michigan Ave.
Chicago, IL 606-4087 USA
Toll Free: 800-874-6500
Web Address: www.realtor.org
The National Association of Realtors (NAR) is composed of realtors involved in residential and commercial real estate as brokers, salespeople, property managers, appraisers and counselors and in other areas of the industry. NAR also sponsors Realtor.com, operated by Move, Inc.

Women's Council of Realtors (WCR)
430 N. Michigan Ave.
Chicago, IL 60611 USA
Fax: 312-329-3290
Toll Free: 800-245-8512
E-mail Address: wcr@wcr.org
Web Address: www.wcr.org
The Women's Council of Realtors (WCR) is a community of women real estate professionals. It promotes the professional growth of its members through networking, leadership development, resources, infrastructure and accessibility

71) Recording & Music Associations

American Federation of Musicians (AFM)
1501 Broadway, Ste. 600
New York, NY 10036 USA
Phone: 212-869-1330
Fax: 212-764-6134
Web Address: www.afm.org
The American Federation of Musicians (AFM) is the largest union in the world for music professionals, serving musicians throughout the U.S. and Canada.

American Society of Composers, Authors & Publishers (ASCAP)
1900 Broadway
New York, NY 10023-7142 USA
Phone: 212-621-6000
Fax: 212-621-8453
Web Address: www.ascap.com
American Society of Composers, Authors & Publishers (ASCAP) is a membership association of U.S. composers, songwriters and publishers of every kind of music, with hundreds of thousands of members worldwide.

Content Delivery & Storage Association (CDSA)
39 N. Bayles Ave.
Port Washington, NY 11050 USA
Phone: 516-767-6720
Fax: 516-883-5793
E-mail Address: mporter@CDSAonline.org
Web Address: www.cdsaonline.org
The Content Delivery & Storage Association (CDSA), formerly the International Recording Media Association, is a worldwide trade association encompassing organizations involved in every facet of recording media, including entertainment, information and software content storage. CDSA is under the management of the Media & Entertainment Services Alliance (MESA).

International Association of Audio Information Services (IAAIS)
Toll Free: 800-280-5325
E-mail Address:
Stuart.Holland@state.mn.us
Web Address: www.iaais.org
International Association of Audio
Information Services (IAAIS) is an
organization that provides audio access to
information for people who are print-
disabled.

Music Publisher's Association of the United States (MPA)
243 5th Ave., Ste. 236
New York, NY 10016 USA
Phone: 212-327-4044
E-mail Address: admin@mpa.org
Web Address: mpa.org
The Music Publisher's Association of the
United States (MPA) serves as a forum
for publishers to deal with the music
industry's vital issues and is actively
involved in supporting and advancing
compliance with copyright law,
combating copyright infringement and
exploring the need for further reform.

Recording Industry Association of America (RIAA)
1025 F St. NW, Fl. 10
Washington, DC 20004 USA
Phone: 202-775-0101
Web Address: www.riaa.com
The Recording Industry Association of
America (RIAA) is the trade group that
represents the U.S. recording industry.

Society of Professional Audio Recording Services (SPARS)
Fax: 214-722-1442
Toll Free: 800-771-7727
E-mail Address: info@spars.com
Web Address: www.spars.com
The Society of Professional Audio
Recording Services (SPARS) is an
organization for members of the recording
industry to share practical business
information about audio and multimedia
facility ownership, management and
operations.

Songwriters Guild of America
5120 Virginia Way, Ste. C22
Brentwood, TN 37027 USA
Phone: 615-742-9945
Fax: 615-630-7501
Toll Free: 800-524-6742
Web Address: www.songwritersguild.com
The Songwriters Guild of America is the
nation's largest and oldest songwriters'
organization, providing its members with
information and programs to further their
careers and understanding of the music
industry.

72) Satellite-Related Professional Organizations

Satellite Broadcasting & Communications Association (SBCA)
1100 17th St. NW, Ste. 1150
Washington, DC 20036 USA
Phone: 202-349-3620
Fax: 202-349-3621
Toll Free: 800-541-5981
E-mail Address: info@sbca.org
Web Address: www.sbca.com
The Satellite Broadcasting &
Communications Association (SBCA) is
the national trade organization
representing all segments of the satellite
consumer services industry in America.

Society of Satellite Professionals International (SSPI)
250 Park Ave., Fl. 7
The New York Information Technology
Ctr.
New York, NY 10177 USA
Phone: 212-809-5199
Fax: 212-825-0075
E-mail Address: rbell@sspi.org
Web Address: www.sspi.org
The Society of Satellite Professionals
International (SSPI) is a nonprofit
member-benefit society that serves
satellite professionals worldwide.

73) Securities Industry Associations

North American Securities Administrators Association, Inc. (NASAA)
750 First St. NE, Ste. 1140
Washington, DC 20002 USA
Phone: 202-737-0900
Fax: 202-783-3571
E-mail Address: ri@nasaa.org
Web Address: www.nasaa.org
The North American Securities
Administrators Association (NASAA) is
the oldest international organization
committed to investor protection. Its web
site provides information on franchising
and raising capital, as well as state blue
sky securities laws and resources for small
investment advisors.

Securities Industry and Financial Markets Association (SIFMA)
120 Broadway, Fl. 35
New York, NY 10271-0080 USA
Phone: 212-313-1200
Fax: 212-313-1301
E-mail Address: inquiry@sifma.org
Web Address: www.sifma.org

The Securities Industry and Financial
Markets Association (SIFMA), formed by
the merger of the Securities Industry
Association (SIA) and the Bond Market
Association, brings together the shared
interests of more than 650 securities and
bond industry firms to accomplish
common goals.

74) Software Industry Associations

Software & Information Industry Association (SIIA)
1090 Vermont Ave. NW, Fl. 6
Washington, DC 20005-4095 USA
Phone: 202-289-7442
Fax: 202-289-7097
Web Address: www.siia.net
The Software & Information Industry
Association (SIIA) is a principal trade
association for the software and digital
content industry.

75) Stocks & Financial Markets Data

Reuters.com
3 Times Sq.
New York, NY 10036 USA
Phone: 646-223-6890
Web Address: www.reuters.com
Reuters.com, a service of Thomson
Reuters, offers information on business
and world markets, political and
international news and company-specific
stock information.

Yahoo! Finance
701 1st Ave.
Yahoo! Inc.
Sunnyvale, CA 94089 USA
Phone: 408-349-3300
Web Address: finance.yahoo.com
Yahoo! Finance provides a wealth of links
and a supreme search guide. Users can
find just about any financial information
concerning both U.S. and world markets.
Tax, insurance information, financial
news and community research can be
conducted through this site, as can
searches for other aspects of the financial
world.

76) Telecommunications Industry Associations

CompTel
900 17th St. NW, Ste. 400
Washington, DC 20006 USA
Phone: 202-296-6650
E-mail Address: gnorris@comptel.org
Web Address: www.comptel.org

CompTel is a trade organization representing voice, data and video communications service providers and their supplier partners. Members are supported through education, networking, policy advocacy and trade shows.

National Association of Telecommunications Officers and Advisors (NATOA)
3213 Duke St., Ste. 695
Alexandria, VA 22314 USA
Phone: 703-519-8035
Fax: 703-997-7080
E-mail Address: info@natoa.org
Web Address: www.natoa.org
The National Association of Telecommunications Officers and Advisors (NATOA) works to support and serve the telecommunications industry's interests and the needs of local governments.

Telecommunications Industry Association (TIA)
1320 N. Courthouse Rd., Ste. 200
Arlington, VA 22201 USA
Phone: 703-907-7700
Fax: 703-907-7727
E-mail Address: smontgomery@tiaonline.org
Web Address: www.tiaonline.org
The Telecommunications Industry Association (TIA) is a leading trade association in the information, communications and entertainment technology industry. TIA focuses on market development, trade promotion, trade shows, domestic and international advocacy, standards development and enabling e-business.

United States Telecom Association (USTelecom)
607 14th St. NW, Ste. 400
Washington, DC 20005 USA
Phone: 202-326-7300
Fax: 202-315-3603
E-mail Address: membership@ustelecom.org
Web Address: www.ustelecom.org
The United States Telecom Association (USTelecom) is a trade association representing service providers and suppliers for the telecom industry.

77) Temporary Staffing Firms

Adecco
Saegereistrasse 10
Glattbrugg, CH-8152 Switzerland
Phone: 41-44-878-88-88
Fax: 41-44-829-88-06
E-mail Address: press.office@adecco.com
Web Address: www.adecco.com
Adecco maintains human resources and staffing services offices in 70 countries. It provides temporary and permanent personnel.

Advantage Resourcing, Inc.
220 Norwood Park S.
Norwood, MA 02062 USA
Phone: 781-251-8000
Toll Free: 800-343-4314
E-mail Address: M
Web Address: www.hirethinking.com
Advantage Resourcing, Inc., formerly Radia Holdings, Inc., provides integrated human resources services throughout Japan, North America, Europe and Australia. It is one of the largest staffing providers, with over 350 branches and satellite offices.

Allegis Group
7301 Parkway Dr.
Hanover, MD 21076 USA
Toll Free: 800-927-8090
Web Address: www.allegisgroup.com
The Allegis Group provides technical, professional and industrial recruiting and staffing services. Allegis specializes in information technology staffing services. The firm operates in the United Kingdom, Germany and The Netherlands as Aerotek and TEKsystems, and in India as Allegis Group India. Aerotek provides staffing solutions for aviation, engineering, automotive and scientific personnel markets.

CDI Corporation
1717 Arch St., Fl. 35
Philadelphia, PA 19103-2768 USA
Phone: 215-636-1240
E-mail Address: vince.webb@cdicorp.com
Web Address: www.cdicorp.com
CDI Corporation specializes in engineering and information technology staffing services. Company segments include CDI IT Solutions, specializing in information technology; CDI Engineering Solutions, specializing in engineering outsourcing services; AndersElite Limited, operating in the United Kingdom and Australia; and MRINetwork, specializing in executive recruitment.

Express Employment Professionals
9701 Boardwalk Blvd.
Oklahoma City, OK 73162 USA
Phone: 405-840-5000
Toll Free: 888-923-3797
Web Address: www.expresspros.com

Express Employment Professionals operates through a network of over 550 locations in the United States, Canada, South Africa and Australia. Services include temporary and flexible staffing, evaluation and direct hire, professional and contract staffing, human resource services and online payroll processing (U.S. only).

Glotel Inc.
8700 W. Bryn Mawr Ave., Ste. 400N
Chicago, IL 60631 USA
Phone: 312-612-7480
E-mail Address: info@glotelinc.com
Web Address: www.glotel.com
Glotel is a global technology staffing and managed projects solutions company specializing in the placement of contract and permanent personnel within all areas of technology. Glotel has a network of offices throughout Europe, the U.S. and Asia-Pacific.

Harvey Nash
110 Bishopgate
London, EC2N 4AY UK
Phone: 44-20-7333-0033
Fax: 44-20-7333-0032
E-mail Address: richard.ashcroft@harveynash.com
Web Address: www.harveynash.com
Harvey Nash provides professional recruitment, interim executive leadership services and outsourcing services. The firm specializes in information technology staffing on a permanent and contract basis in US, UK and Europe. It also offers outsourcing services including offshore software development services, information technology systems management, workforce risk management and managed services for network administration.

Hays plc
250 Euston Rd.
London, NW1 2AF UK
Phone: 44-20-7383-2266
Fax: 44-20-7388-4367
E-mail Address: customerservice@hays.com
Web Address: www.hays.com
Hays plc is a global leader in specialist recruitment. It places professional candidates in permanent, temporary and interim positions across numerous fields, including accountancy and finance; education; health care; IT and telecom; manufacturing and engineering; pharmaceuticals; professional services; retail, sales and marketing; and support services.

Hudson Highland Group, Inc.
1325 Avenue of the Americas, Fl. 12
New York, NY 10019 USA
Phone: 212-351-7400
Fax: 212-351-7401
Web Address: www.hudson.com
Hudson Highland Group, Inc. provides
permanent recruitment, contract and
human resources consulting and inclusion
solutions. Services range from single
placements to total outsourced solutions.
The company employs professionals
serving clients and candidates in 20
countries.

Kelly Services, Inc.
999 W. Big Beaver Rd.
Troy, MI 48084-4782 USA
Phone: 248-362-4444
E-mail Address: kfirst@kellyservices.com
Web Address: www.kellyservices.com
Kelly Services is a workforce solutions
company offering a wide range of
outsourcing and consulting services, as
well as quality staffing on a temporary,
temporary-to-hire and direct-hire basis
both locally and worldwide.

Kforce, Inc.
1001 E. Palm Ave.
Tampa, FL 33605 USA
Toll Free: 800-395-5575
E-mail Address:
internalstaffing@kforce.com
Web Address: www.kforce.com
Kforce, Inc. is one of America's largest
temporary placement firms, with more
than 70 offices in 44 cities across the U.S.
It specializes in employees for the
following types of jobs: finance and
accounting, scientific, technology, health
care, clinical research, mortgages, title
insurance and real estate.

Labor Ready, Inc.
1015 A St.
Tacoma, WA 98402 USA
Phone: 253-383-9101
Fax: 877-733-0399
Toll Free: 877-733-0430
E-mail Address:
customercare@laborready.com
Web Address: www.laborready.com
Labor Ready, Inc. specializes in
temporary staffing in construction,
manufacturing, hospitality services,
transportation, landscaping, warehousing,
retail and more with almost 700 branches
throughout the U.S., Canada and Puerto
Rico.

Manpower, Inc.
100 Manpower Pl.
Milwaukee, WI 53212 USA
Phone: 414-961-1000

Fax: 414-906-7822
E-mail Address:
Britt.Zarling@manpowergroup.com
Web Address: www.manpower.com
One of the largest temporary staffing
providers in the world, Manpower places
approximately 2 million workers annually
in a variety of positions around the world.

Michael Page International plc
Page House, 1 Dashwood Lang Rd.
Addlestone, Weybridge
Surrey, KT15 2QW UK
Phone: 44-207-831-2000
Web Address: www.michaelpage.co.uk
Michael Page International is one of the
world's leading professional recruitment
consultancies specializing in the
placement of candidates in permanent,
contract, temporary and interim positions.
The Group has operations in the US, UK,
Continental Europe, Asia-Pacific and a
regional presence in France and Australia.
In the US, the firm's focus is on the areas
of financial services, supply chain,
executive searches, marketing, legal and
administrative support.

Pasona Group Inc. (Japan)
Otemachi 2-6-4 Chiyoda-ku
Tokyo, 100-8228 Japan
Web Address: www.pasonagroup.co.jp
Pasona, Inc. provides personnel services,
ranging from temporary
staffing/contracting, placement/recruiting
and outplacement to outsourcing and
training.

Randstad USA
2015 S. Park Pl.
Atlanta, GA 30339 USA
Phone: 770-937-7000
Fax: 770-937-7100
Toll Free: 877-922-2468
E-mail Address: info@us.randstad.com
Web Address: www.us.randstad.com
Randstad provides staffing services in the
office, industrial, technical, creative and
professional markets. It specializes in
temporary and permanent staffing;
recruitment and consultant services; and
human resource services. It operates in 83
countries, primarily in Europe, Asia and
the U.S. Brands include Capac, Yacht,
and Tempo-Team.

Robert Half International Inc. (RHI)
2884 Sand Hill Rd.
Menlo Park, CA 94025 USA
Phone: 650-234-6000
E-mail Address: webmaster@rhi.com
Web Address: www.rhi.com
Robert Half International Inc. (RHI)
specializes in accounting and finance
positions. It also places workers in

administrative, information technology,
legal, advertising and marketing positions
on temporary or permanent bases.

Robert Walters plc
11 Slingsby Pl.
St. Martin's Courtyard
London, WC2E 9AB UK
Phone: 44-20-7379-3333
Fax: 44-20-7509-8714
E-mail Address:
london@robertwalters.com
Web Address: www.robertwalters.com
Robert Walters PLC is a professional
recruitment specialist, outsourcing and
human resource consultant. The firm
provides services for the temporary,
contract and permanent placement of
individuals in the sectors of finance,
operations, legal, information technology,
marketing and administration support. It
has offices in 24 countries including the
US.

Spherion Corporation
33625 Cumberland Blvd., Ste. 600
Atlanta, GA 30339 U.S.A.
Phone: 954-308-6266
E-mail Address: gailferro@spherion.com
Web Address: www.spherion.com
Spherion Corp., a subsidiary of SFN
Group, provides temporary staffing,
recruitment and employee consulting,
primarily in administrative, clerical,
customer service and light industrial
fields.

Synergie SA (France)
11 Ave. du Colonel Bonnet
Paris, 75016 France
Phone: 44-14-90-20
Fax: 45-25-97-10
Web Address: www.synergie.fr
Synergie provides human resource
management services that include
temporary placement, consulting and
training. The firm is most active in
France, but also operates through a
network of 550 agencies in throughout
Europe and Canada.

Tempstaff Co., Ltd. (Japan)
Shinjuku Maynds Twr. 2-1-1
Yoyogi, Shibuya-ku
Tokyo, 151-0053 Japan
Phone: 81-3-5350-1212
Web Address: www.tempstaff.co.jp
Tempstaff Co., Ltd. provides temporary
and permanent placement and recruiting
and outsourcing services. It has 263
offices in Japan and 12 overseas offices
located in Los Angeles, Seattle, Shanghai,
Suzhou, Guangzhou, Hong Kong, Taiwan,
Korea, Singapore and Indonesia.

Volt Information Sciences, Inc.
1133 Ave. of the Americas, Fl. 15
New York, NY 10036 USA
Phone: 212-704-2400
Web Address: www.volt.com
Volt Information Sciences, Inc. provides temporary staffing services, professional search, managed services programs, vendor management systems and recruitment process outsourcing, as well as a wealth of additional support services, in North and South America, Europe and Asia through approximately 400 locations.

78) Testing Resources

CPP, Inc.
1055 Joaquin Rd., Ste. 200
Mountain View, CA 94043 USA
Phone: 650-969-8901
Fax: 650-969-8608
Toll Free: 800-624-1765
E-mail Address: custserv@cpp.com
Web Address: www.cpp.com
CPP, Inc. (formerly known as Consulting Psychologists Press) publishes the Meyers-Briggs Type Indicator, Strong Inventory Test and other psychological assessment-related products. CPP also provides information about the tests and, through division Davies-Black Publishing, offers business-related books and services, including those covering career management and leadership development.

79) Textile & Fabric Associations

International Textile and Apparel Association (ITAA)
P.O. Box 70687
Knoxville, TN 37938-0687 USA
Phone: 865-992-1535
E-mail Address: info@itaaonline.org
Web Address: www.itaaonline.org
The International Textile and Apparel Association (ITAA) is a nonprofit educational and scientific corporation dedicated to providing opportunities to scholars in the retail, textile and apparel industries.

80) Travel Business & Professional Associations

American Society of Travel Agents (ASTA)
1101 King St., Ste. 200
Alexandria, VA 22314 USA
Phone: 703-739-2782
Toll Free: 800-275-2782

E-mail Address: askasta@asta.org
Web Address: www.asta.org
The American Society of Travel Agents (ASTA) is one of the world's largest associations of travel professionals.

Association of Corporate Travel Executives (ACTE)
515 King St., Ste. 440
Alexandria, VA 22314 USA
Phone: 703-683-5322
Fax: 703-683-2720
E-mail Address: info@acte.org
Web Address: www.acte.org
The Association of Corporate Travel Executives (ACTE) serves the specialized travel interests of corporate purchasers and travel service suppliers from nearly 50 countries.

Association of Retail Travel Agents (ARTA)
4320 North Miller Rd.
c/o Travel Destinations, Inc.
Scottsdale, AZ 85251-3606 USA
Fax: 866-743-2087
Toll Free: 866-369-8969
Web Address: www.arta.travel
The Association of Retail Travel Agents (ARTA) is one of the largest nonprofit associations in North America to exclusively represent travel agents.

Association of Travel Marketing Executives (ATME)
P.O. Box 3176
West Tisbury, MA 02575 USA
Phone: 508-693-0550
Fax: 508-693-0115
E-mail Address: kzern@atme.org
Web Address: www.atme.org
The Association of Travel Marketing Executives (ATME) is a global professional association of senior-level travel marketing executives dedicated to providing cutting-edge information, education and opportunities for meaningful networking with peers.

National Society of Minorities in Hospitality
6933 Commons Plz., Ste. 537
Chesterfield, VA 23832 USA
Phone: 703-549-9899
Fax: 703-997-7795
E-mail Address: hq@nsmh.org
Web Address: www.nsmh.org
The National Society of Minorities in Hospitality strives to establish a working relationship between the hospitality industry and minority students.

Network of Executive Women in Hospitality, Inc. (NEWH)
P.O. Box 322

Shawano, WI 54166 USA
Fax: 800-693-6394
Toll Free: 800-593-6394
Web Address: www.newh.org
The Network of Executive Women in Hospitality, Inc. (NEWH) brings together professionals from all facets of the hospitality industry by providing opportunities for education, professional development and networking. Although primarily a U.S.-based organization, NEWH does have international chapters in Toronto and London.

Society of Incentive and Travel Executives
401 N. Michigan Ave.
Chicago, IL 60611-4267 USA
Phone: 312-321-5148
Fax: 312-527-6783
E-mail Address: site@siteglobal.com
Web Address: www.site-intl.org
The Society of Incentive and Travel Executives is a worldwide organization of business professionals dedicated to the recognition and development of motivational and performance improvement strategies in the travel industry.

81) Travel Industry Associations

Destination Marketing Association International
2025 M St. NW, Ste. 500
Washington, DC 20036 USA
Phone: 202-296-7888
Fax: 202-296-7889
E-mail Address: info@destinationmarketing.org
Web Address: www.destinationmarketing.org
The Destination Marketing Association International, formerly the International Association of Convention & Visitor Bureaus, strives to enhance the professionalism, effectiveness and image of destination management organizations worldwide. Its members include professionals, industry partners, students and educators from roughly 15 countries.

International Association of Conference Centers (IACC)
243 N. Lindbergh Blvd.
St. Louis, MO 63141 USA
Phone: 314-993-8575
Fax: 314-993-8919
E-mail Address: info@iacconline.org
Web Address: www.iacconline.com
The International Association of Conference Centers (IACC) is a nonprofit, facilities-based organization founded to

promote a greater awareness and understanding of the unique features of conference centers around the world.

National Tour Association (NTA)
101 Prosperous Pl., Ste. 350
Lexington, KY 40509 USA
Phone: 859-264-6540
Fax: 859-266-6570
Toll Free: 800-682-8886
E-mail Address:
NTAwashington@gmail.com
Web Address: www.ntaonline.com
The National Tour Association (NTA) is an association for travel professionals who have an interest in the packaged travel sector of the industry.

U.S. Travel Association
1100 New York Ave. NW, Ste. 450
Washington, DC 20005-3934 USA
Phone: 202-408-8422
Fax: 202-408-1255
E-mail Address: feedback@ustravel.org
Web Address: www.ustravel.org
The U.S. Travel Association is the result of a merger between the Travel Industry Association (TIA) and the Travel Business Roundtable. It is a nonprofit association that represents and speaks for the common interests and concerns of all components of the U.S. travel industry.

82) U.S. Government Agencies

Bureau of Economic Analysis (BEA)
4600 Silver Hill Rd.
Washington, DC 20233 USA
Phone: 301-278-9004
E-mail Address:
customerservice@bea.gov
Web Address: www.bea.gov
The Bureau of Economic Analysis (BEA), an agency of the U.S. Department of Commerce, is the nation's economic accountant, preparing estimates that illuminate key national, international and regional aspects of the U.S. economy.

Bureau of Labor Statistics (BLS)
2 Massachusetts Ave. NE
Washington, DC 20212-0001 USA
Phone: 202-691-5200
Fax: 202-691-7890
Toll Free: 800-877-8339
E-mail Address: blsdata_staff@bls.gov
Web Address: stats.bls.gov
The Bureau of Labor Statistics (BLS) is the principal fact-finding agency for the Federal Government in the field of labor economics and statistics. It is an independent national statistical agency that collects, processes, analyzes and

disseminates statistical data to the American public, U.S. Congress, other federal agencies, state and local governments, business and labor. The BLS also serves as a statistical resource to the Department of Labor.

Equal Employment Opportunity Commission (EEOC)
131 M St. NE
Washington, DC 20507-0100 USA
Phone: 202-663-4900
Fax: 202-633-4679
Toll Free: 800-669-4000
E-mail Address: info@eeoc.gov
Web Address: www.eeoc.gov
The Equal Employment Opportunity Commission (EEOC) is a Federal Government agency focused on practices and programs that foster equal opportunity at work and elsewhere. Its web site features details about various protective laws regarding employment. It also provides information on how to file a discrimination claim.

FedStats
Web Address: fedstats.sites.usa.gov/
FedStats compiles information for statistics from over 100 U.S. federal agencies. Visitors can sort the information by agency, geography and topic, as well as perform searches.

National Labor Relations Board (NLRB)
1015 Half Street SE
Washington, DC 20570-0001 USA
Phone: 2002-273-1000
Toll Free: 866-667-6572
Web Address: www.nlrb.gov
The National Labor Relations Board (NLRB) provides case reports on labor disputes, searchable by company or union.

U.S. Census Bureau
4600 Silver Hill Rd.
Washington, DC 20233-8800 USA
Phone: 301-763-4636
Toll Free: 800-923-8282
E-mail Address: pio@census.gov
Web Address: www.census.gov
The U.S. Census Bureau is the official collector of data about the people and economy of the U.S. Founded in 1790, it provides official social, demographic and economic information. In addition to the Population & Housing Census, which it conducts every 10 years, the U.S. Census Bureau numerous other surveys annually.

U.S. Department of Commerce (DOC)
1401 Constitution Ave. NW
Washington, DC 20230 USA
Phone: 202-482-2000

E-mail Address: TheSec@doc.gov
Web Address: www.commerce.gov
The U.S. Department of Commerce (DOC) regulates trade and provides valuable economic analysis of the economy.

U.S. Department of Labor (DOL)
200 Constitution Ave. NW
Washington, DC 20210 USA
Phone: 202-693-4676
Toll Free: 866-487-2365
Web Address: www.dol.gov
The U.S. Department of Labor (DOL) is the government agency responsible for labor regulations.

U.S. Securities and Exchange Commission (SEC)
100 F St. NE
Washington, DC 20549 USA
Phone: 202-942-8088
Toll Free: 800-732-0330
E-mail Address: help@sec.gov
Web Address: www.sec.gov
The U.S. Securities and Exchange Commission (SEC) is a nonpartisan, quasi-judicial regulatory agency responsible for administering federal securities laws. These laws are designed to protect investors in securities markets and ensure that they have access to disclosure of all material information concerning publicly traded securities. Visitors to the web site can access the EDGAR database of corporate financial and business information.

83) Water Technologies & Resources

American Water Resources Association (AWRA)
P.O. Box 1626
Middleburg, VA 20118 USA
Phone: 540-687-8390
Fax: 540-687-8395
E-mail Address: info@awra.org
Web Address: www.awra.org
The American Water Resources Association (AWRA) represents the interests of professionals involved in water resources and provides a platform for education, research, information exchange on water related issues.

84) Wireless & Cellular Industry Associations

Cellular Telecommunications & Internet Association (CTIA)
1400 16th St. NW, Ste. 600
Washington, DC 20036 USA

Phone: 202-785-0081
Web Address: www.ctia.org
The Cellular Telecommunications &
Internet Association (CTIA) is an
international nonprofit membership
organization that represents a variety of
wireless communications sectors
including cellular service providers,
manufacturers, wireless data and Internet
companies. CTIA's industry committees
study spectrum allocation, homeland
security, taxation, safety and emerging
technology.

Wireless Communications Association International (WCAI)
1333 H St. NW, Ste. 700 W
Washington, DC 20005-4754 USA
Phone: 202-452-7823
Web Address: www.wcai.com
The Wireless Communications
Association International (WCAI) is the
principal nonprofit trade association
representing the wireless broadband
industry.

85) Writers, Photographers & Editors Associations

American Society of Journalists and Authors, Inc. (ASJA)
355 Lexington Ave., Fl. 15
New York, NY 10017 USA
Phone: 212-997-0947
Web Address: www.asja.org
The American Society of Journalists and
Authors (ASJA) is one of the nation's
leading organizations of independent
nonfiction writers.

American Society of Magazine Editors (ASME)
757 Third Ave., Fl. 11
New York, NY 10017 USA
Phone: 212-872-3700
E-mail Address: mpa@magazine.org
Web Address: www.magazine.org/asme
The American Society of Magazine
Editors (ASME) is a professional
organization for editors of print and online
magazines. ASME is part of the Magazine
Publishers of America (MPA).

American Society of News Editors (ASNE)
209 Reynolds Journalism Institute
Missouri School of Journalism
Columbia, MO 65211 USA
Phone: 573-884-2405
Fax: 573-884-3824
Web Address: www.asne.org
The American Society of News Editors
(ASNE) is an association that brings
together editors of daily newspapers and

people directly involved with developing
content for daily newspapers.

Association of Opinion Journalists
801 Third St. South
c/o The Poynter Institute
St. Petersburg, FL 33701 USA
Phone: 518-454-5472
E-mail Address: AOJ@poynter.org
Web Address: https://aoj.wildapricot.org/
The Association of Opinion Journalists,
formerly known as The National
Conference of Editorial Writers (NCEW)
strives to stimulate the conscience and
improve the quality of opinion writing.

International Women's Writing Guild (IWWG)
274 Madison Ave., Ste. 1202
New York, NY 10016 USA
Phone: 917-720-6959
E-mail Address:
iwwgquestions@gmail.com
Web Address: www.iwwg.com
The International Women's Writing Guild
(IWWG) is a network for the personal and
professional empowerment of women
through writing.

Media Communications Association International (MCAI)
c/o MCA-I Chapter
P.O. Box 5135
Madison, WI 53705-0135 USA
Phone: 888-899-6224
E-mail Address:
m_k_schaefer@yahoo.com
Web Address: www.mca-i.org
The Media Communications Association
International (MCAI) is the leading global
community for media communications
professionals seeking to drive the
convergence of communications and
technology for the growth of the
profession.

National Association of Hispanic Journalists (NAHJ)
1050 Connecticut Ave. NW, Fl. 10
Washington, DC 20036 USA
Phone: 202-662-7145
E-mail Address: nahj@nahj.org
Web Address: www.nahj.org
The National Association of Hispanic
Journalists (NAHJ) is dedicated to the
recognition and professional advancement
of Hispanics in the news industry.

National Association of Science Writers, Inc. (NASW)
P.O. Box 7905
Berkley, CA 94707 USA
Phone: 510-647-9500
Web Address: www.nasw.org

The National Association of Science
Writers (NASW) exists to foster the
dissemination of accurate information
regarding science through all media
devoted to informing the public.

National Federation of Press Women (NFPW)
200 Little Falls St., Ste. 405
Falls Church, VA 22046 USA
Phone: 703-237-9804
Fax: 703-237-9808
E-mail Address: presswomen@aol.com
Web Address: www.nfpw.org
The National Federation of Press Women
(NFPW) is an organization of professional
journalists and communicators.

National Writers Union (NWU)
256 W. 38th St., Ste. 703
New York, NY 10018 USA
Phone: 212-254-0279
Fax: 212-254-0673
E-mail Address: nwu@nwu.org
Web Address: www.nwu.org
The National Writers Union (NWU) is a
labor union that represents freelance
writers in all genres, formats and media. It
is committed to improving the economic
and working conditions of freelance
writers.

Society of Children's Book Writers and Illustrators (SCBWI)
4727 Wilshire Blvd., Ste. 301
Los Angeles, CA 90010 USA
Phone: 323-782-1010
Fax: 323-782-1892
E-mail Address: scbwi@scbwi.org
Web Address: www.scbwi.org
The Society of Children's Book Writers
and Illustrators (SCBWI) serves people
who write, illustrate or share a vital
interest in children's literature, including
publishers, librarians, booksellers and
agents.

Chapter 5

THE AMERICAN EMPLOYERS 500:
WHO THEY ARE AND
HOW THEY WERE CHOSEN

Note: financial data given for each of the AMERICAN EMPLOYERS 500 firms is for the year ended December 31, 2016 or the latest figures available to the editors. Telephone numbers, addresses, contact names, Internet addresses and other vital facts were collected in the fall of 2017.

The companies chosen to be listed in THE ALMANAC OF AMERICAN EMPLOYERS are not the same as the "Fortune 500" or any other list of corporations. The AMERICAN EMPLOYERS 500 (the actual number is 503) were chosen specifically for their likelihood to provide new job openings to the greatest number of employees. Complete information about each firm can be found in the "Individual Data Listings," beginning about the middle of this book. They are in alphabetical order.

THE AMERICAN EMPLOYERS 500 includes companies from all parts of the United States and from nearly all industry segments: selected financial services firms, retailers, service companies, wholesalers and distributors, and others, as well as industrial companies, technology firms and manufacturers.

Simply stated, the list contains 500 of the largest, most successful employers in the United States today. In particular, the list contains companies that we have hand-selected to have qualities that we feel will be of greatest interest to job seekers of today who are looking for opportunities to obtain employment with major corporations.

In order to make this reference guide as useful as possible, we are selecting companies for this list by focusing on the type of business, the industry sector served and a company's competitive advantage. To a lesser extent, we are also considering the most recent year's financial performance. We consider industry sector to be a major factor, because some sectors may not offer good career prospects today. Consequently, we have deleted some well-known companies due to the state of their particular markets.

To be included in our list, the firms were selected based on the following criteria:

1) U.S.-based companies. (However, a small number of companies may be subsidiaries of foreign-based firms. Also, a small number of the firms are major U.S. employers that utilize headquarters addresses in other nations.)

2) 2,500 employees or more.

3) These are almost exclusively for-profit companies. However, a small number are major, non-profit health care companies.

4) Selected Type of Business and/or Industry Sector. Companies were chosen based on our analysis of the business potential of their products, services and industrial sectors in light of today's economic conditions and the effects of globalization and technological changes.

The companies were chosen in this manner for the following reasons:

500 COMPANIES so there is a broad base among which to make comparisons and from which you can study potential employers.

LARGER EMPLOYERS (2,500 or more employees) so the information can pertain to as many employees as reasonably possible, and so the companies ranked will tend to create large numbers of job openings. Also, large companies historically have offered significantly higher wages, better benefits and better training than small employers.

FOR-PROFIT so that job seekers using THE ALMANAC OF AMERICAN EMPLOYERS can choose positions in the profit-seeking, private sector, where incentive plans may be available to motivate and reward them, such as profit sharing, stock ownership, bonuses, stock options and the high pay and prestige of top executive posts.

COMPANIES THAT OPERATE IN PROMISING BUSINESS SECTORS because:
1) Companies that are stable or enjoying growing business are much more likely to have job openings. Corporate stability is more important to job seekers today than ever before due to the wave of layoffs and downsizing that continues to sweep through the U.S. (See Chapter 1, "Major Trends Affecting Job Seekers.")
2) These companies are much more likely to offer advancement opportunities. Current employees will benefit from promote-from-within policies when new plants, new stores, new product lines or new offices are opened.

Obviously, some companies are better to work for than others, depending on what you value. Creating this annual list is an arduous task. Generally, our results are very good, but we do occasionally select a company that soon develops problems or announces a layoff. The world of business constantly goes through major changes, and unforeseen events often occur. Nonetheless, it is not easy for a firm to be selected for the AMERICAN EMPLOYERS 500, and the mere presence of a company on the list can be taken as evidence that it has excelled in many ways. To start with, it has to have generated enough business to employ thousands of people–never a simple task. Also, many of these firms are among the dominant companies in their industries.

INDEX OF COMPANIES WITHIN INDUSTRY GROUPS

The industry codes shown below are based on the 2012 NAIC code system (NAIC is used by many analysts as a replacement for older SIC codes because NAIC is more specific to today's industry sectors, see www.census.gov/NAICS). Companies are given a primary NAIC code, reflecting the main line of business of each firm.

Industry Group/Company	Industry Code	2016 Sales	2016 Profits
Advertising Agencies and Marketing Services			
BBDO Worldwide	541810	650,000,000	
Interpublic Group of Companies Inc	541810	7,846,600,192	608,499,968
Omnicom Group Inc	541810	15,416,899,584	1,148,600,064
Advertising, Public Relations and Marketing Services			
Acosta Inc	541800	3,625,000,000	
Alliance Data Systems Corporation	541800	7,138,100,224	515,800,000
Valassis Communications Inc	541800	2,410,000,000	
Aircraft Components, Parts, Assemblies, Interiors and Systems Manufacturing (Aerospace)			
Spirit Aerosystems Holdings Inc	336413	6,792,900,096	469,700,000
TransDigm Group Incorporated	336413	3,171,410,944	586,414,016
Aircraft Engine and Engine Parts Manufacturing			
Honeywell International Inc	336412	39,302,000,640	4,808,999,936
United Technologies Corporation	336412	57,244,000,256	5,055,000,064
Aircraft Manufacturing (Aerospace), including Passenger Airliners and Military Aircraft,			
Boeing Company (The)	336411	94,571,003,904	4,895,000,064
Textron Inc	336411	13,788,000,256	962,000,000
Airlines, Scheduled Passenger Air Transportation			
Alaska Air Group Inc	481111	5,930,999,808	814,000,000
American Airlines Group Inc	481111	40,179,998,720	2,676,000,000
Delta Air Lines Inc	481111	39,638,999,040	4,373,000,192
JetBlue Airways Corporation	481111	6,632,000,000	759,000,000
Southwest Airlines Co	481111	20,425,000,960	2,244,000,000
Spirit Airlines Inc	481111	2,321,956,096	264,879,008
United Continental Holdings Inc	481111	36,556,001,280	2,263,000,064
Ambulatory Health Care Services, Other			
Magellan Health Inc	621999	4,836,883,968	77,879,000
Ambulatory, Outpatient Surgical Clinics, Urgent Care and Emergency Centers			
AMSURG Corporation	621493	2,800,000,000	
Apparel and Clothing Brands, Designers, Importers and Distributors			
Hanesbrands Inc	424300	6,028,198,912	539,382,016
Under Armour Inc	424300	4,825,334,784	256,979,008
VF Corporation	424300	12,019,003,392	1,074,105,984
Asset Management			
BlackRock Inc	523920	11,155,000,320	3,172,000,000
Fidelity Investments Financial Services	523920	15,900,000,000	3,500,000,000
T Rowe Price Group Inc	523920	4,222,899,968	1,215,000,064
Automobile (Car) and Light Truck Dealers, New			
AutoNation Inc	441110	21,609,000,960	430,500,000
Group 1 Automotive Inc	441110	10,887,612,416	147,064,992

Industry Group/Company	Industry Code	2016 Sales	2016 Profits
Hendrick Automotive Group	441110	8,551,253,132	
Larry H Miller Group	441110	4,679,750,795	
Lithia Motors Inc	441110	8,678,157,312	197,058,000
Penske Automotive Group Inc	441110	20,118,499,328	342,900,000
Automobile (Car) and Light Truck Dealers, Used			
CarMax Inc	441120	15,149,674,496	623,427,968
DriveTime Automotive Group Inc	441120	1,600,000,000	
Automobile (Car) and Light Truck Parts and Accessories Stores			
Advance Auto Parts Inc	441310	9,567,679,488	459,622,016
O'Reilly Automotive Inc	441310	8,593,095,680	1,037,691,008
Automobile (Car) and Light Truck Tire Dealers			
Discount Tire Company	441320	4,340,000,000	
Automobile (Car) and Other Motor Vehicle Wholesale Distribution			
JM Family Enterprises Inc	423110	14,900,000,000	
Automobile (Car) and Truck Brake System Manufacturing			
Wabco Holdings Inc	336340	2,809,999,872	223,000,000
Automobile (Car) and Truck Parts, Components and Systems Manufacturing, Including Gasoline Engines, Interiors and Electronics,			
Dana Incorporated	336300	5,825,999,872	640,000,000
Federal-Mogul Corporation	336300		
Gentex Corporation	336300	1,678,924,800	347,591,264
Gentherm Inc	336300	917,600,000	76,598,000
Lear Corporation	336300	18,557,599,744	975,100,032
LKQ Corporation	336300	8,584,031,232	463,975,008
Modine Manufacturing Company	336300	1,352,499,968	-1,600,000
Tenneco Inc	336300	8,599,000,064	363,000,000
Automobile (Car) Manufacturing			
American Honda Motor Co Inc	336111	61,551,806,117	1,525,529,259
Audi of America Inc	336111	12,998,684,059	412,027,737
FCA US LLC	336111	12,000,000,000	1,985,015,213
Ford Motor Co	336111	151,800,004,608	4,595,999,744
General Motors Company (GM)	336111	166,379,995,136	9,427,000,320
Mercedes-Benz USA LLC	336111	43,692,900,000	155,231,879
Tesla Inc	336111	7,000,132,096	-674,913,984
Toyota Motor Sales USA Inc (TMS)	336111	98,245,124,503	
Automobile (Car) Rental			
Avis Budget Group Inc	532111	8,659,000,320	163,000,000
Dollar Thrifty Automotive Group Inc	532111	1,950,000,000	
Enterprise Holdings Inc	532111	20,900,000,000	
Automobile (Car) Reservations (e.g. Uber), Ticket Offices, Time Share and Vacation Club Rentals and Specialty Reservation Services			
ILG Inc	561599	1,356,000,000	265,000,000
Uber Inc	561599	6,500,000,000	-2,800,000,000
Ball Bearing and Roller Bearing Manufacturing			
NN Inc	332991	833,488,000	7,942,000

Industry Group/Company	Industry Code	2016 Sales	2016 Profits
Battery Manufacturing, Including Energy Storage Technologies			
APC by Schneider Electric	335911	4,800,000,000	
Integer Holdings Corporation	335911	1,386,777,984	5,961,000
Building Material Dealers			
BMC Stock Holdings Inc	444190	3,093,743,104	30,880,000
Burial Casket Manufacturing			
Matthews International Corporation	339995	1,480,464,000	66,749,000
Cable TV Programming, Cable Networks and Subscription Video			
Discovery Communications Inc	515210	6,496,999,936	1,194,000,000
Walt Disney Company (The)	515210	55,631,998,976	9,390,999,552
Candy and Chocolate Manufacturing			
Hershey Co	311351	7,440,181,248	720,044,032
Mars Inc	311351	36,000,000,000	
Car Repair (Repair and Maintenance of Automobiles and Trucks)			
Monro Muffler Brake Inc	811100	943,651,008	66,805,000
Carpets (Carpeting and Floor Coverings) and Rugs Mills and Manufacturing			
Mohawk Industries Inc	314110	8,959,086,592	930,361,984
Casino Hotels and Casino Resorts			
Eldorado Resorts Inc	721120	892,896,000	24,802,000
Las Vegas Sands Corp (The Venetian)	721120	11,409,999,872	1,670,000,000
Pinnacle Entertainment Inc	721120	2,378,854,912	-457,409,984
Wynn Resorts Limited	721120	4,466,296,832	241,975,008
Chips (Tortilla, Potato and Corn), Popcorn and Pretzel Manufacturing			
Frito-Lay North America Inc	311919	15,120,000,000	422,002,500
Coffee Shops, Doughnut Shops, Ice Cream Parlors, Canteens and Snack Bars			
Starbucks Corporation	722515	21,315,899,392	2,817,700,096
Commercial Banks (Banking)			
Bank of America Corp	522110	83,700,998,144	17,905,999,872
Bank of New York Mellon Corp	522110	15,237,000,192	3,547,000,064
BB&T Corporation	522110	10,792,999,936	2,425,999,872
Capital One Financial Corp	522110	25,500,999,680	3,751,000,064
Citigroup Inc	522110	69,874,999,296	14,912,000,000
Cullen-Frost Bankers Inc	522110	1,126,044,032	304,260,992
JP Morgan Chase & Co Inc	522110	95,668,002,816	24,732,999,680
US Bancorp	522110	21,105,000,448	5,888,000,000
Wells Fargo & Co	522110	88,266,997,760	21,937,999,872
Commercial Real Estate Investment and Operations, Including Office Buildings, Shopping Centers, Industrial Properties and Related REITs			
Jones Lang LaSalle Inc	531120	6,803,800,064	318,200,000
Computer and Data Systems Design, Consulting and Integration Services			
Accenture LLP	541512	15,653,000,000	
CACI International Inc	541512	3,744,052,992	142,799,008

Industry Group/Company	Industry Code	2016 Sales	2016 Profits
Cognizant Technology Solutions Corporation	541512	13,486,999,552	1,552,999,936
MAXIMUS Inc	541512	2,403,360,000	178,362,000
Sapient Corporation	541512	1,625,000,000	
Science Applications International Corp (SAIC)	541512	4,314,999,808	117,000,000
UST Global Inc	541512	445,200,000	
Computer Manufacturing, Including PCs, Laptops, Mainframes and Tablets			
Dell Technologies Inc	334111	61,000,000,000	
Computer Networking & Related Equipment Manufacturing			
Cisco Systems Inc	334210A	49,246,998,528	10,739,000,320
Juniper Networks Inc	334210A	4,990,099,968	592,700,032
Computer Peripherals and Accessories, including Printers, Monitors and Terminals Manufacturing			
NCR Corporation	334118	6,543,000,064	270,000,000
Computer Programming and Custom Software Development and Consulting			
EPAM Systems Inc	541511	1,160,131,968	99,266,000
Computer Software, Accounting, Banking & Financial			
Concur Technologies Inc	511210Q	1,381,972,534	1,291,875,652
Intuit Inc	511210Q	4,694,000,128	979,000,000
Jack Henry & Associates Inc	511210Q	1,354,646,016	248,867,008
Computer Software, Business Management & ERP			
BMC Software Inc	511210H	2,300,000,000	
Citrix Systems Inc	511210H	3,418,265,088	536,112,000
NetSuite Inc	511210H	855,000,000	
SAS Institute Inc	511210H	3,200,000,000	
TIBCO Software Inc	511210H	1,000,000,000	
Computer Software, Data Base & File Management			
Oracle Corporation	511210J	37,047,001,088	8,901,000,192
Computer Software, Electronic Games, Apps & Entertainment			
Activision Blizzard Inc	511210G	6,608,000,000	966,000,000
Computer Software, Healthcare & Biotechnology			
Allscripts Healthcare Solutions Inc	511210D	1,549,899,008	-25,652,000
Cerner Corporation	511210D	4,796,472,832	636,483,968
eClinicalWorks	511210D	440,000,000	
Epic Systems Corporation	511210D	2,000,000,000	
Computer Software, Multimedia, Graphics & Publishing			
Adobe Systems Inc	511210F	5,854,430,208	1,168,781,952
Computer Software, Network Management, System Testing, & Storage			
F5 Networks Inc	511210B	1,995,033,984	365,855,008
NetScout Systems Inc	511210B	955,419,008	-28,369,000
ServiceNow Inc	511210B	1,390,513,024	-451,804,000
VMware Inc	511210B	7,093,000,192	1,186,000,000
Computer Software, Operating Systems, Languages & Development Tools			
Microsoft Corporation	511210I	85,319,999,488	16,798,000,128

Industry Group/Company	Industry Code	2016 Sales	2016 Profits
Red Hat Inc	511210I	2,052,230,016	199,364,992
Computer Software, Product Lifecycle, Engineering, Design & CAD			
Cadence Design Systems Inc	511210N	1,816,082,944	203,086,000
Mentor Graphics Corp	511210N	1,180,988,032	96,277,000
National Instruments Corporation	511210N	1,228,178,944	82,734,000
Synopsys Inc	511210N	2,422,532,096	266,826,000
Computer Software, Sales & Customer Relationship Management			
SalesForce.com Inc	511210K	6,667,215,872	-47,426,000
Computer Software, Security & Anti-Virus			
McAfee Inc	511210E	2,450,000,000	
Symantec Corp	511210E	3,600,000,000	2,488,000,000
Computer Software, Supply Chain & Logistics			
Manhattan Associates Inc	511210A	604,556,992	124,234,000
Computers, Peripherals, Software and Accessories Distribution			
Anixter International Inc	423430	7,622,799,872	120,500,000
Arrow Electronics Inc	423430	23,825,260,544	522,750,016
Avnet Inc	423430	26,219,278,336	506,531,008
CDW Corporation	423430	13,981,899,776	424,400,000
Ingram Micro Inc	423430	41,770,000,000	
SYNNEX Corporation	423430	14,061,837,312	234,946,000
Tech Data Corp	423430	26,379,782,144	265,736,000
Connectors for Electronics Manufacturing			
Belden Inc	334417	2,356,672,000	128,003,000
Molex LLC	334417	4,000,000,000	
Consrtuction of Oil and Gas Pipelines and Structures			
Team Inc	237120	1,196,696,064	-12,676,000
Construction and Mining (except Oil Well) Machinery and Equipment Wholesale Distribution			
Fastenal Company	423810	3,962,035,968	499,478,016
Construction Equipment and Machinery Manufacturing			
Hillenbrand Inc	333120	1,538,400,000	112,800,000
Construction of Telecommunications Lines and Systems & Electric Power Lines and Systems			
Dycom Industries Inc	237130	2,672,541,952	128,740,000
Quanta Services Inc	237130	7,651,318,784	198,383,008
Consulting Services, Human Resources			
Aon Hewitt	541612	5,845,000,000	
Mercer LLC	541612	4,359,630,000	
Resources Connection Inc	541612	598,521,024	30,443,000
Consulting Services, Marketing			
INC Research/inVentiv Health	541613	1,610,595,968	112,630,000
Contract Electronics Manufacturing Services (CEM) and Printed Circuits Assembly			
Jabil Circuit Inc	334418	18,353,086,464	254,095,008
Sanmina Corp	334418	6,481,181,184	187,838,000

Industry Group/Company	Industry Code	2016 Sales	2016 Profits
Cosmetics; Soaps, Detergents & Cleansers; and Personal Care Products, Perfumes & Colognes Manufacturing			
SC Johnson & Son Inc	325600	10,000,000,000	
Couriers, Express and Overnight Delivery			
FedEx Corporation	492110	50,365,001,728	1,820,000,000
United Parcel Service Inc (UPS)	492110	60,906,000,384	3,431,000,064
CPA Firms (Certified Public Accountants), Accounting			
Deloitte LLP	541211	17,500,000,000	
EY LLP	541211	13,900,000,000	
Grant Thornton LLP	541211	1,650,000,000	
KPMG LLP	541211	11,560,270,498	
PricewaterhouseCoopers (PwC)	541211	35,900,000,000	
Credit Bureaus and Credit Rating Agencies			
Experian North America	561450	2,294,000,000	704,000,000
Moody's Corporation	561450	3,604,199,936	266,600,000
Credit Card Processing, Online Payment Processing, EFT, ACH and Clearinghouses			
American Express Co	522320	32,118,999,040	5,408,000,000
Fidelity National Information Services Inc	522320	9,240,999,936	568,000,000
First Data Corporation	522320	11,584,000,000	420,000,000
Fiserv Inc	522320	5,504,999,936	930,000,000
Fleetcor Technologies Inc	522320	1,831,545,984	452,384,992
Heartland Payment Systems Inc	522320	2,550,500,000	
MasterCard Inc	522320	10,776,000,512	4,059,000,064
Total System Services Inc (TSYS)	522320	4,170,076,928	319,638,016
Vantiv Inc	522320	3,578,991,104	213,208,000
Visa Inc	522320	15,082,000,384	5,991,000,064
Cruise Lines			
Carnival Corporation	483112	16,389,000,192	2,779,000,064
Norwegian Cruise Line Holdings Ltd (NCL)	483112	4,874,339,840	633,084,992
Royal Caribbean Cruises Ltd	483112	8,496,400,896	1,283,388,032
Data Processing, Business Process Outsourcing (BPO) and Internet Content Hosting Services			
Automatic Data Processing Inc (ADP)	518210	11,667,800,064	1,492,499,968
ExlService Holdings Inc	518210	685,987,968	61,733,000
GoDaddy Inc	518210	1,847,900,032	-16,500,000
Syntel Inc	518210	966,550,016	-57,390,000
Web.com Group Inc	518210	710,505,024	3,990,000
Department Stores (except Discount Department Stores)			
Nordstrom Inc	452111	14,437,000,192	600,000,000
Dialysis Centers			
DaVita Healthcare Partners Inc	621492	14,745,105,408	879,873,984
Direct Selling			
Mary Kay Inc	454390	3,500,000,000	
Discount Department Stores			
Kohl's Corporation	452112	19,203,999,744	673,000,000

Industry Group/Company	Industry Code	2016 Sales	2016 Profits
Distributors of Telecommunications Equipment, Telephones, Cellphones and Electronics Components (Wholesale Distribution)			
Brightstar Corporation	423690	7,750,000,000	
Electric Motor and Power & Motor Generator Manufacturing			
Regal-Beloit Corporation	335312	3,224,499,968	203,400,000
Electric Wiring Device Manufacturing			
Hubbell Incorporated	335931	3,505,200,128	293,000,000
Electrical Contractors and Other Wiring Installation Contractors			
EMCOR Group Inc	238210	7,551,523,840	181,935,008
Rosendin Electric	238210	1,400,000,000	
Electricity Control Panels, Circuit Breakers and Power Switches Equipment (Switchgear) Manufacturing			
Littelfuse Inc	335313	1,056,158,976	104,488,000
Engineering Services, Including Civil, Mechanical, Electronic, Computer and Environmental Engineering			
Black & Veatch Holding Company	541330	3,000,000,000	
Burns & McDonnell	541330	2,400,000,000	
Factory Automation, Industrial Process, Thermostat, Flow Meter and Environmental Quality Monitoring and Control Manufacturing			
Ametek Inc	334513	3,840,087,040	512,158,016
Roper Technologies Inc	334513	3,789,925,120	658,644,992
Family Clothing, Apparel and Accessories Stores			
Ross Stores Inc	448140	11,939,998,720	1,020,660,992
TJX Companies Inc (The)	448140	30,944,937,984	2,277,658,112
Fiber Optic Cable, Connectors and Related Products Manufacturing			
Amphenol Corporation	335921	6,286,400,000	822,899,968
CommScope Inc	335921	4,923,620,864	222,838,000
Financial Data Publishing - Print & Online			
Bloomberg LP	511120A	9,400,000,000	
FactSet Research Systems Inc	511120A	1,127,091,968	338,815,008
Fitness Centers, Gyms and Exercise and Fitness Programs			
24 Hour Fitness	713940	1,489,000,000	
Food Manufacturing, Processing and Packaging, Diversified			
Ingredion Inc	311000	6,022,000,128	485,000,000
Food Service Contractors			
Aramark	722310	14,415,828,992	287,806,016
HMSHost Corporation	722310	3,100,000,000	
Sodexo Inc	722310	9,300,000,000	
Fossil Fuel Electric Power Generation			
Berkshire Hathaway Energy Company	221112	17,859,000,000	2,973,000,000
DTE Energy Company	221112	10,629,999,616	868,000,000
Duke Energy Corporation	221112	22,742,999,040	2,152,000,000
FirstEnergy Corporation	221112	14,561,999,872	-6,176,999,936
SCANA Corporation	221112	4,227,000,064	595,000,000

Industry Group/Company	Industry Code	2016 Sales	2016 Profits
Fruit and Vegetable Canning (Including Juices and Sauces)			
TreeHouse Foods Inc	311421	6,175,088,128	-228,594,000
Funeral Homes and Funeral Services			
Service Corporation International Inc	812210	3,031,137,024	177,038,000
General Grocery Products Distributors (Groceries Wholesale Distribution, Excluding Meats, Frozen Foods and Vegetables)			
C&S Wholesale Grocers Inc	424410	30,000,000,000	
SYSCO Corporation	424410	50,366,918,656	949,622,016
United Natural Foods Inc	424410	8,470,285,824	125,766,000
Hazardous Waste Collection			
Stericycle Inc	562112	3,562,341,888	206,359,008
Health Insurance and Medical Insurance Underwriters (Direct Carriers), including Group Health, Supplemental Health and HMOs			
Aetna Inc	524114	63,154,999,296	2,271,000,064
AFLAC Inc	524114	22,559,000,576	2,659,000,064
Amerigroup Corporation	524114	10,000,000,000	
Anthem Inc	524114	84,863,000,576	2,469,799,936
Centene Corporation	524114	40,606,998,528	562,000,000
Cigna Corporation	524114	39,667,998,720	1,867,000,064
Health Care Service Corporation (HCSC)	524114	33,000,000,000	106,300,000
Humana Inc	524114	54,378,999,808	614,000,000
Molina Healthcare Inc	524114	17,781,999,616	52,000,000
UnitedHealth Group Inc	524114	184,839,995,392	7,016,999,936
Unum Group	524114	11,046,500,352	931,400,000
WellCare Health Plans Inc	524114	14,237,100,032	242,100,000
Heavy Construction, Including Civil Engineering-Construction, Major Construction Projects, Land Subdivision, Infrastructure, Utilities, Highways and Bridges			
Fluor Corp	237000	19,036,524,544	281,400,992
Heavy Duty Truck (including Buses) Manufacturing			
Oshkosh Corporation	336120	6,279,199,744	216,400,000
PACCAR Inc	336120	17,033,299,968	521,700,000
Highway, Street, Tunnel & Bridge Construction			
Tutor Perini Corporation	237310	4,973,075,968	95,822,000
Home Centers, Building Materials			
Home Depot Inc (The)	444110	88,519,000,064	7,008,999,936
Lowe's Companies Inc	444110	59,073,998,848	2,545,999,872
Menard Inc	444110	9,500,000,000	
Home Health Care Services			
Almost Family Inc	621610	623,540,992	17,653,000
Chemed Corporation	621610	1,576,881,024	108,743,000
Envision Healthcare Corporation	621610	3,696,000,000	-18,600,000
LHC Group Inc	621610	914,822,976	36,583,000
Lincare Holdings Inc	621610	220,000,000	
Hospitals, General Medical and Surgical			
Adventist Health System	622110	9,651,689,000	89,559,000

Industry Group/Company	Industry Code	2016 Sales	2016 Profits
Ascension Health	622110	21,900,000,000	219,412,440
Catholic Health Initiatives	622110	16,473,769,000	-666,523,000
Cleveland Clinic Foundation (The)	622110	8,037,207,000	139,352,000
Community Health Systems Inc	622110	18,438,000,640	-1,720,999,936
Fairview Health Services	622110	4,363,540,000	213,786,000
HCA Holdings Inc	622110	41,490,001,920	2,889,999,872
Houston Methodist	622110	2,900,000,000	
Kaiser Permanente	622110	64,600,000,000	3,100,000,000
LifePoint Health Inc	622110	6,364,000,256	121,900,000
Mayo Clinic	622110	10,990,000,000	475,000,000
MedStar Health	622110		
Mercy	622110	5,000,000,000	
Providence St Joseph Health	622110	18,878,000,000	5,231,000,000
Spectrum Health	622110	5,220,515,000	212,044,000
Sutter Health Inc	622110	11,873,000,000	554,000,000
Tenet Healthcare Corporation	622110	19,620,999,168	-192,000,000
Trinity Health	622110	15,900,000,000	700,000,000
Universal Health Services Inc	622110	9,766,209,536	702,409,024
Hospitals, Psychiatric and Substance Abuse			
Acadia Healthcare Company Inc	622210	2,810,914,048	6,143,000
Hospitals, Specialty			
HealthSouth Corporation	622310	3,646,000,128	247,600,000
Select Medical Holdings Corporation	622310	4,286,021,120	115,411,000
Hotels, Motels, Inns and Resorts (Lodging and Hospitality)			
Accor North America	721110	621,772,975	
Hilton Inc	721110	11,662,999,552	348,000,000
Hyatt Hotels Corporation	721110	4,429,000,192	204,000,000
Kimpton Hotel & Restaurant Group LLC	721110	1,300,000,000	
La Quinta Holdings Inc	721110	1,006,254,016	-1,288,000
Loews Hotels Holding Corporation	721110	1,293,000,000	12,000,000
Marcus Corporation (The)	721110	543,864,000	37,902,000
Marriott International Inc	721110	17,072,000,000	780,000,000
Ritz-Carlton Hotel Company LLC (The)	721110	2,200,000,000	
Wyndham Worldwide Corporation	721110	5,599,000,064	611,000,000
Household Dishwasher, Disposal, Trash Compactor and Water Heater Manufacturing			
AO Smith Corporation	335228	2,685,900,032	326,500,000
Housewares, including Linen, Bath, Kitchen and Cookware			
Bed Bath & Beyond Inc	442299	12,103,886,848	841,489,024
Container Store Inc (The)	442299	794,630,016	5,142,000
Hydroelectric Power Generation			
PG&E Corporation	221111	17,666,000,896	1,407,000,064
Industrial Equipment and Machinery Distribution			
WW Grainger Inc	423830	10,137,203,712	605,928,000
Industrial Machinery Manufacturing, Other			
Illinois Tool Works Inc	333249	13,598,999,552	2,035,000,064

Industry Group/Company	Industry Code	2016 Sales	2016 Profits
Insurance Agencies, Risk Management Consultants and Insurance Brokers			
Arthur J Gallagher & Co	524210	5,594,800,128	414,400,000
Brown & Brown Inc	524210	1,766,628,992	257,491,008
Hub International Limited	524210	1,470,000,000	
Marsh & McLennan Companies Inc	524210	13,210,999,808	1,768,000,000
Insurance Claims Administration and Services			
Athenahealth Inc	524292	1,082,899,968	21,000,000
Change Healthcare Inc	524292	1,500,000,000	
Internet Search Engines, Online Publishing, Sharing and Consumer Services, Online Radio, TV and Entertainment Sites and Social Media			
Airbnb Inc	519130	1,624,000,000	
CoStar Group Inc	519130	837,630,016	85,071,000
Cox Automotive Inc	519130	7,300,000,000	
Expedia Inc	519130	8,773,564,416	281,848,000
Facebook Inc	519130	27,637,999,616	10,216,999,936
Google (Alphabet Inc)	519130	90,271,997,952	19,477,999,616
IAC/InterActiveCorp	519130	3,139,881,984	-41,280,000
LinkedIn Corp	519130	3,500,000,000	
Match Group Inc	519130	1,222,525,952	171,451,008
Priceline Group Inc (The)	519130	10,743,006,208	2,134,987,008
Sabre Corporation	519130	3,373,387,008	242,562,000
Zillow Inc	519130	846,588,992	-220,438,000
Investment Banking, and Related Stock Brokerage and Investment Services			
Goldman Sachs Group Inc	523110	30,607,998,976	7,398,000,128
Jefferies LLC	523110	3,233,823,000	29,972,000
Legg Mason Inc	523110	2,660,844,032	-25,032,000
Merrill Lynch & Co Inc	523110	16,000,000,000	
Morgan Stanley	523110	34,631,000,064	5,978,999,808
Raymond James Financial Inc	523110	5,403,267,072	529,350,016
Stifel Financial Corp	523110	2,575,495,936	81,520,000
Janitorial Services			
ABM Industries Inc	561720	5,144,699,904	57,200,000
Laboratory Instruments and Lab Equipment Manufacturing			
Waters Corporation	334516	2,167,422,976	521,503,008
Landscaping Services			
ServiceMaster Company LLC (The)	561730	2,745,999,872	155,000,000
Life Insurance and Annuity Underwriters (Direct Carriers)			
Hartford Financial Services Group Inc (The)	524113	18,300,000,256	896,000,000
Lincoln National Corporation	524113	13,329,999,872	1,192,000,000
Mutual of Omaha Companies (The)	524113	7,898,472,000	356,558,000
New York Life Insurance Company	524113	27,908,000,000	1,638,000,000
Northwestern Mutual Life Insurance Company	524113	28,158,000,000	818,000,000
Principal Financial Group Inc	524113	12,394,099,712	1,316,499,968
Prudential Financial Inc	524113	58,779,000,832	4,368,000,000
Trustmark Companies	524113	915,002,500	9,522,536

Industry Group/Company	Industry Code	2016 Sales	2016 Profits
Linen Supply			
Cintas Corporation	812331	4,905,458,176	693,520,000
Machinery and Engines Manufacturing, Including Construction, Agricultural, Mining, Industrial, Commercial and HVAC			
General Electric Co (GE)	333000	123,692,998,656	8,830,999,552
Management Consulting and General Business Consulting (including Human Resources)			
AT Kearney Inc	541610	1,120,000,000	
Bain & Company Inc	541610	2,500,000,000	
Booz Allen Hamilton Holding Corp	541610	5,405,737,984	294,094,016
Boston Consulting Group Inc (The, BCG)	541610	5,600,000,000	
FTI Consulting Inc	541610	1,810,393,984	85,520,000
McKinsey & Company Inc	541610	8,590,500,000	
Oliver Wyman Group	541610	1,803,530,000	
Strategy&	541610	1,194,027,000	
Market Research, Business Intelligence and Opinion Polling			
Gartner Inc	541910	2,444,539,904	193,582,000
Nielsen Holdings plc	541910	6,309,000,192	502,000,000
Mattress Manufacturing			
Select Comfort Corporation	337910	1,311,291,008	51,417,000
Medical Diagnostics, Reagents, Assays and Test Kits Manufacturing			
Bio Rad Laboratories Inc	325413	2,068,172,032	28,125,000
PerkinElmer Inc	325413	2,115,517,056	234,299,008
Medical Equipment and Supplies Manufacturing			
3M Company	339100	30,108,999,680	5,049,999,872
Becton Dickinson & Co	339100	12,483,000,320	976,000,000
Boston Scientific Corp	339100	8,385,999,872	347,000,000
Cooper Companies Inc	339100	1,966,813,952	273,916,992
CR Bard Inc	339100	3,713,999,872	531,400,000
Dentsply Sirona Inc	339100	3,745,299,968	429,900,000
Edwards Lifesciences Corporation	339100	2,963,699,968	569,500,032
Hill-Rom Holdings Inc	339100	2,655,200,000	124,100,000
ResMed Inc	339100	1,838,712,960	352,408,992
Stryker Corporation	339100	11,324,999,680	1,647,000,064
Zimmer Biomet Holdings Inc	339100	7,683,899,904	305,900,000
Medical Imaging and Electromedical (Medical Devices) Equipment, including MRI, Ultrasound, Pacemakers, EKG and CAT			
IDEXX Laboratories Inc	334510	1,775,422,976	222,044,992
Medtronic plc	334510	28,832,999,424	3,537,999,872
Philips Healthcare	334510	20,196,679,771	754,093,072
Varian Medical Systems Inc	334510	3,217,799,936	402,300,000
Medical Laboratories			
Laboratory Corporation of America Holdings	621511	9,641,799,680	732,099,968
Quest Diagnostics Inc	621511	7,514,999,808	645,000,000

Industry Group/Company	Industry Code	2016 Sales	2016 Profits
Medical, Dental and Hospital Equipment and Supplies (Medical Devices) Wholesale Distribution			
Henry Schein Inc	423450	11,571,667,968	506,777,984
Patterson Companies Inc	423450	5,386,702,848	187,184,000
Thermo Fisher Scientific Inc	423450	18,274,099,200	2,021,799,936
Metal Can Manufacturing			
Ball Corporation	332431	9,061,000,192	263,000,000
Crown Holdings Inc	332431	8,284,000,256	496,000,000
Missile (Aerospace Defense) and Space Vehicle Manufacturing			
Orbital ATK Inc	336414	4,455,000,064	293,000,000
Mobile, Modular & Prefabricated Homes and Buildings Manufacturing			
Clayton Homes Inc	321992	4,230,000,000	744,000,000
Mortgage Loan Servicing, Check Cashing and Money Transmission			
Encore Capital Group Inc	522390	1,029,257,984	76,570,000
New Home Builders (Production Builders)			
DR Horton Inc	236117	12,157,400,064	886,300,032
Lennar Corporation	236117	10,949,998,592	911,843,968
NVR Inc	236117	5,830,112,768	425,262,016
PulteGroup Inc	236117	7,668,475,904	602,702,976
Toll Brothers Inc	236117	5,169,507,840	382,095,008
Nuclear Electric Power Generation			
Exelon Corporation	221113	31,360,000,000	1,134,000,000
Nursing Care Facilities (Skilled Nursing Facilities)			
Kindred Healthcare Inc	623110	7,219,518,976	-664,230,016
Online Shopping, B2B and B2C Sales on the Internet (Ecommerce)			
Amazon.com Inc	454111	135,987,003,392	2,371,000,064
Liberty Interactive Corporation	454111	10,218,999,808	473,000,000
Wayfair LLC	454111	3,380,359,936	-194,375,008
Paints and Coatings Manufacturing			
PPG Industries Inc	325510	14,750,999,552	877,000,000
RPM International Inc	325510	4,813,648,896	354,724,992
Sherwin-Williams Company (The)	325510	11,855,601,664	1,132,702,976
Paper Bag and Coated and Treated Paper Manufacturing			
Sonoco Products Company	322220	4,782,877,184	286,433,984
Payroll Services			
Paychex Inc	541214	2,951,899,904	756,800,000
Personal Care Products; Cosmetics and Makeup; Fragrances and Perfumes; and Hair Care Products Manufacturing			
Estee Lauder Companies Inc (The)	325620	11,262,300,160	1,114,599,936
Revlon Inc	325620	2,334,000,128	-21,900,000
Pet and Pet Supplies Stores			
PetSmart Inc	453910	7,050,000,000	
Petrochemicals Manufacturing			
Chevron Phillips Chemical Company LLC	325110	8,455,000,000	1,687,000,000

Industry Group/Company	Industry Code	2016 Sales	2016 Profits
Lubrizol Corporation (The)	325110	6,500,000,000	
Westlake Chemical Corporation	325110	5,075,456,000	398,859,008
Petroleum Refineries			
Phillips 66	324110	85,776,998,400	1,555,000,064
Pharmaceuticals and Drug Manufacturing			
Abbott Laboratories	325412	20,853,000,192	1,400,000,000
AbbVie Inc	325412	25,638,000,640	5,952,999,936
Amgen Inc	325412	22,990,999,552	7,721,999,872
Biogen Inc	325412	11,448,800,256	3,702,799,872
Bristol-Myers Squibb Co	325412	19,427,000,320	4,456,999,936
Celgene Corporation	325412	11,229,200,384	1,999,200,000
Eli Lilly and Company	325412	21,222,100,992	2,737,600,000
Gilead Sciences Inc	325412	30,389,999,616	13,500,999,680
Johnson & Johnson	325412	71,890,001,920	16,540,000,256
Merck & Co Inc	325412	39,807,000,576	3,920,000,000
Pfizer Inc	325412	52,823,998,464	7,215,000,064
Pharmaceuticals and Druggists' Merchandise Distributors			
AmerisourceBergen Corp	424210	146,849,693,696	1,427,928,960
Cardinal Health Inc	424210	121,545,998,336	1,427,000,064
McKesson Corporation	424210	190,884,003,840	2,257,999,872
Pharmacies and Drug Stores			
CVS Health Corporation	446110	177,525,997,568	5,317,000,192
Rite Aid Corporation	446110	30,736,656,384	165,464,992
Walgreens Boots Alliance Inc	446110	117,350,998,016	4,172,999,936
Physicians (except Mental Health Specialists)			
Team Health Holdings Inc	621111	3,700,000,000	
Plastics (Including Packaging Materials, Pipe, Laminated & Unlaminated Film & Sheet, Foam and Bottles) Product Manufacturing			
Berry Global Group Inc	326100	6,488,999,936	236,000,000
Newell Brands Inc	326100	13,264,000,000	527,800,000
Plastics Material and Resin Manufacturing			
Celanese Corporation	325211	5,389,000,192	900,000,000
Plastics Product Manufacturing, Other			
Owens Corning Inc	326199	5,677,000,192	393,000,000
Pottery, Ceramics and Plumbing Fixture Manufacturing			
Kohler Company	327110	6,350,000,000	
Power, Distribution and Specialty Transformer Manufacturing			
AZZ Inc	335311	903,192,000	76,790,000
Power-Driven Handtool Manufacturing			
Stanley Black & Decker Inc	333991	11,406,900,224	965,299,968
Pressed and Blown Glass and Glassware (except Glass Packaging Containers) Manufacturing			
Corning Inc	327212	9,390,000,128	3,695,000,064
Primary Battery Manufacturing			
Spectrum Brands Holdings Inc	335912	5,039,699,968	357,100,000

Industry Group/Company	Industry Code	2016 Sales	2016 Profits
Professional Employer Organizations			
Barrett Business Services Inc	561330	840,585,984	18,799,000
Property and Casualty (P&C) Insurance Underwriters (Direct Carriers)			
American Financial Group Inc	524126	6,497,999,872	649,000,000
AmTrust Financial Services Inc	524126	5,450,456,064	410,985,984
Berkshire Hathaway Inc	524126	223,603,998,720	24,074,000,384
Liberty Mutual Group Inc	524126	38,308,000,000	1,006,000,000
Progressive Corporation (The)	524126	23,441,399,808	1,031,000,000
Safeco Insurance Company of America	524126	1,680,000,000	
State Farm Insurance Companies	524126	76,100,000,000	400,000,000
Travelers Companies Inc (The)	524126	27,625,000,960	3,014,000,128
USAA	524126	27,131,000,000	1,779,000,000
W R Berkley Corporation	524126	7,654,183,936	601,916,032
Pump and Pumping Equipment Manufacturing			
Graco Inc	333911	1,329,293,056	40,674,000
Radar, Navigation, Sonar, Space Vehicle Guidance, Flight Systems and Marine Instrument Manufacturing			
Esterline Technologies Corporation	334511	1,992,631,040	101,685,000
Trimble Navigation Ltd	334511	2,362,200,064	132,400,000
Radio, Television and Other Electronics Stores			
Best Buy Co Inc	443142	39,528,001,536	897,000,000
Real Estate Agents & Brokers			
CBRE Group Inc	531210	13,071,589,376	571,972,992
Cushman & Wakefield Inc	531210	5,000,000,000	
Reconstituted Wood Product Manufacturing			
Patrick Industries Inc	321219	1,221,886,976	55,577,000
Recreational Vehicle (RV) Trailer and Camper Manufacturing			
Thor Industries Inc	336214	4,582,112,256	256,519,008
REITs (Real Estate Investment Trusts) - Residential			
Equity Lifestyle Properties Inc	531110A	870,435,008	173,263,008
Restaurants, Fast-Food, Pizza Delivery, Takeout and Family			
Buffalo Wild Wings Inc	722513	1,986,792,960	94,745,000
Darden Restaurants Inc	722513	6,933,499,904	375,000,000
In-N-Out Burgers Inc	722513	870,000,000	
McDonald's Corp	722513	24,621,899,776	4,686,499,840
Yum! Brands Inc	722513	6,366,000,128	1,619,000,064
Restaurants, Full-Service, Sit Down			
Brinker International Inc	722511	3,257,488,896	200,744,992
Retirement Communities and Assisted Living Facilities for the Elderly			
Brookdale Senior Living Inc	623310	4,976,979,968	-404,396,992
Sales Financing			
Ally Financial Inc	522220	5,437,000,192	1,067,000,000
Scientific Research and Development (R&D) in Life Sciences, Medical Devices, Biotechnology and Pharmaceuticals (Drugs)			
Charles River Laboratories International Inc	541711	1,681,432,064	154,764,992

Industry Group/Company	Industry Code	2016 Sales	2016 Profits
PAREXEL International Corporation	541711	2,426,299,904	154,900,000
Pharmaceutical Product Development Inc	541711	1,300,000,000	
PRA Health Sciences Inc	541711	1,811,710,976	68,175,000
Quintiles IMS Holdings Inc	541711	6,878,000,128	115,000,000
Securities Brokerage, Discount Brokers and Online Stock Brokers			
Charles Schwab Corporation (The)	523120	7,472,999,936	1,888,999,936
Edward D Jones & Co LP	523120	6,557,000,000	746,000,000
Seeds, Pesticides, Herbicides and Other Agricultural Chemical Manufacturing			
Dow AgroSciences LLC	325320	1,006,200,000	
Semiconductor and Solar Cell Manufacturing, Including Chips, Memory, LEDs, Transistors and Integrated Circuits			
Diodes Inc	334413	942,161,984	15,935,000
Intel Corporation	334413	59,386,998,784	10,316,000,256
Qualcomm Inc	334413	23,554,000,896	5,704,999,936
Texas Instruments Inc (TI)	334413	13,370,000,384	3,595,000,064
Semiconductor Manufacturing Equipment and Systems (Including Etching, Wafer Processing & Surface Mount) Manufacturing			
Applied Materials Inc	333242	10,824,999,936	1,720,999,936
Lam Research Corporation	333242	5,885,893,120	914,049,024
Shoe and Footwear Brands, Designers, Importers and Distributors			
Nike Inc	424340	32,376,000,512	3,760,000,000
Soap and Other Detergent Manufacturing			
Clorox Company (The)	325611	5,760,999,936	648,000,000
Soft Drinks (Including Bottled Carbonated and Flavored Water, Bottled Coffee & Tea, Sodas, Pop and Energy Drinks) Manufacturing			
Coca-Cola Bottling Co Consolidated	312111	3,156,428,032	50,146,000
Solid Waste Collection, Treatment, Disposal and Recycling			
Republic Services Inc	562111	9,387,700,224	612,600,000
Specialized Commercial and Service Machinery Manufacturing, Including Cleaning, Laundry and Automobile (Car) Washing Equipment			
Middleby Corporation (The)	333318	2,267,852,032	284,216,000
Spices, Seasonings, Salad Dressing, Mayonnaise, Mustard, Catsup and Condiments Manufacturing			
McCormick & Company Inc	311940	4,411,500,032	471,000,000
Sporting Goods Stores			
Academy Sports & Outdoors Ltd	451110	4,600,000,000	
Cabela's Inc	451110	4,129,359,104	146,947,008
Hibbett Sports Inc	451110	943,104,000	70,528,000
REI (Recreational Equipment Inc)	451110	2,423,221,000	35,372,000
Supermarkets and Grocery (except Convenience) Stores			
HEB Grocery Company LP	445110	24,000,000,000	
Kroger Co (The)	445110	109,829,996,544	2,039,000,064

Industry Group/Company	Industry Code	2016 Sales	2016 Profits
Publix Super Markets Inc	445110	34,274,109,440	2,025,688,064
Safeway Inc	445110	36,000,000,000	
Trader Joe's Company Inc	445110	12,500,000,000	
Talent Agencies, Agents and Managers for Athletes and Entertainers			
IMG Worldwide Inc	711410	1,947,000,000	
William Morris Endeavor Entertainment LLC (WME-IMG)	711410	2,400,000,000	
Telecommunications, Telephone and Network Equipment Manufacturing, including PBX, Routers, Switches and Handsets Manufacturing			
ARRIS Group Inc	334210	6,829,117,952	18,100,000
Telemarketing Bureaus and Other Contact Centers			
Convergys Corporation	561422	2,913,600,000	143,000,000
Telephone, Internet Access, Broadband, Data Networks, Server Facilities and Telecommunications Services Industry			
AT&T Inc	517110	163,785,998,336	12,976,000,000
CenturyLink Inc	517110	17,469,999,104	626,000,000
Charter Communications Inc	517110	29,002,999,808	3,521,999,872
Comcast Corporation	517110	80,402,997,248	8,695,000,064
Cox Communications Inc	517110	10,714,000,000	
DIRECTV	517110	33,703,000,000	32,000,000
EchoStar Corporation	517110	3,056,730,112	179,930,000
Frontier Communications Corporation	517110	8,896,000,000	-373,000,000
HC2 Holdings Inc	517110	1,558,125,952	-94,549,000
Level 3 Communications Inc	517110	8,172,000,256	677,000,000
Liberty Global plc	517110	20,008,800,256	1,705,299,968
Mediacom Communications Corp	517110	741,000,000	
Rackspace Hosting Inc	517110	2,081,000,000	135,200,000
Verizon Communications Inc	517110	125,980,000,256	13,127,000,064
Television Broadcasting			
CBS Corporation	515120	13,166,000,128	1,260,999,936
Cox Enterprises Inc	515120	20,250,000,000	
Fox Entertainment Group Inc	515120	16,500,000,000	
NBCUniversal LLC	515120	31,593,000,000	4,546,000,000
Temporary Staffing, Help and Employment Agencies			
Kelly Services Inc	561320	5,276,800,000	120,800,000
Robert Half International Inc	561320	5,250,399,232	343,388,992
Third-Party Logistics (3PL), Supply Chain and Freight Forwarding			
CH Robinson Worldwide Inc	488510	13,144,413,184	513,384,000
Expeditors International of Washington Inc	488510	6,098,037,248	430,807,008
XPO Logistics Inc	488510	14,619,400,192	69,000,000
Tire and Tube Wholesale Distribution			
American Tire Distributors	423130	5,000,000,000	-92,256,933
Truck, Utility Trailer and RV (Recreational Vehicle) Rental and Leasing			
AMERCO (U-Haul)	532120	3,275,655,936	489,000,992
Penske Corporation	532120	26,000,000,000	
Ryder System Inc	532120	6,786,983,936	262,476,992

Industry Group/Company	Industry Code	2016 Sales	2016 Profits
Trucking and Freight-Long Distance, Full Truckload (FTL)			
JB Hunt Transport Services Inc	484121	6,555,459,072	432,089,984
Trucking and Freight-Long Distance, Less Than Truckload (LTL)			
Old Dominion Freight Line Inc	484122	2,991,516,928	295,764,992
Veterinary Services			
VCA Inc	541940	2,516,863,000	209,196,000
Warehouse Clubs and Super Stores			
Costco Wholesale Corporation	452910	118,718,996,480	2,350,000,128
PriceSmart Inc	452910	2,905,176,064	88,723,000
Sam's Club	452910	56,828,000,000	1,820,000,000
Wal-Mart Stores Inc (Walmart)	452910	482,130,001,920	14,693,999,616
Waste Collection, Recycling, Treatment and Remediation Services			
Waste Management Inc	562000	13,608,999,936	1,182,000,000
Wine Manufacturing (including Wineries with Vineyards)			
Constellation Brands Inc	312130	6,548,400,128	1,054,899,968
Wireless Communications and Radio and TV Broadcasting Equipment Manufacturing, including Cellphones (Handsets)			
Apple Inc	334220	215,638,999,040	45,687,001,088
Harris Corporation	334220	7,466,999,808	324,000,000
Wireless Telecommunications Carriers (except Satellite)			
Agero Inc	517210	675,000,000	
T-Mobile US Inc	517210	37,241,999,360	1,460,000,000
United States Cellular Corporation	517210	3,939,000,064	48,000,000
Women's Clothing, Apparel and Accessories Stores			
Ascena Retail Group Inc	448120	6,995,400,192	-11,900,000
Victoria's Secret	448120	7,781,000,000	1,173,000,000

ALPHABETICAL INDEX

FedEx Corporation
Fidelity Investments Financial Services
Fidelity National Information Services Inc
First Data Corporation
FirstEnergy Corporation
Fiserv Inc
Fleetcor Technologies Inc
Fluor Corp
Ford Motor Co
Fox Entertainment Group Inc
Frito-Lay North America Inc
Frontier Communications Corporation
FTI Consulting Inc
Gartner Inc
General Electric Co (GE)
General Motors Company (GM)
Gentex Corporation
Gentherm Inc
Gilead Sciences Inc
GoDaddy Inc
Goldman Sachs Group Inc
Google (Alphabet Inc)
Graco Inc
Grant Thornton LLP
Group 1 Automotive Inc
Hanesbrands Inc
Harris Corporation
Hartford Financial Services Group Inc
(The)
HC2 Holdings Inc
HCA Holdings Inc
Health Care Service Corporation (HCSC)
HealthSouth Corporation
Heartland Payment Systems Inc
HEB Grocery Company LP
Hendrick Automotive Group
Henry Schein Inc
Hershey Co
Hibbett Sports Inc
Hillenbrand Inc
Hill-Rom Holdings Inc
Hilton Inc
HMSHost Corporation
Home Depot Inc (The)
Honeywell International Inc
Houston Methodist
Hub International Limited
Hubbell Incorporated
Humana Inc
Hyatt Hotels Corporation
IAC/InterActiveCorp
IDEXX Laboratories Inc
ILG Inc
Illinois Tool Works Inc
IMG Worldwide Inc
INC Research/inVentiv Health
Ingram Micro Inc
Ingredion Inc
In-N-Out Burgers Inc
Integer Holdings Corporation
Intel Corporation
Interpublic Group of Companies Inc
Intuit Inc
Jabil Circuit Inc
Jack Henry & Associates Inc

JB Hunt Transport Services Inc
Jefferies LLC
JetBlue Airways Corporation
JM Family Enterprises Inc
Johnson & Johnson
Jones Lang LaSalle Inc
JP Morgan Chase & Co Inc
Juniper Networks Inc
Kaiser Permanente
Kelly Services Inc
Kimpton Hotel & Restaurant Group LLC
Kindred Healthcare Inc
Kohler Company
Kohl's Corporation
KPMG LLP
Kroger Co (The)
La Quinta Holdings Inc
Laboratory Corporation of America
Holdings
Lam Research Corporation
Larry H Miller Group
Las Vegas Sands Corp (The Venetian)
Lear Corporation
Legg Mason Inc
Lennar Corporation
Level 3 Communications Inc
LHC Group Inc
Liberty Global plc
Liberty Interactive Corporation
Liberty Mutual Group Inc
LifePoint Health Inc
Lincare Holdings Inc
Lincoln National Corporation
LinkedIn Corp
Lithia Motors Inc
Littelfuse Inc
LKQ Corporation
Loews Hotels Holding Corporation
Lowe's Companies Inc
Lubrizol Corporation (The)
Magellan Health Inc
Manhattan Associates Inc
Marcus Corporation (The)
Marriott International Inc
Mars Inc
Marsh & McLennan Companies Inc
Mary Kay Inc
MasterCard Inc
Match Group Inc
Matthews International Corporation
MAXIMUS Inc
Mayo Clinic
McAfee Inc
McCormick & Company Inc
McDonald's Corp
McKesson Corporation
McKinsey & Company Inc
Mediacom Communications Corp
MedStar Health
Medtronic plc
Menard Inc
Mentor Graphics Corp
Mercedes-Benz USA LLC
Mercer LLC
Merck & Co Inc

Mercy
Merrill Lynch & Co Inc
Microsoft Corporation
Middleby Corporation (The)
Modine Manufacturing Company
Mohawk Industries Inc
Molex LLC
Molina Healthcare Inc
Monro Muffler Brake Inc
Moody's Corporation
Morgan Stanley
Mutual of Omaha Companies (The)
National Instruments Corporation
NBCUniversal LLC
NCR Corporation
NetScout Systems Inc
NetSuite Inc
New York Life Insurance Company
Newell Brands Inc
Nielsen Holdings plc
Nike Inc
NN Inc
Nordstrom Inc
Northwestern Mutual Life Insurance
Company
Norwegian Cruise Line Holdings Ltd
(NCL)
NVR Inc
Old Dominion Freight Line Inc
Oliver Wyman Group
Omnicom Group Inc
Oracle Corporation
Orbital ATK Inc
O'Reilly Automotive Inc
Oshkosh Corporation
Owens Corning Inc
PACCAR Inc
PAREXEL International Corporation
Patrick Industries Inc
Patterson Companies Inc
Paychex Inc
Penske Automotive Group Inc
Penske Corporation
PerkinElmer Inc
PetSmart Inc
Pfizer Inc
PG&E Corporation
Pharmaceutical Product Development Inc
Philips Healthcare
Phillips 66
Pinnacle Entertainment Inc
PPG Industries Inc
PRA Health Sciences Inc
Priceline Group Inc (The)
PriceSmart Inc
PricewaterhouseCoopers (PwC)
Principal Financial Group Inc
Progressive Corporation (The)
Providence St Joseph Health
Prudential Financial Inc
Publix Super Markets Inc
PulteGroup Inc
Qualcomm Inc
Quanta Services Inc
Quest Diagnostics Inc

Quintiles IMS Holdings Inc
Rackspace Hosting Inc
Raymond James Financial Inc
Red Hat Inc
Regal-Beloit Corporation
REI (Recreational Equipment Inc)
Republic Services Inc
ResMed Inc
Resources Connection Inc
Revlon Inc
Rite Aid Corporation
Ritz-Carlton Hotel Company LLC (The)
Robert Half International Inc
Roper Technologies Inc
Rosendin Electric
Ross Stores Inc
Royal Caribbean Cruises Ltd
RPM International Inc
Ryder System Inc
Sabre Corporation
Safeco Insurance Company of America
Safeway Inc
SalesForce.com Inc
Sam's Club
Sanmina Corp
Sapient Corporation
SAS Institute Inc
SC Johnson & Son Inc
SCANA Corporation
Science Applications International Corp
(SAIC)
Select Comfort Corporation
Select Medical Holdings Corporation
Service Corporation International Inc
ServiceMaster Company LLC (The)
ServiceNow Inc
Sherwin-Williams Company (The)
Sodexo Inc
Sonoco Products Company
Southwest Airlines Co
Spectrum Brands Holdings Inc
Spectrum Health
Spirit Aerosystems Holdings Inc
Spirit Airlines Inc
Stanley Black & Decker Inc
Starbucks Corporation
State Farm Insurance Companies
Stericycle Inc
Stifel Financial Corp
Strategy&
Stryker Corporation
Sutter Health Inc
Symantec Corp
SYNNEX Corporation
Synopsys Inc
Syntel Inc
SYSCO Corporation
T Rowe Price Group Inc
Team Health Holdings Inc
Team Inc
Tech Data Corp
Tenet Healthcare Corporation
Tenneco Inc
Tesla Inc
Texas Instruments Inc (TI)

Textron Inc
Thermo Fisher Scientific Inc
Thor Industries Inc
TIBCO Software Inc
TJX Companies Inc (The)
T-Mobile US Inc
Toll Brothers Inc
Total System Services Inc (TSYS)
Toyota Motor Sales USA Inc (TMS)
Trader Joe's Company Inc
TransDigm Group Incorporated
Travelers Companies Inc (The)
TreeHouse Foods Inc
Trimble Navigation Ltd
Trinity Health
Trustmark Companies
Tutor Perini Corporation
Uber Inc
Under Armour Inc
United Continental Holdings Inc
United Natural Foods Inc
United Parcel Service Inc (UPS)
United States Cellular Corporation
United Technologies Corporation
UnitedHealth Group Inc
Universal Health Services Inc
Unum Group
US Bancorp
USAA
UST Global Inc
Valassis Communications Inc
Vantiv Inc
Varian Medical Systems Inc
VCA Inc
Verizon Communications Inc
VF Corporation
Victoria's Secret
Visa Inc
VMware Inc
W R Berkley Corporation
Wabco Holdings Inc
Walgreens Boots Alliance Inc
Wal-Mart Stores Inc (Walmart)
Walt Disney Company (The)
Waste Management Inc
Waters Corporation
Wayfair LLC
Web.com Group Inc
WellCare Health Plans Inc
Wells Fargo & Co
Westlake Chemical Corporation
William Morris Endeavor Entertainment
LLC (WME-IMG)
WW Grainger Inc
Wyndham Worldwide Corporation
Wynn Resorts Limited
XPO Logistics Inc
Yum! Brands Inc
Zillow Inc
Zimmer Biomet Holdings Inc

INDEX OF U.S. HEADQUARTERS LOCATION BY STATE

To help you locate members of THE AMERICAN EMPLOYERS 500 geographically, the city and state of the headquarters of each company are in the following index.

ALABAMA
HealthSouth Corporation; Birmingham
Hibbett Sports Inc; Birmingham

ARIZONA
Avnet Inc; Phoenix
Discount Tire Company; Scottsdale
DriveTime Automotive Group Inc; Tempe
GoDaddy Inc; Scottsdale
Magellan Health Inc; Scottsdale
PetSmart Inc; Phoenix
Republic Services Inc; Phoenix

ARKANSAS
JB Hunt Transport Services Inc; Lowell
Sam's Club; Bentonville
Wal-Mart Stores Inc (Walmart); Bentonville

CALIFORNIA
24 Hour Fitness; San Ramon
Activision Blizzard Inc; Santa Monica
Adobe Systems Inc; San Jose
Airbnb Inc; San Francisco
American Honda Motor Co Inc; Torrance
Amgen Inc; Thousand Oaks
Apple Inc; Cupertino
Applied Materials Inc; Santa Clara
Bio Rad Laboratories Inc; Hercules
Cadence Design Systems Inc; San Jose
CBRE Group Inc; Los Angeles
Charles Schwab Corporation (The); San Francisco
Cisco Systems Inc; San Jose
Clorox Company (The); Oakland
Cooper Companies Inc; Pleasanton
DIRECTV; El Segundo
Edwards Lifesciences Corporation; Irvine
Encore Capital Group Inc; San Diego
Experian North America; Costa Mesa
Facebook Inc; Menlo Park
Gilead Sciences Inc; Foster City
Google (Alphabet Inc); Mountain View
Ingram Micro Inc; Irvine
In-N-Out Burgers Inc; Irvine
Intel Corporation; Santa Clara
Intuit Inc; Mountain View
Juniper Networks Inc; Sunnyvale
Kaiser Permanente; Oakland
Kimpton Hotel & Restaurant Group LLC; San Francisco
Lam Research Corporation; Fremont
LinkedIn Corp; Mountain View

McAfee Inc; Santa Clara
McKesson Corporation; San Francisco
Molina Healthcare Inc; Long Beach
NetSuite Inc; San Mateo
Oracle Corporation; Redwood City
PG&E Corporation; San Francisco
PriceSmart Inc; San Diego
Qualcomm Inc; San Diego
ResMed Inc; San Diego
Resources Connection Inc; Irvine
Robert Half International Inc; Menlo Park
Rosendin Electric; San Jose
Ross Stores Inc; Dublin
Safeway Inc; Pleasanton
SalesForce.com Inc; San Francisco
Sanmina Corp; San Jose
ServiceNow Inc; Santa Clara
Sutter Health Inc; Sacramento
Symantec Corp; Mountain View
SYNNEX Corporation; Fremont
Synopsys Inc; Mountain View
Tesla Inc; Palo Alto
TIBCO Software Inc; Palo Alto
Trader Joe's Company Inc; Monrovia
Trimble Navigation Ltd; Sunnyvale
Tutor Perini Corporation; Sylmar
Uber Inc; San Francisco
UST Global Inc; Aliso Viejo
Varian Medical Systems Inc; Palo Alto
VCA Inc; Los Angeles
Visa Inc; San Francisco
VMware Inc; Palo Alto
Walt Disney Company (The); Burbank
Wells Fargo & Co; San Francisco
William Morris Endeavor Entertainment LLC (WME-IMG); Beverly Hills

COLORADO
Arrow Electronics Inc; Centennial
Ball Corporation; Broomfield
Catholic Health Initiatives; Englewood
DaVita Healthcare Partners Inc; Denver
EchoStar Corporation; Englewood
Envision Healthcare Corporation; Greenwood Village
Level 3 Communications Inc; Broomfield
Liberty Global plc; Englewood
Liberty Interactive Corporation; Englewood

CONNECTICUT
Aetna Inc; Hartford
Amphenol Corporation; Wallingford
Charter Communications Inc; Stamford
Cigna Corporation; Bloomfield
EMCOR Group Inc; Norwalk
FactSet Research Systems Inc; Norwalk
Frontier Communications Corporation; Norwalk
Gartner Inc; Stamford
General Electric Co (GE); Fairfield
Hartford Financial Services Group Inc (The); Hartford
Hubbell Incorporated; Shelton
Priceline Group Inc (The); Norwalk

Stanley Black & Decker Inc; New Britain
United Technologies Corporation; Farmington
W R Berkley Corporation; Greenwich
XPO Logistics Inc; Greenwich

FLORIDA
Acosta Inc; Jacksonville
Adventist Health System; Altamonte Springs
AutoNation Inc; Fort Lauderdale
Brightstar Corporation; Miami
Brown & Brown Inc; Daytona Beach
Carnival Corporation; Miami
Citrix Systems Inc; Fort Lauderdale
Darden Restaurants Inc; Orlando
Dycom Industries Inc; Palm Beach Gardens
Fidelity National Information Services Inc; Jacksonville
Harris Corporation; Melbourne
ILG Inc; Miami
Jabil Circuit Inc; St. Petersburg
JM Family Enterprises Inc; Deerfield Beach
Lennar Corporation; Miami
Lincare Holdings Inc; Clearwater
Norwegian Cruise Line Holdings Ltd (NCL); Miami
Publix Super Markets Inc; Lakeland
Raymond James Financial Inc; St. Petersburg
Roper Technologies Inc; Sarasota
Royal Caribbean Cruises Ltd; Miami
Ryder System Inc; Miami
Spirit Airlines Inc; Miramar
Tech Data Corp; Clearwater
Web.com Group Inc; Jacksonville
WellCare Health Plans Inc; Tampa

GEORGIA
AFLAC Inc; Columbus
ARRIS Group Inc; Suwanee
BMC Stock Holdings Inc; Atlanta
Cox Automotive Inc; Atlanta
Cox Communications Inc; Atlanta
Cox Enterprises Inc; Atlanta
Delta Air Lines Inc; Atlanta
First Data Corporation; Atlanta
Fleetcor Technologies Inc; Norcross
Home Depot Inc (The); Atlanta
Manhattan Associates Inc; Atlanta
Mercedes-Benz USA LLC; Atlanta
Mohawk Industries Inc; Calhoun
NCR Corporation; Duluth
Newell Brands Inc; Atlanta
PulteGroup Inc; Atlanta
Total System Services Inc (TSYS); Columbus
United Parcel Service Inc (UPS); Atlanta

ILLINOIS
Abbott Laboratories; Abbott Park
AbbVie Inc; North Chicago
Accenture LLP; Chicago

Allscripts Healthcare Solutions Inc;
Chicago
Anixter International Inc; Glenview
Aon Hewitt; Chicago
Arthur J Gallagher & Co; Itasca
AT Kearney Inc; Chicago
Boeing Company (The); Chicago
CDW Corporation; Lincolnshire
Equity Lifestyle Properties Inc; Chicago
Exelon Corporation; Chicago
Grant Thornton LLP; Chicago
Health Care Service Corporation (HCSC);
Chicago
Hill-Rom Holdings Inc; Chicago
Hub International Limited; Chicago
Hyatt Hotels Corporation; Chicago
Illinois Tool Works Inc; Glenview
Ingredion Inc; Westchester
Jones Lang LaSalle Inc; Chicago
Littelfuse Inc; Chicago
LKQ Corporation; Chicago
McDonald's Corp; Oak Brook
Middleby Corporation (The); Elgin
Molex LLC; Lisle
State Farm Insurance Companies;
Bloomington
Stericycle Inc; Lake Forest
Tenneco Inc; Lake Forest
TreeHouse Foods Inc; Oakbrook
Trustmark Companies; Lake Forest
United Continental Holdings Inc; Chicago
United States Cellular Corporation;
Chicago
Walgreens Boots Alliance Inc; Deerfield
WW Grainger Inc; Lake Forest

INDIANA
Anthem Inc; Indianapolis
Berry Global Group Inc; Evansville
Dow AgroSciences LLC; Indianapolis
Eli Lilly and Company; Indianapolis
Hillenbrand Inc; Batesville
Patrick Industries Inc; Elkhart
Thor Industries Inc; Elkhart
Zimmer Biomet Holdings Inc; Warsaw

IOWA
Berkshire Hathaway Energy Company; Des
Moines
Principal Financial Group Inc; Des Moines

KANSAS
Black & Veatch Holding Company;
Overland Park
Spirit Aerosystems Holdings Inc; Wichita

KENTUCKY
Almost Family Inc; Louisville
Humana Inc; Louisville
Kindred Healthcare Inc; Louisville
Yum! Brands Inc; Louisville

LOUISIANA
CenturyLink Inc; Monroe
LHC Group Inc; Lafayette

MAINE
IDEXX Laboratories Inc; Westbrook

MARYLAND
Discovery Communications Inc; Silver
Spring
FTI Consulting Inc; Washington D.C.
HMSHost Corporation; Bethesda
Legg Mason Inc; Baltimore
Marriott International Inc; Bethesda
McCormick & Company Inc; Sparks
MedStar Health; Columbia
Ritz-Carlton Hotel Company LLC (The);
Chevy Chase
Sodexo Inc; Gaithersburg
T Rowe Price Group Inc; Baltimore
Under Armour Inc; Baltimore

MASSACHUSETTS
Agero Inc; Medford
Athenahealth Inc; Watertown
Bain & Company Inc; Boston
Biogen Inc; Cambridge
Boston Consulting Group Inc (The, BCG);
Boston
Boston Scientific Corp; Marlborough
Charles River Laboratories International
Inc; Wilmington
eClinicalWorks; Westborough
Fidelity Investments Financial Services;
Boston
INC Research/inVentiv Health; Boston
Liberty Mutual Group Inc; Boston
NetScout Systems Inc; Westford
PAREXEL International Corporation;
Waltham
PerkinElmer Inc; Waltham
Philips Healthcare; Andover
Sapient Corporation; Boston
Thermo Fisher Scientific Inc; Waltham
TJX Companies Inc (The); Framingham
Waters Corporation; Milford
Wayfair LLC; Boston

MICHIGAN
Ally Financial Inc; Detroit
DTE Energy Company; Detroit
FCA US LLC; Auburn Hills
Federal-Mogul Corporation; Southfield
Ford Motor Co; Dearborn
General Motors Company (GM); Detroit
Gentex Corporation; Zeeland
Gentherm Inc; Northville
Kelly Services Inc; Troy
Lear Corporation; Southfield
Penske Automotive Group Inc; Bloomfield
Hills
Penske Corporation; Bloomfield Hills
Spectrum Health; Grand Rapids
Stryker Corporation; Kalamazoo
Syntel Inc; Troy
Trinity Health; Livonia
Valassis Communications Inc; Livonia
Wabco Holdings Inc; Rochester Hills

MINNESOTA
3M Company; St. Paul
Best Buy Co Inc; Richfield
Buffalo Wild Wings Inc; Minneapolis
CH Robinson Worldwide Inc; Eden Prairie
Fairview Health Services; Minneapolis
Fastenal Company; Winona
Graco Inc; Minneapolis
Mayo Clinic; Rochester
Medtronic plc; Minneapolis
Patterson Companies Inc; St. Paul
Select Comfort Corporation; Minneapolis
UnitedHealth Group Inc; Minnetonka
US Bancorp; Minneapolis

MISSOURI
Ascension Health; St. Louis
Belden Inc; St. Louis
Burns & McDonnell; Kansas City
Centene Corporation; St. Louis
Cerner Corporation; North Kansas City
Edward D Jones & Co LP; Des Peres
Enterprise Holdings Inc; St. Louis
Jack Henry & Associates Inc; Monett
O'Reilly Automotive Inc; Springfield
Stifel Financial Corp; St. Louis

NEBRASKA
Berkshire Hathaway Inc; Omaha
Cabela's Inc; Sidney
Mutual of Omaha Companies (The);
Omaha

NEVADA
AMERCO (U-Haul); Reno
Eldorado Resorts Inc; Reno
Las Vegas Sands Corp (The Venetian); Las
Vegas
Pinnacle Entertainment Inc; Las Vegas
Wynn Resorts Limited; Las Vegas

NEW HAMPSHIRE
C&S Wholesale Grocers Inc; Keene

NEW JERSEY
Ascena Retail Group Inc; Mahwah
Automatic Data Processing Inc (ADP);
Roseland
Avis Budget Group Inc; Parsippany
Becton Dickinson & Co; Franklin Lakes
Bed Bath & Beyond Inc; Union
Celgene Corporation; Summit
Cognizant Technology Solutions
Corporation; Teaneck
CR Bard Inc; Murray Hill
Heartland Payment Systems Inc; Princeton
Honeywell International Inc; Morris Plains
Johnson & Johnson; New Brunswick
Merck & Co Inc; Kenilworth
Prudential Financial Inc; Newark
Quest Diagnostics Inc; Madison
Wyndham Worldwide Corporation;
Parsippany

NEW YORK
ABM Industries Inc; New York
American Express Co; New York
AmTrust Financial Services Inc; New York
Bank of New York Mellon Corp; New York
BBDO Worldwide; New York
BlackRock Inc; New York
Bloomberg LP; New York
Bristol-Myers Squibb Co; New York
CBS Corporation; New York
Citigroup Inc; New York
Constellation Brands Inc; Victor
Corning Inc; Corning
Cushman & Wakefield Inc; New York
Deloitte LLP; New York
Estee Lauder Companies Inc (The); New York
ExlService Holdings Inc; New York
EY LLP; New York
Fox Entertainment Group Inc; New York
Goldman Sachs Group Inc; New York
Henry Schein Inc; Melville
IAC/InterActiveCorp; New York
IMG Worldwide Inc; New York
Interpublic Group of Companies Inc; New York
Jefferies LLC; New York
JetBlue Airways Corporation; Long Island City
JP Morgan Chase & Co Inc; New York
KPMG LLP; New York
Loews Hotels Holding Corporation; New York
Marsh & McLennan Companies Inc; New York
MasterCard Inc; Purchase
McKinsey & Company Inc; New York
Mediacom Communications Corp; Mediacom Park
Mercer LLC; New York
Merrill Lynch & Co Inc; New York
Monro Muffler Brake Inc; Rochester
Moody's Corporation; New York
Morgan Stanley; New York
NBCUniversal LLC; New York
New York Life Insurance Company; New York
Nielsen Holdings plc; New York
Oliver Wyman Group; New York
Omnicom Group Inc; New York
Paychex Inc; Rochester
Pfizer Inc; New York
PricewaterhouseCoopers (PwC); New York
Revlon Inc; New York
Strategy&; New York
Travelers Companies Inc (The); New York
Verizon Communications Inc; New York

NORTH CAROLINA
American Tire Distributors; Huntersville
Bank of America Corp; Charlotte
BB&T Corporation; Winston-Salem
Coca-Cola Bottling Co Consolidated; Charlotte
CommScope Inc; Hickory
Duke Energy Corporation; Charlotte
Hanesbrands Inc; Winston-Salem
Hendrick Automotive Group; Charlotte
Laboratory Corporation of America Holdings; Burlington
Lowe's Companies Inc; Mooresville
Old Dominion Freight Line Inc; Thomasville
Pharmaceutical Product Development Inc; Wilmington
PRA Health Sciences Inc; Raleigh
Quintiles IMS Holdings Inc; Durham
Red Hat Inc; Raleigh
SAS Institute Inc; Cary
VF Corporation; Greensboro

OHIO
American Financial Group Inc; Cincinnati
Cardinal Health Inc; Dublin
Chemed Corporation; Cincinnati
Cintas Corporation; Cincinnati
Cleveland Clinic Foundation (The); Cleveland
Convergys Corporation; Cincinnati
Dana Incorporated; Maumee
FirstEnergy Corporation; Akron
Kroger Co (The); Cincinnati
Lubrizol Corporation (The); Wickliffe
Owens Corning Inc; Toledo
Progressive Corporation (The); Mayfield Village
RPM International Inc; Medina
Sherwin-Williams Company (The); Cleveland
TransDigm Group Incorporated; Cleveland
Vantiv Inc; Symmes Township
Victoria's Secret; Reynoldsburg

OKLAHOMA
Dollar Thrifty Automotive Group Inc; Tulsa
Mercy; Tishomingo

OREGON
Lithia Motors Inc; Medford
Mentor Graphics Corp; Wilsonville
Nike Inc; Beaverton

PENNSYLVANIA
AmerisourceBergen Corp; Chesterbrook
Ametek Inc; Berwyn
Aramark; Philadelphia
Comcast Corporation; Philadelphia
Crown Holdings Inc; Philadelphia
Dentsply Sirona Inc; York
EPAM Systems Inc; Newtown
Hershey Co; Hershey
Lincoln National Corporation; Radnor
Matthews International Corporation; Pittsburgh
PPG Industries Inc; Pittsburgh
Rite Aid Corporation; Camp Hill
Select Medical Holdings Corporation; Mechanicsburg
Toll Brothers Inc; Horsham
Universal Health Services Inc; King Of Prussia

RHODE ISLAND
APC by Schneider Electric; West Kingston
CVS Health Corporation; Woonsocket
Textron Inc; Providence
United Natural Foods Inc; Providence

SOUTH CAROLINA
SCANA Corporation; Cayce
Sonoco Products Company; Hartsville

TENNESSEE
Acadia Healthcare Company Inc; Franklin
AMSURG Corporation; Nashville
Brookdale Senior Living Inc; Brentwood
Change Healthcare Inc; Nashville
Clayton Homes Inc; Maryville
Community Health Systems Inc; Franklin
FedEx Corporation; Memphis
HCA Holdings Inc; Nashville
LifePoint Health Inc; Brentwood
NN Inc; Johnson City
ServiceMaster Company LLC (The); Memphis
Team Health Holdings Inc; Knoxville
Unum Group; Chattanooga

TEXAS
Academy Sports & Outdoors Ltd; Katy
Accor North America; Carrollton
Alliance Data Systems Corporation; Plano
American Airlines Group Inc; Fort Worth
AT&T Inc; Dallas
AZZ Inc; Fort Worth
BMC Software Inc; Houston
Brinker International Inc; Dallas
Celanese Corporation; Irving
Chevron Phillips Chemical Company LLC; The Woodlands
Container Store Inc (The); Coppell
Cullen-Frost Bankers Inc; San Antonio
Dell Technologies Inc; Round Rock
Diodes Inc; Plano
DR Horton Inc; Fort Worth
Fluor Corp; Irving
Frito-Lay North America Inc; Plano
Group 1 Automotive Inc; Houston
HEB Grocery Company LP; San Antonio
Houston Methodist; Houston
Integer Holdings Corporation; Frisco
La Quinta Holdings Inc; Irving
Mary Kay Inc; Dallas
Match Group Inc; Dallas
National Instruments Corporation; Austin
Phillips 66; Houston
Quanta Services Inc; Houston
Rackspace Hosting Inc; San Antonio
Sabre Corporation; Southlake
Service Corporation International Inc; Houston
Southwest Airlines Co; Dallas
SYSCO Corporation; Houston

Team Inc; Sugar Land
Tenet Healthcare Corporation; Dallas
Texas Instruments Inc (TI); Dallas
Toyota Motor Sales USA Inc (TMS); Plano
USAA; San Antonio
Waste Management Inc; Houston
Westlake Chemical Corporation; Houston

Regal-Beloit Corporation; Beloit
SC Johnson & Son Inc; Racine
Spectrum Brands Holdings Inc; Middleton

UTAH
Larry H Miller Group; Sandy

VIRGINIA
Advance Auto Parts Inc; Roanoke
Amerigroup Corporation; Virginia Beach
Audi of America Inc; Herndon
Booz Allen Hamilton Holding Corp;
McLean
CACI International Inc; Arlington
Capital One Financial Corp; McLean
CarMax Inc; Richmond
HC2 Holdings Inc; Herndon
Hilton Inc; McLean
Mars Inc; McLean
MAXIMUS Inc; Reston
NVR Inc; Reston
Orbital ATK Inc; Dulles
Science Applications International Corp
(SAIC); McLean

WASHINGTON
Alaska Air Group Inc; Seattle
Amazon.com Inc; Seattle
Barrett Business Services Inc; Vancouver
Concur Technologies Inc; Bellevue
CoStar Group Inc; Northwest
Costco Wholesale Corporation; Issaquah
Esterline Technologies Corporation;
Bellevue
Expedia Inc; Bellevue
Expeditors International of Washington
Inc; Seattle
F5 Networks Inc; Seattle
Microsoft Corporation; Redmond
Nordstrom Inc; Seattle
PACCAR Inc; Bellevue
Providence St Joseph Health; Renton
REI (Recreational Equipment Inc); Kent
Safeco Insurance Company of America;
Seattle
Starbucks Corporation; Seattle
T-Mobile US Inc; Bellevue
Zillow Inc; Seattle

WISCONSIN
AO Smith Corporation; Milwaukee
Epic Systems Corporation; Verona
Fiserv Inc; Brookfield
Kohler Company; Kohler
Kohl's Corporation; Menomonee Falls
Marcus Corporation (The); Milwaukee
Menard Inc; Eau Claire
Modine Manufacturing Company; Racine
Northwestern Mutual Life Insurance
Company; Milwaukee
Oshkosh Corporation; Oshkosh

Individual Data
Profiles
On Each Of
The AMERICAN EMPLOYERS 500

24 Hour Fitness

www.24hourfitness.com

NAIC Code: 713940

TYPES OF BUSINESS:

Fitness Centers
Online Nutrition Information
Day Spa

BRANDS/DIVISIONS/AFFILIATES:

AEA Investors LP
Active/Express/Fit Lite
Sport
Super-Sport
Ultra-Sport
Training Club 24
Fit:Perks Rewards
Ontario Teachers' Pension Plan

CONTACTS: *Note: Officers with more than one job title may be intentionally listed here more than once.*

Mark Smith, CEO
Jeffrey N. Boyer, COO
Frank Napolitano, Pres.
Patrick Flanagan, CFO
Vicki Davis, Corp. Controller
Danny De La Rosa, Pres., Clubs

GROWTH PLANS/SPECIAL FEATURES:

24 Hour Fitness is one of the world's largest privately owned and operated fitness center chains. The firm has nearly 4 million members and over 400 clubs in 13 U.S. states. The company operates four types of clubs: 24 Hour Fitness Active/Express/Fit Lite club, Sport club, Super-Sport club and Ultra-Sport club. The Fitness/Express/Fit Lite clubs are moderate in size and offer full-body workouts in minutes by using cardio equipment, strength machines and free weights, with most locations offering group exercise classes as well. Sport clubs offer full group exercise schedules, fitness equipment and classes, with most locations providing a sauna, steam room and whirlpool, and some featuring basketball courts and/or swimming pools. Super-Sport clubs offer lots of equipment and functional training areas, with most featuring whirlpools, saunas, towel service, basketball and swimming and some locations offering racquetball. Ultra-Sport clubs are for serious fitness members, offering high-end fitness amenities in prime locations, including group cycling and personal training areas. 24 Hour Fitness offers family memberships, kids' club supervised areas, personal training and Training Club 24, the company's signature group training program. Additionally, members can sign up for the Fit:Perks Rewards program and accumulate points for exclusive rewards such as sweepstakes entries, monthly deals, giveaways and promotions. 24 Hour Fitness is owned by AEA Investors LP, Ontario Teachers' Pension Plan and Fitness Capital Partners.

FINANCIAL DATA: *Note: Data for latest year may not have been available at press time.*

In U.S. $	2016	2015	2014	2013	2012	2011
Revenue	1,489,000,000	1,418,000,000	1,330,000,000	1,300,000,000	1,500,000,000	1,500,000,000
R&D Expense						
Operating Income						
Operating Margin %						
SGA Expense						
Net Income						
Operating Cash Flow						
Capital Expenditure						
EBITDA						
Return on Assets %						
Return on Equity %						
Debt to Equity						

CONTACT INFORMATION:

Phone: 925-543-3100   Fax: 925-543-3200
Toll-Free:
Address: 12647 Alcosta Blvd., Ste. 500, San Ramon, CA 94583 United States

STOCK TICKER/OTHER:

Stock Ticker: Private   Exchange:
Employees: 20,000   Fiscal Year Ends: 12/31
Parent Company: AEA Investors LP

SALARIES/BONUSES:

Top Exec. Salary: $ Bonus: $
Second Exec. Salary: $ Bonus: $

OTHER THOUGHTS:

Estimated Female Officers or Directors: 1
Hot Spot for Advancement for Women/Minorities:

3M Company

NAIC Code: 339100

www.3m.com

TYPES OF BUSINESS:

Health Care Products
Specialty Materials & Textiles
Industrial Products
Safety, Security & Protection Products
Display & Graphics Products
Consumer & Office Products
Electronics & Communications Products
Fuel Cell Technology

BRANDS/DIVISIONS/AFFILIATES:

3M Purification Inc
Thinsulate
Scotch
Command
Filtrete
3M
Semfinder

CONTACTS: Note: Officers with more than one job title may be intentionally listed here more than once.

Inge Thulin, CEO
Khandpur Ashish, Senior VP, Divisional
Michael Roman, Executive VP, Divisional
James Bauman, Executive VP, Divisional
Frank Little, Executive VP, Divisional
Hak Shin, Executive VP, Divisional
Michael Vale, Executive VP, Divisional
Joaquin Delgado, Executive VP, Divisional
Ivan Fong, General Counsel
Marlene McGrath, Senior VP, Divisional
Jon Lindekugel, Senior VP, Divisional
Kimberly Price, Senior VP, Divisional
Paul Keel, Senior VP, Divisional
Julie Bushman, Senior VP, Divisional
Nicholas Gangestad, Senior VP
Ippocratis Vrohidis, Vice President, Divisional
Eric Hammes, Vice President

GROWTH PLANS/SPECIAL FEATURES:

3M Company is involved in the research, manufacturing and marketing of a variety of products. Its operations are organized in five segments: industrial, safety and graphics, electronics and energy, health care and consumer. The industrial business segment serves the automotive, electronics, appliance, paper, printing, food, beverage and construction markets. Its major industrial products include Thinsulate acoustic insulation and 3M paint finishing and detail products. Also, 3M Purification, Inc. provides a line of filtration products. The safety and graphics business segment serves a wide range of markets that increase the safety, security and productivity of people, facilities and systems. Major product offerings include personal protection, traffic safety, border and civil security solutions, commercial graphics sheeting, architectural surface and lighting solutions, cleaning products and roofing granules for asphalt shingles. The electronics and energy business segment serves customers with solutions for electronic devices for telecommunications networks, electrical products, power generation and distribution and infrastructure protection. Major products include LCD computer monitors, LCD televisions, hand-held mobile devices, notebook PCs and automotive displays. The health care business segment serves medical clinics, hospitals, pharmaceuticals, dental and orthodontic practitioners, health information systems and food manufacturing and testing. Products include medical and surgical supplies, skin health, infection prevention, inhalation and transdermal drug delivery systems. The consumer segment serves markets that include consumer retail, office retail, home improvement, building maintenance and other markets. Major products include the Scotch tape, Command adhesive and Filtrete filtration family lines of products. In 2016, the firm sold its temporary protective films business, Polymask, to Pregis, LLC; and acquired Semfinder, a medical coding technology company.

The company offers employees medical and dental insurance, domestic partner benefits, tuition reimbursement, flexible spending accounts, disability coverage, 401(k) and adoption assistance.

FINANCIAL DATA: Note: Data for latest year may not have been available at press time.

In U.S. $	2016	2015	2014	2013	2012	2011
Revenue	30,109,000,000	30,274,000,000	31,821,000,000	30,871,000,000	29,904,000,000	29,611,000,000
R&D Expense	1,735,000,000	1,763,000,000	1,770,000,000	1,715,000,000	1,634,000,000	1,570,000,000
Operating Income	7,223,000,000	6,946,000,000	7,135,000,000	6,666,000,000	6,483,000,000	6,178,000,000
Operating Margin %	23.98%	22.94%	22.42%	21.59%	21.67%	20.86%
SGA Expense	6,111,000,000	6,182,000,000	6,469,000,000	6,384,000,000	6,102,000,000	6,170,000,000
Net Income	5,050,000,000	4,833,000,000	4,956,000,000	4,659,000,000	4,444,000,000	4,283,000,000
Operating Cash Flow	6,662,000,000	6,420,000,000	6,626,000,000	5,817,000,000	5,300,000,000	5,284,000,000
Capital Expenditure	1,420,000,000	1,461,000,000	1,493,000,000	1,665,000,000	1,484,000,000	1,379,000,000
EBITDA	8,726,000,000	8,407,000,000	8,576,000,000	8,078,000,000	7,810,000,000	7,453,000,000
Return on Assets %	15.39%	15.10%	15.29%	13.81%	13.57%	13.86%
Return on Equity %	45.89%	38.94%	32.38%	26.56%	26.93%	27.55%
Debt to Equity	1.04	0.75	0.51	0.25	0.28	0.29

CONTACT INFORMATION:

Phone: 651 733-1110   Fax: 651 733-9973
Toll-Free: 800-364-3577
Address: 3M Center, St. Paul, MN 55144 United States

STOCK TICKER/OTHER:

Stock Ticker: MMM   Exchange: NYS
Employees: 91,584   Fiscal Year Ends: 12/31
Parent Company:

SALARIES/BONUSES:

Top Exec. Salary: $1,483,929   Bonus: $
Second Exec. Salary: Bonus: $
$747,022

OTHER THOUGHTS:

Estimated Female Officers or Directors: 7
Hot Spot for Advancement for Women/Minorities: Y

Sales, profits and employees may be estimates. Financial information, benefits and other data can change quickly and may vary from those stated here.

Abbott Laboratories

NAIC Code: 325412

www.abbott.com

TYPES OF BUSINESS:

Nutritional Products Manufacturing
Immunoassays
Diagnostics
Consumer Health Products
Medical & Surgical Devices
Generic Pharmaceutical Products
LASIK Devices

BRANDS/DIVISIONS/AFFILIATES:

Multi-Link Vision
ARCHITECT
i-STAT
Similac
Ensure
Pediasure
Zone Perfect
St. Jude Medical Inc

CONTACTS: Note: Officers with more than one job title may be intentionally listed here more than once.

Miles White, CEO
Jared Watkin, Senior VP, Divisional
Robert Funck, Chief Accounting Officer
Heather Mason, Executive VP, Divisional
Stephen Fussell, Executive VP, Divisional
John Capek, Executive VP, Divisional
Robert Ford, Executive VP, Divisional
Brian Blaser, Executive VP, Divisional
Hubert Allen, Executive VP
Michael Rousseau, President, Divisional
Eric Fain, President, Divisional
Roger Bird, Senior VP, Divisional
Deepak Nath, Senior VP, Divisional
Andrew Lane, Senior VP, Divisional
Thomas Frinzi, Senior VP, Divisional
Jaime Contreras, Senior VP, Divisional
Brian Yoor, Senior VP, Divisional

GROWTH PLANS/SPECIAL FEATURES:

Abbott Laboratories develops, manufactures and sells health care products and technologies ranging from pharmaceuticals to medical devices marketed in over 150 countries. It operates in four segments: established pharmaceutical, diagnostics, nutrition and vascular products. Established pharmaceuticals deal with gastroenterology issues, women's health, cardiovascular and metabolic illnesses, pain and the central nervous system, respiratory health and immunization. The diagnostics segment develops systems and tests to diagnose infectious diseases, cancer, diabetes and genetic conditions, including the ARCHITECT chemistry system and i-STAT hematology systems, which are marketed to hospitals, laboratories, physicians' offices and plasma protein therapeutic companies. The nutritional segment offers consumer products such as Similac, Ensure, PediaSure and Zone Perfect as well as feeding devices in health care institutions. Vascular products consist of coronary, endovascular and vessel closure devices used in the treatment of vascular disease. Products include the Multi-Link Vision coronary metallic stents, TREK balloon dilatation systems and StarClose vessel closure devices. Other products include the FreeStyle line of diabetes products. In September 2016, Abbott sold Abbott Medical Optics, its vision care business, to Johnson & Johnson for $4.325 billion in cash. The following December, the firm terminated its agreement to acquire Alere, a leading point of care diagnostics company, due to the substantial loss in Alere's value following the merger agreement. In January 2017, Abbott completed its acquisition of St. Jude Medical, Inc. for $25 billion.

The firm offers employees medical, dental and vision insurance; flexible spending accounts; adoption assistance; an employee assistance program; legal services; tuition assistance; and life insurance.

FINANCIAL DATA: Note: Data for latest year may not have been available at press time.

In U.S. $	2016	2015	2014	2013	2012	2011
Revenue	20,853,000,000	20,405,000,000	20,247,000,000	21,848,000,000	39,873,910,000	38,851,260,000
R&D Expense	1,422,000,000	1,405,000,000	1,345,000,000	1,452,000,000	4,322,182,000	4,129,414,000
Operating Income	3,185,000,000	2,867,000,000	2,599,000,000	2,629,000,000	8,084,515,000	5,751,948,000
Operating Margin %	15.27%	14.05%	12.83%	12.03%	20.27%	14.80%
SGA Expense	6,672,000,000	6,785,000,000	6,530,000,000	6,936,000,000	12,059,500,000	12,756,820,000
Net Income	1,400,000,000	4,423,000,000	2,284,000,000	2,576,000,000	5,962,920,000	4,728,449,000
Operating Cash Flow	3,203,000,000	2,966,000,000	3,675,000,000	3,324,000,000	9,314,401,000	8,970,077,000
Capital Expenditure	1,121,000,000	1,110,000,000	1,077,000,000	1,145,000,000	1,795,289,000	1,491,500,000
EBITDA	3,197,000,000	4,818,000,000	4,216,000,000	4,397,000,000	9,638,224,000	8,772,677,000
Return on Assets %	2.98%	10.71%	5.42%	4.67%	9.35%	7.89%
Return on Equity %	6.70%	20.69%	9.78%	9.92%	23.31%	20.19%
Debt to Equity	1.00	0.27	0.15	0.13	0.67	0.49

CONTACT INFORMATION:

Phone: 847 937-6100   Fax: 847 937-1511
Toll-Free:
Address: 100 Abbott Park Rd., Abbott Park, IL 60064-6400 United States

STOCK TICKER/OTHER:

Stock Ticker: ABT
Employees: 75,000
Parent Company:

Exchange: NYS
Fiscal Year Ends: 12/31

SALARIES/BONUSES:

Top Exec. Salary: $1,900,000   Bonus: $
Second Exec. Salary: $999,443   Bonus: $

OTHER THOUGHTS:

Estimated Female Officers or Directors: 5
Hot Spot for Advancement for Women/Minorities: Y

AbbVie Inc

NAIC Code: 325412

www.abbvie.com

TYPES OF BUSINESS:

Pharmaceuticals Manufacturing

BRANDS/DIVISIONS/AFFILIATES:

HUMIRA
VIEKIRA PAK
AndroGel
Lupron
Duopa
KALETRA
Stemcentrx Inc
Rova-T

CONTACTS: Note: Officers with more than one job title may be intentionally listed here more than once.

Richard Gonzalez, CEO
William Chase, CFO
Thomas Hurwich, Chief Accounting Officer
Michael Severino, Chief Scientific Officer
Carlos Alban, Executive VP, Divisional
Laura Schumacher, Executive VP, Divisional
Henry Gosebruch, Executive VP
Timothy Richmond, Senior VP, Divisional
Azita Saleki-Gerhardt, Senior VP, Divisional

GROWTH PLANS/SPECIAL FEATURES:

AbbVie, Inc. is a global biopharmaceutical manufacturing and research firm. The company's core areas of focus include immunology, kidney disease, liver disease, neuroscience, renal disease, Crohn's disease, hepatitis C, endometriosis, thyroid disease, Parkinson's disease, oncology and women's health. It is investigating both small and large molecule approaches, and its research efforts are partnered with external collaborations across industry, academia and health care authorities. AbbVie's leading drugs include HUMIRA, a biologic therapy; VIEKIRA PAK, an all-oral, short-course interferon-free therapy; AndroGel, a testosterone replacement therapy; Lupron, a product for the palliative treatment of advanced prostate cancer, endometriosis and central precocious puberty; Duopa, an intestinal gel for advanced Parkinson's; and KALETRA, a prescription anti-HIV 1 medicine that maintains viral suppression in people with HIV-1. The company operates research centers in Abbott Park and North Chicago, Illinois; Redwood City, South San Francisco and Sunnyvale, California; Worcester and Cambridge, Massachusetts; and Ludwigshafen, Germany. Its products are sold in more than 170 nations worldwide. In June 2016, AbbVie acquired Stemcentrx, Inc. for $5.8 billion, which then added the late-stage asset Rova-T for small cell lung cancer to the firm's product portfolio.

Benefits for U.S. employees include on-site fitness centers or health club memberships, sports and recreation clubs and wellness programs. Time off includes 11 paid holidays per year. Other perks include Work-Life balance programs, adoption assistance and mothers at work programs. Eligible employees may participate in both a 401(k) savings plan and a pension plan.

FINANCIAL DATA: Note: Data for latest year may not have been available at press time.

In U.S. $	2016	2015	2014	2013	2012	2011
Revenue	25,638,000,000	22,859,000,000	19,960,000,000	18,790,000,000	18,380,000,000	17,443,950,000
R&D Expense	4,566,000,000	4,435,000,000	3,649,000,000	3,193,000,000	3,066,000,000	2,617,506,000
Operating Income	9,383,999,000	7,537,000,000	3,411,000,000	5,664,000,000	5,817,000,000	3,620,732,000
Operating Margin %	36.60%	32.97%	17.08%	30.14%	31.64%	20.75%
SGA Expense	5,855,000,000	6,387,000,000	7,724,000,000	5,352,000,000	4,989,000,000	5,893,820,000
Net Income	5,953,000,000	5,144,000,000	1,774,000,000	4,128,000,000	5,275,000,000	3,433,128,000
Operating Cash Flow	7,041,000,000	7,535,000,000	3,549,000,000	6,267,000,000	6,345,000,000	6,246,960,000
Capital Expenditure	479,000,000	532,000,000	612,000,000	491,000,000	333,000,000	355,515,000
EBITDA	10,120,000,000	8,200,000,000	3,584,000,000	6,528,000,000	6,979,000,000	4,892,926,000
Return on Assets %	9.94%	12.76%	6.25%	14.68%	22.60%	16.83%
Return on Equity %	138.04%	180.90%	56.91%	105.10%	67.68%	24.58%
Debt to Equity	7.86	7.41	6.06	3.18	4.35	

CONTACT INFORMATION:

Phone: 847-932-7900   Fax:
Toll-Free: 800-255-5162
Address: 1 N. Waukegan Rd., North Chicago, IL 60064 United States

STOCK TICKER/OTHER:

Stock Ticker: ABBV   Exchange: NYS
Employees: 30,000   Fiscal Year Ends:
Parent Company:

SALARIES/BONUSES:

Top Exec. Salary: $894,523   Bonus: $1,000,000
Second Exec. Salary: Bonus: $
$1,600,000

OTHER THOUGHTS:

Estimated Female Officers or Directors:
Hot Spot for Advancement for Women/Minorities:

ABM Industries Inc

NAIC Code: 561720

www.abm.com

TYPES OF BUSINESS:

Janitorial Services
Parking Facilities
Maintenance Personnel
Security Services
Lighting Services
Billing & Accounting Services
Supplier Management
Energy Efficiency Technology

BRANDS/DIVISIONS/AFFILIATES:

ABM Janitorial Services
Westway Services Holdings Ltd
Mechanical Solutions Inc

CONTACTS: *Note: Officers with more than one job title may be intentionally listed here more than once.*

Diego Scaglione, CFO
Dean Chin, Chief Accounting Officer
James Mcclure, COO
Scott Salmirs, Director
Sarah McConnell, Executive VP
David Goodes, Other Executive Officer
Rene Jacobsen, President, Divisional
Scott Giacobbe, President, Divisional

GROWTH PLANS/SPECIAL FEATURES:

ABM Industries, Inc. is one of the country's largest facility services providers. ABM provides janitorial, parking, engineering, security and mechanical services to commercial, industrial, institutional and retail facilities throughout the U.S. and 20 additional countries. The company operates through several subsidiaries, which are grouped into five segments: janitorial, parking, facility services, building & energy solutions and other. Janitorial services include floor cleaning and finishing, window washing, furniture polishing and carpet cleaning and dusting. Parking provides parking and transportation services for clients such as commercial office buildings, airports and other transportation centers, education institutions, health facilities, hotels, municipalities, retail centers and stadiums. Facility services provides onsite mechanical engineering and technical services and solutions for facilities and infrastructure systems for a variety of client facilities, including transportation centers, commercial infrastructure, corporate office buildings, data centers, educational institutions, high technology manufacturing facilities, museums, resorts, and shopping centers. Building & energy solutions provides heating, ventilation, air-conditioning, electrical, lighting and other general maintenance and repair services. In January 2017, the firm acquired Mechanical Solutions, Inc., a Dallas-based provider of HVAC services, building automation and plumbing.

The firm offers employees dental, medical, vision, disability, life, AD&D and business travel accident insurance; flexible spending accounts; workers compensation insurance; 401(k); employee stock plans; employee assistance; tuition reimbursement; and credit union membership.

FINANCIAL DATA: *Note: Data for latest year may not have been available at press time.*

In U.S. $	2016	2015	2014	2013	2012	2011
Revenue	5,144,700,000	4,897,800,000	5,032,800,000	4,809,281,000	4,300,265,000	4,246,842,000
R&D Expense						
Operating Income	54,700,000	73,600,000	128,600,000	119,025,000	96,566,000	117,568,000
Operating Margin %	1.06%	1.50%	2.55%	2.47%	2.24%	2.76%
SGA Expense	390,100,000	390,000,000	363,900,000	348,274,000	327,855,000	324,762,000
Net Income	57,200,000	76,300,000	75,600,000	72,900,000	62,582,000	68,504,000
Operating Cash Flow	83,500,000	145,300,000	120,700,000	135,313,000	150,612,000	159,990,000
Capital Expenditure	44,000,000	26,500,000	37,400,000	32,593,000	28,052,000	22,124,000
EBITDA	119,800,000	139,600,000	192,400,000	185,734,000	153,545,000	174,141,000
Return on Assets %	2.58%	3.51%	3.50%	3.65%	3.33%	3.99%
Return on Equity %	5.77%	7.72%	8.01%	8.24%	7.60%	8.92%
Debt to Equity	0.27	0.15	0.33	0.34	0.25	0.37

CONTACT INFORMATION:

Phone: 212 297-0200   Fax: 212 297-0375
Toll-Free:
Address: 551 5th Ave., Ste. 300, New York, NY 10176 United States

STOCK TICKER/OTHER:

Stock Ticker: ABM   Exchange: NYS
Employees: 110,000   Fiscal Year Ends: 10/31
Parent Company:

SALARIES/BONUSES:

Top Exec. Salary: $793,333   Bonus: $
Second Exec. Salary: $708,470   Bonus: $

OTHER THOUGHTS:

Estimated Female Officers or Directors: 4
Hot Spot for Advancement for Women/Minorities: Y

Academy Sports & Outdoors Ltd

www.academy.com

NAIC Code: 451110

TYPES OF BUSINESS:

Sporting Goods Stores
Apparel
Footwear
Outdoor Sports Gear
Hunting Licenses

BRANDS/DIVISIONS/AFFILIATES:

KKR & Co LP (Kohlberg Kravis Roberts & Co)

CONTACTS: Note: Officers with more than one job title may be intentionally listed here more than once.

James K. Symancyk, CEO
Rodney Faldyn, Pres.
Beth Menuer, Exec. VP-Footwear
Robert Frennea, Exec. VP-Apparel
Kevin Chapman, Exec. VP-Stores

GROWTH PLANS/SPECIAL FEATURES:

Academy Sports & Outdoors, Ltd., owned by KKR & Co LP, is one of the largest sporting goods retailers in the U.S. The company operates over 225 stores throughout 16 states including Alabama, Arkansas, Florida, Georgia, Illinois, Indiana, Kansas, Kentucky, Louisiana, Mississippi, Missouri, North Carolina, Oklahoma, South Carolina, Tennessee and Texas. Its retail operations also include a full e-commerce retail store. Academy Sports offers a broad selection of sporting equipment, apparel and footwear. The stores, which range in size from 50,000 to 100,000 square feet, are laid out in a racetrack format with soft goods on the inside, including branded and private label athletic and casual apparel; and hard goods, such as camping, hunting, fishing, marine, footwear and fitness and sporting goods on the outside. The company distributes merchandise to its stores from its distribution centers located in Katy, Texas and Twiggs County, Georgia. The center utilizes radio frequency identification devices (RFID), automated inventory and replenishment systems and a state-of-the-art warehouse management system to smoothly operate its large processing and inventory space.

The company offers its employees a 401(k) plan; medical, dental and vision insurance; life insurance; short- and long-term disability benefits; tuition reimbursement; merchandise discounts; bereavement leave; continuing education benefits; and business travel accident insurance.

FINANCIAL DATA: Note: Data for latest year may not have been available at press time.

In U.S. $	2016	2015	2014	2013	2012	2011
Revenue	4,600,000,000	4,500,000,000	4,000,000,000	3,700,000,000	3,254,000,000	2,700,000,000
R&D Expense						
Operating Income						
Operating Margin %						
SGA Expense						
Net Income						
Operating Cash Flow						
Capital Expenditure						
EBITDA						
Return on Assets %						
Return on Equity %						
Debt to Equity						

CONTACT INFORMATION:

Phone: 281-646-5200   Fax: 281-646-5000
Toll-Free: 888-922-2336
Address: 1800 N. Mason Rd., Katy, TX 77449 United States

STOCK TICKER/OTHER:

Stock Ticker: Private   Exchange:
Employees: 22,000   Fiscal Year Ends: 02/28
Parent Company: KKR & Co LP (Kohlberg Kravis Roberts & Co)

SALARIES/BONUSES:

Top Exec. Salary: $ Bonus: $
Second Exec. Salary: $ Bonus: $

OTHER THOUGHTS:

Estimated Female Officers or Directors: 1
Hot Spot for Advancement for Women/Minorities:

Acadia Healthcare Company Inc

www.acadiahealthcare.com

NAIC Code: 622210

TYPES OF BUSINESS:

Psychiatric and Substance Abuse Hospitals
Residential Treatment Facilities
Behavioral Health Care Centers

BRANDS/DIVISIONS/AFFILIATES:

Partnerships in Care (PiC)
Priory Group

CONTACTS: *Note: Officers with more than one job title may be intentionally listed here more than once.*

David Duckworth, CFO
Joey Jacobs, Chairman of the Board
Ronald Fincher, COO
Bruce Shear, Director
Christopher Howard, Executive VP
Scott Schwieger, Other Executive Officer
Brent Turner, President
Randall Goldberg, Vice President, Divisional

GROWTH PLANS/SPECIAL FEATURES:

Acadia Healthcare Company, Inc. provides inpatient behavioral health care services via 573 facilities with more than 17,100 licensed beds in 39 U.S. states, the U.K. and Puerto Rico. Acadia provides psychiatric and chemical dependency services in a variety of settings, including psychiatric hospitals, residential treatment centers, outpatient clinics and therapeutic school-based programs. Treatment specializes in helping children, teenagers and adults suffering from mental health disorders and/or alcohol and drug addiction. Acadia operates through four types of facilities: acute inpatient psychiatric facilities, residential treatment centers, outpatient community-based services and specialty. Acute inpatient psychiatric facilities help stabilize patients that are either a threat to themselves or to others, and have 24-hour observation, daily intervention and residential treatment centers. Residential treatment centers treat patients with behavioral disorders in a non-hospital setting, and balance therapy activities with social, academic and other activities. Certain residential treatment centers provide group home and therapeutic foster care programs. Outpatient community-based services are usually divided between children and adolescents (7-18 years of age) and young children (three months to six years old). Community-based programs provide therapeutic treatment to minors who have clinically-defined emotional, psychiatric or chemical dependency disorders while enabling the youth to remain at home and within their community. Specialty treatment facilities include residential recovery facilities, eating disorder facilities and comprehensive treatment centers (CTCs) for addictive disorders, co-occurring mental disorders and detoxification. Acadia's U.K. operations work under the Partnerships in Care (PiC) name. In early 2016, the firm acquired Priory Group, a provider of behavioral healthcare services in the U.K. The following November, to address the concerns of the Competition and Markets Authority in the U.K. in regards to the acquisition of Priory Group, Acadia sold 21 existing facilities and one de novo behavioral health facility, not yet opened, to funds advised by BC Partners LLP.

FINANCIAL DATA: *Note: Data for latest year may not have been available at press time.*

In U.S. $	2016	2015	2014	2013	2012	2011
Revenue	2,810,914,000	1,794,492,000	1,004,601,000	713,408,000	407,461,000	221,373,000
R&D Expense						
Operating Income	396,819,000	320,810,000	159,113,000	69,245,000	32,829,000	-38,256,000
Operating Margin %	14.11%	17.87%	15.83%	9.70%	8.05%	-17.28%
SGA Expense	307,157,000	153,034,000	78,333,000	134,942,000	34,969,000	57,740,000
Net Income	6,143,000	112,554,000	83,040,000	42,579,000	20,403,000	-34,892,000
Operating Cash Flow	361,478,000	240,403,000	115,286,000	65,562,000	33,898,000	-20,666,000
Capital Expenditure	348,229,000	302,669,000	113,244,000	77,033,000	80,754,000	9,558,000
EBITDA	531,922,000	384,360,000	191,780,000	86,335,000	40,811,000	-24,777,000
Return on Assets %	.11%	3.46%	4.81%	3.85%	2.92%	-8.44%
Return on Equity %	.31%	8.77%	12.19%	9.32%	7.71%	-36.20%
Debt to Equity	1.50	1.30	1.21	1.25	1.07	2.80

CONTACT INFORMATION:

Phone: 615 861-6000   Fax: 615 261-9685
Toll-Free:
Address: 6100 Tower Circle, Ste. 1000, Franklin, TN 37067 United States

STOCK TICKER/OTHER:

Stock Ticker: ACHC   Exchange: NAS
Employees: 40,400   Fiscal Year Ends: 12/31
Parent Company:

SALARIES/BONUSES:

Top Exec. Salary: $1,071,000   Bonus: $
Second Exec. Salary: Bonus: $
$650,000

OTHER THOUGHTS:

Estimated Female Officers or Directors:
Hot Spot for Advancement for Women/Minorities:

Sales, profits and employees may be estimates. Financial information, benefits and other data can change quickly and may vary from those stated here.

Accenture LLP

NAIC Code: 541512

www.accenture.com/us-en

TYPES OF BUSINESS:

IT Consulting
Computer Operations Outsourcing
Supply Chain Technologies
Technology Research
Software Development
Human Resources Consulting
Management Consulting
Research and Development

BRANDS/DIVISIONS/AFFILIATES:

Accenture plc

CONTACTS: Note: Officers with more than one job title may be intentionally listed here more than once.

Pierre Nanterme, CEO
Jo Deblaere, COO
David P. Rowland, CFO
Roxanne Taylor, CMO
Ellyn J. Shook, Chief Human Resources Officer
Paul Daugherty, Chief Technology Officer

GROWTH PLANS/SPECIAL FEATURES:

Accenture, LLP, the U.S. subsidiary of Accenture plc, is a leading provider of management consulting, technology and outsourcing services, with operations in over 30 American cities. The firm delivers services through five operating groups: communications, media and technology; financial services; health and public service; products; and resources. Accenture's communications, media and technology group offers technology, consulting and systems integration to the electronics, communications and media industries. Its financial services group provides consulting and outsourcing strategies to the insurance, capital markets and banking industries. The firm's health and public service group works with local, state, provincial and national governments to deliver better social, economic and health outcomes to the people they serve. Its products group serves the automotive, life sciences, consumer goods, industrial equipment, retail and transportation and travel services industries. The company's resources group works with the chemicals, energy, natural resources and utilities industries. Additionally, Accenture offers management consulting services in finance and enterprise performance, operations, technology, IT security consulting/outsourcing, cloud computing, business, risk management, sales and growth customer services, strategy, sustainability and talent and organization. In June 2017, Accenture acquired the mobile design and development firm, Intrepid.

Accenture offers its employees medical, dental, long-term disability, life and AD&D coverage; nurselines; legal coverage; a profit sharing plan; a 401(k) savings plan; and adoption assistance.

FINANCIAL DATA: Note: Data for latest year may not have been available at press time.

In U.S. $	2016	2015	2014	2013	2012	2011
Revenue	15,653,000,000	14,209,387,000	12,796,847,000	12,035,847,000	10,200,000,000	9,500,000,000
R&D Expense						
Operating Income						
Operating Margin %						
SGA Expense						
Net Income						
Operating Cash Flow						
Capital Expenditure						
EBITDA						
Return on Assets %						
Return on Equity %						
Debt to Equity						

CONTACT INFORMATION:

Phone: 312-693-0161   Fax: 312-693-0507
Toll-Free: 877-889-9009
Address: 161 North Clark Street, Chicago, IL 60601 United States

STOCK TICKER/OTHER:

Stock Ticker: Subsidiary   Exchange:
Employees: 160,000   Fiscal Year Ends: 08/31
Parent Company: Accenture plc

SALARIES/BONUSES:

Top Exec. Salary: $ Bonus: $
Second Exec. Salary: $ Bonus: $

OTHER THOUGHTS:

Estimated Female Officers or Directors:
Hot Spot for Advancement for Women/Minorities: Y

Accor North America

NAIC Code: 721110

www.accorhotels.com/gb/usa/index.shtml

TYPES OF BUSINESS:

Hotels

BRANDS/DIVISIONS/AFFILIATES:

Accor SA
Sofitel
Novotel
Pullman

CONTACTS:
Note: Officers with more than one job title may be intentionally listed here more than once.

Roland de Bonadona, CEO-Americas
Didier Bosc, CFO
Jeff Winslow, CIO
Didier Bosc, Chief Admin. Officer
Alan Rabinowitz, Exec. VP
Jim Amorosia, Pres.
Jeff Winslow, Chief Investment Officer
Robert Moore, Sr. VP-Technical Service

GROWTH PLANS/SPECIAL FEATURES:

Accor North America, a subsidiary of French hotel and human resources conglomerate Accor SA, operates 77 hotels with approximately 20,000 rooms across the U.S., Mexico and Canada. The firm's North American hotel chains include six Sofitel hotels, a French luxury brand that incorporates local culture into its decor. The brand offers visitors first-rate accommodations with upscale restaurants, complete business facilities, fitness centers, fine art and antiques. The Novotel chain is another more upscale offering, which consists of a relaxed modern decor that makes it accessible to both business and leisure travelers. Novotel properties offer rooms with sitting/working areas, mid-scale restaurants and pools and golf course privileges, with nine locations. In addition, the firm operates two Pullman hotels, which offers upscale, executive lodging for business and leisure stays. The Fairmont brand offers luxury lifestyle hotels with 37 properties. Additionally, the North America region contains one Swissotel, one Mama Shelter, one Ibis hotel and three Ibis Styles hotel. Accor incorporates a green policy into all its chains that consists of water-saving shower heads and faucet aerators, Energy Star program participation, power-reducing heating and cooling systems, recycled paper and soy ink for its directories, energy efficient fluorescent lighting and the use of green Ecolab products for laundry and cleaning.

FINANCIAL DATA:
Note: Data for latest year may not have been available at press time.

In U.S. $	2016	2015	2014	2013	2012	2011
Revenue	621,772,975	635,410,802	525,348,522	302,399,520	308,574,820	304,171,460
R&D Expense						
Operating Income						
Operating Margin %						
SGA Expense						
Net Income		255,037,440	269,380,549	153,772,184		
Operating Cash Flow						
Capital Expenditure						
EBITDA						
Return on Assets %						
Return on Equity %						
Debt to Equity						

CONTACT INFORMATION:

Phone: 972-360-9000   Fax: 972-716-6590
Toll-Free: 800-557-3435
Address: 4001 International Pkwy., Carrollton, TX 75007 United States

STOCK TICKER/OTHER:

Stock Ticker: Subsidiary
Employees: 21,563
Parent Company: Accor SA

Exchange:
Fiscal Year Ends: 12/31

SALARIES/BONUSES:

Top Exec. Salary: $ Bonus: $
Second Exec. Salary: $ Bonus: $

OTHER THOUGHTS:

Estimated Female Officers or Directors: 1
Hot Spot for Advancement for Women/Minorities:

Acosta Inc

www.acosta.com

NAIC Code: 541800

TYPES OF BUSINESS:

Marketing Services
Consumer Packaged Goods Sales Research
Retail Sales Support
Integrated Marketing Solutions
Outsourcing
Retail Services

BRANDS/DIVISIONS/AFFILIATES:

Acosta Sales & Marketing
Acosta Marketing Group
Contend
IGNITE Sales Management
Baldwin & Mattson Inc
Neher Sales & Marketing
PacNorth Group (The)
Summit Marketing Canada Ltd

CONTACTS: Note: Officers with more than one job title may be intentionally listed here more than once.

Steve Matthesen, CEO
Steve Kremser, Chief Strategy & Transformation Officer
Robert E. Hill, Jr., Pres.
Tim Bensley, CFO
Kevin George, CMO
Claudia Saenz Amlie, Chief Human Resources Officer
Dilip Lillaney, CIO
Reece Alford, General Counsel
Brian King, Chief Strategy Officer
Vilma Consuegra, VP-Corp. Comm.
Woody Norris, Pres., Client Dev.
Jack Parker, Pres., Grocery Channel Sales
Brian Baldwin, Pres., Strategic Channel Sales
Aidan Tracey, Pres., Acosta Mktg. Group
Gary R. Chartrand, Chmn.

GROWTH PLANS/SPECIAL FEATURES:

Acosta, Inc., which does business as Acosta Sales & Marketing, is an outsourced sales and marketing agency. Founded in 1927 as single-location food broker L.T. Acosta Company, Inc., the firm serves consumer packaged goods companies and retail groups through offices across the U.S. and Canada. Acosta's client roster includes over 60% of the No. 1 and No. 2 grocery store brands. On behalf of its consumer packaged goods clients, the company offers direct sales of new and existing items to retailers such as Safeway and Kroger. As part of this process, Acosta provides services such as the negotiation of volume and price levels. For retail clients, the firm provides in-store stocking services. It seeks to ensure optimal shelf space location and exposure of its customer's brands in order to maximize the sale of their products. Acosta Marketing Group offers enhanced integrated marketing services including buyer trend reports and customer analytics. In 2016, the firm acquired Contend, a data-driven premium content company in Los Angeles; IGNITE Sales Management, which helps manufacturers build and grow profitable brands; Baldwin & Mattson, Inc. and Neher Sales & Marketing, which together will provide personalized service to manufacturers and retailers in the Midwest; and The PacNorth Group, a leading non-food manufacturer agency, which will expand Acosta's non-food coverage in the Northwest region (Washington, Oregon, Idaho and Alaska). In January 2017, Acosta acquired Contemporary Foodservice Marketing, Inc., a leading non-food manufacturer agency in the Midwest representing an extensive selection of manufacturers and products. The following June, the firm acquired Summit Marketing Canada Ltd., marking the firm's entry into the Canadian foodservice market.

Acosta offers its employees medical, vision and dental insurance; a prescription drug plan; life, disability and AD&D insurance; a 401(k) retirement plan; tuition assistance; gym membership; and cell phone, new car and new computer discounts.

FINANCIAL DATA: Note: Data for latest year may not have been available at press time.

In U.S. $	2016	2015	2014	2013	2012	2011
Revenue	3,625,000,000	3,300,000,000	3,300,000,000	3,214,322,800	3,032,380,000	2,834,000,000
R&D Expense						
Operating Income						
Operating Margin %						
SGA Expense						
Net Income						
Operating Cash Flow						
Capital Expenditure						
EBITDA						
Return on Assets %						
Return on Equity %						
Debt to Equity						

CONTACT INFORMATION:

Phone: 904-281-9800   Fax: 904-281-9966
Toll-Free:
Address: 6600 Corporate Center Pkwy., Jacksonville, FL 32216 United States

STOCK TICKER/OTHER:

Stock Ticker: Private
Employees: 35,000
Parent Company: Carlyle Group (The)

Exchange:
Fiscal Year Ends: 07/31

SALARIES/BONUSES:

Top Exec. Salary: $ Bonus: $
Second Exec. Salary: $ Bonus: $

OTHER THOUGHTS:

Estimated Female Officers or Directors: 2
Hot Spot for Advancement for Women/Minorities: Y

Sales, profits and employees may be estimates. Financial information, benefits and other data can change quickly and may vary from those stated here.

Activision Blizzard Inc

www.activisionblizzard.com

NAIC Code: 0

TYPES OF BUSINESS:

Electronic Games, Apps & Entertainment
League-Based, Live Gaming Competition
Apps
TV Distribution of Gaming Events
Merchandising
Licensing Game Content for Movies
Licensing Content to Comic Books

BRANDS/DIVISIONS/AFFILIATES:

Activision Publishing Inc
Blizzard Entertainment Inc
Call of Duty
Skylanders
Destiny
World of Warcraft
King Digital Entertainment plc
Overwatch League

CONTACTS: *Note: Officers with more than one job title may be intentionally listed here more than once.*

Riccardo Zacconi, CEO, Subsidiary
Eric Hirshberg, CEO, Subsidiary
Michael Morhaime, CEO, Subsidiary
Robert Kotick, CEO
Dennis Durkin, CFO
Brian Kelly, Chairman of the Board
Wereb Stephen, Chief Accounting Officer
Thomas Tippl, COO
Brian Stolz, Other Executive Officer
Christopher Walther, Other Executive Officer

GROWTH PLANS/SPECIAL FEATURES:

Activision Blizzard, Inc. is a leading international publisher and developer of subscription-based massively multiplayer online role-playing games (MMORPGs) and other PC-based, console, handheld and mobile games. The company was formed through the merger of Vivendi Games, owner of Blizzard Entertainment, Inc., and Activision, a leading publisher of interactive entertainment. The company operates in two segments: Activision Publishing, Inc. and Blizzard Entertainment, Inc. Activision Publishing and its subsidiaries publish interactive entertainment software products and downloadable content. Its products primarily operate on the PS4 (Playstation), PS3, Xbox One, Xbox 360, Wii U and Wii console systems, as well as on personal computers. This division's intellectual property includes the popular Call of Duty, Skylanders and Destiny game lines. Blizzard Entertainment and its subsidiaries publish real-time strategy games, role-playing games and online subscription-based games in the MMORPG category. This division operates six franchises: World of Warcraft, Diablo, StarCraft, Hearthstone: Heroes of Warcraft, Heroes of the Storm, as well as Legion, which was released in 2016. In 2016, the firm acquired King Digital Entertainment plc for $5.9 billion; and Major League Gaming for $46 million. That December, Blizzard Entertainment announced the creation of a book-publishing label, Blizzard Publishing, dedicated to developing and releasing new Blizzard publications and reissuing out-of-print titles in the company's Warcraft, StarCraft and Diablo settings. A major business initiative is called Overwatch, a console-gaming subscription service with tens of millions of subscribers. The Overwatch League sells tickets to fans who watch teams competing at live events, as well as TV broadcasting of this competition.

FINANCIAL DATA: *Note: Data for latest year may not have been available at press time.*

In U.S. $	2016	2015	2014	2013	2012	2011
Revenue	6,608,000,000	4,664,000,000	4,408,000,000	4,583,000,000	4,856,000,000	4,755,000,000
R&D Expense	958,000,000	646,000,000	571,000,000	584,000,000	604,000,000	646,000,000
Operating Income	1,412,000,000	1,319,000,000	1,183,000,000	1,372,000,000	1,451,000,000	1,328,000,000
Operating Margin %	21.36%	28.28%	26.83%	29.93%	29.88%	27.92%
SGA Expense	1,844,000,000	1,114,000,000	1,129,000,000	1,096,000,000	1,139,000,000	1,001,000,000
Net Income	966,000,000	892,000,000	835,000,000	1,010,000,000	1,149,000,000	1,085,000,000
Operating Cash Flow	2,155,000,000	1,192,000,000	1,292,000,000	1,264,000,000	1,345,000,000	952,000,000
Capital Expenditure	136,000,000	111,000,000	107,000,000	74,000,000	73,000,000	72,000,000
EBITDA	2,562,000,000	1,813,000,000	1,529,000,000	1,692,000,000	1,579,000,000	1,770,000,000
Return on Assets %	5.88%	5.87%	5.80%	7.16%	8.36%	8.13%
Return on Equity %	11.19%	11.51%	12.05%	11.26%	10.53%	10.48%
Debt to Equity	0.53	0.50	0.59	0.70		

CONTACT INFORMATION:

Phone: 310 255-2000　　　Fax: 310 255-2100
Toll-Free:
Address: 3100 Ocean Park Blvd., Santa Monica, CA 90405 United States

STOCK TICKER/OTHER:

Stock Ticker: ATVI
Employees: 9,600
Parent Company:

Exchange: NAS
Fiscal Year Ends: 12/31

SALARIES/BONUSES:

Top Exec. Salary: $2,375,858　　Bonus: $
Second Exec. Salary: $1,360,000　　Bonus: $

OTHER THOUGHTS:

Estimated Female Officers or Directors:
Hot Spot for Advancement for Women/Minorities:

Adobe Systems Inc

www.adobe.com

NAIC Code: 0

TYPES OF BUSINESS:
Computer Software, Multimedia, Graphics & Publishing
Document Management Software
Photo Editing & Management Software
Graphic Design Software

BRANDS/DIVISIONS/AFFILIATES:
Adobe Creative Suite
Adobe Creative Cloud
Adobe Dreamweaver
Adobe InDesign
Adobe Acrobat
Adobe PostScript
Adobe Stock
TubeMogul Inc

CONTACTS: Note: Officers with more than one job title may be intentionally listed here more than once.
Shantanu Narayen, CEO
Mark Garrett, CFO
Ann Lewnes, Chief Marketing Officer
Abhay Parasnis, Chief Technology Officer
Charles Geschke, Co-Chairman
John Warnock, Co-Chairman
Matthew Thompson, Executive VP, Divisional
Bradley Rencher, Executive VP
Michael Dillon, General Counsel
Bryan Lamkin, General Manager, Divisional
John Murphy, Senior VP
Donna Morris, Senior VP, Divisional

GROWTH PLANS/SPECIAL FEATURES:
Adobe Systems, Inc. is one of the largest software companies in the world. It offers a line of creative, business, web and mobile software and services used by creative professionals and developers for creating, managing, delivering, optimizing and engaging with content across multiple operating systems, devices and media. The company operates in three segments: digital media, digital marketing and print and publishing. The digital media division focuses on professional imaging and video products, including the widely used Adobe Creative Suite and Adobe Creative Cloud (CC). Products in this segment also include Adobe Dreamweaver and Adobe InDesign. Digital media's document services business is built around the Adobe Acrobat family of products, the Adobe Reader and a set of integrated cloud-based document services. Adobe PDF documents can be viewed, printed or filled out using the free Adobe Reader. The digital marketing segment consists of the firm's online marketing services including the firm's Adobe Marketing Cloud. The print and publishing segment addresses market opportunities ranging from technical and business publishing to legacy type printing. This segment's Adobe PostScript and Adobe PDF printing technologies provide advanced functionality. Adobe Stock, is an online marketplace for photos, graphics and videos. Creative Cloud members can access digital content through Adobe Stock. Creative Cloud also offers members access to online services to sync, store and share files; participate in Adobe's Behance community of more than 5 million creative professionals; publish and deliver digital content via app stores; develop mobile apps; and create and manage web sites. In December 2016, the firm acquired TubeMogul, Inc. for $540 million, a leader in video advertising.

The firm offers employees life, disability, medical, dental, vision and prescription drug insurance; adoption assistance; employee assistance program; product discounts; and a 401(k).

FINANCIAL DATA: Note: Data for latest year may not have been available at press time.

In U.S. $	2016	2015	2014	2013	2012	2011
Revenue	5,854,430,000	4,795,511,000	4,147,065,000	4,055,240,000	4,403,677,000	4,216,258,000
R&D Expense	975,987,000	862,730,000	844,353,000	826,631,000	742,823,000	738,053,000
Operating Income	1,493,602,000	903,095,000	412,685,000	422,723,000	1,180,191,000	1,099,299,000
Operating Margin %	25.51%	18.83%	9.95%	10.42%	26.80%	26.07%
SGA Expense	2,487,907,000	2,215,161,000	2,195,640,000	2,140,578,000	1,951,141,000	1,800,427,000
Net Income	1,168,782,000	629,551,000	268,395,000	289,985,000	832,775,000	832,847,000
Operating Cash Flow	2,199,728,000	1,469,502,000	1,287,482,000	1,151,686,000	1,499,580,000	1,543,314,000
Capital Expenditure	203,805,000	184,936,000	148,332,000	188,358,000	271,076,000	210,294,000
EBITDA	1,837,115,000	1,277,438,000	734,698,000	744,876,000	1,486,047,000	1,372,387,000
Return on Assets %	9.56%	5.59%	2.53%	2.84%	8.78%	9.72%
Return on Equity %	16.20%	9.13%	3.97%	4.33%	13.37%	15.17%
Debt to Equity	0.25	0.27	0.13	0.22	0.22	0.26

CONTACT INFORMATION:
Phone: 408 536-6000   Fax: 408 536-6799
Toll-Free: 800-833-6687
Address: 345 Park Ave., San Jose, CA 95110 United States

STOCK TICKER/OTHER:
Stock Ticker: ADBE
Employees: 15,706
Parent Company:

Exchange: NAS
Fiscal Year Ends: 11/30

SALARIES/BONUSES:
Top Exec. Salary: $1,010,260   Bonus: $
Second Exec. Salary: $698,977   Bonus: $

OTHER THOUGHTS:
Estimated Female Officers or Directors: 5
Hot Spot for Advancement for Women/Minorities: Y

Advance Auto Parts Inc

www.advanceautoparts.com

NAIC Code: 441310

TYPES OF BUSINESS:

Auto Parts & Accessories Stores
Online Sales

BRANDS/DIVISIONS/AFFILIATES:

Advance Auto Parts
Carquest
Worldpac
Autopart International

CONTACTS: *Note: Officers with more than one job title may be intentionally listed here more than once.*

Thomas Greco, CEO
Thomas Okray, CFO
Jeffrey Smith, Chairman of the Board
Jeffrey Shepherd, Controller
Charles Tyson, Executive VP, Divisional
Robert Cushing, Executive VP, Divisional
Tammy Finley, Executive VP
William Carter, Senior VP, Divisional
Natalie Schechtman, Senior VP, Divisional

GROWTH PLANS/SPECIAL FEATURES:

Advance Auto Parts, Inc. is a leading specialty retailer of automotive aftermarket parts, accessories, batteries and maintenance items. The firm primarily operates in the U.S. and serves both do-it-yourself (DIY) and commercial customers. It operates in a single segment comprised of the company's store and branch operations. Advance Auto serves its customers through a variety of channels ranging from brick-and-mortar store locations to self-service eCommerce sites. The company operates under the following store names: Advance Auto Parts, consisting of 5,200 stores that average 7,500 square feet in size; Carquest, consisting of 873 stores that average 7,400 square feet in size; Worldpac, consisting of 122 stores that average 27,000 square feet in size; and Autopart International, consisting of 184 stores that offer approximately 39,000 SKUs. Primary categories of products offered by the company include: parts such as alternators, batteries, belts, hoses, brakes, brake pads, chassis parts, climate control parts, clutches, drive shafts, engines, engine parts, ignition parts, lighting, radiators, starters, spark plugs, wires, steering and alignment parts, transmissions, water pumps and windshield wiper blades; accessories such as air fresheners, auto paint, anti-theft devices, emergency road kits, floor mats, ice scrapers, mirrors, seat and steering wheel covers and vent shades; chemicals such as antifreeze, brake and power steering fluids, car wash fluids, car waxes, Freon, fuel additives and windshield washer fluid; and oil such as transmission fluid and other automotive petroleum products. The company's 5,293 stores are primarily located in the U.S., with 158 located throughout Canada, 28 throughout Puerto Rico and one in the Virgin Islands.

The firm offers employees medical, dental and vision coverage; a 401(k); stock purchase plans; life and AD&D insurance; short- and long-term disability; flexible spending accounts; employee discounts; an employee assistance program; and dependent scholarships.

FINANCIAL DATA: *Note: Data for latest year may not have been available at press time.*

In U.S. $	2016	2015	2014	2013	2012	2011
Revenue	9,567,679,000	9,737,018,000	9,843,862,000	6,493,814,000	6,205,003,000	6,170,462,000
R&D Expense						
Operating Income	787,598,000	825,780,000	851,710,000	660,318,000	657,315,000	664,642,000
Operating Margin %	8.23%	8.48%	8.65%	10.16%	10.59%	10.77%
SGA Expense	3,468,317,000	3,596,992,000	3,601,903,000	2,591,828,000	2,440,721,000	2,404,648,000
Net Income	459,622,000	473,398,000	493,825,000	391,758,000	387,670,000	394,682,000
Operating Cash Flow	500,874,000	689,642,000	708,991,000	545,250,000	685,281,000	828,849,000
Capital Expenditure	259,559,000	234,747,000	228,446,000	195,757,000	271,182,000	268,129,000
EBITDA	1,057,132,000	1,087,772,000	1,139,495,000	870,811,000	847,459,000	840,134,000
Return on Assets %	5.58%	5.86%	7.30%	7.69%	9.37%	11.26%
Return on Equity %	17.09%	21.13%	28.06%	28.73%	37.66%	41.82%
Debt to Equity	0.35	0.49	0.81	0.69	0.49	0.48

CONTACT INFORMATION:

Phone: 540-362-4911   Fax:
Toll-Free: 877-238-2623
Address: 5008 Airport Rd., Roanoke, VA 24012 United States

STOCK TICKER/OTHER:

Stock Ticker: AAP   Exchange: NYS
Employees: 74,000   Fiscal Year Ends: 12/31
Parent Company:

SALARIES/BONUSES:

Top Exec. Salary: $803,852   Bonus: $3,485,000
Second Exec. Salary: Bonus: $
$785,579

OTHER THOUGHTS:

Estimated Female Officers or Directors: 3
Hot Spot for Advancement for Women/Minorities: Y

Sales, profits and employees may be estimates. Financial information, benefits and other data can change quickly and may vary from those stated here.

Adventist Health System

www.adventisthealthsystem.com

NAIC Code: 622110

TYPES OF BUSINESS:

General Medical and Surgical Hospitals
Nursing Homes
Home Health Care Services

BRANDS/DIVISIONS/AFFILIATES:

Florida Hospital
Seventh-day Adventist Church

CONTACTS: Note: Officers with more than one job title may be intentionally listed here more than once.

Donald L. Jernigan, CEO
Terry D. Shaw, COO
Donald L. Jernigan, Pres.
Terry D. Shaw, CFO
Herb Keller, Sr. VP- CIO
John McLendon, CIO-Information Services
Robert R. Henderschedt, Sr. VP-Admin.
Jeffrey S. Bromme, Chief Legal Officer
Sandra K. Johnson, VP-Bus. Dev., Risk Mgmt. & Compliance
Womack H. Rucker, Jr., VP-Corp. Rel.
Lewis Seifert, Sr. VP-Finance
Amanda Brady, Chief Acct. Officer
Amy L. Zbaraschuk, VP-Finance
T.L. Trimble, VP-Legal Svcs.
Ted Hamilton, VP-Medical Mission
Carlene Jamerson, Sr. VP
John Brownlow, Sr. VP-Managed Care
Celeste M. West, VP-Supply Chain Mgmt.

GROWTH PLANS/SPECIAL FEATURES:

Adventist Health System, sponsored by the Seventh-day Adventist Church, is one of the largest nonprofit Protestant health care organizations in the U.S. The firm operates 45 hospitals in several states, totaling over 8,200 beds, and multiple affiliated extended care centers within the long-term care division. The company serves more than 5 million patients annually. Adventist Health's flagship organization, Florida Hospital, is one of the largest health care providers in central Florida and a national leader in cardiac care. The hospital offers more than 2,500 beds across 16 campuses and provides care in the areas of cancer, neurosciences, orthopedics, kidney disease, limb replantation, sports medicine, rehabilitation and Adventist Health is a world leader in the use of tissue-sparing radiation based on proton beams, rather than traditional photon-based radiation. The firm is guided by its Christian mission, combining disease treatment, preventative medicine, education and advocacy of a wholesome lifestyle. The hospitals in the Adventist Health group provide a wide range of free or reduced-price services in their communities, including free medical vans and community clinics, free screening and education programs, debt forgiveness, abuse shelters and programs for the homeless and jobless. In August 2016, the firm opened a new NICU (neonatal intensive care unit) at its Florida Hospital Memorial Medical Center in Daytona Beach, which includes private family-centered rooms while sick and premature babies are receiving specialized medical treatment.

FINANCIAL DATA: Note: Data for latest year may not have been available at press time.

In U.S. $	2016	2015	2014	2013	2012	2011
Revenue	9,651,689,000	9,116,187,000	7,955,000,000	7,597,799,000	7,346,597,000	6,985,900,000
R&D Expense						
Operating Income						
Operating Margin %						
SGA Expense						
Net Income	89,559,000	-131,403,000	600,000,000	578,818,000	504,958,000	474,200,000
Operating Cash Flow						
Capital Expenditure						
EBITDA						
Return on Assets %						
Return on Equity %						
Debt to Equity						

CONTACT INFORMATION:

Phone: 407-357-1000   Fax:
Toll-Free:
Address: 900 Hope Way, Altamonte Springs, FL 32714 United States

STOCK TICKER/OTHER:

Stock Ticker: Nonprofit   Exchange:
Employees: 80,000   Fiscal Year Ends: 12/31
Parent Company:

SALARIES/BONUSES:

Top Exec. Salary: $ Bonus: $
Second Exec. Salary: $ Bonus: $

OTHER THOUGHTS:

Estimated Female Officers or Directors: 6
Hot Spot for Advancement for Women/Minorities: Y

Aetna Inc

www.aetna.com

NAIC Code: 524114

TYPES OF BUSINESS:

Insurance-Medical & Health
Long-Term Care Insurance
Group Insurance
Pension Products
Dental Insurance
Disability Insurance
Life Insurance

BRANDS/DIVISIONS/AFFILIATES:

CONTACTS: Note: Officers with more than one job title may be intentionally listed here more than once.

Mark Bertolini, CEO
Shawn Guertin, CFO
Harold Paz, Chief Medical Officer
Gary Loveman, Executive VP, Divisional
Francis Soistman, Executive VP, Divisional
Margaret McCarthy, Executive VP, Divisional
Thomas Sabatino, Executive VP
Karen Lynch, President
Karen Lynch, President
Sharon Virag, Vice President

GROWTH PLANS/SPECIAL FEATURES:

Aetna, Inc. is a health care benefits company, providing a broad range of traditional and consumer-directed health insurance products. These include medical, pharmacy, dental, behavioral health, group life & disability plans and Medicaid health care management capabilities to roughly 46.7 million people. Aetna operates in three segments: health care, group insurance and large case pensions. Health care products include medical insurance plans & products, pharmacy benefits management, dental, behavioral health and vision plans offered on both an insured basis and an employee-funded basis. This division's medical plans include point of service, health maintenance organization, preferred provider organization, health savings accounts and indemnity benefits. Group insurance products primarily comprises life insurance, including group term life insurance coverage and accidental death & dismemberment coverage; disability insurance, including short- and long-term disability; and long-term care insurance products, including the cost of care in private home settings, adult day care, assisted living or nursing facilities. The large case pensions segment primarily manages retirement products for tax-qualified pension plans. Customers include employer groups, individuals, college students, part-time/hourly workers, governmental units, labor groups and expatriates. In February 2017, Aetna and Humana mutually agreed to end their merger agreement. Aetna will pay Humana $1 billion as a result of the termination of the merger agreement. Additionally, Aetna has terminated its previously announced agreement to sell certain Medicare Advantage assets to Molina Healthcare, Inc. and will pay the applicable fees associated with that termination.

Employee benefits include medical, dental and vision coverage; flexible spending accounts; life and AD&D insurance; short- and long-term disability; employee assistance programs; 401(k) & employee stock purchase plan; and tuition assistance.

FINANCIAL DATA: Note: Data for latest year may not have been available at press time.

In U.S. $	2016	2015	2014	2013	2012	2011
Revenue	63,155,000,000	60,336,500,000	58,003,200,000	47,294,600,000	36,595,900,000	33,779,800,000
R&D Expense						
Operating Income	4,714,000,000	4,854,600,000	4,253,800,000	3,402,800,000	3,041,100,000	3,445,400,000
Operating Margin %	7.46%	8.04%	7.33%	7.19%	8.30%	10.19%
SGA Expense	12,085,000,000	11,649,300,000	10,837,700,000	8,645,400,000	6,876,400,000	6,804,400,000
Net Income	2,271,000,000	2,390,200,000	2,040,800,000	1,913,600,000	1,657,900,000	1,985,700,000
Operating Cash Flow	3,719,000,000	3,866,100,000	3,372,800,000	2,278,700,000	1,822,000,000	2,507,800,000
Capital Expenditure	270,000,000	362,900,000	369,600,000	479,100,000	338,200,000	372,000,000
EBITDA	5,276,000,000	5,270,500,000	4,458,200,000	3,843,300,000	3,264,100,000	3,771,900,000
Return on Assets %	3.70%	4.47%	3.95%	4.18%	4.14%	5.20%
Return on Equity %	13.36%	15.62%	14.31%	15.66%	16.15%	19.84%
Debt to Equity	1.06	0.48	0.54	0.56	0.62	0.39

CONTACT INFORMATION:

Phone: 860 273-0123   Fax:
Toll-Free: 800-872-3862
Address: 151 Farmington Ave., Hartford, CT 06156 United States

STOCK TICKER/OTHER:

Stock Ticker: AET   Exchange: NYS
Employees: 49,500   Fiscal Year Ends: 12/31
Parent Company:

SALARIES/BONUSES:

Top Exec. Salary: $1,141,762   Bonus: $
Second Exec. Salary: $502,874   Bonus: $600,000

OTHER THOUGHTS:

Estimated Female Officers or Directors: 8
Hot Spot for Advancement for Women/Minorities: Y

AFLAC Inc

NAIC Code: 524114

TYPES OF BUSINESS:

Insurance-Supplemental & Specialty Health
Life Insurance
Cancer Insurance
Long-Term Care Insurance
Accident & Disability Insurance
Vision Plans
Dental Plans

BRANDS/DIVISIONS/AFFILIATES:

American Family Life Assurance Company
Continental American Insurance Company
Aflac Group Insurance
AFLAC Japan
EVER

CONTACTS: Note: Officers with more than one job title may be intentionally listed here more than once.

Daniel Amos, CEO
Charles Lake, President, Subsidiary
June Howard, Chief Accounting Officer
Hiroshi Yamauchi, COO, Divisional
Kriss Cloninger, Director
Paul Amos, Director
Kenneth Janke, Executive VP, Divisional
Eric Kirsch, Executive VP, Subsidiary
Frederick Crawford, Executive VP
Audrey Tillman, Executive VP
Koji Ariyoshi, Executive VP
James Daniels, Executive VP
Teresa White, President, Divisional
Robin Wilkey, Senior VP, Divisional

GROWTH PLANS/SPECIAL FEATURES:

AFLAC, Inc. is a holding company whose principle subsidiary, AFLAC (American Family Life Assurance Company of Columbus), insures more than 50 million people worldwide. The subsidiary is a leading writer of supplemental insurance marketed to employers in the U.S., offering policies for payroll accounts through approximately 13,000 sales agencies, with more than 110,000 sales associates employed by those agencies. AFLAC sells supplemental insurance products, including accident/disability plans, cancer plans, short-term disability plans, sickness & hospital indemnity plans, hospital intensive care plans, fixed-benefit dental plans, vision care plans, long-term care plans and life insurance products. In addition, AFLAC offers specified health event coverage for major medical crises such as heart attack and stroke. U.S. insurance products are designed to provide supplemental coverage to individuals who already have major medical or primary insurance coverage. Through Continental American Insurance Company (branded as Aflac Group Insurance), the company also markets and administers group projects. Subsidiary AFLAC Japan is one of the largest foreign-based insurers in that country. AFLAC Japan's insurance products are designed to help consumers pay for medical and non-medical costs that are not reimbursed under Japan's national health insurance system. EVER, AFLAC Japan's stand-alone medical product, offers a basic level of hospitalization coverage with an affordable premium. AFLAC Japan also sells cancer plans, general medical indemnity plans, medical/sickness riders to its cancer plan, care plans, living benefit life plans, ordinary life insurance plans and annuities. AFLAC Japan accounts for about 71% of AFLAC's annual insurance earnings.

Employee benefits include medical and dental coverage, short- and long-term disability, life insurance, flexible spending accounts, an employee assistance program, employee discount programs and Aflac insurance policies including cancer insurance and hospital confinement indemnity.

FINANCIAL DATA: Note: Data for latest year may not have been available at press time.

In U.S. $	2016	2015	2014	2013	2012	2011
Revenue	22,559,000,000	20,872,000,000	22,728,000,000	23,939,000,000	25,364,000,000	22,171,000,000
R&D Expense						
Operating Income	4,067,000,000	3,862,000,000	4,491,000,000	4,816,000,000	4,302,000,000	2,992,000,000
Operating Margin %	18.02%	18.50%	19.75%	20.11%	16.96%	13.49%
SGA Expense	3,820,000,000	3,517,000,000	3,697,000,000	3,750,000,000	4,159,000,000	3,950,000,000
Net Income	2,659,000,000	2,533,000,000	2,951,000,000	3,158,000,000	2,866,000,000	1,964,000,000
Operating Cash Flow	5,987,000,000	6,776,000,000	6,550,000,000	10,547,000,000	14,952,000,000	10,842,000,000
Capital Expenditure						
EBITDA						
Return on Assets %	2.14%	2.12%	2.44%	2.50%	2.30%	1.80%
Return on Equity %	13.92%	14.05%	17.90%	20.64%	19.44%	15.99%
Debt to Equity	0.26	0.28	0.28	0.33	0.27	0.24

CONTACT INFORMATION:

Phone: 706 323-3431   Fax:
Toll-Free: 800-235-2667
Address: 1932 Wynnton Rd., Columbus, GA 31999 United States

STOCK TICKER/OTHER:

Stock Ticker: AFL   Exchange: NYS
Employees: 10,212   Fiscal Year Ends: 12/31
Parent Company:

SALARIES/BONUSES:

Top Exec. Salary: $1,441,100   Bonus: $
Second Exec. Salary: Bonus: $
$975,000

OTHER THOUGHTS:

Estimated Female Officers or Directors: 8
Hot Spot for Advancement for Women/Minorities: Y

Agero Inc

NAIC Code: 517210

www.agero.com

TYPES OF BUSINESS:

Automotive Telematics
Emergency Response Systems
Stolen Vehicle Tracking
Automobile Operational Analysis
Navigation Tools

BRANDS/DIVISIONS/AFFILIATES:

Cross Country Automotive Services
ATX Group
VehicleAssist
ClaimsAssist
Drive360

CONTACTS: *Note: Officers with more than one job title may be intentionally listed here more than once.*

Dave Ferrick, CEO
Jeffrey Blecher, Sr. VP-Strategy
Kate Sweeney, Exec. VP
Cathy Orrico, Sr. VP-Client Svcs. & Sales
Bernie Gracy, Chief Digital Officer
Peter Necheles, Sr. VP-Corp. Dev.
Michael A. Saxton, Sr. Advisor
Tom Metzger, Sr. VP

GROWTH PLANS/SPECIAL FEATURES:

Agero, Inc., a product of the merger of Cross Country Automotive Services and the ATX Group, is a pioneer in the telematics (location-based voice and data communication services) industry as well as a provider of roadside assistance for motorists and claims management services for insurance carriers. With operations throughout North America, the firm's services are used by more than 100 leading corporations, and its technology is incorporated into 75% of new passenger vehicles sold in the U.S. Agero divides its products and services into four segments: mobile offerings, information services, roadside assistance and claims management. The mobile offerings segment offers products that connect customers with their insurance carriers and roadside assistance companies. Products include VehicleAssist, ClaimsAssist and Drive360. The information services segment leverages data and insights to increase process efficiencies. Agero's roadside assistance segment protects over 75 million drivers through its various scalable services and products, such as VehicleAssist. The claims management segment provides accident scene management and vehicle release services.

FINANCIAL DATA: *Note: Data for latest year may not have been available at press time.*

In U.S. $	2016	2015	2014	2013	2012	2011
Revenue	675,000,000	625,000,000	600,000,000	500,000,000	376,000,000	
R&D Expense						
Operating Income						
Operating Margin %						
SGA Expense						
Net Income						
Operating Cash Flow						
Capital Expenditure						
EBITDA						
Return on Assets %						
Return on Equity %						
Debt to Equity						

CONTACT INFORMATION:

Phone: 781-393-9300   Fax: 781-393-6706
Toll-Free:
Address: One Cabot Rd., Medford, MA 02155 United States

STOCK TICKER/OTHER:

Stock Ticker: Private   Exchange:
Employees: 3,500   Fiscal Year Ends: 12/31
Parent Company: Cross Country Group

SALARIES/BONUSES:

Top Exec. Salary: $ Bonus: $
Second Exec. Salary: $ Bonus: $

OTHER THOUGHTS:

Estimated Female Officers or Directors: 1
Hot Spot for Advancement for Women/Minorities: Y

Airbnb Inc

NAIC Code: 519130

www.airbnb.com

TYPES OF BUSINESS:
Online Homestay Reservations
Room Rental Reservations
Tour Booking Online

BRANDS/DIVISIONS/AFFILIATES:
Airbnb.com
Airbnb for Business

CONTACTS: Note: Officers with more than one job title may be intentionally listed here more than once.
Brian Chesky, CEO
Nathan Blecharczyk, Chief Strategy Officer
Laurence A. Tosi, CFO

GROWTH PLANS/SPECIAL FEATURES:
Airbnb, Inc., founded in 2008, operates a social networking site for travelers and those who have spare housing space. Through Airbnb.com, members who are willing to let travelers stay in their homes, guest houses, resort properties and other accommodations can post their information, including pricing, photos and amenities. In turn, travelers may search in a given market for members who are willing to accommodate them. Airbnb offers more than 3 million listings in 65,000 cities spanning over 192 countries. Since its founding, the company has booked over 160 million guests. Members are encouraged to write reviews describing the positive and/or negative aspects of their stays. These reviews are partially encouraged so that renters and travelers may view profiles and feedback before staying in homes or letting others stay in their homes, thereby reducing the risk of danger or other negative situations. The Airbnb network is also connected to Facebook, allowing members to search the social networking platform for additional information regarding certain hosts and guests. The company expanded its offerings in 2016 to allow booking of tours and events. Airbnb charges room owners a 3% host fee and an additional fee of 6% to 12% per guest. The average commission is about 12% of total revenues. On average, the typical guest stays at their Airbnb accommodation longer than a guest in a typical hotel. The firm has a goal of achieving $10 billion in yearly revenues by 2020. In June 2016, the company launched a feature in Airbnb for Business that allows employees and employers to book business travel for co-workers. In June 2017, the firm, in partnership with the International Rescue Committee, released a new host platform to provide free housing for refugees and evacuees.

About 43% of employees are women.

FINANCIAL DATA: Note: Data for latest year may not have been available at press time.

In U.S. $	2016	2015	2014	2013	2012	2011
Revenue	1,624,000,000	908,000,000	515,000,000	264,000,000	132,000,000	120,000,000
R&D Expense						
Operating Income						
Operating Margin %						
SGA Expense						
Net Income						
Operating Cash Flow						
Capital Expenditure						
EBITDA						
Return on Assets %						
Return on Equity %						
Debt to Equity						

CONTACT INFORMATION:
Phone: 415-728-0000   Fax:
Toll-Free:
Address: 888 Brannan St., Fl. 4, San Francisco, CA 94107 United States

STOCK TICKER/OTHER:
Stock Ticker: Private   Exchange:
Employees: 4,175   Fiscal Year Ends: 12/31
Parent Company:

SALARIES/BONUSES:
Top Exec. Salary: $ Bonus: $
Second Exec. Salary: $ Bonus: $

OTHER THOUGHTS:
Estimated Female Officers or Directors:
Hot Spot for Advancement for Women/Minorities: Y

Alaska Air Group Inc

www.alaskaair.com

NAIC Code: 481111

TYPES OF BUSINESS:
Airlines
Air Cargo

BRANDS/DIVISIONS/AFFILIATES:
Alaska Airlines Inc
Horizon Air Industries Inc
Virgin America Inc

CONTACTS: Note: Officers with more than one job title may be intentionally listed here more than once.
Benito Minicucci, CEO, Subsidiary
David Campbell, CEO, Subsidiary
Bradley Tilden, CEO
Brandon Pedersen, CFO
Christopher Berry, Chief Accounting Officer
Kyle Levine, General Counsel
Andrew Harrison, Other Executive Officer

GROWTH PLANS/SPECIAL FEATURES:
Alaska Air Group, Inc., through its operating subsidiaries Alaska Airlines, Inc. (Alaska), Horizon Air Industries, Inc. (Horizon) and Virgin America, Inc (Virgin America), provides passenger air service to more than 34 million passengers per year to 118 destinations. The firm also provides freight and mail services, primarily to and within Alaska and on the West Coast. Alaska, founded in 1932, operates a fleet of passenger jets and contracts with Horizon, SkyWest Airlines, Inc. and Peninsula Airways, Inc. for regional capacity. Alaska operates an all-Boeing 737 fleet, Virgin America operates as all-Airbus A320 family fleet and Horizon operates an all-Bombardier Q400 turboprop fleet. Alaska offers north/south service within the western USA, Canada and Mexico as well as passenger and dedicated cargo services to and within Alaska. It also provides long-haul east/west service to Hawaii and cities in the mid-continental and eastern USA, primarily from Seattle, where it has its largest concentration of departures. Alaska's leading airports are Seattle and Portland. Horizon is the largest regional airline in the Pacific Northwest, representing 90% of Air Group's regional revenue. The subsidiary serves several cities in the USA, Canada and Mexico. Horizon's leading airports are within the West Coast and Pacific Northwest regions. In December 2016, the firm acquired Virgin America, Inc. for $2.6 billion, adding 60 aircraft serving 23 cities to Alaska Air's business operations.

Both Alaska and Horizon airlines offer employee benefits such as flight privileges, personal time off, health coverage, a 401(k) plan, a profit sharing plan and performance rewards.

FINANCIAL DATA: Note: Data for latest year may not have been available at press time.

In U.S. $	2016	2015	2014	2013	2012	2011
Revenue	5,931,000,000	5,598,000,000	5,368,000,000	5,156,000,000	4,657,000,000	4,317,800,000
R&D Expense						
Operating Income	1,349,000,000	1,298,000,000	962,000,000	838,000,000	532,000,000	448,900,000
Operating Margin %	22.74%	23.18%	17.92%	16.25%	11.42%	10.39%
SGA Expense	1,734,000,000	1,585,000,000	1,705,000,000	1,591,000,000	1,653,000,000	1,237,700,000
Net Income	814,000,000	848,000,000	605,000,000	508,000,000	316,000,000	244,500,000
Operating Cash Flow	1,386,000,000	1,584,000,000	1,030,000,000	981,000,000	753,000,000	696,000,000
Capital Expenditure	678,000,000	831,000,000	694,000,000	566,000,000	518,000,000	387,400,000
EBITDA	1,738,000,000	1,640,000,000	1,297,000,000	1,121,000,000	842,000,000	727,900,000
Return on Assets %	9.86%	13.33%	10.06%	8.95%	5.90%	4.78%
Return on Equity %	30.47%	37.37%	29.11%	29.44%	24.36%	21.46%
Debt to Equity	0.90	0.23	0.32	0.37	0.61	0.93

CONTACT INFORMATION:
Phone: 206 392-5040   Fax:
Toll-Free: 800-252-7522
Address: 19300 Pacific Highway South, Seattle, WA 98188 United States

STOCK TICKER/OTHER:
Stock Ticker: ALK
Employees: 19,112
Parent Company:

Exchange: NYS
Fiscal Year Ends: 12/31

SALARIES/BONUSES:
Top Exec. Salary: $487,600   Bonus: $
Second Exec. Salary: $426,923   Bonus: $

OTHER THOUGHTS:
Estimated Female Officers or Directors: 13
Hot Spot for Advancement for Women/Minorities: Y

Alliance Data Systems Corporation

www.alliancedata.com

NAIC Code: 541800

TYPES OF BUSINESS:

Marketing Services
Credit Services
Transaction Services

BRANDS/DIVISIONS/AFFILIATES:

LoyaltyOne
AIR MILES
Epsilon
World Financial Network National Bank
World Financial Capital Bank
BrandLoyalty Group BV

CONTACTS: *Note: Officers with more than one job title may be intentionally listed here more than once.*

Edward Heffernan, CEO
Charles Horn, CFO
Robert Minicucci, Chairman of the Board
Laura Santillan, Chief Accounting Officer
Melisa Miller, Executive VP
Bryan Kennedy, Executive VP
Bryan Pearson, Executive VP
Joseph Motes, Senior VP

GROWTH PLANS/SPECIAL FEATURES:

Alliance Data Systems Corporation (ADS) is a provider of data-driven and transaction-based marketing and customer loyalty services. The company's products and services are operated through three segments: LoyaltyOne, Epsilon, and card services. The LoyaltyOne segment, which includes the Canadian AIR MILES Reward Program, provides loyalty marketing services, including consumer data, customer-centric retail strategies, direct-to-consumer marketing and loyalty consulting services. More than 170 brand name sponsors participate in the AIR MILES program, including Shell Canada, Jean Coutu, RONA, Amex Bank of Canada, Sobey's and Bank of Montreal. Epsilon provides integrated direct marketing solutions that combine database marketing technology and analytics with a broad range of direct marketing services. The firm uses cooperative databases containing consumer transactional data from multi-channel marketers to develop customer acquisition and retention strategies. The card services segment manages over 160 private label credit cards for various retailers. Its operations include account origination, transaction processing, customer care and collections services for the company's private label and other retail credit card programs. Primary subsidiaries in this segment are World Financial Network National Bank and World Financial Capital Bank. ADS' client base includes companies in the retail, financial services, hospitality, telecommunications and health care markets. The firm has 60% ownership in BrandLoyalty Group B.V., a European marketing and advertising company.

The firm offers its employees medical, dental and vision insurance; a 401(k); disability coverage; life, auto and home insurance; flexible spending accounts; an employee stock purchase program; tuition reimbursement; an employee assistance program; prepaid legal services; and adoption assistance.

FINANCIAL DATA: *Note: Data for latest year may not have been available at press time.*

In U.S. $	2016	2015	2014	2013	2012	2011
Revenue	7,138,100,000	6,439,746,000	5,302,940,000	4,319,063,000	3,641,390,000	3,173,287,000
R&D Expense						
Operating Income	1,265,500,000	1,261,860,000	1,098,467,000	1,098,912,000	974,364,000	812,680,000
Operating Margin %	17.72%	19.59%	20.71%	25.44%	26.75%	25.60%
SGA Expense	143,200,000	203,046,000	141,468,000	109,115,000	108,059,000	95,256,000
Net Income	515,800,000	596,541,000	506,293,000	496,170,000	422,256,000	315,286,000
Operating Cash Flow	2,088,400,000	1,705,841,000	1,344,159,000	1,003,492,000	1,134,190,000	1,011,347,000
Capital Expenditure	207,000,000	191,683,000	158,694,000	135,376,000	116,455,000	73,502,000
EBITDA	1,777,600,000	1,754,000,000	1,411,549,000	1,315,031,000	1,141,240,000	965,833,000
Return on Assets %	1.80%	2.58%	3.02%	3.93%	4.02%	3.65%
Return on Equity %	23.56%	25.03%	31.13%	71.68%	119.88%	316.77%
Debt to Equity	6.09	5.04	3.39	7.01	8.90	21.19

CONTACT INFORMATION:

Phone: 214 494-3000   Fax:
Toll-Free:
Address: 7500 Dallas Pkwy., Ste. 700, Plano, TX 75024 United States

STOCK TICKER/OTHER:

Stock Ticker: ADS   Exchange: NYS
Employees: 17,000   Fiscal Year Ends: 12/31
Parent Company:

SALARIES/BONUSES:

Top Exec. Salary: $1,114,000   Bonus: $
Second Exec. Salary: $627,000   Bonus: $

OTHER THOUGHTS:

Estimated Female Officers or Directors: 5
Hot Spot for Advancement for Women/Minorities: Y

Allscripts Healthcare Solutions Inc   www.allscripts.com

NAIC Code: 0

TYPES OF BUSINESS:

Computer Software, Healthcare & Biotechnology
Interactive Education Services
Clinical Software
Electronic Records Systems
Care Management Software

BRANDS/DIVISIONS/AFFILIATES:

Sunrise Acute EHR
Revenue Cycle Management Services

CONTACTS: *Note: Officers with more than one job title may be intentionally listed here more than once.*

Paul Black, CEO
Dennis Olis, CFO
Michael Klayko, Director
Lisa Khorey, Executive VP
Richard Poulton, President
James Hewitt, Senior VP, Divisional
Brian Farley, Senior VP

GROWTH PLANS/SPECIAL FEATURES:

Allscripts Healthcare Solutions, Inc. provides clinical software, connectivity and information solutions that physicians and health care providers use to improve service delivery. The firm provides software solutions for hospitals, physician practices and post-acute organizations. For hospitals and health systems, these applications include the Sunrise Acute EHR suite of clinical solutions, comprising a full acute care electronic health record (EHR), integrated with financial/administrative solutions including performance management and revenue cycle/access management. Acute care solutions include modules of the Sunrise suite that are available on a stand-alone basis as well as additional stand-alone solutions such as an emergency department information system, care management and discharge management. Allscripts' post-acute tools help smooth the patient transition from hospital to post-acute care facilities, including home health providers, hospices and private duty organizations. For physician practices, the firm's products include integrated EHR and practice management functionality available either via traditional on premise delivery or via Software-as-a-Service; revenue cycle management software and the Revenue Cycle Management Services solution, which enables practices to outsource their full revenue cycle to the firm or address requirements in-house; clearinghouse services; stand-alone electronic prescribing; and document imaging solutions for physician practices. The firm's population health management solution enables hospitals/health systems/ physician practices to connect, transition, analyze, and coordinate care across the entire care community. Additionally, Allscripts offers professional services such as conversion & integration of historical data into its software, training & support services, as well as consulting, remote hosting and IT outsourcing services.

Allscripts offers its employees medical, dental and vision insurance; flex spending accounts; 401(k); adoption assistance; and education assistance.

FINANCIAL DATA: *Note: Data for latest year may not have been available at press time.*

In U.S. $	2016	2015	2014	2013	2012	2011
Revenue	1,549,899,000	1,386,393,000	1,377,873,000	1,373,061,000	1,446,325,000	1,444,077,000
R&D Expense	187,906,000	184,791,000	192,821,000	199,751,000	162,158,000	104,106,000
Operating Income	59,771,000	31,883,000	-39,188,000	-127,601,000	13,271,000	136,544,000
Operating Margin %	3.85%	2.29%	-2.84%	-9.29%	.91%	9.45%
SGA Expense	392,865,000	339,175,000	358,681,000	419,599,000	384,370,000	387,571,000
Net Income	-25,652,000	-2,226,000	-66,453,000	-104,026,000	-1,153,000	73,609,000
Operating Cash Flow	269,004,000	211,579,000	103,496,000	80,987,000	222,670,000	268,754,000
Capital Expenditure	137,982,000	67,586,000	67,099,000	116,156,000	123,131,000	105,054,000
EBITDA	203,982,000	177,865,000	135,443,000	58,524,000	148,961,000	270,629,000
Return on Assets %	-.78%	-.08%	-2.59%	-4.15%	-.04%	2.98%
Return on Equity %	-1.94%	-.16%	-5.10%	-7.99%	-.08%	5.14%
Debt to Equity	1.05	0.43	0.42	0.41	0.28	0.21

CONTACT INFORMATION:

Phone: 866 358-6869   Fax:
Toll-Free: 800-654-0889
Address: 222 Merchandise Mart Plz., Ste. 2024, Chicago, IL 60654
United States

STOCK TICKER/OTHER:

Stock Ticker: MDRX   Exchange: NAS
Employees: 7,500   Fiscal Year Ends: 12/31
Parent Company:

SALARIES/BONUSES:

Top Exec. Salary: $1,000,000   Bonus: $
Second Exec. Salary: Bonus: $
$600,000

OTHER THOUGHTS:

Estimated Female Officers or Directors: 2
Hot Spot for Advancement for Women/Minorities: Y

Sales, profits and employees may be estimates. Financial information, benefits and other data can change quickly and may vary from those stated here.

Ally Financial Inc

NAIC Code: 522220

www.ally.com

TYPES OF BUSINESS:

Automobile Financing
Banking
Corporate Financial Services

BRANDS/DIVISIONS/AFFILIATES:

TradeKing Group Inc

CONTACTS: Note: Officers with more than one job title may be intentionally listed here more than once.

Diane Morais, CEO, Subsidiary
Jeffrey Brown, CEO
Christopher Halmy, CFO
David Debrunner, Chief Accounting Officer
David Shevsky, Chief Risk Officer
Franklin Hobbs, Director
Scott Stengel, General Counsel
Timothy Russi, President, Divisional

GROWTH PLANS/SPECIAL FEATURES:

Ally Financial, Inc. is a global provider of banking and financial services. The company operates in four business segments: automotive financial services, insurance, mortgage finance and corporate finance services. Automotive financial services offer new vehicle financing and leasing, used vehicle financing, vehicle remarketing and protection products through about 4,100 auto dealers across the U.S. The firm's insurance operations offers both consumer finance protection and insurance products sold primarily through automotive dealers, and commercial insurance products sold directly to dealers. The product offering includes vehicle service contracts, vehicle maintenance contracts and guaranteed asset protection products. In addition to its products, the segment also underwrites selected commercial insurance coverages. The mortgage financing segment primarily consists of the management of a held-for-investment consumer mortgage finance loan portfolio, which includes bulk purchases of high-quality jumbo and low-to-moderate income (LMI) mortgage loans originated by third parties. The corporate finance division primarily provides senior secured leveraged cash flow and asset-based loans to mostly U.S.-based middle market companies. This segment primarily focuses on businesses owned by private equity sponsors with loans typically used for leveraged buyouts, mergers and acquisitions, debt refinancing, restructuring and working capital. In June 2016, the firm acquired TradeKing Group, Inc., a digital wealth management company with an online broker/dealer, digital portfolio management platform, as well as educational content and social collaboration channels.

FINANCIAL DATA: Note: Data for latest year may not have been available at press time.

In U.S. $	2016	2015	2014	2013	2012	2011
Revenue	5,437,000,000	4,861,000,000	4,651,000,000	4,263,000,000	4,898,000,000	6,071,000,000
R&D Expense						
Operating Income	1,581,000,000	1,393,000,000	1,246,000,000	357,000,000	-755,000,000	67,000,000
Operating Margin %	29.07%	28.65%	26.78%	8.37%	-15.41%	1.10%
SGA Expense	2,459,000,000	2,352,000,000	2,462,000,000	2,834,000,000	3,348,000,000	4,227,000,000
Net Income	1,067,000,000	1,289,000,000	1,150,000,000	361,000,000	1,196,000,000	-157,000,000
Operating Cash Flow	4,567,000,000	5,095,000,000	3,403,000,000	2,501,000,000	5,049,000,000	5,493,000,000
Capital Expenditure						
EBITDA						
Return on Assets %	.64%	- .82%	.58%	- .41%	.21%	- .51%
Return on Equity %	7.95%	-9.53%	6.50%	-5.31%	3.10%	-7.08%
Debt to Equity	4.06	5.19	4.70	5.36	5.75	7.46

CONTACT INFORMATION:

Phone: 866-710-4623   Fax: 815-282-6156
Toll-Free: 877-247-2559
Address: 200 Renaissance Ctr., Detroit, MI 48265-2000 United States

STOCK TICKER/OTHER:

Stock Ticker: ALLY   Exchange: NYS
Employees: 7,600   Fiscal Year Ends: 12/31
Parent Company:

SALARIES/BONUSES:

Top Exec. Salary: $1,000,000   Bonus: $2,400,000
Second Exec. Salary: $600,000   Bonus: $1,050,000

OTHER THOUGHTS:

Estimated Female Officers or Directors: 7
Hot Spot for Advancement for Women/Minorities: Y

Almost Family Inc

www.almostfamily.com

NAIC Code: 621610

TYPES OF BUSINESS:

Home Health Care Services
Visiting Nurse
Personal Care

BRANDS/DIVISIONS/AFFILIATES:

Community Health Systems Inc

CONTACTS: *Note: Officers with more than one job title may be intentionally listed here more than once.*

William Yarmuth, CEO
C. Guenthner, CFO
Jeffrey Reibel, Chief Accounting Officer
Daniel Schwartz, COO
Rajneesh Kaushal, Other Executive Officer
John Shermyen, Senior VP, Divisional
Patrick Lyles, Senior VP, Divisional

GROWTH PLANS/SPECIAL FEATURES:

Almost Family, Inc. is a regionally focused provider of home health nursing, rehabilitation and personal care services. Almost Family's platform focuses on senior advocacy to address the challenges faced by the aging population. Rehabilitation services include physical therapy, occupational therapy and speech therapy. The firm operates over 340 locations across 26 states. Almost Family has two divisions, Home Health and Healthcare Innovations. The Home Health division is comprised of two reportable segments: visiting nurse services (VN) and personal care services (PC). The VN segment provides a range of Medicare-certified home health nursing services to patients in need of recuperative care, typically following a period of hospitalization or care in another type of inpatient facility. Approximately 95% of the VN segment revenues are generated from the Medicare program, while the remainder is generated from Medicaid and private insurance programs. The PC segment provides services in patients' homes primarily on an as-needed, hourly basis. These services include personal care, medication management, meal preparation, caregiver respite and homemaking. Approximately 83% of the PC segment revenues are generated from Medicaid and other government programs, while the remainder is generated from insurance programs and private pay patients. Healthcare innovations segment includes the company's development activity outside of the traditional home health business platform. In January 2017, Almost Family acquired a controlling interest in the entity holding the home health and hospice assets of Community Health Systems, Inc., a provider of skilled home health and hospice services.

Almost Family offers employees medical, dental and vision insurance; life insurance; AD&D; voluntary short- and long-term disability; flexible spending accounts; and a 401(k).

FINANCIAL DATA: *Note: Data for latest year may not have been available at press time.*

In U.S. $	2016	2015	2014	2013	2012	2011
Revenue	623,541,000	532,214,000	495,829,000	357,812,000	348,524,000	339,853,000
R&D Expense						
Operating Income	34,932,000	32,103,000	24,642,000	14,543,000	28,544,000	34,561,000
Operating Margin %	5.60%	6.03%	4.96%	4.06%	8.19%	10.16%
SGA Expense	253,137,000	218,269,000	201,881,000	152,001,000	139,156,000	138,234,000
Net Income	17,653,000	20,009,000	13,763,000	8,226,000	17,284,000	20,802,000
Operating Cash Flow	24,443,000	21,206,000	6,662,000	19,774,000	17,033,000	25,936,000
Capital Expenditure	6,206,000	3,117,000	1,232,000	2,505,000	2,487,000	2,889,000
EBITDA	39,377,000	36,311,000	28,745,000	17,406,000	31,122,000	37,377,000
Return on Assets %	3.14%	4.86%	3.87%	2.73%	6.91%	8.83%
Return on Equity %	6.15%	7.99%	6.20%	3.93%	8.41%	10.70%
Debt to Equity	0.90	0.44	0.20	0.26		

CONTACT INFORMATION:

Phone: 502 891-1000   Fax: 502 891-8067
Toll-Free:
Address: 9510 Ormsby Station Rd., Louisville, KY 40223 United States

STOCK TICKER/OTHER:

Stock Ticker: AFAM   Exchange: NAS
Employees: 15,500   Fiscal Year Ends: 12/31
Parent Company:

SALARIES/BONUSES:

Top Exec. Salary: $677,000   Bonus: $
Second Exec. Salary: Bonus: $
$450,000

OTHER THOUGHTS:

Estimated Female Officers or Directors: 3
Hot Spot for Advancement for Women/Minorities: Y

Amazon.com Inc

www.amazon.com

NAIC Code: 454111

TYPES OF BUSINESS:

Online Retailing and Related Services
Online Books & Music Retail
Online Videos/DVDs Retail
Online Electronics Retail
Online Auctions
Online Household Goods Retail
Online Auto & Industrial Retail
E-Commerce Support & Hosting

BRANDS/DIVISIONS/AFFILIATES:

Amazon Web Services (AWS)
Kindle
Fire
Fire TV
Fire Phone
Echo
Amazon Market Place
Kindle Direct Publishing

CONTACTS: Note: Officers with more than one job title may be intentionally listed here more than once.

Andrew Jassy, CEO, Divisional
Jeffrey Wilke, CEO, Divisional
Jeffrey Bezos, CEO
Brian Olsavsky, CFO
Shelley Reynolds, Chief Accounting Officer
David Zapolsky, General Counsel
Jeffrey Blackburn, Senior VP, Divisional

GROWTH PLANS/SPECIAL FEATURES:

Amazon.com, Inc. is an internet consumer-shopping site that offers millions of new, used, refurbished and collectible items in categories such as books, movies, music and games, electronics and computers, home and garden, toys, children's goods, grocery, apparel and jewelry, health and beauty, sports, outdoors, digital downloads, tools and auto and industrial. The company, which serves more than 50 million members, operates in three segments: North America (which generates about 60% of annual revenue), international (33%) and Amazon Web Services (AWS) (7%), which offers computing, storage, database and other service offerings globally for start-ups, enterprises, government agencies and academic institutions. The Amazon Marketplace and Merchants programs allow third parties to integrate their products on Amazon web sites and provide related fulfillment and advertising services to third-party merchants; allow customers to shop for products owned by third parties using Amazon's features and technologies; and enable customers to complete transactions that include multiple sellers in a single checkout process. The company also sells proprietary electronic devices, including Kindle e-readers, Fire tablets, Fire TVs, and Fire phones; as well as the Echo personal digital assistant. The firm serves authors and independent publishers with Kindle Direct Publishing, an online platform that lets independent authors and publishers choose a 70% royalty option and make their books available in the Kindle Store. In June 2017, the firm announced plans to acquire Whole Foods Market for $13.7 billion.

Employee benefits include life, disability, accident, medical, dental and vision insurance with domestic partner coverage; flexible spending accounts; relocation assistance; paid holiday/vacations; a 401(k); company stock; and several discount programs.

FINANCIAL DATA: Note: Data for latest year may not have been available at press time.

In U.S. $	2016	2015	2014	2013	2012	2011
Revenue	135,987,000,000	107,006,000,000	88,988,000,000	74,452,000,000	61,093,000,000	48,077,000,000
R&D Expense	16,085,000,000	12,540,000,000	9,275,000,000	6,565,000,000	4,564,000,000	2,909,000,000
Operating Income	4,186,000,000	2,233,000,000	178,000,000	745,000,000	676,000,000	862,000,000
Operating Margin %	3.07%	2.08%	.20%	1.00%	1.10%	1.79%
SGA Expense	27,284,000,000	20,411,000,000	16,650,000,000	12,847,000,000	9,723,000,000	6,864,000,000
Net Income	2,371,000,000	596,000,000	-241,000,000	274,000,000	-39,000,000	631,000,000
Operating Cash Flow	16,443,000,000	11,920,000,000	6,842,000,000	5,475,000,000	4,180,000,000	3,903,000,000
Capital Expenditure	6,737,000,000	4,589,000,000	4,893,000,000	3,444,000,000	3,785,000,000	1,811,000,000
EBITDA	12,492,000,000	8,308,000,000	4,845,000,000	3,900,000,000	2,795,000,000	2,082,000,000
Return on Assets %	3.18%	.99%	-.50%	.75%	-.13%	2.86%
Return on Equity %	14.51%	4.94%	-2.35%	3.05%	-.48%	8.63%
Debt to Equity	0.78	1.05	1.16	0.53	0.46	0.18

CONTACT INFORMATION:

Phone: 206 266-1000   Fax:
Toll-Free:
Address: 410 Terry Ave. N., Seattle, WA 98109 United States

STOCK TICKER/OTHER:

Stock Ticker: AMZN   Exchange: NAS
Employees: 341,400   Fiscal Year Ends: 12/31
Parent Company:

SALARIES/BONUSES:

Top Exec. Salary: $175,000   Bonus: $
Second Exec. Salary: $175,000   Bonus: $

OTHER THOUGHTS:

Estimated Female Officers or Directors: 3
Hot Spot for Advancement for Women/Minorities: Y

AMERCO (U-Haul)
NAIC Code: 532120

TYPES OF BUSINESS:
Truck Rental & Leasing Services
Moving & Storage Services & Supplies
Property & Casualty Insurance
Life Insurance
Annuities
Self-Storage Properties
Propane Tank Refilling
Car Sharing Services

BRANDS/DIVISIONS/AFFILIATES:
U-Haul International Inc
Amerco Real Estate Company
Repwest Insurance Company
Oxford Life Insurance Company
Uhaul.com
Safemove
Safetow
Safestor

CONTACTS: *Note: Officers with more than one job title may be intentionally listed here more than once.*
Edward Shoen, CEO
Jason Berg, CFO
Mary Thompson, Chief Accounting Officer
Samuel Shoen, Director
Laurence Derespino, General Counsel
Mark Haydukovich, President, Subsidiary
John Taylor, President, Subsidiary
Carlos Vizcarra, President, Subsidiary
Douglas Bell, President, Subsidiary

GROWTH PLANS/SPECIAL FEATURES:
AMERCO is a holding company operating through four primary subsidiaries: U-Haul International, Inc.; Amerco Real Estate Company; Repwest Insurance Company; and Oxford Life Insurance Company. Accordingly, the firm has three reportable business segments: moving and storage, property and casualty insurance and life insurance. Moving and storage consists of U-Haul, with its rental equipment fleet of trucks, trailers and tow dollies offered at 1,700 company operated locations and 19,500 independent dealer outlets. It also provides furniture pads, utility dollies and hand trucks; sells a wide selection of moving supplies; and offers protection packages for moving and storage. U-Haul owns more than 139,000 trucks, 108,000 trailers and 38,000 towing devices. The firm's Uhaul.com online reservation portal allows its self-storage customers to make reservations, access all U-Haul storage centers and affiliate partners. This segment is also operated by Amerco Real Estate Company, which manages 536,000 rentable rooms comprising 47.9 million square feet of rentable storage space located in North America. The property and casualty insurance segment, operated by Repwest Insurance Company, provides loss adjusting and claims handling for U-Haul through regional offices across North America. This segment also underwrites components of the Safemove, Safetow, Safestor and Safestor Mobile protection packages to U-Haul customers. The life insurance segment, operated by Oxford Life Insurance Company, provides life and health insurance products primarily to the senior market through the direct writing and reinsuring of life insurance, Medicare supplement and annuity policies.

FINANCIAL DATA: *Note: Data for latest year may not have been available at press time.*

In U.S. $	2016	2015	2014	2013	2012	2011
Revenue	3,275,656,000	3,074,531,000	2,835,252,000	2,558,587,000	2,502,675,000	
R&D Expense						
Operating Income	866,814,000	663,024,000	630,214,000	499,183,000	416,007,000	
Operating Margin %	26.46%	21.56%	22.22%	19.51%	16.62%	
SGA Expense	479,843,000	488,200,000	257,168,000	180,676,000	310,839,000	
Net Income	489,001,000	356,741,000	342,391,000	264,708,000	205,367,000	
Operating Cash Flow	1,041,063,000	808,190,000	709,504,000	661,530,000	664,605,000	
Capital Expenditure	1,509,154,000	1,111,899,000	999,365,000	655,984,000	589,799,000	
EBITDA	1,256,207,000	1,011,739,000	923,383,000	755,542,000	645,796,000	
Return on Assets %	6.51%	5.54%	6.05%	5.31%	4.45%	
Return on Equity %	23.64%	20.91%	24.84%	23.37%	19.37%	
Debt to Equity	1.19	1.16	1.27	1.12	1.43	

CONTACT INFORMATION:
Phone: 775-688-6300   Fax: 775 688-6338
Toll-Free:
Address: 5555 Kietzke Lane, Ste. 100, Reno, NV 89511 United States

STOCK TICKER/OTHER:
Stock Ticker: UHAL   Exchange: NAS
Employees: 28,300   Fiscal Year Ends: 03/31
Parent Company:

SALARIES/BONUSES:
Top Exec. Salary: $700,004   Bonus: $175,000
Second Exec. Salary: Bonus: $
$586,923

OTHER THOUGHTS:
Estimated Female Officers or Directors: 1
Hot Spot for Advancement for Women/Minorities:

American Airlines Group Inc   www.usairways.com

NAIC Code: 481111

TYPES OF BUSINESS:

Airline
Air Freight

BRANDS/DIVISIONS/AFFILIATES:

AMR Corporation
US Airways Group Inc
American Airlines Inc
Piedmont Airlines Inc
Envoy Aviation Group Inc
PSA Airlines Inc
American Eagle

CONTACTS: Note: Officers with more than one job title may be intentionally listed here more than once.

W. Parker, CEO
Derek Kerr, CFO
Stephen Johnson, Executive VP, Divisional
Elise Eberwein, Executive VP, Divisional
Beverly Goulet, Executive VP
Maya Leibman, Executive VP
Robert Isom, President

GROWTH PLANS/SPECIAL FEATURES:

American Airlines Group, Inc., a result of the merger of AMR Corporation and US Airways Group, Inc., operates one of the largest air carriers in the U.S. Its subsidiaries include US Airways Group; American Airlines, Inc.; Piedmont Airlines, Inc.; Envoy Aviation Group, Inc.; and PSA Airlines, Inc. The company operates nearly 6,700 flights per day from its hubs in Charlotte, Chicago, Dallas/Fort Worth, Los Angeles, Miami, New York, Philadelphia, Phoenix and Washington, D.C. The firm offers passenger service to more than 350 destinations in 50 countries. The company's regional airline subsidiaries and affiliates operate under the brand name American Eagle. American Eagle is a network of 10 regional carriers that operate under a codeshare and service agreement with American. Together they operate 606 regional aircraft, servicing 54 million passengers. The cargo division of the firm provides a wide range of freight and mail services, with facilities and interline connections available across the globe. American and US Airways are members of the oneworld alliance whose members and members-elect serve more than 1,000 destinations with 14,250 daily flights to 150 countries.

US Airways provides employees with auto, home, accident, health, long-term care and critical illness insurance; a 401(k); identity theft protection; travel privileges; employee assistance programs; business resource groups; domestic partner programs; paid vacation; and days off.

FINANCIAL DATA: Note: Data for latest year may not have been available at press time.

In U.S. $	2016	2015	2014	2013	2012	2011
Revenue	40,180,000,000	40,990,000,000	42,650,000,000	26,743,000,000	24,855,000,000	23,979,000,000
R&D Expense						
Operating Income	5,284,000,000	6,204,000,000	4,249,000,000	1,399,000,000	107,000,000	-1,054,000,000
Operating Margin %	13.15%	15.13%	9.96%	5.23%	.43%	-4.39%
SGA Expense	12,213,000,000	10,918,000,000	10,052,000,000	6,618,000,000	8,483,000,000	8,633,000,000
Net Income	2,676,000,000	7,610,000,000	2,882,000,000	-1,834,000,000	-1,876,000,000	-1,979,000,000
Operating Cash Flow	6,524,000,000	6,249,000,000	3,080,000,000	675,000,000	1,279,000,000	680,000,000
Capital Expenditure	5,731,000,000	6,151,000,000	5,311,000,000	3,114,000,000	1,888,000,000	1,614,000,000
EBITDA	7,108,000,000	7,105,000,000	5,612,000,000	-304,000,000	-818,000,000	-107,000,000
Return on Assets %	5.36%	16.51%	6.69%	-5.57%	-7.92%	-8.08%
Return on Equity %	56.81%	198.79%				
Debt to Equity	5.94	3.25	8.01			

CONTACT INFORMATION:

Phone: 817-963-1234   Fax:
Toll-Free:
Address: 4333 Amon Carter Blvd, Fort Worth, TX 76155 United States

SALARIES/BONUSES:

Top Exec. Salary: $641,306   Bonus: $
Second Exec. Salary: Bonus: $
$600,936

STOCK TICKER/OTHER:

Stock Ticker: AAL   Exchange: NAS
Employees: 122,300   Fiscal Year Ends: 12/31
Parent Company:

OTHER THOUGHTS:

Estimated Female Officers or Directors: 7
Hot Spot for Advancement for Women/Minorities: Y

American Express Co

NAIC Code: 522320

TYPES OF BUSINESS:

Credit Card Processing and Issuing
Travel-Related Services
Lending & Financing
Transaction Services
Bank Holding Company
International Banking Services
Expense Management
Magazine Publishing

BRANDS/DIVISIONS/AFFILIATES:

American Express Travel Related Services Co Inc
American Express Bank FSB
American Express Centurion Bank

CONTACTS: Note: Officers with more than one job title may be intentionally listed here more than once.

Kenneth Chenault, CEO
Anre Williams, President, Divisional
Jeffrey Campbell, CFO
Marc Gordon, Chief Information Officer
Paul Fabara, Chief Risk Officer
Linda Zukauckas, Controller
Michael ONeill, Executive VP, Divisional
Laureen Seeger, Executive VP
L. Cox, Other Executive Officer
Ashwini Gupta, President, Divisional
Douglas Buckminster, President, Divisional
James Bush, President, Divisional
Susan Sobbott, President, Divisional
Stephen Squeri, Vice Chairman

GROWTH PLANS/SPECIAL FEATURES:

American Express Co. (AmEx), a bank holding company, is a leading global payments and travel firm. Its principal products are charge and credit payment card products and travel-related services. The firm primarily operates through subsidiary American Express Travel Related Services Company, Inc. AmEx's business is organized into four main segments: U.S. card services, international card services, global commercial services and global network & merchant services. The U.S. card services segment operates through AmEx's USA banking subsidiaries American Express Centurion Bank and American Express Bank, FSB. The division provides a wide array of card products and services to consumers and small businesses in the USA. The firm's international card services division offers these services in countries worldwide. The global commercial services segment offers expense management services to firms and organizations worldwide. Its products and services include corporate purchasing cards, corporate cards, corporate meeting cards, buyer initiated payment programs and business travel accounts. The global network & merchant services division operates a global general-purpose charge and credit card network for both proprietary and issued cards; manages merchant services internationally, which includes signing merchants to accept cards and processing and settling card transactions for those merchants; and offers merchants point-of-sale (POS), servicing/settlement and marketing/information products and services. In June 2016, the 16-year partnership between American Express and Costco dissolved, with Costco no longer accepting American Express credit cards.

FINANCIAL DATA: Note: Data for latest year may not have been available at press time.

In U.S. $	2016	2015	2014	2013	2012	2011
Revenue	32,119,000,000	32,818,000,000	34,292,000,000	32,974,000,000	31,582,000,000	29,962,000,000
R&D Expense						
Operating Income	8,096,000,000	7,938,000,000	8,991,000,000	7,888,000,000	6,451,000,000	6,956,000,000
Operating Margin %	25.20%	24.18%	26.21%	23.92%	20.42%	23.21%
SGA Expense	17,137,000,000	16,099,000,000	17,168,000,000	16,458,000,000	16,568,000,000	16,182,000,000
Net Income	5,408,000,000	5,163,000,000	5,885,000,000	5,359,000,000	4,482,000,000	4,935,000,000
Operating Cash Flow	8,224,000,000	10,972,000,000	10,990,000,000	8,547,000,000	7,082,000,000	10,475,000,000
Capital Expenditure	1,375,000,000	1,341,000,000	1,195,000,000	1,006,000,000	1,053,000,000	1,189,000,000
EBITDA						
Return on Assets %	3.30%	3.16%	3.73%	3.49%	2.92%	3.28%
Return on Equity %	25.67%	24.49%	29.07%	27.92%	23.78%	28.18%
Debt to Equity	2.29	2.32	2.80	2.83	3.12	3.16

CONTACT INFORMATION:

Phone: 212 640-2000   Fax: 212 640-2458
Toll-Free: 800-528-4800
Address: 200 Vesey St., World Financial Ctr., New York, NY 10285 United States

STOCK TICKER/OTHER:

Stock Ticker: AXP
Employees: 56,400
Parent Company:

Exchange: NYS
Fiscal Year Ends: 12/31

SALARIES/BONUSES:

Top Exec. Salary: $1,350,000   Bonus: $5,100,000
Second Exec. Salary: $800,000   Bonus: $4,733,000

OTHER THOUGHTS:

Estimated Female Officers or Directors: 4
Hot Spot for Advancement for Women/Minorities: Y

American Financial Group Inc

NAIC Code: 524126

www.afginc.com

TYPES OF BUSINESS:

Insurance, Direct Property & Casualty
Long-Term Care Insurance
Annuities
Supplemental Health Insurance
Specialty Insurance
Multi-Peril Crop & Crop Hail Insurance
Car Insurance
Commercial Real Estate

BRANDS/DIVISIONS/AFFILIATES:

Great American Insurance Group
Great American Life Insurance Company
Annuity Investors Life Insurance Company
National Interstate Corporation

CONTACTS: Note: Officers with more than one job title may be intentionally listed here more than once.

Karl Grafe, Assistant General Counsel
Joseph Consolino, CFO
Michelle Gillis, Chief Administrative Officer
Carl Lindner, Co- President
S. Lindner, Co- President
John Berding, Director
Vito Peraino, General Counsel

GROWTH PLANS/SPECIAL FEATURES:

American Financial Group, Inc. (AFG) is a holding company that, through subsidiary Great American Insurance Group, is engaged primarily in property and casualty insurance. The company focuses on specialized products for businesses, as well as the sale of fixed and fixed-indexed annuities in the retail, financial institutions and education markets. Property & casualty insurance products include a range of commercial coverages through more than 30 niche insurance businesses that make up Great American Insurance Group. This division's specialized products include, but are not limited to, property & transportation insurance for marine, agriculture and commercial automobile sectors; specialty casualty insurance such as executive/professional liability, umbrella/excess liability, excess & surplus, general liability, targeted programs and workers' compensation; and specialty financial products such as fidelity & surety coverage, as well as lease and loan coverage. AFG sells traditional fixed and fixed-indexed annuities in the retail, financial institutions and education markets through independent producers, as well as through direct relationships with certain financial institutions. This division's operations are conducted primarily through subsidiaries: Great American Life Insurance Company (GALIC) and Annuity Investors Life Insurance Company (AILIC). GALIC comprises 384,000 annuity policies in force with ratings of A and A+ for AM Best and S&P, respectively; and AILIC comprises 117,500 annuity policies inforce with the same ratings as GALIC. Annuities are long-term retirement savings instruments that benefit from income accruing on a tax-deferred basis. Annuity contracts are generally classified as either fixed rate (including fixed-indexed) or variable. In November 2016, the firm acquired all the outstanding common shares of National Interstate Corporation that it does not currently own.

The firm offers employees medical, dental, vision, disability and life coverage; paid time off; and onsite fitness centers.

FINANCIAL DATA: Note: Data for latest year may not have been available at press time.

In U.S. $	2016	2015	2014	2013	2012	2011
Revenue	6,498,000,000	6,145,000,000	5,713,000,000	5,092,000,000	5,062,000,000	4,750,000,000
R&D Expense						
Operating Income	787,000,000	565,000,000	626,000,000	689,000,000	537,000,000	560,000,000
Operating Margin %	12.11%	9.19%	10.95%	13.53%	10.60%	11.78%
SGA Expense	1,500,000,000	1,432,000,000	1,254,000,000	1,108,000,000	1,371,000,000	1,269,000,000
Net Income	649,000,000	352,000,000	452,000,000	471,000,000	488,000,000	343,000,000
Operating Cash Flow	1,150,000,000	1,357,000,000	1,222,000,000	760,000,000	817,000,000	667,000,000
Capital Expenditure	49,000,000	102,000,000	47,000,000	52,000,000	71,000,000	86,000,000
EBITDA						
Return on Assets %	1.23%	.72%	1.00%	1.15%	1.29%	1.00%
Return on Equity %	13.65%	7.43%	9.53%	10.26%	10.69%	7.60%
Debt to Equity	0.26	0.22	0.21	0.19	0.20	0.20

CONTACT INFORMATION:

Phone: 513 579-2121   Fax: 513 412-0200
Toll-Free:
Address: 301 E. 4th St., Cincinnati, OH 45202 United States

STOCK TICKER/OTHER:

Stock Ticker: AFG
Employees: 7,000
Parent Company:

Exchange: NYS
Fiscal Year Ends: 12/31

SALARIES/BONUSES:

Top Exec. Salary: $1,150,000   Bonus: $
Second Exec. Salary: Bonus: $
$1,150,000

OTHER THOUGHTS:

Estimated Female Officers or Directors: 3
Hot Spot for Advancement for Women/Minorities: Y

American Honda Motor Co Inc

www.hondainamerica.com

NAIC Code: 336111

TYPES OF BUSINESS:

Automotive Manufacturing
Motorcycles & ATVs
Power Equipment
Marine Engines
Parts Manufacturing & Retail
Research & Development

BRANDS/DIVISIONS/AFFILIATES:

Honda Motor Co Ltd
Honda of America Manufacturing Inc
Honda R&D Americas Inc
Accord
Civic
CR-V
HR-V
Pilot

CONTACTS: Note: Officers with more than one job title may be intentionally listed here more than once.

Takuji Yamada, CEO
Tom Elliott, Exec. VP-Oper.
Tetsuo Iwamura, Pres.
Hiroyuki Suganuma, CFO
Bruce Smith, Sr. VP-Parts & Svcs. Div.
Michael Accavitti, Sr. VP-Auto Oper.
Steven Center, VP-Environmental Bus. Dev. Office
Sage Marie, Sr. Mgr.-Public Rel.
Michael Ryan, VP-Finance
Robyn Eagles, Mgr.-Honda Public Rel..
Gary Robinson, Mgr.-Acura Advertising
Dave Speck, VP-Tech Coordination Product, Regulatory Office
Tom Peyton, Assistant VP-Auto Advertising

GROWTH PLANS/SPECIAL FEATURES:

American Honda Motor Co., Inc. manufactures and sells automobiles, motorcycles, ATVs, personal watercraft, marine engines, lawn care equipment, snow equipment, generators and water pumps. It is the U.S. subsidiary of Honda Motor Co. Ltd. The company's car models include the Accord, Civic, CR-V, HR-V, Odyssey, Pilot and Ridgeline. In addition, Honda owns the Acura brand of vehicles, with 70% of the Honda and Acura vehicles sold in the U.S. being manufactured in the U.S. Other Power Sport products include offroad bikes, ATVs, the Side by Side and scooters. Through Honda of America Manufacturing Inc., the firm operates engine, transmission, automobile, motorcycle, ATV and power equipment plants in Ohio, Indiana, Georgia, Alabama, North Carolina and South Carolina. In 2016, the firm produced 1.29 million cars and light trucks, 1.47 million automobile engines, 1.27 million transmissions, 2 million general purpose engines, 560,000 power equipment products and 82,000 ATVs. Through Honda R&D Americas, Inc., American Honda operates office, testing and research/development facilities in North Carolina, Colorado, Ohio, California, Michigan and Toronto. Its 12 manufacturing plants are in Ohio, Alabama, Georgia, Indiana, South Carolina and North Carolina.

Employee benefits include tuition reimbursement, comprehensive health care plans, pre-tax spending accounts, retirement plans, same-sex domestic-partner benefits and onsite wellness/fitness facilities.

FINANCIAL DATA: Note: Data for latest year may not have been available at press time.

In U.S. $	2016	2015	2014	2013	2012	2011
Revenue	61,551,806,117	60,557,038,000	52,624,765,000	45,043,300,000	45,029,700,000	50,053,100,000
R&D Expense						
Operating Income						
Operating Margin %						
SGA Expense						
Net Income	1,525,529,259	1,801,247,748	3,330,926,576	2,052,150,000	2,706,720,000	3,631,260,000
Operating Cash Flow						
Capital Expenditure						
EBITDA						
Return on Assets %						
Return on Equity %						
Debt to Equity						

CONTACT INFORMATION:

Phone: 310-783-2000   Fax: 310-783-3023
Toll-Free: 800-999-1009
Address: 1919 Torrance Blvd., Torrance, CA 90501 United States

STOCK TICKER/OTHER:

Stock Ticker: Subsidiary   Exchange:
Employees: 30,000   Fiscal Year Ends: 03/31
Parent Company: Honda Motor Co Ltd

SALARIES/BONUSES:

Top Exec. Salary: $ Bonus: $
Second Exec. Salary: $ Bonus: $

OTHER THOUGHTS:

Estimated Female Officers or Directors: 2
Hot Spot for Advancement for Women/Minorities:

American Tire Distributors

NAIC Code: 423130

www.atd-us.com

TYPES OF BUSINESS:
Tires & Related Products, Distribution

BRANDS/DIVISIONS/AFFILIATES:
American Tire Distributors Holdings Inc
ATDOnline
TireBuyer.com

CONTACTS: *Note: Officers with more than one job title may be intentionally listed here more than once.*
Stuart Schuette, CEO
William Berry, Pres.
Bill Williams, CFO
Rebecca Sincair, Chief People Officer
Joyce Vonada, CIO
Michael Gaither, General Counsel
Phillip Marrett, Exec. VP-Product Planning & Positioning
Daniel Brown, Pres., Tire Pros

GROWTH PLANS/SPECIAL FEATURES:
American Tire Distributors (ATD) is one of the nation's largest suppliers of tires and wheels as well as tools and other automotive service equipment. The company serves the replacement tire market through approximately 140 distribution centers in Canada and the U.S., and more than 1,000 delivery vehicles, delivering products to 70,000 customers. ATD distributes more than 40 million replacement tires each year. ATD offers its tire retailers and service shop clients various tires for passenger vehicles and light trucks, tractor-trailers, buses, farm machinery and specialty and recreational vehicles. The company carries brands including Michelin, Continental, Goodyear and Bridgestone. Its wheel selection ranges from 13- to 30-inch rims for passenger vehicles and light trucks. The firm maintains ATDOnline, which offers dealers access to prices, availability and the ability to place orders 24 hours a day, seven days a week; and TireBuyer.com, where customers can buy tires and wheels as well as choose a dealer location for installation. TireBuyer.com also allows potential purchasers to view tires and wheels on their particular vehicle, using the website's 3D visualizer. ATD operates as a subsidiary of American Tire Distributors Holdings, Inc.

FINANCIAL DATA: *Note: Data for latest year may not have been available at press time.*

In U.S. $	2016	2015	2014	2013	2012	2011
Revenue	5,000,000,000	4,800,000,000	5,030,698,000	3,839,269,000	3,455,864,000	1,525,249,000
R&D Expense						
Operating Income						
Operating Margin %						
SGA Expense						
Net Income	-92,256,933	-95,800,000	-94,599,999	-6,357,000	-14,346,000	-36,312,000
Operating Cash Flow						
Capital Expenditure						
EBITDA						
Return on Assets %						
Return on Equity %						
Debt to Equity						

CONTACT INFORMATION:
Phone: 704-992-2000   Fax: 704-992-1384
Toll-Free: 800-222-1167
Address: 12200 Herbert Wayne Ct., Ste. 150, Huntersville, NC 28070 United States

STOCK TICKER/OTHER:
Stock Ticker: Subsidiary   Exchange:
Employees: 4,000   Fiscal Year Ends: 01/04
Parent Company: American Tire Distributors Holdings Inc

SALARIES/BONUSES:
Top Exec. Salary: $ Bonus: $
Second Exec. Salary: $ Bonus: $

OTHER THOUGHTS:
Estimated Female Officers or Directors:
Hot Spot for Advancement for Women/Minorities:

Amerigroup Corporation

NAIC Code: 524114

www.amerigroupcorp.com

TYPES OF BUSINESS:

Managed Health Care

BRANDS/DIVISIONS/AFFILIATES:

Anthem Inc

CONTACTS: *Note: Officers with more than one job title may be intentionally listed here more than once.*

Peter D. Haytaian, Pres.
Richard C. Zoretic, Exec. VP
Scott Anglin, CFO-Anthem
Jenn Crenshaw, VP-Human Resources
Mary T. McCluskey, Exec. VP
Jack Young, VP
Ken Aversa, Sr. VP-Customer Svc. Oper., Medicaid, WellPoint
Georgia Dodds Foley, Chief Compliance Officer, Medicaid, WellPoint
John E. Little, Interim Sr. VP-Gov't Affairs, WellPoint
Aileen McCormick, CEO-Western Region, Medicaid, WellPoint

GROWTH PLANS/SPECIAL FEATURES:

Amerigroup Corporation, the state-sponsored program services division of health benefits company Anthem, Inc., is a managed health care company focused on serving people who receive benefits through publicly-sponsored programs. These programs include Medicaid, Medicare Advantage, Family Care and the Children's Health Insurance Program (CHIP). Since the company does not offer Medicare or commercial products, people served by Amerigroup are generally younger, tend to access health care in an inefficient manner and have a greater percentage of medical expenses related to obstetrics, diabetes, circulatory and respiratory conditions. The firm reduces costs for families and state governments by combining social and behavioral health services to help members obtain health care. Amerigroup's provider networks consist of approximately 136,000 physicians, including primary care physicians, specialists and ancillary providers, and approximately 800 hospitals across all of its markets. The company currently enrolls 3.5 million members in 12 states nationwide.

FINANCIAL DATA: *Note: Data for latest year may not have been available at press time.*

In U.S. $	2016	2015	2014	2013	2012	2011
Revenue	10,000,000,000	10,000,000,000	9,625,000,000	9,125,000,000	219,000,000	6,318,393,856
R&D Expense						
Operating Income						
Operating Margin %						
SGA Expense						
Net Income						
Operating Cash Flow						
Capital Expenditure						
EBITDA						
Return on Assets %						
Return on Equity %						
Debt to Equity						

CONTACT INFORMATION:

Phone: 757 490-6900   Fax:
Toll-Free: 800-600-4441
Address: 4425 Corporation Lane, Virginia Beach, VA 23462 United States

STOCK TICKER/OTHER:

Stock Ticker: Subsidiary   Exchange:
Employees: 8,000   Fiscal Year Ends: 12/31
Parent Company: Anthem Inc

SALARIES/BONUSES:

Top Exec. Salary: $ Bonus: $
Second Exec. Salary: $ Bonus: $

OTHER THOUGHTS:

Estimated Female Officers or Directors: 3
Hot Spot for Advancement for Women/Minorities: Y

AmerisourceBergen Corp

www.amerisourcebergen.com

NAIC Code: 424210

TYPES OF BUSINESS:

Drug Distribution
Pharmacy Management & Consulting Services
Packaging Solutions
Information Technology
Healthcare Equipment

BRANDS/DIVISIONS/AFFILIATES:

AmerisourceBergen Drug Corporation
AmerisourceBergen Specialty Group
AmerisourceBergen Consulting Services
World Courier
St Francis Group

CONTACTS: Note: Officers with more than one job title may be intentionally listed here more than once.

Steven Collis, CEO
Tim Guttman, CFO
Lazarus Krikorian, Chief Accounting Officer
Dale Danilewitz, Chief Information Officer
Sun Park, Executive VP
Gina Clark, Executive VP
John Chou, Executive VP
Kathy Gaddes, Executive VP
Robert Mauch, Executive VP
James Cleary, Executive VP
Peyton Howell, President, Divisional

GROWTH PLANS/SPECIAL FEATURES:

AmerisourceBergen Corp. is one of the largest wholesale distributors of pharmaceutical products and services to a wide variety of health care providers and pharmacies. The firm offers brand name and generic pharmaceuticals, supplies and equipment and serves the U.S., Canada and selected global markets. The company's operations are divided into two segments: pharmaceutical distribution and other. Pharmaceutical distribution provides drug distribution and related services designed to reduce health care costs and improve patient outcomes. This segment comprises two operating divisions: the operations of the AmerisourceBergen Drug Corporation (ABDC) and the AmerisourceBergen Specialty Group (ABSG). ABDC provides pharmacy management including distribution of brand-name & generic pharmaceutical products, staffing/consulting services, scalable automated pharmacy dispensing equipment, medication & supply dispensing cabinets and supply management software to a variety of retail & institutional health care providers. ABSG, through a number of operating businesses, provides pharmaceutical distribution and other services primarily to physician practices who specialize in a variety of disease states, especially oncology, and to other health care providers such as dialysis clinics. This division also distributes plasma and other blood products, injectable pharmaceuticals and vaccines and provides third-party logistics and outcomes research for biotechnology and pharmaceutical manufacturers. The other segment comprises: AmerisourceBergen Consulting Services (ABCS), which provides commercialization support services such as reimbursement support programs, outcomes research, contract field staffing, patient assistance and copay assistance programs; and World Courier, which is a global specialty transportation and logistics provider for the biopharmaceutical industry. Serving more than 50 countries. In 2016, the firm acquired St. Francis Group, the U.K.'s largest animal health buying group.

Employee benefits include health care, retirement, life insurance and disability protection.

FINANCIAL DATA: Note: Data for latest year may not have been available at press time.

In U.S. $	2016	2015	2014	2013	2012	2011
Revenue	146,849,700,000	135,961,800,000	119,569,100,000	87,959,170,000	79,489,600,000	80,217,550,000
R&D Expense						
Operating Income	1,525,774,000	417,370,000	778,884,000	898,399,000	1,252,728,000	1,202,745,000
Operating Margin %	1.03%	.30%	.65%	1.02%	1.57%	1.49%
SGA Expense	2,138,844,000	1,918,045,000	1,587,261,000	1,333,712,000	1,229,495,000	1,197,969,000
Net Income	1,427,929,000	-134,887,000	276,484,000	433,707,000	718,986,000	706,624,000
Operating Cash Flow	3,178,497,000	3,920,379,000	1,463,153,000	788,125,000	1,305,449,000	1,167,948,000
Capital Expenditure	464,616,000	231,585,000	264,457,000	202,450,000	164,041,000	167,954,000
EBITDA	1,927,425,000	625,735,000	943,864,000	1,070,299,000	1,407,550,000	1,335,484,000
Return on Assets %	4.65%	-.54%	1.36%	2.52%	4.72%	4.80%
Return on Equity %	103.36%	-10.41%	12.92%	18.16%	27.01%	24.27%
Debt to Equity	1.81	5.51	1.01	0.60	0.58	0.33

CONTACT INFORMATION:

Phone: 610 727-7000   Fax: 610 647-0141
Toll-Free: 800-829-3132
Address: 1300 Morris Dr., Chesterbrook, PA 19087 United States

STOCK TICKER/OTHER:

Stock Ticker: ABC   Exchange: NYS
Employees: 19,000   Fiscal Year Ends: 09/30
Parent Company:

SALARIES/BONUSES:

Top Exec. Salary: $1,234,231   Bonus: $
Second Exec. Salary: $706,539   Bonus: $

OTHER THOUGHTS:

Estimated Female Officers or Directors: 7
Hot Spot for Advancement for Women/Minorities: Y

Sales, profits and employees may be estimates. Financial information, benefits and other data can change quickly and may vary from those stated here.

Ametek Inc

NAIC Code: 334513

www.ametek.com

TYPES OF BUSINESS:

Monitoring, Testing, Calibration and Display Electronic Device Manufacturing
ElectromechanicalÂ Device Manufacturing

BRANDS/DIVISIONS/AFFILIATES:

Global Tubes
Brookfield Engineering Laboratories
ESP/SurgeX
Laserage Technology Corporation
Rauland-Borg Corporation
Mocon Inc

CONTACTS: *Note: Officers with more than one job title may be intentionally listed here more than once.*

David Zapico, CEO
William Burke, CFO
Frank Hermance, Chairman of the Board
Thomas Montgomery, Chief Accounting Officer
Timothy Jones, President, Divisional
Ronald Oscher, President, Divisional
Thomas Marecic, President, Divisional
Tony Ciampitti, President, Divisional

GROWTH PLANS/SPECIAL FEATURES:

Ametek, Inc. is a global manufacturer of electronic instruments and electromechanical devices, with operations in North America, Europe, Asia and South America. The company markets its products worldwide through two operating groups: the electronic instruments group (EIG) and the electromechanical group (EMG). EIG builds monitoring, testing, calibration and display devices for the process, aerospace, industrial and power markets. The group makes significant use of distributors and sales representatives in marketing its products as well as direct sales in some of its more technically sophisticated products. EMG is a supplier of electromechanical devices. EMG produces highly engineered electromechanical connectors for hermetic (moisture-proof) applications, specialty metals for niche markets and brushless air-moving motors, blowers and heat exchangers. Management believes that the firm has several competitive advantages that assist it in sustaining and enhancing its market positions. The company's marketing efforts are generally organized and carried out at the division level. In general, most of the firm's markets are highly competitive. The principal elements of competition for the company's products are price, product technology, distribution, quality and service. AMETEK owns numerous unexpired U.S. patents and foreign patents, including counterparts of its more important U.S. patents, in the major industrial countries of the world. The firm has 84 operating facilities: 53 in the U.S., nine in the U.K., eight in Germany, three in Canada, two in China, two in France, two in Switzerland and one each in Argentina, Austria, Denmark, Japan, Mexico and Taiwan. In 2016, it acquired Brookfield Engineering Laboratories, a manufacturer of viscometers and rheometers; ESP/SurgeX, a provider of energy intelligence and power protection; and Laserage Technology Corporation, a provider of laser fabrication services for the medical device market. In 2017, the firm acquired Rauland-Borg Corporation, a leading provider of mission critical communication solutions for healthcare and education; and Mocon, Inc., a laboratory and field gas analysis instrumentation provider.

FINANCIAL DATA: *Note: Data for latest year may not have been available at press time.*

In U.S. $	2016	2015	2014	2013	2012	2011
Revenue	3,840,087,000	3,974,295,000	4,021,964,000	3,594,136,000	3,334,213,000	2,989,914,000
R&D Expense						
Operating Income	801,897,000	907,716,000	898,586,000	815,079,000	745,872,000	635,941,000
Operating Margin %	20.88%	22.83%	22.34%	22.67%	22.37%	21.26%
SGA Expense	462,970,000	448,592,000	462,637,000	398,177,000	380,532,000	349,321,000
Net Income	512,158,000	590,859,000	584,460,000	516,999,000	459,132,000	384,464,000
Operating Cash Flow	756,835,000	672,540,000	725,962,000	660,659,000	612,464,000	508,565,000
Capital Expenditure	63,280,000	69,083,000	71,327,000	63,314,000	57,427,000	50,816,000
EBITDA	967,123,000	1,047,635,000	1,023,344,000	917,024,000	843,418,000	712,903,000
Return on Assets %	7.44%	9.03%	9.50%	9.34%	9.65%	9.44%
Return on Equity %	15.73%	18.19%	18.33%	18.23%	20.01%	20.08%
Debt to Equity	0.63	0.47	0.44	0.36	0.44	0.54

CONTACT INFORMATION:

Phone: 610 647-2121   Fax:
Toll-Free:
Address: 1100 Cassatt Rd., Berwyn, PA 19312-1177 United States

STOCK TICKER/OTHER:

Stock Ticker: AME
Employees: 15,700
Parent Company:

Exchange: NYS
Fiscal Year Ends: 12/31

SALARIES/BONUSES:

Top Exec. Salary: $1,300,000   Bonus: $572,000
Second Exec. Salary: $909,891   Bonus: $311,804

OTHER THOUGHTS:

Estimated Female Officers or Directors:
Hot Spot for Advancement for Women/Minorities:

Sales, profits and employees may be estimates. Financial information, benefits and other data can change quickly and may vary from those stated here.

Amgen Inc

NAIC Code: 325412

www.amgen.com

TYPES OF BUSINESS:

Drugs-Diversified
Oncology Drugs
Nephrology Drugs
Inflammation Drugs
Neurology Drugs

BRANDS/DIVISIONS/AFFILIATES:

Aranesp
EPOGEN
Neulasta
NEUPOGEN
Enbrel
Sensipar
Vectibix
Parsabiv

CONTACTS: Note: Officers with more than one job title may be intentionally listed here more than once.

Robert Bradway, CEO
David Piacquad, Senior VP, Divisional
David Meline, CFO
Annette Such, Chief Accounting Officer
Sean Harper, Executive VP, Divisional
Anthony Hooper, Executive VP, Divisional
Brian Mcnamee, Executive VP, Divisional
Esteban Santos, Executive VP, Divisional
Cynthia Patton, Other Executive Officer
Lori Johnston, Senior VP
Jonathan Graham, Senior VP

GROWTH PLANS/SPECIAL FEATURES:

Amgen, Inc. is a global biotechnology medicines company that discovers, develops, manufactures and markets human therapeutics based on cellular and molecular biology. Its products are used for treatment in the fields of supportive cancer care, nephrology and inflammation. Amgen's primary products include Aranesp, EPOGEN, Neulasta, NEUPOGEN, Enbrel, XGEVA and Prolia. Aranesp and EPOGEN stimulate the production of red blood cells to treat anemia and belong to a class of drugs referred to as erythropoiesis-stimulating agents. Aranesp is used for the treatment of anemia both in chronic kidney failure and in concomitant chemotherapy. EPOGEN is used to treat anemia associated with end-stage renal disease. Neulasta and NEUPOGEN selectively stimulate the production of neutrophils, one type of white blood cell that helps the body fight infections. Enbrel inhibits tumor necrosis factor (TNF), a substance induced in response to inflammatory and immunological reactions, such as rheumatoid arthritis and psoriasis. XGEVA is approved for the prevention of skeletal-related events for patients with bone metastases from solid tumors, while Prolia is approved for the treatment of men and postmenopausal women with osteoporosis and a high risk of fracture. Other marketed products include Sensipar/Mimpara, which lowers serum calcium levels; Vectibix, used to treat specific progressions of metastatic colorectal cancer; Nplate, used to treat low platelet count; Kyprolis, used to treat patients with relapsed multiple myeloma; BLINCYTO, to treat certain types of acute lymphoblastic leukemia; Corlanor, used to reduce the risk of worsening heart failure; IMLYGIC, used to treat melanoma; PARSABIV, a calcium-sensing receptor for chronic kidney disease; and Repatha, an inhibitor antibody for cardiovascular diseases. Amgen maintains sales and marketing forces primarily in the U.S., Europe and Canada and markets its products to health care providers such as physicians or their clinics, dialysis centers, hospitals and pharmacies.

Amgen offers its employees health, disability and life insurance; paid time off; home and auto insurance; tuition reimbursement; childcare services; telecommuting options; and recreation/fitness classes.

FINANCIAL DATA: Note: Data for latest year may not have been available at press time.

In U.S. $	2016	2015	2014	2013	2012	2011
Revenue	22,991,000,000	21,662,000,000	20,063,000,000	18,676,000,000	17,265,000,000	15,582,000,000
R&D Expense	3,840,000,000	4,070,000,000	4,297,000,000	4,083,000,000	3,380,000,000	3,167,000,000
Operating Income	9,794,000,000	8,470,000,000	6,191,000,000	5,867,000,000	5,577,000,000	4,312,000,000
Operating Margin %	42.59%	39.10%	30.85%	31.41%	32.30%	27.67%
SGA Expense	5,062,000,000	4,846,000,000	4,699,000,000	5,184,000,000	4,801,000,000	4,486,000,000
Net Income	7,722,000,000	6,939,000,000	5,158,000,000	5,081,000,000	4,345,000,000	3,683,000,000
Operating Cash Flow	10,354,000,000	9,077,000,000	8,555,000,000	6,291,000,000	5,882,000,000	5,119,000,000
Capital Expenditure	837,000,000	649,000,000	1,003,000,000	693,000,000	689,000,000	567,000,000
EBITDA	11,899,000,000	11,181,000,000	8,283,000,000	7,153,000,000	7,150,000,000	5,820,000,000
Return on Assets %	10.35%	9.87%	7.63%	8.43%	8.42%	7.97%
Return on Equity %	26.64%	25.76%	21.54%	24.69%	22.81%	17.14%
Debt to Equity	1.01	1.04	1.17	1.34	1.26	1.12

CONTACT INFORMATION:

Phone: 805 447-1000   Fax: 805 447-1010
Toll-Free: 800-772-6436
Address: 1 Amgen Center Dr., Thousand Oaks, CA 91320 United States

STOCK TICKER/OTHER:

Stock Ticker: AMGN   Exchange: NAS
Employees: 19,200   Fiscal Year Ends: 12/31
Parent Company:

SALARIES/BONUSES:

Top Exec. Salary: $916,789   Bonus: $1,000,000
Second Exec. Salary: $1,531,731   Bonus: $

OTHER THOUGHTS:

Estimated Female Officers or Directors: 4
Hot Spot for Advancement for Women/Minorities: Y

Amphenol Corporation

NAIC Code: 335921

www.amphenol.com

TYPES OF BUSINESS:

Cables & Connectors
Fiber Optic Cable

BRANDS/DIVISIONS/AFFILIATES:

Times Fiber Communications Inc

CONTACTS: *Note: Officers with more than one job title may be intentionally listed here more than once.*

Richard Norwitt, CEO
Craig Lampo, CFO
Martin Loeffler, Director
Lance DAmico, General Counsel
John Treanor, General Manager, Divisional
Luc Walter, General Manager, Divisional
Zachary Raley, General Manager, Divisional
Martin Booker, General Manager, Divisional
William Doherty, General Manager, Divisional
Richard Gu, General Manager, Divisional
David Silverman, Vice President, Divisional
Jean-Luc Gavelle, Vice President
Dieter Ehrmanntraut, Vice President

GROWTH PLANS/SPECIAL FEATURES:

Amphenol Corporation is a leading global designer, manufacturer and marketer of electrical, electronic & fiber optic connectors, interconnect systems and coaxial & flat-ribbon cable. The company has two operating segments: interconnect products & assemblies and cable products & solutions. Interconnect products & assemblies include connectors, which when attached to an electrical, electronic or fiber optic cable; a printed circuit board; or other device, facilitate transmission of power or signal. Value-add systems generally consist of a system of cable, flexible circuits or printed circuit boards and connectors for linking electronic equipment. The cable products & solutions segment primarily designs, manufacturers and markets cable, value-added products and components for use primarily in the broadband communications and information technology markets as well as certain applications in other markets. Amphenol's products are intended for eight primary end markets: automotive, which accounted for 18% of its 2016 sales; broadband communications, 6%; commercial aerospace, 5%; industrial, 18%; information technology and data communications, 21%; military, 9%; mobile devices, 14%; and mobile networks, 9%. Subsidiary Times Fiber Communications, Inc. is one of the world's largest producers of coaxial cable and interconnect products for the cable TV, satellite, data and broadband communications industries. Net sales by geographic region include the U.S., 28%; China, 30%; and other international locations, 42%. Amphenol has international manufacturing and assembly facilities in China, Macedonia, Malaysia, Mexico, India, Indonesia, Eastern Europe and North Africa.

FINANCIAL DATA: *Note: Data for latest year may not have been available at press time.*

In U.S. $	2016	2015	2014	2013	2012	2011
Revenue	6,286,400,000	5,568,700,000	5,345,500,000	4,614,669,000	4,292,065,000	3,939,786,000
R&D Expense						
Operating Income	1,205,200,000	1,104,700,000	1,034,600,000	896,813,000	828,345,000	751,678,000
Operating Margin %	19.17%	19.83%	19.35%	19.43%	19.29%	19.07%
SGA Expense	798,200,000	669,100,000	645,100,000	548,038,000	512,867,000	507,795,000
Net Income	822,900,000	763,500,000	709,100,000	635,672,000	555,317,000	524,191,000
Operating Cash Flow	1,077,600,000	1,030,500,000	880,900,000	769,050,000	674,679,000	565,207,000
Capital Expenditure	190,800,000	172,100,000	209,100,000	158,448,000	129,099,000	100,222,000
EBITDA	1,430,700,000	1,292,700,000	1,221,000,000	1,046,680,000	960,233,000	879,220,000
Return on Assets %	10.31%	10.54%	10.74%	11.16%	11.49%	12.39%
Return on Equity %	23.80%	24.84%	24.59%	24.03%	24.13%	23.33%
Debt to Equity	0.71	0.86	0.91	0.50	0.66	0.63

CONTACT INFORMATION:

Phone: 203 265-8900 Fax: 203 265-8516
Toll-Free: 877-267-4366
Address: 358 Hall Ave., Wallingford, CT 06492 United States

STOCK TICKER/OTHER:

Stock Ticker: APH
Employees: 62,000
Parent Company:

Exchange: NYS
Fiscal Year Ends: 12/31

SALARIES/BONUSES:

Top Exec. Salary: $1,061,000   Bonus: $
Second Exec. Salary: $560,000   Bonus: $

OTHER THOUGHTS:

Estimated Female Officers or Directors: 1
Hot Spot for Advancement for Women/Minorities:

AMSURG Corporation

www.amsurg.com

NAIC Code: 621493

TYPES OF BUSINESS:

Practice-Based Ambulatory Surgery Centers
Physician Services

BRANDS/DIVISIONS/AFFILIATES:

Envision Healthcare Corporation
Envision Healthcare

CONTACTS: *Note: Officers with more than one job title may be intentionally listed here more than once.*

Phillip A. Clendenin, Pres.
Steven Geringer, Chairman of the Board
Phillip Clendenin, Executive VP, Divisional
Robert Coward, Other Executive Officer
Christopher Holden, President
Kevin Eastridge, Senior VP, Divisional

GROWTH PLANS/SPECIAL FEATURES:

AMSURG Corporation, a subsidiary of Envision Healthcare Corporation and operating under the name Envision Healthcare, is a leading physician-centric surgical center and physician services firm. The company operates in two business segments: ambulatory services and physician services. Ambulatory services acquires, develops and operates ambulatory surgery centers (ASCs) in partnerships with physicians. This segment operates more than 245 ASCs in 34 states and the District of Columbia, in partnership with approximately 2,000 physicians. The typical size of a single-specialty ASC is 3,000 to 6,000 square feet; and the size of a multi-specialty ASC is approximately 8,000 to 12,000 square feet. Each center has two or three operating/procedure rooms with areas for reception, preparation, recovery and administration. Each surgery center is specifically tailored to meet the needs of physician partners. Surgery centers perform an average of 7,200 procedures each year. The physician services segment provides outsourced physician services in multiple specialties to hospitals, ASCs and other healthcare facilities, primarily in the areas of anesthesiology, radiology, children's services and emergency medicine.

Employee benefits include medical, vision and dental coverage; a flexible spending account; a health savings account; life and AD&D insurance; short- and long-term disability; long-term care insurance; a 401(k); a wellness program; and employee discounts.

FINANCIAL DATA: *Note: Data for latest year may not have been available at press time.*

In U.S. $	2016	2015	2014	2013	2012	2011
Revenue	2,800,000,000	2,566,884,096	1,621,949,056	1,079,342,976	928,508,992	786,870,016
R&D Expense						
Operating Income						
Operating Margin %						
SGA Expense						
Net Income		162,947,008	53,701,000	72,703,000	62,563,000	49,997,000
Operating Cash Flow						
Capital Expenditure						
EBITDA						
Return on Assets %						
Return on Equity %						
Debt to Equity						

CONTACT INFORMATION:

Phone: 615 665-1283   Fax: 615 665-0755
Toll-Free: 800-945-2301
Address: 1A Burton Hills Blvd., Nashville, TN 37215 United States

SALARIES/BONUSES:

Top Exec. Salary: $ Bonus: $
Second Exec. Salary: $ Bonus: $

STOCK TICKER/OTHER:

Stock Ticker: Subsidiary   Exchange:
Employees: 10,500   Fiscal Year Ends: 12/31
Parent Company: Envision Healthcare Corporation

OTHER THOUGHTS:

Estimated Female Officers or Directors: 2
Hot Spot for Advancement for Women/Minorities: Y

AmTrust Financial Services Inc

NAIC Code: 524126

www.amtrustgroup.com

TYPES OF BUSINESS:

Specialty Property & Casualty Insurance
Underwrites Insurance Policies
Specialty Risk & Extended Warranty
Property and Casualty Insurance

BRANDS/DIVISIONS/AFFILIATES:

ANV Holding BV

CONTACTS: *Note: Officers with more than one job title may be intentionally listed here more than once.*

Max Caviet, CEO, Subsidiary
Barry Zyskind, CEO
Adam Karkowsky, CFO
Christopher Longo, Chief Information Officer
Michael Saxon, Executive VP, Divisional
Stephen Ungar, General Counsel
David Saks, Other Executive Officer

GROWTH PLANS/SPECIAL FEATURES:

AmTrust Financial Services, Inc. underwrites and provides property and casualty insurance in the U.S. and key European locations to niche customer groups that it believes are generally underserved within the broader insurance market. AmTrust manages its business through three primary segments: small commercial business, specialty risk and extended warranty, and specialty program. The small commercial business segment provides workers' compensation to small businesses that operate in low and medium hazard classes, such as restaurants, retail stores, schools, hospitality, light manufacturing, auto service, surety, lumber, community banks, artisan contractors, not-for-profits, physicians and other professional offices. Specialty risk and extended warranty provides custom designed coverages such as accidental damage plans and payment protection plans offered in connection with the sale of consumer and commercial goods in the U.S. and Europe. This division also offers certain niche property, casualty and specialty liability risks in the U.S. and Europe, including general liability, employers' liability and professional and medical liability. Specialty program offers workers' compensation, general liability, commercial auto liability, property coverage, excess and surplus lines programs and other specialty commercial property and casualty insurance to narrowly-defined, homogeneous groups of small and middle market companies. Policyholders in this segment include public entities, retail, wholesale, service operations, artisan contracting, trucking, light and medium manufacturing, habitational and professional employer organizations. In November 2016, the firm acquired ANV Holding BV from Ontario Teachers' Pension Plan Board for $203 million. ANV is a specialty insurance company that underwrites a variety of commercial property and casualty insurance products through its three Lloyd's syndicates and managing general underwriter.

FINANCIAL DATA: *Note: Data for latest year may not have been available at press time.*

In U.S. $	2016	2015	2014	2013	2012	2011
Revenue	5,450,456,000	4,664,340,000	4,084,331,000	2,697,895,000	1,865,156,000	1,357,757,000
R&D Expense						
Operating Income	500,051,000	551,478,000	475,133,000	318,331,000	208,940,000	175,912,000
Operating Margin %	9.17%	11.82%	11.63%	11.79%	11.20%	12.95%
SGA Expense		521,559,000				
Net Income	410,986,000	503,594,000	447,014,000	290,863,000	177,987,000	170,434,000
Operating Cash Flow	916,703,000	990,778,000	1,155,536,000	915,448,000	527,550,000	294,558,000
Capital Expenditure	117,047,000	167,510,000	77,172,000	39,586,000	27,388,000	68,989,000
EBITDA						
Return on Assets %	1.82%	3.04%	3.45%	3.07%	2.71%	3.45%
Return on Equity %	15.18%	22.65%	28.27%	23.14%	17.49%	21.21%
Debt to Equity	0.59	0.48	0.53	0.54	0.41	0.50

CONTACT INFORMATION:

Phone: 212 220-7120   Fax: 212 704-6288
Toll-Free:
Address: 59 Maiden Ln., 43/Fl, New York, NY 10038 United States

STOCK TICKER/OTHER:

Stock Ticker: AFSI   Exchange: NAS
Employees: 8,000   Fiscal Year Ends: 12/31
Parent Company:

SALARIES/BONUSES:

Top Exec. Salary: $550,000   Bonus: $1,176,959
Second Exec. Salary: $975,000   Bonus: $

OTHER THOUGHTS:

Estimated Female Officers or Directors: 1
Hot Spot for Advancement for Women/Minorities:

Sales, profits and employees may be estimates. Financial information, benefits and other data can change quickly and may vary from those stated here.

Anixter International Inc

www.anixter.com

NAIC Code: 423430

TYPES OF BUSINESS:

Wire & Cable Distribution
C Class Inventory Component Distribution
Connectivity Parts Distribution

BRANDS/DIVISIONS/AFFILIATES:

CONTACTS: Note: Officers with more than one job title may be intentionally listed here more than once.

Robert Eck, CEO
Theodore Dosch, CFO
Samuel Zell, Chairman of the Board
William Standish, Executive VP, Divisional
William Galvin, Executive VP, Divisional
Justin Choi, Executive VP

GROWTH PLANS/SPECIAL FEATURES:

Anixter International, Inc. is a leading global distributor of data, voice, video and security network communication products and one of the largest North American distributors of specialty wire and cable products. With approximately 319 sales and warehouse locations in over 50 countries, the firm sells over 450,000 products, such as transmission media (copper and fiber optic cable) and connectivity, support, supply and security surveillance products as well as C-class inventory components (small parts used in manufacturing such as nuts and bolts) to original equipment manufacturers (OEMs). These products, used to connect personal computers, peripheral equipment, mainframe equipment, security equipment and various networks to each other, are incorporated into enterprise networks, physical security networks, central switching offices, web hosting sites and remote transmission sites. In addition, Anixter provides industrial wire and cable products, including electrical and electronic wire and cable, control and instrumentation cable and coaxial cable, used in a wide variety of maintenance, repair and construction-related applications. In 2015, the firm acquired the power solutions segment of HD Supply, Inc. for $825 million; and sold its OEM supply/fasteners business to American Industrial Partners for $380 million. In October 2016, it announced plans to open a new flagship facility in Houston, Texas, scheduled to open in early 2017.

FINANCIAL DATA: Note: Data for latest year may not have been available at press time.

In U.S. $	2016	2015	2014	2013	2012	2011
Revenue	7,622,800,000	6,190,500,000	6,445,500,000	6,226,500,000	6,253,100,000	6,146,900,000
R&D Expense						
Operating Income	285,300,000	267,800,000	360,900,000	354,800,000	282,500,000	362,800,000
Operating Margin %	3.74%	4.32%	5.59%	5.69%	4.51%	5.90%
SGA Expense	1,262,700,000	1,072,700,000	1,107,500,000	1,066,200,000	1,077,700,000	1,044,600,000
Net Income	120,500,000	127,600,000	194,800,000	200,500,000	124,800,000	188,200,000
Operating Cash Flow	278,800,000	91,900,000	104,200,000	334,500,000	141,600,000	144,400,000
Capital Expenditure	32,600,000	28,600,000	40,300,000	32,200,000	34,200,000	26,400,000
EBITDA	341,700,000	295,900,000	378,600,000	373,500,000	301,400,000	387,100,000
Return on Assets %	2.92%	3.30%	6.04%	6.73%	4.07%	6.30%
Return on Equity %	9.75%	11.03%	18.03%	20.07%	12.66%	18.70%
Debt to Equity	1.06	1.39	1.06	0.81	1.01	0.80

CONTACT INFORMATION:

Phone: 224-521-8000   Fax: 224-521-8100
Toll-Free: 800-323-8167
Address: 2301 Patriot Blvd., Glenview, IL 60026 United States

STOCK TICKER/OTHER:

Stock Ticker: AXE
Employees: 8,900
Parent Company:

Exchange: NYS
Fiscal Year Ends: 12/31

SALARIES/BONUSES:

Top Exec. Salary: $980,000   Bonus: $
Second Exec. Salary: Bonus: $
$595,000

OTHER THOUGHTS:

Estimated Female Officers or Directors: 2
Hot Spot for Advancement for Women/Minorities: Y

Anthem Inc

NAIC Code: 524114

www.antheminc.com

TYPES OF BUSINESS:

Health Insurance
Health Maintenance Organizations (HMOs)
Point-of-Service Plans
Dental and Vision Plans
Plan Management (ASO) for Self-Insured Organizations
Prescription Plans
Wellness Programs
Medicare Administrative Services

BRANDS/DIVISIONS/AFFILIATES:

Blue Cross and Blue Shield Association
HealthLink
UniCare
CareMore Health Groups Inc
Blue Cross of California
Anthem Blue Cross Blue Shield
Blue Cross Blue Shield of Georgia
Amerigroup Corporation

CONTACTS: Note: Officers with more than one job title may be intentionally listed here more than once.

Joseph Swedish, CEO
John Gallina, CFO
Ronald Penczek, Chief Accounting Officer
Gloria McCarthy, Chief Administrative Officer
Thomas Zielinski, Executive VP
Jose Tomas, Executive VP
Craig Samitt, Executive VP
Brian Griffin, Executive VP
Peter Haytaian, President, Divisional

GROWTH PLANS/SPECIAL FEATURES:

Anthem, Inc. is a health benefits company, serving roughly 39.9 million medical members through its subsidiaries. The firm is an independent licensee of the Blue Cross and Blue Shield Association, an association of independent health benefit plans, and also serves customers throughout the country under the HealthLink and UniCare brands. Anthem serves certain Arizona, California, Nevada, New York and Virginia markets through subsidiary CareMore Health Group, Inc. The firm offers network-based managed care plans to the large and small employer, individual, Medicaid and senior markets. The managed care plans include preferred provider organizations (PPO), health maintenance organizations (HMO), point-of-service (POS) plans, traditional indemnity plans and other hybrid plans including consumer-driven health plans, hospital-only and limited benefit products. In addition, Anthem provides managed care services to self-insured organizations, including claims processing, underwriting, stop loss insurance, actuarial services, provider network access, medical cost management and other administrative services. The company also provides specialty and other products and services, including life and disability insurance benefits; dental, vision and behavioral health benefit services; long-term care insurance; and flexible spending accounts. Subsidiaries include Blue Cross of California, Anthem Blue Cross Blue Shield and Blue Cross Blue Shield of Georgia as well as non-Blue Cross subsidiaries such as HealthLink, Amerigroup Corporation and HealthCore, Inc. In 2015, Anthem agreed to be acquired by Cigna Corporation in a deal worth $48 billion. In 2016, the U.S. Justice Department challenged the merger, and a District Court blocked the merger in February 2017 on anti-competitive grounds, causing Cigna to call off the agreement.

The firm offers employees tuition assistance; a 401(k) plan; stock purchase plan; paid time off; long-term care coverage; adoption assistance; an employee assistance program; life insurance; medical, dental and vision coverage; and flexible spending accounts.

FINANCIAL DATA: Note: Data for latest year may not have been available at press time.

In U.S. $	2016	2015	2014	2013	2012	2011
Revenue	84,863,000,000	79,156,500,000	73,874,100,000	71,023,500,000	61,711,700,000	60,710,700,000
R&D Expense						
Operating Income	4,555,400,000	4,631,000,000	4,368,100,000	3,840,200,000	3,865,500,000	3,957,900,000
Operating Margin %	5.36%	5.85%	5.91%	5.40%	6.26%	6.51%
SGA Expense	12,557,900,000	12,534,800,000	11,748,400,000	9,952,900,000	8,738,300,000	8,435,600,000
Net Income	2,469,800,000	2,560,000,000	2,569,700,000	2,489,700,000	2,655,500,000	2,646,700,000
Operating Cash Flow	3,204,500,000	4,116,000,000	3,369,300,000	3,052,300,000	2,744,600,000	3,374,400,000
Capital Expenditure	583,600,000	638,200,000	714,600,000	646,500,000	544,900,000	519,500,000
EBITDA						
Return on Assets %	3.89%	4.13%	4.22%	4.20%	4.78%	5.18%
Return on Equity %	10.25%	10.82%	10.48%	10.25%	11.27%	11.23%
Debt to Equity	0.57	0.66	0.58	0.54	0.59	0.36

CONTACT INFORMATION:

Phone: 317 488-6000   Fax:
Toll-Free:
Address: 120 Monument Cir., Indianapolis, IN 46204 United States

STOCK TICKER/OTHER:

Stock Ticker: ANTM   Exchange: NYS
Employees: 53,000   Fiscal Year Ends: 12/31
Parent Company:

SALARIES/BONUSES:

Top Exec. Salary: $1,451,923   Bonus: $
Second Exec. Salary: Bonus: $
$740,371

OTHER THOUGHTS:

Estimated Female Officers or Directors: 1
Hot Spot for Advancement for Women/Minorities: Y

AO Smith Corporation

www.aosmith.com

NAIC Code: 335228

TYPES OF BUSINESS:

Water Heaters
Water Boilers
Solar Water Heating Systems

BRANDS/DIVISIONS/AFFILIATES:

AO Smith
American
GSW
Reliance
State
Takagi
US Craftmaster
Aquasana

CONTACTS: *Note: Officers with more than one job title may be intentionally listed here more than once.*

William Vallett, CEO, Subsidiary
Ajita Rajendra, CEO
John Kita, CFO
Daniel Kempken, Chief Accounting Officer
Peter Martineau, Chief Information Officer
Robert Heideman, Chief Technology Officer
James Stern, Executive VP
Kevin Wheeler, General Manager, Geographical
Wei Ding, General Manager, Subsidiary
Paul Dana, President, Subsidiary
Wilfridus Brouwer, President, Subsidiary
Charles Lauber, Senior VP, Divisional
Mark Petrarca, Senior VP, Divisional

GROWTH PLANS/SPECIAL FEATURES:

A. O. Smith Corporation is a manufacturer of water heating equipment serving a diverse mix of residential, commercial and industrial end markets. The firm markets its products under the brand name AO Smith, American, GSW, John Wood, Reliance, State, Takagi, U.S. Craftmaster, Lochinvar and Aquasana. The company operates in two segments: North America and rest of the world. The North America segment markets products mainly in the U.S. In addition, it manufactures and markets specialty commercial condensing and non-condensing boilers and water system tanks. The rest of the world segment caters to China, Europe and India. Moreover, it manufactures and markets water treatment products, primarily for Asia. Both segments manufacture and market comprehensive lines of residential gas, gas tankless and electric water heaters. The firm's residential and commercial water heaters come in sizes ranging from two and a half-gallon (point-of-use) models to 12,000 gallon products with varying efficiency ranges. It offers electric, natural gas and liquid propane models as well as solar tank units. Typical applications include restaurants, hotels and motels, laundries, car washes and small businesses. The company's commercial and residential boilers come in capacities ranging from 40,000 British Thermal Units (BTUs) to 6.0 million BTUs. The boilers are used in hospitals, schools, hotels and other large commercial buildings. Other products include expansion tanks, commercial solar water heating systems, swimming pool and spa heaters and related products and parts. In 2016, the firm acquired Austin-based water filtration company, Aquasana, from L'Catterton for $87 million. In May 2017, A. O. Smith announced plans to build a new corporate research facility near its Milwaukee headquarters. The 42,700-square-foot technology center will focus on advanced research and development in the areas of potable and hydronic water heating, water treatment and air purification.

FINANCIAL DATA: *Note: Data for latest year may not have been available at press time.*

In U.S. $	2016	2015	2014	2013	2012	2011
Revenue	2,685,900,000	2,536,500,000	2,356,000,000	2,153,800,000	1,939,300,000	1,710,500,000
R&D Expense						
Operating Income	460,400,000	399,100,000	287,200,000	249,300,000	205,400,000	151,000,000
Operating Margin %	17.14%	15.73%	12.19%	11.57%	10.59%	8.82%
SGA Expense	658,900,000	610,700,000	572,100,000	524,500,000	450,500,000	372,800,000
Net Income	326,500,000	282,900,000	207,800,000	169,700,000	158,700,000	305,700,000
Operating Cash Flow	446,600,000	344,400,000	263,900,000	279,600,000	143,800,000	58,700,000
Capital Expenditure	80,700,000	72,700,000	86,100,000	97,700,000	69,900,000	53,500,000
EBITDA	534,900,000	472,900,000	352,200,000	301,800,000	297,600,000	217,800,000
Return on Assets %	11.79%	10.96%	8.46%	7.28%	6.87%	13.70%
Return on Equity %	22.07%	20.03%	15.33%	13.45%	13.92%	31.07%
Debt to Equity	0.20	0.16	0.15	0.13	0.18	0.40

CONTACT INFORMATION:

Phone: 414 359-4000   Fax:
Toll-Free:
Address: 11270 W. Park Place, Milwaukee, WI 53224-9508 United States

STOCK TICKER/OTHER:

Stock Ticker: AOS
Employees: 15,500
Parent Company:

Exchange: NYS
Fiscal Year Ends: 12/31

SALARIES/BONUSES:

Top Exec. Salary: $1,000,000   Bonus: $
Second Exec. Salary: $533,000   Bonus: $

OTHER THOUGHTS:

Estimated Female Officers or Directors:
Hot Spot for Advancement for Women/Minorities:

Sales, profits and employees may be estimates. Financial information, benefits and other data can change quickly and may vary from those stated here.

Aon Hewitt
NAIC Code: 541612

www.aon.com/human-capital-consulting

TYPES OF BUSINESS:
Human Resources Consulting
Human Resources Outsourcing
Employee Benefits Consulting

BRANDS/DIVISIONS/AFFILIATES:
Aon Corporation
Kloud
Modern Survey

CONTACTS: *Note: Officers with more than one job title may be intentionally listed here more than once.*
Kristi Savacool, CEO
Katie Rooney, CFO

GROWTH PLANS/SPECIAL FEATURES:
Aon Hewitt is the human capital consulting and outsourcing division of Aon Corporation. The company's primary goal is to reduce people-related management issues through assessment, succession planning and organizational design. With operations in the U.S., Canada, the U.K., Europe, South Africa, Latin America and the Asia Pacific, Aon Hewitt provides companies with consulting services, benefit administration and human resource business process outsourcing (BPO). Through its consulting services, Aon Hewitt advises large multi-national and mid-size companies on developing strategies to attract and retain talent, such as incentive programs, health insurance and compensation packages; manages personal risk, such as investment initiatives; and implements effective organizational structures. The benefits administration segment advises employers regarding the structure, funding and administration of employee benefit programs, which attract, retain and motivate employees. Human resource BPO services provides clients with assistance in process improvement and design, leadership, organization and human capital development and change management. The firm matches the specific workforce and business needs of a given company with an appropriate business strategy in order to make the most efficient and effective working environment possible. The firm handles client companies of all types and needs, from global corporations and organizations to small businesses operating in a single county. In March 2017, the company launched Fruition, a new investment and governance solution aimed at small pension schemes.

FINANCIAL DATA: *Note: Data for latest year may not have been available at press time.*

In U.S. $	2016	2015	2014	2013	2012	2011
Revenue	5,845,000,000	4,820,000,000	4,264,000,000	4,057,000,000	3,925,000,000	3,501,000,000
R&D Expense						
Operating Income						
Operating Margin %						
SGA Expense						
Net Income			485,000,000	318,000,000		
Operating Cash Flow						
Capital Expenditure						
EBITDA						
Return on Assets %						
Return on Equity %						
Debt to Equity						

CONTACT INFORMATION:
Phone: 847-295-5000   Fax:
Toll-Free:
Address: 4 Overlook Point, Chicago, IL 60069-4302 United States

STOCK TICKER/OTHER:
Stock Ticker: Subsidiary   Exchange:
Employees: 29,000   Fiscal Year Ends: 12/31
Parent Company: Aon Corporation

SALARIES/BONUSES:
Top Exec. Salary: $ Bonus: $
Second Exec. Salary: $ Bonus: $

OTHER THOUGHTS:
Estimated Female Officers or Directors: 1
Hot Spot for Advancement for Women/Minorities: Y

APC by Schneider Electric

www.apc.com

NAIC Code: 335911

TYPES OF BUSINESS:

Back-Up Power Supplies
Power Protection & Management Products
Consulting Services
PC Accessories
Power Management Software
Fuel Cell-Based Power Backup

BRANDS/DIVISIONS/AFFILIATES:

Schneider Electric SA
Fuel Cell Extended Run
InfraStruXure

CONTACTS: Note: Officers with more than one job title may be intentionally listed here more than once.

Jean-Pascal Tricoire, CEO
Luc Remont, Exec.VP-Int'l Operations
Daniel Doimo, Pres.
Emmanuel Babeau, Deputy CEO-Finance
Chris Leong, Exec. VP-Mktg.
Olivier Blum, VP-Human Resources
Neil Rasmussen, Sr. VP-Innovation
Herve Coureil, Exec. VP-IT
Randy Amon, Sr. VP-Customer Care, Quality & Process
Leanne Cunnold, Sr. VP-Bus. Dev. & Strategy
Rob McKernan, Pres., Americas
Mike Maiello, Sr. VP-Home & Bus. Networks
Philippe Arsonneau, Pres., Asia Pacific & Japan
Chenhong Huang, Sr. VP-Greater China
Ed Machala, Sr. VP-Supply Chain, Purchasing & Manufacturing

GROWTH PLANS/SPECIAL FEATURES:

APC by Schneider Electric designs, develops, manufactures and markets power protection and management solutions for computer, communications and electronic applications worldwide. APC stands for American power conversion. The company's products include uninterruptible power supply (UPS) products, electrical surge protection devices, power distribution products, precision cooling equipment, power management software and accessories, racks and enclosures and various desktop and notebook personal computer accessories. These products are primarily used with sensitive electronic devices, which rely on electric utility power, such as home electronics, PCs, high-performance computer workstations, servers, networking equipment, communications equipment, internet equipment, data centers, mainframe computers and facilities. APC's UPS products regulate the flow of utility power to the protected equipment and provide seamless back-up power during power interruptions. Back-up power lasts for enough time to continue computer operations, conduct an orderly shutdown, preserve data, work through short power outages or, in some cases, continue operating for several hours or longer. In addition, the firm's Fuel Cell Extended Run (FCXR) product provides hydrogen-based power backup for its proprietary InfraStruXure power, cooling, environmental monitoring and management data center for modular & mobile configurations. The company's security and environmental appliances and accessories protect against environmental or human threats and monitor valuable systems with sensors, cameras and accessories. APC's precision cooling equipment regulates temperature and humidity. Last, the company provides power management software, consulting services and notebook and PC accessories. Its data center software business is responsible for software creation and development, sales, service and marketing programs. APC is a subsidiary of Schneider Electric SA.

The firm offers employees comprehensive health and dental coverage, short- and long-term disability, flexible spending accounts, life insurance, tuition assistance, a relocation program, leaves of absence, holidays, an employee share plan and a 401(k) plan.

FINANCIAL DATA: Note: Data for latest year may not have been available at press time.

In U.S. $	2016	2015	2014	2013	2012	2011
Revenue	4,800,000,000	4,750,000,000	4,600,000,000	4,450,000,000	4,300,000,000	4,200,000,000
R&D Expense						
Operating Income						
Operating Margin %						
SGA Expense						
Net Income						
Operating Cash Flow						
Capital Expenditure						
EBITDA						
Return on Assets %						
Return on Equity %						
Debt to Equity						

CONTACT INFORMATION:

Phone: 401-789-2208   Fax: 401-789-3710
Toll-Free: 800-788-2208
Address: 132 Fairgrounds Rd., West Kingston, RI 02892 United States

STOCK TICKER/OTHER:

Stock Ticker: Subsidiary   Exchange:
Employees: 7,580   Fiscal Year Ends: 12/31
Parent Company: Schneider Electric SA

SALARIES/BONUSES:

Top Exec. Salary: $ Bonus: $
Second Exec. Salary: $ Bonus: $

OTHER THOUGHTS:

Estimated Female Officers or Directors: 2
Hot Spot for Advancement for Women/Minorities:

Apple Inc

NAIC Code: 334220

TYPES OF BUSINESS:

Electronics Design and Manufacturing
Software
Computers and Tablets
Retail Stores
Smartphones
Online Music Store
Apps Store
Home Entertainment Software & Systems

BRANDS/DIVISIONS/AFFILIATES:

iPhone
iPad
iPod
Apple Watch
Apple TV
watchOS
tvOS
Clips

CONTACTS: Note: Officers with more than one job title may be intentionally listed here more than once.

Timothy Cook, CEO
Luca Maestri, CFO
Arthur Levinson, Chairman of the Board
Chris Kondo, Chief Accounting Officer
Jeffery Williams, COO
D. Sewell, General Counsel
Philip Schiller, Senior VP, Divisional
Craig Federighi, Senior VP, Divisional
Angela Ahrendts, Senior VP, Divisional
Johny Srouji, Senior VP, Divisional
Eduardo Cue, Senior VP, Divisional
Daniel Riccio, Senior VP, Divisional

GROWTH PLANS/SPECIAL FEATURES:

Apple, Inc. designs, manufactures and markets personal computers, portable digital music players and mobile communication devices and sells a variety of related software, services, peripherals and networking applications. The company's products and services include iPhone, iPad, Mac, iPod, Apple Watch, Apple TV, a portfolio of consumer and professional software applications, the iOS, OS X and watchOS operating systems, iCloud, Apple Pay and a variety of accessory, service and support offerings. iOS is the company's multi-touch operating system that serves the foundation for iOS devices. OS X is the firm's Mac operating system, built on an open-source UNIX-based foundation and provides an intuitive and integrated computer experience. watchOS is Apple's operating system for Apple Watch. iCloud provides cloud storage and syncing for a range of data, including email, contacts, calendars, photos and documents. Apple Pay is a mobile payment and digital wallet service. In addition, tvOS is the firm's operating system for Apple TV; and Clips is an app that allows iPad and iPhone users to make and edit short videos for sharing on social media networks. Peripheral products are sold directly to end-users through its retail and online stores and include printers, storage devices, computer memory, digital video and still camera and other computing products and supplies. Apple's retail stores have been a tremendous success. The company sells and delivers digital content and applications through the iTunes Store, App Store, iBookstore, tvOS, Apple TV App Store and Mac App Store. One company goal is to double revenues from digital services, such as the App Store and Apple Music, from $25 billion in 2016 to $50 billion in 2020.

Apple employee benefits include health, life, long-term care and disability insurance; an employee stock purchase and 401(k) plans; paid vacations/holidays; and employee discounts, tuition assistance, counseling services and other perks.

FINANCIAL DATA: Note: Data for latest year may not have been available at press time.

In U.S. $	2016	2015	2014	2013	2012	2011
Revenue	215,639,000,000	233,715,000,000	182,795,000,000	170,910,000,000	156,508,000,000	108,249,000,000
R&D Expense	10,045,000,000	8,067,000,000	6,041,000,000	4,475,000,000	3,381,000,000	2,429,000,000
Operating Income	60,024,000,000	71,230,000,000	52,503,000,000	48,999,000,000	55,241,000,000	33,790,000,000
Operating Margin %	27.83%	30.47%	28.72%	28.66%	35.29%	31.21%
SGA Expense	14,194,000,000	14,329,000,000	11,993,000,000	10,830,000,000	10,040,000,000	7,599,000,000
Net Income	45,687,000,000	53,394,000,000	39,510,000,000	37,037,000,000	41,733,000,000	25,922,000,000
Operating Cash Flow	65,824,000,000	81,266,000,000	59,713,000,000	53,666,000,000	50,856,000,000	37,529,000,000
Capital Expenditure	13,548,000,000	11,488,000,000	9,813,000,000	9,076,000,000	9,402,000,000	7,452,000,000
EBITDA	73,333,000,000	84,505,000,000	61,813,000,000	57,048,000,000	58,518,000,000	35,604,000,000
Return on Assets %	14.92%	20.44%	18.00%	19.33%	28.54%	27.06%
Return on Equity %	36.90%	46.24%	33.61%	30.63%	42.84%	41.67%
Debt to Equity	0.58	0.44	0.25	0.13		

CONTACT INFORMATION:

Phone: 408 996-1010   Fax: 408 974-2483
Toll-Free: 800-692-7753
Address: 1 Infinite Loop, Cupertino, CA 95014 United States

STOCK TICKER/OTHER:

Stock Ticker: AAPL   Exchange: NAS
Employees: 116,000   Fiscal Year Ends: 09/30
Parent Company:

SALARIES/BONUSES:

Top Exec. Salary: $3,000,000   Bonus: $
Second Exec. Salary: Bonus: $
$1,000,000

OTHER THOUGHTS:

Estimated Female Officers or Directors:
Hot Spot for Advancement for Women/Minorities:

Applied Materials Inc

www.appliedmaterials.com

NAIC Code: 333242

TYPES OF BUSINESS:

Semiconductor Manufacturing Equipment
LCD Display Technology Equipment
Automation Software
Energy Generation & Conversion Technologies

BRANDS/DIVISIONS/AFFILIATES:

CONTACTS: Note: Officers with more than one job title may be intentionally listed here more than once.

Gary Dickerson, CEO
Robert Halliday, CFO
James Morgan, Chairman Emeritus
Omkaram Nalamasu, Chief Technology Officer
Thomas Larkins, General Counsel
Ali Salehpour, General Manager, Divisional
Ginetto Addiego, Senior VP, Divisional
Charles Read, Vice President

GROWTH PLANS/SPECIAL FEATURES:

Applied Materials, Inc. (AMI), a global leader in the semiconductor industry, provides manufacturing equipment, services and software to the global semiconductor, flat panel display, solar photovoltaic (PV) and related industries. AMI operates in three segments: semiconductor systems, applied global services and display and adjacent markets. The semiconductor systems division, accounting for 64% of the firm's 2016 revenue, develops, manufactures and sells a range of manufacturing equipment used to fabricate semiconductor chips or integrated circuits. Technologies found in this segment are transistor and interconnect, patterning and packaging, and imaging and process control. The applied global services segment (24%) provides integrated solutions to optimize equipment and fab performance and productivity, including spares, upgrades, services, remanufactured earlier generation equipment and factory automation software for semiconductor, display and other products. Its services encompass the following components: fabrication services, automation systems and software, sub-fabrication systems and equipment, parts programs and abatement control systems. The display and adjacent market segment (11%) is comprised of products for manufacturing liquid crystal displays (LCDs), organic light-emitting diodes (OLEDs), and other display technologies for TVs, personal computers (PCs), tablets, smart phones, and other consumer-oriented devices as well as equipment for flexible substrates. The segment offers a variety of technologies and products, including: array testing, defect review, chemical vapor deposition, physical vapor deposition and flexible technologies.

The company offers employees medical, life, AD&D, disability and business travel accident insurance; flexible spending accounts; an employee assistance program; health appraisals; a 401(k) plan; a stock purchase plan; and credit union membership.

FINANCIAL DATA: Note: Data for latest year may not have been available at press time.

In U.S. $	2016	2015	2014	2013	2012	2011
Revenue	10,825,000,000	9,659,000,000	9,072,000,000	7,509,000,000	8,719,000,000	10,517,000,000
R&D Expense	1,540,000,000	1,451,000,000	1,428,000,000	1,320,000,000	1,237,000,000	1,118,000,000
Operating Income	2,152,000,000	1,693,000,000	1,520,000,000	432,000,000	411,000,000	2,398,000,000
Operating Margin %	19.87%	17.52%	16.75%	5.75%	4.71%	22.80%
SGA Expense	819,000,000	883,000,000	890,000,000	902,000,000	1,076,000,000	901,000,000
Net Income	1,721,000,000	1,377,000,000	1,072,000,000	256,000,000	109,000,000	1,926,000,000
Operating Cash Flow	2,466,000,000	1,163,000,000	1,800,000,000	623,000,000	1,851,000,000	2,426,000,000
Capital Expenditure	253,000,000	215,000,000	241,000,000	197,000,000	162,000,000	209,000,000
EBITDA	2,557,000,000	2,072,000,000	1,918,000,000	855,000,000	833,000,000	2,683,000,000
Return on Assets %	11.51%	9.66%	8.50%	2.12%	.83%	15.52%
Return on Equity %	23.20%	17.78%	14.33%	3.57%	1.35%	23.57%
Debt to Equity	0.43	0.43	0.24	0.27	0.26	0.22

CONTACT INFORMATION:

Phone: 408 727-5555   Fax: 408 727-9943
Toll-Free:
Address: 3050 Bowers Ave., Santa Clara, CA 95052 United States

STOCK TICKER/OTHER:

Stock Ticker: AMAT
Employees: 16,700
Parent Company:

Exchange: NAS
Fiscal Year Ends: 10/31

SALARIES/BONUSES:

Top Exec. Salary: $637,019   Bonus: $2,203,125
Second Exec. Salary: $560,577   Bonus: $1,732,500

OTHER THOUGHTS:

Estimated Female Officers or Directors: 2
Hot Spot for Advancement for Women/Minorities: Y

Aramark

NAIC Code: 722310

www.aramark.com

TYPES OF BUSINESS:

Food Service Contractor
Facilities Management
Uniforms & Career Apparel Rental
Parks & Resorts Concessions & Facilities
Health Care Support Services
Apparel Manufacturing
Clinical Equipment Maintenance

BRANDS/DIVISIONS/AFFILIATES:

Goldman Sachs Capital Partners
CCMP Capital Advisors
JP Morgan Partners
Thomas H Lee Partners LP
Warburg Pincus LLC

CONTACTS: Note: Officers with more than one job title may be intentionally listed here more than once.

Eric Foss, CEO
Stephen Bramlage, CFO
Brian Pressler, Chief Accounting Officer
Lynn McKee, Executive VP, Divisional
Stephen Reynolds, Executive VP
Harrald Kroeker, Senior VP, Divisional
James Tarangelo, Treasurer

GROWTH PLANS/SPECIAL FEATURES:

Aramark is a global provider of food, facilities and uniform services. Serving 19 countries, the company's core market is North America (U.S. and Canada). Aramark operates its business in three segments: food and support services North America (FSS North America), food and support services international (FSS international) and uniform and career apparel (uniform). FSS North America generates 70% of total sales, and FSS international generates 19%. Both serve clients in four principal sectors: education, including colleges, universities, public school districts and private schools; healthcare, including hospitals and nursing homes; business/industry, including office parks/buildings, manufacturing plants, corporate cafeterias, mining operations and oil/gas drilling operations; and sports, leisure and corrections, including professional/collegiate stadiums and arenas, concert venues, national/state parks, convention/civic centers and correctional facilities. To these sectors, Aramark offers dining services, catering, food service management, facilities management, nutrition services, convenience stores, custodial services, grounds keeping, energy management, vending, drinking water filtration, restaurants, clinical equipment maintenance, environmental services, laundry/linen distribution, housekeeping management and much more. The uniform segment provides uniforms and other garments and work clothes and ancillary items such as mats and shop towels in the U.S., Puerto Rico, Canada and Japan. Its clients use uniforms for a variety of reasons, including establishing corporate identity, projecting a professional image and for protection purposes. This division operates more than 2,600 routes, delivering uniforms to its various clients, and generates 11% of total sales. Aramark is owned by a group of investors affiliated with Goldman Sachs Capital Partners, CCMP Capital Advisors, J.P. Morgan Partners, Thomas H. Lee Partners LP and Warburg Pincus, LLC, as well as approximately 250 senior management personnel.

The company offers its employees medical, dental and vision insurance; a pension plan; life and disability insurance; and an employee assistance plan.

FINANCIAL DATA: Note: Data for latest year may not have been available at press time.

In U.S. $	2016	2015	2014	2013	2012	2011
Revenue	14,415,830,000	14,329,140,000	14,832,910,000	13,945,660,000	13,505,430,000	13,082,380,000
R&D Expense						
Operating Income	746,314,000	627,938,000	564,563,000	514,474,000	581,775,000	547,089,000
Operating Margin %	5.17%	4.38%	3.80%	3.68%	4.30%	4.18%
SGA Expense	283,342,000	316,740,000	382,851,000	227,902,000	203,019,000	187,992,000
Net Income	287,806,000	235,946,000	148,956,000	69,356,000	103,551,000	83,846,000
Operating Cash Flow	806,640,000	683,036,000	398,159,000	695,907,000	691,761,000	303,608,000
Capital Expenditure	512,532,000	527,618,000	566,110,000	414,951,000	497,874,000	455,859,000
EBITDA	1,241,862,000	1,132,290,000	1,085,700,000	1,058,390,000	1,113,264,000	1,078,399,000
Return on Assets %	2.76%	2.28%	1.43%	.66%	.98%	
Return on Equity %	14.23%	13.10%	11.36%	7.55%	11.09%	
Debt to Equity	2.41	2.76	3.11	6.37	6.39	

CONTACT INFORMATION:

Phone: 215-238-3000   Fax: 215-238-3333
Toll-Free: 800-272-6275
Address: 1101 Market St., Aramark Tower, Philadelphia, PA 19107 United States

STOCK TICKER/OTHER:

Stock Ticker: ARMK
Employees: 266,500
Parent Company:

Exchange: NYS
Fiscal Year Ends: 09/30

SALARIES/BONUSES:

Top Exec. Salary: $1,700,000   Bonus: $
Second Exec. Salary: $679,804   Bonus: $

OTHER THOUGHTS:

Estimated Female Officers or Directors: 1
Hot Spot for Advancement for Women/Minorities:

Sales, profits and employees may be estimates. Financial information, benefits and other data can change quickly and may vary from those stated here.

ARRIS Group Inc

www.arrisi.com

NAIC Code: 334210

TYPES OF BUSINESS:

Communications Equipment-Cable Systems
Optical & Radio Frequency Transmission Equipment
Internet Access Products
Support & Testing Products
Motorola Home Business

BRANDS/DIVISIONS/AFFILIATES:

ActiveVideo
Pace plc
DOCSIS 3.1 SURFboard SB8200
Ruckus Wireless
ICX Switch

CONTACTS: Note: Officers with more than one job title may be intentionally listed here more than once.

David Potts, CFO
Robert Stanzione, Chairman of the Board
Philip Baldock, Chief Information Officer
Bruce McClelland, Director
Ronald Coppock, Executive VP, Divisional
Stephen McCaffery, Managing Director, Divisional
Daniel Whalen, President, Divisional
Lawrence Robinson, President, Divisional
Timothy OLoughlin, President, Divisional
Victoria Brewster, Senior VP, Divisional
James Brennan, Senior VP, Divisional
Patrick Macken, Senior VP

GROWTH PLANS/SPECIAL FEATURES:

ARRIS Group, Inc. is a global media entertainment and data communications solutions provider. The company is a leading developer, manufacturer and supplier of interactive set-top boxes, end-to-end digital video and Internet protocol television distribution systems, broadband access infrastructure platforms and data and voice customer premises equipment. ARRIS operates through two segments: customer premises equipment (CPE) and network & cloud (N&C). The CPE segment includes set-top boxes, devices installed at the subscriber's television set and connected to the service provider network to decode secure digital video signals; gateways, devices that connect the service provider network and deliver video, voice and data services throughout the subscriber's home; DSL and cable modems, which connect to the cable network to receive and transmit digital information; and embedded multimedia terminal adapters and voice/data modems, equipment that provides telephone service. The N&C segment includes cable operator head-end equipment that communicates with cable modems to control the flow of data; video infrastructure that processes and packages video content for delivery over the service provider; access and transport equipment in the ground and on transmission poles between service providers and subscribers' premises; and technical support and system integration offerings. New products are developed in the firm's R&D laboratories located in Oregon, Pennsylvania, Washington, Illinois, California, Georgia, Connecticut and Massachusetts as well as India, Argentina, Ireland, Sweden, China and Israel. In 2016, ARRIS acquired Pace plc, a developer of digital TV set-top box technology. In February 2017, the firm agreed to acquire the Ruckus Wireless and ICX Switch businesses from Brocade Communication Systems Inc. Additionally, in February 2017, the firm launched its flagship DOCSIS 3.1 SURFboard SB8200 cable modem, which delivers the fastest broadband speeds available.

FINANCIAL DATA: Note: Data for latest year may not have been available at press time.

In U.S. $	2016	2015	2014	2013	2012	2011
Revenue	6,829,118,000	4,798,332,000	5,322,921,000	3,620,902,000	1,353,663,000	1,088,685,000
R&D Expense	584,909,000	534,168,000	556,575,000	425,825,000	170,706,000	146,519,000
Operating Income	110,717,000	210,953,000	341,334,000	-18,013,000	87,271,000	-14,608,000
Operating Margin %	1.62%	4.39%	6.41%	- .49%	6.44%	-1.34%
SGA Expense	454,190,000	417,085,000	410,568,000	338,252,000	161,338,000	148,755,000
Net Income	18,100,000	92,181,000	327,211,000	-48,760,000	53,459,000	-17,662,000
Operating Cash Flow	362,495,000	343,872,000	459,281,000	570,846,000	84,401,000	113,153,000
Capital Expenditure	72,286,000	89,230,000	56,588,000	71,443,000	21,507,000	23,307,000
EBITDA	598,961,000	481,359,000	617,870,000	226,891,000	150,340,000	46,216,000
Return on Assets %	.29%	2.07%	7.53%	-1.70%	3.86%	-1.26%
Return on Equity %	.72%	5.29%	21.74%	-4.27%	5.69%	-1.83%
Debt to Equity	0.68	0.83	0.86	1.28		0.22

CONTACT INFORMATION:

Phone: 678 473-2000   Fax:
Toll-Free:
Address: 3871 Lakefield Dr., Suwanee, GA 30024 United States

STOCK TICKER/OTHER:

Stock Ticker: ARRS   Exchange: NAS
Employees: 7,020   Fiscal Year Ends: 12/31
Parent Company:

SALARIES/BONUSES:

Top Exec. Salary: $933,333   Bonus: $
Second Exec. Salary: Bonus: $
$653,340

OTHER THOUGHTS:

Estimated Female Officers or Directors: 2
Hot Spot for Advancement for Women/Minorities:

Arrow Electronics Inc

www.arrow.com

NAIC Code: 423430

TYPES OF BUSINESS:

Electronic Components-Distributor
Computer Products-Distributor
Technical Support Services
Supply Chain Services
Design Services
Materials Planning
Assembly Services
Inventory Management

BRANDS/DIVISIONS/AFFILIATES:

CONTACTS: Note: Officers with more than one job title may be intentionally listed here more than once.

Michael Long, CEO
Christopher Stansbury, CFO
Vincent Melvin, Chief Information Officer
Mary Morris, Other Executive Officer
Andy King, President, Divisional
Sean Kerins, President, Divisional
Gretchen Zech, Senior VP, Divisional
Gregory Tarpinian, Senior VP

GROWTH PLANS/SPECIAL FEATURES:

Arrow Electronics, Inc. is a global provider of products, services and solutions to industrial and commercial users of electronic components and enterprise computing software. The firm offers its clients products and solutions including materials planning, new product design services, programming and assembly services, inventory management, reverse logistics, electronics asset disposition (EAD) and a variety of online supply chain tools. Arrow serves as a supply channel partner for over 100,000 original equipment manufacturers (OEMs), contract manufacturers and commercial customers through a global network of over 300 sales facilities and 40 distribution centers located in 53 countries. Its operations are divided into two segments: global enterprise computing solutions (ECS), representing 38% of sales, and the global components business, 62%. The global ECS segment distributes enterprise IT products, such as servers, software and storage devices, as well as midrange computing products, services and solutions to value added retailers (VARs) in North America and Europe, the Middle East and Africa (EMEA). This segment also provides unified communications products and related services in North America. The global components business segment distributes electronics components and related products to customers in North and South America, EMEA and the Asia-Pacific. Its sales consist of semiconductors; passive, electro-mechanical and interconnect products, such as capacitors, resistors, potentiometers, power supplies, relays, switches and connectors; and computing, memory and other products. The company maintains an aggressive growth strategy based on acquiring competitors and complementary businesses and has completed 16 strategic acquisitions in the last three years.

FINANCIAL DATA: Note: Data for latest year may not have been available at press time.

In U.S. $	2016	2015	2014	2013	2012	2011
Revenue	23,825,260,000	23,282,020,000	22,768,670,000	21,357,290,000	20,405,130,000	21,390,260,000
R&D Expense						
Operating Income	858,539,000	824,482,000	762,257,000	693,500,000	804,123,000	908,843,000
Operating Margin %	3.60%	3.54%	3.34%	3.24%	3.94%	4.24%
SGA Expense	2,052,863,000	1,986,249,000	1,959,749,000	1,873,638,000	1,849,534,000	1,892,592,000
Net Income	522,750,000	497,726,000	498,045,000	399,420,000	506,332,000	598,810,000
Operating Cash Flow	355,806,000	655,079,000	673,301,000	450,691,000	675,033,000	120,883,000
Capital Expenditure	164,695,000	154,800,000	122,505,000	116,162,000	112,224,000	113,941,000
EBITDA	1,017,734,000	980,236,000	918,305,000	824,641,000	919,473,000	1,019,254,000
Return on Assets %	3.83%	3.90%	4.06%	3.49%	4.91%	6.16%
Return on Equity %	12.21%	11.99%	11.95%	9.78%	13.23%	17.30%
Debt to Equity	0.61	0.55	0.49	0.53	0.39	0.52

CONTACT INFORMATION:

Phone: 300 824-4000   Fax:
Toll-Free:
Address: 9201 E. Dry Creek Rd., Centennial, CO 80112 United States

STOCK TICKER/OTHER:

Stock Ticker: ARW   Exchange: NYS
Employees: 18,700   Fiscal Year Ends: 12/31
Parent Company:

SALARIES/BONUSES:

Top Exec. Salary: $1,150,000   Bonus: $
Second Exec. Salary: Bonus: $
$700,000

OTHER THOUGHTS:

Estimated Female Officers or Directors: 4
Hot Spot for Advancement for Women/Minorities: Y

Arthur J Gallagher & Co

NAIC Code: 524210

www.ajg.com

TYPES OF BUSINESS:

Insurance Brokerage & Management
Risk Management Services
Employee Benefit Services
Investment Operations
Claims Management
Information Management
Insurance Software
Reinsurance

BRANDS/DIVISIONS/AFFILIATES:

CONTACTS: Note: Officers with more than one job title may be intentionally listed here more than once.

J. Gallagher, CEO
Douglas Howell, CFO
Thomas Gallagher, Chairman of the Board, Divisional
Richard Cary, Controller
Walter Bay, General Counsel
Scott Hudson, President, Divisional
William Ziebell, Vice President
Linda Collins, Vice President, Divisional
Susan Pietrucha, Vice President
James Gault, Vice President
James Durkin, Vice President
Joel Cavaness, Vice President

GROWTH PLANS/SPECIAL FEATURES:

Arthur J. Gallagher & Co. and its subsidiaries provide insurance brokerage and third-party claims settlement and administration services to clients in the U.S. and abroad, with Gallagher's brokers, agents and administrators acting as intermediaries between insurers and their customers. The firm operates in three business segments: brokerage, risk management and corporate. The brokerage segment, accounting for 63% of the firm's revenues, is comprised of retail and wholesale brokerage operations. Retail operations focus on property/casualty, employer-provided health and welfare insurance and retirement planning on behalf of middle market commercial, industrial, public, religious and nonprofit clients, while wholesale brokers assist the retail brokers and other non-Gallagher brokers in placing specialized and hard-to-place insurance coverage. The risk management segment (13% of revenues) provides contract claim settlement and administration services for clients that self-insure some or all of their property/casualty coverage and for insurance companies choosing to outsource some or all of their property/casualty claims departments. Gallagher markets its risk management services primarily to Fortune 1000 companies, larger middle market companies, nonprofit organizations and public entities. The corporate segment (24% of revenues) manages the firm's clean energy and tax-advantaged investments and venture capital funds. The majority of the company's revenues are generated in the U.S., with the remaining coming out of the U.K., Australia, Canada and New Zealand.

Employees are offered medical, dental and vision coverage; AD&D; flexible spending account; short- and long-term disability; a 401(k); educational assistance; and an employee stock purchase plan.

FINANCIAL DATA: Note: Data for latest year may not have been available at press time.

In U.S. $	2016	2015	2014	2013	2012	2011
Revenue	5,594,800,000	5,392,400,000	4,626,500,000	3,179,600,000	2,520,300,000	2,134,700,000
R&D Expense						
Operating Income	356,900,000	293,500,000	267,400,000	274,500,000	245,300,000	207,800,000
Operating Margin %	6.37%	5.44%	5.77%	8.63%	9.73%	9.73%
SGA Expense	797,700,000	840,700,000	767,200,000	552,400,000	483,200,000	419,000,000
Net Income	414,400,000	356,800,000	303,400,000	268,600,000	195,000,000	144,100,000
Operating Cash Flow	622,100,000	652,600,000	402,300,000	349,900,000	343,000,000	283,100,000
Capital Expenditure	217,800,000	99,000,000	81,500,000	93,600,000	51,000,000	40,000,000
EBITDA	817,500,000	730,700,000	615,300,000	503,200,000	428,700,000	363,800,000
Return on Assets %	3.69%	3.41%	3.59%	4.39%	3.96%	3.56%
Return on Equity %	11.45%	10.39%	11.41%	14.34%	13.43%	12.26%
Debt to Equity	0.59	0.57	0.65	0.39	0.43	

CONTACT INFORMATION:

Phone: 630 773-3800   Fax: 630 285-4000
Toll-Free:
Address: 2 Pierce Pl., Itasca, IL 60143 United States

STOCK TICKER/OTHER:

Stock Ticker: AJG
Employees: 24,800
Parent Company:

Exchange: NYS
Fiscal Year Ends: 12/31

SALARIES/BONUSES:

Top Exec. Salary: $1,000,000   Bonus: $
Second Exec. Salary: $850,000   Bonus: $

OTHER THOUGHTS:

Estimated Female Officers or Directors: 3
Hot Spot for Advancement for Women/Minorities: Y

Ascena Retail Group Inc

www.ascenaretail.com

NAIC Code: 448120

TYPES OF BUSINESS:

Women's Apparel, Retail
Teen Fashion Stores
Fashion Accessories
Private-Label Credit Cards

BRANDS/DIVISIONS/AFFILIATES:

Justice
Lane Bryant
maurices
dressbarn
Catherines
ANN
Ann Taylor
LOFT

CONTACTS: Note: Officers with more than one job title may be intentionally listed here more than once.

Duane Holloway, Assistant Secretary
David Jaffe, CEO
Robb Giammatteo, CFO
Brian Lynch, COO
Jonathan Pershing, Executive VP
Ernest Laporte, Senior VP

GROWTH PLANS/SPECIAL FEATURES:

Ascena Retail Group, Inc. operates a national chain of value-priced specialty stores offering in-season, moderate to better quality apparel and accessories. The company has approximately 4,900 stores throughout the U.S., Puerto Rico and Canada. It operates in six segments based on a brand-oriented approach: ANN, Justice, Lane Bryant, maurices, dressbarn and Catherines. The ANN segment includes 1,022 specialty retail and outlet stores, ecommerce operations and certain licensed franchises in international territories which allow customers to shop in more than 100 countries worldwide. The ANN segment offers modern feminine classics and versatile fashion choices, sold primarily under the Ann Taylor and LOFT brands. The Justice segment includes 937 specialty retail and outlet stores, e-commerce operations and licensed franchises internationally, offering fashionable apparel to girls ages 6-12, designed for an energetic lifestyle. Lane Bryant includes 772 specialty retail and outlet stores and e-commerce operations, and is a widely-recognized brand name in plus-size fashion. The maurices segment includes 993 specialty retail and outlet stores and e-commerce operations, offering up-to-date fashion for women in their 20s and 30s. The dressbarn segment includes 824 specialty retail and outlet stores and e-commerce operations, offering moderate-to-better quality career and casual fashion for working women ranging from their mid-30's to mid-50's. Catherines includes 373 specialty retail stores and e-commerce operations, and sells plus-size fashion to women 45 years and older who shop in the moderate price range and are concerned with comfort, fit and value. Ascena owns a 695,000-square foot distribution center in Etna Township, Ohio; a 903,000-square foot fulfillment center in Greencastle, Indiana; and 256,000-square foot distribution center in Louisville, Kentucky.

FINANCIAL DATA: Note: Data for latest year may not have been available at press time.

In U.S. $	2016	2015	2014	2013	2012	2011
Revenue	6,995,400,000	4,802,900,000	4,790,600,000	4,714,900,000	3,353,300,000	2,914,000,000
R&D Expense						
Operating Income	93,800,000	-234,900,000	210,800,000	265,300,000	292,600,000	289,800,000
Operating Margin %	1.34%	-4.89%	4.40%	5.62%	8.72%	9.94%
SGA Expense	3,398,800,000	2,347,800,000	2,208,600,000	2,172,200,000	1,478,600,000	852,100,000
Net Income	-11,900,000	-236,800,000	133,400,000	151,300,000	162,200,000	170,500,000
Operating Cash Flow	445,400,000	431,300,000	374,700,000	450,000,000	361,500,000	280,800,000
Capital Expenditure	366,500,000	312,500,000	477,500,000	290,900,000	150,400,000	102,100,000
EBITDA	453,700,000	-16,400,000	403,600,000	432,400,000	390,700,000	376,700,000
Return on Assets %	-.28%	-7.84%	4.45%	5.32%	6.98%	9.76%
Return on Equity %	-.70%	-14.54%	8.09%	10.44%	12.98%	15.68%
Debt to Equity	1.06	0.23	0.09	0.08	0.41	0.14

CONTACT INFORMATION:

Phone: 551-777-6700   Fax:
Toll-Free:
Address: 933 MacArthur Blvd., Mahwah, NJ 07430 United States

STOCK TICKER/OTHER:

Stock Ticker: ASNA   Exchange: NAS
Employees: 48,000   Fiscal Year Ends: 07/31
Parent Company:

SALARIES/BONUSES:

Top Exec. Salary: $1,019,231   Bonus: $
Second Exec. Salary: $557,812   Bonus: $

OTHER THOUGHTS:

Estimated Female Officers or Directors: 2
Hot Spot for Advancement for Women/Minorities: Y

Sales, profits and employees may be estimates. Financial information, benefits and other data can change quickly and may vary from those stated here.

Ascension Health

ascension.org/our-work/subsidiaries/ascension-health

NAIC Code: 622110

TYPES OF BUSINESS:
General Medical and Surgical Hospitals
Acute Care Hospitals
Rehabilitation Hospitals
Psychiatric Hospitals
Pharmacy Management

BRANDS/DIVISIONS/AFFILIATES:
Ascension
Providence Hospital
St. Vincent's Health System
Sacred Heart's Health System
Peyton Manning Children's Hospital
Alexian Brothers
Lourdes Hospital
Nazareth Living Care Center

CONTACTS: Note: Officers with more than one job title may be intentionally listed here more than once.
Anthony R. Tersigni, CEO
Dennis H. Holtschneider, Exec.VP
Robert J. Henkel, Pres.
Anthony J. Speranzo, Exec.VP
Nick Ragone, Sr. VP-Mktg. & Communications
Herbert J. Vallier, Exec. VP-Human Resources
Ziad Haydar, Chief Medical Officer
Christine Kocot McCoy, General Counsel
Patricia A. Maryland, Pres., Health Care Oper.
Eric S. Engler, Sr. VP-Strategic Planning & Dev.
Jon Glaudemans, Chief Advocacy & Communications Officer
Ann Espoito, Sr. VP
Bonnie Phipps, CEO., St. Agnes HealthCare
Susan L. Davis, New York
Scott Caldwell, Chief Supply Chain Officer

GROWTH PLANS/SPECIAL FEATURES:

Ascension Health, a subsidiary of Ascension, is a faith-based, nonprofit health organization in the U.S. Its headquarters are in St. Louis, Missouri, and is comprised of 140 hospitals in 23 states as well as in Washington D.C. It has more than 2,500 sites of care and more than 30 senior care facilities. Ascension Health's facilities include Providence Hospital and St. Vincent's Health System of healthcare facilities in Alabama; Sacred Heart's Health System and St. Vincent's Health facilities in Florida; Peyton Manning Children's Hospital at St. Vincent in Indiana; Saint Thomas Health in Kentucky; St. Mary's of Michigan; Alexian Brothers of Missouri; Lourdes Hospital in New York; Seton Manor in Pennsylvania; Nazareth Living Care Center in Texas; and Ministry Health Care facilities in Wisconsin. In addition to Ascension Health, other Ascension subsidiaries provide services and solutions such as physician practice management, venture capital investing, treasury management, biomedical engineering, clinical care management, information services, risk management and contracting. Ascension Health was formed in 1999 when the four provinces of the Daughters of Charity of St. Vincent de Paul that were sponsors of the Daughters of Charity National Health System (now combined into one, the Province of St. Louise) and the Sisters of St. Joseph of Nazareth brought their health systems together. In May 2017, the firm sold St. Joseph Regional Medical Center to RCCH HealthCare Partners.

Ascension Health offers employee benefits such as medical, dental, vision and life insurance; health care and dependent care reimbursement accounts; a retirement savings program and a pension plan; tuition reimbursement; and an employee assistance program.

FINANCIAL DATA: Note: Data for latest year may not have been available at press time.

In U.S. $	2016	2015	2014	2013	2012	2011
Revenue	21,900,000,000	20,538,803,000	19,901,657,000	16,537,000,000	15,293,000,000	14,071,000,000
R&D Expense						
Operating Income						
Operating Margin %						
SGA Expense						
Net Income	219,412,440	562,596,000	1,803,615,000	451,000,000	931,000,000	415,000,000
Operating Cash Flow						
Capital Expenditure						
EBITDA						
Return on Assets %						
Return on Equity %						
Debt to Equity						

CONTACT INFORMATION:
Phone: 314-733-8000   Fax: 314-733-8013
Toll-Free:
Address: 101 South Hanley Rd., Ste 450, St. Louis, MO 63105 United States

STOCK TICKER/OTHER:
Stock Ticker: Subsidiary   Exchange:
Employees: 153,000   Fiscal Year Ends: 06/30
Parent Company: Ascension

SALARIES/BONUSES:
Top Exec. Salary: $ Bonus: $
Second Exec. Salary: $ Bonus: $

OTHER THOUGHTS:
Estimated Female Officers or Directors: 9
Hot Spot for Advancement for Women/Minorities: Y

AT Kearney Inc

www.atkearney.com

NAIC Code: 541610

TYPES OF BUSINESS:

Management Consulting
Technology Consulting
Retail Consulting
Government Consulting
Manufacturing Consulting
Transportation Consulting
Supply Chain Consulting
Industry Research & Publications

BRANDS/DIVISIONS/AFFILIATES:

Global Retail Development Index
Global Business Policy Council
Executive Agenda
AT Kearney Procurement & Analytic Solutions

CONTACTS: *Note: Officers with more than one job title may be intentionally listed here more than once.*

Johan Aurik, Managing Officer
Daniel Mahler, Head-The Americas
Luca Rossi, Head-EMEA
Laura Gurski, Head-Global Practices
Johan Aurik, Chmn.
John Kurtz, Head-Asia Pacific

GROWTH PLANS/SPECIAL FEATURES:

A.T. Kearney, Inc. is a global consulting firm involved in a wide variety of industries. It maintains 58 offices in major business centers in over 40 countries. The company specializes in CEO-agenda concerns and provides assistance in analytics, marketing & sales, mergers & acquisitions, operations, organization & transformation, procurement, strategic IT, strategy and sustainability. The industries served by the firm include aerospace & defense, automotive, communications/media/technology, consumer products & retail, chemicals, health care, metals & mining, private equity, public sector, financial institutions, transportation/travel/infrastructure and utilities. The company produces research in its various areas of interest, with products including business issue papers, the Global Retail Development Index publications and the Executive Agenda biannual publication. A.T. Kearney created and manages the Global Business Policy Council, designed to give a select group of company's prescient information on global market trends. Subsidiary A.T. Kearney Procurement & Analytic Solutions works with clients to assess their current enterprise-wide supply management capabilities, determine the critical gaps in relation to best practices and build a roadmap for improvement. In April 2016, the company announced a partnership with technology investor, Berlin Technologie Holding to facilitate strategic networking with start-ups.

FINANCIAL DATA: *Note: Data for latest year may not have been available at press time.*

In U.S. $	2016	2015	2014	2013	2012	2011
Revenue	1,120,000,000	1,150,000,000	1,100,000,000	1,135,000,000	1,050,000,000	969,000,000
R&D Expense						
Operating Income						
Operating Margin %						
SGA Expense						
Net Income						
Operating Cash Flow						
Capital Expenditure						
EBITDA						
Return on Assets %						
Return on Equity %						
Debt to Equity						

CONTACT INFORMATION:

Phone: 312-648-0111   Fax: 312-223-6200
Toll-Free:
Address: 222 W. Adams St., Chicago, IL 60606 United States

STOCK TICKER/OTHER:

Stock Ticker: Private   Exchange:
Employees: 3,600   Fiscal Year Ends: 12/31
Parent Company:

SALARIES/BONUSES:

Top Exec. Salary: $ Bonus: $
Second Exec. Salary: $ Bonus: $

OTHER THOUGHTS:

Estimated Female Officers or Directors: 1
Hot Spot for Advancement for Women/Minorities:

AT&T Inc

NAIC Code: 517110

www.att.com

TYPES OF BUSINESS:

Local Telephone Service
Wireless Telecommunications
Long-Distance Telephone Service
Corporate Telecom, Backbone & Wholesale Services
Internet Access
Entertainment & Television via Internet
Satellite TV
VOIP

BRANDS/DIVISIONS/AFFILIATES:

AT&T Mobility LLC
Quickplay Media Inc
INVIDI Technologies
Straight Path Communications
Time Warner Inc

CONTACTS: *Note: Officers with more than one job title may be intentionally listed here more than once.*

John Stankey, CEO, Divisional
Thaddeus Arroyo, CEO, Divisional
Randall Stephenson, CEO
John Stephens, CFO
David McAtee, General Counsel
Lori Lee, Other Corporate Officer
John Donovan, Other Executive Officer
David Huntley, Other Executive Officer
William Blase, Senior Executive VP, Divisional
Robert Quinn, Senior Executive VP, Divisional

GROWTH PLANS/SPECIAL FEATURES:

AT&T, Inc. is one of the world's largest providers of diversified telecommunications services. The company and its subsidiaries offers its communications, digital entertainment services and products to consumers in the U.S., Mexico and Latin America, as well as to businesses and other providers of telecommunications services worldwide. AT&T also owns and operates three regional sports networks. Services & products include wireless communications, data/broadband and internet services, digital video services, local & long-distance telephone services, telecommunications equipment, managed networking and wholesale services. The company operates through four business segments: business solutions, entertainment, consumer mobility and international. Business solutions provides services to businesses, governmental & wholesale customers and individual subscribers who purchase wireless services through employer-sponsored plans. These solutions include virtual private networks, Ethernet-related products, broadband and data/voice products. The entertainment segment provides video, internet and voice communication services to residential customers in the U.S. The consumer mobility business provides nationwide wireless service to consumers, as well as to wireless wholesale & resale subscribers located in the U.S. The international business segment provides entertainment services in Latin America and wireless services in Mexico. Via AT&T Mobility LLC, the firm covers all major metropolitan areas and more than 300 million people with its LTE technology. It also provides 4G coverage using HSPA+ technology. In June 2016, the firm acquired Quickplay Media, Inc. from Madison Dearborn Partners. The following October, AT&T agreed to acquire Time Warner, Inc. The transaction is still to undergo regulatory approval. That November, the firm, DISH Network L.L.C. and WPP jointly acquired INVIDI Technologies, a provider of addressable advertising platforms. In April 2017, AT&T announced plans to acquire Straight Path Communications.

FINANCIAL DATA: *Note: Data for latest year may not have been available at press time.*

In U.S. $	2016	2015	2014	2013	2012	2011
Revenue	163,786,000,000	146,801,000,000	132,447,000,000	128,752,000,000	127,434,000,000	126,723,000,000
R&D Expense						
Operating Income	24,347,000,000	24,785,000,000	11,746,000,000	30,479,000,000	12,997,000,000	9,218,000,000
Operating Margin %	14.86%	16.88%	8.86%	23.67%	10.19%	7.27%
SGA Expense	36,347,000,000	32,954,000,000	41,817,000,000	28,414,000,000	41,079,000,000	38,844,000,000
Net Income	12,976,000,000	13,345,000,000	6,224,000,000	18,249,000,000	7,264,000,000	3,944,000,000
Operating Cash Flow	39,344,000,000	35,880,000,000	31,338,000,000	34,796,000,000	39,176,000,000	34,648,000,000
Capital Expenditure	22,408,000,000	20,015,000,000	21,433,000,000	20,944,000,000	19,465,000,000	20,110,000,000
EBITDA	50,569,000,000	46,828,000,000	31,846,000,000	50,112,000,000	32,026,000,000	28,628,000,000
Return on Assets %	3.21%	3.83%	2.18%	6.63%	2.67%	1.46%
Return on Equity %	10.55%	12.76%	7.01%	19.90%	7.34%	3.63%
Debt to Equity	0.92	0.96	0.88	0.76	0.71	0.58

CONTACT INFORMATION:

Phone: 210 821-4105 Fax:
Toll-Free:
Address: 208 S. Akard St., Dallas, TX 75202 United States

STOCK TICKER/OTHER:

Stock Ticker: T
Employees: 268,000
Parent Company:

Exchange: NYS
Fiscal Year Ends: 12/31

SALARIES/BONUSES:

Top Exec. Salary: $1,791,667 Bonus: $
Second Exec. Salary: Bonus: $
$965,833

OTHER THOUGHTS:

Estimated Female Officers or Directors: 4
Hot Spot for Advancement for Women/Minorities: Y

Athenahealth Inc

www.athenahealth.com

NAIC Code: 524292

TYPES OF BUSINESS:

Outsourced Health Reimbursement Services
Patient Information Management
Billing & Collection Services for Health Care Providers
Automated Messaging

BRANDS/DIVISIONS/AFFILIATES:

athenaNet
athenaCollector
athenaClinicals
athenaCommunicator
athenaCoordinator
Epocrates
Population Health

CONTACTS: Note: Officers with more than one job title may be intentionally listed here more than once.

Jonathan Bush, CEO
Karl Stubelis, CFO
Tim O'Brien, Chief Marketing Officer
Prakash Khot, Chief Technology Officer
Stephen Kahane, Executive VP
Dan Haley, General Counsel
Kyle Armbrester, Other Executive Officer

GROWTH PLANS/SPECIAL FEATURES:

Athenahealth, Inc. is a provider of cloud-based business services to physician practices to reduce their administrative work by combining three components: cloud-based software, networked knowledge and back-office work. The firm offers services through its integrated platform, athenaNet. This platform is comprised of four principal tools: athenaCollector, athenaClinicals, athenaCommunicator and athenaCoordinator. AthenaCollector, the company's flagship product, is a revenue cycle management service that includes a management platform and automates and manages billing-related functions for physicians' practices. The athenaCollector system tracks, controls and executes claims and billing processes. AthenaClinicals, aimed at simplifying electronic medical record (EMR) handling, provides a wholly integrated system for managing the processes of providing and receiving pay for care. AthenaCommunicator is an automated message offering that includes automated patient messaging services, live operator services and a patient web portal. AthenaCoordinator is designed to streamline the order process between practices and hospitals, optimizing order transmission, pre-certification and pre-registration. The firm's Population Health services identifies patients in need of care and analyzes the clinical and financial results of that care to drive improvements in outcomes and costs. Epocrates branded services provide a variety of clinical information & decision support offerings through health care providers' mobile devices, including drug & disease information, medical calculator, tools, clinical guidelines & messaging, market research and formulary hosting. In August 2016, the firm acquired Filament Labs, Inc. (d/b/a Patient IO), a care coordination platform used by providers to engage patients and caregivers outside the four walls of the clinic.

Employee benefits include medical, vision and dental coverage; flexible spending accounts; an employee assistance program; life and AD&D insurance; short- and long-term disability; 401(k); and an employee stock purchase plan.

FINANCIAL DATA: Note: Data for latest year may not have been available at press time.

In U.S. $	2016	2015	2014	2013	2012	2011
Revenue	1,082,900,000	924,728,000	752,599,000	595,003,000	422,271,000	324,067,000
R&D Expense	134,500,000	94,254,000	69,461,000	57,639,000	33,792,000	23,343,000
Operating Income	26,600,000	-4,056,000	955,000	5,853,000	34,627,000	32,733,000
Operating Margin %	2.45%	-.43%	.12%	.98%	8.20%	10.10%
SGA Expense	388,300,000	374,478,000	314,880,000	249,264,000	161,325,000	128,486,000
Net Income	21,000,000	14,027,000	-3,119,000	2,594,000	18,732,000	19,046,000
Operating Cash Flow	182,600,000	163,844,000	149,105,000	93,308,000	70,213,000	60,764,000
Capital Expenditure	158,500,000	184,975,000	129,569,000	67,383,000	39,561,000	24,475,000
EBITDA	169,600,000	142,704,000	94,637,000	67,989,000	63,771,000	53,803,000
Return on Assets %	1.81%	1.36%	-.36%	.42%	4.82%	6.24%
Return on Equity %	3.56%	2.75%	-.71%	.73%	6.83%	9.35%
Debt to Equity	0.43	0.52	0.33	0.44		

CONTACT INFORMATION:

Phone: 617 402-1000   Fax: 617 402-1099
Toll-Free: 800-981-5084
Address: 311 Arsenal St., Watertown, MA 02472 United States

STOCK TICKER/OTHER:

Stock Ticker: ATHN   Exchange: NAS
Employees: 5,305   Fiscal Year Ends: 12/31
Parent Company:

SALARIES/BONUSES:

Top Exec. Salary: $590,000   Bonus: $
Second Exec. Salary: Bonus: $
$519,120

OTHER THOUGHTS:

Estimated Female Officers or Directors: 1
Hot Spot for Advancement for Women/Minorities:

Audi of America Inc

www.audiusa.com

NAIC Code: 336111

TYPES OF BUSINESS:

Automobile Manufacturing
Automotive Accessories
Personal Accessories
Automotive Service

BRANDS/DIVISIONS/AFFILIATES:

Volkswagen Group of America Inc
A3
RS7
A8 L W12
S8 plus
e-tron
Q5 hybrid
Silvercar Inc

CONTACTS: Note: Officers with more than one job title may be intentionally listed here more than once.

Scott Keogh, Pres.
Mark Del Rosso, COO
Christian Schroth, CFO
Filip Brabec, Dir.-Prod. Planning
Ricky Hudi, Chief Exec. Eng. Electrics & Electronics
Reinhard Fischer, Dir.-Strategy
Joe Jacuzzi, Chief Communications Officer
Peter Donnellan, Dir.-After Sales
Pete Hamilton, Regional Dir.-Southern Region
Jeri Ward, Dir.-Customer Exper.
Jeff Tolerico, Dir.-Eastern Region

GROWTH PLANS/SPECIAL FEATURES:

Audi of America, Inc., a subsidiary of Volkswagen Group of America, Inc., is the U.S. sales and marketing branch of the Audi car brand. Audi's 2016-2017 sedan models include the A3, S3, A4, S4, A6, S6, A7, S7, RS7, A8 L, A8 L W12 and S8 plus. SUVs, crossovers and wagon models include the A3 Sportback e-tron, allroad, Q3, Q5, Q5 hybrid, SQ5 and Q7. The models come with various body style options, including sedan, SUVs, crossovers, wagons, coupes and convertibles. Audi vehicles are identifiable through the four-ring logo that appears prominently on the grills of all cars. S models have additional specially-stylized features compared to the A models. Audi equips its luxury cars with options such as Audi MMI Navigation with voice control system, Audi MMI touch, Audi connect, BOSE surround sound and keyless start. Models range in price from about $30,900 (the A3) to roughly $137,900 (the A8 L W12). The Volkswagen Group manufactures a line of car and personal accessories that Audi of America then sells. This line of car accessories allows customers to customize a car at a local dealership as well as from the manufacturer through the company web site's Build Your Audi function. In addition to new cars, the company offers certified pre-owned models that are subject to a 300+ point inspection process. Service and support programs for these vehicles include roadside assistance, no-charge scheduled maintenance and extended warranties. Audi of America imports its cars from five main manufacturing facilities in Brazil, Germany, Italy, Hungary and China. For fiscal 2016-17, the USA division sold 210,213 units, displaying an 4% increase from the previous year. In May 2017, the company acquired Silvercar Inc., a premium car rental company.

FINANCIAL DATA: Note: Data for latest year may not have been available at press time.

In U.S. $	2016	2015	2014	2013	2012	2011
Revenue	12,998,684,059	10,145,871,400	9,291,103,561	8,400,000,000	7,800,000,000	6,478,130,000
R&D Expense						
Operating Income						
Operating Margin %						
SGA Expense						
Net Income	412,027,737	856,793,784	652,541,100	394,760,691	652,241,116	
Operating Cash Flow						
Capital Expenditure						
EBITDA						
Return on Assets %						
Return on Equity %						
Debt to Equity						

CONTACT INFORMATION:

Phone: 703-364-7000   Fax:
Toll-Free: 800-822-8987
Address: 2200 Ferdinand Porsche Drive, Herndon, VA 20171 United States

STOCK TICKER/OTHER:

Stock Ticker: Subsidiary   Exchange:
Employees: 14,809   Fiscal Year Ends: 12/31
Parent Company: Volkswagen Group of America Inc

SALARIES/BONUSES:

Top Exec. Salary: $ Bonus: $
Second Exec. Salary: $ Bonus: $

OTHER THOUGHTS:

Estimated Female Officers or Directors:
Hot Spot for Advancement for Women/Minorities:

Automatic Data Processing Inc (ADP)

NAIC Code: 518210

www.adp.com

TYPES OF BUSINESS:

Data Processing Services
Business Outsourcing Solutions
Information Services
Payroll Processing

BRANDS/DIVISIONS/AFFILIATES:

ADP TotalSource

CONTACTS: Note: Officers with more than one job title may be intentionally listed here more than once.

Carlos Rodriguez, CEO
Jan Siegmund, CFO
Brock Albinson, Chief Accounting Officer
John Jones, Director
Edward Flynn, Executive VP, Divisional
Michael Bonarti, General Counsel
Dermot OBrien, Other Executive Officer
Donald Weinstein, Other Executive Officer
John Ayala, President, Divisional
Douglas Politi, President, Divisional
Maria Black, President, Divisional
Thomas Perrotti, President, Geographical
Michael Eberhard, Treasurer
Stuart Sackman, Vice President, Divisional
Deborah Dyson, Vice President, Divisional

GROWTH PLANS/SPECIAL FEATURES:

Automatic Data Processing, Inc. (ADP) is one of the world's largest providers of cloud-based human capital management (HCM) solutions to employers, as well as business outsourcing services, analytics and compliance expertise. The company serves approximately 650,000 clients in more than 110 countries. ADP operates in two segments: employer services and professional employer organization (PEO) services. The employer services segment offers a comprehensive range of business outsourcing and HCM solutions including payroll services, benefits administration, recruiting and talent management, human resource management, time and attendance management, insurance services, retirement services and compliance and payment solutions. The PEO services segment, which operates as ADP TotalSource, provides small and medium sized businesses with comprehensive employment administration outsourcing solutions (through a co-employment relationship), including payroll, payroll tax filing, human resources guidance, 401(k) plan administration, benefits administration, compliance services, health and workers' compensation coverage and other supplemental benefits for employees. ADP TotalSource has approximately 9,700 clients in all 50 states; the businesses it serves have a combined total of 439,000 worksite employees.

Employee benefits in the U.S. include medical, dental and vision insurance; health care and dependent care flexible spending accounts; life, AD&D and disability coverage; a pension and 401(k) plan; a stock purchase and stock option plan; auto & home insurance programs; tuition reimbursement; and a scholarship program.

FINANCIAL DATA: Note: Data for latest year may not have been available at press time.

In U.S. $	2016	2015	2014	2013	2012	2011
Revenue	11,667,800,000	10,938,500,000	12,206,500,000	11,310,100,000	10,665,200,000	
R&D Expense						
Operating Income	2,190,500,000	2,014,000,000	2,222,700,000	1,997,200,000	1,959,000,000	
Operating Margin %	18.77%	18.41%	18.20%	17.65%	18.36%	
SGA Expense	2,637,000,000	2,496,900,000	2,762,400,000	2,620,600,000	2,466,200,000	
Net Income	1,492,500,000	1,452,500,000	1,515,900,000	1,405,800,000	1,388,500,000	
Operating Cash Flow	1,859,900,000	1,905,600,000	1,821,400,000	1,577,200,000	1,910,200,000	
Capital Expenditure	386,000,000	335,500,000	367,700,000	282,900,000	249,600,000	
EBITDA	2,579,500,000	2,355,100,000	2,616,900,000	2,410,400,000	2,453,100,000	
Return on Assets %	3.88%	4.45%	4.71%	4.45%	4.26%	
Return on Equity %	32.13%	25.30%	23.57%	22.85%	22.90%	
Debt to Equity	0.44					

CONTACT INFORMATION:

Phone: 973 974-5000   Fax: 973 974-5390
Toll-Free: 800-225-5237
Address: 1 ADP Blvd., Roseland, NJ 07068 United States

STOCK TICKER/OTHER:

Stock Ticker: ADP   Exchange: NAS
Employees: 58,000   Fiscal Year Ends: 06/30
Parent Company:

SALARIES/BONUSES:

Top Exec. Salary: $1,000,000   Bonus: $
Second Exec. Salary: Bonus: $
$650,000

OTHER THOUGHTS:

Estimated Female Officers or Directors: 1
Hot Spot for Advancement for Women/Minorities: Y

AutoNation Inc

www.autonation.com

NAIC Code: 441110

TYPES OF BUSINESS:

Auto Dealer
Online Auto Sales
Vehicle Maintenance & Repair Services
Vehicle Parts
Extended Service Contracts
Vehicle Protection Products

BRANDS/DIVISIONS/AFFILIATES:

CONTACTS: Note: Officers with more than one job title may be intentionally listed here more than once.

C. Coleman Edmunds, Assistant Secretary
Cheryl Miller, CFO
Michael Jackson, Chairman of the Board
Lance Iserman, COO
Donna Parlapiano, Executive VP, Divisional
Marc Cannon, Executive VP, Divisional
Jonathan Ferrando, Executive VP, Divisional
Thomas Conophy, Executive VP
Christopher Cade, Vice President

GROWTH PLANS/SPECIAL FEATURES:

AutoNation, Inc. is one of the largest automobile retailers in the U.S. It owns and operates 371 new vehicle franchises from 260 stores located in major metropolitan markets, predominantly in the Sunbelt region of the U.S. The company offers a diversified range of automotive products and services, including new vehicles, which generated 56.7% of the firm's 2016 revenue; used vehicles, 23.1%; parts and automotive services, 14%; and automotive finance, insurance products and other 4.8%. The firm also arranges financing for vehicle purchases through third-party finance sources. The core brands of vehicles, representing approximately 94% of the new vehicles the firm sold in 2016, are manufactured by Toyota, Ford, Honda, Nissan, General Motors, Mercedes-Benz, BMW, Fiat Chrysler and Volkswagen. AutoNation operates in three segments: domestic, import and premium luxury. Domestic is comprised of franchises that sell new General Motors, Jeep, Lincoln, Cadillac, Chevrolet, Ford and Chrysler among other brands. Import includes franchises that sell Toyota, Honda, Infiniti, Hyundai, Subaru, Volvo, Fiat, Acura, Mitsubishi, Mazda, Volkswagen and Nissan vehicles. Premium Luxury includes retailers that sell Land Rover, Mini, smart, Audi, Bentley, Porsche, Maserati, Mercedes, BMW, Alfa Romeo and Lexus franchises. In 2016, the domestic segment accounted for 36% of the company's total new vehicle unit sales; import, 32%; and premium luxury, 31%. The company's website offers prospective buyers the ability to evaluate current trade-in values of vehicles, explore nearby car lots, read automotive reviews and even arrange for the purchase of an automobile online.

The firm offers employees health, dental, life and disability insurance; longevity bonuses; a 401(k) plan; and an employee vehicle purchase program.

FINANCIAL DATA: Note: Data for latest year may not have been available at press time.

In U.S. $	2016	2015	2014	2013	2012	2011
Revenue	21,609,000,000	20,862,000,000	19,108,800,000	17,517,600,000	15,668,800,000	13,832,300,000
R&D Expense						
Operating Income	889,500,000	873,100,000	820,800,000	740,300,000	645,300,000	572,000,000
Operating Margin %	4.11%	4.18%	4.29%	4.22%	4.11%	4.13%
SGA Expense	2,349,400,000	2,263,500,000	2,079,600,000	1,935,000,000	1,749,500,000	1,649,400,000
Net Income	430,500,000	442,600,000	418,700,000	374,900,000	316,400,000	281,400,000
Operating Cash Flow	516,000,000	507,200,000	485,100,000	484,100,000	316,600,000	376,400,000
Capital Expenditure	244,500,000	247,600,000	209,200,000	160,800,000	160,600,000	149,100,000
EBITDA	1,037,700,000	999,300,000	929,200,000	841,400,000	736,500,000	653,700,000
Return on Assets %	4.38%	4.92%	5.13%	4.95%	4.72%	4.62%
Return on Equity %	18.47%	20.02%	20.25%	19.99%	17.66%	14.16%
Debt to Equity	0.69	0.74	1.01	0.87	1.22	0.86

CONTACT INFORMATION:

Phone: 954 769-6000   Fax:
Toll-Free:
Address: 200 SW 1st Ave., Ste.1600, Fort Lauderdale, FL 33301 United States

STOCK TICKER/OTHER:

Stock Ticker: AN   Exchange: NYS
Employees: 26,000   Fiscal Year Ends: 12/31
Parent Company:

SALARIES/BONUSES:

Top Exec. Salary: $1,250,000   Bonus: $
Second Exec. Salary: $771,875   Bonus: $

OTHER THOUGHTS:

Estimated Female Officers or Directors: 2
Hot Spot for Advancement for Women/Minorities:

Avis Budget Group Inc

www.avisbudgetgroup.com

NAIC Code: 532111

TYPES OF BUSINESS:

Automobile Rental
Franchising
Truck Rental

BRANDS/DIVISIONS/AFFILIATES:

Avis
Budget
ZipCar
Payless
Apex
Maggiore
France Cars

CONTACTS: Note: Officers with more than one job title may be intentionally listed here more than once.

Larry De Shon, CEO
Martyn Smith, CFO
Ronald Nelson, Chairman of the Board
David Calabria, Chief Accounting Officer
W. Deaver, Executive VP
Michael Tucker, Executive VP
Edward Linnen, Executive VP
Joseph Ferraro, President, Divisional
Mark Servodidio, President, Divisional

GROWTH PLANS/SPECIAL FEATURES:

Avis Budget Group, Inc. (ABG) operates in the global vehicle rental industry through Avis, Budget, Zipcar, Payless, Apex, Maggiore and France Cars. Avis is a rental car supplier to the premium commercial and leisure segments of the travel industry. Budget is a rental car supplier to the price-conscious segments of the travel industry. Its fleet of approximately 22,000 Budget trucks are rented through a network of approximately 1,000 dealer-operated and 480 company-operated locations throughout the U.S. Zipcar is a car sharing company, with over 1 million members in the U.S., Canada and Europe. Payless is a rental car supplier comprised of 240 vehicle rental locations worldwide. Apex operates in New Zealand and Australia via 20 locations. Maggiore operates in Italy through 130 rental locations. The France Cars operates one of the largest light commercial vehicle fleets in France from more than 60 rental locations. On average, ABG's operations include approximately 11,000 car and truck rental locations throughout the world, with a fleet of more than 600,000 vehicles. It completed more than 39 million vehicle rental transactions worldwide in 2016. The company operates in two segments: Americas, which provides vehicle rentals and ancillary products and services throughout the Americas and the Caribbean, and operates the car sharing business in these markets; and International, which provides and licenses ABG's brands to third parties for vehicle rentals and ancillary products and services primarily in Europe, the Middle East, Asia, Australia and New Zealand, and operates the car sharing business in select markets. In December 2016, ABG completed the acquisition of France Cars.

The company offers its employees medical, dental and vision coverage; life insurance; flexible spending accounts; short-and long-term disability, AD&D; and 401(k).

FINANCIAL DATA: Note: Data for latest year may not have been available at press time.

In U.S. $	2016	2015	2014	2013	2012	2011
Revenue	8,659,000,000	8,502,000,000	8,485,000,000	7,937,000,000	7,357,000,000	5,900,000,000
R&D Expense						
Operating Income	843,000,000	974,000,000	978,000,000	589,000,000	300,000,000	36,000,000
Operating Margin %	9.73%	11.45%	11.52%	7.42%	4.07%	.61%
SGA Expense	1,134,000,000	1,093,000,000	1,080,000,000	1,070,000,000	959,000,000	1,011,000,000
Net Income	163,000,000	313,000,000	245,000,000	16,000,000	290,000,000	-29,000,000
Operating Cash Flow	2,629,000,000	2,584,000,000	2,579,000,000	2,253,000,000	1,889,000,000	1,578,000,000
Capital Expenditure	12,651,000,000	12,127,000,000	12,057,000,000	11,051,000,000	11,199,000,000	8,724,000,000
EBITDA	3,066,000,000	2,750,000,000	3,059,000,000	2,552,000,000	2,461,000,000	2,031,000,000
Return on Assets %	.92%	1.80%	1.47%	.10%	2.06%	-.24%
Return on Equity %	49.39%	56.70%	34.12%	2.09%	49.61%	-7.05%
Debt to Equity	54.85	28.00	17.30	13.80	12.75	21.19

CONTACT INFORMATION:

Phone: 973 496-4700   Fax: 212 413-1924
Toll-Free:
Address: 6 Sylvan Way, Parsippany, NJ 07054 United States

STOCK TICKER/OTHER:

Stock Ticker: CAR   Exchange: NAS
Employees: 30,000   Fiscal Year Ends: 12/31
Parent Company:

SALARIES/BONUSES:

Top Exec. Salary: $1,000,000   Bonus: $
Second Exec. Salary: Bonus: $
$800,000

OTHER THOUGHTS:

Estimated Female Officers or Directors: 2
Hot Spot for Advancement for Women/Minorities:

Sales, profits and employees may be estimates. Financial information, benefits and other data can change quickly and may vary from those stated here.

Avnet Inc

NAIC Code: 423430

www.avnet.com

TYPES OF BUSINESS:
Components-Distributor
Marketing Services
Supply Chain Advisory Services

BRANDS/DIVISIONS/AFFILIATES:
Premier Farnell plc
Hackster Inc

CONTACTS: *Note: Officers with more than one job title may be intentionally listed here more than once.*
William Amelio, CEO
Kevin Moriarty, CFO
William Schumann, Chairman of the Board
Steven Phillips, Chief Information Officer
Michael Buseman, Other Executive Officer
MaryAnn Miller, Other Executive Officer
Erin Lewin, Senior VP

GROWTH PLANS/SPECIAL FEATURES:
Avnet, Inc. is one of the world's largest value-added distributors of electronic components, enterprise computer and storage products, software and embedded subsystems. The firm connects more than 800 suppliers to over 100,000 original equipment manufacturers (OEMs), electronic manufacturing services (EMS) providers, original design manufacturers (ODMs) and value-added resellers (VARs). Additionally, the firm provides engineering design, materials management and logistics services, system integration and configuration and supply chain services. The company divides its business into two divisions, technology solutions and electronics marketing, which operate throughout the Americas, Europe, the Middle East, Africa and Asia/Pacific. The technology solutions division markets and sells servers, data storage, software and related services to resellers and mid to high-end users as well as focusing on the worldwide OEM market. The electronics marketing division markets and sells semiconductors and interconnect, passive and electromechanical devices to a customer base whose end-markets include automotive, communications, computer hardware and peripheral, industrial and manufacturing, medical equipment, military and aerospace. Avnet pursues growth through strategic acquisitions to expand its geographic and market coverage. In late-2016, Avnet acquired Premier Farnell plc; acquired a majority stake in Hackster, Inc.; and agreed to sale its technology solutions unit to Tech Data Corporation for approximately $2.6 billion.

Avnet employees receive life, AD&D, disability, travel accident, medical, dental and vision insurance; flexible spending accounts; a pension plan; a 401(k); an employee stock purchase plan; and tuition reimbursement.

FINANCIAL DATA: *Note: Data for latest year may not have been available at press time.*

In U.S. $	2016	2015	2014	2013	2012	2011
Revenue	26,219,280,000	27,924,660,000	27,499,650,000	25,458,920,000	25,707,520,000	26,534,410,000
R&D Expense						
Operating Income	787,669,000	827,673,000	789,940,000	625,981,000	884,165,000	929,979,000
Operating Margin %	3.00%	2.96%	2.87%	2.45%	3.43%	3.50%
SGA Expense	2,170,524,000	2,274,642,000	2,341,168,000	2,204,319,000	2,092,807,000	2,100,650,000
Net Income	506,531,000	571,913,000	545,604,000	450,073,000	567,019,000	669,069,000
Operating Cash Flow	224,315,000	583,883,000	237,418,000	696,197,000	528,718,000	278,079,000
Capital Expenditure	147,548,000	174,374,000	123,242,000	97,379,000	128,652,000	148,707,000
EBITDA	896,043,000	955,949,000	943,138,000	777,594,000	982,977,000	1,044,807,000
Return on Assets %	4.59%	5.18%	5.02%	4.36%	5.64%	7.56%
Return on Equity %	10.80%	11.94%	11.88%	10.98%	14.24%	18.93%
Debt to Equity	0.28	0.35	0.24	0.28	0.32	0.31

CONTACT INFORMATION:
Phone: 480 643-2000   Fax: 480 643-7370
Toll-Free: 800-409-1483
Address: 2211 South 47th Street, Phoenix, AZ 85034 United States

STOCK TICKER/OTHER:
Stock Ticker: AVT   Exchange: NYS
Employees: 19,000   Fiscal Year Ends: 06/30
Parent Company:

SALARIES/BONUSES:
Top Exec. Salary: $1,000,000   Bonus: $
Second Exec. Salary: $650,000   Bonus: $

OTHER THOUGHTS:
Estimated Female Officers or Directors: 2
Hot Spot for Advancement for Women/Minorities: Y

AZZ Inc

NAIC Code: 335311

www.azz.com

TYPES OF BUSINESS:

Electrical Equipment Manufacturing
Galvanizing Services

BRANDS/DIVISIONS/AFFILIATES:

CONTACTS: *Note: Officers with more than one job title may be intentionally listed here more than once.*

Thomas Ferguson, CEO
Paul Fehlman, CFO
Kevern Joyce, Chairman of the Board
Robert Steines, Chief Accounting Officer
Matthew Emery, Chief Information Officer
Tara Mackey, Other Executive Officer
Tim Pendley, Senior VP, Divisional
Chris Bacius, Vice President, Divisional

GROWTH PLANS/SPECIAL FEATURES:

AZZ, Inc. is a global provider of galvanizing services, welding solutions, specialty electrical equipment and highly engineered services to the power generation, transmission, distribution, refining and industrial markets. The firm operates through two business segments: galvanizing and energy. The galvanizing segment provides hot dip galvanizing to the steel fabrication industry. Hot dip galvanizing is a metallurgical process in which molten zinc is applied to steel. The zinc alloying renders corrosion protection to fabricated steel for extended periods of up to 50 years. AZZ operates 41 galvanizing plants located across 19 states in U.S. and three Canadian provinces. The products are used in agriculture, construction, recreation, electrical utility, petrochemical and bridge and highway application. The energy segment offers specialized products and services designed to support industrial, nuclear and electrical applications. Products under this segment include electrical enclosures, medium and high voltage bus ducts, custom switchgear, explosion proof and hazardous duty lighting, nuclear safety-related equipment and tubular products. The products are also used in oil, gas, petrochemical, power generation, power transmission and utility power distribution. In September 2016, AZZ and Abdulrahman Ababtain Co., Ltd., announced a joint venture agreement to manufacture high voltage gas-insulated transmission line products within the Kingdom of Saudi Arabia. The following October, the firm entered into an agreement to divest its Nuclear Logistics LLC operating business unit to Westinghouse Electric Company.

AZZ offers its employees medical, dental and vision coverage, along with a 401(k) plan and other benefits.

FINANCIAL DATA: *Note: Data for latest year may not have been available at press time.*

In U.S. $	2016	2015	2014	2013	2012	2011
Revenue	903,192,000	816,687,000	751,723,400	570,594,200	469,112,400	
R&D Expense						
Operating Income	122,288,000	106,825,000	100,113,800	94,368,830	75,722,010	
Operating Margin %	13.53%	13.08%	13.31%	16.53%	16.14%	
SGA Expense	107,823,000	98,871,000	105,591,200	66,188,580	48,864,890	
Net Income	76,790,000	64,943,000	59,597,050	60,456,210	40,735,800	
Operating Cash Flow	143,589,000	118,157,000	107,275,300	92,737,620	64,064,830	
Capital Expenditure	39,861,000	29,377,000	43,471,530	24,922,990	19,783,760	
EBITDA	166,940,000	152,780,000	155,622,800	136,804,600	100,174,700	
Return on Assets %	7.99%	6.87%	7.23%	9.29%	6.94%	
Return on Equity %	17.04%	16.31%	16.79%	19.45%	14.98%	
Debt to Equity	0.63	0.75	1.02	0.58	0.73	

CONTACT INFORMATION:

Phone: 817 810-0095   Fax: 817 336-5354
Toll-Free:
Address: One Museum Place, 3100 W. 7th St., Ste. 500, Fort Worth, TX 76107 United States

STOCK TICKER/OTHER:

Stock Ticker: AZZ   Exchange: NYS
Employees: 4,183   Fiscal Year Ends: 02/28
Parent Company:

SALARIES/BONUSES:

Top Exec. Salary: $724,500   Bonus: $
Second Exec. Salary: $373,212   Bonus: $

OTHER THOUGHTS:

Estimated Female Officers or Directors: 1
Hot Spot for Advancement for Women/Minorities:

Bain & Company Inc

NAIC Code: 541610

www.bain.com

TYPES OF BUSINESS:

Management Consulting
Technology Consulting
Merger & Acquisition Consulting

BRANDS/DIVISIONS/AFFILIATES:

CONTACTS: *Note: Officers with more than one job title may be intentionally listed here more than once.*

Bob Bechek, Worldwide Managing Dir.
Dave Johnson, Managing Dir.-The Americas
Dale Cottrell, Managing Dir.-Asia Pacific
Orit Gadiesh, Chmn.
Paul Meehan, Managing Dir.-EMEA

GROWTH PLANS/SPECIAL FEATURES:

Bain & Company, Inc. provides business consulting services on a global level. From 53 offices in 34 countries, the firm's consultants work with top management executives from thousands of companies to help them outperform market competitors and create sustained financial growth and stability. Most of the company's offices are in the heavily industrialized economies of the U.S. and Europe, but offices in locations such as Brazil, Argentina, South Africa, India, China, Japan, Singapore and Australia are also key parts of the firm's business. Consultants typically help executives make important decisions in areas such as corporate strategy, change management, company organization, operations, performance improvement, marketing and sale of a company's unprofitable businesses; develop strategies to create profitable ones; penetrate new product segments; seize new business opportunities; and identify flawed business strategies. Services are provided to clients in industries such as technology, telecom, financial services, retail, media, consumer products, transportation, nonprofit and public sector, energy and utilities, private equity and health care. In appropriate situations, Bain consultants assist clients in implementing the changes they decide to make to their business structures or processes.

The firm tends to hire college graduates with either liberal arts degrees, MBA degrees or both. Positions often involve extensive travel and sometimes major relocation, the costs of which are reimbursed by Bain.

FINANCIAL DATA: *Note: Data for latest year may not have been available at press time.*

In U.S. $	2016	2015	2014	2013	2012	2011
Revenue	2,500,000,000	2,300,000,000	2,100,000,000	2,086,000,000	2,010,000,000	1,863,000,000
R&D Expense						
Operating Income						
Operating Margin %						
SGA Expense						
Net Income						
Operating Cash Flow						
Capital Expenditure						
EBITDA						
Return on Assets %						
Return on Equity %						
Debt to Equity						

CONTACT INFORMATION:

Phone: 617-572-2000   Fax: 617-572-2427
Toll-Free:
Address: 131 Dartmouth St., Boston, MA 02116 United States

STOCK TICKER/OTHER:

Stock Ticker: Private   Exchange:
Employees: 6,000   Fiscal Year Ends: 12/31
Parent Company:

SALARIES/BONUSES:

Top Exec. Salary: $ Bonus: $
Second Exec. Salary: $ Bonus: $

OTHER THOUGHTS:

Estimated Female Officers or Directors: 1
Hot Spot for Advancement for Women/Minorities:

Ball Corporation

www.ball.com

NAIC Code: 332431

TYPES OF BUSINESS:

Metal Can Manufacturing
Civil Space Systems
Defense Systems
Commercial Space Systems
Metal Food and Household Products Packaging
Radio Frequency and Microwave Technology
Metal Beverage Packaging

BRANDS/DIVISIONS/AFFILIATES:

Rexam PLC

CONTACTS: *Note: Officers with more than one job title may be intentionally listed here more than once.*

John Hayes, CEO
Scott Morrison, CFO
Shawn Barker, Controller
James Peterson, COO, Divisional
Daniel Fisher, COO, Divisional
Charles Baker, General Counsel
Robert Strain, President, Subsidiary
Lisa Pauley, Senior VP, Divisional
Jeff Knobel, Treasurer

GROWTH PLANS/SPECIAL FEATURES:

Ball Corporation is a leading manufacturer of metal packaging for the food and beverage, personal care and household products industries. It also supplies aerospace technologies and services to commercial and government customers. The company operates in five business segments: metal beverage packaging, North America and Central America; beverage packaging, South America; beverage packaging, Europe; food & aerosol packaging; and aerospace. The metal beverage packaging, North America and Central America segment, accounting for 40% of the firm's net sales, is involved in the sale of metal beverage containers in multi-year supply contracts to fillers of beer, energy drinks and carbonated soft drinks. The beverage packaging, South America, segment, accounting for 11% of net sales, consists of 14 facilities and produces 60% of South American shipments of containers. The beverage packaging, Europe segment, accounting for 21% of 2016 net sales, supplies two-piece metal beverage containers and ends for beer, energy drink and carbonated soft drink producers as well as aluminum slugs and extruded aerosol containers. The food & aerosol packaging segment, 13% of Ball's net sales, produces two- and three-piece steel food containers and ends for the packaging of pet food, nutritional products, seafood, fruits, vegetables, soups and meats. The aerospace business, 9%, includes national defense hardware, antenna and video tactical solutions, civil space systems and commercial space operations. Products produced include spacecraft sensors, instruments and radio frequency systems. In June 2016, the firm acquired Rexam PLC for $6.1 billion, a U.K.-based beverage can manufacturing company; and sold eight U.S. aluminum can plants and associated assets to Ardagh Group for $3.1 billion in order to settle FTC charges due to the Rexam acquisition.

FINANCIAL DATA: *Note: Data for latest year may not have been available at press time.*

In U.S. $	2016	2015	2014	2013	2012	2011
Revenue	9,061,000,000	7,997,000,000	8,570,000,000	8,468,100,000	8,735,700,000	8,630,900,000
R&D Expense						
Operating Income	463,000,000	605,200,000	838,600,000	795,400,000	790,500,000	836,900,000
Operating Margin %	5.10%	7.56%	9.78%	9.39%	9.04%	9.69%
SGA Expense	512,000,000	451,300,000	466,500,000	418,600,000	385,500,000	381,400,000
Net Income	263,000,000	280,900,000	470,000,000	406,800,000	403,500,000	444,000,000
Operating Cash Flow	194,000,000	1,006,700,000	1,012,500,000	839,000,000	853,200,000	948,400,000
Capital Expenditure	606,000,000	527,900,000	390,800,000	378,300,000	305,000,000	443,800,000
EBITDA	807,000,000	774,200,000	1,086,400,000	1,067,300,000	1,058,300,000	1,138,000,000
Return on Assets %	2.02%	3.23%	6.10%	5.30%	5.45%	6.24%
Return on Equity %	11.22%	24.59%	42.09%	35.15%	34.58%	32.44%
Debt to Equity	2.12	4.03	2.89	2.65	2.76	2.21

CONTACT INFORMATION:

Phone: 303 469-3131   Fax: 303 460-2127
Toll-Free:
Address: 10 Longs Peak Dr., Broomfield, CO 80021 United States

STOCK TICKER/OTHER:

Stock Ticker: BLL   Exchange: NYS
Employees: 18,450   Fiscal Year Ends: 12/31
Parent Company:

SALARIES/BONUSES:

Top Exec. Salary: $1,238,615   Bonus: $
Second Exec. Salary: Bonus: $
$695,243

OTHER THOUGHTS:

Estimated Female Officers or Directors: 2
Hot Spot for Advancement for Women/Minorities: Y

Bank of America Corp

www.bankofamerica.com

NAIC Code: 522110

TYPES OF BUSINESS:

Banking
Asset Management
Investment & Brokerage Services
Mortgages
Credit Cards
Insurance Agency

BRANDS/DIVISIONS/AFFILIATES:

CONTACTS: Note: Officers with more than one job title may be intentionally listed here more than once.

Brian Moynihan, CEO
Thong Nguyen, President, Divisional
Paul Donofrio, CFO
Rudolf Bless, Chief Accounting Officer
Andrea Smith, Chief Administrative Officer
Geoffrey Greener, Chief Risk Officer
Catherine Bessant, CO-COO
Thomas Montag, COO
David Leitch, General Counsel
Ross Jeffries, General Counsel
Dean Athanasia, President, Divisional
Gary Lynch, Vice Chairman
Terrence Laughlin, Vice Chairman, Divisional

GROWTH PLANS/SPECIAL FEATURES:

Bank of America Corp. is a global provider of a diversified range of banking and financial services. The company operates through four primary business segments: consumer banking, global wealth and investment management (GWIM), global banking and global markets. Consumer banking provides deposit and lending services, as well as small business client management services, consumer and small business credit card services, debit card services, consumer vehicle lending and home loan options. GWIM offers Merrill Lynch global wealth management, as well as U.S. trust services and private wealth management services. Global banking offers investment banking, global corporate banking, global commercial banking and business banking services. The global markets segment offers fixed income and equity market products. Other activities by Bank of America include equity investments, international consumer cards, merchant services, liquidating services, residual expense allocation services and more. In December 2016, the firm agreed to sell MBNA Ltd., its consumer credit card business in the U.K., to Lloyds Banking Group. The transaction was expected to close by mid-2017, subject to regulatory approval.

The company offers its employees benefits including tuition and adoption reimbursement; medical, dental and vision insurance plans; employee assistance programs; and health care and dependent care flexible spending accounts.

FINANCIAL DATA: Note: Data for latest year may not have been available at press time.

In U.S. $	2016	2015	2014	2013	2012	2011
Revenue	83,701,000,000	82,507,000,000	84,247,000,000	88,942,000,000	83,334,000,000	93,454,000,000
R&D Expense						
Operating Income	25,153,000,000	22,154,000,000	6,855,000,000	16,172,000,000	3,072,000,000	-230,000,000
Operating Margin %	30.05%	26.85%	8.13%	18.18%	3.68%	-.24%
SGA Expense	46,408,000,000	47,962,000,000	65,324,000,000	58,623,000,000	60,416,000,000	64,474,000,000
Net Income	17,906,000,000	15,888,000,000	4,833,000,000	11,431,000,000	4,188,000,000	1,446,000,000
Operating Cash Flow	18,306,000,000	27,730,000,000	26,739,000,000	92,817,000,000	-13,858,000,000	64,490,000,000
Capital Expenditure			1,160,000,000	521,000,000		1,307,000,000
EBITDA						
Return on Assets %	.74%	.67%	.18%	.46%	.12%	
Return on Equity %	6.82%	6.28%	1.70%	4.60%	1.28%	.04%
Debt to Equity	0.89	1.01	1.08	1.13	1.26	1.75

CONTACT INFORMATION:

Phone: 704 386-5681   Fax:
Toll-Free: 800-432-1000
Address: 100 N. Tryon St., 18th Fl., Charlotte, NC 28255 United States

STOCK TICKER/OTHER:

Stock Ticker: BAC   Exchange: NYS
Employees: 208,000   Fiscal Year Ends: 12/31
Parent Company:

SALARIES/BONUSES:

Top Exec. Salary: $1,000,000   Bonus: $6,400,000
Second Exec. Salary: $850,000   Bonus: $4,160,000

OTHER THOUGHTS:

Estimated Female Officers or Directors: 8
Hot Spot for Advancement for Women/Minorities: Y

Bank of New York Mellon Corp

www.bnymellon.com

NAIC Code: 522110

TYPES OF BUSINESS:

Asset Management & Securities Services
Investment & Wealth Management
Private Banking
Shareowner Services
Broker-Dealer Services
Issuer Services
Treasury Services

BRANDS/DIVISIONS/AFFILIATES:

Bank of New York Mellon (The)
BNY Mellon National Association
Bank of New York Mellon Trust Company, NA (The)
BNY Mellon Trust of Delaware
BNY Mellon Investment Servicing Trust Co
BNY Mellon Trust Company of Illinois
Pershing LLC

CONTACTS: *Note: Officers with more than one job title may be intentionally listed here more than once.*

Mitchell Harris, CEO, Divisional
Gerald Hassell, CEO
Thomas Gibbons, CFO
Kurtis Kurimsky, Chief Accounting Officer
James Wiener, Chief Risk Officer
J. Mccarthy, General Counsel
Michelle Neal, Managing Director
Monique Herena, Other Executive Officer
Brian Shea, Vice Chairman

GROWTH PLANS/SPECIAL FEATURES:

Bank of New York Mellon Corp. (BNYM) is a global investment company providing asset management and securities services for individual investors, institutions and corporations in 35 countries and more than 100 markets. In addition, BNYM offers financial solutions for individuals, including investment and wealth management, private banking and shareowner services. The company works with consultants and advisors to help them select the services that best meet their customers' needs. The firm has two principal banking subsidiaries: The Bank of New York Mellon and BNY Mellon, National Association (NA), which provide trust and custody activities, investment management services, banking services and various securities-related activities. Additionally, the firm has four other U.S. bank and/or trust company subsidiaries concentrating on trust products and services across the nation: The Bank of New York Mellon Trust Company NA, BNY Mellon Trust of Delaware, BNY Mellon Investment Servicing Trust Company and BNY Mellon Trust Company of Illinois. Most of the asset management businesses are direct or indirect non-bank subsidiaries of BNY Mellon. Through Pershing, LLC, the firm offers broker-dealer and advisor services. Pershing is a provider of clearing, execution and financial business solutions to institutional and retail financial organizations and independent registered investment advisors. BNYM's issuer service offerings include global corporate trust services, depositary receipt services and shareowner services. The company also offers treasury services. BNYM has approximately $1.6 trillion in assets under management and $29.9 trillion in assets under administration or custody. Customers include corporations, foundations, governments, unions, endowments, mutual funds and high-net-worth individuals.

Employees are offered medical, vision and dental health plans; life insurance; and an array of retirement plans varying by location.

FINANCIAL DATA: *Note: Data for latest year may not have been available at press time.*

In U.S. $	2016	2015	2014	2013	2012	2011
Revenue	15,237,000,000	15,194,000,000	15,692,000,000	14,983,000,000	14,555,000,000	14,730,000,000
R&D Expense						
Operating Income	4,725,000,000	4,235,000,000	3,563,000,000	3,712,000,000	3,302,000,000	3,617,000,000
Operating Margin %	31.00%	27.87%	22.70%	24.77%	22.68%	24.55%
SGA Expense	7,030,000,000	7,115,000,000	7,447,000,000	7,330,000,000	6,706,000,000	6,627,000,000
Net Income	3,547,000,000	3,158,000,000	2,567,000,000	2,111,000,000	2,445,000,000	2,516,000,000
Operating Cash Flow	6,246,000,000	4,127,000,000	4,484,000,000	-642,000,000	1,629,000,000	2,211,000,000
Capital Expenditure	825,000,000	601,000,000	791,000,000	609,000,000	652,000,000	642,000,000
EBITDA						
Return on Assets %	.92%	.77%	.64%	.55%	.70%	.87%
Return on Equity %	9.53%	8.43%	6.82%	5.74%	7.05%	7.65%
Debt to Equity	0.71	0.62	0.58	0.57	0.56	0.66

CONTACT INFORMATION:

Phone: 212 495-1784   Fax:
Toll-Free:
Address: 1 Wall St., New York, NY 10286 United States

STOCK TICKER/OTHER:

Stock Ticker: BK   Exchange: NYS
Employees: 52,000   Fiscal Year Ends: 12/31
Parent Company:

SALARIES/BONUSES:

Top Exec. Salary: $1,000,000   Bonus: $
Second Exec. Salary: Bonus: $
$650,000

OTHER THOUGHTS:

Estimated Female Officers or Directors: 6
Hot Spot for Advancement for Women/Minorities: Y

Barrett Business Services Inc

www.barrettbusiness.com

NAIC Code: 561330

TYPES OF BUSINESS:

Human Resources Management
Staffing Services
Professional Employer Services (PEO)

BRANDS/DIVISIONS/AFFILIATES:

CONTACTS: Note: Officers with more than one job title may be intentionally listed here more than once.

Michael Elich, CEO
Gary Kramer, CFO
Gerald Blotz, COO, Divisional
Gregory Vaughn, COO, Divisional
Anthony Meeker, Director
Heather Gould, Other Executive Officer

GROWTH PLANS/SPECIAL FEATURES:

Barrett Business Services, Inc. is a human resources management company that provides staffing services and professional employer services. Originally founded in 1951, Barrett is headquartered in Vancouver, Washington and has more than 55 offices in Washington, District of Columbia, California, Oregon, Idaho, Arizona, Nevada, Utah, Colorado, Maryland, Pennsylvania, Virginia, Delaware and North Carolina. The firm's outsourced services help clients deal with issues concerning employment laws and regulations, payroll processing, employee benefits and administration, workers' compensation coverage, effective risk management, workplace safety programs and human resource administration. Barrett's staffing services include short-term, temporary-to-permanent and permanent placements in areas including clerical/administrative work, light industrial assignments, technical work, onsite management assignments and other specialties. The firm has been offering professional employer services (PEO) since 1990, focusing on human resource management services for small and mid-sized companies. The company's professional employer services arrangement allows Barrett to enter a contractual agreement with the client's customer(s), thereby becoming a co-employer with the client company. This enables Barrett to assume responsibility for many or all the human resource management duties, such as payroll/taxes, employee benefits, health insurance, workers' compensation, workplace safety, federal/state employment laws, labor regulatory requirements and other administrative tasks. The firm serves customers in a variety of markets, including electronics manufacturers, various light-manufacturing industries, forest products and agriculture-based companies, transportation and shipping enterprises, food processing, telecommunications, public utilities, general contractors in numerous construction-related fields and various professional services firms.

The company provides its employees medical and dental insurance as well as a 401(k) plan.

FINANCIAL DATA: Note: Data for latest year may not have been available at press time.

In U.S. $	2016	2015	2014	2013	2012	2011
Revenue	840,586,000	740,841,000	636,184,000	532,844,000	402,652,000	314,874,000
R&D Expense						
Operating Income	28,941,000	36,428,000	-45,910,000	24,426,000	18,787,000	3,934,000
Operating Margin %	3.44%	4.91%	-7.21%	4.58%	4.66%	1.24%
SGA Expense	113,342,000	90,177,000	73,821,000	60,061,000	46,450,000	38,174,000
Net Income	18,799,000	25,494,000	-27,084,000	17,892,000	13,131,000	14,318,000
Operating Cash Flow	80,307,000	100,631,000	69,596,000	70,196,000	45,657,000	31,355,000
Capital Expenditure	7,106,000	2,996,000	4,632,000	4,097,000	3,712,000	1,247,000
EBITDA	29,646,000	39,962,000	-42,658,000	27,177,000	20,264,000	5,278,000
Return on Assets %	3.43%	5.39%	-7.11%	6.59%	5.81%	6.96%
Return on Equity %	30.26%	54.70%	-48.70%	28.29%	16.88%	14.53%
Debt to Equity	0.06		0.51	0.06	0.09	

CONTACT INFORMATION:

Phone: 360 828-0700 Fax: 360-828-0701
Toll-Free: 800-494-5669
Address: 8100 NE Parkway Dr., Ste. 200, Vancouver, WA 98662 United States

STOCK TICKER/OTHER:

Stock Ticker: BBSI
Employees: 115,746
Parent Company:

Exchange: NAS
Fiscal Year Ends: 12/31

SALARIES/BONUSES:

Top Exec. Salary: $650,000 Bonus: $350,000
Second Exec. Salary: $400,000 Bonus: $175,000

OTHER THOUGHTS:

Estimated Female Officers or Directors:
Hot Spot for Advancement for Women/Minorities:

Sales, profits and employees may be estimates. Financial information, benefits and other data can change quickly and may vary from those stated here.

BB&T Corporation

NAIC Code: 522110

TYPES OF BUSINESS:

Banking
Mortgages
Consumer Loans
Commercial Loans
Investment Services
Securities Lending
Insurance
Leasing

BRANDS/DIVISIONS/AFFILIATES:

Branch Bank and Trust Company
BB&T Equipment Finance Corporation
BB&T Investment Services Inc
BB&T Insurance Services Inc
CRC Insurance Services Inc
Crump Life Insurance Services Inc
BB&T Commercial Equipment Capital
McGriff Seibels & Williams Inc

CONTACTS: Note: Officers with more than one job title may be intentionally listed here more than once.

Kelly King, CEO
Donna Goodrich, Other Corporate Officer
Daryl Bible, CFO
Cynthia Powell, Chief Accounting Officer
Barbara Duck, Chief Information Officer
Clarke Starnes, Chief Risk Officer
Christopher Henson, COO
Robert Johnson, General Counsel
William Yates, Other Corporate Officer
Brantley Standridge, Other Corporate Officer
W. Bradley, Other Executive Officer
Donta Wilson, Other Executive Officer

GROWTH PLANS/SPECIAL FEATURES:

BB&T Corporation is a financial holding company that conducts the majority of its operations primarily through its commercial bank subsidiary, Branch Bank, and other nonbank subsidiaries. Services and products include those for community banking, residential mortgage banking, dealer financial services, specialized lending, insurance services and financial services. BB&T's largest subsidiary, Branch Bank and Trust Company, provides a wide range of banking and trust services for retail and commercial clients including small and mid-size businesses, public agencies, local governments and individuals, through 2,196 offices. Branch Bank's principal operating subsidiaries include: BB&T Equipment Finance Corporation, providing loan and lease financing to commercial and small businesses; BB&T Investment Services, Inc., offering non-deposit investment alternatives; BB&T Insurance Services, Inc., offering property and casualty, life, health, employee benefits, commercial general liability, surety, title and other insurance products; CRC Insurance Services, Inc., a nationwide wholesale insurance broker; Grandbridge Real Estate Capital, LLC which arranges and services commercial mortgage loans; Crump Life Insurance Services, Inc., a nationwide wholesale insurance broker; BB&T Commercial Equipment Capital (formerly Susquehanna Commercial Finance, Inc.), providing branch banking and trust options; and McGriff, Seibels & Williams, Inc., providing insurance products on an agency basis to large commercial clients. BB&T's non-bank subsidiaries include: BB&T Securities, LLC, a registered investment banking and full-service brokerage firm; Regional Acceptance Corporation, specializing in indirect financing for consumer purchases of primarily mid-model and late-model used automobiles; and Sterling Capital Management, LLC, providing a full range of investment strategies, including domestic and international equity, alternative investment products and strategies and fixed income investing.

Employee benefits include 401(k) and pension options; medical, vision and dental coverage; disability, life and AD&D insurance; health savings account; and wellness program.

FINANCIAL DATA: Note: Data for latest year may not have been available at press time.

In U.S. $	2016	2015	2014	2013	2012	2011
Revenue	10,793,000,000	9,611,000,000	9,158,000,000	9,553,000,000	9,677,000,000	8,620,000,000
R&D Expense						
Operating Income	3,500,000,000	2,917,000,000	2,986,000,000	3,124,000,000	2,792,000,000	1,628,000,000
Operating Margin %	32.42%	30.35%	32.60%	32.70%	28.85%	18.88%
SGA Expense	4,614,000,000	4,047,000,000	3,802,000,000	3,594,000,000	3,705,000,000	3,284,000,000
Net Income	2,426,000,000	2,084,000,000	2,151,000,000	1,679,000,000	1,979,000,000	1,289,000,000
Operating Cash Flow	2,672,000,000	2,915,000,000	3,258,000,000	5,339,000,000	3,698,000,000	4,565,000,000
Capital Expenditure					145,000,000	224,000,000
EBITDA						
Return on Assets %	1.05%	.97%	1.08%	.85%	1.06%	.77%
Return on Equity %	8.76%	8.33%	9.56%	7.96%	10.51%	7.61%
Debt to Equity	0.81	0.96	1.07	1.06	1.00	1.25

CONTACT INFORMATION:

Phone: 336 733-2000   Fax:
Toll-Free: 800-226-5228
Address: 200 W. 2nd St., Winston-Salem, NC 27101 United States

STOCK TICKER/OTHER:

Stock Ticker: BBT   Exchange: NYS
Employees: 37,500   Fiscal Year Ends: 12/31
Parent Company:

SALARIES/BONUSES:

Top Exec. Salary: $1,075,000   Bonus: $
Second Exec. Salary: Bonus: $
$700,000

OTHER THOUGHTS:

Estimated Female Officers or Directors: 3
Hot Spot for Advancement for Women/Minorities: Y

BBDO Worldwide

www.bbdo.com

NAIC Code: 541810

TYPES OF BUSINESS:

Advertising Agency
Marketing Services
Communications Services

BRANDS/DIVISIONS/AFFILIATES:

Omnicom Group Inc
BBDO North America
BBDO EMEA
BBDO Asia Pacific
BBDO Latin America
Proximity Worldwide
Wednesday Agency Group

CONTACTS: Note: Officers with more than one job title may be intentionally listed here more than once.

Andrew Robertson, CEO
Crystal Rix, Chief Strategy Officer
Nicole Martine Hall, SVP
St. John Walsh, Exec. VP
John Osborn, CEO
Chris Thomas, Chmn.

GROWTH PLANS/SPECIAL FEATURES:

BBDO Worldwide is the lead agency network of the Omnicom Group, Inc. and one of the largest agency networks worldwide. The firm provides advertising, marketing and communications planning and execution through an extensive network of 289 offices across the globe. The company's network is structured geographically, and includes BBDO North America, with offices in Canada, Mexico and the U.S.; BBDO EMEA, with offices in 39 countries, including Lebanon, Israel, South Africa, Belgium, France, Germany, the U.K., Greece, Russia, Spain and Switzerland; BBDO Asia Pacific, with offices in 18 countries, including Australia, China, India, Japan and New Zealand; and BBDO Latin America, with offices in 15 countries, including Argentina, Chile, Brazil, Venezuela, Colombia and Guatemala. Within these four geographic arms, the lead agency's activity is supported by a range of subsidiary regional agencies that possess particular expertise and long-standing histories within local markets. Proximity Worldwide, BBDO's spun-off global customer relationship and direct marketing network, provides additional support. A select number of clients, such as Bayer and PepsiCo, utilize BBDO's services on a global basis. Other key accounts include Campbell's, DIAGEO, ExxonMobil, FedEx, Gatorade, General Electric, HP, Hyatt, Johnson & Johnson, Mars, Mercedes-Benz, P&G, Pepsi Max, Lowe's, Sainsbury, Starbucks, VISA, Volkswagen, Wells Fargo and Wrigley. The agency is well-established in developing and delivering campaigns in television, radio, print and interactive and new media formats. In January 2016, the firm acquired a majority stake in luxury marketing powerhouse, Wednesday Agency Group.

FINANCIAL DATA: Note: Data for latest year may not have been available at press time.

In U.S. $	2016	2015	2014	2013	2012	2011
Revenue	650,000,000	603,000,000				
R&D Expense						
Operating Income						
Operating Margin %						
SGA Expense						
Net Income						
Operating Cash Flow						
Capital Expenditure						
EBITDA						
Return on Assets %						
Return on Equity %						
Debt to Equity						

CONTACT INFORMATION:

Phone: 212-459-5000   Fax:
Toll-Free:
Address: 1285 Ave. of the Americas, New York, NY 10019 United States

STOCK TICKER/OTHER:

Stock Ticker: Subsidiary   Exchange:
Employees: 15,000   Fiscal Year Ends: 12/31
Parent Company: Omnicom Group Inc

SALARIES/BONUSES:

Top Exec. Salary: $ Bonus: $
Second Exec. Salary: $ Bonus: $

OTHER THOUGHTS:

Estimated Female Officers or Directors:
Hot Spot for Advancement for Women/Minorities:

Becton Dickinson & Co

NAIC Code: 339100

www.bd.com

TYPES OF BUSINESS:

Medical Equipment-Injection/Infusion
Drug Delivery Systems
Infusion Therapy Products
Diabetes Care Products
Surgical Products
Microbiology Products
Diagnostic Products
Consulting Services

BRANDS/DIVISIONS/AFFILIATES:

BD Medical
BD Life Sciences
CareFusion Corporation
BD Vacutainer
BD Hypak
Cellular Research Inc
CRISI Medical Systems
Vyaire Medical

CONTACTS: Note: Officers with more than one job title may be intentionally listed here more than once.

Vincent Forlenza, CEO
Jeffrey Sherman, General Counsel
Christopher Reidy, CFO
John Gallagher, Chief Accounting Officer
Nabil Shabshab, Chief Marketing Officer
Ellen Strahlman, Chief Medical Officer
Stephen Sichak, Executive VP, Divisional
Linda Tharby, Executive VP
Alberto Mas, Executive VP
Thomas Polen, Executive VP
Gary Cohen, Executive VP
James Lim, Executive VP
Alexandre Conroy, President, Geographical
Gary DeFazio, Secretary
Alexandre Conroy, President, Geographical

GROWTH PLANS/SPECIAL FEATURES:

Becton, Dickinson & Co. (BD) manufactures and sells a broad line of medical supplies, devices and diagnostic systems used by health care professionals, medical research institutions and the public. The company operates in two worldwide business segments: BD Medical and BD Life Sciences. BD Medical offers products, including specially designed devices for diabetes care; pre-fillable drug delivery systems; and infusion therapy products. It also offers anesthesia and surgical products, ophthalmic surgery devices, critical care systems, elastic support products, respiratory ventilation and diagnostic equipment and thermometers. BD Life Sciences offers products for safe collection and transport of diagnostics specimens; instruments and reagent systems to detect a broad range of infectious diseases; and research and clinical tools that facilitate the study of cells in order to get a comprehensive understanding of normal and disease processes. Some of the products are integrated systems for specimen collection, molecular testing systems for infectious diseases and fluorescence-activated cell sorters and analyzers. Two of BD's most popular products are BD Hypak pre-fillable syringes and BD Vacutainer blood-collection products. Outside of the U.S., the company's products are manufactured and sold in Europe, the Middle East, Africa, Japan, Mexico, Brazil, Asia Pacific and Canada. In April 2016, the firm divested its vertebral augmentation solutions business to Stryker Corporation. In October 2016, the company formed a joint venture company with Apax Partners, Vyaire Medical, a standalone, global respiratory solutions company. In April 2017, BD announced that it would acquire C.R. Bard, Inc., a medical supplies manufacturer, for $24 billion.

The firm offers employees medical, dental, vision and prescription drug coverage; a flexible spending account; an employee assistance program; and at select locations, onsite services such as fitness centers, walking trails, banks and cafeterias.

FINANCIAL DATA: Note: Data for latest year may not have been available at press time.

In U.S. $	2016	2015	2014	2013	2012	2011
Revenue	12,483,000,000	10,282,000,000	8,446,000,000	8,054,000,000	7,708,382,000	7,828,904,000
R&D Expense	828,000,000	632,000,000	550,000,000	494,000,000	471,755,000	476,496,000
Operating Income	1,430,000,000	1,074,000,000	1,606,000,000	1,255,000,000	1,557,885,000	1,763,282,000
Operating Margin %	11.45%	10.44%	19.01%	15.58%	20.21%	22.52%
SGA Expense	3,005,000,000	2,563,000,000	2,145,000,000	2,422,000,000	1,923,354,000	1,851,774,000
Net Income	976,000,000	695,000,000	1,185,000,000	1,293,000,000	1,169,927,000	1,270,994,000
Operating Cash Flow	2,559,000,000	1,730,000,000	1,746,000,000	1,717,000,000	1,760,228,000	1,716,000,000
Capital Expenditure	718,000,000	633,000,000	653,000,000	588,000,000	553,644,000	605,257,000
EBITDA	2,576,000,000	2,001,000,000	2,219,000,000	1,849,000,000	2,118,004,000	2,304,371,000
Return on Assets %	3.72%	3.53%	9.63%	10.99%	10.73%	
Return on Equity %	13.19%	11.37%	23.47%	28.17%	26.10%	
Debt to Equity	1.38	1.58	0.74	0.74	0.90	0.51

CONTACT INFORMATION:

Phone: 201 847-6800   Fax:
Toll-Free: 800-284-6845
Address: 1 Becton Dr., Franklin Lakes, NJ 07417 United States

STOCK TICKER/OTHER:

Stock Ticker: BDX   Exchange: NYS
Employees: 50,928   Fiscal Year Ends: 09/30
Parent Company:

SALARIES/BONUSES:

Top Exec. Salary: $1,105,000   Bonus: $
Second Exec. Salary: Bonus: $
$746,568

OTHER THOUGHTS:

Estimated Female Officers or Directors: 6
Hot Spot for Advancement for Women/Minorities: Y

Bed Bath & Beyond Inc

www.bedbathandbeyond.com

NAIC Code: 442299

TYPES OF BUSINESS:

Linens & Housewares, Retail
Small Appliances
Home Accessories
Health & Beauty Care
Baby & Toddler Merchandise

BRANDS/DIVISIONS/AFFILIATES:

Bed Bath & Beyond
buybuy BABY
Christmas Tree Shops
Cost Plus World Market
One Kings Lane
PersonalizationMall.com
Chef Central
Decorist

CONTACTS: Note: Officers with more than one job title may be intentionally listed here more than once.

Steven Temares, CEO
Susan Lattmann, CFO
Warren Eisenberg, Co-Chairman
Leonard Feinstein, Co-Chairman
Eugene Castagna, COO
Arthur Stark, Other Executive Officer
Matthew Fiorilli, Senior VP, Divisional

GROWTH PLANS/SPECIAL FEATURES:

Bed Bath & Beyond, Inc. (BBB) is one of the nation's largest operators of domestic superstores, with approximately 1,546 stores in 50 states as well as Washington D.C., Canada and Puerto Rico. In connection with BBB's retail services, its service marks include: Bed Bath & Beyond, buybuy BABY, Christmas Tree Shops, and That!, Harmon, Face Values, Cost Plus, World Market, Cost Plus World Market, Of a Kind, One Kings Lane, PersonalizationMall.com, PMall, Chef Central and Decorist. Together, these stores sell a wide assortment of domestic merchandise and home furnishings. Domestic merchandise includes categories such as bed linens and related items, bath items and kitchen textiles. Home furnishing include categories such as kitchen and tabletop items, fine tabletop, basic housewares, general home furnishings, consumables and certain juvenile products. Proprietary brands of BBB include Wamsutta, Real Simple and Olivia & Oliver. On an ongoing basis, BBB tests new merchandise categories and adjusts the categories of merchandise carried in-store and online, and may add new product categories or expand its merchandise assortment as appropriate. BBB purchases its merchandise in the U.S., the majority from domestic sources and the balance from importers. It purchases a small amount of merchandise directly from overseas sources. The company buys from approximately 10,800 supppliers. In November 2016, the firm acquired PersonalizationMall.com, LLC, an online retailer of personalized products. In early-2017, it acquired Decorist, Inc., an online interior design platform providing personalized home design services.

FINANCIAL DATA: Note: Data for latest year may not have been available at press time.

In U.S. $	2016	2015	2014	2013	2012	2011
Revenue	12,103,890,000	11,881,180,000	11,503,960,000	10,914,580,000	9,499,890,000	
R&D Expense						
Operating Income	1,414,903,000	1,554,293,000	1,614,587,000	1,638,218,000	1,568,369,000	
Operating Margin %	11.68%	13.08%	14.03%	15.00%	16.50%	
SGA Expense	3,205,407,000	3,065,486,000	2,950,995,000	2,750,537,000	2,362,564,000	
Net Income	841,489,000	957,474,000	1,022,290,000	1,037,788,000	989,537,000	
Operating Cash Flow	1,012,184,000	1,185,848,000	1,383,186,000	1,192,990,000	1,225,284,000	
Capital Expenditure	328,395,000	330,637,000	317,180,000	354,682,000	243,374,000	
EBITDA	1,688,850,000	1,793,486,000	1,833,396,000	1,832,946,000	1,752,242,000	
Return on Assets %	12.69%	14.60%	16.18%	17.29%	17.40%	
Return on Equity %	31.73%	28.64%	25.49%	25.93%	25.19%	
Debt to Equity	0.58	0.54				

CONTACT INFORMATION:

Phone: 908 688-0888   Fax: 908 810-8813
Toll-Free: 800-462-3966
Address: 650 Liberty Ave., Union, NJ 07083 United States

STOCK TICKER/OTHER:

Stock Ticker: BBBY   Exchange: NAS
Employees: 65,000   Fiscal Year Ends: 02/28
Parent Company:

SALARIES/BONUSES:

Top Exec. Salary: $3,967,500   Bonus: $
Second Exec. Salary: Bonus: $
$1,928,846

OTHER THOUGHTS:

Estimated Female Officers or Directors: 1
Hot Spot for Advancement for Women/Minorities:

Belden Inc

NAIC Code: 334417

TYPES OF BUSINESS:

Cable & Wire Connectors Manufacturing
Electronic Products
Broadcasting Equipment
Aerospace & Automotive Electronics
Enclosures

BRANDS/DIVISIONS/AFFILIATES:

Tripwire

CONTACTS: *Note: Officers with more than one job title may be intentionally listed here more than once.*

John Stroup, CEO
Henk Derksen, CFO
Douglas Zink, Chief Accounting Officer
Christopher Gusenleitner, Executive VP, Divisional
Dhrupad Trivedi, Executive VP, Divisional
Glenn Pennycook, Executive VP, Divisional
Roel Vestjens, Executive VP, Divisional
Brian Anderson, General Counsel
Dean McKenna, Senior VP, Divisional
Ross Rosenberg, Senior VP, Divisional

GROWTH PLANS/SPECIAL FEATURES:

Belden, Inc. designs, manufactures and markets signal transmission products, including cable, connectivity and networking components. The company is divided into five segments that offer various solutions: broadcast, enterprise connectivity, industrial connectivity, industrial IT and network security. Broadcast solutions provides production, distribution and connectivity systems for the television broadcast, cable, satellite and internet protocol television (IPTV) industries. Products are used in a variety of applications, including live production signal management, program playout for broadcasters, monitoring for pay-TV operators and broadband connectivity. Broadcast products include camera mounted fiber solutions, interfaces and routers, broadcast and audio-visual cable solutions, monitoring systems, playout systems, outside plant connectivity products and other cable and connectivity products. The enterprise connectivity segment provides infrastructure and connectivity solutions for enterprise customers. Products include fiber and copper connectivity products; fiber optic and copper cable products; and wiring racks, panels and enclosures as well as interconnecting hardware, intelligent patching devices and cable management solutions for complete end-to-end network structured wiring systems. The industrial connectivity solutions segment provides infrastructure components and connectivity systems for industrial automation applications. Products include industrial and input/output (I/O) connectors, industrial cables, IP and networking cables, I/O modules, distribution boxes, ruggedized controls and sensors, wiring solutions and load-moment indicator systems. The industrial IT segment provides mission-critical networking systems. Products include security devices, Ethernet switches and related equipment, routers and gateways, network management software and wireless systems. Last, the network security segment provides the following solutions: controls for protecting enterprises against cyberattacks; automating IT regulatory compliance; and improving operational efficiency. In January 2017, the firm agreed to sell its mobile machine control solutions business, including its 50%-stake in a Chinese joint venture, to WIKA Group.

FINANCIAL DATA: *Note: Data for latest year may not have been available at press time.*

In U.S. $	2016	2015	2014	2013	2012	2011
Revenue	2,356,672,000	2,309,222,000	2,308,265,000	2,069,193,000	1,840,739,000	1,981,953,000
R&D Expense	140,601,000	148,311,000	113,914,000	83,277,000	65,410,000	55,711,000
Operating Income	223,853,000	140,553,000	163,119,000	201,262,000	108,497,000	187,006,000
Operating Margin %	9.49%	6.08%	7.06%	9.72%	5.89%	9.43%
SGA Expense	494,224,000	527,288,000	487,945,000	378,009,000	345,926,000	325,950,000
Net Income	128,003,000	66,204,000	74,449,000	103,313,000	194,490,000	114,345,000
Operating Cash Flow	314,794,000	236,410,000	194,028,000	164,601,000	139,388,000	184,563,000
Capital Expenditure	53,974,000	54,969,000	45,459,000	40,209,000	41,010,000	40,053,000
EBITDA	369,446,000	290,895,000	265,864,000	294,595,000	116,435,000	238,191,000
Return on Assets %	3.16%	2.01%	2.47%	3.87%	8.89%	6.56%
Return on Equity %	9.85%	8.11%	9.05%	12.53%	25.82%	17.15%
Debt to Equity	1.10	2.12	2.18	1.63	1.39	0.79

CONTACT INFORMATION:

Phone: 314 854-8000   Fax: 314 854-8001
Toll-Free: 800-235-3361
Address: 1 N. Brentwood Blvd., 15/Fl, St. Louis, MO 63105 United States

STOCK TICKER/OTHER:

Stock Ticker: BDC   Exchange: NYS
Employees: 8,400   Fiscal Year Ends: 12/31
Parent Company:

SALARIES/BONUSES:

Top Exec. Salary: $868,750   Bonus: $
Second Exec. Salary: $512,820   Bonus: $

OTHER THOUGHTS:

Estimated Female Officers or Directors: 2
Hot Spot for Advancement for Women/Minorities: Y

Berkshire Hathaway Energy Company

www.berkshirehathawayenergyco.com/

NAIC Code: 221112

TYPES OF BUSINESS:

Utilities-Electricity & Natural Gas
Pipelines
Wind Generation
Hydroelectric Generation
Thermal Solar Generation
Real Estate Brokerage
Solar Power

BRANDS/DIVISIONS/AFFILIATES:

Berkshire Hathaway Inc
PacifiCorp
NV Energy Inc
Northern Powergrid
Kern River Gas Transmission Company
BHE Renewables
AltaLink
HomeServices of America Inc

CONTACTS: Note: Officers with more than one job title may be intentionally listed here more than once.

Gregory E. Abel, CEO
Patrick J. Goodman, CFO
Maureen E. Sammon, Chief Admin. Officer
Douglas L. Anderson, General Counsel
Gregory E. Abel, Chmn.

GROWTH PLANS/SPECIAL FEATURES:

Berkshire Hathaway Energy Company generates, transmits, stores, distributes and supplies energy through its subsidiaries to roughly 11.6 million customers. The company has 10 primary subsidiaries. PacifiCorp serves roughly 1.8 million customers, operating in three business units: Rocky Mountain Power, which delivers electricity in Wyoming, Utah and Idaho; Pacific Power, delivering electricity in Oregon, Washington and California; and PacifiCorp Transmission, which constitutes the company's electric generation, energy trading and coal mining operations. MidAmerican Energy Company generates, transmits and sells electricity to over 752,000 customers and supplies natural gas to over 733,000 customers in Illinois, Nebraska, Iowa and South Dakota. NV Energy, Inc. has approximately 1.34 million customers in Nevada, serving approximately 90% of the state with electricity. Northern Powergrid offers 3.9 million users electricity in the Northeastern part of England. Northern Natural Gas Company owns a 14,700-mile interstate natural gas pipeline system extending from Texas to the upper Midwest, serving 81 utility companies. Kern River Gas Transmission Company owns 1,700 miles of interstate pipeline and delivers natural gas to Nevada, Utah and California. BHE Renewables' 4,083 megawatts total capacity of owned and under construction clean energy includes: 1,484 MW solar; 1,153 MW wind; 338 MW geothermal; and 138 MW hydro. AltaLink is the largest regulated transmission company in Alberta, owning more than 8,000 miles of transmission lines and more than 300 substations. BHE U.S. Transmission provides transmission solutions for wholesale customers. HomeServices of America, Inc. is a leading U.S. residential real estate brokerage firm. Berkshire Hathaway Energy is a wholly-owned subsidiary of Berkshire Hathaway, Inc.

The company offers employees medical, dental, vision, disability and life insurance; a 401(k) plan; a profit sharing plan; an employee assistance program; flexible spending accounts; tuition reimbursement; and adoption assistance.

FINANCIAL DATA: Note: Data for latest year may not have been available at press time.

In U.S. $	2016	2015	2014	2013	2012	2011
Revenue	17,859,000,000	18,231,000,000	17,614,000,000	12,743,000,000	11,747,000,000	11,291,000,000
R&D Expense						
Operating Income						
Operating Margin %						
SGA Expense						
Net Income	2,973,000,000	2,851,000,000	2,711,000,000	1,806,000,000	1,644,000,000	1,659,000,000
Operating Cash Flow						
Capital Expenditure						
EBITDA						
Return on Assets %						
Return on Equity %						
Debt to Equity						

CONTACT INFORMATION:

Phone: 515-242-3022   Fax:
Toll-Free:
Address: 666 Grand Ave., Des Moines, IA 50306-0657 United States

STOCK TICKER/OTHER:

Stock Ticker: Subsidiary   Exchange:
Employees: 21,000   Fiscal Year Ends: 12/31
Parent Company: Berkshire Hathaway Inc

SALARIES/BONUSES:

Top Exec. Salary: $ Bonus: $
Second Exec. Salary: $ Bonus: $

OTHER THOUGHTS:

Estimated Female Officers or Directors: 1
Hot Spot for Advancement for Women/Minorities:

Berkshire Hathaway Inc

www.berkshirehathaway.com

NAIC Code: 524126

TYPES OF BUSINESS:

Insurance--Property & Casualty, Specialty, Surety
Retail Operations
Foodservice Operations
Building Products & Services
Apparel & Footwear
Technology Training
Manufactured Housing & RVs
Business Jet Flexible Ownership Services

BRANDS/DIVISIONS/AFFILIATES:

General Re Corporation
GEICO Corporation
Berkshire Hathaway Reinsurance Group
Berkshire Hathaway Primary Group
Clayton Homes Inc
Acme Building Brands
FlightSafety International Inc
Borsheim Jewelry Company Inc

CONTACTS: Note: Officers with more than one job title may be intentionally listed here more than once.

Warren Buffett, CEO
Marc Hamburg, CFO
Daniel Jaksich, Chief Accounting Officer
Charles Munger, Director

GROWTH PLANS/SPECIAL FEATURES:

Berkshire Hathaway, Inc. is a holding company that owns subsidiaries engaged in diverse business activities, most importantly insurance and reinsurance. Berkshire provides property and casualty insurance and reinsurance, as well as life, accident and health reinsurance, through U.S. and foreign businesses. The company conducts its insurance underwriting business through four subsidiary divisions. First, General Re Corporation, through its subsidiaries, conducts global reinsurance business in 45 cities and provides reinsurance worldwide. Second, GEICO Corporation mainly provides private passenger auto insurance to individuals in all 50 U.S. states and Washington, D.C. Third, Berkshire Hathaway Reinsurance Group underwrites excess-of-loss and quota-share reinsurance for insurers and reinsurers. Last, Berkshire Hathaway Primary Group offers insurance for property and casualty. The company's financial subsidiaries include Clayton Homes, Inc., a manufactured housing company; XTRA Corporation, a provider of transportation equipment leases; and CORT Business Services Corporation, a furniture rental company. Berkshire's apparel and footwear businesses include Fruit of the Loom, Russell, Vanity Fair, Garan, Fechheimer Brothers, H.H. Brown Shoe Company, Brooks Sports and Justin Brands. The firm manufactures and distributes building products through Acme Building Brands, Benjamin Moore & Co., Johns Manville, Shaw Industries, Duracell Company and MiTek Industries. Subsidiary FlightSafety International, Inc. provides training to aircraft and ship pilots, while NetJets, Inc. offers fractional ownership programs for aircraft. In addition, subsidiary International Dairy Queen services approximately 6,800 DQ Grill and Chill, Dairy Queen and Orange Julius stores. Borsheim Jewelry Company, Inc. is a retailer of fine jewelry, watches, crystal, china, stemware, flatware, gifts and collectibles. Other non-insurance operations include grocery and foodservice distribution, furniture retailing, carpet manufacturing, utilities and energy, newspapers, cleaning products, confectioneries, agricultural equipment, kitchen tools and recreational vehicles. In June 2017, the firm acquired a nearly 10% stake in real estate investment trust, Store Capital Corporation.

FINANCIAL DATA: Note: Data for latest year may not have been available at press time.

In U.S. $	2016	2015	2014	2013	2012	2011
Revenue	223,604,000,000	210,821,000,000	194,673,000,000	182,150,000,000	162,463,000,000	143,688,000,000
R&D Expense						
Operating Income	32,744,000,000	34,946,000,000	28,105,000,000	28,796,000,000	22,236,000,000	15,314,000,000
Operating Margin %	14.64%	16.57%	14.43%	15.80%	13.68%	10.65%
SGA Expense	47,859,000,000	45,874,000,000	43,099,000,000	11,917,000,000	10,503,000,000	8,670,000,000
Net Income	24,074,000,000	24,083,000,000	19,872,000,000	19,476,000,000	14,824,000,000	10,254,000,000
Operating Cash Flow	32,535,000,000	31,491,000,000	32,010,000,000	27,704,000,000	20,950,000,000	20,476,000,000
Capital Expenditure	12,954,000,000	16,082,000,000	15,185,000,000	11,087,000,000	9,775,000,000	8,191,000,000
EBITDA						
Return on Assets %	4.10%	4.46%	3.93%	4.26%	3.61%	2.68%
Return on Equity %	8.94%	9.71%	8.60%	9.51%	8.41%	6.36%
Debt to Equity	0.35	0.32	0.33	0.32	0.33	0.36

CONTACT INFORMATION:

Phone: 402 346-1400   Fax: 402 346-3375
Toll-Free:
Address: 3555 Farnam St., Omaha, NE 68131 United States

STOCK TICKER/OTHER:

Stock Ticker: BRK.A   Exchange: NYS
Employees: 367,700   Fiscal Year Ends: 12/31
Parent Company:

SALARIES/BONUSES:

Top Exec. Salary: $1,550,000   Bonus: $
Second Exec. Salary: Bonus: $
$100,000

OTHER THOUGHTS:

Estimated Female Officers or Directors:
Hot Spot for Advancement for Women/Minorities:

Berry Global Group Inc

www.berryplastics.com

NAIC Code: 326100

TYPES OF BUSINESS:

Injection Molded Packaging
Open-Top Containers
Closures
Consumer Products
Plastic Housewares
Thermoforming

BRANDS/DIVISIONS/AFFILIATES:

Berry Plastics Group Inc

CONTACTS: Note: Officers with more than one job title may be intentionally listed here more than once.

Mark Miles, CFO
Jonathan Rich, Chairman of the Board
James Till, Chief Accounting Officer
Thomas Salmon, Director
Jason Greene, Executive VP
Jean-Marc Galvez, President, Divisional
Scott Tracey, President, Divisional
Curt Begle, President, Divisional

GROWTH PLANS/SPECIAL FEATURES:

Berry Global Group, Inc., formerly Berry Plastics Group, Inc., operating through Berry Global, Inc., formerly Berry Plastics Corporation, is a leading manufacturer of plastic packaging products, plastic film products, specialty adhesives and coated products. Berry operates through manufacturing facilities in the U. S., Canada, Mexico, India, the Netherlands, Belgium, Germany, Austria, Brazil, Malaysia, China and France. It serves customers ranging from large multinational corporations to small local businesses. The firm manufactures its packaging solutions using a collection of proprietary molds and a set of internally developed processes and technologies. Its principal products include containers, drink cups, bottles, closures and overcaps, tubes and prescription containers, trash bags, stretch films, plastic sheeting and tapes. Berry operates through four divisions: consumer packaging; engineered materials; and health, hygiene & specialties. Its consumer packaging division consists of containers and foodservice items. Additionally, the division's products consist of closures and overcaps, bottles and prescriptions containers as well as tubes. Berry's engineered materials division manufactures and sells primarily polyethylene-based film products, including trash bags, drop cloths, agricultural film, stretch film and custom packaging film. The health, hygiene & specialties segment is organized by geographic regions of North America, South America, Europe and Asia. In each region, the division manufactures and sells a broad range of health and hygiene products such as cable wrap, baby diapers, geosynthetics, adult incontinence, surgical drapes, face masks and specialty filtration products. In January 2017, the firm acquired of AEP Industries, Inc., a manufacturer of flexible plastic packaging films, for an aggregate consideration of $765 million.

FINANCIAL DATA: Note: Data for latest year may not have been available at press time.

In U.S. $	2016	2015	2014	2013	2012	2011
Revenue	6,489,000,000	4,881,000,000	4,958,000,000	4,647,000,000	4,766,000,000	4,561,000,000
R&D Expense						
Operating Income	581,000,000	408,000,000	316,000,000	386,000,000	325,000,000	42,000,000
Operating Margin %	8.95%	8.35%	6.37%	8.30%	6.81%	.92%
SGA Expense	531,000,000	357,000,000	320,000,000	307,000,000	308,000,000	275,000,000
Net Income	236,000,000	86,000,000	62,000,000	57,000,000	2,000,000	-299,000,000
Operating Cash Flow	857,000,000	637,000,000	530,000,000	464,000,000	479,000,000	327,000,000
Capital Expenditure	288,000,000	180,000,000	215,000,000	239,000,000	230,000,000	160,000,000
EBITDA	1,106,000,000	758,000,000	674,000,000	727,000,000	687,000,000	325,000,000
Return on Assets %	3.72%	1.67%	1.19%	1.11%	.03%	-5.73%
Return on Equity %	314.66%					
Debt to Equity	26.20					

CONTACT INFORMATION:

Phone: 812 424-2904   Fax:
Toll-Free:
Address: 101 Oakley St., Evansville, IN 47710 United States

STOCK TICKER/OTHER:

Stock Ticker: BERY   Exchange: NYS
Employees: 21,000   Fiscal Year Ends: 09/30
Parent Company:

SALARIES/BONUSES:

Top Exec. Salary: $1,064,225   Bonus: $
Second Exec. Salary: $550,961   Bonus: $

OTHER THOUGHTS:

Estimated Female Officers or Directors:
Hot Spot for Advancement for Women/Minorities:

Best Buy Co Inc

NAIC Code: 443142

www.bestbuy.com

TYPES OF BUSINESS:

Consumer Electronics Stores
Retail Music & Video Sales
Personal Computers
Office Supplies
Cell Phones and Accessories
Appliances
Cameras
Consumer Electronics Installation & Service

BRANDS/DIVISIONS/AFFILIATES:

Geek Squad
Best Buy Mobile
Best Buy Express
Best Buy Smart Home powered by Vivint
Best Buy Direct
Best Buy
Best Buy Canada

CONTACTS: *Note: Officers with more than one job title may be intentionally listed here more than once.*

Hubert Joly, CEO
Corie Barry, CFO
Mathew Watson, Controller
Keith Nelsen, General Counsel
Paula Baker, Other Executive Officer
Asheesh Saksena, Other Executive Officer
R. Mohan, Other Executive Officer
Shari Ballard, President, Divisional
Trish Walker, President, Divisional

GROWTH PLANS/SPECIAL FEATURES:

Best Buy Co., Inc. is a leading retailer of name-brand consumer electronics, appliances and home office and entertainment products and services. The company conducts business in both the domestic and international markets. The domestic market includes all of the firm's U.S. businesses, operating under such brands as Best Buy; Best Buy Direct; Best Buy Express; Best Buy Mobile; Geek Squad, which provides computer repair and installation services; Magnolia Home Theater; and Pacific Kitchen and Home. The international segment, which is comprised of the firm's businesses in Canada and Mexico, operates under brand names such as Best Buy, Best Buy Express, Best Buy Mobile and Geek Squad. The company's products include home office equipment, cameras, computer and audio/video equipment, computer upgrades and car audio and security system installation. The firm operates 1,200 large-format and 400 small-format Best Buy stores in the U.S. and internationally. In May 2017, the company announced a strategic partnership with Vivint Smart Home, to give customers an easy way to automate and manage their homes through a new platform called Best Buy Smart Home powered by Vivint.

Employee benefits include medical, dental, vision, life, disability, health care and dependent care spending accounts. Wealth benefits include 401(k) accounts, an employee stock purchase plan and bonus/incentive programs.

FINANCIAL DATA: *Note: Data for latest year may not have been available at press time.*

In U.S. $	2016	2015	2014	2013	2012	2011
Revenue	39,528,000,000	40,339,000,000	42,410,000,000	45,085,000,000	50,705,000,000	
R&D Expense						
Operating Income	1,375,000,000	1,450,000,000	1,140,000,000	-125,000,000	1,085,000,000	
Operating Margin %	3.47%	3.59%	2.68%		2.13%	
SGA Expense	7,618,000,000	7,592,000,000	8,391,000,000	9,502,000,000	10,242,000,000	
Net Income	897,000,000	1,233,000,000	532,000,000	-441,000,000	-1,231,000,000	
Operating Cash Flow	1,322,000,000	1,935,000,000	1,094,000,000	1,454,000,000	3,293,000,000	
Capital Expenditure	649,000,000	561,000,000	547,000,000	705,000,000	766,000,000	
EBITDA	2,047,000,000	2,133,000,000	1,903,000,000	758,000,000	2,122,000,000	
Return on Assets %	6.23%	8.42%	3.79%		-7.27%	
Return on Equity %	19.14%	27.45%	13.34%		-23.79%	
Debt to Equity	0.30	0.31	0.40		0.44	

CONTACT INFORMATION:

Phone: 612 291-1000   Fax: 612 292-4001
Toll-Free:
Address: 7601 Penn Ave. S., Richfield, MN 55423 United States

STOCK TICKER/OTHER:

Stock Ticker: BBY   Exchange: NYS
Employees: 125,000   Fiscal Year Ends: 02/28
Parent Company:

SALARIES/BONUSES:

Top Exec. Salary: $1,175,000   Bonus: $
Second Exec. Salary: Bonus: $
$925,000

OTHER THOUGHTS:

Estimated Female Officers or Directors: 5
Hot Spot for Advancement for Women/Minorities: Y

Bio Rad Laboratories Inc

www.bio-rad.com

NAIC Code: 325413

TYPES OF BUSINESS:

Clinical Diagnostics Products
Medical Equipment
Analytical Instruments
Laboratory Devices
Biomaterials
Imaging Products
Assays
Software

BRANDS/DIVISIONS/AFFILIATES:

CONTACTS:
Note: Officers with more than one job title may be intentionally listed here more than once.

John Cassingham, Assistant Secretary
Norman Schwartz, CEO
Christine Tsingos, CFO
James Stark, Chief Accounting Officer
John Goetz, COO
Michael Crowley, Executive VP, Divisional
Giovanni Magni, Executive VP
John Hertia, Executive VP
Shannon Hall, Executive VP
Ronald Hutton, Executive VP

GROWTH PLANS/SPECIAL FEATURES:

Bio-Rad Laboratories, Inc. supplies the research, health care and analytical chemistry markets with a broad range of life science research and clinical diagnostic products and systems. These are used to separate complex chemical and biological materials and to identify, analyze and purify components. The company operates in two industry segments: clinical diagnostics and life science. The clinical diagnostics division encompasses an array of technologies incorporated into a variety of tests used to detect, identify and quantify substances in blood or other body fluids and tissues. The test results are used as aids for medical diagnosis, detection, evaluation, monitoring and treatment of diseases and other conditions. This division is known for diabetes monitoring products, quality control systems, blood virus testing, blood typing, toxicology, genetic disorders products, molecular pathology and Internet-based software. The firm's life science division develops, manufactures and markets more than 5,000 products for applications including electrophoresis, image analysis, molecular detection, chromatography, gene transfer, sample preparation and amplification. Products include a range of laboratory instruments, apparatuses and consumables used for research in genomics, proteomics and food safety. The life science division provides its services to universities, medical schools, pharmaceutical manufacturers, industrial research organizations, food testing laboratories, government agencies and biotechnology researchers.In January 2017, Bio-Rad agreed to acquire RainDance Technologies, Inc., the producer of a proprietary droplet technology that enables research in areas such as non-invasive liquid biopsy.

FINANCIAL DATA:
Note: Data for latest year may not have been available at press time.

In U.S. $	2016	2015	2014	2013	2012	2011
Revenue	2,068,172,000	2,019,441,000	2,175,044,000	2,132,694,000	2,069,235,000	2,073,529,000
R&D Expense	205,864,000	192,972,000	220,333,000	210,952,000	214,040,000	186,439,000
Operating Income	53,194,000	166,708,000	149,984,000	169,456,000	257,200,000	295,156,000
Operating Margin %	2.57%	8.25%	6.89%	7.94%	12.42%	14.23%
SGA Expense	816,724,000	761,990,000	808,200,000	798,070,000	682,898,000	696,294,000
Net Income	28,125,000	113,093,000	88,845,000	77,790,000	163,778,000	178,223,000
Operating Cash Flow	216,410,000	186,210,000	273,312,000	175,476,000	278,898,000	259,816,000
Capital Expenditure	141,571,000	113,372,000	136,478,000	113,698,000	154,197,000	103,324,000
EBITDA	206,402,000	299,339,000	303,588,000	320,856,000	404,443,000	409,897,000
Return on Assets %	.74%	3.20%	2.64%	2.27%	5.01%	5.78%
Return on Equity %	1.10%	4.83%	4.06%	3.70%	8.72%	10.86%
Debt to Equity	0.16	0.17	0.19	0.19	0.36	0.41

CONTACT INFORMATION:

Phone: 510 724-7000   Fax: 510 741-5817
Toll-Free: 800-424-6723
Address: 1000 Alfred Nobel Dr., Hercules, CA 94547 United States

STOCK TICKER/OTHER:

Stock Ticker: BIO
Employees: 8,250
Parent Company:

Exchange: NYS
Fiscal Year Ends: 12/31

SALARIES/BONUSES:

Top Exec. Salary: $914,320   Bonus: $
Second Exec. Salary: $684,184   Bonus: $

OTHER THOUGHTS:

Estimated Female Officers or Directors: 3
Hot Spot for Advancement for Women/Minorities: Y

Biogen Inc

www.biogen.com

NAIC Code: 325412

TYPES OF BUSINESS:

Drugs-Immunology, Neurology & Oncology
Autoimmune & Inflammatory Disease Treatments
Drugs-Multiple Sclerosis
Drugs-Cancer

BRANDS/DIVISIONS/AFFILIATES:

AVONEX
PLEGRIDY
RITUXAN
TECFIDERA
FAMPYRA
ELOCTATE
GAZYVA
Biogen Idec Inc

CONTACTS: Note: Officers with more than one job title may be intentionally listed here more than once.

Michel Vounatsos, CEO
Gregory Covino, CFO
Alfred Sandrock, Chief Medical Officer
Stelios Papadopoulos, Director
Kenneth Dipietro, Executive VP, Divisional
Adriana Karaboutis, Executive VP, Divisional
Michael Ehlers, Executive VP, Divisional
Paul McKenzie, Executive VP, Divisional
Susan Alexander, Executive VP

GROWTH PLANS/SPECIAL FEATURES:

Biogen, Inc. is a biotechnology company focused on discovering, developing, manufacturing and marketing therapies for the treatment of multiple sclerosis (MS), spinal muscular dystrophy and other autoimmune disorders. Biogen's marketed products for MS include: AVONEX, an intramuscular injectable therapy designed to treat relapsing forms of the disease and is one of the most prescribed forms of treatment worldwide; PLEGRIDY, a subcutaneous injectable therapy in the U.S. for the treatment of relapsing forms of MS and in the European Union (EU) for relapsing remitting MS (RRMS); TECFIDERA, an oral therapy in the U.S. for the treatment of relapsing forms of MS and in the EU for people with RRMS; TYSABRI, a monoclonal antibody for the treatment of RRMS and also U.S. approved to treat Crohn's disease; and FAMPYRA, which aids in improving adult patients with MS-related walking disabilities. Biogen collaborates with Genentech, Inc. on the development and commercialization of RITUXAN, a widely prescribed monoclonal antibody used to treat non-Hodgkin's lymphoma, rheumatoid arthritis, chronic lymphocytic leukemia (CLL) and two forms of ANCA-associated vasculitis; and shares operating profits and losses relating to GAZYVA with Genentech. GAZYVA, in combination with chlorambucil, is for the treatment of patients with previously untreated CLL, and is FDA approved. In January 2017, the firm formed a strategic alliance with Siemens Healthineers to jointly develop MRI applications that would quantify key markers of MS disease activity and progression. In February 2017, the company completed the separation of its hemophilia business, Bioverativ Inc., into a fully-independent company.

Biogen offers employees medical, dental and vision insurance; tuition reimbursement; flexible spending accounts; and an employee assistance program.

FINANCIAL DATA: Note: Data for latest year may not have been available at press time.

In U.S. $	2016	2015	2014	2013	2012	2011
Revenue	11,448,800,000	10,763,800,000	9,703,324,000	6,932,199,000	5,516,461,000	5,048,634,000
R&D Expense	1,973,300,000	2,012,800,000	1,893,422,000	1,444,053,000	1,334,919,000	1,219,602,000
Operating Income	5,150,400,000	4,891,000,000	3,955,656,000	2,515,509,000	1,855,849,000	1,724,691,000
Operating Margin %	44.98%	45.43%	40.76%	36.28%	33.64%	34.16%
SGA Expense	2,402,700,000	2,113,100,000	2,232,342,000	1,797,408,000	1,595,360,000	1,373,904,000
Net Income	3,702,800,000	3,547,000,000	2,934,784,000	1,862,341,000	1,380,033,000	1,234,428,000
Operating Cash Flow	4,522,400,000	3,716,100,000	2,942,115,000	2,345,078,000	1,879,897,000	1,727,741,000
Capital Expenditure	727,700,000	643,000,000	287,751,000	3,509,000,000	261,182,000	252,175,000
EBITDA	5,875,700,000	5,463,200,000	4,664,283,000	3,044,219,000	2,257,253,000	2,103,147,000
Return on Assets %	17.47%	20.97%	22.42%	16.93%	14.39%	14.40%
Return on Equity %	34.42%	35.15%	30.21%	23.90%	20.61%	20.88%
Debt to Equity	0.53	0.69	0.05	0.06	0.09	0.16

CONTACT INFORMATION:

Phone: 617-679-2000   Fax: 619 679-2617
Toll-Free:
Address: 225 Binney Street, Cambridge, MA 02142 United States

STOCK TICKER/OTHER:

Stock Ticker: BIIB   Exchange: NAS
Employees: 7,400   Fiscal Year Ends: 12/31
Parent Company:

SALARIES/BONUSES:

Top Exec. Salary: $519,231   Bonus: $1,500,000
Second Exec. Salary: Bonus: $1,170,177
$491,827

OTHER THOUGHTS:

Estimated Female Officers or Directors: 4
Hot Spot for Advancement for Women/Minorities: Y

Black & Veatch Holding Company

www.bv.com

NAIC Code: 541330

TYPES OF BUSINESS:

Heavy & Civil Engineering, Construction
Infrastructure & Energy Services
Environmental & Hydrologic Engineering
Consulting Services
IT Services
Power Plant Engineering and Construction
LNG and Gas Processing Plant Engineering
Climate Change Services

BRANDS/DIVISIONS/AFFILIATES:

CONTACTS: *Note: Officers with more than one job title may be intentionally listed here more than once.*

Steven L. Edwards, CEO
Martin G. Travers, Pres.
Karen L. Daniel, CFO
Lori Kelleher, Chief Human Resources Officer
James R. Lewis, Chief Admin. Officer
Timothy W. Triplett, General Counsel
Cindy Wallis-Lage, Pres., Water
O.H. Oskvig, CEO-Energy Business
William R. Van Dyke, Pres., Federal Svcs.
Steven L. Edwards, Chmn.
Hoe Wai Cheong, Sr. VP-Water-Asia Pacific
John E. Murphy, Pres., Construction & Procurement

GROWTH PLANS/SPECIAL FEATURES:

Black & Veatch Holding Company (B&V) is an engineering, consulting and construction company specializing in infrastructure development for the energy, water, telecommunications, federal, management consulting and environmental markets. The company is employee-owned and operates over 100 offices worldwide. B&V divides its service offerings into 12 categories. The firm's asset management services include power and water asset optimization solutions. Its EPC & Design-build services encompass energy optimization, water planning, greenhouse gas services, climate economics and government services. The company provides construction services for energy facilities, water and wastewater treatment facilities, water distribution systems, desalination facilities, wireless sites and aerospace and defense sites. The construction management service segment offers tailored services aimed at reducing costs while improving quality. Engineering and design services include power delivery, siting, new generation engineering, power plant upgrade and bulk materials handling services. The nexus of water and energy segment addresses the interdependency of water and energy, reducing costs for both. Management consulting services comprise enterprise management and utility efficiency solutions. Procurement services include project procurement strategy, transportation logistics and inspection services. The program management segment manages energy, water, telecom and federal programs. Smart grid/smart utility services include utilities planning, system modeling, distribution automation and field construction. The security services segment offers cyber, electronic and physical security to the communications and utility industries. B&V also offers consulting and planning services.

The company offers employees medical, dental, vision and prescription drug coverage; flexible spending accounts; employee assistance programs; tuition reimbursement; adoption assistance; and credit union membership.

FINANCIAL DATA: *Note: Data for latest year may not have been available at press time.*

In U.S. $	2016	2015	2014	2013	2012	2011
Revenue	3,000,000,000	3,030,000,000	3,600,000,000	3,560,000,000	3,279,000,000	2,600,000,000
R&D Expense						
Operating Income						
Operating Margin %						
SGA Expense						
Net Income						
Operating Cash Flow						
Capital Expenditure						
EBITDA						
Return on Assets %						
Return on Equity %						
Debt to Equity						

CONTACT INFORMATION:

Phone: 913-458-2000   Fax: 913-458-2934
Toll-Free:
Address: 11401 Lamar Ave., Overland Park, KS 66211 United States

STOCK TICKER/OTHER:

Stock Ticker: Private   Exchange:
Employees: 11,350   Fiscal Year Ends: 12/31
Parent Company:

SALARIES/BONUSES:

Top Exec. Salary: $ Bonus: $
Second Exec. Salary: $ Bonus: $

OTHER THOUGHTS:

Estimated Female Officers or Directors: 4
Hot Spot for Advancement for Women/Minorities: Y

BlackRock Inc

NAIC Code: 523920

www.blackrock.com

TYPES OF BUSINESS:

Investment Management
Risk Management Services
Investment System Services

BRANDS/DIVISIONS/AFFILIATES:

Aladdin
iShares
BlackRock Solutions
BlackRock Investment Institute

CONTACTS: *Note: Officers with more than one job title may be intentionally listed here more than once.*

Laurence Fink, CEO
David Blumer, Other Corporate Officer
Ryan Stork, Chairman of the Board, Geographical
Marc Comerchero, Chief Accounting Officer
Robert Goldstein, COO
Robert Kapito, Director
Christopher Meade, General Counsel
J. Kushel, Other Corporate Officer
Jeffrey Smith, Other Corporate Officer
Mark McCombe, Other Corporate Officer
Robert Fairbairn, Other Corporate Officer
Gary Shedlin, Other Corporate Officer

GROWTH PLANS/SPECIAL FEATURES:

BlackRock, Inc. and its subsidiaries form one of the largest investment management firms in the U.S., with $5.1 trillion worth of assets under management. The company manages more than 70 offices in 30 countries. The firm acts as a fiduciary on behalf of institutional and individual investors worldwide through a variety of fixed income, cash management, equity and balanced and alternative investment accounts and funds. The company also provides risk management, investment system outsourcing and financial advisory services. BlackRock's Aladdin platform is an operating system for investment managers that combines risk analytics with portfolio management, trading and operations tools. Its clients include a diverse group of taxable, tax-exempt and official institutions, retail investors and high-net-worth individuals globally. Institutional clients include pension funds, official institutions, foundations, endowments and charities, insurance companies, banks, sub-advisory relationships and private banks. Products are offered directly through intermediaries that include open-end and closed-end mutual funds, iShares exchange-traded funds (ETFs), collective investment funds and separate accounts. The firm also offers risk management, investment systems and advisory services to institutional investors through its BlackRock Solutions (BRS) product line. The firm's global platform, BlackRock Investment Institute, leverages its expertise in markets, asset classes and client segments to produce information that makes the company's portfolio managers better investors.

The company offers employees health care, disability and life coverage; retirement benefits; and tuition assistance.

FINANCIAL DATA: *Note: Data for latest year may not have been available at press time.*

In U.S. $	2016	2015	2014	2013	2012	2011
Revenue	11,155,000,000	11,401,000,000	11,081,000,000	10,180,000,000	9,337,000,000	9,081,000,000
R&D Expense						
Operating Income	4,570,000,000	4,664,000,000	4,474,000,000	3,857,000,000	3,524,000,000	3,249,000,000
Operating Margin %	40.96%	40.90%	40.37%	37.88%	37.74%	35.77%
SGA Expense	5,947,000,000	6,152,000,000	6,030,000,000	5,757,000,000	5,237,000,000	5,177,000,000
Net Income	3,172,000,000	3,345,000,000	3,294,000,000	2,932,000,000	2,458,000,000	2,337,000,000
Operating Cash Flow	2,154,000,000	3,004,000,000	3,081,000,000	3,642,000,000	2,240,000,000	2,826,000,000
Capital Expenditure	119,000,000	221,000,000	66,000,000	94,000,000	150,000,000	247,000,000
EBITDA	4,894,000,000	5,053,000,000	4,905,000,000	4,475,000,000	3,980,000,000	3,610,000,000
Return on Assets %	1.42%	1.43%	1.43%	1.39%	1.29%	1.30%
Return on Equity %	11.01%	11.97%	12.23%	11.30%	9.74%	9.13%
Debt to Equity	0.16	0.17	0.30	0.27	0.31	0.25

CONTACT INFORMATION:

Phone: 212 810-5300   Fax: 212 754-3123
Toll-Free:
Address: 40 E. 52nd St., New York, NY 10022 United States

STOCK TICKER/OTHER:

Stock Ticker: BLK
Employees: 13,000
Parent Company:

Exchange: NYS
Fiscal Year Ends: 12/31

SALARIES/BONUSES:

Top Exec. Salary: $900,000   Bonus: $8,000,000
Second Exec. Salary: Bonus: $6,500,000
$750,000

OTHER THOUGHTS:

Estimated Female Officers or Directors: 5
Hot Spot for Advancement for Women/Minorities: Y

Bloomberg LP

NAIC Code: 0

TYPES OF BUSINESS:

Financial Data Publishing-Print & Online
Magazine Publishing
Management Software
Multimedia Presentation Services
Broadcast Television
Radio Broadcasting
Electronic Exchange Systems
Software

BRANDS/DIVISIONS/AFFILIATES:

QuickTake
Bloomberg Terminal
Bloomberg Tradebook
Bloomberg Vault
Bloomberg Government
Bloomberg New Energy Finance Limited
Bloomberg Television
Bloomberg Content Service

CONTACTS: Note: Officers with more than one job title may be intentionally listed here more than once.

Michael R. Bloomberg, CEO
Daniel L. Doctoroff, Pres.
Jason Schechter, Chief Communications Officer
Matthew Winkler, Editor-in-Chief, Bloomberg News
Thomas Secunda, Vice Chmn.

GROWTH PLANS/SPECIAL FEATURES:

Bloomberg LP is an information services, news and media company, serving the financial services industry, government offices and agencies, corporations and news organizations. The company operates in six segments: communications, financial products, enterprise products, industry products, media and media services. Communications provides press announcements involving Bloomberg through its worldwide press contact centers, including the Americas, Europe/Middle East/Africa and Asia Pacific. Bloomberg's QuickTake franchise offers Q&A-style explainers to help readers quickly navigate breaking news and understand a story's fundamentals as news develops. Financial products is comprised of the Bloomberg Terminal, a platform for financial professionals who need real-time data, news and analytics to make fast and informed decisions; and the Bloomberg Tradebook, a global agency broker that provides anonymous direct market access and algorithmic trading to more than 125 global liquidity venues across 43 countries. This division also includes Bloomberg Briefs, Bloomberg Indexes, Bloomberg SEF (swap execution facility) and Bloomberg Institute. Enterprise provides solutions such as enterprise data, distribution and information; and trading solutions that address workflow with front-end portfolio, inventory, sales and trading, as well as middle and back office operations solutions for buy-side and sell-side firms. This division's Bloomberg Vault is a secure, managed service for information governance, data analytics and trade reconstruction across the enterprise. Industry products include Bloomberg Government, a web-based information service for professionals who interact with the federal government; Bloomberg Law/BNA and Bloomberg Big Law for legal, tax and regulatory professionals; and Bloomberg New Energy Finance Limited for decision-makers in the energy system. Media delivers business and political news through Bloomberg Business, Bloomberg Politics, Bloomberg View, Bloomberg Television, Bloomberg Radio, Bloomberg Mobile Apps and news bureaus. Media Services includes advertising, Bloomberg Content Service and Bloomberg Live Conferences.

FINANCIAL DATA: Note: Data for latest year may not have been available at press time.

In U.S. $	2016	2015	2014	2013	2012	2011
Revenue	9,400,000,000	9,184,000,000	9,000,000,000	8,275,000,000	8,300,000,000	7,700,000,000
R&D Expense						
Operating Income						
Operating Margin %						
SGA Expense						
Net Income			2,650,000,000	2,500,000,000	2,300,000,000	2,150,000,000
Operating Cash Flow						
Capital Expenditure						
EBITDA						
Return on Assets %						
Return on Equity %						
Debt to Equity						

CONTACT INFORMATION:

Phone: 212-318-2000   Fax: 917-369-5000
Toll-Free:
Address: 731 Lexington Ave., New York, NY 10022 United States

STOCK TICKER/OTHER:

Stock Ticker: Private   Exchange:
Employees: 19,000   Fiscal Year Ends: 12/31
Parent Company:

SALARIES/BONUSES:

Top Exec. Salary: $ Bonus: $
Second Exec. Salary: $ Bonus: $

OTHER THOUGHTS:

Estimated Female Officers or Directors: 1
Hot Spot for Advancement for Women/Minorities:

BMC Software Inc

www.bmc.com

NAIC Code: 0

TYPES OF BUSINESS:

Computer Software-Mainframe Related
Systems Management Software
e-Business Software
Consulting & Training Services

BRANDS/DIVISIONS/AFFILIATES:

BMC Remedyforce
BMC HR Case Management
BMC MyIT

CONTACTS: Note: Officers with more than one job title may be intentionally listed here more than once.

Peter Leav, CEO
Stephen B. Solcher, CFO
Paul Appleby, Exec. VP-Mktg. & Sales
Scott Crowder, CTO
Hollie Castro, Sr. VP-Admin.
Patrick K. Tagtow, General Counsel
Steve Goddard, Sr. VP-Bus. Oper.
Ken Berryman, Sr. VP-Strategy & Corp. Dev.
Ann Duhon, Mgr.-Comm.
Derrick Vializ, VP-Investor Rel.
T. Cory Bleuer, Chief Acct. Officer
Patrick K. Tagtow, Chief Compliance Officer
Paul Avenant, Sr. VP-Solutions

GROWTH PLANS/SPECIAL FEATURES:

BMC Software, Inc. is a software vendor company that provides system management, service management and automation solutions primarily for large companies. Its software products span mainframe systems, IT service management, cloud management, IT operations, workload automation and IT automation. The firm offers digital enterprise management, which includes digital service management, digital infrastructure optimization, digital enterprise automations and digital service assurance. The digital service management enhances employee productivity through automation and compliance tracking. Products in this unit include BMC Remedyforce, BMC HR Case Management and BMC MyIT. The digital infrastructure optimization solutions focus on offering services to match digital infrastructure, such as servers, private and hybrid clouds and virtual infrastructures. Digital enterprise automations allow users to centrally orchestrate the automation of services and significantly reduce delivery time across a range of technologies, including networks, mobile devices, middleware, cloud, big data, apps and applications. The digital service assurance combines sophisticated data collection and analytic capabilities allowing businesses to take action based on customer online posts and complaints. BMC's customers include manufacturers, telecommunication companies, financial service providers, educational institutions, retailers, distributors, hospitals, government agencies and channel partners, including resellers, distributors and system integrators. Over 10,000 customers worldwide use BMC products, including 82% of Fortune 500 companies. BMC has 470 patents granted or pending, $2 billion in revenue and employs thousands of people in 30 countries.

FINANCIAL DATA: Note: Data for latest year may not have been available at press time.

In U.S. $	2016	2015	2014	2013	2012	2011
Revenue	2,300,000,000	2,250,000,000	2,205,000,000	2,201,000,000	2,172,000,000	2,065,299,968
R&D Expense						
Operating Income						
Operating Margin %						
SGA Expense						
Net Income			234,000,000	331,000,000	401,000,000	456,200,000
Operating Cash Flow						
Capital Expenditure						
EBITDA						
Return on Assets %						
Return on Equity %						
Debt to Equity						

CONTACT INFORMATION:

Phone: 713 918-8800   Fax: 713 918-8000
Toll-Free: 800-841-2031
Address: 2101 Citywest Blvd., Houston, TX 77042 United States

STOCK TICKER/OTHER:

Stock Ticker: Private   Exchange:
Employees: 6,700   Fiscal Year Ends: 03/31
Parent Company: Bain Capital

SALARIES/BONUSES:

Top Exec. Salary: $ Bonus: $
Second Exec. Salary: $ Bonus: $

OTHER THOUGHTS:

Estimated Female Officers or Directors: 2
Hot Spot for Advancement for Women/Minorities: Y

BMC Stock Holdings Inc

www.buildwithbmc.com

NAIC Code: 444190

TYPES OF BUSINESS:

Building Materials & Hardware Stores, Retail
Building & Construction Services

BRANDS/DIVISIONS/AFFILIATES:

BMC
Ready-Frame
BMC Design
BMC Timber Truss
Building Materials Holding Corp

CONTACTS: *Note: Officers with more than one job title may be intentionally listed here more than once.*

Peter Alexander, CEO
James Major, CFO
Michael McGaugh, COO
David Bullock, Director
Lisa Hamblet, Executive VP, Divisional
Paul Street, General Counsel
Lanesha Minnix, Senior VP
Thomas Barnes, Senior VP, Divisional
William Gay, Senior VP, Divisional
Keith Costello, Senior VP, Divisional
Mike Farmer, Senior VP, Divisional

GROWTH PLANS/SPECIAL FEATURES:

BMC Stock Holdings, Inc. (formerly Building Materials Holding Corp.) is a diversified lumber and building materials distributor and solutions provider that sells to new construction, repair and remodeling contractors. The company carries a wide range of products via operations in 17 U.S. states. Its primary products include lumber, lumber sheet goods, millwork, doors, flooring, windows, structural components (engineered wood products, trusses and wall panels) and other exterior products. BMC's solution-based services include design, product specification, installation and installation management services. The firm also offers a broad range of products sourced through a network of suppliers, which together with various solution-based services, represent approximately 50% of the construction cost of a typical new home. BMC serves its customers from 150 locations, which include 91 distribution and retail operations, 50 millwork fabrication operations, 49 structural components fabrication operations and 12 flooring operations. Brands of the company include BMC, Ready-Frame, BMC Design and BMC Timber Truss.

FINANCIAL DATA: *Note: Data for latest year may not have been available at press time.*

In U.S. $	2016	2015	2014	2013	2012	2011
Revenue	3,093,743,000	1,576,746,000	1,295,716,000	1,197,037,000	942,398,000	759,982,000
R&D Expense						
Operating Income	83,736,000	12,248,000	18,324,000	761,000	-18,907,000	-59,301,000
Operating Margin %	2.70%	.77%	1.41%	.06%	-2.00%	-7.80%
SGA Expense	571,799,000	306,843,000	279,717,000	254,935,000	221,192,000	213,036,000
Net Income	30,880,000	-4,831,000	10,419,000	-4,635,000	-14,533,000	-42,133,000
Operating Cash Flow	106,888,000	743,000	16,941,000	-40,264,000	-12,243,000	-7,001,000
Capital Expenditure	38,067,000	31,319,000	43,306,000	7,448,000	2,741,000	1,339,000
EBITDA	143,957,000	37,621,000	32,454,000	13,694,000	-6,860,000	-44,707,000
Return on Assets %	2.22%	-.55%	3.02%	-2.14%	-8.88%	-18.19%
Return on Equity %	4.71%	-1.25%	7.75%	-7.99%	-56.11%	-90.07%
Debt to Equity	0.53	0.67	0.68	0.50	0.16	0.01

CONTACT INFORMATION:

Phone: 678-222-1219   Fax: 678-222-1316
Toll-Free:
Address: Two Lakeside Commons, 980 Hammond Drive NE, Ste 500, Atlanta, GA 30328 United States

STOCK TICKER/OTHER:

Stock Ticker: BMCH   Exchange: NAS
Employees: 9,000   Fiscal Year Ends: 12/31
Parent Company:

SALARIES/BONUSES:

Top Exec. Salary: $741,667   Bonus: $
Second Exec. Salary: Bonus: $
$450,000

OTHER THOUGHTS:

Estimated Female Officers or Directors: 2
Hot Spot for Advancement for Women/Minorities:

Boeing Company (The)

NAIC Code: 336411

www.boeing.com

TYPES OF BUSINESS:

Aircraft Manufacturing
Aerospace Technology & Manufacturing
Military Aircraft
Satellite Manufacturing
Communications Products & Services
Air Traffic Management Technology
Financing Services
Research & Development

BRANDS/DIVISIONS/AFFILIATES:

Boeing 777
Boeing 737
Boeing 787 Dreamliner
Boeing Capital Corporation
Boeing 747-8
Liquid Robotics

CONTACTS: Note: Officers with more than one job title may be intentionally listed here more than once.

Leanne Caret, CEO, Divisional
Scott Fancher, Senior VP, Divisional
Kevin McAllister, CEO, Divisional
Stanley Deal, CEO, Divisional
Gregory Smith, CFO
Robert Verbeck, Chief Accounting Officer
Theodore Colbert, Chief Information Officer
Gregory Hyslop, Chief Technology Officer
Dennis Muilenburg, Director
J. Luttig, Executive VP
Bertrand-Marc Allen, President, Subsidiary
Heidi Capozzi, Senior VP, Divisional
Patrick Shanahan, Senior VP, Divisional
Diana Sands, Senior VP, Divisional
Thomas Downey, Senior VP, Divisional

GROWTH PLANS/SPECIAL FEATURES:

The Boeing Company is one of the world's major aerospace firms. The company operates in the following segments: commercial airplanes; defense, space & security (BDS), which is further subdivided into Boeing military aircraft (BMA), network & space systems (N&SS) and global services & support (GS&S); and Boeing Capital Corporation (BCC). The commercial airplanes segment develops, produces and markets commercial jet aircraft and related support services. Its family of jet aircraft includes the 737 narrow-body model, the 767 and 777 wide-body models, the 787 Dreamliner and the 747-8 intercontinental and freighter models. On the BDS side, the BMA subdivision is focused on the development of military aircraft and precision engagement as well as mobility products and services. The N&SS subdivision provides products and services to assist customers in transforming operations through network integration, intelligence and surveillance systems, communications and space exploration. The GS&S subdivision is engaged in operations, maintenance and logistics support functions for military platforms. BCC provides financing to commercial aircraft customers. In December 2016, the firm announced it will acquire Liquid Robotics, a market leader in autonomous maritime systems.

The company offers its employees benefits including medical, dental, life, AD&D and disability insurance; flexible spending accounts; pension and retirement savings plans; tuition assistance; and onsite and on-the-job training.

FINANCIAL DATA: Note: Data for latest year may not have been available at press time.

In U.S. $	2016	2015	2014	2013	2012	2011
Revenue	94,571,000,000	96,114,000,000	90,762,000,000	86,623,000,000	81,698,000,000	68,735,000,000
R&D Expense	4,627,000,000	3,331,000,000	3,047,000,000	3,071,000,000	3,298,000,000	3,918,000,000
Operating Income	5,834,000,000	7,443,000,000	7,473,000,000	6,562,000,000	6,311,000,000	5,844,000,000
Operating Margin %	6.16%	7.74%	8.23%	7.57%	7.72%	8.50%
SGA Expense	3,616,000,000	3,525,000,000	3,767,000,000	3,956,000,000	3,717,000,000	3,408,000,000
Net Income	4,895,000,000	5,176,000,000	5,446,000,000	4,585,000,000	3,900,000,000	4,018,000,000
Operating Cash Flow	10,499,000,000	9,363,000,000	8,858,000,000	8,179,000,000	7,508,000,000	4,023,000,000
Capital Expenditure	2,613,000,000	2,450,000,000	2,236,000,000	2,238,000,000	1,710,000,000	1,713,000,000
EBITDA	7,784,000,000	9,263,000,000	9,376,000,000	8,462,000,000	8,184,000,000	7,551,000,000
Return on Assets %	5.30%	5.34%	5.67%	5.05%	4.61%	5.40%
Return on Equity %	136.80%	68.95%	46.21%	44.20%	83.13%	127.94%
Debt to Equity	11.71	1.37	0.93	0.54	1.52	2.85

CONTACT INFORMATION:

Phone: 312 544-2000   Fax:
Toll-Free:
Address: 100 N. Riverside Plz., Chicago, IL 60606 United States

STOCK TICKER/OTHER:

Stock Ticker: BA   Exchange: NYS
Employees: 150,500   Fiscal Year Ends: 12/31
Parent Company:

SALARIES/BONUSES:

Top Exec. Salary: $92,308   Bonus: $2,000,000
Second Exec. Salary: Bonus: $
$1,640,962

OTHER THOUGHTS:

Estimated Female Officers or Directors: 7
Hot Spot for Advancement for Women/Minorities: Y

Booz Allen Hamilton Holding Corp

www.boozallen.com

NAIC Code: 541610

TYPES OF BUSINESS:

Strategy Consulting
Engineering & IT Consulting
Supply Chain Management
Industry Research & Publications
War Gaming & Strategic Simulation

BRANDS/DIVISIONS/AFFILIATES:

Carlyle Group (The)
eGov Holdings Inc

CONTACTS: Note: Officers with more than one job title may be intentionally listed here more than once.

Horacio Rozanski, CEO
Lloyd Howell, CFO
Ralph Shrader, Chairman of the Board
Susan Penfield, Executive VP
Karen Dahut, Executive VP
Joseph Logue, Executive VP
Elizabeth Thompson, Executive VP
Joseph Mahaffee, Executive VP
Nancy Laben, Secretary

GROWTH PLANS/SPECIAL FEATURES:

Booz Allen Hamilton Holding Corp. (BAH), founded in 1914, is a strategy and technology consulting firm, providing services to the U.S. government in the defense, intelligence and civil sectors. BAH's major areas of expertise include business analytics, information technology, cyber security, operations and logistics, organization and change, service innovation, public sector mission effectiveness, strategy and leadership and systems engineering and integration. It derives substantially all of its revenue from services provided under contracts and task orders with the U.S. government. The company's work with national governments around the world has included projects to enhance national security, economic well-being and the health and safety of citizens. Some of BAH's largest clients have included the U.S. Department of Defense; the U.S. Air Force, Army, Navy and Marine Corps; the U.S. Intelligence Community & civil agencies such as the Department of Homeland Security, the Department of Health and Human Services and the Department of the Treasury. The company's international clients are primarily in the Middle East, as well as in south-east Asia. The company also publishes books, reports and studies on industry subjects ranging from information technology to leadership. The firm maintains offices across the U.S. as well as strategic locations overseas. Investment firm, The Carlyle Group, maintains a majority interest in the company. In January 2017, the company acquired eGov Holdings, Inc., a leading provider of .gov solutions for the Federal Government.

The company offers employees dental, medical and vision insurance; life insurance; medical flexible spending accounts; tuition assistance; an employee assistance program; and health and wellness programs.

FINANCIAL DATA: Note: Data for latest year may not have been available at press time.

In U.S. $	2016	2015	2014	2013	2012	2011
Revenue	5,405,738,000	5,274,770,000	5,478,693,000	5,758,059,000	5,859,218,000	
R&D Expense						
Operating Income	444,584,000	458,822,000	460,611,000	446,234,000	387,432,000	
Operating Margin %	8.22%	8.69%	8.40%	7.74%	6.61%	
SGA Expense	2,319,592,000	2,159,439,000	2,229,642,000	2,366,576,000	2,446,543,000	
Net Income	294,094,000	232,569,000	232,188,000	219,058,000	239,955,000	
Operating Cash Flow	249,234,000	309,958,000	332,718,000	464,654,000	360,046,000	
Capital Expenditure	66,635,000	36,041,000	20,905,000	33,113,000	76,925,000	
EBITDA	511,813,000	520,410,000	531,144,000	512,604,000	467,157,000	
Return on Assets %	9.99%	7.87%	7.58%	6.74%	7.57%	
Return on Equity %	98.85%	127.93%	116.55%	31.02%	22.93%	
Debt to Equity	3.63	8.41	9.23	7.31	0.77	

CONTACT INFORMATION:

Phone: 703 902-5000   Fax: 703 902-3333
Toll-Free:
Address: 8283 Greensboro Dr., McLean, VA 22102 United States

STOCK TICKER/OTHER:

Stock Ticker: BAH
Employees: 23,300
Parent Company:

Exchange: NYS
Fiscal Year Ends:

SALARIES/BONUSES:

Top Exec. Salary: $1,437,500   Bonus: $
Second Exec. Salary: $1,000,000   Bonus: $

OTHER THOUGHTS:

Estimated Female Officers or Directors: 4
Hot Spot for Advancement for Women/Minorities: Y

Boston Consulting Group Inc (The, BCG)

NAIC Code: 541610

www.bcg.com

TYPES OF BUSINESS:

Management Consulting
Marketing Consulting
Corporate Strategy Research

BRANDS/DIVISIONS/AFFILIATES:

Center for Health Care Value
BCG Henderson Institute
Center for Customer Insight
Center for Energy Impact
Digital Transformation Accelerator
ValueScience Center

CONTACTS: Note: Officers with more than one job title may be intentionally listed here more than once.

Rich Lesser, CEO
Paul Tranter, Chief of Staff
Debbie Simpson, CFO
Miki Tsusaka, CMO
Jeremy Barton, General Counsel
Miki Tsusaka, Sr. Partner
Sharon Marcil, Sr. Partner
Matthew Krentz, Sr. Partner
Hans-Paul Burkner, Chmn.
Vaishali Rastogi, Partner

GROWTH PLANS/SPECIAL FEATURES:

The Boston Consulting Group, Inc. (BCG) provides international strategy and general management consulting services with the aim of helping businesses create and sustain competitive advantages. With more than 80 offices in 48 countries, BCG is one of the world's largest consulting organizations. Most of its offices are in Europe and Asia, though the firm does have a significant North American presence. Areas of consulting expertise include automotive, consumer markets, corporate development, the energy industry, e-commerce, financial services, globalization, health care, industrial goods, information technology, operations, organization, pricing, retail, strategy, technology, communications, travel and tourism. BCG also publishes extensive reports on many aspects of multiple industries and is constantly developing new ideas on business structure and efficiency. This written material is stored on the company's web site and can be searched from multiple angles. The company also operates the Center for Health Care Value, which collects data to establish fair health care prices in response to the trend of rising costs; include the BCG Henderson Institute (BHI), which attempts to shape business strategy; the Center for Customer Insight, which collects data to determine how to best access the consumer landscape; the Center for Energy Impact, which collects data about the future availability, economics and sustainability of the world's energy sources and the implications for energy companies and their portfolios; the Digital Transformation Accelerator, which helps top management prepare to make fundamental changes in order to remain competitive in the digital age; and the ValueScience Center, which develops and provides advanced valuation techniques for M&A and corporate strategy applications

FINANCIAL DATA: Note: Data for latest year may not have been available at press time.

In U.S. $	2016	2015	2014	2013	2012	2011
Revenue	5,600,000,000	5,000,000,000	4,200,000,000	3,710,000,000	3,625,000,000	3,550,000,000
R&D Expense						
Operating Income						
Operating Margin %						
SGA Expense						
Net Income						
Operating Cash Flow						
Capital Expenditure						
EBITDA						
Return on Assets %						
Return on Equity %						
Debt to Equity						

CONTACT INFORMATION:

Phone: 617-973-1200   Fax: 617-973-1399
Toll-Free:
Address: 1 Exchange Place, 30th & 31st Fl., Boston, MA 02109 United States

STOCK TICKER/OTHER:

Stock Ticker: Private
Employees: 14,000
Parent Company:

Exchange:
Fiscal Year Ends: 12/31

SALARIES/BONUSES:

Top Exec. Salary: $ Bonus: $
Second Exec. Salary: $ Bonus: $

OTHER THOUGHTS:

Estimated Female Officers or Directors: 4
Hot Spot for Advancement for Women/Minorities: Y

Boston Scientific Corp

www.bostonscientific.com

NAIC Code: 339100

TYPES OF BUSINESS:

Supplies-Surgery
Interventional Medical Products
Catheters
Guide wires
Stents
Oncology Research

BRANDS/DIVISIONS/AFFILIATES:

WATCHMAN
CrossBoss
Zurpaz
LithoVue
Dreamwire
AngioJet ZelanteDVT
Precision Spinal Cord Stimulation
Cosman Medical Inc

CONTACTS: Note: Officers with more than one job title may be intentionally listed here more than once.

Michael Mahoney, CEO
Arthur Butcher, President, Divisional
Daniel Brennan, CFO
Timothy Pratt, Chief Administrative Officer
Keith Dawkins, Chief Medical Officer
John Abele, Director Emeritus
Edward Mackey, Executive VP, Divisional
Ian Meredith, Executive VP
Joseph Fitzgerald, Executive VP
Michael Phalen, Executive VP
Kevin Ballinger, Executive VP
Supratim Bose, Executive VP
Jeffrey Mirviss, President, Divisional
David Pierce, President, Divisional
Maulik Nanavaty, President, Divisional
Eric Thepaut, President, Geographical
John Sorenson, Senior VP, Divisional
Wendy Carruthers, Senior VP, Divisional

GROWTH PLANS/SPECIAL FEATURES:

Boston Scientific Corp. is a worldwide developer, manufacturer and marketer of medical devices that are used in a broad range of interventional medical specialties. Boston Scientific operates in seven segments. The cardiac rhythm management segment offers implantable devices that monitor the heart and deliver electricity to treat cardiac abnormalities. The interventional cardiology segment sells coronary stent systems and products for the treatment of peripheral diseases, such as the WATCHMAN appendage closure device or the CrossBoss coronary CTO crossing catheter. The electrophysiology segment develops less-invasive medical technologies used in the diagnosis and treatment of rate and rhythm disorders of the heart. Products in this segment include the ZURPAZ, DIREX, CHANNEL brands of steerable sheaths. The endoscopy segment sells products for the treatment of a variety of digestive diseases, such as the EndoVive endoscopic gastrostomy kit or the Dreamwire high performance guidewire. The urology and pelvic health segment offers products for the treatment of urinary stone disease, benign prostatic hyperplasia (BPH), stress urinary incontinence and other conditions. Products in this segment include LithoVue single-use digital ureteroscope or GreenLight XPS laser therapy. The peripheral interventions segment includes balloon catheters, stents, wires vena cava filters and peripheral embolization devices used to treat patients with peripheral diseases. Brands included in this segment are the ELUVIA vascular stent system and the AngioJet ZelanteDVT thrombectomy catheter. The neuromodulation segment sells the Precision Spinal Cord Stimulation system for the treatment of chronic intractable pain management of the trunk and/or limbs. In 2016, the company made a number of acquisitions: Cosman Medical, Inc., a manufacturer of radiofrequency ablation systems; the Resectr Tissue Resection Device portfolio from Distal Access, LLC; EndoChoice Holdings, Inc.; and the advanced biological tissue business of Neovasc, Inc.

The firm offers employees medical, dental, vision and life insurance; educational assistance; and flexible spending accounts.

FINANCIAL DATA: Note: Data for latest year may not have been available at press time.

In U.S. $	2016	2015	2014	2013	2012	2011
Revenue	8,386,000,000	7,477,000,000	7,380,000,000	7,143,000,000	7,249,000,000	7,622,000,000
R&D Expense	920,000,000	876,000,000	817,000,000	861,000,000	886,000,000	895,000,000
Operating Income	447,000,000	-327,000,000	-301,000,000	120,000,000	-3,868,000,000	904,000,000
Operating Margin %	5.33%	-4.37%	-4.07%	1.67%	-53.35%	11.86%
SGA Expense	3,178,000,000	2,987,000,000	3,013,000,000	2,814,000,000	2,688,000,000	2,659,000,000
Net Income	347,000,000	-239,000,000	-119,000,000	-121,000,000	-4,068,000,000	441,000,000
Operating Cash Flow	972,000,000	600,000,000	1,269,000,000	1,082,000,000	1,260,000,000	1,008,000,000
Capital Expenditure	376,000,000	247,000,000	259,000,000	245,000,000	226,000,000	304,000,000
EBITDA	1,225,000,000	439,000,000	432,000,000	790,000,000	-3,163,000,000	1,640,000,000
Return on Assets %	1.91%	-1.35%	-.70%	-.71%	-21.16%	2.03%
Return on Equity %	5.31%	-3.74%	-1.83%	-1.80%	-44.64%	3.89%
Debt to Equity	0.80	0.89	0.59	0.64	0.61	0.37

CONTACT INFORMATION:

Phone: 508 683-4000   Fax: 508 647-2200
Toll-Free: 888-272-1001
Address: 300 Boston Scientific Way, Marlborough, MA 01752-1234
United States

STOCK TICKER/OTHER:

Stock Ticker: BSX
Employees: 27,000
Parent Company:

Exchange: NYS
Fiscal Year Ends: 12/31

SALARIES/BONUSES:

Top Exec. Salary: $1,042,191   Bonus: $
Second Exec. Salary: $640,017   Bonus: $

OTHER THOUGHTS:

Estimated Female Officers or Directors: 5
Hot Spot for Advancement for Women/Minorities: Y

Brightstar Corporation

www.brightstar.com

NAIC Code: 423690

TYPES OF BUSINESS:

Telecommunication Supply Chain & Distribution Services
Wireless Device & Accessories Distribution
Wireless Device Manufacturing
Supply Chain, Marketing and Retail Consultation

BRANDS/DIVISIONS/AFFILIATES:

Brightstar India
Brightstar Flex
Brightstar Halo
Brightstar Logic
Brightstar Echo
Brightstar Omni
Brightstar Gear
Softbank Commerce & Service Corp

CONTACTS: Note: Officers with more than one job title may be intentionally listed here more than once.

Jaymin Patel, CEO
Dennis J. Strand, Pres., Brightstar Financial Svcs.
Catherine Smith, Sr. VP
Bela Lainck, Pres., Buy-Back & Trade-In Solutions
Rafael M. de Guzman, III, VP-Strategy
Oscar J. Fumagali, Chief Treas. Officer
Oscar J. Rojas, Pres., Brightstar Latin America
Arturo A. Osorio, Pres., Asia Pacific, Middle East & Africa
Jeff Gower, Pres., Brightstar U.S. & Canada
David Leach, CEO-eSecuritel
Ronald D. Fisher, Chmn.
Michael Singer, Sr. VP-Global Strategy & New Bus. Dev.
Ramon Colomina, Pres., Supply Chain Solutions

GROWTH PLANS/SPECIAL FEATURES:

Brightstar Corporation, a wholly-owned subsidiary of SoftBank Group Corp., is a global distributor and provider of managing devices and accessories in the wireless and telecommunications industry. The firm operates facilities in 50 countries worldwide and process over 100 million devices annually. Brightstar's customer base includes more than 50,000 carrier, retail and enterprise customers. Brightstar operates at every stage of the device lifecycle to provide an integrated experience with its customer's business. Some of the operations Brightstar participates in are: designing and manufacturing products under licensing agreements with leading manufacturers, customer return management and device return, recycling and resale. Brightstar's products include: Brightstar Flex, its flexible finance program; Brightstar Halo, a device protection platform that also integrates with carrier billing and POS systems; Brightstar Logic, an integrated supply chain IT platform; Brightstar Echo, its segment for remarketing devices as well as buying back inventory and fixing broken devices; Brightstar Omni, its cloud-based platform for providing a seamless retail experience for the selling, activation and upgrading of devices; and Brightstar Gear, its segment for strategic distribution of premium accessories. Subsidiaries of the firm include Brightstar India, assisting with distribution across India; and Softbank Commerce & Service Corp., a commerce division based in Japan.

FINANCIAL DATA: Note: Data for latest year may not have been available at press time.

In U.S. $	2016	2015	2014	2013	2012	2011
Revenue	7,750,000,000	7,600,000,000	7,200,000,000	7,228,000,000	6,300,000,000	5,700,000,000
R&D Expense						
Operating Income						
Operating Margin %						
SGA Expense						
Net Income						
Operating Cash Flow						
Capital Expenditure						
EBITDA						
Return on Assets %						
Return on Equity %						
Debt to Equity						

CONTACT INFORMATION:

Phone: 305-421-6000   Fax:
Toll-Free:
Address: 9725 NW 117th Ave., #300, Miami, FL 33178 United States

STOCK TICKER/OTHER:

Stock Ticker: Subsidiary   Exchange:
Employees: 9,000   Fiscal Year Ends: 12/31
Parent Company: SoftBank Group Corp

SALARIES/BONUSES:

Top Exec. Salary: $ Bonus: $
Second Exec. Salary: $ Bonus: $

OTHER THOUGHTS:

Estimated Female Officers or Directors: 1
Hot Spot for Advancement for Women/Minorities:

Brinker International Inc

www.brinker.com

NAIC Code: 722511

TYPES OF BUSINESS:

Casual Dining Restaurants

BRANDS/DIVISIONS/AFFILIATES:

Chili's Grill and Bar
Maggiano's Little Italy

CONTACTS: *Note: Officers with more than one job title may be intentionally listed here more than once.*

Thomas Edwards, CFO
David Doyle, Chief Information Officer
Wyman Roberts, Director
Joseph Depinto, Director
John Cywinski, Executive VP, Divisional
Scarlett May, General Counsel
Rick Badgley, Other Executive Officer
Kelli Valade, President, Subsidiary
Steve Provost, President, Subsidiary
Charles Lousignont, Senior VP, Divisional
Joe Taylor, Vice President, Divisional

GROWTH PLANS/SPECIAL FEATURES:

Brinker International, Inc. owns, develops, operates and franchises over 1,600 casual dining restaurant chains in 31 countries under two brands, Chili's Grill & Bar and Maggiano's Little Italy. Chili's Grill & Bar serves lunch and dinner, while also offering a To-Go menu. Entree selections for Chili's range in price from approximately $6 to $18.99. The company owns Chili's restaurants located in 31 countries and two U.S. territories. All company-owned Chili's restaurants are outfitted with Ziosk multi-functional table top tablets that provide entertainment, ordering, guest survey and pay-at-the-table capabilities. Maggiano's Little Italy is a classic Italian-American restaurant, featuring individual and family style menus and extensive banquet facilities. Entree selections for Maggiano's range in price from approximately $13.95 to $42.50. Brinker International's growth plans include expansion through franchises and joint ventures, most revolving around Chili's Grill & Bar. In particular, it plans to focus its international growth in emerging markets, such as India, China, Brazil and Russia. During 2016, the firm opened 12 company-owned and seven franchised Chili's restaurants (domestically), two company-owned Maggiano's restaurants (domestically) and 36 Chili's franchises (internationally). Projected openings for 2017 include up to six company-owned and up to eight franchised domestic Chili's restaurants; two company-owned domestic Maggiano's restaurants; and one company-owned and up to 40 franchised international Chili's restaurants.

The firm offers employees medical, dental, vision, life and short-term disability insurance; disability coverage; prescription discounts; health and dependent care flexible spending accounts; an employee assistance program; a long-term care plan; a 401(k); discounts at company restaurants; and reimbursement programs.

FINANCIAL DATA: *Note: Data for latest year may not have been available at press time.*

In U.S. $	2016	2015	2014	2013	2012	2011
Revenue	3,257,489,000	3,002,278,000	2,905,452,000	2,846,098,000	2,820,722,000	2,761,386,000
R&D Expense						
Operating Income	317,476,000	311,202,000	242,165,000	256,775,000	231,837,000	205,420,000
Operating Margin %	9.74%	10.36%	8.33%	9.02%	8.21%	7.43%
SGA Expense	130,897,000	134,649,000	137,647,000	136,773,000	143,388,000	132,834,000
Net Income	200,745,000	196,694,000	154,039,000	163,359,000	151,232,000	141,060,000
Operating Cash Flow	394,700,000	368,611,000	359,842,000	290,688,000	303,438,000	259,988,000
Capital Expenditure	112,788,000	140,262,000	161,066,000	131,531,000	125,226,000	70,361,000
EBITDA	475,329,000	458,525,000	380,460,000	390,914,000	360,663,000	340,087,000
Return on Assets %	13.80%	13.44%	10.46%	11.31%	10.35%	8.45%
Return on Equity %			145.01%	71.14%	40.39%	24.16%
Debt to Equity			13.19	5.22	1.89	1.14

CONTACT INFORMATION:

Phone: 972 980-9917   Fax: 972 770-9593
Toll-Free:
Address: 6820 LBJ Freeway, Dallas, TX 75240 United States

STOCK TICKER/OTHER:

Stock Ticker: EAT   Exchange: NYS
Employees: 53,000   Fiscal Year Ends: 06/30
Parent Company:

SALARIES/BONUSES:

Top Exec. Salary: $1,030,000   Bonus: $
Second Exec. Salary: Bonus: $
$592,755

OTHER THOUGHTS:

Estimated Female Officers or Directors: 3
Hot Spot for Advancement for Women/Minorities: Y

Bristol-Myers Squibb Co

www.bms.com

NAIC Code: 325412

TYPES OF BUSINESS:

Drugs-Diversified
Medical Imaging Products
Nutritional Products

BRANDS/DIVISIONS/AFFILIATES:

Baraclude
Reyataz
Opdivo
Sprycel
Yervoy
Eliquis
Padlock Therapeutics Inc

CONTACTS: Note: Officers with more than one job title may be intentionally listed here more than once.

Katherine Kelly, Assistant General Counsel
Giovanni Caforio, CEO
Charles Bancroft, CFO
Joseph Caldarella, Chief Accounting Officer
Paul von Autenried, Chief Information Officer
Thomas Lynch, Chief Scientific Officer
Murdo Gordon, Executive VP
Sandra Leung, General Counsel
Anne Nielsen, Other Executive Officer
Emmanuel Blin, Other Executive Officer
Louis Schmukler, President, Divisional
John Elicker, Senior VP, Divisional
Ann Judge, Senior VP, Divisional

GROWTH PLANS/SPECIAL FEATURES:

Bristol-Myers Squibb Co. (BMS) discovers, develops, licenses, manufactures, markets, distributes and sells pharmaceuticals and other health care related products. The company manufactures drugs across multiple therapeutic classes, including cardiovascular; virology, including immunodeficiency virus infection; oncology; affective and other psychiatric disorders; and immunoscience. The firm's pharmaceutical products include chemically-synthesized drugs, or small molecules, and an increasing portion of products produced from biological processes typically involving recombinant DNA technology, or biologics. Small molecule drugs are typically administered orally in the form of a pill, although there are other drug delivery mechanisms that are also used. Biologics are typically administered to patients through injections. Most of the firm's revenues come from products in the following therapeutic classes: cardiovascular; virology, including human immunodeficiency virus (HIV) infection; oncology; neuroscience; immunoscience; and metabolics. Products include Baraclude, Reyataz, Opdivo, Sprycel, Yervoy, Orencia and Eliquis. These products are manufactured at 15 worldwide locations owned by the company. BMS maintains major research and development (R&D) facilities in New Jersey, California, Washington, Massachusetts, Connecticut, Japan, France, England, Belgium and India. BMS invests approximately $4.9 billion in R&D annually. In February 2016, the firm sold its HIV R&D portfolio to ViiV Healthcare for $350 million. In April 2016, BMS acquired Padlock Therapeutics, Inc., a biotechnology company dedicated to treating destructive autoimmune diseases.

The firm offers employees medical and dental insurance, health care reimbursement accounts, a pension plan, a 401(k) plan, short- and long-term disability coverage, life insurance, travel accident insurance, an employee assistance plan and adoption assistance.

FINANCIAL DATA: Note: Data for latest year may not have been available at press time.

In U.S. $	2016	2015	2014	2013	2012	2011
Revenue	19,427,000,000	16,560,000,000	15,879,000,000	16,385,000,000	17,621,000,000	21,244,000,000
R&D Expense	4,940,000,000	5,920,000,000	4,534,000,000	3,731,000,000	3,904,000,000	3,839,000,000
Operating Income	4,630,000,000	1,890,000,000	2,591,000,000	3,096,000,000	2,260,000,000	6,531,000,000
Operating Margin %	23.83%	11.41%	16.31%	18.89%	12.82%	30.74%
SGA Expense	4,911,000,000	4,841,000,000	4,822,000,000	4,939,000,000	5,017,000,000	5,160,000,000
Net Income	4,457,000,000	1,565,000,000	2,004,000,000	2,563,000,000	1,960,000,000	3,709,000,000
Operating Cash Flow	2,850,000,000	1,832,000,000	3,148,000,000	3,545,000,000	6,941,000,000	4,840,000,000
Capital Expenditure	1,215,000,000	820,000,000	526,000,000	537,000,000	548,000,000	367,000,000
EBITDA	6,464,000,000	2,637,000,000	3,051,000,000	3,853,000,000	3,203,000,000	7,927,000,000
Return on Assets %	13.61%	4.77%	5.54%	6.88%	5.69%	11.58%
Return on Equity %	29.28%	10.74%	13.35%	17.81%	13.25%	23.42%
Debt to Equity	0.35	0.45	0.48	0.52	0.48	0.33

CONTACT INFORMATION:

Phone: 212 546-4000 Fax: 212 546-4020
Toll-Free:
Address: 345 Park Ave., New York, NY 10154 United States

STOCK TICKER/OTHER:

Stock Ticker: BMY Exchange: NYS
Employees: 25,000 Fiscal Year Ends: 12/31
Parent Company:

SALARIES/BONUSES:

Top Exec. Salary: $1,513,077 Bonus: $
Second Exec. Salary: $966,115 Bonus: $

OTHER THOUGHTS:

Estimated Female Officers or Directors: 4
Hot Spot for Advancement for Women/Minorities: Y

Brookdale Senior Living Inc

www.brookdaleliving.com

NAIC Code: 623310

TYPES OF BUSINESS:

Assisted Living Facilities
Retirement Communities
Assisted Living Communities
Continued Care Retirement Communities (CCRCs)
Managed Facilities

BRANDS/DIVISIONS/AFFILIATES:

Blackstone Real Estate Partners VIII LP

CONTACTS: Note: Officers with more than one job title may be intentionally listed here more than once.

T. Andrew Smith, CEO
Labeed Diab, COO
Lucinda Baier, CFO
Cedric T. Coco, Exec. VP

GROWTH PLANS/SPECIAL FEATURES:

Brookdale Senior Living, Inc. (BSL) is one of the largest senior living facility operators in the U.S. It operates 1,055 owned, leased or managed senior living facilities in 47 states that can serve approximately 103,000 residents. BSL operates five business segments: retirement centers, assisted living, continuing care retirement communities (CCRCs) rentals, Brookdale ancillary services and management services. It has 129 retirement center communities with 24,339 units, 851 assisted living communities with 58,477 units and 75 rental CCRC communities with 20,558 units. The facilities strive to offer residents a home-like setting and typically feature assistance with daily living, multiple forms of therapy and various home health services. BSL offers a full spectrum of care options, including independent living, personalized assisted living, rehabilitation and skilled nursing. It operates memory care communities, which are freestanding assisted living communities designed for residents with Alzheimer's disease and other dementias. The company maintains its own culinary arts institute, which offers a training ground for chefs and dining staff. Leased communities generated the largest share (49.1%) of 2016 revenues, followed by owned communities (37.9%). BSL generated 82.9% of its 2016 revenue from private pay customers, with the remainder generated by Medicare, Medicaid and other various third-party payer programs. In November 2016, the firm announced a joint venture with Blackstone Real Estate Partners VIII L.P., in which the two companies will acquire a portfolio of 64 communities currently leased to Brookdale by HCP, Inc.

FINANCIAL DATA: Note: Data for latest year may not have been available at press time.

In U.S. $	2016	2015	2014	2013	2012	2011
Revenue	4,976,980,000	4,960,608,000	3,831,706,000	2,891,966,000	2,770,085,000	2,457,918,000
R&D Expense						
Operating Income	-31,083,000	-165,206,000	-84,905,000	131,288,000	82,286,000	90,180,000
Operating Margin %	-.62%	-3.33%	-2.21%	4.53%	2.97%	3.66%
SGA Expense	702,147,000	822,548,000	671,046,000	461,277,000	451,270,000	423,185,000
Net Income	-404,397,000	-457,477,000	-148,990,000	-3,584,000	-65,645,000	-68,175,000
Operating Cash Flow	365,732,000	292,366,000	242,652,000	366,121,000	290,969,000	268,427,000
Capital Expenditure	333,647,000	411,051,000	304,245,000	257,527,000	208,412,000	160,131,000
EBITDA	516,161,000	570,768,000	461,969,000	421,382,000	353,544,000	340,971,000
Return on Assets %	-4.19%	-4.44%	-1.95%	-.07%	-1.43%	-1.51%
Return on Equity %	-17.82%	-17.13%	-7.63%	-.35%	-6.42%	-6.49%
Debt to Equity	2.80	2.52	2.07	2.38	2.16	2.26

CONTACT INFORMATION:

Phone: 615 221-2250   Fax: 615 221-2289
Toll-Free: 866-785-9025
Address: 111 Westwood Place, Ste. 400, Brentwood, TN 37027 United States

STOCK TICKER/OTHER:

Stock Ticker: BKD
Employees: 77,600
Parent Company:

Exchange: NYS
Fiscal Year Ends: 12/31

SALARIES/BONUSES:

Top Exec. Salary: $76,500   Bonus: $1,000,000
Second Exec. Salary: $48,654   Bonus: $1,000,000

OTHER THOUGHTS:

Estimated Female Officers or Directors: 1
Hot Spot for Advancement for Women/Minorities:

Brown & Brown Inc

www.bbinsurance.com

NAIC Code: 524210

TYPES OF BUSINESS:

Insurance-Property & Casualty
Risk Management Services
Professional Liability Insurance
Third-Party Administration & Consulting
Managed Care & Utilization Management Services
Reinsurance
Life Insurance
Health Insurance

BRANDS/DIVISIONS/AFFILIATES:

CONTACTS: Note: Officers with more than one job title may be intentionally listed here more than once.

R. Watts, CFO
J. Brown, Chairman of the Board
Richard Freebourn, Executive VP, Divisional
Robert Lloyd, Executive VP
J. Penny, Other Executive Officer
Anthony Strianese, President, Divisional
Chris Walker, President, Divisional
J. Brown, President

GROWTH PLANS/SPECIAL FEATURES:

Brown & Brown, Inc. is a diversified insurance agency, wholesale brokerage, insurance programs and service organization. The firm markets and sells insurance products and services, primarily in the property, casualty and employee benefit areas. The company operates through 237 locations in 41 states, as well as international offices in London, England; Hamilton, Bermuda; and George Town, Cayman Islands. It operates through four segments: retail, wholesale brokerage, national programs and services. The retail segment provides a range of insurance products and services to commercial, public entity, professional and individual customers. The wholesale brokerage division markets and sells excess and surplus commercial and personal insurance and reinsurance, primarily through independent agents and brokers. The national programs division consists of two units: professional programs, which provides professional liability and related package products for certain medical, financial, real estate and law professionals; and special programs, which markets targeted products and services designated for specific industries, trade groups, public entities and market niches. The services division provides clients with third-party claims administration, consulting for the workers' compensation insurance markets, comprehensive medical utilization management services and Medicare Secondary Payer statute compliance-related services. The retail division generates the majority (52%) of the company's revenue, followed by the national programs division (25.4%), the wholesale brokerage division (13.8%), and the services division (8.8%). In September 2016, Brown & Brown acquired substantially all the assets of Kronholm Insurance Services, Inc. In 2017, the firm acquired the commercial MGA operations of The Insurance House, Inc.; substantially all the assets of Spann Insurance, Inc.; and substantially all the assets of TriCoast Insurance Services, LLC.

FINANCIAL DATA: Note: Data for latest year may not have been available at press time.

In U.S. $	2016	2015	2014	2013	2012	2011
Revenue	1,766,629,000	1,660,509,000	1,575,796,000	1,363,279,000	1,200,032,000	1,013,542,000
R&D Expense						
Operating Income	470,874,000	444,810,000	378,095,000	357,609,000	304,811,000	270,521,000
Operating Margin %	26.65%	26.78%	23.99%	26.23%	25.40%	26.69%
SGA Expense	925,217,000	856,952,000	811,112,000	705,603,000	624,371,000	519,869,000
Net Income	257,491,000	243,318,000	206,896,000	217,112,000	184,045,000	163,995,000
Operating Cash Flow	375,158,000	411,848,000	385,019,000	389,374,000	220,315,000	237,531,000
Capital Expenditure	17,765,000	18,375,000	24,923,000	16,366,000	24,028,000	13,608,000
EBITDA	570,646,000	550,118,000	471,993,000	459,466,000	399,854,000	351,800,000
Return on Assets %	4.86%	4.76%	4.80%	6.40%	6.41%	6.54%
Return on Equity %	11.12%	11.14%	10.04%	11.38%	10.66%	10.41%
Debt to Equity	0.43	0.50	0.54	0.18	0.24	0.15

CONTACT INFORMATION:

Phone: 386 252-9601   Fax: 386 239-7252
Toll-Free:
Address: 220 S. Ridgewood Ave., Daytona Beach, FL 32114 United States

STOCK TICKER/OTHER:

Stock Ticker: BRO
Employees: 8,297
Parent Company:

Exchange: NYS
Fiscal Year Ends: 12/31

SALARIES/BONUSES:

Top Exec. Salary: $1,000,000   Bonus: $
Second Exec. Salary: $500,000   Bonus: $

OTHER THOUGHTS:

Estimated Female Officers or Directors: 3
Hot Spot for Advancement for Women/Minorities: Y

Buffalo Wild Wings Inc

www.buffalowildwings.com

NAIC Code: 722513

TYPES OF BUSINESS:

Limited-Service Restaurants

BRANDS/DIVISIONS/AFFILIATES:

Buffalo Wild Wings Grill & Bar
B-Dubs
Jammin' Jalapeno
Thai Cury
Sweet BBQ
Buffalito
Buzztime Trivia

CONTACTS: *Note: Officers with more than one job title may be intentionally listed here more than once.*

Sally Smith, CEO
Alexander Ware, CFO
Santiago Abraham, Chief Information Officer
James Schmidt, COO
Judith Shoulak, Executive VP
Emily Decker, General Counsel
Lee Patterson, Senior VP, Divisional
Andrew Block, Senior VP, Divisional

GROWTH PLANS/SPECIAL FEATURES:

Buffalo Wild Wings, Inc. is the owner, operator and franchisor of Buffalo Wild Wings Grill & Bar restaurants, also known as B-Dubs. The company operates approximately 1,700 restaurants in the U.S. and Canada. The restaurants' proprietary item is its Buffalo, New York-style chicken wings spun in any of its 16 signature sauces, including Jammin' Jalapeno and Thai Curry; and five signature seasonings, such as Sweet BBQ, Desert Heat, Buffalo and Blazin. Orders can range from 6 wings to 100, with larger orders available for parties. Additionally, the company's menu also features items such as chicken tenders, salads, Wild Flatbreads, sandwiches, popcorn shrimp, specialty hamburgers, wraps, Buffalito soft tacos and appetizers, which are made to order and are available for dine-in and take-out. The restaurants are geared toward both sports fans and families, and designed to make guests feel as if they were in an actual sports stadium. Most restaurants have major sporting events displayed on projection screens, as well as approximately 60 additional televisions either broadcasting various sporting events, or providing the capability to play Buzztime Trivia or other video games. A typical size is approximately 6,200-6,500 square feet. Buffalo Wild Wings restaurants feature anywhere from 20-30 domestic, imported and craft beers on tap, and also sell bottled beers, wines and liquor. Restaurant operations generally are open on a daily basis from 11am-1am, with franchising agreements requiring franchisees to operate the establishments for at least twelve hours a day.

FINANCIAL DATA: *Note: Data for latest year may not have been available at press time.*

In U.S. $	2016	2015	2014	2013	2012	2011
Revenue	1,986,793,000	1,812,722,000	1,516,223,000	1,266,719,000	1,040,530,000	784,478,000
R&D Expense						
Operating Income	136,700,000	138,487,000	135,724,000	100,861,000	82,614,000	72,784,000
Operating Margin %	6.88%	7.63%	8.95%	7.96%	7.93%	9.27%
SGA Expense	131,839,000	143,287,000	131,582,000	110,829,000	98,779,000	87,253,000
Net Income	94,745,000	95,069,000	94,094,000	71,554,000	57,275,000	50,426,000
Operating Cash Flow	282,589,000	237,260,000	217,866,000	179,360,000	145,188,000	148,260,000
Capital Expenditure	141,699,000	172,548,000	137,466,000	138,735,000	130,542,000	130,127,000
EBITDA	290,304,000	265,990,000	234,178,000	185,839,000	150,076,000	122,697,000
Return on Assets %	8.93%	9.87%	12.06%	11.03%	10.54%	11.51%
Return on Equity %	16.14%	15.47%	18.10%	16.85%	16.33%	17.54%
Debt to Equity	0.39	0.10				

CONTACT INFORMATION:

Phone: 952 593-9943   Fax: 952 593-9787
Toll-Free: 800-499-9586
Address: 5500 Wayzata Blvd., Ste. 1600, Minneapolis, MN 55416 United States

STOCK TICKER/OTHER:

Stock Ticker: BWLD   Exchange: NAS
Employees: 37,200   Fiscal Year Ends: 12/31
Parent Company:

SALARIES/BONUSES:

Top Exec. Salary: $841,346   Bonus: $
Second Exec. Salary: $511,837   Bonus: $

OTHER THOUGHTS:

Estimated Female Officers or Directors: 5
Hot Spot for Advancement for Women/Minorities: Y

Burns & McDonnell

NAIC Code: 541330

www.burnsmcd.com

TYPES OF BUSINESS:

Engineering Services
Construction
Consulting
Environmental Consulting
Architecture & Design
Energy Transmission

BRANDS/DIVISIONS/AFFILIATES:

CONTACTS: *Note: Officers with more than one job title may be intentionally listed here more than once.*

Ray Kowalik, CEO
Mark Taylor, Treas.
Don Greenwood, Pres., Construction
Ray Kowalik, VP
John Nobles, Pres., Process & Industrial

GROWTH PLANS/SPECIAL FEATURES:

Burns & McDonnell provides engineering, architectural, construction, environmental and consulting services across the U.S. and worldwide. The company offers more than 350 services, and therefore divides its businesses into the following global practice units. The architecture unit designs and builds plants, facilities and buildings such as federal/military, aviation facilities, facilities, food/consumer factories, health care facilities, information technology facilities and laboratories. The commissioning unit provides verification of new construction, its subsystems for mechanical, plumbing, electrical, fire/life safety, building envelopes, interior systems such as laboratory units, co-generation utility plants, sustainable systems and more. The construction unit, through a general contractor, designs and builds infrastructure for air quality control, aviation, chemicals, oil and gas, electric power generation, electrical transmission/distribution, manufacturing/industrial, environmental, federal/military, food and consumer products and water sectors. The consulting unit provides insight and understanding concerning the engineering, architecture, construction and environmental features of facilities and buildings. The engineering unit provides integrated engineering services across a variety of disciplines and industries. The operations and maintenance unit helps to streamline and optimize the process of operating and maintaining facilities. The planning unit takes the vision and helps put the facilities, operations and systems in place to make it happen. The studies unit provides critical support for business decision, including financial, environmental and functionality. Burns & McDonnell is a 100% employee-owned company, with more than 40 offices worldwide.

The firm offers employees health and life insurance, short- and long-term disability, flexible spending accounts, personal time off, eight paid holidays, educational seminars and tuition assistance. The company is 100% employee-owned through its employee stock ownership plan.

FINANCIAL DATA: *Note: Data for latest year may not have been available at press time.*

In U.S. $	2016	2015	2014	2013	2012	2011
Revenue	2,400,000,000	2,700,000,000	2,645,000,000	2,300,000,000	1,500,000,000	1,174,000,000
R&D Expense						
Operating Income						
Operating Margin %						
SGA Expense						
Net Income						
Operating Cash Flow						
Capital Expenditure						
EBITDA						
Return on Assets %						
Return on Equity %						
Debt to Equity						

CONTACT INFORMATION:

Phone: 816-333-9400   Fax: 816-822-3028
Toll-Free:
Address: 9400 Ward Parkway, Kansas City, MO 64114 United States

STOCK TICKER/OTHER:

Stock Ticker: Private   Exchange:
Employees: 5,499   Fiscal Year Ends: 12/31
Parent Company:

SALARIES/BONUSES:

Top Exec. Salary: $ Bonus: $
Second Exec. Salary: $ Bonus: $

OTHER THOUGHTS:

Estimated Female Officers or Directors:
Hot Spot for Advancement for Women/Minorities:

C&S Wholesale Grocers Inc

www.cswg.com

NAIC Code: 424410

TYPES OF BUSINESS:

Wholesale Food Distribution
Warehousing
Wholesale Food Distribution
Produce
Meat
Health & Beauty Aids
Dairy Products
Fresh/Frozen Bakery Items

BRANDS/DIVISIONS/AFFILIATES:

Par Logistics Management System
FreshKO Produce Services Inc

CONTACTS: *Note: Officers with more than one job title may be intentionally listed here more than once.*

Rick Cohen, CEO
Kevin McNamara, CFO
Bob Palmer, Exec. VP-Procurement & Sales
Asad Husain, Chief Human Resources Officer
George Dramalis, CIO
Mike Newbold, Chief Admin. Officer
Bruce Johnson, Chief Organization Effectiveness Officer
Peter Fiore, Exec. VP-Distribution Services
Rick Cohen, Chmn.
Bob Palmer, Exec. VP-Procurement & Sales

GROWTH PLANS/SPECIAL FEATURES:

C&S Wholesale Grocers, Inc. provides grocery retailers with warehousing, distribution and logistics service solutions. C&S delivers food and non-food items to approximately 6,500 locations in 15 states, including supermarket chains, independent supermarkets, mass marketers and wholesale clubs. It also distributes to military bases and retail stores. The company supplies over 170,000 items including private label products, such as produce, meat, dairy products, delicatessen products, frozen products, tobacco, beauty items and candy. The company's warehouse locations include facilities in Maryland, Alabama, Vermont, New York, Pennsylvania, California, Florida, Indiana, Louisiana, Hawaii, Massachusetts, New Hampshire, South Carolina, New Jersey and Connecticut. C&S has customers that include Giant of Carlisle, Giant of Landover, Safeway, Stop & Shop and Target. Through its subsidiaries and affiliates, C&S provides licensing trademark services and automated warehouse technologies to retail grocery stores and assists large food manufacturers in developing logistical solutions. The company's Par Logistics Management System enables the firm real-time visibility and remote control over all the refrigerated trucks in its fleet. In November 2015, the firm acquired FreshKO Produce Services, Inc.

FINANCIAL DATA: *Note: Data for latest year may not have been available at press time.*

In U.S. $	2016	2015	2014	2013	2012	2011
Revenue	30,000,000,000	29,000,000,000	25,900,000,000	24,200,000,000	23,000,000,000	21,400,000,000
R&D Expense						
Operating Income						
Operating Margin %						
SGA Expense						
Net Income						
Operating Cash Flow						
Capital Expenditure						
EBITDA						
Return on Assets %						
Return on Equity %						
Debt to Equity						

CONTACT INFORMATION:

Phone: 603-354-7000 Fax:
Toll-Free:
Address: 7 Corporate Drive, Keene, NH 03431 United States

STOCK TICKER/OTHER:

Stock Ticker: Private Exchange:
Employees: 17,000 Fiscal Year Ends: 09/30
Parent Company:

SALARIES/BONUSES:

Top Exec. Salary: $ Bonus: $
Second Exec. Salary: $ Bonus: $

OTHER THOUGHTS:

Estimated Female Officers or Directors:
Hot Spot for Advancement for Women/Minorities:

Cabela's Inc

NAIC Code: 451110

www.cabelas.com

TYPES OF BUSINESS:

Sporting Goods Stores
Hunting & Fishing Supplies
Camping Equipment
Outdoor Apparel
Catalog & Online Sales
Credit Card Programs

BRANDS/DIVISIONS/AFFILIATES:

Cabelas.com
Cabelas.ca
World's Foremost Bank
Cabela's CLUB Visa

CONTACTS: *Note: Officers with more than one job title may be intentionally listed here more than once.*

Sean Baker, CEO, Subsidiary
Thomas Millner, CEO
Ralph Castner, CFO
James Cabela, Chairman of the Board
Charles Baldwin, Chief Administrative Officer
Douglas Means, Executive VP
Scott Williams, President
Brent LaSure, Secretary

GROWTH PLANS/SPECIAL FEATURES:

Cabela's, Inc. is a leading retailer of outdoor and hunting supply merchandise. The company's products include merchandise and equipment for hunting, fishing, marine use, camping and recreational sport shooting, as well as casual and outdoor apparel, footwear, optics, vehicle accessories and gifts and home furnishings comprising an outdoor theme. Hunting equipment derives 48.1% of the firm's annual revenue; general outdoor products derive 30.9%; and clothing and footwear derives 21%. Cabela's operates in two segments: merchandising and financial services. The merchandising business operates 85 retail stores and 74 outlet stores in 36 U.S. states; and 11 stores in six Canadian provinces. Retail stores range in size from 40,000 to 246,000 square feet, which either comprise the company's standard format or its large/tourist format. This business segment also includes Cabela's internet and catalog business, which sells products through e-commerce websites (Cabelas.com and Cabelas.ca), mobile devices and print catalog distributions. The financial services business segment provides customers with a rewards program that enhances revenue, operating profitability and customer loyalty within the merchandising segment. Wholly-owned bank subsidiary, World's Foremost Bank (WFB), issues and manages the Cabela's CLUB Visa credit card, a rewards-based program. WFB is a Nebraska state-chartered bank insured by the Federal Deposit Insurance Corporation, and manages more than 2 million active credit card accounts. In October 2016, the firm agreed to be acquired by Bass Pro Shops, Inc. for $4.5 billion.

FINANCIAL DATA: *Note: Data for latest year may not have been available at press time.*

In U.S. $	2016	2015	2014	2013	2012	2011
Revenue	4,129,359,000	3,997,702,000	3,647,650,000	3,599,577,000	3,112,682,000	2,811,166,000
R&D Expense						
Operating Income	273,940,000	307,792,000	335,395,000	361,361,000	275,699,000	231,548,000
Operating Margin %	6.63%	7.69%	9.19%	10.03%	8.85%	8.23%
SGA Expense	1,414,312,000	1,387,647,000	1,251,325,000	1,201,519,000	1,046,861,000	954,125,000
Net Income	146,947,000	189,330,000	201,715,000	224,390,000	173,513,000	142,620,000
Operating Cash Flow	465,400,000	326,991,000	257,979,000	345,004,000	234,629,000	366,468,000
Capital Expenditure	150,948,000	412,716,000	440,891,000	333,009,000	214,267,000	126,740,000
EBITDA	429,258,000	450,214,000	453,434,000	458,824,000	361,106,000	310,237,000
Return on Assets %	1.68%	2.34%	2.86%	3.69%	3.18%	2.95%
Return on Equity %	7.65%	10.38%	11.78%	15.04%	13.57%	12.93%
Debt to Equity	1.55	1.84	1.68	1.72	1.56	1.11

CONTACT INFORMATION:

Phone: 308 254-5505   Fax: 308 254-4800
Toll-Free: 800-237-4444
Address: One Cabela Drive, Sidney, NE 69160 United States

STOCK TICKER/OTHER:

Stock Ticker: CAB
Employees: 19,100
Parent Company:

Exchange: NYS
Fiscal Year Ends: 12/31

SALARIES/BONUSES:

Top Exec. Salary: $1,054,731   Bonus: $392,376
Second Exec. Salary: $541,827   Bonus: $175,339

OTHER THOUGHTS:

Estimated Female Officers or Directors: 2
Hot Spot for Advancement for Women/Minorities:

CACI International Inc

NAIC Code: 541512

www.caci.com

TYPES OF BUSINESS:

Consulting-InfoTech Related
Engineering Simulation Software
Custom Software Engineering
Managed Network Services
Information Management Tools
Knowledge Management
Systems Integration
Radio Frequency Identification (RFID)

BRANDS/DIVISIONS/AFFILIATES:

CACI Limited
CACI BV

CONTACTS: Note: Officers with more than one job title may be intentionally listed here more than once.

Gregory Bradford, CEO, Subsidiary
Kenneth Asbury, CEO
Thomas Mutryn, CFO
J. London, Chairman of the Board
Gregory Buckis, Chief Accounting Officer
John Mengucci, COO
J. Koegel, Executive VP
DeEtte Gray, President, Divisional

GROWTH PLANS/SPECIAL FEATURES:

CACI International, Inc. is a technology development company that provides IT and network services to defense, intelligence and other government departments. Contracts with the U.S. government make up approximately 93.5% of the company's annual revenue. CACI's domestic operations provide business solutions that combine federal domain expertise with technology solutions; command and control (C2) solutions, consisting of hardware, software and interfaces for seamless C2 capabilities; communications solutions for soldier systems, mobile platforms, fixed facilities and the enterprise; cyber security solutions; enterprise IT solutions; health delivery systems, integrating electronic health records, sharpening emergency responsiveness and improving costs; intelligence services that converts data collected into knowledge for decision-making; investigation and litigation support; logistics and material readiness solutions for the secure global flow and storage of goods, services and information in support of U.S. government agencies; and the integration of surveillance and reconnaissance technologies into platforms that enhance soldier and unit situational awareness, mobility, lethality, interoperability and survivability. International operations are conducted primarily through the firm's European subsidiaries, CACI Limited and CACI BV, which provide a diverse mix of IT services and proprietary data and software products. This division serves commercial and government customers throughout the U.K., continental Europe and around the world.

The company offers employees medical, dental and vision insurance; life and AD&D insurance; short- and long-term disability coverage; flexible spending accounts; health club discounts; a 401(k); a discount stock purchase plan; credit union membership; tuition reimbursement; a group legal plan; an employee assistance program; a commuter benefit program; pet care discounts; and merchandise discounts.

FINANCIAL DATA: Note: Data for latest year may not have been available at press time.

In U.S. $	2016	2015	2014	2013	2012	2011
Revenue	3,744,053,000	3,313,452,000	3,564,562,000	3,681,990,000	3,774,473,000	3,577,780,000
R&D Expense						
Operating Income	264,750,000	236,381,000	257,403,000	270,841,000	299,849,000	251,401,000
Operating Margin %	7.07%	7.13%	7.22%	7.35%	7.94%	7.02%
SGA Expense						
Net Income	142,799,000	126,195,000	135,316,000	151,689,000	167,454,000	144,218,000
Operating Cash Flow	242,577,000	223,215,000	198,643,000	249,331,000	266,688,000	225,964,000
Capital Expenditure	20,835,000	17,444,000	15,279,000	15,439,000	18,284,000	14,388,000
EBITDA	329,502,000	302,464,000	322,584,000	324,919,000	355,811,000	307,468,000
Return on Assets %	3.94%	3.81%	4.61%	6.19%	7.10%	6.31%
Return on Equity %	9.25%	8.89%	10.56%	12.81%	13.56%	11.64%
Debt to Equity	0.87	0.69	0.91	0.24	0.45	0.30

CONTACT INFORMATION:

Phone: 703 841-7800   Fax: 703 841-7882
Toll-Free:
Address: 1100 N. Glebe Rd., Arlington, VA 22201 United States

STOCK TICKER/OTHER:

Stock Ticker: CACI   Exchange: NYS
Employees: 16,600   Fiscal Year Ends: 06/30
Parent Company:

SALARIES/BONUSES:

Top Exec. Salary: $862,750   Bonus: $
Second Exec. Salary: $609,000   Bonus: $

OTHER THOUGHTS:

Estimated Female Officers or Directors: 5
Hot Spot for Advancement for Women/Minorities: Y

Cadence Design Systems Inc

www.cadence.com

NAIC Code: 0

TYPES OF BUSINESS:

Software-Electronic Design Automation
Training & Support Services
Design & Methodology Services

BRANDS/DIVISIONS/AFFILIATES:

CONTACTS: *Note: Officers with more than one job title may be intentionally listed here more than once.*

Lip-Bu Tan, CEO
Geoffrey Ribar, CFO
John Shoven, Chairman of the Board
James Cowie, General Counsel
Thomas Beckley, Senior VP, Divisional
Anirudh Devgan, Senior VP, Divisional
Neil Zaman, Senior VP, Divisional
Pieter Vorenkamp, Senior VP, Divisional
Surendra Babu Mandava, Senior VP, Divisional

GROWTH PLANS/SPECIAL FEATURES:

Cadence Design Systems, Inc. is a leading provider of system design enablement solutions and electronic design automation software/hardware used by semiconductor & electronic system customers to develop and design integrated circuits (ICs) and electronic devices. It licenses, sells and leases its hardware technology and provides design and methodology services throughout the world to help manage and accelerate electronic product development processes. Cadence combines its design technologies into platforms for five major design activities: functional verification, digital IC and signoff, custom IC, system interconnect and analysis, and IP (intellectual property). Functional verification products are used to verify that the circuitry designed by customers will perform as intended. Digital IC design offerings are used by customers to create logical representations of a digital circuit or an IC that can be verified for correctness prior to implementation. Once the logic is verified, the design is converted to a format ready for silicon manufacturing. This division's signoff offering is comprised of tools used to signoff the design as ready for manufacture by a silicon foundry, which provides certification for this step. Custom IC design and verification offerings are used to create schematic & physical representations of circuits down to the transistor level for analog, mixed-signal, custom digital, memory and radio frequency designs. System interconnect & analysis offerings are used to develop PCBs and IC packages. IP offerings consist of pre-verified, customizable functional blocks which customers integrate into their system-on-a-chips to accelerate the development process and to reduce the risk of errors in the design process.

Cadence employees receive medical, dental and vision coverage; retiree health access; short- and long-term disability; life insurance; domestic partner coverage; a 401(k); an employee stock purchase plan; and tuition reimbursement.

FINANCIAL DATA: *Note: Data for latest year may not have been available at press time.*

In U.S. $	2016	2015	2014	2013	2012	2011
Revenue	1,816,083,000	1,702,091,000	1,580,932,000	1,460,116,000	1,326,424,000	1,149,835,000
R&D Expense	735,340,000	637,567,000	603,006,000	534,022,000	454,085,000	400,745,000
Operating Income	244,901,000	285,430,000	206,644,000	189,007,000	211,672,000	120,377,000
Operating Margin %	13.48%	16.76%	13.07%	12.94%	15.95%	10.46%
SGA Expense	520,300,000	512,414,000	513,307,000	499,471,000	454,354,000	416,661,000
Net Income	203,086,000	252,417,000	158,898,000	164,243,000	439,948,000	72,229,000
Operating Cash Flow	444,879,000	378,200,000	316,722,000	367,605,000	315,994,000	240,342,000
Capital Expenditure	53,712,000	44,808,000	39,810,000	44,929,000	35,966,000	31,421,000
EBITDA	380,411,000	414,072,000	330,757,000	294,885,000	312,230,000	230,099,000
Return on Assets %	9.13%	9.07%	5.63%	6.96%	21.73%	4.13%
Return on Equity %	19.17%	18.63%	12.76%	15.85%	66.34%	21.00%
Debt to Equity	0.86	0.25	0.26			0.32

CONTACT INFORMATION:

Phone: 408 943-1234   Fax: 408 428-5001
Toll-Free: 800-746-6223
Address: 2655 Seely Ave., Bldg. 5, San Jose, CA 95134 United States

STOCK TICKER/OTHER:

Stock Ticker: CDNS   Exchange: NAS
Employees: 7,100   Fiscal Year Ends: 12/31
Parent Company:

SALARIES/BONUSES:

Top Exec. Salary: $650,000   Bonus: $
Second Exec. Salary: Bonus: $330,000
$275,481

OTHER THOUGHTS:

Estimated Female Officers or Directors: 2
Hot Spot for Advancement for Women/Minorities:

Capital One Financial Corp

www.capitalone.com

NAIC Code: 522110

TYPES OF BUSINESS:

Credit Card Issuing
Credit Card Products & Services
Mortgage Services
Consumer Lending
Health Care Financing
Small Business Loans
Mortgages
Commercial Banking

BRANDS/DIVISIONS/AFFILIATES:

Capital One Bank (USA) National Association
Capital One National Association

CONTACTS: Note: Officers with more than one job title may be intentionally listed here more than once.

Richard Fairbank, CEO
Jonathan Witter, President, Divisional
R. Blackley, CFO
Timothy Golden, Chief Accounting Officer
Robert Alexander, Chief Information Officer
Kevin Borgmann, Chief Risk Officer
John Finneran, General Counsel
Stephen Crawford, Other Corporate Officer
Jory Berson, Other Executive Officer
Frank LaPrade, Other Executive Officer
Noelle Eder, Other Executive Officer
Michael Wassmer, President, Divisional
Christopher Newkirk, President, Divisional
Sanjiv Yajnik, President, Divisional
Michael Slocum, President, Divisional

GROWTH PLANS/SPECIAL FEATURES:

Capital One Financial Corp. is a financial holding company whose banking and non-banking subsidiaries market a variety of financial products and services. The business operates in three segments: credit cards, commercial banking and consumer banking. The credit cards segment includes domestic consumer and small business card lending, domestic small business lending, closed end installment lending and the international card lending businesses in Canada and the U.K. Commercial banking is comprised of lending, deposit gathering and treasury management services provided to commercial real estate and middle market customers. This segment also includes a portfolio of small commercial real estate loans that are in run-off mode. Consumer banking includes branch-based lending and deposit gathering activities for small business customers as well as consumer deposit gathering and lending activities, auto financing and mortgage lending. The company's principle subsidiaries are Capital One Bank (USA), National Association (COBNA) and Capital One, National Association (CONA). COBNA offers consumers credit and debit card services, as well as lending and deposit products. CONA offers banking products and financial services to consumers, small businesses and commercial clients.

Employees of Capital One receive flex spending accounts; medical, dental, vision, prescription drug and employee assistance programs; a 401(k); life, long-term care and disability insurance; military and parental leave; adoption assistance; and an employee discount stock purchase program.

FINANCIAL DATA: Note: Data for latest year may not have been available at press time.

In U.S. $	2016	2015	2014	2013	2012	2011
Revenue	25,501,000,000	23,413,000,000	22,290,000,000	22,384,000,000	21,396,000,000	16,279,000,000
R&D Expense						
Operating Income	5,484,000,000	5,881,000,000	6,569,000,000	6,417,000,000	5,035,000,000	4,587,000,000
Operating Margin %	21.50%	25.11%	29.47%	28.66%	23.53%	28.17%
SGA Expense	9,035,000,000	8,368,000,000	6,952,000,000	7,993,000,000	7,288,000,000	5,041,000,000
Net Income	3,751,000,000	4,050,000,000	4,428,000,000	4,159,000,000	3,517,000,000	3,147,000,000
Operating Cash Flow	11,856,000,000	10,127,000,000	9,304,001,000	9,984,000,000	9,060,000,000	7,455,000,000
Capital Expenditure	779,000,000	532,000,000	502,000,000	818,000,000	560,000,000	315,000,000
EBITDA						
Return on Assets %	1.01%	1.20%	1.43%	1.34%	1.34%	1.54%
Return on Equity %	7.41%	8.38%	10.00%	9.94%	9.93%	11.10%
Debt to Equity	1.25	1.22	1.05	0.95	1.20	0.91

CONTACT INFORMATION:

Phone: 703 720-1000   Fax:
Toll-Free: 800-801-1164
Address: 1680 Capital One Dr., McLean, VA 22102 United States

STOCK TICKER/OTHER:

Stock Ticker: COF
Employees: 47,300
Parent Company:

Exchange: NYS
Fiscal Year Ends: 12/31

SALARIES/BONUSES:

Top Exec. Salary: $ Bonus: $2,677,500
Second Exec. Salary: Bonus: $
$1,592,692

OTHER THOUGHTS:

Estimated Female Officers or Directors: 3
Hot Spot for Advancement for Women/Minorities: Y

Cardinal Health Inc

www.cardinalhealth.com

NAIC Code: 424210

TYPES OF BUSINESS:

Healthcare Products & Services
Supply Chain Services
Medical Products

BRANDS/DIVISIONS/AFFILIATES:

Cardinal.com
Cardinal Health at Home

CONTACTS: *Note: Officers with more than one job title may be intentionally listed here more than once.*

Donald Casey, CEO, Divisional
Jon Giacomin, CEO, Divisional
George Barrett, CEO
Michael Kaufmann, CFO
Stuart Laws, Chief Accounting Officer
Patricia Morrison, Chief Information Officer
Pamela Kimmet, Other Executive Officer
Craig Morford, Other Executive Officer

GROWTH PLANS/SPECIAL FEATURES:

Cardinal Health, Inc. is a provider of products and services that improve the safety and productivity of health care. The company operates in two segments: pharmaceuticals and medical products. The pharmaceutical segment distributes a broad line of branded and generic pharmaceutical products, specialty pharmaceutical, over-the-counter health care products and consumer products. It is also a full-service wholesale distributor to retail customers, hospitals and alternate care providers located throughout the U.S. In addition, this segment operates nuclear pharmacies and cyclotron facilities, provides pharmacy operations, medication therapy management and patient outcomes services to hospitals and other healthcare providers. The segment offers a broad range of support services including computerized order entry provided through Cardinal.com; generic sourcing programs; product movement, inventory and management reports; and consultation on store operations and merchandising. Through its medical products segment, the company distributes a broad range of medical, surgical and laboratory products to hospitals, ambulatory surgery centers, clinical laboratories, physician offices and other healthcare providers in the U.S., Canada and China and to patients in the home in the U.S. through its Cardinal Health at Home division. This segment also manufactures, sources and develops its own line of private brand medical and surgical products which include: single-use surgical drapes, gowns and apparel, exam and surgical gloves and fluid suction and collection systems; and manufactures extravascular closure devices. In April 2017, Cardinal Health agreed to acquire part of the patient monitoring and recovery unit of Medtronic PLC for $6.1 billion.

Employee benefits include medical, dental and vision coverage; a 401(k); flexible spending accounts; short- and long-term disability; life insurance; travel insurance; an employee assistance program; adoption assistance; and tuition reimbursement.

FINANCIAL DATA: *Note: Data for latest year may not have been available at press time.*

In U.S. $	2016	2015	2014	2013	2012	2011
Revenue	121,546,000,000	102,531,000,000	91,084,000,000	101,093,000,000	107,552,000,000	
R&D Expense						
Operating Income	2,459,000,000	2,161,000,000	1,885,000,000	996,000,000	1,792,000,000	
Operating Margin %	2.02%	2.10%	2.06%	.98%	1.66%	
SGA Expense	3,648,000,000	3,240,000,000	3,028,000,000	2,875,000,000	2,677,000,000	
Net Income	1,427,000,000	1,215,000,000	1,166,000,000	334,000,000	1,069,000,000	
Operating Cash Flow	2,971,000,000	2,540,000,000	2,524,000,000	1,727,000,000	1,176,000,000	
Capital Expenditure	465,000,000	300,000,000	249,000,000	195,000,000	263,000,000	
EBITDA	3,100,000,000	2,612,000,000	2,344,000,000	1,393,000,000	2,117,000,000	
Return on Assets %	4.44%	4.32%	4.49%	1.33%	4.53%	
Return on Equity %	22.27%	19.19%	18.84%	5.46%	17.68%	
Debt to Equity	0.75	0.83	0.49	0.61	0.38	

CONTACT INFORMATION:

Phone: 614 757-5000   Fax:
Toll-Free: 800-234-8701
Address: 7000 Cardinal Pl., Dublin, OH 43017 United States

STOCK TICKER/OTHER:

Stock Ticker: CAH   Exchange: NYS
Employees: 49,800   Fiscal Year Ends: 06/30
Parent Company:

SALARIES/BONUSES:

Top Exec. Salary: $1,320,000   Bonus: $
Second Exec. Salary: $721,311   Bonus: $

OTHER THOUGHTS:

Estimated Female Officers or Directors: 8
Hot Spot for Advancement for Women/Minorities: Y

CarMax Inc

NAIC Code: 441120

TYPES OF BUSINESS:

Used Auto Dealers
New Auto Dealers
Online Sales
Vehicle Repair Services
Financial Services

BRANDS/DIVISIONS/AFFILIATES:

CarMax Auto Finance

CONTACTS: Note: Officers with more than one job title may be intentionally listed here more than once.

Thomas Reedy, CFO
Thomas Folliard, Chairman of the Board
Jill Livesay, Chief Accounting Officer
Shamim Mohammad, Chief Information Officer
Edwin Hill, Executive VP, Divisional
William Wood, Executive VP
Eric Margolin, Executive VP
Diane Cafritz, Other Executive Officer
William Nash, President
Jon Daniels, Senior VP, Divisional
James Lyski, Senior VP

GROWTH PLANS/SPECIAL FEATURES:

CarMax, Inc. is a leading retailer of used cars in the U.S. The firm purchases, reconditions and sells used vehicles through 173 used car superstores located in 86 metropolitan markets across the U.S. CarMax vehicles are typically 0 to 10 years old, have more than 100,000 miles and range in price from $11,000 to $34,000. The firm also sells new vehicles at four of its locations under franchise agreements with three car manufacturers. The company offers a wide selection of makes and models of both domestic and imported vehicles to appeal to diverse consumer preferences and budgets, including popular brands from manufacturers such as Chrysler, Ford, General Motors, Honda, Hyundai, Kia, Mazda, Nissan, Toyota and Volkswagen, and luxury brands such as Acura, BMW, Infiniti, Lexus and Mercedes-Benz. The company will also transfer any used vehicle in its nationwide inventory to a local superstore. Vehicles purchased through the company's in-store appraisal process that fall short of retail standards are sold at onsite wholesale auctions restricted to licensed automobile dealers. All store locations provide vehicle repair service and used-car warranty service. In addition, through the company's web site, customers can search new and used cars as well as find information on Kelley Blue Book figures, car buying tips, rebates and incentives. CarMax offers financing options through CarMax Auto Finance, including revolving credit and automobile installment loans. The firm retailed approximately 671,300 used vehicles in fiscal 2017, as well as 391,686 wholesale vehicles it sold through onsite auctions.

CarMax offers its employees a benefits package including educational assistance, a daycare savings account, life insurance, adoption assistance, an associate discount program and an employee assistance program.

FINANCIAL DATA: Note: Data for latest year may not have been available at press time.

In U.S. $	2016	2015	2014	2013	2012	2011
Revenue	15,149,670,000	14,268,720,000	12,574,300,000	10,962,820,000	10,003,600,000	
R&D Expense						
Operating Income	1,058,861,000	997,096,000	493,486,000	732,595,000	700,160,000	
Operating Margin %	6.98%	6.98%	3.92%	6.68%	6.99%	
SGA Expense	1,351,935,000	1,257,725,000	1,155,215,000	1,031,034,000	940,786,000	
Net Income	623,428,000	597,358,000	492,586,000	434,284,000	413,795,000	
Operating Cash Flow	-148,893,000	-968,130,000	-613,163,000	-778,441,000	-62,164,000	
Capital Expenditure	315,584,000	309,817,000	310,317,000	235,707,000	172,616,000	
EBITDA	1,183,662,000	1,108,977,000	930,067,000	828,991,000	783,436,000	
Return on Assets %	4.50%	4.79%	4.56%	4.76%	5.45%	
Return on Equity %	20.56%	18.45%	15.54%	15.25%	16.66%	
Debt to Equity	3.56	2.79	2.21	1.99	1.81	

CONTACT INFORMATION:

Phone: 804 747-0422   Fax: 804 747-5848
Toll-Free: 800-519-1511
Address: 12800 Tuckahoe Creek Pkwy., Richmond, VA 23238 United States

STOCK TICKER/OTHER:

Stock Ticker: KMX
Employees: 24,344
Parent Company:

Exchange: NYS
Fiscal Year Ends: 02/28

SALARIES/BONUSES:

Top Exec. Salary: $902,308   Bonus: $
Second Exec. Salary: $699,039   Bonus: $

OTHER THOUGHTS:

Estimated Female Officers or Directors: 9
Hot Spot for Advancement for Women/Minorities: Y

Carnival Corporation

NAIC Code: 483112

www.carnival.com

TYPES OF BUSINESS:
Cruise Line
On-Board Casinos
Tours
Resort Hotels

BRANDS/DIVISIONS/AFFILIATES:
Carnival Cruise plc
Carnival Cruise Lines
Princess Cruises
Holland America Line
Seabourn Cruise Line
Costa Cruises
P&O Cruises
Cunard

CONTACTS: Note: Officers with more than one job title may be intentionally listed here more than once.
David Noyes, CEO, Geographical
Michael Thamm, CEO, Subsidiary
Stein Kruse, CEO, Subsidiary
Arnold Donald, CEO
David Bernstein, CFO
Micky Arison, Chairman of the Board
Larry Freedman, Chief Accounting Officer
Josh Leibowitz, Chief Strategy Officer
Alan Buckelew, COO
Arnaldo Perez, Secretary

GROWTH PLANS/SPECIAL FEATURES:
Carnival Corporation is a leading provider of cruises and vacation packages to destinations worldwide. The firm is linked with its sister company Carnival plc. The firm divides its cruise brands into two segments: North America, which includes Carnival Cruise Lines, Princess Cruises, Holland America Line and Seabourn Cruise Line; and Europe, Australia & Asia (EAA), comprised of Costa Cruises, P&O Cruises, Cunard and AIDA Cruises. In total, the company operates over 100 ships and 11.5 million guests in 2016. Carnival Cruise Lines operates 25 ships and is based in North America. Princess is a global cruise and tour company operating 17 ships. Holland America Line serves the industry's premium segment, with 14 ships sailing to all seven continents. Seabourn offers luxury cruises on its four luxury yachts. Costa Cruises is a leading cruise company in Europe, Spain and South America, operating a modern fleet of 15 ships. P&O Cruises, which operates from the U.K. and Australia, sails to destinations in the Caribbean, South America, Scandinavia, the Mediterranean and Atlantic Islands as well as Round the World cruises. Cunard operates the Queen Mary 2, Queen Elizabeth and Queen Victoria ships. AIDA operates in the German-speaking cruise market via a fleet of 11 ships. The company also owns Holland America Princess Alaska Tours, a leading tour operator in Alaska and the Canadian Yukon, offering lodging, chartered motorcoaches, glass-domed railcars, luxury day boats and sightseeing packages.

FINANCIAL DATA: Note: Data for latest year may not have been available at press time.

In U.S. $	2016	2015	2014	2013	2012	2011
Revenue	16,389,000,000	15,714,000,000	15,884,000,000	15,456,000,000	15,382,000,000	15,793,000,000
R&D Expense						
Operating Income	3,071,000,000	2,574,000,000	1,792,000,000	1,352,000,000	1,642,000,000	2,255,000,000
Operating Margin %	18.73%	16.38%	11.28%	8.74%	10.67%	14.27%
SGA Expense	2,197,000,000	2,067,000,000	2,054,000,000	1,879,000,000	1,720,000,000	1,717,000,000
Net Income	2,779,000,000	1,757,000,000	1,236,000,000	1,078,000,000	1,298,000,000	1,912,000,000
Operating Cash Flow	5,134,000,000	4,545,000,000	3,430,000,000	2,834,000,000	2,999,000,000	3,766,000,000
Capital Expenditure	3,062,000,000	2,294,000,000	2,583,000,000	2,149,000,000	2,332,000,000	2,696,000,000
EBITDA	4,789,000,000	3,642,000,000	3,168,000,000	2,979,000,000	3,165,000,000	3,799,000,000
Return on Assets %	7.10%	4.46%	3.10%	2.72%	3.33%	5.02%
Return on Equity %	11.98%	7.31%	5.06%	4.44%	5.43%	8.16%
Debt to Equity	0.36	0.31	0.30	0.32	0.29	0.33

CONTACT INFORMATION:
Phone: 305 599-2600   Fax: 305 471-4700
Toll-Free:
Address: 3655 NW 87th Ave., Miami, FL 33178 United States

STOCK TICKER/OTHER:
Stock Ticker: CCL   Exchange: NYS
Employees: 84,600   Fiscal Year Ends: 11/30
Parent Company:

SALARIES/BONUSES:
Top Exec. Salary: $1,000,000   Bonus: $
Second Exec. Salary: Bonus: $
$825,000

OTHER THOUGHTS:
Estimated Female Officers or Directors: 1
Hot Spot for Advancement for Women/Minorities: Y

Catholic Health Initiatives

www.catholichealthinitiatives.org

NAIC Code: 622110

TYPES OF BUSINESS:

General Medical and Surgical Hospitals
Long-Term Care
Assisted & Independent Living Facilities
Community Health Organizations
Home Care Services
Occupational Health Clinic
Cancer Prevention Institute

BRANDS/DIVISIONS/AFFILIATES:

CHI
Centura Health
Mercy Health
KentuckyOne Health
TriHealth
Pathology Associates Medical Laboratories

CONTACTS: *Note: Officers with more than one job title may be intentionally listed here more than once.*

Kevin E. Lofton, CEO
Anthony Jones, Interim Exec.VP-Operations
Kevin E. Lofton, Pres.
J. Dean Swindle, CFO
Patricia G. Webb, Chief Human Resource Officer
Stephen L. Moore, Chief Medical Officer
Mitch H. Melfi, General Counsel
John F. DiCola, Sr. VP-Strategy & Bus. Dev.
Joyce M. Ross, Sr. VP-Comm.
Philip L. Foster, Sr. VP
A. Michelle Cooper, Corp. Responsibility Officer
Kathleen Sanford, Chief Nursing Officer
Joseph W. Wilczek, Sr. VP-Div. Oper.
Christopher Lowney, Chmn.
Steven C. Kehrberg, Sr. VP-Supply Chain

GROWTH PLANS/SPECIAL FEATURES:

Catholic Health Initiatives (CHI) is a national faith-based, nonprofit healthcare organization focused on strengthening and advancing the Catholic health ministry. The organization operates 104 hospitals in 17 states, including academic medical centers and teaching hospitals, critical-access facilities, community health services organizations, accredited nursing colleges, home-health agencies, and other facilities that span the inpatient/outpatient continuum of care. CHI's family of hospitals and facilities comprise the following names: CHI, Centura Health, Mercy Health, KentuckyOne Health, TriHealth, St. Anthony, St. Catherine, St. Mary-Corwin, St. Thomas, St. Rose, Flagnet, and many more. In February 2017, the firm, along with Providence Health & Services agreed to sell their joint venture, Pathology Associates Medical Laboratories, to Laboratory Corporation of America Holdings (LabCorp).

Employee benefits include medical, dental and vision coverage; flexible spending accounts; life and AD&D insurance; short- and long-term disability; a retirement plan; 403(b) and 457(b) plans; and tuition and adoption assistance.

FINANCIAL DATA: *Note: Data for latest year may not have been available at press time.*

In U.S. $	2016	2015	2014	2013	2012	2011
Revenue	16,473,769,000	15,713,280,000	13,888,673,000	10,708,225,000	9,844,271,000	9,004,978,000
R&D Expense						
Operating Income						
Operating Margin %						
SGA Expense						
Net Income	-666,523,000	137,793,000	633,967,000	-54,943,000	311,818,000	335,326,000
Operating Cash Flow						
Capital Expenditure						
EBITDA						
Return on Assets %						
Return on Equity %						
Debt to Equity						

CONTACT INFORMATION:

Phone: 303-298-9100   Fax:
Toll-Free:
Address: 198 Inverness Drive West, Englewood, CO 80112 United States

STOCK TICKER/OTHER:

Stock Ticker: Nonprofit   Exchange:
Employees: 102,466   Fiscal Year Ends: 06/30
Parent Company:

SALARIES/BONUSES:

Top Exec. Salary: $ Bonus: $
Second Exec. Salary: $ Bonus: $

OTHER THOUGHTS:

Estimated Female Officers or Directors: 6
Hot Spot for Advancement for Women/Minorities: Y

CBRE Group Inc

NAIC Code: 531210

www.cbre.com

TYPES OF BUSINESS:

Real Estate Brokerage
Real Estate Management Services
Mortgage Banking
Investment Management
Consulting Services

BRANDS/DIVISIONS/AFFILIATES:

CBRE Inc
CBRE Capital Markets
CBRE Ltd
CBRE Global Investors LLC
Trammell Crow Company LLC
Atrium AS
Skye Group
Capstone Financial Solutions LLC

CONTACTS: Note: Officers with more than one job title may be intentionally listed here more than once.

William Concannon, CEO, Divisional
T. Ferguson, CEO, Divisional
Robert Sulentic, CEO
James Groch, CFO
Ray Wirta, Chairman of the Board
Gil Borok, Chief Accounting Officer
J. Kirk, Chief Administrative Officer
Laurence Midler, Executive VP
Michael Lafitte, President, Divisional
Calvin Frese, President, Geographical

GROWTH PLANS/SPECIAL FEATURES:

CBRE Group, Inc. is one of the world's largest commercial real estate services companies, with over 450 offices in more than 100 countries. It offers services to occupiers, owners, lenders/investors in office, retail, industrial, multi-family and other commercial real estate assets. The firm's core services include commercial property and corporate facilities management, tenant representation, property/agency leasing, property sales, valuation, real estate investment management, commercial mortgage origination and servicing, capital markets (equity and debt), development services and proprietary research. CBRE operates in five segments: Americas, which accounted for 55.3% of its 2016 revenue; Europe, Middle East and Africa (EMEA), 30%; Asia Pacific, 11.4%; global investment management, 2.8%; and development services, 0.5%. Americas operates primarily through CBRE, Inc.; CBRE Capital Markets, Inc.; and CBRE Ltd. EMEA has offices in 60 countries, with its largest located in the France, Germany, Italy, the Netherlands, Russia, Spain and the U.K. Asia Pacific operates in 16 countries, including Australia and New Zealand, China, Hong Kong, India, Japan, Korea and Singapore. In addition, the company has agreements with affiliated offices in Cambodia, Malaysia, the Philippines and Thailand that generate royalty fees and support cross-referral arrangements. Global investment management is handled by subsidiary CBRE Global Investors, LLC. Through the Trammell Crow Company LLC, the firm provides development services primarily in the U.S. to users of and investors in commercial real estate. In 2016, the firm made several acquisitions: Atrium AS, a provider of investment, occupier, valuation and leasing services; Michael Horwitz & Company, a London-based retail property advisor that specializes in the luxury goods sector; Skye Group, a retail project management provider; Floored, Inc., a leading producer of advanced technology for commercial real estate; and Capstone Financial Solutions LLC, a national commercial real estate finance and consulting firm.

The company offers its employees medical, dental and vision insurance; a 401(k); flexible spending accounts; an employee assistance program; and paid vacation and holidays.

FINANCIAL DATA: Note: Data for latest year may not have been available at press time.

In U.S. $	2016	2015	2014	2013	2012	2011
Revenue	13,071,590,000	10,855,810,000	9,049,918,000	7,184,794,000	6,514,099,000	5,905,411,000
R&D Expense						
Operating Income	815,487,000	835,944,000	792,254,000	616,128,000	585,081,000	462,862,000
Operating Margin %	6.23%	7.70%	8.75%	8.57%	8.98%	7.83%
SGA Expense	2,781,310,000	2,633,609,000	2,438,960,000	2,104,310,000	2,002,914,000	1,882,666,000
Net Income	571,973,000	547,132,000	484,503,000	316,538,000	315,555,000	239,162,000
Operating Cash Flow	450,315,000	651,897,000	661,780,000	745,108,000	291,081,000	361,219,000
Capital Expenditure	191,205,000	139,464,000	171,242,000	156,358,000	150,232,000	147,980,000
EBITDA	1,392,504,000	1,312,706,000	1,154,398,000	835,337,000	835,451,000	696,717,000
Return on Assets %	5.24%	5.86%	6.61%	4.27%	4.19%	3.87%
Return on Equity %	19.97%	22.00%	23.31%	18.43%	23.45%	23.22%
Debt to Equity	0.84	0.97	0.81	0.98	1.65	2.26

CONTACT INFORMATION:

Phone: 213-613-3333   Fax: 213 438-4820
Toll-Free:
Address: 400 South Hope Street, 25th Fl, Los Angeles, CA 90071 United States

STOCK TICKER/OTHER:

Stock Ticker: CBG   Exchange: NYS
Employees: 75,000   Fiscal Year Ends: 12/31
Parent Company:

SALARIES/BONUSES:

Top Exec. Salary: $800,000   Bonus: $756,713
Second Exec. Salary: $990,000   Bonus: $500,000

OTHER THOUGHTS:

Estimated Female Officers or Directors: 2
Hot Spot for Advancement for Women/Minorities:

Sales, profits and employees may be estimates. Financial information, benefits and other data can change quickly and may vary from those stated here.

CBS Corporation

www.cbscorporation.com

NAIC Code: 515120

TYPES OF BUSINESS:

Television Broadcasting
News Organization
Outdoor Advertising
Radio Networks & Programming
Television Production
Cable TV Networks
Book Publishing

BRANDS/DIVISIONS/AFFILIATES:

National Amusements Inc
CBS Television Network
CBS Films
CBS All Access
Showtime Networks
CBS Television Stations
CBS Local Digital Media
Simon & Schuster

CONTACTS: Note: Officers with more than one job title may be intentionally listed here more than once.

Leslie Moonves, CEO
Sumner Redstone, Chairman Emeritus
Lawrence Liding, Chief Accounting Officer
Anthony Ambrosio, Chief Administrative Officer
Joseph Ianniello, COO
Shari Redstone, Director
Jonathan Anschell, Executive VP
Richard Jones, Executive VP
Gil Schwartz, Other Executive Officer
Lawrence Tu, Other Executive Officer

GROWTH PLANS/SPECIAL FEATURES:

CBS Corporation is a leading mass media company in the U.S. National Amusements, Inc. owns approximately 80% of the voting stock of CBS. The firm operates through four segments: entertainment, accounting for 67% of 2016 revenues; cable networks, 16%; local media, 14%; and publishing 6%. The entertainment division is composed of the following: CBS Television Network, CBS Television Studios, CBS Studios International, CBS Television Distribution, CBS Interactive and CBS Films; and the digital streaming services of CBS All Access and CBSN. The cable networks segment is composed of Showtime Networks, which operates the firm's premium subscription program services: Showtime, The Movie Channel and Flix; CBS Sports Network, the company's cable network which focuses on college athletics and other sports; and Smithsonian Networks, a venture between Showtime Networks and Smithsonian Institution, which operates Smithsonian Channel, a basic cable program service. The local media segment is composed of CBS Television Stations, the company's 30 owned broadcast television stations; and CBS Local Digital Media, which operates local websites, including content from the company's television stations and news and sports radio stations. The publishing segment is composed of Simon & Schuster, which publishes and distributes consumer books under imprints such as Simon & Schuster, Pocket Books, Scribner, Gallery Books, Touchstone and Atria Books. In February 2017, the firm agreed to combine its radio business with Entercom Communications Corporation in a merger transaction expected to be completed by year's end.

CBS offers its employees health, vision, dental & life insurance; a 401(k) plan; short & long term disability; flexible spending accounts; adoption assistance; eldercare programs; and paid leave to care for a terminally ill family member.

FINANCIAL DATA: Note: Data for latest year may not have been available at press time.

In U.S. $	2016	2015	2014	2013	2012	2011
Revenue	13,166,000,000	13,886,000,000	13,806,000,000	15,284,000,000	14,089,000,000	14,245,000,000
R&D Expense						
Operating Income	2,621,000,000	2,417,000,000	2,896,000,000	3,259,000,000	2,983,000,000	2,529,000,000
Operating Margin %	19.90%	17.40%	20.97%	21.32%	21.17%	17.75%
SGA Expense	2,335,000,000	2,455,000,000	2,462,000,000	2,735,000,000	2,634,000,000	2,755,000,000
Net Income	1,261,000,000	1,413,000,000	2,959,000,000	1,879,000,000	1,574,000,000	1,305,000,000
Operating Cash Flow	1,685,000,000	1,394,000,000	1,275,000,000	1,873,000,000	1,815,000,000	1,749,000,000
Capital Expenditure	196,000,000	193,000,000	206,000,000	270,000,000	254,000,000	265,000,000
EBITDA	2,866,000,000	2,679,000,000	2,808,000,000	3,730,000,000	3,438,000,000	3,067,000,000
Return on Assets %	5.25%	5.90%	11.72%	7.11%	5.97%	4.98%
Return on Equity %	27.25%	22.54%	34.94%	18.62%	15.64%	13.22%
Debt to Equity	2.41	1.47	0.93	0.59	0.57	0.60

CONTACT INFORMATION:

Phone: 212 975-4321   Fax: 212 975-4516
Toll-Free:
Address: 51 W. 52nd St., New York, NY 10019 United States

STOCK TICKER/OTHER:

Stock Ticker: CBS   Exchange: NYS
Employees: 21,270   Fiscal Year Ends: 12/31
Parent Company:

SALARIES/BONUSES:

Top Exec. Salary: $3,500,000   Bonus: $32,000,000
Second Exec. Salary: $2,500,000   Bonus: $12,500,000

OTHER THOUGHTS:

Estimated Female Officers or Directors: 3
Hot Spot for Advancement for Women/Minorities: Y

CDW Corporation

NAIC Code: 423430

TYPES OF BUSINESS:

Direct Selling-Computer Products
Online Sales
Custom Installation & Repair-Computers

BRANDS/DIVISIONS/AFFILIATES:

CDW Government LLC
CDW Canada Inc
CDW Ltd
CDW UK

CONTACTS: Note: Officers with more than one job title may be intentionally listed here more than once.

Thomas Richards, CEO
Ann Ziegler, CFO
Neil Fairfield, Chief Accounting Officer
Jonathan Stevens, Chief Information Officer
Christine Leahy, Other Executive Officer
Dennis Berger, Other Executive Officer
Neal Campbell, Senior VP, Divisional
Christina Rother, Senior VP, Divisional
Matthew Troka, Senior VP, Divisional
Mark Chong, Senior VP, Divisional
Christina Corley, Senior VP, Divisional
Douglas Eckrote, Senior VP, Divisional

GROWTH PLANS/SPECIAL FEATURES:

CDW Corporation is one of the leading providers of multi-branded information technology products and services to business, government, education and healthcare customers in the U.S., Canada and the U.K. The firm offers over 100,000 products from over 1,000 leading technology brands, in addition to customized solution design and management with focus areas including notebooks, desktops, printers, servers and storage, unified communications, security, wireless, power and cooling, networking, software licensing, cloud computing, data center optimization and mobility solutions. The company manages its inventory through a 450,000-square-foot distribution center in Vernon Hills, Illinois; a 513,000-square-foot distribution center in Las Vegas, Nevada; and a 120,000-square foot distribution center in Rugby, Warwickshire, U.K. CDW offers customers free access to certified technicians for telephone support and complete custom installation and repair services via the company's configuration center, in addition to access to a database of frequently asked technical questions and direct links to manufacturers' tech support websites. Its CDW Government, LLC subsidiary provides specialized product offerings and services to federal, state and local governments as well as the educational sector. Subsidiaries CDW Canada, Inc. and CDW Ltd. (doing business as CDW UK) provide IT solutions, serving commercial and public sector customers.

The company offers its employees medical, dental and vision insurance; a 401(k) plan; a profit sharing plan; life and AD&D insurance; flexible spending accounts; tuition reimbursement; short- and long-term disability insurance; and an employee assistance program.

FINANCIAL DATA: Note: Data for latest year may not have been available at press time.

In U.S. $	2016	2015	2014	2013	2012	2011
Revenue	13,981,900,000	12,988,700,000	12,074,500,000	10,768,600,000	10,128,200,000	9,602,400,000
R&D Expense						
Operating Income	819,200,000	742,000,000	673,000,000	508,600,000	510,600,000	470,700,000
Operating Margin %	5.85%	5.71%	5.57%	4.72%	5.04%	4.90%
SGA Expense	1,508,000,000	1,373,800,000	1,248,300,000	1,251,700,000	1,159,000,000	1,116,700,000
Net Income	424,400,000	403,100,000	244,900,000	132,800,000	119,000,000	17,100,000
Operating Cash Flow	604,000,000	277,500,000	435,000,000	366,300,000	317,400,000	214,700,000
Capital Expenditure	63,500,000	90,100,000	55,000,000	47,100,000	41,400,000	45,700,000
EBITDA	1,073,700,000	969,400,000	880,900,000	716,800,000	720,800,000	675,600,000
Return on Assets %	6.19%	6.27%	4.07%	2.28%	2.03%	.28%
Return on Equity %	39.63%	39.66%	29.71%	31.31%	184.21%	
Debt to Equity	3.07	2.94	3.38	4.50	27.33	

CONTACT INFORMATION:

Phone: 847-465-6000   Fax: 847-465-6800
Toll-Free: 800-750-4239
Address: 75 Tri-State International, Lincolnshire, IL 60069 United States

STOCK TICKER/OTHER:

Stock Ticker: CDW   Exchange: NAS
Employees: 8,516   Fiscal Year Ends: 12/31
Parent Company:

SALARIES/BONUSES:

Top Exec. Salary: $851,587   Bonus: $
Second Exec. Salary: Bonus: $
$516,806

OTHER THOUGHTS:

Estimated Female Officers or Directors: 10
Hot Spot for Advancement for Women/Minorities: Y

Celanese Corporation

www.celanese.com

NAIC Code: 325211

TYPES OF BUSINESS:

Manufacturing-Acetyl Intermediate Chemicals
Industrial Products
Technical & High-Performance Polymers
Sweeteners & Sorbates
Ethanol Production
Food Ingredients
Cellulose Derivative Fibers

BRANDS/DIVISIONS/AFFILIATES:

SO.F.TER Group

CONTACTS: Note: Officers with more than one job title may be intentionally listed here more than once.

Mark Rohr, CEO
Kevin Oliver, Chief Accounting Officer
Peter Edwards, Executive VP
Patrick Quarles, Executive VP
Scott Sutton, Executive VP
Christopher Jensen, Senior VP, Divisional

GROWTH PLANS/SPECIAL FEATURES:

Celanese Corporation produces a line of industrial chemicals and advanced materials. It manufactures acetyl products, which are intermediate chemicals for nearly all major industries, and also produces high-performance engineered polymers. The company operates through two segments: materials solutions and the acetyl chain. Together, these segments utilize raw materials, technology, integrated systems and research resources in order to increase efficiency and respond to market needs. Materials solutions is further divided into two units: advanced engineered materials, which includes polyoxymethylene, ultra-high molecular weight polyethylene, polybutylene terephthalate, long-fiber thermoplastics and liquid crystal polymers; and consumer specialties, which includes acetate tow, acetate flake, acetate film, acesulfame potassium, potassium sorbate, sorbic acid and sweetener systems. These materials are used for fuel system components, automotive safety systems, medical applications, industrial applications, battery separators, consumer electronics, filtration, films, packaging, confections, telecommunications and more. The acetyl chain segment is further divided into two units: industrial specialties, which includes conventional emulsions, vinyl acetate ethylene emulsions, ethylene vinyl acetate resins/compounds and low-density polyethylene resins; and acetyl intermediates, which includes acetic acid, vinyl acetate monomer, acetaldehyde, ethyl acetate, fomaldehyde, butyl acetate and ethanol. These materials are used for paints, coatings, adhesives, textiles, paper finishing, packaging, lamination, medical applications, automotive parts, pharmaceuticals, inks and more. Headquartered in Irving, Texas, the company's operations are primarily located in North America, Europe and Asia, consisting of 30 global production facilities and eight affiliate production facilities. In late-2016, the firm acquired Italy-based SO.F.TER Group, a leading independent thermoplastic compounder. In February 2017, it agreed to acquire Nilit Limited's plastics division.

FINANCIAL DATA: Note: Data for latest year may not have been available at press time.

In U.S. $	2016	2015	2014	2013	2012	2011
Revenue	5,389,000,000	5,674,000,000	6,802,000,000	6,510,000,000	6,418,000,000	6,763,000,000
R&D Expense	78,000,000	119,000,000	86,000,000	85,000,000	102,000,000	96,000,000
Operating Income	893,000,000	326,000,000	758,000,000	1,508,000,000	511,000,000	690,000,000
Operating Margin %	16.57%	5.74%	11.14%	23.16%	7.96%	10.20%
SGA Expense	416,000,000	506,000,000	758,000,000	311,000,000	507,000,000	536,000,000
Net Income	900,000,000	304,000,000	624,000,000	1,101,000,000	605,000,000	607,000,000
Operating Cash Flow	893,000,000	862,000,000	962,000,000	762,000,000	722,000,000	638,000,000
Capital Expenditure	246,000,000	520,000,000	678,000,000	377,000,000	410,000,000	204,000,000
EBITDA	1,445,000,000	970,000,000	1,386,000,000	2,100,000,000	1,162,000,000	1,287,000,000
Return on Assets %	10.62%	3.49%	6.99%	12.22%	6.90%	7.22%
Return on Equity %	36.24%	11.70%	22.62%	49.71%	39.40%	53.55%
Debt to Equity	1.11	1.03	0.92	1.06	1.69	2.14

CONTACT INFORMATION:

Phone: 972 443-4000	Fax: 972 332-9373
Toll-Free:
Address: 222 West Las Colinas Blvd, Ste 900N, Irving, TX 75039-5421
United States

STOCK TICKER/OTHER:

Stock Ticker: CE	Exchange: NYS
Employees: 7,293	Fiscal Year Ends: 12/31
Parent Company:

SALARIES/BONUSES:

Top Exec. Salary: $1,142,308	Bonus: $
Second Exec. Salary: $627,692	Bonus: $

OTHER THOUGHTS:

Estimated Female Officers or Directors: 1
Hot Spot for Advancement for Women/Minorities: Y

Celgene Corporation

NAIC Code: 325412

www.celgene.com

TYPES OF BUSINESS:

Cancer & Immune-Inflammatory Related Diseases Drugs

BRANDS/DIVISIONS/AFFILIATES:

Revlimid
Abraxane
Pomalyst/Imnovid
Vidaza
Thalomid
Otezla
Delinia Inc

CONTACTS: Note: Officers with more than one job title may be intentionally listed here more than once.

Mark Alles, CEO
Peter Kellogg, CFO
Robert Hugin, Chairman of the Board
Gerald Masoudi, Executive VP
Rupert Vessey, President, Divisional
Michael Pehl, President, Divisional
Scott Smith, President, Divisional
Jacqualyn Fouse, President

GROWTH PLANS/SPECIAL FEATURES:

Celgene Corporation is a global biopharmaceutical company involved in discovering, developing and commercializing cancer and immune-inflammatory related disease treatment therapies. Celgene's current preclinical and clinical-stage pipeline of new drug candidates and cell therapies include both small molecule and biologic therapeutic agents designed to selectively regulate disease-associated genes and proteins. Celgene's commercial stage products include Revlimid, Abraxane, Pomalyst/Imnovid, Vidaza, Thalomid and Otezla. Revlimid is in several Phase 3 trials across a range of hematological malignances. Abraxane is in various stages of investigation for breast, pancreatic and non-small cell lung cancers. Pomalyst/Imnovid was approved in the U.S., Japan and the European Union for indications in multiple myeloma based on Phase 2 and 3 trial results. Vidaza is a pyrimidine nucleoside analog that has been shown to reverse the effects of DNA hypermethylation and promote subsequent gene re-expression. It is marketed in the U.S. as well as many international markets for the treatment of myelodysplastic syndromes (MDS), chronic myelomonocytic leukemia and acute myeloid leukemia. Thalomid is sold as Thalomid or Thalidomide Celgene outside the U.S., and as Thalomid REMS in the U.S. It is administered orally for the treatment of multiple myeloma and erythema nodosum leprosum. Otezla is administered orally and has been approved for the treatment of psoriatic arthritis and psoriasis. In January 2017, the firm acquired Delinia, Inc., a biotechnology company developing novel therapeutics for autoimmune diseases.

FINANCIAL DATA: Note: Data for latest year may not have been available at press time.

In U.S. $	2016	2015	2014	2013	2012	2011
Revenue	11,229,200,000	9,255,999,000	7,670,400,000	6,493,900,000	5,506,713,000	4,842,070,000
R&D Expense	4,470,100,000	3,697,300,000	2,430,600,000	2,226,200,000	1,724,156,000	1,600,264,000
Operating Income	3,166,600,000	2,254,600,000	2,519,000,000	1,808,900,000	1,746,442,000	1,442,753,000
Operating Margin %	28.19%	24.35%	32.84%	27.85%	31.71%	29.79%
SGA Expense	2,657,700,000	2,305,400,000	2,027,900,000	1,684,500,000	1,373,541,000	1,226,314,000
Net Income	1,999,200,000	1,602,000,000	1,999,900,000	1,449,900,000	1,456,180,000	1,318,150,000
Operating Cash Flow	3,976,300,000	2,483,900,000	2,806,300,000	2,225,900,000	2,018,553,000	1,808,685,000
Capital Expenditure	236,200,000	286,300,000	175,100,000	139,100,000	160,389,000	132,119,000
EBITDA	3,377,300,000	2,743,000,000	2,877,100,000	2,131,100,000	2,028,143,000	1,825,110,000
Return on Assets %	7.25%	7.21%	13.02%	11.54%	13.39%	13.06%
Return on Equity %	31.94%	25.74%	33.01%	25.69%	25.98%	22.93%
Debt to Equity	2.08	2.40	0.96	0.75	0.48	0.23

CONTACT INFORMATION:

Phone: 908 673-9000   Fax: 908 673-9001
Toll-Free:
Address: 86 Morris Ave., Summit, NJ 07901 United States

STOCK TICKER/OTHER:

Stock Ticker: CELG   Exchange: NAS
Employees: 7,132   Fiscal Year Ends: 12/31
Parent Company:

SALARIES/BONUSES:

Top Exec. Salary: $1,500,000   Bonus: $
Second Exec. Salary: Bonus: $
$1,062,583

OTHER THOUGHTS:

Estimated Female Officers or Directors: 3
Hot Spot for Advancement for Women/Minorities: Y

Centene Corporation

www.centene.com

NAIC Code: 524114

TYPES OF BUSINESS:

Insurance-Medical & Health, HMOs & PPOs
Medicaid Managed Care
Specialty Services
Behavioral Health
Disease Management
Managed Vision
Nurse Triage
Pharmacy Benefit Management

BRANDS/DIVISIONS/AFFILIATES:

CentAccount
MemberConnections
Smart For Your Baby

CONTACTS: Note: Officers with more than one job title may be intentionally listed here more than once.

Michael Neidorff, CEO
Jeffrey Schwaneke, CFO
Cynthia Brinkley, Executive VP, Divisional
Christopher Bowers, Executive VP, Divisional
Jesse Hunter, Executive VP, Divisional
Keith Williamson, Executive VP
Mark Brooks, Senior VP
Christopher Isaak, Senior VP

GROWTH PLANS/SPECIAL FEATURES:

Centene Corporation is a multi-line healthcare plan firm operating in two segments: managed care and specialty services. In the managed care segment, the company provides programs and services to people receiving benefits from foster care, Medicaid, the State Children's Health Insurance Program (CHIP), Medicare special needs plans, supplemental security income (SSI), dual eligible individuals (Duals), long term care (LTC) and federally-facilitated and state-based Marketplaces. This segment accounted for 92% of total revenue in 2016. Centene's specialty services segment provides healthcare services to state programs, correctional facilities, healthcare organizations, and to the firm's own subsidiaries. Specialty Services accounted for 8% of total revenue in 2016. The firm's CentAccount program offers financial incentives to members for achieving healthy behavior. Additionally, the company offers a number of education and outreach programs, including MemberConnections, which is designed to create face-to-face links between members and care providers; Start Smart For Your Baby, a prenatal and infant health program; EPSDT (early and periodic screening, diagnostic and treatment) case management, which encourages early and periodic screening, diagnosis and treatment services; and life and health management programs, designed to educate patients on the best and most cost effective treatment options for specific diseases.

The company offers employees health, vision and dental coverage; flexible spending accounts; short- and long-term disability; life and supplemental life insurance; 401(k); an employee stock purchase plan; an employee assistance program; tuition reimbursement; a wellness program; an onsite fitness center; and employee discounts.

FINANCIAL DATA: Note: Data for latest year may not have been available at press time.

In U.S. $	2016	2015	2014	2013	2012	2011
Revenue	40,607,000,000	22,760,000,000	16,560,000,000	10,863,330,000	8,667,612,000	5,340,582,000
R&D Expense						
Operating Income	1,260,000,000	705,000,000	464,000,000	277,417,000	-27,121,000	190,324,000
Operating Margin %	3.10%	3.09%	2.80%	2.55%	-.31%	3.56%
SGA Expense	4,137,000,000	2,041,000,000	1,440,000,000	931,137,000	704,604,000	587,004,000
Net Income	562,000,000	355,000,000	271,000,000	165,099,000	1,859,000	111,218,000
Operating Cash Flow	1,851,000,000	658,000,000	1,223,000,000	382,526,000	278,691,000	261,696,000
Capital Expenditure	306,000,000	150,000,000	103,000,000	67,835,000	82,144,000	73,708,000
EBITDA	1,652,000,000	851,000,000	581,000,000	363,294,000	74,702,000	253,532,000
Return on Assets %	4.08%	5.38%	5.78%	5.26%	.07%	5.38%
Return on Equity %	13.95%	18.20%	18.19%	15.09%	.19%	12.86%
Debt to Equity	0.78	0.56	0.50	0.53	0.56	0.37

CONTACT INFORMATION:

Phone: 314 725-4477   Fax: 314 725-5180
Toll-Free:
Address: 7700 Forsyth Blvd., Centene Plz., St. Louis, MO 63105 United States

STOCK TICKER/OTHER:

Stock Ticker: CNC
Employees: 30,500
Parent Company:

Exchange: NYS
Fiscal Year Ends: 12/31

SALARIES/BONUSES:

Top Exec. Salary: $1,500,000   Bonus: $
Second Exec. Salary: $650,000   Bonus: $

OTHER THOUGHTS:

Estimated Female Officers or Directors: 4
Hot Spot for Advancement for Women/Minorities: Y

CenturyLink Inc

NAIC Code: 517110

www.centurylink.com

TYPES OF BUSINESS:

Local Telephone Service
Long-Distance Services
Internet Service Provider
Business Information Services
Fiber Network Services
Satellite TV
IPTV

BRANDS/DIVISIONS/AFFILIATES:

CenturyLink
Level 3 Communications Inc

CONTACTS: *Note: Officers with more than one job title may be intentionally listed here more than once.*

Glen Post, CEO
R. Ewing, CFO
David Cole, Chief Accounting Officer
Stacey Goff, Chief Administrative Officer
Harvey Perry, Director
Scott Trezise, Executive VP, Divisional
Aamir Hussain, Executive VP
Girish Varma, President, Divisional
Dean Douglas, President, Divisional
Maxine Moreau, President, Divisional

GROWTH PLANS/SPECIAL FEATURES:

CenturyLink, Inc. is an integrated communications company engaged primarily in providing an array of communications services, including local and long distance voice, wholesale local network access, high-speed internet access, other data services and video services. The company divides its operations in two segments: consumer and business. The consumer segment offers strategic and legacy products and services to residential customers that include broadband, wireless, video and Prism TV services. The business segment consists of products and services for commercial, global and governmental customers, and include its private line, broadband, Ethernet, MPLS (multiprotocol label switching), Voice over Internet Protocol (VoIP), network management services, colocation, managed hosting and cloud hosting services. The company provides products and services to customers through its telecommunication network, which consists of voice and data switches, copper cables, fiber-optic cables and other equipment, serving approximately 11.8 million access lines. The company operates around 60 data centers in the U.S., Europe and Asia. Most of CenturyLink's services are sold under the CenturyLink brand, with satellite TV service offered under a co-branded agreement under the DIRECTV brand name and wireless services offered under the firm's agency agreement with Verizon Wireless under the Verizon Wireless name. In November 2016, the firm acquired Level 3 Communications, Inc. in a cash-and-stock deal worth approximately $25 billion.

Employee benefits include medical, dental, prescription and vision coverage; an employee assistance program; retirement plans and a 401(k); flexible spending accounts; life and AD&D insurance; short-and long-term disability; and career development programs.

FINANCIAL DATA: *Note: Data for latest year may not have been available at press time.*

In U.S. $	2016	2015	2014	2013	2012	2011
Revenue	17,470,000,000	17,900,000,000	18,031,000,000	18,095,000,000	18,376,000,000	15,351,000,000
R&D Expense						
Operating Income	2,331,000,000	2,605,000,000	2,410,000,000	1,453,000,000	2,713,000,000	2,025,000,000
Operating Margin %	13.34%	14.55%	13.36%	8.02%	14.76%	13.19%
SGA Expense	3,449,000,000	3,328,000,000	3,347,000,000	3,502,000,000	3,244,000,000	2,975,000,000
Net Income	626,000,000	878,000,000	772,000,000	-239,000,000	777,000,000	573,000,000
Operating Cash Flow	4,608,000,000	5,152,000,000	5,188,000,000	5,559,000,000	6,065,000,000	4,201,000,000
Capital Expenditure	2,981,000,000	2,872,000,000	3,047,000,000	3,048,000,000	2,919,000,000	2,411,000,000
EBITDA	6,254,000,000	6,817,000,000	6,849,000,000	6,063,000,000	7,349,000,000	6,046,000,000
Return on Assets %	1.32%	1.79%	1.51%	- .45%	1.41%	1.46%
Return on Equity %	4.55%	6.03%	4.79%	-1.31%	3.87%	3.76%
Debt to Equity	1.35	1.33	1.33	1.17	1.00	1.02

CONTACT INFORMATION:

Phone: 318 388-9000   Fax: 318 789-8656
Toll-Free:
Address: 100 CenturyLink Dr., Monroe, LA 71203 United States

STOCK TICKER/OTHER:

Stock Ticker: CTL   Exchange: NYS
Employees: 40,000   Fiscal Year Ends: 12/31
Parent Company:

SALARIES/BONUSES:

Top Exec. Salary: $1,250,000   Bonus: $
Second Exec. Salary: Bonus: $125,000
$699,462

OTHER THOUGHTS:

Estimated Female Officers or Directors: 5
Hot Spot for Advancement for Women/Minorities: Y

Sales, profits and employees may be estimates. Financial information, benefits and other data can change quickly and may vary from those stated here.

Cerner Corporation

www.cerner.com

NAIC Code: 0

TYPES OF BUSINESS:

Computer Software, Healthcare & Biotechnology
Medical Information Systems
Application Hosting
Integrated Delivery Networks
Access Management
Consulting Services
Safety & Risk Management

BRANDS/DIVISIONS/AFFILIATES:

Cerner Millennium
HealtheIntent
Cerner Health Services
CernerWorks

CONTACTS: Note: Officers with more than one job title may be intentionally listed here more than once.

Neal Patterson, CEO
Marc Naughton, CFO
Michael Battaglioli, Chief Accounting Officer
Clifford Illig, Co-Founder
Michael Nill, COO
Jeffrey Townsend, Executive VP
Julia Wilson, Other Executive Officer
Randy Sims, Other Executive Officer
Zane Burke, President

GROWTH PLANS/SPECIAL FEATURES:

Cerner Corporation designs, develops, installs and supports information technology and content applications for healthcare organizations, consumers and physicians. Cerner's applications are designed to help eliminate error, variance and waste in the care process as well as provide appropriate health information and knowledge to care givers, clinicians and consumers, and appropriate management information to healthcare administrations. Cerner solutions are offered on the unified Cerner Millennium architecture and on the HealtheIntent cloud-based platform. The Millennium framework combines clinical, financial and management information systems and provides secure access to an individual's electronic medical record at the point of care, and organizes and proactively delivers information to meet the specific needs of the physician, nurse, laboratory technician, pharmacist or other care provider, front- and back-office professionals as well as consumers. The HealtheIntent platform offers EHR-agnostic (electronic health record) solutions based on sophisticated, statistical algorithms to help providers predict and improve outcomes, control costs, improve quality and manage the health of their patients. Cerner also offers a broad range of services including implementation and training, remote hosting, operational management services, revenue cycle services, support and maintenance, healthcare data analysis, clinical process optimization, transaction processing, employer health centers, employee wellness programs and third-party administrator (TPA) services for employer-based health plans. Cerner Health Services offers a portfolio of enterprise-level clinical and financial healthcare information technology solutions, as well as departmental, connectivity, population health and care coordination solutions globally. CernerWorks is the company's remote-hosting business. Roughly more than 25,000 facilities around the world license Cerner's products. These facilities include hospitals; physician practices; ambulatory facilities such as laboratories, ambulatory centers, cardiac facilities, radiology clinics and surgery centers; home health facilities; and retail pharmacies.

FINANCIAL DATA: Note: Data for latest year may not have been available at press time.

In U.S. $	2016	2015	2014	2013	2012	2011
Revenue	4,796,473,000	4,425,267,000	3,402,703,000	2,910,748,000	2,665,436,000	2,203,153,000
R&D Expense	551,418,000	539,799,000	289,358,000	338,786,000	219,639,000	286,801,000
Operating Income	911,013,000	781,136,000	763,084,000	576,012,000	571,662,000	459,798,000
Operating Margin %	18.99%	17.65%	22.42%	19.78%	21.44%	20.87%
SGA Expense	2,464,380,000	2,262,024,000	1,642,437,000	1,481,228,000	1,184,207,000	1,014,882,000
Net Income	636,484,000	539,362,000	525,433,000	398,354,000	397,232,000	306,627,000
Operating Cash Flow	1,155,612,000	947,526,000	847,027,000	695,865,000	708,314,000	546,294,000
Capital Expenditure	771,595,000	648,220,000	467,901,000	584,331,000	306,488,000	208,357,000
EBITDA	1,427,149,000	1,233,361,000	1,080,520,000	855,818,000	815,356,000	687,591,000
Return on Assets %	11.37%	10.68%	12.17%	10.21%	11.84%	11.30%
Return on Equity %	16.32%	14.50%	15.60%	13.27%	15.44%	14.54%
Debt to Equity	0.13	0.14	0.01	0.03	0.04	0.03

CONTACT INFORMATION:

Phone: 816 221-1024   Fax:
Toll-Free:
Address: 2800 Rockcreek Pkwy., North Kansas City, MO 64117 United States

STOCK TICKER/OTHER:

Stock Ticker: CERN
Employees: 24,400
Parent Company:

Exchange: NAS
Fiscal Year Ends: 12/31

SALARIES/BONUSES:

Top Exec. Salary: $1,025,000   Bonus: $
Second Exec. Salary: $657,596   Bonus: $

OTHER THOUGHTS:

Estimated Female Officers or Directors: 13
Hot Spot for Advancement for Women/Minorities: Y

CH Robinson Worldwide Inc

www.chrobinson.com

NAIC Code: 488510

TYPES OF BUSINESS:

3PL Third Party Logistics
Produce Sourcing
Expedited Services
Fuel Purchasing Management Services
Warehousing
Customs Brokerage
Freight Transportation Arrangements

BRANDS/DIVISIONS/AFFILIATES:

Robinson Fresh
ChemSolutions
TMC
APC Logistics

CONTACTS: *Note: Officers with more than one job title may be intentionally listed here more than once.*

John Wiehoff, CEO
Andrew Clarke, CFO
Chad Lindbloom, Chief Information Officer
Christopher OBrien, Other Executive Officer
Angela Freeman, Other Executive Officer
Ben Campbell, Other Executive Officer
James Lemke, President, Divisional
Jordan Kass, President, Divisional
Michael Short, President, Divisional
Robert Biesterfeld, President, Divisional
Jereon Eijsink, President, Divisional

GROWTH PLANS/SPECIAL FEATURES:

C.H. Robinson Worldwide, Inc. (CHRW) is one of the world's largest third-party logistics (3PL) providers and a global provider of multimodal transportation services. It maintains a network of offices in North America, Europe, Asia and South America. CHRW operates in two main sectors: transportation and logistics services and sourcing. In the transportation and logistics services sector, the company (which does not own any of its own equipment) maintains one of the largest global networks of motor carrier by capacity through contracts with approximately 71,000 transportation providers. CHRW serves more than 113,000 customers, handling over 16.9 million shipments annually. The group also contracts air carriers, oceans carriers and specialty motor carriers. In addition, it provides value-added logistics services, supply chain analysis, freight consolidation, core carrier program management and information reporting. The sourcing sector focuses on procuring fresh produce for retailers, wholesalers and foodservice operators nationwide. CHRW markets its own brands of produce under Robinson Fresh, which is sourced through various growers and packed through contract agreements with other packaging firms. Additionally, the company maintains exclusive licensing agreements to distribute fresh produce under various third-party brand names, such as Tropicana, Welch's and Mott's. The company's ChemSolutions division provides logistics services to chemical manufacturing and distribution customers globally. CHRW's division, TMC, offers managed global transportation management system (TMS) software and consulting services, including cloud-based TMS technology. In September 2016, the frim completed the acquisition of APC Logistics, a freight forwarding and customs brokerage service in Australia and New Zealand.

The firm offers employees medical, dental and vision insurance; a 401(k); an employee stock purchase plan; flexible spending accounts; an employee assistance plan; and employee discounts.

FINANCIAL DATA: *Note: Data for latest year may not have been available at press time.*

In U.S. $	2016	2015	2014	2013	2012	2011
Revenue	13,144,410,000	13,476,080,000	13,470,070,000	12,752,080,000	11,359,110,000	10,336,350,000
R&D Expense						
Operating Income	837,531,000	858,310,000	748,418,000	682,650,000	675,320,000	692,730,000
Operating Margin %	6.37%	6.36%	5.55%	5.35%	5.94%	6.70%
SGA Expense	1,439,997,000	1,410,170,000	1,259,234,000	1,153,445,000	1,042,251,000	939,928,000
Net Income	513,384,000	509,699,000	449,711,000	415,904,000	593,804,000	431,612,000
Operating Cash Flow	529,408,000	718,336,000	513,426,000	347,777,000	460,342,000	429,712,000
Capital Expenditure	91,437,000	44,642,000	29,502,000	48,206,000	50,656,000	52,806,000
EBITDA	912,200,000	924,719,000	805,427,000	739,532,000	713,410,000	725,228,000
Return on Assets %	14.94%	15.93%	14.94%	14.83%	24.02%	20.88%
Return on Equity %	42.63%	46.38%	45.27%	34.03%	43.14%	35.19%
Debt to Equity	0.39	0.43	0.47	0.53		

CONTACT INFORMATION:

Phone: 952 937-8500   Fax: 952 937-6714
Toll-Free:
Address: 14701 Charlson Rd., Eden Prairie, MN 55347 United States

STOCK TICKER/OTHER:

Stock Ticker: CHRW   Exchange: NAS
Employees: 14,125   Fiscal Year Ends: 12/31
Parent Company:

SALARIES/BONUSES:

Top Exec. Salary: $1,167,000   Bonus: $
Second Exec. Salary: Bonus: $
$590,000

OTHER THOUGHTS:

Estimated Female Officers or Directors: 4
Hot Spot for Advancement for Women/Minorities: Y

Change Healthcare Inc

www.changehealthcare.com/

NAIC Code: 524292

TYPES OF BUSINESS:

Healthcare Business & Administration Management
Claims Processing & Billing

BRANDS/DIVISIONS/AFFILIATES:

Change Healthcare Holdings Inc
McKesson Corporation
Intelligent Healthcare Network
InterQual

CONTACTS: *Note: Officers with more than one job title may be intentionally listed here more than once.*

Neil de Crescenzo, CEO
Miriam Paramore, Exec. VP-Prod. Mgmt. & Strategy
Gregory T. Stevens, General Counsel
Frank Manzella, Sr. VP-Corp. Dev.
Kevin Mahoney, Exec. VP-Pharmacy Svcs.
Gary D. Stuart, Exec. VP-Payer Svcs.
Sajid Khan, Exec. VP-Ambulatory Svcs.
T. Ulrich Brechbuhl, Exec. VP-Revenue Cycle Solutions

GROWTH PLANS/SPECIAL FEATURES:

Change Healthcare, Inc. is a healthcare information technology company formed by the 2017 merger of former Change Healthcare Holdings, Inc. with McKesson Corporation's IT business. The firm works alongside customers and partners to enable better patient care, choice and outcomes at scale. Change Healthcare provides software, analytics, network solutions and technology-enabled services to serve the needs of stakeholders in the healthcare system, including commercial and governmental payers, employers, hospitals, physicians, providers, laboratories and consumers. The company comprises a 15,000-member team to help customers improve efficiency, reduce costs, increase cash flow and manage complex workflows. Change Healthcare has 2,100 payer connections reaching nearly all U.S. government and commercial payers. It serves 5,500 hospitals and over 800,000 physicians. The firm's Intelligent Healthcare Network has the capability of processing more than 12 billion healthcare-related transactions annually. Change Healthcare's InterQual offering is used by the Centers for Medicare & Medicaid Services and over 4,600 hospitals and facilities to help ensure clinically-appropriate care. Its imaging solutions are used in over 3,300 facilities across the U.S. and internationally.

FINANCIAL DATA: *Note: Data for latest year may not have been available at press time.*

In U.S. $	2016	2015	2014	2013	2012	2011
Revenue	1,500,000,000	1,477,083,000	1,350,413,000	1,242,567,000	1,152,313,000	1,119,648,000
R&D Expense						
Operating Income						
Operating Margin %						
SGA Expense						
Net Income		-96,069,000	-75,854,000	-74,458,000	-78,335,000	-42,144,000
Operating Cash Flow						
Capital Expenditure						
EBITDA						
Return on Assets %						
Return on Equity %						
Debt to Equity						

CONTACT INFORMATION:

Phone: 615-932-3000   Fax:
Toll-Free:
Address: 3055 Lebanon Pike, Nashville, TN 37214 United States

STOCK TICKER/OTHER:

Stock Ticker: Private
Employees: 4,100
Parent Company:

Exchange:
Fiscal Year Ends: 12/31

SALARIES/BONUSES:

Top Exec. Salary: $ Bonus: $
Second Exec. Salary: $ Bonus: $

OTHER THOUGHTS:

Estimated Female Officers or Directors: 1
Hot Spot for Advancement for Women/Minorities:

Charles River Laboratories International Inc

www.criver.com

NAIC Code: 541711

TYPES OF BUSINESS:

Medical and Drug Research Models
Consulting
Bioactivity Software
Biosafety Testing
Contract Staffing
Laboratory Diagnostics
Intellectual Property Consulting
Analytical Testing

BRANDS/DIVISIONS/AFFILIATES:

WRH Inc
Agilux Laboratories Inc
Blue Stream Laboratories

CONTACTS: Note: Officers with more than one job title may be intentionally listed here more than once.

James Foster, CEO
David Smith, CFO
Michael Knell, Chief Accounting Officer
William Barbo, Executive VP
Davide Molho, Executive VP
David Johst, Secretary

GROWTH PLANS/SPECIAL FEATURES:

Charles River Laboratories International, Inc. (CRL) is a global provider of solutions that accelerate the drug discovery and development process, including research models and outsourced preclinical services. CRL operates 75 facilities in 23 countries. The firm's customer base includes global pharmaceutical companies, biotechnology companies, government agencies, hospitals and academic institutions. CRL operates in three segments: research models & services (RMS), discovery & safety assessment (DSA) and manufacturing. RMS supplies research models to the drug development industry, and is a global leader in the production and sale of rodent research model strains, principally genetically and microbiologically defined purpose-bred rats and mice. RMS accounted for 29.4% of 2016 total revenue. DSA (accounting for 49.8% of revenues) provides services that enable clients to outsource their drug discovery research; their critical, regulatory-required safety assessment testing; and related drug discovery and development activities to CRL. Manufacturing (20.9%) helps ensure the safe production and release of products manufactured by the firm's clients. This division's endotoxin and microbial detection business provides non-animal, or in vitro, methods for lot release testing of medical devices and injectable drugs for endotoxin contamination. Its avian vaccine services business provides specific pathogen free (SPF) fertile chicken eggs and chickens for the manufacture of live viruses. Its Biologics Testing Services business provides specialized testing of biologics and devices frequently outsourced by global pharmaceutical and biotechnology companies. In 2016, the firm made several acquisitions: WRH, Inc., a provider of safety assessment and contract development; Agilux Laboratories, Inc., a contract research organization and pharmaceutical lab; and Blue Stream Laboratories, which offers an integrated portfolio of biologic and biosimilar drug development.

The firm offers employees medical, dental, vision and life insurance; flexible spending accounts; short- and long-term disability; a 401(k); an employee stock purchase plan; an employee assistance plan; and more.

FINANCIAL DATA: Note: Data for latest year may not have been available at press time.

In U.S. $	2016	2015	2014	2013	2012	2011
Revenue	1,681,432,000	1,363,302,000	1,297,662,000	1,165,528,000	1,129,530,000	1,142,647,000
R&D Expense						
Operating Income	237,419,000	206,449,000	177,670,000	151,401,000	165,765,000	174,306,000
Operating Margin %	14.12%	15.14%	13.69%	12.98%	14.67%	15.25%
SGA Expense	367,548,000	300,414,000	269,033,000	225,695,000	208,248,000	198,648,000
Net Income	154,765,000	149,313,000	126,698,000	102,828,000	97,295,000	109,566,000
Operating Cash Flow	300,375,000	288,234,000	252,132,000	209,045,000	208,006,000	205,283,000
Capital Expenditure	55,288,000	63,252,000	56,925,000	39,154,000	47,534,000	49,143,000
EBITDA	377,288,000	305,381,000	285,990,000	255,932,000	244,363,000	260,478,000
Return on Assets %	6.47%	7.55%	7.17%	6.36%	6.18%	6.65%
Return on Equity %	19.71%	21.25%	19.29%	16.56%	17.27%	18.06%
Debt to Equity	1.44	1.15	1.10	1.00	0.87	1.33

CONTACT INFORMATION:

Phone: 781 222-6000   Fax: 978 658-7841
Toll-Free:
Address: 251 Ballardvale St., Wilmington, MA 01887 United States

STOCK TICKER/OTHER:

Stock Ticker: CRL   Exchange: NYS
Employees: 11,000   Fiscal Year Ends: 12/31
Parent Company:

SALARIES/BONUSES:

Top Exec. Salary: $1,143,993   Bonus: $
Second Exec. Salary: $607,257   Bonus: $

OTHER THOUGHTS:

Estimated Female Officers or Directors: 3
Hot Spot for Advancement for Women/Minorities: Y

Charles Schwab Corporation (The)

www.schwab.com

NAIC Code: 523120

TYPES OF BUSINESS:

Stock Brokerage-Retail, Online & Discount
Investment Services
Financial Services
Mutual Funds
Wealth Management
Financial Information
Banking
Online Trading Platform

BRANDS/DIVISIONS/AFFILIATES:

Charles Schwab & Co Inc
Charles Schwab Bank
Charles Schwab Investment Management Inc

CONTACTS: Note: Officers with more than one job title may be intentionally listed here more than once.

Joseph Martinetto, CEO, Subsidiary
Marie Chandoha, CEO, Subsidiary
Walter Bettinger, CEO
Charles Schwab, Chairman of the Board
Nigel Murtagh, Executive VP, Divisional
Peter Crawford, Executive VP, Divisional
Terri Kallsen, Executive VP, Divisional
Bernard Clark, Executive VP, Divisional
David Garfield, Executive VP

GROWTH PLANS/SPECIAL FEATURES:

The Charles Schwab Corporation (CSC) engages in securities brokerage, banking, money management and related financial advisory services. The company has managed $2.78 trillion in client brokerage accounts, 10.2 million active brokerage accounts, 1.5 million corporate retirement plan participants and 1.1 million banking accounts through its primary subsidiary, Charles Schwab & Co., Inc. (Schwab). Schwab is a securities broker-dealer with more than 335 domestic branch offices in 46 states, as well as a branch in each of the Commonwealth of Puerto Rico and London, England. It serves clients in Hong Kong through CSC subsidiaries Charles Schwab Bank, a federal savings bank located in Reno, Nevada; and Charles Schwab Investment Management, Inc., an investment advisor for the company's proprietary mutual and exchange-traded funds. CSC provides its financial services and products such as brokerage, banking, trust, advice and mutual/exchange trade funds to individuals and institutional clients through two segments: investor services and advisor services. Investor services provides retail brokerage and banking services to individual investors, retirement plan services and corporate brokerage services. Advisor services provides custodial, trading and support services to independent investment advisors (IAs), and retirement business services to independent retirement plan advisors and record keepers whose plan assets are held at Schwab Bank.

The firm offers employees medical, dental, life, AD&D and vision insurance; health and dependent care flexible spending accounts; disability coverage; a 401(k) plan; a legal services plan; an employee discount program; an employee stock purchase plan; discounts on company products; and an employee assistance program.

FINANCIAL DATA: Note: Data for latest year may not have been available at press time.

In U.S. $	2016	2015	2014	2013	2012	2011
Revenue	7,473,000,000	6,369,000,000	6,054,000,000	5,434,000,000	4,899,000,000	4,709,000,000
R&D Expense						
Operating Income	2,993,000,000	2,279,000,000	2,115,000,000	1,705,000,000	1,450,000,000	1,392,000,000
Operating Margin %	40.05%	35.78%	34.93%	31.37%	29.59%	29.56%
SGA Expense	2,968,000,000	2,723,000,000	2,652,000,000	2,504,000,000	2,264,000,000	2,180,000,000
Net Income	1,889,000,000	1,447,000,000	1,321,000,000	1,071,000,000	928,000,000	864,000,000
Operating Cash Flow	155,000,000	1,246,000,000	2,348,000,000	1,656,000,000	1,266,000,000	2,464,000,000
Capital Expenditure		266,000,000	400,000,000	249,000,000	148,000,000	180,000,000
EBITDA						
Return on Assets %	.85%	.80%	.84%	.72%	.72%	.85%
Return on Equity %	13.65%	11.92%	12.33%	11.07%	10.74%	12.39%
Debt to Equity	0.21	0.24	0.17	0.20	0.18	0.25

CONTACT INFORMATION:

Phone: 415 667-7000   Fax: 415 627-8894
Toll-Free: 800-648-5300
Address: 211 Main Street, San Francisco, CA 94105 United States

STOCK TICKER/OTHER:

Stock Ticker: SCHW
Employees: 16,200
Parent Company:

Exchange: NYS
Fiscal Year Ends: 12/31

SALARIES/BONUSES:

Top Exec. Salary: $1,041,667   Bonus: $
Second Exec. Salary: $625,000   Bonus: $

OTHER THOUGHTS:

Estimated Female Officers or Directors: 6
Hot Spot for Advancement for Women/Minorities: Y

Charter Communications Inc

NAIC Code: 517110

www.charter.com

TYPES OF BUSINESS:

Cable TV Service
Internet Access
Advanced Broadband Cable Services
Telephony Services
Voice Over Internet Protocol

BRANDS/DIVISIONS/AFFILIATES:

Charter Security Suite
Charter.net
Spectrum
Time Warner Cable Inc
Bright House Networks

CONTACTS: *Note: Officers with more than one job title may be intentionally listed here more than once.*

Thomas Rutledge, CEO
Catherine Bohigian, Executive VP, Divisional
Christopher Winfrey, CFO
Kevin Howard, Chief Accounting Officer
Jonathan Hargis, Chief Marketing Officer
John Bickham, COO
Tom Montemagno, Executive VP, Divisional
Michael Baird, Executive VP, Divisional
Kathleen Mayo, Executive VP, Divisional
Thomas Adams, Executive VP, Divisional
James Blackley, Executive VP, Divisional
Scott Weber, Executive VP, Divisional
James Nuzzo, Executive VP, Divisional
Richard DiGeronimo, Executive VP, Divisional
David Kline, Executive VP, Divisional

GROWTH PLANS/SPECIAL FEATURES:

Charter Communications, Inc. operates broadband communications businesses in the U.S., offering traditional cable video programming, high-speed internet access and voice service as well as advanced broadband services. The company serves approximately 4.3 million video customers, 5.2 million high-speed internet customers and 2.6 million telephone customers. Roughly 61% of these customers are bundle service subscribers. The firm's video services include offerings such as basic video, online video, digital video, premium channels, pay-per-view, On Demand and Subscription On Demand, high definition television (HDTV) and digital video recorder (DVR). The firm offers several tiers of high-speed internet services with speeds ranging from 30 megabytes per second (Mbps) to 120 Mbps. The company offers the Charter Security Suite, an internet portal, and Charter.net services. The firm provides voice communications services, primarily using VoIP (voice over internet protocol) technology, as well as telephone services. Residential video, internet and voice services generate approximately 83% of Charter's revenue. Commercial services generate approximately 11% of the company's total revenues and include scalable and tailored broadband communications solutions for business organizations, ranging from small businesses to carrier wholesales. Sale of advertising generates the remainder of Charter's total revenues. In 2016, the company acquired and absorbed both Time Warner Cable, Inc. and Bright House Networks. The Time Warner and Bright House brands were phased out and their services were transitioned to a new brand by Charter called Spectrum.

Employee benefits include medical, dental and vision coverage; a 401(k); flexible spending accounts; health savings accounts; life and AD&D insurance; short- and long-term disability; adoption reimbursement; tuition reimbursement; and employee discounts.

FINANCIAL DATA: *Note: Data for latest year may not have been available at press time.*

In U.S. $	2016	2015	2014	2013	2012	2011
Revenue	29,003,000,000	9,754,000,000	9,108,000,000	8,155,000,000	7,504,000,000	7,204,000,000
R&D Expense						
Operating Income	3,355,000,000	1,114,000,000	971,000,000	925,000,000	916,000,000	1,041,000,000
Operating Margin %	11.56%	11.42%	10.66%	11.34%	12.20%	14.45%
SGA Expense	1,855,000,000	691,000,000	529,000,000		422,000,000	1,426,000,000
Net Income	3,522,000,000	-271,000,000	-183,000,000	-169,000,000	-304,000,000	-369,000,000
Operating Cash Flow	8,041,000,000	2,359,000,000	2,359,000,000	2,158,000,000	1,876,000,000	1,737,000,000
Capital Expenditure	4,722,000,000	1,812,000,000	2,188,000,000	1,749,000,000	1,732,000,000	1,343,000,000
EBITDA	10,262,000,000	3,239,000,000	3,073,000,000	2,779,000,000	2,573,000,000	2,485,000,000
Return on Assets %	3.73%	- .84%	- .87%	-1.02%	-1.94%	-2.35%
Return on Equity %	17.56%	-542.00%	-123.23%	-112.66%	-108.96%	-39.10%
Debt to Equity	1.48		143.99	93.91	85.95	31.43

CONTACT INFORMATION:

Phone: 203-905-7801 Fax:
Toll-Free:
Address: 400 Atlantic Street, Stamford, CT 06901 United States

STOCK TICKER/OTHER:

Stock Ticker: CHTR Exchange: NAS
Employees: 91,500 Fiscal Year Ends: 12/31
Parent Company:

SALARIES/BONUSES:

Top Exec. Salary: $2,000,000 Bonus: $
Second Exec. Salary: Bonus: $
$1,450,962

OTHER THOUGHTS:

Estimated Female Officers or Directors: 1
Hot Spot for Advancement for Women/Minorities:

Chemed Corporation

www.chemed.com

NAIC Code: 621610

TYPES OF BUSINESS:

Home Health Care Services
Plumbing Services

BRANDS/DIVISIONS/AFFILIATES:

VITAS Healthcare Corporation
Roto-Rooter Corporation

CONTACTS: *Note: Officers with more than one job title may be intentionally listed here more than once.*

Nicholas Westfall, CEO, Subsidiary
Kevin Mcnamara, CEO
David Williams, CFO
George Walsh, Chairman of the Board
Michael Witzeman, Chief Accounting Officer
Thomas Hutton, Director
Spencer Lee, Executive VP

GROWTH PLANS/SPECIAL FEATURES:

Chemed Corporation, through its wholly-owned subsidiaries VITAS Healthcare Corporation and Roto-Rooter Corporation, offers hospice care and plumbing services, respectively. VITAS is one of the largest national providers of hospice care and end-of-life services. Its team members include registered nurses, licensed practical nurses, home health aides, physicians, social workers, chaplains and other caregiving professionals. VITAS provides hospice care services in the patient's home, including music therapy and pet visits. Additionally, the firm manages inpatient hospice units, providing service in hospitals, nursing homes and assisted living communities/residential care facilities. More than 95% of VITAS' service revenues consist of payments from Medicare. Roto-Rooter supports the maintenance needs of residential and commercial markets by providing services such as plumbing, drain cleaning, high-pressure water jetting, underground leak and line detection, video camera pipe inspections, grease trap and liquid waste pumping, backflow protection, emergency services, automated drain care programs and pipe repair and replacement. One of the largest businesses of its type in North America, Roto-Rooter operates hundreds of company-owned and franchises throughout the U.S. Concerning revenues, Roto-Rooter's largest share is generated by plumbing repair and maintenance, followed by sewer and drain cleaning, HVAC (heating, ventilation and air conditioning) repair and other products and services.

Employee benefits include medical, prescription and dental coverage; life insurance; short- and long-term disability; a 401(k); profit sharing; flexible spending accounts; and tuition reimbursement.

FINANCIAL DATA: *Note: Data for latest year may not have been available at press time.*

In U.S. $	2016	2015	2014	2013	2012	2011
Revenue	1,576,881,000	1,543,388,000	1,456,282,000	1,413,329,000	1,430,043,000	1,355,970,000
R&D Expense						
Operating Income	178,749,000	184,458,000	168,419,000	133,394,000	156,419,000	153,727,000
Operating Margin %	11.33%	11.95%	11.56%	9.43%	10.93%	11.33%
SGA Expense	243,572,000	237,821,000	220,118,000	212,518,000	208,656,000	202,260,000
Net Income	108,743,000	110,274,000	99,317,000	77,227,000	89,304,000	85,979,000
Operating Cash Flow	135,393,000	171,500,000	110,279,000	150,847,000	131,768,000	174,343,000
Capital Expenditure	39,772,000	44,135,000	43,571,000	29,324,000	35,252,000	29,592,000
EBITDA	215,407,000	217,270,000	204,041,000	171,252,000	191,063,000	183,943,000
Return on Assets %	12.55%	12.88%	11.32%	8.80%	10.78%	10.57%
Return on Equity %	20.96%	22.86%	22.06%	17.12%	20.60%	19.63%
Debt to Equity	0.19	0.16	0.31		0.38	0.40

CONTACT INFORMATION:

Phone: 513 762-6900   Fax: 513 762-6919
Toll-Free:
Address: 255 E. 5th St., Ste. 2600, Cincinnati, OH 45202 United States

STOCK TICKER/OTHER:

Stock Ticker: CHE   Exchange: NYS
Employees: 14,613   Fiscal Year Ends: 12/31
Parent Company:

SALARIES/BONUSES:

Top Exec. Salary: $1,047,013   Bonus: $
Second Exec. Salary: $580,000   Bonus: $

OTHER THOUGHTS:

Estimated Female Officers or Directors: 3
Hot Spot for Advancement for Women/Minorities: Y

Sales, profits and employees may be estimates. Financial information, benefits and other data can change quickly and may vary from those stated here.

Chevron Phillips Chemical Company LLC

www.cpchem.com

NAIC Code: 325110

TYPES OF BUSINESS:

Petrochemical & Plastics Manufacturing
Olefins & Polyolefins
Aromatics & Styrenics
Specialty Chemicals

BRANDS/DIVISIONS/AFFILIATES:

K-Resin SBC
Aromax
Marlex
Scentinel
Soltex
Chevron Corporation
Phillips 66

CONTACTS: *Note: Officers with more than one job title may be intentionally listed here more than once.*

Peter Cella, CEO
Tim D. Leveille, CFO
Greg Wagner, VP-Human Resources
Dennis Holtermann, VP-Research & Tech.
Peggy Colsman, CIO
Rick Roberts, Sr. VP-Mfg.
Tim Hill, General Counsel
Ron Corn, VP-Corp. Planning & Dev.
Brian Cain, Head-Corp. Comm.
Tim D. Leveille, Controller
Dan Coombs, Sr. VP-Specialties, Aromatics & Styrenics
Mark Lashier, Exec. VP-Olefins & Polyolefins
Trevor Roberts, Treas.
David Morgan, VP-Polyethylene

GROWTH PLANS/SPECIAL FEATURES:

Chevron Phillips Chemical Company LLC (CPChem) is the combined petrochemical businesses of Chevron Corporation and Phillips 66, both 50% owners. With 33 production and research centers worldwide, CPChem is an international producer of olefins and polyalphaolefins. It is also a supplier of aromatics, alpha olefins, styrenics, specialty chemicals, polyethylene pipe and proprietary plastics. The company manufactures chemical products that are vital in the various production processes of over 70,000 consumer and industrial products. Its business is separated into two divisions: olefins and polyalphaolefins; and aromatics, styrenics and specialty products. Products in the olefins and polyalphaolefins family consist of ethylene, propylene and their polymer derivatives; olefins and polyalphaolefins; and high-density polyethylene pipe, conduit and pipe fitting. These products are sold as building blocks for other chemicals and as ingredients for use in a variety of end-products, including motor oils, lubricants, plastics, coatings, textiles and packaging. CPChem's aromatics and styrenics include cyclohexane, paraxylene, benzene, styrene, polystyrene and K-Resin SBC, a unique type of copolymer. Aromax is the company's proprietary benzene production process. Aromatics and styrenics are used in the manufacturing of insulation products, housewares, food packaging, electronic parts and media enclosures. Specialty chemicals are used in various applications, including electronics, automobiles, oil and gas well-drilling, appliances, agriculture and pharmaceuticals. Primary brands of the company include Marlex polyethylene, an extrusion and rigid packaging resin; Scentinel gas odorants, which give natural gas a distinctive smell; and Soltex drilling mud additive, for fluid loss control in relation to water-based muds. In October 2016, the firm agreed to sell its K-Resin styrene-butadiene copolymers (SBC) business to INEOS Styrolution, subject to regulatory approvals.

The firm offers employees medical, dental and vision benefits; educational assistance; an employee assistance program; discounts on personal items; and relocation assistance.

FINANCIAL DATA: *Note: Data for latest year may not have been available at press time.*

In U.S. $	2016	2015	2014	2013	2012	2011
Revenue	8,455,000,000	9,248,000,000	13,416,000,000	13,147,000,000	13,243,000,000	13,935,000,000
R&D Expense						
Operating Income						
Operating Margin %						
SGA Expense						
Net Income	1,687,000,000	2,651,000,000	3,288,000,000	2,743,000,000	2,403,000,000	1,970,000,000
Operating Cash Flow						
Capital Expenditure						
EBITDA						
Return on Assets %						
Return on Equity %						
Debt to Equity						

CONTACT INFORMATION:

Phone: 832-813-4100   Fax:
Toll-Free: 800-231-1212
Address: 10001 Six Pines Dr., The Woodlands, TX 77380 United States

STOCK TICKER/OTHER:

Stock Ticker: Joint Venture   Exchange:
Employees: 5,550   Fiscal Year Ends: 12/31
Parent Company: Chevron Corporation

SALARIES/BONUSES:

Top Exec. Salary: $ Bonus: $
Second Exec. Salary: $ Bonus: $

OTHER THOUGHTS:

Estimated Female Officers or Directors: 1
Hot Spot for Advancement for Women/Minorities: Y

Cigna Corporation

NAIC Code: 524114

www.cigna.com

TYPES OF BUSINESS:

Insurance-Medical & Health, HMOs & PPOs
Indemnity Insurance
Investment Management Services
Group Life, Accident & Disability

BRANDS/DIVISIONS/AFFILIATES:

CONTACTS: *Note: Officers with more than one job title may be intentionally listed here more than once.*

David Cordani, CEO
Eric Palmer, CFO
Isaiah Harris, Chairman of the Board
Mary Hoeltzel, Chief Accounting Officer
Mark Boxer, Chief Information Officer
Lisa Bacus, Chief Marketing Officer
John Murabito, Executive VP, Divisional
Alan Muney, Executive VP
Nicole Jones, Executive VP
Jason Sadler, President, Divisional
Christopher Hocevar, President, Divisional
Michael Triplett, President, Divisional
Matthew Manders, President, Divisional

GROWTH PLANS/SPECIAL FEATURES:

Cigna Corporation is a global health services organization. Along with its insurance subsidiaries, the company is a major provider of medical, dental, disability, life and accident insurance and related products and services, the majority of which are offered through employers and other groups. Cigna operates in three segments: global healthcare, global supplemental benefits, and group disability and life. The global healthcare segment accounts for 80% of annual revenue, and is comprised of two divisions: commercial and government. The commercial division consists of global health benefits, products and services designed to meet the needs of local and multinational companies and organizations, along with their domestic and globally mobile employees and dependents. The government division offers Medicare Advantage and Medicare Part D plans to seniors, as well as Medicaid plans. The global supplemental benefits segment accounts for 9% of annual revenue, and offers supplemental health, life and accident insurance products mainly in Asia, Europe and the United States. In addition, it offers services to globally mobile individuals and local citizens through partnerships and local licensing. In China, India and Turkey, products are offered through joint ventures. The group disability and life segment accounts for 11% of annual revenue, and provides group long-term and short-term disability insurance, group life insurance and accident and specialty insurance. These products and services are provided by the firm's subsidiaries. Cigna's other operations include corporate-owned life insurance, deferred gains, run-off reinsurance and its run-off settlement annuity business. In 2015, Cigna agreed to acquire giant competitor Anthem, Inc. in a deal worth $48 billion. In 2016, the U.S. Justice Department challenged the merger, and a District Court blocked the merger in February 2017 on anti-competitive grounds, causing Cigna to call off the agreement.

Employee benefits include child/dependent care, adoption assistance, onsite health centers and an employee assistance program.

FINANCIAL DATA: *Note: Data for latest year may not have been available at press time.*

In U.S. $	2016	2015	2014	2013	2012	2011
Revenue	39,668,000,000	37,876,000,000	34,914,000,000	32,380,000,000	29,119,000,000	21,998,000,000
R&D Expense						
Operating Income	2,979,000,000	3,327,000,000	3,304,000,000	2,176,000,000	2,477,000,000	1,968,000,000
Operating Margin %	7.50%	8.78%	9.46%	6.72%	8.50%	8.94%
SGA Expense	2,468,000,000	2,134,000,000	10,011,000,000	7,566,000,000	7,187,000,000	5,901,000,000
Net Income	1,867,000,000	2,094,000,000	2,102,000,000	1,476,000,000	1,623,000,000	1,327,000,000
Operating Cash Flow	4,026,000,000	2,717,000,000	1,994,000,000	719,000,000	2,350,000,000	1,491,000,000
Capital Expenditure	461,000,000	510,000,000	473,000,000	527,000,000	408,000,000	422,000,000
EBITDA						
Return on Assets %	3.20%	3.70%	3.81%	2.73%	3.09%	2.74%
Return on Equity %	14.49%	18.36%	19.69%	14.51%	17.92%	17.70%
Debt to Equity	0.34	0.41	0.46	0.47	0.51	0.59

CONTACT INFORMATION:

Phone: 860 226-6000   Fax: 215 761-3596
Toll-Free: 800-997-1654
Address: 900 Cottage Grove Rd., Bloomfield, CT 06002 United States

STOCK TICKER/OTHER:

Stock Ticker: CI   Exchange: NYS
Employees: 41,000   Fiscal Year Ends: 12/31
Parent Company:

SALARIES/BONUSES:

Top Exec. Salary: $1,200,000   Bonus: $
Second Exec. Salary: $883,428   Bonus: $

OTHER THOUGHTS:

Estimated Female Officers or Directors: 4
Hot Spot for Advancement for Women/Minorities: Y

Cintas Corporation

NAIC Code: 812331

www.cintas.com

TYPES OF BUSINESS:

Linen & Uniform Supply
Uniform Rental, Sales & Cleaning
Uniform Design & Manufacturing
Outsourcing Services
Dust Control Services
Restroom Cleaning Services
First Aid & Safety Products

BRANDS/DIVISIONS/AFFILIATES:

G&K Services Inc

CONTACTS: Note: Officers with more than one job title may be intentionally listed here more than once.

Scott Farmer, CEO
J. Hansen, CFO
Richard Farmer, Chairman Emeritus
J. Holloman, COO
Thomas Frooman, General Counsel
Paul Adler, Vice President

GROWTH PLANS/SPECIAL FEATURES:

Cintas Corporation provides highly specialized products and services to corporate customers in North America. The company is a leading corporate identity uniform supplier, as well as a supplier of entrance and logo mats, restroom supplies, promotional products, first aid, safety, fire protection products and industrial carpet/tile cleaning services. Cintas operates through two business primary segments: uniform rental & facilities services and first aid & safety services. The uniform rental & facility services segment consists of the rental and servicing of uniforms and other garments, including flame-resistant clothing, mats, mops, shop towels and other ancillary items. This segment also provides restroom cleaning supplies and services; carpet and tile cleaning services; and the sale of items from Cintas' catalogs. The first aid & safety services segment consists of first aid and safety products and services, as well as fire protection products and services. The company provides these products and services to over 900,000 businesses of all types, from small service and manufacturing companies to major corporations that employ thousands of people. In March 2107, the firm acquired G&K Services, Inc. for approximately $2.2 billion.

Employee benefits include flexible spending accounts; medical, prescription drug, dental and vision coverage; disability; and wellness programs.

FINANCIAL DATA: Note: Data for latest year may not have been available at press time.

In U.S. $	2016	2015	2014	2013	2012	2011
Revenue	4,905,458,000	4,476,886,000	4,551,812,000	4,316,471,000	4,102,000,000	
R&D Expense						
Operating Income	781,748,000	696,407,000	567,010,000	565,211,000	539,627,000	
Operating Margin %	15.93%	15.55%	12.45%	13.09%	13.15%	
SGA Expense	1,348,122,000	1,224,930,000	1,302,752,000	1,221,856,000	1,198,981,000	
Net Income	693,520,000	430,618,000	374,442,000	315,442,000	297,637,000	
Operating Cash Flow	465,845,000	580,276,000	607,969,000	552,748,000	469,862,000	
Capital Expenditure	275,385,000	217,720,000	145,580,000	196,486,000	160,802,000	
EBITDA	947,923,000	864,061,000	841,900,000	731,284,000	697,400,000	
Return on Assets %	16.71%	9.95%	8.50%	7.41%	6.99%	
Return on Equity %	36.74%	20.87%	17.04%	14.53%	13.40%	
Debt to Equity	0.56	0.67	0.59	0.59	0.49	

CONTACT INFORMATION:

Phone: 513 459-1200   Fax: 513 573-4030
Toll-Free:
Address: 6800 Cintas Blvd., Cincinnati, OH 45262 United States

STOCK TICKER/OTHER:

Stock Ticker: CTAS   Exchange: NAS
Employees: 42,000   Fiscal Year Ends: 05/31
Parent Company:

SALARIES/BONUSES:

Top Exec. Salary: $1,000,000   Bonus: $
Second Exec. Salary: Bonus: $
$643,966

OTHER THOUGHTS:

Estimated Female Officers or Directors: 1
Hot Spot for Advancement for Women/Minorities:

Cisco Systems Inc

www.cisco.com

NAIC Code: 0

TYPES OF BUSINESS:
Computer Networking Equipment
Routers & Switches
Real-Time Conferencing Technology
Server Virtualization Software
Data Storage Products
Security Products
Teleconference Systems and Technology
Unified Communications Systems

BRANDS/DIVISIONS/AFFILIATES:
Cisco Unified Computing System
Acano Limited
Lancope Inc
OpenDNS

CONTACTS: *Note: Officers with more than one job title may be intentionally listed here more than once.*
Charles Robbins, CEO
John Chambers, Chairman of the Board
Prat Bhatt, Chief Accounting Officer
Karen Walker, Chief Marketing Officer
Chris Dedicoat, Executive VP, Divisional
Kelly Kramer, Executive VP
Mark Chandler, General Counsel
Rebecca Jacoby, Other Executive Officer

GROWTH PLANS/SPECIAL FEATURES:
Cisco Systems, Inc. designs and sells broad lines of products, provides services and delivers integrated solutions to develop and connect networks around the world, building the internet. The company is organized into three geographic segments: the Americas; Europe, Middle East and Africa; and Asia Pacific, Japan and China. Its products and technologies are grouped into: switching, next-generation network routing, collaboration, data center, wireless and security. Switching is an integral networking technology used in campuses, branch offices and data centers. It is used within buildings in local-area networks (LANs) and across great distances in wide-area networks (WANs). Switching products offer forms of connectivity to end users, workstations, IP phones, wireless access points and servers. NGN routing technology interconnects public and private wireline and mobile networks for mobile, data, voice and video applications. This division's portfolio of hardware and software solutions consists of physical and virtual routers, as well as routing and optical systems. Collaboration integrates voice, video, data and mobile applications on fixed and mobile networks across a wide range of devices and related IT equipment. Digital interactive devices enable content originators to deliver entertainment, information and communication services to consumers and businesses worldwide. Data center's Cisco Unified Computing System enables fast IT and scalability for workloads, data analytics and cloud-native applications and infrastructures. Wireless access via wireless fidelity (Wi-Fi) is a technology that provides indoor/outdoor coverage with seamless roaming for voice, video and data applications. Security aims to protect the digital economy of Cisco customers. During 2015, the firm acquired Acano Limited; and sold the customer premises equipment portion of its service provider video connected devices business. In 2016, it acquired Lancope, Inc., a context-aware security analytics company; and OpenDNS, a cloud security platform designed to provide effective security.

FINANCIAL DATA: *Note: Data for latest year may not have been available at press time.*

In U.S. $	2016	2015	2014	2013	2012	2011
Revenue	49,247,000,000	49,161,000,000	47,142,000,000	48,607,000,000	46,061,000,000	43,218,000,000
R&D Expense	6,296,000,000	6,207,000,000	6,294,000,000	5,942,000,000	5,488,000,000	5,823,000,000
Operating Income	12,660,000,000	10,770,000,000	9,345,000,000	11,196,000,000	10,065,000,000	7,674,000,000
Operating Margin %	25.70%	21.90%	19.82%	23.03%	21.85%	17.75%
SGA Expense	11,433,000,000	11,861,000,000	11,437,000,000	11,802,000,000	11,969,000,000	11,720,000,000
Net Income	10,739,000,000	8,981,000,000	7,853,000,000	9,983,000,000	8,041,000,000	6,490,000,000
Operating Cash Flow	13,570,000,000	12,552,000,000	12,332,000,000	12,894,000,000	11,491,000,000	10,079,000,000
Capital Expenditure	1,146,000,000	1,227,000,000	1,275,000,000	1,160,000,000	1,126,000,000	1,174,000,000
EBITDA	15,746,000,000	14,209,000,000	12,711,000,000	14,161,000,000	13,357,000,000	10,939,000,000
Return on Assets %	9.13%	8.21%	7.61%	10.34%	8.99%	7.71%
Return on Equity %	17.42%	15.43%	13.56%	18.08%	16.32%	14.18%
Debt to Equity	0.38	0.35	0.36	0.21	0.31	0.34

CONTACT INFORMATION:
Phone: 408 526-4000   Fax: 408 526-4100
Toll-Free: 800-553-6387
Address: 170 W. Tasman Drive, San Jose, CA 95134 United States

STOCK TICKER/OTHER:
Stock Ticker: CSCO   Exchange: NAS
Employees: 71,833   Fiscal Year Ends: 07/31
Parent Company:

SALARIES/BONUSES:
Top Exec. Salary: $749,135   Bonus: $500,000
Second Exec. Salary: $1,172,115   Bonus: $

OTHER THOUGHTS:
Estimated Female Officers or Directors: 10
Hot Spot for Advancement for Women/Minorities: Y

Sales, profits and employees may be estimates. Financial information, benefits and other data can change quickly and may vary from those stated here.

Citigroup Inc

NAIC Code: 522110

TYPES OF BUSINESS:

Banking
Commercial, Residential & Consumer Lending
Credit Cards
Investment Banking
Insurance
Brokerage Services
Equity
Cash Management

BRANDS/DIVISIONS/AFFILIATES:

Citicorp
Citi Holdings
Citi
Citibank
CitiMortgage
Citibanamex

CONTACTS: Note: Officers with more than one job title may be intentionally listed here more than once.

Stephen Bird, CEO, Divisional
James Forese, CEO, Divisional
William Mills, CEO, Geographical
Jim Cowles, CEO, Geographical
Francisco Aristeguieta, CEO, Geographical
Jane Fraser, CEO, Geographical
Barbara Desoer, CEO, Subsidiary
Michael Corbat, CEO
John Gerspach, CFO
Michael ONeill, Chairman of the Board
Jeffrey Walsh, Chief Accounting Officer
Bradford Hu, Chief Risk Officer
Rohan Weerasinghe, General Counsel
Don Callahan, Other Corporate Officer

GROWTH PLANS/SPECIAL FEATURES:

Citigroup, Inc. is a diversified financial services holding company and one of the largest banking organizations in the world. The firm is organized into two segments: Citicorp and Citi Holdings. Citicorp consists of the company's global consumer banking business, which provides retail banking, local commercial banking, investment services and Citi-branded credit cards; and the institutional clients group, which provides investment banking, debt and equity, lending, real estate, cash management, clearing and trade services. This segment also includes corporate/other, which comprises the firm's treasury operations, its technology and global staff functions, as well as other corporate expenses. Citicorp has operations in North America, Europe, Latin America, Middle East, Africa and Asia. Half of its loans, deposits, revenues and net income are generated from outside the U.S. Citi Holdings operates the company's brokerage and asset management and local consumer lending businesses as well as managing a special asset pool. Citigroup has a number of brands including Citibank, which offers banking services from more than 2,649 branches in 19 countries worldwide; CitiMortgage, which offers a variety of mortgage products; and Citibanamex, a major commercial bank in Mexico. In November 2016, the firm agreed to sell CitiFinancial Canada, Inc. to an investor group led by J.C. Flowers & Co. LLC.

FINANCIAL DATA: Note: Data for latest year may not have been available at press time.

In U.S. $	2016	2015	2014	2013	2012	2011
Revenue	69,875,000,000	76,354,000,000	76,882,000,000	76,366,000,000	70,173,000,000	78,353,000,000
R&D Expense						
Operating Income	21,477,000,000	24,826,000,000	14,364,000,000	19,497,000,000	7,936,000,000	14,624,000,000
Operating Margin %	30.73%	32.51%	18.68%	25.53%	11.30%	18.66%
SGA Expense	29,287,000,000	29,897,000,000	32,239,000,000	31,991,000,000	33,342,000,000	33,167,000,000
Net Income	14,912,000,000	17,242,000,000	7,313,000,000	13,673,000,000	7,541,000,000	11,067,000,000
Operating Cash Flow	53,932,000,000	39,737,000,000	45,434,000,000	57,410,000,000	14,271,000,000	44,741,000,000
Capital Expenditure	2,756,000,000	3,198,000,000	3,386,000,000	3,490,000,000	3,604,000,000	3,448,000,000
EBITDA						
Return on Assets %	.77%	.90%	.35%	.71%	.40%	.58%
Return on Equity %	6.63%	8.02%	3.36%	7.01%	4.12%	6.48%
Debt to Equity	1.00	0.98	1.11	1.11	1.28	1.82

CONTACT INFORMATION:

Phone: 212 559-1000   Fax: 212 816-8913
Toll-Free: 800-285-3000
Address: 388 Greenwich St., New York, NY 10013 United States

STOCK TICKER/OTHER:

Stock Ticker: C   Exchange: NYS
Employees: 219,000   Fiscal Year Ends: 12/31
Parent Company:

SALARIES/BONUSES:

Top Exec. Salary: $500,000   Bonus: $5,920,000
Second Exec. Salary: Bonus: $4,200,000
$1,500,000

OTHER THOUGHTS:

Estimated Female Officers or Directors: 5
Hot Spot for Advancement for Women/Minorities: Y

Citrix Systems Inc

www.citrix.com

NAIC Code: 0

TYPES OF BUSINESS:
Computer Software-Application Server
Consulting Services
Training & Technical Support
Online Services

BRANDS/DIVISIONS/AFFILIATES:
XenApp
XenDesktop
GoTo
XenServer
Citrix NetScaler
ByteMobile Smart Capacity
Citrix Cloud
Subscription Advantage

CONTACTS: Note: Officers with more than one job title may be intentionally listed here more than once.
Robert Calderoni, Chairman of the Board
Jessica Soisson, Chief Accounting Officer
Timothy Minahan, Chief Marketing Officer
David Henshall, COO
Kirill Tatarinov, Director
Carlos Sartorius, Executive VP, Geographical
Klaus Oestermann, General Manager, Divisional
Christopher Hylen, General Manager, Divisional
Jesse Lipson, General Manager, Divisional

GROWTH PLANS/SPECIAL FEATURES:
Citrix Systems, Inc. designs, develops and markets products that allow applications to be delivered, supported and shared on demand. The firm's desktop virtualization solutions, XenApp and XenDesktop, reduce the complexity and cost of desktop management by virtualizing the desktop and applications in the datacenter. XenApp runs the business logic of applications on a central server, transmitting only screen pixels, keystrokes and mouse movements through an encrypted channel to users' computers. XenDesktop streams desktop images through multiple virtual machines. Citrix's software-as-a-service (SaaS) division comprises the GoTo family of products which provide web-based access to office resources for offsite locations. The datacenter and cloud solutions product groups include virtual infrastructure and application networking products. Virtual infrastructure includes the XenServer, a server virtualization solution that aggregates a pool of computing and storage resources. Networking and cloud applications, through products including Citrix NetScalar, ByteMobile Smart Capacity and Citrix Cloud are designed to improve application performance, access datacenter resources in offsite locations and deliver local area network-like performance over a wide area network. The technical services division provides consulting services, technical support and product training to support Citrix products. In addition, Citrix's Subscription Advantage renewable program provides subscribers with immediate access to software upgrades, enhancements and maintenance releases when and if they become available during the term of the contract. In November 2015, the firm announced plans to spin off its GoTo family of products into a separate, publicly-traded company within the first quarter of 2017. In 2016, Citrix sold its CloudPlatform and CloudPortal Business Manager products to Persistent Telecom Solutions, Inc.

Citrix offers employees medical, dental, prescription and vision benefits; on-site fitness centers; 401(k); and paid time off.

FINANCIAL DATA: Note: Data for latest year may not have been available at press time.

In U.S. $	2016	2015	2014	2013	2012	2011
Revenue	3,418,265,000	3,275,594,000	3,142,856,000	2,918,434,000	2,586,123,000	2,206,392,000
R&D Expense	489,265,000	563,975,000	553,817,000	516,338,000	450,571,000	343,727,000
Operating Income	649,158,000	350,085,000	302,311,000	380,717,000	390,778,000	416,966,000
Operating Margin %	18.99%	10.68%	9.61%	13.04%	15.11%	18.89%
SGA Expense	1,563,382,000	1,538,027,000	1,600,187,000	1,476,916,000	1,306,088,000	1,147,088,000
Net Income	536,112,000	319,361,000	251,723,000	339,523,000	352,547,000	356,322,000
Operating Cash Flow	1,115,830,000	1,034,548,000	845,981,000	928,343,000	818,527,000	679,122,000
Capital Expenditure	160,512,000	172,228,000	179,093,000	175,042,000	150,718,000	127,369,000
EBITDA	910,751,000	748,909,000	634,308,000	648,217,000	605,651,000	576,221,000
Return on Assets %	9.03%	5.81%	4.69%	6.78%	7.92%	9.13%
Return on Equity %	23.39%	15.40%	9.16%	10.54%	12.04%	13.48%
Debt to Equity		0.67	0.59			

CONTACT INFORMATION:
Phone: 954 267-3000 Fax: 954 267-9319
Toll-Free: 800-424-8749
Address: 851 W. Cypress Creek Rd., Fort Lauderdale, FL 33309 United States

STOCK TICKER/OTHER:
Stock Ticker: CTXS Exchange: NAS
Employees: 9,600 Fiscal Year Ends: 12/31
Parent Company:

SALARIES/BONUSES:
Top Exec. Salary: $1,000,000 Bonus: $
Second Exec. Salary: $937,500 Bonus: $

OTHER THOUGHTS:
Estimated Female Officers or Directors: 2
Hot Spot for Advancement for Women/Minorities:

Clayton Homes Inc

www.claytonhomes.com

NAIC Code: 321992

TYPES OF BUSINESS:

Construction Services
Manufactured Housing
Insurance & Financing

BRANDS/DIVISIONS/AFFILIATES:

Berkshire Hathaway Inc
Vanderbilt Mortgage and Finance Inc
Clayton

CONTACTS: *Note: Officers with more than one job title may be intentionally listed here more than once.*

Kevin T. Clayton, CEO
Kevin T. Clayton, Pres.
Richard D. Strachan, Pres., Mfg.
Leon Van Tonder, Dir.-Oper.

GROWTH PLANS/SPECIAL FEATURES:

Clayton Homes, Inc., a subsidiary of Berkshire Hathaway, Inc., produces, sells, finances and insures modular and manufactured homes, in addition to commercial and educational relocatable buildings. The company's 35 manufacturing plants produce homes that are marketed in 49 states through over 1,300 independent retailers and approximately 448 company-owned sales centers. Clayton's factory-built manufactured homes are completely-finished dwellings that are constructed under federal code in factories and then transported by truck to its targeted location. The homes are designed to be permanent, owner-occupied residential sites with attached utilities. The firm manufactures a variety of single- and multi-sectional homes from 1,000 to 2,000 square feet and larger under brand names such as Clayton, Buccaneer, Cavalier, Crest, Giles, Golden West, Karsten, Marlette, Norris, Schult and Southern Energy Homes. Standard features offered in Clayton homes include central heating, flooring systems and wall and floor treatments. Customers can choose predesigned homes or custom-design a home by size, number of bedrooms and other features. Through financial subsidiary Vanderbilt Mortgage and Finance, Inc. (VMF), the firm offers financing to manufactured home customers as well as customers purchasing homes from certain third parties. VMF's financing products include manufactured home loans, Federal Housing Authority (FHA) loans, Land Home financing and more. Clayton and its subsidiaries provide financing to 350,000 customers and insurance to 160,000 customers. Additionally, Clayton acts as a reinsurance agent for physical damage, family protection and homebuyer protection insurance and other policies issued by insurance companies in connection with the firm's homes. In 2016, the firm acquired New York-based G&I Homes; Tennessee-based Goodall Homes; and Alabama-based River Birch Homes.

Clayton offers its employees a 401(k) plan; medical, dental, vision and life insurance; training programs; and tuition and fitness reimbursement.

FINANCIAL DATA: *Note: Data for latest year may not have been available at press time.*

In U.S. $	2016	2015	2014	2013	2012	2011
Revenue	4,230,000,000	3,580,000,000	3,310,000,000	3,199,000,000	3,014,000,000	2,932,000,000
R&D Expense						
Operating Income						
Operating Margin %						
SGA Expense						
Net Income	744,000,000	706,000,000	558,000,000	416,000,000	255,000,000	154,000,000
Operating Cash Flow						
Capital Expenditure						
EBITDA						
Return on Assets %						
Return on Equity %						
Debt to Equity						

CONTACT INFORMATION:

Phone: 865-380-3000   Fax: 865-380-3742
Toll-Free: 800-822-0633
Address: 500 Clayton Rd., Maryville, TN 37804 United States

STOCK TICKER/OTHER:

Stock Ticker: Subsidiary   Exchange:
Employees: 13,164   Fiscal Year Ends: 06/30
Parent Company: Berkshire Hathaway Inc

SALARIES/BONUSES:

Top Exec. Salary: $ Bonus: $
Second Exec. Salary: $ Bonus: $

OTHER THOUGHTS:

Estimated Female Officers or Directors:
Hot Spot for Advancement for Women/Minorities:

Cleveland Clinic Foundation (The)   www.clevelandclinic.org

NAIC Code: 622110

TYPES OF BUSINESS:

General Medical and Surgical Hospitals

BRANDS/DIVISIONS/AFFILIATES:

Glickman Urological & Kidney Institute
Lerner Research Institute
Lerner College of Medicine

CONTACTS: Note: Officers with more than one job title may be intentionally listed here more than once.

Delos M. Cosgrove, CEO
William M. Peacock, III, Chief of Oper.
Steven C. Glass, CFO
Paul Matsen, CMO
Linda McHugh, Chief Human Resources Officer
Robert Wyllie, Chief Medical Oper. Officer
Doug Smith, Interim CIO
Cindy Hundorfean, Chief Admin. Officer-Clinical Svcs.
David W. Rowan, Chief Legal Officer
William M. Peacock, III, Chief-Oper.
Michael Harrington, Chief Acct. Officer
Kristen D.W. Morris, Chief Gov't. & Community Rel. Officer
Linda McHugh, Exec. Admin.-CEO & Board of Governors
K. Kelly Hancock, Interim Exec. Chief Nursing Officer
Ann Huston, Chief Strategy Officer
Robert E. Rich, Jr., Chmn.

GROWTH PLANS/SPECIAL FEATURES:

The Cleveland Clinic Foundation is a nonprofit clinic in Ohio that combines medical care with education and research. It is noted for very advanced surgical techniques and advanced care. Founded in 1921, it serves 5.1 million patients per year across the nation and internationally. The Cleveland Clinic has over 4,400 beds across its system, and over 3,500 scientists and physicians work within the system. Facilities include the main hospital; more than 150 outpatient regional care centers, including 18 full-service family health centers and three health & wellness centers in Ohio. Additionally, there are Cleveland Clinics in Florida, comprising hospital, emergency and outpatient services, as well as cancer, neurological care, family health and wellness centers; in Nevada, which has a center for brain health, as well as the Glickman Urological & Kidney Institute; in Canada, with 28,000 square feet of offices in Toronto offering health, sports health and lifestyle management programs; and Abu Dhabi, which has 4.4 million square feet, up to 490 beds, a heart and vascular center, a digestive disease center, an eye center, a neurological center and a respiratory and critical care center. Cleveland's Lerner Research Institute is home of all laboratory-based research by the firm, as well as many translational and clinical studies. The institute comprises 1,200 scientists and support personnel, and is actively involved in programs such as cardiovascular, oncologic, neurologic, allergic, immunologic, musculoskeletal, metabolic, infectious diseases and eye diseases. The Lerner College of Medicine has an enrollment of 160 students obtaining MD degrees with an emphasis on clinical research skills.

Employee benefits include pension and savings plans; health, dental and vision insurance; life insurance; short- and long-term disability; adoption assistance; and an employee wellness program.

FINANCIAL DATA: Note: Data for latest year may not have been available at press time.

In U.S. $	2016	2015	2014	2013	2012	2011
Revenue	8,037,207,000	7,156,972,000	6,687,379,000	6,450,159,000	6,187,137,000	6,000,000,000
R&D Expense						
Operating Income						
Operating Margin %						
SGA Expense						
Net Income	139,352,000	480,224,000	467,543,000	293,995,000	157,069,000	200,000,000
Operating Cash Flow						
Capital Expenditure						
EBITDA						
Return on Assets %						
Return on Equity %						
Debt to Equity						

CONTACT INFORMATION:

Phone: 216-444-2200   Fax:
Toll-Free: 800-223-2273
Address: 9500 Euclid Ave., Cleveland, OH 44195 United States

STOCK TICKER/OTHER:

Stock Ticker: Nonprofit   Exchange:
Employees: 41,000   Fiscal Year Ends: 12/31
Parent Company:

SALARIES/BONUSES:

Top Exec. Salary: $ Bonus: $
Second Exec. Salary: $ Bonus: $

OTHER THOUGHTS:

Estimated Female Officers or Directors: 22
Hot Spot for Advancement for Women/Minorities: Y

Clorox Company (The)
NAIC Code: 325611

www.thecloroxcompany.com

TYPES OF BUSINESS:
Cleaning/Laundry Products-Manufacturing
Automotive Care Products
Pesticides
Cat Litter
Water Filtration Products
Charcoal
Domestic Plastics
Dressings & Sauces

BRANDS/DIVISIONS/AFFILIATES:
Clorox
Clorox 2
Tilex
Liquid-Plumr
Formula 409
Hidden Valley
Ayudin
Renew Life

CONTACTS: Note: Officers with more than one job title may be intentionally listed here more than once.
Benno Dorer, CEO
Kirsten Marriner, Other Executive Officer
Stephen Robb, CFO
Thomas Johnson, Chief Accounting Officer
Manjit Singh, Chief Information Officer
Eric Reynolds, Chief Marketing Officer
Jeff Baker, Controller
Dawn Willoughby, COO, Divisional
Nikolaos Vlahos, COO, Divisional
James Foster, Executive VP, Divisional
Laura Stein, Executive VP, Divisional
Jon Balousek, General Manager, Divisional
Angela Hilt, Other Corporate Officer
Matthew Laszlo, Other Executive Officer
Denise Garner, Other Executive Officer
William Bailey, Senior VP, Divisional

GROWTH PLANS/SPECIAL FEATURES:
The Clorox Company is a leading producer of consumer and institutional products. Its operations consist of four business segments: cleaning, lifestyle, household and international. Cleaning consists of laundry, home-care and professional products that are sold in the U.S. These products include Clorox branded bleaches; Clorox 2 branded color boosters and stain fighters; home-care products sold under the Pine-Sol, S.O.S., Tilex, Liquid-Plumr and Formula 409 brands; and natural cleaning products sold under the Green Works brand name. The lifestyle segment consists of food products, water-filtration systems, filters and all-natural personal care products. These products include sauces and dressing marketed under the KC Masterpiece and Hidden Valley brands, Brita water-filtration systems and filters and Burt's Bees natural personal care products. The household segment consists of charcoal, cat litter, plastic bags, wraps and container products. Brands in this division include Glad, Kingsford, Match Light, Ever Clean, Scoop Away and Fresh Step. The international segment includes brands and products marketed outside the U.S. Clorox sells its products internationally under such brand names as Ayudin, PinoLuz, Bon Bril and Lestoil. Clorox's products are manufactured in over 24 countries and are sold through grocery stores, retail outlets and mass merchandisers to consumers in more than 100 countries. Within the U.S., the company also sells institutional, janitorial, healthcare and food-service versions of many of its products through distributors as well as natural personal care products through the Internet. In May 2016, the firm acquired Renew Life, a leading brand in dietary health, with an emphasis on the digestive system for $290 million.

FINANCIAL DATA: Note: Data for latest year may not have been available at press time.

In U.S. $	2016	2015	2014	2013	2012	2011
Revenue	5,761,000,000	5,655,000,000	5,591,000,000	5,623,000,000	5,468,000,000	5,231,000,000
R&D Expense	141,000,000	136,000,000	125,000,000	130,000,000	121,000,000	115,000,000
Operating Income	1,064,000,000	1,000,000,000	958,000,000	966,000,000	903,000,000	659,000,000
Operating Margin %	18.46%	17.68%	17.13%	17.17%	16.51%	12.59%
SGA Expense	1,393,000,000	1,321,000,000	1,269,000,000	1,307,000,000	1,280,000,000	1,237,000,000
Net Income	648,000,000	580,000,000	558,000,000	572,000,000	541,000,000	557,000,000
Operating Cash Flow	778,000,000	874,000,000	767,000,000	775,000,000	612,000,000	698,000,000
Capital Expenditure	172,000,000	125,000,000	138,000,000	194,000,000	192,000,000	228,000,000
EBITDA	1,236,000,000	1,190,000,000	1,144,000,000	1,157,000,000	1,094,000,000	859,000,000
Return on Assets %	14.92%	13.77%	13.02%	13.20%	12.70%	12.77%
Return on Equity %	312.28%	426.47%	372.00%	10400.00%		
Debt to Equity	6.05	15.22	10.35	14.86		

CONTACT INFORMATION:
Phone: 510 271-7000   Fax: 510 832-1463
Toll-Free:
Address: 1221 Broadway, Oakland, CA 94612-1888 United States

STOCK TICKER/OTHER:
Stock Ticker: CLX   Exchange: NYS
Employees: 8,000   Fiscal Year Ends: 06/30
Parent Company:

SALARIES/BONUSES:
Top Exec. Salary: $976,154   Bonus: $
Second Exec. Salary: Bonus: $
$582,050

OTHER THOUGHTS:
Estimated Female Officers or Directors: 3
Hot Spot for Advancement for Women/Minorities: Y

Coca-Cola Bottling Co Consolidated   www.cokeconsolidated.com

NAIC Code: 312111

TYPES OF BUSINESS:

Beverages-Soft Drink Manufacturing
Bottling Services

BRANDS/DIVISIONS/AFFILIATES:

Coca-Cola Company (The)
POWERade
Dasani
vitaminwater
Minute Maide
Dr Pepper
Monster Energy
Tum-E Yummies

CONTACTS: *Note: Officers with more than one job title may be intentionally listed here more than once.*

J. Harrison, CEO
Clifford Deal, CFO
William Billiard, Chief Accounting Officer
Umesh Kasbekar, Director
Morgan Everett, Director
Robert Chambless, Executive VP, Divisional
James Harris, Executive VP, Divisional
David Katz, Executive VP, Divisional
E. Fisher, Executive VP
Henry Flint, President
Kimberly Kuo, Senior VP, Divisional

GROWTH PLANS/SPECIAL FEATURES:

Coca-Cola Bottling Co. Consolidated (CCB), founded in 1902, is a nonalcoholic beverage manufacturer and distributor. The firm primarily produces, markets and distributes products of The Coca-Cola Company, which owns approximately 34.8% of CCB. The company manufactures products in two categories: sparkling beverages, which consist of beverages with carbonation, including energy drinks; and still beverages, including bottled water, tea, ready-to-drink coffee, enhanced water, juices and sports drinks. CCB distributes and markets still beverages of The Coca-Cola Company such as POWERade, Dasani water, vitaminwater and Minute Maid Juices To Go in certain regions. It also produces and markets Dr. Pepper, Monster Energy and Sundrop in some of its regions. In addition, the company markets and distributes certain products which it owns, including Gold Peak tea; coffee beverages; Fuel in a Bottle power shots; and Tum-E Yummies, a vitamin C enhanced flavored drink. The company's principal soft drink is Coca-Cola classic, and products of The Coca-Cola Company generate more than half of CCB's bottle/can volume to retail customers. CCB holds bottling rights from The Coca-Cola Company covering the majority of North Carolina, South Carolina and West Virginia, as well as portions of Alabama, Mississippi, Tennessee, Kentucky, Illinois, Indiana, Virginia, Pennsylvania, Maryland, Georgia and Florida. The main packaging materials for the firm's beverages are plastic bottles and aluminum cans. In addition, the company provides restaurants and other immediate consumption outlets with fountain products. In February 2017, CCB announced plans to expand its distribution territory in northern Ohio, with wholly-owned Coca-Cola Refreshments USA, Inc. operating this region.

The firm offers employees medical, dental and vision insurance as well as a 401(k) plan.

FINANCIAL DATA: *Note: Data for latest year may not have been available at press time.*

In U.S. $	2016	2015	2014	2013	2012	2011
Revenue	3,156,428,000	2,306,458,000	1,746,369,000	1,641,331,000	1,614,433,000	1,561,239,000
R&D Expense						
Operating Income	127,859,000	98,144,000	85,967,000	73,647,000	88,686,000	87,530,000
Operating Margin %	4.05%	4.25%	4.92%	4.48%	5.49%	5.60%
SGA Expense	1,087,863,000	802,888,000	619,272,000	584,993,000	565,623,000	541,713,000
Net Income	50,146,000	59,002,000	31,354,000	27,675,000	27,217,000	28,608,000
Operating Cash Flow	161,995,000	108,290,000	91,903,000	96,374,000	83,172,000	109,650,000
Capital Expenditure	172,586,000	163,887,000	84,364,000	61,432,000	53,271,000	53,156,000
EBITDA	244,482,000	179,040,000	147,097,000	132,318,000	150,545,000	149,648,000
Return on Assets %	2.33%	3.59%	2.31%	2.16%	2.05%	2.14%
Return on Equity %	19.28%	27.65%	16.72%	16.94%	20.42%	22.07%
Debt to Equity	3.42	2.76	2.70	2.28	3.45	3.60

CONTACT INFORMATION:

Phone: 704 557-4400   Fax: 704 551-4451
Toll-Free: 800-777-2653
Address: 4100 Coca-Cola Plaza, Charlotte, NC 28211 United States

STOCK TICKER/OTHER:

Stock Ticker: COKE   Exchange: NAS
Employees: 13,200   Fiscal Year Ends: 12/31
Parent Company:

SALARIES/BONUSES:

Top Exec. Salary: $1,043,622   Bonus: $
Second Exec. Salary: Bonus: $
$792,788

OTHER THOUGHTS:

Estimated Female Officers or Directors: 3
Hot Spot for Advancement for Women/Minorities: Y

Cognizant Technology Solutions Corporation www.cognizant.com

NAIC Code: 541512

TYPES OF BUSINESS:

Computer Systems Design Services
Outsourced Services
Software Engineering

BRANDS/DIVISIONS/AFFILIATES:

Process Space
Adaptra
KIS Information Services Limited
Mirabeau BV
Frontica Business Solutions
Idea Couture
Heliocentric
ReD Associates

CONTACTS: Note: Officers with more than one job title may be intentionally listed here more than once.

Rajeev Mehta, CEO, Divisional
Brackett Denniston, General Counsel
Francisco DSouza, CEO
Karen McLoughlin, CFO
John Klein, Chairman of the Board
Allen Shaheen, Executive VP, Divisional
Malcolm Frank, Executive VP, Divisional
Srinivasan Veeraraghavachary, Executive VP
Gajakarnan Kandiah, Executive VP
Santosh Thomas, Executive VP
Sumithra Gomatam, Executive VP
Venkat Krishnaswamy, Executive VP
Debashis Chatterjee, Executive VP
Ramakrishna Chintamaneni, Executive VP
Dharmendra Sinha, Executive VP
James Lennox, Other Executive Officer
Robert Telesmanic, Senior VP
Sean Middleton, Senior VP

GROWTH PLANS/SPECIAL FEATURES:

Cognizant Technology Solutions Corporation specializes in custom IT design, development, integration and maintenance services. The firm provides these services primarily to Global 2000 companies located in the U.S., Europe and Asia. The company's core competencies include complex systems development and integration, application maintenance, infrastructure management, enterprise software package implementation and maintenance, technology consulting, data warehousing, business intelligence and analytics, application testing and knowledge process outsourcing. Cognizant operates in four business segments: financial services, which provides services to customers in the banking and insurance industries; healthcare, which provides services to health care and life science industries; manufacturing, retail and logistics, which provides services to those industries; and other, which covers communications, information services, media, entertainment and high technology. Cognizant provides its IT services using an integrated onsite/offshore business model. This business model combines technical and account management teams located onsite at the customer location and offshore at dedicated development centers located primarily in India, Argentina, the U.S., the Philippines, China, France, Canada and Hungary. The firm has developed proprietary methodologies for integrating onsite and offshore teams, including its Process Space software engineering process, which is available to all onsite and offshore programmers. Process Space is used as part of an initial assessment that allows the firm to define the scope and risks of the project and subdivide the project into smaller phases with frequent deliverables and feedback from customers. During 2016, the firm made several acquisitions: Adaptra, KIS Information Services, Mirabeau BV, Frontica Business Solutions, Idea Couture, Heliocentric, Red Associates, KBACE Technologies and Quick Left, Inc. That same year, Cognizant expanded its operations in the Kingdom of Saudi Arabia, with a new office in Riyadh.

FINANCIAL DATA: Note: Data for latest year may not have been available at press time.

In U.S. $	2016	2015	2014	2013	2012	2011
Revenue	13,487,000,000	12,416,000,000	10,262,680,000	8,843,189,000	7,346,472,000	6,121,156,000
R&D Expense						
Operating Income	2,289,000,000	2,142,000,000	1,884,878,000	1,677,910,000	1,361,496,000	1,136,468,000
Operating Margin %	16.97%	17.25%	18.36%	18.97%	18.53%	18.56%
SGA Expense	2,731,000,000	2,508,600,000	2,037,021,000	1,727,609,000	1,557,646,000	1,328,665,000
Net Income	1,553,000,000	1,623,600,000	1,439,267,000	1,228,578,000	1,051,263,000	883,618,000
Operating Cash Flow	1,621,000,000	2,153,300,000	1,473,010,000	1,423,776,000	1,172,583,000	875,152,000
Capital Expenditure	300,000,000	272,800,000	212,203,000	261,626,000	334,465,000	288,221,000
EBITDA	2,755,000,000	2,511,300,000	2,134,566,000	1,857,840,000	1,518,084,000	1,260,643,000
Return on Assets %	11.36%	13.10%	14.44%	16.68%	17.47%	17.51%
Return on Equity %	15.52%	19.08%	20.74%	22.35%	23.87%	23.44%
Debt to Equity	0.07	0.09	0.12			

CONTACT INFORMATION:

Phone: 201 801-0233   Fax: 201 801-0243
Toll-Free: 888-937-3277
Address: 500 Frank W. Burr Blvd., Teaneck, NJ 07666 United States

STOCK TICKER/OTHER:

Stock Ticker: CTSH   Exchange: NAS
Employees: 260,200   Fiscal Year Ends: 12/31
Parent Company:

SALARIES/BONUSES:

Top Exec. Salary: $417,250   Bonus: $566,052
Second Exec. Salary: Bonus: $
$664,300

OTHER THOUGHTS:

Estimated Female Officers or Directors: 1
Hot Spot for Advancement for Women/Minorities:

Comcast Corporation

NAIC Code: 517110

TYPES OF BUSINESS:

Cable Television
VoIP Service
Cable Network Programming
High-Speed Internet Service
Video-on-Demand
Advertising Services
Interactive Program Schedules
Wireless Services

BRANDS/DIVISIONS/AFFILIATES:

XFINITY
NBC
Telemundo
Universal
Comcast Spectator
Philadelphia Flyers
Wells Fargo Center

CONTACTS: Note: Officers with more than one job title may be intentionally listed here more than once.

Neil Smit, CEO, Subsidiary
Stephen Burke, CEO, Subsidiary
Brian Roberts, CEO
Michael Cavanagh, CFO
Lawrence Salva, Chief Accounting Officer
Daniel Murdock, Controller
Dave Watson, COO, Subsidiary
Joseph Collins, Director Emeritus
Judith Rodin, Director Emeritus
Arthur Block, Executive VP
David Cohen, Senior Executive VP

GROWTH PLANS/SPECIAL FEATURES:

Comcast Corporation provides information, entertainment and communications products and services. Comcast operates through five segments: cable communications, cable networks, broadcast television, filmed entertainment and theme parks. The cable communications segment maintains the firm's video, high-speed internet and voice servicing operations, serving residential customers under the XFINITY brand. This division also sells advertising, as well as video, high-speed internet, voice and other services to small- and medium-sized businesses. The cable networks segment includes the firm's national cable networks, its regional sports & news networks, its international cable networks and its cable television production operations. The broadcast television segment consists primarily of the company's NBC and Telemundo broadcast networks, its 10 NBC- and 17 Telemundo-owned local broadcast television stations and its broadcast television production operations. Filmed entertainment is comprised of the studio operations of Universal Pictures, which produces, acquires, markets and distributes filmed entertainment worldwide. Theme parks is comprised of the Universal theme parks in Orlando, Florida; Hollywood, California; and the 51%-owned them park in Osaka, Japan. Additionally, subsidiary Comcast Spectator owns the Philadelphia Flyers and the Wells Fargo Center in Philadelphia, Pennsylvania, and operates arena management-related businesses.

FINANCIAL DATA: Note: Data for latest year may not have been available at press time.

In U.S. $	2016	2015	2014	2013	2012	2011
Revenue	80,403,000,000	74,510,000,000	68,775,000,000	64,657,000,000	62,570,000,000	55,842,000,000
R&D Expense						
Operating Income	16,859,000,000	15,998,000,000	14,904,000,000	13,563,000,000	12,179,000,000	10,721,000,000
Operating Margin %	20.96%	21.47%	21.67%	20.97%	19.46%	19.19%
SGA Expense	29,523,000,000	27,282,000,000	24,940,000,000	23,553,000,000	22,664,000,000	16,727,000,000
Net Income	8,695,000,000	8,163,000,000	8,380,000,000	6,816,000,000	6,203,000,000	4,160,000,000
Operating Cash Flow	19,240,000,000	18,778,000,000	16,945,000,000	14,160,000,000	14,854,000,000	14,345,000,000
Capital Expenditure	10,821,000,000	9,869,000,000	8,542,000,000	7,605,000,000	6,637,000,000	6,261,000,000
EBITDA	26,853,000,000	24,754,000,000	23,101,000,000	21,560,000,000	21,928,000,000	18,348,000,000
Return on Assets %	5.01%	5.00%	5.26%	4.21%	3.84%	3.01%
Return on Equity %	16.37%	15.55%	16.20%	13.62%	12.83%	9.08%
Debt to Equity	1.03	0.93	0.83	0.87	0.77	0.80

CONTACT INFORMATION:

Phone: 215 286-1700   Fax:
Toll-Free: 800-266-2278
Address: One Comcast Center, Philadelphia, PA 19103 United States

STOCK TICKER/OTHER:

Stock Ticker: CMCSA   Exchange: NAS
Employees: 159,000   Fiscal Year Ends: 12/31
Parent Company:

SALARIES/BONUSES:

Top Exec. Salary: $3,013,510   Bonus: $
Second Exec. Salary: Bonus: $
$2,797,499

OTHER THOUGHTS:

Estimated Female Officers or Directors: 16
Hot Spot for Advancement for Women/Minorities: Y

CommScope Inc

www.commscope.com

NAIC Code: 335921

TYPES OF BUSINESS:

Cable-Coaxial & Fiber Optic
Local Area Network Products
Wireless Products

BRANDS/DIVISIONS/AFFILIATES:

CommScope Connectivity Solutions
CommScope Mobility Solutions
Systimax
Uniprise
Andrew

CONTACTS: Note: Officers with more than one job title may be intentionally listed here more than once.

Mark Olson, CFO
Frank Drendel, Chairman of the Board
Robert Granow, Chief Accounting Officer
Randall Crenshaw, COO
Frank Wyatt, General Counsel
Marvin Edwards, President
Peter Karlsson, Senior VP, Divisional
Philip Armstrong, Senior VP, Divisional
Robyn Mingle, Senior VP, Divisional

GROWTH PLANS/SPECIAL FEATURES:

CommScope, Inc. is a global leader in connectivity solutions for communications networks. It provides infrastructure solutions for wireless, residential broadband, business enterprise and carrier wireline networks. CommScope's operations are divided into two segments: CommScope Connectivity Solutions (CCS) and CommScope Mobility Solutions (CMS). The CCS segment provides connectivity and network intelligence for indoor and outdoor network applications. Indoor network solutions are found in commercial buildings and in the network core, which includes data centers, central offices and cable television head-ends. Indoor network solution products are marketed under the Systimax and Uniprise brand names. Outdoor network solutions are found in access and edge networks and include coaxial cabling, fiber optic cable and connectivity solutions, including a robust portfolio of fiber optic connectors and fiber management systems. The CMS segment provides merchant RF wireless network solutions, as well as metro cell, DAS and small cell solutions. Metro cell solutions can be found on street poles and on other urban structures. DAS and small cell solutions allow wireless operators to increase spectral efficiency and enhance cellular coverage and capacity in challenging network conditions such as commercial buildings, urban areas, stadiums and transportation systems. CMS solutions are marketed primarily under the Andrew brand. CommScope's focus on research and innovation has led to over 10,500 patents and patent applications, and approximately 2,700 registered trademarks.

The firm offers employees a 401(k) plan; educational assistance; medical, dental and vision insurance; life and AD&D insurance; short- and long-term disability; and an employee assistance program.

FINANCIAL DATA: Note: Data for latest year may not have been available at press time.

In U.S. $	2016	2015	2014	2013	2012	2011
Revenue	4,923,621,000	3,807,828,000	3,829,614,000	3,480,117,000	3,321,885,000	3,186,446,000
R&D Expense	200,715,000	135,964,000	125,301,000	126,431,000	121,718,000	112,904,000
Operating Income	574,750,000	181,593,000	577,449,000	329,714,000	238,238,000	-134,719,000
Operating Margin %	11.67%	4.76%	15.07%	9.47%	7.17%	-4.22%
SGA Expense	879,495,000	687,389,000	484,891,000	502,275,000	461,149,000	517,903,000
Net Income	222,838,000	-70,875,000	236,772,000	19,396,000	5,353,000	-252,308,000
Operating Cash Flow	606,225,000	302,060,000	289,418,000	237,701,000	286,135,000	135,749,000
Capital Expenditure	68,314,000	56,501,000	36,935,000	36,780,000	27,957,000	38,792,000
EBITDA	949,156,000	476,160,000	755,502,000	541,400,000	488,555,000	120,242,000
Return on Assets %	3.04%	-1.13%	4.88%	.40%	.10%	-4.89%
Return on Equity %	17.03%	-5.60%	19.76%	1.70%	.42%	-18.48%
Debt to Equity	3.26	4.27	2.06	2.30	2.08	1.86

CONTACT INFORMATION:

Phone: 828-324-2200   Fax:
Toll-Free: 800-982-1708
Address: 1100 CommScope Place SE, Hickory, NC 28602 United States

STOCK TICKER/OTHER:

Stock Ticker: COMM   Exchange: NAS
Employees: 25,000   Fiscal Year Ends: 12/31
Parent Company:

SALARIES/BONUSES:

Top Exec. Salary: $1,022,500   Bonus: $
Second Exec. Salary: Bonus: $
$718,795

OTHER THOUGHTS:

Estimated Female Officers or Directors: 2
Hot Spot for Advancement for Women/Minorities:

Community Health Systems Inc

www.chs.net

NAIC Code: 622110

TYPES OF BUSINESS:

General Medical and Surgical Hospitals
Surgical & Emergency Services
Acute Care Services
Internal Medicine
Obstetrics
Emergency Room Services
Diagnostic Services
Ambulatory Surgery Centers

BRANDS/DIVISIONS/AFFILIATES:

GROWTH PLANS/SPECIAL FEATURES:

Community Health Systems, Inc. is one of the largest operators of hospitals in the U.S. The company owns, leases and operates 155 hospitals in 21 states, with an aggregate of 26,222 licensed beds. Community Health Systems provides health care for local residents, offering a wide range of diagnostic, medical and surgical services in in-patient and out-patient settings. In 2016, the firm divested four rural hospitals, three in Mississippi and one in Florida; sold a majority ownership interest in its Home Health division to Almost Family, Inc.; and divested two hospitals in Washington. In 2017, Community Health Systems divested 16 hospitals and had definitive agreements to divest itself of 6 more.

The company offers employees medical, dental and vision insurance; flexible spending accounts; life and disability insurance; and a 401(k) savings plan.

CONTACTS:
Note: Officers with more than one job title may be intentionally listed here more than once.

Wayne Smith, CEO
Kevin Hammons, Chief Accounting Officer
Tim Hingtgen, Executive VP, Divisional
Thomas Aaron, Executive VP
Rachel Seifert, Executive VP
Lynn Simon, Other Executive Officer
Martin Bonick, President, Divisional
Michael Portacci, President, Divisional
Robert Horrar, President, Divisional
P. Smith, President, Divisional
John McClellan, President, Divisional

FINANCIAL DATA: *Note: Data for latest year may not have been available at press time.*

In U.S. $	2016	2015	2014	2013	2012	2011
Revenue	18,438,000,000	19,437,000,000	18,639,000,000	12,997,690,000	13,028,980,000	13,626,170,000
R&D Expense		68,000,000				
Operating Income	-860,000,000	1,337,000,000	1,380,000,000	899,763,000	1,210,124,000	1,134,485,000
Operating Margin %	-4.66%	6.87%	7.40%	6.92%	9.28%	8.32%
SGA Expense	9,074,000,000	9,447,999,000	9,052,000,000	6,505,159,000	6,376,760,000	5,832,706,000
Net Income	-1,721,000,000	158,000,000	92,000,000	141,203,000	265,640,000	201,948,000
Operating Cash Flow	1,137,000,000	921,000,000	1,615,000,000	1,088,719,000	1,280,120,000	1,261,908,000
Capital Expenditure	867,000,000	1,010,000,000	3,944,000,000	613,992,000	768,790,000	1,192,073,000
EBITDA	361,000,000	2,511,000,000	2,501,000,000	1,703,684,000	1,852,262,000	1,780,272,000
Return on Assets %	-7.05%	.58%	.41%	.83%	1.66%	1.35%
Return on Equity %	-61.09%	3.93%	2.60%	4.86%	10.35%	8.80%
Debt to Equity	9.15	4.18	4.16	3.02	3.46	3.66

CONTACT INFORMATION:

Phone: 615 465-7000   Fax: 615 645-7001
Toll-Free:
Address: 4000 Meridian Blvd., Franklin, TN 37067 United States

STOCK TICKER/OTHER:

Stock Ticker: CYH   Exchange: NYS
Employees: 120,000   Fiscal Year Ends: 12/31
Parent Company:

SALARIES/BONUSES:

Top Exec. Salary: $1,600,000   Bonus: $
Second Exec. Salary: Bonus: $
$850,000

OTHER THOUGHTS:

Estimated Female Officers or Directors: 18
Hot Spot for Advancement for Women/Minorities: Y

Concur Technologies Inc

www.concur.com

NAIC Code: 0

TYPES OF BUSINESS:

Software Manufacturer-Expense Reporting
Corporate Expense Management Solutions
Professional Services
Travel and Entertainment Expense Reporting Software
Meeting Expense Reporting Software

BRANDS/DIVISIONS/AFFILIATES:

Concur Travel & Expense
SAP SE

CONTACTS: Note: Officers with more than one job title may be intentionally listed here more than once.

Steve Singh, CEO
Elena Donio, Pres.
Frank Pelzer, CFO
Jessica Shapiro, VP-CMO
Mark Nelson, Chief Technology Officer
John Torrey, Executive VP, Divisional
Robert Cavanaugh, Executive VP
Elena Donio, Executive VP

GROWTH PLANS/SPECIAL FEATURES:

Concur Technologies, Inc. provides business automation process services and software products for the management of travel- and meeting-related corporate expenses. The firm's product solutions cover three primary aspects of corporate travel management: travel procurement, expense management and itinerary management. Travel procurement software automates corporate travel booking and processing functions and can be tailored to a company's specific travel policies and preferred vendors. Employees using Concur's travel procurement solutions are able to set their own travel preferences while organizations set policy through technology filters to retain control. Expense management solutions simplify the expense reporting process, while reducing costs and improving internal controls. Its software automatically imports corporate or personal credit card charges to create expense reports and reconciles transaction data from itinerary data captured at the time of booking, corporate card charges incurred during travel and electronic receipts captured directly from the supplier. Concur's itinerary management solutions enable individual business travelers and their organizations to manage and share travel itinerary information and can be imported into other Concur solutions to provide greater insight and control over travel and expense spend for organizations. Its flagship product, Concur Travel & Expense, integrates online travel booking with automated expense reporting to provide unified end-to-end corporate travel procurement and expense reporting. The firm also offers value-added services and software that integrate with the company's primary products. Additionally, Concur offers professional services including consulting, customer support and training. The company has more than 20,000 customers worldwide. Concur is owned by German software giant SAP SE, and operates as a business unit within SAP.

The firm offers employees life, disability, medical, dental and vision insurance; flexible spending accounts; and a 401(k).

FINANCIAL DATA: Note: Data for latest year may not have been available at press time.

In U.S. $	2016	2015	2014	2013	2012	2011
Revenue	1,381,972,534	724,603,419	702,588,032	545,800,000	439,825,984	349,488,000
R&D Expense						
Operating Income						
Operating Margin %						
SGA Expense						
Net Income	1,291,875,652	-20,571,530	-118,295,000	-24,394,000	-7,006,000	-10,743,000
Operating Cash Flow						
Capital Expenditure						
EBITDA						
Return on Assets %						
Return on Equity %						
Debt to Equity						

CONTACT INFORMATION:

Phone: 425 590-5000   Fax: 425 702-8828
Toll-Free: 800-401-8412
Address: 601 108th Avenue NE, Suite 1000, Bellevue, WA 98004 United States

STOCK TICKER/OTHER:

Stock Ticker: Subsidiary
Employees: 3,183
Parent Company: SAP SE

Exchange:
Fiscal Year Ends: 12/31

SALARIES/BONUSES:

Top Exec. Salary: $ Bonus: $
Second Exec. Salary: $ Bonus: $

OTHER THOUGHTS:

Estimated Female Officers or Directors: 2
Hot Spot for Advancement for Women/Minorities:

Sales, profits and employees may be estimates. Financial information, benefits and other data can change quickly and may vary from those stated here.

Constellation Brands Inc

www.cbrands.com

NAIC Code: 312130

TYPES OF BUSINESS:

Beverages-Wineries
Beer & Distilled Spirits
Wine Distribution
Bottled Water
Import/Export

BRANDS/DIVISIONS/AFFILIATES:

Corona Extra
Modelo Especial
Black Box
Inniskillin
Meiomi
Robert Mondavi
SVEDKA
Black Velvet

CONTACTS: Note: Officers with more than one job title may be intentionally listed here more than once.

Robert Sands, CEO
David Klein, CFO
William Hackett, Chairman of the Board, Divisional
Richard Sands, Chairman of the Board
Jerry Fowden, Directorf
William Newlands, Executive VP
Thomas Mullin, Executive VP
Thomas Kane, Executive VP
F. Hetterich, Executive VP
Christopher Stenzel, Executive VP

GROWTH PLANS/SPECIAL FEATURES:

Constellation Brands, Inc. is one of the largest wine companies in the world as well as a leading alcoholic beverage supplier in the U.S. and Canada, and a major producer and exporter of wine from New Zealand. The firm has three business segments: beer, wine and spirits and corporate operations and other. The beer segment markets and sells popular imported brands, such as Corona Extra, Corona Light, Victoria, Pacifico, Modelo Especial and Negra Modelo. The wine and spirits segment produces and markets premium wines in all major categories, including dessert wine, table wine and sparkling wine in the U.S. and Canada, as well as other countries. Wine brands include Black Box, Clos du Bois, Estancia, Franciscan Estate, Inniskillin, Kim Crawford, Mark West, Meiomi, Mount Veeder, Robert Mondavi, Ruffino, Saved, Simi, The Dreaming Tree and Wild Horse. Spirit products include SVEDKA, a Swedish vodka; and Black Velvet, a Canadian whisky. The corporate and other segment oversees traditional corporate-related activities, such as corporate development, corporate finance, human resources, internal audit, investor relations, legal, public relations and global information technology. In 2016, the firm sold its Canadian wine business; agreed to acquire Charles Smith Wines, LLC for approximately $120 million; and agreed to purchase a brewery operation from Grupo Modelo, a subsidiary of Anheuser-Busch InBev SA/NV, for $500 million. The brewery is expected to become operational by December 2019, with a 132-million-gallon (5 million hectoliters) production capacity.

FINANCIAL DATA: Note: Data for latest year may not have been available at press time.

In U.S. $	2016	2015	2014	2013	2012	2011
Revenue	6,548,400,000	6,028,000,000	4,867,700,000	2,796,100,000	2,654,300,000	
R&D Expense						
Operating Income	1,765,100,000	1,500,200,000	2,437,700,000	522,900,000	486,500,000	
Operating Margin %	26.95%	24.88%	50.07%	18.70%	18.32%	
SGA Expense	1,177,200,000	1,078,400,000	895,100,000	584,700,000	521,500,000	
Net Income	1,054,900,000	839,300,000	1,943,100,000	387,800,000	445,000,000	
Operating Cash Flow	1,413,700,000	1,081,000,000	826,200,000	556,300,000	784,100,000	
Capital Expenditure	891,300,000	719,400,000	223,500,000	62,100,000	68,400,000	
EBITDA	2,036,100,000	1,719,300,000	2,688,500,000	865,700,000	825,300,000	
Return on Assets %	6.57%	5.70%	17.71%	5.25%	6.23%	
Return on Equity %	17.11%	15.61%	49.55%	14.00%	17.02%	
Debt to Equity	1.03	1.23	1.27	1.14	0.90	

CONTACT INFORMATION:

Phone: 585 678-7100   Fax: 585 678-7103
Toll-Free: 888-724-2169
Address: 207 High Point Dr., Bldg. 100, Victor, NY 14564 United States

STOCK TICKER/OTHER:

Stock Ticker: STZ   Exchange: NYS
Employees: 8,700   Fiscal Year Ends: 02/28
Parent Company:

SALARIES/BONUSES:

Top Exec. Salary: $1,310,383   Bonus: $
Second Exec. Salary: Bonus: $
$1,284,849

OTHER THOUGHTS:

Estimated Female Officers or Directors: 2
Hot Spot for Advancement for Women/Minorities:

Container Store Inc (The)

NAIC Code: 442299

TYPES OF BUSINESS:

Household Goods
Luggage
Packing Materials
Specialty Boxes
Online Sales

BRANDS/DIVISIONS/AFFILIATES:

Leonard Green & Partners LP
Container Store (The)
Elfa International AB
Elfa
Contained Home

CONTACTS: Note: Officers with more than one job title may be intentionally listed here more than once.

Anders Rothstein, CEO, Subsidiary
Melissa Reiff, CEO
Jodi Taylor, CFO
William Tindell, Chairman of the Board
Sharon Tindell, Director
Jeffrey Miller, Vice President

GROWTH PLANS/SPECIAL FEATURES:

The Container Store, Inc., controlled by private equity firm Leonard Green & Partners LP, is a national retailer selling organizational and storage products. Products include drawer and cabinet organizers, luggage, tool racks, packing materials, specialty and shipping boxes and locker organizers, among many other household objects designed to manage space efficiently. Store interiors have an open layout which is divided into sections with brightly colored banners such as Closet, Kitchen and Laundry. The company's operations are divided into two segments: The Container Store, made up of retail stores, website and call center; and Elfa, a design and manufacturing business. The firm's stores average 25,000 square feet and carry more than 11,000 items. Most the company's approximately 86 stores are located in 31 states and Washington, D.C. The Container Store processes and ships its entire product line from its 725,000-square-foot distribution center in Coppell, Texas. The company's website allows customers to view and order store products, plan organizational and storage projects and receive free customized assistance from in-store space planning experts. In 2016, this segment made up approximately 92% of the firm's total net sales. The firm is the exclusive distributor of Elfa International AB, a wholly owned Swedish subsidiary, which designs and manufactures component-based shelving and drawer systems, as well as made-to-measure sliding doors. Elfa represented 8% of total net sales, and has four manufacturing facilities located in Sweden (2), Finland and Poland. Contained Home is the firm's in-home, customized design and organization service, where expert organizers go directly to customer homes.

The company offers its employees a 40% discount on merchandise; 401(k); paid vacation; employee assistance program; domestic partner benefits; corporate wellness program; transportation benefits; pet insurance; paid pregnancy disability leave; and medical, life, dental and vision insurance.

FINANCIAL DATA: Note: Data for latest year may not have been available at press time.

In U.S. $	2016	2015	2014	2013	2012	2011
Revenue	794,630,000	781,866,000	748,538,000	706,757,000	633,619,000	
R&D Expense						
Operating Income	24,861,000	46,971,000	31,027,000	24,142,000	-6,628,000	
Operating Margin %	3.12%	6.00%	4.14%	3.41%	-1.04%	
SGA Expense	404,399,000	382,439,000	376,080,000	338,942,000	298,868,000	
Net Income	5,142,000	22,673,000	8,166,000	-130,000	-30,671,000	
Operating Cash Flow	42,307,000	64,625,000	50,762,000	45,186,000	42,203,000	
Capital Expenditure	46,431,000	48,740,000	48,565,000	48,559,000	40,953,000	
EBITDA	59,091,000	77,982,000	60,151,000	46,359,000	20,823,000	
Return on Assets %	.67%	2.92%	-6.71%	-12.06%	-14.63%	
Return on Equity %	2.51%	11.36%	-23.96%	-38.80%	-46.88%	
Debt to Equity	1.55	1.61	1.66	1.18	1.25	

CONTACT INFORMATION:

Phone: 972-538-6900   Fax: 972-538-7623
Toll-Free: 800-733-3532
Address: 500 Freeport Pkwy., Coppell, TX 75019 United States

STOCK TICKER/OTHER:

Stock Ticker: TCS   Exchange: NYS
Employees: 5,100   Fiscal Year Ends: 03/31
Parent Company: Leonard Green & Partners LP

SALARIES/BONUSES:

Top Exec. Salary: $675,000   Bonus: $
Second Exec. Salary: $625,000   Bonus: $

OTHER THOUGHTS:

Estimated Female Officers or Directors: 5
Hot Spot for Advancement for Women/Minorities: Y

Convergys Corporation

www.convergys.com

NAIC Code: 561422

TYPES OF BUSINESS:

Call Centers
Outsourced Customer Care

BRANDS/DIVISIONS/AFFILIATES:

Stream Global Services Inc

CONTACTS: Note: Officers with more than one job title may be intentionally listed here more than once.

Andrea Ayers, CEO
Andre Valentine, CFO
Jeffrey Fox, Chairman of the Board
Taylor Greenwald, Chief Accounting Officer
Jarrod Pontius, Chief Administrative Officer
Marjorie Connelly, COO

GROWTH PLANS/SPECIAL FEATURES:

Convergys Corporation is a global provider of customer care and outsourced contact center services. The firm's customer management business provides outsourced agent-assisted and self-service customer care services as well as consulting and technology services to the in-house customer care market. Phone and web-based agent-assisted service channels provide customers with assistance across the entire customer lifecycle. The company delivers these services using a variety of tools, including computer telephony integration, interactive voice response, advanced speech recognition, knowledge-based management and the internet through agent-assisted and self-service channels. The firm has about 150 contact centers located in 34 countries, assisting customers in approximately 58 languages. These contact centers average approximately 78,000 square feet each, and have approximately 99,700 production workstations that provide service 24 hours a day, 365 days a year. Annually, it handles more than 4 billion customer contacts. Convergys primarily services companies in the automotive, communications, financial services, government, health care, manufacturing, retail, technology and transportation sectors. Its largest client, AT&T, accounts for approximately 15.3% of its annual revenue. Other significant clients include Comcast Corp. and DIRECTV Group, Inc. In 2016, the company acquired buw Holdings, a German customer care agency, expanding Convergys' presence in Germany's growing contact center market. Additionally, in 2016, the firm partnered with Telia Norge AS to supply its Network IVR Solution.

The firm offers its employees life, AD&D, medical, dental and vision insurance; a 401(k) plan; an employee stock purchase plan; tuition reimbursement; an employee assistance program; and an employee discount program.

FINANCIAL DATA: Note: Data for latest year may not have been available at press time.

In U.S. $	2016	2015	2014	2013	2012	2011
Revenue	2,913,600,000	2,950,600,000	2,855,500,000	2,046,100,000	2,005,000,000	2,262,000,000
R&D Expense		7,100,000	7,700,000	8,200,000	10,800,000	49,300,000
Operating Income	204,900,000	194,400,000	150,800,000	137,400,000	38,600,000	168,300,000
Operating Margin %	7.03%	6.58%	5.28%	6.71%	1.92%	7.44%
SGA Expense	688,800,000	695,900,000	714,800,000	467,700,000	477,200,000	527,400,000
Net Income	143,000,000	169,000,000	120,000,000	60,900,000	100,600,000	334,800,000
Operating Cash Flow	305,400,000	249,300,000	261,000,000	210,000,000	113,000,000	196,600,000
Capital Expenditure	87,000,000	109,200,000	116,700,000	63,800,000	98,400,000	88,300,000
EBITDA	354,300,000	363,700,000	316,200,000	233,300,000	131,600,000	559,800,000
Return on Assets %	6.04%	6.93%	5.36%	3.04%	4.61%	15.04%
Return on Equity %	11.03%	13.50%	9.53%	4.57%	7.22%	25.79%
Debt to Equity	0.22	0.26	0.35	0.04	0.04	0.08

CONTACT INFORMATION:

Phone: 513 723-7000   Fax: 513 723-2048
Toll-Free:
Address: 201 E. Foruth St., Cincinnati, OH 45202 United States

STOCK TICKER/OTHER:

Stock Ticker: CVG
Employees: 130,000
Parent Company:

Exchange: NYS
Fiscal Year Ends: 12/31

SALARIES/BONUSES:

Top Exec. Salary: $925,000   Bonus: $
Second Exec. Salary: $575,000   Bonus: $

OTHER THOUGHTS:

Estimated Female Officers or Directors: 3
Hot Spot for Advancement for Women/Minorities: Y

Cooper Companies Inc

www.coopercos.com

NAIC Code: 339100

TYPES OF BUSINESS:

Medical Devices
Contact Lenses
Gynecological Instruments
Diagnostic Products

BRANDS/DIVISIONS/AFFILIATES:

CooperVision Inc
CooperSurgical Inc
Proclear
Phosphorylcholine (PC) Technology
Wallace

CONTACTS: *Note: Officers with more than one job title may be intentionally listed here more than once.*

Robert Weiss, CEO
A. Bender, Chairman of the Board
Carol Kaufman, Chief Administrative Officer
Daniel McBride, COO
Allan Rubenstein, Director
Albert White, Executive VP
Randal Golden, General Counsel
Paul Remmell, President, Subsidiary
Kim Duncan, Vice President, Divisional

GROWTH PLANS/SPECIAL FEATURES:

Cooper Companies, Inc. develops, manufactures and markets healthcare products, primarily medical devices. The company operates through two business units: CooperVision, Inc. (CVI) and CooperSurgical, Inc. (CSI). CVI develops, manufactures and markets a broad range of contact lenses, including disposable spherical and specialty contact lenses. It is a leading manufacturer of toric lenses, which correct astigmatism; multifocal lenses for presbyopia, the blurring of vision due to advancing age; and spherical lenses, including hydrogel lenses, which correct the most common near- and far-sighted visual defects. CVI offers single-use, two-week, monthly and quarterly disposable sphere and toric lenses as well as custom toric lenses to correct a high degree of astigmatism. CVI's Proclear line of spherical, toric and multifocal lenses are manufactured with omafilcon, a material that incorporates its proprietary Phosphorylcholine (PC) Technology to enhance tissue-device compatibility. CVI's products are primarily manufactured at its facilities in the U.S., the U.K., Hungary, Costa Rico and Puerto Rico. It distributes its products out of West Henrietta, New York; Fareham, U.K.; Liege, Belgium; and various smaller international distribution facilities. CSI develops, manufactures and markets medical devices, diagnostic products and surgical instruments and accessories used primarily by gynecologists and obstetricians. The subsidiary manufactures and distributes its products at its facilities in Trumbull, Connecticut; Malov, Denmark; Pasadena, California; Stafford, Texas; and Berlin, Germany. In November 2016, the firm acquired Wallace, the in-vitro fertilization (IVF) segment of Smiths Medical International Ltd.

FINANCIAL DATA: *Note: Data for latest year may not have been available at press time.*

In U.S. $	2016	2015	2014	2013	2012	2011
Revenue	1,966,814,000	1,797,060,000	1,717,776,000	1,587,725,000	1,445,136,000	1,330,835,000
R&D Expense	65,411,000	69,589,000	66,259,000	58,827,000	51,730,000	43,581,000
Operating Income	324,080,000	236,671,000	306,486,000	305,945,000	283,398,000	227,556,000
Operating Margin %	16.47%	13.16%	17.84%	19.26%	19.61%	17.09%
SGA Expense	722,798,000	712,543,000	683,115,000	610,735,000	564,903,000	513,138,000
Net Income	273,917,000	203,523,000	269,856,000	296,151,000	248,339,000	175,430,000
Operating Cash Flow	509,637,000	390,970,000	454,823,000	415,925,000	315,121,000	336,281,000
Capital Expenditure	152,640,000	243,023,000	238,065,000	178,127,000	99,779,000	103,665,000
EBITDA	520,097,000	424,991,000	442,700,000	446,788,000	398,437,000	308,255,000
Return on Assets %	6.13%	4.56%	7.10%	9.74%	8.92%	6.81%
Return on Equity %	10.20%	7.77%	10.84%	12.88%	12.02%	9.73%
Debt to Equity	0.41	0.41	0.49	0.12	0.15	0.16

CONTACT INFORMATION:

Phone: 925 460-3600   Fax: 949 597-0662
Toll-Free:
Address: 6140 Stoneridge Mall Rd., Ste. 590, Pleasanton, CA 94588
United States

STOCK TICKER/OTHER:

Stock Ticker: COO
Employees: 10,600
Parent Company:

Exchange: NYS
Fiscal Year Ends: 10/31

SALARIES/BONUSES:

Top Exec. Salary: $875,000   Bonus: $279,344
Second Exec. Salary: $495,000   Bonus: $108,671

OTHER THOUGHTS:

Estimated Female Officers or Directors: 2
Hot Spot for Advancement for Women/Minorities: Y

Corning Inc

NAIC Code: 327212

www.corning.com

TYPES OF BUSINESS:
Glass & Optical Fiber Manufacturing
Glass Substrates for LCDs
Optical Switching Products
Photonic Modules & Components
Networking Devices
Semiconductor Materials
Laboratory Supplies
Emissions Control Products

BRANDS/DIVISIONS/AFFILIATES:
Samsung Corning Precision Materials Co Ltd
Vascade
LEAF
SMF-28e
ClearCurve
InfiniCor
Alliance Fiber Optic Products Inc
STRAN Technologies

CONTACTS: Note: Officers with more than one job title may be intentionally listed here more than once.
Wendell Weeks, CEO
James Clappin, President, Divisional
R. Tripeny, CFO
Edward Schlesinger, Chief Accounting Officer
Lisa Ferrero, Chief Administrative Officer
David Morse, Chief Technology Officer
Clark Kinlin, Executive VP
Eric Musser, Executive VP, Divisional
Martin Curran, Executive VP
Lewis Steverson, General Counsel
Lawrence McRae, Other Corporate Officer
Jeffrey Evenson, Other Executive Officer
Christine Pambianchi, Senior VP, Divisional
Mark Rogus, Senior VP
Mark Rogus, Senior VP

GROWTH PLANS/SPECIAL FEATURES:
Corning, Inc. is an international technology-based corporation. The firm operates in five business segments: display technologies, optical communications, specialty materials, environmental technologies and life sciences. The display technologies segment manufactures glass substrates for active matrix liquid crystal displays (LCDs), used in notebook computers, flat panel desktop monitor and LCD televisions. Corning owns 57.5% of Samsung Corning Precision Materials Co. Ltd., which produces glass substrates using a proprietary fusion process. The optical communications segment is divided into carrier network and enterprise network. The carrier network products include Vascade submarine optical fibers for use in submarine networks; LEAF optical fiber for long-haul, regional and metropolitan networks; SMF-28e single mode optical fiber for additional transmission wavelengths in metropolitan and access networks, and ClearCurve fiber for use in multiple dwelling units. The enterprise network product portfolio includes ClearCurve ultra-bendable multimode fiber for data centers and other enterprise network applications; InfiniCor fibers for local area networks; and ClearCurve VSDN ultra-bendable optical fiber designed to support emerging high-speed interconnects between computers and other consumer electronics devices. The specialty materials segment offers products such as glass windows for space shuttles and optical components for high-tech industries and includes the firm's Gorilla glass product line of protective cover glass for portable display devices. In its environmental technologies segment, Corning produces ceramic products for emissions and pollution control, such as gasoline/diesel substrate and filter products. The life sciences segment manufactures laboratory products such as consumables (plastic vessels, specialty surfaces and media), as well as general labware and equipment used for cell culture research, bioprocessing, genomics, drug discovery, microbiology and chemistry. In 2016, the firm acquired Alliance Fiber Optic Products, Inc.; and wholly-acquired STRAN Technologies, a U.S.-based producer of harsh environment and tactical interconnect products and services.

FINANCIAL DATA: Note: Data for latest year may not have been available at press time.

In U.S. $	2016	2015	2014	2013	2012	2011
Revenue	9,390,000,000	9,111,000,000	9,715,000,000	7,819,000,000	8,012,000,000	7,890,000,000
R&D Expense	742,000,000	769,000,000	815,000,000	710,000,000	745,000,000	671,000,000
Operating Income	1,391,000,000	1,322,000,000	1,931,000,000	1,371,000,000	1,321,000,000	1,694,000,000
Operating Margin %	14.81%	14.50%	19.87%	17.53%	16.48%	21.47%
SGA Expense	1,472,000,000	1,523,000,000	1,211,000,000	1,126,000,000	1,165,000,000	1,033,000,000
Net Income	3,695,000,000	1,339,000,000	2,472,000,000	1,961,000,000	1,728,000,000	2,805,000,000
Operating Cash Flow	2,521,000,000	2,809,000,000	4,709,000,000	2,787,000,000	3,206,000,000	3,189,000,000
Capital Expenditure	1,130,000,000	1,250,000,000	1,076,000,000	1,019,000,000	1,801,000,000	2,432,000,000
EBITDA	5,046,000,000	2,810,000,000	4,891,000,000	3,595,000,000	3,225,000,000	4,259,000,000
Return on Assets %	12.74%	4.23%	8.44%	6.77%	6.03%	10.45%
Return on Equity %	22.42%	6.93%	12.22%	9.19%	8.11%	13.86%
Debt to Equity	0.23	0.23	0.16	0.15	0.15	0.11

CONTACT INFORMATION:
Phone: 607 974-9000   Fax: 607 974-8688
Toll-Free:
Address: 1 Riverfront Plaza, Corning, NY 14831 United States

STOCK TICKER/OTHER:
Stock Ticker: GLW   Exchange: NYS
Employees: 40,700   Fiscal Year Ends: 12/31
Parent Company:

SALARIES/BONUSES:
Top Exec. Salary: $1,337,740   Bonus: $
Second Exec. Salary: Bonus: $
$731,971

OTHER THOUGHTS:
Estimated Female Officers or Directors: 1
Hot Spot for Advancement for Women/Minorities: Y

Sales, profits and employees may be estimates. Financial information, benefits and other data can change quickly and may vary from those stated here.

CoStar Group Inc

NAIC Code: 519130

www.costar.com

TYPES OF BUSINESS:

Online Commercial Real Estate Information

BRANDS/DIVISIONS/AFFILIATES:

CoStar
LoopNet
Apartments.com
BizBuySell
LandsofAmerica
BizQuest.com
LandAndFarm
Office Underwriting Report

CONTACTS: *Note: Officers with more than one job title may be intentionally listed here more than once.*

Andrew Florance, CEO
Scott Wheeler, CFO
Michael Klein, Chairman of the Board
Rebecca Carr, Chief Marketing Officer
Frank Simuro, Chief Technology Officer
Matthew Linnington, Executive VP, Divisional
Frank Carchedi, Executive VP, Divisional
Giles Newman, Managing Director, Geographical
Frederick Saint, President, Subsidiary
Cameron Stewart, President, Subsidiary
Jonathan Coleman, Secretary
Lisa Ruggles, Senior VP, Divisional
Donna Tanenbaum, Vice President, Divisional

GROWTH PLANS/SPECIAL FEATURES:

CoStar Group, Inc. provides information, analytics and online marketplaces to the commercial real estate industry in the U.S. and the U.K. The firm provides industry professionals and consumers of commercial real estate and apartments ways to explore and complete transactions. The company's five flagship brands include: CoStar, LoopNet, Apartments.com, BizBuySell and LandsofAmerica. Subscription-based information services comprise the CoStar suite, which is sold as a platform consisting of CoStar Property Professional, CoStar COMPS Professional and CoStar Tenant, and through its mobile application, CoStarGo. LoopNet is an online marketplace that enables commercial property owners, landlords and real estate agents working on their behalf to list properties for sale or for lease, and to submit detailed information about property listings. Apartments.com comprises a network of apartment marketing sites, including ApartmentFinder.com and ApartmentHomeLiving.com. This network of subscription-based services offers renters a searchable database of apartment listings and provides professional property management companies and landlords with an advertising destination. BizBuySell and BizQuest.com are leading online marketplaces for operating businesses for sale. Business sellers pay a fee to list their operating businesses for sale, and interested buyers can search the respective sites' listings for free. These sites also allow interested business buyers to search hundreds of franchise opportunities, and franchisors can list their availabilities in the directory on a cost-per-lead basis. LandsofAmerica and LandAndFarm are online marketplaces for rural land for sale. Sellers pay a fee to list their land for sale, and interested buyers can search the listings for free. In addition, CoStar's market analytics platform, Office Underwriting Report, delivers analytics of more than 700,000 office properties in CoStar's database.

The firm offers employees medical, dental and vision insurance; a 401(k); an employee assistance program; tuition reimbursement; life insurance; and disability coverage.

FINANCIAL DATA: *Note: Data for latest year may not have been available at press time.*

In U.S. $	2016	2015	2014	2013	2012	2011
Revenue	837,630,000	711,764,000	575,936,000	440,943,000	349,936,000	251,738,000
R&D Expense	76,400,000	65,760,000	55,426,000	46,757,000	32,756,000	20,037,000
Operating Income	144,905,000	11,455,000	80,878,000	54,154,000	27,440,000	21,771,000
Operating Margin %	17.29%	1.60%	14.04%	12.28%	7.84%	8.64%
SGA Expense	419,780,000	417,733,000	254,221,000	195,664,000	161,267,000	119,526,000
Net Income	85,071,000	-3,465,000	44,869,000	29,734,000	9,915,000	14,656,000
Operating Cash Flow	195,944,000	131,245,000	143,909,000	108,298,000	86,126,000	25,685,000
Capital Expenditure	18,766,000	35,061,000	27,444,000	19,042,000	14,834,000	15,013,000
EBITDA	216,843,000	90,524,000	151,766,000	94,538,000	60,718,000	34,623,000
Return on Assets %	3.98%	-.16%	2.68%	2.45%	1.02%	2.42%
Return on Equity %	5.32%	-.22%	3.67%	3.39%	1.33%	2.81%
Debt to Equity	0.18	0.21	0.24	0.13	0.18	

CONTACT INFORMATION:

Phone: 202-346-6500　　Fax: 202 346-6370
Toll-Free: 800-204-5960
Address: 1331 L Street NW, Northwest, WA 20005 United States

STOCK TICKER/OTHER:

Stock Ticker: CSGP　　　　　　　Exchange: NAS
Employees: 3,064　　　　　　　　Fiscal Year Ends: 12/31
Parent Company:

SALARIES/BONUSES:

Top Exec. Salary: $696,126　　Bonus: $
Second Exec. Salary: $434,194　　Bonus: $200,000

OTHER THOUGHTS:

Estimated Female Officers or Directors:
Hot Spot for Advancement for Women/Minorities: Y

Costco Wholesale Corporation

NAIC Code: 452910

www.costco.com

TYPES OF BUSINESS:

Warehouse Clubs, Retail
Food
Health & Beauty Products
Electronics
Furniture
Apparel
Automotive Supplies
Gasoline Sales

BRANDS/DIVISIONS/AFFILIATES:

Costco Wholesale Industries
Kirkland Signature

CONTACTS: *Note: Officers with more than one job title may be intentionally listed here more than once.*

Jeffrey Brotman, Chairman of the Board
James Sinegal, Co-Founder
Dennis Zook, COO, Divisional
Joseph Portera, COO, Divisional
John McKay, COO, Divisional
James Murphy, COO, Divisional
Roland Vachris, COO, Divisional
W. Jelinek, Director
Timothy Rose, Executive VP, Divisional
Franz Lazarus, Executive VP, Divisional
Richard Galanti, Executive VP
Paul Moulton, Executive VP
Daniel Hines, Senior VP

GROWTH PLANS/SPECIAL FEATURES:

Costco Wholesale Corporation operates membership warehouses based on the concept that offering members very low prices on a limited selection of branded and private-label products will produce high sales volumes and rapid inventory turnover. This rapid turnover, combined with volume purchasing, efficient distribution and reduced handling of merchandise in self-service warehouse facilities, allows the firm to operate at significantly lower margins than traditional discount retailers. Costco buys the majority of its merchandise directly from manufacturers for shipment to warehouses or to consolidation points, minimizing freight and handling costs. Products include health and beauty aids, cleaning supplies, foods, alcohol, appliances, electronics, tools, office supplies, furniture, automotive supplies, apparel, cameras, house wares and books. Stores contain other features, including pharmacies, print shops, photo labs and gas stations. Costco's private products are marketed under the Kirkland Signature label brand. It has three types of memberships: executive, business and gold star. Memberships are designed to build customer loyalty and start at $55 per year (for U.S. and Canadian operations). The firm operates 729 warehouses, including 508 in the U.S. and Puerto Rico; 94 in Canada; 37 in Mexico; 28 in three nations within the U.K.; 25 in Japan; 13 in Taiwan; 13 in South Korea; eight in Australia; two in Spain; and one each in Iceland and France. The stores average approximately 144,000 square feet and stock distinct products including upscale items such as jewelry and wines. Costco Wholesale Industries, a division of the company, operates manufacturing businesses, including special food packaging, optical laboratories, meat processing and jewelry distribution. The company also operates eCommerce websites in the U.S., Canada, the U.K. and Mexico.

Costco offers employees health, dental, vision, life insurance, short- and long-term disability and prescription coverage; 401(k); and employee assistance plans.

FINANCIAL DATA: *Note: Data for latest year may not have been available at press time.*

In U.S. $	2016	2015	2014	2013	2012	2011
Revenue	118,719,000,000	116,199,000,000	112,640,000,000	105,156,000,000	99,137,000,000	88,915,000,000
R&D Expense						
Operating Income	3,672,000,000	3,624,000,000	3,220,000,000	3,053,000,000	2,759,000,000	2,439,000,000
Operating Margin %	3.09%	3.11%	2.85%	2.90%	2.78%	2.74%
SGA Expense	12,146,000,000	11,510,000,000	10,962,000,000	10,155,000,000	9,555,000,000	8,728,001,000
Net Income	2,350,000,000	2,377,000,000	2,058,000,000	2,039,000,000	1,709,000,000	1,462,000,000
Operating Cash Flow	3,292,000,000	4,285,000,000	3,984,000,000	3,437,000,000	3,057,000,000	3,198,000,000
Capital Expenditure	2,649,000,000	2,393,000,000	1,993,000,000	2,083,000,000	1,480,000,000	1,290,000,000
EBITDA	5,007,000,000	4,855,000,000	4,339,000,000	4,096,000,000	3,770,000,000	3,354,000,000
Return on Assets %	7.05%	7.15%	6.50%	7.10%	6.34%	5.78%
Return on Equity %	20.70%	20.74%	17.79%	17.58%	14.02%	12.80%
Debt to Equity	0.33	0.45	0.41	0.46	0.11	0.10

CONTACT INFORMATION:

Phone: 425 313-8100   Fax: 425 313-8103
Toll-Free: 800-774-2678
Address: 999 Lake Dr., Issaquah, WA 98027 United States

STOCK TICKER/OTHER:

Stock Ticker: COST   Exchange: NAS
Employees: 218,000   Fiscal Year Ends: 08/31
Parent Company:

SALARIES/BONUSES:

Top Exec. Salary: $700,000   Bonus: $81,600
Second Exec. Salary: $700,001   Bonus: $52,640

OTHER THOUGHTS:

Estimated Female Officers or Directors: 4
Hot Spot for Advancement for Women/Minorities: Y

Sales, profits and employees may be estimates. Financial information, benefits and other data can change quickly and may vary from those stated here.

Cox Automotive Inc
NAIC Code: 519130

www.coxautoinc.com

TYPES OF BUSINESS:
Internet Search Portals

BRANDS/DIVISIONS/AFFILIATES:
Cox Entertainment Inc
Cox Automotive Australia
Alliance Inspection Management
Dealer-Auction.com
Ready Logistics
Kelley Blue Book
NextGear Capital
AutoTrader

CONTACTS: *Note: Officers with more than one job title may be intentionally listed here more than once.*
Sandy Schwartz, Pres.
Mark O'Neil, COO
Neil Johnston, CFO
John Kovac, CMO
Rock Anderson, Jr., Chief People Officer

GROWTH PLANS/SPECIAL FEATURES:
Cox Automotive, Inc. provides automotive resources and tools for consumers, dealers and manufacturers for the purpose of maximizing value at every step of the car buying and selling process. These sources and tools include leading brands and solutions such as Alliance Inspection Management, a provider of wholesale vehicle inspection services for auto manufacturers, rental fleets, dealers, auctions, finance companies and consumers; Dealer-Auction.com, an online trade-only auction of vehicles direct from franchise dealers; Ready Logistics, offering end-to-end logistics services and solutions for shippers and transporters by connecting auctions, dealers, commercial and consumer clients nationwide; Kelley Blue Book, a provider of new and used vehicle information; and NextGear Capital, a provider of lending products, including lines of credit, for dealers to purchase new and used inventory at over 1,000 auto and specialty auctions and other inventory sources throughout the U.S., Canada, the U.K. and Ireland. Other brands and solutions include BitAuto, DealShield, Jingzhengu, Modix, VINsolutions, AutoStreets, Dealer.com, HomeNet, Motors.co.uk, RMS Automotive, XTime, AutoTrader, Central Dispatch, DealerTrack, Incadea, Mahindra First Choice and Vauto. Cox Automotive, a wholly-owned subsidiary of Cox Entertainment, Inc., partners with more than 40,000 dealers, uniting over 25 brands in order to provide its vehicle buying/selling services on a global scale. In early-2017, the firm combined CarsGuide with DealerSolutions, Sell My Car and certain Manheim businesses to form Cox Automotive Australia.

FINANCIAL DATA: *Note: Data for latest year may not have been available at press time.*

In U.S. $	2016	2015	2014	2013	2012	2011
Revenue	7,300,000,000	7,100,000,000	6,600,000,000	6,200,000,000	7,000,000,000	
R&D Expense						
Operating Income						
Operating Margin %						
SGA Expense						
Net Income						
Operating Cash Flow						
Capital Expenditure						
EBITDA						
Return on Assets %						
Return on Equity %						
Debt to Equity						

CONTACT INFORMATION:
Phone: Fax:
Toll-Free: 855-449-0010
Address: 3003 Summit Blvd., Ste. 200, Atlanta, GA 30319 United States

STOCK TICKER/OTHER:
Stock Ticker: Subsidiary
Employees: 33,000
Parent Company: Cox Entertainment Inc

Exchange:
Fiscal Year Ends: 12/31

SALARIES/BONUSES:
Top Exec. Salary: $ Bonus: $
Second Exec. Salary: $ Bonus: $

OTHER THOUGHTS:
Estimated Female Officers or Directors:
Hot Spot for Advancement for Women/Minorities:

Cox Communications Inc

www.cox.com/residential/home.cox

NAIC Code: 517110

TYPES OF BUSINESS:

Cable TV Service and Internet Access
Digital Cable TV Service
Cable-Based Internet Access
Local & Long-Distance Phone Service
Commercial Telecommunications Services
Data & Video Transport Services

BRANDS/DIVISIONS/AFFILIATES:

Cox Enterprises Inc
Cox Business Services
Managed IP PBX
Cox Media
Valpak
Kudzu.com
Unite Private Networks

CONTACTS: Note: Officers with more than one job title may be intentionally listed here more than once.

Patrick J. Esser, Pres.
Jill Campbell, COO
Mark Bowser, CFO
Mark Greatrex, CMO
Len Barlik, CHRO
Kevin Hart, CTO
Len Barlik, Exec. VP-Prod. Mgmt. & Dev.
Asheesh Saksena, Chief Strategy Officer
Joseph J. Rooney, Sr. VP-Social Media, Advertising & Brand Mktg.
William (Bill) J. Fitzsimmons, Chief Acct. Officer
Philip G. Meeks, Sr. VP-Cox Bus.
Jennifer W. Hightower, Sr. VP-Law & Policy
David Pugliese, Sr. VP-Product Mktg.
Mark A. Kaish, Sr. VP-Tech. Oper.
George Richter, VP-Supply Chain Mgmt.

GROWTH PLANS/SPECIAL FEATURES:

Cox Communications, Inc., owned by Cox Enterprises, Inc., is a broadband communications and entertainment company, serving millions of customers throughout the U.S. Cox offers advanced digital video, high speed internet, and local and long distance telephone services over its own nationwide IP network in 18 states. Cox Business Services provides data, video and voice solutions to small and regional businesses such as schools and universities, government organizations and financial institutions. The firm's Managed IP PBX service provides small business customers that have limited internal information technology departments with telecommunication systems that are monitored and managed around the clock by Cox Business. Cox Media offers national and local cable advertising in traditional spot and new media formats, along with promotional opportunities and production services, and owns Valpak, a leading direct marketing company in the U.S. The company also maintains Kudzu.com, an online directory that aggregates user reviews and ratings on local businesses, merchants and service providers. In July 2016, the company made a strategic investment in Unite Private Networks, a provider of high-bandwidth fiber-based communications networks to the education, government, enterprise business, data centers and healthcare industries.

FINANCIAL DATA: Note: Data for latest year may not have been available at press time.

In U.S. $	2016	2015	2014	2013	2012	2011
Revenue	10,714,000,000	10,650,000,000	10,400,000,000	9,900,000,000	9,600,000,000	9,400,000,000
R&D Expense						
Operating Income						
Operating Margin %						
SGA Expense						
Net Income						
Operating Cash Flow						
Capital Expenditure						
EBITDA						
Return on Assets %						
Return on Equity %						
Debt to Equity						

CONTACT INFORMATION:

Phone: 404-843-5000   Fax: 404-843-5939
Toll-Free: 888-566-7751
Address: 1400 Lake Hearn Dr., Atlanta, GA 30319 United States

STOCK TICKER/OTHER:

Stock Ticker: Subsidiary
Employees: 22,600
Parent Company: Cox Enterprises Inc

Exchange:
Fiscal Year Ends: 12/31

SALARIES/BONUSES:

Top Exec. Salary: $ Bonus: $
Second Exec. Salary: $ Bonus: $

OTHER THOUGHTS:

Estimated Female Officers or Directors: 3
Hot Spot for Advancement for Women/Minorities: Y

Cox Enterprises Inc

www.coxenterprises.com

NAIC Code: 515120

TYPES OF BUSINESS:

Cable Television and Internet Services
Television Broadcasting
Newspaper Publishing
Radio Stations
Online News, Information and Services Sites
Auctions
Automotive E-Commerce
Technology Products

BRANDS/DIVISIONS/AFFILIATES:

Cox Communications Inc
Cox Business Services
Cox Media Group
Cox Automotive
autotrader.com
Kelley Blue Book
motors.co.uk
COMET

CONTACTS: Note: Officers with more than one job title may be intentionally listed here more than once.

John M. Dyer, CEO
Alexander C. Taylor, Exec. VP
Jimmy W. Hayes, Pres.
Dallas S. Clement, CFO
Marybeth N. Leamer, Exec. VP-Admin.
Shauna Sullivan Muhl, VP-Legal
Roberto I. Jimenez, VP-Corp. Comm. & Public Affairs
J. Lacey Lewis, Sr. VP-Finance
Patrick J. Esser, Pres., Cox Comm.
Sanford Schwartz, Pres., Manheim
Bill Hoffman, Pres., Cox Media Group
Kathy Decker, Treas.
James Cox Kennedy, Chmn.

GROWTH PLANS/SPECIAL FEATURES:

Cox Enterprises, Inc., through subsidiary Cox Communications, Inc., is a broadband communications and entertainment company, serving millions of customers throughout the U.S. Cox offers advanced digital video, high-speed internet and local and long distance telephone services over its own nationwide IP network. Cox Business Services provides data, video and voice solutions to small and regional businesses such as schools and universities, government organizations and financial institutions. The firm provides small business customers that have limited internal information technology departments with telecommunication systems that are monitored and managed around the clock by Cox Business. Cox Media Group offers national and local cable advertising in traditional spot and new media formats, along with promotional opportunities and production services. Cox Automotive owns significant automobile industry websites and marketing platforms, including autotrader.com, Kelley Blue Book and motors.co.uk. In April 2017, the firm launched COMET (Cox Media Technology), a unified programmatic platform that connects buyers and sellers across all advertising channels, including desktop, mobile, video and TV. COMET's platform leverages artificial intelligence and anti-fraud technology alongside datasets from Cox Automotive, Cox Communications and Cox Media to provide buyers and sellers with tools that increase return on investment.

FINANCIAL DATA: Note: Data for latest year may not have been available at press time.

In U.S. $	2016	2015	2014	2013	2012	2011
Revenue	20,250,000,000	18,885,000,000	17,450,000,000	15,920,000,000	15,300,000,000	14,700,000,000
R&D Expense						
Operating Income						
Operating Margin %						
SGA Expense						
Net Income						
Operating Cash Flow						
Capital Expenditure						
EBITDA						
Return on Assets %						
Return on Equity %						
Debt to Equity						

CONTACT INFORMATION:

Phone: 678-645-0000   Fax:
Toll-Free:
Address: 6205 Peachtree Dunwoody Rd. 1400 Lake Hearn Dr., Atlanta, GA 30328 United States

STOCK TICKER/OTHER:

Stock Ticker: Private
Employees: 60,000
Parent Company:

Exchange:
Fiscal Year Ends: 12/31

SALARIES/BONUSES:

Top Exec. Salary: $ Bonus: $
Second Exec. Salary: $ Bonus: $

OTHER THOUGHTS:

Estimated Female Officers or Directors: 7
Hot Spot for Advancement for Women/Minorities: Y

CR Bard Inc

www.crbard.com

NAIC Code: 339100

TYPES OF BUSINESS:

Equipment-Urological Catheters
Diagnostic and Interventional Products
Minimally Invasive Vascular Products
Surgical Specialty Products
Supply Chain and Business Services
Oncology Products
Urology Products

BRANDS/DIVISIONS/AFFILIATES:

Unltraverse
LifeStent
PowerPICC
PowerPort
Statlock
PerFix
Ventralex
OptiFix

CONTACTS: *Note: Officers with more than one job title may be intentionally listed here more than once.*

Timothy Ring, CEO
Christopher Holland, CFO
Frank Lupisella, Chief Accounting Officer
Timothy Collins, President, Divisional
Jim Beasley, President, Divisional
John Groetelaars, President, Divisional
John Weiland, President
John DeFord, Senior VP, Divisional
Samrat Khichi, Senior VP
Betty Larson, Vice President, Divisional
Gerard Porreca, Vice President, Divisional
Sharon Luboff, Vice President, Divisional
Patricia Christian, Vice President, Divisional

GROWTH PLANS/SPECIAL FEATURES:

C.R. Bard, Inc. designs, manufactures, packages, distributes and sells medical, surgical, diagnostic and patient care devices. The company markets its products in five categories, four primary ones: vascular, accounting for 27% of 2016 net sales; oncology, 27%, urology, 26%; surgical specialties, 17%; and other, 3%. C.R. Bard's line of minimally-invasive vascular products include percutaneous transluminal angioplasty (PTA) catheters, guidewires, introducers and accessories, peripheral vascular stents, vena cava filters and biopsy devices. Some of the brands in the vascular division are Ultraverse, Crosser CTO, VascuTrakPTA, Flair AV, LifeStar and LifeStent. Additional products include cardiac mapping and electrophysiology laboratory systems as well as diagnostic and temporary pacing electrode catheters, fabrics and meshes and implantable blood vessel replacements. C.R. Bard's oncology products include the PowerPICC and PowerPort devices, which eliminate the need for unnecessary catheters. The urology segment markets products that include the Foley catheter and the Statlock catheter stabilization line. The firm's surgical specialties products include meshes for vessel and hernia repair; irrigation devices for orthopedic, laparoscopic and gynecological procedures; and products for topical hemostasis. These products include the PerFix plug; Ventralex, Ventrio, and Allomax hernia patches; and the OptiFix and Capsure fixation devices. C.R. Bard's products are distributed in the U.S. directly to hospitals and other health care institutions as well as through numerous hospital/surgical supply and other medical specialty distributors. In April 2017, the firm agreed to be acquired by the medical supplies manufacturing firm of Becton, Dickinson & Co. for $24 billion.

U.S. employee benefits include medical, prescription, dental and vision coverage; a wellness program; life and AD&D insurance; short-and long-term disability; flexible spending accounts; a 401(k); and an employee stock purchase plan.

FINANCIAL DATA: *Note: Data for latest year may not have been available at press time.*

In U.S. $	2016	2015	2014	2013	2012	2011
Revenue	3,714,000,000	3,416,000,000	3,323,600,000	3,049,500,000	2,958,100,000	2,896,400,000
R&D Expense	292,800,000	259,200,000	302,000,000	295,700,000	203,200,000	185,400,000
Operating Income	947,600,000	349,400,000	781,500,000	1,265,900,000	812,300,000	560,400,000
Operating Margin %	25.51%	10.22%	23.51%	41.51%	27.46%	19.34%
SGA Expense	1,101,900,000	1,012,100,000	981,500,000	920,300,000	817,300,000	1,041,100,000
Net Income	531,400,000	135,400,000	294,500,000	689,800,000	530,100,000	328,000,000
Operating Cash Flow	546,600,000	798,100,000	660,000,000	1,123,300,000	661,200,000	721,500,000
Capital Expenditure	101,200,000	103,800,000	139,900,000	103,000,000	92,000,000	89,300,000
EBITDA	931,600,000	587,400,000	664,700,000	1,404,800,000	908,300,000	662,300,000
Return on Assets %	10.31%	2.66%	5.81%	15.00%	13.11%	9.23%
Return on Equity %	33.78%	8.18%	15.12%	34.37%	28.59%	19.21%
Debt to Equity	0.98	0.78	0.77	0.67	0.73	0.50

CONTACT INFORMATION:

Phone: 908 277-8000   Fax: 908 277-8278
Toll-Free: 800-367-2273
Address: 730 Central Ave., Murray Hill, NJ 07974 United States

STOCK TICKER/OTHER:

Stock Ticker: BCR
Employees: 16,300
Parent Company:

Exchange: NYS
Fiscal Year Ends: 12/31

SALARIES/BONUSES:

Top Exec. Salary: $1,092,000   Bonus: $
Second Exec. Salary: $913,610   Bonus: $

OTHER THOUGHTS:

Estimated Female Officers or Directors: 6
Hot Spot for Advancement for Women/Minorities: Y

Crown Holdings Inc

NAIC Code: 332431

TYPES OF BUSINESS:

Metal Can Manufacturing
Food and Beverage Cans
Plastic Containers

BRANDS/DIVISIONS/AFFILIATES:

CONTACTS: Note: Officers with more than one job title may be intentionally listed here more than once.

Timothy Donahue, CEO
Thomas Kelly, CFO
John Conway, Chairman of the Board
David Beaver, Controller
Caesar Sweitzer, Independent Director
Djalma Novaes, President, Divisional
Robert Bourque, President, Divisional
Gerard Gifford, President, Divisional
Didier Sourisseau, Senior VP, Divisional

GROWTH PLANS/SPECIAL FEATURES:

Crown Holdings, Inc. is a worldwide leader in the design, manufacture and sale of packaging products for consumer goods. Its primary products include steel and aluminum cans for food, beverage, household and other consumer products and metal vacuum closures and caps. The company operates 146 plants, along with sales and service facilities in 36 countries. Crown is organized geographically within three divisions: Americas, Europe and Asia Pacific. The Americas division includes operations in the U.S., Brazil, Canada, the Caribbean, Colombia and Mexico. Within this region, the company produces aluminum beverage cans and ends and steel crowns, commonly referred to as bottle caps, as well as steel and aluminum food cans and ends and metal vacuum closures. The European division includes operations in Eastern and Western Europe, the Middle East and North Africa, and produces beverage, food and aerosol cans and ends, specialty packaging and metal vacuum closures and caps. This division includes 63 plants in 23 countries. The Asia Pacific division consists of beverage can operations in Cambodia, China, Malaysia, Singapore, Thailand and Vietnam and non-beverage can operations, primarily including food cans and specialty packaging in China, Singapore, Thailand and Vietnam. In this region, Crown operates 31 plants in six countries. The firm supplies beverage cans and ends and other packaging products to a variety of beverage and beer companies, including Anheuser-Busch InBev, Carlsberg, Coca-Cola, Cott Beverages, Dr Pepper Snapple Group, Heineken, Molson Coors, Pepsi-Cola and SAB Miller, among others. Customers for its food packaging products include Abbot Laboratories, Bonduelle, Cecab, Morgan Foods, Mars, Simmons Foods, Nestle and Princes Group, among others. The firm primarily supplies aerosol cans to Colgate Palmolive, Procter & Gamble, Friesland Campina, SC Johnson and Unilever.

FINANCIAL DATA: Note: Data for latest year may not have been available at press time.

In U.S. $	2016	2015	2014	2013	2012	2011
Revenue	8,284,000,000	8,762,000,000	9,097,000,000	8,656,000,000	8,470,000,000	8,644,000,000
R&D Expense						
Operating Income	1,021,000,000	927,000,000	810,000,000	917,000,000	812,000,000	842,000,000
Operating Margin %	12.32%	10.57%	8.90%	10.59%	9.58%	9.74%
SGA Expense	389,000,000	416,000,000	398,000,000	425,000,000	417,000,000	395,000,000
Net Income	496,000,000	393,000,000	387,000,000	324,000,000	557,000,000	282,000,000
Operating Cash Flow	930,000,000	956,000,000	912,000,000	885,000,000	621,000,000	379,000,000
Capital Expenditure	473,000,000	354,000,000	328,000,000	275,000,000	324,000,000	401,000,000
EBITDA	1,259,000,000	1,146,000,000	959,000,000	946,000,000	1,042,000,000	995,000,000
Return on Assets %	5.05%	3.98%	4.36%	4.17%	7.75%	4.09%
Return on Equity %	194.50%	298.85%	629.26%			
Debt to Equity	12.88	36.49	42.07	867.25		

CONTACT INFORMATION:

Phone: 215 698-5100   Fax:
Toll-Free:
Address: One Crown Way, Philadelphia, PA 19154-4599 United States

STOCK TICKER/OTHER:

Stock Ticker: CCK   Exchange: NYS
Employees: 24,000   Fiscal Year Ends: 12/31
Parent Company:

SALARIES/BONUSES:

Top Exec. Salary: $915,000   Bonus: $
Second Exec. Salary: $600,000   Bonus: $

OTHER THOUGHTS:

Estimated Female Officers or Directors: 3
Hot Spot for Advancement for Women/Minorities: Y

Cullen-Frost Bankers Inc

NAIC Code: 522110

www.frostbank.com

TYPES OF BUSINESS:

Banking
Insurance
Loans
Discount Brokerage
Trust Services
Cash Management
Investment Services

BRANDS/DIVISIONS/AFFILIATES:

Frost Bank
Frost Insurance Agency Inc
Frost Brokerage Services Inc
Frost Investment Advisors LLC
Tri-Frost Corporation
Main Plaza Corporation
Cullen-Frost Capital Trust
WNB Capital Trust

CONTACTS: Note: Officers with more than one job title may be intentionally listed here more than once.

Phillip Green, CEO
Paul Bracher, Executive VP, Subsidiary
Jerry Salinas, CFO
Patrick Frost, Director
Robert Berman, Executive VP, Subsidiary
Gary McKnight, Executive VP, Subsidiary
Candace Wolfshohl, Executive VP, Subsidiary
Jimmy Stead, Executive VP, Subsidiary
Paul Olivier, Executive VP, Subsidiary
William Perotti, Executive VP, Subsidiary
Annette Alonzo, Executive VP, Subsidiary

GROWTH PLANS/SPECIAL FEATURES:

Cullen-Frost Bankers, Inc., with $30.2 billion in assets in 2016, is a financial holding company and a bank holding company headquartered in San Antonio, Texas. Through its subsidiaries, Cullen/Frost provides an array of products and services throughout numerous Texas markets, offering commercial and consumer banking services, as well as trust and investment management, insurance, brokerage, mutual funds, leasing, treasury management, capital markets advisory and item processing services. Cullen-Frost serves a variety of industries, including energy, manufacturing, services, construction, retail, telecommunications, healthcare, military and transportation. The company's loan portfolio has a significant concentration of energy-related loans totaling approximately 11.6% of total loans, but is not dependent upon any single industry or customer. Subsidiaries of the firm include Frost Bank, the principal operating subsidiary and sole banking subsidiary of Cullen-Frost; Frost Insurance Agency, Inc.; Frost Brokerage Services, Inc.; Frost Investment Advisors, LLC; Tri-Frost Corporation, which holds securities for investment purposes; Main Plaza Corporation, a loan provider; Cullen-Frost Capital Trust I, II; and WNB Capital Trust I.

Cullen/Frost offers its employees life, medical, dental and vision insurance; long-term disability insurance; a 401(k) plan; a flexible spending account; banking benefits; an employee assistance program; tuition reimbursement; the Tom Frost Scholarship ($5,000 to qualifying child of employee); and a profit sharing plan.

FINANCIAL DATA: Note: Data for latest year may not have been available at press time.

In U.S. $	2016	2015	2014	2013	2012	2011
Revenue	1,126,044,000	1,065,362,000	1,007,078,000	923,373,000	893,648,000	871,778,000
R&D Expense						
Operating Income	341,411,000	319,799,000	336,024,000	290,881,000	308,475,000	286,235,000
Operating Margin %	30.31%	30.01%	33.36%	31.50%	34.51%	32.83%
SGA Expense	466,350,000	451,981,000	365,732,000	347,781,000	327,474,000	317,681,000
Net Income	304,261,000	279,328,000	277,977,000	237,866,000	237,952,000	217,535,000
Operating Cash Flow	437,842,000	393,471,000	286,670,000	173,606,000	299,999,000	274,369,000
Capital Expenditure	53,648,000	147,129,000	131,970,000	39,599,000	24,891,000	26,719,000
EBITDA						
Return on Assets %	1.00%	.95%	1.02%	.97%	1.09%	1.14%
Return on Equity %	10.53%	9.91%	10.63%	9.65%	10.09%	10.01%
Debt to Equity	0.08	0.08	0.08	0.09	0.09	0.09

CONTACT INFORMATION:

Phone: 210 220-4011   Fax: 210 220-5578
Toll-Free: 877-513-7678
Address: 100 W. Houston St., San Antonio, TX 78205 United States

STOCK TICKER/OTHER:

Stock Ticker: CFR   Exchange: NYS
Employees: 4,217   Fiscal Year Ends: 12/31
Parent Company:

SALARIES/BONUSES:

Top Exec. Salary: $950,000   Bonus: $
Second Exec. Salary: Bonus: $
$530,000

OTHER THOUGHTS:

Estimated Female Officers or Directors: 3
Hot Spot for Advancement for Women/Minorities: Y

Cushman & Wakefield Inc

www.cushmanwakefield.com

NAIC Code: 531210

TYPES OF BUSINESS:

Real Estate Brokerage
Property Management
Real Estate Documentation Web Site
Advisory Services
Research Services
Property Valuation

BRANDS/DIVISIONS/AFFILIATES:

DTZ Investment Mangement Limited
Equity Debt & Structured Finance
DTZ Zadelhoff

CONTACTS: Note: Officers with more than one job title may be intentionally listed here more than once.

Brett White, CEO
Edward C. Forst, Pres.
Duncan Palmer, CFO
Mike Daley, CMO
Matthew Bouw, Global Chief Human Resources Officer
Adam Stanley, CIO
Gene Boxer, Global General Counsel
James M. Underhill, CEO-Americas
Sanjay Verma, CEO-Asia Pacific
John Busi, Exec. VP-Valuation & Advisory
Brett White, Chmn.
Carlo Sant'Albano, CEO-Int'l

GROWTH PLANS/SPECIAL FEATURES:

Cushman & Wakefield, Inc. (C&W) is a global commercial real estate brokerage and services company. C&W provides advisory services related to asset buying, selling, financing and leasing; and provides strategic planning, portfolio analysis and space location services. Agency and brokerage services assist clients with marketing and positioning properties through landlord representation, lease advisory, offices, retail services, supply chain, tenant representation and industrial solutions. Its capital markets group offers real estate buying, financing and investment clients various advisory services, including agency execution, investment management and corporate disposition practice. Global consulting services comprise market access, office platform, retail consulting and supply chain solutions for business customers and transaction and portfolio consulting for real estate customers. The practice groups division serves clients in select industries, including energy and resources, health care, hospitality, law firms, life sciences, mission critical facilities and Japanese multinational corporations. The research division offers property research, market analysis and forecasting solutions. The firm's valuation and advisory services include appraisal, portfolio valuation, development strategy, occupancy strategy and property tax services for real estate. C&W's Equity, Debt & Structured Finance platform provides both domestic and international clients customized advisory and integrated capital solutions for all assets classes, including office, multi-family, retail, lodging/leisure, healthcare facilities, senior housing facilities, industrial facilities and land. C&W's corporate occupier and investor services manage real estate portfolios through account, transaction and project management, lease administration and facilities management. C&W is owned by DTZ Investment Management Limited. In November 2016, the firm acquired DTZ Zadelhoff in the Netherlands to provide commercial real estate services in the country.

C&W provides its employees with benefits such as medical, dental, vision, legal, disability and life insurance; domestic partner benefits; educational assistance; 401(k) plans; commuter program; and discounted gym memberships.

FINANCIAL DATA: Note: Data for latest year may not have been available at press time.

In U.S. $	2016	2015	2014	2013	2012	2011
Revenue	5,000,000,000	4,800,000,000	2,849,000,000	2,498,600,000	2,050,000,000	2,000,000,000
R&D Expense						
Operating Income						
Operating Margin %						
SGA Expense						
Net Income			61,600,000	46,200,000	18,202,800	14,900,000
Operating Cash Flow						
Capital Expenditure						
EBITDA						
Return on Assets %						
Return on Equity %						
Debt to Equity						

CONTACT INFORMATION:

Phone: 212-841-7500   Fax: 212-841-5002
Toll-Free:
Address: 1290 Avenue of the Americas, New York, NY 10104 United States

STOCK TICKER/OTHER:

Stock Ticker: Subsidiary   Exchange:
Employees: 43,000   Fiscal Year Ends: 12/31
Parent Company: DTZ Investment Management Limited

SALARIES/BONUSES:

Top Exec. Salary: $ Bonus: $
Second Exec. Salary: $ Bonus: $

OTHER THOUGHTS:

Estimated Female Officers or Directors: 2
Hot Spot for Advancement for Women/Minorities:

CVS Health Corporation

cvshealth.com

NAIC Code: 446110

TYPES OF BUSINESS:

Drug Stores
Pharmacy Benefits Management
Online Pharmacy Services

BRANDS/DIVISIONS/AFFILIATES:

CVS.com
Navarro.com
Onofre.com.br
CVS Pharmacy
Longs Drugs
Navarro Discount Pharmacy
CVS Pharmacy Y mas
SilverScript Insurance Company

CONTACTS: *Note: Officers with more than one job title may be intentionally listed here more than once.*

Larry Merlo, CEO
David Denton, CFO
David Dorman, Chairman of the Board
Eva Boratto, Chief Accounting Officer
Troyen Brennan, Chief Medical Officer
J. Joyner, Executive VP
Thomas Moriarty, Executive VP
Robert Kraft, Executive VP
Jonathan Roberts, Executive VP
Helena Foulkes, Executive VP
Lisa Bisaccia, Other Executive Officer
Steven Gold, Other Executive Officer
Andrew Sussman, Other Executive Officer

GROWTH PLANS/SPECIAL FEATURES:

CVS Health Corporation is a leading provider of prescription and related healthcare services in the U.S. It operates in three segments: corporate, retail/LTC and pharmacy services. The corporate segment provides management and administrative services to support the company's overall operations. The retail/LTC (long-term care) segment includes over 9,709 retail stores, of which 7,980 are stores that operated a pharmacy and 1,674 are CVS pharmacies located within Target Corporation stores. This division also includes CVS online retail pharmacy websites (CVS.com, Navarro.com and Onofre.com.br), 38 on-site pharmacy stores, LTC pharmacy operations and retail healthcare clinics. The retail stores are located in 49 states, the District of Columbia, Puerto Rico and Brazil operating under the CVS Pharmacy, CVS, Longs Drugs, Navarro Discount Pharmacy, CVS Pharmacy Y mas and Drogaria Onofre names. The pharmacy services segment provides a full range of pharmacy benefit management services, including mail order pharmacy services, plan design and administration, formulary management, claims processing and health management programs. Through subsidiary SilverScript Insurance Company, the division is a national provider of drug benefits to eligible beneficiaries under Medicare Part D. The segment operates a national retail pharmacy network with 23 retail specialty pharmacy stores; 13 specialty mail order pharmacies; four mail order dispensing services; and 84 branches with 73 ambulatory infusion suites.

Employee benefits include medical, dental, vision and prescription coverage; free health screenings at MinuteClinic; a 401(k); employee stock purchase plan; short- and long-term disability; employee discounts; education reimbursement; an employee assistance program; and flexible spending accounts.

FINANCIAL DATA: *Note: Data for latest year may not have been available at press time.*

In U.S. $	2016	2015	2014	2013	2012	2011
Revenue	177,526,000,000	153,290,000,000	139,367,000,000	126,761,000,000	123,133,000,000	107,100,000,000
R&D Expense						
Operating Income	10,338,000,000	9,454,000,000	8,799,000,000	8,037,000,000	7,228,000,000	6,330,000,000
Operating Margin %	5.82%	6.16%	6.31%	6.34%	5.87%	5.91%
SGA Expense	18,519,000,000	17,074,000,000	16,568,000,000	15,746,000,000	15,278,000,000	14,231,000,000
Net Income	5,317,000,000	5,237,000,000	4,644,000,000	4,592,000,000	3,877,000,000	3,461,000,000
Operating Cash Flow	10,069,000,000	8,412,000,000	8,137,000,000	5,783,000,000	6,671,000,000	5,856,000,000
Capital Expenditure	2,224,000,000	2,367,000,000	2,136,000,000	1,984,000,000	2,030,000,000	1,872,000,000
EBITDA	12,190,000,000	11,567,000,000	10,224,000,000	9,915,000,000	8,633,000,000	7,902,000,000
Return on Assets %	5.65%	6.23%	6.37%	6.68%	5.94%	5.46%
Return on Equity %	14.36%	13.93%	12.23%	12.14%	10.23%	9.13%
Debt to Equity	0.69	0.70	0.30	0.33	0.24	0.24

CONTACT INFORMATION:

Phone: 401 765-1500   Fax: 401 762-2137
Toll-Free: 888-746-7287
Address: 1 CVS Dr., Woonsocket, RI 02895 United States

STOCK TICKER/OTHER:

Stock Ticker: CVS
Employees: 202,000
Parent Company:

Exchange: NYS
Fiscal Year Ends: 12/31

SALARIES/BONUSES:

Top Exec. Salary: $1,630,000   Bonus: $
Second Exec. Salary: $950,000   Bonus: $

OTHER THOUGHTS:

Estimated Female Officers or Directors: 4
Hot Spot for Advancement for Women/Minorities: Y

Dana Incorporated

NAIC Code: 336300

www.dana.com

TYPES OF BUSINESS:

Automotive Products, Motors & Parts Manufacturing
Engine Systems
Fluid Systems
Heavy Vehicle Technologies
Brake Components
Chassis & Drive Train Components
Filtration Products
Financial Services

BRANDS/DIVISIONS/AFFILIATES:

Dana Holding Corporation

CONTACTS: *Note: Officers with more than one job title may be intentionally listed here more than once.*

Jonathan Collins, CFO
Rodney Filcek, Chief Accounting Officer
George Constand, Chief Technology Officer
James Kamsickas, Director
Mark Wallace, Executive VP
Marc Levin, General Counsel
Aziz Aghili, President, Divisional
Dwayne Matthews, President, Divisional
Robert Pyle, President, Divisional

GROWTH PLANS/SPECIAL FEATURES:

Dana Incorporated (formerly Dana Holding Corporation) supplies high technology driveline, sealing and thermal management products for global vehicle manufacturers. The company operates 91 facilities in 25 countries. Dana divides its operations into four segments: light vehicle, commercial vehicle, off-highway and power technologies. In the light vehicles segment, Dana engages in the manufacturing of component parts for light trucks, crossover utility vehicles, sport utility vehicles, vans and passenger cars. Products include front axles, rear axles, driveshafts, differentials, torque couplings and modular assemblies. Largest customers in this segment are Ford, Fiat Chrysler, Renault-Nissan, Toyota, General Motors and Tata. The commercial vehicle segment manufactures parts for the medium/heavy duty vehicle market, including medium duty trucks, heavy duty trucks, buses and specialty vehicles. Products include axles, driveshafts, steering shafts, suspensions and tire management systems. Major customers include PACCAR, Ford, Volvo, Daimler and Navistar International. The off-highway segment manufactures axels, driveshafts, end-fittings, transmissions, torque converters and electronic controls for off-highway use such as construction, earth moving, agriculture, mining, forestry, rail and material handling. Major customers include Deere & Company, AGCO, Manitou, Sandvik and Oshkosh. Finally, the power technologies segment manufactures parts for the light vehicle, medium/heavy vehicle and off-highway markets. Products include gaskets, cover module, heat shields, engine sealing systems, cooling and heat transfer products. Major customers include Ford, General Motors, Volkswagen, Renault-Nissan and Mahle. In August 2016, the firm changed its name to Dana Incorporated to better reflect how the company conducts its business in the global market as a unified organization. In early-2017, it acquired Brevini Group SpA's power transmission and fluid power businesses; and acquired U.S. Manufacturing Corporation's axle housing and driveline shaft manufacturing operations for $100 million.

FINANCIAL DATA: *Note: Data for latest year may not have been available at press time.*

In U.S. $	2016	2015	2014	2013	2012	2011
Revenue	5,826,000,000	6,060,000,000	6,617,000,000	6,769,000,000	7,224,000,000	7,592,000,000
R&D Expense						
Operating Income	430,000,000	444,000,000	471,000,000	412,000,000	448,000,000	375,000,000
Operating Margin %	7.38%	7.32%	7.11%	6.08%	6.20%	4.93%
SGA Expense	406,000,000	391,000,000	411,000,000	410,000,000	434,000,000	409,000,000
Net Income	640,000,000	159,000,000	319,000,000	244,000,000	300,000,000	219,000,000
Operating Cash Flow	384,000,000	406,000,000	510,000,000	577,000,000	339,000,000	370,000,000
Capital Expenditure	322,000,000	260,000,000	234,000,000	209,000,000	164,000,000	196,000,000
EBITDA	510,000,000	579,000,000	591,000,000	729,000,000	725,000,000	682,000,000
Return on Assets %	13.93%	3.43%	6.20%	-.25%	5.14%	3.61%
Return on Equity %	67.90%	17.58%	30.93%	-1.28%	25.94%	19.71%
Debt to Equity	1.37	2.13	1.49	1.67	0.73	0.84

CONTACT INFORMATION:

Phone: 419 887-3000   Fax: 419 535-4643
Toll-Free: 800-537-8823
Address: 3939 Technology Drive, Maumee, OH 43537 United States

STOCK TICKER/OTHER:

Stock Ticker: DAN   Exchange: NYS
Employees: 24,900   Fiscal Year Ends: 12/31
Parent Company:

SALARIES/BONUSES:

Top Exec. Salary: $1,100,000   Bonus: $500,000
Second Exec. Salary: $580,000   Bonus: $

OTHER THOUGHTS:

Estimated Female Officers or Directors:
Hot Spot for Advancement for Women/Minorities: Y

Darden Restaurants Inc

NAIC Code: 722513

www.darden.com

TYPES OF BUSINESS:

Limited-Service Restaurants

BRANDS/DIVISIONS/AFFILIATES:

Red Lobster
Olive Garden
Capital Grille (The)
Bahama Breeze
LongHorn Steakhouse
Seasons 52
Eddie V's Prime Seafood
Yard House

CONTACTS: Note: Officers with more than one job title may be intentionally listed here more than once.

Eugene Lee, CEO
Ricardo Cardenas, CFO
Charles Sonsteby, Chairman of the Board
John Madonna, Chief Accounting Officer
Matthew Broad, General Counsel
Todd Burrowes, President, Divisional
David George, President, Divisional
Harald Herrmann, Senior VP, Divisional

GROWTH PLANS/SPECIAL FEATURES:

Darden Restaurants, Inc. is a leading publicly-held casual dining company in the U.S. It owns and operates 1,541 restaurants throughout the U.S. and Canada. Darden operates seven restaurant chains: Olive Garden, LongHorn Steakhouse, The Capital Grille, Bahama Breeze, Eddie V's, Yard House and Seasons 52. The company served over 334 million meals in 2016. Olive Garden, with over 800 restaurants, is a casual dining Italian restaurant in the U.S. and Canada. Its menu includes a variety of Italian foods, including antipasti; soups, salad and garlic breadsticks; baked pastas; sauteed chicken, seafood and vegetables; grilled meats; and a variety of desserts. It also offers imported Italian wines, coffee and espresso. LongHorn Steakhouse restaurants, with over 485 locations, are full-service establishments serving both lunch and dinner with American West-themed decor. The Capital Grille is a chain of upscale full-service restaurants that dry-ages its steaks on the premises and flies in fresh seafood daily to its 56 locations as well as featuring a 350-selection wine list. The firm's 36 Bahama Breeze locations offer guests an island dining experience with a menu featuring Caribbean-style beef, chicken and seafood. Eddie V's is a steak and seafood restaurant with 17 locations in Texas, Florida, California, Illinois, Virginia and Arizona. Yard House is a casual American-style restaurant with more than 100 taps of draft beers with over 65 locations. Seasons 52, with 40 restaurants, is a fresh grill and wine bar with seasonally inspired menus, offering nutritionally balanced meals lower in calories than comparable restaurant meals. Additionally, the firm has 50 restaurants operated by independent third parties.

FINANCIAL DATA: Note: Data for latest year may not have been available at press time.

In U.S. $	2016	2015	2014	2013	2012	2011
Revenue	6,933,500,000	6,764,000,000	6,285,600,000	8,551,900,000	7,998,700,000	
R&D Expense						
Operating Income	622,200,000	367,600,000	327,200,000	648,300,000	739,600,000	
Operating Margin %	8.97%	5.43%	5.20%	7.58%	9.24%	
SGA Expense	622,900,000	673,500,000	663,500,000	847,800,000	746,800,000	
Net Income	375,000,000	709,500,000	286,200,000	411,900,000	475,500,000	
Operating Cash Flow	820,400,000	471,000,000	770,100,000	949,300,000	762,200,000	
Capital Expenditure	228,300,000	296,500,000	414,800,000	685,600,000	639,700,000	
EBITDA	913,500,000	687,500,000	631,600,000	1,044,000,000	1,093,500,000	
Return on Assets %	7.09%	10.83%	4.07%	6.39%	8.33%	
Return on Equity %	17.50%	31.60%	13.57%	21.11%	25.17%	
Debt to Equity	0.22	0.62	1.17	1.23	0.81	

CONTACT INFORMATION:

Phone: 407 245-4000   Fax: 407 245-4989
Toll-Free:
Address: 1000 Darden Ctr. Dr., Orlando, FL 32837 United States

STOCK TICKER/OTHER:

Stock Ticker: DRI   Exchange: NYS
Employees: 175,000   Fiscal Year Ends: 05/31
Parent Company:

SALARIES/BONUSES:

Top Exec. Salary: $953,750   Bonus: $
Second Exec. Salary: Bonus: $
$576,539

OTHER THOUGHTS:

Estimated Female Officers or Directors: 7
Hot Spot for Advancement for Women/Minorities: Y

DaVita Healthcare Partners Inc

NAIC Code: 621492

www.davita.com

TYPES OF BUSINESS:

Renal Care Services
Clinical Research

BRANDS/DIVISIONS/AFFILIATES:

HealthCare Partners
DaVita Kidney Care
DaVita (Shandong) Kidney Disease Hospital Co Ltd
WellHealth Quality Care
Mountain View Medical Group
Renal Ventures Management LLC
Purity Dialysis

CONTACTS: *Note: Officers with more than one job title may be intentionally listed here more than once.*

Javier Rodriguez, CEO, Divisional
Kent Thiry, CEO
James Hilger, Chief Accounting Officer
Jeanine Jiganti, Other Executive Officer
Kathleen Waters, Other Executive Officer
Joel Ackerman, Senior VP, Divisional
Leanne Zumwalt, Vice President, Divisional

GROWTH PLANS/SPECIAL FEATURES:

DaVita HealthCare Partners, Inc. is a leading provider of dialysis services in the U.S. for patients suffering from chronic kidney failure, also known as end stage renal disease (ESRD). The company operates through a network of 2,350 outpatient dialysis centers located in 46 states and Washington, D.C., serving approximately 187,700 patients. The firm also provides acute inpatient dialysis services in approximately 900 hospitals and related laboratory services. DaVita's dialysis and related lab services business accounted for approximately 62% of the firm's 2016 revenue. DaVita HealthCare Partners' secondary business is its HealthCare Partners (HCP) services, which provides integrated health care delivery and management. HCP operates through contracts, with 749,300 members under its care in 2016. In addition, HCP also provides a stand-alone dialysis center in Malaysia. DaVita's ancillary services and strategic initiatives include pharmacy services, vascular access services and clinical research, which conduct research trials with dialysis patients. Subsidiary DaVita Kidney Care has a joint venture kidney care specialty hospital chain in Shandong, China, called DaVita (Shandong) Kidney Disease Hospital Co. Ltd. In 2017, the firm finalized its acquisition of Mountain View Medical Group, an independent physicians group; agreed to acquire the medical group Totem Lake Family Medicine through its Everett Clinic; acquired the medical group WellHealth Quality Care through HCP; finalized its acquisition of Renal Ventures Management, LLC; acquired Purity Dialysis through DaVita Kidney Care; and agreed to acquire the medical group Magan Medical Clinic through HCP.

The firm offers employees medical, dental and vision insurance; short- and long-term disability insurance; life insurance; a 401(k) plan; tuition reimbursement; flexible spending accounts; and an employee assistance program.

FINANCIAL DATA: *Note: Data for latest year may not have been available at press time.*

In U.S. $	2016	2015	2014	2013	2012	2011
Revenue	14,745,110,000	13,781,840,000	12,795,110,000	11,764,050,000	8,186,280,000	6,982,214,000
R&D Expense						
Operating Income	1,894,543,000	1,170,695,000	1,815,141,000	1,550,134,000	1,297,084,000	1,130,782,000
Operating Margin %	12.84%	8.49%	14.18%	13.17%	15.84%	16.19%
SGA Expense	1,592,698,000	1,452,135,000	1,261,506,000	1,176,485,000	980,412,000	691,243,000
Net Income	879,874,000	269,732,000	723,114,000	633,446,000	536,017,000	478,001,000
Operating Cash Flow	1,963,444,000	1,557,200,000	1,459,407,000	1,773,341,000	1,100,848,000	1,180,046,000
Capital Expenditure	829,095,000	707,998,000	642,348,000	617,597,000	550,146,000	400,156,000
EBITDA	2,623,529,000	1,769,540,000	2,310,902,000	2,083,658,000	1,633,766,000	1,401,079,000
Return on Assets %	4.72%	1.47%	4.12%	3.82%	4.30%	5.62%
Return on Equity %	18.48%	5.37%	15.06%	15.45%	18.15%	23.20%
Debt to Equity	1.92	1.84	1.62	1.83	2.21	2.06

CONTACT INFORMATION:

Phone: 303 405-2100   Fax: 310 792-8928
Toll-Free:
Address: 2000 16th St., Denver, CO 80202 United States

STOCK TICKER/OTHER:

Stock Ticker: DVA   Exchange: NYS
Employees: 41,000   Fiscal Year Ends: 12/31
Parent Company:

SALARIES/BONUSES:

Top Exec. Salary: $1,273,077   Bonus: $
Second Exec. Salary: Bonus: $740,000
$334,385

OTHER THOUGHTS:

Estimated Female Officers or Directors: 3
Hot Spot for Advancement for Women/Minorities: Y

Dell Technologies Inc

www.delltechnologies.com/en-us/index.htm

NAIC Code: 334111

TYPES OF BUSINESS:

Computer Manufacturing
Direct Sales
Technical & Support Services
Online Music Service
Web Hosting Services
Printers & Accessories
Personal Music Players
Storage Devices

BRANDS/DIVISIONS/AFFILIATES:

Dell
Dell EMC
Pivotal
RSA
Secureworks
VirtuStream
Vmware
EMC Corporation

CONTACTS: Note: Officers with more than one job title may be intentionally listed here more than once.

Michael Dell, CEO
Thomas Sweet, CFO
Jeffrey Clarke, Director
Jeremy Burton, Executive VP, Divisional
Steven Price, Other Executive Officer
Karen Quintos, Other Executive Officer
Rory Read, Other Executive Officer
Marius Haas, Other Executive Officer
John Swainson, President, Divisional
Suresh Vaswani, President, Divisional
Howard Elias, President, Divisional
David Goulden, President, Divisional
Richard Rothberg, Secretary

GROWTH PLANS/SPECIAL FEATURES:

Dell Technologies, Inc. is a multinational information technology corporation. The firm provides transformational devices, processes and services in order to modernize data centers, drive progress and help its clients thrive within the digital era. Dell's products are divided into four groups. Within the digital transformation group, Dell's solutions for the Internet of Things (IoT), cloud-native applications and big data empower companies to reinvent their businesses and transform their IT infrastructure. IoT products are sensor-enabled equipment and smart devices that connect the physical world with the digital world, optimizing operations and delivering enhanced customer experience. Cloud-native applications transform businesses IT into modern and digital enterprises. Big data and analytics help businesses keep up with customer expectations via systems, smart devices and software. The IT transformation group comprises a hybrid cloud IT model modernizes data centers, automates IT processes and transforms operations; a converged infrastructure which streamlines operations and presents an on-demand business culture; and offers all-flash storage architecture. The workforce transformation group provides innovative devices for employees, digital workplace and data security solutions. Last, the security transformation group offers security operations solutions to mitigate advanced threats; identity and access management solutions; perimeter and endpoint security solutions; and governance, risk and compliance solutions. Brands by Dell Technologies include Dell, Dell EMC, Pivotal, RSA, Secureworks, VirtuStream and VMware. In September 2016, the firm acquired EMC Corporation, which became a wholly-owned subsidiary of Dell Technologies. Later that year, Dell Technologies sold Dell Services to NTT Data International, LLC for $3 billion; sold Dell Software Group to Francisco Partners and Elliot Management Corporation for $2.4 billion; and sold its Dell EMC enterprise content division to OpenText Corporation for $1.6 billion.

Dell offers employees medical, dental, vision, life, disability, auto and home insurance; 401(k); and discounts and various assistance programs.

FINANCIAL DATA: Note: Data for latest year may not have been available at press time.

In U.S. $	2016	2015	2014	2013	2012	2011
Revenue		54,142,000,000				
R&D Expense		920,000,000				
Operating Income		-316,000,000				
Operating Margin %		-.58%				
SGA Expense		8,292,000,000				
Net Income		-1,221,000,000				
Operating Cash Flow		2,551,000,000				
Capital Expenditure		478,000,000				
EBITDA		2,569,000,000				
Return on Assets %						
Return on Equity %						
Debt to Equity						

CONTACT INFORMATION:

Phone: 512 338-4400   Fax: 512 283-6161
Toll-Free: 800-289-3355
Address: One Dell Way, Round Rock, TX 78682 United States

SALARIES/BONUSES:

Top Exec. Salary: $826,160   Bonus: $2,957,658
Second Exec. Salary: Bonus: $2,954,633
$496,154

STOCK TICKER/OTHER:

Stock Ticker: DVMT   Exchange: NYS
Employees: 138,000   Fiscal Year Ends: 01/31
Parent Company: Silver Lake Partners

OTHER THOUGHTS:

Estimated Female Officers or Directors: 1
Hot Spot for Advancement for Women/Minorities: Y

Sales, profits and employees may be estimates. Financial information, benefits and other data can change quickly and may vary from those stated here.

Deloitte LLP

NAIC Code: 541211

TYPES OF BUSINESS:

Accounting Services
Management Consulting
Risk Management Services
Financial Advisory Services
Outsourcing Services
Legal & Compliance Advisory Services
Consulting Services

BRANDS/DIVISIONS/AFFILIATES:

Deloitte Touche Tohmatsu Lmited
Deloitte & Touche LLP
M&A Institute
Deloitte Consulting LLP

CONTACTS: Note: Officers with more than one job title may be intentionally listed here more than once.

Catherine M. Engelbert, CEO
Mike Fucci, Chmn.

GROWTH PLANS/SPECIAL FEATURES:

Deloitte, LLP, the U.S. division of global accounting firm Deloitte Touche Tohmatsu Limited, offers a variety of financial and consulting services. The company divides its services into five business segments: auditing, consulting, risk and financial advisory, tax and mergers and acquisitions. The auditing segment provides independent financial statement and internal control audits, in accordance with the latest professional standards. The consulting segment provides human capital, strategy and operations and technology business performance knowledge. The risk and financial advisory segment provides services that cover financial transactions, regulatory/forensics compliance and risk/resilience. The tax segment provides tax compliance, controversy and co-sourcing services, federal tax advisory, multistate tax and tax management consulting services, among others. The mergers and acquisitions segment provides services and analytics concerning mergers and acquisitions; and Deloitte's M&A Institute can help merger/acquisition professionals enhance their capabilities and readiness within a collaborative environment where they can build on connections and access relevant trainings. Industries served by Deloitte include consumer and industrial products, life sciences and healthcare, real estate, construction, energy/resources, manufacturing, technology, media/telecommunications, financial services, public sector and many more. Subsidiary Deloitte & Touche, LLP provides accounting services. A related company, Deloitte Consulting LLP, provides consulting services in areas such as human resources, business strategy and technology.

Deloitte, LLP offers employees medical, dental and prescription drug coverage; short- and long-term disability; life and travel accident insurance; a group legal plan; tuition assistance; flexible work arrangements; an employee assistance program; adoption assistance and reimbursement; emergency backup daycare; sabbaticals; flexible spending accounts; and a professional development program.

FINANCIAL DATA: Note: Data for latest year may not have been available at press time.

In U.S. $	2016	2015	2014	2013	2012	2011
Revenue	17,500,000,000	16,147,000,000	14,910,000,000	13,894,000,000	13,067,000,000	11,939,000,000
R&D Expense						
Operating Income						
Operating Margin %						
SGA Expense						
Net Income						
Operating Cash Flow						
Capital Expenditure						
EBITDA						
Return on Assets %						
Return on Equity %						
Debt to Equity						

CONTACT INFORMATION:

Phone: 212-489-1600   Fax: 212-489-1687
Toll-Free:
Address: 1633 Broadway, Paramount Bldg., New York, NY 10019-6754 United States

STOCK TICKER/OTHER:

Stock Ticker: Subsidiary   Exchange:
Employees: 78,642   Fiscal Year Ends: 05/31
Parent Company: Deloitte Touche Tohmatsu Limited

SALARIES/BONUSES:

Top Exec. Salary: $ Bonus: $
Second Exec. Salary: $ Bonus: $

OTHER THOUGHTS:

Estimated Female Officers or Directors: 18
Hot Spot for Advancement for Women/Minorities: Y

Delta Air Lines Inc

www.delta.com

NAIC Code: 481111

TYPES OF BUSINESS:

Airline
Air Freight

BRANDS/DIVISIONS/AFFILIATES:

Virgin Atlantic Airways Ltd

CONTACTS: Note: Officers with more than one job title may be intentionally listed here more than once.

Paul Jacobson, CFO
Edward Bastian, Director
Francis Blake, Director
Peter Carter, Executive VP
Glen Hauenstein, President
Wayne West, Senior Executive VP

GROWTH PLANS/SPECIAL FEATURES:

Delta Air Lines, Inc. is a major air carrier that provides scheduled air transportation domestically and internationally for freight and more than 180 million passengers annually. From its multiple hubs (Atlanta, Cincinnati, Detroit, Los Angeles, Boston, Minneapolis/St. Paul, New York-JFK, New York-LaGuardia, Salt Lake City, Seattle, Amsterdam, Paris-Charles de Gaulle and Tokyo-Narita), the company serves 335 destinations in 62 countries. The firm has a total 832 aircraft in fleet, with 639 being company owned and 193 being leased. Delta is a founding member of the SkyTeam international alliance, a global airline alliance that provides customers with 1,000 worldwide destinations, flights and services. Delta also has trans-Atlantic joint ventures with both Air France KLM Group and Alitalia in addition to a trans-Pacific joint venture with Virgin Australia. The company also holds a 49% interest in Virgin Atlantic Airways Ltd., giving Delta a more competitive stance in the vital New York City to London Heathrow route.

Delta offers its employees medical, dental, vision and life insurance; flexible spending accounts; a 401(k) plan; profit sharing; credit union membership; employee assistance programs; adoption assistance, paid holiday and vacation; and free and reduced rate travel benefits for employees and their close family members.

FINANCIAL DATA: Note: Data for latest year may not have been available at press time.

In U.S. $	2016	2015	2014	2013	2012	2011
Revenue	39,639,000,000	40,704,000,000	40,362,000,000	37,773,000,000	36,670,000,000	35,115,000,000
R&D Expense						
Operating Income	6,952,000,000	7,802,000,000	2,206,000,000	3,400,000,000	2,175,000,000	1,975,000,000
Operating Margin %	17.53%	19.16%	5.46%	9.00%	5.93%	5.62%
SGA Expense	11,744,000,000	11,938,000,000	10,905,000,000	9,829,000,000	9,228,000,000	8,839,999,000
Net Income	4,373,000,000	4,526,000,000	659,000,000	10,540,000,000	1,009,000,000	854,000,000
Operating Cash Flow	7,205,000,000	7,927,000,000	4,947,000,000	4,504,000,000	2,476,000,000	2,834,000,000
Capital Expenditure	3,391,000,000	2,945,000,000	2,249,000,000	2,568,000,000	1,968,000,000	1,254,000,000
EBITDA	8,854,000,000	9,637,000,000	3,977,000,000	5,058,000,000	3,402,000,000	3,193,000,000
Return on Assets %	8.37%	8.43%	1.23%	21.77%	2.29%	1.97%
Return on Equity %	37.80%	46.03%	6.44%	221.61%		
Debt to Equity	0.50	0.62	0.97	0.84		

CONTACT INFORMATION:

Phone: 404 715-2600   Fax: 404 715-1400
Toll-Free: 866-715-2170
Address: 1030 Delta Blvd., Atlanta, GA 30320 United States

STOCK TICKER/OTHER:

Stock Ticker: DAL   Exchange: NYS
Employees: 84,000   Fiscal Year Ends: 12/31
Parent Company:

SALARIES/BONUSES:

Top Exec. Salary: $741,669   Bonus: $
Second Exec. Salary: Bonus: $
$633,333

OTHER THOUGHTS:

Estimated Female Officers or Directors: 2
Hot Spot for Advancement for Women/Minorities: Y

Dentsply Sirona Inc

www.sirona.com

NAIC Code: 339100

TYPES OF BUSINESS:

Dental Device Manufacturing

BRANDS/DIVISIONS/AFFILIATES:

Dentsply Sirona Academy

CONTACTS: Note: Officers with more than one job title may be intentionally listed here more than once.

Ulrich Michel, CFO
Bret Wise, Chairman of the Board
Christopher Clark, COO, Divisional
James Mosch, COO, Divisional
Jeffrey Slovin, Director
Rainer Berthan, Executive VP, Divisional
Jonathan Friedman, General Counsel
Maureen MacInnis, Other Executive Officer

GROWTH PLANS/SPECIAL FEATURES:

Dentsply Sirona, Inc. manufactures professional dental products and technologies. The firm's products and solutions include leading positions and platforms across consumables, equipment, technology and specialty products. Products include general dental supplies and devices, computer-aided design and computer-aided manufacturing (CAD/CAM) restoration systems, a full suite of dental restorative products, digital intra-oral, panoramic and 3D imaging systems, dental treatment centers, hand pieces, hygiene systems and dental specialty products in orthodontics, endodontics and implants. Dentsply Sirona's global consumable healthcare product team provides innovative urological and surgical solutions designed to improve quality of life for patients. Dentsply Sirona's global headquarters are based in York, Pennsylvania, and its international headquarters are located in Salzburg, Austria. In July 2017, the firm opened Dentsply Sirona Academy, a new facility in Weybridge, London, U.K., which will address the continuing educational needs of all dental professionals. The academy provides worldwide access to more than 11,000 courses covering a range of clinical, technical and practice excellence programs.

FINANCIAL DATA: Note: Data for latest year may not have been available at press time.

In U.S. $	2016	2015	2014	2013	2012	2011
Revenue	3,745,300,000	2,674,300,000	2,922,620,000	2,950,770,000	2,928,429,000	2,537,718,000
R&D Expense						
Operating Income	454,700,000	375,200,000	445,600,000	419,166,000	381,939,000	300,728,000
Operating Margin %	12.14%	14.02%	15.24%	14.20%	13.04%	11.85%
SGA Expense	1,523,000,000	1,077,300,000	1,143,106,000	1,144,890,000	1,148,731,000	936,847,000
Net Income	429,900,000	251,200,000	322,854,000	313,192,000	314,213,000	244,520,000
Operating Cash Flow	563,400,000	497,400,000	560,401,000	417,846,000	369,685,000	393,469,000
Capital Expenditure	126,100,000	72,000,000	105,767,000	101,421,000	95,401,000	74,254,000
EBITDA	748,500,000	508,500,000	580,360,000	546,863,000	516,729,000	384,960,000
Return on Assets %	5.35%	5.54%	6.63%	6.23%	6.46%	6.10%
Return on Equity %	8.22%	10.78%	13.29%	13.20%	15.49%	13.26%
Debt to Equity	0.18	0.48	0.49	0.46	0.55	0.80

CONTACT INFORMATION:

Phone: Fax:
Toll-Free: 800-877-0020
Address: 221 W. Philadelphia Street, Ste. 60W, York, PA 17401 United States

STOCK TICKER/OTHER:

Stock Ticker: XRAY Exchange: NAS
Employees: 15,700 Fiscal Year Ends: 09/30
Parent Company:

SALARIES/BONUSES:

Top Exec. Salary: $912,500 Bonus: $
Second Exec. Salary: $802,919 Bonus: $

OTHER THOUGHTS:

Estimated Female Officers or Directors: 1
Hot Spot for Advancement for Women/Minorities:

Sales, profits and employees may be estimates. Financial information, benefits and other data can change quickly and may vary from those stated here.

Diodes Inc

NAIC Code: 334413

www.diodes.com

TYPES OF BUSINESS:
Semiconductor Manufacturing
Semiconductor Design
Semiconductor Marketing

BRANDS/DIVISIONS/AFFILIATES:
Diodes FabTech Inc
Shanghai Kaihong Technology Electronic Co Ltd
Diodes Hong Kong Holding Company Limited
Pericom Semiconductor Corporation

CONTACTS: Note: Officers with more than one job title may be intentionally listed here more than once.
Keh-Shew Lu, CEO
Richard White, CFO
Raymond Soong, Chairman of the Board
Julie Holland, General Manager, Divisional
Hans Rohrer, Senior VP, Divisional
Mark King, Senior VP, Divisional
C.H. Chen, Vice Chairman of the Board
Clemente Beltran, Vice President, Divisional
Francis Tang, Vice President, Divisional
Edmund Tang, Vice President, Divisional

GROWTH PLANS/SPECIAL FEATURES:
Diodes, Inc. designs, manufactures and markets discrete and analogue semiconductor products. The semiconductors are found in a variety of end-user products in the consumer electronics, computing, industrial, communications and automotive sectors. Diodes' product line includes more than 10,000 offerings, such as diodes, rectifiers, transistors, metal oxide semiconductor field-effect transistors (MOSFETs), protection devices and functional specific arrays. The company also produces amplifiers and comparators, Hall effect and temperature sensors, power management devices (including light emitting diode drivers), DC-DC switching and linear voltage regulators, voltage references, special function devices (including USB power switch, load switch, voltage supervisor and motor controllers) and silicon wafers used to manufacture these products. The main headquarters, logistic center and sales center are located in Plano, Texas. Manufacturing, engineering, assembly and warehouse facilities are located in China, Germany, Taiwan, South Korea, Hong Kong, the U.K. and the U.S. The firm conducts a number of operations through its subsidiaries, including Diodes FabTech, Inc., which is responsible for wafer fabrication, research and development, engineering and sales; Shanghai Kaihong Technology Electronic Co. Ltd., which also handles packaging, assembly, testing, research and development and engineering; and Diodes Hong Kong Holding Company Limited, which contains a logistical center and handles sales and marketing. Diodes has approximately 250 direct customers worldwide, including original equipment manufacturers and electronic manufacturing services providers. The firm also has roughly 150 distributor customers around the world, through which it indirectly serves more than 50,000 customers. In November 2015, the firm acquired Pericom Semiconductor Corporation for $413 million.

FINANCIAL DATA: Note: Data for latest year may not have been available at press time.

In U.S. $	2016	2015	2014	2013	2012	2011
Revenue	942,162,000	848,904,000	890,651,000	826,846,000	633,806,000	635,251,000
R&D Expense	69,937,000	57,027,000	52,136,000	48,302,000	33,761,000	27,231,000
Operating Income	38,056,000	42,102,000	84,511,000	42,281,000	24,896,000	71,989,000
Operating Margin %	4.03%	4.95%	9.48%	5.11%	3.92%	11.33%
SGA Expense	158,256,000	139,245,000	133,701,000	132,106,000	101,363,000	89,974,000
Net Income	15,935,000	24,274,000	63,678,000	26,532,000	24,152,000	50,737,000
Operating Cash Flow	124,742,000	118,111,000	134,272,000	109,891,000	64,221,000	61,650,000
Capital Expenditure	58,549,000	133,244,000	57,766,000	47,054,000	58,166,000	80,941,000
EBITDA	137,257,000	124,927,000	167,095,000	117,772,000	95,876,000	128,241,000
Return on Assets %	1.01%	1.74%	5.43%	2.54%	2.81%	6.18%
Return on Equity %	2.02%	3.10%	8.65%	3.84%	3.68%	8.63%
Debt to Equity	0.53	0.57	0.18	0.26	0.06	

CONTACT INFORMATION:
Phone: 972 987-3900   Fax: 972-731-3510
Toll-Free:
Address: 4949 Hedgcoxe Road, Ste. 200, Plano, TX 75024 United States

STOCK TICKER/OTHER:
Stock Ticker: DIOD
Employees: 7,693
Parent Company:

Exchange: NAS
Fiscal Year Ends: 12/31

SALARIES/BONUSES:
Top Exec. Salary: $633,792   Bonus: $
Second Exec. Salary: $384,708   Bonus: $

OTHER THOUGHTS:
Estimated Female Officers or Directors: 1
Hot Spot for Advancement for Women/Minorities:

DIRECTV
NAIC Code: 517110

www.directv.com

TYPES OF BUSINESS:
Satellite Broadcasting
Commercial Satellite Fleet
Satellite-Based Internet Services
Digital Television

BRANDS/DIVISIONS/AFFILIATES:
AT&T Inc
DIRECTV Holdings LLC
DIRECTV Latin American Holdings Inc
DIRECTV Sports Networks LLC
Sky Brasil Servicos Ltda
PanAmericana
Sky Mexico
Game Show Network LLC

CONTACTS: *Note: Officers with more than one job title may be intentionally listed here more than once.*
Michael White, CEO
Patrick Doyle, CFO
Romulo Pontual, Chief Technology Officer
Larry Hunter, Executive VP
Joseph Bosch, Executive VP
Bruce Churchill, Executive VP
Steven Adams, Senior VP
Fazal Merchant, Senior VP

GROWTH PLANS/SPECIAL FEATURES:
DIRECTV, a wholly-owned subsidiary of AT&T, Inc., is a leading provider of digital television entertainment throughout the U.S. and Latin America. The company's three business segments, DIRECTV U.S., DIRECTV Latin America and DIRECTV Sports Networks, and their subsequent subsidiaries are engaged in digital entertainment programming via satellite for residential and commercial subscribers. DIRECTV U.S., operating through DIRECTV Holdings LLC, provides direct-to-home digital television services, with approximately 40 million subscribers. It offers one of the nation's most comprehensive selections of over 190 HD channels, 3D programming and Video on Demand services. It has a fleet of owned and leased satellites. DIRECTV Latin America, operated by DIRECTV Latin American Holdings, Inc., is comprised of PanAmericana; its 93%-owned subsidiary Sky Brasil Servicos Ltda.; and its 41% investment in Innova, S de RL de CV (known as Sky Mexico). DIRECTV Sports Networks, operating through DIRECTV Sports Networks LLC, is comprised primarily of three regional sports television networks based in Seattle, Denver and Pittsburgh, each of which operates under the Root Sports brand name. Additionally, DIRECTV owns a 42% interest in Game Show Network LLC, a basic television network dedicated to game-related programming and internet interactive game playing.

Employees receive medical, dental and vision coverage; flexible spending accounts; wellness plans; employee assistance programs; free DIRECTV service; discounted DIRECTV services for friends and family; and a 401(k) savings plan with a matching contribution opportunity.

FINANCIAL DATA: *Note: Data for latest year may not have been available at press time.*

In U.S. $	2016	2015	2014	2013	2012	2011
Revenue	33,703,000,000	34,000,000,000	33,260,000,000	31,754,000,000		
R&D Expense						
Operating Income						
Operating Margin %						
SGA Expense						
Net Income	32,000,000	-100,000	3,102,000,000	2,995,000,000		
Operating Cash Flow						
Capital Expenditure						
EBITDA						
Return on Assets %						
Return on Equity %						
Debt to Equity						

CONTACT INFORMATION:
Phone: 310-964-5000   Fax:
Toll-Free:
Address: 2260 E. Imperial Hwy., El Segundo, CA 90245 United States

STOCK TICKER/OTHER:
Stock Ticker: Subsidiary   Exchange:
Employees: 33,500   Fiscal Year Ends: 12/31
Parent Company: AT&T Inc

SALARIES/BONUSES:
Top Exec. Salary: $ Bonus: $
Second Exec. Salary: $ Bonus: $

OTHER THOUGHTS:
Estimated Female Officers or Directors: 3
Hot Spot for Advancement for Women/Minorities: Y

Discount Tire Company

www.discounttire.com

NAIC Code: 441320

TYPES OF BUSINESS:

Tire Stores
Mail-Order & Online Tire Sales
Roadside Assistance

BRANDS/DIVISIONS/AFFILIATES:

Discount Tire
America's Tire Co
CarCareONE

CONTACTS: Note: Officers with more than one job title may be intentionally listed here more than once.

Michael Zuieback, CEO
Michael Zuieback, Pres.
Christian Roe, CFO
Don G. Majors, Jr., VP-Mktg.
Charlie Baugh, CIO
Bruce T. Halle, Chmn.

GROWTH PLANS/SPECIAL FEATURES:

Discount Tire Company, based in Arizona, is one of the largest independent tire dealers in the U.S. The firm operates over 1,000 stores in 31 U.S. states. These stores operate under the Discount Tire name as well as under the America's Tire Co. name in certain parts of California. Discount Tire carries leading tire brands such as BF Goodrich, Michelin, Goodyear, Pirelli and GT Radial as well in-house exclusive brands Road Hugger, Arizonian, MB Wheels and Pathfinder tires and wheels. Types of tires offered by the company are lawn & garden, ATV/UTV, trailer, temporary spares, winter, performance truck, ribbed, highway all-season, mud-terrain, all-terrain, all-purpose, track and competition, summer performance, all-season performance, grand touring and the standard all-season touring. The company also repairs tires, offers tire rotations and balancing and provides free air pressure checking to its customers. In addition, the firm sells and delivers tires through its mail-order/online division (Discount Tire direct), which provides fast free shipping to a customer's door as well as through its web site. This web site also provides extensive information for its customers on all aspects of wheel and tire care. The company offers a Discount Tire/America's Tire CarCareONE card, a credit card that also provides emergency roadside assistance. The CarCareONE card is underwritten by Synchrony Financial.

Discount Tires offers its employees benefits including flexible spending accounts; an employee assistance program; medical, vision, life and dental insurance; paid vacation; a 401(k) plan; and profit sharing plans. Part-time employees are eligible for medical insurance and a 401(k).

FINANCIAL DATA: Note: Data for latest year may not have been available at press time.

In U.S. $	2016	2015	2014	2013	2012	2011
Revenue	4,340,000,000	4,200,000,000	3,900,000,000	3,500,000,000	3,300,000,000	3,100,000,000
R&D Expense						
Operating Income						
Operating Margin %						
SGA Expense						
Net Income						
Operating Cash Flow						
Capital Expenditure						
EBITDA						
Return on Assets %						
Return on Equity %						
Debt to Equity						

CONTACT INFORMATION:

Phone: 480-606-6000   Fax: 480-951-8619
Toll-Free:
Address: 20225 N. Scottsdale Rd., Scottsdale, AZ 85254 United States

STOCK TICKER/OTHER:

Stock Ticker: Private   Exchange:
Employees: 18,635   Fiscal Year Ends: 12/31
Parent Company:

SALARIES/BONUSES:

Top Exec. Salary: $ Bonus: $
Second Exec. Salary: $ Bonus: $

OTHER THOUGHTS:

Estimated Female Officers or Directors:
Hot Spot for Advancement for Women/Minorities:

Discovery Communications Inc

corporate.discovery.com

NAIC Code: 515210

TYPES OF BUSINESS:

Cable TV Networks
Digital Media
Catalog & Online Sales
Educational Products
E-commerce
Merchandising

BRANDS/DIVISIONS/AFFILIATES:

Discovery Channel
TLC
Eurosport
Oprah Winfrey Network (OWN, The)
DMAX
Investigation Discovery
American Heroes Channel
Velocity

CONTACTS: Note: Officers with more than one job title may be intentionally listed here more than once.

Jean-Briac Perrette, CEO, Divisional
David Zaslav, CEO
Gunnar Wiedenfels, CFO
Robert Miron, Chairman of the Board
Kurt Wehner, Chief Accounting Officer
Adria Romm, Other Corporate Officer
Paul Guyardo, Other Executive Officer
David Leavy, Other Executive Officer
Bruce Campbell, Other Executive Officer

GROWTH PLANS/SPECIAL FEATURES:

Discovery Communications, Inc. is a global media and entertainment company that produces and distributes original and purchased programming across multiple platforms to 2.8 billion cumulative subscribers across the globe. Discovery spans a variety of diverse genres, including exploration, survival, natural history, environment, technology, docu-series, health and wellness and space. The firm operates in four segments: U.S. networks, international networks, education and other. The U.S. networks segment operates and owns ten national TV networks: Discovery Channel, TLC, Animal Planet, Investigation Discovery, Science, American Heroes Channel and Velocity. The division also includes the firm's interests in The Oprah Winfrey Network (OWN) and Discovery Family (formerly The Hub). The firm's international networks reach more than 220 countries and territories around the world and are distributed in over 40 languages. Networks include Discovery Channel, Animal Planet, Eurosport, Turbo, DMAX and Discovery Kids. Education offers a suite of curriculum-based tools and educator enhancement resources that promote the integration of media and technology in the classroom. Other is largely comprised of production studios that develop television content for our networks and television service providers throughout the world. The company's portfolio also includes web sites, retail, merchandising and various digital media products and services. In August 2017, Discovery agreed to acquire Scripps Networks Interactive, Inc., a lifestyle programming firm that specializes in comfort-food television, for $11.9 billion. The deal is expected to close in early 2018, pending regulatory approval.

FINANCIAL DATA: Note: Data for latest year may not have been available at press time.

In U.S. $	2016	2015	2014	2013	2012	2011
Revenue	6,497,000,000	6,394,000,000	6,265,000,000	5,535,000,000	4,487,000,000	4,235,000,000
R&D Expense						
Operating Income	2,058,000,000	1,985,000,000	2,061,000,000	1,998,000,000	1,855,000,000	1,799,000,000
Operating Margin %	31.67%	31.04%	32.89%	36.09%	41.34%	42.47%
SGA Expense	1,690,000,000	1,669,000,000	1,692,000,000	1,575,000,000	1,291,000,000	1,183,000,000
Net Income	1,194,000,000	1,034,000,000	1,139,000,000	1,075,000,000	943,000,000	1,132,000,000
Operating Cash Flow	1,373,000,000	1,277,000,000	1,318,000,000	1,285,000,000	1,099,000,000	1,100,000,000
Capital Expenditure	88,000,000	103,000,000	120,000,000	115,000,000	77,000,000	58,000,000
EBITDA	2,346,000,000	2,219,000,000	2,404,000,000	2,318,000,000	1,883,000,000	2,732,000,000
Return on Assets %	5.79%	5.08%	5.82%	7.70%	7.59%	9.87%
Return on Equity %	17.26%	14.66%	15.29%	17.22%	14.72%	17.77%
Debt to Equity	1.51	1.39	1.07	1.04	0.82	0.64

CONTACT INFORMATION:

Phone: 240 662-2000   Fax: 240 662-1868
Toll-Free:
Address: 1 Discovery Pl., Silver Spring, MD 20910 United States

STOCK TICKER/OTHER:

Stock Ticker: DISCA
Employees: 7,000
Parent Company:

Exchange: NAS
Fiscal Year Ends: 12/31

SALARIES/BONUSES:

Top Exec. Salary: $3,000,000   Bonus: $
Second Exec. Salary: Bonus: $
$1,544,423

OTHER THOUGHTS:

Estimated Female Officers or Directors: 1
Hot Spot for Advancement for Women/Minorities: Y

Dollar Thrifty Automotive Group Inc

www.thrifty.com/AboutUs/content.aspx

NAIC Code: 532111

TYPES OF BUSINESS:

Automobile Rental
Used Car Sales
Financial Services

BRANDS/DIVISIONS/AFFILIATES:

Hertz Global Holdings Inc
Dollar
Thrifty

CONTACTS: Note: Officers with more than one job title may be intentionally listed here more than once.

Scott L. Thompson, Pres.
H. Clofford Buster, CFO
Rick L. Morris, CIO
Scott L. Thompson, Chmn.

GROWTH PLANS/SPECIAL FEATURES:

Dollar Thrifty Automotive Group, Inc. (DTG) is a holding company for rental car agencies that operate under the brand names Dollar and Thrifty. These agencies comprise one of the largest car rental networks in the world. DTG itself is a wholly-owned subsidiary of Hertz Global Holdings, Inc. There are more than 1,000 corporately-owned and franchised Dollar and Thrifty stores strategically located in 77 countries throughout North, Central and South America, Africa, the Middle East, the Caribbean, Asia and the Pacific. DTG also sells vehicle rental franchises worldwide, and provides sales and marketing, reservations, data processing systems, insurance and other services to franchisees. DTG offers customers supplemental equipment and optional products, including global positioning system equipment, ski racks, infant/child seats, as well as rent-a-toll products for electronic toll payments.

The company offers employees medical, dental and vision coverage; domestic partner benefits; flexible spending accounts; a wellness program; short- and long-term disability; life and AD&D insurance; an employee assistance program; a 401(k); tuition reimbursement; and employee discounts.

FINANCIAL DATA: Note: Data for latest year may not have been available at press time.

In U.S. $	2016	2015	2014	2013	2012	2011
Revenue	1,950,000,000	1,900,000,000	1,910,000,000	1,875,000,000	1,700,000,000	1,548,928,000
R&D Expense						
Operating Income						
Operating Margin %						
SGA Expense						
Net Income						
Operating Cash Flow						
Capital Expenditure						
EBITDA						
Return on Assets %						
Return on Equity %						
Debt to Equity						

CONTACT INFORMATION:

Phone: 918-660-7700   Fax: 918-669-2934
Toll-Free: 888-700-9803
Address: 5330 E. 31st St., Tulsa, OK 74135 United States

SALARIES/BONUSES:

Top Exec. Salary: $ Bonus: $
Second Exec. Salary: $ Bonus: $

STOCK TICKER/OTHER:

Stock Ticker: Subsidiary   Exchange:
Employees: 5,942   Fiscal Year Ends: 12/31
Parent Company: Hertz Global Holdings Inc

OTHER THOUGHTS:

Estimated Female Officers or Directors: 2
Hot Spot for Advancement for Women/Minorities:

Dow AgroSciences LLC

www.dowagro.com

NAIC Code: 325320

TYPES OF BUSINESS:

Agricultural Chemicals
Agricultural Biotechnology Products
Herbicides, Pesticides & Fungicides
Plant Genetics

BRANDS/DIVISIONS/AFFILIATES:

Dow Chemical Company (The)
Herculex
WideStrike
SpinTor
Triumph

CONTACTS: *Note: Officers with more than one job title may be intentionally listed here more than once.*

Tim Hassinger, CEO
Susan Lewis, COO
Antonio Galindez, Pres.
Beth Nicholas, CFO
Audrey Grimm, Human Resources

GROWTH PLANS/SPECIAL FEATURES:

Dow AgroSciences LLC, a wholly-owned subsidiary of The Dow Chemical Company, is a global provider of pest management and biotechnology products for agricultural and specialty markets. Dow ArgoSciences produces more than 25 product lines, which encompass the Herculex, WideStrike, SpinTor, Triumph brands, among others. The firm operates in two business units: crop protection and seeds. The crop protection unit offers insecticide, herbicide, fungicide and fumigant technologies for vegetation management, range and pastureland, turf and ornamental plants, as well as pest management products and solutions for the prevention of structural damages to homes and buildings. The seeds business unit includes seeds and trait research, production of seeds for a wide range of crops, plant biotechnology for crop improvement and disease management and investments in canola and sunflower seeds for production of omega-9 healthy oils. The firm has engaged in many collaboration ventures with companies such as Monsanto, a global provider of agricultural products and technology-based solutions; KeyGene, a research and development company focused on developing and applying DNA expertise in the molecular genetics of crop plants; Chromatin, Inc., which develops and markets proprietary technology that allows whole chromosomes to be designed and integrated into plant cells; and NemGenix, an agricultural biotechnology company based in Perth, Australia.

Dow AgroSciences offers its employees medical and dental plans, life and AD&D insurance, annual bonuses linked to company performance, a profit sharing plan, an employee stock purchase plan, a 401(k) savings plan and a pension.

FINANCIAL DATA: *Note: Data for latest year may not have been available at press time.*

In U.S. $	2016	2015	2014	2013	2012	2011
Revenue	1,006,200,000	860,000,000	850,000,000	840,000,000	800,000,000	700,000,000
R&D Expense						
Operating Income						
Operating Margin %						
SGA Expense						
Net Income						
Operating Cash Flow						
Capital Expenditure						
EBITDA						
Return on Assets %						
Return on Equity %						
Debt to Equity						

CONTACT INFORMATION:

Phone: 317-337-3000   Fax:
Toll-Free:
Address: 9330 Zionsville Rd., Indianapolis, IN 46268 United States

STOCK TICKER/OTHER:

Stock Ticker: Subsidiary   Exchange:
Employees: 7,700   Fiscal Year Ends: 12/31
Parent Company: Dow Chemical Company (The)

SALARIES/BONUSES:

Top Exec. Salary: $ Bonus: $
Second Exec. Salary: $ Bonus: $

OTHER THOUGHTS:

Estimated Female Officers or Directors:
Hot Spot for Advancement for Women/Minorities:

DR Horton Inc

NAIC Code: 236117

www.drhorton.com

TYPES OF BUSINESS:

Construction, Home Building and Residential
Mortgages
Title Insurance

BRANDS/DIVISIONS/AFFILIATES:

DHI Mortgage
Wilson Parker Homes

CONTACTS: Note: Officers with more than one job title may be intentionally listed here more than once.

Thomas Montano, Assistant Secretary
Bill Wheat, CFO
Donald Horton, Chairman of the Board
Michael Murray, COO
David Auld, President

GROWTH PLANS/SPECIAL FEATURES:

D.R. Horton, Inc. is a leading national builder of single-family homes with a diversified set of holdings and operating divisions in 26 states and 78 metropolitan markets. The firm generally builds homes between 1,000 to 4,000 square feet, ranging in price from $100,000 to over 1 million. In 2016, the company closed approximately 36,648 homes, with an average closing sales price approximating $285,700. The company is divided into six regional homebuilding segments and one financial services segment. The homebuilding segments are East, operating in eight states; Midwest, three states; Southeast, five states; South Central, three states; Southwest, two states; and West, six states. The building services section constructs residences, tailored to the particular community where they are being built, including single-family residential homes, townhouses, condominiums, duplexes and triplexes. Detached homes sales accounted for 89% of the firm's 2016 revenues. Subcontractors under the supervision of D. R. Horton do substantially all the actual building. The financial services segment of the company provides mortgage financing and title insurance through its wholly-owned subsidiary, DHI Mortgage. The home builder's current business strategy is to enter new lot option contracts to purchase finished lots in selected communities to potentially increase sales volumes and profitability. The firm plans to renegotiate existing lot option contracts as necessary to reduce lot costs and better match the scheduled lot purchases with new home demand in each community. The company also manages inventory of homes under construction by selectively starting construction on unsold homes to capture new home demand while monitoring the number and aging of unsold homes and aggressively marketing its unsold, completed homes in inventory. In September 2016, the firm acquired Wilson Parker Homes, whose operations are in Georgia, North Carolina, South Carolina and Arizona.

FINANCIAL DATA: Note: Data for latest year may not have been available at press time.

In U.S. $	2016	2015	2014	2013	2012	2011
Revenue	12,157,400,000	10,824,000,000	8,024,900,000	6,259,300,000	4,354,000,000	3,636,800,000
R&D Expense						
Operating Income	1,334,500,000	1,092,500,000	790,900,000	654,400,000	242,900,000	12,100,000
Operating Margin %	10.97%	10.09%	9.85%	10.45%	5.57%	.33%
SGA Expense	1,320,300,000	1,186,000,000	965,400,000	766,300,000	614,100,000	556,300,000
Net Income	886,300,000	750,700,000	533,500,000	462,700,000	956,300,000	71,800,000
Operating Cash Flow	618,000,000	700,400,000	-661,400,000	-1,231,100,000	-298,100,000	14,900,000
Capital Expenditure	86,100,000	56,100,000	100,200,000	58,000,000	33,600,000	16,300,000
EBITDA	1,395,500,000	1,177,500,000	852,600,000	685,600,000	288,600,000	83,900,000
Return on Assets %	7.80%	7.03%	5.59%	5.74%	15.17%	1.27%
Return on Equity %	13.97%	13.63%	11.63%	12.09%	30.78%	2.74%
Debt to Equity	0.48	0.64	0.71	0.86	0.69	0.65

CONTACT INFORMATION:

Phone: 817-390-8200   Fax: 817 856-8429
Toll-Free:
Address: 301 Commerce St., Ste. 500, Fort Worth, TX 76102 United States

STOCK TICKER/OTHER:

Stock Ticker: DHI
Employees: 6,976
Parent Company:

Exchange: NYS
Fiscal Year Ends: 09/30

SALARIES/BONUSES:

Top Exec. Salary: $500,000   Bonus: $1,100,000
Second Exec. Salary: $1,000,000   Bonus: $

OTHER THOUGHTS:

Estimated Female Officers or Directors: 1
Hot Spot for Advancement for Women/Minorities:

DriveTime Automotive Group Inc

www.drivetime.com

NAIC Code: 441120

TYPES OF BUSINESS:

Used Auto Dealers
Auto Financing
Auto Leasing

BRANDS/DIVISIONS/AFFILIATES:

DriveCare Powertrain Protection Plan
Bridgecrest Acceptance Company

CONTACTS: Note: Officers with more than one job title may be intentionally listed here more than once.

Ray Fidel, CEO
Ray Fidel, Pres.
Mark G. Sauder, CFO
Scott Worthington, VP-Mktg.
Chris Braddock, VP-Sales
Paul I. Kaplan, CIO
Jon Ehlinger, General Counsel
Jon Ehlinger, VP-Public Rel.
Al Appelman, VP-Risk & Customer Analytics
Ernest C. Garcia II, Chmn.

GROWTH PLANS/SPECIAL FEATURES:

DriveTime Automotive Group, Inc. is a leading chain of buy-here-pay-here used car dealerships. The company targets its products and services to the sub-prime segment of the automobile financing industry. This segment serves customers with limited credit histories, low income or past credit problems who cannot access traditional financing. Advantages of buy-here-pay-here dealerships include the ability to offer customers expanded credit opportunities and flexible payment terms as well as the ability to make payments at the dealership. For each used vehicle sold, the company offers a 30-day limited warranty, 5-day return guarantee, autocheck history report and a certified multi-point inspection. The firm finances all the used cars through retail installment contracts. DriveTime currently operates 144 dealerships nationwide. The dealerships are located in high-visibility, high-traffic commercial areas and comprise more than 11,000 available vehicles (all DriveTime dealerships combined), featuring a wide selection of makes and models. The ages of the cars typically range from three to seven years. DriveTime acquires its inventory primarily from used vehicle auctions. After purchase, the cars are delivered to one of the company's centers, where they are inspected thoroughly and reconditioned for sale. The company offers its DriveCare Powertrain Protection Plan to customers interested in extended protection coverage. Besides flexible auto loan financing, no-commitment lease options are also offered. Subsidiary Bridgecrest Acceptance Company is a licensed third-party servicer that services loans for DriveTime and other affiliated finance companies. All credit scoring, risk decision analytics and verifications remain the responsibility of DriveTime.

DriveTime offers its employees benefits including medical, dental, vision, disability and life insurance; paid time off; a 401(k); flexible spending accounts; and tuition reimbursement.

FINANCIAL DATA: Note: Data for latest year may not have been available at press time.

In U.S. $	2016	2015	2014	2013	2012	2011
Revenue	1,600,000,000	1,525,000,000	1,475,000,000	1,400,896,000	1,221,064,000	1,121,967,000
R&D Expense						
Operating Income						
Operating Margin %						
SGA Expense						
Net Income						
Operating Cash Flow						
Capital Expenditure						
EBITDA						
Return on Assets %						
Return on Equity %						
Debt to Equity						

CONTACT INFORMATION:

Phone: Fax:
Toll-Free: 888-418-1212
Address: 1720 W. Rio Salado Pkwy, Tempe, AZ 85281 United States

STOCK TICKER/OTHER:

Stock Ticker: Private   Exchange:
Employees: 4,430   Fiscal Year Ends: 12/31
Parent Company:

SALARIES/BONUSES:

Top Exec. Salary: $ Bonus: $
Second Exec. Salary: $ Bonus: $

OTHER THOUGHTS:

Estimated Female Officers or Directors:
Hot Spot for Advancement for Women/Minorities:

DTE Energy Company

www.dteenergy.com

NAIC Code: 221112

TYPES OF BUSINESS:
Utilities-Electricity & Natural Gas
Energy Management
Wholesale Energy Trading
Fuel Supply Services
Hydroelectric Power
Nuclear Power
Coal Shipping-Rail & Boat
Consulting Services

BRANDS/DIVISIONS/AFFILIATES:
DTE Electric
DTE Gas

CONTACTS: Note: Officers with more than one job title may be intentionally listed here more than once.
Gerard Anderson, CEO
Peter Oleksiak, CFO
Donna England, Chief Accounting Officer
David Meador, Chief Administrative Officer
Mark Stiers, COO, Subsidiary
Trevor Lauer, COO, Subsidiary
Gerardo Norcia, COO
Bruce Peterson, General Counsel
Lisa Muschong, Other Executive Officer
David Ruud, President, Divisional
Larry Steward, Senior VP, Divisional
Steve Kurmas, Vice Chairman

GROWTH PLANS/SPECIAL FEATURES:
DTE Energy Company is a diversified energy and energy technology company that develops merchant power and industrial energy projects and works in energy trading, selling electricity, natural gas, coal, chilled water, landfill gas and steam. DTE is also one of the nation's largest purchasers, transporters and marketers of coal. The company's operations are divided into four segments: electric, gas, non-utility operations and corporate & other. The electric segment consists of DTE Electric, which is engaged in the generation, purchase, distribution and sale of electricity to approximately 2.2 million residential, commercial and industrial customers in southeastern Michigan. The gas segment is represented by DTE Gas, which buys, stores, transports and distributes natural gas to 1.3 million residential, commercial and industrial customers. The firm's non-utility operations segment include gas storage & pipelines, encompassing DTE's interstate gas transmission pipelines and storage facilities; power & industrial projects, primarily consisting of energy product delivery, coal transportation, as well as marketing and electricity provided by biomass-fueled energy projects; and energy trading, which buys, sells and trades electricity, coal and natural gas, and provides risk management services such as energy marketing and trading operations. The corporate & other segment consists of various holding company activities, certain non-utility debt and energy-related investments. In 2016, the firm retired three coal-fired generating units among its plants, and announced plans to close eight additional coal-fired generators at three plants in Michigan by 2023, replacing them with renewable energy.

DTE offers its employees medical, dental and vision coverage; comprehensive wellness programs; a 401(k) plan; flexible spending accounts; an employee assistance program; long-term care insurance; life, disability and AD&D insurance; and flex time.

FINANCIAL DATA: Note: Data for latest year may not have been available at press time.

In U.S. $	2016	2015	2014	2013	2012	2011
Revenue	10,630,000,000	10,337,000,000	12,301,000,000	9,661,000,000	8,791,000,000	8,897,000,000
R&D Expense						
Operating Income	1,445,000,000	1,239,000,000	1,590,000,000	1,203,000,000	1,279,000,000	1,423,000,000
Operating Margin %	13.59%	11.98%	12.92%	12.45%	14.54%	15.99%
SGA Expense						
Net Income	868,000,000	727,000,000	905,000,000	661,000,000	610,000,000	711,000,000
Operating Cash Flow	2,084,000,000	1,911,000,000	1,839,000,000	2,154,000,000	2,209,000,000	2,008,000,000
Capital Expenditure	2,045,000,000	2,020,000,000	2,049,000,000	1,876,000,000	1,820,000,000	1,484,000,000
EBITDA	2,553,000,000	2,252,000,000	2,849,000,000	2,452,000,000	2,418,000,000	2,476,000,000
Return on Assets %	2.85%	2.56%	3.35%	2.52%	2.33%	2.79%
Return on Equity %	9.76%	8.50%	11.13%	8.64%	8.48%	10.35%
Debt to Equity	1.25	1.00	1.00	0.91	0.95	1.02

CONTACT INFORMATION:
Phone: 313 235-4000 Fax: 313 235-6743
Toll-Free: 866-966-5555
Address: 1 Energy Plaza, Detroit, MI 48226 United States

STOCK TICKER/OTHER:
Stock Ticker: DTE Exchange: NYS
Employees: 10,000 Fiscal Year Ends: 12/31
Parent Company:

SALARIES/BONUSES:
Top Exec. Salary: $1,293,519 Bonus: $
Second Exec. Salary: $694,815 Bonus: $

OTHER THOUGHTS:
Estimated Female Officers or Directors: 8
Hot Spot for Advancement for Women/Minorities: Y

Sales, profits and employees may be estimates. Financial information, benefits and other data can change quickly and may vary from those stated here.

Duke Energy Corporation

www.duke-energy.com

NAIC Code: 221112

TYPES OF BUSINESS:
Utilities-Electricity & Natural Gas
Merchant Power Generation
Natural Gas Transportation & Storage
Electricity Transmission
Energy Marketing
Real Estate
Telecommunications
Facility & Plant Services

BRANDS/DIVISIONS/AFFILIATES:
Duke Energy Carolinas
Duke Energy Progress
Duke Energy Florida
Duke Energy Indiana
Duke Energy Ohio
Duke-American Transmission Co
Piedmont Natural Gas

CONTACTS: Note: Officers with more than one job title may be intentionally listed here more than once.
Lynn Good, CEO
Steven Young, CFO
William Currens, Chief Accounting Officer
Melissa Anderson, Executive VP, Divisional
Lloyd Yates, Executive VP, Divisional
Douglas Esamann, Executive VP, Divisional
Dhiaa Jamil, Executive VP
Julie Janson, Executive VP
Franklin Yoho, Executive VP

GROWTH PLANS/SPECIAL FEATURES:
Duke Energy Corporation is an energy services provider that offers delivery and management of electricity and natural gas throughout the U.S. The company operates in three segments: Electric Utilities and Infrastructure (EUI), Gas Utilities and Infrastructure (GUI) and Commercial Renewables. EUI conducts operations primarily through the regulated public utilities of Duke Energy Carolinas, Duke Energy Progress, Duke Energy Florida, Duke Energy Indiana and Duke Energy Ohio. This segment provides retail electric service through the generation, transmission, distribution and sale of electricity to approximately 7.5 million customers within the Southeast and Midwest regions of the U.S. EUI also has a 50% stake in Duke-American Transmission Co., a partnership with American Transmission Company, formed to design, build and operate transmission infrastructure. GUI conducts natural gas operations primarily through the regulated public utilities of Piedmont and Duke Energy Ohio. This segment serves 1.5 million residential, commercial, industrial and power generation natural gas customers. GUI also owns, operates and has investments in various pipeline transmission and natural gas storage facilities. The Commercial Renewables segment primarily acquires, builds, develops and operates wind and solar renewable generation throughout the continental U.S. The portfolio includes nonregulated renewable energy and energy storage businesses. Included within the segment is utility-scale wind and solar generation assets which total 2,900 megawatts across 14 states from 21 wind farms and 63 commercial solar farms. In 2016, Duke Energy completed the acquisition of Piedmont Natural Gas, adding a million natural gas customers and 7.4 million electric customers to its customer base; sold its Brazilian holdings to China Three Gorges Corporation; and sold its international businesses in Peru, Chile, Ecuador, El Salvador and Argentina to I Square Capital.

The firm offers employees life, disability, medical, dental and vision insurance; retirement benefits; and wellness programs.

FINANCIAL DATA: Note: Data for latest year may not have been available at press time.

In U.S. $	2016	2015	2014	2013	2012	2011
Revenue	22,743,000,000	23,459,000,000	23,925,000,000	24,598,000,000	19,624,000,000	14,529,000,000
R&D Expense						
Operating Income	5,341,000,000	5,367,000,000	5,258,000,000	4,982,000,000	3,110,000,000	2,777,000,000
Operating Margin %	23.48%	22.87%	21.97%	20.25%	15.84%	19.11%
SGA Expense						
Net Income	2,152,000,000	2,816,000,000	1,883,000,000	2,665,000,000	1,768,000,000	1,706,000,000
Operating Cash Flow	6,798,000,000	6,676,000,000	6,586,000,000	6,382,000,000	5,244,000,000	3,672,000,000
Capital Expenditure	7,901,000,000	6,766,000,000	5,384,000,000	5,526,000,000	5,501,000,000	4,372,000,000
EBITDA	9,530,000,000	9,363,000,000	9,263,000,000	8,695,000,000	6,345,000,000	5,350,000,000
Return on Assets %	1.69%	2.32%	1.59%	2.33%	2.00%	2.80%
Return on Equity %	5.32%	6.98%	4.58%	6.49%	5.56%	7.53%
Debt to Equity	1.11	0.94	0.91	0.92	0.89	0.82

CONTACT INFORMATION:
Phone: 704-382-3853 Fax: 704-382-3814
Toll-Free: 800-873-3853
Address: 550 S. Tryon St., Charlotte, NC 28202 United States

STOCK TICKER/OTHER:
Stock Ticker: DUK Exchange: NYS
Employees: 28,798 Fiscal Year Ends: 12/31
Parent Company:

SALARIES/BONUSES:
Top Exec. Salary: $1,291,667 Bonus: $
Second Exec. Salary: $737,500 Bonus: $

OTHER THOUGHTS:
Estimated Female Officers or Directors: 8
Hot Spot for Advancement for Women/Minorities: Y

Dycom Industries Inc

www.dycomind.com

NAIC Code: 237130

TYPES OF BUSINESS:

Construction, Maintenance & Installation Services
Engineering Services
Utility Maintenance Services

BRANDS/DIVISIONS/AFFILIATES:

CONTACTS: Note: Officers with more than one job title may be intentionally listed here more than once.

Laurie Thomsen,
Eitan Gertel,
Steven Nielsen, CEO
H. Deferrari, CFO
Timothy Estes, Executive VP
Kimberly Dickens, Other Executive Officer
Richard Vilsoet, Secretary
Rebecca Roach, Vice President

GROWTH PLANS/SPECIAL FEATURES:

Dycom Industries, Inc. is a leading provider of specialty contracting services. Dycom provides services throughout the U.S. and on a limited basis in Canada. Services include engineering, construction, maintenance and installation services to telecommunications providers; underground locating services to various utilities including telecommunications providers; and other construction and maintenance services to electric utilities. The company's top five customers accounted for approximately 69.7% of its 2016 revenue and received 24.4% of its revenue from AT&T, 14.5% from Century Link Inc., 13.6% from Comcast Corporation, 11% from Verizon Communications and 6.2% from another significant customer. Dycom provides outside plant engineers and drafters to telecommunication providers who design aerial, underground and buried fiber optic, copper and coaxial cable systems that extend from the telephone company's central office, or cable operator headend, to the consumer's home or business. Engineering services the firm provides to telephone companies include fiber cable routing and design; the design of service area concept boxes, terminals, drops and transmission and central office equipment; and the proper administration of feeder and distribution cable pairs. For cable television multiple system operators, Dycom performs make-ready studies, strand mapping, field walk-out, computer-aided radio frequency design and fiber cable routing and design. The firm's construction, maintenance and installation services include placing and splicing fiber, copper and coaxial cables; excavating trenches in which to place cables; placing related structures such as poles, anchors, conduits, manholes, cabinets and closures; placing drop lines from main distribution lines to the consumer's home or business; and maintaining and removing these facilities. It also provides premise wiring services to various corporations and state and local governments, predominantly limited to the installation, repair and maintenance of telecommunications infrastructure within improved structures.

FINANCIAL DATA: Note: Data for latest year may not have been available at press time.

In U.S. $	2016	2015	2014	2013	2012	2011
Revenue	2,672,542,000	2,022,312,000	1,811,593,000	1,608,612,000	1,201,119,000	1,035,868,000
R&D Expense						
Operating Income	246,874,000	154,318,000	81,918,000	76,944,000	65,453,000	41,594,000
Operating Margin %	9.23%	7.63%	4.52%	4.78%	5.44%	4.01%
SGA Expense	217,149,000	178,700,000	161,858,000	145,771,000	104,024,000	94,622,000
Net Income	128,740,000	84,324,000	39,978,000	35,188,000	39,378,000	16,107,000
Operating Cash Flow	261,488,000	141,900,000	84,185,000	106,744,000	65,125,000	43,857,000
Capital Expenditure	186,011,000	102,997,000	89,136,000	64,650,000	77,612,000	61,457,000
EBITDA	371,814,000	250,362,000	174,690,000	162,425,000	143,971,000	107,034,000
Return on Assets %	8.36%	6.55%	3.37%	3.65%	5.26%	2.29%
Return on Equity %	24.18%	16.99%	8.75%	8.56%	10.57%	4.31%
Debt to Equity	1.26	1.02	0.92	1.03	0.47	0.53

CONTACT INFORMATION:

Phone: 561 627-7171   Fax: 561 627-7709
Toll-Free:
Address: 11780 U.S. Highway 1, Ste. 600, Palm Beach Gardens, FL 33408 United States

STOCK TICKER/OTHER:

Stock Ticker: DY   Exchange: NYS
Employees: 11,159   Fiscal Year Ends: 07/31
Parent Company:

SALARIES/BONUSES:

Top Exec. Salary: $910,000   Bonus: $
Second Exec. Salary: $450,000   Bonus: $400,000

OTHER THOUGHTS:

Estimated Female Officers or Directors:
Hot Spot for Advancement for Women/Minorities:

EchoStar Corporation

NAIC Code: 517110

www.echostar.com

TYPES OF BUSINESS:
Digital Set-Top Boxes & Related Products
Fixed Satellite Services

BRANDS/DIVISIONS/AFFILIATES:
EchoStar Technologies
Echostar Satellite Services
Hughes Communications Inc
EchoStar Mobile Limited
EchoStar XXI
EchoStar XXII
EchoStar XIX

CONTACTS: *Note: Officers with more than one job title may be intentionally listed here more than once.*
Michael Dugan, CEO
David Rayner, CFO
Charles Ergen, Chairman of the Board
Pradman Kaul, Director
Kranti Kilaru, Executive VP, Divisional
Dean Manson, Executive VP
Anders Johnson, Other Executive Officer

GROWTH PLANS/SPECIAL FEATURES:
EchoStar Corp. is a global provider of satellite operations, video delivery solutions and broadband satellite technologies and services for home and office, delivering innovative network technologies, managed services and solutions for enterprises and governments. The company operates in three business segments: Hughes Communications, Inc.; EchoStar Technologies; and EchoStar Satellite Services. Hughes provides satellite broadband internet to North American consumers and broadband network services and equipment to domestic and international enterprise markets. The Hughes segment also offers managed services to large enterprises, as well as solutions to customers for mobile satellite systems. EchoStar Technologies designs, develops, and distributes set-top boxes technology primarily for satellite TV service providers, telecommunication and international cable companies and directly to consumers. This segment additionally provides digital broadcast operations such as satellite uplinking/downlinking and transmission services. EchoStar Technologies offer its TV Anywhere technology through Slingbox units directly to consumers via retail outlets and online, as well as to the pay-TV operator market. EchoStar Satellite Services provides satellite services on a full-time and occasional-use basis primarily to DISH Network, Dish Mexico, U.S. government service providers, internet service providers, broadcast news organizations, programmers and private enterprise customers. Subsidiary EchoStar Mobile Limited is based in Ireland and licensed by the European Union (EU) to provide mobile satellite service/complementary ground component (MSS/CGC) services covering the entire EU using S-band spectrum. Due to delays with its launch provider, this division is scheduled to launch EchoStar XXI and EchoStar XXII in mid to late-2017, to provide space segment capacity to EchoStar Mobile. In December 2016, the EchoStar XIX was launched and provides additional capacity for the Hughes broadband services segment.

The firm offers employees medical, dental and vision plans; tuition reimbursement; discounted employee products and services; disability and life insurance; a 401(k) plan; and an employee stock purchase program.

FINANCIAL DATA: *Note: Data for latest year may not have been available at press time.*

In U.S. $	2016	2015	2014	2013	2012	2011
Revenue	3,056,730,000	3,143,714,000	3,445,578,000	3,282,452,000	3,121,704,000	2,761,431,000
R&D Expense	76,024,000	73,717,000	60,886,000	67,942,000	69,649,000	50,966,000
Operating Income	364,398,000	356,033,000	328,090,000	103,587,000	99,886,000	80,838,000
Operating Margin %	11.92%	11.32%	9.52%	3.15%	3.19%	2.92%
SGA Expense	385,634,000	378,686,000	372,010,000	358,499,000	372,644,000	303,276,000
Net Income	179,930,000	153,357,000	152,874,000	2,525,000	211,048,000	3,639,000
Operating Cash Flow	803,343,000	776,451,000	840,131,000	450,507,000	505,149,000	447,018,000
Capital Expenditure	721,506,000	729,275,000	680,026,000	433,621,000	611,482,000	377,172,000
EBITDA	905,542,000	871,796,000	906,358,000	665,629,000	805,039,000	494,262,000
Return on Assets %	2.23%	2.25%	2.36%	.03%	3.21%	.07%
Return on Equity %	4.77%	4.52%	4.89%	.07%	6.82%	.12%
Debt to Equity	0.92	0.59	0.65	0.73	0.77	0.81

CONTACT INFORMATION:
Phone: 303 706-4000   Fax:
Toll-Free:
Address: 100 Inverness Terrace E., Englewood, CO 80112 United States

STOCK TICKER/OTHER:
Stock Ticker: SATS   Exchange: NAS
Employees: 4,000   Fiscal Year Ends: 12/31
Parent Company:

SALARIES/BONUSES:
Top Exec. Salary: $850,013   Bonus: $
Second Exec. Salary: $769,621   Bonus: $

OTHER THOUGHTS:
Estimated Female Officers or Directors: 1
Hot Spot for Advancement for Women/Minorities:

Sales, profits and employees may be estimates. Financial information, benefits and other data can change quickly and may vary from those stated here.

eClinicalWorks

NAIC Code: 0

www.eclinicalworks.com

TYPES OF BUSINESS:

Computer Software, Healthcare & Biotechnology
Electronic Prescription Filing
Patient Flow Management
Claims Submission & Management Software
Business Optimization Software

BRANDS/DIVISIONS/AFFILIATES:

Enterprise Business Optimizer
eClinicalWorks HMS
eClinicalWorks CCMR

CONTACTS: *Note: Officers with more than one job title may be intentionally listed here more than once.*

Girish Kumar Navani, CEO

GROWTH PLANS/SPECIAL FEATURES:

eClinicalWorks is a private company operating in the ambulatory clinical systems market. The company primarily provides electronic medical record (EMR) and practice management tools for its clients, including physicians; large and small health systems; large and medium medical group practices, including federally qualified health centers and community health centers; and small, solo provider practices. The firm's customer base consists of more than 125,000 physicians and over 850,000 medical professionals in all 50 states and 24 countries. eClinicalWorks' EMR cloud solution provides patient flow management, patient record access, registry reporting, electronic prescription request, referring physician communication and clinical data transfers, all while keeping the data private. When used with the firm's PM system, this system enables clients to review patient history, current medications, allergies and diagnostic tests; streamline medical billing management; check patient insurance eligibility; electronically submit and manage claims; and perform clinical and financial analyses through its Enterprise Business Optimizer (eBO) tool. eClinicalWorks HMS is a web-based product that covers the clinical, administrative and financial areas of an integrated healthcare delivery system. Other suites include eClinicalWorks CCMR, a population health program across all functional accountable care organization (ACO) categories; the health and online wellness suite, which offer tools that facilitates secure communication between providers and patients; and the revenue cycle management console, which assists in processing claims, financial analytics, reimbursement evaluation and six levels of clearinghouse integrations. The company also maintains a web-based patient portal, eClinicalWorks' patient portal allows patients to access their physician's systems to view their own lab results and appointment information as well as request prescription refills and communicate with doctors and nurses.

eClinicalWorks offers its employees health, dental, vision, life and disability insurance; flexible spending accounts; and a 401(k) plan.

FINANCIAL DATA: *Note: Data for latest year may not have been available at press time.*

In U.S. $	2016	2015	2014	2013	2012	2011
Revenue	440,000,000	358,000,000	333,000,000	300,000,000	255,000,000	204,700,000
R&D Expense						
Operating Income						
Operating Margin %						
SGA Expense						
Net Income						
Operating Cash Flow						
Capital Expenditure						
EBITDA						
Return on Assets %						
Return on Equity %						
Debt to Equity						

CONTACT INFORMATION:

Phone: 508-836-2700   Fax: 508-836-4466
Toll-Free: 866-888-6929
Address: 2 Technology Dr., Westborough, MA 01581 United States

STOCK TICKER/OTHER:

Stock Ticker: Private   Exchange:
Employees: 4,500   Fiscal Year Ends: 12/31
Parent Company:

SALARIES/BONUSES:

Top Exec. Salary: $ Bonus: $
Second Exec. Salary: $ Bonus: $

OTHER THOUGHTS:

Estimated Female Officers or Directors:
Hot Spot for Advancement for Women/Minorities:

Edward D Jones & Co LP

www.edwardjones.com

NAIC Code: 523120

TYPES OF BUSINESS:

Stock Brokerage
Financial Planning
Retirement & Estate Planning
Life Insurance
Banking Services
Annuities

BRANDS/DIVISIONS/AFFILIATES:

Jones Financial Companies LLLP (The)
Edward Jones

CONTACTS: *Note: Officers with more than one job title may be intentionally listed here more than once.*

James D. Weddle, Managing Partner
Kavin D. Bastien, CFO
Norman Eaker, Principal-Firm Admin.
James A. Tricarico, General Counsel

GROWTH PLANS/SPECIAL FEATURES:

Edward D. Jones & Co. LP, which trades under the name Edward Jones, is an investment brokerage network specifically focused on individual investors, most of whom are retired, as well as small-business owners in rural communities and suburbs. The firm serves nearly 7 million clients and has a network of approximately 12,700 offices in the U.S. and Canada. Edward Jones keeps its offices continuously connected through satellite uplinks. Edward Jones brokers focus on conservative long-term investors with the intention of buying and holding stocks in relatively low-risk investment portfolios in government bonds, blue-chip stocks and high-quality mutual funds. Other products from the company include annuities, college saving programs, estate planning, life insurance, retirement plans and traditional banking services, such as savings and checking accounts. The firm also maintains a research department to provide specific investment recommendations and market information for retail customers. Edward Jones' web site offers financial planning for life events, including buying a home, expecting a child, changing jobs and the loss of a loved one. Edward D. Jones & Co. is a wholly-owned subsidiary of Jones Financial Companies LLLP.

The company offers employees medical and dental benefits, 401(k) plans, life and disability insurance, a profit sharing plan and tuition reimbursement.

FINANCIAL DATA: *Note: Data for latest year may not have been available at press time.*

In U.S. $	2016	2015	2014	2013	2012	2011
Revenue	6,557,000,000	6,619,000,000	6,278,000,000	5,657,000,000	4,965,200,000	4,509,861,000
R&D Expense						
Operating Income						
Operating Margin %						
SGA Expense						
Net Income	746,000,000	838,000,000	770,000,000	674,338,000	555,000,000	481,783,000
Operating Cash Flow						
Capital Expenditure						
EBITDA						
Return on Assets %						
Return on Equity %						
Debt to Equity						

CONTACT INFORMATION:

Phone: 314-515-2000   Fax: 314-515-2622
Toll-Free:
Address: 12555 Manchester Rd., Des Peres, MO 63131 United States

STOCK TICKER/OTHER:

Stock Ticker: Subsidiary   Exchange:
Employees: 43,000   Fiscal Year Ends: 12/31
Parent Company: Jones Financial Companies LLLP (The)

SALARIES/BONUSES:

Top Exec. Salary: $ Bonus: $
Second Exec. Salary: $ Bonus: $

OTHER THOUGHTS:

Estimated Female Officers or Directors: 3
Hot Spot for Advancement for Women/Minorities: Y

Edwards Lifesciences Corporation

www.edwards.com

NAIC Code: 339100

TYPES OF BUSINESS:

Supplies-Cardiovascular Disease Related
Cardiac Surgery Products
Critical Care Products
Vascular Products
Heart Valve Implants

BRANDS/DIVISIONS/AFFILIATES:

PERIMOUNT
Edwards Intuity Valve System
Edwards SAPIEN
Swan-Ganz
FloTrac
ClearSight
EV1000
Valtech Cardio Ltd

CONTACTS: Note: Officers with more than one job title may be intentionally listed here more than once.

Michael Mussallem, CEO
Scott Ullem, CFO
Robert Sellers, Chief Accounting Officer
Larry Wood, Vice President, Divisional
Catherine Szyman, Vice President, Divisional
Donald Bobo, Vice President, Divisional
Bernard Zovighian, Vice President, Divisional
Huimin Wang, Vice President, Geographical
Patrick Verguet, Vice President, Geographical

GROWTH PLANS/SPECIAL FEATURES:

Edwards Lifesciences Corporation designs products for cardiovascular diseases, such as heart valve disease, coronary artery disease, peripheral vascular disease (PVD) and congestive heart failure. The firm operates in three main areas: surgical heart valve therapy (23% of 2016 net sales), transcatheter heart valves (55%) and critical care (12%). Surgical heart valve products include the PERIMOUNT line of pericardial heart valves made from biologically inert porcine tissue, often on a wire-form stent; and valve repair therapies, such as the Edwards Intuity Valve System, a minimally-invasive aortic system designed to enable a faster procedure and a smaller incision. Transcatheter heart valves are designed to treat heart valves disease using catheter-based approaches. Its main products are the Edwards SAPIEN, Sapien XT and Sapien 3 transcatheter aortic heart valves and delivery systems used to treat heart valve disease using catheter-based approaches for patients deemed at high risk for traditional open-heart surgery. The aortic heart valves are available for sale in more than 65 countries. The company's critical care products include the Swan-Ganz brand hemodynamic monitoring devices used during surgery; FloTrac, a minimally invasive continuous cardiac output monitoring system; ClearSight hemodynamic monitor that provides real-time, beat-to-beat information; and EV1000 clinical monitoring platform which displays a patient's physiological status and integrates many of the firm's sensors and catheters into one platform. The firm sells its products in approximately 100 countries, including Australia, Brazil, Canada, France, Germany, Italy, Japan, the Netherlands, Spain and the U.K.In January 2017, Edwards acquired Valtech Cardio Ltd., the developer of the Cardioband System for transcatheter repair of the mitral and tricuspid valves, for $340 million.

Employee benefits include medical, dental and vision coverage; 401(k); an employee stock purchase plan; short- and long-term disability; and adoption assistance.

FINANCIAL DATA: Note: Data for latest year may not have been available at press time.

In U.S. $	2016	2015	2014	2013	2012	2011
Revenue	2,963,700,000	2,493,700,000	2,322,900,000	2,045,500,000	1,899,600,000	1,678,600,000
R&D Expense	443,300,000	383,100,000	346,500,000	323,000,000	291,300,000	246,300,000
Operating Income	785,700,000	635,700,000	1,233,200,000	454,500,000	408,400,000	278,500,000
Operating Margin %	26.51%	25.49%	53.08%	22.21%	21.49%	16.59%
SGA Expense	904,700,000	850,700,000	858,000,000	745,600,000	705,300,000	642,400,000
Net Income	569,500,000	494,900,000	811,100,000	391,700,000	293,200,000	236,700,000
Operating Cash Flow	704,400,000	549,700,000	1,022,300,000	472,700,000	373,800,000	314,500,000
Capital Expenditure	217,400,000	106,500,000	93,700,000	110,100,000	127,700,000	90,600,000
EBITDA	828,300,000	705,400,000	1,229,800,000	593,800,000	452,800,000	344,700,000
Return on Assets %	13.29%	13.05%	25.95%	15.83%	13.95%	12.63%
Return on Equity %	22.23%	21.08%	43.25%	25.78%	20.81%	17.89%
Debt to Equity	0.31	0.23	0.27	0.38	0.12	0.11

CONTACT INFORMATION:

Phone: 949 250-2500   Fax: 949 250-2525
Toll-Free: 800-424-3278
Address: 1 Edwards Way, Irvine, CA 92614 United States

STOCK TICKER/OTHER:

Stock Ticker: EW   Exchange: NYS
Employees: 11,100   Fiscal Year Ends: 12/31
Parent Company:

SALARIES/BONUSES:

Top Exec. Salary: $976,731   Bonus: $
Second Exec. Salary: $557,668   Bonus: $

OTHER THOUGHTS:

Estimated Female Officers or Directors: 3
Hot Spot for Advancement for Women/Minorities: Y

Sales, profits and employees may be estimates. Financial information, benefits and other data can change quickly and may vary from those stated here.

Eldorado Resorts Inc

www.eldoradoresorts.com

NAIC Code: 721120

TYPES OF BUSINESS:

Casino Hotel Properties

BRANDS/DIVISIONS/AFFILIATES:

Eldorado Resort Casino Shreveport
Eldorado Hotel and Casino Reno
Mountaineer Casino, Racetrack & Resort
Presque Isle Downs & Casino
Eldorado Gaming Scioto Downs
Silver Legacy Resort Casino
RacelineBet Inc
Racelinebet.com

CONTACTS: *Note: Officers with more than one job title may be intentionally listed here more than once.*

Gary Carano, CEO
Stephanie Lepori, Chief Accounting Officer
Thomas Reeg, Director
Anthony Carano, Executive VP

GROWTH PLANS/SPECIAL FEATURES:

Eldorado Resorts, Inc. is a gaming and hospitality company established in 1973 that owns and operates gaming facilities located in Louisiana (LA), Nevada (NV), Ohio (OH), Pennsylvania (PA) and West Virginia (WV). The firm's primary source of revenue is gaming, but its hotels, restaurants, bars, shops and other venues are used to attract customers to its properties. Eldorado's properties consist of Eldorado Resort Casino Shreveport, a 403-room, all suite art deco-style hotel and tri-level riverboat dockside casino situated on the Red River in Shreveport, LA; Eldorado Hotel and Casino Reno, an 814-room hotel, casino and entertainment facility located in downtown Reno, NV; Mountaineer Casino, Racetrack & Resort, a 354-room resort with a casino and live thoroughbred horse racing located on the Ohio River at the northern tip of WV's northwestern panhandle; Presque Isle Downs & Casino, a casino and live thoroughbred horse racing facility with slot machines, table games and poker located in Erie, PA; Eldorado Gaming Scioto Downs, a live thoroughbred horse racing facility with video lottery terminals (VLTs) located in Columbus, OH; Circus Circus Reno, a circus-themed hotel-casino with slot machines, table games and 1,571 hotel rooms in NV; and Silver Legacy Resort Casino, a 1,711-room themed hotel and casino which is located adjacent to the Eldorado Hotel and Casino, Reno. Through subsidiary RacelineBet, Inc., Eldorado operates Racelinebet.com, a national account wagering service that offers online and telephone wagering on horse races. Additionally, Eldorado established Columbus Southeast Hotel Group LLC, a joint venture with Vista Host, Inc. to develop a new Hampton Inn & Suites hotel that will be attached to Eldorado's Scioto Downs. In September 2016, the firm agreed to acquire Isle of Capri Casinos, Inc., a regional gaming and entertainment company, for $1.7 billion. The transaction is awaiting regulatory approval.

FINANCIAL DATA: *Note: Data for latest year may not have been available at press time.*

In U.S. $	2016	2015	2014	2013	2012	2011
Revenue	892,896,000	719,784,000	361,823,000	247,186,000	254,740,000	
R&D Expense						
Operating Income	89,118,000	72,516,000	17,555,000	22,582,000	15,841,000	
Operating Margin %	9.98%	10.07%	4.85%	9.13%	6.21%	
SGA Expense	190,652,000	144,566,000	85,337,000	61,453,000	63,660,000	
Net Income	24,802,000	114,183,000	-14,425,000	18,897,000	-991,000	
Operating Cash Flow	97,570,000	56,715,000	33,879,000	23,536,000	28,366,000	
Capital Expenditure	47,380,000	36,762,000	10,564,000	7,413,000	9,181,000	
EBITDA	152,567,000	163,082,000	46,841,000	51,609,000	32,729,000	
Return on Assets %	1.89%	9.13%	-1.99%	6.99%		
Return on Equity %	8.71%	54.09%	-12.70%	25.00%		
Debt to Equity	2.66	3.18	5.14	2.22		

CONTACT INFORMATION:

Phone: 775 328-0100   Fax:
Toll-Free:
Address: 100 W. Liberty St., Reno, NV 89501 United States

STOCK TICKER/OTHER:

Stock Ticker: ERI   Exchange: NAS
Employees: 7,400   Fiscal Year Ends: 12/31
Parent Company:

SALARIES/BONUSES:

Top Exec. Salary: $750,000   Bonus: $
Second Exec. Salary: Bonus: $
$650,000

OTHER THOUGHTS:

Estimated Female Officers or Directors:
Hot Spot for Advancement for Women/Minorities:

Eli Lilly and Company

www.lilly.com

NAIC Code: 325412

TYPES OF BUSINESS:

Pharmaceuticals Discovery & Development
Veterinary Products

BRANDS/DIVISIONS/AFFILIATES:

Humulin
Tragenta
Alimta
Cyramza
Effient
Rumensin
Duramune
CoLucid Pharmaceuticals Inc

CONTACTS: *Note: Officers with more than one job title may be intentionally listed here more than once.*

Derica Rice, CFO
Jeffrey Simmons, President, Divisional
John Lechleiter, Chairman of the Board
Donald Zakrowski, Chief Accounting Officer
Jan Lundberg, Executive VP, Divisional
Michael Harrington, General Counsel
Melissa Barnes, Other Executive Officer
Maria Crowe, President, Divisional
Alfonso Zulueta, President, Divisional
Enrique Conterno, President, Divisional
Susan Mahony, President, Divisional
David Ricks, President
Barton Peterson, Senior VP, Divisional

GROWTH PLANS/SPECIAL FEATURES:

Eli Lilly and Company researches, develops, manufactures and sells pharmaceuticals designed to treat a variety of conditions. The firm operates through two segments: human pharmaceutical products and animal health products. Human pharmaceutical products are grouped into four divisions: endocrinology, neuroscience, oncology and cardiovascular. Endocrinology products include Humalog, Humulin, Trajenta, Jentadueto, Jardiance, Trulicity and Glyxambi, for the treatment of diabetes; Forteo and Evista, for osteoporosis in women; Humatrope, for human growth hormone deficiency; and Axiron, a topical solution of testosterone. Neuroscience products include Cymbalta and Prozac, for major depressive disorder; Zyprexa, for schizophrenia; Strattera, for attention-deficit hyperactivity disorder; and Amyvid, a radioactive diagnostic agent for brain imaging of people with cognitive decline. Oncology products include Alimta, for non-small cell lung cancer; Erbitux, for colorectal cancers; Gemzar, for pancreatic cancer/metastatic breast cancer/ovarian cancer/bladder cancer; and Cyramza, for advanced or metastatic gastric cancer. Cardiovascular products include Cialis, for erectile dysfunction; and Effient, for reduction of thrombotic cardiovascular events. Animal health products are grouped into two divisions: food animals and companion animals. Food animal products include Rumensin, a cattle feed additive; Posilac, a protein supplement; Paylean and Optaflexx, leanness and/or performance enhancers; and Tylan and Denagard, antibiotics. Companion animal products include Trifexis and Comfortis chewable tablets are manufactured for flea prevention; and Duramune, Bronchi-Shield, Fel-O and Rabvac, vaccines. In early-2017, the firm acquired Boehringer Ingelheim Vetmedica, Inc.'s U.S. feline, canine and rabies vaccines portfolio; and CoLucid Pharmaceuticals, Inc., which is developing lasmiditan oral tablets and intravenous lasmiditan for the acute treatment of headache and migraine pain in adults.

Eli Lilly offers employees life, health, prescription drug and dental insurance; domestic partner benefits; an employee assistance program; paid maternity leave; a 401(k); flexible spending accounts; adoption assistance; and tuition reimbursement.

FINANCIAL DATA: *Note: Data for latest year may not have been available at press time.*

In U.S. $	2016	2015	2014	2013	2012	2011
Revenue	21,222,100,000	19,958,700,000	19,615,600,000	23,113,100,000	22,603,400,000	24,286,500,000
R&D Expense	5,273,900,000	5,331,400,000	4,733,600,000	5,531,300,000	5,278,100,000	5,020,800,000
Operating Income	3,841,300,000	3,057,100,000	3,328,700,000	5,370,400,000	5,408,200,000	5,528,500,000
Operating Margin %	18.10%	15.31%	16.96%	23.23%	23.92%	22.76%
SGA Expense	6,452,000,000	6,533,000,000	6,620,800,000	7,125,600,000	7,513,500,000	7,879,900,000
Net Income	2,737,600,000	2,408,400,000	2,390,500,000	4,684,800,000	4,088,600,000	4,347,700,000
Operating Cash Flow	4,851,000,000	2,772,800,000	4,367,100,000	5,735,000,000	5,304,800,000	7,234,500,000
Capital Expenditure	1,037,000,000	1,066,200,000	1,470,900,000	1,093,300,000	1,044,200,000	1,692,900,000
EBITDA	5,055,800,000	4,484,800,000	4,528,100,000	7,495,000,000	7,048,200,000	6,909,100,000
Return on Assets %	7.36%	6.62%	6.60%	13.45%	12.01%	13.44%
Return on Equity %	19.15%	16.08%	14.48%	28.92%	28.88%	33.49%
Debt to Equity	0.59	0.54	0.34	0.23	0.37	0.40

CONTACT INFORMATION:

Phone: 317 276-2000   Fax:
Toll-Free:
Address: Lilly Corporate Center, Indianapolis, IN 46285 United States

STOCK TICKER/OTHER:

Stock Ticker: LLY   Exchange: NYS
Employees: 41,975   Fiscal Year Ends: 12/31
Parent Company:

SALARIES/BONUSES:

Top Exec. Salary: $1,500,000   Bonus: $
Second Exec. Salary: Bonus: $
$1,067,805

OTHER THOUGHTS:

Estimated Female Officers or Directors: 8
Hot Spot for Advancement for Women/Minorities: Y

Sales, profits and employees may be estimates. Financial information, benefits and other data can change quickly and may vary from those stated here.

EMCOR Group Inc

www.emcorgroup.com

NAIC Code: 238210

TYPES OF BUSINESS:

Electric, Heating and AC Contractors
Mechanical Contracting
Technical Consulting Services
Facilities Management

BRANDS/DIVISIONS/AFFILIATES:

Ardent Services LLC
Rabalais Constructors LLC

CONTACTS: Note: Officers with more than one job title may be intentionally listed here more than once.

Anthony Guzzi, CEO
Mark Pompa, CFO
Stephen Bershad, Chairman of the Board
R. Matz, Executive VP, Divisional
Maxine Mauricio, Executive VP

GROWTH PLANS/SPECIAL FEATURES:

EMCOR Group, Inc. is a global leader in mechanical and electrical contracting and facilities services. The company offers its services through more than 75 subsidiaries and joint ventures and more than 170 offices located throughout the U.S., as well as in Canada, the U.K. and the Middle East. Services provided to its customers include the design, integration, installation, start up, operation and maintenance of systems for generation and distribution of electrical power; lighting systems; low-voltage systems, such as fire alarm, security, communications and process control systems; voice and data communication systems; heating, ventilation, air conditioning, refrigeration and clean-room process ventilation systems; plumbing, process and high-purity piping systems; water and wastewater treatment systems; and central plant heating and cooling systems. In addition to its construction services, EMCOR offers facilities services, such as site-based operations and maintenance, mobile maintenance and service, facilities management, installation and support for building systems, technical consulting and diagnostic services, small modification and retrofit projects and program development and management for energy systems. Most of the firm's business is done with corporations, municipalities and other government agencies, owner/developers and building tenants. Additional services are provided to a range of general and specialty contractors, with EMCOR operating as a subcontractor. In April 2016, the company acquired Ardent Services, LLC and Rabalais Constructors, LLC (collectively Ardent), leading providers of instrumentation and critical electrical services for $205 million.

EMCOR offers its employees benefits including medical, vision and dental coverage; life insurance; flexible spending accounts; disability income; employee wellness and assistance programs; and a 401(k) and stock purchase options.

FINANCIAL DATA: Note: Data for latest year may not have been available at press time.

In U.S. $	2016	2015	2014	2013	2012	2011
Revenue	7,551,524,000	6,718,726,000	6,424,965,000	6,417,158,000	6,346,679,000	5,613,459,000
R&D Expense						
Operating Income	308,458,000	287,082,000	289,878,000	210,292,000	249,967,000	210,793,000
Operating Margin %	4.08%	4.27%	4.51%	3.27%	3.93%	3.75%
SGA Expense	725,538,000	656,573,000	626,478,000	591,063,000	556,242,000	518,121,000
Net Income	181,935,000	172,286,000	168,664,000	123,792,000	146,584,000	130,826,000
Operating Cash Flow	264,561,000	266,666,000	246,657,000	150,069,000	184,408,000	149,425,000
Capital Expenditure	39,648,000	35,460,000	38,035,000	35,497,000	37,875,000	29,581,000
EBITDA	388,910,000	361,944,000	365,210,000	278,758,000	312,489,000	266,389,000
Return on Assets %	4.89%	4.96%	4.92%	3.76%	4.78%	4.53%
Return on Equity %	12.07%	11.91%	11.70%	8.80%	11.35%	10.95%
Debt to Equity	0.26	0.20	0.22	0.22	0.11	0.12

CONTACT INFORMATION:

Phone: 203 849-7800   Fax: 203 849-7900
Toll-Free: 866-890-7794
Address: 301 Merritt Seven, Norwalk, CT 06851 United States

STOCK TICKER/OTHER:

Stock Ticker: EME
Employees: 31,000
Parent Company:

Exchange: NYS
Fiscal Year Ends: 12/31

SALARIES/BONUSES:

Top Exec. Salary: $1,071,000   Bonus: $
Second Exec. Salary: $670,000   Bonus: $

OTHER THOUGHTS:

Estimated Female Officers or Directors: 3
Hot Spot for Advancement for Women/Minorities: Y

Encore Capital Group Inc

www.encorecapital.com

NAIC Code: 522390

TYPES OF BUSINESS:

Credit Card Receivables
Debt Collections

BRANDS/DIVISIONS/AFFILIATES:

Atlantic Credit & Finance Inc
Cabot Credit Management Limited
Refinancia SA
Propel Acquisition LLC
Grove Holdings

CONTACTS: Note: Officers with more than one job title may be intentionally listed here more than once.

Ashish Masih, CEO
Jonathan Clark, CFO
Paul Grinberg, Chairman of the Board, Subsidiary
Willem Mesdag, Chairman of the Board
Gregory Call, General Counsel

GROWTH PLANS/SPECIAL FEATURES:

Encore Capital Group, Inc. is an international specialty finance company providing debt recovery solutions for consumers and property owners across a broad range of financial assets. Encore operates through two business segments: portfolio purchasing & recovery (PP&R) and tax liens. PP&R acquires portfolios of defaulted consumer receivables at deep discounts to face value and manage them by working with individuals as they repay their obligations and work toward financial recovery. Defaulted receivables are consumers' unpaid financial commitments to credit originators, including banks, credit unions, consumer finance companies, commercial retailers and telecommunication companies. Subsidiaries within this division include wholly-owned Atlantic Credit & Finance Inc., a U.S.-based firm that specializes in collecting high-balance receivables by forging collaborative relationships with consumers majority-owned; majority-owned Cabot Credit Management Limited, a market leader in debt management in the U.K. and Ireland; majority-owned Grove Holdings, a U.K.-based specialty investment firm focused on consumer non-performing loans in the U.K. and bank and non-bank receivables in Spain; and majority-owned Refinancia SA, a market leader in the management of non-performing loans in Colombia and Peru. The tax lien segment is operated through subsidiary Propel Acquisition LLC, and its subsidiaries, which acquire and service residential and commercial tax liens on real property. Propel works directly with property owns to structure affordable payment plans by paying delinquent property taxes on behalf of the property owners in exchange for payment agreements collateralized by a tax lien on the property. Propel also purchases tax liens directly from taxing authorities in various other states. This segment's portfolio of tax liens and other assets extends through 22 U.S. states.

FINANCIAL DATA: Note: Data for latest year may not have been available at press time.

In U.S. $	2016	2015	2014	2013	2012	2011
Revenue	1,029,258,000	1,161,572,000	1,072,789,000	773,364,000	555,872,000	467,371,000
R&D Expense						
Operating Income	241,514,000	245,302,000	319,444,000	198,359,000	154,176,000	120,774,000
Operating Margin %	23.46%	21.11%	29.77%	25.64%	27.73%	25.84%
SGA Expense	652,139,000	734,866,000	631,537,000	494,809,000	346,917,000	302,160,000
Net Income	76,570,000	45,135,000	103,726,000	75,299,000	69,477,000	60,958,000
Operating Cash Flow	130,332,000	114,425,000	111,544,000	74,775,000	98,520,000	84,579,000
Capital Expenditure	31,668,000	28,647,000	23,238,000	13,423,000	6,265,000	5,564,000
EBITDA	290,610,000	281,482,000	347,506,000	207,684,000	164,997,000	126,874,000
Return on Assets %	1.94%	1.13%	3.22%	3.90%	7.00%	7.87%
Return on Equity %	13.25%	7.40%	17.36%	15.40%	17.87%	18.08%
Debt to Equity	5.01	5.39	4.45	3.23	1.73	1.04

CONTACT INFORMATION:

Phone: 877 445-4581 Fax:
Toll-Free: 877-445-4581
Address: 3111 Camino Del Rio N., Ste. 103, San Diego, CA 92108 United States

STOCK TICKER/OTHER:

Stock Ticker: ECPG
Employees: 6,700
Parent Company:

Exchange: NAS
Fiscal Year Ends: 12/31

SALARIES/BONUSES:

Top Exec. Salary: $860,000 Bonus: $
Second Exec. Salary: $563,750 Bonus: $

OTHER THOUGHTS:

Estimated Female Officers or Directors: 2
Hot Spot for Advancement for Women/Minorities:

Sales, profits and employees may be estimates. Financial information, benefits and other data can change quickly and may vary from those stated here.

Enterprise Holdings Inc

www.enterpriseholdings.com

NAIC Code: 532111

TYPES OF BUSINESS:

Car & Truck Rental
Vanpool Services

BRANDS/DIVISIONS/AFFILIATES:

Alamo Rent A Car
National Car Rental
Enterprise Rent-A-Car
Enterprise Car Sales
Enterprise Truck Rental
Exotic Car Collection by Enterprise
Enterprise CarShre
Zimride

CONTACTS: *Note: Officers with more than one job title may be intentionally listed here more than once.*

Pamela Nicholson, Pres.
Christine Taylor, Exec. VP
Pamela Nicholson, Pres.
Rick Short, CFO
Patrick T. Farrell, CMO
Edward Adams, Sr. VP-Human Resources
Craig Kennedy, CIO
Lee Kaplan, Chief Admin. Officer
Matthew G. Darrah, Exec. VP-North American Oper.
Greg Stubblefield, Chief Strategy Officer
Patrick T. Farrell, Chief Comm. Officer
Rose Langhorst, Treas.
Steve Bloom, Pres., Enterprise Fleet Mgmt.
Jo Ann Taylor Kindle, Pres., Enterprise Holdings Foundation
Andrew C. Taylor, Chmn.
Greg Stubblefield, Exec. VP-Global Sales & Mktg.

GROWTH PLANS/SPECIAL FEATURES:

Enterprise Holdings, Inc. is the parent company of Alamo Rent A Car, National Car Rental and Enterprise Rent-A-Car car rental agencies. The company also owns Enterprise Car Sales, Enterprise Truck Rental and Exotic Car Collection by Enterprise, as well as car/ride sharing programs Enterprise CarShare, Enterprise Rideshare and Zimride by Enterprise. The company's combined rental fleet is the largest in the world, at 1.9 million vehicles. It serves more than 9,600 fully-staffed neighborhood and airport locations in more than 90 countries worldwide. Alamo Rent A Car is a budget rental car company catering to leisure and vacation customers, particularly international travelers visiting North America. It operates self-service kiosks at 71 U.S. locations. National Car Rental is a premium rental brand that serves frequent business travelers and offers the Emerald Club frequent-renter benefits program. Enterprise Rent-A-Car boasts over 5,800 retail and airport offices in the U.S. Enterprise Car Sales is a used-car reseller that provides non-negotiable pricing and after-market warranties on used cars acquired through trade-in or extracted from the rental fleet. Enterprise Truck Rental provides commercial-grade trucks such as ¾- to 1-ton pickups, cargo vans, straight trucks, as well as stakebed trucks (from 16 to 26 feet long), all equipped for commercial use. Exotic Car Collection enables customers to rent vehicles such as exotic sports cars and luxury sedans, including Ferrari, Maserati, Porsche, Bentley, Range Rover and more. Enterprise CarShare is a car sharing program that allows customers to rent a car for flexible periods of time through an online membership portal. Enterprise Rideshare specializes in customized vanpool programs and commuter services for individuals and/or companies. Zimride is a ride-sharing platform for companies and universities.

Enterprise Holdings offers its employees medical, dental and vision insurance; prescription drug coverage; flexible spending accounts; life insurance; and long-term disability plans.

FINANCIAL DATA: *Note: Data for latest year may not have been available at press time.*

In U.S. $	2016	2015	2014	2013	2012	2011
Revenue	20,900,000,000	19,400,000,000	17,800,000,000	16,400,000,000	15,400,000,000	14,100,000,000
R&D Expense						
Operating Income						
Operating Margin %						
SGA Expense						
Net Income						
Operating Cash Flow						
Capital Expenditure						
EBITDA						
Return on Assets %						
Return on Equity %						
Debt to Equity						

CONTACT INFORMATION:

Phone: 314-512-2880   Fax: 314-512-4706
Toll-Free:
Address: 600 Corporate Park Dr., St. Louis, MO 63105 United States

STOCK TICKER/OTHER:

Stock Ticker: Private   Exchange:
Employees: 93,070   Fiscal Year Ends: 03/31
Parent Company:

SALARIES/BONUSES:

Top Exec. Salary: $ Bonus: $
Second Exec. Salary: $ Bonus: $

OTHER THOUGHTS:

Estimated Female Officers or Directors: 5
Hot Spot for Advancement for Women/Minorities: Y

Envision Healthcare Corporation

www.evhc.net

NAIC Code: 621610

TYPES OF BUSINESS:

Home Health Care Services
Other Human Health Activities

BRANDS/DIVISIONS/AFFILIATES:

AmSurg Corporation
Envision Healthcare Holdings Inc

CONTACTS: *Note: Officers with more than one job title may be intentionally listed here more than once.*

Claire Gulmi, CFO
William Sanger, Chairman of the Board
Randel Owen, Executive VP
Robert Coward, Executive VP
Craig Wilson, General Counsel
Patrick Solomon, Other Executive Officer
Christopher Holden, President
Kevin Eastridge, Senior VP

GROWTH PLANS/SPECIAL FEATURES:

Envision Healthcare Corporation (formerly Envision Healthcare Holdings, Inc.) is a healthcare services provider. The firm offers an array of clinical solutions such as physician-led services, medical transportation services and ambulatory services. Envision Healthcare helps physicians align with health systems, payors and communities to form efficient and effective clinical networks. The physician-led services segment comprises the company's hospital-based and non-hospital-based physician services. Its service contracts cover more than 1,500 clinical departments at healthcare facilities in 45 U.S. states and the District of Columbia. Over 46,000 physicians and other healthcare providers are employed by or affiliated with Envision Healthcare. The medical transportation services segment includes community-based medical transportation services, including emergency (911), non-emergency, managed transportation, air ambulance and disaster response services. This division provides medical transportation services pursuant to more than 4,100 contracts and arrangements in 38 states and the District of Columbia. The ambulatory services segment includes Envision Healthcare's ambulatory surgery business, which acquires, develops, owns and operates ambulatory surgery centers (ASCs) and surgical hospitals in partnership with physicians and health systems. This division owns and operates 260 ASCs in 35 states and the District of Columbia. In December 2016, Envision Healthcare Holdings was acquired by AmSurg Corporation. AmSurg subsequently merged itself into Envision Healthcare, creating Envision Healthcare Corporation.

FINANCIAL DATA: *Note: Data for latest year may not have been available at press time.*

In U.S. $	2016	2015	2014	2013	2012	2011
Revenue	3,696,000,000	2,566,884,000	1,621,949,000	1,079,343,000	928,509,000	786,870,000
R&D Expense						
Operating Income	376,300,000	617,505,000	394,364,000	338,065,000	281,945,000	242,448,000
Operating Margin %	10.18%	24.05%	24.31%	31.32%	30.36%	30.81%
SGA Expense	2,308,300,000	1,322,716,000	728,466,000	333,190,000		
Net Income	-18,600,000	162,947,000	53,701,000	72,703,000	62,563,000	49,997,000
Operating Cash Flow	419,800,000	537,959,000	412,371,000	332,824,000	295,652,000	243,423,000
Capital Expenditure	99,500,000	60,305,000	40,217,000	28,856,000	28,864,000	22,170,000
EBITDA	526,200,000	714,998,000	454,708,000	371,093,000	312,023,000	268,623,000
Return on Assets %	-.23%	2.54%	1.27%	3.44%	3.45%	3.65%
Return on Equity %	-.62%	8.45%	4.32%	10.00%	9.58%	8.47%
Debt to Equity	0.86	1.13	1.47	0.76	0.90	0.72

CONTACT INFORMATION:

Phone: 303 495-1200   Fax:
Toll-Free:
Address: 6363 S. Fiddlers Green Cir., 14/Fl, Greenwood Village, CO 80111 United States

STOCK TICKER/OTHER:

Stock Ticker: EVHC
Employees: 65,200
Parent Company:

Exchange: NYS
Fiscal Year Ends: 12/31

SALARIES/BONUSES:

Top Exec. Salary: $1,670,131   Bonus: $
Second Exec. Salary: $1,040,000   Bonus: $

OTHER THOUGHTS:

Estimated Female Officers or Directors:
Hot Spot for Advancement for Women/Minorities:

EPAM Systems Inc

NAIC Code: 541511

www.epam.com

TYPES OF BUSINESS:

Software Engineering
Customer Relationship Management
Consulting
Technical Writing

BRANDS/DIVISIONS/AFFILIATES:

Dextrys

CONTACTS: Note: Officers with more than one job title may be intentionally listed here more than once.

Arkadiy Dobkin, CEO
Anthony Conte, CFO
Gary Abrahams, Chief Accounting Officer
Elaina Shekhter, Chief Marketing Officer
Ginger Mosier, General Counsel
Balazs Fejes, Other Corporate Officer
Boris Shnayder, Other Corporate Officer
Lawrence Solomon, Other Executive Officer

GROWTH PLANS/SPECIAL FEATURES:

EPAM Systems, Inc. is a global software product development and digital platform engineering services provider. The company serves clients worldwide, primarily in North America, Europe, Asia and Australia. EPAM comprises a strong focus on innovative and scalable software solutions, and a continually-evolving mix of advanced capabilities. The firm's services include software product development, custom application development, application testing, enterprise application platform development, application management and support, and infrastructure management. Vertical markets served by EPAM include financial services, which derives 25.2% of annual revenues; travel and consumer, 22.4%; software and high-tech, 20.5%; media and entertainment; 15%; and life sciences and healthcare, 9.1%. Emerging vertical industries derive the remaining percentage of revenues. EPAM's clients primarily consist of Forbes Global 2000 corporations, with North American clients representing more than 57% of annual revenue; and Europe representing more than 35%. In 2016, the firm acquired Dextrys, a software engineering and application development provider.

FINANCIAL DATA: Note: Data for latest year may not have been available at press time.

In U.S. $	2016	2015	2014	2013	2012	2011
Revenue	1,160,132,000	914,128,000	730,027,000	555,117,000	433,799,000	334,528,000
R&D Expense						
Operating Income	133,696,000	105,967,000	86,183,000	76,493,000	66,006,000	55,008,000
Operating Margin %	11.52%	11.59%	11.80%	13.77%	15.21%	16.44%
SGA Expense	264,658,000	222,759,000	163,666,000	116,497,000	85,868,000	64,930,000
Net Income	99,266,000	84,456,000	69,641,000	61,994,000	54,484,000	44,353,000
Operating Cash Flow	164,817,000	76,393,000	104,874,000	58,225,000	48,499,000	54,520,000
Capital Expenditure	29,317,000	17,964,000	15,840,000	15,920,000	27,077,000	17,093,000
EBITDA	157,083,000	123,362,000	103,666,000	91,613,000	76,888,000	60,367,000
Return on Assets %	11.64%	12.30%	13.56%	15.82%	17.44%	5.78%
Return on Equity %	14.23%	15.67%	16.57%	18.71%	26.82%	14.58%
Debt to Equity	0.03	0.05				

CONTACT INFORMATION:

Phone: 267 759-9000   Fax: 267 759-8989
Toll-Free:
Address: 41 University Dr., Ste. 202, Newtown, PA 18940 United States

STOCK TICKER/OTHER:

Stock Ticker: EPAM   Exchange: NYS
Employees: 22,383   Fiscal Year Ends: 12/31
Parent Company:

SALARIES/BONUSES:

Top Exec. Salary: $437,500   Bonus: $222,833
Second Exec. Salary: Bonus: $166,988
$310,000

OTHER THOUGHTS:

Estimated Female Officers or Directors: 2
Hot Spot for Advancement for Women/Minorities:

Epic Systems Corporation

www.epic.com

NAIC Code: 0

TYPES OF BUSINESS:

Computer Software, Healthcare & Biotechnology
Information Networks
Support Services

BRANDS/DIVISIONS/AFFILIATES:

Epicenter
EpicCare
Epic Europe BV
Lucy
Community Library Exchange

CONTACTS: Note: Officers with more than one job title may be intentionally listed here more than once.

Judy Faulkner, CEO
Carl D. Dvorak, COO
Robert M. Fahrenbach, CFO
Carl Dvorak, Exec. VP

GROWTH PLANS/SPECIAL FEATURES:

Epic Systems Corporation is a developer of health industry clinical, access and revenue software for mid-size and large medical groups, hospitals, academic facilities, children's organizations, multi-hospital systems and integrated healthcare organizations. All Epic software applications are designed to share a single database, called Epicenter, so that each viewer can access all available patient data through a single interface from anywhere in the organization. The firm's clinical software products include integrated inpatient and ambulatory systems under the EpicCare brand as well as health information management tools and specialty information systems. The firm's interoperability service, Lucy, personal health record that allows patients to organize and access their medical history independently of any one facility. Other products offer access services, including scheduling, inpatient and ambulatory registration, call management and nurse triage; revenue cycle services, such as hospital and professional billing; health plan and managed care administration systems; clinical and financial data repositories; enterprise reporting; patient medical record access systems; and connectivity tools, including voice recognition, interfacing and patient monitoring devices. In conjunction with its software applications, the company provides extensive client services, including training, process engineering, tailoring of applications to the client's situation and access to network specialists who plan and implement client systems. In addition, Epic hosts Community Library Exchange, an online collection of application tools and pre-made content that allows clients to share report and registration templates, custom forms, enterprise report formats and documentation shortcuts. Epic also operates in the Netherlands under Epic Europe BV.

Employees of the firm are offered medical, dental, vision, life and disability insurance; a 401(k) plan; and flexible spending accounts.

FINANCIAL DATA: Note: Data for latest year may not have been available at press time.

In U.S. $	2016	2015	2014	2013	2012	2011
Revenue	2,000,000,000	1,978,000,000	1,856,000,000	1,750,000,000	1,526,000,000	1,190,000,000
R&D Expense						
Operating Income						
Operating Margin %						
SGA Expense						
Net Income						
Operating Cash Flow						
Capital Expenditure						
EBITDA						
Return on Assets %						
Return on Equity %						
Debt to Equity						

CONTACT INFORMATION:

Phone: 608-271-9000   Fax: 608-271-7237
Toll-Free:
Address: 1979 Milky Way, Verona, WI 53593 United States

STOCK TICKER/OTHER:

Stock Ticker: Private   Exchange:
Employees: 9,000   Fiscal Year Ends: 12/31
Parent Company:

SALARIES/BONUSES:

Top Exec. Salary: $ Bonus: $
Second Exec. Salary: $ Bonus: $

OTHER THOUGHTS:

Estimated Female Officers or Directors: 1
Hot Spot for Advancement for Women/Minorities:

Equity Lifestyle Properties Inc

www.equitylifestyleproperties.com

NAIC Code: 0

TYPES OF BUSINESS:

Real Estate Investment Trust
Manufactured Home & RV Communities

BRANDS/DIVISIONS/AFFILIATES:

MHC Operating Limited Partnership

CONTACTS: *Note: Officers with more than one job title may be intentionally listed here more than once.*

Thomas Heneghan, CEO, Subsidiary
Paul Seavey, CFO
Samuel Zell, Chairman of the Board
Patrick Waite, COO
Howard Walker, Director
Roger Maynard, Executive VP, Divisional
Marguerite Nader, President

GROWTH PLANS/SPECIAL FEATURES:

Equity Lifestyle Properties, Inc. (ELS) is an integrated real estate investment trust (REIT) that owns and operates communities of developed residential sites as well as recreational vehicle (RV) resorts. The company primarily operates through MHC Operating Limited Partnership. The firm owns or has an interest in 391 properties throughout the U.S. and Canada, consisting of about 146,610 residential sites. The heaviest concentrations of these properties are located in Florida, California and Arizona, with 122, 49 and 42 properties, respectively. Additional U.S. sites are located in Texas, Pennsylvania, Washington, Colorado, Wisconsin, Oregon, North Carolina, Delaware, Indiana, Nevada, New York, Virginia, New Jersey, Illinois, Maine, Massachusetts, Idaho, Michigan, Minnesota, New Hampshire, South Carolina, Utah, Maryland, North Dakota, Ohio, Tennessee, Alabama, Connecticut and Kentucky. These communities are designed and improved for the placement of detached, single-family manufactured homes (MH) that are produced offsite, then installed and set on residential sites within the communities. The owner of each home leases the site on which it is located, while the firm handles property infrastructure issues, such as water, sewage and power. Sites typically contain centralized entrances, paved streets, curbs, gutters, parkways, clubhouses for social activities and recreation, swimming pools, shuffleboard courts, tennis courts, laundry facilities and cable television service, among other amenities. Each community is designed to attract, and is marketed to, retirees, empty-nesters, families or first-time homeowners. The company focuses on owning properties in or near large metropolitan markets as well as popular retirement and vacation destinations. In 2016, the firm acquired four properties: three RV resorts and one MH community.

FINANCIAL DATA: *Note: Data for latest year may not have been available at press time.*

In U.S. $	2016	2015	2014	2013	2012	2011
Revenue	870,435,000	821,654,000	776,809,000	728,375,000	709,877,000	580,073,000
R&D Expense						
Operating Income	184,527,000	146,423,000	137,520,000	75,208,000	67,963,000	40,556,000
Operating Margin %	21.19%	17.82%	17.70%	10.32%	9.57%	6.99%
SGA Expense	50,621,000	47,016,000	42,476,000	43,493,000	37,302,000	51,354,000
Net Income	173,263,000	139,371,000	128,005,000	116,199,000	69,391,000	36,598,000
Operating Cash Flow	353,348,000	352,882,000	285,745,000	255,349,000	236,459,000	175,641,000
Capital Expenditure	217,681,000	117,486,000	145,112,000	182,421,000	99,473,000	713,121,000
EBITDA	407,683,000	370,941,000	367,418,000	308,214,000	310,314,000	226,818,000
Return on Assets %	4.75%	3.79%	3.47%	3.14%	1.58%	.82%
Return on Equity %	19.74%	16.63%	15.48%	14.44%	7.55%	4.77%
Debt to Equity	2.39	2.71	2.85	2.89	3.13	3.14

CONTACT INFORMATION:

Phone: 312 279-1400   Fax: 312 279-1710
Toll-Free:
Address: 2 N. Riverside Plz., Ste. 800, Chicago, IL 60606 United States

STOCK TICKER/OTHER:

Stock Ticker: ELS   Exchange: NYS
Employees: 4,100   Fiscal Year Ends: 12/31
Parent Company:

SALARIES/BONUSES:

Top Exec. Salary: $400,000   Bonus: $
Second Exec. Salary: Bonus: $
$360,000

OTHER THOUGHTS:

Estimated Female Officers or Directors: 3
Hot Spot for Advancement for Women/Minorities: Y

Estee Lauder Companies Inc (The)

www.elcompanies.com

NAIC Code: 325620

TYPES OF BUSINESS:

Cosmetics
Cosmetic & Fragrance Sales
Retail Cosmetics Stores
Hair Care Products

BRANDS/DIVISIONS/AFFILIATES:

Aveda
La Mer
Clinique
Estee Lauder
Bobbie Brown
Aramis
Becca Cosmetics
Too Faced

CONTACTS: *Note: Officers with more than one job title may be intentionally listed here more than once.*

Fabrizio Freda, CEO
John Demsey, President, Divisional
Tracey Travis, CFO
Leonard Lauder, Chairman Emeritus
William Lauder, Chairman of the Board
Ronald Lauder, Chairman, Divisional
Michael OHare, Executive VP, Divisional
Carl Haney, Executive VP, Divisional
Gregory Polcer, Executive VP, Divisional
Alexandra Trower, Executive VP, Divisional
Sara Moss, Executive VP
Spencer Smul, Other Corporate Officer
Cedric Prouve, President, Divisional

GROWTH PLANS/SPECIAL FEATURES:

The Estee Lauder Companies, Inc. is a global manufacturer and marketer of skin care, cosmetic, fragrance and hair care products. The company's products are sold in over 150 countries and territories under brand names such as Estee Lauder, Aramis, Clinique, Origins, M.A.C., Bobbi Brown, La Mer and Aveda. The firm is also the global licensee for fragrances and cosmetics sold under the Tommy Hilfiger, Donna Karan, Michael Kors, Tom Ford, Tory Burch and Coach brand names. Estee Lauder sells its products principally through 46,000 points of sale, including upscale department stores, specialty retailers, upscale perfumeries and pharmacies and prestige salons and spas as well as freestanding company-owned stores and spas, authorized retailer web sites, stores on cruise ships, television direct marketing, in-flight and duty-free shops and self-select outlets. The founding Lauder family still controls 86.7% of the company's voting shares. The firm operates on a global basis, with over half of its sales generated outside the U.S. Skin care products currently account for roughly 39% of the company's sales; makeup products, 42%; fragrance products, 13%; and hair care items, 5%. In December 2016, the company acquired Becca Cosmetics, a prestige makeup brand, offering innovative color and complexion products that complement a wide range of skin tones, for $235 million; and Too Faced Cosmetics, a high-quality, cruelty-free cosmetics company with a large millennial following, for $1.45 billion.

FINANCIAL DATA: *Note: Data for latest year may not have been available at press time.*

In U.S. $	2016	2015	2014	2013	2012	2011
Revenue	11,262,300,000	10,780,400,000	10,968,800,000	10,181,700,000	9,713,601,000	8,810,000,000
R&D Expense						
Operating Income	1,610,300,000	1,606,300,000	1,827,600,000	1,526,000,000	1,311,700,000	1,089,400,000
Operating Margin %	14.29%	14.90%	16.66%	14.98%	13.50%	12.36%
SGA Expense	7,337,800,000	7,073,500,000	6,985,900,000	6,597,000,000	6,324,800,000	5,696,700,000
Net Income	1,114,600,000	1,088,900,000	1,204,100,000	1,019,800,000	856,900,000	700,800,000
Operating Cash Flow	1,788,700,000	1,943,300,000	1,535,200,000	1,226,300,000	1,126,700,000	1,027,000,000
Capital Expenditure	525,300,000	473,000,000	510,200,000	461,000,000	420,700,000	351,000,000
EBITDA	2,040,600,000	2,029,900,000	2,212,200,000	1,886,000,000	1,618,000,000	1,383,800,000
Return on Assets %	12.76%	13.51%	16.03%	14.84%	13.31%	12.07%
Return on Equity %	30.89%	29.04%	33.71%	33.87%	31.95%	30.61%
Debt to Equity	0.53	0.44	0.34	0.40	0.39	0.41

CONTACT INFORMATION:

Phone: 212 572-4200   Fax: 212 572-3941
Toll-Free:
Address: 767 5th Ave., New York, NY 10153 United States

STOCK TICKER/OTHER:

Stock Ticker: EL
Employees: 44,000
Parent Company:

Exchange: NYS
Fiscal Year Ends: 06/30

SALARIES/BONUSES:

Top Exec. Salary: $1,900,000   Bonus: $
Second Exec. Salary: $1,500,000   Bonus: $

OTHER THOUGHTS:

Estimated Female Officers or Directors: 10
Hot Spot for Advancement for Women/Minorities: Y

Esterline Technologies Corporation

NAIC Code: 334511

www.esterline.com

TYPES OF BUSINESS:

Aerospace Systems
Avionics

BRANDS/DIVISIONS/AFFILIATES:

CONTACTS: Note: Officers with more than one job title may be intentionally listed here more than once.

Curtis Reusser, CEO
Robert George, CFO
Gary Posner, Controller
Marcia Mason, Executive VP
Paul Benson, Executive VP
Roger Ross, Executive VP
Albert Yost, Executive VP

GROWTH PLANS/SPECIAL FEATURES:

Esterline Technologies Corporation is a specialized manufacturing company principally serving aerospace and defense customers. It also serves the industrial/commercial and medical markets. Its current business and strategic growth plan focuses on three key technology segments: avionics and controls; sensors and systems; and advanced materials, including thermally engineered components and specialized high-performance elastomers and other complex materials. The avionics and controls business segment includes avionics systems, control systems, interface technologies and communication systems capabilities. This segment primarily designs and develops cockpit systems integration and avionics solutions for commercial and military applications. Esterline's sensors and systems business segment includes power systems and advanced sensors capabilities. It develops and manufactures high-precision temperature, pressure and speed sensors; electrical power switching; control and data communication devices; and other related systems principally for aerospace and defense customers. Last, the advanced materials business segment includes engineered materials and defense technologies capabilities. It develops and manufactures high-performance elastomer products used in a wide range of commercial aerospace, space and military applications, and highly-engineered thermal components for commercial aerospace and industrial applications.

FINANCIAL DATA: Note: Data for latest year may not have been available at press time.

In U.S. $	2016	2015	2014	2013	2012	2011
Revenue	1,992,631,000	1,774,449,000	2,051,169,000	1,969,754,000	1,992,318,000	1,717,985,000
R&D Expense	95,939,000	91,491,000	98,901,000	95,736,000	107,745,000	94,505,000
Operating Income	170,159,000	156,985,000	243,822,000	237,923,000	189,306,000	197,914,000
Operating Margin %	8.53%		11.88%	12.07%	9.50%	11.52%
SGA Expense	395,274,000	346,781,000	364,259,000	391,147,000	382,887,000	304,154,000
Net Income	101,685,000	59,612,000	102,418,000	164,734,000	112,535,000	133,040,000
Operating Cash Flow	167,158,000	144,295,000	216,364,000	250,772,000	194,171,000	192,429,000
Capital Expenditure	68,472,000	49,341,000	45,678,000		49,446,000	49,507,000
EBITDA	270,784,000	236,687,000	359,871,000	349,648,000	297,563,000	283,356,000
Return on Assets %	3.35%		3.17%	5.07%	3.40%	4.45%
Return on Equity %	6.35%		5.44%	9.45%	7.09%	8.94%
Debt to Equity	0.53		0.32	0.35	0.52	0.65

CONTACT INFORMATION:

Phone: 425 453-9400   Fax: 425 453-2916
Toll-Free:
Address: 500 108th Ave. NE, Bellevue, WA 98004 United States

STOCK TICKER/OTHER:

Stock Ticker: ESL   Exchange: NYS
Employees: 13,572   Fiscal Year Ends: 10/31
Parent Company:

SALARIES/BONUSES:

Top Exec. Salary: $850,000   Bonus: $
Second Exec. Salary: Bonus: $
$520,962

OTHER THOUGHTS:

Estimated Female Officers or Directors:
Hot Spot for Advancement for Women/Minorities:

Exelon Corporation

NAIC Code: 221113

www.exeloncorp.com

TYPES OF BUSINESS:

Electric Power Generation-Nuclear
Energy Marketing

BRANDS/DIVISIONS/AFFILIATES:

Exelon Generation Company LLC
Pepco Holdings LLC
Commonwealth Edison Company
PECO Energy Company
Baltimore Gas and Electric Company
Potomac Electric Power Company
Delmarva Power & Light Company
Atlantic City Electric Company

CONTACTS: Note: Officers with more than one job title may be intentionally listed here more than once.

Denis OBrien, CEO, Divisional
Michael Innocenzo, COO, Subsidiary
Calvin Butler, CEO, Subsidiary
Joseph Nigro, CEO, Subsidiary
Kenneth Cornew, CEO, Subsidiary
Anne Pramaggiore, CEO, Subsidiary
Craig Adams, CEO, Subsidiary
David Velazquez, CEO, Subsidiary
Christopher Crane, CEO
Donna Kinzel, CFO, Subsidiary
Bryan Wright, CFO, Subsidiary
Joseph Trpik, CFO, Subsidiary
Phillip Barnett, CFO, Subsidiary
David Vahos, CFO, Subsidiary
Scott Bailey, Chief Accounting Officer, Subsidiary
Matthew Bauer, Chief Accounting Officer, Subsidiary
Andrew Holmes, Chief Accounting Officer, Subsidiary
Robert Aiken, Chief Accounting Officer, Subsidiary
Gerald Kozel, Chief Accounting Officer, Subsidiary
Duane DesParte, Chief Accounting Officer
Terence Donnelly, COO, Subsidiary
Michael Pacilio, COO, Subsidiary
Stephen Woerner, COO, Subsidiary
J. Anthony, COO, Subsidiary

GROWTH PLANS/SPECIAL FEATURES:

Exelon Corporation is a Fortune 100 utility services holding company, delivering electricity and natural gas to customers in 48 U.S. states and Canada. The firm's primary subsidiaries include Exelon Generation Company, LLC (ExGen); Pepco Holdings, LLC (PH); Commonwealth Edison Company (ComEd); PECO Energy Company; Baltimore Gas and Electric Company (BGE); Potomac Electric Power Company (PepCo); Delmarva Power & Light Company; and Atlantic City Electric Company (Atlanta Electric). ExGen's business consists of the generation, delivery and marketing of power across multiple geographical regions through its 50.01%-owned Constellation Energy Nuclear Group, Inc. This division's total generating capacity is nearly 40,000 megawatts of power. PH is a utility services holding company engaged in the energy delivery business, and is based in Washington, D.C. ComEd purchases and sells regulated retail electricity, and also provides electric transmission and distribution services to retail customers in northern Illinois. PECO, BGE, PepCo, Delmarva and Atlanta Electric operate the same as ComEd: PECO serves retail customers in southeastern Pennsylvania; BGE serves central Maryland; PepCo serves the District of Columbia and major portions of Montgomery County and Prince George's County; Delmarva serves portions of Delaware and Maryland; and Atlantic Electric serves portions of southern New Jersey.

Exelon offers employees health and life insurance, disability coverage, a 401(k) and an employee stock purchase plan.

FINANCIAL DATA: Note: Data for latest year may not have been available at press time.

In U.S. $	2016	2015	2014	2013	2012	2011
Revenue	31,360,000,000	29,447,000,000	27,429,000,000	24,888,000,000	23,489,000,000	18,924,000,000
R&D Expense						
Operating Income	3,112,000,000	4,409,000,000	3,096,000,000	3,656,000,000	2,380,000,000	4,480,000,000
Operating Margin %	9.92%	14.97%	11.28%	14.68%	10.13%	23.67%
SGA Expense						
Net Income	1,134,000,000	2,269,000,000	1,623,000,000	1,719,000,000	1,160,000,000	2,495,000,000
Operating Cash Flow	8,445,000,000	7,616,000,000	4,457,000,000	6,343,000,000	6,131,000,000	4,853,000,000
Capital Expenditure	8,553,000,000	7,624,000,000	6,077,000,000	5,395,000,000	5,810,000,000	4,042,000,000
EBITDA	7,606,000,000	8,396,000,000	7,419,000,000	6,593,000,000	6,805,000,000	6,982,000,000
Return on Assets %	1.07%	2.49%	1.94%	2.16%	1.73%	4.64%
Return on Equity %	4.39%	9.37%	7.15%	7.78%	6.47%	17.85%
Debt to Equity	1.24	0.94	0.88	0.80	0.85	0.84

CONTACT INFORMATION:

Phone: 312 394-7398   Fax: 312 394-7945
Toll-Free: 800-483-3220
Address: 10 S. Dearborn St., 48/Fl., Chicago, IL 60680-5379 United States

STOCK TICKER/OTHER:

Stock Ticker: EXC   Exchange: NYS
Employees: 34,396   Fiscal Year Ends: 12/31
Parent Company:

SALARIES/BONUSES:

Top Exec. Salary: $1,255,515   Bonus: $
Second Exec. Salary: $857,477   Bonus: $

OTHER THOUGHTS:

Estimated Female Officers or Directors: 6
Hot Spot for Advancement for Women/Minorities: Y

ExlService Holdings Inc

www.exlservice.com

NAIC Code: 518210

TYPES OF BUSINESS:

Business Process Outsourcing
Contact Center Operations
Collections, Cash Management & Loan Servicing
Customer Support Services
Claims Processing & Servicing

BRANDS/DIVISIONS/AFFILIATES:

LISS Systems Limited
IQR Consulting Inc
Datasource Consulting LLC

CONTACTS: Note: Officers with more than one job title may be intentionally listed here more than once.

Rohit Kapoor, CEO
Vishal Chhibbar, CFO
Pavan Bagai, COO
Garen Staglin, Director
Nancy Saltzman, Executive VP
Vikas Bhalla, Executive VP
Rembert de Villa, Executive VP
Nalin Miglani, Executive VP

GROWTH PLANS/SPECIAL FEATURES:

ExlService Holdings, Inc. is an operations management and analytics company that helps businesses enhance growth and profitability. Its proprietary platforms, methodologies and tools are utilized to improve global operations, enhance data-driven insights, increase customer satisfaction and manage risk and compliance. The firm operates in five business segments: insurance; healthcare; travel, transportation and logistics; finance and accounting; and analytics. The insurance segment serves property and casualty insurance, life insurance, disability insurance, annuity and retirement services companies. It provides business process management (BPM) services in relation to claims processing, subrogation, premium and benefit administration, agency management, account reconciliation, policy research, underwriting support, new business processing, policy servicing, premium audit, surveys, billing and collection and commercial/residential survey. The healthcare segment primarily serves U.S.-based healthcare payers and providers in relation to care management, population health, payment integrity, revenue optimization and customer engagement, reduced claims and administration costs and improved access to the healthcare system. The travel, transportation and logistics segment serves clients within the less-than-truckload, truckload and intermodal logistics sectors. Its services include business processes in corporate and leisure travel, such as reservations, customer service, fulfillment and finance/accounting. The finance and accounting segment provides services such as procure-to-pay, order-to-cash, hire-to-retire, record-to-report, regulatory reporting, financial planning and analysis, audit and assurance, treasury and tax processes. Last, the analytics segment focuses on improving business outcomes via generating data-driven insights across the entire business. Its services include predictive and prescriptive analytics in the areas of customer acquisition and lifecycle management, risk underwriting and pricing, operational effectiveness, credit and operational risk monitoring and governance, regulatory reporting and data management. In 2016, the firm acquired LISS Systems Limited; IQR Consulting, Inc.; and Datasource Consulting, LLC.

FINANCIAL DATA: Note: Data for latest year may not have been available at press time.

In U.S. $	2016	2015	2014	2013	2012	2011
Revenue	685,988,000	628,492,000	499,278,000	478,452,000	442,930,000	360,541,000
R&D Expense						
Operating Income	64,222,000	67,343,000	34,040,000	67,420,000	57,232,000	41,318,000
Operating Margin %	9.36%	10.71%	6.81%	14.09%	12.92%	11.46%
SGA Expense	139,230,000	126,767,000	104,675,000	95,173,000	88,199,000	76,242,000
Net Income	61,733,000	51,565,000	32,445,000	48,097,000	41,836,000	34,780,000
Operating Cash Flow	100,258,000	96,691,000	66,659,000	82,792,000	65,782,000	56,235,000
Capital Expenditure	25,850,000	25,585,000	27,678,000	15,916,000	18,804,000	19,468,000
EBITDA	119,807,000	108,579,000	62,068,000	92,337,000	82,855,000	64,312,000
Return on Assets %	9.09%	8.42%	6.25%	10.69%	10.28%	10.18%
Return on Equity %	12.37%	11.65%	8.26%	13.53%	13.43%	13.19%
Debt to Equity	0.06	0.12	0.12			0.01

CONTACT INFORMATION:

Phone: 212 277-7100   Fax: 212 277-7111
Toll-Free:
Address: 280 Park Ave., 38/Fl., New York, NY 10017 United States

STOCK TICKER/OTHER:

Stock Ticker: EXLS   Exchange: NAS
Employees: 26,000   Fiscal Year Ends: 12/31
Parent Company:

SALARIES/BONUSES:

Top Exec. Salary: $615,027   Bonus: $
Second Exec. Salary: $411,054   Bonus: $

OTHER THOUGHTS:

Estimated Female Officers or Directors: 2
Hot Spot for Advancement for Women/Minorities:

Sales, profits and employees may be estimates. Financial information, benefits and other data can change quickly and may vary from those stated here.

Expedia Inc

www.expedia.com

NAIC Code: 519130

TYPES OF BUSINESS:

Online Travel Services
Online Reservations
Corporate Travel Services
Vacation Packages
Retail Travel Services Kiosks
Destination Activities & Tours
Online Travel Information
Inventory-Based Hotel Room Offerings

BRANDS/DIVISIONS/AFFILIATES:

Expedia.com
Hotwire.com
Classic Vacations
Expedia CruiseShipCenters
trivago GmbH
Travelocity
HomeAway Inc
Orbtiz Worldwide Inc

CONTACTS: *Note: Officers with more than one job title may be intentionally listed here more than once.*

Dara Khosrowshahi, CEO
Mark Okerstrom, CFO
Barry Diller, Chairman of the Board
Lance Soliday, Chief Accounting Officer
Victor Kaufman, Director
Robert Dzielak, Executive VP

GROWTH PLANS/SPECIAL FEATURES:

Expedia, Inc. is an online travel service offering travel shopping and reservation services, publishing schedules, pricing and availability information for numerous airlines, lodging properties, car rental companies, cruise lines and multiple-destination service providers, including restaurants, attractions and tours. The company's travel portfolio includes more than 350,000 properties, 1.2 million live vacation rental listings in 200 countries, as well as 500 airlines. The Expedia brand web sites, for both USA (Expedia.com) and international travelers, offer a large variety of travel products and services available directly to travelers. It also operates as a merchant by directly contracting from suppliers and selling discounted products directly to the consumer. The firm owns Hotels.com, which provides a full portfolio of hotel contacts around the world, and Hotwire.com, a web site that offers travelers discount airfare. Other subsidiaries include Classic Vacations, a premium vacation packaging agency; eLong, an online travel service based in Beijing, China; Egencia, a travel management service for corporate customers; Expedia CruiseShipCenters, a network of cruise vacation retail locations; Expedia Local Expert, which specializes in local tours and attractions; Expedia Affiliate Network, which powers bookings for leading airlines and hotels; trivago GmbH, an online hotel metasearch company; wotif.com Holdings Limited, an operator of travel brands in the Asia Pacific; and CarRentals.com, an online car rental booking company. Recently, Expedia acquired Travelocity, HomeAway, Inc. and Orbitz Worldwide, Inc.

The company offers employees medical, life, AD&D, disability, dental and vision insurance; flexible spending accounts; onsite flu shots; a 401(k); adoption assistance; an employee assistance program; a group legal program; tuition reimbursement; travel assistance; business travel accident insurance; pet insurance; and discounts for auto and home insurance.

FINANCIAL DATA: *Note: Data for latest year may not have been available at press time.*

In U.S. $	2016	2015	2014	2013	2012	2011
Revenue	8,773,564,000	6,672,317,000	5,763,485,000	4,771,259,000	4,030,347,000	3,449,009,000
R&D Expense	1,235,019,000	830,244,000	686,154,000		484,898,000	380,999,000
Operating Income	461,702,000	413,566,000	517,764,000	366,060,000	431,724,000	479,609,000
Operating Margin %	5.26%	6.19%	8.98%	7.67%	10.71%	13.90%
SGA Expense	5,072,207,000	3,850,412,000	3,275,241,000	3,151,043,000	2,183,416,000	1,805,204,000
Net Income	281,848,000	764,465,000	398,097,000	232,850,000	280,171,000	472,294,000
Operating Cash Flow	1,564,334,000	1,368,045,000	1,366,959,000	763,200,000	1,229,575,000	1,030,072,000
Capital Expenditure	749,348,000	787,041,000	328,387,000	308,581,000	235,697,000	207,837,000
EBITDA	1,243,950,000	1,552,502,000	908,162,000	671,526,000	633,797,000	647,724,000
Return on Assets %	1.80%	6.23%	4.75%	3.14%	4.12%	7.17%
Return on Equity %	6.26%	22.99%	20.26%	10.52%	12.50%	19.38%
Debt to Equity	0.76	0.65	0.97	0.58	0.54	0.56

CONTACT INFORMATION:

Phone: 425 679-7200   Fax: 425 564-7240
Toll-Free: 800-397-3342
Address: 333 108th Ave. NE, Bellevue, WA 98004 United States

STOCK TICKER/OTHER:

Stock Ticker: EXPE   Exchange: NAS
Employees: 20,075   Fiscal Year Ends: 12/31
Parent Company:

SALARIES/BONUSES:

Top Exec. Salary: $1,000,000   Bonus: $1,375,000
Second Exec. Salary: Bonus: $750,000
$750,000

OTHER THOUGHTS:

Estimated Female Officers or Directors: 1
Hot Spot for Advancement for Women/Minorities:

Expeditors International of Washington Inc www.expeditors.com

NAIC Code: 488510

TYPES OF BUSINESS:

Freight Transportation Arrangement
Online Services
Logistics Software
Freight Consolidation
Customs Brokerage

BRANDS/DIVISIONS/AFFILIATES:

exp.o
exp.o Booking
exp.o ISF
TradeFlow
Expeditors Tradewin LLC

CONTACTS: Note: Officers with more than one job title may be intentionally listed here more than once.

Tay Yoshitani,
Jeffrey Musser, CEO
Bradley Powell, CFO
Christopher McClincy, Chief Information Officer
Robert Wright, Director
Richard Rostan, Executive VP, Geographical
Benjamin Clark, General Counsel
Philip Coughlin, President, Divisional
Daniel Wall, President, Divisional
Eugene Alger, President, Divisional

GROWTH PLANS/SPECIAL FEATURES:

Expeditors International of Washington, Inc. provides global logistics services through an international network spanning 331 locations in 109 countries, which includes four regional headquarters in London, Sao Paulo, Beirut and Shanghai. The company's services include consolidation or forwarding of air and ocean freight, customs brokerage, distribution management, vendor consolidation, cargo insurance, purchase order management and customized logistics information. Ocean freight services account for 33% of the firm's revenue, airfreight accounts for 41%, and customs brokerage and other services account for 26%. Expeditors International does not compete for domestic freight, overnight courier or small parcel business and does not own aircraft or steamships. The company provides many services over the internet. Expeditors International's web-based tracking system, exp.o, offers query capabilities to find the status of inbound shipments or orders and to view customs details. Linked to exp.o, exp.o Booking is the company's web-based electronic booking tool that provides notifications, pick-up arrangements, shipment tracking and document generation. Exp.o ISF (importer security filing) assists importers in fulfilling U.S. Customs Importer Security Filing requirements. Through web access to international tariff data and rules, TradeFlow helps international companies reduce the risks and manage the costs associated with importing and exporting. Subsidiary Expeditors Tradewin LLC provides customs consulting services.

Expeditors International offers its employees a comprehensive benefits package, a 401(k) plan and a stock purchase plan.

FINANCIAL DATA: Note: Data for latest year may not have been available at press time.

In U.S. $	2016	2015	2014	2013	2012	2011
Revenue	6,098,037,000	6,616,632,000	6,564,721,000	6,080,257,000	5,980,943,000	6,150,498,000
R&D Expense						
Operating Income	670,163,000	721,484,000	594,648,000	552,073,000	530,798,000	618,327,000
Operating Margin %	10.98%	10.90%	9.05%	9.07%	8.87%	10.05%
SGA Expense	1,308,210,000	1,287,971,000	1,206,264,000	1,164,281,000	1,117,280,000	1,116,997,000
Net Income	430,807,000	457,223,000	376,888,000	348,526,000	333,360,000	385,679,000
Operating Cash Flow	529,099,000	564,712,000	394,966,000	407,536,000	370,126,000	457,131,000
Capital Expenditure	59,316,000	44,383,000	37,472,000	53,411,000	47,626,000	78,115,000
EBITDA	716,959,000	767,496,000	643,940,000	600,144,000	591,584,000	676,930,000
Return on Assets %	16.03%	16.70%	12.76%	11.67%	11.45%	13.90%
Return on Equity %	24.36%	25.68%	19.06%	16.94%	16.53%	20.59%
Debt to Equity						

CONTACT INFORMATION:

Phone: 206 674-3400   Fax: 206 674-3459
Toll-Free:
Address: 1015 3rd Ave., Fl. 12, Seattle, WA 98104 United States

SALARIES/BONUSES:

Top Exec. Salary: $100,000   Bonus: $
Second Exec. Salary: Bonus: $
$100,000

STOCK TICKER/OTHER:

Stock Ticker: EXPD   Exchange: NAS
Employees: 16,000   Fiscal Year Ends: 12/31
Parent Company:

OTHER THOUGHTS:

Estimated Female Officers or Directors: 2
Hot Spot for Advancement for Women/Minorities:

Experian North America

www.experian.com

NAIC Code: 561450

TYPES OF BUSINESS:

Credit Bureau
Customer Relationship Software & Solutions
Marketing Software & Solutions
Business & Consumer Internet Sites
Online Services
Risk Management Services, Automotive

BRANDS/DIVISIONS/AFFILIATES:

Experian plc
Experian.com
CreditReport.com
freecreditscore.com

CONTACTS: Note: Officers with more than one job title may be intentionally listed here more than once.

Craig Boundy, CEO
Don Robert, CEO-Experian plc
Kerry Williams, Pres., Credit Svcs. & Experian Latin America
Brian Cassin, CFO-Experian plc
John Peace, Chmn.-Experian plc

GROWTH PLANS/SPECIAL FEATURES:

Experian North America, a subsidiary of Experian plc, is a leading credit-reporting agency in the U.S., Canada and Mexico. It also helps organizations find, develop and manage customer relationships by providing information, decision-making solutions and processing services. Experian operates through four segments: credit services, decision analytics, marketing services and consumer services. The credit services unit provides clients with solutions that optimize processes in acquiring new customers, prospecting for customers, customer portfolio management tools and collections services. Decision analytics provides analytical software and services to help clients optimize their lending strategies, allowing companies to manage credit risk, maintain regulatory compliance, predict behavior, prevent and detect fraud and allow for more efficient decision making. The marketing services unit provides customer acquisition, retention and growth and marketing strategy services to the advertising and media, automotive, banking, catalog, retail, financial services, consumer products and travel and hospitality markets. Finally, the consumer services segment offers consumers access to their credit histories and financial management tools through various websites, including Experian.com, CreditReport.com and freecreditscore.com.

Parent company Experian offers its employees health, dental and vision care plans; flexible spending accounts; education assistance; credit union membership; an employee assistance program; referral bonuses; employee discounts; adoption assistance; and fitness reimbursement.

FINANCIAL DATA: Note: Data for latest year may not have been available at press time.

In U.S. $	2016	2015	2014	2013	2012	2011
Revenue	2,294,000,000	2,390,000,000	2,404,000,000	2,258,000,000	2,092,000,000	1,905,000,000
R&D Expense						
Operating Income						
Operating Margin %						
SGA Expense						
Net Income	704,000,000	741,000,000	757,000,000	718,000,000	658,000,000	556,000,000
Operating Cash Flow						
Capital Expenditure						
EBITDA						
Return on Assets %						
Return on Equity %						
Debt to Equity						

CONTACT INFORMATION:

Phone: 714-830-7000   Fax: 714-830-2449
Toll-Free: 888-397-3742
Address: 475 Anton Blvd., Costa Mesa, CA 92626 United States

SALARIES/BONUSES:

Top Exec. Salary: $ Bonus: $
Second Exec. Salary: $ Bonus: $

STOCK TICKER/OTHER:

Stock Ticker: Subsidiary   Exchange:
Employees: 6,700   Fiscal Year Ends: 03/31
Parent Company: Experian plc

OTHER THOUGHTS:

Estimated Female Officers or Directors:
Hot Spot for Advancement for Women/Minorities:

EY LLP

NAIC Code: 541211

www.ey.com

TYPES OF BUSINESS:

Accounting
Risk Management
Tax Preparation Services
Human Resources Management
IT Services
Transaction Support Services
Industry Publications

BRANDS/DIVISIONS/AFFILIATES:

EY

CONTACTS: Note: Officers with more than one job title may be intentionally listed here more than once.

Steve Howe, Managing Partner-Americas
Michael Inserra, Regional Managing Partner-Financial Svcs.
Tom Hough, Vice Chair-Assurance Svcs.
Richard Jeanneret, Vice Chair-Transaction Advisory Svcs.
Jean-Yves, Vice Chair-Quality & Risk Mgmt.
Tom McGrath, Sr. Vice Chair-Accounts
Ronen Barel, Chmn.

GROWTH PLANS/SPECIAL FEATURES:

EY, LLP, the U.S. branch of the global accounting firm EY (Ernst & Young), is a professional services company. The firm provides advisory, tax, assurance and transactions. Advisory services include actuarial, customer, cyber security, finance, risk management, internal audit, people advisory, program management, risk assurance, risk transformation, strategy, supply chain & operations and technology. Tax services include global tax, country tax, cross border tax, global trade, global compliance and reporting, human capital, private client, law, tax accounting, tax performance, tax policy and controversy, transaction tax, sales tax, transfer pricing and operating model effectiveness. Assurance services include accounting compliance, reporting, climate change, sustainability, financial accounting, financial statement audit, fraud investigation and dispute services. Transactions service include corporate development, divesture, lead advisory, operational transaction, restructuring, strategy, transaction support, transaction tax, valuation and business modeling. Industries served by EY, LLP include automotive, transportation, health, oil and gas, technology, consumer products and retail, life sciences, power and utilities, telecommunications, financial services, media and entertainment, private equity, government and public sector, mining and metals, real estate, hospitality and construction.

FINANCIAL DATA: Note: Data for latest year may not have been available at press time.

In U.S. $	2016	2015	2014	2013	2012	2011
Revenue	13,900,000,000	12,701,000,000	11,542,000,000	10,750,000,000	9,820,000,000	8,981,000,000
R&D Expense						
Operating Income						
Operating Margin %						
SGA Expense						
Net Income						
Operating Cash Flow						
Capital Expenditure						
EBITDA						
Return on Assets %						
Return on Equity %						
Debt to Equity						

CONTACT INFORMATION:

Phone: 212-773-3000   Fax: 212-773-6350
Toll-Free:
Address: 5 Times Sq., 14th Fl., New York, NY 10036 United States

STOCK TICKER/OTHER:

Stock Ticker: Subsidiary   Exchange:
Employees: 39,400   Fiscal Year Ends: 06/30
Parent Company: EY

SALARIES/BONUSES:

Top Exec. Salary: $ Bonus: $
Second Exec. Salary: $ Bonus: $

OTHER THOUGHTS:

Estimated Female Officers or Directors: 5
Hot Spot for Advancement for Women/Minorities: Y

F5 Networks Inc

www.f5.com

NAIC Code: 0

TYPES OF BUSINESS:

Computer Software, Network Management, System Testing & Storage
Internet Traffic Management Solutions
Firewall Software
File Virtualization

BRANDS/DIVISIONS/AFFILIATES:

BIG-IP
VIPRION
Silverline
iRules
iControl
iApps
iCall

CONTACTS: *Note: Officers with more than one job title may be intentionally listed here more than once.*

Andrew Reinland, CFO
Benjamin Gibson, Chief Marketing Officer
Ryan Kearny, Chief Technology Officer
Alan Higginson, Director
John McAdam, Director
John Dilullo, Executive VP, Divisional
Edward Eames, Executive VP
Scot Rogers, Executive VP

GROWTH PLANS/SPECIAL FEATURES:

F5 Networks, Inc. provides application delivery networking products that improve the security, availability and performance of network applications. The core technology of the firm is the full-proxy, programmable, massively-scalable software platform called TMOS (Traffic Management Operating System). The TMOS platform supports a broadest array of application services, including local and global traffic management, network and application security, access management, web acceleration and several other network and application services. These services are available as software modules that can run individually or as part of an integrated solution on the high-performance, scalable, purpose-built BIG-IP appliances and chassis-based VIPRION systems; or as software-only Virtual Editions that run on major hypervisors in public and private clouds. The cloud-based Silverline software-as-a-service (SaaS) offerings allow customers to subscribe to online denial-of-service protection and application security services. The core features and functions of TMOS enable the firm's products to inspect and modify the content of IP traffic flows at network speeds and sessions between users and applications and support a broad and growing array of services. The built-in scripting language, iRules, enables customers and third parties to write customized rules to inspect and modify traffic. TMOS also has an open software interface called iControl, which allows the firm's products to communicate with one another and with third-party products; a set of features called iApps that speed deployment of services and give users an application-centric view of how applications are managed and delivered; and a scripting framework called iCall that lets users configure their F5 devices inline. The company sells its products and services to large enterprise customers and service providers through a variety of channels, including distributors, value-added resellers and systems integrators.

Employee benefits include medical, dental and vision coverage; flexible spending accounts; life and disability insurance; employee stock and employee assistance programs; 401(k); and tuition assistance.

FINANCIAL DATA: *Note: Data for latest year may not have been available at press time.*

In U.S. $	2016	2015	2014	2013	2012	2011
Revenue	1,995,034,000	1,919,823,000	1,732,046,000	1,481,314,000	1,377,247,000	1,151,834,000
R&D Expense	334,227,000	296,583,000	263,792,000	209,614,000	177,406,000	138,910,000
Operating Income	547,377,000	552,899,000	493,557,000	430,818,000	426,303,000	350,662,000
Operating Margin %	27.43%	28.79%	28.49%	29.08%	30.95%	30.44%
SGA Expense	767,174,000	738,080,000	664,738,000	585,442,000	537,370,000	454,258,000
Net Income	365,855,000	365,014,000	311,183,000	277,314,000	275,186,000	241,397,000
Operating Cash Flow	711,535,000	684,541,000	548,992,000	499,693,000	495,437,000	416,938,000
Capital Expenditure	68,238,000	67,086,000	22,718,000	26,583,000	30,117,000	36,160,000
EBITDA	604,153,000	605,482,000	539,678,000	470,823,000	461,442,000	371,549,000
Return on Assets %	15.84%	16.23%	14.09%	13.39%	15.81%	16.47%
Return on Equity %	29.24%	27.17%	21.40%	19.33%	22.60%	22.89%
Debt to Equity						

CONTACT INFORMATION:

Phone: 206 272-5555   Fax: 206 272-5556
Toll-Free: 888-882-4447
Address: 401 Elliott Ave. W., Seattle, WA 98119 United States

STOCK TICKER/OTHER:

Stock Ticker: FFIV   Exchange: NAS
Employees: 4,395   Fiscal Year Ends: 09/30
Parent Company:

SALARIES/BONUSES:

Top Exec. Salary: $727,416   Bonus: $
Second Exec. Salary: Bonus: $
$551,000

OTHER THOUGHTS:

Estimated Female Officers or Directors: 3
Hot Spot for Advancement for Women/Minorities: Y

Facebook Inc

NAIC Code: 519130

TYPES OF BUSINESS:

Social Networking
Advertising Services
Developer Tools
Online Video
3-D Headset Manufacturing
Apps

BRANDS/DIVISIONS/AFFILIATES:

Facebook Platform
Instagram
Messenger
WhatsApp Messenger

CONTACTS: *Note: Officers with more than one job title may be intentionally listed here more than once.*

Jan Koum, CEO, Subsidiary
Mark Zuckerberg, CEO
David Wehner, CFO
Susan Taylor, Chief Accounting Officer
Michael Schroepfer, Chief Technology Officer
Sheryl Sandberg, COO
Christopher Cox, Other Executive Officer
David Fischer, Vice President, Divisional
Colin Stretch, Vice President

GROWTH PLANS/SPECIAL FEATURES:

Facebook, Inc. owns and operates a free social networking utility for communicating online with family, friends and acquaintances. As of the end of 2016, the company had 1.79 billion monthly active users in general, and 1.18 billion daily active users who specifically used the company's mobile products. Some of the site's core functions and applications include individual profiles and home pages; friend lists; group pages; and photos, videos, events and other shared items. Communication is enabled through means such as in-site instant messaging, personal messages, public posts and status updates. Third-party applications (such as games, quizzes and personality tests) can also be added to users' pages to further personalize the site. For privacy, the firm gives users the ability to limit, to some extent, who can view their profile, postings and other personal information. The company's Facebook Platform is a set of development tools and application programming interfaces that enable developers to integrate with Facebook to create social apps and web sites. More than 10 million apps and web sites have been integrated as part of the platform. Facebook generates the majority of its revenues from advertising, which can be customized to reach specifically targeted audiences by accessing information users provide the company on their individual profiles. Subsidiary Instagram is a mobile phone-based photo-sharing service that makes it simple for users to upload photos to their profiles; Messenger is a mobile-to-mobile messaging application available on Android, iOS and Windows Phone devices; and WhatsApp Messenger is a cross-platform mobile messaging app that allows people to exchange messages on iOS, Android, BlackBerry, Windows Phone and Nokia devices.

Facebook provides its employees with health coverage; life and disability insurance; 401(k); parental leave and daycare reimbursements; vacation pay; and an employee assistance program. The firm's headquarters features an onsite cafeteria serving free breakfast, lunch and dinner daily. Bout 32% of employees are women.

FINANCIAL DATA: *Note: Data for latest year may not have been available at press time.*

In U.S. $	2016	2015	2014	2013	2012	2011
Revenue	27,638,000,000	17,928,000,000	12,466,000,000	7,872,000,000	5,089,000,000	3,711,000,000
R&D Expense	5,919,000,000	4,816,000,000	2,666,000,000	1,415,000,000	1,399,000,000	388,000,000
Operating Income	12,427,000,000	6,225,000,000	4,994,000,000	2,804,000,000	538,000,000	1,756,000,000
Operating Margin %	44.96%	34.72%	40.06%	35.61%	10.57%	47.31%
SGA Expense	5,503,000,000	4,020,000,000	2,653,000,000	1,778,000,000	1,788,000,000	707,000,000
Net Income	10,217,000,000	3,688,000,000	2,940,000,000	1,500,000,000	53,000,000	1,000,000,000
Operating Cash Flow	16,108,000,000	8,599,000,000	5,457,000,000	4,222,000,000	1,612,000,000	1,549,000,000
Capital Expenditure	4,491,000,000	2,523,000,000	1,831,000,000	1,362,000,000	1,235,000,000	606,000,000
EBITDA	14,870,000,000	8,162,000,000	6,176,000,000	3,821,000,000	1,194,000,000	2,060,000,000
Return on Assets %	17.81%	8.19%	10.07%	9.03%	.29%	14.33%
Return on Equity %	19.70%	9.13%	11.34%	10.95%	.39%	22.91%
Debt to Equity				0.01	0.16	0.09

CONTACT INFORMATION:

Phone: 650 543-4800   Fax:
Toll-Free:
Address: 1601 Willow Rd., Menlo Park, CA 94025 United States

STOCK TICKER/OTHER:

Stock Ticker: FB   Exchange: NAS
Employees: 17,048   Fiscal Year Ends: 12/31
Parent Company:

SALARIES/BONUSES:

Top Exec. Salary: $738,077   Bonus: $1,293,635
Second Exec. Salary: $662,692   Bonus: $940,421

OTHER THOUGHTS:

Estimated Female Officers or Directors: 2
Hot Spot for Advancement for Women/Minorities: Y

FactSet Research Systems Inc

www.factset.com

NAIC Code: 0

TYPES OF BUSINESS:

Online Financial & Economic Data
Financial Software
Consulting Services

BRANDS/DIVISIONS/AFFILIATES:

BISAM Technologies SA
Interactive Data Managed Solutions

CONTACTS: Note: Officers with more than one job title may be intentionally listed here more than once.

Maurizio Nicolelli, CFO
Philip Hadley, Chairman of the Board
Matthew McNulty, Controller
John Wiseman, Executive VP, Divisional
Mark Hale, Executive VP
Scott Miller, Executive VP
Rachel Stern, General Counsel
Edward Baker-Greene, Other Executive Officer
Philip Snow, President

GROWTH PLANS/SPECIAL FEATURES:

FactSet Research Systems, Inc. supplies financial information and analytical applications to global investors, including portfolio managers, performance analysts, risk managers, sell-side equity researchers, investment bankers and fixed income professionals. Headquartered in Norwalk, Connecticut, the company operates 38 locations in 21 countries. FactSet has more than 86,000 users and 3,500 clients in over 50 countries worldwide, with access to data from more than 220 data suppliers, 115 news sources and 85 exchanges. It combines the content of tens of thousands of companies from multiple sources (stock markets, research firms, governments and others) into a single online platform of information and analytics. The firm integrates content from premier providers such as Thomson Reuters, Standard & Poor's, Axioma, Interactive Data Corporation, Dow Jones & Company, Northfield Information Services, Barclays Capital, Intex Solutions and many more. FactSet's operations are organized into three reportable segments based on geographic operations: the U.S., Europe and Asia Pacific. The majority of fiscal revenue is derived from its U.S. clients, with Europe being next and Asia Pacific the remainder. The U.S. segment services finance professionals including financial institutions throughout the Americas, while the European and Asia Pacific segments service investment professionals located throughout Europe and Asia, respectively. The European segment is headquartered in London, England and maintains offices in France, Germany, the Netherlands, Latvia, Dubai and Italy. The Asia Pacific segment is headquartered in Tokyo, Japan with offices in Hong Kong, Australia and India. FactSet's client retention rate is over 95%. In 2017, the firm acquired BISAM Technologies SA; and the Interactive Data Managed Solutions business from Intercontinental Exchange.

FactSet offers U.S. employees medical, dental, life, disability, vision, AD&D and business travel insurance; wellness programs; disability and maternity leave; counseling services; flexible spending accounts; 401(k) and employee stock purchase plans; and tuition reimbursement.

FINANCIAL DATA: Note: Data for latest year may not have been available at press time.

In U.S. $	2016	2015	2014	2013	2012	2011
Revenue	1,127,092,000	1,006,768,000	920,335,000	858,112,000	805,793,000	726,510,000
R&D Expense						
Operating Income	349,676,000	331,918,000	302,219,000	269,419,000	272,990,000	238,335,000
Operating Margin %	31.02%	32.96%	32.83%	31.39%	33.87%	32.80%
SGA Expense	290,007,000	269,511,000	264,430,000	282,314,000	257,266,000	243,552,000
Net Income	338,815,000	241,051,000	211,543,000	198,637,000	188,809,000	171,046,000
Operating Cash Flow	331,140,000	306,442,000	265,023,000	269,809,000	231,965,000	207,136,000
Capital Expenditure	47,740,000	25,682,000	17,743,000	18,517,000	22,520,000	29,343,000
EBITDA	387,728,000	363,267,000	336,654,000	305,198,000	306,769,000	275,182,000
Return on Assets %	38.59%	34.43%	31.26%	28.69%	27.93%	26.27%
Return on Equity %	64.59%	46.23%	40.18%	36.31%	35.37%	33.61%
Debt to Equity	0.57	0.06				

CONTACT INFORMATION:

Phone: 203 810-1000   Fax: 203 810-1001
Toll-Free:
Address: 601 Merritt 7, 3/Fl., Norwalk, CT 06851 United States

STOCK TICKER/OTHER:

Stock Ticker: FDS   Exchange: NYS
Employees: 8,375   Fiscal Year Ends: 08/31
Parent Company:

SALARIES/BONUSES:

Top Exec. Salary: $350,000   Bonus: $800,000
Second Exec. Salary: Bonus: $600,000
$275,000

OTHER THOUGHTS:

Estimated Female Officers or Directors: 3
Hot Spot for Advancement for Women/Minorities: Y

Fairview Health Services

NAIC Code: 622110

www.fairview.org

TYPES OF BUSINESS:

General Medical and Surgical Hospitals
Specialty Clinics
Home Care
Hospice Services
Children's Services
Cancer Care
Senior Care
Academic Teaching Hospital

BRANDS/DIVISIONS/AFFILIATES:

Fairview Lakes Medical Center
Maple Grove Medical Center
Fairview Northland Medical Center
Fairview Ridges Hospital
Grand Itasca Clinic & Hospital
Fairview Southdale Hospital
University of Minnesota Academic Health Center
Ebenezer

CONTACTS: Note: Officers with more than one job title may be intentionally listed here more than once.

James Hereford, CEO
Daniel Fromm, CFO
Carolyn Jacobson, Chief Human Resources Officer
Brent Asplin, Chief Clinical Officer
Alistair Jacques, CIO
Mark Hansberry, VP-Strategic Planning
Mark Hansberry, VP-Comm.
Brent Asplin, Pres., Fairview Medical Group
Daniel K. Anderson, Pres., Fairview Community Hospitals
Bob Beacher, Pres., Fairview Pharmacy Services
Richard Howard, Pres., Fairview Foundation
David Murphy, Chmn.
Mark Thomas, Pres., Senior Services

GROWTH PLANS/SPECIAL FEATURES:

Fairview Health Services is an integrated health network. It serves the Minneapolis-St. Paul area of Minnesota and suburbs; the Red Wing, Northland, Lakes and Range areas of Minnesota; the Minnesota Valley; and Wyoming. The system contains acute care hospitals; urgent care facilities; primary care, specialty care and occupational health clinics; senior care and housing facilities; freestanding surgery centers; ambulatory care facilities; retail and specialty pharmacies; counseling centers, home healthcare programs; and various foundations supporting health-related services. The company's hospitals include Fairview Lakes Medical Center, Maple Grove Hospital, Fairview Northland Medical Center, Fairview Ridges Hospital, Grand Itasca Clinic & Hospital and Fairview Southdale Hospital. Fairview also has an academic partnership with the University of Minnesota and University of Minnesota Physicians. Through these partnerships, Fairview Health operates from the University of Minnesota Academic Health Center, which consists of six schools and colleges that educate and train researchers, physicians and other healthcare professionals; the University of Minnesota Physicians, a group practice with more than 800 physicians and 1,600 healthcare professionals who apply clinical breakthroughs for patients at University of Minnesota Medical Center and University of Minnesota Masonic Children's Hospital, as well as hospitals and clinics throughout the community. Through its subsidiary Ebenezer, Fairview provides senior housing facilities such as apartments, assisted living complexes, cooperatives, condominiums, a memory care facility for patients living with Alzheimer's or other early-stage dementias and adult and intergenerational daycare programs. The Fairview Foundation is the group's funding entity for operations, special projects, programs, allocations and endowments. In March 2017, the firm opened a new Fairview Urgent Care location in Edina, Minnesota.

Fairview offers its employees life, disability, health and dental insurance; assistance program; wellness options; various employee assistance programs; 403(b) and 401(k) and medical mission grants.

FINANCIAL DATA: Note: Data for latest year may not have been available at press time.

In U.S. $	2016	2015	2014	2013	2012	2011
Revenue	4,363,540,000	3,867,550,000	3,560,832,000	3,318,513,000	3,218,081,000	3,011,509,000
R&D Expense						
Operating Income						
Operating Margin %						
SGA Expense						
Net Income	213,786,000	64,908,000	166,695,000	244,300,000	108,039,000	16,667,000
Operating Cash Flow						
Capital Expenditure						
EBITDA						
Return on Assets %						
Return on Equity %						
Debt to Equity						

CONTACT INFORMATION:

Phone: 612-672-7272   Fax: 612-672-7186
Toll-Free: 800-824-1953
Address: 2450 Riverside Ave., Minneapolis, MN 55454 United States

STOCK TICKER/OTHER:

Stock Ticker: Nonprofit   Exchange:
Employees: 32,000   Fiscal Year Ends: 12/31
Parent Company:

SALARIES/BONUSES:

Top Exec. Salary: $ Bonus: $
Second Exec. Salary: $ Bonus: $

OTHER THOUGHTS:

Estimated Female Officers or Directors: 9
Hot Spot for Advancement for Women/Minorities: Y

Fastenal Company

www.fastenal.com

NAIC Code: 423810

TYPES OF BUSINESS:

Construction and Mining Equipment Wholesalers
Office Equipment Merchant Wholesalers

BRANDS/DIVISIONS/AFFILIATES:

Fastenal

CONTACTS: *Note: Officers with more than one job title may be intentionally listed here more than once.*

Daniel Florness, CEO
Sheryl Lisowski, Controller
Willard Oberton, Director
Reyne Wisecup, Director
James Jansen, Executive VP, Divisional
Nicholas Lundquist, Executive VP, Divisional
Gary Polipnick, Executive VP, Divisional
John Soderberg, Executive VP, Divisional
William Drazkowski, Executive VP, Divisional
Jeffery Watts, Executive VP, Divisional
Charles Miller, Executive VP, Divisional
Holden Lewis, Executive VP
Terry Owen, Senior Executive VP, Divisional
Leland Hein, Senior Executive VP, Divisional

GROWTH PLANS/SPECIAL FEATURES:

Fastenal Company is a retailer and wholesaler of industrial and construction supplies, many of which are sold under the Fastenal name. The firm's fastener product line consists of two broad categories: threaded fasteners, such as bolts, nuts, screws, studs and related washers; and miscellaneous supplies and hardware, such as pins and machinery keys, concrete anchors, metal framing systems, wire rope, strut, rivets and related accessories. Fastenal operates roughly 2,503 store locations in 21 countries, supported by 14 distribution centers in North America (11 in the U.S., two in Canada and one in Mexico). In March 2017, the firm agreed to acquire certain assets of industrial and fastener supply distributor, Manufacturer's Supply Company.

Fastenal offers its employees medical, dental, life, disability and AD&D insurance; a retirement savings plan; company profit sharing; and employee discount programs.

FINANCIAL DATA: *Note: Data for latest year may not have been available at press time.*

In U.S. $	2016	2015	2014	2013	2012	2011
Revenue	3,962,036,000	3,869,187,000	3,733,507,000	3,326,106,000	3,133,577,000	2,766,859,000
R&D Expense						
Operating Income	795,839,000	828,755,000	787,590,000	712,657,000	673,691,000	574,609,000
Operating Margin %	20.08%	21.41%	21.09%	21.42%	21.49%	20.76%
SGA Expense	1,169,470,000	1,121,590,000	1,110,776,000	1,007,431,000	941,236,000	859,369,000
Net Income	499,478,000	516,361,000	494,150,000	448,636,000	420,536,000	357,929,000
Operating Cash Flow	513,999,000	546,940,000	499,392,000	416,120,000	396,292,000	268,489,000
Capital Expenditure	189,451,000	155,168,000	189,474,000	206,540,000	138,406,000	120,043,000
EBITDA	900,285,000	915,726,000	861,021,000	777,772,000	727,743,000	619,315,000
Return on Assets %	19.20%	21.11%	22.28%	23.05%	24.02%	22.70%
Return on Equity %	26.75%	27.78%	26.79%	26.92%	27.85%	26.11%
Debt to Equity	0.19	0.16				

CONTACT INFORMATION:

Phone: 507 454-5374   Fax: 507 453-8049
Toll-Free:
Address: 2001 Theurer Blvd., Winona, MN 55987-0978 United States

STOCK TICKER/OTHER:

Stock Ticker: FAST   Exchange: NAS
Employees: 19,624   Fiscal Year Ends: 12/31
Parent Company:

SALARIES/BONUSES:

Top Exec. Salary: $577,500   Bonus: $
Second Exec. Salary: $439,167   Bonus: $

OTHER THOUGHTS:

Estimated Female Officers or Directors: 2
Hot Spot for Advancement for Women/Minorities:

FCA US LLC   www.fcanorthamerica.com/company/AboutUs/Pages/AboutUs.aspx

NAIC Code: 336111

TYPES OF BUSINESS:

Automobile Manufacturing
Research & Development
Nanotechnology-Coatings
Light Truck Manufacturing
Financial Services

BRANDS/DIVISIONS/AFFILIATES:

Fiat Chrysler Automobiles NV
Chrysler
Jeep
Alfa Romeo
Mopar
Uconnect
AppleCarPlay
Vehicle-to-X

CONTACTS: Note: Officers with more than one job title may be intentionally listed here more than once.

Sergio Marchionne, CEO
Richard K. Palmer, CFO
Ralph V. Gilles, Sr. VP-Prod. Design
Mark M. Chernoby, Sr. VP-Eng.
Mauro Pino, Sr. VP-Mfg. & World Class Mfg.
Peter Grady, VP-Network Dev. & Fleet
Marjorie Loeb, General Counsel
Barbara J. Pilarski, VP-Bus. Dev.
Gualberto Ranieri, Sr. VP-Comm.
Laurie A. Macaddino, VP-Audit
Doug D. Betts, Sr. VP-Quality
Alistair Gardner, Pres.
Reid Bigland, Head-U.S. Sales
Sergio Marchionne, Chmn.
Steven G. Beahm, Sr. VP-Supply Chain Mgmt.

GROWTH PLANS/SPECIAL FEATURES:

FCA US LLC, also known as Chrysler, is a North American automaker headquartered in Michigan. It is a member of the Fiat Chrysler Automobiles NV family of companies. FCA US designs, engineers, manufactures and sells vehicles under the Chrysler, Jeep, Dodge, Ram and Fiat brands, as well as the street and racing technology (SRT) performance vehicle designation. The company also distributes the Alfa Romeo model and Mopar products. FCA is one of the largest automakers in the world based on total annual vehicle sales, shipping 2.6 million vehicles in 2016 from its 37 worldwide manufacturing sites. Recent vehicle models feature AppleCarPlay and Android Auto, providing a safer way to use a smartphone inside a car. Its fourth-generation Uconnect system brings interactive ability to the in-car radio and telemetric-like controls to car settings. Other concepts FCA is exploring for future Uconnect models include predictive technology that monitors the driver's daily habits; Vehicle-to-X communication, enabling vehicles to communicate with each other and the roadside; and privacy mode, which detects when a passenger is present in the vehicle. FCA's 2017 Chrysler Pacifica and Pacifica Hybrid models have been re-engineered from the ground up on an all-new platform for class-leading ride, handling and noise, vibration and harshness, and boast 115 minivan innovations. The hybrid offers up to 80 miles per gallon equivalent (MPGe) in city driving. The firm maintains 12 regional business centers, 23 parts distribution centers and eight training and test facilities.

The firm offers employees medical, prescription, vision and dental coverage; life insurance; discounted auto and home insurance; discount new vehicle purchase programs; and educational and personal development programs.

FINANCIAL DATA: Note: Data for latest year may not have been available at press time.

In U.S. $	2016	2015	2014	2013	2012	2011
Revenue	12,000,000,000	11,676,910,000	10,913,000,000	72,140,000,000	65,800,000,000	55,000,000,000
R&D Expense						
Operating Income						
Operating Margin %						
SGA Expense						
Net Income	1,985,015,213	1,747,498,195	1,587,005,793	2,760,000,000	1,700,000,000	183,000,000
Operating Cash Flow						
Capital Expenditure						
EBITDA						
Return on Assets %						
Return on Equity %						
Debt to Equity						

CONTACT INFORMATION:

Phone: 248-576-5741   Fax:
Toll-Free: 800-992-1997
Address: 1000 Chrysler Dr., Auburn Hills, MI 48326-2766 United States

STOCK TICKER/OTHER:

Stock Ticker: Private   Exchange:
Employees: 83,800   Fiscal Year Ends: 12/31
Parent Company: Fiat Chrysler Automobiles NV

SALARIES/BONUSES:

Top Exec. Salary: $ Bonus: $
Second Exec. Salary: $ Bonus: $

OTHER THOUGHTS:

Estimated Female Officers or Directors: 3
Hot Spot for Advancement for Women/Minorities: Y

Federal-Mogul Corporation

www.federalmogul.com

NAIC Code: 336300

TYPES OF BUSINESS:

Aftermarket Products & Services
Powertrain Products
Sealing Systems
Vehicle Safety & Performance Products

BRANDS/DIVISIONS/AFFILIATES:

IEH BA LLC (Beck Arnley)

CONTACTS: Note: Officers with more than one job title may be intentionally listed here more than once.

Michelle Taigman, Assistant Secretary
Rainer Jueckstock, CEO, Divisional
Daniel Ninivaggi, CEO, Subsidiary
Martin Hendricks, President, Divisional
Scott Pepin, Senior VP, Divisional
Jerome Rouquet, Senior VP
John Patouhas, Vice President

GROWTH PLANS/SPECIAL FEATURES:

Federal-Mogul Corporation is a supplier of vehicle and industrial products for fuel economy, alternative energies, environment and safety systems. The company operates two divisions: powertrain, which accounted for 57% of annual sales; and motorparts, 43%. Powertrain focuses on original equipment (OE) products for automotive, heavy duty and industrial applications. This segment offers its customers a diverse array of market-leading products for OE applications, including pistons, piston rings, piston pins, cylinder liners, valve seats & guides, ignition products, dynamic seals, bonded piston seals, combustion & exhaust gaskets, static gaskets & seals, rigid heat shields, engine bearings, industrial bearings, brushings & washers, plus element resistant systems protection sleeving products, acoustic shielding and flexible heat shields. The motorparts segment sells and distributes a broad portfolio of products manufactured by Powertrain. Motorparts' products include brake disc pads, brake linings, brake linings, brake blocks, brake system components, chassis products, wipers and other product lines to OE and aftermarket customers. Federal-Mogul maintains manufacturing facilities and distribution centers in 24 countries. In December 2016, the firm acquired IEH BA, LLC (known as Beck Arnley), a provider of original equipment quality parts and fluids for foreign nameplate vehicles in North America; and agreed to sell certain assets and liabilities related to its wipers business in the motorparts segment.

The firm offers employees medical, dental, prescription drug, vision and hearing insurance; flexible spending accounts; life and AD&D insurance; disability coverage; a 401(k) plan; tuition assistance; and a pension plan.

FINANCIAL DATA: Note: Data for latest year may not have been available at press time.

In U.S. $	2016	2015	2014	2013	2012	2011
Revenue		7,418,999,808	7,317,000,192	6,785,999,872	6,664,000,000	6,910,000,128
R&D Expense						
Operating Income						
Operating Margin %						
SGA Expense						
Net Income		-110,000,000	-168,000,000	41,000,000	-117,000,000	-90,000,000
Operating Cash Flow						
Capital Expenditure						
EBITDA						
Return on Assets %						
Return on Equity %						
Debt to Equity						

CONTACT INFORMATION:

Phone: 248 354-7700   Fax: 248 354-8950
Toll-Free:
Address: 27300 West 11 Mile road, Southfield, MI 48034 United States

STOCK TICKER/OTHER:

Stock Ticker: FDML   Exchange: NAS
Employees: 53,700   Fiscal Year Ends: 12/31
Parent Company:

SALARIES/BONUSES:

Top Exec. Salary: $ Bonus: $
Second Exec. Salary: $ Bonus: $

OTHER THOUGHTS:

Estimated Female Officers or Directors: 1
Hot Spot for Advancement for Women/Minorities:

FedEx Corporation

NAIC Code: 492110

www.fedex.com

TYPES OF BUSINESS:

Couriers and Express Delivery Services
Ground Delivery Services
Freight Services
Document Solutions & Business Services
International Trade Services

BRANDS/DIVISIONS/AFFILIATES:

Federal Express Corp
FedEx Ground Package System Inc
FedEx Freight Inc
TNT
FedEx SupplyChain System
FedEx Trade Networks Inc
FedEx SmartPost Inc
FedEx Custom Critical Inc

CONTACTS: Note: Officers with more than one job title may be intentionally listed here more than once.

David Bronczek, CEO, Subsidiary
Michael Ducker, CEO, Subsidiary
Henry Maier, CEO, Subsidiary
Frederick Smith, CEO
Robert Carter, Chief Information Officer
T. Glenn, Executive VP, Divisional
Alan Graf, Executive VP
Christine Richards, Executive VP
John Merino, Vice President

GROWTH PLANS/SPECIAL FEATURES:

FedEx Corporation is a global provider of shipping, transportation, e-commerce and business services. It operates through a number of subsidiaries, including Federal Express Corp. (FedEx Express); TNT Express B.V., an international express transportation company acquired in late 2016; FedEx Ground Package System, Inc. (FedEx Ground); FedEx Freight, Inc. (FedEx Freight); and FedEx Corporate Services, Inc. (FedEx Services). FedEx Express is an express transportation company offering time-certain delivery within one to three business days. The division also includes FedEx SupplyChain System; FedEx Trade Networks, Inc., which provides international trade services, specializing in custom brokerage; and FedEx CrossBorder (formerly known as Bongo International LLC), which provides cross-border enablement technology and solutions. FedEx Ground offers small-package ground delivery service. It provides service to almost every business address in the U.S. and Canada as well as residential delivery to nearly 100% of U.S. residents through FedEx Home Delivery. Other subsidiaries are FedEx SmartPost, Inc., which specializes in the consolidation and delivery of high volumes of low-weight, less time-sensitive business-to-consumer packages using the U.S. Postal Service or Canada Post for final delivery to residences; and GENCO Distribution System, Inc., a third-party logistics provider. FedEx Freight provides less-than-truckload (LTL) freight services through its FedEx Freight Priority and its FedEx Freight Economy. The division also includes FedEx Custom Critical, Inc., a time-specific, critical shipment carrier. FedEx Services serves other FedEx companies with sales, marketing and IT support in addition to customer service, as well as document and business services through FedEx Office and Print Services.

FedEx Corporation offers its employees medical, dental and vision care insurance; short- and long-term disability; worker's compensation; life insurance; a pension plan; and a retirement savings plan.

FINANCIAL DATA: Note: Data for latest year may not have been available at press time.

In U.S. $	2016	2015	2014	2013	2012	2011
Revenue	50,365,000,000	47,453,000,000	45,567,000,000	44,287,000,000	42,680,000,000	
R&D Expense						
Operating Income	3,077,000,000	1,867,000,000	3,446,000,000	2,551,000,000	3,186,000,000	
Operating Margin %	6.10%	3.93%	7.56%	5.76%	7.46%	
SGA Expense	20,079,000,000	19,576,000,000	16,555,000,000	17,230,000,000	16,099,000,000	
Net Income	1,820,000,000	1,050,000,000	2,097,000,000	1,561,000,000	2,032,000,000	
Operating Cash Flow	5,708,000,000	5,366,000,000	4,264,000,000	4,688,000,000	4,835,000,000	
Capital Expenditure	4,818,000,000	4,347,000,000	3,533,000,000	3,375,000,000	4,007,000,000	
EBITDA	5,707,000,000	4,473,000,000	6,036,000,000	4,923,000,000	5,306,000,000	
Return on Assets %	4.37%	2.99%	6.29%	4.91%	7.09%	
Return on Equity %	12.63%	6.93%	12.83%	9.71%	13.57%	
Debt to Equity	1.00	0.48	0.31	0.15	0.08	

CONTACT INFORMATION:

Phone: 901 818-7500   Fax: 901 346-1013
Toll-Free:
Address: 942 S. Shady Grove Rd., Memphis, TN 38120 United States

STOCK TICKER/OTHER:

Stock Ticker: FDX   Exchange: NYS
Employees: 169,000   Fiscal Year Ends: 05/31
Parent Company:

SALARIES/BONUSES:

Top Exec. Salary: $1,279,632   Bonus: $
Second Exec. Salary: Bonus: $
$960,936

OTHER THOUGHTS:

Estimated Female Officers or Directors: 3
Hot Spot for Advancement for Women/Minorities: Y

Fidelity Investments Financial Services

www.fidelity.com

NAIC Code: 523920

TYPES OF BUSINESS:

Mutual Funds
Human Resources Administration Services
Employee Benefits Services
Online Brokerage
Outsourced Staffing and Recruiting Services
Clearing and Execution Products and Services
Real Estate Investments
Institutional Account Management and Services

BRANDS/DIVISIONS/AFFILIATES:

Fidelity Insitutional Asset Management
Fidelity Charitable

CONTACTS: Note: Officers with more than one job title may be intentionally listed here more than once.

Kathleen Murphy, Pres.
Jim Speros, Chief Creative Officer
Steve A. Scullen, III, Pres., Corp. Oper.
Lori Kalahar Johnson, VP-Online Strategy
Michael A. Jones, CEO
Jacques Perold, Pres., Fidelity Management & Research Company
Charles Morrison, Pres., Asset Mgmt.
Nancy D. Prior, Pres., Fixed Income Div.

GROWTH PLANS/SPECIAL FEATURES:

Fidelity Investments Financial Services (FIFS) is one of the world's largest providers of financial services. With over $2.3 trillion in assets under management, the company offers personal investment services, workplace investment services, institutional solutions and asset management. The personal investment division offers financial planning and retirement options such as independent retirement accounts (IRAs), annuities and managed accounts; brokerage and cash management products; college savings accounts; and other financial services for individual investors. The workplace investment division works with employers to build benefit programs for their employees. This segment provides recordkeeping, investments and servicing in relation to contributions, benefits, health and welfare and stock plans. For financial institutions, FIFS provides technology and personalized service such as clearing, custody, investment products, brokerage and trading services to a wide range of financial firms. Fidelity Institutional Asset Management is a distribution organization dedicated to the institutional marketplace. It serves as a gateway to Fidelity's broad and deep institutional investment management capabilities, including U.S. equity, international equity, fixed income and asset allocation. In addition, Fidelity Charitable is an independent public charity that allows donors to establish a dedicated donor-advised fund to support their favorite charities in the short-term, and create a systematic plan for longer-term philanthropic goals. Headquartered in Boston, Massachusetts, FIS serves customers through 10 regional offices and more than 190 investor centers in the U.S. Globally, the company spans eight other countries via 40,000 associates.

The company is owned approximately 50% by the founding family and 50% by employees.

FINANCIAL DATA: Note: Data for latest year may not have been available at press time.

In U.S. $	2016	2015	2014	2013	2012	2011
Revenue	15,900,000,000	15,350,000,000	14,900,000,000	13,600,000,000	13,000,000,000	12,800,000,000
R&D Expense						
Operating Income						
Operating Margin %						
SGA Expense						
Net Income	3,500,000,000	3,000,000,000	3,400,000,000	2,600,000,000	3,400,000,000	3,300,000,000
Operating Cash Flow						
Capital Expenditure						
EBITDA						
Return on Assets %						
Return on Equity %						
Debt to Equity						

CONTACT INFORMATION:

Phone: 617-563-7000   Fax:
Toll-Free: 800-343-3548
Address: 82 Devonshire St., Boston, MA 02109 United States

STOCK TICKER/OTHER:

Stock Ticker: Private   Exchange:
Employees: 45,000   Fiscal Year Ends: 12/31
Parent Company:

SALARIES/BONUSES:

Top Exec. Salary: $ Bonus: $
Second Exec. Salary: $ Bonus: $

OTHER THOUGHTS:

Estimated Female Officers or Directors: 2
Hot Spot for Advancement for Women/Minorities:

Fidelity National Information Services Inc   www.fisglobal.com

NAIC Code: 522320

TYPES OF BUSINESS:

Payment & Transaction Processing Services
IT Consulting
Outsourcing Services
Due Diligence Services
Mortgage Loan Processing

BRANDS/DIVISIONS/AFFILIATES:

Capco

CONTACTS: *Note: Officers with more than one job title may be intentionally listed here more than once.*

Gary Norcross, CEO
James Woodall, CFO
Frank Martire, Chairman of the Board
Katy Thompson, Chief Accounting Officer
Michael Oates, Chief Administrative Officer
Gregory Montana, Chief Risk Officer
Marianne Brown, Co-COO
Anthony Jabbour, Co-COO

GROWTH PLANS/SPECIAL FEATURES:

Fidelity National Information Services, Inc. (FIS) offers banking/payments technology solutions, processing services and information-based services. Headquartered in Jacksonville, Florida, FIS maintains a global presence, serving more than 20,000 financial institutions through offices in over 130 countries worldwide. Through its Capco brand, the firm provides core financial institution processing, card issuer and transaction processing services as well as outsourcing services to financial institutions and retailers worldwide. The company operates in three segments: integrated financial solutions (IFS), global financial solutions (GFS) and corporate and other. IFS serves the North America regional and community bank market for transaction and account processing, payment solutions, channel solutions, digital channels, risk and compliance solutions and services. This segment's solutions include core processing and ancillary applications, digital solutions (internet, mobile and eBanking), fraud and risk management, compliance, electronic funds transfer, credit cards, item processing, output services, government payment, ePayment and retail check authorization. GFS serves the largest financial institutions worldwide with banking and payments solutions, as well as consulting and transformation services. This segment also delivers an array of capital markets and asset management solutions and services, as well as insurance and public sector and education solutions and services. GFS solutions include retail banking, payment services, securities processing, finance, asset management, global trading, corporate liquidity, insurance, wealth management, global commercial services, strategic consulting, as well as domain-specific, mission critical enterprise resource planning and administrative software to state and local governments and K-12 educational institutions. The corporate and other segment consists of overhead expense, leveraged functions and miscellaneous expenses not included in the operating segments. In May 2017, the firm agreed to sell a majority stake (approximately 60%) in Capco to Clayton, Dubilier & Rice.

FINANCIAL DATA: *Note: Data for latest year may not have been available at press time.*

In U.S. $	2016	2015	2014	2013	2012	2011
Revenue	9,241,000,000	6,595,200,000	6,413,800,000	6,070,700,000	5,807,600,000	5,745,700,000
R&D Expense						
Operating Income	1,298,000,000	1,099,200,000	1,270,600,000	1,064,400,000	1,079,200,000	1,066,800,000
Operating Margin %	14.04%	16.66%	19.81%	17.53%	18.58%	18.56%
SGA Expense	1,710,000,000	1,102,800,000	810,500,000	920,700,000	781,500,000	671,800,000
Net Income	568,000,000	631,500,000	679,100,000	493,100,000	461,200,000	469,600,000
Operating Cash Flow	1,925,000,000	1,136,900,000	1,164,900,000	1,060,300,000	1,046,700,000	1,171,500,000
Capital Expenditure	616,000,000	415,300,000	371,200,000	336,200,000	296,100,000	300,300,000
EBITDA	2,483,000,000	1,905,500,000	1,852,500,000	1,638,200,000	1,695,300,000	1,646,300,000
Return on Assets %	2.17%	3.09%	4.76%	3.58%	3.36%	3.35%
Return on Equity %	5.95%	7.95%	10.33%	7.45%	7.01%	7.27%
Debt to Equity	1.04	1.23	0.77	0.65	0.63	0.69

CONTACT INFORMATION:

Phone: 904 438-6000   Fax: 904 357-1105
Toll-Free: 888-323-0310
Address: 601 Riverside Ave., Jacksonville, FL 32204 United States

STOCK TICKER/OTHER:

Stock Ticker: FIS   Exchange: NYS
Employees: 55,000   Fiscal Year Ends: 12/31
Parent Company:

SALARIES/BONUSES:

Top Exec. Salary: $1,000,000   Bonus: $
Second Exec. Salary: Bonus: $
$800,000

OTHER THOUGHTS:

Estimated Female Officers or Directors: 3
Hot Spot for Advancement for Women/Minorities: Y

Sales, profits and employees may be estimates. Financial information, benefits and other data can change quickly and may vary from those stated here.

First Data Corporation

www.firstdatacorp.com

NAIC Code: 522320

TYPES OF BUSINESS:
Credit Card Processing
Electronic Payment Processing
Check Verification
Prepaid Card Services
Private-Label Credit Card Services
ATMs
Terminals

BRANDS/DIVISIONS/AFFILIATES:
Clover
VisionPLUS

CONTACTS: *Note: Officers with more than one job title may be intentionally listed here more than once.*

Frank Bisignano, CEO
Himanshu Patel, CFO
Matthew Cagwin, Chief Accounting Officer
Thomas Higgins, Chief Administrative Officer
Joseph Plumeri, Director
Christine Larsen, EVP
Barry McCarthy, Executive VP, Divisional
Adam Rosman, Executive VP
Daniel Charron, Executive VP
Gustavo Marin, Executive VP
Anthony Marino, Executive VP
Michael Neborak, Executive VP
Andrew Gelb, Executive VP
Christopher Foskett, Executive VP
Ivo Distelbrink, Executive VP
Cynthia Armine-Klein, Executive VP
Guy Chiarello, President

GROWTH PLANS/SPECIAL FEATURES:

First Data Corporation is a provider of electronic commerce and payment solutions for merchants, financial institutions and card issuers globally and has operations in 118 countries, serving approximately 6 million merchant locations. The company also develops, implements and manages prepaid stored-value gift card services for retailers, general use credit cards and private-label credit cards for businesses. The firm's operations are organized in three segments: global business solutions (GBS), global financial solutions (GFS) and network and security solutions (NSS). GBS provides retail point-of-sale merchant acquiring and eCommerce services, as well as next-generation offerings such as mobile payment services, webstore-in-a-box solutions, and the cloud-based Clover point-of-sale operating system, which includes a marketplace for proprietary and third-party business applications. GFS provides credit solutions for bank and non-bank issuers. These include credit and retail private-label card processing within the U.S. and international markets; and licensed financial software systems, such as First Data's VisionPLUS bank processing application, and lending solutions. This segment also provides financial institutions services such as card personalization and embossing, statement printing, client service and remittance processing. NSS provides a wide range of value-added solutions sold to GBS and GFS clients, smaller financial institutions and other enterprise clients. These solutions include electronic transfer of funds solutions, debit card processing solutions, stored value network solutions and security and fraud solutions. This division also supports digital strategies such as online and mobile banking, and mobile wallets. First Data processes approximately 80 billion transactions globally, which accounts for more than 25% of the world's eCommerce volume.

First Data offers its employees medical, dental and vision insurance; life, accident and disability insurance; flexible spending accounts; tuition reimbursement; adoption assistance; employee discounts; and a 401(k) plan.

FINANCIAL DATA: *Note: Data for latest year may not have been available at press time.*

In U.S. $	2016	2015	2014	2013	2012	2011
Revenue	11,584,000,000	11,451,000,000	11,151,800,000	10,808,900,000	10,680,300,000	10,713,600,000
R&D Expense						
Operating Income	1,602,000,000	1,170,000,000	1,439,300,000	1,122,600,000	1,073,800,000	941,500,000
Operating Margin %	13.82%	10.21%	12.90%	10.38%	10.05%	8.78%
SGA Expense	2,045,000,000	2,292,000,000	1,961,800,000	1,888,800,000	1,825,400,000	1,693,700,000
Net Income	420,000,000	-1,481,000,000	-457,800,000	-869,100,000	-700,900,000	-516,100,000
Operating Cash Flow	2,111,000,000	795,000,000	1,013,200,000	672,700,000	767,400,000	1,115,600,000
Capital Expenditure	477,000,000	602,000,000	566,500,000	378,500,000	370,300,000	404,800,000
EBITDA	2,663,000,000	2,303,000,000	2,514,300,000	2,298,700,000	2,319,200,000	2,417,700,000
Return on Assets %	1.12%	-4.31%	-1.31%	-2.37%	-1.79%	-1.32%
Return on Equity %	44.49%	-1370.66%				-149.39%
Debt to Equity	14.98	28.30				233.14

CONTACT INFORMATION:
Phone: 404-890-2000   Fax:
Toll-Free: 800-735-3362
Address: 5565 Glenridge Connector NE, Ste. 2000, Atlanta, GA 30342 United States

STOCK TICKER/OTHER:
Stock Ticker: FDC   Exchange: NYS
Employees: 24,000   Fiscal Year Ends: 12/31
Parent Company: KKR & Co LP (Kohlberg Kravis Roberts & Co)

SALARIES/BONUSES:
Top Exec. Salary: $750,000   Bonus: $3,471,210
Second Exec. Salary: $1,320,000   Bonus: $1,287,000

OTHER THOUGHTS:
Estimated Female Officers or Directors: 1
Hot Spot for Advancement for Women/Minorities:

FirstEnergy Corporation

www.firstenergycorp.com

NAIC Code: 221112

TYPES OF BUSINESS:

Electric Utility
Power Generation
Energy Management
Telecommunications

BRANDS/DIVISIONS/AFFILIATES:

FirstEnergy Solutions Corporation

CONTACTS: *Note: Officers with more than one job title may be intentionally listed here more than once.*

Charles Jones, CEO
M. Dowling, Senior VP, Subsidiary
James Pearson, CFO
K. Taylor, Chief Accounting Officer
George Smart, Director
Leila Vespoli, Executive VP, Divisional
James Lash, Executive VP
Robert Reffner, General Counsel
Lynn Cavalier, Other Executive Officer
Bennett Gaines, Other Executive Officer
Donald Schneider, President, Subsidiary
Steven Strah, President, Subsidiary
Gary Benz, Senior VP, Subsidiary
Charles Lasky, Senior VP, Subsidiary
Dennis Chack, Senior VP, Subsidiary
M. Dowling, Senior VP, Subsidiary

GROWTH PLANS/SPECIAL FEATURES:

FirstEnergy Corporation is an investor-owned electric system with more than 24,000 miles of transmission lines that connect the Midwest and Mid-Atlantic regions. The company's generating fleet comprises and total capacity of nearly 17,000 megawatts. FirstEnergy's 10 regulated distribution companies serve 6 million customers, operating an infrastructure of more than 269,000 miles of distribution lines stretching from the Ohio-Indiana border to the New Jersey shore. The firm's generation subsidiaries control nearly 17,000 megawatts of capacity from a diverse fleet of carbon-free nuclear, scrubbed coal, natural gas, hydro and other renewables. FirstEnergy Solutions Corporation supplies energy to residential, commercial and industrial customers located in Illinois, Maryland, Michigan, New Jersey, Ohio and Pennsylvania. In 2017, in an effort to exit the competitive power business and focus on being a regulated company, FirstEnergy Corporation agreed to sell four competitive natural gas generating plants in Pennsylvania, as well as its competitive portion of a Virginia hydroelectric power station to LS Power Equity Partners. It also agreed to sell Hatfield's Ferry Power Station in Pennsylvania, to APV Renaissance Partners Opco, LLC.

Employee benefits include medical, prescription, dental and vision coverage; flexible spending accounts; life insurance; long-term care insurance; long-term disability; a 401(k) savings plan; pension plan; education assistance; adoption assistance; an employee assistance program; and employee discounts.

FINANCIAL DATA: *Note: Data for latest year may not have been available at press time.*

In U.S. $	2016	2015	2014	2013	2012	2011
Revenue	14,562,000,000	15,026,000,000	15,049,000,000	14,917,000,000	15,303,000,000	16,258,000,000
R&D Expense						
Operating Income	-8,262,000,000	2,292,000,000	1,062,000,000	1,607,000,000	2,176,000,000	1,698,000,000
Operating Margin %	-56.73%	15.25%	7.05%	10.77%	14.21%	10.44%
SGA Expense	4,005,000,000	3,991,000,000	4,797,000,000	3,337,000,000	4,378,000,000	3,909,000,000
Net Income	-6,177,000,000	578,000,000	299,000,000	392,000,000	770,000,000	885,000,000
Operating Cash Flow	3,371,000,000	3,447,000,000	2,713,000,000	2,662,000,000	2,320,000,000	3,063,000,000
Capital Expenditure	3,067,000,000	2,894,000,000	3,312,000,000	2,638,000,000	2,678,000,000	2,278,000,000
EBITDA	-6,181,000,000	3,744,000,000	2,626,000,000	2,713,000,000	3,377,000,000	3,572,000,000
Return on Assets %	-12.95%	1.10%	.58%	.77%	1.57%	2.15%
Return on Equity %	-66.19%	4.65%	2.38%	3.04%	5.84%	8.11%
Debt to Equity	2.91	1.54	1.54	1.24	1.16	1.18

CONTACT INFORMATION:

Phone: 800 736-3402   Fax:
Toll-Free: 800-633-4766
Address: 76 S. Main St., Akron, OH 44308 United States

STOCK TICKER/OTHER:

Stock Ticker: FE
Employees: 15,707
Parent Company:

Exchange: NYS
Fiscal Year Ends: 12/31

SALARIES/BONUSES:

Top Exec. Salary: $1,133,840   Bonus: $
Second Exec. Salary: $758,606   Bonus: $

OTHER THOUGHTS:

Estimated Female Officers or Directors: 6
Hot Spot for Advancement for Women/Minorities: Y

Fiserv Inc

NAIC Code: 522320

www.fiserv.com

TYPES OF BUSINESS:

Financial Services
Investment Services
Online Banking
Electronic Billing & Payment
Software Applications & Investment Management Solutions

BRANDS/DIVISIONS/AFFILIATES:

CONTACTS: *Note: Officers with more than one job title may be intentionally listed here more than once.*

Jeffery Yabuki, CEO
Kenneth Best, Chief Accounting Officer
Robert Hau, Chief Financial Officer
Mark Ernst, COO
Glenn Renwick, Director
Steven Tait, Other Executive Officer
Byron Vielehr, President, Divisional
Kevin Schultz, President, Divisional
Devin McGranahan, President, Divisional
Kevin Gregoire, President, Divisional
Lynn McCreary, Secretary

GROWTH PLANS/SPECIAL FEATURES:

Fiserv, Inc. provides integrated data processing and information management systems to more than 12,000 financial services providers, including banks, thrifts, credit unions, investment management firms, leasing and finance companies, retailers, merchants and government agencies. It operates in two primary segments: financial institution services (financial) and payments and industry products (payments). The financial segment provides banks, thrifts and credit unions with account processing services, item processing services, loan origination and servicing products, cash management and consulting services as well as other products and services that support a variety of financial transactions. The payments segment provides products and services that address a range of technology needs for the financial services industry, including internet banking, electronic bill payment, electronic funds transfer and debit processing, fraud and risk management capabilities, card and print personalization services, check imaging and investment account processing services for separately managed accounts. The company operates centers nationwide for full-service data processing, software development, item processing and check imaging, technology support and related product businesses. It operates support centers located in approximately 120 cities located in South America, Europe and the Asia Pacific. In June 2017, the firm agreed to acquire Monitise plc, a provider of digital banking solutions for financial institutions.

FINANCIAL DATA: *Note: Data for latest year may not have been available at press time.*

In U.S. $	2016	2015	2014	2013	2012	2011
Revenue	5,505,000,000	5,254,000,000	5,066,000,000	4,814,000,000	4,482,000,000	4,337,000,000
R&D Expense						
Operating Income	1,445,000,000	1,311,000,000	1,210,000,000	1,061,000,000	1,056,000,000	996,000,000
Operating Margin %	26.24%	24.95%	23.88%	22.03%	23.56%	22.96%
SGA Expense	1,101,000,000	1,034,000,000	975,000,000	977,000,000	829,000,000	799,000,000
Net Income	930,000,000	712,000,000	754,000,000	648,000,000	611,000,000	472,000,000
Operating Cash Flow	1,431,000,000	1,346,000,000	1,307,000,000	1,039,000,000	835,000,000	953,000,000
Capital Expenditure	290,000,000	359,000,000	292,000,000	236,000,000	195,000,000	192,000,000
EBITDA	1,856,000,000	1,643,000,000	1,615,000,000	1,465,000,000	1,417,000,000	1,266,000,000
Return on Assets %	9.74%	7.62%	7.99%	7.19%	7.16%	5.60%
Return on Equity %	35.76%	23.91%	21.91%	18.50%	18.30%	14.55%
Debt to Equity	1.75	1.61	1.12	1.04	0.94	0.98

CONTACT INFORMATION:

Phone: 262 879-5000   Fax: 262 879-5275
Toll-Free: 800-872-7882
Address: 255 Fiserv Dr., Brookfield, WI 53045 United States

STOCK TICKER/OTHER:

Stock Ticker: FISV   Exchange: NAS
Employees: 23,000   Fiscal Year Ends: 12/31
Parent Company:

SALARIES/BONUSES:

Top Exec. Salary: $499,599   Bonus: $500,000
Second Exec. Salary: Bonus: $
$840,000

OTHER THOUGHTS:

Estimated Female Officers or Directors: 1
Hot Spot for Advancement for Women/Minorities:

Fleetcor Technologies Inc

www.fleetcor.com

NAIC Code: 522320

TYPES OF BUSINESS:

Payment & Transaction Processing Services

BRANDS/DIVISIONS/AFFILIATES:

CONTACTS: *Note: Officers with more than one job title may be intentionally listed here more than once.*

Ronald Clarke, CEO
Eric Dey, CFO
John Reed, Chief Information Officer
Charles Freund, Executive VP, Divisional
John Coughlin, Executive VP, Divisional
Ashley Thekkekara, Other Corporate Officer
Pedro Donda, President, Divisional
Andrew Blazye, President, Divisional
David Maxsimic, President, Divisional
Todd House, President, Divisional
Gregory Secord, President, Divisional
Kurt Adams, President, Divisional
Alexey Gavrilenya, President, Geographical
Armando Netto, President, Geographical
Alan King, President, Geographical

GROWTH PLANS/SPECIAL FEATURES:

FleetCor Technologies, Inc. is a leading independent global provider of fuel cards, workforce payment products and services to businesses, commercial fleets, major oil companies, petroleum marketers and government entities in countries throughout North America, Latin America and Europe. The company's payment programs enable customers to better manage and control employee spending and provide card-accepting merchants with a high-volume customer base that can increase their sales. In 2016, FleetCor processed approximately 2.2 billion transactions on its proprietary networks and third-party networks. The company sells a range of customized fleet and lodging payment programs directly and indirectly through partners such as major oil companies and petroleum marketers. It provides customers with various card products that typically function like a charge card to purchase fuel, lodging and related products and services at participating locations. Depending on the customer's and partner's needs, the firm provides these services in a variety of outsourced solutions ranging from end-to-end solutions (encompassing issuing, processing and network services) to limited back office processing services. Other services include the company's proprietary equipment which, when installed at the fueling site and on the vehicle, reduces the chances of unauthorized or fraudulent transactions; a telematics solution in Europe that combines GPS, satellite tracking and other wireless technology to allow fleet operators to monitor their vehicles; and prepaid fuel and food vouchers in Mexico. In order to deliver its payment programs and services, FleetCor owns and operates proprietary closed-loop networks in North America and internationally. In May 2017, the firm agreed to acquire Cambridge Global Payments, a business-to-business international payments provider. That June, it agreed to sell subsidiary and telematics provider, NexTraq, to Michelin.

FINANCIAL DATA: *Note: Data for latest year may not have been available at press time.*

In U.S. $	2016	2015	2014	2013	2012	2011
Revenue	1,831,546,000	1,702,865,000	1,199,390,000	895,171,000	707,534,000	519,591,000
R&D Expense						
Operating Income	754,153,000	667,534,000	565,449,000	420,632,000	324,928,000	226,334,000
Operating Margin %	41.17%	39.20%	47.14%	46.98%	45.92%	43.56%
SGA Expense	415,068,000	406,790,000	281,490,000	199,629,000	156,551,000	121,371,000
Net Income	452,385,000	362,431,000	368,707,000	284,501,000	216,199,000	147,335,000
Operating Cash Flow	705,912,000	754,584,000	608,334,000	375,685,000	135,460,000	279,625,000
Capital Expenditure	59,011,000	41,875,000	27,070,000	20,785,000	19,111,000	13,454,000
EBITDA	957,409,000	860,987,000	677,810,000	493,369,000	375,843,000	260,425,000
Return on Assets %	5.16%	4.37%	5.84%	8.55%	8.56%	7.73%
Return on Equity %	15.29%	12.98%	18.44%	26.37%	25.06%	20.50%
Debt to Equity	0.81	0.72	0.78	0.38	0.53	0.34

CONTACT INFORMATION:

Phone: 770 449-0479   Fax: 770 449-3471
Toll-Free: 800-877-9019
Address: 5445 Triangle Pkwy, Ste. 400, Norcross, GA 30092 United States

STOCK TICKER/OTHER:

Stock Ticker: FLT
Employees: 7,100
Parent Company:

Exchange: NYS
Fiscal Year Ends: 12/31

SALARIES/BONUSES:

Top Exec. Salary: $1,000,000   Bonus: $
Second Exec. Salary: $398,077   Bonus: $70,000

OTHER THOUGHTS:

Estimated Female Officers or Directors:
Hot Spot for Advancement for Women/Minorities:

Fluor Corp

NAIC Code: 237000

TYPES OF BUSINESS:

Heavy Construction and Engineering
Power Plant Construction and Management
Facilities Management
Procurement Services
Consulting Services
Project Management
Asset Management
Staffing Services

BRANDS/DIVISIONS/AFFILIATES:

ServiTrade
Ameco
Fluor Constructors International Inc
Stork Holding BV

CONTACTS: Note: Officers with more than one job title may be intentionally listed here more than once.

David Seaton, CEO
Biggs Porter, CFO
Robin Chopra, Chief Accounting Officer
Ray Barnard, Executive VP, Divisional
Jose Luis Bustamante, Executive VP, Divisional
Garry Flowers, Executive VP, Divisional
Carlos Hernandez, Executive VP
Bruce Stanski, President, Divisional
Mark Landry, Senior VP, Divisional

GROWTH PLANS/SPECIAL FEATURES:

Fluor Corp., through its subsidiaries, is a global provider of engineering, procurement, construction and maintenance services, with offices in over 60 countries. The company provides logistics services in both Afghanistan and Iraq. Besides being a primary service provider to the U.S. federal government, Fluor serves a diverse set of industries including oil and gas, chemical and petrochemicals, transportation, mining and metals, power, life sciences and manufacturing. It operates in four business segments: energy, chemicals and mining (ECM); industrial, power and infrastructure (IPI); maintenance, modification and asset integrity (MMAI); and government. ECM focuses on opportunities in the upstream, downstream, chemical, petrochemical, offshore and onshore oil and gas production, liquefied natural gas, pipeline, metals and mining markets. IPI provides design, engineering, procurement, construction and project management services to the transportation, life sciences, advanced manufacturing, water and power sectors. The government segment is a provider of engineering, construction, logistics, base and facilities operations and maintenance, contingency response and environmental and nuclear services to U.S. and international governments. MMAI provides facility start-up and management, plant and facility maintenance, operations support and asset management services to the oil and gas, chemicals, life sciences, mining and metals, consumer products and manufacturing industries. The firm focuses on asset management solutions, as well as providing services in diverse areas such as electrical and instrumentation, fabric maintenance, mechanical and piping. In addition, Fluor Constructors International, Inc. provides unionized management and construction services in the U.S. and Canada. Subsidiary Ameco provides integrated mobile equipment and tool solutions and includes Mozambique construction equipment company, Servitrade. In March 2016, the firm acquired Stork Holding B.V., a Netherland-based provider of maintenance, modification and asset integrity services.

Fluor offers its employees health, dental, vision, life and accident insurance; disability coverage; savings and retirement plans; a tax savings account; and educational assistance.

FINANCIAL DATA: Note: Data for latest year may not have been available at press time.

In U.S. $	2016	2015	2014	2013	2012	2011
Revenue	19,036,520,000	18,114,050,000	21,531,580,000	27,351,570,000	27,577,140,000	23,381,400,000
R&D Expense						
Operating Income	599,243,000	926,367,000	1,216,322,000	1,190,043,000	733,987,000	985,456,000
Operating Margin %	3.14%	5.11%	5.64%	4.35%	2.66%	4.21%
SGA Expense	191,073,000	168,329,000	182,711,000	175,148,000	151,010,000	163,460,000
Net Income	281,401,000	412,512,000	510,909,000	667,711,000	456,330,000	593,728,000
Operating Cash Flow	705,919,000	849,132,000	642,574,000	788,906,000	628,378,000	889,769,000
Capital Expenditure	235,904,000	240,220,000	324,704,000	288,487,000	254,747,000	338,167,000
EBITDA	842,202,000	961,060,000	1,427,184,000	1,411,584,000	974,124,000	1,219,356,000
Return on Assets %	3.34%	5.21%	6.18%	8.04%	5.51%	7.47%
Return on Equity %	9.19%	13.50%	14.87%	18.81%	13.54%	17.22%
Debt to Equity	0.48	0.33	0.31	0.13	0.15	0.15

CONTACT INFORMATION:

Phone: 469 398-7000   Fax: 469 398-7255
Toll-Free:
Address: 6700 Las Colinas Blvd., Irving, TX 75039 United States

STOCK TICKER/OTHER:

Stock Ticker: FLR   Exchange: NYS
Employees: 61,551   Fiscal Year Ends: 12/31
Parent Company:

SALARIES/BONUSES:

Top Exec. Salary: $1,295,029   Bonus: $
Second Exec. Salary: $841,318   Bonus: $

OTHER THOUGHTS:

Estimated Female Officers or Directors: 3
Hot Spot for Advancement for Women/Minorities: Y

Sales, profits and employees may be estimates. Financial information, benefits and other data can change quickly and may vary from those stated here.

Ford Motor Co

NAIC Code: 336111

www.ford.com

TYPES OF BUSINESS:

Automobile Manufacturing
Automobile Financing
Fuel-Cell & Hybrid Research

BRANDS/DIVISIONS/AFFILIATES:

Ford
Lincoln
Ford Motor Credit Co
Ford Mustang
Ford F150
Ford Focus
Lincoln Navigator SUV
Ford Escape Hybrid SUV

CONTACTS: Note: Officers with more than one job title may be intentionally listed here more than once.

Nancy Falotico, CEO, Subsidiary
Ray Day, Vice President, Divisional
James Hackett, CEO
Robert Shanks, CFO
William Ford, Chairman of the Board
Raj Nair, Chief Technology Officer
Stephen Odell, Executive VP, Divisional
Marcy Klevorn, Executive VP
Joseph Hinrichs, Executive VP
James Farley, Executive VP
Paul Ballew, Other Executive Officer
Dave Schoch, President, Geographical
Felicia Fields, Vice President, Divisional
Ziad Ojakli, Vice President, Divisional
John Casesa, Vice President, Divisional

GROWTH PLANS/SPECIAL FEATURES:

Ford Motor Co. is a designer and manufacturer of automobiles and automotive systems. The firm operates in two segments: automotive and financial services. The automotive segment designs, manufactures, sells and services cars and trucks under the brands Ford and Lincoln. The company sells its vehicles to the public via independently owned dealerships, including roughly 10,608 Ford; 214 Lincoln; and 915 Ford/Lincoln dealerships. These dealerships are in North America, South America, Europe, Asia Pacific and Africa. In addition to new car sales, the firm also sells vehicles to its dealerships for sale to fleet customers, including commercial fleet customers, daily rental car companies and governments, and sells parts and accessories to authorized parts distributors. The firm's financial services segment, operating through Ford Motor Credit Co., offers vehicle-related financing, leasing and insurance. Some of Ford's most popular vehicles include the Ford Mustang sports car, the Ford F150 truck, the compact Ford Focus, the Lincoln Navigator SUV and the Ford Escape Hybrid SUV. The company hopes to quickly introduce fully electric vehicles to the U.S. market. In January 2017, the firm announced the production of 13 new electric vehicles in the next five years, including hybrid versions of the F-150 and Mustang, as well as a fully electric small SUV with a projected EPA-estimated range of over 300 miles. In May 2017, Ford announced that it plans to reduce its global workforce by about 10% as part of an effort to reduce its total cost structure and boost profitability.

FINANCIAL DATA: Note: Data for latest year may not have been available at press time.

In U.S. $	2016	2015	2014	2013	2012	2011
Revenue	151,800,000,000	149,558,000,000	144,077,000,000	146,917,000,000	134,252,000,000	136,264,000,000
R&D Expense						
Operating Income	4,116,000,000	8,064,000,000	3,745,000,000	5,647,000,000	6,377,000,000	11,341,000,000
Operating Margin %	2.71%	5.39%	2.59%	3.84%	4.74%	8.32%
SGA Expense	12,196,000,000	14,999,000,000	14,117,000,000	13,176,000,000	12,182,000,000	11,578,000,000
Net Income	4,596,000,000	7,373,000,000	3,187,000,000	7,155,000,000	5,665,000,000	20,213,000,000
Operating Cash Flow	19,792,000,000	16,170,000,000	14,507,000,000	10,444,000,000	9,045,000,000	9,784,001,000
Capital Expenditure	6,992,000,000	7,196,000,000	7,463,000,000	6,597,000,000	5,488,000,000	4,293,000,000
EBITDA	16,412,000,000	18,991,000,000	12,575,000,000	14,286,000,000	13,637,000,000	17,368,000,000
Return on Assets %	1.98%	3.40%	1.55%	3.64%	3.07%	11.78%
Return on Equity %	15.89%	27.58%	12.45%	33.80%	36.57%	281.61%
Debt to Equity	3.19	3.13	3.22	2.90	4.15	3.93

CONTACT INFORMATION:

Phone: 313 322-3000   Fax: 313 222-4177
Toll-Free: 800-392-3673
Address: 1 American Rd., Dearborn, MI 48126 United States

STOCK TICKER/OTHER:

Stock Ticker: F
Employees: 201,000
Parent Company:

Exchange: NYS
Fiscal Year Ends: 12/31

SALARIES/BONUSES:

Top Exec. Salary: $1,787,500   Bonus: $
Second Exec. Salary: $1,625,000   Bonus: $

OTHER THOUGHTS:

Estimated Female Officers or Directors: 4
Hot Spot for Advancement for Women/Minorities: Y

Fox Entertainment Group Inc

www.fox.com

NAIC Code: 515120

TYPES OF BUSINESS:

Broadcast Television
Film Distribution and Production
Television Programming
Online Communities and Game Sites
Professional Sports
Electronic Games
Cable TV Programming
Online Entertainment

BRANDS/DIVISIONS/AFFILIATES:

Twenty-First Century Fox Inc
FX
National Geographic Channel
Fox News
Fox Sports
20th Century Fox
Fox Home Entertainment
Fox International Channels

CONTACTS: *Note: Officers with more than one job title may be intentionally listed here more than once.*

Roger Ailes, CEO

GROWTH PLANS/SPECIAL FEATURES:

Fox Entertainment Group, Inc., a wholly-owned subsidiary of Twenty-First Century Fox, Inc., is a conglomerate focused on film and television entertainment. The company engages in feature film and television production and distribution principally through the following businesses: filmed entertainment, television stations, a television broadcast network and cable networks. The filmed entertainment business finances, develops, produces, distributes and markets motion pictures, as well as television and home entertainment programming. The television stations business owns and operates network broadcast groups, comprised of stations in more than 15 markets, covering over 37% of U.S. television homes. These markets include: New York, Los Angeles, Chicago, Dallas, San Francisco, Washington, D.C. and Houston. The television broadcast network operates entertainment channels in the U.S. and internationally. The network provides nearly 20 hours of regularly-scheduled network programming on a weekly basis; 15 hours of prime-time programming; an hour of late-night programming; and weekend programming timeslots. Programming includes, but is not limited to, adult animation, children's programming, news and sports. The cable networks business includes domestic programming services that together reach more than 550 million subscribing television homes. Fox networks include FX, National Geographic Channel, Fox News, Fox Sports, 20th Century Fox, Fox Studios, Fox Home Entertainment, 21st Century Fox, Fox International Channels, Fox Music and Fox Searchlight.

FINANCIAL DATA: *Note: Data for latest year may not have been available at press time.*

In U.S. $	2016	2015	2014	2013	2012	2011
Revenue	16,500,000,000	14,500,000,000	13,300,000,000			
R&D Expense						
Operating Income						
Operating Margin %						
SGA Expense						
Net Income						
Operating Cash Flow						
Capital Expenditure						
EBITDA						
Return on Assets %						
Return on Equity %						
Debt to Equity						

CONTACT INFORMATION:

Phone: 212-852-7111   Fax: 212-852-7145
Toll-Free:
Address: 1211 Avenue of the Americas, New York, NY 10036 United States

STOCK TICKER/OTHER:

Stock Ticker: Subsidiary   Exchange:
Employees: 12,500   Fiscal Year Ends: 06/30
Parent Company: Twenty-First Century Fox Inc

SALARIES/BONUSES:

Top Exec. Salary: $ Bonus: $
Second Exec. Salary: $ Bonus: $

OTHER THOUGHTS:

Estimated Female Officers or Directors:
Hot Spot for Advancement for Women/Minorities:

Frito-Lay North America Inc

www.fritolay.com

NAIC Code: 311919

TYPES OF BUSINESS:

Snack Products
Salsas/Dips
Chips
Cookies

BRANDS/DIVISIONS/AFFILIATES:

PepsiCo Inc
Doritos
Cheetos
Lay's
Rold Gold
SunChips
Grandma's
Smartfood

CONTACTS: *Note: Officers with more than one job title may be intentionally listed here more than once.*

Vivek Sankaran, Pres.
Hari Avula, CFO
Ted Herrod, Sr. VP-Sales
Michael Hourihan, VP-Procurement
Mike Zbuchalski, Sr. VP-R&D
Kristen Blum, CIO
Marc Kesselman, General Counsel
Christopher Wyse, VP-Public Affairs
Randy Melville, Gen. Mgr.-Central Bus. Unit
Vivek Sankaran, Chief Customer Officer
Dave Scalera, Sr. VP-Go-to-Market Capability & Productivity
Ted Herrod, Gen. Mgr.-West Bus. Unit
Marc Guay, Pres., PepsiCo Foods Canada
Leslie Starr Keating, Sr. VP-Supply Chain

GROWTH PLANS/SPECIAL FEATURES:

Frito-Lay North America, Inc., a subsidiary of PepsiCo, Inc., manufactures, markets, sells and distributes branded snacks. The firm's proprietary products include: Lay's potato chips, Doritos tortilla chips, Tostitos tortilla chips, Cheetos cheese-flavored snacks, Fritos corn chips, Ruffles potato chips, SunChips and multigrain snacks. Additionally, the company's brand portfolio includes: Rold Gold pretzels; Baked! Cheetos, Lay's, Ruffles and Tostitos chips; Grandma's cookies; Cracker Jack candy-coated popcorn; Matador beef jerky; Funyuns onion rings; Sabritones puffed wheat snacks; El Isleno plantain chips; Smartfood popcorn; Stacy's pita chips and 100 calorie mini bite portion control snack packs. The firm's joint venture with Strauss Group markets refrigerated spreads and dips under the Sabra brand name, including hummus, salsas and guacamole. The firm recently updated the Lay's Classic Potato Chips recipe to feature only potatoes, healthier oils such as corn and sunflower oil and a dash of salt; and updated the Tostitos and SunChips brands to feature healthier recipes with no MSG, artificial preservatives or artificial flavorings. The company offers a gluten-free recipe section on its web site for customers with Celiac Disease or gluten sensitivities.

Employee benefits include medical, dental and vision coverage; life insurance; disability coverage; a flexible spending account; wellness programs; an employee assistance program; tuition reimbursement; a pension plan; a retirement plan; a discount stock purchase plan; discounts on electronics, entertainment and automobiles; childcare and elderly care; and commuter reimbursement.

FINANCIAL DATA: *Note: Data for latest year may not have been available at press time.*

In U.S. $	2016	2015	2014	2013	2012	2011
Revenue	15,120,000,000	14,950,000,000	14,502,000,000	14,126,000,000	13,574,000,000	13,322,000,000
R&D Expense						
Operating Income						
Operating Margin %						
SGA Expense						
Net Income	422,002,500	4,304,000,000	4,054,000,000	3,877,000,000	3,646,000,000	3,621,000,000
Operating Cash Flow						
Capital Expenditure						
EBITDA						
Return on Assets %						
Return on Equity %						
Debt to Equity						

CONTACT INFORMATION:

Phone: 972-334-7000   Fax: 972-334-2019
Toll-Free: 800-352-4477
Address: 7701 Legacy Dr., Plano, TX 75024 United States

STOCK TICKER/OTHER:

Stock Ticker: Subsidiary   Exchange:
Employees: 49,120   Fiscal Year Ends: 12/31
Parent Company: PepsiCo Inc

SALARIES/BONUSES:

Top Exec. Salary: $ Bonus: $
Second Exec. Salary: $ Bonus: $

OTHER THOUGHTS:

Estimated Female Officers or Directors: 3
Hot Spot for Advancement for Women/Minorities: Y

Frontier Communications Corporation

www.frontier.com

NAIC Code: 517110

TYPES OF BUSINESS:

Telecommunications
Internet Services
Long-Distance Phone Services
Directory Service
Access Services
Wireless Internet Services

BRANDS/DIVISIONS/AFFILIATES:

Vantage

CONTACTS: Note: Officers with more than one job title may be intentionally listed here more than once.

Cecilia McKenney, Executive VP

GROWTH PLANS/SPECIAL FEATURES:

Frontier Communications Corporation provides communication services to rural, small and medium-sized towns throughout the U.S. The firm operates as an incumbent local exchange carrier with 5.4 million customers. It provides local and long distance voice, data and internet access and video services. Local services include basic telephone wireline services as well as call forwarding, conference calling, caller ID, voicemail and call waiting. Long distance services use external interexchange carrier facilities. Data and internet services offer a variety of wireline and satellite broadband services to residential, commercial and carrier customers. Residential services include broadband, dial up internet, portal and e-mail products. Commercial services include Ethernet, dedicated internet, multiprotocol label switching (MPLS), time division multiplexing (TDM) data transport services and optical transport services. These services are all supported by a 24/7 help desk and an advanced network. Access services enable other carriers to use Frontier's facilities to originate and terminate their local and long distance voice traffic. The firm offers small and medium enterprise (SME) business customers third-party telecommunications equipment produced to fit their specific business operation needs. Frontier's video services are provided through its agency relationship with DISH. The company offers its customers fiber optic video services throughout Washington, Indiana and Oregon. Frontier's Vantage brand is a premium, all-digital platform that includes TV HD offerings, ultra-fast broadband and enhanced voice over internet protocol (VoIP).

Employees receive medical, dental and vision coverage; life insurance; tuition reimbursement; flexible spending accounts; and corporate discounts.

FINANCIAL DATA: Note: Data for latest year may not have been available at press time.

In U.S. $	2016	2015	2014	2013	2012	2011
Revenue	8,896,000,000	5,576,000,000	4,772,490,000	4,761,576,000	5,011,853,000	5,243,043,000
R&D Expense						
Operating Income	888,000,000	745,000,000	819,941,000	980,721,000	987,168,000	899,621,000
Operating Margin %	9.98%	13.36%	17.18%	20.59%	19.69%	17.15%
SGA Expense	2,093,000,000	1,348,000,000	1,088,180,000	1,188,611,000		
Net Income	-373,000,000	-196,000,000	132,893,000	112,835,000	136,636,000	149,614,000
Operating Cash Flow	1,666,000,000	1,301,000,000	1,270,072,000	1,495,627,000	1,552,473,000	1,572,681,000
Capital Expenditure	1,401,000,000	863,000,000	688,096,000	634,685,000	802,504,000	824,839,000
EBITDA	2,939,000,000	2,072,000,000	1,997,879,000	1,999,618,000	2,183,744,000	2,314,322,000
Return on Assets %	-2.10%	-1.38%	.74%	.65%	.77%	.84%
Return on Equity %	-11.64%	-6.88%	3.44%	2.76%	3.19%	3.10%
Debt to Equity	3.88	2.76	2.59	1.94	2.04	1.84

CONTACT INFORMATION:

Phone: 203 614-5600   Fax: 203 614-4602
Toll-Free:
Address: 401 Merritt 7, Norwalk, CT 06851 United States

STOCK TICKER/OTHER:

Stock Ticker: FTR   Exchange: NAS
Employees: 28,300   Fiscal Year Ends: 12/31
Parent Company:

SALARIES/BONUSES:

Top Exec. Salary: $458,750   Bonus: $1,000,000
Second Exec. Salary: Bonus: $840,000
$415,000

OTHER THOUGHTS:

Estimated Female Officers or Directors: 7
Hot Spot for Advancement for Women/Minorities: Y

FTI Consulting Inc

NAIC Code: 541610

www.fticonsulting.com

TYPES OF BUSINESS:

Bankruptcy & Restructuring Consulting
Interim Management Staffing
Corporate Recovery Services
Litigation Assistance
Forensic Accounting
Data Mining
Technology Consulting
Software Development

BRANDS/DIVISIONS/AFFILIATES:

Ringtail

CONTACTS: Note: Officers with more than one job title may be intentionally listed here more than once.

Steven Gunby, CEO
Ajay Sabherwal, CFO
Gerard Holthaus, Chairman of the Board
Catherine Freeman, Chief Accounting Officer
Matthew Pachman, Chief Risk Officer
Curtis Lu, General Counsel
Joanne Catanese, Other Corporate Officer
Holly Paul, Other Executive Officer
Paul Linton, Other Executive Officer

GROWTH PLANS/SPECIAL FEATURES:

FTI Consulting, Inc. is a global consulting firm that provides turnaround, restructuring, bankruptcy and other related consulting services. The firm works in industries including retail, insurance, media and entertainment and energy and utilities. It operates 48 U.S. offices in 19 states and 34 foreign countries, including the U.K., Russia, France, Japan and China. FTI divides its operations into five segments: corporate finance and restructuring, forensic and litigation consulting, economic consulting, technology and strategic communications. The corporate finance and restructuring segment's services include turnaround and restructuring services, which consist of providing advisory services to debtors, creditors and stakeholders confronted with liquidity problems, underperformance and over-expansion; interim key executive staffing; and mergers and acquisitions services, which include financial accounting, investment banking and tax advice. Forensic and litigation consulting includes forensic accounting and financial investigations; trial services, which include providing advice and support for clients in complex civil trials; and pre-, in- and post-trial dispute advisory services. Economic consulting includes analyses of complex economic issues in legal and regulatory proceedings. The technology segment includes FTI's proprietary Ringtail software for document review, litigation support and information management. Strategic communications include financial and brand communications, media relations, public affairs and business consulting.

The firm offers employees life, disability, AD&D, medical, dental and vision insurance; health and dependent care flexible spending accounts; a 401(k); and an employee assistance program.

FINANCIAL DATA: Note: Data for latest year may not have been available at press time.

In U.S. $	2016	2015	2014	2013	2012	2011
Revenue	1,810,394,000	1,779,149,000	1,756,212,000	1,652,432,000	1,576,871,000	1,566,768,000
R&D Expense						
Operating Income	142,156,000	164,511,000	147,426,000	81,439,000	59,036,000	205,447,000
Operating Margin %	7.85%	9.24%	8.39%	4.92%	3.74%	13.11%
SGA Expense	434,552,000	432,668,000	433,845,000	394,681,000	378,016,000	373,295,000
Net Income	85,520,000	66,053,000	58,807,000	-10,594,000	-36,986,000	103,903,000
Operating Cash Flow	233,488,000	139,920,000	135,401,000	193,271,000	120,188,000	173,828,000
Capital Expenditure	28,935,000	31,399,000	39,256,000	42,544,000	27,759,000	31,091,000
EBITDA	201,628,000	191,272,000	202,743,000	138,779,000	116,350,000	262,704,000
Return on Assets %	3.83%	2.83%	2.45%	-.45%	-1.57%	4.30%
Return on Equity %	7.26%	5.87%	5.48%	-1.00%	-3.40%	9.14%
Debt to Equity	0.30	0.43	0.63	0.68	0.67	0.58

CONTACT INFORMATION:

Phone: 202-312-9100   Fax: 202-312-9101
Toll-Free: 800-334-5701
Address: 1101 K Street NW, Washington D.C., MD 20005 United States

STOCK TICKER/OTHER:

Stock Ticker: FCN
Employees: 4,718
Parent Company:

Exchange: NYS
Fiscal Year Ends: 12/31

SALARIES/BONUSES:

Top Exec. Salary: $182,692   Bonus: $875,000
Second Exec. Salary: $1,000,000   Bonus: $

OTHER THOUGHTS:

Estimated Female Officers or Directors: 3
Hot Spot for Advancement for Women/Minorities: Y

Gartner Inc

www.gartner.com

NAIC Code: 541910

TYPES OF BUSINESS:

Research-Computer Hardware & Software
Industry Research
IT Symposia & Conferences
Measurement & Advisory Services

BRANDS/DIVISIONS/AFFILIATES:

Symposium/Itxpo
SCM World

CONTACTS: Note: Officers with more than one job title may be intentionally listed here more than once.

Eugene Hall, CEO
Craig Safian, CFO
James Smith, Chairman of the Board
Michael Diliberto, Chief Information Officer
Alwyn Dawkins, Senior VP, Divisional
Per Waern, Senior VP, Divisional
Robin Kranich, Senior VP, Divisional
Peter Sondergaard, Senior VP, Divisional
David McVeigh, Senior VP, Divisional
David Godfrey, Senior VP, Divisional
Thomas Christopher, Senior VP, Divisional
Kendall Davis, Senior VP, Divisional
Daniel Peale, Senior VP

GROWTH PLANS/SPECIAL FEATURES:

Gartner, Inc. is a research and advisory firm that offers independent research and analysis on IT, computer hardware, software, communications and related technology industries. With consultants in more than 90 countries, it provides coverage of the IT industry to nearly 11,000 organizations. The company operates in three segments: research, consulting and events. The research segment, the main service of the company, provides research content and advice for IT professionals, technology companies and the investment community in the form of reports and briefings, as well as peer networking services and membership programs designed specifically for CIOs and other senior executives. The consulting division provides customized solutions to unique client needs through on-site, day-to-day support, as well as proprietary tools for measuring and improving IT performance with a focus on coast, performance, efficiency and quality. The events group provides IT, supply chain, digital marketing and other business professionals the opportunity to attend various symposia, conferences and exhibitions to learn, contribute and network with their peers. Its flagship event, Symposium/ITxpo, as well as summits, focus on specific technologies and industries and offer experimental workshop-style seminars. This division also provides the latest Gartner research into applicable insight and advice at its events. In 2016, Gartner acquired SCM World, a leading cross-industry peer network and learning community that provides subscription-based research and conferences; and increased its presence in South Africa, becoming a direct sales channel effective January 1, 2017. In early 2017, the firm agreed to acquire CEB, Inc. for $2.6 billion; and announced it would increase its presence in Thailand by transitioning to a direct business operation effective February 1, 2017.

FINANCIAL DATA: Note: Data for latest year may not have been available at press time.

In U.S. $	2016	2015	2014	2013	2012	2011
Revenue	2,444,540,000	2,163,056,000	2,021,441,000	1,784,213,000	1,615,808,000	1,468,588,000
R&D Expense						
Operating Income	305,141,000	287,997,000	286,162,000	275,492,000	245,707,000	214,062,000
Operating Margin %	12.48%	13.31%	14.15%	15.44%	15.20%	14.57%
SGA Expense	1,089,184,000	962,677,000	876,067,000	760,458,000	678,843,000	613,707,000
Net Income	193,582,000	175,635,000	183,766,000	182,801,000	165,903,000	136,902,000
Operating Cash Flow	365,632,000	345,561,000	346,779,000	315,654,000	279,813,000	255,566,000
Capital Expenditure	49,863,000	46,128,000	38,486,000	36,498,000	44,337,000	41,954,000
EBITDA	377,965,000	341,890,000	326,395,000	311,269,000	275,272,000	245,464,000
Return on Assets %	8.52%	8.61%	9.96%	10.73%	11.05%	10.27%
Return on Equity %		1220.91%	70.34%	54.73%	67.92%	74.23%
Debt to Equity	10.91		2.38	0.37	0.37	0.82

CONTACT INFORMATION:

Phone: 203 316-1111   Fax:
Toll-Free:
Address: 56 Top Gallant Road, Stamford, CT 06902-7700 United States

STOCK TICKER/OTHER:

Stock Ticker: IT
Employees: 8,813
Parent Company:

Exchange: NYS
Fiscal Year Ends: 12/31

SALARIES/BONUSES:

Top Exec. Salary: $901,584   Bonus: $
Second Exec. Salary: Bonus: $
$503,260

OTHER THOUGHTS:

Estimated Female Officers or Directors: 3
Hot Spot for Advancement for Women/Minorities: Y

General Electric Co (GE)

NAIC Code: 333000

TYPES OF BUSINESS:

Machinery and Equipment Manufacturing
Energy Systems & Consulting
Business Leasing & Finance
Industrial & Electrical Equipment
Transportation, Aircraft Engines, Rail Systems & Truck Fleet Management
Real Estate Investments & Finance
Medical Equipment

BRANDS/DIVISIONS/AFFILIATES:

GE Capital
GE Capital Aviation Services

CONTACTS: *Note: Officers with more than one job title may be intentionally listed here more than once.*

Elizabeth Comstock, CEO, Divisional
David Joyce, CEO, Divisional
John Rice, CEO, Divisional
John Flannery, CEO, Subsidiary
Kieran Murphy, CEO, Subsidiary
Jeffrey Immelt, CEO
Jeffrey Bornstein, CFO
Jan Hauser, Chief Accounting Officer
Alexander Dimitrief, General Counsel
Susan Peters, Senior VP, Divisional

GROWTH PLANS/SPECIAL FEATURES:

General Electric Co. (GE) is one of the largest technology, media and financial services corporations in the world. The firm operates through several divisions: power & water, oil & gas, energy management, aviation, health care, transportation, appliances & lighting and GE Capital. Power & water is a leader in the field of development, implementation and improvement of products and technologies that harness resources such as wind, oil, gas and water to produce electric power. Oil & gas helps oil and gas companies make more efficient and sustainable use of the world's energy resources. Energy management designs, manufactures and services leading technology solutions for the delivery, management, conversion and optimization of electrical power for customers across multiple energy-intensive industries. Aviation is one of the world's leading providers of jet engines and related services with operations in North America, Europe, Asia and South America. Health care provides essential health care technologies to developed, developing and emerging countries. Transportation is a global technology leader and supplier to the railroad, marine, drilling and mining industries. Appliances & lighting manufactures, sells and services major home appliances, including refrigerators, freezers and residential water systems; and lighting products such as automotive, decorative and specialty bulbs. GE Capital manages all of the lending and financial services units of GE, including commercial lending and leasing, consumer lending, real estate activities, energy financial services and commercial aircraft leasing and finance (through GE Capital Aviation Services). In late 2016, GE announced plans to merge its oil & gas industry business units with Baker Hughes, Inc.

FINANCIAL DATA: *Note: Data for latest year may not have been available at press time.*

In U.S. $	2016	2015	2014	2013	2012	2011
Revenue	123,693,000,000	117,386,000,000	148,589,000,000	146,045,000,000	147,359,000,000	147,300,000,000
R&D Expense						
Operating Income	17,833,000,000	16,862,000,000	26,711,000,000	26,267,000,000	29,914,000,000	34,643,000,000
Operating Margin %	14.41%	14.36%	17.97%	17.98%	20.30%	23.51%
SGA Expense	18,377,000,000	17,831,000,000	30,572,000,000	37,819,000,000	39,244,000,000	40,296,000,000
Net Income	8,831,000,000	-6,126,000,000	15,233,000,000	13,057,000,000	13,641,000,000	14,151,000,000
Operating Cash Flow	-244,000,000	19,891,000,000	27,710,000,000	28,579,000,000	31,331,000,000	33,359,000,000
Capital Expenditure	7,199,000,000	7,309,000,000	13,727,000,000	13,458,000,000	15,126,000,000	12,650,000,000
EBITDA	19,052,000,000	16,496,000,000	35,994,000,000	36,029,000,000	39,260,000,000	43,828,000,000
Return on Assets %	1.90%	-1.07%	2.33%	1.94%	1.94%	1.78%
Return on Equity %	9.39%	-5.41%	11.77%	10.29%	11.39%	11.14%
Debt to Equity	1.39	1.50	1.73	1.85	2.08	2.25

CONTACT INFORMATION:

Phone: 203 373-2211　　　　Fax: 203 373-3131
Toll-Free:
Address: 3135 Easton Turnpike, Fairfield, CT 06828 United States

STOCK TICKER/OTHER:

Stock Ticker: GE　　　　　　　　　　　Exchange: NYS
Employees: 295,000　　　　　　　　　　Fiscal Year Ends: 12/31
Parent Company:

SALARIES/BONUSES:

Top Exec. Salary: $3,800,000　　　Bonus: $4,320,000
Second Exec. Salary: $2,575,000　　Bonus: $3,784,000

OTHER THOUGHTS:

Estimated Female Officers or Directors: 10
Hot Spot for Advancement for Women/Minorities: Y

General Motors Company (GM)

NAIC Code: 336111

www.gm.com

TYPES OF BUSINESS:

Automobile Manufacturing
Security & Information Services
Automotive Electronics
Financing & Insurance
Parts & Service
Transmissions
Engines
Locomotives

BRANDS/DIVISIONS/AFFILIATES:

Chevrolet
Buick
Cadillac
GMC
Opel
Vauxhall
Holden

CONTACTS: *Note: Officers with more than one job title may be intentionally listed here more than once.*

Mary Barra, CEO
Alan Batey, Executive VP
Charles Stevens, CFO
Karl-Thomas Neumann, Chairman of the Board, Subsidiary
Thomas Timko, Chief Accounting Officer
Vinit Sethi, Director
Mark Reuss, Executive VP, Divisional
Alicia Boler-Davis, Executive VP, Divisional
Stefan Jacoby, Executive VP, Divisional
Craig Glidden, Executive VP
Matthew Tsien, Executive VP
Carel De Nysschen, Executive VP
Barry Engle, Executive VP
Daniel Ammann, President
John Quattrone, Senior VP, Divisional

GROWTH PLANS/SPECIAL FEATURES:

General Motors Company (GM) is engaged in the worldwide development, production and marketing of cars, trucks, automotive systems and locomotives. The firm's major North American brands include Chevrolet, Buick, Cadillac and GMC. Besides its North American brands, GM markets vehicles internationally under the following brands: Opel, via Adam Opel AG; Vauxhall, via Vauxhall Motors Ltd.; and Holden, via GM. The company is organized into four geographically-based segments: General Motors North America (GMNA), focused on U.S., Canada, and Mexico; General Motors international operations (GMIO), focused primarily on Egypt, Australia, the Middle East and Asia; General Motors Europe (GME), centered on European operations; and General Motors South America (GMSA), with operations primarily in Brazil, Argentina, Colombia and Venezuela. GM's equity ownership stakes through various regional subsidiaries in Asia design, manufacture and market vehicles under the Baojun, Buick, Cadillac, Chevrolet, Jiefang and Wuling brands. The firm has 19,452 dealerships worldwide, with 4,857 locations in North America.

FINANCIAL DATA: *Note: Data for latest year may not have been available at press time.*

In U.S. $	2016	2015	2014	2013	2012	2011
Revenue	166,380,000,000	152,356,000,000	155,929,000,000	155,427,000,000	152,256,000,000	150,276,000,000
R&D Expense						
Operating Income	9,545,000,000	4,897,000,000	1,530,000,000	5,131,000,000	-30,363,000,000	5,656,000,000
Operating Margin %	5.73%	3.21%	.98%	3.30%	-19.94%	3.76%
SGA Expense	11,710,000,000	13,405,000,000	12,158,000,000	12,382,000,000	13,593,000,000	12,163,000,000
Net Income	9,427,000,000	9,687,000,000	3,949,000,000	5,346,000,000	6,188,000,000	9,190,000,000
Operating Cash Flow	16,545,000,000	11,978,000,000	10,058,000,000	12,630,000,000	10,605,000,000	8,166,000,000
Capital Expenditure	29,166,000,000	7,874,000,000	7,091,000,000	7,565,000,000	9,118,000,000	7,078,000,000
EBITDA	22,664,000,000	16,178,000,000	11,887,000,000	15,833,000,000	8,994,000,000	13,869,000,000
Return on Assets %	4.52%	5.20%	1.63%	2.38%	3.30%	5.35%
Return on Equity %	22.52%	25.71%	7.48%	11.53%	18.13%	28.34%
Debt to Equity	1.26	1.09	0.89	0.55	0.40	0.42

CONTACT INFORMATION:

Phone: 313 556-5000   Fax:
Toll-Free:
Address: 300 Renaissance Ctr., Detroit, MI 48265-3000 United States

STOCK TICKER/OTHER:

Stock Ticker: GM   Exchange: NYS
Employees: 135,000   Fiscal Year Ends: 12/31
Parent Company:

SALARIES/BONUSES:

Top Exec. Salary: $1,750,000   Bonus: $
Second Exec. Salary: Bonus: $
$1,200,000

OTHER THOUGHTS:

Estimated Female Officers or Directors: 8
Hot Spot for Advancement for Women/Minorities: Y

Gentex Corporation

NAIC Code: 336300

TYPES OF BUSINESS:

Specialty Automobile Parts Manufacturer
Electro-Optic Technology
Rearview Mirrors & Mirror Sub-Assemblies
Headlight Systems
Smoke Alarms & Smoke Detectors
Electrochromic Window Shades

BRANDS/DIVISIONS/AFFILIATES:

SmartBeam
HomeLink
Alteos

CONTACTS: Note: Officers with more than one job title may be intentionally listed here more than once.

Scott Ryan, Assistant General Counsel
Fred Bauer, CEO
Kevin Nash, Chief Accounting Officer
James Hollars, Independent Director
Steve Downing, Senior VP
Joseph Matthews, Vice President, Divisional

GROWTH PLANS/SPECIAL FEATURES:

Gentex Corporation designs, develops, manufactures and markets proprietary products for the automotive, aviation and fire protection industry. The automotive division is the firm's largest business segment and builds products such as interior and exterior electrochromic automatic-dimming rearview mirrors and automotive electronics. The company also has an exterior auto-dimming mirror sub-assembly, which works as a complete glare-control system with the interior mirror. Automatic-dimming mirrors include the SmartBeam driver-assist feature for headlamp lighting control; HomeLink mirror electronics; LED (light-emitting diode) map lamps; compass and temperature displays; telematics; hands-free communication; rear camera display and full display interior mirrors; CMOS (complementary metal-oxide semiconductor) imager-based video cameras for rear vision with high dynamic range; proprietary exterior turn signals; and side blind zone indicators. Gentex supplies automatic-dimming rearview mirrors for Rolls Royce, Renault, Ford, Kia, General Motors, Honda, Audi, BMW, Toyota and other manufacturers. The fire protection segment produces photoelectric smoke detectors and alarms; visual signaling alarms; electrochemical carbon monoxide alarms and detectors; audible and visual signaling alarms; and bells and speakers for use in fire detection systems in commercial and residential buildings. The firm's aviation segment manufactures dimmable aircraft windows under the brand name Alteos for the passenger compartment of the Boeing 787 Dreamliner series.

Gentex offers its employees health, dental, life and disability insurance; a 401(k) plan; tuition reimbursement; profit sharing bonus; adoption assistance; access to a wellness center; and an employee stock purchase plan.

FINANCIAL DATA: Note: Data for latest year may not have been available at press time.

In U.S. $	2016	2015	2014	2013	2012	2011
Revenue	1,678,925,000	1,543,618,000	1,375,501,000	1,171,864,000	1,099,560,000	1,023,762,000
R&D Expense	94,238,030	88,392,920	84,175,740	76,495,050	85,003,600	81,634,160
Operating Income	511,742,900	458,766,400	398,834,200	304,741,800	234,455,200	231,367,900
Operating Margin %	30.48%	29.72%	28.99%	26.00%	21.32%	22.59%
SGA Expense	62,471,280	56,616,700	55,879,780	49,496,040	48,359,720	48,578,250
Net Income	347,591,300	318,469,900	288,604,600	222,930,000	168,586,800	164,668,200
Operating Cash Flow	471,464,800	351,578,400	327,223,100	317,338,800	257,846,000	141,668,700
Capital Expenditure	120,955,600	97,941,760	72,518,980	55,380,460	117,474,400	120,177,700
EBITDA	600,330,400	539,365,600	476,210,500	367,596,000	284,635,000	274,002,600
Return on Assets %	15.59%	15.26%	15.24%	14.71%	13.80%	15.11%
Return on Equity %	19.13%	19.33%	19.91%	18.20%	15.69%	17.14%
Debt to Equity	0.09	0.13	0.16	0.20		

CONTACT INFORMATION:

Phone: 616 772-1800   Fax: 616 772-7348
Toll-Free:
Address: 600 N. Centennial St., Zeeland, MI 49464 United States

STOCK TICKER/OTHER:

Stock Ticker: GNTX   Exchange: NAS
Employees: 5,315   Fiscal Year Ends: 12/31
Parent Company:

SALARIES/BONUSES:

Top Exec. Salary: $542,195   Bonus: $159,983
Second Exec. Salary: Bonus: $98,609
$335,949

OTHER THOUGHTS:

Estimated Female Officers or Directors: 1
Hot Spot for Advancement for Women/Minorities:

Gentherm Inc

NAIC Code: 336300

TYPES OF BUSINESS:

Automobile Parts Manufacturing
Thermoelectric Devices
Climate Control Seats
Temperature Controlled Mattresses

BRANDS/DIVISIONS/AFFILIATES:

Gentherm GmbH
Gentherm Global Power Technologies
Gentherm North America
Gentherm Asia Electronics
Global Thermoelectric Inc
Cincinnati Sub-Zero Products

CONTACTS: *Note: Officers with more than one job title may be intentionally listed here more than once.*

Barry Steele, CFO
Francois Castaing, Chairman of the Board
Frithjof Oldorff, COO, Subsidiary
Kenneth Phillips, General Counsel
Erin Ascher, Other Executive Officer
Daniel Coker, President
Ryan Gaul, Vice President, Divisional
Darren Schumacher, Vice President, Divisional

GROWTH PLANS/SPECIAL FEATURES:

Gentherm, Inc. designs, develops and markets products based on its advanced, proprietary thermoelectric device (TED) technologies for a wide range of global markets and heating and cooling applications. The firm's current principal product is its climate control seat (CCS), which it sells to automobile and light truck original equipment manufacturers (OEMs) or Tier 1 suppliers. The CCS actively heats and cools the passenger by using TED technologies. The CCS product is currently offered as a standard or optional feature on automobiles produced by Ford, General Motors, Toyota, Nissan, Hyundai, Volkswagen, Fiat Chrysler, BMW, Daimler, Honda and Jaguar/Land Rover. The firm also offers a heated-only variant of the CCS, which has a lower price and is targeted to certain lower cost vehicle models and certain geographical markets. Other products the firm has developed include a line of actively heated and cooled luxury mattresses and an automotive heated and cooled cup holder for the 2011 Dodge Charger. Additionally, through its majority-owned subsidiary Gentherm GmbH, the firm produces automotive cable systems used to connect automotive components to sources of power. Subsidiary Gentherm Global Power Technologies is a global market leader and developer of thermoelectric generators, and is also the company's advanced research and product development division. Other subsidiaries include Gentherm North America and Gentherm Asia Electronics. Gentherm holds 513 issued patents, of which 216 are U.S. and 297 are non-U.S. patents. In 2016, the firm acquired Cincinnati Sub-Zero Products, a manufacturer of patient temperature systems for the healthcare industry.

FINANCIAL DATA: *Note: Data for latest year may not have been available at press time.*

In U.S. $	2016	2015	2014	2013	2012	2011
Revenue	917,600,000	856,445,000	811,300,000	662,082,000	554,979,000	369,588,000
R&D Expense	72,923,000	59,604,000	57,526,000	49,873,000	40,950,000	28,440,000
Operating Income	106,119,000	121,319,000	98,434,000	49,580,000	36,058,000	18,881,000
Operating Margin %	11.56%	14.16%	12.13%	7.48%	6.49%	5.10%
SGA Expense	115,252,000	95,456,000	84,647,000	72,895,000	64,919,000	42,110,000
Net Income	76,598,000	95,393,000	70,119,000	33,820,000	17,872,000	10,344,000
Operating Cash Flow	108,400,000	104,712,000	80,335,000	59,794,000	36,865,000	35,370,000
Capital Expenditure	66,316,000	55,490,000	38,887,000	35,861,000	26,793,000	11,816,000
EBITDA	151,584,000	162,577,000	132,512,000	80,829,000	67,435,000	42,233,000
Return on Assets %	10.28%	15.83%	13.48%	6.99%	2.73%	.92%
Return on Equity %	18.13%	28.11%	26.64%	16.34%	9.90%	3.49%
Debt to Equity	0.36	0.24	0.29	0.26	0.24	0.97

CONTACT INFORMATION:

Phone: 248-504-0500   Fax: 248-348-9735
Toll-Free:
Address: 21680 Haggerty Rd., Ste. 101, Northville, MI 48167 United States

STOCK TICKER/OTHER:

Stock Ticker: THRM
Employees: 11,685
Parent Company:

Exchange: NAS
Fiscal Year Ends: 12/31

SALARIES/BONUSES:

Top Exec. Salary: $750,000   Bonus: $637,500
Second Exec. Salary: $437,750   Bonus: $196,626

OTHER THOUGHTS:

Estimated Female Officers or Directors: 1
Hot Spot for Advancement for Women/Minorities:

Gilead Sciences Inc

www.gilead.com

NAIC Code: 325412

<table>
<tr><td>

TYPES OF BUSINESS:

Viral & Bacterial Infections Drugs
Respiratory & Cardiopulmonary Diseases Drugs

BRANDS/DIVISIONS/AFFILIATES:

Atripla
Complera
Harvoni
Zydelig
Letairis
Ranexa
Cayston
AmBisome

CONTACTS: *Note: Officers with more than one job title may be intentionally listed here more than once.*

John Milligan, CEO
Robin Washington, CFO
John Martin, Chairman of the Board
Kevin Young, COO
Gregg Alton, Executive VP, Divisional
James Meyers, Executive VP, Divisional
Norbert Bischofberger, Executive VP, Divisional

</td><td>

GROWTH PLANS/SPECIAL FEATURES:

Gilead Sciences, Inc. is a biopharmaceutical company that discovers, develops and commercializes therapeutics for the treatment of life-threatening diseases such as viral and bacterial infections as well as respiratory and cardiopulmonary diseases. The firm maintains research, development, manufacturing, sales and marketing facilities in the U.S., Europe and Australia and operates through its subsidiaries in over 30 countries. Gilead's current products on the market consist of: Atripla, Complera, Emtriva, Stribild, Truvada, Tybost, Viread and Vitekta, which are oral medicines used as part of a combination therapy to treat HIV/AIDS; Harvoni, Hepsera, Sovaldi and Viread, which are oral medicines to treat liver diseases; Zydelig, an oral medicine for oncology purposes; Letairis, Ranexa (oral medicines) and Lexiscan (injection medicine), for cardiovascular purposes; Cayston inhalation solution and oral medicine Tamiflu, for respiratory and inflammation purposes; AmBisome, an injection medicine to treat meningitis in HIV infected patients; and Macugen, an injection medicine to treat neovascular age-related macular degeneration.

The company offers its employees medical, vision, dental, disability, life and AD&D insurance; a 401(k); a stock purchase plan; an entertainment discount program; an employee assistance plan; and tuition reimbursement.

</td></tr>
</table>

FINANCIAL DATA: *Note: Data for latest year may not have been available at press time.*

In U.S. $	2016	2015	2014	2013	2012	2011
Revenue	30,390,000,000	32,639,000,000	24,890,000,000	11,201,690,000	9,702,517,000	8,385,385,000
R&D Expense	5,098,000,000	3,014,000,000	2,854,000,000	2,119,756,000	1,759,945,000	1,229,151,000
Operating Income	17,633,000,000	22,193,000,000	15,265,000,000	4,523,999,000	4,010,175,000	3,789,841,000
Operating Margin %	58.02%	67.99%	61.32%	40.38%	41.33%	45.19%
SGA Expense	3,398,000,000	3,426,000,000	2,983,000,000	1,699,431,000	1,461,034,000	1,241,983,000
Net Income	13,501,000,000	18,108,000,000	12,101,000,000	3,074,808,000	2,591,566,000	2,803,637,000
Operating Cash Flow	16,669,000,000	20,329,000,000	12,818,000,000	3,104,988,000	3,194,716,000	3,639,010,000
Capital Expenditure	748,000,000	747,000,000	557,000,000	190,782,000	397,046,000	131,904,000
EBITDA	19,219,000,000	23,445,000,000	16,318,000,000	4,859,817,000	4,251,102,000	4,158,654,000
Return on Assets %	24.81%	41.86%	42.34%	14.06%	13.44%	19.40%
Return on Equity %	72.15%	106.64%	90.32%	29.73%	32.29%	44.49%
Debt to Equity	1.39	1.14	0.77	0.34	0.75	1.12

CONTACT INFORMATION:

Phone: 650 574-3000   Fax: 650 578-9264
Toll-Free: 800-445-3235
Address: 333 Lakeside Dr., Foster City, CA 94404 United States

STOCK TICKER/OTHER:

Stock Ticker: GILD   Exchange: NAS
Employees: 9,000   Fiscal Year Ends: 12/31
Parent Company:

SALARIES/BONUSES:

Top Exec. Salary: $1,737,000   Bonus: $
Second Exec. Salary: Bonus: $
$1,465,385

OTHER THOUGHTS:

Estimated Female Officers or Directors: 4
Hot Spot for Advancement for Women/Minorities: Y

GoDaddy Inc

www.godaddy.com

NAIC Code: 518210

TYPES OF BUSINESS:

Domain Name Registration
Domain Name Reselling
Research & Development, Internet Services

BRANDS/DIVISIONS/AFFILIATES:

CONTACTS: Note: Officers with more than one job title may be intentionally listed here more than once.

Blake Irving, CEO
Ray Winborne, CFO
Arne Josefsberg, Chief Information Officer
Barbara Rechterman, Chief Marketing Officer
Charles Robel, Director
Bob Parsons, Director
James Carroll, Executive VP, Divisional
Nima Kelly, Executive VP
Steven Aldrich, Other Executive Officer
Auguste Goldman, Other Executive Officer
Scott Wagner, President

GROWTH PLANS/SPECIAL FEATURES:

GoDaddy, Inc. provides domain name registration and related services. The company has 13.8 million customers made up of individuals and organizations. GoDaddy operates the world's largest domain marketplace where customers can find a domain name to match their idea, with approximately 63 million domains under management. The firm is a leading technology provider to small businesses, web design professionals and individuals, offering easy-to-use cloud-based products. GoDaddy provides web site building, hosting and security tools to construct and protect each customer's online presence. Products are developed internally, and include shared web site hosting, web site hosting on virtual dedicated servers and dedicated services, managed hosting services, cloud services, cloud applications, web site builder, eCommerce solutions, search engine visibility, email accounts, office solutions via Microsoft Office 365 and email marketing solutions. GoDaddy provides localized solutions in 63 countries, with 26% of its total bookings attributable to customers outside the U.S. In May 2016, the company acquired FreedomVoice, a virtual phone services company for small businesses, for $42 million. Later that year, in December, the firm acquired Host Europe Group, a web services provider for small businesses, for $1.79 billion.

The firm offers employees 100% paid medical and dental premiums, employee appreciation outings, a 401(k) plan, life and disability insurance, maternity and paternity leave, adoption assistance, subsidized lunches and employee discounts.

FINANCIAL DATA: Note: Data for latest year may not have been available at press time.

In U.S. $	2016	2015	2014	2013	2012	2011
Revenue	1,847,900,000	1,607,300,000	1,387,262,000	1,130,845,000	910,903,000	31,349,000
R&D Expense	287,800,000	270,200,000	254,440,000	207,941,000	175,406,000	8,078,000
Operating Income	50,100,000	-31,000,000	-61,876,000	-131,925,000	-202,504,000	-49,492,000
Operating Margin %	2.71%	-1.92%	-4.46%	-11.66%	-22.23%	-157.87%
SGA Expense	692,100,000	643,400,000	523,557,000	440,394,000	369,082,000	50,818,000
Net Income	-16,500,000	-47,400,000	-143,305,000	-199,884,000	-279,052,000	-53,574,000
Operating Cash Flow	386,500,000	259,400,000	180,568,000	153,313,000	106,110,000	-35,090,000
Capital Expenditure	62,800,000	79,300,000	67,901,000	52,089,000	44,230,000	2,297,000
EBITDA	195,800,000	107,400,000	91,627,000	10,519,000	-61,558,000	-44,609,000
Return on Assets %	- .45%	-1.40%	-4.42%	-6.40%	-9.21%	
Return on Equity %	-3.33%	-11.33%	-23.43%	-21.89%	-27.52%	
Debt to Equity	1.84	2.44	3.44	1.33	0.97	

CONTACT INFORMATION:

Phone: 480-505-8800   Fax: 480-505-8844
Toll-Free:
Address: 14455 N. Hayden Rd., Ste. 219, Scottsdale, AZ 85260 United States

STOCK TICKER/OTHER:

Stock Ticker: GDDY   Exchange: NYS
Employees: 4,749   Fiscal Year Ends: 12/31
Parent Company:

SALARIES/BONUSES:

Top Exec. Salary: $1,000,000   Bonus: $
Second Exec. Salary: Bonus: $
$750,000

OTHER THOUGHTS:

Estimated Female Officers or Directors: 3
Hot Spot for Advancement for Women/Minorities: Y

Goldman Sachs Group Inc

www.goldmansachs.com

NAIC Code: 523110

TYPES OF BUSINESS:

Investment Banking
Securities & Investment Management
Financial Services
Asset Management
Bank Holding Company

BRANDS/DIVISIONS/AFFILIATES:

GS Bank
Honest Dollar

CONTACTS: *Note: Officers with more than one job title may be intentionally listed here more than once.*

Richard Gnodde, CEO, Subsidiary
Lloyd Blankfein, CEO
Harvey Schwartz, CFO
Sarah Smith, Chief Accounting Officer
David Solomon, Co- President
Gregory Palm, Executive VP
Alan Cohen, Executive VP
Edith Cooper, Executive VP
John Rogers, Executive VP
Pablo Salame, Other Corporate Officer

GROWTH PLANS/SPECIAL FEATURES:

Goldman Sachs Group, Inc. is a financial holding company regulated by the Board of Governors of the Federal Reserve System, operating in over 30 countries. The firm has four main business divisions: institutional client services, investment management, investment banking and investing & lending. The institutional client services division accounts for the majority of the company's annual profits, more than 40%. It provides clients with services regarding fixed income currency and commodities execution on a variety of products such as interest rate and credit products, mortgages, currencies and commodities. The investment management segment provides investment and wealth advisory services on a range of asset classes and investment plans, including equity, fixed income, hedge funds, private equity, real estate, currencies, commodities and asset allocation of strategies to institutions and high-net-worth individuals who access the companies' products through third-party distributors. The investment banking division provides financial advisory services including strategic advisory assignments with respect to mergers and acquisitions, divestitures, corporate defense activities, risk management, debt and equity underwriting, restructurings and spin-offs to corporate and government clients around the world. The investing & lending sector manages a portfolio of investments consisting of equity and debt securities in addition to other investments in privately negotiated transactions, leveraged buyouts, acquisitions and investment funds managed by external parties. In addition, the Goldman Sachs Prime Brokerage program in Europe and the U.S. delivers investment research, products and execution services to brokerage firms. In 2016, the firm launched an online-only U.S. savings bank, GS Bank; acquired the online deposit platform of GE Capital Bank, assuming approximately $16 billion of deposits; and acquired Honest Dollar, a web and mobile-based retirement savings platform for Americans without access to employer-sponsored retirement plans.

Goldman Sachs offers employees medical, prescription, life, disability, accident, travel, dental and vision insurance; 401(k); adoption assistance; and investing services.

FINANCIAL DATA: *Note: Data for latest year may not have been available at press time.*

In U.S. $	2016	2015	2014	2013	2012	2011
Revenue	30,608,000,000	33,820,000,000	34,528,000,000	34,206,000,000	34,163,000,000	28,811,000,000
R&D Expense						
Operating Income	10,304,000,000	8,778,000,000	12,357,000,000	11,737,000,000	11,207,000,000	6,169,000,000
Operating Margin %	33.66%	25.95%	35.78%	34.31%	32.80%	21.41%
SGA Expense	12,913,000,000	14,041,000,000	14,019,000,000	14,106,000,000	14,833,000,000	14,220,000,000
Net Income	7,398,000,000	6,083,000,000	8,477,000,000	8,040,000,000	7,475,000,000	4,442,000,000
Operating Cash Flow	5,570,000,000	6,961,000,000	-7,623,000,000	4,543,000,000	12,879,000,000	21,645,000,000
Capital Expenditure	2,876,000,000	1,833,000,000	678,000,000	706,000,000	961,000,000	1,184,000,000
EBITDA						
Return on Assets %	.82%	.64%	.91%	.83%	.78%	.27%
Return on Equity %	9.37%	7.46%	11.15%	10.97%	10.66%	3.64%
Debt to Equity	2.78	2.65	2.58	2.60	2.86	3.13

CONTACT INFORMATION:

Phone: 212 902-1000   Fax: 212 902-3000
Toll-Free:
Address: 200 West St., New York, NY 10282 United States

STOCK TICKER/OTHER:

Stock Ticker: GS   Exchange: NYS
Employees: 34,400   Fiscal Year Ends: 12/31
Parent Company:

SALARIES/BONUSES:

Top Exec. Salary: $1,850,000   Bonus: $5,445,000
Second Exec. Salary: Bonus: $5,445,000
$1,850,000

OTHER THOUGHTS:

Estimated Female Officers or Directors: 5
Hot Spot for Advancement for Women/Minorities: Y

Google (Alphabet Inc)

www.google.com

NAIC Code: 519130

TYPES OF BUSINESS:

Search Engine-Internet
Paid Search Listing Advertising Services
Online Software and Productivity Tools
Online Video and Photo Services
Travel Booking
Analytical Tools
Venture Capital
Online Maps

BRANDS/DIVISIONS/AFFILIATES:

Alphabet Inc
Google.com
AdSense
Google Chrome
Google TV
Google Books
Google Docs
Gmail

CONTACTS: *Note: Officers with more than one job title may be intentionally listed here more than once.*

Sundar Pichai, CEO, Subsidiary
Larry Page, CEO
Ruth Porat, CFO
Eric Schmidt, Chairman of the Board
Sergey Brin, Director
Diane Greene, Director
David Drummond, Other Executive Officer
James Campbell, Vice President

GROWTH PLANS/SPECIAL FEATURES:

Google (Alphabet, Inc.) operates Google.com, a global leader in technology and a provider of the world's most used search engine, which connects people to information by indexing the content of billions of internet pages. While end-users can use Google's search engine for free, the company profits from charging fees to other sites that use its search technology through an auction-based program that enables business clients to bid for ad space. Businesses use the AdWords program to promote their products and services. In addition, third-party web sites that comprise the Google network use the AdSense program to deliver ads that generate revenue and are relevant to search results. Advertising revenue is also generated from other web-based applications that provide clients with delivery of display services; advertising technology that creates a real-time auction marketplace where advertisers can trade display ad space; a free and open source smartphone operating system; and tools that allow users to locate local information via the web. The company's business operates in four different areas: search, advertising, operating systems and platforms and enterprise. The company's operating systems and platforms division develops proprietary products such as the Android market, Google Chrome, Google TV and Google Books. The enterprise division creates productivity and content sharing tools, such as Google Docs, Gmail, Blogger, Google Play, Google+ and YouTube. Google operates 70 offices in more than 40 countries. In August 2015, the firm created holding company Alphabet. Google's search business, YouTube and the Android and Chrome software units operate as one unit under Alphabet. Other businesses, mainly in development stage, operate as separate units under Alphabet. These businesses include Nest, Google Ventures, Google Fiber and Calico.

FINANCIAL DATA: *Note: Data for latest year may not have been available at press time.*

In U.S. $	2016	2015	2014	2013	2012	2011
Revenue	90,272,000,000	74,989,000,000	66,001,000,000	59,825,000,000	50,175,000,000	37,905,000,000
R&D Expense	13,948,000,000	12,282,000,000	9,831,999,000	7,952,000,000	6,793,000,000	5,162,000,000
Operating Income	23,716,000,000	19,360,000,000	16,496,000,000	13,966,000,000	12,760,000,000	11,742,000,000
Operating Margin %	26.27%	25.81%	24.99%	23.34%	25.43%	30.97%
SGA Expense	17,470,000,000	15,183,000,000	13,982,000,000	12,049,000,000	9,988,000,000	7,813,000,000
Net Income	19,478,000,000	16,348,000,000	14,444,000,000	12,920,000,000	10,737,000,000	9,737,000,000
Operating Cash Flow	36,036,000,000	26,024,000,000	22,376,000,000	18,659,000,000	16,619,000,000	14,565,000,000
Capital Expenditure	10,212,000,000	9,915,000,000	10,959,000,000	7,358,000,000	3,273,000,000	3,438,000,000
EBITDA	30,418,000,000	24,818,000,000	22,339,000,000	18,518,000,000	16,432,000,000	14,235,000,000
Return on Assets %	12.36%	11.36%	11.93%	12.62%	12.90%	14.93%
Return on Equity %	15.01%	14.07%	15.06%	16.24%	16.53%	18.65%
Debt to Equity	0.02	0.01	0.03	0.02	0.04	0.05

CONTACT INFORMATION:

Phone: 650 253-0000   Fax: 650 253-0001
Toll-Free:
Address: 1600 Amphitheatre Pkwy., Mountain View, CA 94043 United States

STOCK TICKER/OTHER:

Stock Ticker: GOOG
Employees: 72,053
Parent Company:

Exchange: NAS
Fiscal Year Ends: 12/31

SALARIES/BONUSES:

Top Exec. Salary: $1,250,000   Bonus: $
Second Exec. Salary: $650,000   Bonus: $

OTHER THOUGHTS:

Estimated Female Officers or Directors: 3
Hot Spot for Advancement for Women/Minorities: Y

Graco Inc

NAIC Code: 333911

www.graco.com

TYPES OF BUSINESS:

Pump and Pumping Equipment Manufacturing

BRANDS/DIVISIONS/AFFILIATES:

CONTACTS: *Note: Officers with more than one job title may be intentionally listed here more than once.*

Patrick McHale, CEO
Lee Mitau, Chairman of the Board
Caroline Chambers, Chief Accounting Officer
David Lowe, Executive VP, Divisional
Mark Sheahan, General Manager, Divisional
Mark Eberlein, General Manager, Divisional
Peter OShea, General Manager, Divisional
Brian Zumbolo, General Manager, Geographical
Bernard Moreau, General Manager, Geographical
Jeffrey Johnson, General Manager, Geographical
Dale Johnson, President, Divisional
Christian Rothe, Treasurer
David Ahlers, Vice President, Divisional
Charles Rescorla, Vice President, Divisional
Karen Gallivan, Vice President

GROWTH PLANS/SPECIAL FEATURES:

Graco, Inc. provides fluid handling solutions to customers in the manufacturing, processing, construction and maintenance industries throughout the world. The company operates in three segments: industrial, contractor and process. The industrial segment includes the industrial products and the applied fluid technologies divisions. The industrial products division markets equipment and services to customers who manufacture, assemble, maintain, repair and refinish products such as appliances, vehicles, airplanes, electronics, cabinets and furniture. The applied fluid technologies division designs and sells equipment for use by industrial customers, including systems used to spray polyurethane foam and polyuria coatings. The contractor segment markets a complete line of airless paint and texture sprayers; accessories such as spray guns, hoses and filters; and spare parts such as tips and seals. The process segment includes process, oil and natural gas and lubrication divisions. Process markets pumps, valves, meters and accessories to move and dispense chemicals, oil and natural gas, water, wastewater, petroleum, food lubricants and other fluids. Markets served include food, beverage, dairy, oil and natural gas, pharmaceutical, cosmetics, semi-conductor, electronics, wastewater, mining, fast oil change facilities, service garages, fleet service centers, automobile dealerships and industrial lubrication applications. Oil and natural gas markets chemical injection pumping solutions, high pressure and ultra-high pressure valves. The lubrication division designs and sells equipment for use in vehicle servicing, supplying pumps, hose reels, meters, valves and accessories. It also offers systems, components and accessories for the automatic lubrication of bearings, gears and generators in industrial and commercial equipment, compressors, turbines and on- and off-road vehicles.

FINANCIAL DATA: *Note: Data for latest year may not have been available at press time.*

In U.S. $	2016	2015	2014	2013	2012	2011
Revenue	1,329,293,000	1,286,485,000	1,221,130,000	1,104,024,000	1,012,456,000	895,283,000
R&D Expense	60,606,000	58,559,000	54,246,000	51,428,000	48,921,000	41,554,000
Operating Income	113,879,000	302,125,000	308,925,000	279,769,000	224,677,000	219,514,000
Operating Margin %	8.56%	23.48%	25.29%	25.34%	22.19%	24.51%
SGA Expense	341,734,000	324,016,000	303,565,000	276,258,000	276,932,000	239,137,000
Net Income	40,674,000	345,713,000	225,573,000	210,822,000	149,126,000	142,328,000
Operating Cash Flow	269,093,000	189,639,000	241,255,000	243,055,000	189,682,000	162,044,000
Capital Expenditure	42,113,000	41,749,000	30,636,000	23,319,000	18,234,000	24,785,000
EBITDA	162,535,000	536,963,000	369,321,000	344,285,000	275,361,000	251,342,000
Return on Assets %	3.08%	23.54%	15.70%	15.91%	13.58%	20.26%
Return on Equity %	6.72%	56.14%	36.66%	38.73%	38.39%	48.50%
Debt to Equity	0.53	0.61	1.03	0.64	1.22	0.92

CONTACT INFORMATION:

Phone: 612 623-6000   Fax: 612 623-6777
Toll-Free:
Address: 88 11th Ave. NE, Minneapolis, MN 55413 United States

STOCK TICKER/OTHER:

Stock Ticker: GGG   Exchange: NYS
Employees: 3,300   Fiscal Year Ends: 12/31
Parent Company:

SALARIES/BONUSES:

Top Exec. Salary: $772,900   Bonus: $
Second Exec. Salary: Bonus: $2,259
$380,700

OTHER THOUGHTS:

Estimated Female Officers or Directors:
Hot Spot for Advancement for Women/Minorities:

Grant Thornton LLP

www.grantthornton.com

NAIC Code: 541211

TYPES OF BUSINESS:

Accounting & Auditing Services
Financial Services
Administration Consulting

BRANDS/DIVISIONS/AFFILIATES:

Grant Thornton International Ltd

CONTACTS: Note: Officers with more than one job title may be intentionally listed here more than once.

Mike McGuire, CEO
Jim Brady, COO
J. Michael McGuire, Nat'l Managing Partner-Oper.
Trent Gazzaway, Managing Partner-Audit Svcs.
Doreen Griffith, Managing Partner-Tax Svcs.
Steve Lukens, Managing Partner-Advisory Svcs.

GROWTH PLANS/SPECIAL FEATURES:

Grant Thornton, LLP is the U.S. arm of Grant Thornton International Ltd., and provides advisory, audit and tax services to both public and private corporations. The company's advisory services include business consulting; forensic, investigative and dispute services; governance, risk and compliance; restructuring and turnaround; technology solutions; transaction advisory; and valuation. Its audit solutions include employee benefit plan audit, financial statement audit, fresh start accounting, international financial reporting standards reporting and resources and public finance. Tax services include the Affordable Care Act, compensation and benefits consulting, international tax, private wealth services, SALT alerts, state and local tax, strategic federal tax, tax accounting/risk advisory, tax compliance and tax hot topics. Industries served by the firm include construction, distribution, energy, financial services, food and beverage, health care, hospitality and restaurants, life sciences, manufacturing, not-for-profit organizations, private equity, public sector, real estate, retail, technology and transportation. Grant Thornton, LLP has 59 offices nationwide, with revenues in excess of $1.6 billion. During 2016, the firm signed a multi-year agreement with the National Center for the Middle Market (NCMM), which provides critical data analysis, insights and perspectives for companies, policymakers and other key stakeholders, to help accelerate growth, increase competitiveness and create middle market jobs. Grant Thornton will help fund and publish NCMM's research. In April 2017, Grant Thornton, LLP opened a new office in Austin, Texas, to serve executives and managers at all levels of the public sector.

Grant Thornton's employee benefits include medical and dental plans, reimbursement accounts and a 401(k) plan.

FINANCIAL DATA: Note: Data for latest year may not have been available at press time.

In U.S. $	2016	2015	2014	2013	2012	2011
Revenue	1,650,000,000	1,450,000,000	1,354,000,000	1,300,000,000	1,260,000,000	1,175,000,000
R&D Expense						
Operating Income						
Operating Margin %						
SGA Expense						
Net Income						
Operating Cash Flow						
Capital Expenditure						
EBITDA						
Return on Assets %						
Return on Equity %						
Debt to Equity						

CONTACT INFORMATION:

Phone: 312-856-0200   Fax: 412-602-8099
Toll-Free:
Address: 171 N. Clark St., Ste. 200, Chicago, IL 60601 United States

STOCK TICKER/OTHER:

Stock Ticker: Private   Exchange:
Employees: 8,000   Fiscal Year Ends: 07/31
Parent Company: Grant Thornton International Ltd

SALARIES/BONUSES:

Top Exec. Salary: $ Bonus: $
Second Exec. Salary: $ Bonus: $

OTHER THOUGHTS:

Estimated Female Officers or Directors: 2
Hot Spot for Advancement for Women/Minorities:

Group 1 Automotive Inc
NAIC Code: 441110

TYPES OF BUSINESS:
Auto Dealers
Auto Repair Services
Insurance Services
Automotive Replacement Parts
Financing Services
Collision Service Centers

BRANDS/DIVISIONS/AFFILIATES:
Spire Automotive Group
Think Ford Reading
Cedar Park Nissan

CONTACTS: *Note: Officers with more than one job title may be intentionally listed here more than once.*
Earl Hesterberg, CEO
John Rickel, CFO
Stephen Quinn, Director
Darryl Burman, General Counsel
Frank Grese, Senior VP, Divisional
Peter DeLongchamps, Vice President, Divisional
Daryl Kenningham, Vice President, Divisional

GROWTH PLANS/SPECIAL FEATURES:
Group 1 Automotive, Inc. is a leading operator in the U.S., U.K. and Brazil automotive retailing industries. The company, through its subsidiaries, sells new and used cars and light trucks, provides maintenance and repair services, sells replacement parts and arranges vehicle financing and insurance through its 210 franchises. The franchises include 159 dealership locations and 38 collision centers. The dealerships offer 31 different brands, which include Toyota, BMW, Ford, Mercedes-Benz, Honda, Nissan, Lexus, Chevrolet, Audi, Hyundai, Acura, Jeep, MINI, GMC, Volkswagen, RAM, Kia, Cadillac, Dodge, Subaru, Land Rover, Buick, Sprinter, Chrysler, Scion, Peugeot, Mazda, Lincoln, Porsche, smart, Volvo and Jaguar. Group 1's dealerships have taken several steps toward building customer confidence in their used vehicle inventory, including participation in manufacturer certification processes. These processes make used vehicles eligible for new vehicle benefits such as new vehicle finance rates and extended manufacturer warranties. In 2016, the firm acquired Spire Automotive Group, based in London, England; and sold three U.S. dealerships, which included Mercedes-Benz and Volkswagen of Freehold, New Jersey and Ira Toyota of Milford, Massachusetts. In 2017, the firm acquired a BMW motorcycle franchise in Brazil; opened Think Ford Reading, the firm's seventh dealership in the U.K.; opened Cedar Park Nissan, in Austin, Texas; and disposed of two Nissan dealerships in Brazil.

FINANCIAL DATA: *Note: Data for latest year may not have been available at press time.*

In U.S. $	2016	2015	2014	2013	2012	2011
Revenue	10,887,610,000	10,632,510,000	9,937,889,000	8,918,581,000	7,476,100,000	6,079,765,000
R&D Expense						
Operating Income	340,234,000	278,338,000	302,110,000	273,322,000	229,996,000	193,503,000
Operating Margin %	3.12%	2.61%	3.04%	3.06%	3.07%	3.18%
SGA Expense	1,170,763,000	1,120,833,000	1,061,964,000	976,856,000	848,446,000	735,229,000
Net Income	147,065,000	93,999,000	93,004,000	113,992,000	100,209,000	82,394,000
Operating Cash Flow	384,857,000	141,047,000	198,288,000	52,372,000	-75,322,000	199,316,000
Capital Expenditure	156,521,000	120,252,000	150,392,000	102,858,000	88,491,000	60,558,000
EBITDA	391,468,000	325,577,000	298,051,000	308,359,000	261,530,000	220,566,000
Return on Assets %	3.18%	2.11%	2.33%	3.18%	3.64%	3.52%
Return on Equity %	15.27%	9.53%	9.23%	11.50%	12.01%	10.35%
Debt to Equity	1.30	1.31	1.03	0.64	0.64	0.59

CONTACT INFORMATION:
Phone: 713 647-5700   Fax: 713 647-5858
Toll-Free:
Address: 800 Gessner, Ste. 500, Houston, TX 77024 United States

STOCK TICKER/OTHER:
Stock Ticker: GPI   Exchange: NYS
Employees: 13,500   Fiscal Year Ends: 12/31
Parent Company:

SALARIES/BONUSES:
Top Exec. Salary: $1,100,000   Bonus: $
Second Exec. Salary: Bonus: $
$583,500

OTHER THOUGHTS:
Estimated Female Officers or Directors:
Hot Spot for Advancement for Women/Minorities: Y

Hanesbrands Inc

www.hanesbrands.com

NAIC Code: 424300

TYPES OF BUSINESS:
Apparel and Clothing Brands, Designers, Importers and Distributors
Outerwear
Hosiery
Internet Sales
Catalogs

BRANDS/DIVISIONS/AFFILIATES:
Champion
Hanes
Playtex
Lilyette
Just My Size
Wonderbra
Maidenform
Knights Apparel

CONTACTS: Note: Officers with more than one job title may be intentionally listed here more than once.
Gerald Evans, CEO
Richard Noll, Chairman of the Board
M. Scott Lewis, Chief Accounting Officer
Joia Johnson, General Counsel
Elizabeth Burger, Other Executive Officer
Michael Faircloth, Other Executive Officer
John Marsh, President, Divisional
W. Upchurch, President, Divisional

GROWTH PLANS/SPECIAL FEATURES:
Hanesbrands, Inc. designs, manufactures, sources and sells apparel including t-shirts, bras, panties, men's underwear, kids' underwear, socks, hosiery, casual wear and active wear. The company is organized into four operating segments: innerwear, which accounted for 43% of its 2016 revenue; activewear, 26%; direct-to-consumer, 5%; and international, 26%. Hanesbrands' innerwear segment produces bras, panties, men's underwear, kids' underwear and socks marketed under the Hanes, Playtex, Bali, Just My Size, Maidenform, L'eggs, Lilyette, Donna Karan and Wonderbra brands. Hanesbrands also maintains a licensing agreement with Polo Ralph Lauren to produce underwear. The activewearwear segment produces t-shirts, fleece, athletic uniforms, thermals sleepwear and casual wear marketed under the Hanes, Champion, Hanes Beefy-T, Duofold and Just My Size brands. The direct-to-consumer segment operates 252 outlet stores as well as catalogs and e-commerce channels. The international segment includes sales in Europe, Asia, Latin America, Canada, Australia, the Middle East, Africa and the Caribbean, with the company's largest international markets comprising Europe, Canada, Japan, Mexico, Brazil and Australia. Its largest customers are Wal-Mart and Target, which accounted for 20% and 15%, respectively, of total revenue. Hanesbrands engages in manufacturing through both company-owned and operated facilities and third-party contractors. The firm's design, research and product development activities are primarily located in a North Carolina facility, with some activities in New York City and Lenexa, Kansas. In July 2016, the company acquired Pacific Brands Limited, an intimate apparel and underwear company in Australia. Additionally, in December 2016, the firm divested its Australian Dunlop Flooring and Tontine pillow business, a noncore operation acquired from Pacific Brands.

FINANCIAL DATA: Note: Data for latest year may not have been available at press time.

In U.S. $	2016	2015	2014	2013	2012	2011
Revenue	6,028,199,000	5,731,549,000	5,324,746,000	4,627,802,000	4,525,721,000	4,637,143,000
R&D Expense						
Operating Income	775,649,000	595,118,000	563,954,000	515,186,000	440,115,000	478,281,000
Operating Margin %	12.86%	10.38%	10.59%	11.13%	9.72%	10.31%
SGA Expense	1,500,399,000	1,541,214,000	1,340,453,000	1,096,507,000	979,932,000	1,062,090,000
Net Income	539,382,000	428,855,000	404,519,000	330,494,000	164,681,000	266,688,000
Operating Cash Flow	605,607,000	227,007,000	508,090,000	591,281,000	548,902,000	167,957,000
Capital Expenditure	83,399,000	99,375,000	64,311,000	43,627,000	40,994,000	90,099,000
EBITDA	878,824,000	699,021,000	662,156,000	606,076,000	533,151,000	569,006,000
Return on Assets %	8.61%	7.91%	8.68%	8.56%	4.29%	6.81%
Return on Equity %	43.15%	32.21%	30.91%	31.21%	21.00%	42.88%
Debt to Equity	2.86	1.76	1.16	1.19	1.48	2.65

CONTACT INFORMATION:
Phone: 336 519-8080   Fax: 312 726-3712
Toll-Free:
Address: 1000 E. Hanes Mill Rd., Winston-Salem, NC 27105 United States

STOCK TICKER/OTHER:
Stock Ticker: HBI
Employees: 67,800
Parent Company:

Exchange: NYS
Fiscal Year Ends: 12/31

SALARIES/BONUSES:
Top Exec. Salary: $1,200,000   Bonus: $
Second Exec. Salary: $912,500   Bonus: $

OTHER THOUGHTS:
Estimated Female Officers or Directors: 4
Hot Spot for Advancement for Women/Minorities: Y

Harris Corporation

NAIC Code: 334220

TYPES OF BUSINESS:

Communications Equipment Manufacturing
Wireless Communications Equipment
Healthcare IT Systems
Managed Satellite Communications
Integrated IT Systems

BRANDS/DIVISIONS/AFFILIATES:

Single Channel Ground and Airborne Radio System

CONTACTS: Note: Officers with more than one job title may be intentionally listed here more than once.

William Brown, CEO
Rahul Ghai, CFO
Todd Taylor, Chief Accounting Officer
Scott Mikuen, General Counsel
Dana Mehnert, Other Executive Officer
Christopher Young, President, Divisional
Carl DAlessandro, President, Divisional
Edward Zoiss, President, Divisional
William Gattle, President, Divisional
Robert Duffy, Senior VP, Divisional
Sheldon Fox, Senior VP, Divisional

GROWTH PLANS/SPECIAL FEATURES:

Harris Corporation is an international communications and information technology company. The firm, along with its subsidiaries, serves government and commercial markets in over 125 countries. Harris operates through four divisions: communication systems, space and intelligence systems, electronic systems and critical networks. The communication systems segment is a global supplier of secure radio communications products and systems for defense and government operations, and also performs advanced research, primarily for the U.S. Department of Defense and for international customers in government, defense and peacekeeping organizations. Its products include the Single Channel Ground and Airborne Radio System (SINCGARS), a widely-used radio system. Its space and intelligence systems provide complete Earth observation, environmental, geospatial, space protection and intelligence solutions from advanced sensors and payloads, as well as ground processing and information analytics for national security, defense, civil and commercial customers. Products include space antenna systems and reflectors. It also provides optic, environmental and geospatial solutions. The electronic systems segment offers a portfolio of electronic warfare, avionics, wireless technology, C4I and undersea systems for aviation, defense and maritime applications. It offers electronic warfare solutions such as sensor fusion for multispectral situational awareness, ESM systems for threat detection, radar systems and satellite-based communication systems. The critical networks division provides managed services supporting air traffic management, energy and maritime communications, and ground network operation and sustainment, as well as IT and engineering services, to government and commercial customers. In April 2016, the firm sold its aerostructures business to Albany International Corp. In January 2017, Harris Corporation sold its CapRock Communications business to SpeedCast International Limited. Additionally, in January 2017, the company agreed to sell its government IT services division to Veritas Capital.

The firm offers employees benefits including medical, dental and vision insurance; a 401(k); paid time off; tuition reimbursement; and health and dependent care spending accounts.

FINANCIAL DATA: Note: Data for latest year may not have been available at press time.

In U.S. $	2016	2015	2014	2013	2012	2011
Revenue	7,467,000,000	5,083,000,000	5,012,000,000	5,111,700,000	5,451,300,000	5,924,600,000
R&D Expense						
Operating Income	1,149,000,000	713,000,000	881,900,000	812,200,000	941,100,000	970,200,000
Operating Margin %	15.38%	14.02%	17.59%	15.88%	17.26%	16.37%
SGA Expense	1,186,000,000	1,008,000,000	819,600,000	914,500,000	940,900,000	1,143,900,000
Net Income	324,000,000	334,000,000	534,800,000	113,000,000	30,600,000	588,000,000
Operating Cash Flow	924,000,000	854,000,000	849,200,000	833,000,000	852,900,000	833,100,000
Capital Expenditure	152,000,000	148,000,000	212,600,000	178,200,000	233,800,000	324,900,000
EBITDA	1,155,000,000	851,000,000	1,093,300,000	994,300,000	1,215,400,000	1,183,100,000
Return on Assets %	2.57%	3.69%	10.92%	2.16%	.52%	10.78%
Return on Equity %	10.04%	12.78%	31.57%	6.45%	1.37%	25.06%
Debt to Equity	1.34	1.48	0.86	1.01	0.97	0.75

CONTACT INFORMATION:

Phone: 321 727-9100   Fax: 321 724-3973
Toll-Free: 800-442-7747
Address: 1025 W. NASA Blvd., Melbourne, FL 32919 United States

STOCK TICKER/OTHER:

Stock Ticker: HRS   Exchange: NYS
Employees: 22,300   Fiscal Year Ends: 06/30
Parent Company:

SALARIES/BONUSES:

Top Exec. Salary: $1,172,913   Bonus: $
Second Exec. Salary: Bonus: $
$527,770

OTHER THOUGHTS:

Estimated Female Officers or Directors: 2
Hot Spot for Advancement for Women/Minorities: Y

Hartford Financial Services Group Inc (The) www.thehartford.com

NAIC Code: 524113

TYPES OF BUSINESS:

Life Insurance
Mutual Funds
Property & Casualty Insurance
Group Life & Accident Insurance
Reinsurance
Employee Benefits Administration
Asset Management
Bank Holding Company

BRANDS/DIVISIONS/AFFILIATES:

Hartford Life Insurance Company
Talcott Resolution
Northern Homelands Company
Lattice Strategies LLC

CONTACTS: Note: Officers with more than one job title may be intentionally listed here more than once.

Christopher Swift, CEO
Beth Bombara, CFO
Scott Lewis, Chief Accounting Officer
Kathleen Bromage, Chief Marketing Officer
Robert Rupp, Chief Risk Officer
William Bloom, Executive VP, Divisional
Martha Gervasi, Executive VP, Divisional
David Robinson, Executive VP
Brion Johnson, Executive VP
James Davey, Executive VP
John Wilcox, Other Executive Officer
Douglas Elliot, President

GROWTH PLANS/SPECIAL FEATURES:

The Hartford Financial Services Group, Inc. is a diversified insurance and financial services company that offers insurance and investment products. Through Hartford Life Insurance Company and its many subsidiaries, it is a leading provider of investment products, individual life, group life and group disability insurance products and property and casualty insurance products in the U.S., Canada and select overseas markets. The Hartford is organized into six major divisions: commercial lines, personal lines, group benefits, mutual funds, Talcott Resolution and corporate. Commercial lines provides standard workers' compensation, property, automobile, liability, marine, livestock and umbrella coverages as well as a variety of customized insurance products and risk management services. Personal lines provides standard automobile, homeowners and home-based business coverages, including a special program designed for members of AARP. Group benefits offers group life, accident and disability coverage as well as group retiree health and voluntary benefits to individual members of employer groups. Mutual funds offers investment management, administration, distribution and related services to investors through investment products in both domestic and international markets. Talcott Resolution is comprised of run-off business from the company's U.S. annuity, international annuity and institutional and private-placement life insurance businesses. The corporate division includes Hartford's capital raising activities, including debt financing and interest expense; purchase accounting adjustments; and other expenses. In 2016, the firm acquired Northern Homelands Company; acquired Lattice Strategies, LLC; and sold its U.K. property and casualty run-off subsidiaries, Downlands Liability Management Limited and Hartford Financial Products International Limited to Catalina Holdings U.K. Limited.

The firm offers employees medical, dental and vision insurance; a wellness program; investment, savings, stock & bond purchase plans; and short- and long-term disability.

FINANCIAL DATA: Note: Data for latest year may not have been available at press time.

In U.S. $	2016	2015	2014	2013	2012	2011
Revenue	18,300,000,000	18,377,000,000	18,614,000,000	26,236,000,000	26,412,000,000	21,859,000,000
R&D Expense						
Operating Income	804,000,000	1,978,000,000	1,699,000,000	63,000,000	-527,000,000	230,000,000
Operating Margin %	4.39%	10.76%	9.12%	.24%	-1.99%	1.05%
SGA Expense	3,633,000,000	3,772,000,000	4,028,000,000	4,280,000,000	5,237,000,000	4,398,000,000
Net Income	896,000,000	1,682,000,000	798,000,000	176,000,000	-38,000,000	662,000,000
Operating Cash Flow	2,066,000,000	2,756,000,000	1,886,000,000	1,237,000,000	2,681,000,000	2,274,000,000
Capital Expenditure	224,000,000	307,000,000	121,000,000			
EBITDA						
Return on Assets %	.39%	.71%	.30%	.05%	- .02%	.19%
Return on Equity %	5.18%	9.25%	4.24%	.81%	- .36%	2.94%
Debt to Equity	0.27	0.28	0.30	0.32	0.31	0.29

CONTACT INFORMATION:

Phone: 860 547-5000   Fax: 860 720-6097
Toll-Free:
Address: 690 Asylum Ave., 1 Hartford Plaza, Hartford, CT 06115 United States

STOCK TICKER/OTHER:

Stock Ticker: HIG   Exchange: NYS
Employees: 16,900   Fiscal Year Ends: 12/31
Parent Company:

SALARIES/BONUSES:

Top Exec. Salary: $1,075,000   Bonus: $
Second Exec. Salary: $918,750   Bonus: $

OTHER THOUGHTS:

Estimated Female Officers or Directors: 1
Hot Spot for Advancement for Women/Minorities: Y

HC2 Holdings Inc

NAIC Code: 517110

www.hc2.com

TYPES OF BUSINESS:

International & Long-Distance Telephone Service
Internet Service Provider
Cellular Phone Service
Prepaid Calling Cards
Virtual Private Networks
Managed Hosting Services
e-Commerce Applications
Co-Location Services

BRANDS/DIVISIONS/AFFILIATES:

DBM Global Inc
Global Marine Systems Limited
American Natural Gas
Continental Insurance Group Ltd
Continental General Insurance Company
PTGi-International Carrier Services Inc
Pansend Life Sciences Ltd
MediBeacon Inc

CONTACTS: Note: Officers with more than one job title may be intentionally listed here more than once.

Andrea Mancuso, Assistant General Counsel
Philip Falcone, CEO
Michael Sena, CFO
Suzi Herbst, Chief Administrative Officer
Andrew Backman, Managing Director, Divisional
Paul Voigt, Other Corporate Officer
Paul Robinson, Other Executive Officer

GROWTH PLANS/SPECIAL FEATURES:

HC2 Holdings, Inc. is a diversified holding company that operates in six primary business segments: construction, marine services, energy, insurance, telecommunications and life sciences. These business segments are carried out through the company's subsidiaries. DBM Global, Inc. makes up the firm's construction segment, and is a fully integrated fabricator and erector of structural steel and heavy steel plate for commercial and industrial construction projects. Global Marine Systems Limited (GMSL) makes up HC2's marine services segment, offering global offshore engineering with a focus on specialist subsea services across the market sectors of telecommunications, oil & gas and offshore power. American Natural Gas (ANG) makes up the energy segment. It is a premier retailer of compressed natural gas which designs, builds, owns, operates and maintains natural gas fueling stations for transportation. Continental Insurance Group Ltd. provides a platform for HC2's run-off long-term care business, which is performed through the insurance company: Continental General Insurance Company. PTGi-International Carrier Services, Inc. provides internet-based protocol and time-division multiplexing access, and provides transport of long distance voice minutes. Last, Pansend Life Sciences Ltd. focuses on supporting health care and biotechnology product development. In June 2016, HC2 subsidiary MediBeacon, Inc. acquired Mannheim Pharma & Diagnostics, a life science company based in Mannheim, Germany.

FINANCIAL DATA: Note: Data for latest year may not have been available at press time.

In U.S. $	2016	2015	2014	2013	2012	2011
Revenue	1,558,126,000	1,120,806,000	543,202,000	230,686,000	260,554,000	989,259,000
R&D Expense						
Operating Income	-1,421,000	2,229,000	-14,426,000	-39,136,000	-8,663,000	12,751,000
Operating Margin %	-.09%	.19%	-2.65%	-16.96%	-3.32%	1.28%
SGA Expense	152,890,000	111,957,000	81,396,000	34,692,000	102,760,000	214,585,000
Net Income	-94,549,000	-35,565,000	-12,107,000	111,606,000	27,887,000	-38,730,000
Operating Cash Flow	79,148,000	-32,561,000	32,813,000	-20,315,000	23,569,000	42,932,000
Capital Expenditure	29,048,000	21,324,000	5,819,000	12,577,000	31,747,000	31,533,000
EBITDA	26,445,000	23,333,000	-17,524,000	-1,082,000	16,810,000	70,454,000
Return on Assets %	-3.77%	-2.29%	-3.48%	57.40%	6.60%	-7.31%
Return on Equity %	-152.47%	-55.40%	-27.16%	181.60%	34.37%	-44.73%
Debt to Equity	9.69	3.95	6.68		1.85	2.62

CONTACT INFORMATION:

Phone: 703-865-0700   Fax:
Toll-Free:
Address: 505 Huntmar Park Dr., Ste. 325, Herndon, VA 20170 United States

STOCK TICKER/OTHER:

Stock Ticker: HCHC
Employees: 2,744
Parent Company:

Exchange: NYS
Fiscal Year Ends: 12/31

SALARIES/BONUSES:

Top Exec. Salary: $229,615   Bonus: $600,000
Second Exec. Salary: $294,231   Bonus: $150,000

OTHER THOUGHTS:

Estimated Female Officers or Directors:
Hot Spot for Advancement for Women/Minorities:

HCA Holdings Inc

NAIC Code: 622110

www.hcahealthcare.com

TYPES OF BUSINESS:

General Medical and Surgical Hospitals
Outpatient Surgery Centers
Sub-Acute Care
Psychiatric Hospitals
Rehabilitation Services
Hospital Management Services

BRANDS/DIVISIONS/AFFILIATES:

CONTACTS: *Note: Officers with more than one job title may be intentionally listed here more than once.*

R. Johnson, CEO
Victor Campbell, Senior VP
William Rutherford, CFO
Martin Paslick, Chief Information Officer
Jonathan Perlin, Chief Medical Officer
Samuel Hazen, COO
Robert Waterman, General Counsel
Joseph Sowell, Other Executive Officer
Alan Yuspeh, Other Executive Officer
Jane Englebright, Other Executive Officer
Jon Foster, President, Divisional
A. Moore, President, Divisional
Michael Cuffe, President, Divisional
Charles Hall, President, Divisional
Jana Davis, Senior VP, Divisional
Ravi Chari, Senior VP, Divisional
Sandra Morgan, Senior VP, Divisional

GROWTH PLANS/SPECIAL FEATURES:

HCA Holdings, Inc. owns and operates approximately 170 hospitals and 118 freestanding surgery centers in 20 states and the U.K. The company's acute care hospitals provide a full range of services, including internal medicine, general surgery, neurosurgery, orthopedics, obstetrics, cardiac care, diagnostic services, emergency services, radiology, respiratory therapy, cardiology and physical therapy. The psychiatric hospitals provide therapeutic programs including child, adolescent and adult psychiatric care and adult and adolescent alcohol and drug abuse treatment and counseling. The outpatient healthcare facilities operated by HCA include surgery centers, diagnostic and imaging centers, comprehensive outpatient rehabilitation and physical therapy centers. The company's hospitals do not engage in extensive medical research and education programs; however, some facilities are affiliated with medical schools and may participate in the clinical rotation of medical interns and residents. In addition, HCA provides a variety of management services to healthcare facilities such as patient safety programs; ethics and compliance programs; national supply contracts; equipment purchasing and leasing contracts; and accounting, financial and clinical systems. Other services include governmental reimbursement assistance, construction planning and coordination, information technology systems, legal counsel, human resource services and internal audit. In May 2017, the firm agreed to acquire three Houston hospitals from Tenet Healthcare; and agreed to acquire two Texas hospitals from Community Health Systems.

Employee benefits include medical, vision and dental coverage; a 401(k); life insurance; disability; and financial education resources.

FINANCIAL DATA: *Note: Data for latest year may not have been available at press time.*

In U.S. $	2016	2015	2014	2013	2012	2011
Revenue	41,490,000,000	39,678,000,000	36,918,000,000	34,182,000,000	33,013,000,000	32,506,000,000
R&D Expense						
Operating Income	6,186,000,000	5,918,000,000	5,565,000,000	2,946,000,000	4,852,000,000	4,338,000,000
Operating Margin %	14.90%	14.91%	15.07%	8.61%	14.69%	13.34%
SGA Expense	18,897,000,000	18,115,000,000	16,641,000,000	15,646,000,000	15,089,000,000	13,440,000,000
Net Income	2,890,000,000	2,129,000,000	1,875,000,000	1,556,000,000	1,605,000,000	2,465,000,000
Operating Cash Flow	5,653,000,000	4,734,000,000	4,448,000,000	3,680,000,000	4,175,000,000	3,933,000,000
Capital Expenditure	2,760,000,000	2,375,000,000	2,176,000,000	1,943,000,000	1,862,000,000	1,679,000,000
EBITDA	8,483,000,000	7,526,000,000	7,044,000,000	6,547,000,000	6,371,000,000	7,063,000,000
Return on Assets %	8.69%	6.65%	6.24%	5.46%	5.83%	9.71%
Return on Equity %						
Debt to Equity						

CONTACT INFORMATION:

Phone: 615 344-9551   Fax: 615 320-2266
Toll-Free:
Address: 1 Park Plaza, Nashville, TN 37203 United States

STOCK TICKER/OTHER:

Stock Ticker: HCA   Exchange: NYS
Employees: 241,000   Fiscal Year Ends: 12/31
Parent Company:

SALARIES/BONUSES:

Top Exec. Salary: $1,391,667   Bonus: $
Second Exec. Salary: $995,834   Bonus: $

OTHER THOUGHTS:

Estimated Female Officers or Directors: 2
Hot Spot for Advancement for Women/Minorities:

Health Care Service Corporation (HCSC)

NAIC Code: 524114

www.hcsc.com

TYPES OF BUSINESS:

Insurance-Medical & Health, HMOs & PPOs
Traditional Indemnity Plans
Medicare Supplemental Health
Life Insurance
Dental & Vision Insurance
Electronic Claims & Information Network
Workers' Compensation
Retirement Services

BRANDS/DIVISIONS/AFFILIATES:

Blue Cross and Blue Shield of Illinois
Blue Cross and Blue Shield of Montana
Blue Cross and Blue Shield of Texas
Blue Cross and Blue Shield of New Mexico
Blue Cross and Blue Shield of Oklahoma
Dental Netowrk of America Inc
Availity LLC
TMG Health Inc

CONTACTS: Note: Officers with more than one job title may be intentionally listed here more than once.

Paula Steiner, CEO
Colleen Reitan, Exec.VP-Plan Oper.
Eric Feldstein, Sr. VP
Nazneen Razi, Chief Human Resources Officer
Stephen Ondra, Chief Medical Officer
John Cannon, Chief Admin. Officer
Deborah Dorman-Rodriguez, Corp. Sec.
Martin G. Foster, Pres., Plan Oper.
Paula A. Steiner, Chief Strategy Officer
Ross Blackstone, Contact-Media
Ted Haynes, Pres., Oklahoma Div.
Kurt Shipley, Pres., New Mexico Div.
Karen M. Atwood, Pres., Illinois Div.
Bert E. Marshall, Pres., Texas Div.

GROWTH PLANS/SPECIAL FEATURES:

Health Care Service Corporation (HCSC) is a customer-owned health insurer which operates through its Blue Cross and Blue Shield divisions in Illinois, Montana, Texas, New Mexico and Oklahoma. The company provides PPOs, HMOs, POS plans, traditional indemnity and Medicare supplemental health plans to over 15 million members. HCSC also has several subsidiaries that offer a variety of health and life insurance products and related services to employers and individuals. Through its non-Blue Cross and Blue Shield subsidiaries, the firm offers prescription drug plans, Medicare supplemental insurance, dental and vision coverage, life and disability insurance, workers' compensation, retirement services and medical financial services. One such subsidiary, Dental Network of America, Inc., functions as a third-party administrator for all company dental programs and is registered in every state except Florida. It also offers a dental discount card program. Availity, LLC, a partially-owned subsidiary, operates a healthcare clearinghouse and provides internet-based health information services. TMG Health, Inc. offers business process outsourcing (BPO) for Medicare and Medicaid. Dearborn National operates as the brand name for HCSC's ancillary benefits subsidiaries, offering group life, disability, dental, worksite and voluntary products. Other subsidiaries include Medecision, Inc.; HCSC Insurance Service Company; Prime Therapeutics, LLC; and TriWest Healthcare Alliance.

Employee benefits include medical coverage, 401(k), a pension plan, life & AD&D insurance, dependent life coverage, short- and long-term disability, educational assistance, flexible spending accounts, transportation reimbursement, group legal service, an employee assistance program, adoption assistance and a wellness program.

FINANCIAL DATA: Note: Data for latest year may not have been available at press time.

In U.S. $	2016	2015	2014	2013	2012	2011
Revenue	33,000,000,000	35,000,000,000	31,200,000,000	22,690,000,000	20,714,282,000	19,958,096,000
R&D Expense						
Operating Income						
Operating Margin %						
SGA Expense						
Net Income	106,300,000	-65,800,000	-281,000,000	684,300,000	1,007,066,000	1,203,879,000
Operating Cash Flow						
Capital Expenditure						
EBITDA						
Return on Assets %						
Return on Equity %						
Debt to Equity						

CONTACT INFORMATION:

Phone: 312-653-6000   Fax: 312-819-1220
Toll-Free: 800-654-7385
Address: 300 E. Randolph St., Chicago, IL 60601 United States

STOCK TICKER/OTHER:

Stock Ticker: Mutual Company   Exchange:
Employees: 21,000   Fiscal Year Ends: 12/31
Parent Company:

SALARIES/BONUSES:

Top Exec. Salary: $ Bonus: $
Second Exec. Salary: $ Bonus: $

OTHER THOUGHTS:

Estimated Female Officers or Directors: 6
Hot Spot for Advancement for Women/Minorities: Y

HealthSouth Corporation

www.healthsouth.com

NAIC Code: 622310

TYPES OF BUSINESS:

Rehabilitation Facilities
Long-term Care Hospitals
Home Health Programs

BRANDS/DIVISIONS/AFFILIATES:

CONTACTS: Note: Officers with more than one job title may be intentionally listed here more than once.

April Anthony, CEO, Subsidiary
Mark Tarr, CEO
Douglas Coltharp, CFO
Andrew Price, Chief Accounting Officer
Elissa Charbonneau, Chief Medical Officer
Leo Higdon, Director
Barbara Jacobsmeyer, Executive VP, Divisional
Cheryl Levy, Other Executive Officer
John Darby, Secretary
Edmund Fay, Senior VP

GROWTH PLANS/SPECIAL FEATURES:

HealthSouth Corporation is a major provider of post-acute healthcare services. The company offers both facility-based and home-based post-acute services in 35 U.S. states and Puerto Rico through its network of inpatient rehabilitation hospitals, home health agencies and hospice agencies. HealthSouth manages its operations via two segments: inpatient rehabilitation, and home health and hospice. Inpatient rehabilitation comprises 123 hospitals with more than 8,500 licensed beds. This segment provides specialized rehabilitation treatment on both an inpatient and outpatient basis. Inpatient rehabilitation hospitals offer specialized rehabilitative care across an array of diagnosis and deliver comprehensive, high-quality, cost-effective patient care services. During 2016, this segment discharged more than 165,000 patients and had over 640,700 outpatient visits. Home health and hospice comprises 186 home health locations and 35 hospice locations. It is the nation's fourth largest provider of Medicare-certified home nursing services to adult patients in need of care. These services include, among others, skilled nursing, physical/occupational/speech therapy, medical social work and home health aide services. Home health admitted more than 106,000 patients and home hospice admitted 3,337 patients in 2016. In November 2016, HealthSouth sold seven pediatric home health locations.

The firm offers employees medical, dental and vision insurance; flexible spending accounts; life and disability insurance; a 401(k) plan; a 529 college savings plan; pre-paid legal services; and an employee assistance plan.

FINANCIAL DATA: Note: Data for latest year may not have been available at press time.

In U.S. $	2016	2015	2014	2013	2012	2011
Revenue	3,646,000,000	3,115,700,000	2,374,300,000	2,247,200,000	2,134,900,000	2,026,900,000
R&D Expense						
Operating Income	648,800,000	546,700,000	467,400,000	482,300,000	416,900,000	386,400,000
Operating Margin %	17.79%	17.54%	19.68%	21.46%	19.52%	19.06%
SGA Expense	2,332,500,000	1,997,200,000	1,449,300,000	1,347,200,000	1,331,700,000	1,252,400,000
Net Income	247,600,000	183,100,000	222,000,000	323,600,000	185,000,000	208,700,000
Operating Cash Flow	605,500,000	484,800,000	444,900,000	470,300,000	411,500,000	342,700,000
Capital Expenditure	202,900,000	156,500,000	187,900,000	216,500,000	159,700,000	109,100,000
EBITDA	826,700,000	678,200,000	603,800,000	590,300,000	516,600,000	441,100,000
Return on Assets %	5.33%	4.52%	7.25%	9.31%	6.82%	7.86%
Return on Equity %	36.75%	33.46%	59.53%	230.07%		
Debt to Equity	4.04	5.12	4.46	5.98		

CONTACT INFORMATION:

Phone: 205 967-7116   Fax: 205 969-4740
Toll-Free: 800-765-4772
Address: 3660 Grandview Pkwy., Ste. 200, Birmingham, AL 35243
United States

STOCK TICKER/OTHER:

Stock Ticker: HLS   Exchange: NYS
Employees: 27,968   Fiscal Year Ends: 12/31
Parent Company:

SALARIES/BONUSES:

Top Exec. Salary: $1,000,000   Bonus: $
Second Exec. Salary: Bonus: $
$645,833

OTHER THOUGHTS:

Estimated Female Officers or Directors: 8
Hot Spot for Advancement for Women/Minorities: Y

Heartland Payment Systems Inc
www.heartlandpaymentsystems.com

NAIC Code: 522320

TYPES OF BUSINESS:

Financial Processing Services
Credit/Debit Processing
Payroll Processing Services
Processing Equipment Provider
Micropayments

BRANDS/DIVISIONS/AFFILIATES:

Global Payments Inc
Heartland Payroll Company
Heartland Marketing Solutions
HPS Exchange

CONTACTS: Note: Officers with more than one job title may be intentionally listed here more than once.

Jeffrey Sloan, CEO
David Mangum, COO
Samir Zabaneh, CFO
Cameron Bready, CFO
Jane Elliot, Chief Administrative Offer
Guido Sacchi, CIO
Charles Kallenbach, General Counsel
David Gilbert, President, Divisional
Michael Lawler, President, Divisional
Robert Baldwin, Vice Chairman

GROWTH PLANS/SPECIAL FEATURES:

Heartland Payment Systems, Inc. (HPS), a wholly-owned subsidiary of Global Payments, Inc., is a provider of credit/debit card, payroll and other associated processing services to more than 300,000 U.S. bankcard merchants. HPS primarily serves restaurant, hospitality, hotel and retail merchants throughout the U.S. The firm's services include credit/debit card processing, payroll services and the HPS Exchange, while products include gift cards (with company logos), terminals, printers and other processing equipment. Its credit/debit card processing services allow clients to extend a variety of payment options to customers; the firm processes all major credit cards, including Visa, MasterCard, American Express, Diners Club, JCB and Discover, 24 hours per day, 365 days a year. The company's payroll services, which it provides through Heartland Payroll Company, entail calculation of payroll checks (which includes taxes, voluntary reductions, retirement plans and direct deposit), tax returns/filing concerns and additional services, such as reimbursement checks and automated check signing. The HPS Exchange is a company-developed transaction processing platform with added features unique to HPS. The platform features fast transaction processing, customized reports/receipts and online merchant management, which allows retailers to immediately view transaction processing details in real time. Additional products and services offered by the firm include K-12 school solutions, primarily school nutrition programs and point of sale (POS) systems at over 34,000 schools; micropayment services; campus solutions, which include networked payment solutions for college campuses; and loyalty and Heartland Marketing Solutions, which comprise loyalty and gift card programs. In April 2016, the merger between the company and Global Payments, Inc., was completed.

HPS offers its employees health, dental and life insurance; short- and long-term disability; flexible spending and dependent care accounts; and the option to add additional life insurance for spouses and dependents.

FINANCIAL DATA: Note: Data for latest year may not have been available at press time.

In U.S. $	2016	2015	2014	2013	2012	2011
Revenue	2,550,500,000	2,682,395,904	2,311,380,992	2,135,372,032	2,013,436,032	1,985,577,000
R&D Expense						
Operating Income						
Operating Margin %						
SGA Expense						
Net Income		84,732,000	33,879,000	78,626,000	65,889,000	43,939,000
Operating Cash Flow						
Capital Expenditure						
EBITDA						
Return on Assets %						
Return on Equity %						
Debt to Equity						

CONTACT INFORMATION:

Phone: 609 683-3831   Fax: 609 683-3815
Toll-Free: 888-963-3600
Address: 90 Nassau St., Princeton, NJ 08542 United States

STOCK TICKER/OTHER:

Stock Ticker: Subsidiary   Exchange:
Employees: 3,734   Fiscal Year Ends: 12/31
Parent Company: Global Payments Inc

SALARIES/BONUSES:

Top Exec. Salary: $ Bonus: $
Second Exec. Salary: $ Bonus: $

OTHER THOUGHTS:

Estimated Female Officers or Directors: 2
Hot Spot for Advancement for Women/Minorities:

HEB Grocery Company LP

NAIC Code: 445110

www.heb.com

TYPES OF BUSINESS:
Supermarkets
Grocery Stores
Gourmet Food Stores
Dairy Processing
Bakery
Pharmacy Services

BRANDS/DIVISIONS/AFFILIATES:
H-E-B
Central Market
H-E-B plus!
Joe V's Smart Shop
Temple Retail Support Center

CONTACTS: *Note: Officers with more than one job title may be intentionally listed here more than once.*
Craig Boyan, CEO
Craig Boyan, COO
Craig Boyan, Pres.
Martin Otto, CFO
Judy Lindquist, General Counsel
Lynette Padalecki, VP-Corp. Planning & Analysis
Winell Herron, VP-Public Affairs & Diversity
Scott McClelland, Pres., Houston Food & Drug Stores Div.
Suzanne Wade, Pres., San Antonio Food & Drug Stores Div.
William Fry, VP-Quality Assurance & Environmental Affairs
Roxanne Orsak, Exec. VP-Drug
Mike Graham, Sr. VP-Logistics & Supply Chain

GROWTH PLANS/SPECIAL FEATURES:

HEB Grocery Company, LP is one of the largest regional food retailers in the southwestern U.S. and Mexico. It operates over 355 grocery stores in 150 communities in Texas and Mexico under the H-E-B brand name. The firm owns one of the largest milk plants in Texas as well as a large bread bakery, a meat plant, a pastry bakery, an ice cream plant, a chip plant and a photo processing lab. The stores carry a wide variety of merchandise, including a line of products under the H-E-B brand. H-E-B also operates nine Central Market stores, with locations in Houston, Dallas, Fort Worth, Plano, San Antonio, Southlake and Austin. Central Markets are gourmet specialty stores featuring large prepared foods-to-go areas, eat-in areas, comprehensive wine departments, specialty butcher and fish counters, a European bakery, a deli with meats, a large selection of cheeses from around the globe and a juice and ice cream bar. H-E-B plus! stores offer additional departments including Cook & Grill, Card & Party and a Tortilleria. The firm also owns a series of seven discount stores in the Houston and Baytown, Texas area known as Joe V's Smart Shop. HEB Grocery owns and operates a retail support center in Monterrey, Mexico, as well as the Temple Retail Support Center, a 450,000-square-foot warehouse and transportation facility in central Texas.

Employees of the firm are offered a variety of benefits, including discounts on groceries and a prescription plan. In 2015, the company launched a benefit whereby qualified employees receive an annual grant of shares of nonvoting stock equal to 3% of wages.

FINANCIAL DATA: *Note: Data for latest year may not have been available at press time.*

In U.S. $	2016	2015	2014	2013	2012	2011
Revenue	24,000,000,000	23,000,000,000	22,000,000,000	20,400,000,000	19,750,000,000	19,125,000,000
R&D Expense						
Operating Income						
Operating Margin %						
SGA Expense						
Net Income						
Operating Cash Flow						
Capital Expenditure						
EBITDA						
Return on Assets %						
Return on Equity %						
Debt to Equity						

CONTACT INFORMATION:
Phone: 210-938-8000   Fax: 210-938-8169
Toll-Free: 800-432-3113
Address: 646 S. Main Ave, San Antonio, TX 78204 United States

STOCK TICKER/OTHER:
Stock Ticker: Private   Exchange:
Employees: 98,000   Fiscal Year Ends: 10/31
Parent Company:

SALARIES/BONUSES:
Top Exec. Salary: $ Bonus: $
Second Exec. Salary: $ Bonus: $

OTHER THOUGHTS:
Estimated Female Officers or Directors: 5
Hot Spot for Advancement for Women/Minorities: Y

Hendrick Automotive Group

www.hendrickauto.com

NAIC Code: 441110

TYPES OF BUSINESS:

Auto Dealers
Parts & Service
Accessories
Racing & Motorsports

BRANDS/DIVISIONS/AFFILIATES:

Hendrick Autoguard
Hendrick Marrow Program
Hendrick Motorsports

CONTACTS: *Note: Officers with more than one job title may be intentionally listed here more than once.*

Edward J. Brown, III, CEO
Edward J. Brown, III, Pres.
Brian Williams, VP-Mktg. & Advertising
Veronica Zayatz, VP-Acct., Audits & Taxes
Rick Hendrick, Chmn.

GROWTH PLANS/SPECIAL FEATURES:

Hendrick Automotive Group sells new and used automobiles from 29 automakers such as Acura, Lincoln, Subaru, Toyota, Ford, Audi, KIA, Fiat, Scion, Hyundai, Honda, GMC, Porsche, BMW, Cadillac and Volvo. It boasts a network of 102 dealerships in 14 states across the U.S., as well as 143 franchise locations. The firm's automobile offerings include cars as well as light trucks. Hendrick Automotive offers other services, including financing, maintenance, body repair and parts and accessories. The group has 30 collision centers and four accessories distributor installers located across the U.S. Customers can access a database of pre-owned and new cars on the company web site. Through Hendrick Autoguard, the company offers warranty and vehicle protection plans for new and used cars and trucks. Hendrick Automotive also supports charitable operations including the Hendrick Marrow Program, which recruits potential matching marrow donors, raises funds for tissue typing and offers support for those suffering from leukemia and other blood-related diseases. In addition, Hendrick Automotive operates Hendrick Motorsports, which sponsors a number of NASCAR teams.

FINANCIAL DATA: *Note: Data for latest year may not have been available at press time.*

In U.S. $	2016	2015	2014	2013	2012	2011
Revenue	8,551,253,132	7,088,366,765	7,500,000,000	7,000,000,000	5,900,000,000	4,900,000,000
R&D Expense						
Operating Income						
Operating Margin %						
SGA Expense						
Net Income						
Operating Cash Flow						
Capital Expenditure						
EBITDA						
Return on Assets %						
Return on Equity %						
Debt to Equity						

CONTACT INFORMATION:

Phone: 704-568-5550   Fax: 704-566-3295
Toll-Free:
Address: 6000 Monroe Rd., Ste. 100, Charlotte, NC 28212 United States

STOCK TICKER/OTHER:

Stock Ticker: Private   Exchange:
Employees: 13,500   Fiscal Year Ends: 12/31
Parent Company:

SALARIES/BONUSES:

Top Exec. Salary: $ Bonus: $
Second Exec. Salary: $ Bonus: $

OTHER THOUGHTS:

Estimated Female Officers or Directors: 1
Hot Spot for Advancement for Women/Minorities:

Henry Schein Inc

www.henryschein.com

NAIC Code: 423450

TYPES OF BUSINESS:

Health Care Products Distribution
Dental Supplies Distribution
Veterinary Products Distribution
Electronic Catalogs

BRANDS/DIVISIONS/AFFILIATES:

Henry Schein Animal Health
Oasis
Dentrix
EXACT
Easy Dental
DVM Manager
AVImark
Southern Anesthesia + Surgical

CONTACTS: Note: Officers with more than one job title may be intentionally listed here more than once.

James Breslawski, CEO, Divisional
Michael Ettinger, Secretary
Karen Prange, CEO, Divisional
Stanley Bergman, CEO
Steven Paladino, CFO
Gerald Benjamin, Chief Administrative Officer
James Harding, Chief Technology Officer
Mark Mlotek, Director
Walter Siegel, General Counsel
David McKinley, Other Executive Officer
Michael Racioppi, Other Executive Officer
Robert Minowitz, President, Divisional
Peter McCarthy, President, Divisional
Bridget Ross, President, Divisional
Lorelei McGlynn, Senior VP, Divisional
Paul Rose, Senior VP, Divisional
Paul Rose, Senior VP, Divisional

GROWTH PLANS/SPECIAL FEATURES:

Henry Schein, Inc. distributes products and services to office-based healthcare practitioners in North America and Europe. The firm has more than 1 million customers worldwide and distributes more than 120,000 national and Henry Schein private-brand products and 180,000 special-order items. The company operates in two segments: healthcare distribution and technology. The healthcare distribution segment, which accounts for roughly 96.3% of annual revenue, aggregates the dental, medical and animal health divisions. This segment distributes branded and generic pharmaceuticals, small equipment, laboratory products, large dental equipment, consumable products, infection-control products, vaccines, diagnostic tests, surgical products and vitamins. Through Henry Schein Animal Health, a majority-owned subsidiary, the firm distributes animal health products in Europe as well as the U.S., Australia and New Zealand. The technology segment provides software, technology and other value-added services to healthcare practitioners, primarily in the U.S. and Canada. Value-added solutions include practice-management software systems for dental and medical practitioners and animal health clinics. Practice-management software solutions include Oasis, Dentrix, EXACT and Easy Dental for dental practices; DVM Manager and AVImark for veterinary clinics; and MicroMD for physician usage. The technology group also provides financial services and continuing education for practitioners. In May 2017, the firm acquired Southern Anesthesia + Surgical, a U.S. distributor of anesthesia and surgical supplies to oral surgeons, dental anesthesiologists and periodontists.

The company offers employees medical, dental, vision, life, AD&D and disability insurance; flexible spending accounts; 401(k); college savings plan; tuition assistance; and paid time off.

FINANCIAL DATA: Note: Data for latest year may not have been available at press time.

In U.S. $	2016	2015	2014	2013	2012	2011
Revenue	11,571,670,000	10,629,720,000	10,371,390,000	9,560,647,000	8,939,967,000	8,530,242,000
R&D Expense						
Operating Income	771,574,000	733,972,000	715,142,000	677,054,000	618,961,000	582,149,000
Operating Margin %	6.66%	6.90%	6.89%	7.08%	6.92%	6.82%
SGA Expense	2,416,504,000	2,243,356,000	2,196,173,000	1,978,960,000	1,873,360,000	1,835,906,000
Net Income	506,778,000	479,058,000	466,077,000	431,554,000	388,076,000	367,661,000
Operating Cash Flow	615,461,000	586,841,000	592,504,000	664,175,000	408,099,000	554,625,000
Capital Expenditure	70,179,000	71,684,000	82,116,000	60,215,000	51,237,000	45,176,000
EBITDA	957,508,000	905,893,000	885,607,000	820,267,000	760,412,000	715,580,000
Return on Assets %	7.65%	7.57%	7.92%	7.87%	7.70%	7.91%
Return on Equity %	17.85%	16.81%	16.64%	15.98%	15.38%	15.18%
Debt to Equity	0.25	0.16	0.19	0.16	0.18	0.14

CONTACT INFORMATION:

Phone: 631 843-5500   Fax: 631 843-5665
Toll-Free:
Address: 135 Duryea Rd., Melville, NY 11747 United States

STOCK TICKER/OTHER:

Stock Ticker: HSIC   Exchange: NAS
Employees: 21,000   Fiscal Year Ends: 12/31
Parent Company:

SALARIES/BONUSES:

Top Exec. Salary: $1,342,385   Bonus: $
Second Exec. Salary: Bonus: $400,000
$410,000

OTHER THOUGHTS:

Estimated Female Officers or Directors: 6
Hot Spot for Advancement for Women/Minorities: Y

Hershey Co

NAIC Code: 311351

www.hersheys.com

TYPES OF BUSINESS:

Candy Manufacturing
Baking Supplies
Chocolate Products
Confectionaries & Snacks
Amusement Parks
Resorts/Hotels

BRANDS/DIVISIONS/AFFILIATES:

Kit Kat
Reese's
Hershey Kisses
Hershey's Chocolate World
Scharffen Berger
Artisan Confections Company
Hershey India Confectionery Private Limited
barkTHINS

CONTACTS: Note: Officers with more than one job title may be intentionally listed here more than once.

Michele Buck, CEO
Javier Idrovo, Chief Accounting Officer
D. Wege, Chief Administrative Officer
Waheed Zaman, Chief Technology Officer
John Bilbrey, Director
Leslie Turner, General Counsel
Terence ODay, Other Executive Officer
Kevin Walling, Other Executive Officer
Patricia Little, Senior VP

GROWTH PLANS/SPECIAL FEATURES:

Hershey Co. is one of the largest candy makers in the U.S., manufacturing more than 80 brand names in the chocolate, sweets and refreshment business. The company's products are marketed in approximately 70 countries worldwide. Its operations are aggregated into two segments: North America and International & Other. Hershey's principal product groups include chocolate and non-chocolate confectionery products such as Reese's, Kit Kat, Hershey Bars and Hershey Kisses; packaged items; and grocery products, such as baking ingredients, chocolate drink mixes, peanut butter, dessert toppings and beverages. Its products are sold primarily to wholesale distributors, chain grocery stores, mass merchandisers, chain drug stores, vending companies, wholesale clubs, convenience stores, dollar stores, concessionaires, department stores and natural food stores. Its direct retail operations, including Hershey's Chocolate World in Hershey, Pennsylvania, and Hershey's retail stores in New York City, Chicago, Niagara Falls (Ontario), Shanghai, Dubai and Singapore, are managed by The Hershey Experience. Wholly-owned subsidiary Artisan Confections Company produces Scharffen Berger high-cacao dark chocolate products and Dagoba natural and organic chocolate products. Hershey also produces products in China through Lotte Shanghai Foods Company; markets its Van Houten brand products in the Middle East and Asia; and also markets through Godrej Hershey Ltd., a wholly-owned subsidiary known as Hershey India Confectionery Private Limited. In April 2016, the frim acquired Ripple Brand Collective, LLC, owner of the barkTHINS snacking chocolate bar, for an undisclosed amount.

The firm offers employees health, dental and vision insurance; an employee assistance program; life insurance; disability coverage; onsite fitness centers; gym membership reimbursement; a 401(k) plan; retirement contributions; an employee stock purchase plan; health care and dependent care spending accounts; store discounts; adoption assistance; and tuition reimbursement.

FINANCIAL DATA: Note: Data for latest year may not have been available at press time.

In U.S. $	2016	2015	2014	2013	2012	2011
Revenue	7,440,181,000	7,386,626,000	7,421,768,000	7,146,079,000	6,644,252,000	6,080,788,000
R&D Expense						
Operating Income	1,205,783,000	1,037,759,000	1,389,575,000	1,339,675,000	1,111,148,000	1,055,028,000
Operating Margin %	16.20%	14.04%	18.72%	18.74%	16.72%	17.35%
SGA Expense	1,947,904,000	2,064,114,000	1,900,970,000	1,922,508,000	1,703,796,000	1,477,750,000
Net Income	720,044,000	512,951,000	846,912,000	820,470,000	660,931,000	628,962,000
Operating Cash Flow	983,475,000	1,214,456,000	838,221,000	1,188,405,000	1,094,827,000	580,867,000
Capital Expenditure	269,476,000	356,810,000	370,789,000	350,911,000	277,966,000	347,567,000
EBITDA	1,493,266,000	1,227,758,000	1,605,173,000	1,543,866,000	1,324,125,000	1,273,388,000
Return on Assets %	13.24%	9.34%	15.41%	16.22%	14.41%	14.48%
Return on Equity %	80.72%	41.82%	55.35%	62.11%	70.09%	71.82%
Debt to Equity	2.98	1.56	1.06	1.11	1.47	2.05

CONTACT INFORMATION:

Phone: 717 534-4200   Fax: 717 531-6161
Toll-Free: 800-468-1714
Address: 100 Crystal A Dr., Hershey, PA 17033 United States

STOCK TICKER/OTHER:

Stock Ticker: HSY   Exchange: NYS
Employees: 17,980   Fiscal Year Ends: 12/31
Parent Company:

SALARIES/BONUSES:

Top Exec. Salary: $1,240,753   Bonus: $
Second Exec. Salary: $720,352   Bonus: $

OTHER THOUGHTS:

Estimated Female Officers or Directors: 4
Hot Spot for Advancement for Women/Minorities: Y

Hibbett Sports Inc

www.hibbett.com

NAIC Code: 451110

TYPES OF BUSINESS:

Sporting Goods Stores
Sports Apparel
Athletic Shoes
Training Equipment

BRANDS/DIVISIONS/AFFILIATES:

Hibbett Sports
Hibbett Team Sales Inc
Sports Additions

CONTACTS: *Note: Officers with more than one job title may be intentionally listed here more than once.*

Jeffry Rosenthal, CEO
Scott Bowman, CFO
Michael Newsome, Chairman of the Board
Jared Briskin, Other Executive Officer
Cathy Pryor, Senior VP, Divisional

GROWTH PLANS/SPECIAL FEATURES:

Hibbett Sports, Inc. is an operator of sporting goods stores in small to mid-sized markets predominantly in the Southeast, Southwest, Midwest and Mid-Atlantic U.S. Its stores offer a broad assortment of athletic equipment, footwear and apparel. The company's merchandise assortment features a broad selection of brand name merchandise emphasizing team sports complemented by localized apparel and accessories designed to appeal to a wide range of customers. Hibbett operates a total of 1,044 stores in 33 states. The firm's primary retail format is Hibbett Sports, a 5,000-square-foot store model located in strip centers frequently near Wal-Mart stores. The firm has 20 Sports Addition stores, which are mall-based establishments averaging 2,500 square feet with roughly 90% of merchandise consisting of athletic footwear and the remainder consisting of caps and a limited assortment of apparel. Sports Additions stores offer a broader assortment of athletic footwear, with a greater emphasis on fashion than the athletic footwear choices offered by traditional Hibbett Sports stores. Subsidiary Hibbett Team Sales, Inc. supplies customized athletic apparel, equipment and footwear to school, athletic and youth programs in Georgia, Mississippi and Florida. It sells its merchandise directly to educational institutions and youth associations.

The firm offers employees life, disability, medical and dental insurance; a vision care plan; a stock purchase plan; a 401(k) plan; employee discounts; and a 529 college savings plan.

FINANCIAL DATA: *Note: Data for latest year may not have been available at press time.*

In U.S. $	2016	2015	2014	2013	2012	2011
Revenue	943,104,000	913,486,000	851,965,000	818,700,000	732,645,000	
R&D Expense						
Operating Income	112,004,000	118,146,000	113,891,000	115,981,000	93,531,000	
Operating Margin %	11.87%	12.93%	13.36%	14.16%	12.76%	
SGA Expense	203,673,000	192,648,000	181,527,000	169,872,000	155,672,000	
Net Income	70,528,000	73,584,000	70,877,000	72,582,000	59,060,000	
Operating Cash Flow	58,479,000	102,392,000	53,301,000	87,124,000	54,921,000	
Capital Expenditure	25,147,000	22,873,000	50,507,000	21,970,000	12,997,000	
EBITDA	129,073,000	134,158,000	127,749,000	129,024,000	106,761,000	
Return on Assets %	15.76%	16.94%	17.86%	21.00%	18.81%	
Return on Equity %	22.19%	23.40%	26.09%	32.77%	29.24%	
Debt to Equity						

CONTACT INFORMATION:

Phone: 205 942-4292   Fax: 205 912-7290
Toll-Free:
Address: 2700 Milan Court, Birmingham, AL 35211 United States

STOCK TICKER/OTHER:

Stock Ticker: HIBB
Employees: 9,300
Parent Company:

Exchange: NAS
Fiscal Year Ends: 01/31

SALARIES/BONUSES:

Top Exec. Salary: $515,000   Bonus: $
Second Exec. Salary: $400,000   Bonus: $

OTHER THOUGHTS:

Estimated Female Officers or Directors: 3
Hot Spot for Advancement for Women/Minorities: Y

Hillenbrand Inc

www.hillenbrandinc.com

NAIC Code: 333120

GROWTH PLANS/SPECIAL FEATURES:

Hillenbrand, Inc. is a holding company involved in funeral products and bulk solid material handling equipment. The firm operates through two primary business platforms: Batesville and process equipment group. Batesville, which includes subsidiary Batesville Casket Company, manufactures and sells non-gasketed steel, hardwood and veneer hardwood caskets as well as cloth-covered and all-wood caskets. Additional products include urns, containers and other similar products. The company's hardwood caskets are made from mahogany, cherry, walnut, maple, pile, oak, pecan, poplar and sycamore woods, and are manufactured to resist the entrance of outside elements as well as rust and corrosion. Urns and containers are primarily made of hardwoods, fiberboard, bronze, acrylic and marble. Brands within this segment include Batesville, Marsellus, Dimensions and Cremation Options. The process equipment group segment designs, produces, markets, sells and services feeders and pneumatic conveying equipment as well as equipment that is used to reduce materials in size, such as coal-crushing tools. The segment consists of four companies: Coperion Capital GmbH, which is involved in compounding and extruding equipment, bulk materials handling systems and related engineering services, as well as in feeding and pneumatic conveying equipment; Rotex Global, LLC, which manufactures separation equipment, such as gyratory and vibratory screeners and sifters; and TerraSource Global, a creator of size reduction equipment, conveying systems and screening equipment, operating under the Pennsylvania Crusher, Gundlach and Jeffrey Rader brands. In March 2017, the firm announced plans to construct a Hillenbrand Health and Wellness Center in Manchester, Tennessee, to provide wellness and primary care at no extra cost to eligible employees. The center was scheduled to open by year's end.

FINANCIAL DATA: *Note: Data for latest year may not have been available at press time.*

In U.S. $	2016	2015	2014	2013	2012	2011
Revenue	1,538,400,000	1,596,800,000	1,667,200,000	1,553,400,000	983,200,000	883,400,000
R&D Expense						
Operating Income	191,100,000	194,000,000	174,500,000	118,100,000	148,800,000	158,600,000
Operating Margin %	12.42%	12.14%	10.46%	7.60%	15.13%	17.95%
SGA Expense	346,500,000	348,300,000	414,700,000	409,100,000	240,100,000	211,300,000
Net Income	112,800,000	111,400,000	109,700,000	63,400,000	104,800,000	106,100,000
Operating Cash Flow	238,200,000	105,000,000	179,600,000	127,200,000	138,200,000	189,500,000
Capital Expenditure	21,200,000	31,000,000	23,600,000	29,900,000	20,900,000	21,900,000
EBITDA	249,800,000	240,400,000	241,600,000	207,100,000	187,700,000	204,900,000
Return on Assets %	5.98%	5.97%	5.59%	4.10%	9.24%	9.50%
Return on Equity %	18.39%	18.92%	19.05%	11.79%	22.07%	26.03%
Debt to Equity	0.94	0.87	0.93	1.15	0.53	0.97

CONTACT INFORMATION:

Phone: 812 934-7500   Fax: 812 934-7613
Toll-Free:
Address: 1 Batesville Blvd., Batesville, IN 47006 United States

STOCK TICKER/OTHER:

Stock Ticker: HI   Exchange: NYS
Employees: 6,100   Fiscal Year Ends: 09/30
Parent Company:

SALARIES/BONUSES:

Top Exec. Salary: $690,356   Bonus: $
Second Exec. Salary: Bonus: $
$493,683

OTHER THOUGHTS:

Estimated Female Officers or Directors: 3
Hot Spot for Advancement for Women/Minorities: Y

Hill-Rom Holdings Inc

www.hill-rom.com

NAIC Code: 339100

TYPES OF BUSINESS:

Equipment-Hospital Beds & Related Products
Specialized Therapy Products
Rentals

BRANDS/DIVISIONS/AFFILIATES:

Mortara Instrument Inc

CONTACTS: Note: Officers with more than one job title may be intentionally listed here more than once.

John J. Greisch, CEO
John J. Greisch, Pres.
Ken Meyers, Sr. VP
Brian Lawrence, Sr. VP

GROWTH PLANS/SPECIAL FEATURES:

Hill-Rom Holdings, Inc. is a global medical technology company. Hill-Rom partners with healthcare providers in more than 100 countries, with a focus on patient care solutions. The firm operates and manages its business within four segments, each aligned by region and/or product type: North America patient support systems, international patient support systems, front line care and surgical solutions. North America patient support systems sells and rents Hill-Rom's specialty frames, surfaces and mobility solutions, as well as its clinical workflow solutions in the U.S. and Canada. Frames and surfaces include medical surgical beds, intensive care unit beds and bariatric patient beds; and mobility solutions include lifts and other devices used to safely move patients. Clinical workflow solutions include communications technologies and software solutions. International patient support systems sells and rents similar products as the North America segment, but in regions outside the U.S. and Canada. Front line care globally sells and rents respiratory care products, and sells medical diagnostic equipment and a varied portfolio of devices that assess, diagnose, treat and manage a wide variety of illnesses and diseases. Surgical solutions sells Hill-Rom's surgical products globally, and include surgical tables, lights and pendants utilized within the operating room setting. This segment also offers a range of positioning devices for use in shoulder, hip, spinal and lithotomy surgeries, as well as platform-neutral positioning accessories for nearly every model of operating room table. In February 2017, the firm acquired Mortara Instrument, Inc., a producer of diagnostic cardiology devices. That June, it agreed to sell its Volker business, which serves the European long-term care bed market, to CoBe Capital.

FINANCIAL DATA: Note: Data for latest year may not have been available at press time.

In U.S. $	2016	2015	2014	2013	2012	2011
Revenue	2,655,200,000	1,988,200,000	1,686,100,000	1,716,200,000	1,634,300,000	1,591,700,000
R&D Expense	133,500,000	91,800,000	71,900,000	70,200,000	66,900,000	63,800,000
Operating Income	230,300,000	83,100,000	122,600,000	154,900,000	168,800,000	166,800,000
Operating Margin %	8.67%	4.17%	7.27%	9.02%	10.32%	10.47%
SGA Expense	853,300,000	664,200,000	548,300,000	549,500,000	496,400,000	502,000,000
Net Income	124,100,000	47,700,000	60,600,000	105,000,000	120,800,000	133,300,000
Operating Cash Flow	281,200,000	213,800,000	210,300,000	263,200,000	261,700,000	222,500,000
Capital Expenditure	83,300,000	121,300,000	62,700,000	65,300,000	77,800,000	68,900,000
EBITDA	437,700,000	201,700,000	231,400,000	224,700,000	281,700,000	272,100,000
Return on Assets %	2.84%	1.53%	3.62%	6.53%	8.25%	10.47%
Return on Equity %	10.45%	4.88%	7.27%	12.56%	15.54%	18.39%
Debt to Equity	1.57	1.89	0.45	0.26	0.29	0.06

CONTACT INFORMATION:

Phone: 3120819-7200   Fax:
Toll-Free:
Address: Two Prudential Plz., Ste. 4100, Chicago, IL 60601 United States

STOCK TICKER/OTHER:

Stock Ticker: HRC
Employees: 10,000
Parent Company:

Exchange: NYS
Fiscal Year Ends: 09/30

SALARIES/BONUSES:

Top Exec. Salary: $337,500   Bonus: $750,000
Second Exec. Salary: $1,065,000   Bonus: $

OTHER THOUGHTS:

Estimated Female Officers or Directors: 1
Hot Spot for Advancement for Women/Minorities: Y

Sales, profits and employees may be estimates. Financial information, benefits and other data can change quickly and may vary from those stated here.

Hilton Inc

NAIC Code: 721110

TYPES OF BUSINESS:

Hotels & Resorts
Management Services
Conference Centers
Franchising

BRANDS/DIVISIONS/AFFILIATES:

Waldorf Astoria
Hhonors
Hilton Worldwide, Inc.
Tapestry Collection by Hilton
DoubleTree
Embassy Suites
Homewood Suites
Hampton Inn

CONTACTS: Note: Officers with more than one job title may be intentionally listed here more than once.

Mark Wang, CEO, Subsidiary
Christopher Nassetta, CEO
Kevin Jacobs, CFO
Jonathan Gray, Chairman of the Board
Michael Duffy, Chief Accounting Officer
James Holthouser, Executive VP, Divisional
Kristin Campbell, Executive VP
Matthew Schuyler, Executive VP
Christopher Silcock, Executive VP
Ian Carter, Executive VP

GROWTH PLANS/SPECIAL FEATURES:

Hilton Inc. (formerly Hilton Worldwide, Inc.) is one of the largest hospitality companies in the world. Hilton Worldwide consists of more than 13 hotel brands and 4,900 hotels in 104 countries, ranging from affordable focus-service hotels to luxury extended stay suites. Hotel brands include Hilton, Hilton Garden Inn, DoubleTree, Embassy Suites, Homewood Suites, Home2 Suites, Hampton Inn, Conrad Hotels, Curio A Collection by Hilton, Tapestry Collection by Hilton, tru by Hilton, Canopy by Hilton and The Waldorf Astoria Collection. Hhonors, the firm's loyalty enrollment program for returning customers, has tens of millions of members worldwide and includes partner benefits with several airlines. In addition, Hilton offers architecture and construction and management services to individuals interested in developing their own Hilton-branded properties. In January 2017, Hilton announced the completion of the spin-offs of Park Hotels & Resorts Inc. (Park) and Hilton Grand Vacations Inc. (HGV), resulting in three independent, publicly traded companies. Park and HGV will both trade on the New York Stock Exchange.

Hilton has been recognized with awards for 100 Best Workplaces, World's 25 Best Multinational Workplaces, Best Workplaces for Women and Best Workplaces for Millennials.

FINANCIAL DATA: Note: Data for latest year may not have been available at press time.

In U.S. $	2016	2015	2014	2013	2012	2011
Revenue	11,663,000,000	11,272,000,000	10,502,000,000	9,735,000,000	9,276,000,000	8,783,000,000
R&D Expense						
Operating Income	1,861,000,000	2,071,000,000	1,673,000,000	1,102,000,000	1,100,000,000	975,000,000
Operating Margin %	15.95%	18.37%	15.93%	11.32%	11.85%	11.10%
SGA Expense	616,000,000	547,000,000	491,000,000	748,000,000	460,000,000	416,000,000
Net Income	348,000,000	1,404,000,000	673,000,000	415,000,000	352,000,000	253,000,000
Operating Cash Flow	1,350,000,000	1,394,000,000	1,366,000,000	2,101,000,000	1,110,000,000	1,167,000,000
Capital Expenditure	398,000,000	372,000,000	337,000,000	332,000,000	536,000,000	482,000,000
EBITDA	2,528,000,000	2,763,000,000	2,393,000,000	1,921,000,000	1,692,000,000	1,403,000,000
Return on Assets %	1.34%	5.41%	2.55%	1.54%	1.29%	.92%
Return on Equity %	5.85%	26.15%	14.76%	12.45%	16.88%	13.54%
Debt to Equity	1.80	1.72	2.43	2.90	6.77	8.78

CONTACT INFORMATION:

Phone: 703-883-1000   Fax:
Toll-Free: 800-445-8667
Address: 7930 Jones Branch Dr., Ste. 1100, McLean, VA 22102 United States

STOCK TICKER/OTHER:

Stock Ticker: HLT   Exchange: NYS
Employees: 169,000   Fiscal Year Ends: 12/31
Parent Company:

SALARIES/BONUSES:

Top Exec. Salary: $1,200,000   Bonus: $
Second Exec. Salary: Bonus: $
$743,404

OTHER THOUGHTS:

Estimated Female Officers or Directors: 2
Hot Spot for Advancement for Women/Minorities: Y

HMSHost Corporation

www.hmshost.com

NAIC Code: 722310

TYPES OF BUSINESS:

Food Service Contractors
Food, Beverage & Retail Concessions
Travel Plazas
Food Courts

BRANDS/DIVISIONS/AFFILIATES:

Autogrill SpA
Ciao Gourmet Market
La Tapenade Mediterranean
Z Market
Wicker Park Seafood & Sushi Bar
Beaudevin
Jose Cuervo Tequileria

CONTACTS: Note: Officers with more than one job title may be intentionally listed here more than once.

Steve Johnson, CEO
Jeff Yablun, COO
Tom Fricke, Pres.
Mark Ratych, CFO
Laura E. FitzRandolph, Exec. VP-Human Resources
Sarah Naqvi, Exec. VP-CIO

GROWTH PLANS/SPECIAL FEATURES:

HMSHost Corporation, a wholly-owned subsidiary of Italy-based Autogrill SpA, is a leading provider of food and beverage concessions for travelers. The firm operates facilities in over 120 airports worldwide as well as 99 roadside travel plazas along major U.S. and Canada toll roads and turnpikes in the Northeast and Midwest. HMSHost also serves tourist destinations such as Space Center Houston and the Empire State Building. The company's international airport operations include food service outlets at major and regional airports in Canada, Australia, Singapore, Ireland, India, Denmark, Sweden, the Netherlands, the U.K., Malaysia, France, Finland, Russia, the Middle East, Vietnam, Indonesia and New Zealand. HMSHost is engaged in a range of national and local brand licensing and franchising relationships, providing its food service with well-known brands ranging from Wolfgang Puck, Landry's Seafood, Quiznos Sub to Starbucks, Pizza Hut, SmashBurger and the Chili's Too. The company also develops proprietary branded concepts including Ciao Gourmet Market, La Tapenade Mediterranean, Z Market, Wicker Park Seafood & Sushi Bar, Beaudevin and Jose Cuervo Tequileria.

FINANCIAL DATA: Note: Data for latest year may not have been available at press time.

In U.S. $	2016	2015	2014	2013	2012	2011
Revenue	3,100,000,000	2,800,000,000	2,704,700,000	2,759,400,000	2,700,000,000	2,679,000,000
R&D Expense						
Operating Income						
Operating Margin %						
SGA Expense						
Net Income			86,500,000	76,900,000		
Operating Cash Flow						
Capital Expenditure						
EBITDA						
Return on Assets %						
Return on Equity %						
Debt to Equity						

CONTACT INFORMATION:

Phone: 240-694-4100   Fax: 240-694-4790
Toll-Free:
Address: 6905 Rockledge Dr., Bethesda, MD 20817 United States

STOCK TICKER/OTHER:

Stock Ticker: Subsidiary   Exchange:
Employees: 39,500   Fiscal Year Ends: 12/31
Parent Company: Autogrill SpA

SALARIES/BONUSES:

Top Exec. Salary: $ Bonus: $
Second Exec. Salary: $ Bonus: $

OTHER THOUGHTS:

Estimated Female Officers or Directors: 1
Hot Spot for Advancement for Women/Minorities:

Home Depot Inc (The)

www.homedepot.com

NAIC Code: 444110

TYPES OF BUSINESS:

Home Centers, Retail
Home Improvement Products
Building Materials
Lawn & Garden Products
Online & Catalog Sales
Tool & Truck Rental
Installation & Design Services

BRANDS/DIVISIONS/AFFILIATES:

Hampton Bay Lighting
Husky
Vigoro
RIDGID
Ryobi
Glacier Bay
HDX

CONTACTS: *Note: Officers with more than one job title may be intentionally listed here more than once.*

Carol Tome, CFO
Matthew Carey, Chief Information Officer
William Lennie, Executive VP, Divisional
Timothy Crow, Executive VP, Divisional
Mark Holifield, Executive VP, Divisional
Edward Decker, Executive VP, Divisional
Ann-Marie Campbell, Executive VP, Divisional
Teresa Roseborough, Executive VP
Craig Menear, President

GROWTH PLANS/SPECIAL FEATURES:

The Home Depot, Inc. is one of the world's largest home improvement retailers. The company operates approximately 2,278 Home Depot stores throughout the U.S., Canada, Guam, Puerto Rico, the Virgin Islands and Mexico. A typical store encompasses 104,000-square-feet of enclosed space with a 24,000-square-foot outdoor garden center; these locations usually stock between 30,000 and 40,000 items. These stores sell an assortment of building materials, plumbing materials, electrical materials, kitchen products, hardware, seasonal items, paint, flooring and wall coverings. The firm's proprietary brands include Hampton Bay lighting, Husky hand tools, Vigoro lawn care products, RIDGID and Ryobi power tools, Glacier Bay bath fixtures and HDX storage and cleaning products. Home Depot markets its products primarily to three types of customers: professional customers, such as remodelers, contractors, repairmen and small business owners; do-it-for-me shoppers, who are homeowners that personally purchase Home Depot products but hire third-party individuals for installation and/or project completion; and do-it-yourself (DIY) customers, who are homeowners that both shop for and personally install and/or utilize the firm's materials. In April 2017, the firm acquired the naming rights to a 13-acre park to be built adjacent to the Atlanta Falcons NFL franchise's new stadium. The Home Depot Backyard is set to be built once the former Georgia Dome is demolished.

The company offers its employees medical, dental, vision, life, AD&D and disability insurance; a 401(k) plan; a stock purchase plan; adoption, education and relocation assistance; flexible spending accounts; a legal services plan; auto and homeowners insurance; and veterinary coverage.

FINANCIAL DATA: *Note: Data for latest year may not have been available at press time.*

In U.S. $	2016	2015	2014	2013	2012	2011
Revenue	88,519,000,000	83,176,000,000	78,812,000,000	74,754,000,000	70,395,000,000	
R&D Expense						
Operating Income	11,774,000,000	10,469,000,000	9,166,000,000	7,766,000,000	6,661,000,000	
Operating Margin %	13.30%	12.58%	11.63%	10.38%	9.46%	
SGA Expense	16,801,000,000	16,834,000,000	16,597,000,000	16,508,000,000	16,028,000,000	
Net Income	7,009,000,000	6,345,000,000	5,385,000,000	4,535,000,000	3,883,000,000	
Operating Cash Flow	9,373,000,000	8,242,000,000	7,628,000,000	6,975,000,000	6,651,000,000	
Capital Expenditure	1,503,000,000	1,442,000,000	1,389,000,000	1,312,000,000	1,221,000,000	
EBITDA	13,803,000,000	12,592,000,000	10,935,000,000	9,537,000,000	8,356,000,000	
Return on Assets %	16.99%	15.77%	13.19%	11.11%	9.63%	
Return on Equity %	89.64%	58.09%	35.54%	25.42%	21.11%	
Debt to Equity	3.30	1.80	1.17	0.53	0.60	

CONTACT INFORMATION:

Phone: 770 433-8211   Fax: 770 431-2707
Toll-Free: 800-553-3199
Address: 2455 Paces Ferry Rd. N.W., Atlanta, GA 30339 United States

STOCK TICKER/OTHER:

Stock Ticker: HD   Exchange: NYS
Employees: 406,000   Fiscal Year Ends: 01/31
Parent Company:

SALARIES/BONUSES:

Top Exec. Salary: $1,300,000   Bonus: $
Second Exec. Salary: Bonus: $
$1,079,231

OTHER THOUGHTS:

Estimated Female Officers or Directors: 7
Hot Spot for Advancement for Women/Minorities: Y

Honeywell International Inc

www.honeywell.com

NAIC Code: 336412

TYPES OF BUSINESS:

Aircraft Engine and Engine Parts Manufacturing
Automation & Control Systems
Turboprop Engines
Performance Polymers
Specialty Chemicals
Nuclear Services
Life Sciences

BRANDS/DIVISIONS/AFFILIATES:

UOP Russell LLC
Xtralis International Holdings Limited
COM DEV International
Intelligrated

CONTACTS: Note: Officers with more than one job title may be intentionally listed here more than once.

Timothy Mahoney, CEO, Divisional
Terrence Hahn, CEO, Divisional
Rajeev Gautam, CEO, Divisional
John Waldron, CEO, Divisional
David Cote, CEO
Thomas Szlosek, CFO
Darius Adamczyk, COO
Katherine Adams, General Counsel
Mark James, Senior VP, Divisional
Krishna Mikkilineni, Senior VP, Divisional
Andreas Kramvis, Vice Chairman
Roger Fradin, Vice Chairman

GROWTH PLANS/SPECIAL FEATURES:

Honeywell International, Inc. invents and commercializes technologies that address critical challenges related to energy, safety, security, productivity and global urbanization. The firm operates through four segments: aerospace, home and building technologies (HBT), performance materials and technologies (PMT), and safety and productivity solutions (SPS). The aerospace segment supplies products, software and services for aircraft and vehicles that it sells to original equipment manufacturers (OEMs) and other customers in a variety of end markets. These markets include aircraft/aviation, defense and space contractors, and automotive and truck manufacturers. Its products consist of aircraft engines, integrated avionics, systems and service solutions; related products and services for aircraft manufacturers; and turbochargers for the performance improvement and efficiency of passenger cars and commercial vehicles. HBT provides products, software, solutions and technologies that help owners of homes stay connected and in control of their comfort, security and energy use; enable commercial building owners and occupants to ensure their facilities are safe, energy efficient, sustainable and productive; and help electricity, gas and water providers to serve customers and communities. PMT develops and manufactures advanced materials, process technologies and automation solutions. Its products include catalysts, absorbents, equipment and consulting. Last, SPS provides products, software and connected solutions that improve productivity, workplace safety and asset performance. Safety products include equipment and footwear designed for work, play and outdoor activities; and productivity products include gas detection technology, mobile devices, software, supply chain/warehouse automation equipment, sensors, switches and controls. In 2016, it acquired the 30% stake in UOP Russell, LLC that it did not already own, which develops technology and manufactures modular equipment to process natural gas; Xtralis International Holdings Limited, a global provider of aspiration smoke detection and perimeter security technologies; COM DEV International, a satellite and space components provider; and Intelligrated, a provider of supply chain and warehouse automation technologies.

FINANCIAL DATA: Note: Data for latest year may not have been available at press time.

In U.S. $	2016	2015	2014	2013	2012	2011
Revenue	39,302,000,000	38,581,000,000	40,306,000,000	39,055,000,000	37,665,000,000	36,529,000,000
R&D Expense						
Operating Income	6,683,000,000	6,828,000,000	5,831,000,000	5,501,000,000	4,226,000,000	2,686,000,000
Operating Margin %	17.00%	17.69%	14.46%	14.08%	11.21%	7.35%
SGA Expense	5,469,000,000	5,006,000,000	5,518,000,000	5,190,000,000	5,218,000,000	5,399,000,000
Net Income	4,809,000,000	4,768,000,000	4,239,000,000	3,924,000,000	2,926,000,000	2,067,000,000
Operating Cash Flow	5,498,000,000	5,454,000,000	5,024,000,000	4,335,000,000	3,517,000,000	2,833,000,000
Capital Expenditure	1,095,000,000	1,073,000,000	1,094,000,000	947,000,000	884,000,000	798,000,000
EBITDA	7,815,000,000	7,779,000,000	7,060,000,000	6,728,000,000	5,152,000,000	3,615,000,000
Return on Assets %	9.29%	10.06%	9.32%	8.99%	7.16%	5.32%
Return on Equity %	25.54%	26.53%	24.13%	25.78%	24.60%	19.25%
Debt to Equity	0.62	0.30	0.34	0.38	0.49	0.63

CONTACT INFORMATION:

Phone: 973 455-2000 Fax:
Toll-Free: 877-841-2840
Address: 115 Tabor Road, Morris Plains, NJ 07950 United States

STOCK TICKER/OTHER:

Stock Ticker: HON Exchange: NYS
Employees: 131,000 Fiscal Year Ends: 12/31
Parent Company:

SALARIES/BONUSES:

Top Exec. Salary: $1,890,000 Bonus: $5,700,000
Second Exec. Salary: $1,120,383 Bonus: $1,450,000

OTHER THOUGHTS:

Estimated Female Officers or Directors: 2
Hot Spot for Advancement for Women/Minorities: Y

Sales, profits and employees may be estimates. Financial information, benefits and other data can change quickly and may vary from those stated here.

Houston Methodist

NAIC Code: 622110

www.methodisthealth.com

TYPES OF BUSINESS:

General Medical and Surgical Hospitals

BRANDS/DIVISIONS/AFFILIATES:

Houston Methodist Hospital Central
Houston Methodist Sugar Land Hospital
Houston Methodist West Hospital
Houston Methodist Willowbrook Hospital
Houston San Jacinto Methodist Hospital
Houston Methodist St John Hospital
Houston Methodist The Woodlands Hospital
Houston Methodist Specialty Physician Group

CONTACTS: Note: Officers with more than one job title may be intentionally listed here more than once.

Marc L. Boom, CEO
Marc L. Boom, Pres.
Gregory Nelson, Sec.
Carlton Caucum, Treas.
Joseph Walter III, Assistant Treas.
Robert K. Moses, Jr., Assistant Sec.
Ewing Werlein, Jr., Chmn.

GROWTH PLANS/SPECIAL FEATURES:

Houston Methodist is a nonprofit healthcare organization that owns and operates several hospitals and facilities located in Houston. Its hospitals include Houston Methodist Hospital Central, Houston Methodist Sugar Land Hospital, Houston Methodist West Hospital, Houston Methodist Willowbrook Hospital, Houston San Jacinto Methodist Hospital, Houston Methodist St. John Hospital and Houston Methodist The Woodlands Hospital. Each campus is staffed by highly-trained specialists who provide advanced treatment as well as follow-up care. Some of the Methodist hospital's areas of focus include breast care, heart care, neuroscience, orthopedics and oncology. Houston Methodist Hospital, the system's flagship, is among U.S. News & World Report's best hospitals. Houston Methodist Research Institute is home to physicians that collaborate on more than 800 clinical trials. The Houston Methodist Institute for Technology, Innovation and Education is a 35,000-square-foot surgical training center and virtual hospital which provides ongoing education. Houston Methodist Hospital Foundation accepts all gifts on Houston Methodist's behalf and views donor contribution as essential to its growth and success. Houston Methodist Community Benefits support individuals and organizations that provide financial and medical assistance to more than 150,000 patients on an annual basis. Houston Methodist Specialty Physician Group are physicians employed by Houston Methodist that are rooted in an academic and research environment where teaching and continued education are encouraged. Houston Methodist Primary Care Group is dedicated to providing patient care for the entire family. Other centers include long-term acute care hospitals, emergency care centers and a comprehensive care center.

FINANCIAL DATA: Note: Data for latest year may not have been available at press time.

In U.S. $	2016	2015	2014	2013	2012	2011
Revenue	2,900,000,000	2,800,000,000	2,616,170,000	2,616,169,000	2,331,041,000	2,285,000,000
R&D Expense						
Operating Income						
Operating Margin %						
SGA Expense						
Net Income						
Operating Cash Flow						
Capital Expenditure						
EBITDA						
Return on Assets %						
Return on Equity %						
Debt to Equity						

CONTACT INFORMATION:

Phone: 713-790-3311 Fax:
Toll-Free:
Address: 6565 Fannin St., Houston, TX 77030 United States

STOCK TICKER/OTHER:

Stock Ticker: Nonprofit Exchange:
Employees: 20,000 Fiscal Year Ends: 12/31
Parent Company:

SALARIES/BONUSES:

Top Exec. Salary: $ Bonus: $
Second Exec. Salary: $ Bonus: $

OTHER THOUGHTS:

Estimated Female Officers or Directors: 5
Hot Spot for Advancement for Women/Minorities: Y

Hub International Limited

NAIC Code: 524210

www.hubinternational.com

TYPES OF BUSINESS:

Insurance Brokerage & Management
Risk Management
Property & Casualty Insurance
Employee Benefit Services
Investments & Financial Planning
Life Insurance
Health & Disability Insurance

BRANDS/DIVISIONS/AFFILIATES:

Hellman & Friedman LLC

CONTACTS: *Note: Officers with more than one job title may be intentionally listed here more than once.*

Martin P. Hughes, CEO
Marc I. Cohen, Pres.
Joseph C. Hyde, CFO
Trey Biggs, Chief Sales Officer
Carla Moradi, Exec. VP-IT
Scott Goodreau, Chief Legal Officer
Roy H. Taylor, Pres., West Region
Lawrence J. Lineker, Pres., Canadian Region
Scott Goodreau, Pres., Central Region
Deborah Deters, Sr. VP
Martin P. Hughes, Chmn.
James Barton, Pres., Canada & Midwest Regions

GROWTH PLANS/SPECIAL FEATURES:

Hub International Limited is an insurance brokerage providing an array of property, casualty, life and health insurance as well as employee benefits, investment and risk management products and services. The company focuses primarily on middle-market commercial accounts in the U.S. and Canada, and operates through more than 400 integrated broker offices using a variety of retail and wholesale distribution channels. Hub operates through four divisions: personal insurance, business insurance, employee benefits and risk services. Personal insurance includes homeowner's, condominiums, co-op housing, health and renter's insurance; auto, boat, collector car, recreational vehicle and travel insurance; and specialty insurance such as personal excess liability and aviation. Business insurance includes aviation, business owners, commercial auto, employment practices, marine, professional liability, boiler and machinery, business property, cyber liability, director/officer liability, executive liability, environmental protection, financial services, workers' compensation, business travel, trade credit and political risk, surety bonds, mergers & acquisitions, general liability and contest and prize insurance. Employee benefits comprises group medical plans, disability, group life insurance, voluntary benefits, dental plans, individual health, employee benefits consulting, absence management, wellness programs, health advocacy and benefits administration. Risk services include regulatory compliance assistance, safety management, emergency response planning, business continuity, fleet safety management, property protection, claim data analysis, disability management, claim reporting guidance, return-to-work planning, crisis management and webinars. Hub International is privately-owned by Hellman & Friedman, LLC. In June 2017, the firm, along with USI Insurance Services, LLC were currently the frontrunners to acquire Wells Fargo's insurance brokerage and consulting business.

FINANCIAL DATA: *Note: Data for latest year may not have been available at press time.*

In U.S. $	2016	2015	2014	2013	2012	2011
Revenue	1,470,000,000	1,260,000,000	1,230,000,000	1,147,560,000	988,700,000	878,321,552
R&D Expense						
Operating Income						
Operating Margin %						
SGA Expense						
Net Income						
Operating Cash Flow						
Capital Expenditure						
EBITDA						
Return on Assets %						
Return on Equity %						
Debt to Equity						

CONTACT INFORMATION:

Phone: 312-922-5000   Fax: 877-402-6606
Toll-Free: 877-402-4187
Address: 300 N. LaSalle St., 17/F, Chicago, IL 60654 United States

STOCK TICKER/OTHER:

Stock Ticker: Private   Exchange:
Employees: 10,000   Fiscal Year Ends: 12/31
Parent Company: Hellman & Friedman LLC

SALARIES/BONUSES:

Top Exec. Salary: $ Bonus: $
Second Exec. Salary: $ Bonus: $

OTHER THOUGHTS:

Estimated Female Officers or Directors: 1
Hot Spot for Advancement for Women/Minorities: Y

Hubbell Incorporated

NAIC Code: 335931

www.hubbell.com

TYPES OF BUSINESS:

Current-Carrying Wiring Device Manufacturing

BRANDS/DIVISIONS/AFFILIATES:

Hubbell
Raco
Wiegmann
Hubbell Building Automation
Alera Lighting
Hubbell Outdoor Lighting
Ohio Brass
iDevices LLC

CONTACTS: Note: Officers with more than one job title may be intentionally listed here more than once.

David Nord, CEO
William Sperry, CFO
Joseph Capozzoli, Chief Accounting Officer
An-Ping Hsieh, General Counsel
Darrin Wegman, President, Divisional
Gerben Bakker, President, Divisional
Kevin Poyck, President, Divisional
Rodd Ruland, President, Divisional
Stephen Mais, Senior VP, Divisional
Maria Lee, Treasurer

GROWTH PLANS/SPECIAL FEATURES:

Hubbell Incorporated designs, manufactures and distributes electrical and electronic products for a range of non-residential and residential construction, industrial and utility applications. The company operates in two segments: electrical and power. The electrical segment is comprised of businesses that sell stock and custom products including standard and special application wiring device products, rough-in electrical products, connector and grounding products, lighting fixtures and controls, as well as other electrical equipment. The products are typically used in and around industrial, commercial and institutional facilities by electrical contractors, maintenance personnel, electricians and telecommunications companies. Hubbell's products are supplied principally to industrial, non-residential and residential customers. These products are sold under brand and trademarks including, such as Hubbell, Raco, Kellems, Bell, Wiegmann, Gleason Reel, Hawke, Hipotronics, Chalmit and Austdac. Hubbell manufactures and sells lighting fixtures and controls for indoor and outdoor applications within residential, commercial, institutional and industrial markets. These products are sold under a number of brand and trademarks, such as Kim Lighting, Sportsliter Solutions, Kurt Versen, Beacon Products, Hubbell Building Automation, Spaulding Lighting, Alera Lighting, Dual-Lite and Hubbell Outdoor Lighting. The power segment consists of operations that design and manufacture various transmission, distribution, substation and telecommunications products mainly used by the electrical utility industry. Hubbell manufactures and sells a number of electrical distribution, transmission, and substation products. These products are sold under a number of brand and trademarks, such as Ohio Brass, Chance, Anderson, Fargo, Hubbell, Quazite, Electro Composites, Hot Box, PCORE and Delmar. In April 2017, the firm acquired iDevices, LLC, a producer of home automation products.

FINANCIAL DATA: Note: Data for latest year may not have been available at press time.

In U.S. $	2016	2015	2014	2013	2012	2011
Revenue	3,505,200,000	3,390,400,000	3,359,400,000	3,183,900,000	3,044,400,000	2,871,600,000
R&D Expense						
Operating Income	477,800,000	474,600,000	517,400,000	507,600,000	471,800,000	423,800,000
Operating Margin %	13.63%	13.99%	15.40%	15.94%	15.49%	14.75%
SGA Expense	622,900,000	617,200,000	591,600,000	562,900,000	540,400,000	499,900,000
Net Income	293,000,000	277,300,000	325,300,000	326,500,000	299,700,000	267,900,000
Operating Cash Flow	398,200,000	331,100,000	391,500,000	381,800,000	349,100,000	335,000,000
Capital Expenditure	67,200,000	77,100,000	60,300,000	58,800,000	49,100,000	55,400,000
EBITDA	566,100,000	534,800,000	595,900,000	575,200,000	539,400,000	488,900,000
Return on Assets %	8.67%	8.46%	9.99%	10.64%	10.34%	9.61%
Return on Equity %	17.52%	15.08%	16.97%	18.30%	19.15%	18.23%
Debt to Equity	0.62	0.34	0.31	0.31	0.35	0.40

CONTACT INFORMATION:

Phone: 475 882-4000   Fax: 203 799-4333
Toll-Free:
Address: 40 Waterview Dr., Shelton, CT 06484 United States

STOCK TICKER/OTHER:

Stock Ticker: HUBB
Employees: 17,400
Parent Company:

Exchange: NYS
Fiscal Year Ends: 12/31

SALARIES/BONUSES:

Top Exec. Salary: $1,000,000   Bonus: $
Second Exec. Salary: Bonus: $
$525,000

OTHER THOUGHTS:

Estimated Female Officers or Directors:
Hot Spot for Advancement for Women/Minorities:

Humana Inc

NAIC Code: 524114

www.humana.com

TYPES OF BUSINESS:

Insurance-Medical & Health, HMOs & PPOs
Insurance-Dental
Employee Benefit Plans
Insurance-Group Life
Wellness Programs

BRANDS/DIVISIONS/AFFILIATES:

CONTACTS: Note: Officers with more than one job title may be intentionally listed here more than once.

Bruce Broussard, CEO
Brian Kane, CFO
Kurt Hilzinger, Chairman of the Board
Cynthia Zipperle, Chief Accounting Officer
Brian LeClaire, Chief Information Officer
Roy Beveridge, Chief Medical Officer
Jody Bilney, Other Executive Officer
Timothy Huval, Other Executive Officer
Christopher Hunter, Other Executive Officer
Heidi Margulis, Senior VP, Divisional
Christopher Todoroff, Senior VP
Christopher Kay, Senior VP

GROWTH PLANS/SPECIAL FEATURES:

Humana, Inc. is a leading health benefits company in the U.S., serving approximately 14.2 million medical benefit plan members and 7 million specialty products members in the U.S. and Puerto Rico. It operates in three segments: retail, employer group and healthcare services. The retail segment consists of Medicare and commercial fully-insured medical and specialty health insurance benefits, including dental, vision and other supplemental health and financial protection products, marketed directly to individuals. The employer group segment consists of Medicare and commercial fully-insured medical and specialty health insurance benefits, including dental, vision and other supplemental health and financial protection products as well as administrative services-only products marketed to employer groups. Humana provides health benefits and related services to companies ranging from fewer than 10 to over 10,000 employees. The healthcare services segment includes services offered to health plan members as well as to third parties that promote health and wellness, including provider services, pharmacies, integrated wellness and home care services. Other businesses consist of military services, primarily the TRICARE South Region, Medicaid and closed-block long-term care businesses as well as the firm's contract with the Centers for Medicare and Medicaid Services to administer the Limited Income Newly Eligible Transition program, known as LI-NET. Many of its products are offered through HMOs (health maintenance organizations), private fee-for-service (PFFS) and preferred provider organizations (PPOs). In February 2017, Humana and Aetna terminated their merger agreement.

The firm offers employees an array of comprehensive benefits.

FINANCIAL DATA: Note: Data for latest year may not have been available at press time.

In U.S. $	2016	2015	2014	2013	2012	2011
Revenue	54,379,000,000	54,289,000,000	48,500,000,000	41,313,000,000	39,126,000,000	36,832,000,000
R&D Expense						
Operating Income	1,552,000,000	2,431,000,000	2,170,000,000	1,921,000,000	1,911,000,000	2,235,000,000
Operating Margin %	2.85%	4.47%	4.47%	4.64%	4.88%	6.06%
SGA Expense	7,277,000,000	7,318,000,000	7,639,000,000	6,355,000,000	5,830,000,000	5,395,000,000
Net Income	614,000,000	1,276,000,000	1,147,000,000	1,231,000,000	1,222,000,000	1,419,000,000
Operating Cash Flow	1,936,000,000	868,000,000	1,618,000,000	1,716,000,000	1,923,000,000	2,079,000,000
Capital Expenditure	527,000,000	523,000,000	528,000,000	441,000,000	410,000,000	346,000,000
EBITDA						
Return on Assets %	2.45%	5.29%	5.18%	6.04%	6.48%	8.39%
Return on Equity %	5.83%	12.76%	12.09%	13.55%	14.45%	18.93%
Debt to Equity	0.35	0.36	0.39	0.27	0.29	0.20

CONTACT INFORMATION:

Phone: 502 580-1000   Fax: 502 580-1441
Toll-Free:
Address: 500 W. Main St., Louisville, KY 40202 United States

STOCK TICKER/OTHER:

Stock Ticker: HUM
Employees: 54,200
Parent Company:

Exchange: NYS
Fiscal Year Ends: 12/31

SALARIES/BONUSES:

Top Exec. Salary: $1,235,446   Bonus: $
Second Exec. Salary: $835,470   Bonus: $

OTHER THOUGHTS:

Estimated Female Officers or Directors: 3
Hot Spot for Advancement for Women/Minorities: Y

Sales, profits and employees may be estimates. Financial information, benefits and other data can change quickly and may vary from those stated here.

Hyatt Hotels Corporation

www.hyatt.com

NAIC Code: 721110

TYPES OF BUSINESS:

Hotel Ownership & Management
Timeshares
Golf Courses
Gaming
Retirement Communities
Motels & Inns
Hotel Franchising

BRANDS/DIVISIONS/AFFILIATES:

Hyatt Regency
Grand Hyatt
Hyatt Place
Hyatt Gold Passport
Andaz
Hyatt House
Hyatt Residence Club
Park Hyatt

CONTACTS: Note: Officers with more than one job title may be intentionally listed here more than once.

Mark Hoplamazian, CEO
Thomas Pritzker, Chairman of the Board
Bradley OBryan, Chief Accounting Officer
Patrick Grismer, Executive VP
Maryam Banikarim, Executive VP
Rena Reiss, Executive VP
H. Floyd, Executive VP
Peter Sears, Executive VP
David Udell, Executive VP
Peter Fulton, Executive VP
Stephen Haggerty, Other Corporate Officer
Anne-Marie Law, Other Executive Officer

GROWTH PLANS/SPECIAL FEATURES:

Hyatt Hotels Corporation (Hyatt) owns, operates, manages and franchises full-service luxury hotels in 56 countries across the globe. The company owns, manages or franchises approximately 698 hotels with approximately 156,336 rooms. Hyatt's operations consist of several brands. Hyatt and Hyatt Regency host business and leisure travelers, although Hyatt Regency caters mainly to larger groups. Grand Hyatt hotels cater to leisure and business travelers and include accommodations for banquets and conferences. Park Hyatt hotels are smaller, full-service luxury hotels featuring world class art and restaurants in a few of the world's most visited cities. The Andaz branded hotels are boutique-style hotels that feature restaurants and bars aimed at local clientele as well as single travelers. The two select service brands, Hyatt House and Hyatt Place, are extended-stay brands designed to feel more like home. Hyatt Residence Club provides vacation ownership and vacation rental opportunities, offering members timeshare or points-based resort vacation opportunities. Hyatt Ziva and Hyatt Zilara are the company's all-inclusive resort brands which are developed, sold and managed as part of the Hyatt Residence club. Hyatt's guest loyalty program, Hyatt Gold Passport, has over 20 million members. In 2016, the firm acquired Thompson Miami Beach Hotel, which will be rebranded as The Confidante and join The Unbound Collection within the Hyatt brands. In 2017, the firm acquired Miraval Group, a leading provider of wellness resorts and spas.

The firm offers employees complementary hotel rooms; medical, dental, vision and prescription drug coverage; and tuition assistance.

FINANCIAL DATA: Note: Data for latest year may not have been available at press time.

In U.S. $	2016	2015	2014	2013	2012	2011
Revenue	4,429,000,000	4,328,000,000	4,415,000,000	4,184,000,000	3,949,000,000	3,698,000,000
R&D Expense						
Operating Income	299,000,000	323,000,000	279,000,000	233,000,000	159,000,000	153,000,000
Operating Margin %	6.75%	7.46%	6.31%	5.56%	4.02%	4.13%
SGA Expense	345,000,000	308,000,000	349,000,000	323,000,000	316,000,000	283,000,000
Net Income	204,000,000	124,000,000	344,000,000	207,000,000	88,000,000	113,000,000
Operating Cash Flow	489,000,000	538,000,000	473,000,000	456,000,000	499,000,000	393,000,000
Capital Expenditure	211,000,000	269,000,000	253,000,000	232,000,000	301,000,000	331,000,000
EBITDA	707,000,000	582,000,000	950,000,000	731,000,000	518,000,000	445,000,000
Return on Assets %	2.65%	1.57%	4.21%	2.61%	1.16%	1.53%
Return on Equity %	5.16%	2.87%	7.32%	4.31%	1.82%	2.27%
Debt to Equity	0.37	0.26	0.29	0.27	0.25	0.25

CONTACT INFORMATION:

Phone: 312 750-1234   Fax:
Toll-Free: 800-323-7249
Address: 71 S. Wacker Dr., 12th Fl., Chicago, IL 60606 United States

STOCK TICKER/OTHER:

Stock Ticker: H   Exchange: NYS
Employees: 45,000   Fiscal Year Ends: 12/31
Parent Company:

SALARIES/BONUSES:

Top Exec. Salary: $1,135,833   Bonus: $
Second Exec. Salary: Bonus: $
$746,667

OTHER THOUGHTS:

Estimated Female Officers or Directors: 3
Hot Spot for Advancement for Women/Minorities: Y

IAC/InterActiveCorp

www.iac.com

NAIC Code: 519130

TYPES OF BUSINESS:

E-Commerce, Online Advertising & Search Engines
Online Personals & Dating Services
Online Entertainment & Shopping Directories
Service Provider Listings Online

BRANDS/DIVISIONS/AFFILIATES:

Match Group Inc
HomeAdvisor
OKCupid
BlackPeople Meet
Princeton Review (The)
About.com
Ask.com
Vimeo

CONTACTS: Note: Officers with more than one job title may be intentionally listed here more than once.

Barry Diller, Chairman of the Board
Joseph Levin, Director
Glenn Schiffman, Executive VP
Mark Stein, Executive VP
Gregg Winiarski, General Counsel
Michael Schwerdtman, Senior VP
Victor Kaufman, Vice Chairman

GROWTH PLANS/SPECIAL FEATURES:

IAC/InterActiveCorp is a leading media and internet company. It is organized into six segments: Match Group, HomeAdvisor, publishing, applications, video and other. Match Group is comprised of the dating and non-dating businesses of 84.6%-owned Match Group, Inc. The dating business consists of more than 45 brands, available in 38 languages in 190 countries, and include the key brands of Match, OKCupid, PlentyOfFish, Tinder, Meetic, Twoo, OurTime, BlackPeopleMeet and FriendScout24. All of the dating products enable users to establish a profile and review other people's profiles free of charge. This segment's non-dating business includes The Princeton Review, offering a variety of educational test preparation, academic tutoring and college counseling services. HomeAdvisor is a nationwide home services digital marketplace that helps connect consumers with home professionals in the U.S., as well as in France and the Netherlands under various brands. Its network of home services professionals consisted of more than 100,000 paying service professionals in the U.S., offering services in more than 500 categories. The publishing segment is divided into premium brands and ask/other. Premium brands include About.com, Dictionary.com, Investopedia and The Daily Beast; and ask/other includes Ask.com, CityGrid and ASKfm, as well as a labs division focused on accelerating growth within the publishing segment. This segment publishes digital content and/or provides search services to users. The applications segment provides search services and utility applications to users. These include direct-to-consumer downloadable desktop applications such as SlimWare and Apalon, as well as IAC's business-to-business partnership operations. The video segment operates a global video sharing platform for creators and their audiences. These primarily consist of Vimeo, DailyBurn, Electus, IAC Films, CollegeHumor and Notional. Last, the other segment is comprised of ShoeBuy, an online retailer of footwear and related apparel. In November 2015, the firm went public with its Match Group segment. In 2016, it sold its PriceRunner web site.

FINANCIAL DATA: Note: Data for latest year may not have been available at press time.

In U.S. $	2016	2015	2014	2013	2012	2011
Revenue	3,139,882,000	3,230,933,000	3,109,547,000	3,022,987,000	2,800,933,000	2,059,444,000
R&D Expense	197,885,000	185,766,000	160,515,000	141,330,000	101,869,000	78,760,000
Operating Income	-32,625,000	179,588,000	378,727,000	426,203,000	323,568,000	197,762,000
Operating Margin %	-1.03%	5.55%	12.17%	14.09%	11.55%	9.60%
SGA Expense	1,792,423,000	1,871,205,000	1,568,047,000	1,336,601,000	1,294,774,000	942,902,000
Net Income	-41,280,000	119,472,000	414,873,000	285,784,000	159,266,000	174,233,000
Operating Cash Flow	292,377,000	349,405,000	424,048,000	410,961,000	351,055,000	372,386,000
Capital Expenditure	78,039,000	62,049,000	57,233,000	80,311,000	51,201,000	39,954,000
EBITDA	178,938,000	418,666,000	445,325,000	568,649,000	383,463,000	255,728,000
Return on Assets %	-.83%	2.51%	9.75%	7.10%	4.41%	5.08%
Return on Equity %	-2.24%	6.29%	22.55%	17.10%	8.94%	8.03%
Debt to Equity	0.84	0.96	0.54	0.64	0.35	0.05

CONTACT INFORMATION:

Phone: 212 314-7300   Fax: 212 314-7399
Toll-Free:
Address: 555 W. 18th St., New York, NY 10011 United States

STOCK TICKER/OTHER:

Stock Ticker: IAC   Exchange: NAS
Employees: 9,100   Fiscal Year Ends: 12/31
Parent Company:

SALARIES/BONUSES:

Top Exec. Salary: $1,000,000   Bonus: $2,500,000
Second Exec. Salary: $500,000   Bonus: $2,000,000

OTHER THOUGHTS:

Estimated Female Officers or Directors: 6
Hot Spot for Advancement for Women/Minorities: Y

IDEXX Laboratories Inc

www.idexx.com

NAIC Code: 334510

TYPES OF BUSINESS:

Veterinary Laboratory Testing Equipment
Point-of-Care Diagnostic Products
Veterinary Pharmaceuticals
Information Management Software
Food & Water Testing Products
Laboratory Testing Services
Consulting

BRANDS/DIVISIONS/AFFILIATES:

VetTest
VetLyte
VetStat
LaserCyte Dx
SNAPshot DX
Coag Dx Analyzer
Colisure
ProCyte Dx Hematology Analyzer

CONTACTS: *Note: Officers with more than one job title may be intentionally listed here more than once.*

Jonathan Ayers, CEO
Brian Mckeon, CFO
Jay Mazelsky, Executive VP
Giovani Twigge, Other Executive Officer
Jacqueline Studer, Vice President

GROWTH PLANS/SPECIAL FEATURES:

IDEXX Laboratories, Inc. develops, manufactures and distributes products and provides services for the veterinary and the food and water testing markets. The company operates in three business segments: companion animal group, which provides diagnostic and information technology-based products and services for the veterinary markets; water quality products; and livestock, poultry and diary, which provides diagnostic products and services for livestock and poultry health, and to ensure the quality and safety of milk and food. IDEXX markets an integrated and flexible suite of in-house laboratory analyzers for use in veterinary practices, which is referred to as the VetLab suite of analyzers. The suite includes several instrument systems as well as associated proprietary consumable products such as VetTest, VetLyte, VetStat and LaserCyte Dx analyzers; the IDEXX SNAPshot Dx; the ProCyte Dx Hematology Analyzer; and the Coag Dx Analyzer, among other offerings. In addition, the company provides assay kits, software and instrumentation for accurate assessment of infectious disease in production animals, such as cattle, swine and poultry. Water quality products include Colilert, Colilert-18 and Colisure tests, which simultaneously detect total coliforms and E. coli in water. IDEXX's principal product for use in testing for antibiotic residue in milk is the SNAP Beta-Lactam test, which detects penicillin, amoxicillin, ampicillin, ceftiofur and cephapirin residues. SNAPduo Beta-Tetra ST detects certain tetracycline antibiotic residues in addition to those detected by the Beta-Lactam test kits. Moreover, IDEXX's other operating segment combines and presents products for the human point-of-care medical diagnostics market with its pharmaceutical product line and out-licensing arrangements. Sales of products and services to customers outside the U.S. account for 39% of the company's overall revenue.

IDEXX offers its employees health, dental and life insurance; a401(k) and employee stock purchase plans; short- and long-term disability; flexible spending accounts; and sick days, vacation and paid holidays.

FINANCIAL DATA: *Note: Data for latest year may not have been available at press time.*

In U.S. $	2016	2015	2014	2013	2012	2011
Revenue	1,775,423,000	1,601,892,000	1,485,807,000	1,377,058,000	1,293,338,000	1,218,689,000
R&D Expense	101,122,000	99,681,000	98,263,000	88,003,000	82,014,000	76,042,000
Operating Income	350,239,000	299,912,000	260,255,000	266,762,000	262,563,000	236,225,000
Operating Margin %	19.72%	18.72%	17.51%	19.37%	20.30%	19.38%
SGA Expense	524,075,000	482,465,000	457,598,000	401,353,000	354,571,000	334,239,000
Net Income	222,045,000	192,078,000	181,906,000	187,800,000	178,267,000	161,786,000
Operating Cash Flow	334,571,000	216,364,000	235,846,000	245,996,000	230,282,000	220,700,000
Capital Expenditure	64,787,000	82,921,000	60,698,000	78,636,000	66,392,000	53,464,000
EBITDA	432,113,000	371,336,000	320,872,000	323,243,000	316,873,000	286,171,000
Return on Assets %	14.77%	13.43%	13.91%	16.09%	16.70%	16.78%
Return on Equity %		1150.47%	57.23%	32.53%	30.32%	29.05%
Debt to Equity			2.97	0.29		

CONTACT INFORMATION:

Phone: 207 556-0300　　　Fax: 207 856-0346
Toll-Free: 800-548-6733
Address: 1 Idexx Dr., Westbrook, ME 04092 United States

STOCK TICKER/OTHER:

Stock Ticker: IDXX　　　　　　Exchange: NAS
Employees: 7,365　　　　　　　Fiscal Year Ends: 12/31
Parent Company:

SALARIES/BONUSES:

Top Exec. Salary: $800,000　　Bonus: $
Second Exec. Salary: $533,538　　Bonus: $

OTHER THOUGHTS:

Estimated Female Officers or Directors: 2
Hot Spot for Advancement for Women/Minorities: Y

Sales, profits and employees may be estimates. Financial information, benefits and other data can change quickly and may vary from those stated here.

ILG Inc

NAIC Code: 561599

www.iilg.com

TYPES OF BUSINESS:

Timeshare Exchange Broker

BRANDS/DIVISIONS/AFFILIATES:

Interval Network
Hyatt Residence Club
Vistana Signature Experiences Inc

CONTACTS: Note: Officers with more than one job title may be intentionally listed here more than once.

Sergio Rivera, CEO, Subsidiary
William Harvey, CFO
Craig Nash, Chairman of the Board
John Galea, Chief Accounting Officer
Marie Lee, Chief Information Officer
Stephen Williams, COO, Subsidiary
Jeanette Marbert, COO
Victoria Kincke, General Counsel
Kelly Frank, Other Executive Officer
David Gilbert, President, Divisional
Kelvin Bloom, President, Subsidiary

GROWTH PLANS/SPECIAL FEATURES:

ILG, Inc. is a membership-based travel and vacation management company. The firm operates in two primary segments: exchange and rental and vacation ownership. Exchange and rental offers access to vacation accommodations and other travel-related transactions and services to leisure travelers. The segment works with resort developers, and operates vacation rental properties, providing owners of vacation interests with flexibility and choice by delivering access to alternate accommodations through exchange networks encompassing a variety of resorts. Its principal exchange network is the Interval Network, in which more than 3,000 resorts located in over 80 nations participated. Hyatt Residence Club encompasses 16 resorts within the network exchange program. Vacation ownership engages in the management of vacation ownership resorts; sales, marketing and financing of vacation ownership interests; and related services to owners and associations. This segment provides services to nearly 200 vacation ownership properties as well as sales and marketing of vacation ownership interests in the Hyatt Residence Club resorts. Additionally, the firm operates Trading Places International, a timeshare exchange and rental network; Aqua-Aston Hospitality, a Honolulu-based property-management company; and Vacation Resorts International and VRI Europe, a provider of resort and homeowners' association management services. In May 2016, the firm completed its acquisition of Vistana Signature Experiences, Inc., a leading operator and developer of high-end ownership resorts.

FINANCIAL DATA: Note: Data for latest year may not have been available at press time.

In U.S. $	2016	2015	2014	2013	2012	2011
Revenue	1,356,000,000	697,436,000	614,373,000	501,215,000	473,339,000	428,794,000
R&D Expense						
Operating Income	185,000,000	128,144,000	127,094,000	132,745,000	109,781,000	98,784,000
Operating Margin %	13.64%	18.37%	20.68%	26.48%	23.19%	23.03%
SGA Expense	392,000,000	221,128,000	194,785,000	166,296,000	158,829,000	148,012,000
Net Income	265,000,000	73,315,000	78,930,000	81,217,000	40,702,000	41,126,000
Operating Cash Flow	-7,000,000	142,722,000	110,658,000	109,864,000	80,438,000	95,907,000
Capital Expenditure	95,000,000	20,297,000	19,087,000	14,700,000	15,040,000	13,038,000
EBITDA	409,000,000	169,139,000	162,161,000	156,030,000	127,060,000	142,205,000
Return on Assets %	11.56%	5.62%	6.71%	8.40%	4.32%	4.19%
Return on Equity %	26.51%	17.96%	21.68%	26.37%	15.63%	17.37%
Debt to Equity	0.57	0.96	1.27	0.73	0.95	1.36

CONTACT INFORMATION:

Phone: 305 666-1861   Fax: 305 667-0653
Toll-Free: 888-784-3447
Address: 6262 Sunset Dr., Miami, FL 33143 United States

STOCK TICKER/OTHER:

Stock Ticker: ILG   Exchange: NAS
Employees: 10,500   Fiscal Year Ends: 12/31
Parent Company:

SALARIES/BONUSES:

Top Exec. Salary: $318,187   Bonus: $549,005
Second Exec. Salary: Bonus: $
$823,866

OTHER THOUGHTS:

Estimated Female Officers or Directors: 3
Hot Spot for Advancement for Women/Minorities: Y

Illinois Tool Works Inc

NAIC Code: 333249

www.itw.com

TYPES OF BUSINESS:

Industrial Products & Equipment
Steel, Plastic & Paper Products
Power Systems & Electronics
Transportation-Related Components, Fasteners, Fluids & Polymers
Construction-Related Fasteners & Tools
Food Equipment & Adhesives
Decorative Surfacing Materials
Adhesives, Sealants & Lubrication

BRANDS/DIVISIONS/AFFILIATES:

CONTACTS: *Note: Officers with more than one job title may be intentionally listed here more than once.*

E. Santi, CEO
Christopher OHerlihy, Vice Chairman
Michael Larsen, CFO
Randall Scheuneman, Chief Accounting Officer
John Hartnett, Executive VP
Michael Zimmerman, Executive VP
Lei Zhang Schlitz, Executive VP
Juan Valls, Executive VP
Roland Martel, Executive VP
Steven Martindale, Executive VP
Sundaram Nagarajan, Executive VP
Norman Finch, General Counsel
Mary Lawler, Other Executive Officer
David Parry, Vice Chairman

GROWTH PLANS/SPECIAL FEATURES:

Illinois Tool Works, Inc. is a multinational manufacturer of a diversified range of industrial products and equipment, with operations in 57 countries. It operates in seven primary segments: automotive OEM, test and measurement and electronics, food equipment, polymers and fluids, welding, construction products and specialty products. The automotive OEM segment produces components and fasteners for automotive-related applications. Products include plastic and metal components, fasteners and assemblies for automobiles, light trucks and other industrial uses. The test and measurement segment produces equipment, consumables and related software for testing and measuring of materials and structures as well as equipment and consumables used in the production of electronic subassemblies and microelectronics. The food equipment division provides commercial food equipment and related services. Products include warewashing equipment; cooking and refrigeration equipment; food processing equipment; and kitchen exhaust, ventilation and pollution control systems. The polymer and fluids segment offers adhesives, sealants, lubrication and cutting fluids, janitorial and hygiene products and fluids and polymers for auto aftermarket maintenance and appearance. The welding segment produces arc welding equipment, consumables and accessories for a wide array of industrial and commercial applications. The construction products segment produces tools, fasteners and other products for construction applications. Products include packaged hardware, fasteners, anchors and other products for retail. Finally, the specialty products segment produces beverage packaging equipment and consumables; product coding and marking equipment and consumables; and appliance components and fasteners. In July 2016, the company acquired the engineered fasteners and components business from ZF TRW.

FINANCIAL DATA: *Note: Data for latest year may not have been available at press time.*

In U.S. $	2016	2015	2014	2013	2012	2011
Revenue	13,599,000,000	13,405,000,000	14,484,000,000	14,135,000,000	17,924,000,000	17,786,580,000
R&D Expense						
Operating Income	3,064,000,000	2,867,000,000	2,888,000,000	2,514,000,000	2,847,000,000	2,731,008,000
Operating Margin %	22.53%	21.38%	19.93%	17.78%	15.88%	15.35%
SGA Expense	2,415,000,000	2,417,000,000	2,678,000,000	2,815,000,000	3,332,000,000	3,282,352,000
Net Income	2,035,000,000	1,899,000,000	2,946,000,000	1,679,000,000	2,870,000,000	2,071,384,000
Operating Cash Flow	2,302,000,000	2,299,000,000	1,616,000,000	2,528,000,000	2,072,000,000	1,956,008,000
Capital Expenditure	273,000,000	284,000,000	361,000,000	368,000,000	382,000,000	353,408,000
EBITDA	3,615,000,000	3,422,000,000	3,456,000,000	3,199,000,000	4,430,000,000	3,378,856,000
Return on Assets %	13.15%	11.36%	15.65%	8.55%	15.39%	12.10%
Return on Equity %	42.94%	31.53%	35.66%	16.57%	27.89%	21.36%
Debt to Equity	1.68	1.32	0.87	0.28	0.43	0.34

CONTACT INFORMATION:

Phone: 847 724-7500   Fax: 847 657-4261
Toll-Free:
Address: 155 Harlem Avenue, Glenview, IL 60025 United States

STOCK TICKER/OTHER:

Stock Ticker: ITW   Exchange: NYS
Employees: 50,000   Fiscal Year Ends: 12/31
Parent Company:

SALARIES/BONUSES:

Top Exec. Salary: $1,205,313   Bonus: $
Second Exec. Salary: Bonus: $
$769,558

OTHER THOUGHTS:

Estimated Female Officers or Directors: 4
Hot Spot for Advancement for Women/Minorities: Y

IMG Worldwide Inc

img.com

NAIC Code: 711410

TYPES OF BUSINESS:

Agents-Athletes
Agents-Models
Agents-Writers, Artists & Musicians
Event Marketing
Corporate Marketing Consulting Services
Sports Television Programming
Sports Schools & Training

BRANDS/DIVISIONS/AFFILIATES:

William Morris Endeavor Entertainment LLC
Trans World International
CSI Sports
Tigress Productions Limited
Nunet AG
WME/IMG
Kovert Creative
Ultimate Fighting Championship

CONTACTS: Note: Officers with more than one job title may be intentionally listed here more than once.

Ari Emanuel, Co-CEO
Patrick Whitesell, Co-CEO
Michel Masquelier, Pres., IMG Media
George Pyne, Pres., IMG Sports & Entertainment

GROWTH PLANS/SPECIAL FEATURES:

IMG Worldwide, Inc. is one of largest sports and lifestyle marketing and management agencies in the world. The company represents some of the world's top athletes, broadcasters, models, classical musicians, authors and newsmakers from offices in over 25 countries. The agency operates in a number of industries, including professional sports, college sports, fashion, entertainment, media and other various entertainment categories. Its sports operations handle everything from events and sponsorships to client representation and training. The company owns, produces and manages several prestigious sporting events, including events at Wimbledon and Nobel Prize functions. Sports clients have included tennis player Venus Williams, baseball player Derek Jeter, basketball player Charles Barkley and hockey player Jaromir Jagr. IMG's fashion and entertainment operations handle a multitude of events and personalities, including models Gisele Bundchen and Cindy Crawford. Its media operations create, distribute, sell and represent content across every medium. IMG's media division, along with the firm's subsidiaries TWI (Trans World International), CSI Sports, Tigress Productions Limited and Nunet AG, is one of the world's largest independent producers and distributors of televised sports programming. Annually, the company produces and distributes original programming to over 130 countries. IMG is a subsidiary of William Morris Endeavor Entertainment, LLC (WME), with some of its work and solutions branded as WME/IMG. In 2016, WME/IMG partnered with Joseph Assad and Lewis Kay to form Kovert Creative, a creative agency that brings together brands and talent in the core areas of digital services, personal and brand marketing and communications. Kovert Creative has offices in New York and Los Angeles. That same year, WME/IMG acquired Ultimate Fighting Championship (UFC), the professional mixed martial arts organization, for $4 billion.

FINANCIAL DATA: Note: Data for latest year may not have been available at press time.

In U.S. $	2016	2015	2014	2013	2012	2011
Revenue	1,947,000,000	1,800,000,000	1,705,000,000	1,650,000,000	1,500,000,000	1,400,000,000
R&D Expense						
Operating Income						
Operating Margin %						
SGA Expense						
Net Income		400,000,000				
Operating Cash Flow						
Capital Expenditure						
EBITDA						
Return on Assets %						
Return on Equity %						
Debt to Equity						

CONTACT INFORMATION:

Phone: 212-489-8300   Fax: 646-558-8399
Toll-Free:
Address: 200 5th Ave., Fl. 7, New York, NY 10010 United States

STOCK TICKER/OTHER:

Stock Ticker: Subsidiary   Exchange:
Employees: 5,000   Fiscal Year Ends: 12/31
Parent Company: William Morris Endeavor Entertainment LLC

SALARIES/BONUSES:

Top Exec. Salary: $ Bonus: $
Second Exec. Salary: $ Bonus: $

OTHER THOUGHTS:

Estimated Female Officers or Directors:
Hot Spot for Advancement for Women/Minorities:

INC Research/inVentiv Health

www.inventivhealth.com

NAIC Code: 541613

TYPES OF BUSINESS:

Marketing-Life Sciences & Pharmaceuticals
Sales & Marketing Outsourcing
Clinical Staffing
Health Care Communications
Advertising Services
Data Services
Sales Force Deployment
Clinical Research Services

BRANDS/DIVISIONS/AFFILIATES:

inVentiv Health Clinical Division
Addison Whitney
inVentiv Health Public Relations Group
Navicor
Adheris Health
inVentiv Group Holdings Inc
inVentiv Therapeutics Institute
inVentiv Recruitment Solutions

CONTACTS: *Note: Officers with more than one job title may be intentionally listed here more than once.*

Alistair Macdonald, CEO
Gregory Rush, CFO
Christopher Gaenzle, Chief Administrative Officer
Michael Gibertini, COO
David Norton, Director

GROWTH PLANS/SPECIAL FEATURES:

INC Research/inVentiv Health is a clinical and marketing services provider for the pharmaceutical and life sciences industries. The company operates in six core business units: commercial, clinical, communication, consulting, patient outcomes and selling solutions. Commercial specializes in providing sales teams and sales support services, including clinical educators, medical science liaisons and sales staffing and training; marketing and communications, such as advertising, branding, PR, patient education and digital and social media strategies; and patient outcomes, which include services related to patient adherence, assistance and reimbursement as well as disease management and cost containment. Clinical is comprised of inVentiv Health Clinical Division, which is a clinical research organization (CRO) that provides global drug development services to pharmaceutical, biotechnology, generic drug and medical device companies, with capabilities in Phase I-IV clinical development, bioanalytical services and strategic resourcing. The communications unit includes Addison Whitney, a full-service brand identity consultancy; GSW Worldwide, a full-service healthcare communications agency; inVentiv Health Public Relations Group, comprised of four global health communications agencies: Allidura Consumer, Biosector 2, Chamberlain Healthcare PR and Chandler Chicco Agency; Navicor, a healthcare advertising agency; and PALIO advertising agency. Consulting, through InVentiv Health Consulting, offers specialized services to clients in the pharmaceutical and biotech industries. Patient outcomes consists of Adheris Health, a provider of tailored, direct-to-patient medication adherence programs. The selling solutions unit is comprised of inVentiv Health Selling Solutions; inVentiv Recruitment Solutions; and inVentiv Therapeutics Institute. In August 2017, the firm and INC Research Holdings, Inc., a Phase I-IV CRO, announced the completion of their merger, creating a fully integrated biopharmaceutical solutions organization. In the interim the firm will be known as INC Research/inVentiv Health until a relaunch under a new brand in 2018. INC Research/inVentiv Health will trade on the Nasdaq under the symbol INCR.

FINANCIAL DATA: *Note: Data for latest year may not have been available at press time.*

In U.S. $	2016	2015	2014	2013	2012	2011
Revenue	1,610,596,000	1,399,239,000	1,178,799,000	995,090,000	868,600,000	655,986,000
R&D Expense						
Operating Income	155,359,000	152,360,000	63,644,000	31,458,000	-37,530,000	-40,195,000
Operating Margin %	9.64%	10.88%	5.39%	3.16%	-4.32%	-6.12%
SGA Expense	175,529,000	158,246,000	153,045,000	118,398,000	109,428,000	105,385,000
Net Income	112,630,000	117,047,000	-23,470,000	-41,529,000	-59,114,000	-59,547,000
Operating Cash Flow	109,332,000	204,740,000	131,447,000	37,270,000	42,999,000	-18,533,000
Capital Expenditure	31,353,000	21,111,000	25,551,000	17,714,000	9,591,000	4,763,000
EBITDA	205,338,000	202,628,000	79,375,000	88,592,000	46,199,000	35,611,000
Return on Assets %	9.01%	9.53%	-2.19%	-.43%	-4.74%	
Return on Equity %	43.41%	38.39%	-8.14%	-1.81%	-18.81%	
Debt to Equity	1.61	2.17	1.05	2.12	1.85	

CONTACT INFORMATION:

Phone: 800-416-0555   Fax:
Toll-Free:
Address: 470 Atlantic Ave., Fl. 11, Boston, MA 02210 United States

STOCK TICKER/OTHER:

Stock Ticker: INCR   Exchange: NAS
Employees: 15,000   Fiscal Year Ends: 12/31
Parent Company:

SALARIES/BONUSES:

Top Exec. Salary: $770,785   Bonus: $
Second Exec. Salary: Bonus: $
$583,262

OTHER THOUGHTS:

Estimated Female Officers or Directors: 1
Hot Spot for Advancement for Women/Minorities: Y

Sales, profits and employees may be estimates. Financial information, benefits and other data can change quickly and may vary from those stated here.

Ingram Micro Inc

www.ingrammicro.com

NAIC Code: 423430

TYPES OF BUSINESS:

Microcomputers, Distribution
Networking Equipment
Software & Accessories Distribution
Supply Chain Management Services
Online Marketing Services

BRANDS/DIVISIONS/AFFILIATES:

Tianjin Tianhai Investment Company Ltd

CONTACTS: Note: Officers with more than one job title may be intentionally listed here more than once.

Alain Monie, CEO
William Humes, CFO
Gina Mastantuono, CFO
Larry Boyd, Executive VP
Shailendra Gupta, President, Divisional
Scott Sherman, Vice President, Divisional

GROWTH PLANS/SPECIAL FEATURES:

Ingram Micro, Inc. is a global distributor of IT products. The company markets microcomputer hardware, networking equipment and software products to over 200,000 resellers in approximately 160 countries. Ingram provides a comprehensive inventory of hundreds of thousands of distinct items from approximately 1,700 vendors. Its products are sold in five primary segments: IT peripherals, systems, software, networking and mobility. IT peripherals include printers, scanners, displays, projectors, monitors, panels, mass storage, tape, digital signage products, digital cameras, digital video disc players, game consoles, TVs, audio products, small appliances, media management, home control systems, barcode/card printers, AIDC scanners and software, wireless infrastructure products, physical security products, processors, motherboards, hard drives, memory, as well as ink and toner supplies, paper, carrying cases and anti-glare screens. Systems products include rack, tower and blade servers; desktops; and portable personal computers and tablets. Software products include business application software, operating system software, entertainment software, middleware, developer software tools, security software, storage software and virtualization software. Networking products include networking hardware, communication products and network security hardware such as switches, hubs, routers, wireless local area networks, wireless wide area networks, network interface cards, cellular data cards, network-attached storage and storage area networks. Mobility products include mobile handsets, tablets, navigation devices, aircards, SIM cards, flash memory and other mobile companion products, including health and fitness bands, wearables, accessories and services. Ingram also offers supply chain management services such as sales and marketing, customer care, financial services and logistics to suppliers and resellers. In December 2016, the firm was acquired by Tianjin Tianhai Investment Company, Ltd., a China-based shipping and distribution group for approximately $6 billion. Ingram subsequently ceased from public trading, and operates as a private subsidiary of Tianjin Tianhai.

FINANCIAL DATA: Note: Data for latest year may not have been available at press time.

In U.S. $	2016	2015	2014	2013	2012	2011
Revenue	41,770,000,000	43,025,850,368	46,487,425,024	42,553,917,440	37,827,297,280	36,328,701,952
R&D Expense						
Operating Income						
Operating Margin %						
SGA Expense						
Net Income		215,104,992	266,691,008	310,583,008	305,908,992	244,240,000
Operating Cash Flow						
Capital Expenditure						
EBITDA						
Return on Assets %						
Return on Equity %						
Debt to Equity						

CONTACT INFORMATION:

Phone: 714 566-1000   Fax: 714 566-7604
Toll-Free:
Address: 3351 Michelson Dr., Ste. 100, Irvine, CA 92612-0697 United States

STOCK TICKER/OTHER:

Stock Ticker: Subsidiary   Exchange:
Employees: 30,000   Fiscal Year Ends: 12/31
Parent Company: HNA Group

SALARIES/BONUSES:

Top Exec. Salary: $ Bonus: $
Second Exec. Salary: $ Bonus: $

OTHER THOUGHTS:

Estimated Female Officers or Directors: 2
Hot Spot for Advancement for Women/Minorities: Y

Ingredion Inc

NAIC Code: 311000

www.ingredion.us/Pages/default.aspx

TYPES OF BUSINESS:

Food Products, Manufacturing
Wet Milling
Food Ingredients
Starch-Based Products
Cornstarch
Liquid Sweeteners

BRANDS/DIVISIONS/AFFILIATES:

CONTACTS: *Note: Officers with more than one job title may be intentionally listed here more than once.*

Ilene Gordon, CEO
James Zallie, Executive VP, Divisional
Jack Fortnum, Executive VP
Christine Castellano, General Counsel
Anthony Delio, Other Executive Officer
Robert Stefansic, Other Executive Officer
Jorgen Kokke, President, Geographical
Martin Sonntag, Senior VP, Divisional
Diane Frisch, Senior VP, Divisional
James Gray, Vice President, Divisional
Stephen Latreille, Vice President

GROWTH PLANS/SPECIAL FEATURES:

Ingredion Inc. is one of the world's largest corn refiners and a major supplier of food ingredients and industrial products derived from wet milling and processing of corn and other starch-based materials such as tapioca, potatoes and rice. Corn processing is a two-step process. During the front-end process, corn is steeped in a water-based solution and separated into starch and other co-products such as animal feed and germ. The starch is then dried for sale or further processed to make sweeteners and other ingredients that serve the particular needs of various industries. The company's sweetener products, which account for 44% of sales, include high fructose corn syrup, glucose corn syrups, high maltose corn syrups, caramel color, dextrose, polyols, maltodextrins and glucose and corn syrup solids. Starch-based products (43% of sales) include both industrial and food-grade starches. Ingredion's specialty ingredients (25% of sales) comprise select starch and sweetener ingredients that provide clean-label solutions that enable front-of-pack claims for customers. The firm serves customers in many diverse industries, including the food and beverage, pharmaceutical, paper products, laminated paper, textile and brewing industries as well as the global animal feed and corn oil markets. Ingredion supplies a broad range of customers, including food, beverage, brewing, pharmaceutical, paper/corrugated products, textile, personal care, animal feed and corn oil markets. Ingredion owns and operates 43 manufacturing facilities worldwide.

FINANCIAL DATA: *Note: Data for latest year may not have been available at press time.*

In U.S. $	2016	2015	2014	2013	2012	2011
Revenue	6,022,000,000	5,958,000,000	5,668,000,000	6,653,000,000	6,868,000,000	6,219,000,000
R&D Expense						
Operating Income	808,000,000	660,000,000	581,000,000	613,000,000	668,000,000	671,000,000
Operating Margin %	13.41%	11.07%	10.25%	9.21%	9.72%	10.78%
SGA Expense	579,000,000	562,000,000	525,000,000	534,000,000	556,000,000	543,000,000
Net Income	485,000,000	402,000,000	355,000,000	396,000,000	428,000,000	416,000,000
Operating Cash Flow	771,000,000	686,000,000	731,000,000	619,000,000	732,000,000	300,000,000
Capital Expenditure	284,000,000	280,000,000	276,000,000	298,000,000	313,000,000	263,000,000
EBITDA	1,011,000,000	862,000,000	788,000,000	815,000,000	889,000,000	885,000,000
Return on Assets %	8.93%	7.90%	6.79%	7.23%	7.84%	8.00%
Return on Equity %	20.59%	18.60%	15.49%	16.36%	18.85%	20.39%
Debt to Equity	0.72	0.84	0.82	0.71	0.70	0.85

CONTACT INFORMATION:

Phone: 708-551-2600   Fax: 708-551-2700
Toll-Free: 800-443-2746
Address: 5 Westbrook Corporate Ctr., Westchester, IL 60154 United States

STOCK TICKER/OTHER:

Stock Ticker: INGR
Employees: 11,000
Parent Company:

Exchange: NYS
Fiscal Year Ends: 12/31

SALARIES/BONUSES:

Top Exec. Salary: $1,189,404   Bonus: $
Second Exec. Salary: $611,252   Bonus: $

OTHER THOUGHTS:

Estimated Female Officers or Directors: 7
Hot Spot for Advancement for Women/Minorities: Y

In-N-Out Burgers Inc

in-n-out.com

NAIC Code: 722513

TYPES OF BUSINESS:

Fast-Food Restaurants
Hamburger Restaurants

BRANDS/DIVISIONS/AFFILIATES:

In-N-Out Burger
Animal Style

CONTACTS:
Note: Officers with more than one job title may be intentionally listed here more than once.

Lynsi Snyder, Pres.
Mark Taylor, COO
Roger Kotch, CFO
Michelle Guzman, Dir-Mktg
Katherine Sauls, Dir.-Human Resources
Rob Howards, Dir-IT

GROWTH PLANS/SPECIAL FEATURES:

In-N-Out Burgers, Inc. is a chain of fast food restaurants that began in 1948 and primarily serve hamburgers, French fries, ice cream shakes and beverages. Founded in Baldwin Park, California, it has slowly expanded outside of the state and into Arizona, Nevada, Utah, Oregon and Texas with over 325 locations. Hamburgers and cheeseburgers consist of 100% pure beef, American cheese, leaf lettuce, tomato, a special spread, with or without onions and stacked high on a freshly-baked bun. The restaurants have an extras menu where hamburger choices include double meat; 3x3, containing three patties and three slices of cheese; 4x4, four patties and four slices of cheese; protein style, the burger wrapped in lettuce instead of a bun; and Animal Style, which is any size burger choice with the patties cooked with mustard and all the fixings. All hamburger patties are free of additives, fillers and preservatives of any kind. The firm pays a premium to purchase fresh, high quality beef chuck, and has in-house butchers that remove the bones, grind the meat and make every patty ready for cooking. Potatoes are shipped directly from farms, individually cut in the firm's stores, then cooked in 100% pure vegetable oil. Shakes are made with milk and real ice cream. In-N-Out's web site offers products to purchase such as apparel, gift cards and other items, as well as limited time offers.

Typical fast food equipment such as heat lamps, microwaves and freezers are never found in their kitchens. The firm offers employees a comprehensive wellness plan; paid holidays and vacations; and a 401(k) plan. It receives high ranks in many surveys of top employers. Pay is above average for this industry. Employees also enjoy flexible work schedules, ongoing training programs (In-N-Out University) and promote-from-within opportunities.

FINANCIAL DATA:
Note: Data for latest year may not have been available at press time.

In U.S. $	2016	2015	2014	2013	2012	2011
Revenue	870,000,000	740,000,000	630,000,000	558,200,000	470,000,000	394,800,000
R&D Expense						
Operating Income						
Operating Margin %						
SGA Expense						
Net Income						
Operating Cash Flow						
Capital Expenditure						
EBITDA						
Return on Assets %						
Return on Equity %						
Debt to Equity						

CONTACT INFORMATION:

Phone: 949-509-6200   Fax: 949-509-6389
Toll-Free: 800-786-1000
Address: 4199 Campus Dr., Fl. 9, Irvine, CA 92612 United States

STOCK TICKER/OTHER:

Stock Ticker: Private
Employees: 22,000
Parent Company:

Exchange:
Fiscal Year Ends: 12/31

SALARIES/BONUSES:

Top Exec. Salary: $ Bonus: $
Second Exec. Salary: $ Bonus: $

OTHER THOUGHTS:

Estimated Female Officers or Directors:
Hot Spot for Advancement for Women/Minorities: Y

Integer Holdings Corporation

integer.net

NAIC Code: 335911

TYPES OF BUSINESS:

Medical Device Contract Manufacturing
Implantable Medical Device Components
Specialty Battery Manufacturing

BRANDS/DIVISIONS/AFFILIATES:

Greatbatch
Lake Region Medical
Electrochem

CONTACTS: *Note: Officers with more than one job title may be intentionally listed here more than once.*

Michael Dinkins, CFO
Jeremy Friedman, COO
Bill Sanford, Director
Joseph Dziedzic, Director
Timothy McEvoy, General Counsel
Declan Smyth, President, Divisional
Jennifer Bolt, President, Divisional
Antonio Gonzalez, President, Divisional
Thomas Mazza, Treasurer

GROWTH PLANS/SPECIAL FEATURES:

Integer Holdings Corporation is one of the largest medical device outsource manufacturers in the world. The firm's two business segments are medical and non-medical. The medical segment comprises advanced surgical, orthopedic, portable medical, cardio/vascular and cardiac/neuromodulation product lines marketed under the Greatbatch and Lake Region Medical brands. These products include arthroscopic devices and components, laparoscopic and general surgical devices, biopsy and drug delivery products, components for a range of cardiac and endovascular procedures, devices used during the treatment of peripheral arterial disease and more. The non-medical segment includes power solutions such as customized battery power and management systems marketed under the Electrochem brand. In addition to primary power solutions, Electrochem offers customized secondary or rechargeable battery packs in a diverse range of chemistries for critical applications. Integer has offices strategically located worldwide, including North America, South America, Europe and Asia Pacific.

FINANCIAL DATA: *Note: Data for latest year may not have been available at press time.*

In U.S. $	2016	2015	2014	2013	2012	2011
Revenue	1,386,778,000	800,414,000	687,787,000	663,945,000	646,177,000	568,822,000
R&D Expense	55,001,000	52,995,000	49,845,000	54,077,000	52,490,000	45,513,000
Operating Income	108,270,000	13,146,000	75,654,000	61,339,000	25,821,000	61,699,000
Operating Margin %	7.80%	1.64%	10.99%	9.23%	3.99%	10.84%
SGA Expense	153,291,000	102,530,000	90,602,000	88,107,000	80,992,000	72,548,000
Net Income	5,961,000	-7,594,000	55,458,000	36,267,000	-4,799,000	33,122,000
Operating Cash Flow	105,532,000	12,479,000	81,276,000	56,755,000	64,831,000	89,921,000
Capital Expenditure	58,632,000	44,616,000	24,823,000	18,558,000	41,069,000	22,489,000
EBITDA	202,979,000	62,445,000	118,288,000	96,065,000	71,153,000	113,015,000
Return on Assets %	.20%	-.38%	6.00%	4.07%	-.54%	3.99%
Return on Equity %	.75%	-1.03%	9.59%	7.09%	-1.01%	7.40%
Debt to Equity	2.34	1.98	0.28	0.36	0.46	0.50

CONTACT INFORMATION:

Phone: 716 759-5600   Fax: 716 759-5654
Toll-Free:
Address: 2595 Dallas Parkway, Ste. 310, Frisco, TX 75034 United States

STOCK TICKER/OTHER:

Stock Ticker: ITGR   Exchange: NYS
Employees: 9,400   Fiscal Year Ends: 12/31
Parent Company:

SALARIES/BONUSES:

Top Exec. Salary: $491,417   Bonus: $1,592,000
Second Exec. Salary: Bonus: $
$800,000

OTHER THOUGHTS:

Estimated Female Officers or Directors:
Hot Spot for Advancement for Women/Minorities:

Intel Corporation

www.intel.com

NAIC Code: 334413

TYPES OF BUSINESS:

Microprocessors
Semiconductors
Circuit Boards
Flash Memory Products
Software Development
Home Network Equipment
Digital Imaging Products
Healthcare Products

BRANDS/DIVISIONS/AFFILIATES:

Altera Corporation
Nervana Systems

CONTACTS: Note: Officers with more than one job title may be intentionally listed here more than once.

Brian Krzanich, CEO
Robert Swan, CFO
Andy Bryant, Chairman of the Board
Stacy Smith, Executive VP, Divisional
Diane Bryant, Executive VP
Venkata Renduchintala, Executive VP
Richard Taylor, Other Corporate Officer

GROWTH PLANS/SPECIAL FEATURES:

Intel Corporation designs and manufactures products and technologies that power the cloud and smart connectivity. The company produces computer, networking and communications platforms to a broad set of customers, including original equipment manufacturers (OEMs), original design manufacturers (ODMs), cloud and communications service providers, as well as industrial, communications and automotive equipment manufacturers. Intel's business across the cloud and data center are accelerated by memory and field-programmable gate array technologies. Its devices include everything smart: personal computers (PCs), sensors, consoles and other edge devices that are connected to the cloud. Memory and programmable solutions make possible new classes of products for the data center and Internet of Things. Intel is a leader in silicon manufacturing process technology, of which its products are manufactured in the company's own facilities. Its intellectual property can be shared across its platforms and operating segments, providing cost reduction and seamless production capabilities. Intel also offers software and services for consumer and corporate environments, as well as for assisting software developers in creating software applications via Intel platforms. Intel's client computing product group includes platforms for notebooks, 2-in-1 systems, desktops, tablets, phones, wired/wireless connectivity products and mobile communications components. Its non-volatile memory solutions (NAND) flash memory products are primarily used it solid-state drives. During 2016, the firm acquired Altera Corporation; acquired deep-learning startup, Nervana Systems; and sold a majority stake in its computer-security unit to TPG Capital. In March 2017, Intel agreed to acquire Mobileye NV, an Israeli developer of autonomous driving systems, for more than $15 billion.

FINANCIAL DATA: Note: Data for latest year may not have been available at press time.

In U.S. $	2016	2015	2014	2013	2012	2011
Revenue	59,387,000,000	55,355,000,000	55,870,000,000	52,708,000,000	53,341,000,000	53,999,000,000
R&D Expense	12,740,000,000	12,128,000,000	11,537,000,000	10,611,000,000	10,148,000,000	8,350,000,000
Operating Income	12,874,000,000	14,002,000,000	15,347,000,000	12,291,000,000	14,638,000,000	17,477,000,000
Operating Margin %	21.67%	25.29%	27.46%	23.31%	27.44%	32.36%
SGA Expense	8,397,000,000	7,930,000,000	8,136,000,000	8,088,000,000	8,057,000,000	7,670,000,000
Net Income	10,316,000,000	11,420,000,000	11,704,000,000	9,620,000,000	11,005,000,000	12,942,000,000
Operating Cash Flow	21,808,000,000	19,017,000,000	20,418,000,000	20,776,000,000	18,884,000,000	20,963,000,000
Capital Expenditure	9,625,000,000	7,446,000,000	10,197,000,000	10,747,000,000	11,842,000,000	10,764,000,000
EBITDA	21,459,000,000	23,260,000,000	23,896,000,000	20,887,000,000	22,485,000,000	23,886,000,000
Return on Assets %	9.53%	11.71%	12.70%	10.88%	14.15%	19.27%
Return on Equity %	16.20%	19.52%	20.51%	17.57%	22.66%	27.14%
Debt to Equity	0.31	0.32	0.21	0.22	0.25	0.15

CONTACT INFORMATION:

Phone: 408 765-8080   Fax: 408 765-2633
Toll-Free: 800-628-8686
Address: 2200 Mission College Blvd., Santa Clara, CA 95054 United States

STOCK TICKER/OTHER:

Stock Ticker: INTC   Exchange: NAS
Employees: 106,000   Fiscal Year Ends: 12/31
Parent Company:

SALARIES/BONUSES:

Top Exec. Salary: $900,000   Bonus: $2,700,000
Second Exec. Salary: $194,800   Bonus: $2,750,000

OTHER THOUGHTS:

Estimated Female Officers or Directors: 10
Hot Spot for Advancement for Women/Minorities: Y

Interpublic Group of Companies Inc

www.interpublic.com

NAIC Code: 541810

TYPES OF BUSINESS:

Advertising Services
Marketing & Branding
Market Research
Public Relations
Online Marketing
Direct Marketing
Promotions & Events
Sports & Entertainment Marketing

BRANDS/DIVISIONS/AFFILIATES:

Foote, Cone & Belding
IPG Mediabrands
MullenLowe Group
McCann Worldgroup
Weber Shandwick
Cassidy
Golin
FutureBrand

CONTACTS: Note: Officers with more than one job title may be intentionally listed here more than once.

Michael Roth, CEO
Frank Mergenthaler, CFO
Christopher Carroll, Chief Accounting Officer
Philippe Krakowsky, Executive VP
Andrew Bonzani, General Counsel

GROWTH PLANS/SPECIAL FEATURES:

Interpublic Group of Companies, Inc. (IPG) is a group comprising of hundreds of advertising and specialized marketing and communications services companies that combined represent one of the largest resources of advertising and marketing expertise in the world, with offices and affiliations in over 100 countries. The firm has three global networks: McCann Worldgroup; Foot, Cone & Belding; and MullenLowe Group. IPG operates through two divisions: integrated agency networks (IAN) and constituency management group (CMG). IAN is comprised of its three global networks and IPG Mediabrands. IAN agencies provide an array of global communications and marketing services, each offering a distinctive range of solutions for clients. Its digital specialist agencies provide digital capabilities, and its domestic integrated agencies provide advertising, marketing, communications services and/or marketing services and partner with the firm's global operating divisions as needed. CMG is comprised of a number of specialist marketing service offerings which includes Weber Shandwick, Cassidy, Golin, FutureBrand, Jack Morton and Octagon Worldwide. These marketing service subsidiaries provide clients with public relations, meeting and event production, sports and entertainment marketing, corporate and brand identity and marketing consulting. IPG's five largest clients are General Motors, Johnson & Johnson, L'Oreal, Samsung and Unilever.

FINANCIAL DATA: Note: Data for latest year may not have been available at press time.

In U.S. $	2016	2015	2014	2013	2012	2011
Revenue	7,846,600,000	7,613,800,000	7,537,100,000	7,122,300,000	6,956,200,000	7,014,600,000
R&D Expense						
Operating Income	938,000,000	871,900,000	788,400,000	598,300,000	678,300,000	687,200,000
Operating Margin %	11.95%	11.45%	10.46%	8.40%	9.75%	9.79%
SGA Expense	6,908,600,000	6,742,700,000	6,748,500,000	6,463,400,000	6,277,900,000	6,326,400,000
Net Income	608,500,000	454,600,000	477,100,000	267,900,000	446,700,000	532,300,000
Operating Cash Flow	513,400,000	674,000,000	669,500,000	592,900,000	357,200,000	273,500,000
Capital Expenditure	200,700,000	161,100,000	148,700,000	173,000,000	169,200,000	140,300,000
EBITDA	1,081,000,000	1,005,000,000	968,600,000	748,100,000	956,000,000	1,026,100,000
Return on Assets %	4.85%	3.58%	3.71%	1.96%	3.29%	4.01%
Return on Equity %	30.55%	22.27%	22.02%	11.74%	19.60%	22.89%
Debt to Equity	0.63	0.81	0.76	0.51	0.93	0.54

CONTACT INFORMATION:

Phone: 212 704-1200   Fax: 212 399-8130
Toll-Free:
Address: 909 Third Ave., New York, NY 10022 United States

STOCK TICKER/OTHER:

Stock Ticker: IPG   Exchange: NYS
Employees: 49,800   Fiscal Year Ends: 12/31
Parent Company:

SALARIES/BONUSES:

Top Exec. Salary: $1,500,000   Bonus: $
Second Exec. Salary: Bonus: $
$1,000,000

OTHER THOUGHTS:

Estimated Female Officers or Directors: 9
Hot Spot for Advancement for Women/Minorities: Y

Intuit Inc

NAIC Code: 0

TYPES OF BUSINESS:

Computer Software-Financial Management
Business Accounting Software
Consumer Finance Software
Tax Preparation Software
Online Financial Services

BRANDS/DIVISIONS/AFFILIATES:

ProConnect
QuickBooks Online
Lacerte
ProSeries
ProConnect Tax Online
ProFile
ProSeries Professional Edition
ProSeries Basic Edition

CONTACTS: *Note: Officers with more than one job title may be intentionally listed here more than once.*

R. Williams, CFO
William Campbell, Chairman Emeritus
Brad Smith, Chairman of the Board
Mark Flournoy, Chief Accounting Officer
H. Stansbury, Chief Technology Officer
Daniel Wernikoff, Executive VP
Laura Fennell, Executive VP
Scott Cook, Founder
Sasan Goodarzi, General Manager, Divisional

GROWTH PLANS/SPECIAL FEATURES:

Intuit, Inc. is a provider of software and web-based services, specializing in financial management and tax solutions. The company has three business segments: small business, consumer tax and ProConnect. The small business segment targets small businesses, as well as the accounting professionals who serve them. This division's products include QuickBooks Online, which offers financial management tools; online payroll solutions; online payment solutions; an Intuit developer group, which provides tools that third-party developers need to create online and mobile applications that personalize and add value to QuickBooks; desktop payments solutions; technical support; and financial supplies. The consumer tax segment targets consumers, and includes TurboTax income tax preparation products and services. TurboTax products and services are designed to enable individuals to prepare and file their own federal and state personal income tax returns quickly and accurately. The ProConnect segment targets professional accountants in the U.S. and Canada, who are essential to both small business success and doing the nations' taxes. ProConnect professional tax offerings include Lacerte, ProSeries, ProConnect Tax Online and ProFile. Lacerte is designed for full-service accounting firms who handle more complex returns. ProSeries offers two software versions: ProSeries Professional Edition, designed for year-round tax practices handling moderately complex tax returns; and ProSeries Basic Edition, for the needs of smaller and seasonal tax practices. ProConnect Tax Online is a cloud-based solution designed for year-round practices who prepare moderately complex consumer and small business returns, and integrates with QuickBooks Online offerings. Last, ProFile is Intuit's Canadian tax offering which serves year-round, full-service accounting firms for both consumer and business tax returns. This division's services include year-round document storage and access, collaboration services, e-signature and bank products. During 2016, the firm sold its Demandforce, QuickBase and Quicken businesses.

Intuit employees receive health, dental and life insurance; and 401(k) and employee stock purchase plans.

FINANCIAL DATA: *Note: Data for latest year may not have been available at press time.*

In U.S. $	2016	2015	2014	2013	2012	2011
Revenue	4,694,000,000	4,192,000,000	4,506,000,000	4,171,000,000	4,151,000,000	3,851,000,000
R&D Expense	881,000,000	798,000,000	758,000,000	685,000,000	669,000,000	634,000,000
Operating Income	1,242,000,000	738,000,000	1,314,000,000	1,233,000,000	1,177,000,000	1,007,000,000
Operating Margin %	26.45%	17.60%	29.16%	29.56%	28.35%	26.14%
SGA Expense	1,807,000,000	1,771,000,000	1,746,000,000	1,641,000,000	1,506,000,000	1,465,000,000
Net Income	979,000,000	365,000,000	907,000,000	858,000,000	792,000,000	634,000,000
Operating Cash Flow	1,401,000,000	1,504,000,000	1,446,000,000	1,366,000,000	1,246,000,000	1,013,000,000
Capital Expenditure	522,000,000	261,000,000	201,000,000	209,000,000	196,000,000	228,000,000
EBITDA	1,476,000,000	970,000,000	1,542,000,000	1,472,000,000	1,443,000,000	1,267,000,000
Return on Assets %	21.24%	7.17%	16.97%	16.87%	16.17%	12.30%
Return on Equity %	56.05%	13.49%	27.44%	27.34%	29.55%	23.32%
Debt to Equity						

CONTACT INFORMATION:

Phone: 650 944-6000   Fax: 650 944-3060
Toll-Free: 800-446-8848
Address: 2700 Coast Ave., Mountain View, CA 94043 United States

SALARIES/BONUSES:

Top Exec. Salary: $1,000,000   Bonus: $
Second Exec. Salary: $725,000   Bonus: $

STOCK TICKER/OTHER:

Stock Ticker: INTU   Exchange: NAS
Employees: 7,900   Fiscal Year Ends: 07/31
Parent Company:

OTHER THOUGHTS:

Estimated Female Officers or Directors: 5
Hot Spot for Advancement for Women/Minorities: Y

Jabil Circuit Inc

NAIC Code: 334418

www.jabil.com

TYPES OF BUSINESS:

Contract Electronics Manufacturing
Maintenance & Support Services
Custom Design Services

BRANDS/DIVISIONS/AFFILIATES:

CONTACTS: *Note: Officers with more than one job title may be intentionally listed here more than once.*

Michael Loparco, CEO, Divisional
Alessandro Parimbelli, CEO, Divisional
Erich Hoch, CEO, Divisional
Steven Borges, CEO, Divisional
Mark Mondello, CEO
Forbes Alexander, CFO
Timothy Main, Chairman of the Board
Meheryar Dastoor, Controller
William Muir, COO
Thomas Sansone, Director
Joseph Mcgee, Executive VP, Divisional
Courtney Ryan, Executive VP, Divisional
Robert Katz, Executive VP
William Peters, President
Sergio Cadavid, Senior VP

GROWTH PLANS/SPECIAL FEATURES:

Jabil Circuit, Inc. (JBL) is a provider of worldwide electronic manufacturing services. It provides electronics design, production and product management services to a broad range of companies. JBL divides its operations into two segments: diversified manufacturing services (DMS) and electronics manufacturing services (EMS). DMS is focused on providing engineering solutions and on material sciences and technologies. This segment includes customers primarily in the consumer lifestyles and wearable technologies, defense & aerospace, emerging growth, health care, mobility and packaging industries. EMS is focused around leveraging information technology, supply chain design and engineering, technologies largely centered on core electronics, sharing of JBL's large-scale manufacturing infrastructure and the ability to serve a broad range of end markets. This segment includes customers primarily in the automotive, digital home, industrial and energy, networking and telecommunications, point of sale, printing and storage industries. The firm maintains facilities located worldwide, including Austria, Belgium, Brazil, Canada, China, Finland, France, Germany, Hungary, India, Ireland, Israel, Italy, Japan, Malaysia, Mexico, The Netherlands, Poland, Russia, Scotland, Singapore, South Korea, Spain, Taiwan, Ukraine, the U.S. and Vietnam. Its largest customers include Apple, Inc.; Cisco Systems, Inc.; LM Ericsson Telephone Company; General Electric Company; Hewlett-Packard Company; Ingenico SA; NetApp, Inc.; Dell Technologies.; Valeo SA; and Zebra Technologies Corporation.

FINANCIAL DATA: *Note: Data for latest year may not have been available at press time.*

In U.S. $	2016	2015	2014	2013	2012	2011
Revenue	18,353,090,000	17,899,200,000	15,762,150,000	18,336,890,000	17,151,940,000	16,518,830,000
R&D Expense	31,954,000	27,645,000	28,611,000	28,468,000	25,837,000	25,034,000
Operating Income	522,833,000	555,411,000	204,074,000	511,438,000	621,931,000	578,734,000
Operating Margin %	2.84%	3.10%	1.29%	2.78%	3.62%	3.50%
SGA Expense	924,427,000	862,647,000	675,730,000	688,752,000	644,452,000	604,179,000
Net Income	254,095,000	284,019,000	241,313,000	371,482,000	394,687,000	381,063,000
Operating Cash Flow	916,207,000	1,240,282,000	498,857,000	1,213,889,000	634,226,000	828,009,000
Capital Expenditure	924,239,000	963,145,000	624,060,000	736,858,000	497,697,000	458,989,000
EBITDA	1,220,333,000	1,088,913,000	687,456,000	925,243,000	968,521,000	898,059,000
Return on Assets %	2.55%	3.14%	2.73%	4.38%	5.31%	5.67%
Return on Equity %	10.69%	12.46%	10.54%	16.73%	19.87%	22.12%
Debt to Equity	0.85	0.58	0.74	0.72	0.78	0.59

CONTACT INFORMATION:

Phone: 727 577-9749   Fax: 727 579-8529
Toll-Free:
Address: 10560 Dr. Martin Luther King Jr. St. N., St. Petersburg, FL 33716 United States

STOCK TICKER/OTHER:

Stock Ticker: JBL
Employees: 161,000
Parent Company:

Exchange: NYS
Fiscal Year Ends: 08/31

SALARIES/BONUSES:

Top Exec. Salary: $1,100,000   Bonus: $
Second Exec. Salary: $700,000   Bonus: $

OTHER THOUGHTS:

Estimated Female Officers or Directors:
Hot Spot for Advancement for Women/Minorities: Y

Jack Henry & Associates Inc

www.jackhenry.com

NAIC Code: 0

TYPES OF BUSINESS:

Software-Data Processing
Financial Services Software
Consulting Services
Hardware Sales

BRANDS/DIVISIONS/AFFILIATES:

Jack Henry Banking
Symitar
ProfitStars
SilverLake
CIF 20/20
Core Director
Episys
Bayside Business Solutions

CONTACTS: Note: Officers with more than one job title may be intentionally listed here more than once.

Kevin Williams, CFO
John Prim, Chairman of the Board
Mark Forbis, Chief Technology Officer
Matthew Flanigan, Director
David Foss, President
Robert Schendel, Secretary

GROWTH PLANS/SPECIAL FEATURES:

Jack Henry & Associates, Inc. is a provider of integrated computer systems relating to data processing and management information for banks, credit unions and other financial institutions in the U.S. The company serves nearly 10,500 financial institutions and corporate entities. It provides products and services through three marketed brands: Jack Henry Banking, Symitar and ProfitStars. Jack Henry Banking currently supports more than 1,100 commercial banks with information and transaction processing platforms that provide enterprise-wide automation. Its core banking software platforms include SilverLake, an IBM System i-based product designed for commercial-focused banks with assets ranging from $500 million to $30 billion, as well as some progressive smaller banks and startup banks; CIF 20/20, an IBM-System i-based system that supports nearly 530 banks ranging from new institutions to those with assets exceeding $2 billion; and Core Director, a Windows-based client/server system that serves more than 200 banks ranging from new institutions to banks with assets over $1 billion. The Symitar brand supports credit unions through its two core platforms: Episys, an IBM power system-based program designed for credit unions with more than $50 million in assets; and CruiseNet, designed for credit unions with less than $50 million in assets. ProfitStars provides specialized products and services to nearly 10,200 financial services organizations. Products include business intelligence and management applications, retail delivery products, business banking systems, electronic funds transfer products, internet banking products, risk management and protection programs, document imaging products and professional services and education products. In 2016, the firm acquired Bayside Business Solutions, a portfolio management systems provider.

The firm offers employees medical, dental and vision insurance; flexible spending accounts; and education assistance.

FINANCIAL DATA: Note: Data for latest year may not have been available at press time.

In U.S. $	2016	2015	2014	2013	2012	2011
Revenue	1,354,646,000	1,256,190,000	1,210,053,000	1,129,386,000	1,027,109,000	966,897,000
R&D Expense	81,234,000	71,495,000	66,748,000	63,202,000	60,876,000	63,395,000
Operating Income	361,659,000	317,865,000	311,999,000	265,547,000	236,235,000	216,317,000
Operating Margin %	26.69%	25.30%	25.78%	23.51%	23.00%	22.37%
SGA Expense	157,593,000	146,494,000	139,882,000	148,243,000	126,619,000	119,622,000
Net Income	248,867,000	211,221,000	201,136,000	176,645,000	154,984,000	137,471,000
Operating Cash Flow	365,116,000	373,790,000	341,659,000	309,174,000	264,550,000	240,132,000
Capital Expenditure	164,562,000	145,301,000	111,667,000	97,774,000	80,034,000	59,039,000
EBITDA	491,614,000	437,030,000	420,147,000	366,528,000	332,030,000	306,956,000
Return on Assets %	13.62%	12.20%	12.36%	10.87%	9.91%	8.95%
Return on Equity %	25.04%	20.81%	19.06%	17.18%	16.63%	16.86%
Debt to Equity		0.05			0.10	0.14

CONTACT INFORMATION:

Phone: 417 235-6652   Fax:
Toll-Free: 800-299-4222
Address: 663 W. Highway 60, Monett, MO 65708 United States

STOCK TICKER/OTHER:

Stock Ticker: JKHY   Exchange: NAS
Employees: 5,822   Fiscal Year Ends: 06/30
Parent Company:

SALARIES/BONUSES:

Top Exec. Salary: $620,000   Bonus: $
Second Exec. Salary: Bonus: $
$493,881

OTHER THOUGHTS:

Estimated Female Officers or Directors: 3
Hot Spot for Advancement for Women/Minorities: Y

JB Hunt Transport Services Inc

www.jbhunt.com

NAIC Code: 484121

TYPES OF BUSINESS:

General Trucking
Logistics Services
Intermodal Services
Dedicated Fleet Services

BRANDS/DIVISIONS/AFFILIATES:

CONTACTS: *Note: Officers with more than one job title may be intentionally listed here more than once.*

Kevin Bracy, Assistant Secretary
John Roberts, CEO
David Mee, CFO
Kirk Thompson, Chairman of the Board
John Kuhlow, Chief Accounting Officer
Stuart Scott, Chief Information Officer
Shelley Simpson, Chief Marketing Officer
Craig Harper, Executive VP
Nicholas Hobbs, Executive VP
Terrence Matthews, Executive VP

GROWTH PLANS/SPECIAL FEATURES:

J.B. Hunt Transport Services, Inc. is a North American truckload transportation and logistics company serving the U.S., Canada and Mexico. The firm's operations are organized into four business segments: intermodal (JBI), dedicated contract services (DCS), full truckload dry-van freight (JBT) and integrated capacity solutions (ICS). The JBI segment utilizes agreements with rail carriers under which those carriers provide for railway movement of goods, while J.B. Hunt provides for the drayage (i.e. transport of goods by truck to and from rail terminals). The segment operates 73,957 company-controlled containers system wide. It also manages a fleet of 4,276 company-owned tractors. The DCS segment involves the provision of customized services governed by long-term contracts and currently includes dry-van, flatbed, temperature-controlled, dump trailers and local inner-city operations. This segment specializes in the design, development and execution of customer-specific fleet services, including private fleet conversion, dedicated fleet creation and transportation system augmentation. It operates 6,762 company-owned trucks, 436 customer-owned trucks and 10 independent contractor trucks. The JBT segment consists of conventional truck transport services in which company-controlled tractors pick up, transport and deliver cargo. J.B. Hunt dedicates 1,462 company-owned tractors to this segment. The segment also has 687 independent contractors, some of whom lease company-owned tractors. The ICS division provides non-asset and asset-light transportation solutions to customers through relationships with third-party carriers and integration with company-owned equipment.

The firm offers employees life, disability, auto, home, medical, dental and vision insurance; a 401(k) plan; and health care and dependent care reimbursement accounts.

FINANCIAL DATA: *Note: Data for latest year may not have been available at press time.*

In U.S. $	2016	2015	2014	2013	2012	2011
Revenue	6,555,459,000	6,187,646,000	6,165,441,000	5,584,571,000	5,054,980,000	4,526,842,000
R&D Expense						
Operating Income	721,020,000	715,694,000	631,542,000	576,708,000	530,200,000	444,233,000
Operating Margin %	10.99%	11.56%	10.24%	10.32%	10.48%	9.81%
SGA Expense	1,634,650,000	1,466,761,000	1,341,000,000	1,183,682,000	1,064,757,000	1,030,853,000
Net Income	432,090,000	427,235,000	374,792,000	342,382,000	310,354,000	257,006,000
Operating Cash Flow	854,143,000	873,308,000	646,779,000	574,351,000	548,044,000	635,692,000
Capital Expenditure	638,430,000	725,122,000	808,569,000	493,431,000	439,494,000	502,282,000
EBITDA	1,082,601,000	1,055,393,000	926,125,000	830,157,000	759,367,000	658,184,000
Return on Assets %	11.57%	12.14%	12.05%	12.95%	13.11%	12.15%
Return on Equity %	31.83%	34.11%	33.81%	37.95%	45.66%	45.06%
Debt to Equity	0.69	0.77	0.56	0.45	0.73	1.23

CONTACT INFORMATION:

Phone: 479 820-0000   Fax:
Toll-Free: 800-643-3622
Address: 615 J.B. Hunt Corporate Dr., Lowell, AR 72745-0130 United States

STOCK TICKER/OTHER:

Stock Ticker: JBHT
Employees: 22,190
Parent Company:

Exchange: NAS
Fiscal Year Ends: 12/31

SALARIES/BONUSES:

Top Exec. Salary: $807,747   Bonus: $
Second Exec. Salary: $480,660   Bonus: $

OTHER THOUGHTS:

Estimated Female Officers or Directors: 4
Hot Spot for Advancement for Women/Minorities: Y

Sales, profits and employees may be estimates. Financial information, benefits and other data can change quickly and may vary from those stated here.

Jefferies LLC

www.jefferies.com

NAIC Code: 523110

TYPES OF BUSINESS:

Stock Brokerage/Investment Banking
Corporate Finance
Asset Management
Mergers & Acquisitions Advising
Execution Services

BRANDS/DIVISIONS/AFFILIATES:

Leucadia National Corporation
Jefferies Investment Advisers LLC
Jefferies International Limited

CONTACTS: *Note: Officers with more than one job title may be intentionally listed here more than once.*

Richard B. Handler, CEO
Peregrine Broadbent, CFO
Michael J. Sharp, General Counsel
Steven R. Black, Global Head-Equities Research
Patrice Blanc, CEO-Jefferies Bache
Tim Cronin, Head-Int'l Fixed Income
Benjamin D. Lorello, Global Head-Investment Banking & Capital Markets
Richard B. Handler, Chmn.
David Weaver, Head-European Capital Markets

GROWTH PLANS/SPECIAL FEATURES:

Jefferies LLC, a wholly-owned subsidiary of Leucadia National Corporation, is an international full-service investment banking firm. The company serves investors, companies and government entities. Jefferies offers expertise in investment banking, equities, fixed income, commodities and wealth management in the Americas, Europe, the Middle East and Asia. For corporate clients, the firm is a merger and acquisition (M&A) and restructuring advisor and underwriter of debt and equity issues. For institutional investors and high-end individuals, the firm is a leading provider of trade execution and liquidity in equity, convertible and high yield securities and a market maker of fixed income and commodity-linked products. Jefferies also offers top-tier wealth management, prime services and securities finance. The company's investment banking division offers debt capital markets, equity capital markets, M&As, restructuring and recapitalization and U.K. corporate brokering. This segment's deep sector products include consumer and retail, energy, financial institutions, financial sponsors, health care, industrials, media and telecom, public finance, real estate, gaming, lodging and technology. Its equities division provide cash equities, electronic trading solutions, equity derivatives, convertibles, prime services and corporate access. Fixed income products consist of government securities, mortgage- and asset-backed securities, corporate credit, emerging markets, municipal securities and capital markets. Jefferies' research and strategy division offers insight to clients on market strategy, economics, equity, fixed income, foreign exchange and commodities in the Americas, Europe and Asia. Asset management is provided through various investment advisory entities including Jefferies Investment Advisers, LLC and Jefferies International Limited. Wealth management services include portfolio management services, executive services and family office services.

FINANCIAL DATA: *Note: Data for latest year may not have been available at press time.*

In U.S. $	2016	2015	2014	2013	2012	2011
Revenue	3,233,823,000	3,274,904,000	3,846,265,000	2,930,000,000	2,998,784,000	2,545,190,912
R&D Expense						
Operating Income						
Operating Margin %						
SGA Expense						
Net Income	29,972,000	114,227,000	303,021,000	341,000,000	323,149,000	284,617,984
Operating Cash Flow						
Capital Expenditure						
EBITDA						
Return on Assets %						
Return on Equity %						
Debt to Equity						

CONTACT INFORMATION:

Phone: 212 284-2300   Fax: 212 284-2111
Toll-Free:
Address: 520 Madison Ave., New York, NY 10022 United States

STOCK TICKER/OTHER:

Stock Ticker: Subsidiary   Exchange:
Employees: 3,797   Fiscal Year Ends: 11/30
Parent Company: Leucadia National Corporation

SALARIES/BONUSES:

Top Exec. Salary: $ Bonus: $
Second Exec. Salary: $ Bonus: $

OTHER THOUGHTS:

Estimated Female Officers or Directors:
Hot Spot for Advancement for Women/Minorities:

JetBlue Airways Corporation

www.jetblue.com

NAIC Code: 481111

TYPES OF BUSINESS:

Airline
In-Flight Entertainment

BRANDS/DIVISIONS/AFFILIATES:

JetBlue Vacations
TrueBlue
Mint
Blue
Blue Plus
Blue Flex

CONTACTS: *Note: Officers with more than one job title may be intentionally listed here more than once.*

Stephen Priest, CFO
Joel Peterson, Chairman of the Board
Alexander Chatkewitz, Chief Accounting Officer
Frank Sica, Director
Martin St George, Executive VP, Divisional
James Hnat, Executive VP, Divisional
Robin Hayes, President

GROWTH PLANS/SPECIAL FEATURES:

JetBlue Airways Corporation is a low-fare, low-cost passenger airline. It primarily operates on point-to-point routes with its fleet of Airbus A321, Airbus A320 and EMBRAER 190 aircraft types. It serves 100 cities in the U.S., Caribbean and Latin America. Most of its average 925 daily flights have as an origin or destination one of the company's six focus cities: Boston, Fort Lauderdale, Los Angeles/Long Beach, New York, Orlando and San Juan, Puerto Rico. The company's flights are single-class, but feature leather seats and seat-back televisions with 36 channels of free DirecTV programming, 100 stations of free SiriusXM satellite radio and movie channel offerings from JetBlue Features. JetBlue sells vacation packages through JetBlue Vacations, a one-stop website designed to meet customers' demand for packaged travel planning. The firm also participates in three major global distribution systems: Sabre, Galileo and Amadeus; and four major online travel agents (OTAs): Expedia, Travelocity, Orbitz and Priceline. JetBlue also offers customers a choice to purchase tickets from three branded fares: Blue, Blue Plus and Blue Flex. Each fare includes different offerings such as free checked bags, reduced change fees and additional TrueBlue rewards points. The company's premium transcontinental product, Mint, includes 16 fully lie-flat seats in select Airbus aircraft, four of which are in suites with a privacy door.

JetBlue offers employees medical, dental, vision and life insurance; short- and long-term disability insurance; a group legal plan; flexible spending accounts; pilot loss of license; health risk assessments; disease management programs; an airline credit union; a 401(k) plan; a Roth 401(k) plan; self-directed accounts; a profit sharing plan; a stock purchase plan; and free and reduced rate standby travel on JetBlue flights.

FINANCIAL DATA: *Note: Data for latest year may not have been available at press time.*

In U.S. $	2016	2015	2014	2013	2012	2011
Revenue	6,632,000,000	6,416,000,000	5,817,000,000	5,441,000,000	4,982,000,000	4,504,000,000
R&D Expense						
Operating Income	1,312,000,000	1,216,000,000	515,000,000	428,000,000	376,000,000	322,000,000
Operating Margin %	19.78%	18.95%	8.85%	7.86%	7.54%	7.14%
SGA Expense	1,957,000,000	1,804,000,000	1,525,000,000	1,358,000,000	1,248,000,000	1,146,000,000
Net Income	759,000,000	677,000,000	401,000,000	168,000,000	128,000,000	86,000,000
Operating Cash Flow	1,632,000,000	1,598,000,000	912,000,000	758,000,000	698,000,000	614,000,000
Capital Expenditure	850,000,000	941,000,000	857,000,000	637,000,000	828,000,000	528,000,000
EBITDA	1,712,000,000	1,562,000,000	1,082,000,000	733,000,000	646,000,000	566,000,000
Return on Assets %	8.36%	8.20%	5.28%	2.33%	1.81%	1.25%
Return on Equity %	21.01%	23.59%	17.19%	8.35%	7.02%	5.04%
Debt to Equity	0.29	0.43	0.77	0.99	1.30	1.62

CONTACT INFORMATION:

Phone: 718 286-7900   Fax: 718 709-3621
Toll-Free: 800-538-2583
Address: 27-01 Queens Plaza North, Long Island City, NY 11101 United States

STOCK TICKER/OTHER:

Stock Ticker: JBLU   Exchange: NAS
Employees: 18,406   Fiscal Year Ends: 12/31
Parent Company:

SALARIES/BONUSES:

Top Exec. Salary: $550,000   Bonus: $61,050
Second Exec. Salary: $425,000   Bonus: $23,637

OTHER THOUGHTS:

Estimated Female Officers or Directors: 5
Hot Spot for Advancement for Women/Minorities: Y

JM Family Enterprises Inc

www.jmfamily.com

NAIC Code: 423110

TYPES OF BUSINESS:

Automobile Distribution-Wholesale
Automobile Dealer
Parts Distribution
Financing & Insurance
Dealership Financing
Consulting Services

BRANDS/DIVISIONS/AFFILIATES:

JM Lexus
JM Lexus Certified Pre-owned Superstore
JM&A Group
Southeast Toyota Distributors LLC
World Omni Financial Corp
DataScan
Southeast Toyota Finance

CONTACTS: Note: Officers with more than one job title may be intentionally listed here more than once.

Colin Brown, CEO
Brent Burns, Pres.
Carmen Johnson, General Counsel
Frank Armstrong, Exec. VP
Ron Coombs, Sr. VP
Forrest Heathcott, Exec. VP
Ed Sheehy, Exec. VP

GROWTH PLANS/SPECIAL FEATURES:

JM Family Enterprises, Inc. is a leading family-owned diversified automotive company. Through its subsidiaries, JM is a distributor of Toyotas and Scions, a diversified financial services company, a provider of finance and insurance products, a provider of integrated software systems for automotive dealers and a Lexus dealership. Subsidiaries JM Lexus and the JM Lexus Certified Pre-owned Superstore, located in Margate and Coconut Creek, Florida, generate the highest sales volume among all Lexus dealers worldwide, and has done so for 25 consecutive years. Subsidiary JM&A Group is an independent provider of finance and insurance products to more than 3,800 automobile dealerships. Southeast Toyota Distributors, LLC is an independent distributor of Toyotas, distributing vehicles, parts and accessories to more than 175 independent Toyota dealers in Alabama, Florida, Georgia, North Carolina and South Carolina. Last, World Omni Financial Corp. is a diversified financial services company offering a wide range of products and services to automotive dealers, consumers and lenders. World Omni comprises: DataScan, a provider of wholesale floorplan accounting and risk management systems; and Southeast Toyota Finance, a finance company for Toyota dealers in the Southeast U.S., servicing nearly 650,000 finance and lease accounts.

JM offers its employees educational assistance and development programs; flextime; adoption assistance; an onsite fitness center and access to a cafeteria and credit union; massage therapy; health and dependent care spending accounts; and medical, dental, vision, prescription, life and disability insurance.

FINANCIAL DATA: Note: Data for latest year may not have been available at press time.

In U.S. $	2016	2015	2014	2013	2012	2011
Revenue	14,900,000,000	14,500,000,000	13,750,000,000	12,500,000,000	11,500,000,000	9,300,000,000
R&D Expense						
Operating Income						
Operating Margin %						
SGA Expense						
Net Income						
Operating Cash Flow						
Capital Expenditure						
EBITDA						
Return on Assets %						
Return on Equity %						
Debt to Equity						

CONTACT INFORMATION:

Phone: 954-429-2000   Fax: 954-429-2300
Toll-Free:
Address: 100 Jim Moran Blvd., Deerfield Beach, FL 33442 United States

STOCK TICKER/OTHER:

Stock Ticker: Private   Exchange:
Employees: 4,203   Fiscal Year Ends: 12/31
Parent Company:

SALARIES/BONUSES:

Top Exec. Salary: $ Bonus: $
Second Exec. Salary: $ Bonus: $

OTHER THOUGHTS:

Estimated Female Officers or Directors: 1
Hot Spot for Advancement for Women/Minorities:

Johnson & Johnson

NAIC Code: 325412

www.jnj.com

TYPES OF BUSINESS:

Personal Health Care & Hygiene Products
Sterilization Products
Surgical Products
Pharmaceuticals
Skin Care Products
Baby Care Products
Contact Lenses
Medical Equipment

BRANDS/DIVISIONS/AFFILIATES:

Motrin
Band-Aid
Listerine
Tylenol
Neosporin
Pepcid AC
Risperdal Consta
Abbott Medical Optics

CONTACTS: Note: Officers with more than one job title may be intentionally listed here more than once.

Alex Gorsky, CEO
Dominic Caruso, CFO
Sandra Peterson, Chairman of the Board, Divisional
Jorge Mesquita, Chairman of the Board, Divisional
Joaquin Duato, Chairman of the Board, Divisional
Gary Pruden, Chairman of the Board, Divisional
Ronald Kapusta, Chief Accounting Officer
Paulus Stoffels, Executive VP
Peter Fasolo, Executive VP
Michael Ullmann, General Counsel

GROWTH PLANS/SPECIAL FEATURES:

Johnson & Johnson, founded in 1886, is one of the world's most comprehensive and well-known researchers, developers and manufacturers of health care products. Johnson & Johnson's worldwide operations are divided into three segments: consumer, pharmaceuticals and medical devices. The company's principal consumer goods are personal care and hygiene products, including baby care, skin care, oral care, wound care and women's health care products as well as nutritional and over-the-counter pharmaceutical products. Major consumer brands include Motrin, Band-Aid, Listerine, Tylenol, Neosporin, Aveeno and Pepcid AC. The pharmaceutical segment covers a wide spectrum of health fields, including anti-infective, antipsychotic, contraceptive, dermatology, gastrointestinal, hematology, immunology, neurology, oncology, pain management and virology. Among its pharmaceutical products are Risperdal Consta, an antipsychotic used to treat schizophrenia, and Remicade for the treatment of immune mediated inflammatory diseases. In the medical devices segment, Johnson & Johnson makes a number of products including orthopedic joint reconstruction devices, surgical care, advanced sterilization products, blood glucose monitoring devices, diagnostic products and disposable contact lenses. The firm owns more than 230 companies across 60 countries, and is headquartered in New Brunswick, New Jersey. In January 2017, Johnson & Johnson agreed to acquire Actelion Ltd., Europe's largest biotech firm by sales and market capitalization, for $30 billion. The deal does not include the drug discovery operations of Actelion. That February, it acquired Abbott Medical Optics, which provides ophthalmic products in three areas of patient care: cataract surgery, laser refractive surgery and consumer eye health. These product lines were combined with ACUVUE contact lenses business, and the combined organization will operate under the name Jonson & Johnson Vision.

FINANCIAL DATA: Note: Data for latest year may not have been available at press time.

In U.S. $	2016	2015	2014	2013	2012	2011
Revenue	71,890,000,000	70,074,000,000	74,331,000,000	71,312,000,000	67,224,000,000	65,030,000,000
R&D Expense	9,095,000,000	9,046,000,000	8,672,000,000	8,183,000,000	7,665,000,000	7,548,000,000
Operating Income	21,165,000,000	18,065,000,000	20,959,000,000	18,377,000,000	15,869,000,000	16,153,000,000
Operating Margin %	29.44%	25.77%	28.19%	25.76%	23.60%	24.83%
SGA Expense	19,945,000,000	21,203,000,000	21,954,000,000	21,830,000,000	20,869,000,000	20,969,000,000
Net Income	16,540,000,000	15,409,000,000	16,323,000,000	13,831,000,000	10,853,000,000	9,671,999,000
Operating Cash Flow	18,767,000,000	19,279,000,000	18,471,000,000	17,414,000,000	15,396,000,000	14,298,000,000
Capital Expenditure	3,226,000,000	3,463,000,000	3,714,000,000	3,595,000,000	2,934,000,000	2,893,000,000
EBITDA	24,283,000,000	23,494,000,000	24,991,000,000	20,057,000,000	17,973,000,000	16,090,000,000
Return on Assets %	12.04%	11.65%	12.37%	10.88%	9.23%	8.93%
Return on Equity %	23.36%	21.87%	22.70%	19.91%	17.80%	17.01%
Debt to Equity	0.31	0.18	0.21	0.17	0.17	0.22

CONTACT INFORMATION:

Phone: 732 524-0400   Fax: 732 214-0332
Toll-Free:
Address: 1 Johnson & Johnson Plaza, New Brunswick, NJ 08933 United States

STOCK TICKER/OTHER:

Stock Ticker: JNJ   Exchange: NYS
Employees: 126,400   Fiscal Year Ends: 12/31
Parent Company:

SALARIES/BONUSES:

Top Exec. Salary: $1,600,000   Bonus: $
Second Exec. Salary: $1,144,000   Bonus: $

OTHER THOUGHTS:

Estimated Female Officers or Directors: 4
Hot Spot for Advancement for Women/Minorities: Y

Jones Lang LaSalle Inc

www.us.jll.com

NAIC Code: 531120

TYPES OF BUSINESS:

Real Estate Rental, Leasing & Management
Investment Management
Project Management
Consulting Services
Real Estate Investment Banking
Properties Brokerage

BRANDS/DIVISIONS/AFFILIATES:

LaSalle Investment Management
Bill Goold Realty
Washington Partners Inc
Integral UK Ltd

CONTACTS: *Note: Officers with more than one job title may be intentionally listed here more than once.*

John Forrest, CEO, Divisional
Bryan Duncan, Other Corporate Officer
Gregory OBrien, CEO, Geographical
Anthony Couse, CEO, Geographical
Guy Grainger, CEO, Geographical
Jeff Jacobson, CEO, Subsidiary
Christie Kelly, CFO
David Johnson, Chief Information Officer
Louis Bowers, Controller
Sheila Penrose, Director
Parikshat Suri, Executive VP
Allan Frazier, Executive VP
Patricia Maxson, Executive VP
James Jasionowski, Executive VP
Mark Ohringer, Executive VP
Grace Chang, Managing Director, Divisional
Christian Ulbrich, President

GROWTH PLANS/SPECIAL FEATURES:

Jones Lang LaSalle, Inc. (JLL) is a real estate money management firm that provides integrated real estate and investment management expertise on a local, regional and global level to owner, occupier and investor clients. The firm is active in property and corporate facility management services, with a portfolio encompassing roughly 4 billion square feet worldwide. JLL offers its real estate services across three geographically-aligned business segments: the Americas; Europe, the Middle East and Africa (EMEA); and Asia Pacific. The company's range of real estate service areas includes agency leasing, property management, project and development management, valuations, brokerage of properties, capital markets, real estate investment banking and merchant banking, corporate finance, hotel advisory, space acquisition and disposition, facilities management, strategic consulting, energy management and sustainability, value recovery and receivership services as well as money management. These services are offered to for-profit and not-for-profit firms as well as to governmental entities and public-private partnerships across a wide variety of property categories, including offices, hotels, industrial, retail, multi-family residential, hospitals, data centers, sporting facilities, cultural institutions and transportation centers. A fourth business segment encompasses the operations of subsidiary LaSalle Investment Management, a diversified real estate investment management firm with $60.1 billion in assets under management. JLL has operations in over 1,000 locations in 80 countries worldwide, including 280 corporate offices. In 2016, the firm acquired Bill Goold Realty; Washington Partners, Inc.; and Integral UK Ltd.

FINANCIAL DATA: *Note: Data for latest year may not have been available at press time.*

In U.S. $	2016	2015	2014	2013	2012	2011
Revenue	6,803,800,000	5,965,671,000	5,429,603,000	4,461,591,000	3,932,830,000	3,584,544,000
R&D Expense						
Operating Income	440,600,000	529,798,000	465,664,000	368,819,000	289,403,000	251,205,000
Operating Margin %	6.47%	8.88%	8.57%	8.26%	7.35%	7.00%
SGA Expense	6,152,900,000	5,293,615,000	4,827,097,000	3,994,604,000	3,519,196,000	3,194,380,000
Net Income	318,200,000	438,672,000	386,063,000	269,865,000	208,050,000	164,384,000
Operating Cash Flow	214,500,000	375,769,000	498,861,000	293,167,000	327,698,000	211,338,000
Capital Expenditure	312,600,000	196,703,000	156,927,000	110,684,000	94,758,000	91,538,000
EBITDA	629,500,000	715,415,000	608,266,000	448,672,000	424,346,000	374,424,000
Return on Assets %	4.59%	7.77%	7.97%	6.02%	5.01%	4.50%
Return on Equity %	11.60%	17.27%	16.89%	13.04%	11.39%	10.06%
Debt to Equity	0.42	0.19	0.11	0.19	0.22	0.27

CONTACT INFORMATION:

Phone: 312 782-5800   Fax: 312 782-4339
Toll-Free:
Address: 200 E. Randolph Dr., Chicago, IL 60601 United States

STOCK TICKER/OTHER:

Stock Ticker: JLL   Exchange: NYS
Employees: 77,000   Fiscal Year Ends: 12/31
Parent Company:

SALARIES/BONUSES:

Top Exec. Salary: $750,000   Bonus: $
Second Exec. Salary: Bonus: $
$481,619

OTHER THOUGHTS:

Estimated Female Officers or Directors: 2
Hot Spot for Advancement for Women/Minorities: Y

JP Morgan Chase & Co Inc

www.jpmorganchase.com

NAIC Code: 522110

TYPES OF BUSINESS:

Banking
Mortgages
Investment Banking
Stock Brokerage
Credit Cards
Business Finance
Mutual Funds
Annuities

BRANDS/DIVISIONS/AFFILIATES:

JPMorgan Chase Bank NA
Chase Bank USA NA
JP Morgan Securities LLC

CONTACTS: *Note: Officers with more than one job title may be intentionally listed here more than once.*

Gordon Smith, CEO, Divisional
Mary Erdoes, CEO, Divisional
Douglas Petno, CEO, Divisional
Mark ODonovan, CEO, Divisional
Daniel Pinto, CEO, Divisional
James Dimon, CEO
Marianne Lake, CFO
Nicole Giles, Chief Accounting Officer
Ashley Bacon, Chief Risk Officer
Stacey Friedman, General Counsel
John Donnelly, Other Corporate Officer

GROWTH PLANS/SPECIAL FEATURES:

J.P. Morgan Chase & Co., Inc. (JPM) is one of the largest banking institutions in the world, with operations in over 60 countries and over $2.5 trillion in assets. JPM's principal subsidiaries include JPMorgan Chase Bank, NA, a national banking association with operations in 23 states; Chase Bank USA, NA, a leading provider of retail banking services and credit cards; and J.P. Morgan Securities LLC, an investment banking firm. JPM operates its business through five segments: consumer and community banking (CCB), corporate and investment banking (CIB), commercial banking, asset management and corporate/private equity. The CCB segment serves consumers and businesses through personal service at bank branches and through ATMs, online, mobile and telephone banking. The CIB segment, comprised of banking and markets and investor services, offers a broad range of investment banking, market-making, prime brokerage, and treasury and securities products and services to a global client base. The commercial banking segment provides local expertise and service to U.S. and U.S. multinational clients, including corporations, municipalities, financial institutions and nonprofit entities with annual revenue generally ranging from $20 million to $2 billion. The asset management segment is a global leader in investment and wealth management. The corporate/private equity segment measures, monitors, reports and manages the firm's liquidity, funding and structural interest rate and foreign exchange risks.

The company offers employees benefits including medical, dental, vision, life, disability and accident insurance; adoption assistance; an employee assistance program; tuition assistance; 401(k) and retirement plans; an employee stock purchase plan; and discounts on banking services.

FINANCIAL DATA: *Note: Data for latest year may not have been available at press time.*

In U.S. $	2016	2015	2014	2013	2012	2011
Revenue	95,668,000,000	93,543,000,000	94,205,000,000	96,606,000,000	97,031,000,000	97,234,000,000
R&D Expense						
Operating Income	34,536,000,000	30,702,000,000	29,792,000,000	25,914,000,000	28,917,000,000	26,749,000,000
Operating Margin %	36.09%	32.82%	31.62%	26.82%	29.80%	27.50%
SGA Expense	39,722,000,000	38,651,000,000	38,514,000,000	38,735,000,000	38,386,000,000	37,127,000,000
Net Income	24,733,000,000	24,442,000,000	21,762,000,000	17,923,000,000	21,284,000,000	18,976,000,000
Operating Cash Flow	20,196,000,000	73,466,000,000	36,593,000,000	107,953,000,000	25,079,000,000	95,932,000,000
Capital Expenditure						
EBITDA						
Return on Assets %	.95%	.90%	.80%	.69%	.85%	.80%
Return on Equity %	10.26%	10.33%	9.75%	8.40%	10.72%	10.21%
Debt to Equity	1.39	1.39	1.44	1.47	1.41	1.46

CONTACT INFORMATION:

Phone: 212 270-6000   Fax: 212 270-1648
Toll-Free: 877-242-7372
Address: 270 Park Ave., New York, NY 10017 United States

STOCK TICKER/OTHER:

Stock Ticker: JPM   Exchange: NYS
Employees: 251,196   Fiscal Year Ends: 12/31
Parent Company:

SALARIES/BONUSES:

Top Exec. Salary: $8,303,234   Bonus: $
Second Exec. Salary: Bonus: $7,300,000
$750,000

OTHER THOUGHTS:

Estimated Female Officers or Directors: 3
Hot Spot for Advancement for Women/Minorities: Y

Juniper Networks Inc

www.juniper.net

NAIC Code: 0

TYPES OF BUSINESS:

Networking Equipment
IP Networking Systems
Internet Routers
Network Security Products
Internet Software
Intrusion Prevention
Application Acceleration

BRANDS/DIVISIONS/AFFILIATES:

ACX
MX
M
PTX
Cloud CPE
NorthStar
Junos
OCX1100

CONTACTS: *Note: Officers with more than one job title may be intentionally listed here more than once.*

Rami Rahim, CEO
Ken Miller, CFO
Scott Kriens, Chairman of the Board
Terrance Spidell, Chief Accounting Officer
Pradeep Sindhu, Chief Technology Officer
Vincent Molinaro, Executive VP
Andy Athreya, Other Executive Officer
Kevin Hutchins, Senior VP, Divisional
Brian Martin, Senior VP

GROWTH PLANS/SPECIAL FEATURES:

Juniper Networks, Inc. designs, develops and sells products and services for high-performance networks. These products help customers build highly scalable, reliable, secure and cost-effective networks for their businesses. Juniper sells its products in more than 100 countries in three geographic regions: Americas; Europe, Middle East and Africa (EMEA); and Asia Pacific. The company's offerings address high-performance network requirements for global service providers, cloud environments, enterprises, governments and research and public sector organizations who view the network as critical to its business success. Routing products include the firm's ACX, MX, M, PTX and T series, as well as its Cloud CPE end-to-end solution and NorthStar wide-area network controller. Switching products include the EX and QFX series, as well as the disaggregated version of Junos software, and the OCX1100 open networking switch designed to combine a cloud-optimized open compute project with the Junos operating system. Security products include the SRX series for data center gateway services, and for campus and branch gateway services; the vSRX virtual firewall; advanced malware protection; and Spotlight Secure threat intelligence platform. Juniper's Junos platform enables customers to expand network software into the application space, deploy software clients to control delivery and accelerate the pace of innovation with an ecosystem of developers. Juniper Networks owns over 2,480 issued or pending technology patents. In December 2016, the firm announced its intent to acquire AppFormix in order to bolster Juniper's cloud portfolio with machine learning and telemetry technology.

The firm offers its employees medical, dental, prescription and vision insurance; a savings plan; paid time off and holidays; and a stock purchase plan.

FINANCIAL DATA: *Note: Data for latest year may not have been available at press time.*

In U.S. $	2016	2015	2014	2013	2012	2011
Revenue	4,990,100,000	4,857,800,000	4,627,100,000	4,669,100,000	4,365,400,000	4,448,709,000
R&D Expense	1,013,700,000	994,500,000	1,006,200,000	1,043,200,000	1,101,600,000	1,026,790,000
Operating Income	889,700,000	912,000,000	-419,700,000	565,900,000	308,100,000	618,524,000
Operating Margin %	17.82%	18.77%	-9.07%	12.12%	7.05%	13.90%
SGA Expense	1,197,800,000	1,172,700,000	1,254,700,000	1,293,200,000	1,245,600,000	1,180,192,000
Net Income	592,700,000	633,700,000	-334,300,000	439,800,000	186,500,000	425,136,000
Operating Cash Flow	1,106,000,000	892,500,000	763,400,000	842,300,000	642,400,000	986,726,000
Capital Expenditure	214,700,000	210,300,000	192,900,000	243,100,000	414,000,000	266,314,000
EBITDA	1,096,400,000	1,112,000,000	166,700,000	773,800,000	531,400,000	791,254,000
Return on Assets %	6.48%	7.44%	-3.56%	4.36%	1.88%	4.60%
Return on Equity %	12.42%	13.35%	-5.47%	6.15%	2.64%	6.20%
Debt to Equity	0.42	0.36	0.27	0.13	0.15	0.14

CONTACT INFORMATION:

Phone: 408 745-2000   Fax: 408 745-2100
Toll-Free: 888-586-4737
Address: 1133 Innovation Way, Sunnyvale, CA 94089 United States

STOCK TICKER/OTHER:

Stock Ticker: JNPR   Exchange: NYS
Employees: 9,832   Fiscal Year Ends: 12/31
Parent Company:

SALARIES/BONUSES:

Top Exec. Salary: $1,000,000   Bonus: $
Second Exec. Salary: $610,000   Bonus: $

OTHER THOUGHTS:

Estimated Female Officers or Directors: 3
Hot Spot for Advancement for Women/Minorities: Y

Kaiser Permanente

NAIC Code: 622110

TYPES OF BUSINESS:

General Medical and Surgical Hospitals
General & Specialty Hospitals
Outpatient Facilities
HMO
Health Insurance
Integrated Health Care System
Physician Networks
Clinical Record Management

BRANDS/DIVISIONS/AFFILIATES:

Kaiser Foundation Health Plan Inc
Kaiser Foundation Hospitals
Permanente Medical Groups
Kaiser Permanente Health Research
KP HealthConnect

CONTACTS: Note: Officers with more than one job title may be intentionally listed here more than once.

Bernard Tyson, CEO
Kathy Lancaster, CFO
Chuck Columbus, Chief Human Resources Officer
Raymond J. Baxter, Sr. VP-Community Benefit, Research & Health Policy
Richard D. Daniels, CIO
Mark S. Zemelman, General Counsel
Arthur M. Southam, Exec. VP-Health Plan Oper.
Chris Grant, Sr. VP-Corp. Dev. & Care Delivery Strategy
Diane Gage Lofgren, Sr. VP
Cynthia Powers Overmyer, Sr. VP-Internal Audit Svcs.
Daniel P. Garcia, Chief Compliance Officer
Anthony Barrueta, Sr. VP-Gov't Rel.
Amy Compton-Phillips, Associate Exec. Dir.-Quality, Permanente
Bernard Tyson, Chmn.

GROWTH PLANS/SPECIAL FEATURES:

Kaiser Permanente is a nonprofit company dedicated to providing integrated healthcare coverage. The firm operates in California, Colorado, Georgia, Hawaii, Maryland, Washington D.C., Oregon, Virginia and Washington. It serves 11.8 million members, most of which are in California (more than 8.4 million). Kaiser has three main operating divisions: Kaiser Foundation Health Plan, Inc., which contracts with individuals and groups to provide medical coverage; Kaiser Foundation Hospitals and their subsidiaries, operating community hospitals and outpatient facilities in several states; and Permanente Medical Groups, the company's network of physicians providing healthcare to its members. The company's resources include approximately 38 medical centers, including hospitals and outpatient facilities; 673 medical offices; and 21,200 physicians. Kaiser Foundation Hospitals also fund medical- and health-related research. In addition, Kaiser Permanente Health Research has eight research centers across the country, which conduct clinical trials of new drugs and medical devices and specialize in epidemiological studies. The firm, as a participant in the Medicare program, cares for over 1.3 million Medicare members, making it one of the largest health plans serving the Medicare program. The KP HealthConnect program integrates clinical records with appointments, registration and billing, thereby significantly improving care delivery and patient satisfaction.

Employees of the firm are offered medical, vision, dental and life insurance; a prescription plan; paid time off for vacations; designated holidays; sick leave; disability benefits; retirement plans; tuition reimbursement; employee assistance programs; and transit spending account options. Kaiser Permanente's employee health care coverage extends to spouses, domestic partners and unmarried children.

FINANCIAL DATA: Note: Data for latest year may not have been available at press time.

In U.S. $	2016	2015	2014	2013	2012	2011
Revenue	64,600,000,000	60,700,000,000	56,400,000,000	53,100,000,000	50,600,000,000	47,900,000,000
R&D Expense						
Operating Income						
Operating Margin %						
SGA Expense						
Net Income	3,100,000,000	1,900,000,000	3,100,000,000	2,700,000,000	2,600,000,000	1,600,000,000
Operating Cash Flow						
Capital Expenditure						
EBITDA						
Return on Assets %						
Return on Equity %						
Debt to Equity						

CONTACT INFORMATION:

Phone: 510-271-5910   Fax: 510-267-7524
Toll-Free:
Address: 1 Kaiser Plaza, 19/Fl., Oakland, CA 94612 United States

STOCK TICKER/OTHER:

Stock Ticker: Nonprofit   Exchange:
Employees: 186,497   Fiscal Year Ends: 12/31
Parent Company:

SALARIES/BONUSES:

Top Exec. Salary: $ Bonus: $
Second Exec. Salary: $ Bonus: $

OTHER THOUGHTS:

Estimated Female Officers or Directors: 9
Hot Spot for Advancement for Women/Minorities: Y

Kelly Services Inc

www.kellyservices.com

NAIC Code: 561320

TYPES OF BUSINESS:

Staffing & Temporary Help
Human Resources Consulting
Outsourcing Solutions
Permanent Hiring Programs
Call Center Services
Benefits & Payroll Outsourcing

BRANDS/DIVISIONS/AFFILIATES:

CONTACTS: *Note: Officers with more than one job title may be intentionally listed here more than once.*

George Corona, CEO
Terence Adderley, Chairman of the Board
Laura Lockhart, Chief Accounting Officer
Teresa Carroll, Executive VP
Peter Quigley, Executive VP
Natalia Shuman-Fabbri, General Manager, Geographical
Steven Armstrong, General Manager, Geographical
Antonina Ramsey, Other Executive Officer
Olivier Thirot, Senior VP

GROWTH PLANS/SPECIAL FEATURES:

Kelly Services, Inc. is a staffing and services company that offers temporary staffing services, staff leasing, outsourcing and full-time placement. Kelly's workforce solutions are provided to customers through offices in three regions: the Americas; Europe, the Middle East and Africa (EMEA); and Asia Pacific (APAC). It operates in seven segments: Americas commercial, Americas professional and technical (Americas PT), EMEA commercial, EMEA PT, APAC commercial, APAC PT and the outsourcing and consulting group (OCG). Americas commercial specialties include providing trained staff, employees and support roles for offices, including data entry, clerical and administrative; contact centers, including technical support hotlines and telemarketing units; education, supplying schools; marketing, including seminars, as well as sales and trade shows; electronic assembly, including assemblers, quality control inspectors and technicians; and light industrial, including maintenance workers, material handlers and assemblers. Americas PT provides staffing services for the following sectors: science, engineering, IT, creative services, finance/accounting, health care and law. EMEA commercial provides staffing services similar to Americas commercial, including the following sectors: office, contact center, temporary-to-hire, catering, hospitality and industrial. EMEA PT provides staffing services similar to Americas PT, including engineering, finance/accounting, health care, IT and science. APAC (Asia Pacific) commercial provides staffing similar to the Americas and EMEA commercial, including permanent placement, temporary staffing and temporary-to-full-time staffing. APAC PT provides similar staffing as Americas and EMEA PT, including engineering, IT and science. OCG delivers integrated talent management solutions to meet customer needs across multiple regions, skill sets and the entire spectrum of talent categories. Services in this segment include contingent workforce outsourcing, business process outsourcing, recruitment process outsourcing, independent contractor solutions, payroll process outsourcing, career transition and executive coaching/development and executive search.

FINANCIAL DATA: *Note: Data for latest year may not have been available at press time.*

In U.S. $	2016	2015	2014	2013	2012	2011
Revenue	5,276,800,000	5,518,200,000	5,562,700,000	5,413,100,000	5,450,500,000	5,551,000,000
R&D Expense						
Operating Income	63,200,000	66,700,000	21,900,000	53,300,000	72,300,000	57,700,000
Operating Margin %	1.19%	1.20%	.39%	.98%	1.32%	1.03%
SGA Expense	843,100,000	853,600,000	886,500,000	834,500,000	821,200,000	836,400,000
Net Income	120,800,000	53,800,000	23,700,000	58,900,000	50,100,000	63,700,000
Operating Cash Flow	37,400,000	23,500,000	-70,000,000	115,300,000	61,100,000	19,100,000
Capital Expenditure	12,700,000	16,900,000	21,700,000	20,000,000	21,500,000	15,400,000
EBITDA	174,800,000	88,600,000	41,300,000	72,000,000	94,500,000	92,400,000
Return on Assets %	6.08%	2.78%	1.27%	3.43%	3.15%	4.37%
Return on Equity %	12.66%	6.22%	2.86%	7.53%	7.07%	9.80%
Debt to Equity						

CONTACT INFORMATION:

Phone: 248 362-4444   Fax: 248 362-2258
Toll-Free:
Address: 999 W. Big Beaver Rd., Troy, MI 48084 United States

SALARIES/BONUSES:

Top Exec. Salary: $1,000,000   Bonus: $
Second Exec. Salary: $655,000   Bonus: $

STOCK TICKER/OTHER:

Stock Ticker: KELYA   Exchange: NAS
Employees: 507,500   Fiscal Year Ends: 12/31
Parent Company:

OTHER THOUGHTS:

Estimated Female Officers or Directors: 11
Hot Spot for Advancement for Women/Minorities: Y

Kimpton Hotel & Restaurant Group LLC   www.kimptonhotels.com

NAIC Code: 721110

TYPES OF BUSINESS:

Hotels
Restaurants
Hotel Management Services

BRANDS/DIVISIONS/AFFILIATES:

InterContinental Hotels Group PLC
Hotel Vintage Plaza
Hotel Burnham
Café Pescatore
Area 31
Silverleaf Tavern
Kimpton Seafire Resort + Spa
Kimpton De Witt Hotel

CONTACTS: *Note: Officers with more than one job title may be intentionally listed here more than once.*

Mike DeFrino, CEO
Judy Miles, General Counsel
Joe Long, Exec. VP-Dev.
Lisa Demoney, Sr. Dir.-Digital Mktg. & Media
Stephanie Moustirats, Dir.-Hotel Public Rel.
James Alderman, Sr. VP-Acquisitions & Dev.
James Lin, Sr. VP-Restaurant Oper.
Barry Pollard, Sr. VP-Hotel Oper.
Christine Lawson, Sr. VP-Hotel Sales & Catering

GROWTH PLANS/SPECIAL FEATURES:

Kimpton Hotel & Restaurant Group, LLC, based in San Francisco, owns 63 lifestyle boutique hotels in 33 primarily in the U.S., but is emerging internationally. Its holdings also consist of more than 60 restaurants and bars next to or within its hotels. The firm specializes in renovating old, disused buildings to transform them into unique hotels as well as small, European-style restaurants. Its themed hotels include Hotel Vintage Plaza in Portland, Oregon, which has an Italian romance theme; Hotel Vintage in Seattle, highlighting local Washington wines; and Hotel Burnham in Chicago, which focuses on its significance in Chicago's history. Notable restaurants run by Kimpton include San Francisco bistros Cafe Pescatore, Scala's Bistro and Puccini & Pinetti; Sazerac in Seattle; Atwood Cafe in Chicago; Area 31 in Miami; Firefly in Washington, D.C.; Ruby Room in Boston; and Silverleaf Tavern in New York City. The company also offers full service spas at some of its locations. Special services offered by its hotels include the Mind, Body, Spa Program, which offers in-room massage, yoga, Pilates and meditation; pet packages, which include pet-friendly amenities and services; and Hosted Evening Wine Hour. The company is also engaged in comprehensive management services for other companies, offering everything from financial management to facilities renovation. The company is owned by hotel giant InterContinental Hotels Group PLC. Kimpton plans to open eight additional hotels, located in California, Colorado, Illinois, North Carolina, Ohio, Wisconsin, as well as in the Cayman Islands. The firm's Kimpton Seafire Resort + Spa, its first international hotel, opened in Grand Cayman, Cayman Islands in November 2016. Its second international hotel, Kimpton De Witt Hotel, in Amsterdam, Netherlands, was due to open in 2017.

The firm offers employees medical, dental, vision and life insurance; long- and short-term disability; paid vacation time; tuition reimbursement; and employee discounts.

FINANCIAL DATA: *Note: Data for latest year may not have been available at press time.*

In U.S. $	2016	2015	2014	2013	2012	2011
Revenue	1,300,000,000	1,200,000,000	1,049,880,000	1,000,000,000	945,000,000	905,000,000
R&D Expense						
Operating Income						
Operating Margin %						
SGA Expense						
Net Income						
Operating Cash Flow						
Capital Expenditure						
EBITDA						
Return on Assets %						
Return on Equity %						
Debt to Equity						

CONTACT INFORMATION:

Phone: 415-397-5572   Fax: 415-296-8031
Toll-Free: 800-546-7866
Address: 222 Kearny St., Ste. 200, San Francisco, CA 94108 United States

STOCK TICKER/OTHER:

Stock Ticker: Subsidiary   Exchange:
Employees: 7,754   Fiscal Year Ends: 12/31
Parent Company: InterContinental Hotels Group PLC

SALARIES/BONUSES:

Top Exec. Salary: $ Bonus: $
Second Exec. Salary: $ Bonus: $

OTHER THOUGHTS:

Estimated Female Officers or Directors: 9
Hot Spot for Advancement for Women/Minorities: Y

Kindred Healthcare Inc

www.kindredhealthcare.com

NAIC Code: 623110

TYPES OF BUSINESS:

Nursing Care Facilities
Nursing Centers
Contract Rehabilitation Services

BRANDS/DIVISIONS/AFFILIATES:

Kindred at Home
Kindred Rehabilitation Services

GROWTH PLANS/SPECIAL FEATURES:

Kindred Healthcare, Inc. is a healthcare services company. The firm is organized into four operating divisions: hospital, Kindred at Home, Kindred Rehabilitation Services and nursing center. The hospital division operates 82 transitional care hospitals (certified as long-term acute care (LTAC) under the Medicare program) in 18 U.S. states. Kindred at Home provides home health, hospice and community care services from 635 locations in 40 states. Kindred Rehabilitation Services operates 19 inpatient rehabilitation hospitals (IRFs) and 102 hospital-based acute rehabilitation units, providing rehabilitation services primarily in hospitals and long-term care settings in 46 states. The nursing center division operates 91 nursing centers and seven assisted-living facilities in 19 states. In June 2017, the firm agreed to sell its skilled nursing facility business to BM Eagle Holdings, LLC for $700 million.

The firm offers employees medical, dental and vision coverage; flexible spending accounts; and a 401(k) plan.

CONTACTS:
Note: Officers with more than one job title may be intentionally listed here more than once.

Stephen Farber, CFO
Stephen Cunanan, Chief Administrative Officer
Kent Wallace, COO
Phyllis Yale, Director
William Altman, Executive VP, Divisional
David Causby, Executive VP
Joseph Landenwich, General Counsel
Michael Beal, President, Divisional
Pete Kalmey, President, Divisional
Jason Zachariah, President, Divisional
Benjamin Breier, President
John Lucchese, Senior VP
Paul Diaz, Vice Chairman of the Board

FINANCIAL DATA:
Note: Data for latest year may not have been available at press time.

In U.S. $	2016	2015	2014	2013	2012	2011
Revenue	7,219,519,000	7,054,907,000	5,027,599,000	4,900,510,000	6,181,291,000	5,521,763,000
R&D Expense						
Operating Income	380,854,000	134,929,000	170,125,000	-58,016,000	113,583,000	5,322,000
Operating Margin %	5.27%	1.91%	3.38%	-1.18%	1.83%	.09%
SGA Expense	1,693,962,000	1,777,897,000	1,290,862,000	318,077,000	428,979,000	399,257,000
Net Income	-664,230,000	-93,384,000	-79,837,000	-168,492,000	-40,367,000	-53,481,000
Operating Cash Flow	184,962,000	163,262,000	105,471,000	199,412,000	262,562,000	153,706,000
Capital Expenditure	130,877,000	141,862,000	96,338,000	112,732,000	165,497,000	220,558,000
EBITDA	91,081,000	296,109,000	335,071,000	232,422,000	316,121,000	183,138,000
Return on Assets %	-10.51%	-1.53%	-1.66%	-4.11%	-.96%	-1.65%
Return on Equity %	-57.44%	-6.34%	-6.32%	-14.40%	-3.17%	-4.60%
Debt to Equity	3.95	2.09	1.97	1.45	1.31	1.18

CONTACT INFORMATION:

Phone: 502 596-7300   Fax: 502 596-4170
Toll-Free: 800-545-0749
Address: 680 S. Fourth St., Louisville, KY 40202 United States

STOCK TICKER/OTHER:

Stock Ticker: KND   Exchange: NYS
Employees: 100,100   Fiscal Year Ends: 12/31
Parent Company:

SALARIES/BONUSES:

Top Exec. Salary: $563,417   Bonus: $1,000,000
Second Exec. Salary: $1,045,098   Bonus: $

OTHER THOUGHTS:

Estimated Female Officers or Directors: 4
Hot Spot for Advancement for Women/Minorities: Y

Kohler Company

NAIC Code: 327110

TYPES OF BUSINESS:

Plumbing Fixtures
Resorts
Kitchen & Bath Products
Building Materials

BRANDS/DIVISIONS/AFFILIATES:

Kohler
Sterling
Kallista
Ann Sacks
Robern
Kohler Engines
Lombardini
Somo

CONTACTS: Note: Officers with more than one job title may be intentionally listed here more than once.

K. David Kohler, CEO
Herbert V. Kohler, Jr., Chmn.

GROWTH PLANS/SPECIAL FEATURES:

Kohler Company founded in 1873, is an American manufacturer that operates on six continents worldwide. The firm has four divisions: kitchen and bath, power, decorative products and hospitality. The kitchen and bath division offers products under the Kohler, Sterling, Kallista, Ann Sacks and Robern brands. Products include fashionable sinks, faucets, toilets, bidets, vanities, medicine cabinets, accessories and commercial products. The products can include a number of features including luxury design, automated systems, stainless steel and touchless products. The power division include: Kohler Engines, Lombardini, Kohler Power, Somo and Kohler Power Uninterruptible. Products include private and commercial agricultural equipment, including lawn mowers; maritime equipment, such as marine generators; home generators; and uninterruptible power solutions. The decorative products division include the Ann Sacks, Kallista and Robern brands. Products include furniture, lighting, home accessories, textiles, artesian stone design, plumbing products and high-end hospitality furnishings. Hospitality includes golf destinations and hospitality products. The hospitality division includes the American Club Resort (Kohler, Wisconsin) and Old Course Hotel (St. Andrews, Scotland) offer spa services, golf, lodgings and high-end cuisine to their guests. Additional hospitality services include Kohler Original Chocolates and Kohler At Home, offering high end bedding and spa-like products for home use. In February 2017, the firm sold its Baker, Milling Road and McGuire furniture brands to Samson Investment Holding Company.

Kohler offers its employees medical, dental, life and prescription insurance; dependent and health care spending accounts; a wellness program; a pension plan; a 401(k) plan with company matching; annual bonuses; paid time off; and employee discounts.

FINANCIAL DATA: Note: Data for latest year may not have been available at press time.

In U.S. $	2016	2015	2014	2013	2012	2011
Revenue	6,350,000,000	6,000,000,000	5,210,000,000	5,000,000,000	4,800,000,000	4,500,000,000
R&D Expense						
Operating Income						
Operating Margin %						
SGA Expense						
Net Income						
Operating Cash Flow						
Capital Expenditure						
EBITDA						
Return on Assets %						
Return on Equity %						
Debt to Equity						

CONTACT INFORMATION:

Phone: 920-457-4441   Fax:
Toll-Free: 800-456-4537
Address: 444 Highland Dr., Kohler, WI 53044 United States

STOCK TICKER/OTHER:

Stock Ticker: Private   Exchange:
Employees: 30,000   Fiscal Year Ends:
Parent Company:

SALARIES/BONUSES:

Top Exec. Salary: $ Bonus: $
Second Exec. Salary: $ Bonus: $

OTHER THOUGHTS:

Estimated Female Officers or Directors:
Hot Spot for Advancement for Women/Minorities:

Kohl's Corporation

NAIC Code: 452112

www.kohls.com

TYPES OF BUSINESS:

Discount Department Stores
Online Sales

GROWTH PLANS/SPECIAL FEATURES:

Kohl's Corporation operates family-oriented specialty department stores. The company currently operates 1,154 Kohl's department stores, 12 FILA outlets and three Off-Aisle clearance centers throughout the U.S., as well as an e-commerce site, Kohls.com. Store formats include prototype, approximately 88,000 square feet of retail space; small, approximately 68,000 square feet of retail space; and urban, approximately 125,000 square feet of retail space. Kohl's stores offer apparel, shoes and accessories for women, children and men; soft home products, such as sheets and pillows; and other home products, such as small electronics and luggage. Brands sold include Apt. 9, Croft & Barrow, Jumping Beans, Food Network, Jennifer Lopez, Simply Vera Want and Rock & Republic. Approximately 30% of Kohl's' merchandise is marketed towards women, 20% is marketed towards men, 19% is comprised of home furnishing products, 13% is designed for children, 9% is comprised of accessories and 9% is comprised of footwear. The firm maintains nine retail distribution centers located in Ohio, Texas, Virginia, Missouri, New York, California, Georgia and Illinois; and e-commerce fulfillment centers in Ohio, Maryland, Texas and California.

The company offers its employees medical, dental and vision insurance; long-term disability and life insurance; a 401(k) plan; tuition reimbursement; onsite fitness classes, child care, dry cleaning and food service; adoption assistance; parental leave.

BRANDS/DIVISIONS/AFFILIATES:

Kohl's
FILA
Off-Aisle
Kohls.com

CONTACTS: Note: Officers with more than one job title may be intentionally listed here more than once.

Kevin Mansell, CEO
Richard Schepp, Chief Administrative Officer
Sona Chawla, COO
Michelle Gass, Other Executive Officer

FINANCIAL DATA: Note: Data for latest year may not have been available at press time.

In U.S. $	2016	2015	2014	2013	2012	2011
Revenue	19,204,000,000	19,023,000,000	19,031,000,000	19,279,000,000	18,804,000,000	
R&D Expense						
Operating Income	1,553,000,000	1,689,000,000	1,742,000,000	1,890,000,000	2,158,000,000	
Operating Margin %	8.08%	8.87%	9.15%	9.80%	11.47%	
SGA Expense	4,452,000,000	4,350,000,000	4,313,000,000	4,267,000,000	4,243,000,000	
Net Income	673,000,000	867,000,000	889,000,000	986,000,000	1,167,000,000	
Operating Cash Flow	1,474,000,000	2,024,000,000	1,884,000,000	1,265,000,000	2,143,000,000	
Capital Expenditure	690,000,000	682,000,000	643,000,000	785,000,000	927,000,000	
EBITDA	2,487,000,000	2,575,000,000	2,631,000,000	2,723,000,000	2,940,000,000	
Return on Assets %	4.80%	6.01%	6.28%	7.04%	8.43%	
Return on Equity %	11.72%	14.48%	14.78%	15.70%	15.97%	
Debt to Equity	0.83	0.77	0.78	0.73	0.63	

CONTACT INFORMATION:

Phone: 262 703-7000   Fax: 262 703-6373
Toll-Free:
Address: N56 W17000 Ridgewood Dr., Menomonee Falls, WI 53051 United States

STOCK TICKER/OTHER:

Stock Ticker: KSS
Employees: 138,000
Parent Company:

Exchange: NYS
Fiscal Year Ends: 01/31

SALARIES/BONUSES:

Top Exec. Salary: $1,400,441   Bonus: $
Second Exec. Salary: $1,113,750   Bonus: $

OTHER THOUGHTS:

Estimated Female Officers or Directors:
Hot Spot for Advancement for Women/Minorities: Y

KPMG LLP
NAIC Code: 541211

www.kpmg.com/US/en/Pages/default.aspx

TYPES OF BUSINESS:
Accounting Services
Human Resource Advisory Services
Accounting Technology
Publications
Risk Management

BRANDS/DIVISIONS/AFFILIATES:
KPMG International
Audit Committee Institute
KPMG TaxWatch

CONTACTS: *Note: Officers with more than one job title may be intentionally listed here more than once.*
Lynne M. Doughtie, CEO
George Ledwith, Dir.-Global Comm.

GROWTH PLANS/SPECIAL FEATURES:

KPMG, LLP, a subsidiary of global accounting cooperative KPMG International, is a leading provider of audit, advisory and tax services within the U.S. The firm's audit operations are based on a multidisciplinary approach focused on compliance tools, technological assistance and cultural values. KPMG founded and maintains the Audit Committee Institute, designed to educate audit committee members about governance, accounting, financial reporting and other audit issues. KPMG's tax services segment provides tax assistance in the following areas: economic and valuation services, exempt organizations tax, federal tax, inbound tax services, international corporate tax, international executive services, legislative and regulatory services, mergers and acquisitions, state and local tax and trade and customs. The company also provides tax-related news through its KPMG TaxWatch podcast series and tax-related newsletters and publications. The firm's advisory services division assists its clients in achieving strengthened governance, reporting and internal controls; early identification and assessment of risk and control issues; improved efficiency and effectiveness of key business processes; and informed responses to existing and proposed regulatory requirements. With offices across the country, KPMG serves companies and organizations in such major industry sectors as alternative investments, private capital, communications/media, consumer markets, energy, financial services, government, healthcare, life sciences, middle market and technology. The firm also maintains a special focus group that has industry experience with the issues Japanese companies face in the U.S., as well as both Japanese and U.S. business cultures, practices and standards.

KPMG offers employees medical, dental and vision coverage; short- and long-term disability; life and long-term care insurance; a 401(k) plan; a pension plan; flexible spending accounts; and discounts on cars, insurance, jewelry, retailers, transit passes and other programs.

FINANCIAL DATA: *Note: Data for latest year may not have been available at press time.*

In U.S. $	2016	2015	2014	2013	2012	2011
Revenue	11,560,270,498	9,340,000,000	8,376,440,000	7,880,000,000	7,450,000,000	7,050,000,000
R&D Expense						
Operating Income						
Operating Margin %						
SGA Expense						
Net Income						
Operating Cash Flow						
Capital Expenditure						
EBITDA						
Return on Assets %						
Return on Equity %						
Debt to Equity						

CONTACT INFORMATION:
Phone: 212-758-9700   Fax: 212-751-2109
Toll-Free:
Address: 345 Par Ave., New York, NY 10154-0102 United States

STOCK TICKER/OTHER:
Stock Ticker: Subsidiary   Exchange:
Employees: 23,000   Fiscal Year Ends: 09/30
Parent Company: KPMG International

SALARIES/BONUSES:
Top Exec. Salary: $ Bonus: $
Second Exec. Salary: $ Bonus: $

OTHER THOUGHTS:
Estimated Female Officers or Directors:
Hot Spot for Advancement for Women/Minorities:

Kroger Co (The)

www.kroger.com

NAIC Code: 445110

TYPES OF BUSINESS:

Grocery Stores
Convenience Stores
Jewelry Stores
Pharmacies
Food Processing
Gas Stations
Department Stores

BRANDS/DIVISIONS/AFFILIATES:

Kroger
City Market
Dillons
Food 4 Less
Fred Meyer
Quik Stop
Modern HC Holdings Inc
Murray's Cheese

CONTACTS: *Note: Officers with more than one job title may be intentionally listed here more than once.*

W. Mcmullen, CEO
Mary Adcock, Vice President, Divisional
J. Schlotman, CFO
Christopher Hjelm, Chief Information Officer
Frederick Morganthall, Executive VP, Divisional
Michael Donnelly, Executive VP, Divisional
Yael Cosset, Other Executive Officer
Sukanya Madlinger, Senior VP
Mark Tuffin, Senior VP
Alessandro Tosolini, Senior VP, Divisional
Robert Clark, Senior VP, Divisional
Todd Foley, Treasurer
Stuart Aitken, Vice President
Jessica Adelman, Vice President, Divisional
Erin Sharp, Vice President, Divisional
Timothy Massa, Vice President, Divisional
Christine Wheatley, Vice President, Divisional

GROWTH PLANS/SPECIAL FEATURES:

The Kroger Co. is one of the largest supermarket operators in the U.S. The company operates 2,796 supermarkets under a variety of names such as Kroger, City Market, Dillons, Jay C, Food 4 Less, Fred Meyer, Fry's and Smith's. More than 1,440 of these stores have fuel centers, and more than 2,250 have pharmacies. Kroger's supermarkets operate under one of four store formats: combination food and drug stores, multi-department stores, marketplace stores and price impact warehouses. The combo stores are the primary food store format and typically draw customers from a 2- to 2.5-mile radius; multi-department stores are larger in size than combos and sell merchandise such as apparel, home furnishings, dÃ©cor, outdoor living, electronics, automotive products, toys and fine jewelry; marketplace stores offer full-service grocery, pharmacy and beauty care departments, as well as general merchandise; and price impact warehouses offer low cost promotions for grocery, health and beauty items. The firm also operates 784 convenience stores under the Quik Stop, Loaf N' Jug, Tom Thumb, Turkey Hill, Kwik Shop and Smith's Express names. Kroger's 319 fine jewelry stores operate under the Fred Meyer brand. Kroger manages a number of walk-in medical clinics located in its stores. The company operates 38 manufacturing plants, which supply approximately 40% of the corporate brand units sold in its retail outlets. These plants consist of 17 dairies, 10 deli or bakery plants, five grocery product plants, two beverage plants, two meat plants and two cheese plants. In September 2016, the firm acquired Modern HC Holdings, Inc., and merged it with wholly-owned Axium Pharmacy Holdings, Inc. to create a combined specialty pharmacy company. In February 2017, Kroger acquired Murray's Cheese, a producer and distributor of fine cheeses, meats and specialty food items.

FINANCIAL DATA: *Note: Data for latest year may not have been available at press time.*

In U.S. $	2016	2015	2014	2013	2012	2011
Revenue	109,830,000,000	108,465,000,000	98,375,000,000	96,751,000,000	90,374,000,000	
R&D Expense						
Operating Income	3,576,000,000	3,137,000,000	2,725,000,000	2,764,000,000	1,278,000,000	
Operating Margin %						
SGA Expense	18,669,000,000	17,868,000,000	15,809,000,000	15,477,000,000	15,964,000,000	
Net Income	2,039,000,000	1,728,000,000	1,519,000,000	1,497,000,000	602,000,000	
Operating Cash Flow	4,833,000,000	4,163,000,000	3,380,000,000	2,833,000,000	2,658,000,000	
Capital Expenditure	3,349,000,000	2,831,000,000	2,330,000,000	2,062,000,000	1,898,000,000	
EBITDA	5,665,000,000	5,085,000,000	4,428,000,000	4,416,000,000	2,916,000,000	
Return on Assets %	6.32%	5.77%	5.63%	6.22%	2.56%	
Return on Equity %	33.33%	32.01%	31.67%	36.56%	12.97%	
Debt to Equity	1.42	1.80	1.79	1.46	1.72	

CONTACT INFORMATION:

Phone: 513 762-4000   Fax: 513 762-1575
Toll-Free: 866-221-4141
Address: 1014 Vine St., Cincinnati, OH 45202 United States

STOCK TICKER/OTHER:

Stock Ticker: KR   Exchange: NYS
Employees: 443,000   Fiscal Year Ends: 01/31
Parent Company:

SALARIES/BONUSES:

Top Exec. Salary: $1,251,781   Bonus: $
Second Exec. Salary: $850,360   Bonus: $

OTHER THOUGHTS:

Estimated Female Officers or Directors: 5
Hot Spot for Advancement for Women/Minorities: Y

La Quinta Holdings Inc

NAIC Code: 721110

www.lq.com

TYPES OF BUSINESS:

Hotels, Motels & Suites
Hotel Management
Franchising

BRANDS/DIVISIONS/AFFILIATES:

Blackstone Group LP
La Quinta Inns
La Quinta Inns and Suites

CONTACTS: Note: Officers with more than one job title may be intentionally listed here more than once.

James Forson, CFO
Mitesh Shah, Chairman of the Board
Julie Cary, Chief Marketing Officer
John Cantele, COO
Mark Chloupek, Executive VP
Rajiv Trivedi, Executive VP
Keith Cline, President

GROWTH PLANS/SPECIAL FEATURES:

La Quinta Holdings, Inc. is the operator of the La Quinta motels and suites properties. La Quinta is a leading limited-service lodging brand that provides comfortable guest rooms in convenient locations at affordable prices. The firm is one of the largest owners and operators of limited-service hotels in the U.S. It maintains 888 hotels and 87,200 rooms in 48 states, as well as Canada, Mexico, Honduras and Columbia, under the brands La Quinta Inns and La Quinta Inns and Suites. The firm also licenses its brand name to franchisees for royalties and other fees. The company markets its services to both leisure guests and business travelers. A typical La Quinta Inn features approximately 130 guest rooms with amenities including movies-on-demand, interactive video games, free high-speed Internet, complimentary continental breakfast, a swimming pool, fax services and 24-hour front desk message services. La Quinta Inn and Suites properties also feature deluxe two-room suites with microwaves and refrigerators as well as fitness centers, courtyards and expanded food offerings. The Blackstone Group LP holds a 30.1% interest in the company and can currently appoint 20% of the company's directors. Currently, La Quinta has a pipeline of 248 franchised hotels to be in the U.S., Mexico, Columbia, Nicaragua, Guatemala, Chile and El Salvador. In January 2017, the firm began discussions on whether to separate into two stand-alone, publicly traded companies by spinning off its real estate assets as a separate company.

The firm offers employees medical, dental and vision coverage; life insurance; long-term disability; an employee assistance program; flexible spending accounts; a 401(k) plan; tuition reimbursement; an internal referral bonus program; and room rate discounts.

FINANCIAL DATA: Note: Data for latest year may not have been available at press time.

In U.S. $	2016	2015	2014	2013	2012	2011
Revenue	1,006,254,000	1,029,974,000	976,938,000	873,893,000	818,012,000	751,541,000
R&D Expense						
Operating Income	78,464,000	128,071,000	136,669,000	156,181,000	129,595,000	101,849,000
Operating Margin %	7.79%	12.43%	13.98%	17.87%	15.84%	13.55%
SGA Expense	246,323,000	250,677,000	261,781,000	190,055,000	180,987,000	154,949,000
Net Income	-1,288,000	26,365,000	-337,297,000	3,976,000	-30,954,000	63,513,000
Operating Cash Flow	262,794,000	290,495,000	286,082,000	232,858,000	248,187,000	220,429,000
Capital Expenditure	143,752,000	100,776,000	78,630,000	115,632,000	102,899,000	96,152,000
EBITDA	228,784,000	311,489,000	311,690,000	321,570,000	292,328,000	267,571,000
Return on Assets %	-.04%	.84%	-10.48%	.12%	-.90%	1.82%
Return on Equity %	-.18%	3.40%	-59.99%	1.25%	-12.26%	33.50%
Debt to Equity	2.56	2.27	2.31		9.00	15.17

CONTACT INFORMATION:

Phone: 214-492-6600 Fax: 214-492-6616
Toll-Free:
Address: 909 Hidden Ridge, Ste. 600, Irving, TX 75038 United States

STOCK TICKER/OTHER:

Stock Ticker: LQ Exchange: NYS
Employees: 7,333 Fiscal Year Ends: 12/31
Parent Company: Blackstone Group LP

SALARIES/BONUSES:

Top Exec. Salary: $714,984 Bonus: $500,000
Second Exec. Salary: $383,607 Bonus: $150,000

OTHER THOUGHTS:

Estimated Female Officers or Directors: 2
Hot Spot for Advancement for Women/Minorities:

Laboratory Corporation of America Holdings   www.labcorp.com

NAIC Code: 621511

TYPES OF BUSINESS:

Clinical Laboratory Testing
Diagnostics
Urinalyses
Blood Cell Counts
Blood Chemistry Analysis
HIV Tests
Genetic Testing
Specialty & Niche Tests

BRANDS/DIVISIONS/AFFILIATES:

LabCorp Diagnostics
Covance Drug Development
Sequenom Inc
ClearPath Diagnostics
Pathology Associates Medical Laboratories

CONTACTS: Note: Officers with more than one job title may be intentionally listed here more than once.

John Ratliff, CEO, Divisional
David King, CEO
Lance Berberian, Chief Information Officer
Glenn Eisenberg, Executive VP
Lisa Uthgenannt, Other Executive Officer
F. Eberts, Other Executive Officer
Edward Dodson, Senior VP

GROWTH PLANS/SPECIAL FEATURES:

Laboratory Corporation of America Holdings (LabCorp) is a leading independent clinical laboratory company based in the U.S. LabCorp's 52,000+ employees serve customers in approximately 60 countries, providing diagnostic, drug development and technology-enabled solutions for more than 110 million patient encounters annually. The firm operates in two business segments: LabCorp Diagnostics, a clinical laboratory business; and Covance Drug Development, a provider of end-to-end drug development services, from early-stage research to regulatory approval and beyond. LabCorp processes tests on approximately 500,000 patient specimens daily, and has clinical laboratory locations throughout the U.S. and other countries, including Canada and the U.K. It offers a menu of more than 4,800 tests, with several hundred used in general patient care by physicians to establish or support a diagnosis, to monitor treatment or to search for an otherwise undiagnosed condition. Most frequent tests include blood chemistry analysis, blood cell counts, thyroid tests, Pap tests, Hemoglobin A1C, prostate-specific antigen, tests for sexually-transmitted diseases, hepatitis C, Vitamin D and substance-abuse tests. Covance's global network comprises offices in 30 countries and business in approximately 60 countries. It has deep expertise in clinical trials, and has collaborated on all the novel oncology drugs, as well as most (95%) of the drugs servicing the rare and orphan disease space that were approved in 2016. LabCorp Diagnostics derives approximately 70% of annual sales revenue and Covance derives about 30%. In late-2016, the firm acquired Sequenom, Inc., a provider of non-invasive prenatal testing; and ClearPath Diagnostics. In 2017, it acquired assets of Mount Sinai Health System Clinical Outreach Laboratories; and acquired Pathology Associates Medical Laboratories.

Employee benefits include medical, dental and vision coverage; flexible spending accounts; 401(k) and stock purchase plan; life and AD&D insurance; and short- and long-term disability.

FINANCIAL DATA: Note: Data for latest year may not have been available at press time.

In U.S. $	2016	2015	2014	2013	2012	2011
Revenue	9,641,800,000	8,680,100,000	6,011,600,000	5,808,300,000	5,671,400,000	5,542,300,000
R&D Expense						
Operating Income	1,312,400,000	1,002,900,000	910,400,000	990,900,000	1,023,500,000	948,400,000
Operating Margin %	13.61%	11.55%	15.14%	17.06%	18.04%	17.11%
SGA Expense	1,630,200,000	1,622,000,000	1,198,200,000	1,128,800,000	1,114,600,000	1,159,600,000
Net Income	732,100,000	436,900,000	511,200,000	573,800,000	583,100,000	519,700,000
Operating Cash Flow	1,175,900,000	982,400,000	739,000,000	818,700,000	841,400,000	855,600,000
Capital Expenditure	278,900,000	255,800,000	203,500,000	202,200,000	176,300,000	145,700,000
EBITDA	1,823,800,000	1,464,800,000	1,181,700,000	1,242,200,000	1,268,500,000	1,185,000,000
Return on Assets %	5.14%	4.05%	7.16%	8.33%	9.01%	8.43%
Return on Equity %	14.01%	11.25%	19.24%	22.03%	22.33%	20.91%
Debt to Equity	0.97	1.21	0.95	1.15	0.80	0.83

CONTACT INFORMATION:

Phone: 336 229-1127   Fax: 336 229-7717
Toll-Free:
Address: 358 S. Main St., Burlington, NC 27215 United States

STOCK TICKER/OTHER:

Stock Ticker: LH   Exchange: NYS
Employees: 52,000   Fiscal Year Ends: 12/31
Parent Company:

SALARIES/BONUSES:

Top Exec. Salary: $1,133,333   Bonus: $
Second Exec. Salary: Bonus: $
$653,438

OTHER THOUGHTS:

Estimated Female Officers or Directors: 3
Hot Spot for Advancement for Women/Minorities: Y

Lam Research Corporation

NAIC Code: 333242

www.lamrc.com

TYPES OF BUSINESS:

Semiconductor Manufacturing Equipment
Etch Processing Systems
Chemical Mechanical Planarization Systems
Wafer Cleaning Equipment & Services
Support Services

BRANDS/DIVISIONS/AFFILIATES:

Flex
Versys
Kiyo
Syndion
VECTOR
ALTUS
SABRE
SOLA

CONTACTS: *Note: Officers with more than one job title may be intentionally listed here more than once.*

Martin Anstice, CEO
Douglas Bettinger, CFO
Richard Gottscho, Chief Technology Officer
Timothy Archer, COO
Stephen Newberry, Director
Sarah ODowd, Other Executive Officer

GROWTH PLANS/SPECIAL FEATURES:

Lam Research Corporation supplies wafer fabrication equipment and services to semiconductor companies worldwide. The firm designs, manufactures, markets and services semiconductor processing equipment used in semiconductor device fabrication. The company's etch products are used to deposit special films on silicon wafers and to selectively etch away portions of these films utilizing plasma-based technologies, creating an integrated circuit (IC). Its products include the Flex product family for dielectric etch, the Versys metal and Kiyo product families for conductor etch and the Syndion product family for three-dimensional ICs. Lam's VECTOR family of plasma-enhanced chemical vapor deposition and atomic layer deposition systems delivers superior thin film quality, wafer-to-water uniformity, productivity and low cost of ownership. The firm also offers wafer cleaning services and equipment that employs proprietary technology and can be used throughout the semiconductor manufacturing process. Lam's ALTUS product family deposits a highly conformal atomic layer for advanced tungsten metallization applications. The patented multi-station sequential deposition architecture enables a layer to be formed using pulsed nucleation layer technology. The SABRE electrochemical deposition (ECD) product family is a system for copper damascene manufacturing. SABRE 3D addresses through-silicon via (TSV) and wafer-level packaging (WLP) applications, such as copper pillar, redistribution layers, high-density fanout, underbump metallization, bumping and microbumps used in post-TSV processing. The SPEED family of products are designed to provide void-free gapfill of high-quality dielectric films with throughput and reliability. And the SOLA product family is used for treatment of back-end-of-line low-k dielectric films and front-end-of-line silicon nitride strained films.

The firm offers employees life, disability, AD&D, medical, dental and vision insurance; flexible spending accounts; educational and employee assistance programs; adoption aid; and access to a credit union.

FINANCIAL DATA: *Note: Data for latest year may not have been available at press time.*

In U.S. $	2016	2015	2014	2013	2012	2011
Revenue	5,885,893,000	5,259,312,000	4,607,309,000	3,598,916,000	2,665,192,000	3,237,693,000
R&D Expense	913,712,000	825,242,000	716,471,000	683,688,000	444,559,000	373,293,000
Operating Income	1,074,256,000	788,039,000	677,669,000	118,071,000	237,733,000	804,285,000
Operating Margin %	18.25%	14.98%	14.70%	3.28%	8.91%	24.84%
SGA Expense	630,954,000	591,611,000	613,341,000	599,487,000	400,052,000	308,075,000
Net Income	914,049,000	655,577,000	632,289,000	113,879,000	168,723,000	723,748,000
Operating Cash Flow	1,350,277,000	785,503,000	717,049,000	719,933,000	499,028,000	881,028,000
Capital Expenditure	175,330,000	198,265,000	145,503,000	160,795,000	107,272,000	127,495,000
EBITDA	1,385,918,000	1,092,452,000	1,077,309,000	431,182,000	344,205,000	881,015,000
Return on Assets %	8.44%	7.55%	8.29%	1.49%	2.79%	22.11%
Return on Equity %	16.62%	12.93%	13.28%	2.36%	4.43%	34.15%
Debt to Equity	0.57	0.19	0.16	0.17	0.14	0.29

CONTACT INFORMATION:

Phone: 510 572-0200   Fax: 510 572-6454
Toll-Free: 800-526-7678
Address: 4650 Cushing Parkway, Fremont, CA 94538 United States

STOCK TICKER/OTHER:

Stock Ticker: LRCX   Exchange: NAS
Employees: 7,500   Fiscal Year Ends: 06/30
Parent Company:

SALARIES/BONUSES:

Top Exec. Salary: $937,789   Bonus: $
Second Exec. Salary: Bonus: $
$624,061

OTHER THOUGHTS:

Estimated Female Officers or Directors: 3
Hot Spot for Advancement for Women/Minorities: Y

Larry H Miller Group

www.lhm.com

NAIC Code: 441110

TYPES OF BUSINESS:

Auto Dealers, Retail
Auto Financing & Service
Sports Arenas
Movie Theaters
Professional Sports Teams
TV Station
Sports Apparel Stores

BRANDS/DIVISIONS/AFFILIATES:

Larry H Miller Dealerships
Prestige Financial
Total Care Auto Powered by Lancar
Larry H Miller Megaplex Theaters
FANZZ
Zone
Jordan Commons
Larry H Miller Real Estate

CONTACTS: Note: Officers with more than one job title may be intentionally listed here more than once.

Clark Whitworth, CEO
David Smith, Exec. VP-Oper.
Michael Wankier, Exec. VP-Finance
Lynda Jeppesen, Sr. VP-Human Resources
Robert Tingey, General Counsel
Jay Francis, Exec. VP-Oper.
Clark Whitworth, CFO-Automotive
Robert Hyde, CFO-Sports & Entertainment
Steve Starks, Exec. VP-Oper.
Gail Miller, Owner

GROWTH PLANS/SPECIAL FEATURES:

Larry H. Miller Group is a holding company that operates a large number of subsidiary companies engaged in automotive dealerships, finance, insurance, sports and entertainment, and retail. LMG has more than 80 businesses and properties operating in 46 U.S. states. Larry H. Miller Dealerships sell a wide variety of automotive brands including Ford, Cadillac, Lexus, Toyota, Honda, Chevrolet and Jeep via 60 dealership locations under 20 different automotive brands in seven western states. Prestige Financial is a provider of consumer financial solutions for both franchised and independent automobile dealerships across America. Total Care Auto Powered by Landcar provides vehicle insurance coverage. Within the sports and entertainment and retail divisions, Larry H. Miller Megaplex Theaters comprise more than 180 screens at 17 locations within Nevada and Utah; FANZZ and Just Sports comprise the company's sports apparel stores, with nearly 100 locations in 14 states; the Larry H. Miller's Tour of Utah showcases professional cyclists for a week of racing during the month of August; the Salt Lake Bees are a triple-A affiliate of the Los Angeles Angels; and the Zone (1280 AM) and FOX Sports Radio (97.5 FM) are 60,000-watt sports radio stations in Utah. In addition, Jordan Commons comprises restaurants, offices, a theatre and an event complex in Sandy, Utah; and Larry H. Miller Real Estate purchases, develops and manages properties for the firm's group of companies. In February 2017, Larry H. Miller Dealerships acquired Corona Nissan in California.

The company offers employees a 401(k); medical, dental and life insurance; employee discounts; an employee assistance program; a flexible spending account; and a scholarship program.

FINANCIAL DATA: Note: Data for latest year may not have been available at press time.

In U.S. $	2016	2015	2014	2013	2012	2011
Revenue	4,679,750,795	3,933,621,552	4,565,000,000	4,300,000,000	3,500,000,000	2,500,000,000
R&D Expense						
Operating Income						
Operating Margin %						
SGA Expense						
Net Income						
Operating Cash Flow						
Capital Expenditure						
EBITDA						
Return on Assets %						
Return on Equity %						
Debt to Equity						

CONTACT INFORMATION:

Phone: 801-563-4100   Fax: 801-563-4198
Toll-Free:
Address: 9350 S.150 E., Ste. 1000, Sandy, UT 84070 United States

STOCK TICKER/OTHER:

Stock Ticker: Private   Exchange:
Employees: 7,800   Fiscal Year Ends: 12/31
Parent Company:

SALARIES/BONUSES:

Top Exec. Salary: $ Bonus: $
Second Exec. Salary: $ Bonus: $

OTHER THOUGHTS:

Estimated Female Officers or Directors:
Hot Spot for Advancement for Women/Minorities:

Las Vegas Sands Corp (The Venetian)

www.lasvegassands.com

NAIC Code: 721120

TYPES OF BUSINESS:

Hotel Casinos
Convention & Conference Centers
Shopping Center Development
Casino Property Development

BRANDS/DIVISIONS/AFFILIATES:

Venetian Resort Hotel Casino (The)
Sands Expo and Convention Center (The)
Sands China Ltd
Sands Macao Casino (The)
Palazzo Resort Hotel Casino (The)
Venetian Macao Resort Hotel (The)
Marina Bay Sands Pte Ltd
Parisian Macao

CONTACTS: Note: Officers with more than one job title may be intentionally listed here more than once.

Sheldon Adelson, CEO
Patrick Dumont, CFO
Randy Hyzak, Chief Accounting Officer
Robert Goldstein, COO
Lawrence Jacobs, Executive VP

GROWTH PLANS/SPECIAL FEATURES:

Las Vegas Sands Corp. (LVSC) is an international hotel, resort and casino firm. Its flagship property is The Venetian Resort Hotel Casino, which is connected to The Palazzo Resort Hotel Casino. Together, The Venetian and The Palazzo offer 225,000 square feet of gaming space, with 240 table games and 2,350 slot machines, as well as 7,092 hotel suites. LVSC also runs the 1.2 million square foot convention and trade show facility, The Sands Expo and Convention Center, and a supplemental event and conference center. Additionally, the firm operates the Sands Casino Resort Bethlehem in eastern Pennsylvania, which features 145,000 square feet of gaming space, a 300-room hotel, 150,000 square feet of retail space and other amenities. Outside the U.S., LVSC has operations in Macao, through majority-owned subsidiary Sands China Ltd., and Singapore, through Marina Bay Sands Pte. Ltd. The company's largest development project, the multi-billion dollar Cotai Strip, is a collection of hotel properties, casinos and entertainment venues in Macao. Sands China runs The Sands Macao and The Venetian Macao Resort Hotel, the anchor property on the Cotai Strip. Other properties on the Cotai Strip include the Four Seasons Macao, the Plaza Casino and Parisian Macao. Its Singapore property, Marina Bay Sands features three 55-story hotel towers, gaming space, convention space, two state-of-the-art theaters and The Shoppes at Marina Bay Sands. In September 2016, LVSC celebrated the opening of the Parisian Macao on the Cotai Strip. The Parisian Macao features approximately 253,000 square feet of gaming space with approximately 385 table games and 1,560 slot machines, as well as approximately 3,000 rooms and suites and the Shoppes at Parisian, approximately 300,000 square feet of unique retail shopping.

FINANCIAL DATA: Note: Data for latest year may not have been available at press time.

In U.S. $	2016	2015	2014	2013	2012	2011
Revenue	11,410,000,000	11,688,460,000	14,583,850,000	13,769,880,000	11,131,130,000	9,410,745,000
R&D Expense	9,000,000	10,372,000	14,325,000	15,809,000	19,958,000	11,309,000
Operating Income	2,493,000,000	2,841,475,000	4,099,226,000	3,408,243,000	2,311,382,000	2,389,887,000
Operating Margin %	21.84%	24.31%	28.10%	24.75%	20.76%	25.39%
SGA Expense	1,670,000,000	1,491,093,000	1,459,113,000	1,532,614,000	1,412,760,000	1,131,809,000
Net Income	1,670,000,000	1,966,236,000	2,840,629,000	2,305,997,000	1,524,093,000	1,560,123,000
Operating Cash Flow	4,043,000,000	3,449,971,000	4,832,844,000	4,439,412,000	3,057,757,000	2,662,496,000
Capital Expenditure	1,445,000,000	1,528,642,000	1,178,656,000	943,982,000	1,449,234,000	1,508,593,000
EBITDA	3,640,000,000	3,924,666,000	5,138,481,000	4,422,191,000	3,213,186,000	3,172,176,000
Return on Assets %	8.05%	9.07%	12.60%	10.27%	6.86%	5.86%
Return on Equity %	25.70%	28.02%	38.18%	31.31%	20.44%	18.39%
Debt to Equity	1.52	1.37	1.37	1.22	1.43	1.21

CONTACT INFORMATION:

Phone: 702 414-1000   Fax: 702 414-4884
Toll-Free:
Address: 3355 Las Vegas Blvd. S., Las Vegas, NV 89109 United States

STOCK TICKER/OTHER:

Stock Ticker: LVS
Employees: 49,000
Parent Company:

Exchange: NYS
Fiscal Year Ends: 12/31

SALARIES/BONUSES:

Top Exec. Salary: $3,400,000   Bonus: $
Second Exec. Salary: Bonus: $
$1,200,000

OTHER THOUGHTS:

Estimated Female Officers or Directors:
Hot Spot for Advancement for Women/Minorities:

Lear Corporation

NAIC Code: 336300

www.lear.com

TYPES OF BUSINESS:

Automobile Components
Automotive Interiors
Electrical Systems
Instrument Panels
Seat Systems
Flooring Systems
Entertainment & Wireless Systems
Keyless Entry Systems

BRANDS/DIVISIONS/AFFILIATES:

CONTACTS: Note: Officers with more than one job title may be intentionally listed here more than once.

Matthew Simoncini, CEO
Jeffrey Vanneste, CFO
Henry Wallace, Chairman of the Board
Amy Doyle, Chief Accounting Officer
Terrence Larkin, Executive VP, Divisional
Raymond Scott, Executive VP
Shari Burgess, Other Executive Officer
Frank Orsini, President, Divisional
Jay Kunkel, President, Divisional
Melvin Stephens, Senior VP, Divisional
Thomas DiDonato, Senior VP, Divisional
James Murawski, Vice President, Divisional

GROWTH PLANS/SPECIAL FEATURES:

Lear Corporation is one of the world's largest automotive interior systems suppliers. The firm serves every major automotive manufacturer, including General Motors, Ford, BMW, Fiat Chrysler and Daimler. The company currently operates 143 facilities in 22 countries. Its business is conducted through two segments: seating and e-systems. The seating segment consists of the design, engineering, just-in-time assembly and delivery of complete seat systems as well as the manufacture of all major seat components, including seat structures and mechanisms, seat covers, seat forms and headrests. The segment produces seat systems that are fully assembled and ready for installation in automobiles and light trucks. These include luxury and performance automotive seating required by premium automakers, including Alfa Romeo, Audi, Lamborghini, BMW, Cadillac, Ferrari, Jaguar Land Rover, Lincoln, Maserati, Mercedes-Benz and Porsche. The e-systems segment consists of the design, manufacture, assembly and supply of electrical distribution systems, electronic modules and related components and software for light vehicles globally. Its electrical distribution systems route electrical signals and manage electrical power within the vehicle for traditional vehicle architectures, as well as high power and hybrid electric systems. Electronics control various functions within the vehicle, and include body control modules, smart junction boxes, gateway modules, wireless control modules, lighting control modules and audio amplifiers. Connectivity capabilities facilitate secure, wireless communication between the vehicle's systems and external networks, as well as other vehicles. As of December 2016, the company had 22 operating joint ventures located in six countries, of which 15 operated in Asia and seven in North America. In February 2017, Lear Corporation agreed to acquire Grupo Antolin's automotive seating business.

FINANCIAL DATA: Note: Data for latest year may not have been available at press time.

In U.S. $	2016	2015	2014	2013	2012	2011
Revenue	18,557,600,000	18,211,400,000	17,727,300,000	16,234,000,000	14,567,000,000	14,156,500,000
R&D Expense						
Operating Income	1,427,200,000	1,186,800,000	929,200,000	736,600,000	705,200,000	679,600,000
Operating Margin %	7.69%	6.51%	5.24%	4.53%	4.84%	4.80%
SGA Expense	621,900,000	580,500,000	529,900,000	528,700,000	479,300,000	485,600,000
Net Income	975,100,000	745,500,000	672,400,000	431,400,000	1,282,800,000	540,700,000
Operating Cash Flow	1,619,300,000	1,271,100,000	927,800,000	820,100,000	729,800,000	790,300,000
Capital Expenditure	528,300,000	485,800,000	424,700,000	460,600,000	458,300,000	329,500,000
EBITDA	1,799,000,000	1,466,000,000	1,165,800,000	964,000,000	938,300,000	901,700,000
Return on Assets %	10.10%	8.03%	7.69%	5.22%	16.87%	7.93%
Return on Equity %	32.58%	25.33%	22.39%	13.20%	43.31%	22.08%
Debt to Equity	0.62	0.65	0.49	0.34	0.17	0.28

CONTACT INFORMATION:

Phone: 248 447-1500   Fax:
Toll-Free: 800-413-5327
Address: 21557 Telegraph Road, Southfield, MI 48033 United States

STOCK TICKER/OTHER:

Stock Ticker: LEA   Exchange: NYS
Employees: 148,400   Fiscal Year Ends: 12/31
Parent Company:

SALARIES/BONUSES:

Top Exec. Salary: $1,354,500   Bonus: $
Second Exec. Salary: Bonus: $
$855,098

OTHER THOUGHTS:

Estimated Female Officers or Directors: 1
Hot Spot for Advancement for Women/Minorities:

Legg Mason Inc
NAIC Code: 523110

TYPES OF BUSINESS:
Stock Brokerage/Investment Banking
Mutual Funds

BRANDS/DIVISIONS/AFFILIATES:
Legg Mason Funds
Royce Funds (The)
Western Asset Funds
RARE Infrastructure Limited
Financial Guard LLC
EnTrustPermal
Clarion Partners

CONTACTS: *Note: Officers with more than one job title may be intentionally listed here more than once.*
Joseph Sullivan, CEO
Peter Nachtwey, CFO
Ursula Schliessler, Chief Administrative Officer
Thomas Merchant, Executive VP
Terence Johnson, Executive VP
John Kenney, Other Corporate Officer
Frances Cashman, Other Corporate Officer
Thomas Hoops, Other Corporate Officer
Patricia Lattin, Other Executive Officer

GROWTH PLANS/SPECIAL FEATURES:
Legg Mason, Inc. is a global asset management company with consolidated assets under management totaling $696.6 billion. Operating through its subsidiaries, the firm provides investment management and related services to institutional and individual clients, company-sponsored mutual funds and other pooled investment vehicles. The company offers these products and services directly and through various financial intermediaries. The firm conducts its business primarily through several asset managers, housed in independent subsidiaries owned by Legg Mason. Asset managers provide a range of separate account investment management services to institutional clients, including pension and other retirement plans, corporations, insurance companies, endowments, foundations and governments as well as to high-net-worth individuals and families. Asset managers also sponsor and manage various groups of U.S. mutual funds, including the Legg Mason Funds and The Royce Funds. The Legg Mason Funds consist of 128 mutual funds and 32 closed-end funds in the U.S., all of which are sub-advised by subsidiary asset managers. The Royce Funds consist of 20 mutual funds and three closed-end funds, most of which invest primarily in smaller-cap company stocks using a value approach. Funds which previously comprised the company's Western Asset Funds are now included in the Legg Mason Funds. Outside the U.S., the firm manages, supports and distributes funds across a wide array of global fixed income, liquidity and equity investment strategies. International funds include a broad range of cross border funds that are domiciled in Ireland and Luxembourg and are sold in a number of countries across Asia, Europe and Latin America. In October 2015, it acquired a majority stake in RARE Infrastructure Limited, based in Sydney, Australia. In 2016, Legg Manon acquired an 82% in Financial Guard LLC; sold its interest in LMM LCC; completed the combination of EnTrust and Permal businesses, owning 65% of the combined EnTrustPermal; and acquired an 82% equity interest in Clarion Partners.

The company offers employees paid time off, health care coverage, commuter discounts, a 401(k) plan, a profit sharing plan, a stock purchase plan, adoption assistance and tuition reimbursement.

FINANCIAL DATA: *Note: Data for latest year may not have been available at press time.*

In U.S. $	2016	2015	2014	2013	2012	2011
Revenue	2,660,844,000	2,819,106,000	2,741,757,000	2,612,650,000	2,662,574,000	
R&D Expense						
Operating Income	50,831,000	498,219,000	430,893,000	-434,499,000	338,753,000	
Operating Margin %	1.91%	17.67%	15.71%	-16.63%	12.72%	
SGA Expense	2,070,994,000	2,119,704,000	2,102,563,000	2,110,700,000	2,113,576,000	
Net Income	-25,032,000	237,080,000	284,784,000	-353,327,000	220,817,000	
Operating Cash Flow	454,451,000	568,118,000	437,324,000	303,332,000	496,769,000	
Capital Expenditure	40,330,000	45,773,000	40,452,000	38,351,000	31,822,000	
EBITDA	83,542,000	481,353,000	535,397,000	-359,840,000	484,462,000	
Return on Assets %	-.37%	3.25%	3.96%	-4.46%	2.55%	
Return on Equity %	-.62%	5.01%	5.96%	-6.73%	3.85%	
Debt to Equity	0.41	0.23	0.21	0.27	0.24	

CONTACT INFORMATION:
Phone: 410 539-0000   Fax: 410 454-4174
Toll-Free: 800-822-5544
Address: 100 International Dr., Baltimore, MD 21202 United States

STOCK TICKER/OTHER:
Stock Ticker: LM   Exchange: NYS
Employees: 3,338   Fiscal Year Ends: 02/28
Parent Company:

SALARIES/BONUSES:
Top Exec. Salary: $500,000   Bonus: $3,320,000
Second Exec. Salary: $294,075   Bonus: $1,667,972

OTHER THOUGHTS:
Estimated Female Officers or Directors: 2
Hot Spot for Advancement for Women/Minorities:

Sales, profits and employees may be estimates. Financial information, benefits and other data can change quickly and may vary from those stated here.

Lennar Corporation

www.lennar.com

NAIC Code: 236117

TYPES OF BUSINESS:

Construction, Home Building and Residential
Mortgages
Title Insurance & Services

BRANDS/DIVISIONS/AFFILIATES:

Universal American Mortgage Company LLC
Eagle Home Mortgage LLC
Railto Investments
Lennar
WCI Communities Inc

CONTACTS: Note: Officers with more than one job title may be intentionally listed here more than once.

Stuart Miller, CEO
Bruce Gross, CFO
David Collins, Chief Accounting Officer
Jonathan Jaffe, COO
Richard Beckwitt, President
Mark Sustana, Secretary
Diane Bessette, Vice President

GROWTH PLANS/SPECIAL FEATURES:

Lennar Corporation is a U.S. homebuilder and provider of financial services operating in 17 states. The firm sells single-family attached and detached homes and, to a lesser extent, multi-level residential buildings primarily under the Lennar brand name in communities targeted to first-time, move-up and active adult homebuyers. The company also purchases, develops and sells residential land. Lennar divides its homebuilding operations into seven segments: East (which includes Florida, Georgia, Maryland, New Jersey, North Carolina, South Carolina and Virginia); Central (including Arizona, Colorado and Texas); West (California and Nevada); other (including Illinois, Minnesota, Tennessee, Oregon and Washington); Lennar Financial Services; Rialto Investments; and Lennar Multifamily. Lennar Financial Services operates through its financial services subsidiaries, Universal American Mortgage Company, LLC and Eagle Home Mortgage, LLC, the firm provides mortgage financing, title insurance and closing services for both buyers of its homes and third parties. Lennar's subsidiaries provide loans to 82% of its homebuyers who obtain mortgage financing in areas where it offers services. The Rialto Investments division provides advisory services, ongoing asset management services and acquisition and monetization services related to distressed loans and securities portfolios. The Lennar multifamily segment, currently under development, will focus on developing a portfolio of multifamily rental properties in select U.S. markets. Lennar's homes have an average sale price of about $362,000. In 2016, it delivered 26,563 homes to buyers. Lennar generally supervises and controls the development of land and the design and building of its residential communities with a relatively small labor force, hiring subcontractors for site improvements and virtually all of the work involved in the construction of homes. In February 2017, Lennar completed the acquisition of WCI Communities, Inc., a luxury lifestyle community developer and homebuilder for $643 million.

The company offers employees medical, dental and vision insurance; home and auto insurance; mortgage and title benefits; short-and long-term disability; and life insurance.

FINANCIAL DATA: Note: Data for latest year may not have been available at press time.

In U.S. $	2016	2015	2014	2013	2012	2011
Revenue	10,950,000,000	9,474,008,000	7,779,812,000	5,935,095,000	4,104,706,000	3,095,385,000
R&D Expense						
Operating Income	1,262,363,000	1,086,016,000	922,038,000	685,836,000	322,176,000	103,934,000
Operating Margin %	11.52%	11.46%	11.85%	11.55%	7.84%	3.35%
SGA Expense	232,562,000	216,244,000	177,161,000	146,060,000	127,338,000	95,256,000
Net Income	911,844,000	802,894,000	638,916,000	479,674,000	679,124,000	92,199,000
Operating Cash Flow	507,804,000	-419,646,000	-788,488,000	-807,714,000	-424,648,000	-259,135,000
Capital Expenditure	51,151,000	17,623,000	14,278,000	8,126,000	2,822,000	9,936,000
EBITDA	1,385,314,000	1,265,736,000	1,044,877,000	806,203,000	344,548,000	210,124,000
Return on Assets %	6.06%	5.80%	5.20%	4.43%	6.95%	1.02%
Return on Equity %	14.24%	15.16%	14.03%	12.65%	22.22%	3.47%
Debt to Equity	0.63	0.89	0.93	0.99	1.18	1.40

CONTACT INFORMATION:

Phone: 305 559-4000   Fax: 305 227-7115
Toll-Free: 800-741-4663
Address: 700 NW 107th Ave., Ste. 400, Miami, FL 33172 United States

STOCK TICKER/OTHER:

Stock Ticker: LEN   Exchange: NYS
Employees: 8,335   Fiscal Year Ends: 11/30
Parent Company:

SALARIES/BONUSES:

Top Exec. Salary: $1,000,000   Bonus: $
Second Exec. Salary: Bonus: $180,525
$650,000

OTHER THOUGHTS:

Estimated Female Officers or Directors: 3
Hot Spot for Advancement for Women/Minorities: Y

Sales, profits and employees may be estimates. Financial information, benefits and other data can change quickly and may vary from those stated here.

Level 3 Communications Inc

www.level3.com

NAIC Code: 517110

TYPES OF BUSINESS:

Private Data Networks-Fiber Optic
Broadband Network Services
Managed Modem Access Services
Digital Media Capture and Distribution
High-Speed Content Upload
Server Facilities

BRANDS/DIVISIONS/AFFILIATES:

Softswitch

CONTACTS: *Note: Officers with more than one job title may be intentionally listed here more than once.*

Jeffrey Storey, CEO
Sunit Patel, CFO
Eric Mortensen, Chief Accounting Officer
James Ellis, Director
Hector Alonso, President, Divisional
Laurinda Pang, President, Geographical
John Ryan, Secretary

GROWTH PLANS/SPECIAL FEATURES:

Level 3 Communications, Inc. is a leading provider of integrated communications services. Its primary business is the provision of communications services over its extensive broadband networks in North America, Europe and Latin America, consisting of approximately 106,000 intercity route miles. The networks supply a portfolio of services including internet protocol (IP) services (internet access, Ethernet and virtual private network services), broadband transport and colocation services to enterprises and other organization in more than 60 countries. Its patented Softswitch-based managed modem and voice services, which use a distributed computer system to emulate traditional circuit switches, provide customers with voice over IP (VoIP) technology. Level 3 divides its services into two segments: Core Network Services and Wholesale Voice Services. Core Network Services consist of IP and data services, transport and fiber services, voice services, colocation and datacenter services and security services. IP and data services include Internet Services, virtual private network, content delivery network, media delivery, Vyvx broadcast service and Managed Services. Transport and fiber services include wavelengths, private lines, transoceanic services and dark fiber, as well as related professional services. Voice services offer a range of local and enterprise voice services including VoIP services and traditional circuit-switch based services. Colocation and Data Center services include data center facilities and services including cloud, hosting and application management solutions. Security services uses the firm's view of the threat landscape to enable customers to address the escalating risk of cyber-attacks. The Wholesale Voice Services include voice termination and toll free service. Wholesale long distance includes domestic and international voice termination services. The wholesale Toll Free service terminates toll free calls that are originated on the traditional telephone network. In November 2016, the firm agreed to be acquired by CenturyLink, Inc. for approximately $25 billion.

FINANCIAL DATA: *Note: Data for latest year may not have been available at press time.*

In U.S. $	2016	2015	2014	2013	2012	2011
Revenue	8,172,000,000	8,229,000,000	6,777,000,000	6,313,000,000	6,376,000,000	4,333,000,000
R&D Expense						
Operating Income	1,444,000,000	1,331,000,000	1,013,000,000	666,000,000	575,000,000	52,000,000
Operating Margin %	17.67%	16.17%	14.94%	10.54%	9.01%	1.20%
SGA Expense	1,407,000,000	1,467,000,000	1,181,000,000	2,376,000,000	2,416,000,000	1,759,000,000
Net Income	677,000,000	3,433,000,000	314,000,000	-109,000,000	-422,000,000	-756,000,000
Operating Cash Flow	2,343,000,000	1,855,000,000	1,161,000,000	713,000,000	578,000,000	384,000,000
Capital Expenditure	1,334,000,000	1,229,000,000	910,000,000	760,000,000	743,000,000	494,000,000
EBITDA	2,638,000,000	2,091,000,000	1,700,000,000	1,378,000,000	1,108,000,000	735,000,000
Return on Assets %	2.76%	15.22%	1.85%	-.83%	-3.18%	-7.01%
Return on Equity %	6.43%	41.63%	8.07%	-8.44%	-35.70%	-145.94%
Debt to Equity	0.99	1.08	1.72	5.90	7.27	7.02

CONTACT INFORMATION:

Phone: 720 888-1000 Fax: 720 888-5088
Toll-Free: 877-253-8353
Address: 1025 Eldorado Blvd., Broomfield, CO 80021 United States

STOCK TICKER/OTHER:

Stock Ticker: LVLT Exchange: NYS
Employees: 12,600 Fiscal Year Ends: 12/31
Parent Company:

SALARIES/BONUSES:

Top Exec. Salary: $1,200,000 Bonus: $3,150,000
Second Exec. Salary: Bonus: $1,488,040
$637,998

OTHER THOUGHTS:

Estimated Female Officers or Directors: 2
Hot Spot for Advancement for Women/Minorities: Y

LHC Group Inc

NAIC Code: 621610

www.lhcgroup.com

TYPES OF BUSINESS:
Home Health Care Services
Hospices
Long-Term Acute Care Hospitals

BRANDS/DIVISIONS/AFFILIATES:

CONTACTS: *Note: Officers with more than one job title may be intentionally listed here more than once.*
Keith Myers, CEO
Joshua Proffitt, CFO
Donald Stelly, COO

GROWTH PLANS/SPECIAL FEATURES:
LHC Group, Inc. provides post-acute healthcare services to patients through its home nursing agencies, community-based service agencies, hospice agencies and long-term acute care hospitals (LTACHs) in the U.S. Through its subsidiaries, LHC operates 372 service providers in 26 states within the continental U.S. The company operates through four segments: home health services, hospice services, community-based services and facility-based services (via LTACHs). Home health services include skilled nursing, medically-oriented social services, as well as physical, occupational and speech therapy. This division operates 283 home health service locations, of which 164 are wholly-owned, 114 are majority-owned by LHC and the rest are under license lease arrangements. Hospice services provides end-of-life care to patients with terminal illnesses through interdisciplinary teams of physicians, nurses, home health aides, counselors and volunteers. This division operates 65 hospice locations, of which 49 are wholly-owned, 14 are majority-owned by LHC and two are under license lease arrangements. Community-based services provides assistance with activities of daily living to elderly, chronically ill and disabled patients. This division operates 11 locations, of which 10 are wholly-owned and one is majority-owned by LHC. LTACH/facility-based services are provided to patients with complex medical conditions who have transitioned out of a hospital intensive care unit but whose conditions remain too severe for treatment in a non-acute setting. This division owns and operates six LTACHs, of which all but one are located within host hospitals; and owns and operates a pharmacy, a family health center, a family health clinic and physical therapy clinics.

FINANCIAL DATA: *Note: Data for latest year may not have been available at press time.*

In U.S. $	2016	2015	2014	2013	2012	2011
Revenue	914,823,000	816,366,000	733,632,000	658,283,000	637,569,000	633,872,000
R&D Expense						
Operating Income	70,562,000	66,343,000	45,486,000	46,757,000	54,305,000	-6,382,000
Operating Margin %	7.71%	8.12%	6.20%	7.10%	8.51%	-1.00%
SGA Expense	270,622,000	248,629,000	233,945,000	214,133,000	205,637,000	275,588,000
Net Income	36,583,000	32,335,000	21,837,000	22,342,000	27,440,000	-13,244,000
Operating Cash Flow	67,472,000	59,934,000	38,657,000	45,915,000	74,772,000	-3,376,000
Capital Expenditure	16,009,000	13,283,000	8,105,000	8,343,000	8,415,000	7,945,000
EBITDA	83,214,000	78,755,000	55,322,000	55,325,000	62,295,000	2,920,000
Return on Assets %	6.19%	6.11%	4.77%	5.52%	7.00%	-3.51%
Return on Equity %	9.75%	9.60%	7.14%	7.96%	10.31%	-4.92%
Debt to Equity	0.22	0.27	0.19	0.07	0.07	0.13

CONTACT INFORMATION:
Phone: 337 233-1307   Fax: 337 235-8037
Toll-Free:
Address: 901 Hugh Wallis Rd. S., Lafayette, LA 70508 United States

STOCK TICKER/OTHER:
Stock Ticker: LHCG   Exchange: NAS
Employees: 11,598   Fiscal Year Ends: 12/31
Parent Company:

SALARIES/BONUSES:
Top Exec. Salary: $550,000   Bonus: $150,000
Second Exec. Salary: $700,000   Bonus: $

OTHER THOUGHTS:
Estimated Female Officers or Directors: 6
Hot Spot for Advancement for Women/Minorities: Y

Liberty Global plc

NAIC Code: 517110

www.lgi.com

TYPES OF BUSINESS:

Video, Voice & Broadband Internet Access Services
Telephony Services
VoIP Services
Mobile Telephony Services
Video on Demand Services

BRANDS/DIVISIONS/AFFILIATES:

Virgin Media Inc
Ziggo Group Holdings BV
Unitymedia GmbH
Telenet Group Holdings NV
UPC Holding BV
VTR GlobalCom SpA
Liberty Cablevision of Puerto Rico LLC
BASE Company NV

CONTACTS: *Note: Officers with more than one job title may be intentionally listed here more than once.*

Michael Fries, CEO
John Malone, Chairman of the Board
Balan Nair, Chief Technology Officer
Bernard Dvorak, Co-CFO
Charles Bracken, Co-CFO
Bryan Hall, Executive VP
Diederik Karsten, Executive VP
Leonard Stegman, Managing Director

GROWTH PLANS/SPECIAL FEATURES:

Liberty Global plc is an international provider of video, voice, mobile and broadband internet services, serving 27.5 million customers across 14 countries. Wholly-owned Virgin Media, Inc. offers these services in the U.K. and Ireland. Ziggo Group Holdings BV, Unitymedia GmbH and Telenet Group Holdings NV provide services in the Netherlands, Germany and Belgium. UPC Holding BV provides services in several European countries. VTR GlobalCom SpA provides services to Chile; and Liberty Cablevision of Puerto Rico, LLC provides services to Puerto Rico. A variety of broadband services are offered over Liberty Global's cable distribution systems, including video, broadband internet and fixed-line telephone; and in certain areas of operations, it offers mobile services. In 2015, the firm acquired Puerto Rico Cable Acquisition Company, Inc., which does business as Choice Cable TV; and sold its Film1 channels to Sony Pictures Television Networks. In 2016, it acquired BASE Company NV, a major mobile network operator in Belgium.

FINANCIAL DATA: *Note: Data for latest year may not have been available at press time.*

In U.S. $	2016	2015	2014	2013	2012	2011
Revenue	20,008,800,000	17,062,700,000	18,248,300,000	14,474,200,000	10,310,800,000	9,510,800,000
R&D Expense						
Operating Income	2,801,300,000	2,101,100,000	2,228,200,000	2,012,100,000	1,983,100,000	1,818,400,000
Operating Margin %	14.00%	12.31%	12.21%	13.90%	19.23%	19.11%
SGA Expense	3,566,900,000	2,973,500,000	3,172,800,000	2,616,500,000	1,936,100,000	1,780,400,000
Net Income	1,705,300,000	-1,196,400,000	-695,000,000	-963,900,000	322,800,000	-772,700,000
Operating Cash Flow	5,935,500,000	5,399,300,000	5,603,200,000	3,931,300,000	2,919,700,000	2,736,300,000
Capital Expenditure	2,644,300,000	2,272,300,000	2,684,400,000	2,481,500,000	1,883,600,000	1,927,000,000
EBITDA	8,988,900,000	7,116,600,000	6,988,900,000	6,036,800,000	3,885,200,000	3,336,400,000
Return on Assets %	2.91%	-1.74%	-.98%	-1.81%	.86%	-2.21%
Return on Equity %	16.03%	-9.51%	-5.19%	-13.54%	12.87%	-26.41%
Debt to Equity	2.96	4.03	3.03	3.63	12.29	8.75

CONTACT INFORMATION:

Phone: 303 220-6600   Fax: 720 875-5401
Toll-Free:
Address: 12300 Liberty Blvd., Englewood, CO 80112 United States

STOCK TICKER/OTHER:

Stock Ticker: LBTYA
Employees: 41,000
Parent Company:

Exchange: NAS
Fiscal Year Ends: 12/31

SALARIES/BONUSES:

Top Exec. Salary: $2,115,000   Bonus: $
Second Exec. Salary: $1,057,500   Bonus: $

OTHER THOUGHTS:

Estimated Female Officers or Directors: 3
Hot Spot for Advancement for Women/Minorities: Y

Liberty Interactive Corporation

www.libertyinteractive.com

NAIC Code: 454111

TYPES OF BUSINESS:

Online and Internet Businesses
e-Commerce

BRANDS/DIVISIONS/AFFILIATES:

QVC Inc
zulily LLC
Bodybuilding.com LLC
CommerceHub
Evite Inc
HSN Inc
FTD Companies Inc
Leisure Group Inc

CONTACTS: *Note: Officers with more than one job title may be intentionally listed here more than once.*

Michael George, CEO, Subsidiary
Gregory Maffei, CEO
Mark Carleton, CFO
John Malone, Chairman of the Board
Pamela Coe, Other Corporate Officer
Richard Baer, Other Executive Officer
Albert Rosenthaler, Other Executive Officer

GROWTH PLANS/SPECIAL FEATURES:

Liberty Interactive Corporation is a holding company with interests primarily in e-commerce businesses. The firm's largest business is QVC, Inc., which markets and sells a wide variety of consumer products in the U.S., and several foreign countries, primarily through live televised shopping programs and via the internet through its U.S. and international web sites. Other significant consolidated subsidiaries include zulily, LLC, an online retailer offering fun and entertainment shopping with new product styles launched daily; Bodybuilding.com, LLC, an e-retailer of nutritional and dietary supplements; CommerceHub, a provider of cloud-based e-commerce fulfillment and marketing software platform of integrated supply, demand and delivery solutions for a wide variety of marketing channels; and Evite, Inc., an online invitation and social event planning service on the web. Liberty Interactive's equity investments include HSN, Inc., an interactive multichannel retailer comprised of the HSN and Cornerstone Brands operating segments; FTD Companies, Inc., a premier floral and gifting company; Interval Leisure Group, Inc., a global provider of non-traditional lodging, including vacation rental and vacation ownership; and LendingTree, Inc., the owner of several brands and businesses that provide information, tools, advice, products and services for critical transactions in their customers' lives. In November 2016, the firm split-off Liberty Expedia Holdings, Inc. into a separate, publicly-traded company. In July 2017, Liberty Interactive agreed to acquire the remaining shares of HSN for approximately $2.6 billion. The firm plans to merge HSN with QVC. Following the merger, the Liberty Interactive plans to spin off its cable operations into an independent company and rename itself QVC Group.

FINANCIAL DATA: *Note: Data for latest year may not have been available at press time.*

In U.S. $	2016	2015	2014	2013	2012	2011
Revenue	10,219,000,000	9,169,000,000	10,028,000,000	10,307,000,000	10,018,000,000	9,616,000,000
R&D Expense						
Operating Income	1,011,000,000	1,170,000,000	1,206,000,000	1,131,000,000	1,124,000,000	1,133,000,000
Operating Margin %	9.89%	12.76%	12.02%	10.97%	11.21%	11.78%
SGA Expense	1,716,000,000	1,495,000,000	1,794,000,000	1,909,000,000	1,810,000,000	1,728,000,000
Net Income	473,000,000	640,000,000	520,000,000	438,000,000	466,000,000	912,000,000
Operating Cash Flow	1,273,000,000	981,000,000	1,204,000,000	972,000,000	1,470,000,000	914,000,000
Capital Expenditure	206,000,000	218,000,000	226,000,000	295,000,000	338,000,000	312,000,000
EBITDA	1,947,000,000	1,918,000,000	1,835,000,000	1,745,000,000	1,799,000,000	2,007,000,000
Return on Assets %	3.20%	4.54%	3.73%	2.92%	2.87%	5.42%
Return on Equity %	9.40%	13.50%	9.75%	6.54%	6.90%	14.27%
Debt to Equity	1.30	1.18	1.36	0.79	0.61	0.74

CONTACT INFORMATION:

Phone: 720 875-5400   Fax: 720 875-7469
Toll-Free: 866-876-0461
Address: 12300 Liberty Blvd., Englewood, CO 80112 United States

STOCK TICKER/OTHER:

Stock Ticker: QVCA
Employees: 21,080
Parent Company:

Exchange: NAS
Fiscal Year Ends: 12/31

SALARIES/BONUSES:

Top Exec. Salary: $1,125,509   Bonus: $
Second Exec. Salary: $960,750   Bonus: $

OTHER THOUGHTS:

Estimated Female Officers or Directors: 1
Hot Spot for Advancement for Women/Minorities:

Liberty Mutual Group Inc

NAIC Code: 524126

www.libertymutualgroup.com

TYPES OF BUSINESS:

Insurance, Direct Property & Casualty
Rehabilitation Services
Disability Care Management
Homeowners' Insurance
Auto Insurance
Group Life Insurance
Asset Management & Investment Products
Workers' Compensation

BRANDS/DIVISIONS/AFFILIATES:

Liberty Mutual
Safeco Insurance
Liberty International Underwriters
Liberty Mutual Surety
Liberty Specialty Markets
Ironshore Inc

CONTACTS: Note: Officers with more than one job title may be intentionally listed here more than once.

David H. Long, CEO
Dennis J. Langwell, CFO
Melanie M. Foley, Sr. VP-Human Resources
James M. McGlennon, CIO
Melanie M. Foley, Sr. VP-Admin.
James F. Kelleher, Sr. VP
Paul G. Alexander, Mgr.-Comm.
Laurance H.S. Yahia, Treas.
J. Paul Condrin III, Exec. VP
A. Alexander Fontanes, Exec. VP
Christopher L. Peirce, Exec. VP
Timothy M. Sweeney, Exec. VP
David H. Long, Chmn.
Luis Bonell, Exec. VP

GROWTH PLANS/SPECIAL FEATURES:

Liberty Mutual Group, Inc. is a group of insurance companies with offices worldwide. The company offers personal insurance for private passenger automobile, homeowners and other property-casualty insurance product in the U.S. through the Liberty Mutual and Safeco Insurance brands. Liberty Life Assurance Company of Boston offers a wide range of life insurance and annuity products. For businesses, Liberty Mutual offers a variety of flexible commercial insurance coverages, including property, casualty, employee benefits and specialty lines for companies of all types and sizes. Worldwide specialty coverages are offered through three operations: Liberty International Underwriters, Liberty Mutual Surety and Liberty Specialty Markets. Liberty International writes a variety of specialty and commercial insurance products, including casualty, marine, construction, energy, directors and officers, trade credit, professional liability, aviation, property and crisis management. Liberty Mutual Surety works with independent agents and brokers to underwrite all types of contractors and corporations for local, regional, national and multinational customers. Last, Liberty Specialty Markets provides specialty, commercial and reinsurance specialty products for specialty markets worldwide. In May 2017, the firm acquired Ironshore, Inc., a premier global specialty insurance company.

Employees are offered medical, dental and vision insurance; a 401(k) plan; a pension plan; tuition reimbursement; flexible spending accounts; disability insurance; and life insurance.

FINANCIAL DATA: Note: Data for latest year may not have been available at press time.

In U.S. $	2016	2015	2014	2013	2012	2011
Revenue	38,308,000,000	37,617,000,000	37,721,000,000	36,556,000,000	36,325,000,000	34,671,000,000
R&D Expense						
Operating Income						
Operating Margin %						
SGA Expense						
Net Income	1,006,000,000	514,000,000	1,833,000,000	1,743,000,000	829,000,000	365,000,000
Operating Cash Flow						
Capital Expenditure						
EBITDA						
Return on Assets %						
Return on Equity %						
Debt to Equity						

CONTACT INFORMATION:

Phone: 617-357-9500   Fax: 617-350-7648
Toll-Free: 800-837-5254
Address: 175 Berkeley St., Boston, MA 02116 United States

STOCK TICKER/OTHER:

Stock Ticker: Mutual Company   Exchange:
Employees: 51,000   Fiscal Year Ends: 12/31
Parent Company:

SALARIES/BONUSES:

Top Exec. Salary: $ Bonus: $
Second Exec. Salary: $ Bonus: $

OTHER THOUGHTS:

Estimated Female Officers or Directors: 4
Hot Spot for Advancement for Women/Minorities: Y

LifePoint Health Inc

www.lifepointhealth.net/

NAIC Code: 622110

TYPES OF BUSINESS:

General Medical and Surgical Hospitals

BRANDS/DIVISIONS/AFFILIATES:

LHC Group Inc
In-Home Healthcare Partnership
LifePoint Hospitals Inc

CONTACTS: *Note: Officers with more than one job title may be intentionally listed here more than once.*

William Carpenter, CEO
Michael Coggin, CFO
John Bumpus, Chief Administrative Officer
Russell Holman, Chief Medical Officer
David Dill, COO
Jennifer Peters, General Counsel
Jeffrey Seraphine, Other Executive Officer
Melissa Waddey, President, Divisional
Victor Giovanetti, President, Divisional
Robert Klein, President, Divisional
R. Raplee, President, Divisional

GROWTH PLANS/SPECIAL FEATURES:

LifePoint Health, Inc., formerly LifePoint Hospitals, Inc., is a holding company that owns and operates general acute care hospitals in non-urban communities in the U.S. The firm operates 72 hospitals, with over 9,400 beds, as well as 1,700 physician practices, 40 post-acute facilities and 30 outpatient centers located in 22 states across the country. The company's hospitals typically provide the range of medical and surgical services commonly available in hospitals in non-urban markets. These services generally include internal medicine; obstetrics; general surgery; emergency room, psychiatric, diagnostic and coronary care; radiology; oncology; rehabilitation and pediatric services; and, in some hospitals, specialized services such as open-heart surgery, skilled nursing and neuro-surgery. In many markets, LifePoint also provides outpatient services such as one-day surgery, laboratory, x-ray, respiratory therapy, imaging, sports medicine and lithotripsy. Post-acute services and facilities include long-term care services, nursing homes and assisted living establishments. Outpatient centers and services include urgent care centers, diagnostic imaging centers, ambulatory surgery centers and radiation oncology programs. In January 2017, the firm created a joint venture with wholly-owned subsidiary LHC Group, Inc. to form In-Home Healthcare Partnership, which owns and operates all of LifePoint's home health agencies and hospices, and some of LHC's home health agencies and hospices.

The company offers its employees medical, dental, vision, life and disability insurance; adoption assistance; flexible spending accounts; a wellness program; a Wells Fargo Employee Home Mortgage Program; and a 401(k) plan.

FINANCIAL DATA: *Note: Data for latest year may not have been available at press time.*

In U.S. $	2016	2015	2014	2013	2012	2011
Revenue	6,364,000,000	5,214,300,000	4,483,100,000	3,678,300,000	3,391,800,000	3,026,100,000
R&D Expense						
Operating Income	347,300,000	426,700,000	383,700,000	308,500,000	352,500,000	370,400,000
Operating Margin %	5.45%	8.18%	8.55%	8.38%	10.39%	12.24%
SGA Expense	4,068,900,000	3,439,500,000	2,134,500,000	2,628,300,000	586,000,000	514,800,000
Net Income	121,900,000	181,900,000	126,100,000	128,200,000	151,900,000	162,900,000
Operating Cash Flow	435,200,000	627,100,000	412,300,000	354,000,000	382,200,000	401,500,000
Capital Expenditure	399,500,000	274,700,000	207,100,000	185,200,000	221,400,000	219,900,000
EBITDA	691,900,000	705,700,000	634,200,000	553,900,000	565,200,000	556,000,000
Return on Assets %	1.97%	3.17%	2.28%	2.48%	3.34%	3.82%
Return on Equity %	5.48%	8.23%	5.77%	6.01%	7.60%	8.50%
Debt to Equity	1.32	1.16	1.02	0.81	0.82	0.82

CONTACT INFORMATION:

Phone: 615 920-7000   Fax:
Toll-Free:
Address: 330 Seven Springs Way, Brentwood, TN 37027 United States

STOCK TICKER/OTHER:

Stock Ticker: LPNT
Employees: 47,000
Parent Company:

Exchange: NAS
Fiscal Year Ends: 12/31

SALARIES/BONUSES:

Top Exec. Salary: $1,179,000   Bonus: $
Second Exec. Salary: $687,000   Bonus: $

OTHER THOUGHTS:

Estimated Female Officers or Directors: 1
Hot Spot for Advancement for Women/Minorities: Y

Lincare Holdings Inc

www.lincare.com

NAIC Code: 621610

TYPES OF BUSINESS:

Home Health Care-Oxygen & Other Respiratory Therapy Services
Durable Medical Equipment
Home Infusion Therapies

BRANDS/DIVISIONS/AFFILIATES:

Linde AG

CONTACTS: *Note: Officers with more than one job title may be intentionally listed here more than once.*

Kristen Hoefer, CEO
Shawn S. Schabel, Pres.

GROWTH PLANS/SPECIAL FEATURES:

Lincare Holdings, Inc. provides oxygen and other respiratory therapy services to in-home patients throughout the U.S. and Canada. The company also provides durable medical equipment and home infusion therapies in certain geographic markets. The firm's customers typically suffer from chronic obstructive pulmonary diseases (COPD), such as emphysema, chronic bronchitis or asthma, and require supplemental oxygen or other respiratory therapy services in order to alleviate the symptoms and discomfort of respiratory dysfunction. Lincare's home oxygen equipment comes in two variations: oxygen concentrators and liquid oxygen systems. Oxygen concentrators are stationary units that provide a continuous flow of oxygen by filtering ordinary room air and are often supplemented with portable gaseous oxygen cylinders or liquid oxygen systems to meet the ambulatory or emergency needs of the customer. Liquid oxygen systems are thermally insulated containers of liquid oxygen; they generally consist of a stationary unit and a portable unit. Other respiratory therapy services offered by the company include nebulizers and associated respiratory medications; non-invasive ventilation; ventilators and continuous positive airway pressure devices, which maintain open airways in customers suffering from obstructive sleep apnea by providing airflow at prescribed pressures during sleep. Lincare's home infusion therapy products and services include chemotherapy, continuous pain management, intravenous antibiotic therapy, parenteral nutrition, dobutamine infusions, enteral nutrition, immunoglobulin therapy and central catheter management. Therapies for enteral therapy are available at certain Lincare locations with a licensed dietitian on staff. The firm also offers pediatric respiratory services, where medical professionals work hand in hand with a child and its caregivers to instruct the child on how to treat their illness. Lincare is a subsidiary of German technology firm, Linde AG.

FINANCIAL DATA: *Note: Data for latest year may not have been available at press time.*

In U.S. $	2016	2015	2014	2013	2012	2011
Revenue	220,000,000	220,000,000	2,100,000,000	2,000,000,000	1,900,000,000	1,847,520,000
R&D Expense						
Operating Income						
Operating Margin %						
SGA Expense						
Net Income						
Operating Cash Flow						
Capital Expenditure						
EBITDA						
Return on Assets %						
Return on Equity %						
Debt to Equity						

CONTACT INFORMATION:

Phone: 727-530-7700   Fax: 727-532-9692
Toll-Free:
Address: 19387 US 19 N., Clearwater, FL 33764 United States

STOCK TICKER/OTHER:

Stock Ticker: Subsidiary   Exchange:
Employees: 11,000   Fiscal Year Ends: 12/31
Parent Company: Linde AG

SALARIES/BONUSES:

Top Exec. Salary: $ Bonus: $
Second Exec. Salary: $ Bonus: $

OTHER THOUGHTS:

Estimated Female Officers or Directors:
Hot Spot for Advancement for Women/Minorities:

Lincoln National Corporation

www.lfg.com

NAIC Code: 524113

TYPES OF BUSINESS:

Life Insurance
Investment Management
Retirement Plans
Mutual Funds
Financial Planning
Annuities

BRANDS/DIVISIONS/AFFILIATES:

Lincoln Financial Group

CONTACTS: Note: Officers with more than one job title may be intentionally listed here more than once.

Dennis Glass, CEO
Randal Freitag, CFO
Christine Janofsky, Chief Accounting Officer
Kenneth Solon, Chief Information Officer
William Cunningham, Director
Kirkland Hicks, Executive VP
Ellen Cooper, Executive VP
Lisa Buckingham, Executive VP
Wilford Fuller, President, Subsidiary
Andrea Goodrich, Secretary

GROWTH PLANS/SPECIAL FEATURES:

Lincoln National Corporation is a holding company operating multiple insurance and retirement businesses. The operations of the firm's subsidiaries, collectively known as Lincoln Financial Group, are divided into four operating businesses: retirement plan services, life insurance, annuities and group protection. Retirement plan services provides employers with retirement plan products and services, with a focus on defined contribution retirement plans. The life insurance segment offers life insurance products including term insurances, a linked-benefit product, indexed Universal Life (UL) insurance and both single and survivorship versions of UL and variable UL (VUL) products. In a UL contract, contract holders typically have flexibility in the timing and amount of premium payments and the amount of death benefit, provided there is sufficient account value to cover all policy charges. VUL products are UL products that provide a return on account values linked to an underlying investment portfolio of variable funds offered through the products. The annuities segment offers fixed and variable annuities to its clients. Group protection offers employers non-medical insurance products, principally term life, disability and dental. The company's other operations include financial data for operations that are not directly related to the business segments, investment income and its run-off institutional pension business.

Lincoln National offers its employees benefits including disability, life, medical, dental and vision insurance; domestic partner benefits; tuition reimbursement; a 401(k) with matching contributions; an employee assistance program; and flexible work arrangements.

FINANCIAL DATA: Note: Data for latest year may not have been available at press time.

In U.S. $	2016	2015	2014	2013	2012	2011
Revenue	13,330,000,000	13,572,000,000	13,554,000,000	11,969,000,000	11,532,000,000	10,636,000,000
R&D Expense						
Operating Income	1,458,000,000	1,430,000,000	1,997,000,000	1,631,000,000	1,568,000,000	599,000,000
Operating Margin %	10.93%	10.53%	14.73%	13.62%	13.59%	5.63%
SGA Expense	4,277,000,000	4,318,000,000	4,079,000,000	3,701,000,000		
Net Income	1,192,000,000	1,154,000,000	1,515,000,000	1,244,000,000	1,313,000,000	294,000,000
Operating Cash Flow	1,272,000,000	2,243,000,000	2,526,000,000	799,000,000	1,269,000,000	1,277,000,000
Capital Expenditure						
EBITDA						
Return on Assets %	.46%	.45%	.61%	.54%	.62%	.14%
Return on Equity %	8.48%	7.86%	10.37%	8.75%	9.01%	2.18%
Debt to Equity	0.36	0.40	0.33	0.39	0.36	0.38

CONTACT INFORMATION:

Phone: 484 583-1400   Fax: 215 448-3962
Toll-Free: 877-275-5462
Address: 150 N. Radnor Chester Rd., Ste. A305, Radnor, PA 19087 United States

STOCK TICKER/OTHER:

Stock Ticker: LNC   Exchange: NYS
Employees: 9,057   Fiscal Year Ends: 12/31
Parent Company:

SALARIES/BONUSES:

Top Exec. Salary: $1,200,000   Bonus: $
Second Exec. Salary: $575,000   Bonus: $125,000

OTHER THOUGHTS:

Estimated Female Officers or Directors: 2
Hot Spot for Advancement for Women/Minorities: Y

LinkedIn Corp

NAIC Code: 519130

www.linkedin.com

TYPES OF BUSINESS:

Business-Oriented Social Networking
Advertising Services
Recruiting Tools

BRANDS/DIVISIONS/AFFILIATES:

LinkedIn.com
lynda.com
Microsoft Corp

CONTACTS: *Note: Officers with more than one job title may be intentionally listed here more than once.*

Jeffrey Weiner, CEO
Reid Hoffman, Chairman of the Board
Susan Taylor, Chief Accounting Officer
Michael Gamson, Senior VP, Divisional
Patricia Wadors, Senior VP, Divisional
James Scott, Senior VP, Divisional
Shannon Stubo, Senior VP, Divisional
Steven Sordello, Senior VP
Michael Callahan, Senior VP

GROWTH PLANS/SPECIAL FEATURES:

LinkedIn Corp. is an online social networking site targeting the business and professional community. Through its web site, LinkedIn.com, users can post profiles, connect with co-workers, post resumes and search for job openings. Other features on the site include Company Pages, which allows companies to showcase brands and products; and a suite of products for corporate recruitment initiatives, including sourcing and pipelining, a referral engine, career pages and recruitment ads. The site generates revenue through ad sales, user subscription fees on premium accounts and enterprise hiring software licensing fees. The company offers a range of solutions to its members, including free solutions, such as stay connected and informed, advance my career and ubiquitous access; and monetized solutions, such as talent, marketing and premium subscription. Its membership base exceeds more than 467 million users in over 200 countries and territories and is available in multiple languages including English, French, German, Italian, Portuguese, Spanish, Japanese, Korean, Russian, Arabic and Turkish. It is currently expanding its international scope, opening offices in London, Amsterdam, Singapore, Tokyo and Mumbai. In December 2016, LinkedIn was acquired by Microsoft for $26 billion.

FINANCIAL DATA: *Note: Data for latest year may not have been available at press time.*

In U.S. $	2016	2015	2014	2013	2012	2011
Revenue	3,500,000,000	2,990,910,976	2,218,767,104	1,528,545,024	972,308,992	522,188,992
R&D Expense						
Operating Income						
Operating Margin %						
SGA Expense						
Net Income		-166,144,000	-15,747,000	26,769,000	21,610,000	11,912,000
Operating Cash Flow						
Capital Expenditure						
EBITDA						
Return on Assets %						
Return on Equity %						
Debt to Equity						

CONTACT INFORMATION:

Phone: 650 687-3600   Fax:
Toll-Free:
Address: 2029 Stierlin Ct., Mountain View, CA 94043 United States

STOCK TICKER/OTHER:

Stock Ticker: Subsidiary   Exchange:
Employees: 9,372   Fiscal Year Ends: 12/31
Parent Company: Microsoft Corp

SALARIES/BONUSES:

Top Exec. Salary: $ Bonus: $
Second Exec. Salary: $ Bonus: $

OTHER THOUGHTS:

Estimated Female Officers or Directors: 4
Hot Spot for Advancement for Women/Minorities: Y

Lithia Motors Inc

www.lithia.com

NAIC Code: 441110

TYPES OF BUSINESS:

Auto Dealers
Automotive Repair & Maintenance
Insurance & Financing

BRANDS/DIVISIONS/AFFILIATES:

MyLithia

CONTACTS: *Note: Officers with more than one job title may be intentionally listed here more than once.*

Bryan Deboer, CEO
John North, CFO
Sidney Deboer, Chairman of the Board
Christopher Holzshu, Executive VP
Scott Hillier, Senior VP, Divisional
Chun-Wai Liang, Senior VP, Subsidiary

GROWTH PLANS/SPECIAL FEATURES:

Lithia Motors, Inc. is a leading operator of automotive dealerships, retailing both new and used vehicles through 154 stores in the U.S. and over the Internet. The company operates stores in Oregon, California, Texas, Washington, Hawaii, Iowa, Idaho, Alaska, Montana, North Dakota, Nevada and New Mexico. California and Oregon represent the firm's two largest markets, with 35 and 25 locations respectively. The firm sells new and used cars and light trucks; sells replacement parts; provides vehicle maintenance, warranty, paint and repair services; and arranges related financing, service contracts, protection products and credit insurance for its automotive customers. Lithia's dealerships offer customers vehicles in 30 domestic and imported brands, including Ford, Toyota, BMW, Suzuki and Hyundai. Lithia also operates 22 collision repair centers. The company markets its parts and service products by notifying the owners of vehicles purchased at its franchises when their vehicles are due for periodic service. The firm's other marketing efforts include direct-mail ads to previous customers as well as newspaper, television and radio ads. The Lithia web site offers users several services, such as viewing new and used vehicle inventories and scheduling service appointments. Additionally, the firm has an app available for download, the MyLithia app. The company also offers financing and insurance to customers that purchase new or used vehicles. In 2016, Lithia Motors sold 145,772 new vehicles.

Lithia offers employees medical, dental and vision insurance; short- and long-term disability coverage; life insurance; an employee stock purchase plan; a 401(k) plan; and employee discounts.

FINANCIAL DATA: *Note: Data for latest year may not have been available at press time.*

In U.S. $	2016	2015	2014	2013	2012	2011
Revenue	8,678,157,000	7,864,252,000	5,390,326,000	4,005,749,000	3,316,487,000	2,699,360,000
R&D Expense						
Operating Income	338,364,000	302,735,000	231,899,000	183,518,000	148,369,000	111,991,000
Operating Margin %	3.89%	3.84%	4.30%	4.58%	4.47%	4.14%
SGA Expense	899,590,000	811,175,000	563,207,000	427,400,000	373,688,000	327,545,000
Net Income	197,058,000	182,999,000	138,720,000	106,000,000	80,362,000	58,860,000
Operating Cash Flow	86,516,000	74,209,000	30,319,000	32,059,000	-212,476,000	-766,000
Capital Expenditure	100,761,000	83,244,000	85,983,000	50,025,000	64,584,000	31,673,000
EBITDA	381,630,000	343,329,000	261,461,000	206,546,000	168,208,000	129,635,000
Return on Assets %	5.57%	5.99%	6.02%	6.58%	6.09%	5.55%
Return on Equity %	22.66%	24.37%	22.97%	22.01%	20.21%	17.12%
Debt to Equity	0.84	0.73	0.90	0.45	0.67	0.75

CONTACT INFORMATION:

Phone: 541 776-6401   Fax: 541 776-6362
Toll-Free: 877-331-3084
Address: 150 N. Bartlett St., Medford, OR 97501 United States

STOCK TICKER/OTHER:

Stock Ticker: LAD
Employees: 11,170
Parent Company:

Exchange: NYS
Fiscal Year Ends: 12/31

SALARIES/BONUSES:

Top Exec. Salary: $950,000   Bonus: $
Second Exec. Salary: Bonus: $
$485,100

OTHER THOUGHTS:

Estimated Female Officers or Directors:
Hot Spot for Advancement for Women/Minorities:

Littelfuse Inc

www.littelfuse.com

NAIC Code: 335313

TYPES OF BUSINESS:

Electrical Switches, Sensors, Microelectronics, Optomechanicals

BRANDS/DIVISIONS/AFFILIATES:

CONTACTS: *Note: Officers with more than one job title may be intentionally listed here more than once.*

Meenal Sethna, CFO
Gordon Hunter, Chairman of the Board
Ian Highley, Chief Technology Officer
Ryan Stafford, Executive VP
Deepak Nayar, General Manager, Divisional
Dieter Roeder, General Manager, Divisional
Matthew Cole, General Manager, Divisional
David Heinzmann, President
Michael Rutz, Senior VP, Divisional

GROWTH PLANS/SPECIAL FEATURES:

Littelfuse, Inc. designs, manufactures and sells circuit-protection devices for the electronics, automotive and industrial markets. The firm operates through three segments: electronics, automotive and industrial. Electronics is the firm's largest segment, supplying manufacturers with circuit protection devices used in products such as mobile phones, computers and LCD (liquid crystal display) televisions. Some of the firm's customers in the electronics business include Cisco, Huawei, Samsung, Panasonic, IBM and Intel. The automotive segment supplies fuses for original equipment manufacturers (OEMs) and aftermarket customers. The segment's customers range from Ford and General Motors to O'Reilly Auto Parts and Pep Boys. Littelfuse's smallest segment, industrial, provides a broad range of low-voltage and medium-voltage circuit protection products to electrical distributors and their customers in the construction, OEM and industrial maintenance, repair and operating supplies markets. Common uses for the products are in mining and wet environments where power sources are exposed to water. The firm attempts to offer an array of circuit-protection solutions, rather than specializing in one product area. In late-2016, the firm acquired certain assets of ON Semiconductor Corporation, which includes the electronics segment, consisting of transient voltage suppression diodes, switching thyristors and insulated-gate bipolar transistors (IGBTs).

FINANCIAL DATA: *Note: Data for latest year may not have been available at press time.*

In U.S. $	2016	2015	2014	2013	2012	2011
Revenue	1,056,159,000	867,864,000	851,995,000	757,853,000	667,913,000	664,955,000
R&D Expense	42,198,000	30,802,000	31,122,000	24,415,000	21,231,000	19,439,000
Operating Income	130,644,000	104,157,000	133,830,000	129,881,000	106,870,000	113,904,000
Operating Margin %	12.36%	12.00%	15.70%	17.13%	16.00%	17.12%
SGA Expense	206,129,000	153,714,000	146,975,000	132,657,000	124,277,000	116,740,000
Net Income	104,488,000	82,466,000	99,418,000	88,784,000	75,332,000	87,024,000
Operating Cash Flow	180,133,000	165,826,000	153,141,000	117,367,000	116,170,000	120,750,000
Capital Expenditure	46,228,000	44,019,000	32,281,000	34,953,000	22,529,000	17,555,000
EBITDA	185,039,000	152,638,000	178,424,000	161,632,000	133,186,000	146,156,000
Return on Assets %	8.17%	7.72%	9.49%	9.85%	10.34%	13.39%
Return on Equity %	13.40%	11.20%	14.05%	13.93%	13.84%	18.25%
Debt to Equity	0.54	0.11	0.14	0.13		

CONTACT INFORMATION:

Phone: 773 628-1000   Fax: 847 391-0434
Toll-Free:
Address: 8755 W. Higgins Rd, Chicago, IL 60631 United States

STOCK TICKER/OTHER:

Stock Ticker: LFUS   Exchange: NAS
Employees: 10,300   Fiscal Year Ends: 12/31
Parent Company:

SALARIES/BONUSES:

Top Exec. Salary: $780,231   Bonus: $ 700
Second Exec. Salary: Bonus: $ 150
$522,917

OTHER THOUGHTS:

Estimated Female Officers or Directors:
Hot Spot for Advancement for Women/Minorities:

LKQ Corporation

www.lkqcorp.com

NAIC Code: 336300

TYPES OF BUSINESS:

Remanufactured OEM Parts
Aftermarket Replacement Parts
Vehicle Salvage
Scrap/Bulk Automotive Parts
Refurbished Aluminum Wheels

BRANDS/DIVISIONS/AFFILIATES:

Andrew Page Limited

CONTACTS:
Note: Officers with more than one job title may be intentionally listed here more than once.

John Quinn, CEO, Divisional
Sukhpal Ahluwahlia, Chairman of the Board, Subsidiary
Ashley Brooks, Chief Information Officer
Michael Clark, Controller
Joseph Holsten, Director
Victor Casini, General Counsel
Dominick Zarcone, President
Justin Jude, Senior VP, Divisional
Matthew McKay, Senior VP, Divisional
Walter Hanley, Senior VP, Divisional

GROWTH PLANS/SPECIAL FEATURES:

LKQ Corporation is a global distributor of vehicle products, including replacement parts, components and systems used in the repair and maintenance of vehicles. The company also distributes specialty vehicle products and accessories. LKQ operates through three segments: North America, Europe and specialty. The North America segment comprises the company's wholesale operations, which include aftermarket, recycled, remanufactured, refurbished and original equipment manufacturer (OEM) parts supplied to professional collision and mechanical automobile repair businesses throughout the U.S. and Canada. The Europe segment provides mechanical aftermarket parts for the repair of vehicles 3 to 15 years old. Top-selling products within this division include brake pads, discs, sensors, clutches, spark plugs, batteries, steering systems and components, suspension systems and components, filters, and oil/automotive fluids. Last, the specialty segment sells and distributes recreational vehicle appliances, vehicle air conditioners, tow hitches, truck bed covers, vehicle protection products, cargo management products, wheels, tires and suspension products. This division primarily supplies small- to medium-sized businesses that focus on a narrow product or market niche. In February 2017, the firm agreed to acquire an equity interest in Mekonomen AB from Axel Johnson AB; acquired Andrew Page Limited; and agreed to sell its OEM glass manufacturing business to Vitro.

FINANCIAL DATA:
Note: Data for latest year may not have been available at press time.

In U.S. $	2016	2015	2014	2013	2012	2011
Revenue	8,584,031,000	7,192,633,000	6,740,064,000	5,062,528,000	4,122,930,000	3,269,862,000
R&D Expense						
Operating Income	763,398,000	704,627,000	649,868,000	530,180,000	437,953,000	361,483,000
Operating Margin %	8.89%	9.79%	9.64%	10.47%	10.62%	11.05%
SGA Expense	2,359,110,000	1,987,271,000	1,866,520,000	1,454,080,000	1,219,343,000	972,991,000
Net Income	463,975,000	423,223,000	381,519,000	311,623,000	261,225,000	210,264,000
Operating Cash Flow	635,014,000	529,837,000	370,897,000	428,056,000	206,190,000	211,772,000
Capital Expenditure	207,074,000	170,490,000	140,950,000	90,186,000	88,255,000	86,416,000
EBITDA	971,630,000	835,082,000	777,867,000	613,474,000	510,761,000	414,583,000
Return on Assets %	6.65%	7.54%	7.56%	7.56%	7.54%	7.64%
Return on Equity %	14.15%	14.50%	15.04%	14.44%	14.47%	13.75%
Debt to Equity	0.95	0.49	0.66	0.53	0.53	0.56

CONTACT INFORMATION:

Phone: 312 621-1950   Fax: 312 621-1969
Toll-Free: 877-557-2677
Address: 500 W. Madison St., Ste. 2800, Chicago, IL 60661 United States

STOCK TICKER/OTHER:

Stock Ticker: LKQ
Employees: 42,500
Parent Company:

Exchange: NAS
Fiscal Year Ends: 12/31

SALARIES/BONUSES:

Top Exec. Salary: $1,000,000   Bonus: $
Second Exec. Salary: $565,000   Bonus: $

OTHER THOUGHTS:

Estimated Female Officers or Directors:
Hot Spot for Advancement for Women/Minorities:

Loews Hotels Holding Corporation

www.loewshotels.com

NAIC Code: 721110

TYPES OF BUSINESS:

Hotels, Luxury
Hotel Management Services

BRANDS/DIVISIONS/AFFILIATES:

Loews Corporation
Loews Miami Beach Hotel
Loews Santa Monica Beach Hotel
Loews Royal Pacific Resort at Universal Orlando
Loews Portofino Bay Hotel at Universal Orlando
Loews Sapphire Falls Resort at Universal Orlando
YouFirst Loyalty Program

CONTACTS: Note: Officers with more than one job title may be intentionally listed here more than once.

Jonathan M. Tisch, CEO
Shawn Hauver, VP-Oper.
Lark-Marie Anton, Sr. VP-Public Rel. & Mktg. Comm.

GROWTH PLANS/SPECIAL FEATURES:

Loews Hotels Holding Corporation, a subsidiary of the Loews Corporation, currently has a portfolio of 24 owned and/or operated luxury hotels and resorts. Located in select cities throughout the U.S. and Canada, the firm's properties include the 790-room Loews Miami Beach Hotel in Florida, the 581-room Loews Philadelphia Hotel, the 347-room Loews Santa Monica Beach Hotel in Southern California and the 142-room Loews Hotel Vogue in Montreal. Loews Hotels operates three joint venture hotels with Universal Studios in Orlando, Florida: Loews Royal Pacific Resort at Universal Orlando, one of its largest hotels with 1,000 rooms; the 750-room Loews Portofino Bay Hotel at Universal Orlando; and the 1,000-room Loews Sapphire Falls Resort at Universal Orlando Resort (opened in 2016). Loews Hotels' business amenities include high-speed Internet access, a power breakfast with notable business leaders, notarization services, private dining rooms, boardrooms and concierge services. The YouFirst Loyalty Program rewards guests based on number of stays and offers free Internet access, late checkout, guaranteed rooms and upgrades for guests who visit at least twice a year. Loews Hotels offers facilities for weddings, meetings and special events; and special programs and services designed for people traveling with pets, children and teenagers.

FINANCIAL DATA: Note: Data for latest year may not have been available at press time.

In U.S. $	2016	2015	2014	2013	2012	2011
Revenue	1,293,000,000	604,000,000	472,659,000	380,000,000	397,938,000	337,000,000
R&D Expense						
Operating Income						
Operating Margin %						
SGA Expense						
Net Income	12,000,000	12,000,000	11,000,000	141,000,000	61,000,000	13,000,000
Operating Cash Flow						
Capital Expenditure						
EBITDA						
Return on Assets %						
Return on Equity %						
Debt to Equity						

CONTACT INFORMATION:

Phone: 212-521-2000   Fax: 212-521-2525
Toll-Free: 800-235-6397
Address: 667 Madison Ave., New York, NY 10021 United States

STOCK TICKER/OTHER:

Stock Ticker: Subsidiary
Employees: 4,775
Parent Company: Loews Corporation

Exchange:
Fiscal Year Ends: 12/31

SALARIES/BONUSES:

Top Exec. Salary: $ Bonus: $
Second Exec. Salary: $ Bonus: $

OTHER THOUGHTS:

Estimated Female Officers or Directors: 2
Hot Spot for Advancement for Women/Minorities: Y

Lowe's Companies Inc

www.lowes.com

NAIC Code: 444110

TYPES OF BUSINESS:

Home Centers, Retail
Home Improvement Products
Home Installation Services
Special Order Sales

BRANDS/DIVISIONS/AFFILIATES:

Orchard Supply Hardware
Maintenance Supply Headquarters

CONTACTS: *Note: Officers with more than one job title may be intentionally listed here more than once.*

Marshall Croom, CFO
Paul Ramsay, Chief Information Officer
Rick Damron, COO
Ross Mccanless, General Counsel
N. Peace, Other Corporate Officer
Richard Maltsbarger, Other Corporate Officer
Michael McDermott, Other Executive Officer
Jennifer Weber, Other Executive Officer
Robert Niblock, President
Matthew Hollifield, Senior VP

GROWTH PLANS/SPECIAL FEATURES:

Lowe's Companies, Inc. is one of the largest home improvement retailers in the world. The company owns roughly 2,129 stores in 50 U.S. states, Mexico and Canada, each carrying approximately 37,000 products and 213 million square feet of retail space. The company also operates 87 stores under the Orchard Supply Hardware name in California, Oregon and Florida. Hundreds of thousands of items are also available through the firm's special order system. Lowe's stores chiefly serve do-it-yourself (DIY) homeowners and commercial business customers, including contractors, landscapers, electricians, painters and plumbers. Its home improvement product categories include building materials, lighting, cabinets and countertops, seasonal living, millwork, lumber, flooring, lawn and landscaping items, hardware, fashion and rough plumbing, appliances, paint, tools, plants and plant pots, outdoor power equipment, rough electrical, home environment and organization and windows and walls. Each Lowe's store carries a wide selection of national brand name merchandise such as Samsung, Whirlpool, Stainmaster, GE, Valspar, Sylvania, Dewalt and Owens Corning; and exclusive brand names such as Kobalt, allen+roth, Blue Hawk, Utilitech and Aquasource. The company's Lowes.com web site facilitates customers researching, comparing and buying Lowe's products, and also allows customers to special order products not carried in its physical store locations. Lowe's entered the smarthome market with Iris, an affordable, cloud-based home management system, which allows users to interact and control their home's security cameras, thermostat, locks, lighting and appliances remotely from a smart phone or computer. In June 2017, the firm acquired Maintenance Supply Headquarters, a distributor of maintenance, repair and operations products serving the multifamily housing industry.

Lowe's offers its employees life, short- and long-term disability, accident, auto, home, medical, dental and vision insurance; family assistance programs; stock purchase plan; tuition reimbursement; paid time off; 401(k); and flexible spending accounts.

FINANCIAL DATA: *Note: Data for latest year may not have been available at press time.*

In U.S. $	2016	2015	2014	2013	2012	2011
Revenue	59,074,000,000	56,223,000,000	53,417,000,000	50,521,000,000	50,208,000,000	
R&D Expense						
Operating Income	4,971,000,000	4,792,000,000	4,149,000,000	3,560,000,000	3,277,000,000	
Operating Margin %	8.41%	8.52%	7.76%	7.04%	6.52%	
SGA Expense	14,115,000,000	13,281,000,000	12,865,000,000	12,244,000,000	12,593,000,000	
Net Income	2,546,000,000	2,698,000,000	2,286,000,000	1,959,000,000	1,839,000,000	
Operating Cash Flow	4,784,000,000	4,929,000,000	4,111,000,000	3,762,000,000	4,349,000,000	
Capital Expenditure	1,197,000,000	880,000,000	940,000,000	1,211,000,000	1,829,000,000	
EBITDA	6,563,000,000	6,385,000,000	5,719,000,000	5,211,000,000	4,862,000,000	
Return on Assets %	8.03%	8.30%	6.99%	5.91%	5.46%	
Return on Equity %	28.75%	24.58%	17.78%	12.89%	10.61%	
Debt to Equity	1.50	1.08	0.85	0.65	0.42	

CONTACT INFORMATION:

Phone: 704 758-1000   Fax: 336 658-4766
Toll-Free: 800-445-6937
Address: 1000 Lowe's Blvd., Mooresville, NC 28117 United States

STOCK TICKER/OTHER:

Stock Ticker: LOW   Exchange: NYS
Employees: 290,000   Fiscal Year Ends: 01/31
Parent Company:

SALARIES/BONUSES:

Top Exec. Salary: $1,300,000   Bonus: $
Second Exec. Salary: $790,000   Bonus: $

OTHER THOUGHTS:

Estimated Female Officers or Directors: 3
Hot Spot for Advancement for Women/Minorities: Y

Lubrizol Corporation (The)

NAIC Code: 325110

TYPES OF BUSINESS:

Manufacturing-Specialty Chemicals
Fuel & Lubricant Additives
Polymers
Performance Coatings, Resins & Additives
Plastic Plumbing, Automobile Molded Parts & Film
Rubber, Plastic & Lubricants Additives

BRANDS/DIVISIONS/AFFILIATES:

Bershire Hathaway Inc
Lubrizol Advanced Materials Inc
Lubrizol Additives

CONTACTS: *Note: Officers with more than one job title may be intentionally listed here more than once.*

Eric R. Schnur, CEO
Eric R. Schnur, Chmn.

GROWTH PLANS/SPECIAL FEATURES:

The Lubrizol Corporation, a subsidiary of Berkshire Hathaway, Inc., is a manufacturer and marketer of specialty chemicals and additives for the transportation, consumer and industrial markets. The company maintains production facilities throughout the Americas, Europe, the Middle East & Africa and Asia Pacific. It operates through two segments: Lubrizol Additives and Lubrizol Advanced Materials, Inc. The Lubrizol Additives segment partners with customers and original equipment manufacturers to solve end-user challenges through additives for engine oils, driveline applications, gasoline and diesel fuel, and other transportation-related fluids and industrial applications. Engine oil additives are useful in heavy duty diesel vehicles, passenger cars, marine vehicles, motorcycles, recreational vehicles, power tools and stationary natural gas equipment. Driveline additives are useful in axle oil, transmission fluids, construction and mining fluids and agriculture processes. Industrial lubricant additives are useful in grease, metalworking, industrial gear oil, hydraulic fluids, emulsion explosives, turbine and circulating oils and compressor lubricants. Fuel additives are useful in diesel, home heating oil, gasoline, industrial, marine and biofuel processes and applications. The Lubrizol Advanced Materials segment (and subsidiary) provides formulations that enable the distinct characteristics in customer's products, such as enhanced durability, nourishment in products and better quality in digital printing. Products lines include: engineered polymers, personal and home care, performance coatings, CPVC (chlorinated polyvinyl chloride) piping systems (flexible and withstand temperatures) and life sciences (such as medical devices and pharmaceuticals). In March 2017, the firm began construction of a new polyisobutylene (PIB) unit at its Deer Park, Texas facility. It is a 10-year phase investment plan with Daelim Industrial to produce high reactive PIB, a key raw material for next-generation dispersants and lubricants. The new unit is expected to be fully operational in the first half of 2019.

Lubrizol employee benefits vary by country but include healthcare and disability coverage and retirement planning.

FINANCIAL DATA: *Note: Data for latest year may not have been available at press time.*

In U.S. $	2016	2015	2014	2013	2012	2011
Revenue	6,500,000,000	7,000,000,000	7,000,000,000	6,400,000,000	6,100,000,000	5,800,000,000
R&D Expense						
Operating Income						
Operating Margin %						
SGA Expense						
Net Income						
Operating Cash Flow						
Capital Expenditure						
EBITDA						
Return on Assets %						
Return on Equity %						
Debt to Equity						

CONTACT INFORMATION:

Phone: 440-943-4200   Fax: 440-943-5337
Toll-Free:
Address: 29400 Lakeland Blvd., Wickliffe, OH 44092 United States

SALARIES/BONUSES:

Top Exec. Salary: $ Bonus: $
Second Exec. Salary: $ Bonus: $

STOCK TICKER/OTHER:

Stock Ticker: Subsidiary   Exchange:
Employees: 9,043   Fiscal Year Ends: 12/31
Parent Company: Berkshire Hathaway Inc

OTHER THOUGHTS:

Estimated Female Officers or Directors: 1
Hot Spot for Advancement for Women/Minorities:

Magellan Health Inc

www.magellanhealth.com

NAIC Code: 621999

TYPES OF BUSINESS:

Specialty Managed Health Care Services
Psychiatric Hospitals
Residential Treatment Centers

BRANDS/DIVISIONS/AFFILIATES:

Magellan Complete Care

CONTACTS: Note: Officers with more than one job title may be intentionally listed here more than once.

Sanjeev Srivastava, CEO, Divisional
Mostafa Kamal, CEO, Subsidiary
Barry Smith, CEO
Jonathan Rubin, CFO
Caskie Lewis-Clapper, Other Executive Officer
Daniel Gregoire, Secretary
Jeffrey West, Senior VP

GROWTH PLANS/SPECIAL FEATURES:

Magellan Health, Inc. is engaged in the healthcare management business. Magellan develops innovative solutions that combine advanced analytics, agile technology and clinical excellence to promote best decision-making capabilities for its clients. The firm serves health plans, managed care organizations, employers, labor unions, various military & governmental agencies and third-party administrators. Magellan operates in two business segments: Magellan healthcare and Magellan Rx management. Magellan healthcare includes the firm's management of behavioral healthcare services and employee assistance program services; management of specialty areas such as diagnostic imaging and musculoskeletal management; and the integrated management of physical, behavioral and pharmaceutical health care for special populations delivered via Magellan Complete Care. Special populations include individuals with serious mental illness, dual eligible, long-term services and supports and other populations with unique and often complex health care needs. Magellan Rx management comprises products and solutions that provide clinical and financial management of pharmaceuticals paid under medical and pharmacy benefit programs. Its services include pharmacy benefit management, pharmacy benefit administration for state Medicaid & other government-sponsored programs, pharmaceutical dispensing operations, clinical & formulary management programs, medical pharmacy management programs, as well as programs for the integrated management of specialty drugs across both the medical & pharmacy benefit that treat complex conditions. In July 2016, the firm acquired Armed Forces Services Corporation, behavioral health and specialty services provider to various agencies of the federal government, including all five branches of the U.S. Armed Forces. That November, Magellan agreed to acquire the privately held pharmacy Veridicus Holdings, LLC.

Magellan offers employees medical, dental, disability, AD&D and life insurance; an employee assistance program; 401(k); educational assistance; adoption assistance; telecommuting; and flexible spending accounts.

FINANCIAL DATA: Note: Data for latest year may not have been available at press time.

In U.S. $	2016	2015	2014	2013	2012	2011
Revenue	4,836,884,000	4,597,400,000	3,760,118,000	3,546,317,000	3,207,397,000	2,799,400,000
R&D Expense						
Operating Income	152,892,000	75,532,000	124,006,000	166,200,000	189,093,000	194,381,000
Operating Margin %	3.16%	1.64%	3.29%	4.68%	5.89%	6.94%
SGA Expense	876,612,000	822,392,000	723,498,000	619,546,000	557,512,000	529,634,000
Net Income	77,879,000	31,413,000	79,404,000	125,261,000	151,027,000	129,623,000
Operating Cash Flow	66,699,000	239,185,000	211,044,000	183,161,000	181,293,000	112,003,000
Capital Expenditure	60,881,000	71,584,000	62,337,000	64,542,000	69,549,000	54,394,000
EBITDA	261,756,000	180,541,000	216,377,000	240,179,000	251,600,000	255,785,000
Return on Assets %	3.45%	1.50%	4.12%	7.65%	10.58%	8.96%
Return on Equity %	7.19%	2.85%	6.93%	11.52%	16.21%	13.75%
Debt to Equity	0.19	0.22	0.22	0.02		

CONTACT INFORMATION:

Phone: 602-572-6050   Fax:
Toll-Free: 800-410-8312
Address: 4800 Scottsdale Rd, Ste 4000, Scottsdale, AZ 85251 United States

STOCK TICKER/OTHER:

Stock Ticker: MGLN   Exchange: NAS
Employees: 9,700   Fiscal Year Ends: 12/31
Parent Company:

SALARIES/BONUSES:

Top Exec. Salary: $1,000,000   Bonus: $
Second Exec. Salary: $609,000   Bonus: $

OTHER THOUGHTS:

Estimated Female Officers or Directors: 3
Hot Spot for Advancement for Women/Minorities: Y

Sales, profits and employees may be estimates. Financial information, benefits and other data can change quickly and may vary from those stated here.

Manhattan Associates Inc

www.manh.com

NAIC Code: 0

TYPES OF BUSINESS:

Computer Software, Supply Chain & Logistics
Consulting & Support
RFID System Integration
Consulting Services

BRANDS/DIVISIONS/AFFILIATES:

CONTACTS: *Note: Officers with more than one job title may be intentionally listed here more than once.*

Eddie Capel, CEO
Dennis Story, CFO
John Huntz, Chairman of the Board
Linda Pinne, Chief Accounting Officer
Bruce Richards, Other Executive Officer
Robert Howell, Senior VP, Divisional

GROWTH PLANS/SPECIAL FEATURES:

Manhattan Associates, Inc. develops and provides technology-based supply chain software services. Its products consist of software and hardware and are used for both the managing and execution of supply chain activities. The company serves various industries, including consumer goods, food, government, high-tech/electronics, industrial/wholesale, life science, logistics service providers, retail and transportation, and specializes in demand forecasting and inventory replenishment, warehouse and labor management, performance analysis and event planning. Manhattan Associates' software solutions platform provides three major benefits: cross-functional business solutions, total cost of ownership and the power of shared components. Its software solutions modules are comprised of planning, including assortment, omni-channel, financial and item planning; inventory optimization; omni-channel central, including customer service, enterprise inventory and order management; omni-channel local, including point of sale, clienteling, store fulfillment & inventory and tablet retailing; distribution management; transportation management; supply chain convergence; and visibility. Outside of the U.S., the firm has offices in Australia, China, France, India, Japan, the Netherlands, Singapore and the U.K., as well as representatives in Mexico and reseller partnerships in Latin America, Eastern Europe, the Middle East, South Africa and Asia.

Manhattan Associates offers its employees medical, dental, vision and prescription drug coverage; flexible spending accounts; life and AD&D insurance; short- and long-term disability; a 401(k) plan; access to a credit union; discounted health club membership; and educational assistance.

FINANCIAL DATA: *Note: Data for latest year may not have been available at press time.*

In U.S. $	2016	2015	2014	2013	2012	2011
Revenue	604,557,000	556,371,000	492,104,000	414,518,000	376,248,000	329,253,000
R&D Expense	54,736,000	53,859,000	48,953,000	44,549,000	44,704,000	42,372,000
Operating Income	194,307,000	161,446,000	127,124,000	101,287,000	80,073,000	61,363,000
Operating Margin %	32.14%	29.01%	25.83%	24.43%	21.28%	18.63%
SGA Expense	96,545,000	97,874,000	97,072,000	81,706,000	84,096,000	81,652,000
Net Income	124,234,000	103,475,000	82,000,000	67,296,000	51,853,000	44,907,000
Operating Cash Flow	139,346,000	120,153,000	94,162,000	89,387,000	75,271,000	55,824,000
Capital Expenditure	6,843,000	11,492,000	9,415,000	4,740,000	7,873,000	5,074,000
EBITDA	203,397,000	169,210,000	133,501,000	107,112,000	85,711,000	68,647,000
Return on Assets %						
Return on Equity %						
Debt to Equity						

CONTACT INFORMATION:

Phone: 770 955-7070   Fax: 770 995-0302
Toll-Free:
Address: 2300 Windy Ridge Pkwy., 10/Fl, Atlanta, GA 30339 United States

STOCK TICKER/OTHER:

Stock Ticker: MANH
Employees: 3,020
Parent Company:

Exchange: NAS
Fiscal Year Ends: 12/31

SALARIES/BONUSES:

Top Exec. Salary: $575,000   Bonus: $
Second Exec. Salary: $350,167   Bonus: $

OTHER THOUGHTS:

Estimated Female Officers or Directors:
Hot Spot for Advancement for Women/Minorities:

Marcus Corporation (The)

NAIC Code: 721110

www.marcuscorp.com

TYPES OF BUSINESS:

Hotels & Motels
Movie & IMAX Theaters
Hotels/Resorts

BRANDS/DIVISIONS/AFFILIATES:

Marcus Theatres Corp
MCS Capital LLC
Funset Boulevard

CONTACTS: Note: Officers with more than one job title may be intentionally listed here more than once.

Rolando Rodriguez, CEO, Subsidiary
Gregory Marcus, CEO
Douglas Neis, CFO
Stephen Marcus, Chairman of the Board
Thomas Kissinger, General Counsel

GROWTH PLANS/SPECIAL FEATURES:

The Marcus Corporation is an owner and operator of movie theaters, hotels and resorts. Through its Marcus Theatres Corp. subsidiary, the company owns or operates 69 movie theaters, with 878 screens in Wisconsin, Ohio, Illinois, Minnesota, North Dakota, Nebraska and Iowa. Marcus also operates a family entertainment center, Funset Boulevard, adjacent to its theater in Appleton, Wisconsin. In addition, Marcus Corporation owns or manages approximately 18 hotels and 5,500 rooms, and also manages hotels and other properties for third parties. Owned hotels and resorts include the Pfister Hotel, the InterContinental Milwaukee and The Hilton Milwaukee City Center in Milwaukee, Wisconsin; the Hilton Madison at Monona Terrace in Madison, Wisconsin; The Grand Geneva Resort & Spa in Lake Geneva, Wisconsin; the Hotel Phillips in Kansas City, Missouri; the Four Points by Sheraton Chicago Downtown/Magnificent Mile in Chicago, Illinois; and the Skirvin Hilton in Oklahoma City, Oklahoma. Subsidiary MCS Capital, LLC acquires and develops new hotel investments. In 2016, the firm acquired the Wehrenberg Theatres chain, adding 197 screens at 14 locations in four states to its portfolio.

FINANCIAL DATA: Note: Data for latest year may not have been available at press time.

In U.S. $	2016	2015	2014	2013	2012	2011
Revenue	543,864,000	488,067,000	447,939,000	412,836,000	413,898,000	
R&D Expense						
Operating Income	69,954,000	50,194,000	48,382,000	38,204,000	46,515,000	
Operating Margin %	12.86%	10.28%	10.80%	9.25%	11.23%	
SGA Expense	93,586,000	87,103,000	80,324,000	77,255,000	74,623,000	
Net Income	37,902,000	23,995,000	25,001,000	17,506,000	22,734,000	
Operating Cash Flow	82,655,000	80,452,000	66,440,000	63,202,000	69,028,000	
Capital Expenditure	83,606,000	74,988,000	56,673,000	23,491,000	38,017,000	
EBITDA	111,875,000	87,941,000	81,948,000	78,151,000	81,570,000	
Return on Assets %	4.15%	3.04%	3.29%	2.36%	3.18%	
Return on Equity %	9.71%	7.16%	7.90%	5.38%	6.65%	
Debt to Equity	0.76	0.72	0.78	0.84	0.40	

CONTACT INFORMATION:

Phone: 414 905-1000   Fax: 414 905-2879
Toll-Free:
Address: 100 E. Wisconsin Ave., Ste. 1900, Milwaukee, WI 53202-4125
United States

STOCK TICKER/OTHER:

Stock Ticker: MCS   Exchange: NYS
Employees: 7,900   Fiscal Year Ends: 05/31
Parent Company:

SALARIES/BONUSES:

Top Exec. Salary: $676,112   Bonus: $
Second Exec. Salary: $510,288   Bonus: $40,000

OTHER THOUGHTS:

Estimated Female Officers or Directors: 2
Hot Spot for Advancement for Women/Minorities: Y

Marriott International Inc

NAIC Code: 721110

www.marriott.com

TYPES OF BUSINESS:

Hotels & Resorts
Suites Hotels
Corporate Apartments
Extended Stay Lodging
Luxury Hotels
Business Hotels

BRANDS/DIVISIONS/AFFILIATES:

Marriott Hotels
Ritz-Carlton (The)
Starwood Hotels & Resorts Worldwide Inc
Renaissance Hotels
Courtyard by Marriott
Fairfield Inn & Suites
TownePlace Suites by Marriott
JW Marriott

CONTACTS: *Note: Officers with more than one job title may be intentionally listed here more than once.*

Arne Sorenson, CEO
Argiris Kyriakidis, Managing Director, Geographical
Kathleen Oberg, CFO
J. Marriott, Chairman of the Board
Stephanie Linnartz, Chief Marketing Officer
Bao Giang Val Bauduin, Controller
Sterling Colton, Director Emeritus
William Shaw, Director Emeritus
Edward Ryan, Executive VP
Anthony Capuano, Executive VP
David Rodriguez, Executive VP
Amy McPherson, Managing Director, Geographical
Craig Smith, Managing Director, Geographical
David Grissen, President, Divisional

GROWTH PLANS/SPECIAL FEATURES:

Marriott International, Inc. operates 6,080 hotels and related lodging facilities in 120 countries and territories, totaling nearly 1.2 million rooms. The company operates through three segments: North American full-service lodging, North American limited-service lodging and international. Marriott develops, operates and franchises hotels under various brand names, including Marriott Hotels, JW Marriott, The Ritz-Carlton, BuVLGARI Hotels and Resorts, Renaissance Hotels, Courtyard by Marriott, Residence Inn by Marriott, Fairfield Inn & Suites, SpringHill Suites by Marriott, EDITION, Autograph Collection Hotels, Marriott Executive Apartments, Marriott Vacation Club, Gaylor Hotels, AC Hotels by Marriott, Protea Hotels, Moxy Hotels and TownePlace Suites by Marriott. The firm also operates 44 home and condominium projects and 28 Marriott Executive Apartments located in 15 countries. Additionally, Marriott Golf manages 35 golf resorts worldwide. The company operates 24 system-wide hotel reservation centers: nine in the U.S. and Canada and 15 in other countries and territories. In February 2016, it expanded its footprint in Chhattisgarh, India with Courtyard by Marriott Raipur; signed for five hotels to open in Japan by 2018 with Mori Trust Group, which will be under the Marriott Hotels brand; and announced plans to open two new hotels in Cartagena, Colombia by 2018. In September 2016, Marriott completed the acquisition of Starwood Hotels & Resorts Worldwide, Inc.

FINANCIAL DATA: *Note: Data for latest year may not have been available at press time.*

In U.S. $	2016	2015	2014	2013	2012	2011
Revenue	17,072,000,000	14,486,000,000	13,796,000,000	12,784,000,000	11,814,000,000	12,317,000,000
R&D Expense						
Operating Income	1,368,000,000	1,350,000,000	1,159,000,000	988,000,000	940,000,000	526,000,000
Operating Margin %	8.01%	9.31%	8.40%	7.72%	7.95%	4.27%
SGA Expense	1,090,000,000	634,000,000	659,000,000	726,000,000	645,000,000	752,000,000
Net Income	780,000,000	859,000,000	753,000,000	626,000,000	571,000,000	198,000,000
Operating Cash Flow	1,582,000,000	1,430,000,000	1,224,000,000	1,140,000,000	989,000,000	1,089,000,000
Capital Expenditure	279,000,000	426,000,000	476,000,000	465,000,000	690,000,000	257,000,000
EBITDA	1,586,000,000	1,561,000,000	1,351,000,000	1,144,000,000	1,131,000,000	688,000,000
Return on Assets %	5.16%	13.26%	11.02%	9.53%	9.32%	2.65%
Return on Equity %	88.28%					49.25%
Debt to Equity	1.53					

CONTACT INFORMATION:

Phone: 301 380-3000   Fax: 301 380-3967
Toll-Free: 800-721-7033
Address: 10400 Fernwood Rd., Bethesda, MD 20817 United States

STOCK TICKER/OTHER:

Stock Ticker: MAR   Exchange: NAS
Employees: 226,500   Fiscal Year Ends: 12/31
Parent Company:

SALARIES/BONUSES:

Top Exec. Salary: $3,000,000   Bonus: $
Second Exec. Salary: Bonus: $
$1,236,000

OTHER THOUGHTS:

Estimated Female Officers or Directors: 7
Hot Spot for Advancement for Women/Minorities: Y

Mars Inc

www.mars.com

NAIC Code: 311351

TYPES OF BUSINESS:

Chocolate & Confectionery Manufacturing
Snack Foods & Candy Bars
Pet Nutrition
Drink Vending Systems
Prepared Foods
Information Technology Services

BRANDS/DIVISIONS/AFFILIATES:

M&Ms
M&M World
Milky Way
Twix
Seeds of Change
Cesar
Uncle Ben's
Starburst

CONTACTS: Note: Officers with more than one job title may be intentionally listed here more than once.

Grant F. Reid, Pres.
Reuben Gamoran, CFO
Bruce McColl, CMO
Richard Ware, VP-R&D
John Donofrio, General Counsel
David Kamenetzky, VP-Corp. Affairs
Frank Mars, Pres., Symbioscience
Martin Radvan, Pres., Wrigley
Grant Reid, Pres., Chocolate
Poul Weihrauch, Pres., Food
Steven Badger, Chmn.
Richard Ware, VP-Supply & Procurement

GROWTH PLANS/SPECIAL FEATURES:

Mars, Inc., founded in 1911, is a family-owned company that operates through six business divisions: chocolate, pet care, food, drinks, Symbioscience and Wm. Wrigley Jr. Company, which produces Wrigley gum and sugar. The company's chocolate segment makes some of the world's most popular and widely available snacks and confectionery products, including M&Ms, Mars, Snickers, Milky Way, Twix, Dove and 3 Musketeers. The company has a branded retail store called M&M World, with three locations in the U.S., one in London and one in Shanghai. The pet care unit offers products for cats and dogs, including such brands as Cesar, Whiskas, Pedigree, Royal Canine, Banfield Pet Hospital, Sheba, Iams, Temptations and Wisdom Panel. In the food division, Mars produces rice, entrees, sauces and condiments under the Uncle Ben's, Dolmio, Suzi-Wan, Royco, Raris, Seeds of Change and Ebly brands. The firm's drinks segment distributes Mars' KLIX, Bright Tea Co., Dove/Galaxy hot chocolate, Alterra coffee and FLAVIA drink vending machine systems, which are industry leading products that provide in-cup drinks such as fresh ground coffee, leaf tea and hot chocolate. The Symbioscience unit offers products such as Mars Botanical Cocoapro, Cocoa-Via, and Mars Veterinary-Wisdom Panel MX. The Wrigley Gum and Sugar division offers snacks such as Starburst, Skittles, Juicy Fruit gum, Life Savers and Altoids. Mars operates manufacturing facilities throughout the U.S., as well as facilities in Bolton and Newmarket, Ontario. In January 2017, Mars agreed to acquire VCA, Inc., a veterinary and dog day-care company, for approximately $9.1 billion including $1.4 billion in outstanding debt. VCA will operate as a separate and distinct business unit within the pet care division.

FINANCIAL DATA: Note: Data for latest year may not have been available at press time.

In U.S. $	2016	2015	2014	2013	2012	2011
Revenue	36,000,000,000	35,500,000,000	34,000,000,000	33,200,000,000	31,500,000,000	31,000,000,000
R&D Expense						
Operating Income						
Operating Margin %						
SGA Expense						
Net Income						
Operating Cash Flow						
Capital Expenditure						
EBITDA						
Return on Assets %						
Return on Equity %						
Debt to Equity						

CONTACT INFORMATION:

Phone: 703-821-4900   Fax: 703-448-9678
Toll-Free: 800-627-7852
Address: 6885 Elm St., McLean, VA 22101 United States

STOCK TICKER/OTHER:

Stock Ticker: Private
Employees: 80,000
Parent Company:

Exchange:
Fiscal Year Ends: 12/31

SALARIES/BONUSES:

Top Exec. Salary: $ Bonus: $
Second Exec. Salary: $ Bonus: $

OTHER THOUGHTS:

Estimated Female Officers or Directors: 1
Hot Spot for Advancement for Women/Minorities:

Marsh & McLennan Companies Inc

http://www.mmc.com/

NAIC Code: 524210

TYPES OF BUSINESS:

Insurance Brokerage
Consulting Services
Risk Management
Benefits Administration
Human Resources Services

BRANDS/DIVISIONS/AFFILIATES:

Marsh Inc
Guy Carpenter & Company LLC
Mercer Inc
Oliver Wyman Group
Lippincott
NERA Economic Consulting
Insurance Partners of Texas

CONTACTS: *Note: Officers with more than one job title may be intentionally listed here more than once.*

Carey Roberts, Assistant General Counsel
Peter Zaffino, CEO, Subsidiary
Julio Portalatin, CEO, Subsidiary
Scott McDonald, CEO, Subsidiary
Mark McGivney, CFO
E. Gilbert, Chief Information Officer
Robert Rapport, Controller
H. Hanway, Director
Daniel Glaser, Director
Peter Beshar, Executive VP
Laurie Ledford, Other Executive Officer
John Doyle, President, Subsidiary

GROWTH PLANS/SPECIAL FEATURES:

Marsh & McLennan Companies, Inc. (MMC) is a global professional services firm. The company provides insurance and management and consulting services in the areas of risk, strategy and human capital to clients in over 130 countries. It is the parent company of a number of leading risk experts and specialty consultants, including Marsh, Inc., an insurance broker, intermediary and risk advisor; Guy Carpenter & Company, LLC, a risk and reinsurance specialist; Mercer, Inc., a provider of HR and related financial advice and services; and Oliver Wyman Group, a management consultancy. MMC operates in two divisions: risk and insurance services, and consulting. The risk and insurance services segment generated 54% of the firm's total revenue and is primarily composed of Marsh and Guy Carpenter. The consulting segment was responsible for 46% of the firm's total revenue and operates through Mercer and Oliver Wyman. The Mercer division offers investment consulting services and specialized management and economic consulting services as well as human resources consulting and related outsourcing. Oliver Wyman includes Lippincott, a consulting firm that helps clients with branding and corporate image; and NERA Economic Consulting, one of the world's largest consulting groups that focuses on economics and deploys professional economists. In May 2017, MMC acquired Insurance Partners of Texas, an Abilene-based employee benefits consulting firm.

MMC offers employees medical, dental and vision insurance; spending accounts; life insurance; business travel accident insurance; disability coverage; an employee stock purchase plan; a 401(k) plan; a retirement plan; tuition assistance; auto and home insurance; pet insurance; a legal assistance plan; and an employee assistance program.

FINANCIAL DATA: *Note: Data for latest year may not have been available at press time.*

In U.S. $	2016	2015	2014	2013	2012	2011
Revenue	13,211,000,000	12,893,000,000	12,951,000,000	12,261,000,000	11,924,000,000	11,526,000,000
R&D Expense						
Operating Income	2,664,000,000	2,419,000,000	2,301,000,000	2,077,000,000	1,829,000,000	1,638,000,000
Operating Margin %	20.16%	18.76%	17.76%	16.93%	15.33%	14.21%
SGA Expense	7,461,000,000	7,334,000,000	7,515,000,000	7,226,000,000	7,134,000,000	6,969,000,000
Net Income	1,768,000,000	1,599,000,000	1,465,000,000	1,357,000,000	1,176,000,000	993,000,000
Operating Cash Flow	2,007,000,000	1,888,000,000	2,112,000,000	1,341,000,000	1,322,000,000	1,705,000,000
Capital Expenditure	253,000,000	325,000,000	368,000,000	401,000,000	320,000,000	280,000,000
EBITDA	3,107,000,000	2,893,000,000	2,610,000,000	2,498,000,000	2,226,000,000	1,935,000,000
Return on Assets %	9.71%	8.86%	8.41%	8.15%	7.40%	6.45%
Return on Equity %	27.83%	23.57%	19.58%	18.78%	18.92%	16.21%
Debt to Equity	0.72	0.67	0.47	0.33	0.40	0.45

CONTACT INFORMATION:

Phone: 212 345-5000   Fax: 212 345-4809
Toll-Free:
Address: 1166 Ave. of the Americas, New York, NY 10036 United States

STOCK TICKER/OTHER:

Stock Ticker: MMC   Exchange: NYS
Employees: 60,000   Fiscal Year Ends: 12/31
Parent Company:

SALARIES/BONUSES:

Top Exec. Salary: $1,400,000   Bonus: $
Second Exec. Salary: Bonus: $
$1,000,000

OTHER THOUGHTS:

Estimated Female Officers or Directors: 3
Hot Spot for Advancement for Women/Minorities: Y

Mary Kay Inc

NAIC Code: 454390

www.marykay.com

TYPES OF BUSINESS:

Cosmetics & Beauty Supplies, Direct Selling
Online Retail
Fragrances
Over-the-Counter Drugs
Cosmetics & Beauty Supplies, Manufacturing

BRANDS/DIVISIONS/AFFILIATES:

Modern Maven
Cityscape
Forever Diamonds
Belara
Thinking of You
Domain
MK High Intensity
Tribute

CONTACTS: *Note: Officers with more than one job title may be intentionally listed here more than once.*

David Holl, CEO
David B. Holl, Pres.
Deborah Gibbins, CFO
Sheryl Adkins-Green, CMO
Melinda Foster Sellers, Chief People Officer
Kregg Jodie, CIO
Nathan Moore, Chief Legal Officer
Darrell Overcash, Pres., North America Region
Tara Eustace, Pres., European Region
Jose Smeke, Pres., Latin American Region
Richard R. Rogers, Exec. Chmn.
K.K. Chua, Pres., Asia Pacific Region
Dennis Greaney, Chief Supply Chain Officer

GROWTH PLANS/SPECIAL FEATURES:

Mary Kay, Inc. is one of the largest direct sellers of skin care products in the U.S. The company's merchandise includes more than 200 products across several categories, including skin care, color cosmetics, spa and body care and fragrances. Skin care includes anti-aging creams; cleansers; moisturizers; basic skin care for different skin types; products for specific needs, such as acne treatment and oil control; and lip and eye care. Color cosmetics products include lip, eyes, cheeks, nails, foundations and powder color enhancers as well as travel sets and applicators. The Mary Kay fragrance line has specialty scents for both men and women, including Modern Maven, Cityscape, Forever Diamonds, Belara and Thinking of You for women, and Domain, MK High Intensity and Tribute for men. Mary Kay develops, tests, manufactures and packages the majority of its products at its own plants. Most inventory is manufactured at the Dallas site, where the company headquarters and the Mary Kay Museum are located. An additional manufacturing facility is located in China. With FDA approval, the company also manufactures and distributes certain products classified as over-the-counter drugs, such as sunscreens and acne treatment products. There are about 3.5 million Mary Kay independent beauty consultants serving customers in more than 35 countries worldwide. About 40% of new sales recruits are relatively young, aged 18 to 30. A new recruit pays $100 for a basic starter kit in order to begin selling Mary Kay products. Independent beauty consultants may eventually become independent sales directors and/or independent national sales directors. Mary Kay has more than 1,200 patents for products, technologies and packaging designs in its global portfolio.

FINANCIAL DATA: *Note: Data for latest year may not have been available at press time.*

In U.S. $	2016	2015	2014	2013	2012	2011
Revenue	3,500,000,000	3,700,000,000	3,200,000,000	3,100,000,000	3,000,000,000	2,900,000,000
R&D Expense						
Operating Income						
Operating Margin %						
SGA Expense						
Net Income						
Operating Cash Flow						
Capital Expenditure						
EBITDA						
Return on Assets %						
Return on Equity %						
Debt to Equity						

CONTACT INFORMATION:

Phone: 972-687-6300   Fax: 972-687-1611
Toll-Free: 800-627-9529
Address: 16251 Dallas Pkwy., Dallas, TX 75001 United States

STOCK TICKER/OTHER:

Stock Ticker: Private   Exchange:
Employees: 5,000   Fiscal Year Ends: 12/31
Parent Company:

SALARIES/BONUSES:

Top Exec. Salary: $ Bonus: $
Second Exec. Salary: $ Bonus: $

OTHER THOUGHTS:

Estimated Female Officers or Directors: 3
Hot Spot for Advancement for Women/Minorities: Y

MasterCard Inc

NAIC Code: 522320

TYPES OF BUSINESS:

Credit Card Issuer
Transaction Processing Services

BRANDS/DIVISIONS/AFFILIATES:

MasterCard
Maestro
Cirrus

CONTACTS: *Note: Officers with more than one job title may be intentionally listed here more than once.*

Michael Miebach,
Ajay Bhalla, President, Divisional
Ajaypal Banga, CEO
Martina Hund-Mejean, CFO
Walt Macnee, Chairman of the Board, Subsidiary
Richard Haythornthwaite, Chairman of the Board
Andrea Forster, Chief Accounting Officer
Raja Rajamannar, Chief Marketing Officer
Sandra Arkell, Controller
Timothy Murphy, General Counsel
Michael Fraccaro, Other Executive Officer
Garry Lyons, Other Executive Officer
Raghu Malhotra, President, Divisional
Javier Perez, President, Divisional
Andrea Scerch, President, Divisional
Raj Seshadri, President, Divisional
Kevin Stanton, President, Divisional

GROWTH PLANS/SPECIAL FEATURES:

MasterCard, Inc. is a global payment solutions company that provides services to support the credit, debit and related payment programs of thousands of financial institutions. The company develops and markets payment solutions and processes payment transactions; it also provides consulting services to customers and merchants. MasterCard manages payment card brands including MasterCard, Maestro and Cirrus. A typical transaction processed over the MasterCard network involves four parties in addition to the firm: the cardholder, the merchant, the issuer (the cardholder's financial institution) and the acquirer (the merchant's financial institution). The company's customers are the financial institutions that act as issuers and acquirers. MasterCard generates revenues from the fees that it charges customers for providing these transaction processing and other payment-related services by assessing their customers based on their volume of dollar activity. The company's credit and debit cards are accepted at more than 150 currencies in 210 countries and territories worldwide.

The firm offers employees medical, dental and vision coverage; life, disability and AD&D insurance; child care options; flexible work hours; adoption assistance; financial wellness programs; and personal services and discounts.

FINANCIAL DATA: *Note: Data for latest year may not have been available at press time.*

In U.S. $	2016	2015	2014	2013	2012	2011
Revenue	10,776,000,000	9,667,000,000	9,473,000,000	8,346,000,000	7,391,000,000	6,714,000,000
R&D Expense						
Operating Income	5,761,000,000	5,078,000,000	5,106,000,000	4,503,000,000	3,937,000,000	2,713,000,000
Operating Margin %	53.46%	52.52%	53.90%	53.95%	53.26%	40.40%
SGA Expense	4,525,000,000	4,244,000,000	4,046,000,000	3,490,000,000	3,204,000,000	3,037,000,000
Net Income	4,059,000,000	3,808,000,000	3,617,000,000	3,116,000,000	2,759,000,000	1,906,000,000
Operating Cash Flow	4,484,000,000	4,043,000,000	3,407,000,000	4,135,000,000	2,948,000,000	2,684,000,000
Capital Expenditure	382,000,000	342,000,000	334,000,000	299,000,000	218,000,000	177,000,000
EBITDA	6,114,000,000	5,385,000,000	5,448,000,000	4,772,000,000	4,182,000,000	2,965,000,000
Return on Assets %	23.23%	24.10%	24.46%	23.33%	23.83%	19.51%
Return on Equity %	69.47%	59.41%	50.67%	43.27%	43.16%	34.42%
Debt to Equity	0.91	0.54	0.22			

CONTACT INFORMATION:

Phone: 914 249-2000   Fax: 914 249-4206
Toll-Free: 800-627-8372
Address: 2000 Purchase St., Purchase, NY 10577 United States

STOCK TICKER/OTHER:

Stock Ticker: MA   Exchange: NYS
Employees: 11,300   Fiscal Year Ends: 12/31
Parent Company:

SALARIES/BONUSES:

Top Exec. Salary: $1,200,000   Bonus: $
Second Exec. Salary: Bonus: $
$1,200,000

OTHER THOUGHTS:

Estimated Female Officers or Directors: 2
Hot Spot for Advancement for Women/Minorities: Y

Match Group Inc

www.match.com

NAIC Code: 519130

TYPES OF BUSINESS:

Internet Dating Sites

BRANDS/DIVISIONS/AFFILIATES:

IAC/InterActiveCorp
Match
OkCupid
PlentyofFish
Tinger
BlackPeopleMeet
FriendScout24
Princeton Review (The)

CONTACTS: *Note: Officers with more than one job title may be intentionally listed here more than once.*

Gregory Blatt, CEO
Gary Swidler, CFO
Sandra Martin, Chief Accounting Officer
Jared Sine, General Counsel
Amarnath Thombre, Other Executive Officer
Sam Yagan, Vice Chairman of the Board

GROWTH PLANS/SPECIAL FEATURES:

Match Group, Inc., a subsidiary of IAC/InterActiveCorp, is a global provider of dating products. The company operates a portfolio of over 45 brands, including Match, OkCupid, PlentyOfFish, Tinder, Meetic, Twoo, OurTime, BlackPeopleMeet and FriendScout24, each designed to increase user's likelihood of finding a romantic connection. Its target market includes all adults in North America, Western Europe and other select countries who are not in a committed relationship and who have access to the internet. Match Group currently offers its dating products in 38 languages across more than 190 countries. Match features include the ability to both search profiles, receive algorithmic matches and the ability to attend live events, promoted by Match, with other members. OkCupid attracts users through a mathematical and question/answer approach. PlentyofFish has the ability to search profiles and receive algorithmic matches. Tinder is a mobile-only offering with location-based features. Meetic serves users in France, Spain, Italy and the Netherlands and is similar to Match. Twoo is a dating product seeded through existing social networks, with its user base being primarily concentrated in Europe, Asia and South America. OurTime and BlackPeopleMeet serve the needs of individuals for whom commonalities around age, religion, ethnicity or circumstance are of fundamental importance when making a romantic connection. FriendScout24 is the market leader in dating products in Germany, with a strong presence in Austria and Switzerland. It is characterized by its search-based product offering. Additionally, Match Group operates a non-dating business through its ownership of The Princeton Review, which provides a variety of test preparation, academic tutoring and college counseling services. In late 2015, the firm went public on the NASDAQ exchange under the ticker, MTCH.

FINANCIAL DATA: *Note: Data for latest year may not have been available at press time.*

In U.S. $	2016	2015	2014	2013	2012	2011
Revenue	1,222,526,000	1,020,431,000	888,268,000	803,089,000	713,449,000	
R&D Expense	83,065,000	67,348,000	49,738,000	42,973,000	38,921,000	
Operating Income	305,908,000	193,556,000	228,567,000	221,333,000	186,630,000	
Operating Margin %	25.02%	18.96%	25.73%	27.56%	26.15%	
SGA Expense	545,351,000	535,455,000	452,997,000	415,511,000	381,308,000	
Net Income	171,451,000	120,383,000	147,764,000	125,003,000	85,675,000	
Operating Cash Flow	234,106,000	209,082,000	173,615,000	174,797,000	164,371,000	
Capital Expenditure	48,903,000	29,156,000	21,793,000	19,807,000	19,853,000	
EBITDA	368,056,000	251,527,000	278,119,000	258,877,000	212,998,000	
Return on Assets %	8.62%	7.44%	11.36%	9.67%		
Return on Equity %	44.22%	22.32%	18.07%	14.96%		
Debt to Equity	2.36	4.28	0.23	0.09		

CONTACT INFORMATION:

Phone: 214-576-9352   Fax:
Toll-Free:
Address: 8300 Douglas Ave., Ste. 800, Dallas, TX 75225 United States

STOCK TICKER/OTHER:

Stock Ticker: MTCH   Exchange: NAS
Employees: 5,100   Fiscal Year Ends:
Parent Company: IAC/InterActiveCorp

SALARIES/BONUSES:

Top Exec. Salary: $1,000,000   Bonus: $3,000,000
Second Exec. Salary: $550,000   Bonus: $1,100,000

OTHER THOUGHTS:

Estimated Female Officers or Directors:
Hot Spot for Advancement for Women/Minorities:

Matthews International Corporation   www.matw.com

NAIC Code: 339995

TYPES OF BUSINESS:

Burial Caskets and Cases Manufacturing

BRANDS/DIVISIONS/AFFILIATES:

SGK Brand Solutions
Schawk Inc
A + E Ungricht GmbH + Co KG
Equator Ltd

CONTACTS: Note: Officers with more than one job title may be intentionally listed here more than once.

Joseph Bartolacci, CEO
Steven Nicola, CFO
John Turner, Chairman of the Board
Gregory Babe, Chief Technology Officer
David Beck, Controller
David Schawk, Director
Brian Dunn, Executive VP, Divisional
Brian Walters, General Counsel
Steven Gackenbach, President, Divisional
Paul Rahill, President, Divisional
Robert Marsh, Treasurer
Marcy Campbell, Vice President, Divisional

GROWTH PLANS/SPECIAL FEATURES:

Matthews International Corporation is a designer, manufacturer and marketer of memorialization products and brand solutions. Memorialization products consist primarily of bronze memorials and other memorialization products, caskets and cremation equipment for the cemetery and funeral home industries. The company's products and operations are comprised of three business segments: SGK Brand Solutions, memorialization and industrial technologies. SGK Brand Solutions is comprised of the graphics imaging business, including wholly-owned Schawk, Inc., and Matthews' merchandising solutions operations. This segment provides brand development, brand management, pre-media services, printing plates and cylinders, embossing tools and creative design services to consumer packaged goods, retail and packaging industries. The memorialization segment manufactures and markets a full line of memorialization products used primarily in cemeteries, funeral homes and crematories. These products are sold primarily in the U.S., Europe, Canada and Australia, and include cast bronze memorials, granite memorials, caskets, cremation equipment and other memorialization products. This division also manufactures and markets architectural products used to identify or commemorate people, places, events and accomplishments. The industrial technologies segment designs, manufactures and distributes an array of marking, coding and industrial automation solutions, order fulfillment systems and related consumables. Manufacturers, suppliers and distributors worldwide rely on Matthews' integrated systems to identify, track, control and pick their products. During 2017, the firm acquired A. + E. Ungricht GmbH + Co KG, a European provider of pre-press services and gravure printing forms; and Equator Ltd., a design agency specializing in the grocery retail and consumer product goods sectors.

FINANCIAL DATA: Note: Data for latest year may not have been available at press time.

In U.S. $	2016	2015	2014	2013	2012	2011
Revenue	1,480,464,000	1,426,068,000	1,106,597,000	985,357,000	900,317,000	898,821,000
R&D Expense						
Operating Income	118,815,000	105,023,000	82,891,000	95,792,000	93,577,000	118,516,000
Operating Margin %	8.02%	7.36%	7.49%	9.72%	10.39%	13.18%
SGA Expense	437,639,000	424,352,000	309,605,000	260,726,000	242,993,000	233,144,000
Net Income	66,749,000	63,449,000	43,674,000	54,888,000	55,843,000	72,372,000
Operating Cash Flow	140,274,000	141,064,000	92,399,000	109,326,000	82,123,000	95,564,000
Capital Expenditure	41,682,000	48,251,000	29,237,000	24,924,000	33,236,000	22,440,000
EBITDA	185,058,000	172,882,000	123,288,000	132,226,000	124,218,000	147,918,000
Return on Assets %	3.13%	3.02%	2.69%	4.68%	5.01%	6.92%
Return on Equity %	9.27%	8.40%	6.57%	10.68%	11.85%	15.62%
Debt to Equity	1.19	1.21	0.91	0.63	0.62	0.64

CONTACT INFORMATION:

Phone: 412-442-8200   Fax: 412-442-8290
Toll-Free:
Address: Two Northshore Center, Pittsburgh, PA 15212-5851 United States

STOCK TICKER/OTHER:

Stock Ticker: MATW   Exchange: NAS
Employees: 10,300   Fiscal Year Ends: 09/30
Parent Company:

SALARIES/BONUSES:

Top Exec. Salary: $800,267   Bonus: $
Second Exec. Salary: $475,692   Bonus: $

OTHER THOUGHTS:

Estimated Female Officers or Directors:
Hot Spot for Advancement for Women/Minorities:

MAXIMUS Inc

www.maximus.com

NAIC Code: 541512

TYPES OF BUSINESS:

Consulting-Government Agencies
Outsourced Program Management
IT Systems Management
Consulting

BRANDS/DIVISIONS/AFFILIATES:

Ascend
Assessments Australia

CONTACTS: *Note: Officers with more than one job title may be intentionally listed here more than once.*

Richard Montoni, CEO
Richard Nadeau, CFO
Peter Pond, Chairman of the Board
Raymond Ruddy, Director
David Francis, General Counsel
Mark Andrekovich, Other Executive Officer
Bruce Caswell, President

GROWTH PLANS/SPECIAL FEATURES:

MAXIMUS, Inc. provides business process services (BPS) to government health and human services agencies. MAXIMUS is one of the largest pure-play health and human services BPS providers to governments in the U.S., the U.K., Australia, Canada, Saudi Arabia and New Zealand. The company is divided into three segments: health services, accounting for 54% of 2016 revenue; human services, 21%; and U.S. federal services, 25%. Health services provides BPS and consulting services for state, provincial and federal government programs, such as Medicaid, CHIP (children's health insurance programs) and the Affordable Care Act, in the U.S.; Health Insurance BC (British Columbia), in Canada; and Health Assessment Advisory Service and Fit for Work Services, in the U.K. Human services provides national, state and local human services agencies with a variety of BPS and related consulting services for government programs such as welfare-to-work, child support higher education and K-12 special education. The U.S. federal services segment provides BPS and program management for large government programs, independent health review and appeals services for both the U.S. federal government and similar state-based programs. This division also offers technology solutions for civilian federal programs. In 2016, the firm acquired independent and specialized health assessment provider Ascend; and Assessments Australia, a provider of support service assessments.

The company offers its employees medical, dental, vision, life and AD&D insurance; flexible spending accounts; long-term care policies; legal services; employee assistance; 401(k); paid time off; discounts on childcare; and credit union accounts.

FINANCIAL DATA: *Note: Data for latest year may not have been available at press time.*

In U.S. $	2016	2015	2014	2013	2012	2011
Revenue	2,403,360,000	2,099,821,000	1,700,912,000	1,331,279,000	1,050,145,000	929,633,000
R&D Expense						
Operating Income	286,603,000	259,832,000	225,308,000	186,208,000	127,575,000	122,401,000
Operating Margin %	11.92%	12.37%	13.24%	13.98%	12.14%	13.16%
SGA Expense	268,259,000	238,792,000	226,815,000	197,859,000	157,402,000	132,866,000
Net Income	178,362,000	157,772,000	145,440,000	116,731,000	76,133,000	81,168,000
Operating Cash Flow	180,026,000	206,217,000	213,600,000	120,938,000	115,160,000	96,860,000
Capital Expenditure	46,391,000	105,149,000	47,148,000	62,176,000	23,148,000	26,114,000
EBITDA	361,883,000	317,414,000	273,976,000	222,024,000	154,035,000	145,246,000
Return on Assets %	13.56%	14.46%	16.53%	15.03%	12.07%	14.85%
Return on Equity %	26.20%	27.00%	26.79%	23.80%	18.44%	22.76%
Debt to Equity	0.22	0.34				

CONTACT INFORMATION:

Phone: 703 251-8500   Fax:
Toll-Free: 800-629-4687
Address: 1891 Metro Center Dr., Reston, VA 20190 United States

STOCK TICKER/OTHER:

Stock Ticker: MMS   Exchange: NYS
Employees: 18,800   Fiscal Year Ends: 09/30
Parent Company:

SALARIES/BONUSES:

Top Exec. Salary: $725,000   Bonus: $
Second Exec. Salary: Bonus: $225,000
$425,000

OTHER THOUGHTS:

Estimated Female Officers or Directors: 3
Hot Spot for Advancement for Women/Minorities: Y

Mayo Clinic

NAIC Code: 622110

TYPES OF BUSINESS:

General Medical and Surgical Hospitals
Physician Practice Management
Medical Research
Health Care Education

BRANDS/DIVISIONS/AFFILIATES:

Mayo Clinic
St. Marys Hospital
Dan Abraham Healthy Living Center
Birdsall Medical Research Building
Mayo Clinic Hospital
Mayo Clinic Specialty Building

CONTACTS: Note: Officers with more than one job title may be intentionally listed here more than once.

John H. Noseworthy, CEO
John H. Noseworthy, Pres.
Kedrick D. Adkins Jr, CFO
Shirley A. Weis, Chief Admin. Officer
Jonathan J. Oviatt, Chief Legal Officer
Harry N. Hoffman, Treas.
William C. Rupp, VP
Wyatt W. Decker, VP
Robert F. Brigham, Assistant Sec.
Sherry L. Hubert, Assistant Sec.
Samuel A. Di Piazza Jr., Chmn.

GROWTH PLANS/SPECIAL FEATURES:

Mayo Clinic is a nonprofit healthcare organization founded in 1864, and part of the Mayo Foundation for Medical Education and Research. Mayo Clinic provides medical treatment, physician management, healthcare education, research and other specialized medical services through a network of clinics and hospitals in Minnesota, Arizona and Florida. The organization's primary clinics, which house physician group practices, are located in Rochester, Minnesota; Jacksonville, Florida; and Scottsdale and Phoenix, Arizona. The Rochester campus comprises a fully-integrated medical research and education center, and includes the Mayo Clinic, The Hilton and Stabile buildings, as well as St. Mary's Hospital. The Dan Abraham Healthy Living Center, also located on the Rochester campus, is a state-of-the-art wellness and fitness facility. The Jacksonville campus is centered around the Davis and Mayo buildings, in conjunction with the Birdsall Medical Research Building. The Mayo Clinic Hospital, located on the Jacksonville campus, offers 304 beds and 22 operating rooms. In addition, it offers care in more than 35 medical and surgical specialties. The Scottsdale campus is centered around a five-story outpatient clinic. The Mayo Clinic Hospital, located in Phoenix, contains 268 beds, 21 operating rooms, an outpatient surgery center, a patient education library, a pharmacy, a full-service laboratory and an endoscopy suite. The Mayo Clinic Specialty Building is an outpatient clinic building connected to the Mayo Clinic Hospital on the Phoenix campus. In 2016-17, Mayo Clinic, Rochester, was ranked as the #1 overall hospital in the U.S. by U.S. News & World Report, including its treatment related to diabetes, gastroenterology, geriatrics, gynecology, nephrology, neurology, pulmonology and urology.

Doctors are paid by salary, rather than fee for service. Employees of the firm are offered medical, dental, vision, AD&D, life, disability and prescription drug plans; employee and tuition assistance; flexible spending accounts; and pension plans.

FINANCIAL DATA: Note: Data for latest year may not have been available at press time.

In U.S. $	2016	2015	2014	2013	2012	2011
Revenue	10,990,000,000	10,315,000,000	9,760,600,000	9,420,800,000	8,843,900,000	8,475,700,000
R&D Expense						
Operating Income						
Operating Margin %						
SGA Expense						
Net Income	475,000,000	526,000,000	834,800,000	612,100,000	395,400,000	610,200,000
Operating Cash Flow						
Capital Expenditure						
EBITDA						
Return on Assets %						
Return on Equity %						
Debt to Equity						

CONTACT INFORMATION:

Phone: 507-284-2511   Fax: 507-284-0161
Toll-Free: 800-660-4582
Address: 200 First St. SW, Rochester, MN 55905 United States

STOCK TICKER/OTHER:

Stock Ticker: Nonprofit   Exchange:
Employees: 64,000   Fiscal Year Ends: 12/31
Parent Company:

SALARIES/BONUSES:

Top Exec. Salary: $ Bonus: $
Second Exec. Salary: $ Bonus: $

OTHER THOUGHTS:

Estimated Female Officers or Directors: 5
Hot Spot for Advancement for Women/Minorities: Y

McAfee Inc

www.mcafee.com

NAIC Code: 0

TYPES OF BUSINESS:

Computer Software, Security & Anti-Virus
Virus Protection Software
Network Management Software

BRANDS/DIVISIONS/AFFILIATES:

Intel Corporation
Intel Secutrity-McAfee
McAfee Total Protection
McAfee LiveSafe
McAfee AntiVirus Plus
Intel Security Partner Program

CONTACTS: Note: Officers with more than one job title may be intentionally listed here more than once.

Christopher Young, CEO
Michael Fey, CTO
Bryan Reed Barney, Exec. VP-Prod. Dev.
Ari Jaaksi, Sr. VP
Louis Riley, General Counsel
Tom Fountain, Sr. VP
Edward Hayden, Sr. VP-Finance & Acct.
Steve Redman, Exec. VP-Global Sales
Ken Levine, Sr. VP
Gert-Jan Schenk, Pres., EMEA
Barry McPherson, Exec. VP-Worldwide Delivery & Support Svcs.
Jean-Claude Broido, Pres., McAfee Japan
Barry McPherson, Exec. VP-Supply Chain & Facilities

GROWTH PLANS/SPECIAL FEATURES:

McAfee, Inc., operating under the brand Intel Security-McAfee, is a subsidiary of Intel Corporation. The firm is a global developer and supplier of software-based computer security systems that prevent intrusions on networks and protect computer systems from attacks. It allows home users, businesses, government agencies, service providers and partners to block attacks, prevent disruptions and continuously track and improve their security. The company's products are categorized for consumers, small business, partners and enterprise. Consumer products are geared toward users who work from home on one or multiple devices such as computers, tablets, laptops and smartphones. Products consist of PC protection software such as McAfee Total Protection, which works as an anti-virus and maintains an enhanced firewall, McAfee LiveSafe and McAfee AntiVirus Plus. Small business products are designed for businesses with 250 or less devices ranging from PCs, tablets, servers and smartphones. Products categories in this segment includes desktops, email and web and popular products are Security for Business, SaaS Email Security and SaaS Web & Email Protection among others. Partners consists of Intel Security Partner Program, which offers special security solutions through resale or technology partnerships. The resale partnerships include resellers and managed service providers and the technology partnerships include global, OEM and security innovation alliances. Enterprise security products are geared toward companies with hundreds to tens of thousands computers. Products cover email and web security, mobile and network security, endpoint protection, database security and data protection and encryption. In September 2016, parent Intel partnered with TPG Capital to convert Intel Security-McAfee into a joint venture called McAfee. TPG will be the majority owner (51%) of McAfee.

FINANCIAL DATA: Note: Data for latest year may not have been available at press time.

In U.S. $	2016	2015	2014	2013	2012	2011
Revenue	2,450,000,000	2,375,000,000	2,216,000,000	2,190,000,000	2,072,000,000	2,200,000,000
R&D Expense						
Operating Income						
Operating Margin %						
SGA Expense						
Net Income			55,000,000	24,000,000	12,000,000	
Operating Cash Flow						
Capital Expenditure						
EBITDA						
Return on Assets %						
Return on Equity %						
Debt to Equity						

CONTACT INFORMATION:

Phone: 972-963-8000 Fax:
Toll-Free: 855-380-6445
Address: 2821 Mission College Blvd., Santa Clara, CA 95054 United States

STOCK TICKER/OTHER:

Stock Ticker: Subsidiary
Employees: 8,001
Parent Company: Intel Corporation

Exchange:
Fiscal Year Ends: 12/31

SALARIES/BONUSES:

Top Exec. Salary: $ Bonus: $
Second Exec. Salary: $ Bonus: $

OTHER THOUGHTS:

Estimated Female Officers or Directors: 3
Hot Spot for Advancement for Women/Minorities: Y

McCormick & Company Inc

www.mccormick.com

NAIC Code: 311940

TYPES OF BUSINESS:

Herbs, Spices & Seasonings

BRANDS/DIVISIONS/AFFILIATES:

Stubb's
McCormick
Simply Asia
Zatarain's
Thai Kitchen
Lawry's
Club House
Ducros

CONTACTS: *Note: Officers with more than one job title may be intentionally listed here more than once.*

Christina Mcmullen, Chief Accounting Officer
Lawrence Kurzius, Director
Michael Smith, Executive VP
Brendan Foley, President, Divisional
Malcolm Swift, President, Divisional
Lisa Manzone, Senior VP, Divisional
Nneka Rimmer, Senior VP, Divisional
Jeffery Schwartz, Vice President

GROWTH PLANS/SPECIAL FEATURES:

McCormick & Company, Inc. is a global manufacturer, marketer and distributor of spices, seasonings and flavorings to the entire food industry, including retail outlets, food manufacturers and food service businesses. The firm operates in two segments: consumer and industrial. The consumer segment sells spices, herbs, seasoning blends and other flavors to retail outlets, including grocery, mass merchandise, warehouse clubs, discount and drug stores. Its leading brands are McCormick, Lawry's and Club House, with ethnic brands consisting of Zatarain's, Simply Asia, Thai Kitchen and Stubb's, as well as global brands such as Ducros, Kamis, Kohinoor and Schwartz. The industrial segment sells seasoning blends, natural spices and herbs, wet flavors, coating systems and compound flavors to other food manufacturers and the food service industry, both directly and indirectly through distributors. The company's major sales, distribution and production facilities are located in the North America, Europe and China as well as additional facilities in Australia, Mexico, India, Singapore, Central America, Thailand and South Africa.

McCormick offers its employees medical and dental insurance, life and disability insurance, adoption assistance, a profit sharing plan, an employee stock purchase plan, an employee assistance program and tuition assistance.

FINANCIAL DATA: *Note: Data for latest year may not have been available at press time.*

In U.S. $	2016	2015	2014	2013	2012	2011
Revenue	4,411,500,000	4,296,300,000	4,243,200,000	4,123,400,000	4,014,200,000	3,697,600,000
R&D Expense						
Operating Income	641,000,000	548,400,000	603,000,000	550,500,000	578,300,000	540,300,000
Operating Margin %	14.53%	12.76%	14.21%	13.35%	14.40%	14.61%
SGA Expense	1,175,000,000	1,127,400,000	1,122,000,000	1,075,000,000	1,039,500,000	982,200,000
Net Income	471,000,000	402,100,000	437,900,000	387,700,000	407,800,000	374,200,000
Operating Cash Flow	658,100,000	590,000,000	503,600,000	465,200,000	455,000,000	340,000,000
Capital Expenditure	153,800,000	128,400,000	132,700,000	99,900,000	110,300,000	96,700,000
EBITDA	753,900,000	655,400,000	706,800,000	658,700,000	683,500,000	640,900,000
Return on Assets %	10.30%	9.01%	9.88%	9.00%	9.88%	9.96%
Return on Equity %	28.57%	23.22%	23.51%	21.44%	24.83%	24.49%
Debt to Equity	0.64	0.63	0.56	0.52	0.46	0.64

CONTACT INFORMATION:

Phone: 410-771-7301 Fax:
Toll-Free:
Address: 18 Loveton Cir., Sparks, MD 21152 United States

STOCK TICKER/OTHER:

Stock Ticker: MKC
Employees: 10,500
Parent Company:

Exchange: NYS
Fiscal Year Ends: 11/30

SALARIES/BONUSES:

Top Exec. Salary: $1,050,000 Bonus: $
Second Exec. Salary: $861,374 Bonus: $

OTHER THOUGHTS:

Estimated Female Officers or Directors: 1
Hot Spot for Advancement for Women/Minorities: Y

McDonald's Corp

www.mcdonalds.com

NAIC Code: 722513

TYPES OF BUSINESS:

Fast Food Restaurants
Home-Meal Replacement Restaurants
Franchising

BRANDS/DIVISIONS/AFFILIATES:

Big Mac
Quarter Pounder
Filet O'Fish
Happy Meal
Egg McMuffin
McDonald's Next
Create Your Taste

CONTACTS: *Note: Officers with more than one job title may be intentionally listed here more than once.*

Brian Mullens, Chief Accounting Officer
Catherine Hoovel, Vice President
Enrique Hernandez, Director
Stephen Easterbrook, Director
Jim Sappington, Executive VP, Divisional
Robert Gibbs, Executive VP, Divisional
Kevin Ozan, Executive VP
Silvia Lagnado, Executive VP
David Fairhurst, Executive VP
Gloria Santona, Executive VP
Joseph Erlinger, President, Divisional
Ian Borden, President, Divisional
Christopher Kempczinski, President, Geographical
Douglas Goare, President, Geographical
Jerome Krulewitch, Senior VP, Divisional

GROWTH PLANS/SPECIAL FEATURES:

McDonald's Corp. operates more than 36,500 fast-food restaurants in over 100 countries, serving approximately 70 million customers per day. McDonald's has expanded by its franchising model, whereby independent businessmen and women provide capital by initially investing in equipment, signs, seating and decor of restaurants and personally operating them. The company shares the investment by owning or leasing the land and buildings. Approximately 80% of McDonald's worldwide restaurants are franchises, the rest being operated directly by the company or under joint-venture agreements. The McDonald's menu includes items such as hamburgers, cheeseburgers, fish and chicken sandwiches, chicken nuggets, French fries, salads, milkshakes, desserts and soft drinks. McDonald's restaurants are also open during breakfast hours and offer egg sandwiches, hotcakes, biscuit and bagel sandwiches and muffins. Brand names include the Big Mac, Quarter Pounder, Filet O'Fish, Happy Meal and Egg McMuffin. As part of a multi-year beverage business strategy designed to take advantage of the significant and growing beverage category, the company is introducing hot specialty coffee offerings on a market-by-market basis, all of which serve as a platform for the recent introduction of smoothies, frappes and other beverage options in a number of markets. The company is continually working to provide nutritious additions to its menu, including salads, apple slices, oatmeal and low fat yogurt.

The firm offers qualified employees medical, dental and vision insurance; short- and long-term disability; profit sharing and savings plans; adoption assistance; vacation and holiday pay; and a child care discount.

FINANCIAL DATA: *Note: Data for latest year may not have been available at press time.*

In U.S. $	2016	2015	2014	2013	2012	2011
Revenue	24,621,900,000	25,413,000,000	27,441,300,000	28,105,700,000	27,567,000,000	27,006,000,000
R&D Expense						
Operating Income	7,744,500,000	7,145,500,000	7,949,200,000	8,764,300,000	8,604,600,000	8,529,700,000
Operating Margin %	31.45%	28.11%	28.96%	31.18%	31.21%	31.58%
SGA Expense	2,384,500,000	2,434,300,000	2,487,900,000	2,385,600,000	2,455,200,000	2,393,700,000
Net Income	4,686,500,000	4,529,300,000	4,757,800,000	5,585,900,000	5,464,800,000	5,503,100,000
Operating Cash Flow	6,059,600,000	6,539,100,000	6,730,300,000	7,120,700,000	6,966,100,000	7,150,100,000
Capital Expenditure	1,821,100,000	1,813,900,000	2,583,400,000	2,824,700,000	3,049,200,000	2,729,800,000
EBITDA	9,267,300,000	8,749,700,000	9,587,000,000	10,311,500,000	10,084,100,000	9,920,000,000
Return on Assets %	13.59%	12.54%	13.41%	15.51%	15.98%	16.94%
Return on Equity %	191.92%	45.42%	32.96%	35.68%	36.82%	37.92%
Debt to Equity		3.40	1.16	0.88	0.89	0.84

CONTACT INFORMATION:

Phone: 630 623-3000   Fax: 630 623-5700
Toll-Free: 800-244-6227
Address: 1 McDonald's Plz., Oak Brook, IL 60523 United States

STOCK TICKER/OTHER:

Stock Ticker: MCD
Employees: 375,000
Parent Company:

Exchange: NYS
Fiscal Year Ends: 12/31

SALARIES/BONUSES:

Top Exec. Salary: $1,266,667   Bonus: $
Second Exec. Salary: $615,000   Bonus: $337,500

OTHER THOUGHTS:

Estimated Female Officers or Directors: 4
Hot Spot for Advancement for Women/Minorities: Y

McKesson Corporation

www.mckesson.com

NAIC Code: 424210

TYPES OF BUSINESS:

Pharmaceutical Distribution
Medical-Surgical Products Distribution
Health Care Management Software
Consulting
Outsourcing

BRANDS/DIVISIONS/AFFILIATES:

Change Healthcare LLC

CONTACTS: *Note: Officers with more than one job title may be intentionally listed here more than once.*

John Hammergren, CEO
James Beer, CFO
Kathleen McElligott, Chief Information Officer
Jorge Figueredo, Executive VP, Divisional
Bansi Nagji, Executive VP, Divisional
Lori Schechter, Executive VP
Paul Julian, Executive VP
John Saia, Secretary
Paul Smith, Senior VP, Divisional
Erin Lampert, Senior VP
Brian Moore, Senior VP

GROWTH PLANS/SPECIAL FEATURES:

McKesson Corporation provides medicines, pharmaceutical supplies, information and care management products and services to the healthcare industry. The company operates in two segments: distribution solutions and technology solutions. The distribution solutions segment distributes branded and generic pharmaceutical drugs and other healthcare-related products internationally; and provides practice management, technology, clinical support and business solutions to community-based oncology and other specialty practices. The technology solutions segment provides clinical, financial and supply chain management solutions to healthcare organizations. This division also includes 70%-owned Change Healthcare, LLC, a provider of software and analytics, network solutions and technology-enabled services that deliver wide-ranging financial, operational and clinical benefits to payers, providers and consumers. During 2017, McKesson (70% ownership) and Change Healthcare Holdings, Inc. (30%) created healthcare information technology company, Change Healthcare, combining all of Change Healthcare's business and the majority of McKesson's technology solutions business.

Employee benefits include medical, dental, vision, AD&D and dependent life insurance; an employee assistance program; and flexible spending accounts.

FINANCIAL DATA: *Note: Data for latest year may not have been available at press time.*

In U.S. $	2016	2015	2014	2013	2012	2011
Revenue	190,884,000,000	179,045,000,000	137,609,000,000	122,455,000,000	122,734,000,000	
R&D Expense	392,000,000	392,000,000	456,000,000	480,000,000	440,000,000	
Operating Income	3,545,000,000	2,968,000,000	2,367,000,000	2,315,000,000	2,149,000,000	
Operating Margin %	1.85%	1.65%	1.72%	1.89%	1.75%	
SGA Expense	7,276,000,000	7,901,000,000	5,418,000,000	4,198,000,000	3,829,000,000	
Net Income	2,258,000,000	1,476,000,000	1,263,000,000	1,338,000,000	1,403,000,000	
Operating Cash Flow	3,672,000,000	3,112,000,000	3,136,000,000	2,483,000,000	2,950,000,000	
Capital Expenditure	677,000,000	545,000,000	415,000,000	406,000,000	403,000,000	
EBITDA	4,488,000,000	4,048,000,000	3,103,000,000	2,750,000,000	2,721,000,000	
Return on Assets %	4.08%	2.79%	2.91%	3.94%	4.38%	
Return on Equity %	26.68%	17.86%	16.20%	19.25%	19.97%	
Debt to Equity	0.73	1.02	1.05	0.63	0.44	

CONTACT INFORMATION:

Phone: 415 983-8300   Fax: 415 983-8453
Toll-Free: 800-826-9360
Address: 1 Post St., San Francisco, CA 94104 United States

STOCK TICKER/OTHER:

Stock Ticker: MCK   Exchange: NYS
Employees: 78,000   Fiscal Year Ends: 03/31
Parent Company:

SALARIES/BONUSES:

Top Exec. Salary: $1,680,000   Bonus: $
Second Exec. Salary: $765,500   Bonus: $775,000

OTHER THOUGHTS:

Estimated Female Officers or Directors: 4
Hot Spot for Advancement for Women/Minorities: Y

McKinsey & Company Inc

NAIC Code: 541610

www.mckinsey.com

TYPES OF BUSINESS:

Management Consulting
Strategic & Logistics Consulting
Industry-Specific Consulting
Business Research
Business Publications

BRANDS/DIVISIONS/AFFILIATES:

McKinsey Global Institute
McKinsey Quarterly

CONTACTS: *Note: Officers with more than one job title may be intentionally listed here more than once.*

Dominic Barton, Managing Dir.

GROWTH PLANS/SPECIAL FEATURES:

McKinsey & Company, Inc. is a privately-held international management consulting firm established in 1926. Headquartered in New York, the firm maintains more than 100 offices in over 50 countries. McKinsey provides consulting services for leading businesses, governments, non-governmental organizations and non-profits. The company helps clients make improvements to their performance at every level of their organization. Business functions include analytics, business technology, digital technology, implementation, learning programs for clients, marketing and sales, operations, organization, recover and transformation services, risk, strategy and corporate finance, as well as sustainability and resource productivity. Industries served by McKinsey include advanced electronics, aerospace and defense, automotive and assembly, chemicals, consumer packaged goods, electric power and natural gas, financial services, healthcare systems and services, high tech, infrastructure, media and entertainment, metals and mining, oil and gas, paper and forest products, pharmaceuticals and medical products, private equity and principal investors, public sector, retail, semiconductors, social sector, telecommunications and travel/transport/logistics. The McKinsey Global Institute helps leaders in multiple sectors develop deeper understanding of the global economy. The firm's flagship business publication, McKinsey Quarterly, has been defining and informing the senior-management agenda since 1964.

FINANCIAL DATA: *Note: Data for latest year may not have been available at press time.*

In U.S. $	2016	2015	2014	2013	2012	2011
Revenue	8,590,500,000	8,300,000,000	8,000,000,000	7,150,000,000	6,375,000,000	5,450,000,000
R&D Expense						
Operating Income						
Operating Margin %						
SGA Expense						
Net Income						
Operating Cash Flow						
Capital Expenditure						
EBITDA						
Return on Assets %						
Return on Equity %						
Debt to Equity						

CONTACT INFORMATION:

Phone: 212-446-7000   Fax: 212-446-8575
Toll-Free:
Address: 55 E. 52nd St., Fl. 21, New York, NY 10022 United States

STOCK TICKER/OTHER:

Stock Ticker: Private   Exchange:
Employees: 17,000   Fiscal Year Ends: 12/31
Parent Company:

SALARIES/BONUSES:

Top Exec. Salary: $ Bonus: $
Second Exec. Salary: $ Bonus: $

OTHER THOUGHTS:

Estimated Female Officers or Directors: 2
Hot Spot for Advancement for Women/Minorities: Y

Mediacom Communications Corp

www.mediacomcc.com

NAIC Code: 517110

TYPES OF BUSINESS:

Cable TV Service
Internet Service
Digital Cable
Telephone Service

BRANDS/DIVISIONS/AFFILIATES:

Mediacom Online
Mediacom Online Ultra
Mediacom Phone
Home Controller

CONTACTS: Note: Officers with more than one job title may be intentionally listed here more than once.

Rocco B. Commisso, CEO
John G. Pascarelli, VP-Operations
Mark E. Stephan, CFO
David M. McNaughton, Sr. VP-Mktg.
Italia Commisso Weinand, Sr. VP-Human Resources & Programming
J.R. Walden, CTO
Joseph E. Young, General Counsel
John G. Pascarelli, Exec. VP-Oper.
Jack Griffin, Dir.-Corp. Finance
Edward S. Pardini, Sr. VP-Divisional Oper.-North Central Division
Brian M. Walsh, Sr. VP
Tapan Dandnaik, Sr. VP-Customer Service & Financial Oper.
Steve Litwer, Sr. VP-Advertising Sales, OnMedia Div.
Rocco B. Commisso, Chmn.

GROWTH PLANS/SPECIAL FEATURES:

Mediacom Communications Corp., a leading cable company, supplies an array of broadband products and services to more than 1,500 communities throughout the U.S., reaching over 1.4 million homes. The firm offers its customers a full array of traditional video services, which includes basic service, digital video service, pay-per-view service, high definition television, digital video recorders and video-on-demand. In addition, the company offers five types of high-speed internet access: Internet 60, allows for download speeds up to 60 Mbps; Internet 100, speeds up to 100 Mbps; Internet 200, up to 200 Mbps; Internet 500, caps at 500 Mbps; and 1GIG, which allows for up to 1,000 Mbps of download speeds. The firm's Mediacom Phone offers customers unlimited local, regional and long-distance calling within the U.S., Puerto Rico, U.S. Virgin Islands and Canada. It is delivered over voice over internet protocol (VoIP) that digitizes voice signals and routes them as data packets through Mediacom's controlled broadband cable systems. It includes features such as Caller ID with name and number, call waiting, three-way calling and enhanced Emergency 911 dialing. Mediacom also offers video, HSD (high speed data), phone, network and transport services to commercial and large enterprise customers. It offers large enterprise customers who require high-bandwidth connections solutions such as the point-to-point circuits required by wireless communications providers. Additionally, Mediacom offers a home security product, Home Controller, which provides 24-hour-a-day monitoring from a UL-approved facility. In May 2016, the firm announced it would be adding a wide variety of foreign language programming, including Filipino, French, German, Italian, Korean, Russian, South-Asian and Vietnamese. Each of the channels can be purchased a la carte by any Mediacom customer subscribing to the LocalPlus TV or higher tier of video service.

FINANCIAL DATA: Note: Data for latest year may not have been available at press time.

In U.S. $	2016	2015	2014	2013	2012	2011
Revenue	741,000,000	738,710,000	711,634,000	698,861,000	681,683,000	1,550,400,000
R&D Expense						
Operating Income						
Operating Margin %						
SGA Expense						
Net Income		123,009,000	75,219,000	90,446,000	68,491,000	
Operating Cash Flow						
Capital Expenditure						
EBITDA						
Return on Assets %						
Return on Equity %						
Debt to Equity						

CONTACT INFORMATION:

Phone: 855-633-4226   Fax: 845-698-4069
Toll-Free: 800-479-2082
Address: 1 Mediacom Way, Mediacom Park, NY 10918 United States

STOCK TICKER/OTHER:

Stock Ticker: Private   Exchange:
Employees: 4,441   Fiscal Year Ends: 12/31
Parent Company:

SALARIES/BONUSES:

Top Exec. Salary: $ Bonus: $
Second Exec. Salary: $ Bonus: $

OTHER THOUGHTS:

Estimated Female Officers or Directors: 1
Hot Spot for Advancement for Women/Minorities:

MedStar Health

www.medstarhealth.org

NAIC Code: 622110

TYPES OF BUSINESS:

General Medical and Surgical Hospitals
Assisted Living Services
Home Health Services
Ambulatory Centers
Rehabilitation Centers
Nursing Homes
Physician Network Management
Research

BRANDS/DIVISIONS/AFFILIATES:

MedStar Franklin Square Medical Center
MedStar Good Samaritan Hospital
MedStar Harbor Hospital
MedStar Montgomery Medical Center
MedStar Southern Maryland Hospital Center
MedStar National Rehabilitation Hospital
MedStar Physician Partners
MedStar Health Research Institute

CONTACTS: *Note: Officers with more than one job title may be intentionally listed here more than once.*

Kenneth A. Samet, CEO
Joy Drass, COO
Kenneth A. Samet, Pres.
Michael J. Curran, CFO
Kevin P. Kowalski, Exec. VP-Mktg.
Loretta Young Walker, VP-Chief Human Resources Officer
Stephen R.T. Evans, Chief Medical Officer
Michael J. Curran, Chief Admin. Officer
Oliver M. Johnson, II, General Counsel
Eric R. Wagner, Exec. VP-Diversified Oper. & External Affairs
Christine M. Swearingen, Exec. VP-Planning & Community Rel.
Jean Hitchcock, VP-Public Affairs & Mktg.
Susan K. Nelson, VP-Finance & Acct. Oper.
Carl Schindelar, Exec. VP-Oper., Baltimore Region
Jennie P. McConagha, Chief of Staff
Joel N. Bryan, Treas.
Pegeen Townsend, VP-Gov't Affairs
William R. Roberts, Chmn.

GROWTH PLANS/SPECIAL FEATURES:

MedStar Health is a nonprofit, community-based health care organization primarily composed of several integrated businesses, including 10 major hospitals, with 30,000 associates and 6,000 affiliated physicians. The hospitals are located within proximity of the Baltimore/Washington, D.C. area and include the following: MedStar Franklin Square Medical Center, MedStar Good Samaritan Hospital, MedStar Harbor Hospital, MedStar Montgomery Medical Center, MedStar Southern Maryland Hospital Center, MedStar St. Mary's Hospital, MedStar Union Memorial Hospital, MedStar Georgetown University Hospital, MedStar Washington Hospital Center and MedStar National Rehabilitation Hospital. The hospitals' services include primary, urgent and sub-acute care; behavioral health and psychiatric services; medical education; and research. MedStar also provides assisted living, home health, hospice and long-term care and operates nursing homes, senior housing, adult day care, rehabilitation and ambulatory centers. MedStar serves roughly 140,000 inpatients, over 4.3 million outpatients and conducts 266,778 home health visits annually. The organization manages MedStar Physician Partners, a comprehensive physician network serving in the region. Its MedStar Health Research Institute conducts research and clinical trials; and MedStar Health has one of the largest graduate medical education programs in the country, training more than 1,100 medical residents annually, and is the medical education and clinical partner of Georgetown University.

MedStar's employees are offered health, dental and vision insurance; flexible spending accounts; an employee assistance program; paid leave; a tax deferred retirement savings plan; life & disability insurance; and tuition assistance.

FINANCIAL DATA: *Note: Data for latest year may not have been available at press time.*

In U.S. $	2016	2015	2014	2013	2012	2011
Revenue		5,030,000,000	4,628,100,000	4,200,000,000	4,175,900,000	4,017,200,000
R&D Expense						
Operating Income						
Operating Margin %						
SGA Expense						
Net Income		359,000,000	304,700,000	185,700,000	69,900,000	312,200,000
Operating Cash Flow						
Capital Expenditure						
EBITDA						
Return on Assets %						
Return on Equity %						
Debt to Equity						

CONTACT INFORMATION:

Phone: 410-772-6500   Fax: 410-715-3905
Toll-Free: 877-772-6505
Address: 10980 Grantchester Way, Columbia, MD 21044 United States

STOCK TICKER/OTHER:

Stock Ticker: Nonprofit   Exchange:
Employees: 31,000   Fiscal Year Ends: 06/30
Parent Company:

SALARIES/BONUSES:

Top Exec. Salary: $ Bonus: $
Second Exec. Salary: $ Bonus: $

OTHER THOUGHTS:

Estimated Female Officers or Directors: 15
Hot Spot for Advancement for Women/Minorities: Y

Medtronic plc

www.medtronic.com

NAIC Code: 334510

TYPES OF BUSINESS:

Equipment-Defibrillators & Pacing Products
Neurological Devices
Diabetes Management Devices
Ear, Nose & Throat Surgical Equipment
Pain Management Devices
Cardiac Surgery Equipment

BRANDS/DIVISIONS/AFFILIATES:

Bellco Health
Heartware International Inc

CONTACTS: *Note: Officers with more than one job title may be intentionally listed here more than once.*

Bryan Hanson,
Omar Ishrak, CEO
Karen Parkhill, CFO
Michael Coyle, Executive VP
Hooman Hakami, Executive VP
Robert Hoedt, Executive VP
Bradley Lerman, General Counsel
Richard Kuntz, Other Executive Officer
Carol Surface, Other Executive Officer
Geoffrey Martha, President, Divisional

GROWTH PLANS/SPECIAL FEATURES:

Medtronic plc is a global leader in medical device technology, serving physicians, clinicians and patients in approximately 160 countries worldwide. Its operations consist of four primary segments: the cardiac and vascular group, which includes the cardiac rhythm and heart failure disease management (CRHF), as well as coronary, structural heart and endovascular therapies; the restorative therapies group, which includes the spinal, neuromodulation, diabetes and surgical technologies divisions; the minimally invasive technologies group, which includes surgical and patient monitoring and recovery solutions; and the diabetes group, which includes advanced diabetes management solutions. Products in the CRHF division manage cardiac rhythm disorders and include pacemakers, implantable defibrillators, ablation products and products for the treatment of atrial fibrillation (AF). The coronary, structural heart and endovascular therapies makes technology that supports the interventional treatment of coronary artery disease to help improve blood flow, and includes products such as stents, guide wires, and catheters. The spinal division offers medical devices used to treat spinal and cranial conditions. The neuromodulation division develops devices for the treatment of neurological, urological and gastroenterological disorders. The surgical technologies division develops and manufactures minimally invasive products to treat ear, nose and throat and neurological diseases. The patient monitoring and recovery develops and markets sensors, monitors and temperature management products, as well as products and therapies for complication-free recovery. The diabetes unit develops integrated diabetes management systems, insulin pump therapies, continuous glucose monitoring systems and therapy management software. In 2016, the firm acquired Bellco Health, a pioneer in hemodialysis treatment solutions; the gynecology business from Smith & Nephew plc for approximately $350 billion; and Heartware International, Inc., a leading innovator of minimally invasive technologies for treating advanced heart failure. In April 2017, Medtronic sold part of its patient monitoring and recovery unit to Cardinal Health, Inc, for $6.1 billion.

The firm offers employees health care and disability, adoption and elder care assistance, retirement plans and stock options.

FINANCIAL DATA: *Note: Data for latest year may not have been available at press time.*

In U.S. $	2016	2015	2014	2013	2012	2011
Revenue	28,833,000,000	20,261,000,000	17,005,000,000	16,590,000,000	16,184,000,000	
R&D Expense	2,224,000,000	1,640,000,000	1,477,000,000	1,557,000,000	1,490,000,000	
Operating Income	5,291,000,000	3,766,000,000	3,813,000,000	4,251,000,000	4,658,000,000	
Operating Margin %	18.35%	18.58%	22.42%	25.62%	28.78%	
SGA Expense	9,469,000,000	6,904,000,000	5,847,000,000	5,698,000,000	5,623,000,000	
Net Income	3,538,000,000	2,675,000,000	3,065,000,000	3,467,000,000	3,617,000,000	
Operating Cash Flow	5,218,000,000	4,902,000,000	4,959,000,000	4,883,000,000	4,470,000,000	
Capital Expenditure	1,046,000,000	571,000,000	396,000,000	457,000,000	499,000,000	
EBITDA	8,542,000,000	5,458,000,000	4,934,000,000	5,221,000,000	5,327,000,000	
Return on Assets %	3.42%	3.69%	8.42%	10.20%	11.39%	
Return on Equity %	6.72%	7.36%	16.08%	19.37%	21.86%	
Debt to Equity	0.58	0.63	0.53	0.52	0.43	

CONTACT INFORMATION:

Phone: 763 514-4000   Fax: 763 514-4000
Toll-Free: 800-633-8766
Address: 710 Medtronic Pkwy., Minneapolis, MN 55432 United States

STOCK TICKER/OTHER:

Stock Ticker: MDT   Exchange: NYS
Employees: 91,000   Fiscal Year Ends: 04/30
Parent Company:

SALARIES/BONUSES:

Top Exec. Salary: $1,548,216   Bonus: $
Second Exec. Salary: Bonus: $250,000
$749,039

OTHER THOUGHTS:

Estimated Female Officers or Directors: 5
Hot Spot for Advancement for Women/Minorities: Y

Sales, profits and employees may be estimates. Financial information, benefits and other data can change quickly and may vary from those stated here.

Menard Inc

NAIC Code: 444110

TYPES OF BUSINESS:

Home Improvement Stores
Lumber
Housing Materials
Building Materials Manufacturing
Prefabricated Houses

BRANDS/DIVISIONS/AFFILIATES:

Menards
Midwest Manufacturing
MasterForce
MasterCraft
Dakota
Grip Fast
Tuscany
Tool Shop

CONTACTS: Note: Officers with more than one job title may be intentionally listed here more than once.

John R. Menard, Jr., Pres.
Charlie Menard, General Manager

GROWTH PLANS/SPECIAL FEATURES:

Menard, Inc. is a family-owned company that began in 1960, headquartered in Eau Claire, Wisconsin and has 300 home improvement stores. The company's Menards-branded stores are located throughout the Midwest in a 14-state region: Illinois, Indiana, Iowa, Kansas, Kentucky, Michigan, Minnesota, Missouri, Nebraska, North Dakota, Ohio, South Dakota, Wisconsin and Wyoming. The firm's departments include appliances; bath; building materials; doors, windows and millwork; electrical; flooring and rugs; grocery and pet; heating and cooling; home and decor; kitchen; lighting and ceiling fans; maintenance, repair and operations; outdoors; paint; plumbing; home and patio; storage and organization; and tools and hardware. Menards provides a number of quality brands such as Midwest Manufacturing, Masterforce, Dakota, Mastercraft, Grip Fast, Tuscany, Tool Shop and Enchanted Garden/Enchanted Forest. The company's subsidiary, Midwest Manufacturing, operates a number of manufacturing facilities in Wisconsin, Illinois, Ohio, Nebraska, Iowa and Minnesota. Menard has four distribution centers in Plato, Illinois; Shelby, Iowa; Holiday City, Ohio; and Eau Claire, Wisconsin.

The company offers employees medical, dental and disability insurance; a profit sharing program; advancement opportunities; 401(k); store discounts; and bonuses.

FINANCIAL DATA: Note: Data for latest year may not have been available at press time.

In U.S. $	2016	2015	2014	2013	2012	2011
Revenue	9,500,000,000	8,970,000,000	8,710,000,000	7,775,000,000	7,600,000,000	7,475,000,000
R&D Expense						
Operating Income						
Operating Margin %						
SGA Expense						
Net Income						
Operating Cash Flow						
Capital Expenditure						
EBITDA						
Return on Assets %						
Return on Equity %						
Debt to Equity						

CONTACT INFORMATION:

Phone: 715-876-5911   Fax: 715-876-2868
Toll-Free:
Address: 5101 Menard Drive, Eau Claire, WI 54703 United States

STOCK TICKER/OTHER:

Stock Ticker: Private   Exchange:
Employees: 46,500   Fiscal Year Ends: 01/31
Parent Company:

SALARIES/BONUSES:

Top Exec. Salary: $ Bonus: $
Second Exec. Salary: $ Bonus: $

OTHER THOUGHTS:

Estimated Female Officers or Directors:
Hot Spot for Advancement for Women/Minorities:

Mentor Graphics Corp

www.mentor.com

NAIC Code: 0

TYPES OF BUSINESS:

Software-Component Design, Simulation & Testing
Electronic Design Automation Tools
Consulting Services

BRANDS/DIVISIONS/AFFILIATES:

Veloce
Calibre
Questa
Olympus-SoC
Xpedition Series (The)
Flexras Technologies
Tanner EDA
Calypto Design Systems Inc

CONTACTS: Note: Officers with more than one job title may be intentionally listed here more than once.

Walden Rhines, CEO
Gregory Hinckley, CFO
Richard Trebing, Chief Accounting Officer
Michael Ellow, Senior VP, Divisional
Brian Derrick, Vice President, Divisional
Dean Freed, Vice President

GROWTH PLANS/SPECIAL FEATURES:

Mentor Graphics Corp. is a supplier of electronic design automation (EDA) systems, advanced computer software and emulation hardware products used to automate the design, analysis and testing of electronic hardware and embedded systems and components. These products are primarily marketed to large companies in the military, aerospace, communications, computer, consumer electronics, semiconductor, networking, multimedia and transportation industries. The company's offerings include Scalable Verification products, integrated circuit (IC) design and integrated system design. Scalable Verification products help engineers verify that their IC designs function as needed. Products in this category include Questa, a scalable verification platform that includes support, simulation and verification technologies for extended verification of systems and ICs, and hardware emulation systems, such as the Veloce product family. IC design products consist of the Calibre and Olympus-SoC (system-on-chip) product lines. Calibre tools are designed to aid customers in the design process of ICs at the nanometer (nm) level. Olympus-SoC products are designed for creating ICs with geometries of 65 nm and below. Integrated system design products support the printed circuit board (PCB) and field-programmable gate array (FPGA) design process with products such as The Xpedition Series, PADS, HyperLynx, and XtremePCB. Mentor sells and licenses its products through a direct sales force as well as distributors and sales representatives. In 2015, the firm acquired Flexras Technologies, Tanner EDA and Calypto Design Systems, Inc. In November 2016, Mentor Graphics agreed to be acquired by Siemens AG for $37.25 a share in cash.

Employees of Mentor receive a 401(k); adoption assistance; a discount stock purchase plan; medical, dental, vision and prescription drug coverage; life and AD&D insurance; and tuition reimbursement.

FINANCIAL DATA: Note: Data for latest year may not have been available at press time.

In U.S. $	2016	2015	2014	2013	2012	2011
Revenue	1,180,988,032	1,244,132,992	1,156,372,992	1,088,727,040	1,014,638,016	914,753,024
R&D Expense						
Operating Income						
Operating Margin %						
SGA Expense						
Net Income	96,277,000	147,139,008	155,258,000	138,736,000	83,872,000	28,584,000
Operating Cash Flow						
Capital Expenditure						
EBITDA						
Return on Assets %						
Return on Equity %						
Debt to Equity						

CONTACT INFORMATION:

Phone: 503 685-7000   Fax: 503 685-1202
Toll-Free: 800-592-2210
Address: 8005 SW Boeckman Rd., Wilsonville, OR 97070 United States

STOCK TICKER/OTHER:

Stock Ticker: MENT   Exchange: NAS
Employees: 5,558   Fiscal Year Ends: 01/31
Parent Company:

SALARIES/BONUSES:

Top Exec. Salary: $ Bonus: $
Second Exec. Salary: $ Bonus: $

OTHER THOUGHTS:

Estimated Female Officers or Directors:
Hot Spot for Advancement for Women/Minorities:

Mercedes-Benz USA LLC

www.mbusa.com

NAIC Code: 336111

TYPES OF BUSINESS:

Automobile Manufacturing
Marketing & Sales Services
Dealership

BRANDS/DIVISIONS/AFFILIATES:

Daimler AG
Mercedex-Benz US International Inc
AMG Driving Academy

CONTACTS: Note: Officers with more than one job title may be intentionally listed here more than once.

Dietmar Exler, CEO
Harald Henn, CFO
Ola Kallenius, VP-Mktg. & Sales
Norbert H. Litzkow, Chief Technology Officer
Matthew E. Roy, VP-Admin.
Michelle D. Spreitzer, General Counsel
Donna Boland, Mgr.-Corp. Comm.

GROWTH PLANS/SPECIAL FEATURES:

Mercedes-Benz USA LLC (MBUSA), a wholly-owned subsidiary of Daimler AG, sells, services, distributes and markets Mercedes-Benz cars and light trucks and Maybach super-luxury sedans throughout the U.S. MBUSA's vehicles include the C-, E- and S-Class and Maybach sedans; C-, E- and S-Class, CLA, CLS and AMG GT S coupes; G- and E-Class, GLA, GLC, GLE, GLE Coupe and GLS sport utility vehicles (SUVs) and wagons; SLC- and SL-Class roadsters; the E- and S-Class Cabriolet convertibles; and the B-Class, C-Class, S-Class and GLE hybrid and electric sedans and SUVs. The firm sells these vehicles through a network of more than 300 independently owned dealerships in the U.S. MBUSA also provides sales, marketing and other services to Mercedes-Benz dealerships. Company certified collision centers are located in Alabama, Alaska, Arizona, California, Colorado, Connecticut, Delaware, District of Columbia, Florida, Georgia, Hawaii and Idaho. Mercedes-Benz U.S. International, Inc. (MBUSI), a division of Mercedes-Benz and a subsidiary of Daimler AG, operates a Mercedes-Benz automobile manufacturing plant near Vance, Alabama, which is approximately 5 million square feet in size and sits on a 966-acre plot. The factory produces more than 300,000 vehicles annually. In addition, the company operates the AMG Driving Academy, a teen driving school in Los Angeles; and a 71,000-square-foot research and development facility in Sunnyvale, California.

Employee benefits include medical, dental, vision, short- and long-term disability, life, AD&D, automobile, home and pet insurance; domestic partner benefits; flexible spending accounts; paid holidays; and a 401(k). The firm has been listed in Fortune magazine's 100 Best Companies to Work For, and noted by the Great Place to Work Institute.

FINANCIAL DATA: Note: Data for latest year may not have been available at press time.

In U.S. $	2016	2015	2014	2013	2012	2011
Revenue	43,692,900,000	43,260,000,000	41,197,513,000	38,394,700,000	33,556,967,000	
R&D Expense						
Operating Income						
Operating Margin %						
SGA Expense						
Net Income	155,231,879	152,378,099	219,621,273	94,128,328	409,015,739	
Operating Cash Flow						
Capital Expenditure						
EBITDA						
Return on Assets %						
Return on Equity %						
Debt to Equity						

CONTACT INFORMATION:

Phone: 201-573-0600   Fax: 201-573-0117
Toll-Free: 800-367-6372
Address: 303 Perimeter Ctr. N., Atlanta, GA 30346 United States

STOCK TICKER/OTHER:

Stock Ticker: Subsidiary   Exchange:
Employees: 16,000   Fiscal Year Ends: 12/31
Parent Company: Daimler AG

SALARIES/BONUSES:

Top Exec. Salary: $ Bonus: $
Second Exec. Salary: $ Bonus: $

OTHER THOUGHTS:

Estimated Female Officers or Directors: 2
Hot Spot for Advancement for Women/Minorities:

Mercer LLC

NAIC Code: 541612

www.mercer.com

TYPES OF BUSINESS:

Consulting-Human Resources
Investment/Financial Consulting
Health and Benefits Management
Human Capital Consulting
Outsourced Human Resources Services (BPO)
Investment Management
Retirement Plan Administration
Merger/Acquisition Consulting

BRANDS/DIVISIONS/AFFILIATES:

Marsh & McLennan Companies Inc

CONTACTS: Note: Officers with more than one job title may be intentionally listed here more than once.

Julio A. Portalatin, CEO
Ken Haderer, COO
Julio A. Portalatin, Pres.
Helen Shan, CFO
Rian Miller, General Counsel
David Rahill, Pres., Health & Benefits
Phil de Cristo, Pres., Investments
Patricia Milligan, Pres., North America
Orlando Ashford, Pres., Talent
Simon O'Regan, Pres., EuroPac

GROWTH PLANS/SPECIAL FEATURES:

Mercer, LLC, a subsidiary of Marsh & McLennan Companies, Inc., offers a broad range of human resource advice and solutions in 42 countries. The firm divides its services into four categories: health and benefits, wealth and investments, workforce and careers and mergers and acquisitions. Health and benefits include private health exchange, employee benefits, global benefits, health benefits administration and affinity benefits. Wealth and investments include retirement plan administration, defined benefit pension plans, pension risk management, defined contribution plans, employee financial wellness, alternative investments, endowments and foundations and financial intermediary partnerships. Workforce and careers include talent strategy, executive compensation, workforce rewards, talent mobility, human resource transformation and employee communication. Mergers and acquisitions (MA) include M&A due diligence, M&A project management office, post-merger integration and private equity advisory. Mercer provides its solutions and services for those in business roles such as CEOs, boards, CFOs, talent leaders, benefits managers, financial advisors, trustees and fiduciaries and employees; for organizations such as corporations, multinational corporations, endowments and foundations, affinity, public sector, wealth management and private equity; and for industries such as energy, insurance, health care, financial services, higher education and retail. Based in New York, USA, the firm has offices throughout the world, including North America, Latin America, Europe, the Middle East, Africa, Asia-Pacific, Australia and New Zealand.

Employees of the firm receive benefits including medical, dental, life, disability and vision coverage; health club discounts; legal assistance; eldercare; continuing education programs; an employee stock purchase plan; paid vacations; tuition reimbursement; and family resource programs.

FINANCIAL DATA: Note: Data for latest year may not have been available at press time.

In U.S. $	2016	2015	2014	2013	2012	2011
Revenue	4,359,630,000	4,313,000,000	4,350,000,000	4,241,000,000	4,147,000,000	3,782,000,000
R&D Expense						
Operating Income						
Operating Margin %						
SGA Expense						
Net Income						
Operating Cash Flow						
Capital Expenditure						
EBITDA						
Return on Assets %						
Return on Equity %						
Debt to Equity						

CONTACT INFORMATION:

Phone: 212-345-7000   Fax: 212-345-7414
Toll-Free:
Address: 1166 Ave. of the Americas, New York, NY 10036 United States

STOCK TICKER/OTHER:

Stock Ticker: Subsidiary   Exchange:
Employees: 21,000   Fiscal Year Ends: 12/31
Parent Company: Marsh & McLennan Companies Inc

SALARIES/BONUSES:

Top Exec. Salary: $ Bonus: $
Second Exec. Salary: $ Bonus: $

OTHER THOUGHTS:

Estimated Female Officers or Directors: 2
Hot Spot for Advancement for Women/Minorities: Y

Merck & Co Inc

www.merck.com

NAIC Code: 325412

TYPES OF BUSINESS:

Drugs-Diversified
Anti-Infective & Anti-Cancer Drugs
Dermatologicals
Cardiovascular Drugs
Animal Health Products

BRANDS/DIVISIONS/AFFILIATES:

Merck Sharp & Dohme Corp
IOmet Pharma
Afferent Phamaceuticals

CONTACTS: Note: Officers with more than one job title may be intentionally listed here more than once.

Kenneth Frazier, CEO
Rita Karachun, Chief Accounting Officer
Mirian Graddick-Weir, Executive VP, Divisional
Julie Gerberding, Executive VP, Divisional
Robert Davis, Executive VP
Michael Holston, Executive VP
Roger Perlmutter, Executive VP
Richard DeLuca, Executive VP
Sanat Chattopadhyay, Executive VP
Adam Schechter, Executive VP
Adele Ambrose, Other Executive Officer

GROWTH PLANS/SPECIAL FEATURES:

Merck & Co., Inc., known as Merck Sharp & Dohme Corp. outside of the U.S. and Canada, is a global healthcare company that develops and manufactures medicines, vaccines and biologics. The firm operates through four segments: pharmaceutical, animal health, healthcare services and alliances. Pharmaceutical, the company's primary segment, markets human health pharmaceutical and vaccine products either directly or through joint ventures. Merck & Co. markets and develops human health pharmaceutical products for the treatment of bone, respiratory, dermatology, immunology, cardiovascular, diabetes, obesity, infectious disease, neurological, ophthalmology and oncology conditions. These products are sold primarily to drug wholesalers and retailers, hospitals, government agencies and managed healthcare providers such as health maintenance organizations (HMOs), pharmacy benefit managers and other institutions. Vaccine products are primarily sold to physicians, wholesalers, physician distributors and government entities. This segment also offers certain women's health products, including contraceptives and fertility treatments. The animal health segment offers vaccine, anti-infective and anti-parasitic products for disease prevention, treatment and control in farm and companion animals. The healthcare services segment provides services and solutions that focus on engagement, health analytics and clinical services to improve the value of care delivered to patients. The alliances segment consists of revenue derived from the company's relationship with AstraZeneca LP. Merck continues to pursue opportunities for establishing external alliances to complement its internal research capabilities, including research collaborations as well as licensing preclinical and clinical compounds and technology platforms. In 2016, the firm announced two new partnerships: with Quartet Medicine and its small molecule pain treatments, and with Complix in order to investigate intracellular cancer targets; acquired IOmet Pharma; and acquired Afferent Pharmaceuticals.

FINANCIAL DATA: Note: Data for latest year may not have been available at press time.

In U.S. $	2016	2015	2014	2013	2012	2011
Revenue	39,807,000,000	39,498,000,000	42,237,000,000	44,033,000,000	47,267,000,000	48,047,000,000
R&D Expense	10,124,000,000	6,704,000,000	7,180,000,000	7,503,000,000	8,168,000,000	8,467,000,000
Operating Income	6,030,000,000	6,928,000,000	5,670,000,000	6,360,000,000	9,855,000,000	7,670,000,000
Operating Margin %	15.14%	17.54%	13.42%	14.44%	20.84%	15.96%
SGA Expense	9,762,000,000	10,313,000,000	11,606,000,000	11,911,000,000	12,776,000,000	13,733,000,000
Net Income	3,920,000,000	4,442,000,000	11,920,000,000	4,404,000,000	6,168,000,000	6,272,000,000
Operating Cash Flow	10,376,000,000	12,421,000,000	7,860,000,000	11,654,000,000	10,022,000,000	12,383,000,000
Capital Expenditure	1,614,000,000	1,283,000,000	2,317,000,000	1,548,000,000	1,954,000,000	1,723,000,000
EBITDA	10,793,000,000	12,448,000,000	24,706,000,000	13,334,000,000	16,431,000,000	15,510,000,000
Return on Assets %	3.97%	4.43%	11.68%	4.15%	5.83%	5.93%
Return on Equity %	9.24%	9.51%	24.22%	8.56%	11.46%	11.49%
Debt to Equity	0.60	0.53	0.38	0.41	0.30	0.28

CONTACT INFORMATION:

Phone: 908 423-1000   Fax: 908 735-1253
Toll-Free:
Address: 2000 Galloping Hill Road, Kenilworth, NJ 07033 United States

STOCK TICKER/OTHER:

Stock Ticker: MRK   Exchange: NYS
Employees: 68,000   Fiscal Year Ends: 12/31
Parent Company:

SALARIES/BONUSES:

Top Exec. Salary: $991,654   Bonus: $1,250,000
Second Exec. Salary: Bonus: $
$1,527,404

OTHER THOUGHTS:

Estimated Female Officers or Directors: 4
Hot Spot for Advancement for Women/Minorities: Y

Sales, profits and employees may be estimates. Financial information, benefits and other data can change quickly and may vary from those stated here.

Mercy
NAIC Code: 622110

TYPES OF BUSINESS:
General Medical and Surgical Hospitals
Outpatient Care
Health Classes
Long-Term Care
Community Service & Outreach

BRANDS/DIVISIONS/AFFILIATES:
IBM Watson Health
Mercy Virtual Care Center
MyMercy
Mercy SafeWatch

CONTACTS: Note: Officers with more than one job title may be intentionally listed here more than once.
Lynn Britton, Pres.
Michael McCurry, Exec.VP
Shannon Sock, Exec. VP
Donn Sorensen, Regional Pres., East Communities
Diana Smalley, Regional Pres., West Communities
Shannon Sock, Exec. VP-Organizational Effectiveness
Kim Day, Regional Pres., Central Communities
Donn Sorenson, Exec. VP-Operations

GROWTH PLANS/SPECIAL FEATURES:
Mercy, established in 1986, is one of the largest U.S. health systems, serving millions of people annually. Mercy includes 44 acute care and specialty hospitals (heart, children's, orthopedic and rehabilitation), more than 700 physician practices and outpatient facilities, 40,000 co-workers and more than 2,000 Mercy Clinic physicians in Arkansas, Kansas, Missouri and Oklahoma. It also has outreach ministries in Arkansas, Louisiana, Mississippi and Texas. The Mercy Virtual Care Center monitors patients 24/7/365 using high-speed data and video connections. MyMercy is a free service that allows patients to connect online with their doctors; provides access to their medical information and test results; renew subscriptions; and schedule office appointments as well as schedule e-visits via personal computer, tablet or smartphone. Mercy SafeWatch is an electronic intensive care unit (ICU) that provides 24-hour vigilance to critically-ill patients. As of 2016, Mercy operates as a wholly-owned subsidiary of IBM Watson Health.

The company offers employees medical, dental, vision, life and long-term disability coverage; a retirement program; tuition reimbursement; and a co-worker assistance plan for full- and part-time employees and their immediate family members.

FINANCIAL DATA: Note: Data for latest year may not have been available at press time.

In U.S. $	2016	2015	2014	2013	2012	2011
Revenue	5,000,000,000	5,000,000,000	4,510,184,000	4,380,885,000	4,200,000,000	4,300,000,000
R&D Expense						
Operating Income						
Operating Margin %						
SGA Expense						
Net Income						
Operating Cash Flow						
Capital Expenditure						
EBITDA						
Return on Assets %						
Return on Equity %						
Debt to Equity						

CONTACT INFORMATION:
Phone: 580-371-2592   Fax:
Toll-Free:
Address: 1000 S. Byrd St., Tishomingo, OK 73460 United States

STOCK TICKER/OTHER:
Stock Ticker: Subsidiary   Exchange:
Employees: 40,000   Fiscal Year Ends: 06/30
Parent Company: IBM Watson Health

SALARIES/BONUSES:
Top Exec. Salary: $ Bonus: $
Second Exec. Salary: $ Bonus: $

OTHER THOUGHTS:
Estimated Female Officers or Directors: 10
Hot Spot for Advancement for Women/Minorities: Y

Merrill Lynch & Co Inc

NAIC Code: 523110

www.ml.com

TYPES OF BUSINESS:

Stock Brokerage & Investment Banking
Research Services
Financial Planning Services

BRANDS/DIVISIONS/AFFILIATES:

Bank of America Corporation
Merrill Edge

CONTACTS: *Note: Officers with more than one job title may be intentionally listed here more than once.*

John Thiel, Head-Merrill Lynch Wealth Management
John Hogarty, COO-GWIM
Alexandre Bettamio, CEO-Brazilian Oper.
Manuel Ebner, CEO-Merrill Lynch Capital Markets AG
Brian T. Moynihan, Chmn.

GROWTH PLANS/SPECIAL FEATURES:

Merrill Lynch & Co., Inc., a wholly owned subsidiary of Bank of America Corporation, is a wealth management, capital markets and advisory firm. The firm is one of the largest brokerages in the world, managing over $2 trillion in client assets. The company provides banking, investing, asset management and other financial and risk management products and services to its clients. The company's services include corporate and investment banking services, such as commercial lending, high-yield debt, equity and mergers and acquisitions review; personal wealth management; private banking; and retail brokerage. Merrill Lynch operates in three segments: global wealth and investment management (GWIM), global research and global banking and markets. GWIM primarily provides wealth management services to high-net-worth individuals and institutions, with a focus on retirement plans, philanthropic planning and asset management. This division utilizes Merrill Edge, a self-directing electronic platform that provides clients with access to Merrill Lynch investing and Bank of America banking. GWIM also comprises a fiduciary and special needs group to help caregivers of individuals with special needs ensure a lifetime of financial security. The global research segment informs and supports customer decisions by analyzing prospective companies, hedge funds, mutual funds, pension funds, wealth management funds and other investment targets. The global banking and markets segment services corporations, institutions and government entities with debt underwriting, financing and other banking services.

FINANCIAL DATA: *Note: Data for latest year may not have been available at press time.*

In U.S. $	2016	2015	2014	2013	2012	2011
Revenue	16,000,000,000	14,898,000,000	15,256,000,000	14,771,000,000	13,800,000,000	13,500,000,000
R&D Expense						
Operating Income						
Operating Margin %						
SGA Expense						
Net Income			2,465,000,000	2,469,000,000	1,876,000,000	1,270,000,000
Operating Cash Flow						
Capital Expenditure						
EBITDA						
Return on Assets %						
Return on Equity %						
Debt to Equity						

CONTACT INFORMATION:

Phone: 212-449-1000   Fax: 212-449-9418
Toll-Free: 800-637-7455
Address: 250 Vesey St., 4 World Financial Center, New York, NY 10080
United States

STOCK TICKER/OTHER:

Stock Ticker: Subsidiary   Exchange:
Employees: 52,000   Fiscal Year Ends: 12/31
Parent Company: Bank of America Corporation

SALARIES/BONUSES:

Top Exec. Salary: $ Bonus: $
Second Exec. Salary: $ Bonus: $

OTHER THOUGHTS:

Estimated Female Officers or Directors: 2
Hot Spot for Advancement for Women/Minorities:

Microsoft Corporation

NAIC Code: 0

www.microsoft.com

TYPES OF BUSINESS:

Computer Software, Operating Systems, Languages & Development Tools
Enterprise Software
Game Consoles
Operating Systems
Software as a Service (SAAS)
Search Engine and Advertising
E-Mail Services
Instant Messaging

BRANDS/DIVISIONS/AFFILIATES:

Office 365
Dynamics
SQL
Windows
Visual Studio
Azure

CONTACTS: *Note: Officers with more than one job title may be intentionally listed here more than once.*

Satya Nadella, CEO
Amy Hood, CFO
John Thompson, Chairman of the Board
Frank Brod, Chief Accounting Officer
William Gates, Co-Founder
Kathleen Hogan, Executive VP, Divisional
Margaret Johnson, Executive VP, Divisional
Christopher Capossela, Executive VP
Jean-Philippe Courtois, Executive VP
Bradford Smith, Other Executive Officer

GROWTH PLANS/SPECIAL FEATURES:

Microsoft Corporation develops, license and supports software products, services and devices. It is a technology company that builds best-in-class platforms and productivity services for a mobile-first, cloud-first world. The firm's products include operating systems; cross-device productivity applications; server applications; business solution applications; desktop and server management tools; software development tools; video games; and training and certification of computer system integrators and developers. Microsoft also designs, manufactures and sells devices such as personal computers (PCs), tablets, gaming and entertainment consoles, phones, other intelligent devices and related accessories that integrate with its cloud-based offerings. The company operates its business in two segments: productivity and business processes, which consists of products and services in its portfolio of productivity, communication and information services through its devices and platforms; and intelligent cloud, which consists of the company's public, private and hybrid server products and cloud services that can power modern businesses. Products offered through the productivity and business processes segment include Office 365 and Dynamics. Products offered through the intelligent cloud segment include SQL servers, Windows servers, Visual Studio, system centers and Azure, as well as enterprise and consulting services. In 2016, the firm sold its entry-level phone business.

Microsoft offers its employees health, dental and vision coverage; onsite health screenings; adoption assistance; childcare service discounts; a 401(k) plan; an employee stock purchase plan; and tuition assistance.

FINANCIAL DATA: *Note: Data for latest year may not have been available at press time.*

In U.S. $	2016	2015	2014	2013	2012	2011
Revenue	85,320,000,000	93,580,000,000	86,833,000,000	77,849,000,000	73,723,000,000	
R&D Expense	11,988,000,000	12,046,000,000	11,381,000,000	10,411,000,000	9,811,000,000	
Operating Income	20,182,000,000	18,161,000,000	27,759,000,000	26,764,000,000	21,763,000,000	
Operating Margin %	23.65%	19.40%	31.96%	34.37%	29.51%	
SGA Expense	19,260,000,000	20,324,000,000	20,632,000,000	20,425,000,000	18,426,000,000	
Net Income	16,798,000,000	12,193,000,000	22,074,000,000	21,863,000,000	16,978,000,000	
Operating Cash Flow	33,325,000,000	29,080,000,000	32,231,000,000	28,833,000,000	31,626,000,000	
Capital Expenditure	8,343,000,000	5,944,000,000	5,485,000,000	4,257,000,000	2,305,000,000	
EBITDA	27,616,000,000	25,245,000,000	33,629,000,000	31,236,000,000	25,614,000,000	
Return on Assets %	9.08%	6.99%	14.02%	16.58%	14.76%	
Return on Equity %	22.09%	14.35%	26.16%	30.09%	27.50%	
Debt to Equity	0.56	0.34	0.22	0.15	0.16	

CONTACT INFORMATION:

Phone: 425 882-8080   Fax: 425 936-7329
Toll-Free: 800-642-7676
Address: One Microsoft Way, Redmond, WA 98052 United States

STOCK TICKER/OTHER:

Stock Ticker: MSFT   Exchange: NAS
Employees: 124,000   Fiscal Year Ends: 06/30
Parent Company:

SALARIES/BONUSES:

Top Exec. Salary: $1,200,000   Bonus: $4,464,000
Second Exec. Salary: Bonus: $2,384,000
$866,667

OTHER THOUGHTS:

Estimated Female Officers or Directors: 4
Hot Spot for Advancement for Women/Minorities: Y

Middleby Corporation (The)

www.middleby.com

NAIC Code: 333318

TYPES OF BUSINESS:

Commercial Kitchen Equipment

BRANDS/DIVISIONS/AFFILIATES:

Blodgett
Bloomfield
CTX
Carter-Hoffman
FriFri
Toastmaster
Alkar
RapidPak

CONTACTS: *Note: Officers with more than one job title may be intentionally listed here more than once.*

Martin Lindsay, Assistant Secretary
Selim Bassoul, CEO
Timothy Fitzgerald, CFO
David Brewer, COO, Divisional

GROWTH PLANS/SPECIAL FEATURES:

The Middleby Corporation is engaged in the design, manufacture, marketing, distribution and service of a line of cooking and warming equipment. The company conducts its business through three main business segments: commercial foodservice equipment (CFE), food processing equipment (FPE) and residential kitchen equipment (RKE). CFE has a broad portfolio of brands and cooking and warming equipment, which enable it to serve virtually any cooking or warming application within a commercial restaurant or institutional kitchen. This equipment is used across all types of foodservice operations, including quick-service restaurants, full-service restaurants, convenience stores, retail outlets, hotels and other institutions. Brands include Blodgett, Bloomfield, CTX, Carter-Hoffmann, FriFri, Lang, MagiKitch'n, Middleby Marshall, Southbend, Star, Toastmaster and Wells. FPE provides an array of products designed for the food processing industry. Products include cooking equipment, including batch ovens, belt ovens and convey cooking systems marketed under the Alkar brand; food preparation equipment, such as breading, battering, mixing, forming and slicing machines, marketed under the MP Equipment brand; and packaging and food safety equipment marketed under the RapidPak brand. RKE manufactures, sells and distributes kitchen equipment for the residential market. Its products include ranges, ovens, refrigerators, dishwashers, microwaves, cooktops and outdoor equipment sold under the Brigade, Jade, TurboChef, U-Line and Viking brands. During 2017, the firm acquired Buford Corporation, a manufacturer of industrial baking equipment; Sveba Dahlen Group, a developer and manufacturer of ovens and baking equipment for the commercial foodservice and industrial baking industries; and CVP Systems, a manufacturer of high-speed packaging systems for the meat processing industry.

FINANCIAL DATA: *Note: Data for latest year may not have been available at press time.*

In U.S. $	2016	2015	2014	2013	2012	2011
Revenue	2,267,852,000	1,826,598,000	1,636,538,000	1,428,685,000	1,038,174,000	855,907,000
R&D Expense						
Operating Income	446,225,000	302,603,000	300,432,000	244,462,000	188,084,000	148,710,000
Operating Margin %	19.67%	16.56%	18.35%	17.11%	18.11%	17.37%
SGA Expense	444,431,000	375,148,000	346,672,000	305,549,000	214,905,000	195,427,000
Net Income	284,216,000	191,610,000	193,312,000	153,928,000	120,697,000	95,473,000
Operating Cash Flow	294,110,000	249,592,000	233,882,000	146,158,000	128,346,000	130,393,000
Capital Expenditure	24,817,000	22,362,000	13,143,000	19,640,000	7,652,000	7,840,000
EBITDA	503,419,000	352,208,000	337,634,000	284,846,000	210,581,000	168,659,000
Return on Assets %	10.01%	7.93%	9.95%	10.04%	10.09%	9.45%
Return on Equity %	23.37%	17.63%	20.95%	20.68%	20.79%	20.40%
Debt to Equity	0.57	0.62	0.58	0.68	0.39	

CONTACT INFORMATION:

Phone: 847 741-3300   Fax:
Toll-Free:
Address: 1400 Toastmaster Dr., Elgin, IL United States

STOCK TICKER/OTHER:

Stock Ticker: MIDD
Employees: 8,026
Parent Company:

Exchange: NAS
Fiscal Year Ends: 12/31

SALARIES/BONUSES:

Top Exec. Salary: $1,000,000   Bonus: $
Second Exec. Salary: $600,000   Bonus: $

OTHER THOUGHTS:

Estimated Female Officers or Directors:
Hot Spot for Advancement for Women/Minorities:

Modine Manufacturing Company

www.modine.com

NAIC Code: 336300

TYPES OF BUSINESS:

Automobile Parts Manufacturer
Heat Exchangers & Systems
Oil Cores
Electronics Cooling
Heating & Air Conditioning Products
Radiator Cores
Fuel Cells

BRANDS/DIVISIONS/AFFILIATES:

Luvata Heat Transfer Solutions Inc

CONTACTS: Note: Officers with more than one job title may be intentionally listed here more than once.

Thomas Burke, CEO
Michael Lucareli, CFO
Thomas Marry, COO
Margaret Kelsey, General Counsel
Scott Bowser, Vice President, Divisional
Scott Miller, Vice President, Divisional
Dennis Appel, Vice President, Divisional
Matthew McBurney, Vice President, Divisional
Holger Schwab, Vice President, Geographical
Scott Wollenberg, Vice President, Geographical

GROWTH PLANS/SPECIAL FEATURES:

Modine Manufacturing Company is a worldwide leader in thermal management technology. The firm serves the vehicular; industrial; commercial; fuel cell; and building heating, ventilating, air conditioning and refrigeration (HVAC&R) markets. Modine develops, produces and markets thermal management products, components and systems such as radiators, stainless steel heat exchangers, charge air coolers, exhaust gas recirculation (EGR) coolers and oil coolers. Its primary customers are original equipment manufacturers (OEMs) in various industries, including the commercial truck, bus and specialty vehicle markets; the firm also caters to construction contractors and wholesalers of plumbing and heating equipment. Modine is organized into four segments: Americas (North and South), Asia, Europe and building HVAC. The three geographic units represent the company's original equipment segments and serve the commercial vehicle, off-highway and automotive markets. These divisions sell radiators, charge-air-coolers, heat exchangers, EGR coolers, fan shrouds, engine oil coolers, fuel coolers, intake air coolers and HVAC system modules such as condensers, evaporators and heater cores. The firm's building HVAC segment includes unit heaters such as gas-fired, hydronic, electric and oil-fired; duct furnaces, both indoor and outdoor; infrared units, both high- and low-intensity; hydronic products, including commercial fin-tube radiation, cabinet unit heaters and convectors; roof-mounted direct- and indirect-fired makeup air units; commercial packaged rooftop ventilation units; unit ventilators; single packaged vertical units; geothermal and water-source heat pumps; precision air conditioning units for data center applications; air-handling units; chillers; ceiling cassettes; and condensing units. In November 2016, the firm acquired Luvata Heat Transfer Solutions, Inc., a global supplier of coils, coolers and coatings.

Modine offers employees medical benefits, educational assistance, retirement plans, life insurance and flexible spending accounts.

FINANCIAL DATA: Note: Data for latest year may not have been available at press time.

In U.S. $	2016	2015	2014	2013	2012	2011
Revenue	1,352,500,000	1,496,400,000	1,477,600,000	1,376,000,000	1,577,152,000	
R&D Expense						
Operating Income	-7,500,000	52,700,000	37,200,000	-600,000	67,524,000	
Operating Margin %	-.55%	3.52%	2.51%	-.04%	4.28%	
SGA Expense	204,500,000	184,500,000	181,700,000	166,300,000	189,046,000	
Net Income	-1,600,000	21,800,000	130,400,000	-24,200,000	38,461,000	
Operating Cash Flow	72,400,000	63,500,000	104,500,000	48,800,000	45,758,000	
Capital Expenditure	62,800,000	58,300,000	53,100,000	49,800,000	64,352,000	
EBITDA	51,400,000	104,500,000	94,500,000	55,400,000	118,084,000	
Return on Assets %	-.17%	2.22%	14.08%	-2.82%	4.24%	
Return on Equity %	-.43%	5.58%	37.76%	-8.19%	11.18%	
Debt to Equity	0.33	0.36	0.30	0.49	0.43	

CONTACT INFORMATION:

Phone: 262 636-1200   Fax: 262 636-1424
Toll-Free:
Address: 1500 DeKoven Ave., Racine, WI 53403 United States

STOCK TICKER/OTHER:

Stock Ticker: MOD   Exchange: NYS
Employees: 11,200   Fiscal Year Ends: 02/28
Parent Company:

SALARIES/BONUSES:

Top Exec. Salary: $917,869   Bonus: $
Second Exec. Salary: Bonus: $
$530,538

OTHER THOUGHTS:

Estimated Female Officers or Directors: 4
Hot Spot for Advancement for Women/Minorities: Y

Mohawk Industries Inc

www.mohawkind.com

NAIC Code: 314110

TYPES OF BUSINESS:

Floor Covering Stores
Tile & Stone Products
Extrusion
Laminate Flooring Technology
Roofing Systems

BRANDS/DIVISIONS/AFFILIATES:

Mohawk Carpet Distribution Inc
Dal-Tile Corporation
Unilin BVBA
Aladdin
Pergo
American Olean
Marazzi
Quick-Step

CONTACTS: *Note: Officers with more than one job title may be intentionally listed here more than once.*

Jeffrey Lorberbaum, CEO
Frank Boykin, CFO
James Brunk, Chief Accounting Officer
W. Wellborn, COO
Rodney Patton, General Counsel
Brian Carson, President, Divisional
John Turner, President, Divisional
Bernard Thiers, President, Subsidiary

GROWTH PLANS/SPECIAL FEATURES:

Mohawk Industries, Inc. is a leading producer of floor-covering products for residential and commercial applications in the U.S. and residential applications in Europe. Its primary subsidiaries are Mohawk Carpet Distribution, Inc.; Dal-Tile Corporation; and Unilin BVBA. Mohawk's operating segments include flooring NA, global ceramic, and flooring ROW. The flooring NA segment designs, manufactures, sources, distributes and markets its carpet and rug product line in a broad range of colors, textures and patterns. It also markets and distributes ceramic tile, laminate, hardwood, resilient floor covering, carpet pad and flooring accessories. Its brands include Aladdin, Bigelow, Karastan, Horizon, IVC, Pergo, Quickstep, Portico and SmartStrand. It sells through independent floor covering retailers, home centers, mass merchandisers, department stores, shop at home, buying groups, commercial dealers and commercial end users. The global ceramic segment designs, manufactures, sources, distributes and markets a broad line of ceramic tile, porcelain tile and natural stone products. Its brands include American Olean, Dal-Tile, Marazzi, Kerama Marazzi, KAI, Ragno and Mohawk Tile. The flooring ROW segment designs, manufactures, sources, licenses, distributes and markets laminate and hardwood flooring. This segment also licenses certain patents related to laminate flooring installation. Its brands include IVC, Moduleo, Quickstep, Pergo and Magnum brands. In Europe, the laminate and wood segment also produces roofing elements, insulation boards, medium-density fiberboard, chipboards and other wood products. Subsidiary Pergo is a manufacturer of laminate flooring in the U.S. and Europe.

FINANCIAL DATA: *Note: Data for latest year may not have been available at press time.*

In U.S. $	2016	2015	2014	2013	2012	2011
Revenue	8,959,087,000	8,071,563,000	7,803,446,000	7,348,754,000	5,787,980,000	5,642,258,000
R&D Expense						
Operating Income	1,279,943,000	837,566,000	772,796,000	546,931,000	379,508,000	315,542,000
Operating Margin %	14.28%	10.37%	9.90%	7.44%	6.55%	5.59%
SGA Expense	1,532,882,000	1,573,120,000	1,381,396,000	1,373,878,000	1,110,550,000	1,101,337,000
Net Income	930,362,000	615,302,000	531,965,000	348,786,000	250,258,000	173,922,000
Operating Cash Flow	1,327,553,000	911,873,000	662,188,000	525,163,000	587,590,000	300,993,000
Capital Expenditure	672,125,000	503,657,000	561,804,000	366,550,000	208,294,000	275,573,000
EBITDA	1,691,139,000	1,182,594,000	1,107,668,000	846,688,000	659,498,000	599,225,000
Return on Assets %	9.22%	6.75%	6.34%	4.71%	4.00%	2.82%
Return on Equity %	17.50%	13.27%	11.98%	8.52%	7.01%	5.20%
Debt to Equity	0.19	0.24	0.31	0.47	0.35	0.35

CONTACT INFORMATION:

Phone: 706 629-7721   Fax: 706 625-3851
Toll-Free: 800-241-4494
Address: 160 S. Industrial Blvd., Calhoun, GA 30701 United States

STOCK TICKER/OTHER:

Stock Ticker: MHK
Employees: 37,800
Parent Company:

Exchange: NYS
Fiscal Year Ends: 12/31

SALARIES/BONUSES:

Top Exec. Salary: $1,142,473   Bonus: $
Second Exec. Salary: $987,186   Bonus: $

OTHER THOUGHTS:

Estimated Female Officers or Directors: 1
Hot Spot for Advancement for Women/Minorities:

Molex LLC

NAIC Code: 334417

TYPES OF BUSINESS:

Electronic Connector Manufacturing
Transportation Products
Commercial Products
Micro Products
Automation & Electrical Products
Integrated Products
Global Sales & Marketing Organization

BRANDS/DIVISIONS/AFFILIATES:

Koch Industries Inc
Woodhead
Phillips-Medisize Corporation

CONTACTS: *Note: Officers with more than one job title may be intentionally listed here more than once.*

Martin P. Slark, CEO
Liam McCarthy, COO
David D. Johnson, CFO
Graham C. Brock, Pres., Global Sales & Mktg.
Ana G. Rodriguez, Sr. VP-Global Human Resources
Gary J. Matula, CIO
Robert J. Zeitler, General Counsel
Tim Ruff, Sr. VP-Bus. Dev. & Corp. Strategy
David D. Johnson, Treas.
John H. Krehbiel, Jr., Co-Chmn.
Junichi Kaji, Pres., Global Mirco Prod. Div.
J. Michael Nauman, Pres., Global Integrated Prod. Div.
Joseph Nelligan, Pres., Commercial Prod. Division

GROWTH PLANS/SPECIAL FEATURES:

Molex, LLC, a subsidiary of Koch Industries, Inc., is a manufacturer of electronic components. It designs, manufactures and sells more than 100,000 products, including terminals, connectors, planar cables, cable assemblies, interconnection systems, backplanes, integrated products and mechanical and electronic switches. The company also provides manufacturing services to integrate specific components into a customer's product. The firm's products are sold primarily within seven markets: IT, telecommunications, consumer, industrial, automotive, mobile devices and other. In the IT market, Molex develops signal, power and optical connectors and cables for usage in desktop computers, personal computers, mobile devices and peripheral equipment. The telecommunications division produces products such as backplane connector systems, optical signal products and transmission equipment. The consumer segment specializes in micro-miniature connector engineering, high wattage products and cable and wire application equipment. This unit manufactures the world's smallest connectors for audio players, DVD players and video cameras as well as products for large computer game facilities and machines. The firm's industrial products include network interface cards, cord sets and software for industrial networks. The Woodhead electrical solutions product line is designed to increase worker safety. Automotive products are designed for use in all automobile systems, including infotainment and navigation, powertrain and safety. The mobile devices division produces connectors for mobile phones, tablets and notebook computers. Other offerings include products such as connectors and integrated systems for the military and medical industries. This includes the Solid State Lighting market, which focuses on developing products for general illumination purposes. The firm operates 50 manufacturing facilities in 18 countries throughout the Americas, Asia Pacific and Europe. In October 2016, the firm acquired Phillips-Medisize Corporation, and will operate as an indirect subsidiary of Molex.

FINANCIAL DATA: *Note: Data for latest year may not have been available at press time.*

In U.S. $	2016	2015	2014	2013	2012	2011
Revenue	4,000,000,000	3,900,000,000	3,862,540,000	3,620,446,976	3,489,189,120	3,587,333,888
R&D Expense						
Operating Income						
Operating Margin %						
SGA Expense						
Net Income			260,189,372	243,623,008	281,376,992	298,808,000
Operating Cash Flow						
Capital Expenditure						
EBITDA						
Return on Assets %						
Return on Equity %						
Debt to Equity						

CONTACT INFORMATION:

Phone: 630 969-4550   Fax: 630 969-1352
Toll-Free: 800-786-6539
Address: 2222 Wellington Court, Lisle, IL 60532-1682 United States

STOCK TICKER/OTHER:

Stock Ticker: Subsidiary   Exchange:
Employees: 35,983   Fiscal Year Ends: 06/30
Parent Company: Koch Industries Inc

SALARIES/BONUSES:

Top Exec. Salary: $ Bonus: $
Second Exec. Salary: $ Bonus: $

OTHER THOUGHTS:

Estimated Female Officers or Directors: 2
Hot Spot for Advancement for Women/Minorities:

Molina Healthcare Inc

www.molinahealthcare.com

NAIC Code: 524114

TYPES OF BUSINESS:

HMO-Low Income Patients
Medicaid HMO
SCHIP HMO

BRANDS/DIVISIONS/AFFILIATES:

Molina Medicaid Solutions
Universal American's Total Care Medicaid

CONTACTS: *Note: Officers with more than one job title may be intentionally listed here more than once.*

Dale Wolf, Chairman of the Board
Terry Bayer, COO
Jeff Barlow, Other Executive Officer
Joseph White, Treasurer

GROWTH PLANS/SPECIAL FEATURES:

Molina Healthcare, Inc. is a multi-stage managed care organization participating in government-sponsored health care programs for low-income persons, such as the Medicaid program and Children's Health Insurance Program (CHIP, including Perinatal). The company also focuses on a small number of persons who are dually eligible under the Medicaid and Medicare programs. Molina operates in two segments: health plans and Molina Medicaid Solutions. Health plans consists of operational health plans in 12 states and Molina's direct delivery business. The health plans are operated by the firm's wholly-owned subsidiaries in those states, each of which is licensed as a health maintenance organization (HMO). Molina Medicaid Solutions provides design, development, implementation and business process outsourcing (BPO) solutions to state governments for their Medicaid management information systems (MMIS). MMIS is a core tool used to support the administration of state Medicaid and other health care entitlement programs. Molina Medicaid currently holds MMIS contracts in Idaho, Louisiana, Maine, New Jersey, West Virginia and the U.S. Virgin Islands; and also holds a contract to provide pharmacy rebate administration services for the Florida Medicaid program. In August 2016, the firm acquired the Universal American's Total Care Medicaid plan from Universal American Corp., adding approximately 38,000 Total Care Medicaid members to Molina Healthcare. Happening in the month, Molina Healthcare agreed to acquire certain Medicaid Advantage assets from both Aetna, Inc. and Humana, Inc.

Molina offers employees medical, dental and vision plans; life insurance; disability; employee assistance; flexible spending accounts; 401(k); and an employee stock purchase plan.

FINANCIAL DATA: *Note: Data for latest year may not have been available at press time.*

In U.S. $	2016	2015	2014	2013	2012	2011
Revenue	17,782,000,000	14,178,000,000	9,666,601,000	6,588,934,000	6,028,763,000	4,769,940,000
R&D Expense						
Operating Income	306,000,000	387,000,000	192,917,000	136,560,000	35,473,000	80,173,000
Operating Margin %	1.72%	2.72%	1.99%	2.07%	.58%	1.68%
SGA Expense	1,610,000,000	1,303,000,000	853,284,000	665,996,000	532,627,000	415,932,000
Net Income	52,000,000	143,000,000	62,223,000	52,929,000	9,790,000	20,818,000
Operating Cash Flow	673,000,000	1,125,000,000	1,060,257,000	190,083,000	347,784,000	225,395,000
Capital Expenditure	176,000,000	132,000,000	114,934,000	98,049,000	78,145,000	60,581,000
EBITDA	488,000,000	514,000,000	326,519,000	227,083,000	114,598,000	154,556,000
Return on Assets %	.74%	2.58%	1.66%	2.14%	.54%	1.31%
Return on Equity %	3.24%	11.13%	6.53%	6.31%	1.27%	2.82%
Debt to Equity	0.71	0.74	0.89	0.67	0.33	0.31

CONTACT INFORMATION:

Phone: 562 435-3666   Fax: 562 499-0790
Toll-Free: 888-562-5442
Address: 200 Oceangate, Ste. 100, Long Beach, CA 90802 United States

STOCK TICKER/OTHER:

Stock Ticker: MOH
Employees: 21,000
Parent Company:

Exchange: NYS
Fiscal Year Ends: 12/31

SALARIES/BONUSES:

Top Exec. Salary: $1,170,000   Bonus: $
Second Exec. Salary: $878,000   Bonus: $

OTHER THOUGHTS:

Estimated Female Officers or Directors: 2
Hot Spot for Advancement for Women/Minorities: Y

Sales, profits and employees may be estimates. Financial information, benefits and other data can change quickly and may vary from those stated here.

Monro Muffler Brake Inc

www.monro.com

NAIC Code: 811100

TYPES OF BUSINESS:

Automotive Repair & Maintenance
Under-Car Repair Services
Inspection Services
Tires

BRANDS/DIVISIONS/AFFILIATES:

Monro Service Corporation
Car-X LLC
Monro Muffler Brake & Service
Tread Quarters Discount tire
Mr Tire
Autotire Car Care Center
Ken Towery's Tire & Auto Care
McGee Tire

CONTACTS: *Note: Officers with more than one job title may be intentionally listed here more than once.*

John Van Heel, CEO
Brian DAmbrosia, CFO
Robert Gross, Chairman of the Board
Christopher Hoornbeck, President, Subsidiary
Maureen Mulholland, Secretary
Craig Hoyle, Senior VP, Divisional
Raymond Pickens, Vice President, Divisional
John Lamb, Vice President, Divisional

GROWTH PLANS/SPECIAL FEATURES:

Monro Muffler Brake, Inc. operates through a chain of 1,118 company-operated stores, 114 franchised locations, five wholesale locations, two retread facilities and 14 dealer-operated stores, providing automotive under-car repair and tire services in 27 U.S. states. These stores are typically located in high-visibility locations in suburban areas and small towns, and operate under the names Monro Muffler Brake & Service, Tread Quarters Discount Tire, Mr. Tire, Autotire Car Care Center, Tire Warehouse, Tire Barn Warehouse, Ken Towery's Tire & Auto Care, The Tire Choice, Car-X and McGee Tire. The firm's stores service approximately 5.9 million vehicles annually. Monro provides a range of services on passenger cars, light trucks and vans for brakes; mufflers and exhaust systems; and steering, drive train, suspension and wheel alignment. Other products and services offered by the company include tires and routine maintenance services, such as state inspections. It specializes in the repair and replacement of parts that must be periodically replaced due to normal wear and tear. Typically, the firm does not perform under-the-hood repair, except for oil change services, heating and cooling system flush and fill services and some minor tune-ups. Monro operates two subsidiaries: Monro Service Corporation, which provides purchasing, distribution, merchandising, advertising, accounting and other store support functions; and Car-X, LLC, which operates as a franchisor, with 113 Car-X franchised locations.

Monro offers its employees Automotive Service Excellence (ASE) certification reimbursement; recreational discounts; an employee assistance program; tool insurance; and medical, dental, life and disability insurance.

FINANCIAL DATA: *Note: Data for latest year may not have been available at press time.*

In U.S. $	2016	2015	2014	2013	2012	2011
Revenue	943,651,000	894,492,000	831,432,000	731,997,000	686,552,000	
R&D Expense						
Operating Income	120,589,000	109,789,000	95,347,000	73,705,000	91,416,000	
Operating Margin %	12.77%	12.27%	11.46%	10.06%	13.31%	
SGA Expense	265,114,000	243,561,000	224,627,000	204,442,000	184,981,000	
Net Income	66,805,000	61,799,000	54,459,000	42,567,000	54,612,000	
Operating Cash Flow	126,504,000	126,349,000	93,943,000	84,436,000	82,626,000	
Capital Expenditure	36,834,000	34,750,000	32,150,000	34,185,000	28,556,000	
EBITDA	160,358,000	145,510,000	127,035,000	101,205,000	115,497,000	
Return on Assets %	6.95%	7.41%	7.40%	6.96%	11.35%	
Return on Equity %	13.14%	13.89%	13.94%	12.29%	17.97%	
Debt to Equity	0.50	0.53	0.44	0.51	0.15	

CONTACT INFORMATION:

Phone: 585-647-6400   Fax: 585-647-0945
Toll-Free:
Address: 200 Holleder Pkwy., Rochester, NY 14615 United States

STOCK TICKER/OTHER:

Stock Ticker: MNRO   Exchange: NAS
Employees: 7,535   Fiscal Year Ends: 03/31
Parent Company:

SALARIES/BONUSES:

Top Exec. Salary: $550,000   Bonus: $
Second Exec. Salary: Bonus: $150,000
$270,000

OTHER THOUGHTS:

Estimated Female Officers or Directors: 1
Hot Spot for Advancement for Women/Minorities:

Moody's Corporation

NAIC Code: 561450

TYPES OF BUSINESS:

Credit Bureau
Credit Risk Assessment Products & Services
Credit Processing Software
Credit Training Services

BRANDS/DIVISIONS/AFFILIATES:

Korea Investors Service
Euler Hermes Rating GmbH

CONTACTS: *Note: Officers with more than one job title may be intentionally listed here more than once.*

Raymond Mcdaniel, CEO
Michael Crimmins, Chief Accounting Officer
Richard Cantor, Chief Risk Officer
Henry McKinnell, Director
Linda Huber, Executive VP
John Goggins, Executive VP
Robert Fauber, President, Divisional
Mark Almeida, President, Subsidiary
Blair Worrall, Senior VP, Divisional
Lisa Westlake, Senior VP

GROWTH PLANS/SPECIAL FEATURES:

Moody's Corporation is a provider of credit ratings; credit and economic related research, data and analytical tools; risk management software; quantitative credit risk measures, credit portfolio management solutions, training and financial credentialing and certification services; and outsourced research and analytical services to institutional customers. The company maintains offices worldwide. Moody's operates in two segments: Moody's investors service (MIS) and Moody's analytics (MA). MIS publishes rating opinions on a broad range of credit obligors and credit obligations issued in domestic and international markets, including various corporate and governmental obligations, structured finance securities and commercial paper programs. Ratings are distributed via press releases through a variety of print and electronic media, including the internet and other real-time information systems used by securities traders and investors. MIS has ratings relationships with approximately 11,000 corporate issuers and approximately 18,000 public finance issuers. Additionally, the company has rated and currently monitors ratings on approximately 64,000 structured finance obligations. MA offers a range of products that support the risk management activities of institutional participants in global financial markets. These products and services include in-depth research on major debt issuers, industry studies and commentary on topical credit related events as well as economic research, credit data and analytical tools such as quantitative credit risk scores. MA's customers represent more than 4,600 institutions worldwide operating in approximately 145 countries. During 2016, Moody's research website was accessed by over 258,000 individuals, including 36,000 client users. In 2016, the firm acquired Korea Investors Service, a provider of domestic credit ratings; and an approximate 5% stake in Euler Hermes Rating GmbH, a ratings agency that provides credit ratings for small- and medium-sized enterprises across Europe.

FINANCIAL DATA: *Note: Data for latest year may not have been available at press time.*

In U.S. $	2016	2015	2014	2013	2012	2011
Revenue	3,604,200,000	3,484,500,000	3,334,300,000	2,972,500,000	2,730,300,000	2,280,700,000
R&D Expense						
Operating Income	638,700,000	1,473,400,000	1,439,100,000	1,234,600,000	1,077,400,000	888,400,000
Operating Margin %	17.72%	42.28%	43.16%	41.53%	39.46%	38.95%
SGA Expense	1,800,200,000	921,300,000	869,300,000	822,100,000	752,200,000	629,600,000
Net Income	266,600,000	941,300,000	988,700,000	804,500,000	690,000,000	571,400,000
Operating Cash Flow	1,226,100,000	1,153,600,000	1,018,600,000	926,800,000	823,100,000	803,300,000
Capital Expenditure	115,200,000	89,000,000	74,600,000	42,300,000	45,000,000	67,700,000
EBITDA	833,600,000	1,618,600,000	1,680,800,000	1,360,000,000	1,191,300,000	986,400,000
Return on Assets %	5.10%	19.22%	21.81%	19.25%	20.18%	21.09%
Return on Equity %			1325.33%	222.79%	638.29%	
Debt to Equity				6.23	4.17	

CONTACT INFORMATION:

Phone: 212 553-0300   Fax: 212 553-4820
Toll-Free:
Address: 250 Greenwich St., 7 World Trade Center, New York, NY 10007 United States

STOCK TICKER/OTHER:

Stock Ticker: MCO
Employees: 10,600
Parent Company:

Exchange: NYS
Fiscal Year Ends: 12/31

SALARIES/BONUSES:

Top Exec. Salary: $1,000,000   Bonus: $
Second Exec. Salary: $609,000   Bonus: $

OTHER THOUGHTS:

Estimated Female Officers or Directors: 2
Hot Spot for Advancement for Women/Minorities: Y

Morgan Stanley

NAIC Code: 523110

TYPES OF BUSINESS:

Stock Brokerage/Investment Banking
Institutional Securities
Wealth Management
Asset Management
Bank Holding Company

BRANDS/DIVISIONS/AFFILIATES:

CONTACTS: *Note: Officers with more than one job title may be intentionally listed here more than once.*

James Gorman, CEO
Jonathan Pruzan, CFO
Paul Wirth, Chief Accounting Officer
Keishi Hotsuki, Chief Risk Officer
Jeffrey Brodsky, Executive VP
Eric Grossman, Executive VP
Daniel Simkowitz, Other Corporate Officer
Thomas Kelleher, President

GROWTH PLANS/SPECIAL FEATURES:

Morgan Stanley is a global financial services firm with approximately $1.1 billion in assets under management or supervision and over 1,300 offices in 43 countries. Morgan Stanley provides a wide variety of products and services to a large and diversified group of clients, including corporations, governments, financial institutions and individuals. The firm operates in three business segments: institutional securities, investment management and wealth management. The institutional securities division incorporates activities such as capital raising; financial advisory services, including advice on mergers and acquisitions, restructurings, real estate and project finance; corporate lending; sales, trading, financing and market-making activities in equity and fixed income securities; risk management analytics; research; and investment activities. The investment management division provides global asset management products and services in fixed income; alternative investments, including hedge funds and funds of funds; equity; and merchant banking, which includes real estate, private equity and infrastructure, to institutional clients through proprietary and third-party distribution channels. The wealth management division provides comprehensive financial services to clients through a network of global representatives in more than 600 locations. This segment serves individual investors and small-to-medium sized businesses and institutions with an emphasis on ultra-high net worth, high net worth and affluent investors. Its advisory services cover equities, options, futures, foreign currencies, precious metals, fixed income securities, mutual funds, structured products, alternative investments, unit investment trusts, managed futures and mutual fund asset allocation programs. Wealth management also engages in fixed income principal trading. In October 2016, Morgan Stanley invested in digital human capital management firm, 24 Seven, Inc.

FINANCIAL DATA: *Note: Data for latest year may not have been available at press time.*

In U.S. $	2016	2015	2014	2013	2012	2011
Revenue	34,631,000,000	35,155,000,000	34,275,000,000	32,417,000,000	26,112,000,000	32,403,000,000
R&D Expense						
Operating Income	8,848,000,000	8,495,000,000	3,591,000,000	4,482,000,000	515,000,000	6,114,000,000
Operating Margin %	25.54%	24.16%	10.47%	13.82%	1.97%	18.86%
SGA Expense	18,252,000,000	18,464,000,000	20,117,000,000	18,683,000,000	18,137,000,000	18,820,000,000
Net Income	5,979,000,000	6,127,000,000	3,467,000,000	2,932,000,000	68,000,000	4,110,000,000
Operating Cash Flow	2,447,000,000	3,674,000,000	1,131,000,000	35,553,000,000	24,548,000,000	6,684,000,000
Capital Expenditure	1,276,000,000	1,373,000,000	992,000,000	1,316,000,000	1,312,000,000	1,304,000,000
EBITDA						
Return on Assets %	.68%	.71%	.38%	.32%		.26%
Return on Equity %	8.08%	8.55%	4.94%	4.30%	-.04%	3.82%
Debt to Equity	2.56	2.41	2.54	2.67	3.05	3.38

CONTACT INFORMATION:

Phone: 212 761-4000   Fax: 212 761-0086
Toll-Free:
Address: 1585 Broadway, New York, NY 10036 United States

STOCK TICKER/OTHER:

Stock Ticker: MS
Employees: 55,311
Parent Company:

Exchange: NYS
Fiscal Year Ends: 12/31

SALARIES/BONUSES:

Top Exec. Salary: $1,666,041   Bonus: $10,949,130
Second Exec. Salary: $1,500,000   Bonus: $9,698,750

OTHER THOUGHTS:

Estimated Female Officers or Directors: 3
Hot Spot for Advancement for Women/Minorities: Y

Mutual of Omaha Companies (The)

www.mutualofomaha.com

NAIC Code: 524113

TYPES OF BUSINESS:

Life Insurance
Asset Management
Annuities
Medical & Dental Insurance
Supplemental Health Insurance
IT Services & Consulting

BRANDS/DIVISIONS/AFFILIATES:

Mutual of Omaha Insurance Company
Mutual of Omaha Investor Services Inc
Mutual of Omaha Bank
Mutual of Omaha Mortgage LLC
Wild Kingdom

CONTACTS: Note: Officers with more than one job title may be intentionally listed here more than once.

James T. Blackledge, CEO
Stacy A. Scholtz, Exec.VP-Oper.
David A. Diamond, CFO
Richard Hrabchak, Exec. VP-CIO
Richard C. Anderl, General Counsel
Stacy A. Scholtz, Exec. VP-Corp. Oper.
David A. Diamond, Treas.
Daniel P. Martin, Exec. VP-Group Benefit Svcs.
Michael C. Weekly, Exec. VP-Individual Financial Svcs.
Richard A. Witt, Chief Investment Officer
Kenneth R. Cook, Pres., East Campus Realty
Daniel P. Neary, Chmn.

GROWTH PLANS/SPECIAL FEATURES:

The Mutual of Omaha Companies provide insurance, annuities and asset management products through several affiliated companies. Mutual of Omaha Insurance Company offers insurance products and services, and is licensed nationwide. Products include Medicare supplement insurance, life insurance and employer-based plans. Mutual of Omaha Investor Services, Inc. offers securities and advisory services, and is a registered broker-dealer and FINRA/SIPC (Financial Industry Regulatory Authority/Securities Investor Protection Corporation) member. Each of the firm's underwriting companies are responsible for their own contractual and financial obligations. Mutual of Omaha Bank offers banking services to individuals, businesses and community associations, including bank accounts, bank cards, mortgage lending products, credit lines, wealth management and online/mobile banking, as well as document management. Mutual of Omaha Mortgage, LLC is a joint venture between Mutual of Omaha Bank and PrimeLending Ventures Management and offers a variety of residential lending options and mortgage loan advisory services. Last, Mutual of Omaha's Wild Kingdom is a wildlife program that broadcasts a series on Animal Planet. Its hosts programs, via television and online, that relate to nature and the animal world.

The firm offers employees benefits including medical, dental, vision, life and disability insurance; flexible spending accounts; and a 401(k).

FINANCIAL DATA: Note: Data for latest year may not have been available at press time.

In U.S. $	2016	2015	2014	2013	2012	2011
Revenue	7,898,472,000	7,235,734,000	6,878,021,000	6,602,152,000	6,378,107,000	5,974,057,000
R&D Expense						
Operating Income						
Operating Margin %						
SGA Expense						
Net Income	356,558,000	333,006,000	291,701,000	359,248,000	283,797,000	130,050,000
Operating Cash Flow						
Capital Expenditure						
EBITDA						
Return on Assets %						
Return on Equity %						
Debt to Equity						

CONTACT INFORMATION:

Phone: 402-342-7600   Fax: 402-351-2775
Toll-Free: 800-775-6000
Address: Mutual of Omaha Plz., Omaha, NE 68175 United States

STOCK TICKER/OTHER:

Stock Ticker: Mutual Company   Exchange:
Employees: 5,100   Fiscal Year Ends: 12/31
Parent Company:

SALARIES/BONUSES:

Top Exec. Salary: $ Bonus: $
Second Exec. Salary: $ Bonus: $

OTHER THOUGHTS:

Estimated Female Officers or Directors: 3
Hot Spot for Advancement for Women/Minorities: Y

National Instruments Corporation

NAIC Code: 0

TYPES OF BUSINESS:

Software-Instrumentation
Virtual Instrumentation
Signal Conditioning Hardware
Test & Measurement Software
Motion Control Products
Analysis & Visualization Software
Automation Software
Image Acquisition Products

BRANDS/DIVISIONS/AFFILIATES:

LabVIEW
LabVIEW Real-Time
LabVIEW Communications System Design Suite
LabWindows/CVI and Measurement Studio
LabVIEW for LEGO MINDSTORMS

CONTACTS: Note: Officers with more than one job title may be intentionally listed here more than once.

John Roiko, Chief Accounting Officer
James Truchard, Co-Founder
Jeffrey Kodosky, Co-Founder
Alexander Davern, Director
Eric Starkloff, Executive VP, Divisional
Scott Rust, Senior VP, Divisional

GROWTH PLANS/SPECIAL FEATURES:

National Instruments Corporation (NI) supplies test, measurement and automation products used by engineers and scientists from numerous industries. Its key markets range from the automotive, aerospace, electronics, semiconductors and defense sectors, to the education, government, medical research and telecommunications industries, among others. Products and services include system design software; programming tools; application software; hardware products and related driver software; the Ni education platform, including software and hardware products for teaching; NI services, including hardware services and maintenance; software maintenance services; and training and certification. The company's flagship product is LabVIEW, a system design software for measurement and control. With LabVIEW, users program graphically and can design custom virtual instruments by connecting icons with software wires to create block diagrams, which are natural design notations for scientists and engineers. Users can customize front panels with knobs, buttons, dials and graphs to emulate control panels of instruments or add custom graphics to visually represent the control and operation of processes. Add-on LabVIEW Real-Time enables users to easily configure their application program to execute using a real-time operating system kernel instead of a general purpose operating system. LabVIEW Communications System Design Suite is specifically for wireless prototyping, and also provides a plug-in architecture to offer productive starting points with open application frameworks for LTE, 802.11 and other key standards. LabWindows/CVI and Measurement Studio is designed for alternative programming environments. NI software products are complimentary to LabVIEW. The company's education platform combines software, hardware and courseware designed to create engaging, authentic learning experiences that prepare students for the next generation of innovation. LabVIEW for LEGO MINDSTORMS is used in the development of robotics projects in secondary school.

The company offers employees 401(k), stock purchase and profit sharing plans; health, dental and vision coverage; life and disability insurance; tuition assistance and more.

FINANCIAL DATA: Note: Data for latest year may not have been available at press time.

In U.S. $	2016	2015	2014	2013	2012	2011
Revenue	1,228,179,000	1,225,456,000	1,243,862,000	1,172,558,000	1,143,692,000	1,024,173,000
R&D Expense	235,706,000	225,131,000	227,433,000	234,796,000	222,994,000	199,071,000
Operating Income	119,726,000	137,172,000	145,187,000	98,617,000	116,934,000	112,712,000
Operating Margin %	9.74%	11.19%	11.67%	8.41%	10.22%	11.00%
SGA Expense	559,626,000	546,197,000	553,110,000	535,218,000	523,490,000	471,426,000
Net Income	82,734,000	95,262,000	126,333,000	80,513,000	90,137,000	94,072,000
Operating Cash Flow	195,840,000	162,637,000	195,110,000	169,479,000	132,516,000	169,899,000
Capital Expenditure	78,626,000	68,154,000	73,559,000	67,861,000	102,684,000	71,930,000
EBITDA	193,116,000	210,501,000	215,393,000	166,591,000	175,620,000	162,609,000
Return on Assets %	5.60%	6.54%	9.02%	6.12%	7.39%	8.90%
Return on Equity %	7.53%	8.66%	11.80%	8.20%	10.06%	11.78%
Debt to Equity	0.02	0.03				

CONTACT INFORMATION:

Phone: 512 338-9119   Fax: 512 683-9300
Toll-Free: 800-433-3488
Address: 11500 N. Mopac Expressway, Austin, TX 78759-3504 United States

STOCK TICKER/OTHER:

Stock Ticker: NATI   Exchange: NAS
Employees: 7,552   Fiscal Year Ends: 12/31
Parent Company:

SALARIES/BONUSES:

Top Exec. Salary: $550,000   Bonus: $
Second Exec. Salary: $356,250   Bonus: $

OTHER THOUGHTS:

Estimated Female Officers or Directors: 1
Hot Spot for Advancement for Women/Minorities:

NBCUniversal LLC

www.nbcuni.com

NAIC Code: 515120

TYPES OF BUSINESS:

Television Broadcasting
Online News & Information
TV & Movie Production
Radio Broadcasting
Interactive Online Content
Cable Television Programming
Theme Parks
Film, TV & Home Video Distribution

BRANDS/DIVISIONS/AFFILIATES:

Comcast Corporation
Bravo Media
Weather Channel (The)
NBC Entertainment
Universal Studios Hollywood
Hulu
DreamWorks Animation
Olympic Channel: Home of Team USA

CONTACTS: *Note: Officers with more than one job title may be intentionally listed here more than once.*

Stephen B. Burke, CEO
Anand Kini, CFO
Jeff Shell, Chmn.-Universal Filmed Entertainment
Kimberley D. Harris, General Counsel
Maggie McLean Suniewick, Sr. VP-Strategic Integration
Cameron Blanchard, Exec. VP-Comm.
Patricia Fili-Krushel, Chmn.-NBCUniversal News Group
Robert Greenblatt, Chmn., NBC Entertainment
Bonnie Hammer, Chmn., NBCUniversal Cable Entertainment Group
Ted Harbert, Chmn., NBC Broadcasting
Matt Bond, Chmn.
Kevin MacLellan, Chmn., NBCUniversal Int'l
Matt Bond, Exec. VP-Content Dist.

GROWTH PLANS/SPECIAL FEATURES:

NBCUniversal, LLC is one of the world's largest entertainment and media companies in the development, production and marketing of news, entertainment and information to a global audience. The company is a product of a 2004 merger of Vivendi Universal Entertainment and NBC (National Broadcasting Company). The firm is a wholly owned subsidiary of Comcast Corporation. The firm operates in eight divisions: cable, broadcast, digital, film, parks, local media, TV studios production and international. The cable division includes Bravo Media, chiller, Cloo, CNBC, E! Entertainment, Golf Channel, MSNBC, NBC Sports Network, NBC UNIVERSO, Oxygen Media, Sprout, Spyfy, The Weather Channel Company, Universal HD and USA Network. The broadcast division includes NBC Entertainment, NBC News, NBC Sports, Telemundo and NBC Olympics. The digital division consists of Fandango, GolfNow, Hulu and Seeso. The film division includes Focus Features, Universal Pictures, Universal Pictures International and Universal Pictures Home Entertainment. The parks division includes Universal Orlando Resort, Universal Studios Japan, Universal Studios Singapore and Universal Studios Hollywood. The local media division consists of Cozi TV, NBC Sports Regional Networks, TeleXitos and NBCUniversal-owned television stations. The international division includes CNBC International, NBCUniversal International Television, hayu and CNBC International. The TV studios production division consists of Universal Cable Productions, Telemundo Studios and Universal Television. In August 2016, the firm acquired DreamWorks Animation for $3.8 billion, which now operates as a wholly-owned subsidiary of Comcast-NBCUniversal. That December, NBCUniversal launched a new cable television network focused on Olympic sports, athletes and stores, the Olympic Channel: Home of Team USA.

NBC Universal offers its employees medical, dental, vision and prescription drug coverage; a 401(k) plan; health club discounts; same-sex domestic partner benefits; life insurance; and flexible spending accounts.

FINANCIAL DATA: *Note: Data for latest year may not have been available at press time.*

In U.S. $	2016	2015	2014	2013	2012	2011
Revenue	31,593,000,000	28,462,000,000	25,428,000,000	23,650,000,000	23,812,000,000	20,234,000,000
R&D Expense						
Operating Income						
Operating Margin %						
SGA Expense						
Net Income	4,546,000,000	3,624,000,000	3,297,000,000	2,122,000,000	3,231,000,000	1,836,000,000
Operating Cash Flow						
Capital Expenditure						
EBITDA						
Return on Assets %						
Return on Equity %						
Debt to Equity						

CONTACT INFORMATION:

Phone: 212-664-4444   Fax: 212-664-4085
Toll-Free:
Address: 30 Rockefeller Plaza, New York, NY 10112 United States

STOCK TICKER/OTHER:

Stock Ticker: Subsidiary   Exchange:
Employees: 40,000   Fiscal Year Ends: 12/31
Parent Company: Comcast Corporation

SALARIES/BONUSES:

Top Exec. Salary: $ Bonus: $
Second Exec. Salary: $ Bonus: $

OTHER THOUGHTS:

Estimated Female Officers or Directors: 12
Hot Spot for Advancement for Women/Minorities: Y

NCR Corporation

NAIC Code: 334118

www.ncr.com

TYPES OF BUSINESS:

Computer Manufacturing
Barcode Scanning Equipment
Automatic Teller Machines (ATMs)
Transaction Processing Equipment
Point-of-Sale & Store Automation
Data Warehousing
Printer Consumables

BRANDS/DIVISIONS/AFFILIATES:

Blackstone Group LP (The)

CONTACTS: *Note: Officers with more than one job title may be intentionally listed here more than once.*

William Nuti, CEO
Robert Fishman, CFO
Frederick Marquardt, Executive VP, Divisional
Michael Bayer, Executive VP, Divisional
Paul Langenbahn, Executive VP, Divisional
Robert Ciminera, Executive VP, Divisional
Edward Gallagher, General Counsel
Andrea Ledford, Other Executive Officer
Mark Benjamin, President

GROWTH PLANS/SPECIAL FEATURES:

NCR Corporation is a global technology company that provides information technology and related services to various industries, enabling client companies to interact more efficiently with customers. The company offers financial-oriented self-service technologies, such as ATMs, cash dispensers, self-checkout kiosks and software solutions. Its operations are divided into three operating segments: software, services and hardware. The software segment includes a portfolio of industry-based software applications and application suites for the financial services, retail, hospitality and small business industries. Moreover, the firm offers other industry-oriented software applications including cash management software, video banking software, fraud and loss prevention applications, check and document imaging, remote-deposit capture and customer-facing digital banking applications for the financial services industry; and secure electronic and mobile payment solutions, sector-specific point of sale software applications, and back-office inventory and store and restaurant management applications for the retail and hospitality industries. The services segment provides global end-to-end services solutions including assessment and preparation, staging, installation, implementation, and maintenance and support for its hardware solutions. The firm also provides systems management and complete managed services for its product offerings. In addition, it provides servicing for third party networking products and computer hardware from select manufacturers. The hardware solutions segment includes its suite of financial-oriented self-service ATM-related hardware, and its retail- and hospitality-oriented point of sale terminal, self-checkout kiosk and related hardware. The company also offers other self-service kiosks, such as self-check in kiosks for airlines, and wayfinding solutions for buildings and campuses. In May 2016, NCR completed the sale of its Interactive Printer Solutions (IPS) business to Atlas Holdings LLC for $47 million. In August 2016, the firm launched the NCR Innovation Lab, its new R&D branch, which will focus on cross-functional research for areas of mobile, big-data, cloud, internet, machines and predictive analytics.

FINANCIAL DATA: *Note: Data for latest year may not have been available at press time.*

In U.S. $	2016	2015	2014	2013	2012	2011
Revenue	6,543,000,000	6,373,000,000	6,591,000,000	6,123,000,000	5,730,000,000	5,443,000,000
R&D Expense	242,000,000	230,000,000	263,000,000	203,000,000	219,000,000	177,000,000
Operating Income	599,000,000	135,000,000	353,000,000	666,000,000	232,000,000	65,000,000
Operating Margin %	9.15%	2.11%	5.35%	10.87%	4.04%	1.19%
SGA Expense	926,000,000	1,042,000,000	1,012,000,000	871,000,000	894,000,000	805,000,000
Net Income	270,000,000	-178,000,000	191,000,000	443,000,000	146,000,000	53,000,000
Operating Cash Flow	894,000,000	681,000,000	524,000,000	281,000,000	-294,000,000	351,000,000
Capital Expenditure	227,000,000	229,000,000	258,000,000	226,000,000	160,000,000	163,000,000
EBITDA	893,000,000	386,000,000	602,000,000	865,000,000	390,000,000	230,000,000
Return on Assets %	2.88%	-2.24%	2.28%	6.11%	2.44%	1.06%
Return on Equity %	71.63%	-20.30%	10.49%	29.37%	14.27%	6.30%
Debt to Equity	4.31		1.85	1.87	1.51	1.06

CONTACT INFORMATION:

Phone: 937 445-5000   Fax: 937 445-5541
Toll-Free: 800-225-5627
Address: 3097 Satellite Blvd., Duluth, GA 30096 United States

STOCK TICKER/OTHER:

Stock Ticker: NCR   Exchange: NYS
Employees: 33,500   Fiscal Year Ends: 12/31
Parent Company:

SALARIES/BONUSES:

Top Exec. Salary: $1,000,000   Bonus: $
Second Exec. Salary: $611,539   Bonus: $

OTHER THOUGHTS:

Estimated Female Officers or Directors: 3
Hot Spot for Advancement for Women/Minorities: Y

Sales, profits and employees may be estimates. Financial information, benefits and other data can change quickly and may vary from those stated here.

NetScout Systems Inc

www.netscout.com

NAIC Code: 0

TYPES OF BUSINESS:

Computer Software, Network Management, System Testing & Storage Application Management Solutions

BRANDS/DIVISIONS/AFFILIATES:

Adaptive Service Intelligence
nGeniusONE
InfiniStream

CONTACTS: Note: Officers with more than one job title may be intentionally listed here more than once.

Anil Singhal, CEO
Jean Bua, CFO
Michael Szabados, COO
John Downing, Executive VP, Divisional

GROWTH PLANS/SPECIAL FEATURES:

NetScout Systems, Inc. designs, develops, manufactures, markets, sells and supports a family of products that assures the performance and availability of critical business applications and services in complex, high-speed networks. Powered by NetScout's proprietary Adaptive Service Intelligence technology, its solutions are used to monitor customers' service delivery environment in order to identify performance issues and provide insight into network-based security threats. The firm markets its core service assurance and cybersecurity solutions into two primary markets: enterprise and service provider. Within the enterprise market, NetScout's nGeniusONE and InfiniStream technologies enable IT and government organizations to improve service issues and security threats before they become serious and affect large numbers of users. These products are based on real-time analytic information platforms that can be managed across both virtual and physical environments. The service provider market serves customers categorized into three groups: mobile operators, fixed-line and cable operators, and internet service providers. For mobile operators, NetScout products monitor radio access networks, and provide analytics that present insight into subscriber trends and their customer experiences. For fixed-line and cable operators, products and solutions enable them to monitor and manage their local area WiFi connectivity services as well as broadband and telephone services targeting small- and medium-sized businesses. These products and solutions provide comprehensive insight into IP services, service usage, service availability, application awareness, traffic load, network availability and network performance. Last, for internet service providers, products and solutions help protect their networks against distributed denial of service (DDos) attacks, and assist in rapidly locating and isolating advanced network threats.

FINANCIAL DATA: Note: Data for latest year may not have been available at press time.

In U.S. $	2016	2015	2014	2013	2012	2011
Revenue	955,419,000	453,669,000	396,647,000	350,550,000	308,679,000	
R&D Expense	208,630,000	75,242,000	70,454,000	61,546,000	49,478,000	
Operating Income	-25,550,000	96,773,000	78,014,000	64,529,000	53,683,000	
Operating Margin %	-2.67%	21.33%	19.66%	18.40%	17.39%	
SGA Expense	411,049,000	183,742,000	160,234,000	146,525,000	137,112,000	
Net Income	-28,369,000	61,192,000	49,106,000	40,609,000	32,428,000	
Operating Cash Flow	95,285,000	106,933,000	110,946,000	95,412,000	68,307,000	
Capital Expenditure	30,370,000	12,982,000	14,152,000	11,948,000	11,288,000	
EBITDA	113,961,000	115,447,000	96,884,000	82,491,000	69,326,000	
Return on Assets %	-1.33%	9.58%	8.46%	7.25%	5.92%	
Return on Equity %	-1.97%	14.48%	12.57%	11.37%	9.79%	
Debt to Equity	0.12				0.18	

CONTACT INFORMATION:

Phone: 978 614-4000   Fax: 978 614-4004
Toll-Free: 800-357-7666
Address: 310 Littleton Rd., Westford, MA 01886 United States

STOCK TICKER/OTHER:

Stock Ticker: NTCT   Exchange: NAS
Employees: 3,113   Fiscal Year Ends: 02/28
Parent Company:

SALARIES/BONUSES:

Top Exec. Salary: $325,000   Bonus: $
Second Exec. Salary: $275,000   Bonus: $

OTHER THOUGHTS:

Estimated Female Officers or Directors: 2
Hot Spot for Advancement for Women/Minorities:

NetSuite Inc

NAIC Code: 0

www.netsuite.com

TYPES OF BUSINESS:

Business Management Application Suites
Enterprise Resource Planning
Customer Relationship Management
E-Commerce Capabilities

BRANDS/DIVISIONS/AFFILIATES:

Oracle Corporation
NetSuite OneWorld
NetSuite CRM
SuiteCommerce

CONTACTS: Note: Officers with more than one job title may be intentionally listed here more than once.

Zach Nelson, CEO
Jim McGeever, Pres.
Ronald Gill, CFO
Marc Huffman, Worldwide Sales Distribution
Kathy Zwickert, Chief People Officer
Evan Goldberg, Chief Technology Officer
Douglas Solomon, General Counsel
Marc Huffman, President, Divisional

GROWTH PLANS/SPECIAL FEATURES:

NetSuite, Inc. is a leading vendor of cloud-based financials, enterprise resource planning (ERP) and omnichannel commerce software. It provides a suite of cloud enterprise resource planning (ERP), customer relationship management (CRM) and e-commerce capabilities that enables customers to manage their back-office, front-office and web operations in a single application. From comprehensive financial management capabilities to inventory, supply chain and warehouse management solutions, NetSuite empowers businesses of all sizes, across all industries. NetSuite's cloud ERP solution is used by more than 30,000 companies, organizations and subsidiaries across 160+ countries. NetSuite OneWorld delivers a real-time, unified global business management platform for enterprises that manages multi-national and multi-subsidiary operations at a fraction of the cost of traditional on-premise ERP solutions. NetSuite CRM software delivers a real-time, 360-degree view of a business' customers. It provides a seamless flow of information across the entire customer lifecycle, from lead to sales order, fulfillment, upsell, cross-sell and support. NetSuite's professional services automation solutions meet the needs of fledgling startups to growing enterprises. SuiteCommerce unifies every step of the multichannel, multi-location business, from e-commerce, point of sale and order management, to marketing, merchandising, inventory, financials and support. NetSuite products offer a variety of management and procurement solutions, including financial, order, production, supply chain, warehouse/fulfillment and human capital management. Industries served by the company include software/internet companies, wholesale distribution, advertising/digital marketing, media/publishing, financial services, healthcare, non-profit, retail, manufacturing, IT services, professional services, consulting, energy and education. In November 2016, NetSuite was acquired by Oracle Corporation for $9.3 billion, and subsequently ceased from public trading.

FINANCIAL DATA: Note: Data for latest year may not have been available at press time.

In U.S. $	2016	2015	2014	2013	2012	2011
Revenue	855,000,000	741,148,992	556,284,032	414,508,000	308,824,992	236,326,000
R&D Expense						
Operating Income						
Operating Margin %						
SGA Expense						
Net Income		-124,743,000	-100,037,000	-70,409,000	-35,229,000	-32,007,000
Operating Cash Flow						
Capital Expenditure						
EBITDA						
Return on Assets %						
Return on Equity %						
Debt to Equity						

CONTACT INFORMATION:

Phone: 650 627-1000   Fax: 650 627-1001
Toll-Free: 877-638-7848
Address: 2955 Campus Drive, Ste. 100, San Mateo, CA 94403-2511
United States

STOCK TICKER/OTHER:

Stock Ticker: Subsidiary   Exchange:
Employees: 3,357   Fiscal Year Ends: 12/31
Parent Company: Oracle Corporation

SALARIES/BONUSES:

Top Exec. Salary: $ Bonus: $
Second Exec. Salary: $ Bonus: $

OTHER THOUGHTS:

Estimated Female Officers or Directors: 3
Hot Spot for Advancement for Women/Minorities: Y

New York Life Insurance Company

www.newyorklife.com

NAIC Code: 524113

TYPES OF BUSINESS:

Life Insurance
Annuities
Mutual Funds
Asset Management
Life Insurance
Real Estate

BRANDS/DIVISIONS/AFFILIATES:

NYLIFE Securities LLC
NYLIFE Distributors LLC
MainStay Investments

CONTACTS: *Note: Officers with more than one job title may be intentionally listed here more than once.*

Theodore A. Mathas, CEO
John Y. Kim, Chief Investment Officer
Tony Malloy, Chief Investment Officer
Frank M. Boccio, Chief Admin. Officer
Sheila K. Davidson, General Counsel
Barry Schub, Sr. VP-Strategy & Communications
George Nichols, III, Sr. VP-Office of Gov't Affairs
Christopher O. Blunt, Exec. VP
Mark W. Pfaff, Exec. VP
Susan A. Thrope, Deputy General Counsel

GROWTH PLANS/SPECIAL FEATURES:

New York Life Insurance Company provides life insurance, investments, retirement income and long-term care insurance. The firm has approximately $537.7 billion assets under management. New York Life operates through two segments: insurance products and investment products. Insurance products include life insurance and long-term care insurance. Types of life insurance includes term life, whole life, universal life, variable universal life, corporate sponsored plans and group membership associations. Wholly-owned subsidiaries within this unit include NYLIFE Securities, LLC and NYLIFE Distributors, LLC. Long-term insurance helps provide for the cost of long-term care generally not covered by health insurance, Medicare or Medicaid. Investment products include retirement income, investment annuities and mutual funds. Retirement income offers several guaranteed income annuity products such as lifetime income annuities, future income annuities, lifetime mutual income annuities and future mutual income annuities. Investment annuities are types of savings plans that help prepare individuals for retirement, and come in the form of variable annuities and fixed deferred annuities. Mutual funds are provided under New York Life's MainStay Investments registered service mark and name, offering a broad selection of mutual funds across multiple asset classes and investment styles. These investments include U.S./international/global stock funds; investment grade, high yield and municipal bond funds; and asset allocation funds that invest in a mix of asset classes and investment styles.

FINANCIAL DATA: *Note: Data for latest year may not have been available at press time.*

In U.S. $	2016	2015	2014	2013	2012	2011
Revenue	27,908,000,000	26,127,000,000	27,451,000,000	24,781,000,000	24,709,000,000	23,653,000,000
R&D Expense						
Operating Income						
Operating Margin %						
SGA Expense						
Net Income	1,638,000,000	1,785,000,000	2,455,000,000	2,045,000,000	2,090,000,000	1,171,000,000
Operating Cash Flow						
Capital Expenditure						
EBITDA						
Return on Assets %						
Return on Equity %						
Debt to Equity						

CONTACT INFORMATION:

Phone: 212-576-7000   Fax: 212-576-8145
Toll-Free: 800-692-3086
Address: 51 Madison Ave., New York, NY 10010 United States

STOCK TICKER/OTHER:

Stock Ticker: Mutual Company   Exchange:
Employees: 12,000   Fiscal Year Ends: 12/31
Parent Company:

SALARIES/BONUSES:

Top Exec. Salary: $ Bonus: $
Second Exec. Salary: $ Bonus: $

OTHER THOUGHTS:

Estimated Female Officers or Directors: 4
Hot Spot for Advancement for Women/Minorities: Y

Newell Brands Inc

NAIC Code: 326100

TYPES OF BUSINESS:
Consumer & Commercial Products Manufacturer
Markers & Writing Instruments
Cookware, Bakeware & Cutlery
Tools & Hardware Products
Infant Products
Industrial Products

BRANDS/DIVISIONS/AFFILIATES:
Jarden
Rubbermaid
Calphalon
PaperMate
Yankee Candle
Mr Coffee
WoodWick Candle
Sistema Plastics

CONTACTS: *Note: Officers with more than one job title may be intentionally listed here more than once.*
Michael Polk, CEO
Michael Cowhig, Chairman of the Board
James Cunningham, Chief Accounting Officer
William Burke, COO
Ralph Nicoletti, Executive VP
Richard Davies, Executive VP
Fiona Laird, Executive VP
Mark Tarchetti, President
Bradford Turner, Secretary

GROWTH PLANS/SPECIAL FEATURES:
Newell Brands, Inc. is a global manufacturer and marketer of a variety of consumer and commercial products. The company divides its operations into eight business groups: home solutions, consisting of Rubbermaid, Calphalon, Contigo, bubba, and Goody brands; writing, including Sharpie, PaperMate, Expo, Prismacolor, Mr. Sketch, Elmer's, X-Acto, Parker, Dymo Office and Waterman; commercial products, consisting of Rubbermaid Commercial Products; baby and parenting products, including Graco, Baby Jogger, Aprica and Teutonia; branded consumables, consisiting of Yankee Candle and First Alert; consumer solutions, such as Crock-Pot, FoodSaver, Mr. Coffee, Oster and Sunbeam; outdoor solutions, consisting of Coleman, Jostens, Berkley and Marmot; and process solutions, which consists of Jarden Plastic Solutions, Jarden Applied Materials and Jarden Zinc Products. During 2016, Newell Brands divested its decor business, which included brands Levolor and Kirsch, to Hunter Douglas for $270 million; and divested its tools business to Stanley Black & Decker for approximately $2 billion. In early-2017, the firm acquired Smith Mountain Industries, a provider of premium home fragrance products, primarily marketed under the WoodWick Candle brand, for $100 million; acquired Sistema Plastics, a leader of innovative food storage containers for $460 million; and divested its fire starter and fire log business, which includes the Pine Mountain and Diamond brands, to Royal Oak Enterprises LLC.

Newell employees receive benefits including medical, dental, vision, life, AD&D and disability coverage; flexible spending accounts; an educational assistance program; adoption assistance; and a 401(k).

FINANCIAL DATA: *Note: Data for latest year may not have been available at press time.*

In U.S. $	2016	2015	2014	2013	2012	2011
Revenue	13,264,000,000	5,915,700,000	5,727,000,000	5,692,500,000	5,902,700,000	5,864,600,000
R&D Expense						
Operating Income	1,100,100,000	601,400,000	604,700,000	621,000,000	651,900,000	257,200,000
Operating Margin %	8.29%	10.16%	10.55%	10.90%	11.04%	4.38%
SGA Expense	3,223,800,000	1,626,000,000	1,545,900,000	1,446,100,000	1,521,100,000	1,515,300,000
Net Income	527,800,000	350,000,000	377,800,000	474,600,000	401,300,000	125,200,000
Operating Cash Flow	1,828,500,000	565,800,000	634,100,000	605,200,000	618,500,000	561,300,000
Capital Expenditure	441,400,000	211,400,000	161,900,000	138,200,000	177,200,000	222,900,000
EBITDA	1,537,300,000	597,200,000	682,500,000	761,400,000	810,000,000	402,500,000
Return on Assets %	2.56%	5.01%	5.92%	7.72%	6.48%	1.99%
Return on Equity %	8.01%	19.05%	19.26%	23.33%	20.86%	6.67%
Debt to Equity	0.99	1.47	1.12	0.80	0.85	0.97

CONTACT INFORMATION:
Phone: 770 418-7000   Fax: 815 233-8060
Toll-Free:
Address: 3 Glenlake Pkwy., Atlanta, GA 30328 United States

STOCK TICKER/OTHER:
Stock Ticker: NWL
Employees: 53,400
Parent Company:

Exchange: NYS
Fiscal Year Ends: 12/31

SALARIES/BONUSES:
Top Exec. Salary: $493,845   Bonus: $1,900,000
Second Exec. Salary: $1,312,500   Bonus: $

OTHER THOUGHTS:
Estimated Female Officers or Directors: 3
Hot Spot for Advancement for Women/Minorities: Y

Nielsen Holdings plc

www.nielsen.com

NAIC Code: 541910

TYPES OF BUSINESS:

Market Research
Magazine Publishing
Media/Entertainment Audience Research
Trade Publications
Directories
Business Consulting
Internet Audience Research

BRANDS/DIVISIONS/AFFILIATES:

eXelate
Pointlogic
Informate Mobile Intelligence
Repucom

CONTACTS: *Note: Officers with more than one job title may be intentionally listed here more than once.*

Dwight Barns, CEO
Jamere Jackson, CFO
Jeffrey Charlton, Chief Accounting Officer
James Powell, Chief Technology Officer
Stephen Hasker, COO
James Attwood, Director
Eric Dale, Other Executive Officer
Nancy Phillips, Other Executive Officer
Giovanni Tavolieri, President, Divisional

GROWTH PLANS/SPECIAL FEATURES:

Nielsen Holdings plc is a leading global provider of marketing information, audience measurement and business media products and services with operations in over 100 countries and data measurements of 10 million consumers worldwide. The firm has two major segments: what consumers watch (watch) and what consumers buy (buy). Accounting for 46% the company's 2015 revenues, the watch segment provides viewership data and analytics primarily to the media industry, and advertising across three primary platforms that include mobile screens, online and television. Clients of this segment use Nielsen's data to plan and optimize their advertising spending and to better ensure that their advertisements reach the intended audience. The buy segment (responsible for 54% of 2015 revenue) provides consumer behavior information and analytics primarily to businesses in the consumer packaged goods industry. Clients use the data to manage their brands, find new sources of demand, launch and grow new products, improve their marketing mix and establish more effective consumer relationships. In 2015, the firm acquired eXelate, a leading provider of data and technology to facilitate the buying and selling of advertising across programmatic platforms. In 2016, it acquired Pointlogic, a global leader in marketing decision support systems via innovative software; Mumbai-based mobile usage measure Informate Mobile Intelligence; and Repucom, a leader in sports measurement, evaluation and intelligence.

FINANCIAL DATA: *Note: Data for latest year may not have been available at press time.*

In U.S. $	2016	2015	2014	2013	2012	2011
Revenue	6,309,000,000	6,172,000,000	6,288,000,000	5,703,000,000	5,612,000,000	5,532,000,000
R&D Expense						
Operating Income	1,143,000,000	1,093,000,000	1,089,000,000	861,000,000	952,000,000	794,000,000
Operating Margin %	18.11%	17.70%	17.31%	15.09%	16.96%	14.35%
SGA Expense	1,851,000,000	1,915,000,000	1,917,000,000	1,815,000,000	1,778,000,000	1,888,000,000
Net Income	502,000,000	570,000,000	384,000,000	740,000,000	273,000,000	84,000,000
Operating Cash Flow	1,296,000,000	1,179,000,000	1,093,000,000	901,000,000	784,000,000	641,000,000
Capital Expenditure	433,000,000	408,000,000	412,000,000	374,000,000	358,000,000	367,000,000
EBITDA	1,752,000,000	1,846,000,000	1,494,000,000	1,350,000,000	1,341,000,000	1,110,000,000
Return on Assets %	3.23%	3.71%	2.48%	4.91%	1.87%	.58%
Return on Equity %	11.76%	12.01%	7.12%	13.88%	5.70%	2.23%
Debt to Equity	1.88	1.58	1.27	1.13	1.26	1.42

CONTACT INFORMATION:

Phone: 646 654-5000 Fax:
Toll-Free: 800-864-1224
Address: 85 Broad Street, New York, NY 10004 United States

STOCK TICKER/OTHER:

Stock Ticker: NLSN
Employees: 43,000
Parent Company:

Exchange: NYS
Fiscal Year Ends: 12/31

SALARIES/BONUSES:

Top Exec. Salary: $741,154   Bonus: $325,000
Second Exec. Salary: Bonus: $
$1,000,000

OTHER THOUGHTS:

Estimated Female Officers or Directors: 4
Hot Spot for Advancement for Women/Minorities: Y

Nike Inc
NAIC Code: 424340

TYPES OF BUSINESS:
Footwear Distribution
Athletic Equipment
Sports Accessories
Retail Stores
Sports Apparel
Plastic Products
Hockey Products
Swimwear

BRANDS/DIVISIONS/AFFILIATES:
Virgin Mega USA
Chuck Taylor
Converse Inc
Hurley International LLC
One Star
Jordan
NIKE IHM Inc
Jack Purcell

CONTACTS: *Note: Officers with more than one job title may be intentionally listed here more than once.*
Mark Parker, CEO
Philip Knight, Chairman Emeritus
Chris Abston, Chief Accounting Officer
Hilary Krane, Chief Administrative Officer
Eric Sprunk, COO
John Slusher, Executive VP, Divisional
David Ayre, Executive VP, Divisional
Andrew Campion, Executive VP
Michael Spillane, President, Divisional
Trevor Edwards, President, Divisional
John Coburn, Vice President

GROWTH PLANS/SPECIAL FEATURES:
Nike, Inc. designs, develops and markets footwear, apparel, equipment and accessories. It is one of the largest sellers of athletic footwear and athletic apparel in the world. The company's athletic footwear products are designed primarily for specific athletic use, although a large percentage of its products are worn for casual or leisure purposes. Running, training, basketball and soccer sport-inspired urban shoes and children's shoes are the firm's top-selling product categories. Nike also markets shoes designed for tennis, golf, baseball, football, lacrosse, walking, outdoor activities, skateboarding, bicycling, volleyball, wrestling, cheerleading, aquatic activities and other athletic and recreational uses. The firm maintains several wholly-owned subsidiaries: Converse, Inc., which distributes and licenses footwear, apparel and accessories through brand names Converse, All Star, One Star, Chuck Taylor, Star Chevron and Jack Purcell; Hurley International LLC, which is headquartered in the U.K. and designs/distributes a collection of action sports apparel sold under the Hurley brand; and Jordan, which sells a line of basketball shoes, clothing and gear for men. Another subsidiary, NIKE IHM, Inc. sells small amounts of various plastic products to other manufacturers. Nike sells its products to retail accounts, through Nike-owned retail stores and through a mix of independent distributors and licensees worldwide. Within the U.S., the firm operates 362 Nike Brand and subsidiary retail stores: 230 Nike locations, 103 Converse stores including factory outlets and 29 Hurley locations. In the international market, which includes countries within Europe, Asia, South America and Africa, the firm maintains 683 retail stores (660 Nike and 23 Converse). In 2016, Nike acquired Virgin Mega USA, a mobile shopping company.

FINANCIAL DATA: *Note: Data for latest year may not have been available at press time.*

In U.S. $	2016	2015	2014	2013	2012	2011
Revenue	32,376,000,000	30,601,000,000	27,799,000,000	25,313,000,000	24,128,000,000	
R&D Expense						
Operating Income	4,502,000,000	4,175,000,000	3,680,000,000	3,254,000,000	3,040,000,000	
Operating Margin %	13.90%	13.64%	13.23%	12.85%	12.59%	
SGA Expense	10,469,000,000	9,892,000,000	8,766,000,000	7,780,000,000	7,431,000,000	
Net Income	3,760,000,000	3,273,000,000	2,693,000,000	2,485,000,000	2,223,000,000	
Operating Cash Flow	3,096,000,000	4,680,000,000	3,003,000,000	3,027,000,000	1,899,000,000	
Capital Expenditure	1,143,000,000	963,000,000	880,000,000	636,000,000	597,000,000	
EBITDA	5,164,000,000	4,824,000,000	4,312,000,000	3,767,000,000	3,445,000,000	
Return on Assets %	17.48%	16.28%	14.88%	15.03%	14.59%	
Return on Equity %	30.12%	27.81%	24.50%	23.07%	21.98%	
Debt to Equity	0.16	0.08	0.11	0.10	0.02	

CONTACT INFORMATION:
Phone: 503 671-6453   Fax: 503 671-6300
Toll-Free: 800-344-6453
Address: 1 Bowerman Dr., Beaverton, OR 97005 United States

STOCK TICKER/OTHER:
Stock Ticker: NKE
Employees: 74,400
Parent Company:

Exchange: NYS
Fiscal Year Ends: 05/31

SALARIES/BONUSES:
Top Exec. Salary: $1,550,000   Bonus: $
Second Exec. Salary: $990,000   Bonus: $

OTHER THOUGHTS:
Estimated Female Officers or Directors: 2
Hot Spot for Advancement for Women/Minorities: Y

NN Inc

www.nninc.com/

NAIC Code: 332991

TYPES OF BUSINESS:

Ball and Roller Bearing Manufacturing

BRANDS/DIVISIONS/AFFILIATES:

CONTACTS: *Note: Officers with more than one job title may be intentionally listed here more than once.*

Richard Holder, CEO
Thomas Burwell, CFO
Matthew Heiter, General Counsel
John Manzi, General Manager, Divisional
Warren Veltman, General Manager, Divisional

GROWTH PLANS/SPECIAL FEATURES:

NN, Inc. is a global manufacturer of high precision bearing components, industrial plastic products and precision metal components to a wide array of markets. The company has 40 manufacturing plants in North America, Western & Eastern Europe, South America and China. NN operates through three segments: precision bearing components, precision engineered products and autocam precision components. The precision bearing components segment derives 30% of annual net sales, and manufactures and supplies high precision bearing components, consisting of balls, cylindrical rollers, tapered rollers, spherical rollers and metal retainers for leading bearing and CV-joint (constant velocity) manufacturers on a global basis. The precision engineered products segment (31%) manufactures highly-engineered, difficult-to-manufacture precision metal components and subassemblies for the automotive, HVAC (heating, ventilation and air conditioning), fluid power and diesel engine end markets. Products within this division include surgical knives, bioresorbable implants, surgical staples, orthopedic system tools, laparoscopic devices, drug delivery devices, catheter components, electrical connectors, precision stampings, optical grade plastics, thermally-conductive plastics, as well as titanium, Inconel, magnesium and gold electroplating. The autocam precision components segment (39%) sells a wide range of highly-engineered, extremely close tolerance, precision-machined metal components and subassemblies primarily to the consumer transportation, industrial technology, HVAC, fluid power and diesel engine end markets. This division has developed an expertise in manufacturing highly-complex, system critical components for fuel systems, engines, transmissions, power steering systems and electromechanical motors.

FINANCIAL DATA: *Note: Data for latest year may not have been available at press time.*

In U.S. $	2016	2015	2014	2013	2012	2011
Revenue	833,488,000	667,280,000	488,601,000	373,206,000	370,084,000	424,691,000
R&D Expense						
Operating Income	59,400,000	26,797,000	27,687,000	27,827,000	25,071,000	29,432,000
Operating Margin %	7.12%	4.01%	5.66%	7.45%	6.77%	6.93%
SGA Expense	80,266,000	51,745,000	43,756,000	33,281,000	31,561,000	30,657,000
Net Income	7,942,000	-7,431,000	8,217,000	17,178,000	24,268,000	20,937,000
Operating Cash Flow	69,303,000	33,310,000	30,708,000	31,751,000	37,358,000	14,955,000
Capital Expenditure	43,820,000	38,553,000	27,602,000	15,250,000	17,089,000	20,329,000
EBITDA	118,333,000	51,431,000	48,442,000	44,509,000	41,862,000	48,645,000
Return on Assets %	.57%	-.70%	1.68%	6.50%	9.24%	8.24%
Return on Equity %	2.52%	-3.04%	5.03%	12.21%	21.26%	23.55%
Debt to Equity	2.51	2.60	1.97	0.19	0.52	0.75

CONTACT INFORMATION:

Phone: 423 743-9151   Fax: 423 743-2670
Toll-Free:
Address: 207 Mockingbird Lane, Johnson City, TN 37604 United States

STOCK TICKER/OTHER:

Stock Ticker: NNBR   Exchange: NAS
Employees: 5,299   Fiscal Year Ends: 12/31
Parent Company:

SALARIES/BONUSES:

Top Exec. Salary: $634,616   Bonus: $118,680
Second Exec. Salary: $326,014   Bonus: $

OTHER THOUGHTS:

Estimated Female Officers or Directors:
Hot Spot for Advancement for Women/Minorities:

Sales, profits and employees may be estimates. Financial information, benefits and other data can change quickly and may vary from those stated here.

Nordstrom Inc

www.nordstrom.com

NAIC Code: 452111

TYPES OF BUSINESS:

Department Stores
Outlet Stores
Online Retailing
Catalog Sales
Financial Services
Federal Savings Bank

BRANDS/DIVISIONS/AFFILIATES:

Nordstrom.com
Nordstromrack.com/HauteLook
TrunkClub.com
Nordstrom Rack
Jeffrey
Last Chance
Nordstrom fsb
Nordstrom

CONTACTS: *Note: Officers with more than one job title may be intentionally listed here more than once.*

Philip Satre, Chairman of the Board
James Howell, Chief Accounting Officer
Daniel Little, Chief Information Officer
Scott Meden, Chief Marketing Officer
Peter Nordstrom, Director
Erik Nordstrom, Director
Blake Nordstrom, Director
Christine Deputy Ott, Executive VP, Divisional
Robert Sari, Executive VP
Geevy Thomas, Executive VP
Ken Worzel, Executive VP
James Nordstrom, Executive VP
Karen McKibbin, Executive VP
Michael Maher, Senior VP, Divisional

GROWTH PLANS/SPECIAL FEATURES:

Nordstrom, Inc., founded in 1901, is an upscale fashion apparel and shoe retailer. Nordstrom operates a total of 344 stores in 40 U.S. states, as well as an e-Commerce business through Nordstrom.com, Nordstromrack.com/HauteLook and TrunkClub.com. The retailer also operates five Nordstrom full-line stores in Canada. The company sells a wide selection of apparel, shoes and accessories for women, men and children. The west and east coasts of the U.S. are the areas where the company has its largest presence. Nordstrom operates through two segments: retail and credit. The retail segment includes 117 Nordstrom branded full-line stores, 216 off-price Nordstrom Rack stores, five Canadian full-line stores, as well as other retail channels Trunk Club showrooms, Jeffrey boutiques and a clearance store that operates under the Last Chance name. The credit segment includes Nordstrom's wholly-owned federal savings bank, Nordstrom fsb, through which it offers a private label credit card, Nordstrom VISA credit cards and a debit card. It generates income through finance charges and fees on these cards and saves on interchange fees that the retail segment would incur when its customers use third-party cards. In May 2017, the firm announced plans to open six Nordstrom Rack stores in Canada in 2018, including Vaughan Mills and One Bloor in Toronto; Deerfoot Meadows in Calgary; South Edmonton Common in Edmonton; The Ottawa Train Yards in Ottawa; and the Heartfeld Town Centre in Mississauga.

Nordstrom offers employees benefits including medical, dental, vision, AD&D, life and short- and long-term disability insurance; wellness programs; 401(k) plan & profit sharing; employee stock purchase plan; access to the company bank and credit union; employee assistance programs; adoption financial assistance; and merchandise discounts.

FINANCIAL DATA: *Note: Data for latest year may not have been available at press time.*

In U.S. $	2016	2015	2014	2013	2012	2011
Revenue	14,437,000,000	13,506,000,000	12,540,000,000	12,148,000,000	10,877,000,000	
R&D Expense						
Operating Income	1,101,000,000	1,323,000,000	1,350,000,000	1,345,000,000	1,249,000,000	
Operating Margin %	7.62%	9.79%	10.76%	11.07%	11.48%	
SGA Expense	4,168,000,000	3,777,000,000	3,453,000,000	3,371,000,000	3,036,000,000	
Net Income	600,000,000	720,000,000	734,000,000	735,000,000	683,000,000	
Operating Cash Flow	2,451,000,000	1,220,000,000	1,320,000,000	1,110,000,000	1,177,000,000	
Capital Expenditure	1,082,000,000	861,000,000	803,000,000	513,000,000	511,000,000	
EBITDA	1,677,000,000	1,832,000,000	1,805,000,000	1,713,000,000	1,576,000,000	
Return on Assets %	7.08%	8.08%	8.80%	8.86%	8.56%	
Return on Equity %	36.24%	31.85%	36.76%	37.99%	34.34%	
Debt to Equity	3.20	1.27	1.49	1.63	1.60	

CONTACT INFORMATION:

Phone: 206 628-2111   Fax: 206 628-1795
Toll-Free: 888-282-6060
Address: 1617 Sixth Ave., Seattle, WA 98101 United States

STOCK TICKER/OTHER:

Stock Ticker: JWN   Exchange: NYS
Employees: 72,500   Fiscal Year Ends: 01/31
Parent Company:

SALARIES/BONUSES:

Top Exec. Salary: $782,223   Bonus: $
Second Exec. Salary: Bonus: $
$751,152

OTHER THOUGHTS:

Estimated Female Officers or Directors: 8
Hot Spot for Advancement for Women/Minorities: Y

Northwestern Mutual Life Insurance Company

www.northwesternmutual.com

NAIC Code: 524113

TYPES OF BUSINESS:

Life Insurance
Disability Insurance
Employee Benefit Plans
Long-Term Care Insurance
Investment Products & Services
Financial Planning Services

BRANDS/DIVISIONS/AFFILIATES:

Northwestern Long Term Care Insurance Company
Northwestern Mutual Investment Services LLC
Northwestern Mutual Wealth Management Company

CONTACTS: Note: Officers with more than one job title may be intentionally listed here more than once.

John E. Schlifske, CEO
Gregory C. Oberland, Pres.
Michael G. Carter, CFO
Joann M. Esienhart, Sr.VP-Human Resources
Ronald P. Joelson, Chief Investment Officer
Jean M. Maier, Exec. VP-Tech.
Raymond J. Manista, General Counsel
Jean M. Maier, Exec. VP-Enterprise Oper.
Ronald P. Joelson, Exec. VP
Todd M. Schoon, Exec. VP-Agencies
John E. Schlifske, Chmn.

GROWTH PLANS/SPECIAL FEATURES:

Northwestern Mutual Life Insurance Company (NMLIC) is a financial network company. It offers network services, insurance products, investment products and advisory services to 4.4 million policy owners, and has $250 billion in assets, $28 billion in revenues and more than $1.6 trillion worth of life insurance protection in force. NMLIC's network services include asset and income protection, personal needs analysis, investment services, education funding and retirement products. The firm also offers permanent, term and combination life insurance plans, providing individual and group disability plans to approximately 500,000 policy holders. Long-term care insurance is offered to more than 150,000 policy holders through NMLIC's Northwestern Long Term Care Insurance Company subsidiary. Northwestern Mutual Investment Services, LLC is a broker-dealer and registered investment advisor that serves the investment planning and product needs of individuals and businesses. This company's special account services include electronic transfers, dividend reinvestment, a mutual fund purchase program, account protection, direct deposit, check writing privileges and online account access. It also offers a variety of individual investment services such as college education funding and IRA (individual retirement account) solutions. Northwestern Mutual Wealth Management Company is a limited purpose federal savings bank that also provides investment management, trust services and fee-based financial planning. This subsidiary is not a broker-dealer or insurance company.

NMLIC offers its employees flexible spending accounts, training programs, flexible work schedules, adoption assistance, an onsite fitness center, credit union membership, educational assistance and a business casual work environment.

FINANCIAL DATA: Note: Data for latest year may not have been available at press time.

In U.S. $	2016	2015	2014	2013	2012	2011
Revenue	28,158,000,000	27,880,000,000	26,707,000,000	25,909,000,000	24,621,000,000	23,595,000,000
R&D Expense						
Operating Income						
Operating Margin %						
SGA Expense						
Net Income	818,000,000	815,000,000	679,000,000	802,000,000	783,000,000	645,000,000
Operating Cash Flow						
Capital Expenditure						
EBITDA						
Return on Assets %						
Return on Equity %						
Debt to Equity						

CONTACT INFORMATION:

Phone: 414-271-1444   Fax: 414-299-7022
Toll-Free:
Address: 720 E. Wisconsin Ave., Milwaukee, WI 53202 United States

SALARIES/BONUSES:

Top Exec. Salary: $ Bonus: $
Second Exec. Salary: $ Bonus: $

STOCK TICKER/OTHER:

Stock Ticker: Mutual Company   Exchange:
Employees: 5,000   Fiscal Year Ends: 12/31
Parent Company:

OTHER THOUGHTS:

Estimated Female Officers or Directors: 5
Hot Spot for Advancement for Women/Minorities: Y

Norwegian Cruise Line Holdings Ltd (NCL)   www.ncl.com
NAIC Code: 483112

TYPES OF BUSINESS:
Cruise Line
Luxury Cruise Lines

BRANDS/DIVISIONS/AFFILIATES:
Regent Seven Seas
Oceania Cruises
Prestige Cruises International

CONTACTS: Note: Officers with more than one job title may be intentionally listed here more than once.
Daniel Farkas, Assistant Secretary
Jason Montague, CEO, Divisional
Andrew Stuart, CEO, Subsidiary
Robert Binder, CEO, Subsidiary
Frank Del Rio, CEO
Wendy Beck, CFO
Faye Ashby, Chief Accounting Officer
Walter Revell, Director
Harry Sommer, Executive VP,Divisional
T. Lindsay, Executive VP,Divisional

GROWTH PLANS/SPECIAL FEATURES:
Norwegian Cruise Line Holdings Ltd. (NCLH) is one of the largest cruise line operators in the world. It offers a wide variety of cruises ranging in length from one day to three weeks and itineraries originating from 19 ports (of which 13 are in North America). In addition to the traditional cruise markets in the Caribbean and Mexico, Norwegian sails to destinations in Europe, including the Mediterranean and the Baltic, Bermuda, Alaska and Hawaii. The firm owns Prestige Cruises International, which in turn owns Oceania Cruises and Regent Seven Seas Cruises. These two brands operate a total of eight ships with over 6,400 berths. Oceania operates a fleet of five mid-size ships, providing customers with an upscale and sophisticated experience including personalized service and elegant accommodations. It offers destination-oriented cruises to approximately 330 ports around the globe. Regent offers a luxury all-inclusive cruise vacation experience, including free air transportation, a pre-cruise hotel night stay, premium wines and top shelf liquors, gratuities and unlimited shore excursions. The brand operates three all-suite ships, with itineraries to approximately 300 ports worldwide. Overall, the company has a combined fleet of 22 ships, which offer itineraries to more than 520 destinations worldwide. By 2019, the firm's fleet of major ships will total 27. Additionally, four more ships will be added to the fleet between 2022 and 2025.

FINANCIAL DATA: Note: Data for latest year may not have been available at press time.

In U.S. $	2016	2015	2014	2013	2012	2011
Revenue	4,874,340,000	4,345,048,000	3,125,881,000	2,570,294,000	2,276,246,000	2,219,324,000
R&D Expense						
Operating Income	925,464,000	702,486,000	502,941,000	395,887,000	357,093,000	316,112,000
Operating Margin %	18.98%	16.16%	16.08%	15.40%	15.68%	14.24%
SGA Expense	666,156,000	554,999,000	403,169,000	301,155,000	251,183,000	251,351,000
Net Income	633,085,000	427,137,000	338,352,000	101,714,000	168,556,000	126,859,000
Operating Cash Flow	1,239,666,000	1,041,178,000	635,601,000	475,281,000	398,594,000	356,990,000
Capital Expenditure	1,092,091,000	1,122,734,000	1,051,974,000	894,851,000	303,840,000	184,797,000
EBITDA	1,371,099,000	1,152,821,000	807,818,000	640,998,000	574,623,000	527,161,000
Return on Assets %	5.01%	3.58%	3.71%	1.61%	2.93%	2.28%
Return on Equity %	15.22%	11.70%	11.04%	4.39%	8.72%	7.09%
Debt to Equity	1.28	1.52	1.59	1.08	1.36	1.53

CONTACT INFORMATION:
Phone: 305-436-4000   Fax: 305-436-4140
Toll-Free:
Address: 7665 Corporate Center Dr., Miami, FL 33126 United States

STOCK TICKER/OTHER:
Stock Ticker: NCLH   Exchange: NAS
Employees: 30,000   Fiscal Year Ends: 12/31
Parent Company:

SALARIES/BONUSES:
Top Exec. Salary: $1,500,000   Bonus: $
Second Exec. Salary: Bonus: $250,000
$650,000

OTHER THOUGHTS:
Estimated Female Officers or Directors: 4
Hot Spot for Advancement for Women/Minorities: Y

NVR Inc

NAIC Code: 236117

TYPES OF BUSINESS:

Construction, Home Building and Residential Mortgages
Townhouse Construction
Condominium Construction

BRANDS/DIVISIONS/AFFILIATES:

Ryan Homes
NVHomes
Heartland Homes
NVR Mortgage Finance Inc

CONTACTS: Note: Officers with more than one job title may be intentionally listed here more than once.

Paul Saville, CEO
Daniel Malzahn, CFO
Dwight Schar, Chairman of the Board
Eugene Bredow, Chief Accounting Officer
Jeffrey Martchek, President, Divisional
Robert Henley, President, Subsidiary

GROWTH PLANS/SPECIAL FEATURES:

NVR, Inc. is primarily engaged in the construction and sale of single-family detached homes, townhomes and condominium buildings. Additionally, NVR offers mortgage banking services through its subsidiary NVR Mortgage Finance, Inc. (NVRM). NVRM originates mortgage loans for NVR's homebuilding customers and sells all mortgage loans it closes to investors in the secondary markets on a servicing released basis. The company operates in 14 states, with concentration in the Washington, D.C. and Baltimore, Maryland metropolitan areas, which accounted for 30% and 13% of its 2016 homebuilding revenues. NVR's homebuilding operations include the sale and construction of single-family detached homes, townhomes and condominium buildings under four brand names: Ryan Homes, NVHomes and Heartland Homes. The Ryan Homes products are moderately priced and marketed primarily to first-time homeowners and first-time move-up buyers. Ryan Homes are currently sold in 29 metropolitan areas located primarily in the eastern U.S. NVHomes are marketed primarily to move-up and upscale buyers and are sold in Delaware, Washington, D.C., Baltimore and Philadelphia metropolitan areas. Heartland Homes are sold in Pittsburgh. The firm's houses range from approximately 1,000 to 9,000 square feet, typically including two to four bedrooms, and are priced between $140,000 and $1.8 million. NVR also provides mortgage-related services through its mortgage banking operations, which include subsidiaries that broker title insurance and perform title searches.

FINANCIAL DATA: Note: Data for latest year may not have been available at press time.

In U.S. $	2016	2015	2014	2013	2012	2011
Revenue	5,830,113,000	5,169,562,000	4,449,508,000	4,220,908,000	3,193,204,000	2,663,906,000
R&D Expense						
Operating Income	678,932,000	626,771,000	473,055,000	441,081,000	282,606,000	185,605,000
Operating Margin %	11.64%	12.12%	10.63%	10.44%	8.85%	6.96%
SGA Expense	443,320,000	424,009,000	407,867,000	355,623,000	334,959,000	294,515,000
Net Income	425,262,000	382,927,000	281,630,000	266,477,000	180,588,000	129,420,000
Operating Cash Flow	384,465,000	203,391,000	184,549,000	270,222,000	264,384,000	1,463,000
Capital Expenditure	22,369,000	18,277,000	31,672,000	19,016,000	12,365,000	11,444,000
EBITDA	705,673,000	648,305,000	494,300,000	454,472,000	290,706,000	216,140,000
Return on Assets %	16.48%	15.73%	11.64%	10.46%	8.23%	6.40%
Return on Equity %	33.43%	32.40%	23.61%	19.43%	12.64%	8.30%
Debt to Equity	0.45	0.48	0.53	0.47	0.40	

CONTACT INFORMATION:

Phone: 703 956-4000   Fax: 703 956-4750
Toll-Free:
Address: 11700 Plz. America Dr., Ste. 500, Reston, VA 20190 United States

STOCK TICKER/OTHER:

Stock Ticker: NVR   Exchange: NYS
Employees: 4,900   Fiscal Year Ends: 12/31
Parent Company:

SALARIES/BONUSES:

Top Exec. Salary: $1,566,375   Bonus: $
Second Exec. Salary: $539,000   Bonus: $

OTHER THOUGHTS:

Estimated Female Officers or Directors:
Hot Spot for Advancement for Women/Minorities:

Old Dominion Freight Line Inc

NAIC Code: 484122

TYPES OF BUSINESS:

Trucking
LTL Trucking
Freight Logistics

BRANDS/DIVISIONS/AFFILIATES:

Mallory Alexander International Logistics LLC

CONTACTS: Note: Officers with more than one job title may be intentionally listed here more than once.

Adam Satterfield, Assistant Secretary
John Congdon, CEO, Subsidiary
Earl Congdon, Chairman of the Board
Kimberly Maready, Chief Accounting Officer
Greg Gantt, COO
David Congdon, Director
Ross Parr, General Counsel
Cecil Overbey, Senior VP, Divisional
Kevin Freeman, Senior VP, Divisional
David Bates, Senior VP, Divisional

GROWTH PLANS/SPECIAL FEATURES:

Old Dominion Freight Line, Inc. is a less-than-truckload (LTL) multi-regional motor carrier. The firm provides one- to five-day service among six regions in the U.S. and next-day and second-day service within these regions. LTL carriers pick up multiple shipments from multiple customers on a single truck and then route the goods through service centers where freight may be transferred to other trucks for delivery. Old Dominion offers its services through five groups: domestic, offering domestic shipping solutions; household services, providing booking, and receiving the trailer for loading and delivery; expedited, for time-sensitive deliveries; global, providing direct service to Alaska, Hawaii, Canada, Mexico and Puerto Rico, as well as international shipping throughout the Caribbean, Europe, the Far East, Central America and South America via Mallory Alexander International Logistics, LLC; and technology, for tracking the progress and delivery times of shipments. Old Dominion conducts its operations through approximately 225 U.S. service center locations, with major break-bulk facilities in Atlanta, Georgia; Rialto, California; Indianapolis, Indiana; Greensboro, North Carolina; Harrisburg, Pennsylvania; Memphis and Morristown, Tennessee; and Dallas, Texas. The firm uses roughly 21,540 trailers (most of which are 28 feet in length) in its line haul operations, often combined into tractor-trailer-trailer combinations, allowing goods to be shipped with minimal unloading and reloading. Old Dominion operates approximately 7,688 tractors. Tractors are generally used in long-distance operations for roughly three to five years and are then transferred to less demanding pickup and delivery operations.

FINANCIAL DATA: Note: Data for latest year may not have been available at press time.

In U.S. $	2016	2015	2014	2013	2012	2011
Revenue	2,991,517,000	2,972,442,000	2,787,897,000	2,337,648,000	2,110,483,000	1,882,541,000
R&D Expense						
Operating Income	483,835,000	498,240,000	441,307,000	338,438,000	285,254,000	234,072,000
Operating Margin %	16.17%	16.76%	15.82%	14.47%	13.51%	12.43%
SGA Expense	1,774,505,000	1,695,632,000	1,518,575,000	1,306,510,000	1,188,634,000	1,065,465,000
Net Income	295,765,000	304,690,000	267,514,000	206,113,000	169,452,000	139,470,000
Operating Cash Flow	565,583,000	553,880,000	391,674,000	350,666,000	328,056,000	277,380,000
Capital Expenditure	417,941,000	462,059,000	367,680,000	295,606,000	373,193,000	250,214,000
EBITDA	671,786,000	660,570,000	585,590,000	465,378,000	395,382,000	324,971,000
Return on Assets %	11.45%	12.95%	12.83%	11.31%	10.50%	10.13%
Return on Equity %	16.72%	19.17%	19.62%	18.25%	18.00%	18.28%
Debt to Equity	0.05	0.06	0.08	0.12	0.19	0.26

CONTACT INFORMATION:

Phone: 336 889-5000   Fax: 336 822-5239
Toll-Free: 800-432-6335
Address: 500 Old Dominion Way, Thomasville, NC 27360 United States

STOCK TICKER/OTHER:

Stock Ticker: ODFL   Exchange: NAS
Employees: 17,543   Fiscal Year Ends: 12/31
Parent Company:

SALARIES/BONUSES:

Top Exec. Salary: $594,313   Bonus: $
Second Exec. Salary: Bonus: $
$594,313

OTHER THOUGHTS:

Estimated Female Officers or Directors:
Hot Spot for Advancement for Women/Minorities:

Oliver Wyman Group

www.oliverwymangroup.com

NAIC Code: 541610

TYPES OF BUSINESS:

Management Consulting
Business Strategy Consulting
Financial Services Consulting
Risk Management & Insurance Consulting

BRANDS/DIVISIONS/AFFILIATES:

Marsh & McLennan Companies Inc
Oliver Wyman
Lippincott
NERA Economic Consulting
Mercer LLC
Guy Carpenter
Marsh

CONTACTS: *Note: Officers with more than one job title may be intentionally listed here more than once.*

Scott McDonald, CEO
Matthew Cunningham, CFO
Nicky Dingemans, Chief Human Capital Officer
Paula McGlarry, General Counsel
Simon Harris, Chief Strategy & Corp. Dev. Officer
David Fishbaum, Actuarial
Rachel Kirsh, Chief Risk Officer

GROWTH PLANS/SPECIAL FEATURES:

Oliver Wyman Group (OWG), a subsidiary of Marsh & McLennan Companies, Inc., is a global consulting group with offices in over 50 cities in 25 countries. The company operates in three units. The largest part of the group is its Oliver Wyman unit, a management consulting firm offering general business consulting with specialized expertise in strategy, operations, risk management, organizational transformation and leadership development. The second unit is Lippincott, a firm offering services related to corporate brand strategy and design consultancy. The group's third unit, NERA Economic Consulting, provides economic analysis and advice related to complex business and legal issues arising from regulation, public policy, litigation, strategy and competition. In addition, as part of the Marsh & McLennan group, OWG works in partnership with sister companies such as Mercer, LLC, a health, retirement, talent and investment consulting services firm; Guy Carpenter, a provider of risk and reinsurance advisory services; and Marsh, which provides insurance broking and risk management consulting. OWG's clients are primarily the CEOs and top management of Fortune 1000 firms across a number of key industries, including automotive, aviation and aerospace, defense, energy, communications and media, financial services, retail and consumer products, healthcare, life sciences, technology and transportation. Special projects of the firm include the Oliver Wyman Institute, a collaborative group that conducts market research; and the Delta Organization & Leadership Executive Learning Center, which implements custom leadership development and education programs.

FINANCIAL DATA: *Note: Data for latest year may not have been available at press time.*

In U.S. $	2016	2015	2014	2013	2012	2011
Revenue	1,803,530,000	1,751,000,000	1,710,000,000	1,483,000,000	1,466,000,000	1,483,000,000
R&D Expense						
Operating Income						
Operating Margin %						
SGA Expense						
Net Income						
Operating Cash Flow						
Capital Expenditure						
EBITDA						
Return on Assets %						
Return on Equity %						
Debt to Equity						

CONTACT INFORMATION:

Phone: 212-345-8000   Fax: 212-345-8075
Toll-Free:
Address: 1166 Ave. of the Americas, New York, NY 10036 United States

STOCK TICKER/OTHER:

Stock Ticker: Subsidiary   Exchange:
Employees: 4,000   Fiscal Year Ends: 12/31
Parent Company: Marsh & McLennan Companies Inc

SALARIES/BONUSES:

Top Exec. Salary: $ Bonus: $
Second Exec. Salary: $ Bonus: $

OTHER THOUGHTS:

Estimated Female Officers or Directors: 3
Hot Spot for Advancement for Women/Minorities: Y

Omnicom Group Inc

NAIC Code: 541810

www.omnicomgroup.com

TYPES OF BUSINESS:

Advertising Services
Public Relations
Market Research
Marketing & Brand Consulting
Interactive & Search Engine Marketing
Media Planning & Buying
Health Care Communications

BRANDS/DIVISIONS/AFFILIATES:

Diversified Agency Services
DDB Worldwide Communications Group Inc
DDB Worldwide Inc
TBWA Worldwide Inc
OMD Worldwide
Lucky Generals
Wednesday Agency Group
BioPharm Communications

CONTACTS: *Note: Officers with more than one job title may be intentionally listed here more than once.*

Jonathan Nelson, CEO, Divisional
John Wren, CEO
Bruce Crawford, Chairman of the Board
Peter Swiecicki, Controller
Philip Angelastro, Executive VP
Michael OBrien, General Counsel
Andrew Castellaneta, Senior VP
Dennis Hewitt, Treasurer

GROWTH PLANS/SPECIAL FEATURES:

Omnicom Group, Inc. is a holding company that, through its subsidiaries, is one of the largest advertising, marketing and corporate communications companies in the world. The firm owns over a thousand subsidiary agencies that operate in over 100 countries, serving over 5,000 clients. Its agencies provide an extensive range of services, mainly focusing on four fundamental disciplines: advertising, customer relationship management, public relations and specialty communications. The company's holdings are managed by the Diversified Agency Services (DAS) group of companies; this sector includes over 200 public relations, marketing, consulting and special communications firms, such as Ketchum, Inc. and Porter Novelli. Omnicom's advertising is based in three areas: global advertising brands, national advertising agencies and media services. Its global network consists of three advertising agencies: BBDO Worldwide Communications Group, Inc., DDB Worldwide, Inc. and TBWA Worldwide, Inc. National advertising agencies include Arnell Group, Goodby Silverstein & Partners, GSD&M, Martin/Williams, Merkley and Partners and Zimmerman Partners. Media services operate as the Omnicom Media Group, which include two full service media companies, OMD Worldwide and PHD Network, and several media specialist companies. Other group activities of note include experiential marketing, mobile marketing, package design, custom printing, reputation consulting and search engine marketing. Omnicom digital oversees the company's digital operations. In 2016, BBDO Worldwide acquired a majority stake in Wednesday Agency Group, a fashion and luxury lifestyle brand-focused creative agency. Additionally, in 2016, Omnicom Health Group acquired BioPharm Communications, the largest healthcare marketing and communications group in the world. In February 2017, TBWA Worldwide acquired a majority stake in Lucky Generals, an independent UK creative agency.

FINANCIAL DATA: *Note: Data for latest year may not have been available at press time.*

In U.S. $	2016	2015	2014	2013	2012	2011
Revenue	15,416,900,000	15,134,400,000	15,317,800,000	14,584,500,000	14,219,400,000	13,872,500,000
R&D Expense						
Operating Income	2,008,900,000	1,920,100,000	1,944,100,000	1,825,300,000	1,804,200,000	1,671,100,000
Operating Margin %	13.03%	12.68%	12.69%	12.51%	12.68%	12.04%
SGA Expense	443,900,000	1,852,400,000	2,023,700,000	1,993,400,000	2,034,500,000	1,950,800,000
Net Income	1,148,600,000	1,093,900,000	1,104,000,000	991,100,000	998,300,000	952,600,000
Operating Cash Flow	1,931,200,000	2,172,300,000	1,476,500,000	1,809,000,000	1,451,300,000	1,315,300,000
Capital Expenditure	165,500,000	202,700,000	213,000,000	212,000,000	226,300,000	185,500,000
EBITDA	2,333,900,000	2,250,800,000	2,281,600,000	2,142,900,000	2,122,000,000	1,980,800,000
Return on Assets %	5.04%	4.95%	4.96%	4.47%	4.68%	4.75%
Return on Equity %	49.50%	40.79%	33.69%	28.14%	28.66%	26.89%
Debt to Equity	2.27	1.45	1.60	1.12	1.28	0.90

CONTACT INFORMATION:

Phone: 212 415-3600   Fax: 212 415-3393
Toll-Free:
Address: 437 Madison Ave., New York, NY 10022 United States

STOCK TICKER/OTHER:

Stock Ticker: OMC   Exchange: NYS
Employees: 78,500   Fiscal Year Ends: 12/31
Parent Company:

SALARIES/BONUSES:

Top Exec. Salary: $1,000,000   Bonus: $13,640,000
Second Exec. Salary: $850,000   Bonus: $3,600,000

OTHER THOUGHTS:

Estimated Female Officers or Directors: 6
Hot Spot for Advancement for Women/Minorities: Y

Oracle Corporation

www.oracle.com

NAIC Code: 0

TYPES OF BUSINESS:

Computer Software, Data Base & File Management
e-Business Applications Software
Internet-Based Software
Consulting Services
Human Resources Management Software
CRM Software
Middleware

BRANDS/DIVISIONS/AFFILIATES:

Oracle Saas
Oracle PaaS
Oracle Applications
Oracle Database
Java
Oracle Fusion Middleware
AddThis
NetSuite

CONTACTS: *Note: Officers with more than one job title may be intentionally listed here more than once.*

Lawrence Ellison, Chairman of the Board
William West, Chief Accounting Officer
Safra Catz, Co-CEO
Mark Hurd, Co-CEO
Jeffrey Henley, Director
John Fowler, Executive VP, Divisional
Dorian Daley, Executive VP
Thomas Kurian, President, Divisional

GROWTH PLANS/SPECIAL FEATURES:

Oracle Corporation is a leading enterprise software company, providing hardware products and services to over 400,000 customers throughout the world. The firm markets its integrated hardware and software systems directly to corporations. Oracle's products can be categorized into three broad areas: software and cloud, hardware systems and services. The software and cloud division is further divided into new software licenses & cloud software subscriptions, which includes Oracle's Software-as-a-Service (SaaS) and Platform-as-a-Service (PaaS) offerings; cloud infrastructure as a service; and software license updates & product support. This division represents 78% of total revenues. Hardware systems is comprised of hardware systems products and hardware systems support services, representing 13% of total revenues. Services (9% or revenues) offers consulting services, enhanced support services and education services. Applications and technologies of the firm include Oracle SaaS, providing software applications delivered via a cloud-based IT environment that the company hosts, manages and supports; Oracle Applications software are licensed for use in on-premise, data center and related IT environments to manage and automate core business functions across the enterprise; Oracle PaaS is designed to deliver Oracle Database, Java and other platform services in the cloud to enable developers to extend applications; Oracle Database software is licensed to customers and designed to enable reliable & secure storage, retrieval and manipulation of all forms of data; Oracle Fusion Middleware is a broad family of integrated application infrastructure software products; and Java is a software development language platform. During 2016, the firm acquired the following: application companies, including AddThis, Crosswise, LogFire and NetSuite; industry solution companies, including Textura and Opower; and middleware companies, including Palerra and Ravello Systems. That November, it agreed to acquire Dyn.

Oracle offers employees a 401(k) plan; employee assistance and employee stock purchase plans; and a Live and Work Well program.

FINANCIAL DATA: *Note: Data for latest year may not have been available at press time.*

In U.S. $	2016	2015	2014	2013	2012	2011
Revenue	37,047,000,000	38,226,000,000	38,275,000,000	37,180,000,000	37,121,000,000	
R&D Expense	5,787,000,000	5,524,000,000	5,151,000,000	4,850,000,000	4,523,000,000	
Operating Income	12,604,000,000	13,871,000,000	14,759,000,000	14,684,000,000	13,706,000,000	
Operating Margin %	34.02%	36.28%	38.56%	39.49%	36.92%	
SGA Expense	9,039,000,000	8,732,000,000	8,605,000,000	8,400,000,000	8,253,000,000	
Net Income	8,901,000,000	9,938,000,000	10,955,000,000	10,925,000,000	9,981,000,000	
Operating Cash Flow	13,561,000,000	14,336,000,000	14,921,000,000	14,224,000,000	13,743,000,000	
Capital Expenditure	1,189,000,000	1,391,000,000	580,000,000	650,000,000	648,000,000	
EBITDA	15,418,000,000	16,838,000,000	17,526,000,000	17,626,000,000	16,644,000,000	
Return on Assets %	7.98%	9.87%	12.72%	13.64%	13.14%	
Return on Equity %	18.55%	20.80%	23.93%	24.73%	23.91%	
Debt to Equity	0.84	0.82	0.48	0.41	0.30	

CONTACT INFORMATION:

Phone: 650 506-7000   Fax: 650 506-7200
Toll-Free: 800-392-2999
Address: 500 Oracle Parkway, Redwood City, CA 94065 United States

STOCK TICKER/OTHER:

Stock Ticker: ORCL   Exchange: NYS
Employees: 138,000   Fiscal Year Ends: 05/31
Parent Company:

SALARIES/BONUSES:

Top Exec. Salary: $950,000   Bonus: $
Second Exec. Salary: $950,000   Bonus: $

OTHER THOUGHTS:

Estimated Female Officers or Directors: 6
Hot Spot for Advancement for Women/Minorities: Y

Sales, profits and employees may be estimates. Financial information, benefits and other data can change quickly and may vary from those stated here.

Orbital ATK Inc

NAIC Code: 336414

www.orbitalatk.com

TYPES OF BUSINESS:

Aerospace Technology & Manufacturing

BRANDS/DIVISIONS/AFFILIATES:

CONTACTS: *Note: Officers with more than one job title may be intentionally listed here more than once.*

David Thompson, CEO
Christine Wolf, Senior VP, Divisional
Garrett Pierce, CFO
Ronald Fogleman, Chairman of the Board
Christopher Voci, Chief Accounting Officer
Antonio Elias, Chief Technology Officer
Blake Larson, COO
Frank Culbertson, Executive VP
Scott Lehr, Executive VP
Michael Kahn, Executive VP
Thomas McCabe, General Counsel
Hollis Thompson, Vice President, Divisional

GROWTH PLANS/SPECIAL FEATURES:

Orbital ATK, Inc. designs, builds and delivers space, defense and aviation-related systems to customers around the world both as a prime contractor and as a merchant supplier. The company's products include launch vehicles and related propulsion systems; satellites and associated components and services; composite aerospace structures; tactical missiles, subsystems and defense electronics; and precision weapons, armament systems and ammunition. Orbital ATK reports its business in three segments: flight systems, defense systems and space systems. The flight systems group produces solid rocket propulsion systems and specialty energetic products; provider of small- and medium-class space launch vehicles for civil, military and commercial missions; supplier of interceptor boosters and target vehicles for missile defense applications; and manufacturer of composite structures for commercial and military aircraft and launch vehicles. The defense systems group produces propulsion and controls for a tactical missiles and missile defense interceptors as well as fusing and warheads for tactical missiles and munitions; supplies advanced defense electronics for strike weapon systems, missile-warning and aircraft survivability as well as special-mission aircraft; and produces medium- and large-caliber ammunition, medium-caliber gun systems and precision munitions guidance kits as well as mall-caliber ammunition. The space systems group provides small- and medium-class commercial satellites used for global communications and high-resolution Earth imaging; provider of small- and medium-class spacecraft that perform scientific research and national security missions for government customers; provider of commercial cargo delivery services to the International Space Station and developer of advanced space systems; and provider of spacecraft components and subsystems and specialized engineering services.

FINANCIAL DATA: *Note: Data for latest year may not have been available at press time.*

In U.S. $	2016	2015	2014	2013	2012	2011
Revenue	3,113,000,000	3,173,967,000	4,775,128,000	4,362,145,000	4,613,399,000	
R&D Expense	49,000,000	49,349,000	62,520,000	64,678,000	66,403,000	
Operating Income	223,000,000	231,953,000	590,306,000	469,643,000	495,586,000	
Operating Margin %	7.16%	7.30%	12.36%	10.76%	10.74%	
SGA Expense	395,000,000	388,500,000	486,816,000	406,548,000	432,907,000	
Net Income	195,000,000	202,484,000	340,915,000	271,805,000	262,612,000	
Operating Cash Flow	311,000,000	311,331,000	388,020,000	273,592,000	372,307,000	
Capital Expenditure	113,000,000	112,704,000	145,964,000	96,889,000	122,292,000	
EBITDA	305,000,000	316,980,000	708,334,000	564,147,000	605,147,000	
Return on Assets %		3.59%	6.71%	6.09%	5.84%	
Return on Equity %		10.97%	19.97%	19.92%	22.03%	
Debt to Equity		0.86	0.96	0.68	1.03	

CONTACT INFORMATION:

Phone: 703 406-5000   Fax:
Toll-Free:
Address: 45101 Warp Dr., Dulles, VA 20166 United States

STOCK TICKER/OTHER:

Stock Ticker: OA   Exchange: NYS
Employees: 12,700   Fiscal Year Ends: 03/31
Parent Company:

SALARIES/BONUSES:

Top Exec. Salary: $945,688   Bonus: $
Second Exec. Salary: $654,231   Bonus: $286,808

OTHER THOUGHTS:

Estimated Female Officers or Directors:
Hot Spot for Advancement for Women/Minorities:

O'Reilly Automotive Inc

www.oreillyauto.com

NAIC Code: 441310

TYPES OF BUSINESS:

Auto Parts Stores
Tools
Auto Accessories

BRANDS/DIVISIONS/AFFILIATES:

O'Reilly Auto Parts
Power Torque
BrakeBest
Prestone
Master Pro
Omnispark
Super Start
Ultima

CONTACTS: *Note: Officers with more than one job title may be intentionally listed here more than once.*

Gregory Henslee, CEO
Charles OReilly, Vice Chairman of the Board
Thomas McFall, CFO
David OReilly, Chairman of the Board
Jeremy Fletcher, Controller
Gregory Johnson, Co-President
Jeff Shaw, Co-President
Larry Ellis, Senior VP, Divisional
Randy Johnson, Senior VP, Divisional
Tony Bartholomew, Senior VP, Divisional
Brad Beckham, Senior VP, Divisional
Byron Childers, Senior VP, Divisional
Jeffrey Lauro, Senior VP, Divisional
Scott Kraus, Senior VP, Divisional
Carl Wilbanks, Senior VP, Divisional
Robert Dumas, Senior VP, Divisional
Jeffrey Groves, Senior VP, Divisional
Lawrence OReilly, Vice Chairman of the Board

GROWTH PLANS/SPECIAL FEATURES:

O'Reilly Automotive, Inc. is one of the largest specialty retailers of automotive aftermarket parts, tools, supplies, equipment and accessories in the U.S., selling products to both do-it-yourself (DIY) customers and professional installers. The company operates 4,829 stores under the O'Reilly Auto Parts name in 47 states across the U.S. Stores carry an average of 45,000 stock keeping units (SKUs) with an extensive product line consisting of new and remanufactured automotive hard parts, such as alternators, starters, brake system components, batteries, chassis parts and engine parts; maintenance items, such as oil, antifreeze, fluids, wiper blades, lighting, engine additives and appearance products; accessories, such as floor mats, truck accessories and seat covers; and a complete line of auto body paint and related materials, automotive tools and professional service equipment. Store merchandise generally consists of nationally recognized, well-advertised, name-brand products such as AC Delco, Armor All, Bosch, BWD, Cardone, Castrol, Gates Rubber, Monroe, Moog, Pennzoil, Prestone, Quaker State, STP, Turtle Wax, Valvoline, Wagner and Wix. In addition to name-brand products, stores carry a wide variety of high-quality private-label products under the BestTest, BrakeBest, Import Direct, Master Pro, Micro-Gard, Murray, Omnispark, Precision, Power Torque, Super Start and Ultima brands. O'Reilly operates 27 distribution centers and 312 hub stores, each equipped with highly automated material handling equipment that expedites the movement of products to loading areas for shipment to individual stores on a nightly basis. O'Reilly Automotive opened 210 new stores in 2016, with plans to open another 190 stores in 2017, in an effort to penetrate existing markets and expand into new, contiguous ones. In addition to its expansions, the firm acquired 48 Bond Auto Parts store locations.

O'Reilly offers its employees medical, dental, vision, pharmacy and life insurance; a credit union membership; a 401(k) plan with company match; a profit sharing plan; paid time off; a discount stock purchase plan; and an employee assistance program.

FINANCIAL DATA: *Note: Data for latest year may not have been available at press time.*

In U.S. $	2016	2015	2014	2013	2012	2011
Revenue	8,593,096,000	7,966,674,000	7,216,081,000	6,649,237,000	6,182,184,000	5,788,816,000
R&D Expense						
Operating Income	1,699,206,000	1,514,021,000	1,270,374,000	1,103,485,000	977,393,000	866,766,000
Operating Margin %	19.77%	19.00%	17.60%	16.59%	15.80%	14.97%
SGA Expense	2,809,805,000	2,648,622,000	2,438,527,000	2,265,516,000	2,120,025,000	1,973,381,000
Net Income	1,037,691,000	931,216,000	778,182,000	670,292,000	585,746,000	507,673,000
Operating Cash Flow	1,454,167,000	1,281,476,000	1,190,430,000	908,026,000	1,251,555,000	1,118,991,000
Capital Expenditure	476,344,000	414,020,000	429,987,000	395,881,000	300,719,000	328,319,000
EBITDA	1,925,988,000	1,727,751,000	1,469,677,000	1,291,196,000	1,158,827,000	1,009,818,000
Return on Assets %	14.95%	14.09%	12.34%	11.34%	10.41%	9.62%
Return on Equity %	57.83%	46.79%	39.05%	32.90%	23.65%	16.76%
Debt to Equity	1.15	0.70	0.69	0.71	0.51	0.28

CONTACT INFORMATION:

Phone: 417 862-6708 Fax: 417 863-2242
Toll-Free: 800-755-6759
Address: 233 S. Patterson Ave., Springfield, MO 65802 United States

STOCK TICKER/OTHER:

Stock Ticker: ORLY Exchange: NAS
Employees: 74,580 Fiscal Year Ends: 12/31
Parent Company:

SALARIES/BONUSES:

Top Exec. Salary: $1,238,461 Bonus: $
Second Exec. Salary: $713,846 Bonus: $

OTHER THOUGHTS:

Estimated Female Officers or Directors: 1
Hot Spot for Advancement for Women/Minorities: Y

Oshkosh Corporation

www.oshkoshcorporation.com

NAIC Code: 336120

TYPES OF BUSINESS:

Fire & Emergency Vehicles
Military Trucks
Truck Bodies
Specialty Trucks
Cement Mixers
Refuse Trucks

BRANDS/DIVISIONS/AFFILIATES:

JerrDan
JLG Industries Inc
Pierce
Oshkosh Defense

CONTACTS: *Note: Officers with more than one job title may be intentionally listed here more than once.*

William Jones, CEO
Colleen Moynihan, Senior VP, Divisional
James Freeders, Chief Accounting Officer
Joseph Kimmitt, Executive VP, Divisional
David Sagehorn, Executive VP
Ignacio Cortina, Executive VP
Robert Sims, Executive VP
Mark Radue, Executive VP
James Johnson, Executive VP
Frank Nerenhausen, Executive VP
Bradley Nelson, President, Divisional
John Bryant, President, Divisional
Marek May, Senior VP, Divisional
Robert Messina, Senior VP, Divisional

GROWTH PLANS/SPECIAL FEATURES:

Oshkosh Corporation is a leading designer, manufacturer and marketer of specialty vehicles and vehicle bodies. The company operates in four segments: defense, access equipment, fire and emergency and commercial. The access equipment segment, accounting for 56% of the firm's sales, is formed through JLG, a global manufacturer of aerial work platforms and telehandlers used in a wide variety of construction, agricultural, industrial, institutional and general maintenance applications to position workers and materials at elevated heights. Through its Jerr-Dan subsidiary, the segment also manufactures towing and recovery equipment in the U.S. The defense segment, accounting for roughly 15% of the company's sales, supplies severe-duty, heavy-payload tactical trucks to the U.S. Department of Defense (DoD). The fire and emergency segment (13%), through subsidiary Pierce, is a leading domestic manufacturer of fire apparatus assembled on custom chassis. It also manufactures fire apparatus assembled on commercially-available chassis, snow removal vehicles and emergency vehicles, including pumpers; aerial and ladder trucks; tankers; light-, medium- and heavy-duty rescue vehicles; rough terrain response vehicles; mobile command and control centers; bomb squad vehicles; and hazardous materials control vehicles. The segment sells aircraft rescue and fire fighting (ARFF) vehicles to domestic and international airports. The commercial segment (16%), manufactures rear- and front-discharge concrete mixers, refuse collection vehicles, mobile and stationary compactors and waste transfer units, portable and stationary concrete batch plants and vehicle components. JLG markets its products in over 3,500 locations worldwide.

The firm offers employees medical, prescription, dental, vision, AD&D, disability and life insurance; a flexible spending account; a 401(k); tuition reimbursement; an employee stock purchase program; and a pension plan.

FINANCIAL DATA: *Note: Data for latest year may not have been available at press time.*

In U.S. $	2016	2015	2014	2013	2012	2011
Revenue	6,279,200,000	6,098,100,000	6,808,200,000	7,665,100,000	8,180,900,000	7,584,700,000
R&D Expense						
Operating Income	364,000,000	398,600,000	503,300,000	505,700,000	366,000,000	500,900,000
Operating Margin %	5.79%	6.53%	7.39%	6.59%	4.47%	6.60%
SGA Expense	612,400,000	587,400,000	624,100,000	620,500,000	567,300,000	513,200,000
Net Income	216,400,000	229,500,000	309,300,000	318,000,000	230,800,000	273,400,000
Operating Cash Flow	577,700,000	82,500,000	170,400,000	438,000,000	268,300,000	387,700,000
Capital Expenditure	127,300,000	158,000,000	124,900,000	59,900,000	64,300,000	86,200,000
EBITDA	496,200,000	520,700,000	630,100,000	637,800,000	493,600,000	651,600,000
Return on Assets %	4.74%	4.97%	6.58%	6.54%	4.72%	5.73%
Return on Equity %	11.13%	11.75%	15.05%	16.05%	13.37%	18.70%
Debt to Equity	0.41	0.44	0.44	0.42	0.51	0.63

CONTACT INFORMATION:

Phone: 920 235-9151   Fax:
Toll-Free:
Address: 2307 Oregon St., Oshkosh, WI 54902 United States

STOCK TICKER/OTHER:

Stock Ticker: OSK
Employees: 13,800
Parent Company:

Exchange: NYS
Fiscal Year Ends: 09/30

SALARIES/BONUSES:

Top Exec. Salary: $946,708   Bonus: $
Second Exec. Salary: Bonus: $
$672,433

OTHER THOUGHTS:

Estimated Female Officers or Directors: 5
Hot Spot for Advancement for Women/Minorities: Y

Owens Corning Inc

www.owenscorning.com

NAIC Code: 326199

TYPES OF BUSINESS:

Building Materials (e.g., Fascia, Panels, Siding, Soffit), Plastics, Manufacturing
Glass Fiber Reinforcements
Manufactured Stone Veneer Products
Glass Fiber Fabrics
Construction Services

BRANDS/DIVISIONS/AFFILIATES:

Owens Corning PINK FIBERGLAS Insulation

CONTACTS: Note: Officers with more than one job title may be intentionally listed here more than once.

Michael McMurray, CFO
Michael Thaman, Chairman of the Board
Kelly Schmidt, Controller
Ava Harter, General Counsel
Julian Francis, President, Divisional
Arnaud Genis, President, Divisional
Brian Chambers, President, Divisional
Daniel Smith, Senior VP, Divisional

GROWTH PLANS/SPECIAL FEATURES:

Owens Corning is a producer of residential and commercial building materials and glass fiber reinforcements and other similar materials for composite systems. The company operates through three business segments: composites, insulation and roofing. Composites includes the firm's reinforcements and downstream businesses, and accounted for 33% of total net sales in 2016. This division's glass fiber materials can be found in over 40,000 end-use applications within the following five markets: building and construction, transportation, consumer, industrial, and power and energy. End-use applications include pipe, roofing shingles, sporting goods, consumer electronics, telecommunications cables, boats, aviation, defense, automotive, industrial containers and wind-energy. Composites manufactures, fabricates and sells glass reinforcements in the form of fiber and of fabrics. Insulation comprises 30% net sales, and its products help customers conserve energy, provide improved acoustical performance and offer convenience of installation and use for new home construction and remodeling purposes. These products include thermal and acoustical batts, loosefill insulation, foam sheathing and accessories, and are sold under the brand and trademark name Owens Corning PINK FIBERGLASS Insulation. Roofing products (37%) include laminate and strip asphalt roofing shingles, as well as oxidized asphalt and roofing accessories. In late-2016, the firm acquired the glass non-wovens and fabrics businesses of Ahlstrom of Helsinki, Finland. In May 2017, it agreed to acquire Pittsburgh Corning, a leading producer of cellular glass insulation systems for commercial and industrial markets.

The company offers employees medical, dental and vision insurance; a wellness program; short- and long-term disability coverage; health care and dependent care spending accounts; relocation assistance; life insurance; personal accident insurance; and auto and home insurance.

FINANCIAL DATA: Note: Data for latest year may not have been available at press time.

In U.S. $	2016	2015	2014	2013	2012	2011
Revenue	5,677,000,000	5,350,000,000	5,276,000,000	5,295,000,000	5,172,000,000	5,335,000,000
R&D Expense	82,000,000	73,000,000	76,000,000	77,000,000	79,000,000	77,000,000
Operating Income	699,000,000	548,000,000	392,000,000	385,000,000	148,000,000	461,000,000
Operating Margin %	12.31%	10.24%	7.42%	7.27%	2.86%	8.64%
SGA Expense	584,000,000	525,000,000	487,000,000	530,000,000	509,000,000	525,000,000
Net Income	393,000,000	330,000,000	226,000,000	204,000,000	-19,000,000	276,000,000
Operating Cash Flow	943,000,000	742,000,000	441,000,000	418,000,000	330,000,000	289,000,000
Capital Expenditure	373,000,000	393,000,000	363,000,000	353,000,000	332,000,000	442,000,000
EBITDA	1,042,000,000	848,000,000	696,000,000	717,000,000	423,000,000	779,000,000
Return on Assets %	5.19%	4.41%	2.97%	2.68%	-.25%	3.75%
Return on Equity %	10.35%	8.88%	6.03%	5.56%	-.52%	7.51%
Debt to Equity	0.54	0.45	0.53	0.53	0.58	0.52

CONTACT INFORMATION:

Phone: 419 248-8000   Fax: 419 248-8445
Toll-Free: 800-438-7465
Address: 1 Owens Corning Pkwy., Toledo, OH 43659 United States

STOCK TICKER/OTHER:

Stock Ticker: OC   Exchange: NYS
Employees: 16,000   Fiscal Year Ends: 12/31
Parent Company:

SALARIES/BONUSES:

Top Exec. Salary: $1,140,500   Bonus: $
Second Exec. Salary: $596,667   Bonus: $

OTHER THOUGHTS:

Estimated Female Officers or Directors: 2
Hot Spot for Advancement for Women/Minorities: Y

PACCAR Inc

NAIC Code: 336120

www.paccar.com

TYPES OF BUSINESS:

Truck Manufacturing
Premium Truck Manufacturer
Parts Distribution
Finance, Lease and Insurance Services

BRANDS/DIVISIONS/AFFILIATES:

Kenworth Truck Company
DAF Trucks
Peterbilt Motors
PACCAR Financial Services
PACCAR Leasing
Carco
Braden
Gearmatic

CONTACTS: *Note: Officers with more than one job title may be intentionally listed here more than once.*

Ronald Armstrong, CEO
Harrie Schippers, CFO
Mark Pigott, Chairman of the Board
Michael Barkley, Chief Accounting Officer
A Ley, Chief Information Officer
Gary Moore, Executive VP
James Clack, General Counsel
T. Quinn, General Manager, Divisional
Michael Dozier, General Manager, Subsidiary
Preston Feight, President, Subsidiary
Darrin Siver, Senior VP
Robert Bengston, Senior VP, Divisional
Marco Davila, Vice President
Jack LeVier, Vice President, Divisional

GROWTH PLANS/SPECIAL FEATURES:

PACCAR, Inc. is a leading manufacturer of premium light-, medium- and heavy-duty trucks. The firm operates in three major divisions: trucks, parts and financial services. Truck division subsidiaries include Kenworth Truck Company, Peterbilt Motors and DAF Trucks. The vehicles are used worldwide for over-the-road and off-highway hauling of freight, petroleum, wood products, construction and other materials. The Kenworth and Peterbilt nameplates are manufactured and distributed by separate divisions in the U.S. and foreign plants in Canada, Mexico and Australia. Headquartered in the Netherlands, DAF Trucks comprises the European component of PACCAR, with distribution throughout Europe, Asia and Africa. Products and services are available worldwide, with customer call centers operating continuously. Substantially all trucks and related parts are sold to independent dealers, and this division accounts for 75% of net sales. The parts division includes the distribution of aftermarket parts for trucks and related commercial vehicles in the U.S., Canada, Europe, Australia, Mexico and South America. Aftermarket truck parts are sold and delivered to the company's independent dealers through the firm's 17 strategically-located distribution centers. The parts segment accounts for 18% of net sales. The company's financial services segment (7% of net sales), which operates through wholly-owned subsidiaries PACCAR Financial Services and PACCAR Leasing, maintains a presence in over 23 countries. This division provides financing and leasing arrangements, mainly for its manufactured trucks. The company's share of the U.S. and Canadian Class 8 truck market is roughly 28.5%. In addition, other businesses (less than 1% of net sales) consists of a manufacturing division, which makes industrial winches in two U.S. plants and markets them under the Braden, Carco and Gearmatic nameplates.

FINANCIAL DATA: *Note: Data for latest year may not have been available at press time.*

In U.S. $	2016	2015	2014	2013	2012	2011
Revenue	17,033,300,000	19,115,100,000	18,997,000,000	17,123,800,000	17,050,500,000	16,355,200,000
R&D Expense	247,200,000	239,800,000	215,600,000	251,400,000	279,300,000	288,200,000
Operating Income	1,241,600,000	2,445,600,000	2,134,500,000	1,827,600,000	1,753,900,000	1,660,700,000
Operating Margin %	7.28%	12.79%	11.23%	10.67%	10.28%	10.15%
SGA Expense	1,373,200,000	541,500,000	561,400,000	559,500,000	571,600,000	546,900,000
Net Income	521,700,000	1,604,000,000	1,358,800,000	1,171,300,000	1,111,600,000	1,042,300,000
Operating Cash Flow	2,300,800,000	2,556,000,000	2,123,600,000	2,375,700,000	1,519,000,000	1,592,600,000
Capital Expenditure	1,964,900,000	1,725,200,000	1,537,300,000	1,872,800,000	1,803,400,000	1,647,300,000
EBITDA	2,250,700,000	3,374,500,000	3,074,500,000	2,661,600,000	2,488,200,000	2,362,000,000
Return on Assets %	2.49%	7.68%	6.57%	5.95%	6.21%	6.63%
Return on Equity %	7.60%	23.42%	20.29%	18.76%	19.83%	19.44%
Debt to Equity	0.88	0.83	0.82	0.90	0.77	0.55

CONTACT INFORMATION:

Phone: 425 468-7400   Fax: 425 468-8216
Toll-Free:
Address: 777 106th Ave. NE, Bellevue, WA 98004 United States

STOCK TICKER/OTHER:

Stock Ticker: PCAR
Employees: 23,000
Parent Company:

Exchange: NAS
Fiscal Year Ends: 12/31

SALARIES/BONUSES:

Top Exec. Salary: $1,210,000   Bonus: $
Second Exec. Salary: $800,000   Bonus: $

OTHER THOUGHTS:

Estimated Female Officers or Directors:
Hot Spot for Advancement for Women/Minorities:

PAREXEL International Corporation

www.parexel.com

NAIC Code: 541711

TYPES OF BUSINESS:

Clinical Trial & Data Management
Biostatistical Analysis & Reporting
Medical Communications Services
Clinical Pharmacology Services
Consulting Services

BRANDS/DIVISIONS/AFFILIATES:

ClinPhone
Epro
Health Advances LLC
ExecuPharm Inc
Medical Affairs Company (The)

CONTACTS: Note: Officers with more than one job title may be intentionally listed here more than once.

Emma Reeve, CFO
Sybrand Pretorius, Chief Scientific Officer
Mark Goldberg, COO
Josef Von Rickenbach, Founder
Michelle Graham, Other Executive Officer
Xavier Flinois, President, Divisional
Gadi Saarony, Senior VP, Divisional
Roland Andersson, Senior VP, Divisional
Joshua Schultz, Senior VP, Divisional
David Godwin, Senior VP, Divisional
Douglas Batt, Senior VP

GROWTH PLANS/SPECIAL FEATURES:

PAREXEL International Corporation is a leading biopharmaceutical outsourcing services company, providing a broad range of expertise in clinical research, clinical logistics, medical communications, consulting, commercialization and advanced technology products and services to the worldwide pharmaceutical, biotechnology and medical device industries. Operating in more than 80 locations throughout 52 countries, PAREXEL has three business segments: clinical research services (CRS), PAREXEL consulting services (PC) and PAREXEL informatics (PI). CRS, accounting for 77.6% of revenue, includes all phases of clinical research from first-in-man trials through post-marketing studies. CRS service offerings include clinical trials management, observational studies, patient/disease registries and post-marketing surveillance, data management and biostatistics, epidemiology and health economics/outcomes research, clinical logistics, pharmacovigilance and clinical pharmacology as well as related medical affairs, patient recruitment and investigator site services. PC provides technical expertise and advice in such areas as drug development, regulatory affairs and good manufacturing practice compliance consulting. In addition, it provides market development, product development, commercialization and targeted communications services in support of product launch. PC consultants also identify alternatives and propose solutions to address clients' product development, registration and commercialization issues. The segment provides information technology solutions designed to improve product development processes. Products and services include ClinPhone randomization and trial supply management services, medical imaging services, ePRO (electronic patient reported outcomes), clinical trial management systems, electronic data capture systems, web-based portals, systems integration and patient diary applications. In 2016, the firm acquired Health Advances, LLC, a life sciences strategy consulting firm; and ExecuPharm, Inc., a global functional service provider. In February 2017, it acquired The Medical Affairs Company, a provider of outsourced medical affairs services to the pharmaceutical, biotechnology and medical device industries.

FINANCIAL DATA: Note: Data for latest year may not have been available at press time.

In U.S. $	2016	2015	2014	2013	2012	2011
Revenue	2,426,300,000	2,330,274,000	2,266,342,000	1,995,966,000	1,618,234,000	1,422,425,000
R&D Expense						
Operating Income	224,000,000	199,852,000	199,498,000	136,123,000	88,802,000	81,630,000
Operating Margin %	9.23%	8.57%	8.80%	6.81%	5.48%	5.73%
SGA Expense	385,300,000	367,192,000	379,800,000	318,806,000	263,462,000	271,049,000
Net Income	154,900,000	147,821,000	129,094,000	95,972,000	63,158,000	48,786,000
Operating Cash Flow	261,300,000	157,843,000	287,201,000	183,815,000	234,457,000	-1,455,000
Capital Expenditure	95,500,000	80,167,000	72,585,000	81,089,000	74,403,000	60,153,000
EBITDA	320,900,000	284,791,000	280,826,000	217,403,000	158,262,000	141,124,000
Return on Assets %	7.94%	7.99%	7.14%	5.79%	4.26%	3.68%
Return on Equity %	23.85%	23.78%	23.12%	16.71%	10.74%	9.70%
Debt to Equity	0.76	0.51	0.57	0.78	0.35	0.42

CONTACT INFORMATION:

Phone: 781 487-9900   Fax: 781 487-0525
Toll-Free:
Address: 195 West St., Waltham, MA 02451 United States

STOCK TICKER/OTHER:

Stock Ticker: PRXL   Exchange: NAS
Employees: 18,660   Fiscal Year Ends: 06/30
Parent Company:

SALARIES/BONUSES:

Top Exec. Salary: $966,874   Bonus: $679,400
Second Exec. Salary: $622,263   Bonus: $317,400

OTHER THOUGHTS:

Estimated Female Officers or Directors: 1
Hot Spot for Advancement for Women/Minorities: Y

Sales, profits and employees may be estimates. Financial information, benefits and other data can quickly and may vary from those stated here.

Patrick Industries Inc

NAIC Code: 321219

www.patrickind.com

TYPES OF BUSINESS:

Reconstituted Wood Product Manufacturing

BRANDS/DIVISIONS/AFFILIATES:

Leisure Product Enterprises LLC
Marine Concepts/Design Concepts
Florida Marine Tanks Inc
Marine Electrical Products Inc

CONTACTS: Note: Officers with more than one job title may be intentionally listed here more than once.

Joshua Boone, CFO
Todd Cleveland, Director
Paul Hassler, Director
Kip Ellis, Executive VP, Divisional
Jeff Rodino, Executive VP, Divisional
Courtney Blosser, Executive VP, Divisional
Andy Nemeth, President

GROWTH PLANS/SPECIAL FEATURES:

Patrick Industries, Inc. is a manufacturer and supplier of building products and materials to the manufactured housing and recreational vehicle industries. Additionally, it is a supplier to certain other industrial markets such as furniture manufacturing, marine, architectural and the automotive aftermarket. Through the firm's manufacturing divisions, it manufactures and fabricates a variety of products: decorative vinyl and paper laminated panels, solid surface countertops, fabricated aluminum products, profile moldings, slide-out trims, cabinet doors, hardwood furniture, fiberglass bath fixtures, fiberglass and plastic components, softwoods, interior passage doors, RV painting and slotwall panels. In conjunction with its manufacturing capabilities, Patrick Industries also provide value added processes, including custom fabrication, edge-banding, drilling, boring and cut-to-size capabilities. The company also distributes pre-finished wall and ceiling panels, drywall products, electrical systems components, audio systems components, cement siding, raw and processed lumber, fiber-reinforced polyester, interior passage doors, roofing products, laminate and ceramic flooring, shower doors, furniture, fireplaces and surrounds, interior/exterior lighting products and miscellaneous products. Patrick Industries' annual sales by market include 75% to the recreational vehicle industry, 13% to the manufactured housing industry and 12% to the industrial industry. The company maintains 56 manufacturing plants and 22 warehouse and distribution facilities in 16 U.S. states. In May 2017, the firm acquired Leisure Product Enterprises, LLC, a holding company of three manufacturing subsidiaries: Marine Concepts/Design Concepts, Florida Marine Tanks, Inc. and Marine Electrical Products, Inc.

FINANCIAL DATA: Note: Data for latest year may not have been available at press time.

In U.S. $	2016	2015	2014	2013	2012	2011
Revenue	1,221,887,000	920,333,000	735,717,000	594,931,000	437,367,000	307,822,000
R&D Expense						
Operating Income	90,837,000	69,918,000	51,471,000	40,945,000	27,040,000	13,475,000
Operating Margin %	7.43%	7.59%	6.99%	6.88%	6.18%	4.37%
SGA Expense	98,264,000	73,523,000	62,525,000	48,137,000	37,419,000	30,248,000
Net Income	55,577,000	42,219,000	30,674,000	24,040,000	28,095,000	8,470,000
Operating Cash Flow	97,147,000	65,630,000	45,741,000	22,431,000	20,997,000	11,815,000
Capital Expenditure	15,406,000	7,958,000	6,542,000	8,669,000	7,895,000	2,436,000
EBITDA	115,199,000	86,693,000	61,904,000	48,242,000	30,895,000	17,692,000
Return on Assets %	12.06%	13.16%	14.27%	15.13%	24.51%	10.54%
Return on Equity %	35.39%	36.49%	33.14%	33.45%	62.26%	36.05%
Debt to Equity	1.38	1.50	0.98	0.66	0.80	1.10

CONTACT INFORMATION:

Phone: 574 294-7511   Fax: 574 522-5213
Toll-Free:
Address: 107 West Franklin Street, Elkhart, IN 46515 United States

STOCK TICKER/OTHER:

Stock Ticker: PATK   Exchange: NAS
Employees: 4,497   Fiscal Year Ends: 12/31
Parent Company:

SALARIES/BONUSES:

Top Exec. Salary: $541,539   Bonus: $
Second Exec. Salary: $422,475   Bonus: $

OTHER THOUGHTS:

Estimated Female Officers or Directors:
Hot Spot for Advancement for Women/Minorities:

Patterson Companies Inc

www.pattersoncompanies.com

NAIC Code: 423450

TYPES OF BUSINESS:

Dental Products & Related Services
Veterinary Products
Non-Wheelchair Assistive Products

BRANDS/DIVISIONS/AFFILIATES:

Patterson Dental Supply Inc
Animal Health International Inc

CONTACTS: *Note: Officers with more than one job title may be intentionally listed here more than once.*

John Adent, CEO, Divisional
Paul Guggenheim, CEO, Subsidiary
Ann Gugino, CFO
John Buck, Director
Kelly Baker, Other Executive Officer
James Wiltz, President
Les Korsh, Vice President

GROWTH PLANS/SPECIAL FEATURES:

Patterson Companies, Inc. is a value-added specialty distributor serving the U.S. and Canadian dental supply markets and the U.S., Canadian and U.K. animal health supply markets. The company operates through these two segments: dental supply and animal health. The dental supply segment comprises subsidiary Patterson Dental Supply, Inc., which is one of the largest distributors of dental products in North America, offering full-service, value-added supplies to more than 114,000 dentists, dental laboratories, institutions and other healthcare professionals. The division provides consumable products, including X-ray film, restorative materials, hand instruments and sterilization products; basic and advanced technology dental equipment; practice management and clinical software; patient education systems; and office forms and stationery. Patterson Dental also offers related services including dental equipment installation, maintenance and repair, dental office design and equipment financing. The animal health segment comprises subsidiary Animal Health International, Inc., which distributes biologicals, pharmaceuticals, parasticides, supplies and equipment to the animal health supply market. This market is engaged in beef and dairy cattle, poultry and swine, and other food-producing animals. It also includes the companion animal supply market, which primarily consists of dogs, cats and horses. This segment offers over 189,000 stock keeping units (SKUs) to its customers, including many proprietary branded products, which provide a competitive edge in relation to price as well as to customer loyalty.

Employee benefits include medical, dental and vision coverage; flexible spending accounts; short- and long-term disability; life and accident insurance; a 401(k); employee stock purchase and ownership plans; education and employee assistance; and employee discounts.

FINANCIAL DATA: *Note: Data for latest year may not have been available at press time.*

In U.S. $	2016	2015	2014	2013	2012	2011
Revenue	5,386,703,000	4,375,020,000	4,063,715,000	3,637,212,000	3,535,661,000	
R&D Expense						
Operating Income	347,713,000	373,427,000	345,756,000	354,455,000	358,009,000	
Operating Margin %	6.45%	8.53%	8.50%	9.74%	10.12%	
SGA Expense	975,035,000		852,522,000			
Net Income	187,184,000	223,261,000	200,612,000	210,272,000	212,815,000	
Operating Cash Flow	156,329,000	262,691,000	195,836,000	299,195,000	321,158,000	
Capital Expenditure	79,354,000	62,945,000	40,387,000	21,983,000	29,650,000	
EBITDA	434,141,000	427,694,000	398,611,000	403,516,000	402,364,000	
Return on Assets %	5.78%	7.68%	7.23%	7.75%	8.02%	
Return on Equity %	12.66%	14.95%	13.99%	15.18%	14.49%	
Debt to Equity	0.70	0.47	0.49	0.51	0.52	

CONTACT INFORMATION:

Phone: 651 686-1600   Fax: 651 686-9331
Toll-Free: 800-328-5536
Address: 1031 Mendota Heights Rd., St. Paul, MN 55120 United States

STOCK TICKER/OTHER:

Stock Ticker: PDCO   Exchange: NAS
Employees: 7,500   Fiscal Year Ends: 04/30
Parent Company:

SALARIES/BONUSES:

Top Exec. Salary: $770,477   Bonus: $
Second Exec. Salary: Bonus: $
$399,167

OTHER THOUGHTS:

Estimated Female Officers or Directors: 4
Hot Spot for Advancement for Women/Minorities: Y

Paychex Inc

NAIC Code: 541214

TYPES OF BUSINESS:

Payroll Processing Services
Payroll & Tax Preparation
Internal Accounting Records
Human Resources Outsourcing
Employee Benefits Outsourcing
Regulatory Compliance
Workers' Compensation Insurance Services
Online Payroll Services

BRANDS/DIVISIONS/AFFILIATES:

Paychex Online Payroll
Paychex Flex
Paychex Insurance Agency Inc
SurePayroll
Paychex Flex Enterprise

CONTACTS: *Note: Officers with more than one job title may be intentionally listed here more than once.*

Martin Mucci, CEO
Efrain Rivera, CFO
B. Golisano, Chairman of the Board
Jennifer Vossler, Controller
Stephanie Schaeffer, Other Executive Officer
Michael Gioja, Senior VP, Divisional
Mark Bottini, Senior VP, Divisional
John Gibson, Senior VP, Divisional
Laurie Zaucha, Vice President, Divisional

GROWTH PLANS/SPECIAL FEATURES:

Paychex, Inc. provides comprehensive payroll and integrated human resource and employee benefits outsourcing solutions for small- to medium-sized businesses. It serves approximately 605,000 clients through more than 100 offices in the U.S. and approximately 2,000 customers in Germany through four offices located in Hamburg, Berlin, Munich and Dusseldorf. Paychex mainly targets businesses with fewer than 100 employees, which represents 99% of the company's operations. Paychex primarily offers human capital management (HCM) services through Paychex Flex, a software-as-a-service (SaaS) platform, which provides an integrated product suite offering solutions including applicant tracking, employee onboarding, payroll, employee benefits and human resource administration, time and attendance, performance management and retirement services. The firm's payroll processing services, which form the foundation of its service portfolio, include the calculation, preparation and delivery of employee payroll checks; production of internal accounting records and management reports; preparation of federal, state and local payroll tax returns; and collection and remittance of clients' payroll obligations. Additionally, Paychex offers professional employer organization (PEO) services and insurance offerings through the Paychex Insurance Agency, Inc. For small businesses, products include Paychex Online Payroll, a suite of self-service and interactive services available twenty-four hours a day, seven days a week; and SurePayroll, do-it-yourself, self-service SaaS solution, as well as mobile applications. For mid-market businesses, products include Paychex Flex Enterprise solution set, which offers an integrated suite of HCM solutions tied together by the Paychex Flex platform. In April 2016, Paychex announced a strategic alliance with LPL Financial, a leading independent broker-dealer, to offer the Small Market Solution, a solution intended to minimize investment fiduciary risk and offers increased productivity for plan sponsors and advisors.

Employees of Paychex receive medical, vision and dental coverage; a prescription drug plan; flexible spending accounts; child care and employee assistance programs; and tuition reimbursement.

FINANCIAL DATA: *Note: Data for latest year may not have been available at press time.*

In U.S. $	2016	2015	2014	2013	2012	2011
Revenue	2,951,900,000	2,739,600,000	2,518,900,000	2,326,200,000	2,229,800,000	
R&D Expense						
Operating Income	1,146,600,000	1,053,600,000	982,700,000	904,800,000	853,900,000	
Operating Margin %	38.84%	38.45%	39.01%	38.89%	38.29%	
SGA Expense	948,200,000	878,000,000	803,700,000	750,100,000	695,100,000	
Net Income	756,800,000	674,900,000	627,500,000	569,000,000	548,000,000	
Operating Cash Flow	1,018,200,000	895,200,000	880,900,000	675,300,000	706,600,000	
Capital Expenditure	97,700,000	102,800,000	95,400,000	98,700,000	89,600,000	
EBITDA	1,261,700,000	1,167,300,000	1,087,700,000	1,003,000,000	951,700,000	
Return on Assets %	11.71%	10.50%	10.01%	9.00%	9.23%	
Return on Equity %	40.93%	37.88%	35.34%	33.68%	35.34%	
Debt to Equity						

CONTACT INFORMATION:

Phone: 585-385-6666   Fax: 585 383-3428
Toll-Free: 800-322-7292
Address: 911 Panorama Trail S., Rochester, NY 14625-0397 United States

STOCK TICKER/OTHER:

Stock Ticker: PAYX   Exchange: NAS
Employees: 13,700   Fiscal Year Ends: 05/31
Parent Company:

SALARIES/BONUSES:

Top Exec. Salary: $900,000   Bonus: $
Second Exec. Salary: $450,000   Bonus: $75,000

OTHER THOUGHTS:

Estimated Female Officers or Directors: 6
Hot Spot for Advancement for Women/Minorities: Y

Sales, profits and employees may be estimates. Financial information, benefits and other data can change quickly and may vary from those stated here.

Penske Automotive Group Inc

www.penskeautomotive.com

NAIC Code: 441110

TYPES OF BUSINESS:
Auto Dealers
Automotive Leasing
Parts & Service

BRANDS/DIVISIONS/AFFILIATES:
Western Star Trucks Australia
Penske Truck Leasing Co LP
CarSense
CarShop

CONTACTS: Note: Officers with more than one job title may be intentionally listed here more than once.
Roger Penske, CEO
J. Carlson, Chief Accounting Officer
Robert Kurnick, Director
Bud Denker, Executive VP, Divisional
Shane Spradlin, Executive VP

GROWTH PLANS/SPECIAL FEATURES:
Penske Automotive Group, Inc. (PAG) is an international transportation services company operating automotive dealerships and commercial vehicle distribution principally in the U.S., Western Europe, Australia and New Zealand. It operates 355 automotive retail franchises, of which 164 are located in the U.S. and 191 outside of the U.S. The franchises outside the U.S. are located primarily in the U.K. In 2016, the company retailed and wholesaled more than 556,000 vehicles. The commercial vehicle segment includes the operations of subsidiary Western Star Trucks Australia, the exclusive importer and distributor of Western Star heavy duty trucks (a Daimler brand), MAN heavy and medium duty trucks and buses (a VW Group brand), and Dennis Eagle refuse collection vehicles, together with associated parts across Australia, New Zealand and portions of Southeast Asia. The company also holds a 23.4% interest in Penske Truck Leasing Co., L.P. (PTL), a leading provider of transportation services and supply chain management. PTL operates and maintains approximately 240,000 vehicles and serves customers in North America, South America, Europe, Australia and Asia, and is one of the largest purchasers of commercial trucks in North America. In January 2017, the firm acquired CarSense, a stand-alone specialty retailer of used vehicles in the U.S. dedicated to reconditioning and retailing high quality, late model used vehicles. That following month, the company acquired the U.K.-based company, CarShop, a leading retailer of used vehicles.

Employee benefits include medical, dental, prescription, vision and life insurance; a 401(k) with company match; flexible spending accounts; an employee assistance program; and paid time off.

FINANCIAL DATA: Note: Data for latest year may not have been available at press time.

In U.S. $	2016	2015	2014	2013	2012	2011
Revenue	20,118,500,000	19,284,900,000	17,177,200,000	14,705,400,000	13,163,520,000	11,556,230,000
R&D Expense						
Operating Income	574,900,000	566,500,000	504,100,000	436,200,000	364,858,000	298,190,000
Operating Margin %						
SGA Expense	2,302,000,000	2,223,000,000	1,999,600,000	1,761,900,000	1,594,095,000	1,478,297,000
Net Income	342,900,000	326,100,000	286,700,000	244,200,000	185,540,000	176,881,000
Operating Cash Flow	367,100,000	391,500,000	366,600,000	314,800,000	323,400,000	63,475,000
Capital Expenditure	203,100,000	199,500,000	174,800,000	256,300,000	161,286,000	133,115,000
EBITDA	734,100,000	683,800,000	630,900,000	528,600,000	428,672,000	370,826,000
Return on Assets %	4.06%	4.27%	4.20%	4.14%	3.75%	4.12%
Return on Equity %	19.36%	18.94%	18.16%	17.38%	15.20%	16.24%
Debt to Equity	1.04	0.70	0.79	0.68	0.70	0.74

CONTACT INFORMATION:
Phone: 248 648-2500   Fax: 248 648-2525
Toll-Free:
Address: 2555 Telegraph Rd., Bloomfield Hills, MI 48302 United States

STOCK TICKER/OTHER:
Stock Ticker: PAG   Exchange: NYS
Employees: 24,000   Fiscal Year Ends: 12/31
Parent Company:

SALARIES/BONUSES:
Top Exec. Salary: $1,200,000   Bonus: $
Second Exec. Salary: $500,000   Bonus: $265,000

OTHER THOUGHTS:
Estimated Female Officers or Directors: 2
Hot Spot for Advancement for Women/Minorities:

Penske Corporation

NAIC Code: 532120

www.penske.com

TYPES OF BUSINESS:

Truck Rental
Auto Racing
Auto Sales & Service
Supply Chain Solutions
Auto Accessories Manufacturing & Retail
Fuel Management Systems
Fleet Management Services
Vehicle Components & Systems

BRANDS/DIVISIONS/AFFILIATES:

Penske Automotive Group
Penske Motor Group
Penske Truck Rental
Penske Logistics
Truck-Lite
Penske Racing
Truck-Lite Co LLC
Davco Technology LLC

CONTACTS: Note: Officers with more than one job title may be intentionally listed here more than once.

Roger S. Penske, CEO
Robert H. Kurnick Jr., Pres.
Gregory J. Houfley, CFO
Robert H. Kurnick, Jr., Pres., Penske Automotive Group
Calvin C. Sharp, Exec. VP-Human Resources, Penske Automotive Group
David K. Jones, CFO
Shane M. Spradlin, General Counsel
Roger S. Penske, Chmn.
Marc Althen, Pres., Penske Logistics

GROWTH PLANS/SPECIAL FEATURES:

Penske Corporation is a diversified transportation company that participates in a variety of automotive markets through its network of subsidiaries. Its markets include auto sales and service, truck rental, supply chain solutions, vehicle headlight design and development, vehicle lighting and harness safety systems, fluid management and automobile racing. Penske Automotive Group (PAG) is an international transportation services company that operates retail automotive dealerships, Hertz car rental franchises and commercial vehicle distribution. It operates primarily in the U.S., Western Europe, Australia and New Zealand. Penske Motor Group owns and operates automobile dealerships in California. Penske Truck Leasing is a partnership between the firm and General Electricals. It operates over 240,000 vehicles and consists of Penske Truck Rental, which offers fleet management services including service leasing, truck rentals, logistics, used trucks for sale and felt services for utility and transit companies with municipalities at almost 1,000 Penske facilities nationwide. Penske Logistics focuses on supply chain solutions, providing services designed to cut costs, reduce cycle time, improve service and integrate technology into the operations of its customers. Truck-Lite is responsible for creating vehicle lighting and harness safety systems for fleet vehicles through its affiliated subsidiaries: Truck-Lite Co., LLC and Truck-Lite Europe Limited. Davco Technology, LLC provides diesel fuel management with its line of filters, fuel/water separators and fuel warmers. Davco products include the Sea Pro for marine applications, Diesel Pro for medium trucks and the Industrial Pro for fuel filtration and water separation for industrial applications such as power generation, mining, oil and gas exploration. Penske Racing's operations include teams competing in NASCAR Sprint Cup Series, IndyCar Series, NASCAR Nationwide Series and American Le Mans Series.

FINANCIAL DATA: Note: Data for latest year may not have been available at press time.

In U.S. $	2016	2015	2014	2013	2012	2011
Revenue	26,000,000,000	23,000,000,000	20,500,000,000	20,000,000,000	19,000,000,000	17,000,000,000
R&D Expense						
Operating Income						
Operating Margin %						
SGA Expense						
Net Income						
Operating Cash Flow						
Capital Expenditure						
EBITDA						
Return on Assets %						
Return on Equity %						
Debt to Equity						

CONTACT INFORMATION:

Phone: 248-648-2000   Fax: 248-648-2525
Toll-Free:
Address: 2555 Telegraph Rd., Bloomfield Hills, MI 48302 United States

STOCK TICKER/OTHER:

Stock Ticker: Private   Exchange:
Employees: 51,500   Fiscal Year Ends: 12/31
Parent Company:

SALARIES/BONUSES:

Top Exec. Salary: $ Bonus: $
Second Exec. Salary: $ Bonus: $

OTHER THOUGHTS:

Estimated Female Officers or Directors:
Hot Spot for Advancement for Women/Minorities:

PerkinElmer Inc

NAIC Code: 325413

TYPES OF BUSINESS:

Diagnostic Systems
Mechanical Components
Optoelectronics
Pharmaceutical Manufacturing
Life Science Systems
Environmental Safety Equipment

BRANDS/DIVISIONS/AFFILIATES:

Aanalyst
AxION
Glutomatic
OilExpress
Supra-clean
DELFIA
NeoGram
EnLite

CONTACTS: Note: Officers with more than one job title may be intentionally listed here more than once.

Robert Friel, CEO
Andrew Okun, Chief Accounting Officer
James Corbett, Executive VP
Joel Goldberg, General Counsel
Deborah Butters, Other Executive Officer
Prahlad Singh, President, Divisional
Daniel Tereau, Senior VP, Divisional
Frank Wilson, Senior VP

GROWTH PLANS/SPECIAL FEATURES:

PerkinElmer, Inc. provides technology, services and solutions for the diagnostics, food, environmental, industrial, life sciences research and laboratory services markets. The company operates through two segments: discovery and analytical solutions, and diagnostics. The discovery and analytical solutions segment comprises a portfolio of technologies that help life sciences researchers better understand diseases and develop treatments. This division also helps the ability to detect, monitor and manage contaminants and toxic chemicals impacting the environment and food supply. Just a few of the many product, services and application solutions developed by this segment include: gas chromatographs, mass spectrometers, sample-handling equipment, advanced liquid chromatography systems, analyzers, quantitative pathology research solutions, radiometric detection solutions, screening systems and plate readers. The diagnostics segment offers instruments, reagents, assay platforms and software to hospitals, medical labs, clinicians and medical research professionals. This division focuses on reproductive health, emerging market diagnostics and applied genomics. Products, services and application solutions include screening platforms, in vitro diagnostic kits, blood analyzing kits, informatics data management, X-ray detectors, umbilical cord blood banking services, automated liquid handling platforms, next-generation sequencing automation and nucleic acid quantitation and automated small scale purification. Brand names include AAnalyst, AxION, Glutomatic, OilExpress, Supra-clean, DELFIA, NeoGram, XRD and EnLite. PerkinElmer is headquartered in Waltham, Massachusetts, and markets its products and services in more than 150 countries. In 2017, the firm sold its medical imaging business to Varex Imaging Corporation; and agreed to acquire EUROIMMUN Medical Laboratory Diagnostics AG, a global leader in autoimmune testing.

FINANCIAL DATA: Note: Data for latest year may not have been available at press time.

In U.S. $	2016	2015	2014	2013	2012	2011
Revenue	2,115,517,000	2,262,359,000	2,237,219,000	2,166,232,000	2,115,205,000	1,921,287,000
R&D Expense	124,278,000	125,928,000	121,141,000	133,023,000	132,639,000	115,821,000
Operating Income	283,066,000	286,134,000	210,742,000	217,442,000	98,543,000	91,128,000
Operating Margin %	13.38%	12.64%	9.41%	10.03%	4.65%	4.74%
SGA Expense	600,885,000	598,848,000	659,335,000	585,850,000	632,734,000	627,172,000
Net Income	234,299,000	212,425,000	157,778,000	167,212,000	69,940,000	7,655,000
Operating Cash Flow	350,615,000	287,098,000	281,597,000	158,591,000	152,170,000	224,874,000
Capital Expenditure	31,702,000	29,632,000	29,072,000	38,991,000	42,408,000	30,592,000
EBITDA	385,568,000	395,515,000	322,609,000	331,727,000	223,239,000	200,058,000
Return on Assets %	5.55%	5.11%	3.90%	4.26%	1.80%	.21%
Return on Equity %	10.98%	10.23%	7.81%	8.50%	3.69%	.40%
Debt to Equity	0.48	0.47	0.51	0.46	0.48	0.51

CONTACT INFORMATION:

Phone: 781 663-6900   Fax:
Toll-Free: 800-762-4000
Address: 940 Winter St., Waltham, MA 02451 United States

STOCK TICKER/OTHER:

Stock Ticker: PKI   Exchange: NYS
Employees: 8,000   Fiscal Year Ends: 01/31
Parent Company:

SALARIES/BONUSES:

Top Exec. Salary: $1,054,615   Bonus: $
Second Exec. Salary: $524,692   Bonus: $

OTHER THOUGHTS:

Estimated Female Officers or Directors: 1
Hot Spot for Advancement for Women/Minorities: Y

PetSmart Inc

NAIC Code: 453910

www.petsmart.com

TYPES OF BUSINESS:

Pets & Pet Supplies, Retail
Online & Catalog Sales
Pet Training
In-Store Adoption Centers
Veterinary Services
Pet Boarding
Pet Grooming

BRANDS/DIVISIONS/AFFILIATES:

Argos Holdings Inc
PetSmart.com
PetPerks
Medical Management International Inc
Banfield Pet Hospital
PetSmart PetHotels
Chewy.com

CONTACTS: *Note: Officers with more than one job title may be intentionally listed here more than once.*

Michael J. Massey, CEO
David Lenhardt, CEO
Alan Schnaid, Exec.VP
Erick Goldberg, Sr. VP-Human Resources
Donald Beaver, Chief Information Officer
Michael Goodwin, Sr. VP-CIO
Paulette Dodson, General Counsel
Erick Goldberg, Senior VP, Divisional
Bruce Thorn, Senior VP, Divisional
Jaye Perricone, Senior VP, Divisional
Matthew McAdam, Senior VP, Divisional
Melvin Tucker, Senior VP, Divisional
Gene Burt, Senior VP, Divisional

GROWTH PLANS/SPECIAL FEATURES:

PetSmart, Inc. is a leading operator of superstores specializing in pet food, supplies and services. The company operates over 1,500 stores in the U.S., Puerto Rico and Canada, which offer an assortment of pet services and products. Its stores range in size from 12,000 to 27,500 square feet and carry roughly 11,000 distinct items in store and 9,000 additional items online through PetSmart.com. These items include nationally recognized brand names and a selection of proprietary or private label brands. PetSmart stores sell supplies for dogs, cats, fresh-water tropical fish, reptiles, birds and other small pets. The firm offers a PetPerks loyalty program to its customers. PetSmart stores also offer value-added pet services including grooming, training, boarding and day camp; and it operates full-service veterinary hospitals in many of its stores. Medical Management International, Inc., an operator of veterinary hospitals, operates more than 800 of PetSmart's hospitals under the name Banfield Pet Hospital. The remaining seven hospitals are located in Canada and operated by other third parties. PetSmart offers pet boarding in more than 200 stores through its PetSmart PetsHotels. PetsHotels provide boarding for dogs and cats, which includes 24-hour supervision by caregivers who are PetSmart-trained to provide personalized pet care, temperature controlled rooms and suites and play time as well as day camp for dogs. The company also actively supports pet adoption through its in-store adoption centers. PetSmart is privately-owned by Argos Holdings, Inc. In April 2017, PetSmart agreed to acquire online retailer Chewy.com for $3.35 billion.

PetSmart offers its employees medical, dental and vision insurance; life and AD&D insurance; short- and long-term disability; a 401(k) plan; an employee stock purchase plan; adoption assistance; associate discount; tuition assistance; flexible spending accounts; and a work/life balance program.

FINANCIAL DATA: *Note: Data for latest year may not have been available at press time.*

In U.S. $	2016	2015	2014	2013	2012	2011
Revenue	7,050,000,000	7,000,000,000	6,916,626,944	6,758,237,184	6,113,304,064	5,693,796,864
R&D Expense						
Operating Income						
Operating Margin %						
SGA Expense						
Net Income			419,520,000	389,528,992	290,243,008	239,867,008
Operating Cash Flow						
Capital Expenditure						
EBITDA						
Return on Assets %						
Return on Equity %						
Debt to Equity						

CONTACT INFORMATION:

Phone: 623 580-6100　　　　Fax:
Toll-Free: 800-738-1385
Address: 19601 N. 27th Ave., Phoenix, AZ 85027 United States

STOCK TICKER/OTHER:

Stock Ticker: Private　　　　　　　　　　Exchange:
Employees: 53,000　　　　　　　　　　　Fiscal Year Ends: 01/31
Parent Company: Argos Holdings Inc

SALARIES/BONUSES:

Top Exec. Salary: $　　　　Bonus: $
Second Exec. Salary: $　　　Bonus: $

OTHER THOUGHTS:

Estimated Female Officers or Directors: 3
Hot Spot for Advancement for Women/Minorities: Y

Pfizer Inc

NAIC Code: 325412

www.pfizer.com

TYPES OF BUSINESS:

Pharmaceuticals
Infusion Technologies

BRANDS/DIVISIONS/AFFILIATES:

Prevnar 13
Xeljanz
Eliquis
Lyrica
Enbrel
Xtandi
Medivation Inc
Anacor Pharmaceuticals Inc

CONTACTS: Note: Officers with more than one job title may be intentionally listed here more than once.

Ian Read, CEO
John Young, President, Divisional
Frank DAmelio, CFO
Loretta Cangialosi, Chief Accounting Officer
Freda Lewis-Hall, Chief Medical Officer
Rady Johnson, Chief Risk Officer
Laurie Olson, Executive VP, Divisional
Charles Hill, Executive VP, Divisional
Sally Susman, Executive VP, Divisional
Douglas Lankler, Executive VP
Alexander Mackenzie, Executive VP
Margaret Madden, Other Executive Officer
Albert Bourla, President, Divisional
Mikael Dolsten, President, Divisional
Kirsten Lund-Jurgensen, President, Divisional
Brenton Saunders, President

GROWTH PLANS/SPECIAL FEATURES:

Pfizer, Inc. is a research-based, global pharmaceutical company. It discovers, develops, manufactures and markets health care products. The company operates in two business segments: innovative health and essential health. The innovative health segment focuses on developing and commercializing novel, value-creating medicines and vaccines that significantly improve patients' lives, as well as products for consumer healthcare. Key therapeutic areas within this division include internal medicine, vaccines, oncology, inflammation/immunology, rare diseases and consumer healthcare. Leading brands within this segment include Prevnar 13, Xeljanz, Eliquis, Lyrica, Enbrel, Viagra, Ibrance, Xtandi and several over-the-counter (OTC) consumer products. The essential health segment comprises legacy brands that have lost or will soon lose market exclusivity in both developed and emerging markets. These branded products include generics, generic sterile injectable products and biosimilars. This division also includes a research and development organization, as well as the company's manufacturing business. Brands within this segment include Lipitor, Premarin, Norvasc, Lyrica (within Europe, Russia, Turkey, Israel and Central Asia countries), Celebrex and Pristiq, as well as several sterile injectable products. In 2016, Pfizer acquired Medivation, Inc., a biopharmaceutical company focused on developing and commercializing small molecules for oncology; Anacor Pharmaceuticals, Inc., which focuses on novel small-molecule therapeutics derived from its boron chemistry platform; and acquired the development and commercialization rights to AstraZeneca's small molecule anti-infectives business, primarily outside the U.S. In February 2017, Pfizer sold its global infusion therapy assets (HIS) to ICU Medical for approximately $900 million.

FINANCIAL DATA: Note: Data for latest year may not have been available at press time.

In U.S. $	2016	2015	2014	2013	2012	2011
Revenue	52,824,000,000	48,851,000,000	49,605,000,000	51,584,000,000	58,986,000,000	67,425,000,000
R&D Expense	7,872,000,000	7,690,000,000	8,393,000,000	6,678,000,000	7,870,000,000	9,112,001,000
Operating Income	13,730,000,000	11,824,000,000	13,249,000,000	16,727,000,000	13,221,000,000	15,241,000,000
Operating Margin %	25.99%	24.20%	26.70%	32.42%	22.41%	22.60%
SGA Expense	14,837,000,000	14,809,000,000	14,097,000,000	14,355,000,000	16,616,000,000	19,468,000,000
Net Income	7,215,000,000	6,960,000,000	9,135,000,000	22,003,000,000	14,570,000,000	10,009,000,000
Operating Cash Flow	15,901,000,000	14,512,000,000	16,883,000,000	17,765,000,000	17,054,000,000	20,240,000,000
Capital Expenditure	1,999,000,000	1,496,000,000	1,583,000,000	1,465,000,000	1,327,000,000	1,660,000,000
EBITDA	15,294,000,000	15,321,000,000	19,137,000,000	23,540,000,000	21,215,000,000	23,469,000,000
Return on Assets %	4.25%	4.13%	5.35%	12.29%	7.79%	5.22%
Return on Equity %	11.61%	10.23%	12.38%	27.94%	17.83%	11.78%
Debt to Equity	0.52	0.44	0.44	0.39	0.38	0.42

CONTACT INFORMATION:

Phone: 212 733-2323   Fax: 212 573-7851
Toll-Free:
Address: 235 E. 42nd Street, New York, NY 10017 United States

STOCK TICKER/OTHER:

Stock Ticker: PFE   Exchange: NYS
Employees: 96,500   Fiscal Year Ends: 12/31
Parent Company:

SALARIES/BONUSES:

Top Exec. Salary: $1,905,250   Bonus: $
Second Exec. Salary: Bonus: $
$1,324,000

OTHER THOUGHTS:

Estimated Female Officers or Directors: 7
Hot Spot for Advancement for Women/Minorities: Y

PG&E Corporation

www.pgecorp.com

NAIC Code: 221111

TYPES OF BUSINESS:

Hydroelectric Power Generation
Electric and Gas Utility
Electricity Generation
Pipelines
Nuclear Generation
Natural Gas

BRANDS/DIVISIONS/AFFILIATES:

Pacific Gas and Electric Company

CONTACTS: Note: Officers with more than one job title may be intentionally listed here more than once.

David Thomason, CFO, Subsidiary
Desmond Bell, Senior VP, Divisional
Jason Wells, CFO
Anthony Earley, Chairman of the Board
Nickolas Stavropoulos, COO, Subsidiary
John Simon, Executive VP
Hyun Park, General Counsel
Edward Halpin, Other Executive Officer
Loraine Giammona, Other Executive Officer
Karen Austin, Other Executive Officer
Dinyar Mistry, Other Executive Officer
Julie Kane, Other Executive Officer
Geisha Williams, President
Fong Wan, Senior VP, Subsidiary
Steven Malnight, Senior VP, Subsidiary
Jesus Soto, Senior VP, Subsidiary

GROWTH PLANS/SPECIAL FEATURES:

PG&E Corporation is a holding company that markets energy services and products in northern and central California through subsidiary Pacific Gas and Electric Company. The subsidiary is one of the largest electric and natural gas utilities in the U.S., serving roughly 16 million customers. With approximately 142,000 circuit miles of distribution lines, the company's electricity distribution network extends through most of northern and central California. Pacific owns and operates power plants producing nearly half of the power it sells including 104 hydroelectric, one nuclear (with two units), 13 photovoltaic and 12 fossil fuel facilities. The company's hydroelectric generation system covers 16 counties in northern and central California. This system consists of approximately 6,700 miles of backbone and local transmission pipelines, 42,800 miles of distribution pipelines and eight natural gas compressor and storage facilities. Through interconnections with various interstate pipelines, the company can receive gas from every major natural gas basin in western North America, including basins in Canada, the southwestern U.S. and the Rocky Mountains.

The company offers employees supplemental life, disability, medical, dental and vision insurance; flexible spending accounts for health care and dependent care; paid time off; paid sick leave; a wellness program; GlobalFit program; a 401(k); retiree medical and life insurance; post-retirement life insurance; an employee assistance program; adoption reimbursement; and tuition reimbursement opportunities. Other benefits include a company-matching program for educational or environmental charitable contributions, employee organized activities and employee discounts and volunteer opportunities.

FINANCIAL DATA: Note: Data for latest year may not have been available at press time.

In U.S. $	2016	2015	2014	2013	2012	2011
Revenue	17,666,000,000	16,833,000,000	17,090,000,000	15,598,000,000	15,040,000,000	14,956,000,000
R&D Expense						
Operating Income	2,177,000,000	1,508,000,000	2,450,000,000	1,762,000,000	1,693,000,000	1,942,000,000
Operating Margin %	12.32%	8.95%	14.33%	11.29%	11.25%	12.98%
SGA Expense						
Net Income	1,407,000,000	888,000,000	1,450,000,000	828,000,000	830,000,000	858,000,000
Operating Cash Flow	4,409,000,000	3,753,000,000	3,677,000,000	3,427,000,000	4,882,000,000	3,739,000,000
Capital Expenditure	5,709,000,000	5,173,000,000	4,833,000,000	5,207,000,000	4,624,000,000	4,038,000,000
EBITDA	5,046,000,000	4,246,000,000	4,962,000,000	3,888,000,000	4,042,000,000	4,213,000,000
Return on Assets %	2.11%	1.41%	2.48%	1.50%	1.59%	1.76%
Return on Equity %	8.07%	5.40%	9.54%	5.93%	6.48%	7.21%
Debt to Equity	0.90	0.96	0.95	0.88	0.95	0.97

CONTACT INFORMATION:

Phone: 415 973-8200   Fax: 415 973-8719
Toll-Free: 800-719-9056
Address: 77 Beale Street, 24/F, San Francisco, CA 94177 United States

SALARIES/BONUSES:

Top Exec. Salary: $1,318,750   Bonus: $
Second Exec. Salary: Bonus: $
$695,833

STOCK TICKER/OTHER:

Stock Ticker: PCG   Exchange: NYS
Employees: 22,000   Fiscal Year Ends: 12/31
Parent Company:

OTHER THOUGHTS:

Estimated Female Officers or Directors: 15
Hot Spot for Advancement for Women/Minorities: Y

Pharmaceutical Product Development Inc

www.ppdi.com

NAIC Code: 541711

TYPES OF BUSINESS:

Contract Research
Drug Discovery & Development Services
Clinical Data Consulting Services
Medical Marketing & Information Support Services
Drug Discovery Services
Medical Device Development

BRANDS/DIVISIONS/AFFILIATES:

Carlyle Group (The)
Hellman & Friedman

CONTACTS: Note: *Officers with more than one job title may be intentionally listed here more than once.*

David Simmons, CEO
Christine A. Dingivan, Chief Medical Officer
B. Judd Hartman, General Counsel
William W. Richardson, Sr. VP-Global Bus. Dev.
Randy Buckwalter, Head-Media
Luke Heagle, Head-Investor Rel.
Lee E. Babiss, Chief Science Officer
David Johnston, Exec. VP-Global Lab Svcs.
David Simmons, Chmn.
Paul Colvin, Exec. VP-Global Clinical Dev.

GROWTH PLANS/SPECIAL FEATURES:

Pharmaceutical Product Development, Inc. (PPD), jointly owned by The Carlyle Group and Hellman & Friedman, provides drug discovery and development services to pharmaceutical, biotechnology, medical device, academic and government organizations. PPD's services are divided into seven segments: early development, which offers a range of early development services, phase 1 clinical trial services and non-clinical consulting; clinical development, which helps advance drug research and development for products; PPD Laboratories, which provides comprehensive lab services; post-approval, which provides post-approval studies and late-stage clinical trials management; PPD Consulting, which acts as a consulting partner that assists companies with their biopharmaceutical product's success from pre-clinical through post-approval; functional service partnerships, provides customizable outsourcing solutions, including full-time equivalent models, units-based contracts and geographical-aligned agreements; and technology/innovation/performance, which helps companies deliver life-changing medicines, cutting-edge technologies, real-time analytics and customized training. Therapeutic areas of studies include cardiovascular, critical care, dermatology, dental pain research, endocrine and metabolics, gastroenterology, hemotology and oncology, immunology, infectious diseases, neuroscience, ophthalmology, respiratory and urology. PPD is headquartered in North Carolina, USA, with additional offices spanning 47 countries. In early-2017, the firm announced plans to open a new 24-bed clinical research unit in Las Vegas, to conduct complex, procedurally-intensive Phase I and early development clinical research on behalf of pharmaceutical and biotechnology clients.

FINANCIAL DATA: Note: *Data for latest year may not have been available at press time.*

In U.S. $	2016	2015	2014	2013	2012	2011
Revenue	1,300,000,000	1,200,000,000	1,222,000,000	1,023,100,000	749,100,032	700,000,000
R&D Expense						
Operating Income						
Operating Margin %						
SGA Expense						
Net Income						
Operating Cash Flow						
Capital Expenditure						
EBITDA						
Return on Assets %						
Return on Equity %						
Debt to Equity						

CONTACT INFORMATION:

Phone: 910-251-0081   Fax: 910-762-5820
Toll-Free:
Address: 929 N. Front Street, Wilmington, NC 28401-3331 United States

STOCK TICKER/OTHER:

Stock Ticker: Private   Exchange:
Employees: 18,500   Fiscal Year Ends: 12/31
Parent Company: Carlyle Group (The)

SALARIES/BONUSES:

Top Exec. Salary: $ Bonus: $
Second Exec. Salary: $ Bonus: $

OTHER THOUGHTS:

Estimated Female Officers or Directors: 2
Hot Spot for Advancement for Women/Minorities:

Philips Healthcare

NAIC Code: 334510

www.healthcare.philips.com

TYPES OF BUSINESS:

Manufacturing-Medical Equipment
Diagnostic & Treatment Equipment
Imaging Equipment
Equipment Repair & Maintenance
Healthcare Consulting

BRANDS/DIVISIONS/AFFILIATES:

Koninklijke Philips NV
SmartPath
Skolkovo Innovation Center

CONTACTS: Note: Officers with more than one job title may be intentionally listed here more than once.

Frans van Houten, CEO-Koninklijke Philips
Eric Silfen, Chief Medical Officer
Clement Revetti, Chief Legal Officer
Michael Dreher, Global Head-Oper. & Customer Svcs.
Diego Olego, Chief Strategy & Innovation Officer
Rachel Bloom-Baglin, Media Contact-Global
Frans van Houten, CEO-Royal Philips Electronics NV
Steve Laczynski, Pres., Americas
Desmond Thio, Pres., China
Brent Shafer, CEO-Home Health Care Solutions
Arjen Radder, Pres., Asia Pacific

GROWTH PLANS/SPECIAL FEATURES:

Philips Healthcare, a subsidiary of Koninklijke Philips NV, manufactures medical diagnostic and treatment equipment and distributes products to more than 100 countries throughout the world. The company operates in three business segments: products, consulting and customer service solutions. The products segment includes the products and services such as advance molecular imaging, clinical informatics, computed tomography, diagnostic ECG (electrocardiogram), emergency care, resuscitation, fluoroscopy, hospital respiratory care, interventional X-ray, magnetic resonance, mammography, mother and child care, patient monitoring, radiation oncology, radiography, refurbished systems, sleep and respiratory care, and ultrasound. The consulting segment provides clinical and business performance improvement solutions, manages services, experience solutions and population health solutions. The customer service solutions segment includes customer care support, remote management, dashboard solutions, power solutions and lifecycle solutions. Philips Healthcare also provides education and training via courses that are clinically relevant. The company's business specialties include clinical specialties such as anesthesia, cardiology, critical care, home respiratory care, mother and child care, radiology and sleep apnea care; business and government specialties such as military care and workplace/community automated external defibrillator (AED); and non-clinical specialties such as healthcare management and IT management. Philips Healthcare's SmartPath offering enables healthcare providers to optimize, enhance and transform existing equipment in order to have like-new/current functionality. It is a partnership program that helps extend the life of equipment for a fraction of the cost. In 2016, parent Koninklijke Philips spun off its lighting business to focus on healthcare. In May 2017, it agreed to acquire Respiratory Technologies, Inc., a U.S. provider of an innovative airway clearance solution for patients with chronic respiratory conditions. That June, it opened its first innovation center in Russia, Skolkovo Innovation Center, to develop next-generation health technologies based on computer and data science, as well as healthcare-related artificial intelligence.

FINANCIAL DATA: Note: Data for latest year may not have been available at press time.

In U.S. $	2016	2015	2014	2013	2012	2011
Revenue	20,196,679,771	14,406,749,346	12,100,715,917	12,574,865,989	13,632,240,000	11,462,000,000
R&D Expense						
Operating Income						
Operating Margin %						
SGA Expense						
Net Income	754,093,072	-39,000,000	11,791,810	976,696,340	1,805,250,000	1,482,600,000
Operating Cash Flow						
Capital Expenditure						
EBITDA						
Return on Assets %						
Return on Equity %						
Debt to Equity						

CONTACT INFORMATION:

Phone: 978-659-3000   Fax:
Toll-Free: 800-722-9377
Address: 3000 Minuteman Rd., Andover, MA 01810 United States

STOCK TICKER/OTHER:

Stock Ticker: Subsidiary   Exchange:
Employees: 71,000   Fiscal Year Ends: 12/31
Parent Company: Koninklijke Philips NV

SALARIES/BONUSES:

Top Exec. Salary: $ Bonus: $
Second Exec. Salary: $ Bonus: $

OTHER THOUGHTS:

Estimated Female Officers or Directors: 2
Hot Spot for Advancement for Women/Minorities:

Phillips 66

NAIC Code: 324110

www.phillips66.com

TYPES OF BUSINESS:

Petroleum Refineries
Natural Gas Gathering
Gasoline Marketing
Chemicals Interests

BRANDS/DIVISIONS/AFFILIATES:

DCP Midstream LLC
Phillips 66 Partners LP
Chevron Phillips Chemical Company LLC

CONTACTS: Note: Officers with more than one job title may be intentionally listed here more than once.

Greg Garland, CEO
Kevin Mitchell, CFO
Lawrence Ziemba, Executive VP, Divisional
Robert Herman, Executive VP, Divisional
Paula Johnson, Executive VP, Divisional
Timothy Taylor, President
Chukwuemeka Oyolu, Vice President

GROWTH PLANS/SPECIAL FEATURES:

Phillips 66 is a downstream energy company engaged in refining, marketing and distributing petroleum products as well as power generation. Previously a unit of ConocoPhillips, Phillips 66 is organized into four operating segments: refining, marketing & specialties (M&S), midstream and chemicals. The company's refining operations include 13 refineries with a net crude oil capacity of 2.2 million barrels per day (bpd). This segment buys, sells and refines crude oil and other feedstocks into petroleum products such as gasolines, distillates and aviation fuels. The M&S segment purchases refined petroleum products such as gasolines, distillates and aviation fuels for resale and markets, mainly in the U.S. and Europe. This segment includes the manufacturing and marketing of specialty products as well as power generation operations. The midstream segment comprises three business lines: transportation, which transports crude oil and other feedstocks to refineries and other locations, delivers refined and specialty products to market and provides storage services for crude oil and petroleum products; DCP Midstream LLC, which gathers, processes, transports and markets natural gas and transports, fractionates and markets natural gas liquids (NGL); and NGL, which transports, fractionates and markets NGL. The midstream segment also includes subsidiary Phillips 66 Partners LP, which owns, operates, develops and acquires fee-based crude oil, refined petroleum product and NGL pipelines and terminals as well as other transportation and midstream assets. The chemicals segment manufactures and markets petrochemicals and plastics on a worldwide basis. This segments includes its 50% interest in Chevron Phillips Chemical Company LLC, one of the world's top producers of olefins and polyolefins.

FINANCIAL DATA: Note: Data for latest year may not have been available at press time.

In U.S. $	2016	2015	2014	2013	2012	2011
Revenue	85,777,000,000	100,949,000,000	164,093,000,000	174,809,000,000	182,922,000,000	200,614,000,000
R&D Expense						
Operating Income	2,519,000,000	6,410,000,000	6,188,000,000	5,761,000,000	8,006,000,000	7,079,000,000
Operating Margin %	2.93%	6.34%	3.77%	3.29%	4.37%	3.52%
SGA Expense	1,638,000,000	1,670,000,000	1,663,000,000	1,478,000,000	1,722,000,000	1,409,000,000
Net Income	1,555,000,000	4,227,000,000	4,762,000,000	3,726,000,000	4,124,000,000	4,775,000,000
Operating Cash Flow	2,963,000,000	5,713,000,000	3,529,000,000	6,027,000,000	4,296,000,000	5,006,000,000
Capital Expenditure	2,844,000,000	5,764,000,000	3,773,000,000	1,779,000,000	1,721,000,000	1,022,000,000
EBITDA	3,697,000,000	7,405,000,000	7,007,000,000	6,748,000,000	7,790,000,000	7,549,000,000
Return on Assets %	3.09%	8.68%	9.66%	7.60%	9.03%	10.83%
Return on Equity %	6.81%	18.91%	21.87%	17.41%	18.71%	19.38%
Debt to Equity	0.42	0.38	0.36	0.27	0.33	0.01

CONTACT INFORMATION:

Phone: 281-293-6600   Fax:
Toll-Free:
Address: 3010 Briarpark Dr., Houston, TX 77042 United States

STOCK TICKER/OTHER:

Stock Ticker: PSX
Employees: 14,800
Parent Company:

Exchange: NYS
Fiscal Year Ends: 12/31

SALARIES/BONUSES:

Top Exec. Salary: $1,616,816   Bonus: $
Second Exec. Salary: $1,071,376   Bonus: $

OTHER THOUGHTS:

Estimated Female Officers or Directors: 4
Hot Spot for Advancement for Women/Minorities: Y

Pinnacle Entertainment Inc

www.pnkinc.com

NAIC Code: 721120

TYPES OF BUSINESS:

Casinos
Hospitality & Entertainment Facilities
Racetrack Facilities

BRANDS/DIVISIONS/AFFILIATES:

Gaming and Leisure Properties Inc
L'Auberge Casino Resort
L'Auberge Baton Rouge
River City Casino & Hotel
Belterra Casino Resort
Boomtown Casino Hotel
Cactus Petes and The Horseshu Jackpot
Heartland Poker Tour

CONTACTS: Note: Officers with more than one job title may be intentionally listed here more than once.

Anthony Sanfilippo, CEO
Carlos Ruisanchez, CFO
James Martineau, Chairman of the Board
Virginia Shanks, Chief Administrative Officer
Neil Walkoff, Executive VP, Divisional
Troy Stremming, Executive VP, Divisional
Donna Negrotto, Executive VP

GROWTH PLANS/SPECIAL FEATURES:

Pinnacle Entertainment, Inc. is a developer, owner and operator of casinos and other hospitality facilities. The company owns and operates 16 gaming entertainment properties, located in Colorado, Indiana, Iowa, Louisiana, Mississippi, Missouri, Nevada and Texas. The company's largest casino resort, L'Auberge Casino Resort located in Lake Charles, Louisiana, offers 995 guestrooms, suites and villas, as well as 1,547 slot machines, 75 table games, a golf course and a full-service spa. L'Auberge Casino Hotel in Baton Rouge, Louisiana, features 1,440 slot machines, 49 table games, a hotel with 205 guestrooms and a rooftop pool, nine dining outlets, an amphitheater style event lawn feature and a multi-purpose event center. The River City Casino & Hotel in St. Louis, Missouri includes 200 hotel rooms, 1.938 slot machines and 52 table games. Other properties include Belterra Casino Resort located near Florence, Indiana; six Ameristar Casino Hotels in Iowa, Indiana, Missouri, Mississippi and Colorado; two Boomtown Casino Hotels featuring dockside riverboat casinos in New Orleans and Bossier City, Louisiana; and Cactus Petes and The Horseshu Jackpot, featuring a hotel, gaming, dining, golf course and showroom entertainment. The company also owns the Heartland Poker Tour, a live and televised poker tournament series; and owns a majority interest in Retama Park Racetrack outside of San Antonio, Texas.

FINANCIAL DATA: Note: Data for latest year may not have been available at press time.

In U.S. $	2016	2015	2014	2013	2012	2011
Revenue	2,378,855,000	2,291,848,000	2,210,543,000	1,487,836,000	1,002,836,000	
R&D Expense		14,247,000	12,962,000	89,009,000	21,508,000	
Operating Income	-146,325,000	301,166,000	310,473,000	104,387,000	136,695,000	
Operating Margin %	-6.15%	13.14%	14.04%	7.01%	13.63%	
SGA Expense	510,770,000	426,064,000	421,399,000	287,381,000	181,175,000	
Net Income	-457,410,000	48,887,000	43,843,000	-255,870,000	-31,805,000	
Operating Cash Flow	255,747,000	408,226,000	328,486,000	161,067,000	186,906,000	
Capital Expenditure	97,932,000	109,032,000	255,815,000	292,623,000	300,521,000	
EBITDA	67,151,000	543,933,000	543,536,000	142,773,000	201,831,000	
Return on Assets %	-11.03%	-1.74%	.87%	-4.95%		
Return on Equity %		-33.65%	17.83%	-119.73%		
Debt to Equity		4.78	14.30	20.42		

CONTACT INFORMATION:

Phone: 702 541-7777   Fax:
Toll-Free:
Address: 3980 Howard Hughes Pkwy, Las Vegas, NV 89169 United States

STOCK TICKER/OTHER:

Stock Ticker: PNK   Exchange: NAS
Employees: 16,092   Fiscal Year Ends: 12/31
Parent Company: Gaming and Leisure Properties Inc

SALARIES/BONUSES:

Top Exec. Salary: $1,200,000   Bonus: $
Second Exec. Salary: $800,000   Bonus: $

OTHER THOUGHTS:

Estimated Female Officers or Directors: 3
Hot Spot for Advancement for Women/Minorities: Y

PPG Industries Inc

NAIC Code: 325510

www.ppg.com

TYPES OF BUSINESS:

Automotive Paints
Coatings
Glass
Chemicals
Fiberglass
Industrial Products

BRANDS/DIVISIONS/AFFILIATES:

PPG
Glidden
Comex
Olympic
Dulux
Homax
MetoKote
Taiwan Chlorine Industries Ltd

CONTACTS: Note: Officers with more than one job title may be intentionally listed here more than once.

Michael McGarry, CEO
Frank Sklarsky, CFO
Vincent Morales, Controller
Viktoras Sekmakas, Executive VP
Glenn Bost, General Counsel
Jean-Marie Greindl, President, Divisional
Timothy Knavish, Senior VP, Divisional
Ramaparasad Vadlamannati, Senior VP, Divisional

GROWTH PLANS/SPECIAL FEATURES:

PPG Industries, Inc. is a global manufacturer of decorative and protective coatings that operates in three business segments: performance coatings, industrial coatings and glass. The performance coatings and industrial coatings reportable segments supply coatings and specialty materials for customers in a wide array of end-use markets, including industrial equipment and components, packaging material; aircraft and marine equipment; automotive original equipment; as well as for other industrial and consumer products. In addition to supplying coatings to the automotive original equipment market, PPG supplies refinishes to the automotive aftermarket. PPG also serves commercial and residential new build and maintenance markets by supplying coatings to painting and maintenance contractors and directly to consumers for decoration and maintenance. These coatings are sold under the PPG, Glidden, Comex, Olympic, Dulux, Sikkens, Mulco, Flood, Liquid Nails, Sico, CIL, Renner, Taubman's, White Knight, Bristol and Homax brands. The glass business consists of flat glass and fiber glass, supplying its products to commercial and residential construction companies, as well as the wind energy, energy infrastructure, transportation and electronics industries. Most glass products are sold directly to manufacturing companies. In 2016, PPG acquired MetoKote, a coatings service business; sold its flat glass manufacturing and glass coatings operations to Vitro S.A.B. de C.V.; sold its European fiber glass operations to glass manufacturer Nippon Electric Glass Co. Ltd.; and sold its 50% ownership interest in its two PFG Fiber Glass joint ventures to Nan Ya Plastics Corp. In 2017, the firm acquired a Romanian paint and architectural coatings manufacturer from DEUTEK S.A., the remaining 50% ownership interest in its Asian joint ventures comprising IVC (Malaysia) Sdn Bhd and IVC-OPS (Singapore) Pte. Ltd. from Omni-Plus System Pte. Ltd. and a 40% ownership interest in Taiwan Chlorine Industries Ltd. from China Petrochemical Development Corporation.

FINANCIAL DATA: Note: Data for latest year may not have been available at press time.

In U.S. $	2016	2015	2014	2013	2012	2011
Revenue	14,751,000,000	15,330,000,000	15,360,000,000	15,108,000,000	15,200,000,000	14,885,000,000
R&D Expense	466,000,000	486,000,000	492,000,000	488,000,000	455,000,000	430,000,000
Operating Income	2,098,000,000	2,079,000,000	1,843,000,000	1,701,000,000	1,573,000,000	1,673,000,000
Operating Margin %	14.22%	13.56%	11.99%	11.25%	10.34%	11.23%
SGA Expense	3,662,000,000	3,679,000,000	3,758,000,000	3,699,000,000	3,335,000,000	3,234,000,000
Net Income	877,000,000	1,406,000,000	2,102,000,000	3,231,000,000	941,000,000	1,095,000,000
Operating Cash Flow	1,325,000,000	1,837,000,000	1,528,000,000	1,791,000,000	1,787,000,000	1,436,000,000
Capital Expenditure	402,000,000	476,000,000	587,000,000	515,000,000	411,000,000	390,000,000
EBITDA	1,414,000,000	2,503,000,000	2,079,000,000	2,160,000,000	2,077,000,000	2,274,000,000
Return on Assets %	5.34%	8.11%	12.56%	20.35%	6.21%	7.45%
Return on Equity %	17.88%	27.66%	41.57%	71.83%	25.73%	31.79%
Debt to Equity	0.78	0.81	0.68	0.68	0.82	1.10

CONTACT INFORMATION:

Phone: 412 434-3131   Fax: 412 434-2571
Toll-Free:
Address: 1 PPG Pl., Pittsburgh, PA 15272 United States

STOCK TICKER/OTHER:

Stock Ticker: PPG   Exchange: NYS
Employees: 47,000   Fiscal Year Ends: 12/31
Parent Company:

SALARIES/BONUSES:

Top Exec. Salary: $1,100,000   Bonus: $
Second Exec. Salary: $966,667   Bonus: $

OTHER THOUGHTS:

Estimated Female Officers or Directors: 6
Hot Spot for Advancement for Women/Minorities: Y

PRA Health Sciences Inc

NAIC Code: 541711

prahs.com

TYPES OF BUSINESS:

Clinical Research & Testing Services
Clinical Development Services
Clinical Trials
Data Management Services

BRANDS/DIVISIONS/AFFILIATES:

Kohlberg Kravis Roberts & Co LP

CONTACTS: Note: Officers with more than one job title may be intentionally listed here more than once.

Colin Shannon, CEO
Linda Baddour, CFO
David Dockhorn, Executive VP

GROWTH PLANS/SPECIAL FEATURES:

PRA Health Sciences is a contract research organization (CRO) that provides clinical drug development services to pharmaceutical and biotechnology companies around the world. It is owned by Kohlberg Kravis Roberts & Co. LP. CROs typically assist companies in developing drug compounds, biologics, drug delivery devices and the attainment of certain regulatory approvals necessary to market these technologies. PRA Health Sciences specializes in the categories of oncology, central nervous system (CNS), respiratory, inflammation and infectious diseases. In addition, the firm provides a broad array of services in clinical development programs, including the creation of drug development and regulatory strategy plans, the utilization of bioanalytical laboratory testing and the development of integrated global clinical databases. The company also provides data management services such as electronic data capture, data monitoring and database development. Clinical trials in the USA are largely centered on PRA Health Sciences' facilities in Kansas. The firm has approximately 70 offices and has conducted more than 700 high-level, complex early development clinical trials and over 1,500 bioanalytical studies.

The firm offers employees comprehensive medical benefits, life insurance, retirement programs, holidays and paid time off, tuition advance payment programs and a scholarship program for employee dependents.

FINANCIAL DATA: Note: Data for latest year may not have been available at press time.

In U.S. $	2016	2015	2014	2013	2012	2011
Revenue	1,811,711,000	1,613,883,000	1,459,586,000	1,390,161,000	699,736,000	
R&D Expense						
Operating Income	162,349,000	164,298,000	56,839,000	12,499,000	45,610,000	
Operating Margin %	8.96%	10.18%	3.89%	.89%	6.51%	
SGA Expense	314,727,000	246,417,000	253,970,000	270,703,000	160,643,000	
Net Income	68,175,000	81,765,000	-35,742,000	-62,234,000	-2,707,000	
Operating Cash Flow	160,047,000	153,676,000	22,747,000	-23,939,000	99,259,000	
Capital Expenditure	33,143,000	32,814,000	27,323,000	4,910,000	18,067,000	
EBITDA	231,855,000	242,250,000	153,403,000	102,565,000	76,297,000	
Return on Assets %	3.08%	3.66%	-1.54%	-3.68%	-.27%	
Return on Equity %	9.52%	11.85%	-6.24%	-19.34%	-1.53%	
Debt to Equity	1.09	1.26	1.40	2.66	2.56	

CONTACT INFORMATION:

Phone: 919-786-8200   Fax: 919-786-8201
Toll-Free:
Address: 4130 Park Lake Ave., Ste. 400, Raleigh, NC 27612 United States

STOCK TICKER/OTHER:

Stock Ticker: PRAH   Exchange: NAS
Employees: 13,000   Fiscal Year Ends: 12/31
Parent Company: Kohlberg Kravis Roberts & Co LP

SALARIES/BONUSES:

Top Exec. Salary: $746,500   Bonus: $345,000
Second Exec. Salary: $436,000   Bonus: $150,000

OTHER THOUGHTS:

Estimated Female Officers or Directors: 2
Hot Spot for Advancement for Women/Minorities: Y

Priceline Group Inc (The)

www.priceline.com

NAIC Code: 519130

TYPES OF BUSINESS:

Online Retail-Travel Services
Auction-Based Travel Sales
Online Financial Services
Commission-Based Travel Bookings (Travel Agency Model)

BRANDS/DIVISIONS/AFFILIATES:

Priceline.com
Name Your Own Price
Booking.com
Agoda.com
RentalCars.com
OpenTable
KAYAK Software Corporation

CONTACTS: Note: Officers with more than one job title may be intentionally listed here more than once.

Gillian Tans, CEO, Subsidiary
Daniel Finnegan, CFO
Jeffery Boyd, Chairman of the Board
Glenn Fogel, Director
Peter Millones, Executive VP

GROWTH PLANS/SPECIAL FEATURES:

The Priceline Group, Inc. is a leading online travel company that offers its customers a broad range of travel services, including airline tickets, hotel rooms, car rentals, vacation packages, cruises and destination services primarily through its proprietary Priceline.com and Booking.com websites. Within the U.S., the firm offers customers the ability to purchase travel services in a traditional, price-disclosed manner or the opportunity to use the Name Your Own Price service, which allows customers to make offers on travel goods and services at discounted prices. To make an offer, a customer specifies the origin and destination of the trip, the dates on which the customer wishes to depart and return, the price the customer is willing to pay and the customer's valid credit card to guarantee the offer. The company enables customers to make hotel reservations on a worldwide basis, primarily under the Booking.com and Agoda.com brands internationally, and primarily under the Priceline.com brand in the U.S. Through these operations, Priceline works with more than 600,000 chain-owned and independently owned hotels, offering hotel reservations on various web sites and in 42 different languages. Through subsidiary RentalCars.com, the company offers retail price-disclosed rental car reservations through over 46,000 locations. OpenTable is the company's brand for booking online restaurant reservations, and primarily operates in the U.S. The firm's international business represents approximately 88% of the company's gross bookings and contributes more than 94% of Priceline's consolidated operating income. Subsidiary KAYAK Software Corporation provides a price comparison service allowing consumers to search and compare prices for travel services.

Employee benefits include annual bonuses; medical, life, AD&D, disability and dental coverage; a 401(k) savings and investment plan with company match; tuition reimbursement; an employee assistance plan; flexible spending accounts; and travel agent discount benefits.

FINANCIAL DATA: Note: Data for latest year may not have been available at press time.

In U.S. $	2016	2015	2014	2013	2012	2011
Revenue	10,743,010,000	9,223,987,000	8,441,971,000	6,793,306,000	5,260,956,000	4,355,610,000
R&D Expense	142,393,000	113,617,000	97,498,000	71,890,000	43,685,000	33,813,000
Operating Income	2,906,313,000	3,258,907,000	3,073,312,000	2,412,414,000	1,829,793,000	1,398,922,000
Operating Margin %	27.05%	35.33%	36.40%	35.51%	34.78%	32.11%
SGA Expense	6,016,151,000	4,946,789,000	4,205,500,000	3,113,607,000	2,145,062,000	1,593,321,000
Net Income	2,134,987,000	2,551,360,000	2,421,753,000	1,892,663,000	1,419,566,000	1,056,371,000
Operating Cash Flow	3,924,697,000	3,102,231,000	2,914,397,000	2,301,436,000	1,785,750,000	1,341,812,000
Capital Expenditure	268,383,000	173,915,000	131,504,000	84,445,000	55,158,000	46,833,000
EBITDA	3,230,273,000	3,561,043,000	3,285,621,000	2,497,801,000	1,889,074,000	1,453,339,000
Return on Assets %	11.46%	15.76%	19.08%	22.24%	26.93%	30.72%
Return on Equity %	22.93%	29.38%	31.29%	35.02%	43.87%	48.15%
Debt to Equity	0.62	0.70	0.44	0.25	0.22	0.03

CONTACT INFORMATION:

Phone: 203-2998000   Fax:
Toll-Free:
Address: 800 Connecticut Ave., Norwalk, CT 06854 United States

STOCK TICKER/OTHER:

Stock Ticker: PCLN   Exchange: NAS
Employees: 18,500   Fiscal Year Ends:
Parent Company:

SALARIES/BONUSES:

Top Exec. Salary: $498,356   Bonus: $
Second Exec. Salary: Bonus: $
$373,013

OTHER THOUGHTS:

Estimated Female Officers or Directors: 1
Hot Spot for Advancement for Women/Minorities: Y

PriceSmart Inc

www.pricesmart.com

NAIC Code: 452910

TYPES OF BUSINESS:

Warehouse Clubs, Retail
Merchandise
Warehouse Club Membership

BRANDS/DIVISIONS/AFFILIATES:

CONTACTS: Note: Officers with more than one job title may be intentionally listed here more than once.

John Heffner, CFO
Robert Price, Chairman of the Board
William Naylon, COO
Jose Laparte, Director
Sherry Bahrambeygui, Director
Rodrigo Calvo, Executive VP, Divisional
Frank Diaz, Executive VP, Divisional
Brud Drachman, Executive VP, Divisional
John Hildebrandt, Executive VP, Divisional
Francisco Velasco, Executive VP
Jesus Von Chong, Executive VP

GROWTH PLANS/SPECIAL FEATURES:

PriceSmart, Inc. is one of the largest operators of warehouse membership clubs in Central America, the Caribbean and South America. The company serves over 2.9 million cardholders at 39 owned and operated warehouse clubs in Central America, South America and the Caribbean. PriceSmart's membership club model is similar to U.S. clubs like Costco and Sam's, with some differences: smaller store size, lower membership fees (average $30), and merchandise is tailored to local preferences as well as for retail and wholesale customers. PriceSmart warehouse clubs can be found in Colombia, 7; Costa Rica, 6; Panama, 5; Trinidad and Tobago, 4; Guatemala, 3; Dominican Republic, 3; Honduras, 3; El Salvador, 2; Nicaragua, 2; and one each in Aruba, Barbados, Jamaica and the U.S. Virgin Islands. Online shopping is available to its members in all countries. Merchandise departments include electronics, computers, baby, automotive, restaurant/institutional, sporting goods, outdoor, hardware, toys and games, appliances, housewares, bed and bath, luggage, healthcare, furniture, office and fashion accessories.

FINANCIAL DATA: Note: Data for latest year may not have been available at press time.

In U.S. $	2016	2015	2014	2013	2012	2011
Revenue	2,905,176,000	2,802,603,000	2,517,567,000	2,299,812,000	2,050,745,000	1,714,247,000
R&D Expense						
Operating Income	136,723,000	146,366,000	136,707,000	127,935,000	107,926,000	90,880,000
Operating Margin %	4.70%	5.22%	5.43%	5.56%	5.26%	5.30%
SGA Expense	317,665,000	301,393,000	265,751,000	242,449,000	224,039,000	192,663,000
Net Income	88,723,000	89,124,000	92,886,000	84,265,000	67,621,000	61,750,000
Operating Cash Flow	139,862,000	110,503,000	137,275,000	130,633,000	89,889,000	75,599,000
Capital Expenditure	77,700,000	89,185,000	118,101,000	69,927,000	52,705,000	47,033,000
EBITDA	176,925,000	177,481,000	167,019,000	151,871,000	132,644,000	114,426,000
Return on Assets %	8.35%	9.10%	10.51%	10.79%	9.65%	9.98%
Return on Equity %	14.49%	15.78%	18.04%	18.72%	17.01%	17.34%
Debt to Equity	0.11	0.12	0.14	0.12	0.17	0.16

CONTACT INFORMATION:

Phone: 858 404-8800   Fax: 858 404-8848
Toll-Free:
Address: 9740 Scranton Rd., San Diego, CA 92121 United States

STOCK TICKER/OTHER:

Stock Ticker: PSMT   Exchange: NAS
Employees: 7,835   Fiscal Year Ends: 08/31
Parent Company:

SALARIES/BONUSES:

Top Exec. Salary: $724,200   Bonus: $
Second Exec. Salary: Bonus: $
$516,120

OTHER THOUGHTS:

Estimated Female Officers or Directors: 4
Hot Spot for Advancement for Women/Minorities: Y

PricewaterhouseCoopers (PwC)

www.pwc.com

NAIC Code: 541211

TYPES OF BUSINESS:

Accounting Services
Business Advisory
Corporate Finance Services
Employee Benefits Services
Tax Services
Business Publications
Management Consulting

BRANDS/DIVISIONS/AFFILIATES:

CONTACTS: *Note: Officers with more than one job title may be intentionally listed here more than once.*

Martyn Curragh, CFO
Mike Fenlon, Chief People Officer
Gary Price, Chief Admin. Officer
Diana Weiss, General Counsel
Robert E. Moritz, Chmn.
Mitch Cohen, Vice Chmn.
Terri McClements, Head-U.S. Human Capital & Public Policy
Laura Cox Kaplan, Head-Regulation Affairs & Public Policy
Tim Ryan, Chmn.

GROWTH PLANS/SPECIAL FEATURES:

PricewaterhouseCoopers (PwC) is a global accounting firm with over 220,000 employees across 155+ countries. PwC provides the following services: advisory, audit/assurance, entrepreneurial/private clients, family business, IFRS (a global financial reporting language), legal, people/organization, sustainability/climate change and tax. The company serves a wide array of industry sectors, including aerospace/defense, asset and wealth management, automotive, banking/capital markets, capital projects, infrastructure, chemicals, communications, energy, utilities, mining, engineering, construction, entertainment/media, financial services, forest/paper/packaging, government services, public services, healthcare, hospitality/leisure, industrial manufacturing, insurance, metals, pharmaceuticals, life sciences, private equity, real estate, retail, consumer, sovereign wealth funds, technology and transportation and logistics.

The company offers employees a formal work-life balance program; substantial sick leave and family care leave; flexible work arrangements that may include job-sharing, flex time, sabbaticals and a compressed work week; and access to training at the PwC Open University.

FINANCIAL DATA: *Note: Data for latest year may not have been available at press time.*

In U.S. $	2016	2015	2014	2013	2012	2011
Revenue	35,900,000,000	35,400,000,000	34,000,000,000	32,100,000,000	31,500,000,000	29,200,000,000
R&D Expense						
Operating Income						
Operating Margin %						
SGA Expense						
Net Income						
Operating Cash Flow						
Capital Expenditure						
EBITDA						
Return on Assets %						
Return on Equity %						
Debt to Equity						

CONTACT INFORMATION:

Phone: 646-471-3000   Fax: 813-286-6000
Toll-Free:
Address: 300 Madison Ave., New York, NY 10017-6204 United States

STOCK TICKER/OTHER:

Stock Ticker: Private   Exchange:
Employees: 223,468   Fiscal Year Ends: 06/30
Parent Company:

SALARIES/BONUSES:

Top Exec. Salary: $ Bonus: $
Second Exec. Salary: $ Bonus: $

OTHER THOUGHTS:

Estimated Female Officers or Directors: 5
Hot Spot for Advancement for Women/Minorities: Y

Principal Financial Group Inc

www.principal.com

NAIC Code: 524113

TYPES OF BUSINESS:

Asset Management
Life Insurance
Health Insurance
Annuities
Disability Insurance
Investment Services
Specialty Benefits Insurance

BRANDS/DIVISIONS/AFFILIATES:

CONTACTS: *Note: Officers with more than one job title may be intentionally listed here more than once.*

Daniel Houston, CEO
Deanna Strable-Soethout, CFO
Gary Scholten, Chief Information Officer
Gregory Elming, Chief Risk Officer
Terrance Lillis, Executive VP
Timothy Dunbar, Executive VP
Luis Valdes, Other Corporate Officer
Nora Everett, President, Divisional
James Mccaughan, President, Divisional
Karen Shaff, Secretary

GROWTH PLANS/SPECIAL FEATURES:

The Principal Financial Group is a leading provider of retirement savings, investment and insurance products and services. It holds a total of $591.6 billion in assets and serves 22.1 million customers globally, with a focus on small and medium sized businesses (companies with less than 1,000 employees). The company is organized into four segments: retirement and income solutions, principal global investors, principal international and U.S. insurance solutions. The retirement and income solutions segment offers products and services for retirement savings and retirement income: to small- and medium-sized businesses, including 401k and 403b plans, benefit pension plans, non-qualified executive benefit plants, employee stock ownership plans, as well as SIMPLE individual retirement accounts (IRA) and payroll deduction plans; to large institutional clients, offering investment-only products such as guaranteed investment contracts; and employees of businesses and other individuals, offering accumulate savings for retirement plans, as well as mutual funds, individual annuities and bank products. The principal global investors segment manages assets for sophisticated investors worldwide, including equity, fixed income, real estate and other alternative investments. This division maintains offices worldwide, including Australia, China, Germany, Japan, the Netherlands, Singapore, Switzerland, the U.K. and the U.S. The principal international segment focuses on countries and territories with growing middle classes, favorable demographics and increasing long-term savings. This division has operations in Brazil, Chile, China, Hong Kong Special Administrative Region, India, Mexico and Southeast Asia. The U.S. insurance solutions segment offers group and individual insurance solutions, providing comprehensive insurance solutions for small- and medium-sized businesses and their owners and executives. These solutions include both group and individual dental, vision, life and disability insurance; and both group and individual life insurance options.

Employee benefits include medical, dental and vision coverage; retirement plans and 401(k); employee stock purchase plan; financial services; and health and wellness programs.

FINANCIAL DATA: *Note: Data for latest year may not have been available at press time.*

In U.S. $	2016	2015	2014	2013	2012	2011
Revenue	12,394,100,000	11,964,400,000	10,477,600,000	9,289,500,000	9,215,100,000	8,709,600,000
R&D Expense						
Operating Income	1,591,700,000	1,430,800,000	1,494,900,000	1,124,000,000	959,400,000	987,600,000
Operating Margin %	12.84%	11.95%	14.26%	12.09%	10.41%	11.33%
SGA Expense	3,732,600,000	3,672,400,000	3,574,300,000			3,057,700,000
Net Income	1,316,500,000	1,234,000,000	1,144,100,000	912,700,000	805,900,000	715,000,000
Operating Cash Flow	3,857,800,000	4,377,100,000	3,102,900,000	2,221,200,000	3,080,900,000	2,713,300,000
Capital Expenditure	154,900,000	136,400,000	136,000,000	59,400,000	38,900,000	56,900,000
EBITDA						
Return on Assets %	.58%	.55%	.52%	.47%	.49%	.46%
Return on Equity %	13.47%	12.40%	11.18%	9.05%	7.97%	7.04%
Debt to Equity	0.30	0.35	0.24	0.26	0.27	0.16

CONTACT INFORMATION:

Phone: 515 247-5111   Fax:
Toll-Free: 800-986-3343
Address: 711 High St., Des Moines, IA 50392 United States

STOCK TICKER/OTHER:

Stock Ticker: PFG   Exchange: NYS
Employees: 14,854   Fiscal Year Ends: 12/31
Parent Company:

SALARIES/BONUSES:

Top Exec. Salary: $795,192   Bonus: $
Second Exec. Salary: Bonus: $
$663,500

OTHER THOUGHTS:

Estimated Female Officers or Directors: 10
Hot Spot for Advancement for Women/Minorities: Y

Sales, profits and employees may be estimates. Financial information, benefits and other data can change quickly and may vary from those stated here.

Progressive Corporation (The)

www.progressive.com

NAIC Code: 524126

TYPES OF BUSINESS:

Insurance, Direct Property & Casualty
Automobile Insurance

BRANDS/DIVISIONS/AFFILIATES:

American Strategic Insurance Corp
Progressive Home Advantage
Progressive Commercial Advantage

CONTACTS: *Note: Officers with more than one job title may be intentionally listed here more than once.*

John Auer, CEO, Subsidiary
John Sauerland, CFO
Glenn Renwick, Chairman of the Board
Jeffrey Basch, Chief Accounting Officer
Steven Broz, Chief Information Officer
Jeffrey Charney, Chief Marketing Officer
William Cody, Other Executive Officer
Lori Niederst, Other Executive Officer
Daniel Mascaro, Other Executive Officer
Michael Sieger, President, Divisional
Patrick Callahan, President, Divisional
John Murphy, President, Divisional
John Barbagallo, President, Divisional
Susan Griffith, President

GROWTH PLANS/SPECIAL FEATURES:

The Progressive Corporation, together with its subsidiaries and affiliates, is one of the largest auto insurers in the U.S. Progressive is divided into seven business segments. The personal lines segment writes insurance for personal autos and recreational and other vehicles in all 50 states and the District of Columbia. This division also writes personal auto insurance in Australia. The commercial lines segment primarily writes liability, physical damage and other auto-related insurance for automobiles and trucks owned and/or operated predominantly by small businesses as a part of the commercial auto market. This division offers its products in 49 states. The property segment, through American Strategic Insurance Corp. (ASI), is one of the 20 largest homeowners carriers in the U.S. ASI specializes in personal and commercial property insurance, personal umbrella insurance and primary and excess flood insurance. The other indemnity segment consists of managing The Progressive Corporation's run-off businesses, including the run-off of its professional liability business, with five professional liability policies currently in force. The service businesses segment includes the servicing of the company's commercial auto insurance procedures and plans, as well as the company's two commission-based service businesses: Progressive Home Advantage and Progressive Commercial Advantage. Progressive Home Advantage offers home, condominium and renter's insurance; and Progressive Commercial Advantage offers customers the ability to package their auto coverage with other commercial coverages that are written by unaffiliated insurance companies or placed with additional companies through unaffiliated insurance agencies. The reinsurance segment participates in mandatory state pools; acts as a servicing agent for state-mandated involuntary plans for commercial vehicles; and participates in federally regulated write-your-own plans for flood. Last, the claims segment manages the vehicle claims handling on a company-wide basis through approximately 220 stand-alone claims offices throughout the U.S.

Progressive offers health insurance; 401(k); wellness, maternity and other assistive programs.

FINANCIAL DATA: *Note: Data for latest year may not have been available at press time.*

In U.S. $	2016	2015	2014	2013	2012	2011
Revenue	23,441,400,000	20,853,800,000	19,391,400,000	18,170,900,000	17,083,900,000	15,508,100,000
R&D Expense						
Operating Income	1,470,700,000	1,911,600,000	1,907,400,000	1,720,000,000	1,317,700,000	1,487,000,000
Operating Margin %	6.27%	9.16%	9.83%	9.46%	7.71%	9.58%
SGA Expense	92,000,000	77,500,000	69,800,000	38,800,000	36,100,000	19,400,000
Net Income	1,031,000,000	1,267,600,000	1,281,000,000	1,165,400,000	902,300,000	1,015,500,000
Operating Cash Flow	2,701,900,000	2,292,900,000	1,725,600,000	1,899,900,000	1,691,400,000	1,497,900,000
Capital Expenditure	215,000,000	130,700,000	108,100,000	140,400,000	127,700,000	78,900,000
EBITDA						
Return on Assets %	3.26%	4.55%	5.10%	4.94%	4.05%	4.72%
Return on Equity %	13.52%	17.83%	19.53%	19.11%	15.27%	17.13%
Debt to Equity	0.39	0.37	0.31	0.30	0.34	0.42

CONTACT INFORMATION:

Phone: 440 461-5000   Fax:
Toll-Free: 800-776-4737
Address: 6300 Wilson Mills Rd., Mayfield Village, OH 44143 United States

STOCK TICKER/OTHER:

Stock Ticker: PGR   Exchange: NYS
Employees: 31,721   Fiscal Year Ends: 12/31
Parent Company:

SALARIES/BONUSES:

Top Exec. Salary: $633,654   Bonus: $
Second Exec. Salary: $616,346   Bonus: $

OTHER THOUGHTS:

Estimated Female Officers or Directors: 2
Hot Spot for Advancement for Women/Minorities: Y

Sales, profits and employees may be estimates. Financial information, benefits and other data can change quickly and may vary from those stated here.

Providence St Joseph Health

NAIC Code: 622110

TYPES OF BUSINESS:

General Medical and Surgical Hospitals
Assisted Living Facilities
Low Income Living Facilities
Counseling

BRANDS/DIVISIONS/AFFILIATES:

Providence Health & Services
St. Joseph Health
Covenant Health
Facey Medical Foundation
Hoag Memorial Presbyterian
Kadlec
Pacific Medical Centers
Institute for Mental Health and Wellness

CONTACTS: *Note: Officers with more than one job title may be intentionally listed here more than once.*

Rodney F. Hochman, CEO
Mike Butler, Pres.-Operations
Jo Ann Escasa-Haigh, Interim-CFO
Myron Berdischewsky, Chief Medical & Quality Officer
Cindy Strauss, Sr. VP
Mike Butler, Pres., Oper. & Svcs.
David Brown, VP-Strategy & Bus. Dev.
Deborah Burton, VP
Jack Friedman, Sr. VP-Accountable Care & Payor Relations
Joel Gilbertson, VP-Gov't. & Public Affairs
John O. Mudd, Sr. VP-Mission leadership
Dave Hunter, VP-Supply Chain Mgmt.

GROWTH PLANS/SPECIAL FEATURES:

Providence St. Joseph Health, formed by the 2016 merger of Providence Health & Services and St. Joseph Health, comprises 50 hospitals, 829 clinics, 23,000 physicians, supportive housing facilities and 111,000 caregivers with the goal of improving the health of the communities it serves, especially the poor and the vulnerable. The faith-based firm provides a comprehensive range of services across Alaska, California, Montana, New Mexico, Oregon, Texas and Washington. The Providence St. Joseph Health family includes: Providence Health & Services (Alaska, Washington, Montana, Oregon and California), St. Joseph Health (California, New Mexico and Texas), Covenant Health (Texas), Facey Medical Group (California), Hoag Memorial Presbyterian (California), Kadlec (Washington), Pacific Medical Centers (Washington), as well as Swedish Health Services (Washington). The company established the Institute for Mental Health and Wellness in order to provide effective mental health services for those who struggle with mental health stigmatization, diagnosis and treatment. The Foundation for Mental Health and Wellness will oversee this work, and the funds derived by the foundation will support research and startup operations for mental health awareness, diagnosis and treatment.

FINANCIAL DATA: *Note: Data for latest year may not have been available at press time.*

In U.S. $	2016	2015	2014	2013	2012	2011
Revenue	18,878,000,000	14,434,000,000	12,261,825,000	11,099,009,000	10,608,249,000	8,420,847,000
R&D Expense						
Operating Income						
Operating Margin %						
SGA Expense						
Net Income	5,231,000,000	77,000,000	771,422,000	253,270,000	1,216,516,000	361,727,000
Operating Cash Flow						
Capital Expenditure						
EBITDA						
Return on Assets %						
Return on Equity %						
Debt to Equity						

CONTACT INFORMATION:

Phone: 425-525-3355   Fax:
Toll-Free:
Address: 1801 Lind Avenue SW, Renton, WA 98057 United States

STOCK TICKER/OTHER:

Stock Ticker: Nonprofit   Exchange:
Employees: 100,000   Fiscal Year Ends: 12/31
Parent Company:

SALARIES/BONUSES:

Top Exec. Salary: $ Bonus: $
Second Exec. Salary: $ Bonus: $

OTHER THOUGHTS:

Estimated Female Officers or Directors: 5
Hot Spot for Advancement for Women/Minorities: Y

Prudential Financial Inc

NAIC Code: 524113

TYPES OF BUSINESS:

Insurance-Life
Property & Casualty Insurance
Asset Management
Life Insurance

BRANDS/DIVISIONS/AFFILIATES:

CONTACTS: Note: Officers with more than one job title may be intentionally listed here more than once.

John Strangfeld, CEO
Robert Falzon, CFO
Robert Axel, Chief Accounting Officer
Barbara Koster, Chief Information Officer
Nicholas Silitch, Chief Risk Officer
Charles Lowrey, COO, Divisional
Stephen Pelletier, COO, Geographical
Mark Grier, Director
Timothy Harris, Executive VP
Scott Sleyster, Other Executive Officer
Richard Lambert, Other Executive Officer
Sharon Taylor, Senior VP, Divisional

GROWTH PLANS/SPECIAL FEATURES:

Prudential Financial, Inc. provides financial products and services, including life insurance, annuities, retirement-related services, mutual funds and investment management. Prudential is a financial leader with approximately $1.264 trillion of assets under management, and has operations in the U.S., Asia, Europe and Latin America. The company's products and services are offered to individual and institutional customers through proprietary and third party distribution networks. The businesses of Prudential are divided into the financial services businesses and the closed block businesses. The financial business consists of four operating divisions, which together has seven segments, as well as corporate and other operations. The U.S. retirement solutions and investment management division, contains the individual annuities, retirement and asset management segments. The U.S. individual life and group insurance division consists of its individual life and group insurance segments. The international insurance division contains the international insurance segment. The closed block division is designed to provide for the reasonable expectations for future policy dividends after demutualization of holders of participating individual life insurance policies and annuities by allocating assets that will be used exclusively for payment of benefits, including policy-holder dividends, expenses and taxes with respect to these products. The corporate and other operations include items and initiatives that are not allocated to business segments, as well as businesses that have been or will be divested.

Employee benefits include medical, dental, disability, life and accident insurance; a 401(k); fitness and wellness centers; and employee discounts.

FINANCIAL DATA: Note: Data for latest year may not have been available at press time.

In U.S. $	2016	2015	2014	2013	2012	2011
Revenue	58,779,000,000	57,119,000,000	54,105,000,000	41,461,000,000	84,815,000,000	49,045,000,000
R&D Expense						
Operating Income	5,705,000,000	7,769,000,000	1,759,000,000	-1,684,000,000	676,000,000	5,117,000,000
Operating Margin %	9.70%	13.60%	3.25%	-4.06%	.79%	10.43%
SGA Expense	11,779,000,000	10,912,000,000	11,807,000,000	11,011,000,000	11,094,000,000	9,815,000,000
Net Income	4,368,000,000	5,642,000,000	1,381,000,000	-667,000,000	469,000,000	3,666,000,000
Operating Cash Flow	14,778,000,000	13,895,000,000	19,396,000,000	8,445,000,000	20,909,000,000	12,377,000,000
Capital Expenditure						
EBITDA						
Return on Assets %	.56%	.74%	.19%	-.09%	.07%	.62%
Return on Equity %	9.95%	13.48%	3.84%	-1.80%	1.23%	10.52%
Debt to Equity	0.44	0.67	0.47	0.76	0.68	0.66

CONTACT INFORMATION:

Phone: 973 802-6000   Fax: 973 367-6476
Toll-Free: 877-998-7625
Address: 751 Broad St., Newark, NJ 07102 United States

STOCK TICKER/OTHER:

Stock Ticker: PRU   Exchange: NYS
Employees: 49,739   Fiscal Year Ends: 12/31
Parent Company:

SALARIES/BONUSES:

Top Exec. Salary: $1,400,000   Bonus: $
Second Exec. Salary: Bonus: $
$1,190,000

OTHER THOUGHTS:

Estimated Female Officers or Directors: 6
Hot Spot for Advancement for Women/Minorities: Y

Publix Super Markets Inc

www.publix.com

NAIC Code: 445110

TYPES OF BUSINESS:

Grocery Stores
Dairy, Deli & Bakery Products
Convenience Stores
Liquor Stores
Restaurants

BRANDS/DIVISIONS/AFFILIATES:

CONTACTS: *Note: Officers with more than one job title may be intentionally listed here more than once.*

Sharon Miller, Assistant Secretary
David Bornmann, Vice President
William Crenshaw, CEO
David Phillips, CFO
Laurie Zeitlin, Chief Information Officer
Charles Jenkins, Director
Hoyt Barnett, Director
Randall Jones, President
John Hrabusa, Senior VP
John Attaway, Senior VP
Linda Hall, Vice President
Dale Myers, Vice President
David Duncan, Vice President
David Bridges, Vice President
Michael Smith, Vice President
Thomas Mclaughlin, Vice President
William Fauerbach, Vice President
Alfred Ottolino, Vice President
Mark Irby, Vice President
John Frazier, Vice President
Marc Salm, Vice President

GROWTH PLANS/SPECIAL FEATURES:

Publix Super Markets, Inc. is a leading operator of supermarkets, with 1,147 locations in Alabama, Florida, Georgia, South Carolina, North Carolina, Tennessee and Virginia. The firm's supermarkets sell groceries, dairy products, produce, deli foods, bakery items, meat, seafood, housewares and health and beauty merchandise. Many stores also feature pharmacies, floral departments, photo labs, liquor stores and in-store banking areas. It also owns several pharmacy and convenience store locations under various names. Publix's lines of merchandise include a variety of nationally advertised and private label brands as well as some unbranded merchandise, such as produce, meat and seafood. In addition to its retail operations, Publix manufactures dairy, bakery and deli products. Manufacturing facilities are located in: Florida, including Lakeland, Miami, Jacksonville, Orlando, Deerfield Beach and Boynton Beach; and Georgia, including Atlanta and Lawrenceville. The firm is one of the largest employee-owned grocery stores in the U.S.

Publix offers its employees health, dental and vision coverage; quarterly retail bonuses; an employee stock ownership plan; holiday bonuses; free hot lunches; prescription discounts; a 401(k) plan; a profit sharing plan; access to a credit union; tuition reimbursement; and an employee assistance plan.

FINANCIAL DATA: *Note: Data for latest year may not have been available at press time.*

In U.S. $	2016	2015	2014	2013	2012	2011
Revenue	34,274,110,000	32,618,760,000	30,802,470,000	29,147,520,000	27,706,770,000	27,178,760,000
R&D Expense						
Operating Income	2,751,651,000	2,678,241,000	2,400,861,000	2,319,738,000	2,165,251,000	2,134,925,000
Operating Margin %	8.02%	8.21%	7.79%	7.95%	7.81%	7.85%
SGA Expense	6,788,153,000	6,480,908,000	6,168,955,000	5,890,461,000	5,630,537,000	5,523,469,000
Net Income	2,025,688,000	1,965,048,000	1,735,308,000	1,653,954,000	1,552,255,000	1,491,966,000
Operating Cash Flow	3,252,955,000	2,941,365,000	2,777,232,000	2,567,303,000	2,604,207,000	2,341,187,000
Capital Expenditure	1,443,827,000	1,235,648,000	1,374,124,000	668,485,000	697,112,000	602,952,000
EBITDA	3,375,854,000	3,260,133,000	2,914,254,000	2,821,427,000	2,795,833,000	2,627,564,000
Return on Assets %	11.97%	12.49%	12.12%	12.80%	13.18%	13.92%
Return on Equity %	15.66%	16.58%	16.12%	17.13%	20.36%	22.23%
Debt to Equity	0.01	0.01	0.01	0.01	0.01	0.01

CONTACT INFORMATION:

Phone: 863 688-1188　　　　Fax: 863 688-5532
Toll-Free: 800-242-1227
Address: 3300 Publix Corporate Pkwy., Lakeland, FL 33811 United States

STOCK TICKER/OTHER:

Stock Ticker: PUSH
Employees: 191,000
Parent Company:

Exchange: GREY
Fiscal Year Ends: 12/31

SALARIES/BONUSES:

Top Exec. Salary: $610,870　　　Bonus: $
Second Exec. Salary: $　　　　　Bonus: $

OTHER THOUGHTS:

Estimated Female Officers or Directors: 5
Hot Spot for Advancement for Women/Minorities: Y

Sales, profits and employees may be estimates. Financial information, benefits and other data can change quickly and may vary from those stated here.

PulteGroup Inc

pultegroupinc.com

NAIC Code: 236117

TYPES OF BUSINESS:

Construction, Home Building and Residential
Financial Services
Mortgages
Land Development

BRANDS/DIVISIONS/AFFILIATES:

Pulte Home Corp
Del Webb Corp
Centex Corp
Pulte Mortgage LLC
DiVosta Homes Sales Inc
John Wieland Homes and Neighborhoods

CONTACTS: *Note: Officers with more than one job title may be intentionally listed here more than once.*

Robert OShaughnessy, CFO
James Ossowski, Chief Accounting Officer
James Ellinghausen, Executive VP, Divisional
Harmon Smith, Executive VP
Steven Cook, Executive VP
Ryan Marshall, President

GROWTH PLANS/SPECIAL FEATURES:

PulteGroup, Inc. is a holding company with subsidiaries in the homebuilding and financial services industries. These subsidiaries include Del Webb Corp.; Pulte Home Corp.; Centex Corp.; DiVosta Homes Sales, Inc.; John Wieland Homes and Neighborhoods; and Pulte Mortgage LLC. PulteGroup's core homebuilding business is engaged in the acquisition and development of land, primarily for residential purposes within the U.S. The firm builds a wide variety of homes targeted for first-time, first and second move-up and active adult home buyers, including detached units, townhouses, condominium apartments and duplexes, with varying prices, models, options and lot sizes. Its homebuilding business operates in 49 markets spanning 25 states and offers homes in about 726 communities. During 2015, the firm closed 19,951 homes, with the average unit selling price of $373,000. Sales prices range from less than $100,000 to more than $1,000,000, 85% of which fall between $150,000 and $500,000. PulteGroup's homebuilding operations consist of six geographic segments: Northeast (including Connecticut, Maryland, Massachusetts, New Jersey, New York, Pennsylvania and Virginia), Florida, Texas, Midwest (including Illinois, Indiana, Kentucky, Michigan, Minnesota, Missouri and Ohio), Southeast (consisting of Georgia, North Carolina, South Carolina and Tennessee) and West (including Arizona, California, Nevada, New Mexico and Washington). The firm's strategy is based on extensive market research that reveals well-defined buying profiles, job demographics and lifestyle choices. PulteGroup's financial services segment consists principally of mortgage operations conducted through Pulte Mortgage LLC and its subsidiaries.

The company offers employees medical, dental and vision insurance; a 401(k); life and AD&D insurance; business travel accident insurance; short- and long-term disability; tuition reimbursement; an employee assistance program; and time off for volunteering.

FINANCIAL DATA: *Note: Data for latest year may not have been available at press time.*

In U.S. $	2016	2015	2014	2013	2012	2011
Revenue	7,668,476,000	5,981,964,000	5,822,363,000	5,679,595,000	4,819,998,000	4,136,690,000
R&D Expense						
Operating Income	968,864,000	820,486,000	703,279,000	587,540,000	241,699,000	-24,236,000
Operating Margin %	12.63%	13.71%	12.07%	10.34%	5.01%	-.58%
SGA Expense	957,150,000	589,780,000	667,815,000	568,500,000	514,457,000	519,583,000
Net Income	602,703,000	494,090,000	474,338,000	2,620,116,000	206,145,000	-210,388,000
Operating Cash Flow	68,270,000	-348,129,000	309,249,000	881,136,000	760,140,000	17,222,000
Capital Expenditure	39,295,000	45,440,000	48,790,000	28,899,000	13,942,000	21,238,000
EBITDA	988,543,000	863,033,000	730,471,000	560,121,000	214,400,000	-276,889,000
Return on Assets %	6.24%	5.59%	5.44%	33.87%	3.02%	-2.88%
Return on Equity %	12.69%	10.26%	9.96%	76.62%	9.98%	-10.32%
Debt to Equity	0.73	0.49	0.40	0.46	1.14	1.59

CONTACT INFORMATION:

Phone: 404-978-6400   Fax:
Toll-Free: 866-785-8325
Address: 3350 Peachtree Road NE, Ste 150, Atlanta, GA 30326 United States

STOCK TICKER/OTHER:

Stock Ticker: PHM
Employees: 4,623
Parent Company:

Exchange: NYS
Fiscal Year Ends: 12/31

SALARIES/BONUSES:

Top Exec. Salary: $1,200,000   Bonus: $
Second Exec. Salary: $742,307   Bonus: $

OTHER THOUGHTS:

Estimated Female Officers or Directors: 4
Hot Spot for Advancement for Women/Minorities: Y

Qualcomm Inc

NAIC Code: 334413

TYPES OF BUSINESS:

Telecommunications Equipment
Digital Wireless Communications Products
Integrated Circuits
Mobile Communications Systems
Wireless Software & Services
E-Mail Software
Code Division Multiple Access

BRANDS/DIVISIONS/AFFILIATES:

Guizhou Huaxintong Semi-Conductor Technology Co
RF360 Holdings Singapore Pte Ltd
NXP Semiconductors NV

CONTACTS: Note: Officers with more than one job title may be intentionally listed here more than once.

Steven Mollenkopf, CEO
George Davis, CFO
Paul Jacobs, Chairman of the Board
John Murphy, Chief Accounting Officer
Matthew Grob, Chief Technology Officer
Michelle Sterling, Executive VP, Divisional
Brian Modoff, Executive VP, Divisional
James Thompson, Executive VP, Subsidiary
Cristiano Amon, Executive VP, Subsidiary
Donald Rosenberg, Executive VP
Alexander Rogers, Executive VP
Derek Aberle, President

GROWTH PLANS/SPECIAL FEATURES:

Qualcomm, Inc. provides digital wireless communications products, technologies and services. Its operations are divided into three segments: Qualcomm CDMA Technologies (QCT), Qualcomm Technology Licensing (QTL) and Qualcomm Strategic Initiatives (QSI). QCT designs application-specific integrated circuits based on Code Division Multiple Access (CDMA), Orthogonal Frequency-Division Multiple Access (OFDMA), Time Division Multiple Access (TDMA) and other technologies for use in voice and data communications, networking, application processing, multimedia functions and GPS products. QTL grants licenses and provides rights to use portions of Qualcomm's intellectual property portfolio to third-party manufacturers of wireless products and networking equipment. QSI makes strategic investments in various companies and technologies that Qualcomm believes will open new opportunities for its technologies. Joint venture (with Guizhou Province), Guizhou Huaxintong Semi-Conductor Technology Co. Ltd., designs and sells world-class server chipset technology in China; and joint venture (with TDK Corporation), RF360 Holdings Singapore Pte. Ltd., delivers radio frequency (RF) front-end modules and RF filters into fully integrated systems for mobile devices and fast-growing business segments such as the Internet of Things, drones, robotics, automotive applications and more. In November 2016, Qualcomm acquired NXP Semiconductors NV, a provider of secure connectivity solutions for embedded applications.

U.S. employees of the company receive medical, dental and vision insurance; dependent/health care reimbursement accounts; tuition reimbursement; a 401(k); and an employee stock purchase plan.

FINANCIAL DATA: Note: Data for latest year may not have been available at press time.

In U.S. $	2016	2015	2014	2013	2012	2011
Revenue	23,554,000,000	25,281,000,000	26,487,000,000	24,866,000,000	19,121,000,000	14,957,000,000
R&D Expense	5,151,000,000	5,490,000,000	5,477,000,000	4,967,000,000	3,915,000,000	2,995,000,000
Operating Income	6,495,000,000	5,776,000,000	7,550,000,000	7,230,000,000	5,682,000,000	5,026,000,000
Operating Margin %	27.57%	22.84%	28.50%	29.07%	29.71%	33.60%
SGA Expense	2,385,000,000	2,344,000,000	2,290,000,000	2,518,000,000	2,324,000,000	1,945,000,000
Net Income	5,705,000,000	5,271,000,000	7,967,000,000	6,853,000,000	6,109,000,000	4,260,000,000
Operating Cash Flow	7,400,000,000	5,506,000,000	8,887,000,000	8,778,000,000	5,998,000,000	4,900,000,000
Capital Expenditure	539,000,000	994,000,000	1,185,000,000	1,048,000,000	1,284,000,000	593,000,000
EBITDA	8,558,000,000	7,805,000,000	8,700,000,000	9,234,000,000	7,549,000,000	6,862,000,000
Return on Assets %	11.06%	10.60%	16.93%	15.48%	15.38%	12.71%
Return on Equity %	18.05%	14.93%	21.17%	19.68%	20.20%	17.82%
Debt to Equity	0.31	0.31				

CONTACT INFORMATION:

Phone: 858 587-1121   Fax: 858 658-2100
Toll-Free:
Address: 5775 Morehouse Dr., San Diego, CA 92121 United States

SALARIES/BONUSES:

Top Exec. Salary: $889,438   Bonus: $1,375,000
Second Exec. Salary: Bonus: $1,000,000
$542,324

STOCK TICKER/OTHER:

Stock Ticker: QCOM   Exchange: NAS
Employees: 33,000   Fiscal Year Ends: 09/30
Parent Company:

OTHER THOUGHTS:

Estimated Female Officers or Directors: 2
Hot Spot for Advancement for Women/Minorities: Y

Quanta Services Inc

www.quantaservices.com

NAIC Code: 237130

TYPES OF BUSINESS:

Construction, Power & Communication Lines
Network Installation & Support Services
Network Design Services
Electric Power Transmission Systems
Gas Pipeline Systems

BRANDS/DIVISIONS/AFFILIATES:

CONTACTS: *Note: Officers with more than one job title may be intentionally listed here more than once.*

Earl Austin, CEO
Derrick Jensen, CFO
Jerry Lemon, Chief Accounting Officer
Randall Wisenbaker, Executive VP, Divisional
Jesse Morris, Executive VP, Divisional
Paul Gregory, Other Executive Officer
Nicholas Grindstaff, Treasurer
Dorothy Upperman, Vice President, Divisional

GROWTH PLANS/SPECIAL FEATURES:

Quanta Services, Inc. is a specialty contract provider of infrastructure services. The company designs, installs and maintains networks for the electric power, natural gas and oil pipeline industries. Quanta Services operates in two segments: electric power infrastructure services (EPIS) and oil and gas infrastructure services (OGIS). EPIS derives the majority of the firm's annual revenue and provides comprehensive network solutions to customers in the electric power industry. Services performed by this segment include the design, installation, upgrade, repair and maintenance of electric power transmissions and distribution infrastructure and substation facilities along with other engineering and technical services. It also provides emergency restoration services, including the repair of infrastructure damaged by inclement weather, the energized installation, maintenance and upgrade of electric power infrastructure utilizing unique bare hand and hot stick methods and Quanta's proprietary robotic arm technologies, as well as the installation of smart grid technologies on electric power networks. OGIS provides infrastructure solutions to customers involved in the development and transportation of natural gas, oil and other pipeline products. Services performed by this segment include the design, installation, repair and maintenance of pipeline transmission and distribution systems, gathering systems, production systems and compressor and pump stations, as well as related trenching, directional boring and automatic welding services. This division also provides pipeline protection, integrity testing, rehabilitation and replacement and fabrication of pipeline support systems and related structures and facilities.

FINANCIAL DATA: *Note: Data for latest year may not have been available at press time.*

In U.S. $	2016	2015	2014	2013	2012	2011
Revenue	7,651,319,000	7,572,436,000	7,851,250,000	6,522,842,000	5,920,269,000	4,623,829,000
R&D Expense						
Operating Income	320,813,000	237,503,000	475,575,000	526,928,000	465,122,000	217,683,000
Operating Margin %	4.19%	3.13%	6.05%	8.07%	7.85%	4.70%
SGA Expense	653,338,000	592,863,000	722,038,000	501,010,000	434,894,000	372,963,000
Net Income	198,383,000	310,907,000	296,714,000	401,921,000	306,629,000	132,515,000
Operating Cash Flow	381,176,000	618,183,000	310,824,000	446,592,000	106,217,000	218,030,000
Capital Expenditure	212,555,000	210,179,000	301,728,000	263,558,000	210,986,000	172,005,000
EBITDA	524,498,000	434,392,000	671,899,000	803,542,000	626,320,000	364,212,000
Return on Assets %	3.75%	5.39%	4.90%	7.35%	6.23%	2.93%
Return on Equity %	6.17%	8.18%	6.78%	10.04%	8.57%	3.92%
Debt to Equity	0.10	0.15	0.01			

CONTACT INFORMATION:

Phone: 713 629-7600   Fax: 713 629-7676
Toll-Free:
Address: 2800 Post Oak Blvd, Ste 2600, Houston, TX 77056 United States

STOCK TICKER/OTHER:

Stock Ticker: PWR   Exchange: NYS
Employees: 28,100   Fiscal Year Ends: 12/31
Parent Company:

SALARIES/BONUSES:

Top Exec. Salary: $979,924   Bonus: $
Second Exec. Salary: $600,000   Bonus: $

OTHER THOUGHTS:

Estimated Female Officers or Directors:
Hot Spot for Advancement for Women/Minorities:

Sales, profits and employees may be estimates. Financial information, benefits and other data can change quickly and may vary from those stated here.

Quest Diagnostics Inc

www.questdiagnostics.com

NAIC Code: 621511

TYPES OF BUSINESS:

Services-Testing & Diagnostics
Clinical Laboratory Testing
Clinical Trials Testing
Esoteric Testing Laboratories

BRANDS/DIVISIONS/AFFILIATES:

Nichols Institute
Athena Diagnostics

CONTACTS: *Note: Officers with more than one job title may be intentionally listed here more than once.*

Stephen Rusckowski, CEO
Mark Guinan, CFO
Michael Prevoznik, General Counsel
Catherine Doherty, Other Corporate Officer
Jon Cohen, Other Corporate Officer
James Davis, Other Corporate Officer
Carrie Eglinton Manner, Senior VP, Divisional
Everett Cunningham, Senior VP, Divisional
Robert Klug, Vice President

GROWTH PLANS/SPECIAL FEATURES:

Quest Diagnostics, Inc. is a U.S. clinical laboratory testing company, offering diagnostic testing and related services to the health care industry. The firm's operations consist of routine, esoteric and clinical trials testing. Quest operates through its national network of over 2,200 patient service centers, principal laboratories in several major metropolitan areas, rapid-response laboratories, outpatient anatomic pathology centers, hospital-based laboratories and esoteric testing laboratories on both coasts. Routine tests measure various important bodily health parameters. Tests in this category include blood cholesterol level tests, complete blood cell counts, urinalyses, pregnancy and prenatal tests, substance-abuse tests and allergy tests such. The company also provides cancer diagnostics, including anatomic pathology services in the U.S. Gene-based and other esoteric tests require more sophisticated technology and highly skilled personnel. Quest's two esoteric testing laboratories, comprising the Nichols Institute and Athena Diagnostics, are among the leading esoteric clinical testing laboratories in the world. Esoteric tests involve endocrinology, genetics, immunology, microbiology, oncology, serology, endocrinology, hematology and toxicology. Clinical trial testing primarily involves assessing the safety and efficacy of new drugs to meet FDA requirements. The company has clinical trials testing centers in the U.S. and the U.K., and provides clinical trials testing in Argentina, Brazil, China and Singapore through affiliated laboratories. Additionally, Quest provides risk management services to the life insurance industry in the U.S. and Canada as well as many other countries.

The firm offers employees medical, dental and life insurance; employee assistance program; and flexible spending accounts.

FINANCIAL DATA: *Note: Data for latest year may not have been available at press time.*

In U.S. $	2016	2015	2014	2013	2012	2011
Revenue	7,515,000,000	7,493,000,000	7,435,000,000	7,146,000,000	7,382,562,000	7,510,490,000
R&D Expense						
Operating Income	1,277,000,000	1,399,000,000	983,000,000	1,475,000,000	1,200,797,000	995,048,000
Operating Margin %	16.99%	18.67%	13.22%	20.64%	16.26%	13.24%
SGA Expense	1,681,000,000	1,679,000,000	1,728,000,000	1,704,000,000	1,745,200,000	1,814,315,000
Net Income	645,000,000	709,000,000	556,000,000	849,000,000	555,721,000	470,567,000
Operating Cash Flow	1,069,000,000	810,000,000	938,000,000	652,000,000	1,187,168,000	895,474,000
Capital Expenditure	293,000,000	263,000,000	308,000,000	231,000,000	182,234,000	161,556,000
EBITDA	1,526,000,000	1,561,000,000	1,330,000,000	1,793,000,000	1,522,679,000	1,310,683,000
Return on Assets %	6.40%	7.14%	5.90%	9.31%	5.97%	5.27%
Return on Equity %	13.78%	15.78%	13.48%	20.93%	14.14%	12.18%
Debt to Equity	0.80	0.74	0.75	0.79	0.80	0.91

CONTACT INFORMATION:

Phone: 973 520-2700   Fax:
Toll-Free: 800-222-0446
Address: 3 Giralda Farms, Madison, NJ 07940 United States

STOCK TICKER/OTHER:

Stock Ticker: DGX   Exchange: NYS
Employees: 43,000   Fiscal Year Ends: 12/31
Parent Company:

SALARIES/BONUSES:

Top Exec. Salary: $1,100,000   Bonus: $
Second Exec. Salary: Bonus: $
$586,538

OTHER THOUGHTS:

Estimated Female Officers or Directors: 3
Hot Spot for Advancement for Women/Minorities: Y

Quintiles IMS Holdings Inc

www.quintiles.com

NAIC Code: 541711

TYPES OF BUSINESS:

Contract Research
Pharmaceutical, Biotech & Medical Device Research
Consulting & Training Services
Sales & Marketing Services

BRANDS/DIVISIONS/AFFILIATES:

Quintiles Transnational Holdings Inc
IMS Health Holdings Inc

CONTACTS: Note: Officers with more than one job title may be intentionally listed here more than once.

Michael Mcdonnell, CFO
Ari Bousbib, Chairman of the Board
Charles Williams, Chief Accounting Officer
James Erlinger, Executive VP
W. Staub, President, Divisional
Kevin Knightly, President, Divisional

GROWTH PLANS/SPECIAL FEATURES:

Quintiles IMS Holdings, Inc. (formerly Quintiles Transnational Holdings, Inc.) provides integrated information and technology-enabled healthcare services. The company's offerings help clients improve clinical, scientific and commercial results, with operations in more than 100 countries. Quintiles IMS' range of healthcare information, technology and service solutions span the entire product lifecycle, from clinical to commercial operations. Its information includes more than 530 million comprehensive and anonymous patient records spanning sales, prescription and promotional data; medical claims; electronic medical records; and social media. The firm's proprietary assets develop clinical and commercial capabilities. These assets and capabilities include: healthcare-specific global IT infrastructure, data-enriched clinical development, real-world insights ecosystem, proprietary commercial applications, as well as a global staff of more than 50,000 employees. In October 2016, Quintiles Transnational merged with IMS Health Holdings, Inc. in an all-stock deal worth about $8.75 billion.

FINANCIAL DATA: Note: Data for latest year may not have been available at press time.

In U.S. $	2016	2015	2014	2013	2012	2011
Revenue	6,878,000,000	5,737,619,000	5,459,998,000	5,099,545,000	4,865,513,000	4,327,748,000
R&D Expense				604,663,000		548,784,000
Operating Income	642,000,000	646,612,000	590,390,000	462,333,000	396,435,000	345,251,000
Operating Margin %	9.33%	11.26%	10.81%	9.06%	8.14%	7.97%
SGA Expense	1,011,000,000	920,985,000	882,338,000	255,847,000	817,755,000	213,515,000
Net Income	115,000,000	387,205,000	356,383,000	226,591,000	177,546,000	241,772,000
Operating Cash Flow	860,000,000	475,691,000	431,754,000	397,370,000	335,701,000	160,953,000
Capital Expenditure	164,000,000	78,391,000	82,650,000	92,346,000	71,336,000	75,679,000
EBITDA	912,000,000	768,529,000	723,791,000	554,128,000	500,087,000	385,744,000
Return on Assets %	.91%	10.70%	11.18%	8.14%	7.36%	10.40%
Return on Equity %	2.85%					
Debt to Equity	0.82					

CONTACT INFORMATION:

Phone: 919-998-2000   Fax:
Toll-Free: 866-267-4479
Address: 4820 Emperor Blvd., Durham, NC 27703 United States

STOCK TICKER/OTHER:

Stock Ticker: Q   Exchange: NYS
Employees: 50,000   Fiscal Year Ends: 12/31
Parent Company:

SALARIES/BONUSES:

Top Exec. Salary: $650,000   Bonus: $500,000
Second Exec. Salary: Bonus: $
$1,055,091

OTHER THOUGHTS:

Estimated Female Officers or Directors: 3
Hot Spot for Advancement for Women/Minorities: Y

Rackspace Hosting Inc
NAIC Code: 517110

www.rackspace.com

TYPES OF BUSINESS:
Web Hosting Services
Data Centers
Cloud Computing Services
Server Farms

BRANDS/DIVISIONS/AFFILIATES:
Apollo Global Management LLC
RackConnect
OpenStack

CONTACTS: *Note: Officers with more than one job title may be intentionally listed here more than once.*
Taylor Rhodes, CEO
Mark Roenigk, COO
Karl Pichler, CFO
Carla Pineyro Sublett, CMO
Aimee Hoyt, Sr. VP-Human Resources
Ryan Neading, CIO

GROWTH PLANS/SPECIAL FEATURES:
Rackspace Hosting, Inc. provides hosting services for businesses, specializing in web sites, web-based information technology (IT) systems and computing-as-a-service. It actively offers four service categories: dedicated cloud, public cloud, private cloud and hybrid cloud. Dedicated cloud is known as managed hosting, referring to IT services provided on a server or servers reserved for specific customers. A subscription-based business, this service provides a management portal and tools. Public cloud services deliver pooled computing resources on-demand over the internet. This division offers cloud servers for computing; cloud sites for website hosting; cloud block storage and cloud files for storage; cloud databases for hosting MySQL instances; cloud load balances for traffic management; cloud backup for file protection; cloud monitoring for infrastructure control; cloud Domain Name System (DNS) for domain management; and cloud applications, which includes email, collaboration and file back-ups. Private cloud, used widely by large corporate customers, refers to a pool of computing resources that is virtualized for greater efficiency and nimbleness, but that is dedicated to one particular customer rather than being used by multiple customers. The hardware can be located in data centers or in the customer's facilities. Hybrid cloud allows customers to seamlessly utilize the benefits of both dedicated and public cloud through its RackConnect service. Through the hybrid cloud, the technologies can be combined to address each customer's changing needs. Rackspace serves more than 300,000 customers in over 120 countries. Additionally, the firm is the co-founder, with NASA, of OpenStack, the world's fastest-growing open cloud platform and developer community. In November 2016, Rackspace was acquired by the private equity firm Apollo Global Management LLC for $4.3 billion.

The firm offers employees medical, dental and vision insurance; a 401(k) plan; profit sharing; employee training; and an onsite fitness facility.

FINANCIAL DATA: *Note: Data for latest year may not have been available at press time.*

In U.S. $	2016	2015	2014	2013	2012	2011
Revenue	2,081,000,000	2,001,299,968	1,794,356,992	1,534,786,048	1,309,239,040	1,025,064,000
R&D Expense						
Operating Income						
Operating Margin %						
SGA Expense						
Net Income	135,200,000	126,200,000	110,553,000	86,737,000	105,418,000	76,411,000
Operating Cash Flow						
Capital Expenditure						
EBITDA						
Return on Assets %						
Return on Equity %						
Debt to Equity						

CONTACT INFORMATION:
Phone: 210 312-4000   Fax: 210 312-4300
Toll-Free: 800-961-2888
Address: 5000 Walzem Rd., San Antonio, TX 78218 United States

STOCK TICKER/OTHER:
Stock Ticker: Private   Exchange:
Employees: 6,200   Fiscal Year Ends: 12/31
Parent Company: Apollo Global Management LLC

SALARIES/BONUSES:
Top Exec. Salary: $ Bonus: $
Second Exec. Salary: $ Bonus: $

OTHER THOUGHTS:
Estimated Female Officers or Directors: 1
Hot Spot for Advancement for Women/Minorities:

Raymond James Financial Inc

www.raymondjames.com

NAIC Code: 523110

TYPES OF BUSINESS:

Stock Brokerage/Investment Banking
Trust Services
Asset Management
Banking

BRANDS/DIVISIONS/AFFILIATES:

Raymond James & Associates Inc
Raymond James Financial Services Inc
Raymond James Financial Services Advisors Inc
Raymond James Bank NA
Raymond James Ltd
Eagle Asset Management Inc
Raymond James Investment Services Limited
Raymond James Financial International Ltd

CONTACTS: *Note: Officers with more than one job title may be intentionally listed here more than once.*

Paul Allison, CEO, Subsidiary
John Carson, President
Dennis Zank, CEO, Subsidiary
Steven Raney, CEO, Subsidiary
Paul Reilly, CEO
Jeffrey Julien, CFO
Thomas James, Chairman of the Board
Jennifer Ackart, Chief Accounting Officer
George Catanese, Chief Risk Officer
Francis Godbold, Director
Jeffrey Dowdle, Executive VP, Divisional
Bella Allaire, Executive VP, Subsidiary
Jonathan Santelli, General Counsel
Scott Curtis, President, Subsidiary
Tashtego Elwyn, President, Subsidiary
Jeffrey Trocin, President, Subsidiary

GROWTH PLANS/SPECIAL FEATURES:

Raymond James Financial, Inc. (RJF) is a diversified financial services holding company with subsidiaries engaged in investment and financial planning primarily in the U.S. and Canada. Services include securities, brokerage, investment banking, asset management, banking and cash management and trust products. The firm's principal subsidiaries are Raymond James & Associates, Inc. (RJ&A); Raymond James Financial Services, Inc. (RJFS); Raymond James Financial Services Advisors, Inc. (RJFSA); Raymond James, Ltd. (RJ Ltd); Eagle Asset Management, Inc. (Eagle); and Raymond James Bank, NA (RJ Bank). RJF operates through five segments: private client group, capital markets, asset management, RJ Bank and other. The private client group provides securities transaction and financial planning services to roughly 2.9 million client accounts through the branch office systems of RJ&A, RJFS, RJFSA, RJ Ltd. and in the U.K, through Raymond James Investment Services Limited (RJIS). The capital markets segment's activities consist primarily of equity and fixed income products and services in which institutional clients are serviced through the RJ&A fixed income department and its European offices; Raymond James Financial International, Ltd. (headquartered in London); and James European Securities, Inc. The asset management segment includes proprietary asset management operations, internally sponsored mutual funds, non-affiliated private account portfolio management alternatives, a national bank and other fee based programs. The segment includes Eagle, the Eagle Family of Funds, the asset management operations of RJ&A, Raymond James Trust, National Association (RJT) and other fee-based programs. RJ Bank is a federally-chartered bank that provides residential, consumer and commercial loans, as well as deposit accounts, to clients of the company's broker-dealer subsidiaries and to the general public. The other segment includes principal capital and private equity activities as well as various corporate overhead costs of RJF. In September 2016, the firm acquired Deutsche Bank Wealth Management's U.S. private client services unit.

FINANCIAL DATA: *Note: Data for latest year may not have been available at press time.*

In U.S. $	2016	2015	2014	2013	2012	2011
Revenue	5,403,267,000	5,200,210,000	4,861,369,000	4,485,427,000	3,806,531,000	3,334,056,000
R&D Expense			139,672,000			
Operating Income	777,371,000	776,712,000	715,948,000	593,910,000	467,921,000	450,745,000
Operating Margin %	14.38%	14.93%	14.72%	13.24%	12.29%	13.51%
SGA Expense	4,112,836,000	3,851,343,000	3,617,741,000	3,472,892,000	2,845,163,000	2,438,440,000
Net Income	529,350,000	502,140,000	480,248,000	367,154,000	295,869,000	278,353,000
Operating Cash Flow	-518,324,000	899,177,000	507,587,000	659,805,000	391,289,000	1,558,441,000
Capital Expenditure	121,733,000	74,111,000	60,149,000	72,879,000	77,515,000	37,200,000
EBITDA						
Return on Assets %	1.81%	2.00%	2.06%	1.65%	1.51%	1.55%
Return on Equity %	11.19%	11.55%	12.30%	10.59%	10.10%	11.38%
Debt to Equity	0.46	0.41	0.45	0.36	0.43	0.27

CONTACT INFORMATION:

Phone: 727 567-1000   Fax:
Toll-Free: 800-248-8863
Address: 880 Carillon Parkway, St. Petersburg, FL 33716 United States

STOCK TICKER/OTHER:

Stock Ticker: RJF
Employees: 11,900
Parent Company:

Exchange: NYS
Fiscal Year Ends: 09/30

SALARIES/BONUSES:

Top Exec. Salary: $445,000   Bonus: $4,575,034
Second Exec. Salary: $330,000   Bonus: $2,450,012

OTHER THOUGHTS:

Estimated Female Officers or Directors: 1
Hot Spot for Advancement for Women/Minorities: Y

Red Hat Inc

NAIC Code: 0

TYPES OF BUSINESS:

Computer Software-Linux Operating Systems
Open-Source Software

BRANDS/DIVISIONS/AFFILIATES:

Red Hat JBoss Middleware Suite
Red Hat Satellite
Red Hat Virtualization
Red Hat Enterprise Linux
Ansible Inc
3scale

CONTACTS: *Note: Officers with more than one job title may be intentionally listed here more than once.*

James Whitehurst, CEO
Eric Shander, CFO
Henry Shelton, Chairman of the Board
Arun Oberoi, Executive VP, Divisional
Michael Cunningham, Executive VP
DeLisa Alexander, Executive VP
Paul Cormier, President, Divisional

GROWTH PLANS/SPECIAL FEATURES:

Red Hat, Inc. is a provider of open-source software solutions. The firm's solutions include its core enterprise operating system platform Red Hat Enterprise Linux, the enterprise middleware platform Red Hat JBoss Middleware Suite, virtual solutions, cloud storage and other Red Hat enterprise technologies. The company offers a choice of operating system platforms for servers, work stations and desktops that support multiple application areas, including the data center, edge-of-the-network applications, IT infrastructure, corporate desktop and technical/developer workstation. Red Hat JBoss Middleware delivers a suite of middleware products for service-oriented architectures, permitting web-enabled applications to run on open source and other platforms. The software provides an application infrastructure for building and deploying distributed applications that are accessible via the internet, corporate intranets, extranets and virtual private networks. Applications deployed on JBoss include online e-business, hotel and airline reservations, online banking, credit card processing, securities trading, health care systems, customer and partner portals, retail and point of sale systems (POS), telecommunications network infrastructure and grid-based systems. The integrated management service, Red Hat Satellite, permit Red Hat enterprise technologies to be updated and configured as well as the performance of these and other technologies to be monitored and managed in an automated fashion. Red Hat Virtualization allows a single system to run more than one operating systems by abstracting the operating systems and application software from the underlying hardware infrastructure. The firm's suite of training and other professional service offerings enable enterprise customers to adapt Red Hat's technologies to their needs. In 2015, Red Hat acquired Ansible, Inc., a provider of powerful IT automation solutions. In June 2016, the firm acquired 3scale, a leading provider of application programming interface management technology.

FINANCIAL DATA: *Note: Data for latest year may not have been available at press time.*

In U.S. $	2016	2015	2014	2013	2012	2011
Revenue	2,052,230,000	1,789,489,000	1,534,615,000	1,328,817,000	1,133,103,000	
R&D Expense	413,322,000	367,856,000	317,263,000	263,150,000	208,662,000	
Operating Income	288,048,000	249,994,000	232,289,000	201,038,000	199,913,000	
Operating Margin %	14.03%	13.97%	15.13%	15.12%	17.64%	
SGA Expense	1,041,231,000	898,440,000	752,463,000	664,029,000	545,980,000	
Net Income	199,365,000	180,201,000	178,292,000	150,204,000	146,626,000	
Operating Cash Flow	716,092,000	622,795,000	540,580,000	465,297,000	391,883,000	
Capital Expenditure	55,517,000	51,771,000	97,559,000	120,038,000	51,618,000	
EBITDA	374,074,000	341,155,000	306,694,000	263,379,000	251,285,000	
Return on Assets %	5.01%	5.21%	6.02%	5.66%	6.25%	
Return on Equity %	15.20%	12.69%	11.61%	10.29%	10.90%	
Debt to Equity	0.54	0.55		0.03		

CONTACT INFORMATION:

Phone: 919 754-3700   Fax: 919 754-3701
Toll-Free: 888-733-4281
Address: 1801 Varsity Dr., Raleigh, NC 27606 United States

SALARIES/BONUSES:

Top Exec. Salary: $1,000,000   Bonus: $
Second Exec. Salary: $700,000   Bonus: $

STOCK TICKER/OTHER:

Stock Ticker: RHT   Exchange: NYS
Employees: 10,500   Fiscal Year Ends: 02/28
Parent Company:

OTHER THOUGHTS:

Estimated Female Officers or Directors: 3
Hot Spot for Advancement for Women/Minorities: Y

Regal-Beloit Corporation

www.regal-beloit.com

NAIC Code: 335312

TYPES OF BUSINESS:

Mechanical Products Manufacturing
HVAC Components

BRANDS/DIVISIONS/AFFILIATES:

CONTACTS: Note: Officers with more than one job title may be intentionally listed here more than once.

Mark Gliebe, CEO
Charles Hinrichs, CFO
Jonathan Schlemmer, COO
Thomas Valentyn, General Counsel
Terry Colvin, Vice President, Divisional
John Avampato, Vice President
Robert Lazzerini, Vice President

GROWTH PLANS/SPECIAL FEATURES:

Regal-Beloit Corporation is a U.S.-based multinational corporation that manufactures electric motors and controls, electric generators and power transmission products. The company operates through three segments: commercial & industrial systems (CIS), climate solutions and power transmission solutions. CIS designs, manufactures and sells fractional, integral and large horsepower AC and DC motors and controls for commercial and industrial applications. These motors are sold directly to original equipment manufacturer (OEM) and end-user customers through direct and independent sales representatives, as well as through regional and national distributors. Climate solutions designs, manufactures and sells fractional motors, electronic variable speed controls and blowers used in a variety of residential and light commercial air moving applications including HVAC systems and commercial refrigeration. Power transmission solutions designs, manufactures and markets standard, modified and highly engineered enclosed gear drives, gearmotors, transmissions and custom open gearing used for motion control within complex equipment systems. This gearing reduces the speed and increases the torque from an electric motor or other prime mover to meet the requirements of equipment such as a conveyor drive. Regal manufactures many the products that it sells at its facilities located in the U.S., Canada, Mexico, India, China, Thailand and Europe.

FINANCIAL DATA: Note: Data for latest year may not have been available at press time.

In U.S. $	2016	2015	2014	2013	2012	2011
Revenue	3,224,500,000	3,509,700,000	3,257,100,000	3,095,700,000	3,166,900,000	2,808,332,000
R&D Expense						
Operating Income	320,600,000	252,800,000	121,500,000	208,000,000	312,800,000	255,713,000
Operating Margin %	9.94%	7.20%	3.73%	6.71%	9.87%	9.10%
SGA Expense				494,200,000		
Net Income	203,400,000	143,300,000	31,000,000	120,000,000	195,600,000	152,290,000
Operating Cash Flow	439,600,000	381,100,000	298,200,000	305,000,000	351,700,000	265,296,000
Capital Expenditure	65,200,000	92,200,000	88,200,000	91,000,000	82,300,000	57,621,000
EBITDA	480,500,000	416,500,000	268,100,000	341,400,000	440,400,000	355,691,000
Return on Assets %	4.54%	3.58%	.87%	3.32%	5.72%	5.32%
Return on Equity %	10.23%	7.40%	1.55%	5.98%	11.21%	10.51%
Debt to Equity	0.64	0.88	0.32	0.29	0.38	0.59

CONTACT INFORMATION:

Phone: 608 364-8800   Fax: 608 364-8818
Toll-Free:
Address: 200 State Street, Beloit, WI 53511 United States

STOCK TICKER/OTHER:

Stock Ticker: RBC   Exchange: NYS
Employees: 23,000   Fiscal Year Ends: 12/31
Parent Company:

SALARIES/BONUSES:

Top Exec. Salary: $955,000   Bonus: $
Second Exec. Salary: $590,000   Bonus: $

OTHER THOUGHTS:

Estimated Female Officers or Directors:
Hot Spot for Advancement for Women/Minorities:

REI (Recreational Equipment Inc)

www.rei.com

NAIC Code: 451110

TYPES OF BUSINESS:

Outdoor Gear & Clothing, Retail
Sporting Equipment Retail & Rental
Adventure Travel Services
Catalog & Online Sales

BRANDS/DIVISIONS/AFFILIATES:

REI
REI Adventures
REI Gear and Apparel
Novara

CONTACTS: Note: Officers with more than one job title may be intentionally listed here more than once.

Jerry Stritzke, CEO
Eric Artz, Exec. VP
Jerry Stritzke, Pres.
Tracie Winbigler, CFO
Craig Rowley, VP-Mktg.
Raquel Karls, Sr. VP-Human Resources
Julie Averill, CIO
Susan Viscon, VP-Merch.
Catherine Walker, General Counsel
Brad Brown, Sr. VP-e-Commerce & Direct Sales
Michael Collins, VP-Public Affairs
Sue Sallee, VP-Finance & Acct.
Tim Spangler, Sr. VP-Retail
Kathleen Peterson, VP-REI Private Brands
Cheryl Scott, Chmn.
Rick Bingle, VP-Supply Chain

GROWTH PLANS/SPECIAL FEATURES:

Recreational Equipment, Inc. (REI) is one of the largest consumer cooperatives in the U.S. The firm offers quality outdoor gear, clothing and footwear selected for performance and durability in outdoor recreation, including hiking, climbing, camping, bicycling, paddling and winter sports. Today, REI has more than 6 million active members served by 149 retail stores located throughout the U.S. Stores include a variety of facilities for testing equipment, including bike test trails, climbing pinnacles and camp stove demonstration tables. While anyone may shop at the stores, customers who pay a small fee to become members receive special discounts and a share in the company's profits through an annual patronage refund based on their purchases. REI's e-commerce site is one of the largest outdoor online stores, offering a comprehensive library of product information, expert gear advice and outdoor recreation information. In addition to nationally-recognized brands, the company sells private label apparel and accessories under the REI Gear and Apparel brand. It also offers mountain, road and touring bikes under the private Novara name. Through REI Adventures, the company has been operating small group tours throughout the world for more than 20 years, avoiding standard tourist routes and emphasizing outdoor activities. Each year, REI Adventures plans domestic and international bicycling, trekking, kayaking, hiking, camping and mountaineering adventures. The firm invests millions of dollars on an annual basis to build trails, clean up the environment and teach children outdoor ethics.

The firm offers employees health, life and disability plans; tuition reimbursement; adoption and relocation assistance; an employee discount program; and a public transit subsidy.

FINANCIAL DATA: Note: Data for latest year may not have been available at press time.

In U.S. $	2016	2015	2014	2013	2012	2011
Revenue	2,423,221,000	2,217,130,000	2,017,476,000	2,000,000,000	1,900,000,000	1,800,000,000
R&D Expense						
Operating Income						
Operating Margin %						
SGA Expense						
Net Income	35,372,000	44,183,000	19,031,000	153,300,000	132,600,000	116,200,000
Operating Cash Flow						
Capital Expenditure						
EBITDA						
Return on Assets %						
Return on Equity %						
Debt to Equity						

CONTACT INFORMATION:

Phone: 253-891-2500   Fax: 253-891-2523
Toll-Free: 800-426-4840
Address: 6750 S. 228th Street, Kent, WA 98032 United States

STOCK TICKER/OTHER:

Stock Ticker: Private   Exchange:
Employees: 12,000   Fiscal Year Ends: 01/02
Parent Company:

SALARIES/BONUSES:

Top Exec. Salary: $ Bonus: $
Second Exec. Salary: $ Bonus: $

OTHER THOUGHTS:

Estimated Female Officers or Directors: 7
Hot Spot for Advancement for Women/Minorities: Y

Republic Services Inc

www.republicservices.com

NAIC Code: 562111

TYPES OF BUSINESS:

Solid Waste Collection
Recycling

BRANDS/DIVISIONS/AFFILIATES:

BlackRock Advisors LLC

CONTACTS: Note: Officers with more than one job title may be intentionally listed here more than once.

Donald Slager, CEO
Brian Goebel, Chief Accounting Officer
Jeffrey Hughes, Chief Administrative Officer
Manuel Kadre, Director
Charles Serianni, Executive VP
Catharine Ellingsen, Executive VP

GROWTH PLANS/SPECIAL FEATURES:

Republic Services, Inc. provides non-hazardous solid waste collection services for commercial, industrial, municipal and residential customers through 340 collection operations in 41 states and Puerto Rico. It owns or operates 201 transfer stations, 193 active landfills, 67 recycling centers, eight treatment/recovery/disposal facilities and 12 salt water disposal wells. The company's operations primarily consist of providing collection, transfer station and disposal of non-hazardous solid waste and the recovery and recycling of certain materials. The firm provides solid waste collection services to commercial, industrial, municipal and residential customers through its collection operations. In 2016, it generated 76% of its revenue from collection services. Republic Services deposits waste at its transfer stations, as do other private haulers and municipal haulers. The waste is compacted and then transferred to trailers for transport to disposal sites or recycling facilities. The company's disposal and materials recovery activities generate revenue through the collection, processing and sale of corrugated cardboard, newspaper, aluminum, glass and other materials. Republic Services' facilities and operations are subject to a variety of federal, state and local requirements that regulate the environment, public health, safety, zoning and land use. In January 2017, BlackRock Advisors, LLC increased its stake in Republic Services by 3.4%, now owning more than 5.5% in the company.

FINANCIAL DATA: Note: Data for latest year may not have been available at press time.

In U.S. $	2016	2015	2014	2013	2012	2011
Revenue	9,387,700,000	9,115,000,000	8,788,300,000	8,417,200,000	8,118,300,000	8,192,900,000
R&D Expense						
Operating Income	1,537,500,000	1,558,800,000	1,233,100,000	1,210,300,000	1,320,600,000	1,552,700,000
Operating Margin %	16.37%	17.10%	14.03%	14.37%	16.26%	18.95%
SGA Expense	975,400,000	983,100,000	920,400,000	853,800,000	820,900,000	825,400,000
Net Income	612,600,000	749,900,000	547,600,000	588,900,000	571,800,000	589,200,000
Operating Cash Flow	1,847,800,000	1,679,700,000	1,529,800,000	1,548,200,000	1,513,800,000	1,766,700,000
Capital Expenditure	927,800,000	945,600,000	862,500,000	880,800,000	903,500,000	936,500,000
EBITDA	2,407,400,000	2,610,800,000	2,218,900,000	2,165,200,000	2,139,300,000	2,190,100,000
Return on Assets %	2.97%	3.68%	2.73%	2.97%	2.91%	3.02%
Return on Equity %	7.92%	9.66%	6.99%	7.54%	7.43%	7.58%
Debt to Equity	0.99	0.97	0.91	0.88	0.91	0.89

CONTACT INFORMATION:

Phone: 480 627-2700   Fax:
Toll-Free:
Address: 18500 North Allied Way, Phoenix, AZ 85054 United States

STOCK TICKER/OTHER:

Stock Ticker: RSG
Employees: 33,000
Parent Company:

Exchange: NYS
Fiscal Year Ends: 12/31

SALARIES/BONUSES:

Top Exec. Salary: $1,100,000   Bonus: $
Second Exec. Salary: Bonus: $
$511,779

OTHER THOUGHTS:

Estimated Female Officers or Directors:
Hot Spot for Advancement for Women/Minorities:

ResMed Inc

NAIC Code: 339100

www.resmed.com

TYPES OF BUSINESS:

Sleep Disordered Breathing Medical Equipment
Diagnosis & Treatment Products

BRANDS/DIVISIONS/AFFILIATES:

AirSense 10
S9
Conduit Technology LLC

CONTACTS: *Note: Officers with more than one job title may be intentionally listed here more than once.*

Michael Farrell, CEO
Brett Sandercock, CFO
Peter Farrell, Chairman of the Board
David Pendarvis, Chief Administrative Officer
Robert Douglas, COO
Anne Reiser, President, Geographical
James Hollingshead, President, Geographical

GROWTH PLANS/SPECIAL FEATURES:

ResMed, Inc. is an Australian-founded company that develops, manufactures and distributes medical equipment and cloud-based software applications for treating, diagnosing and managing sleep disordered breathing (SDB) and other respiratory disorders. SDB includes obstructive sleep apnea (OSA) and other related respiratory disorders that occur during sleep. The company was originally founded to commercialize a continuous positive airway pressure (CPAP) treatment for OSA, which delivers pressurized air, typically through a nasal mask, to prevent collapse of the upper airway during sleep. Since the introduction of nasal CPAP, the firm has developed a number of innovative products for SDB, including mask systems, headgear, airflow generators, diagnostic products and other accessories. The firm's CPAP include AirSense 10 Elite and AirSense 10 CPAP. Its variable positive airway pressure (VPAP) products include the S9 family: VPAP ST-A and COPD (chronic obstructive pulmonary disease; and the AirCurve 10 family: S, V Auto, ST, ASV and CS. Other product categories include automatic positive airway pressure (APAP) products, diagnostic products and data/patient management products. The company's business strategy includes expanding into new clinical applications by seeking to identify new uses for its technologies, as well as increasing consumer awareness of the little-known condition, which may afflict up to 20% of Americans. The firm sells products in over 100 countries through wholly-owned subsidiaries and independent distributors. ResMed's market is divided into three regions, North & Latin America, Europe and Asia Pacific. Through various subsidiaries, the company owns approximately 1,043 issued U.S. patents (including approximately 413 design patents) and approximately 2,020 issued foreign patents. In June 2017, the firm acquired Conduit Technology, LLC, a provider of documentation and workflow solutions.

FINANCIAL DATA: *Note: Data for latest year may not have been available at press time.*

In U.S. $	2016	2015	2014	2013	2012	2011
Revenue	1,838,713,000	1,678,912,000	1,554,973,000	1,514,457,000	1,368,515,000	
R&D Expense	118,651,000	114,865,000	118,226,000	144,889,000	109,733,000	
Operating Income	428,952,000	409,236,000	405,087,000	354,824,000	294,407,000	
Operating Margin %	23.32%	24.37%	26.05%	23.42%	21.51%	
SGA Expense	488,057,000	478,627,000	450,414,000	430,802,000	401,621,000	
Net Income	352,409,000	352,886,000	345,273,000	307,133,000	254,850,000	
Operating Cash Flow	547,933,000	383,180,000	391,268,000	402,823,000	383,159,000	
Capital Expenditure	67,829,000	71,944,000	81,156,000	71,782,000	61,107,000	
EBITDA	537,621,000	514,750,000	510,661,000	469,786,000	422,587,000	
Return on Assets %	12.94%	15.52%	15.10%	14.12%	12.11%	
Return on Equity %	21.47%	21.09%	20.49%	19.08%	15.26%	
Debt to Equity	0.51	0.18	0.17		0.15	

CONTACT INFORMATION:

Phone: 858 836-5000   Fax: 858 746-2900
Toll-Free: 800-424-0737
Address: 9001 Spectrum Ctr. Blvd., San Diego, CA 92123 United States

STOCK TICKER/OTHER:

Stock Ticker: RMD
Employees: 6,080
Parent Company:

Exchange: NYS
Fiscal Year Ends: 06/30

SALARIES/BONUSES:

Top Exec. Salary: $845,000   Bonus: $
Second Exec. Salary: $694,606   Bonus: $

OTHER THOUGHTS:

Estimated Female Officers or Directors: 2
Hot Spot for Advancement for Women/Minorities:

Resources Connection Inc

www.resourcesglobal.com

NAIC Code: 541612

TYPES OF BUSINESS:

Business Process Outsourcing
Accounting
Human Resources Outsourcing
IT Outsourcing
Supply Chain Management
Legal Services
Risk Management & Internal Audit Services
Corporate Advisory

BRANDS/DIVISIONS/AFFILIATES:

Resources Global Professionals
Sitrick Brincko Group
policyIQ

CONTACTS: Note: Officers with more than one job title may be intentionally listed here more than once.

Kate Duchene, CEO
Herbert Mueller, CFO
Donald Murray, Chairman of the Board
John Bower, Chief Accounting Officer

GROWTH PLANS/SPECIAL FEATURES:

Resources Connection, Inc., operating primarily as Resources Global Professionals (RGP), is an international professional services firm that assists its clients with projects requiring specialized expertise in a number of fields. Resources Connection maintains 45 offices in the U.S. and 23 abroad, serving a diverse base of more than 1,800 clients. The firm's service offerings include finance and accounting services; information management; corporate governance, risk and compliance (GRC); corporate advisory, communications and restructuring; supply chain management; human capital; and legal services. In the finance and accounting segment, the company provides assistance for corporate reorganizations; financial analyses, such as product cost and margin analyses; budgeting and forecasting; public-entity reporting; and audit preparation. The information management services segment offers financial system/enterprise resource planning implementation and post-implementation optimization. The corporate GRC segment provides compliance reviews, assistance services and internal audit co-sourcing. This division's proprietary policyIQ offering is a cloud-based GRC software application, enabling the management of a wide range of processes, including risk assessment, compliance, procedure management, internal audit programs, anti-corruption compliance and contract administration. The corporate advisory, communications and restructuring segment operates through the Sitrick Brincko Group, which offers a combination of strategic counsel, execution and organizational and logistical support critical to companies undergoing restructuring and change. The firm's supply chain management services include leading strategic sourcing efforts, negotiating contracts and purchasing strategies. The human capital segment includes change management, organization development and effectiveness, as well as optimization of human resources technology and operations. The firm offers legal services by providing attorneys, paralegals and contract managers to assist clients, including law firms, with project-based or peak period needs.

The company offers employees continuing education and training, certification programs, comprehensive benefits and bonus programs and participation in the employee stock purchase plan.

FINANCIAL DATA: Note: Data for latest year may not have been available at press time.

In U.S. $	2016	2015	2014	2013	2012	2011
Revenue	598,521,000	590,589,000	567,181,000	556,334,000	571,763,000	
R&D Expense						
Operating Income	53,803,000	50,258,000	37,975,000	39,702,000	73,092,000	
Operating Margin %	8.98%	8.50%	6.69%	7.13%	12.78%	
SGA Expense	174,806,000	173,797,000	172,531,000	168,318,000	170,992,000	
Net Income	30,443,000	27,508,000	19,886,000	20,504,000	41,142,000	
Operating Cash Flow	38,262,000	31,751,000	32,018,000	34,959,000	36,370,000	
Capital Expenditure	2,381,000	2,364,000	3,725,000	3,147,000	2,786,000	
EBITDA	57,360,000	54,565,000	43,291,000	45,976,000	82,187,000	
Return on Assets %	7.25%	6.57%	4.74%	4.83%	9.07%	
Return on Equity %	8.91%	8.01%	5.69%	5.70%	11.14%	
Debt to Equity						

CONTACT INFORMATION:

Phone: 714 430-6400   Fax: 714 433-6100
Toll-Free: 800-900-1131
Address: 17101 Armstrong Ave., Irvine, CA 92614 United States

SALARIES/BONUSES:

Top Exec. Salary: $583,000   Bonus: $
Second Exec. Salary: $397,308   Bonus: $

STOCK TICKER/OTHER:

Stock Ticker: RECN   Exchange: NAS
Employees: 3,301   Fiscal Year Ends: 05/31
Parent Company:

OTHER THOUGHTS:

Estimated Female Officers or Directors: 6
Hot Spot for Advancement for Women/Minorities: Y

Revlon Inc

NAIC Code: 325620

TYPES OF BUSINESS:
Cosmetics
Fragrances
Hair Care Products
Skin Care Products

BRANDS/DIVISIONS/AFFILIATES:
Revlon Consumer Products Corp
Almay
Pure Ice
Revlon Professional
CND
American Crew
Cutex
Elizabeth Arden Inc

CONTACTS: Note: Officers with more than one job title may be intentionally listed here more than once.
Fabian Garcia, CEO
Christopher Peterson, CFO
Ronald Perelman, Chairman of the Board
Giovanni Pieraccioni, COO, Divisional
E. Beattie, Director

GROWTH PLANS/SPECIAL FEATURES:
Revlon, Inc., through its subsidiary Revlon Consumer Products Corp., manufactures, markets and sells an extensive array of cosmetics, skin care, fragrances and personal care products. Revlon is one of the world's best-known names in cosmetics and is a leading mass-market brand. The firm's products are marketed under names including Almay, UniqOneCharlie, Mitchum, Gatineau, Pure Ice, Revlon, Llongueras, Natural Honey, ColorSilk and Jean Nate. These products are sold in more than 130 countries worldwide. Revlon operates in four segments: consumer, professional, Elizabeth Arden and other. The consumer segment is comprised of products manufactured, marketed and sold primarily within the mass channel in the USA and internationally, as well as certain department stores and other specialty stores outside the USA. The professional segment manufactures, markets and sells professional products primarily to hair and nail salons and distributors in the USA, as well as internationally. Products in this division are marketed under such brands as Revlon Professional, for hair color, hair care and hair treatments; Creme of Nature for multi-cultural hair care; CND in nail polishes and enhancements such as CND Shellac and CND Vinylux nail polishes; and American Crew in men's grooming products. The Elizabeth Arden segment markets, distributes and sells fragrances, skin care and color cosmetics to prestige retailers, specialty stores, the mass retail channel, distributors, perfumeries, department stores, boutiques, travel retailers and other retailers in the U.S. and internationally. The other segment includes the results of the CBB Beauty Group. In June 2016, Revlon acquired from Coty, Inc. its international Cutex business, completing the global consolidation of the Cutex brand's worldwide operations under Revlon management. The following September, the firm acquired Elizabeth Arden, Inc., a global prestige beauty company.

FINANCIAL DATA: Note: Data for latest year may not have been available at press time.

In U.S. $	2016	2015	2014	2013	2012	2011
Revenue	2,334,000,000	1,914,300,000	1,941,000,000	1,494,700,000	1,426,100,000	1,381,400,000
R&D Expense						
Operating Income	155,300,000	215,800,000	235,500,000	189,000,000	188,700,000	203,300,000
Operating Margin %	6.65%	11.27%	12.13%	12.64%	13.23%	14.71%
SGA Expense	1,161,000,000	1,002,500,000	1,009,500,000	731,700,000	710,200,000	685,500,000
Net Income	-21,900,000	56,100,000	40,900,000	-5,800,000	51,100,000	53,400,000
Operating Cash Flow	116,900,000	155,300,000	174,000,000	123,300,000	104,100,000	88,000,000
Capital Expenditure	59,300,000	48,300,000	55,500,000	28,600,000	20,900,000	13,900,000
EBITDA	236,900,000	297,200,000	304,400,000	226,100,000	245,000,000	241,700,000
Return on Assets %	-.86%	2.83%	2.01%	-.34%	4.26%	4.75%
Return on Equity %						
Debt to Equity						

CONTACT INFORMATION:
Phone: 212 527-4000   Fax: 212 527-4130
Toll-Free:
Address: 1 New York Plaza, New York, NY 10004 United States

STOCK TICKER/OTHER:
Stock Ticker: REV   Exchange: NYS
Employees: 7,300   Fiscal Year Ends: 12/31
Parent Company:

SALARIES/BONUSES:
Top Exec. Salary: $1,044,231   Bonus: $3,500,000
Second Exec. Salary: Bonus: $
$924,615

OTHER THOUGHTS:
Estimated Female Officers or Directors: 6
Hot Spot for Advancement for Women/Minorities: Y

Rite Aid Corporation

www.riteaid.com

NAIC Code: 446110

TYPES OF BUSINESS:

Drug Stores

BRANDS/DIVISIONS/AFFILIATES:

Riteaid.com
Rite Aid
GNC

CONTACTS: *Note: Officers with more than one job title may be intentionally listed here more than once.*

Kenneth Martindale, CEO, Divisional
John Standley, CEO
Darren Karst, CFO
Anthony Montini, Executive VP, Divisional
David Abelman, Executive VP, Divisional
Bryan Everett, Executive VP, Divisional
Jocelyn Konrad, Executive VP, Divisional
Douglas Donley, Senior VP

GROWTH PLANS/SPECIAL FEATURES:

Rite Aid Corporation is a U.S.-based retail drugstore company which operates over 4,536 drug stores in 31 states and Washington, D.C. Rite Aid stores primarily markets prescription drugs, which account for approximately 68.3% of its revenues. Other marketed merchandise, which accounts for the remaining 31.7% of revenues, includes non-prescription medications, health and beauty aids, personal care items, cosmetics, household items, beverages, convenience foods, greeting cards and seasonal merchandise. In addition to its marketed products, the firm offers an automated refill option for customers with ongoing prescriptions; and it also makes prescription refill reminder phone calls. Customers can order prescription refills through the company's e-commerce site Riteaid.com. The firm's average store size is approximately 12,600 square feet. Its larger stores are located in the western U.S. Rite Aid offers approximately 3,000 products under the Rite Aid private brand. The company maintains a strategic alliance with GNC, which enables Rite Aid to sell GNC branded and co-branded products. Rite Aid operates more than 2,300 GNC store-within-Rite Aid-stores. Approximately 63% of Rite Aid's stores are freestanding, 56% include a drive-through pharmacy, and 52% include a GNC store-within-Rite Aid-store. A majority of stores also include one-hour photo shops. In June 2017, Walgreens canceled its deal to buy Rite Aid after a long-term struggle concerning regulatory approvals, and replaced it with a new deal: purchasing more than 2,100 stores, three distribution centers and related inventory. Rite Aid signed an agreement with Walgreens to sell these assets for $5.175 billion.

The company offers its employees health, dental, vision and prescription plans; vision discount plan; basic and supplemental life and AD&D insurances; flexible spending accounts; bereavement leave; employee assistance; 401(k); stock purchase plan; and more.

FINANCIAL DATA: *Note: Data for latest year may not have been available at press time.*

In U.S. $	2016	2015	2014	2013	2012	2011
Revenue	30,736,660,000	26,528,380,000	25,526,410,000	25,392,260,000	26,121,220,000	
R&D Expense						
Operating Income	764,486,000	839,145,000	721,268,000	646,652,000	161,871,000	
Operating Margin %	2.48%	3.16%	2.82%	2.54%	.61%	
SGA Expense	7,013,346,000	6,695,642,000	6,561,162,000	6,600,765,000	6,531,411,000	
Net Income	165,465,000	2,109,173,000	249,414,000	118,105,000	-368,571,000	
Operating Cash Flow	997,402,000	648,959,000	702,046,000	819,588,000	266,537,000	
Capital Expenditure	669,995,000	539,386,000	421,223,000	382,980,000	250,137,000	
EBITDA	1,237,190,000	1,241,060,000	1,078,550,000	937,037,000	577,580,000	
Return on Assets %	1.64%	26.68%	3.07%	1.48%	-5.07%	
Return on Equity %	51.83%					
Debt to Equity	11.98	97.17				

CONTACT INFORMATION:

Phone: 717 761-2633   Fax: 717 975-5905
Toll-Free: 800-748-3243
Address: 30 Hunter Lane, Camp Hill, PA 17011 United States

STOCK TICKER/OTHER:

Stock Ticker: RAD   Exchange: NYS
Employees: 90,000   Fiscal Year Ends: 02/28
Parent Company:

SALARIES/BONUSES:

Top Exec. Salary: $1,184,500   Bonus: $
Second Exec. Salary: Bonus: $
$927,000

OTHER THOUGHTS:

Estimated Female Officers or Directors: 3
Hot Spot for Advancement for Women/Minorities: Y

Ritz-Carlton Hotel Company LLC (The)　　　www.ritzcarlton.com

NAIC Code: 721110

TYPES OF BUSINESS:

Hotels, Luxury
Condominiums
Golf Courses
Spas
Time Share Units

BRANDS/DIVISIONS/AFFILIATES:

Marriott International Inc
Six Senses
La Prairie
ESPA
Ritz-Carlton Destination Club (The)
Residencies at the Ritz-Carlton (The)

CONTACTS: Note: Officers with more than one job title may be intentionally listed here more than once.

Herve Humler, Pres.

GROWTH PLANS/SPECIAL FEATURES:

The Ritz-Carlton Hotel Company, LLC, a subsidiary of Marriott International, Inc., is one of the world's best-known luxury hotel chains, operating 91 hotels in 30 countries and territories. The firm maintains international sales offices in locations such as Chicago, New York, Los Angeles, Dubai, Shanghai, Tokyo and London. To cater toward an upscale client base, full-service luxury spas are offered at most Ritz-Carlton resorts. Some spas operate under the brand names Six Senses, La Prairie and ESPA. Besides its hotels, the firm provides vacation properties and residential suites under The Ritz-Carlton Destination Club and The Residencies at the Ritz-Carlton. The Ritz-Carlton Destination Club is the firm's time-share ownership unit, offering a flexible alternative to a second home. Membership is currently available in locations such as Aspen Highlands, Bachelor Gulch and Vail, Colorado; St. Thomas, U.S. Virgin Islands; San Francisco and North Lake Tahoe, California; Jupiter, Florida; Abaco, Bahamas; and Kauai Lagoons and Maui, Hawaii. The Residencies at the Ritz-Carlton offer luxury condominiums and estate homes throughout the U.S. and in Canada, Thailand, Israel, the Bahamas and Malaysia. Ritz-Carlton also markets its 12 luxury golf courses (many designed by leading names in the golf world such as Greg Norman and Jack Nicklaus) and fitness facilities to both local residents and visitors, and hosts many PGA and Senior PGA tournaments. Partner hotels include Bulgari Hotels and Resorts, EDITION hotels and The Cosmopolitan (Las Vegas).

The firm offers employees health care & dependent care spending accounts; tuition reimbursement; dental & vision insurance; short- and long-term disability coverage; credit union membership; and employee assistance programs.

FINANCIAL DATA: Note: Data for latest year may not have been available at press time.

In U.S. $	2016	2015	2014	2013	2012	2011
Revenue	2,200,000,000	2,400,000,000	2,355,320,000	2,222,213,400	2,126,520,000	2,217,060,000
R&D Expense						
Operating Income						
Operating Margin %						
SGA Expense						
Net Income						
Operating Cash Flow						
Capital Expenditure						
EBITDA						
Return on Assets %						
Return on Equity %						
Debt to Equity						

CONTACT INFORMATION:

Phone: 301-547-4700　　Fax:
Toll-Free: 888-241-3333
Address: 4445 Willard Ave., Ste. 800, Chevy Chase, MD 20815 United States

STOCK TICKER/OTHER:

Stock Ticker: Subsidiary　　　　　Exchange:
Employees: 40,000　　　　　　　　Fiscal Year Ends: 12/31
Parent Company: Marriott International Inc

SALARIES/BONUSES:

Top Exec. Salary: $　　　Bonus: $
Second Exec. Salary: $　　Bonus: $

OTHER THOUGHTS:

Estimated Female Officers or Directors: 1
Hot Spot for Advancement for Women/Minorities:

Robert Half International Inc

www.rhi.com

NAIC Code: 561320

TYPES OF BUSINESS:

Staffing
Risk Consulting
Internal Audit Services
Litigation Consulting & Forensic Accounting

BRANDS/DIVISIONS/AFFILIATES:

Accountemps
Robert Half Finance & Accounting
Robert Half Management Resources
Robert Half Technology
OfficeTeam
Robert Half Legal
Creative Group (The)
Protiviti Inc

CONTACTS: Note: Officers with more than one job title may be intentionally listed here more than once.

Harold Messmer, CEO
M. Waddell, CFO
Michael Buckley, Chief Accounting Officer
Paul Gentzkow, COO, Divisional
Robert Glass, Executive VP, Divisional
Evelyn Crane-Oliver, Secretary

GROWTH PLANS/SPECIAL FEATURES:

Robert Half International, Inc. (RHI) is a staffing firm that provides professional staffing and risk consulting services. RHI operates through more than 400 company-operated or -owned locations around the world. It provides temporary, project and full-time workers to firms in areas such as accounting, finance, administrative and legal support, IT, advertising and marketing. RHI consists of seven staffing divisions: Accountemps, for the staffing of accounting, tax and finance professionals; Robert Half Finance & Accounting and Robert Half Management Resources, for senior-level accounting and finance professionals; OfficeTeam, a division for highly skilled temporary administrative support staff; Robert Half Technology, for IT professionals; Robert Half Legal, which provides attorneys, paralegals and legal support personnel; and The Creative Group, for advertising, marketing and web design professionals. RHI has increased its focus on providing workers for small to mid-size businesses, and it has a growing number of highly-experienced, older workers on its list. Protiviti, Inc., the company's wholly-owned subsidiary, provides internal audit and risk consulting services by aiding clients in identifying, measuring and managing operational and technology-related risks in areas such as the media, hospitality, communications, energy, financial services, real estate, healthcare, government, education, non-profit, manufacturing, distribution and technology. Business risk consultations involve areas such as anti-money laundering, capital projects and construction, energy commodity risks, fraud investigation and forensic accounting. Technology risk consultations provide solutions for security and privacy, continuity, change management, IT assets and application effectiveness.

The firm offers employees medical, dental, vision and life insurance; a savings plan; short- and long-term disability coverage; an employee assistance program; and travel accident insurance.

FINANCIAL DATA: Note: Data for latest year may not have been available at press time.

In U.S. $	2016	2015	2014	2013	2012	2011
Revenue	5,250,399,000	5,094,933,000	4,695,014,000	4,245,895,000	4,111,213,000	3,776,976,000
R&D Expense						
Operating Income	553,222,000	580,480,000	496,625,000	396,577,000	343,048,000	250,216,000
Operating Margin %	10.53%	11.39%	10.57%	9.34%	8.34%	6.62%
SGA Expense	1,606,217,000	1,533,799,000	1,425,734,000	1,324,815,000	1,305,614,000	1,240,184,000
Net Income	343,389,000	357,796,000	305,928,000	252,195,000	209,942,000	149,922,000
Operating Cash Flow	442,081,000	438,236,000	340,698,000	309,217,000	289,177,000	256,316,000
Capital Expenditure	82,956,000	75,057,000	62,830,000	53,725,000	64,449,000	56,535,000
EBITDA	617,537,000	633,945,000	546,306,000	445,349,000	394,166,000	301,631,000
Return on Assets %	19.72%	21.35%	19.50%	17.56%	15.59%	11.42%
Return on Equity %	32.85%	36.07%	32.21%	28.63%	25.56%	18.07%
Debt to Equity						

CONTACT INFORMATION:

Phone: 650 234-6000   Fax:
Toll-Free:
Address: 2884 Sand Hill Rd., Menlo Park, CA 94025 United States

STOCK TICKER/OTHER:

Stock Ticker: RHI
Employees: 16,400
Parent Company:

Exchange: NYS
Fiscal Year Ends: 12/31

SALARIES/BONUSES:

Top Exec. Salary: $525,000   Bonus: $
Second Exec. Salary: $265,000   Bonus: $

OTHER THOUGHTS:

Estimated Female Officers or Directors: 1
Hot Spot for Advancement for Women/Minorities:

Roper Technologies Inc

www.ropertech.com

NAIC Code: 334513

TYPES OF BUSINESS:

Controls Manufacturing
Energy Controls
Medical Systems
Flow Controls

BRANDS/DIVISIONS/AFFILIATES:

Roper Industries Inc
iSqFt Holdings Inc (ConstructConenct)
Deltek Inc

CONTACTS: Note: Officers with more than one job title may be intentionally listed here more than once.

Brian Jellison, CEO
John Humphrey, CFO
Paul Soni, Controller
Neil Hunn, Executive VP
John Stipancich, General Counsel
Jason Conley, Vice President
Robert Crisci, Vice President, Divisional

GROWTH PLANS/SPECIAL FEATURES:

Roper Technologies, Inc., formerly known as Roper Industries, Inc., designs, manufactures and distributes energy systems and controls, scientific and industrial imaging products and software, industrial technology products and radio frequency (RF) products and services. The firm's operations are reported in four segments: Medical & Scientific Imaging, Energy Systems & Controls, Industrial Technology and RF Technology. The Medical & Scientific Imaging segment principally offers products and software in medical applications and high performance digital imaging products. The Energy Systems & Controls segment mainly produces control systems, fluid properties testing equipment, industrial valves and controls, vibration sensors and other non-destructive inspection and measurement products and solutions, which are provided through six reporting units. The Industrial Technology segment produces industrial pumps, equipment and consumables for materials analysis, industrial leak testing equipment, flow measurement and metering equipment and water meter and automatic meter reading (AMR) products and systems. The RF Technology segment provides radio frequency identification (RFID) and other communication related technology and software solutions that are used mainly in comprehensive toll and traffic systems and processing, security and access control, campus card systems, freight matching, food industries, metering and remote monitoring applications. Roper markets its products and services to selected segments of a range of industries, including healthcare, transportation, food, water, RF applications, energy, research and medical, education, security and other niche markets. In October 2016, the acquired iSqFt Holdings, Inc. (d/b/a ConstructConenct), a leading provider of cloud-based data, collaboration, and workflow automation solutions to the commercial construction industry. The following December, Roper acquired Deltek, Inc., a provider of software and information solutions for project-based businesses serving niche markets, for $2.8 billion.

FINANCIAL DATA: Note: Data for latest year may not have been available at press time.

In U.S. $	2016	2015	2014	2013	2012	2011
Revenue	3,789,925,000	3,582,395,000	3,549,494,000	3,238,128,000	2,993,489,000	2,797,089,000
R&D Expense						
Operating Income	1,054,563,000	1,027,918,000	999,473,000	842,361,000	757,587,000	660,539,000
Operating Margin %	27.82%	28.69%	28.15%	26.01%	25.30%	23.61%
SGA Expense	1,277,847,000	1,136,728,000	1,102,426,000	1,040,567,000	914,130,000	855,025,000
Net Income	658,645,000	696,067,000	646,033,000	538,293,000	483,360,000	427,247,000
Operating Cash Flow	963,785,000	928,825,000	840,441,000	802,553,000	677,852,000	601,618,000
Capital Expenditure	40,106,000	36,260,000	37,644,000	42,528,000	38,405,000	40,702,000
EBITDA	1,295,016,000	1,232,179,000	1,196,757,000	1,031,359,000	908,954,000	800,682,000
Return on Assets %	5.37%	7.49%	7.78%	7.05%	7.80%	8.22%
Return on Equity %	11.88%	13.84%	14.40%	13.62%	14.04%	14.37%
Debt to Equity	1.00	0.61	0.46	0.58	0.40	0.31

CONTACT INFORMATION:

Phone: 941 556-2601   Fax: 941 556-2670
Toll-Free:
Address: 6901 Professional Parkway East, Sarasota, FL 34240 United States

STOCK TICKER/OTHER:

Stock Ticker: ROP   Exchange: NYS
Employees: 14,155   Fiscal Year Ends: 12/31
Parent Company:

SALARIES/BONUSES:

Top Exec. Salary: $1,225,000   Bonus: $
Second Exec. Salary: $767,000   Bonus: $

OTHER THOUGHTS:

Estimated Female Officers or Directors:
Hot Spot for Advancement for Women/Minorities:

Rosendin Electric

www.rosendin.com

NAIC Code: 238210

TYPES OF BUSINESS:

Electrical Contractor

BRANDS/DIVISIONS/AFFILIATES:

KST Electric Ltd

CONTACTS: *Note: Officers with more than one job title may be intentionally listed here more than once.*

Tom Sorley, CEO
Larry Beltramo, Pres.
Sam Lamonica, CIO

GROWTH PLANS/SPECIAL FEATURES:

Rosendin Electric is a San Jose, California-based employee-owned electrical contractor that has been operating since the early 1900s. Services provided by the firm include preconstruction services that assist general contractors and owners during the development phase of a project. These services include design-build engineering, prefabrication, 24-hour/seven-days-a-week service response, network services, electric utility work along highways, service and maintenance, as well as the construction of solar & wind farms. Rosendin's project portfolio includes services for the following industries: biotechnology, pharmaceuticals, data centers, education, healthcare, high tech, institutions, multi-family residences, solar power, transportation, commercial, design-build, entertainment, heavy industrial, hotels, power, telecom and wind energy. Rosendin is also experienced in meeting LEED regulations. Subsidiary KST Electric Ltd. is a Texas-based electrical, data and communication contracting company.

Rosendin offers employees an employee stock ownership plan, 401(k) matching program, health/life/disability insurance and various employee assistance program options.

FINANCIAL DATA: *Note: Data for latest year may not have been available at press time.*

In U.S. $	2016	2015	2014	2013	2012	2011
Revenue	1,400,000,000	1,300,000,000	1,100,000,000	935,000,000	887,000,000	820,000,000
R&D Expense						
Operating Income						
Operating Margin %						
SGA Expense						
Net Income						
Operating Cash Flow						
Capital Expenditure						
EBITDA						
Return on Assets %						
Return on Equity %						
Debt to Equity						

CONTACT INFORMATION:

Phone: 480-286-2800   Fax:
Toll-Free:
Address: 880 Mabury Rd., San Jose, CA 95133 United States

STOCK TICKER/OTHER:

Stock Ticker: Private   Exchange:
Employees: 5,300   Fiscal Year Ends:
Parent Company:

SALARIES/BONUSES:

Top Exec. Salary: $ Bonus: $
Second Exec. Salary: $ Bonus: $

OTHER THOUGHTS:

Estimated Female Officers or Directors:
Hot Spot for Advancement for Women/Minorities:

Ross Stores Inc

NAIC Code: 448140

www.rossstores.com

TYPES OF BUSINESS:

Discount Apparel Stores
Home Furnishings

BRANDS/DIVISIONS/AFFILIATES:

Ross Dress for Less
dd's DISCOUNTS

CONTACTS: *Note: Officers with more than one job title may be intentionally listed here more than once.*

Barbara Rentler, CEO
Michael Hartshorn, CFO
Norman Ferber, Chairman Emeritus
Michael OSullivan, Co- President
James Fassio, Co- President
Michael Balmuth, Director
John Call, Executive VP, Divisional
Brian Morrow, Other Executive Officer
Bernard Brautigan, President, Divisional
Lisa Panattoni, President, Divisional

GROWTH PLANS/SPECIAL FEATURES:

Ross Stores, Inc. operates 1,340 off-price retail apparel and home accessories stores in 36 states, Washington, D.C. and Guam, most of which operate under the Ross Dress for Less brand. The company also operates 193 dd's DISCOUNTS locations in 15 states. Most of the stores are located in community and neighborhood strip shopping centers in heavily populated urban and suburban areas. The company's chains target value-conscious women and men ages 18-54. Ross offers new, in-season, name-brand and designer apparel, accessories, footwear and home merchandise at savings of 20%-60% off department and specialty store regular prices, while dd's DISCOUNTS, targeting lower-income customers, offers similar merchandise, but at savings of up to 70% off department and specialty store prices. The company's stores are supplied by four distribution processing facilities. Ross has combined a network of approximately 8,000 vendors and manufacturers, purchasing the vast majority of its merchandise directly from the manufacturer. By purchasing later in the merchandise buying cycle than department and specialty stores, Ross takes advantage of imbalances between retailers' demand for products and manufacturers' supply of those products. In addition, the company typically does not require that manufacturers provide promotional and markdown allowances, return privileges, split shipments, drop shipments to stores or delayed deliveries of merchandise, further enabling Ross to provide significant discounts on in-season merchandise. Sales of ladies products account for approximately 28% of the firm's revenues; home accents/bed and bath, 25%; men's products, 13%; accessories, lingerie, jewelry and fragrances, 13%; shoes, 13%; and children's products, 8%.

Ross offers its employees medical, dental, vision and life insurance; sick pay; health care spending accounts; holiday and personal days; a commuter reimbursement account; a 401(k) plan; and an employee stock purchasing plan.

FINANCIAL DATA: *Note: Data for latest year may not have been available at press time.*

In U.S. $	2016	2015	2014	2013	2012	2011
Revenue	11,940,000,000	11,041,680,000	10,230,350,000	9,721,065,000	8,608,291,000	
R&D Expense						
Operating Income	1,624,371,000	1,488,350,000	1,343,063,000	1,271,751,000	1,053,144,000	
Operating Margin %	13.60%	13.47%	13.12%	13.08%	12.23%	
SGA Expense	1,738,755,000	1,615,371,000	1,526,366,000	1,437,886,000	1,304,065,000	
Net Income	1,020,661,000	924,724,000	837,304,000	786,763,000	657,170,000	
Operating Cash Flow	1,326,252,000	1,372,865,000	1,022,003,000	979,644,000	820,105,000	
Capital Expenditure	366,960,000	646,691,000	550,515,000	424,434,000	416,271,000	
EBITDA	1,899,877,000	1,721,720,000	1,549,674,000	1,457,842,000	1,224,036,000	
Return on Assets %	21.32%	21.50%	22.12%	22.57%	20.48%	
Return on Equity %	42.96%	43.14%	44.37%	48.26%	46.51%	
Debt to Equity	0.16	0.17	0.07	0.08	0.10	

CONTACT INFORMATION:

Phone: 925 965-4400   Fax:
Toll-Free:
Address: 5130 Hacienda Drive, Dublin, CA 94568-7579 United States

STOCK TICKER/OTHER:

Stock Ticker: ROST   Exchange: NAS
Employees: 78,600   Fiscal Year Ends: 01/31
Parent Company:

SALARIES/BONUSES:

Top Exec. Salary: $1,317,907   Bonus: $700,000
Second Exec. Salary: Bonus: $
$1,301,875

OTHER THOUGHTS:

Estimated Female Officers or Directors: 4
Hot Spot for Advancement for Women/Minorities: Y

Royal Caribbean Cruises Ltd

www.royalcaribbean.com

NAIC Code: 483112

TYPES OF BUSINESS:
Cruise Line
Rail Tours
Online Travel Services
Academic Tours

BRANDS/DIVISIONS/AFFILIATES:
Royal Caribbean International
Celebrity Cruises
Azamara Club Cruises
Celebrity Xpedition
TUI Cruises
Pullmantur
SkySea Cruises

CONTACTS: *Note: Officers with more than one job title may be intentionally listed here more than once.*
Lawrence Pimentel, CEO, Subsidiary
Michael Bayley, CEO, Subsidiary
Lisa Lutoff-Perlo, CEO, Subsidiary
Richard Fain, CEO
Jason Liberty, CFO
Henry Pujol, Chief Accounting Officer
Adam Goldstein, COO
Harri Kulovaara, Executive VP, Divisional
Bradley Stein, General Counsel

GROWTH PLANS/SPECIAL FEATURES:
Royal Caribbean Cruises, Ltd. is a global cruise vacation firm, serving the contemporary, premium and deluxe cruise markets, including the budget and luxury segments. With 49 ships offering 123,270 berths, the firm operates five brand names: Royal Caribbean International (RCI), Celebrity Cruises and Azamara Club Cruises. Royal Caribbean's ships have itineraries that call on approximately 535 destinations worldwide. RCI operates 25 ships with 78,150 berths, offering cruise itineraries that range from 2-24 nights. Its destinations include Alaska, Asia, Australia, Bahamas, Bermuda, Canada, the Caribbean, Europe, the Panama Canal, South America and New Zealand. Celebrity Cruises operates 12 ships with 23,170 berths targeted toward higher-end clientele. It also operates Celebrity Xpedition, a ship that travels to the Galapagos Islands and offers pre-cruise tours of Ecuador. This cruise line has four ships on order, comprising a new generation known as Project Edge, with a capacity of 11,600 berths which are expected to enter service in late-2018 through 2022, respectively. Azamara Club Cruises serves the up-market and consists of two smaller ships, of about 1,400 passengers each, that focus on cruises to unique destinations, with an emphasis on on-board lectures and fine dining. Its ships sail in Asia, the Mediterranean, South America and less traveled Caribbean Islands. Partner brands are complemented by 50%-owned TUI Cruises, which is tailored for the German market; 49%-owned Pullmantur, which serves the Spanish, Portuguese and Latin American cruise markets; and 35%-owned SkySea Cruises, which offers a custom-tailored product for Chinese cruise guests.

FINANCIAL DATA: *Note: Data for latest year may not have been available at press time.*

In U.S. $	2016	2015	2014	2013	2012	2011
Revenue	8,496,401,000	8,299,074,000	8,073,855,000	7,959,894,000	7,688,024,000	7,537,263,000
R&D Expense						
Operating Income	1,477,205,000	874,902,000	941,859,000	798,148,000	403,110,000	931,628,000
Operating Margin %	17.38%	10.54%	11.66%	10.02%	5.24%	12.36%
SGA Expense	1,100,290,000	1,086,504,000	1,048,952,000	1,044,819,000	1,011,543,000	960,602,000
Net Income	1,283,388,000	665,783,000	764,146,000	473,692,000	18,287,000	607,421,000
Operating Cash Flow	2,516,690,000	1,946,366,000	1,743,759,000	1,412,068,000	1,381,734,000	1,455,739,000
Capital Expenditure	2,494,363,000	1,613,340,000	1,811,398,000	763,777,000	1,291,499,000	1,173,626,000
EBITDA	2,485,673,000	1,770,516,000	1,794,890,000	1,560,825,000	1,104,565,000	1,634,054,000
Return on Assets %	5.93%	3.19%	3.74%	2.37%	.09%	3.07%
Return on Equity %	14.93%	8.14%	8.94%	5.53%	.21%	7.43%
Debt to Equity	0.88	0.96	0.92	0.73	0.83	0.93

CONTACT INFORMATION:
Phone: 305 539-6000   Fax: 305 539-0562
Toll-Free:
Address: 1050 Caribbean Way, Miami, FL 33132 United States

STOCK TICKER/OTHER:
Stock Ticker: RCL
Employees: 66,000
Parent Company:

Exchange: NYS
Fiscal Year Ends: 12/31

SALARIES/BONUSES:
Top Exec. Salary: $1,092,308   Bonus: $
Second Exec. Salary: $823,077   Bonus: $

OTHER THOUGHTS:
Estimated Female Officers or Directors: 3
Hot Spot for Advancement for Women/Minorities: Y

RPM International Inc

NAIC Code: 325510

www.rpminc.com

TYPES OF BUSINESS:

Home & Industrial Maintenance Products
Specialty Paints
Protective Coatings
Roofing Systems
Sealants & Adhesives

BRANDS/DIVISIONS/AFFILIATES:

Tremco
Stonhard
Carboline
Dap
Rust-Oleum
Varathane
Holton Food Products Company
Seal-Krete

CONTACTS: Note: Officers with more than one job title may be intentionally listed here more than once.

Frank Sullivan, CEO
Russell Gordon, CFO
Keith Smiley, Chief Accounting Officer
Ronald Rice, COO
Edward Moore, General Counsel
Matthew Ratajczak, Treasurer
Janeen Kastner, Vice President, Divisional
Barry Slifstein, Vice President, Divisional

GROWTH PLANS/SPECIAL FEATURES:

RPM International, Inc., through its subsidiaries, manufactures, markets and sells specialty paints, protective coatings and roofing systems and sealants and adhesives. The firm focuses on maintenance and improvement needs of both the industrial, specialty and consumer markets. The industrial segment includes maintenance and protection products for roofing and waterproofing systems; flooring; corrosion control; and other specialty applications such as fluorescent pigments, industrial gratings and industrial sealants. These products are sold under brand names including Tremco, Stonhard, Carboline and Tremco illbruck. The specialty segment includes fluorescent colorants and pigments, fire and water damage restoration, wood treatment and fuel additives. Products in this segment are sold under the Day-Glo, Radiant, Unsmoke, Kop-Coat, Sapphire and NatureSeal brand names, among others. The consumer segment includes rust-preventative, special purpose and decorative paints, caulks, sealants, primers and other consumer products. This segment sells products under a variety of brand names, including Dap, Rust-Oleum, Varathane and Zinsser. The firm markets its products in roughly 164 countries and territories and operates manufacturing facilities in 120 locations in the U.S., Argentina, Belgium, Brazil Canada, Chile, Colombia, France, Germany, India, Italy, Malaysia, Mexico, the Netherlands, Norway, Poland, Saudi Arabia, South Africa, Spain, Sweden, Turkey, the UAE and the U.K. In 2016, the firm acquired Holton Food Products Company; Seal-Krete; the remaining 51% interest in Carboline Dalian Paint Production Co., Ltd.; Duram Industries Pty Limited; Applied Polymerics, Inc. & Marketing Associates, Inc.; Specialty Polymer Coatings, Inc.; and the foam division of Clayton Corp. In 2017, RPM acquired two businesses, a manufacturer of commercial floor cleaning equipment and chemicals and a manufacturer of specialty chemical raw materials, and Prime Resin, a manufacturer of specialty chemicals and equipment for infrastructure construction and repair.

FINANCIAL DATA: Note: Data for latest year may not have been available at press time.

In U.S. $	2016	2015	2014	2013	2012	2011
Revenue	4,813,649,000	4,594,550,000	4,376,353,000	4,078,655,000	3,777,416,000	
R&D Expense						
Operating Income	566,071,000	518,425,000	485,640,000	308,278,000	386,549,000	
Operating Margin %	11.75%	11.28%	11.09%	7.55%	10.23%	
SGA Expense	1,520,977,000	1,422,944,000	1,390,128,000	1,309,235,000	1,155,714,000	
Net Income	354,725,000	239,484,000	291,660,000	98,603,000	215,936,000	
Operating Cash Flow	474,706,000	330,448,000	278,149,000	368,454,000	294,872,000	
Capital Expenditure	117,183,000	85,363,000	93,792,000	91,367,000	71,615,000	
EBITDA	686,188,000	640,044,000	595,507,000	340,481,000	474,032,000	
Return on Assets %	7.49%	5.17%	6.86%	2.56%	6.10%	
Return on Equity %	26.63%	17.54%	22.57%	8.27%	17.65%	
Debt to Equity	1.19	1.28	0.97	1.14	0.94	

CONTACT INFORMATION:

Phone: 330 273-5090   Fax: 330 225-8743
Toll-Free:
Address: 2628 Pearl Rd., Medina, OH 44258 United States

STOCK TICKER/OTHER:

Stock Ticker: RPM   Exchange: NYS
Employees: 14,318   Fiscal Year Ends: 05/31
Parent Company:

SALARIES/BONUSES:

Top Exec. Salary: $960,000   Bonus: $
Second Exec. Salary: $720,000   Bonus: $

OTHER THOUGHTS:

Estimated Female Officers or Directors: 2
Hot Spot for Advancement for Women/Minorities:

Ryder System Inc

NAIC Code: 532120

www.ryder.com

TYPES OF BUSINESS:

Truck Rental & Leasing
Trucking
Logistics & Consulting Services
Supply Chain Management
Dedicated Fleet Services
Fleet Management Services

BRANDS/DIVISIONS/AFFILIATES:

CONTACTS: Note: Officers with more than one job title may be intentionally listed here more than once.

Art Garcia, CFO
Robert Sanchez, Chairman of the Board
Melvin Kirk, Chief Information Officer
Karen Jones, Chief Marketing Officer
John Gleason, Executive VP
Robert Fatovic, Executive VP
Francisco Lopez, Other Executive Officer
Dennis Cooke, President, Divisional
John Diez, President, Divisional
John Sensing, President, Divisional

GROWTH PLANS/SPECIAL FEATURES:

Ryder System, Inc. is a global provider of transportation and supply chain management solutions. It operates in three segments: fleet management solutions (FMS), supply chain solutions (SCS) and dedicated transportation solutions (DTS). FMS, which accounts for 61% of Ryder's revenue, provides full service leasing, contract maintenance, contract-related maintenance and commercial rental of trucks, tractors and trailers to customers principally in the U.S., Canada and the U.K. The division also offers transaction fleet solutions, including commercial truck rental; maintenance services; and value-added fleet support services, such as insurance, vehicle administration and fuel services. In addition, it provides customers with access to a large selection of used trucks, tractors and trailers through its used vehicle sales program. SCS derives 24% of revenue, provides a broad range of innovative logistics management services designed to optimize a customer's supply chain and address its key business requirements. Supply chain solutions include distribution and transportation services for industry verticals such as automotive, technology, healthcare, consumer packaged goods, retail and industrial, which are primarily in located North America and Asia. DTS derives 15% of revenue, and provides vehicles and drivers as part of a dedicated transportation solution within the U.S. This segment combines the equipment, maintenance and administrative services of a full-service lease with drivers, along with other services, in order to offer solutions designed to increase Ryder customers' competitive position, improve risk management and integrate transportation needs with their overall supply chain. This division's additional services include routing and scheduling, fleet sizing, safety, regulatory compliance, risk management, technology and communications support and other technical support. DTS offers a high degree of specialization to meet customer needs.

FINANCIAL DATA: Note: Data for latest year may not have been available at press time.

In U.S. $	2016	2015	2014	2013	2012	2011
Revenue	6,786,984,000	6,571,893,000	6,638,774,000	6,419,285,000	6,256,967,000	6,050,534,000
R&D Expense						
Operating Income	545,258,000	505,909,000	451,031,000	490,249,000	350,909,000	344,234,000
Operating Margin %	8.03%	7.69%	6.79%	7.63%	5.60%	5.68%
SGA Expense	842,697,000	844,497,000	816,975,000	790,681,000	766,704,000	771,244,000
Net Income	262,477,000	304,768,000	218,575,000	237,792,000	209,979,000	169,777,000
Operating Cash Flow	1,601,022,000	1,441,788,000	1,369,991,000	1,223,082,000	1,130,905,000	1,041,456,000
Capital Expenditure	1,905,157,000	2,667,978,000	2,259,164,000	2,140,464,000	2,133,235,000	1,698,589,000
EBITDA	1,809,534,000	1,830,333,000	1,568,146,000	1,519,621,000	1,432,560,000	1,324,741,000
Return on Assets %	2.40%	2.95%	2.32%	2.72%	2.63%	2.37%
Return on Equity %	12.99%	16.03%	11.76%	14.13%	15.07%	12.47%
Debt to Equity	2.24	2.45	2.47	2.07	2.35	2.35

CONTACT INFORMATION:

Phone: 305 500-3726   Fax: 305 500-4129
Toll-Free:
Address: 11690 NW 105th St., Miami, FL 33178 United States

STOCK TICKER/OTHER:

Stock Ticker: R   Exchange: NYS
Employees: 34,500   Fiscal Year Ends: 12/31
Parent Company:

SALARIES/BONUSES:

Top Exec. Salary: $785,225   Bonus: $
Second Exec. Salary: $543,750   Bonus: $

OTHER THOUGHTS:

Estimated Female Officers or Directors: 4
Hot Spot for Advancement for Women/Minorities: Y

Sabre Corporation

www.sabre-holdings.com

NAIC Code: 519130

TYPES OF BUSINESS:

Travel Reservations System for Airlines
Travel Marketing Solutions
Distribution & Technology Solutions
Consulting Services

BRANDS/DIVISIONS/AFFILIATES:

SabreSonic
Sabre AirVision Marketing & Planning
Sabre AirCentre Enterprise
SynXis
SynXis Property Manager Solutions
Trust Group of Companies

CONTACTS: *Note: Officers with more than one job title may be intentionally listed here more than once.*

Sean Menke, CEO
Richard Simonson, CFO
Lawrence Kellner, Chairman of the Board
Rachel Gonzalez, Executive VP
William Robinson, Executive VP
Dave Shirk, Executive VP
Wade Jones, Executive VP
Hugh Jones, Executive VP
Steve Milton, Secretary

GROWTH PLANS/SPECIAL FEATURES:

Sabre Corporation is a provider of travel products and services through two business segments: travel network and airline and hospitality solutions. The travel network segment comprises Sabre's global business-to-business travel marketplace, consisting primarily of its global distribution system (GDS) and solutions that add value for travel suppliers and travel buyers. GDS facilitates travel via inventory, prices and availability from its travel suppliers, including airlines, hotels, car rental brands, rail carriers, cruise lines and tour operators, with travel buyers, including online travel agencies, offline travel agencies, travel management companies and corporate travel departments. The airline and hospitality solutions business offers a broad portfolio of software technology products, through a software-as-a-service (Saas) and hosted delivery model, to airlines, hotel properties and other travel suppliers. The airline solutions division provide software that helps Sabre's airline customers better market, sell, serve and operate. Its SabreSonic suite provides capabilities and managing sales and customer service across an airline's touch points. Sabre AirVision Marketing & Planning is a suite of airline commercial planning solutions that focus on helping Sabre airline customers improve profitability and develop their brand. Sabre AirCentre Enterprise is a suite of solutions that drive operational effectiveness through holistic planning and management of airline, airport and customer operations. The hospitality solutions division provides software and solutions to hotel properties worldwide. Solutions include distribution through Sabre's SynXis central reservation system, property management through SynXis Property Manager Solutions, marketing services and consulting services that optimize distribution and marketing. In 2016, the firm acquired the Trust Group of Companies, a central reservation, revenue management and hotel marketing provider.

FINANCIAL DATA: *Note: Data for latest year may not have been available at press time.*

In U.S. $	2016	2015	2014	2013	2012	2011
Revenue	3,373,387,000	2,960,896,000	2,631,417,000	3,049,525,000	3,039,060,000	2,855,961,000
R&D Expense						
Operating Income	459,572,000	459,769,000	421,345,000	176,760,000	-618,785,000	128,245,000
Operating Margin %	13.62%	15.52%	16.01%	5.79%	-20.36%	4.49%
SGA Expense	626,153,000	557,077,000	468,152,000	792,929,000	547,928,000	806,435,000
Net Income	242,562,000	545,482,000	69,223,000	-100,494,000	-611,356,000	-66,074,000
Operating Cash Flow	699,400,000	529,207,000	387,659,000	157,188,000	305,754,000	356,444,000
Capital Expenditure	327,647,000	286,697,000	227,227,000	226,026,000	193,262,000	164,638,000
EBITDA	873,558,000	811,249,000	710,975,000	487,559,000	-274,102,000	424,562,000
Return on Assets %	4.36%	10.78%	1.21%	-2.89%	-12.96%	-1.87%
Return on Equity %	43.87%	192.59%				
Debt to Equity	5.25	6.56	36.54			

CONTACT INFORMATION:

Phone: 682-605-1000   Fax:
Toll-Free:
Address: 3150 Sabre Drive, Southlake, TX 76092 United States

STOCK TICKER/OTHER:

Stock Ticker: SABR   Exchange: NAS
Employees: 10,000   Fiscal Year Ends: 12/31
Parent Company:

SALARIES/BONUSES:

Top Exec. Salary: $975,000   Bonus: $
Second Exec. Salary: Bonus: $
$671,539

OTHER THOUGHTS:

Estimated Female Officers or Directors: 1
Hot Spot for Advancement for Women/Minorities:

Safeco Insurance Company of America

www.safeco.com

NAIC Code: 524126

TYPES OF BUSINESS:

Direct Property & Casualty Insurance
Personal Insurance

BRANDS/DIVISIONS/AFFILIATES:

Liberty Mutual Group Inc
Safeco Package
Liberty Northwest
Colorado Casualty Insurance
America First Insurance
Golden Eagle Insurance
Ohio Casualty Montgomery Insurance
Safeco Insurance Fund

CONTACTS: Note: Officers with more than one job title may be intentionally listed here more than once.

Gary R. Gregg, CEO
Donald J. DeShaw, General Counsel

GROWTH PLANS/SPECIAL FEATURES:

Safeco Insurance Company of America (Safeco) is a property and casualty insurance provider for homeowners and drivers. The company is a subsidiary of life, auto and home insurance provider Liberty Mutual Group, Inc. Safeco's personal insurance services include auto, homeowners, condo, rental and specialty insurance products for individuals. Specialty insurance products include umbrella, classic car, motorcycle, recreational vehicle and boat/watercraft owners' insurance coverage for individuals. The company also offers The Safeco Package, a combined auto and home property insurance product. Safeco maintains regional offices in California, Texas, Indiana, Ohio, Colorado, Washington, New Hampshire and Georgia. It also has service offices in Missouri, Oregon, Illinois and Connecticut; and customer care centers in Indiana, Washington and Colorado. The firm's business insurance activities are operated by Safeco's sister companies, such as Liberty Northwest, Colorado Casualty Insurance, America First Insurance, Golden Eagle Insurance, Ohio Casualty, Montgomery Insurance and Peerless Insurance. These companies provide business-owner policies, surety bonds, commercial auto, commercial multi-peril, workers' compensation, commercial property and general liability policies for small- and mid-sized businesses. The Safeco Insurance Fund, a fund within the Liberty Mutual Foundation, supports nonprofit organizations within the state of Washington. The fund's grands program focuses on educational opportunities of underprivileged youth, ensuring security through life-saving basic services to homeless persons and promoting accessibility for individuals of all abilities. In addition, Safeco held naming rights to the Seattle Mariners' baseball stadium, Safeco Field, for 20 years, from 1998 up to the 2018 season.

Through Liberty Mutual Group, Safeco offers its employees benefits including a 401(k) plan; flexible spending accounts; medical, vision, disability, life, AD&D, dependent life and long-term care insurance; paid time off; and tuition reimbursement.

FINANCIAL DATA: Note: Data for latest year may not have been available at press time.

In U.S. $	2016	2015	2014	2013	2012	2011
Revenue	1,680,000,000	1,650,000,000	1,595,200,000	1,461,447,245	1,631,937,130	1,709,915,290
R&D Expense						
Operating Income						
Operating Margin %						
SGA Expense						
Net Income						
Operating Cash Flow						
Capital Expenditure						
EBITDA						
Return on Assets %						
Return on Equity %						
Debt to Equity						

CONTACT INFORMATION:

Phone: 206-545-5000 Fax:
Toll-Free:
Address: 1001 Fourth Ave., Safeco Plz., Seattle, WA 98185 United States

STOCK TICKER/OTHER:

Stock Ticker: Subsidiary Exchange:
Employees: 3,000 Fiscal Year Ends: 12/31
Parent Company: Liberty Mutual Group Inc

SALARIES/BONUSES:

Top Exec. Salary: $ Bonus: $
Second Exec. Salary: $ Bonus: $

OTHER THOUGHTS:

Estimated Female Officers or Directors:
Hot Spot for Advancement for Women/Minorities: Y

Safeway Inc

NAIC Code: 445110

www.safeway.com

TYPES OF BUSINESS:

Grocery Stores
Food Processing & Packaging
Online Grocery Sales & Home Delivery
Pharmacies
Gift Cards & Payment Processing Technology

BRANDS/DIVISIONS/AFFILIATES:

AB Acquisition LLC
Safeway
Carrs
Pavilions
Tom Thumb
Randall's
Vons
GroceryWorks

CONTACTS: *Note: Officers with more than one job title may be intentionally listed here more than once.*

Robert G. Miller, CEO
Larree Renda, Executive VP
Kelly Griffith, Executive VP, Divisional
Diane Dietz, Executive VP
Melissa Plaisance, Senior VP, Divisional
David Stern, Senior VP, Divisional
Donald Wright, Senior VP, Divisional
Jerry Tidwell, Senior VP, Divisional
Russell Jackson, Senior VP, Divisional
Robert Gordon, Senior VP
Robert G. Miller, Chmn.

GROWTH PLANS/SPECIAL FEATURES:

Safeway, Inc. is one of the largest food retailers in the U.S., operating stores in 33 states and the District of Columbia. These stores operate regionally under the names Safeway, Carrs, Pavilions, Tom Thumb, Randall's and Vons, each of which offer a wide selection of both food and general merchandise and feature a variety of special departments such as bakery, delicatessen, pharmacy and floral departments. In addition, the company offers online grocery shopping and home delivery through its wholly-owned subsidiary GroceryWorks. Safeway has developed a line of Safeway SELECT brand products, ranging from packaged foods to laundry detergent, and offers corporate-branded products under the Safeway labels: O Organics, Eating Right, Bright Green and Open Nature. Beyond these operations, Safeway manages its Blackhawk Network subsidiary, which is one of the largest providers of third-party prepaid gift cards in the country. In 2015, AB Acquisition LLC (Albertson's) completed a merger with Safeway. The combined companies have more than 2,200 stores, 27 distribution centers and 19 manufacturing plants, with 265,000 employees nationwide.

Safeway offers its employees medical, prescription drug, vision and dental coverage; an employee assistance plan; flexible spending accounts; life insurance; short- and long-term disability; paid time off; a stock purchase plan; a retirement plan; and a 401(k) plan.

FINANCIAL DATA: *Note: Data for latest year may not have been available at press time.*

In U.S. $	2016	2015	2014	2013	2012	2011
Revenue	36,000,000,000	36,980,000,000	36,330,200,000	35,064,900,000	35,161,500,000	43,630,198,784
R&D Expense						
Operating Income						
Operating Margin %						
SGA Expense						
Net Income			113,400,000	3,507,500,032	596,499,968	516,700,000
Operating Cash Flow						
Capital Expenditure						
EBITDA						
Return on Assets %						
Return on Equity %						
Debt to Equity						

CONTACT INFORMATION:

Phone: 925 467-3000   Fax: 925 467-3323
Toll-Free: 877-723-3929
Address: 5918 Stoneridge Mall Rd., Pleasanton, CA 94588-3229 United States

STOCK TICKER/OTHER:

Stock Ticker: Private   Exchange:
Employees: 138,000   Fiscal Year Ends: 12/31
Parent Company: AB Acquisition LLC

SALARIES/BONUSES:

Top Exec. Salary: $ Bonus: $
Second Exec. Salary: $ Bonus: $

OTHER THOUGHTS:

Estimated Female Officers or Directors: 4
Hot Spot for Advancement for Women/Minorities: Y

SalesForce.com Inc

www.salesforce.com

NAIC Code: 0

TYPES OF BUSINESS:

Software-Sales & Marketing Automation
Customer Relationship Management Software
Software Subscription Services

BRANDS/DIVISIONS/AFFILIATES:

Sales Cloud
Service Cloud
Marketing Cloud
Community Cloud
Analytics Cloud
IoT Cloud
Salesforce Quip
Salesforce Platform

CONTACTS: *Note: Officers with more than one job title may be intentionally listed here more than once.*

Marc Benioff, CEO
Mark Hawkins, CFO
Joe Allanson, Chief Accounting Officer
Parker Harris, Chief Technology Officer
Keith Block, Director
Cynthia Robbins, Executive VP, Divisional
Amy Weaver, General Counsel
Burke Norton, Other Executive Officer
Maria Martinez, President, Divisional
Alexandre Dayon, President, Divisional

GROWTH PLANS/SPECIAL FEATURES:

SalesForce.com, Inc. builds and delivers customer relationship management (CRM) applications through an on-demand web services platform. The firm's web-based services enable clients to track sales and marketing by delivering enterprise software as an online service, making software purchases similar to paying for a utility as opposed to a packaged product. The firm offers core cloud based services such as sales force automation, customer service and support, marketing automation, community management, analytics, as well as a platform for building custom application. Products include Sales Cloud, Service Cloud, Marketing Cloud, Community Cloud, Analytics Cloud, IoT (Internet of Things) Cloud, Commerce Cloud, Salesforce Quip and Salesforce Platform. Sales Cloud is a platform for sales force automation and solutions for partner relationship management; Service Cloud addresses customer service and support needs; Marketing Cloud is a digital marketing platform that manages customer interactions across email, mobile, social, web and connected products; Community Cloud creates trusted, branded destinations for customers, partners and employees to collaborate; Analytics Cloud is an app and platform for business intelligence; IoT Cloud connects billions of events from devices, sensors, apps and more from the IoT to SalesForce, enabling companies to take action with the connected world; Commerce Cloud empowers brands to deliver a comprehensive digital commerce experience across web, mobile, social and store; Salesforce Quip is a next-generation productivity solution designed for teams with a mobile-first strategy; and Salesforce Platform (formerly App Cloud) is for building enterprise apps quickly via tools, frameworks and services. In February 2017, the firm acquired Sequence, a user experience design agency that works with brands like Best Buy, Peets, Apple, Google and many more.

SalesForce.com offers its employees paid time off, parental/family care, employee stock purchase plans, educational reimbursement, wellness allowances, volunteer time off and a 401(k) plan.

FINANCIAL DATA: *Note: Data for latest year may not have been available at press time.*

In U.S. $	2016	2015	2014	2013	2012	2011
Revenue	6,667,216,000	5,373,586,000	4,071,003,000	3,050,195,000	2,266,539,000	
R&D Expense	946,300,000	792,917,000	623,798,000	429,479,000	295,347,000	
Operating Income	114,923,000	-145,633,000	-286,074,000	-110,710,000	-35,085,000	
Operating Margin %	1.72%	-2.71%	-7.02%	-3.62%	-1.54%	
SGA Expense	3,988,062,000	3,437,032,000	2,764,851,000	2,047,847,000	1,517,391,000	
Net Income	-47,426,000	-262,688,000	-232,175,000	-270,445,000	-11,572,000	
Operating Cash Flow	1,612,585,000	1,173,714,000	875,469,000	736,897,000	591,507,000	
Capital Expenditure	709,852,000	416,889,000	299,110,000	179,707,000	171,300,000	
EBITDA	662,514,000	308,448,000	88,699,000	119,949,000	141,014,000	
Return on Assets %	-.40%	-2.64%	-3.16%	-5.58%	-.31%	
Return on Equity %	-1.05%	-7.49%	-8.66%	-13.85%	-.80%	
Debt to Equity	0.29	0.37	0.44			

CONTACT INFORMATION:

Phone: 415 901-7000 Fax: 415 901-7040
Toll-Free:
Address: 1 Market St., Ste. 300, The Landmark, San Francisco, CA 94105 United States

STOCK TICKER/OTHER:

Stock Ticker: CRM Exchange: NYS
Employees: 25,000 Fiscal Year Ends: 01/31
Parent Company:

SALARIES/BONUSES:

Top Exec. Salary: $1,550,000 Bonus: $
Second Exec. Salary: $900,000 Bonus: $271,438

OTHER THOUGHTS:

Estimated Female Officers or Directors: 4
Hot Spot for Advancement for Women/Minorities: Y

Sales, profits and employees may be estimates. Financial information, benefits and other data can change quickly and may vary from those stated here.

Sam's Club
NAIC Code: 452910

TYPES OF BUSINESS:
Warehouse Clubs, Retail

BRANDS/DIVISIONS/AFFILIATES:
Wal-Mart Stores Inc
Member's Mark
Bakers & Chefs
Sam's Club
Sam's Club 5-3-1 MasterCard

CONTACTS: *Note: Officers with more than one job title may be intentionally listed here more than once.*
John Furner, CEO
Kelly Thompson, Sr.VP
Rosalind G. Brewer, Pres.
Maarten Jager, Sr.VP
Ashley Buchanan, CMO
David Galloreese, Sr.VP-People
Hsiao Wang, Sr. VP-IT
Charles Redfield, Exec. VP-Merch.
Whitney Head, General Counsel
P. Todd Harbaugh, Exec. VP-Oper.
Don Frieson, Sr. VP-Planning & Replenishment
John Boswell, Sr. VP-e-Commerce
Bill Durling, Sr. Dir.-Corp. Comm.
Mike Turner, Sr. VP-Sam's Club Membership
Whitney Head, Sr. VP- Asset Protection & Compliance

GROWTH PLANS/SPECIAL FEATURES:
Sam's Club, a subsidiary of Wal-Mart Stores, Inc., is an American chain of membership-only retail warehouse clubs. There are more than 650 clubs across the U.S. and Puerto Rico, with in-club benefits including pharmacy, fuel stations, optical centers, hearing aid centers, photo centers, tire and battery centers, daily taste sampling, demonstrations and free monthly health screenings. Sam's Club offers discounted prices on items, including appliances, electronics, office supplies, food, clothing, optical and pharmacy services, home furnishings, books and auto supplies. It also sells selected private-label items under the Member's Mark, Bakers & Chefs and Sam's Club brands. Most locations also offer fresh departments such as bakery, meat, produce, floral and Sam's Cafe. Sam's Club requires a customer to become a member, providing three options for an annual fee: Sam's Savings ($45 annual fee), Sam's Business ($45 annual fee) and Sam's Plus ($100 annual fee). In addition to merchandise discounts, the firm offers its members discounted services that include various types of insurance, a travel club, an auto purchase program, discount credit card processing, mail-order pharmacy services, internet access and long-distance services. Sam's Club 5-3-1 MasterCard option is a credit card cash back program issued by Synchrony Financial. Sam's Club stores, averaging 70,000-190,000 square feet, are designed to resemble a warehouse, with merchandise displayed on shipping pallets or in large freezer/cooler units. The company's merchandise consists of five categories: grocery and consumables; fuel and other categories; technology, office and entertainment; home and apparel; and health and wellness. During 2016, Sam's Club began accepting Visa credit cards at most of its stores; and rolled out a mobile application that allows customers to scan items while they shop and pay for them, skipping the checkout line. As of December 2016, the app can be used at all U.S. locations.

FINANCIAL DATA: *Note: Data for latest year may not have been available at press time.*

In U.S. $	2016	2015	2014	2013	2012	2011
Revenue	56,828,000,000	58,020,000,000	57,157,000,000	56,423,000,000	53,795,000,000	49,459,000,000
R&D Expense						
Operating Income						
Operating Margin %						
SGA Expense						
Net Income	1,820,000,000	1,976,000,000	1,843,000,000	1,960,000,000	1,865,000,000	1,711,000,000
Operating Cash Flow						
Capital Expenditure						
EBITDA						
Return on Assets %						
Return on Equity %						
Debt to Equity						

CONTACT INFORMATION:
Phone: 479-277-7000   Fax:
Toll-Free: 888-746-7726
Address: 2101 S. E. Simple Savings Drive, Bentonville, AR 72716 United States

STOCK TICKER/OTHER:
Stock Ticker: Subsidiary   Exchange:
Employees: 112,000   Fiscal Year Ends: 01/31
Parent Company: Wal-Mart Stores Inc

SALARIES/BONUSES:
Top Exec. Salary: $ Bonus: $
Second Exec. Salary: $ Bonus: $

OTHER THOUGHTS:
Estimated Female Officers or Directors: 3
Hot Spot for Advancement for Women/Minorities: Y

Sanmina Corp

NAIC Code: 334418

TYPES OF BUSINESS:

Printed Circuit Assembly (Electronic Assembly) Manufacturing
Assembly & Testing
Logistics Services
Support Services
Product Design & Engineering
Repair & Maintenance Services

BRANDS/DIVISIONS/AFFILIATES:

Viking Technology
SCI Technology Inc

CONTACTS: *Note: Officers with more than one job title may be intentionally listed here more than once.*

Jure Sola, CEO
Robert Eulau, CFO
David Anderson, Chief Accounting Officer
Dennis Young, Executive VP, Divisional
Alan Reid, Executive VP, Divisional
Christopher Sadeghian, Secretary

GROWTH PLANS/SPECIAL FEATURES:

Sanmina Corp. is a global provider of customized, integrated electronics manufacturing services (EMS). With production facilities in 23 countries, the firm is one of the largest global EMS providers. The firm has two business segments: integrated manufacturing solutions (IMS) and components, products and services (CPS). The IMS includes printed circuit board assembly and test, which involves attaching electronic components such as integrated circuits, capacitors, microprocessors to printed circuit boards; final system assembly and test, which consists of combining assemblies and modules to form finished products; and direct-order-fulfillment, which involves receiving customer orders, configuring products and delivering the products either to the OEM, a distribution channel. The CPS segment include interconnect systems (printed circuit board fabrication, backplane and cable assemblies) and mechanical systems (enclosures, precision machining and plastic injection molding). This segment also includes the operations of Viking Technology, a manufacturer of flash memory and related storage products and SCI Technology, Inc.'s defense and aerospace products, as well as logistics and repair services. The company caters to defense and aerospace, computing and storage, automotive, multi-media, clean technology, medical systems and communications network industries.

Employee benefits include a 401(k); tuition reimbursement; credit union membership; an employee assistance program; flexible spending accounts; and medical, prescription, dental, vision, life and AD&D insurance.

FINANCIAL DATA: *Note: Data for latest year may not have been available at press time.*

In U.S. $	2016	2015	2014	2013	2012	2011
Revenue	6,481,181,000	6,374,541,000	6,215,106,000	5,917,124,000	6,093,334,000	6,602,411,000
R&D Expense	37,746,000	33,083,000	32,495,000	25,571,000	21,899,000	20,802,000
Operating Income	224,785,000	203,101,000	199,682,000	157,629,000	137,490,000	211,997,000
Operating Margin %	3.46%	3.18%	3.21%	2.66%	2.25%	3.21%
SGA Expense	244,604,000	239,288,000	242,288,000	238,072,000	240,863,000	247,127,000
Net Income	187,838,000	377,261,000	197,165,000	79,351,000	180,234,000	68,917,000
Operating Cash Flow	390,116,000	174,896,000	307,382,000	317,889,000	215,413,000	234,908,000
Capital Expenditure	120,400,000	119,097,000	69,507,000	75,950,000	78,631,000	107,574,000
EBITDA	341,438,000	301,771,000	290,220,000	240,431,000	221,164,000	303,223,000
Return on Assets %	5.27%	11.08%	6.25%	2.57%	5.52%	2.07%
Return on Equity %	12.00%	27.26%	16.86%	7.72%	20.78%	9.62%
Debt to Equity	0.26	0.27	0.31	0.51	0.86	1.53

CONTACT INFORMATION:

Phone: 408-964-3500   Fax: 408-964-3636
Toll-Free:
Address: 2700 N. First St., San Jose, CA 95134 United States

STOCK TICKER/OTHER:

Stock Ticker: SANM
Employees: 45,397
Parent Company:

Exchange: NAS
Fiscal Year Ends: 09/30

SALARIES/BONUSES:

Top Exec. Salary: $900,000   Bonus: $
Second Exec. Salary: $510,000   Bonus: $

OTHER THOUGHTS:

Estimated Female Officers or Directors:
Hot Spot for Advancement for Women/Minorities:

Sapient Corporation

NAIC Code: 541512

publicis.sapient.com

TYPES OF BUSINESS:

IT Consulting
Internet Strategy Consulting
Interactive Marketing Software

BRANDS/DIVISIONS/AFFILIATES:

Publicis Groupe
Sapient Global Markets
SapientRazorfish
Sapient Government Services

CONTACTS: Note: Officers with more than one job title may be intentionally listed here more than once.

Alan Herrick, CEO
Joseph Tibbetts, CFO
Alan Wexler, Executive VP
J. Moore, Founder
Joseph LaSala, General Counsel
Harry Register, Managing Director, Divisional
Christian Oversohl, Managing Director, Geographical
Laurie MacLaren, Senior VP, Divisional

GROWTH PLANS/SPECIAL FEATURES:

Sapient Corporation is a business consulting and technology services firm that designs and manages information technology to improve business performance for clients in the U.S. and abroad. Sapient has offices in the U.S., Europe, Asia, Australia and South America. The firm operates through three primary business units: SapientRazorfish, Sapient Global Markets and Sapient Government Services. SapientRazorfish, a leading global interactive marketing agency, provides interactive marketing and creative services, web site and interactive development, media planning and buying, strategic planning and market analytics and marketing technologies. Sapient Global Markets offers financial and commodity market customer advisory services, analytics, technology and business process solutions. Sapient Government Services provides consulting, technology and marketing services to several agencies of the U.S. government, including the Library of Congress, Federal Bureau of Investigation, National Institutes of Health and U.S. Department of Homeland Security. The group also serves provincial and other governmental entities in Canada and Europe. Sapient works on both long- and short-term consulting projects. It operates through a proprietary Global Distributed Delivery (GDD) model, which allows associates in widely disparate locations to work together efficiently. The firm's clients consist of companies within the following industries: financial services, technology, communications, consumer, automotive, energy services, government, health and education.

FINANCIAL DATA: Note: Data for latest year may not have been available at press time.

In U.S. $	2016	2015	2014	2013	2012	2011
Revenue	1,625,000,000	1,562,781,000	1,451,000,000	1,305,232,000	1,161,548,032	1,062,204,032
R&D Expense						
Operating Income						
Operating Margin %						
SGA Expense						
Net Income						
Operating Cash Flow						
Capital Expenditure						
EBITDA						
Return on Assets %						
Return on Equity %						
Debt to Equity						

CONTACT INFORMATION:

Phone: 617 621-0200   Fax: 617 621-1300
Toll-Free: 877-454-9860
Address: 131 Dartmouth St., Boston, MA 02116 United States

STOCK TICKER/OTHER:

Stock Ticker: Subsidiary   Exchange:
Employees: 11,900   Fiscal Year Ends: 12/31
Parent Company: PUBLICIS GROUPE

SALARIES/BONUSES:

Top Exec. Salary: $ Bonus: $
Second Exec. Salary: $ Bonus: $

OTHER THOUGHTS:

Estimated Female Officers or Directors: 2
Hot Spot for Advancement for Women/Minorities:

SAS Institute Inc

www.sas.com

NAIC Code: 0

TYPES OF BUSINESS:

Software-Statistical Analysis
Business Intelligence Software
Data Warehousing
Online Bookstore
Consulting

BRANDS/DIVISIONS/AFFILIATES:

CONTACTS: Note: Officers with more than one job title may be intentionally listed here more than once.

James Goodnight, CEO
Don Parker, VP
Randy Guard, VP
Jenn Mann, VP-Human Resources
Keith Collins, VP
John Boswell, Chief Legal Officer
Carl Farrell, Exec. VP-SAS Americas
John Sall, Exec. VP
Mikael Hagstrom, Exec. VP-EMEA & Asia Pacific

GROWTH PLANS/SPECIAL FEATURES:

SAS Institute, Inc. provides statistical analysis software. The company's products are designed to extract, manage and analyze large volumes of data, often assisting in financial reporting and credit analysis. Individual contracts can be tailored to specific global and local industries, such as banking, manufacturing and government. SAS' advanced analytics software is infused with cutting-edge, innovative algorithms that help its clients solve their most intractable problems, make the best decisions possible and capture new opportunities. The software comprises data mining, statistical analysis, forecasting, text analysis, optimization and stimulation features. Other products that provide enterprise solutions include business intelligence, cloud analytics, customer intelligence, data management, fraud & security intelligence, in-memory analytics, performance management, risk management, solutions for Hadoop and supply chain intelligence. Industries that utilize SAS products and solutions include automotive, banking, capital markets, casinos, communications, consumer goods, defense/security, government, healthcare, high-tech manufacturing, education, hotels, insurance, life science, manufacturing, media, oil and gas, retail, sports, travel, transportation and utilities. SAS serves more than 80,000 business, government and university sites in over 149 different countries, including 90 of the top 100 companies on the Fortune Global 500 list.

SAS offers its employees life, disability, medical, dental, auto, home and vision insurance; flexible spending accounts; onsite health care and fitness centers; an employee assistance program; adoption assistance; scholarship programs; a 401(k); and a profit sharing plan.

FINANCIAL DATA: Note: Data for latest year may not have been available at press time.

In U.S. $	2016	2015	2014	2013	2012	2011
Revenue	3,200,000,000	3,160,000,000	3,090,000,000	3,020,000,000	2,870,000,000	2,725,000,000
R&D Expense						
Operating Income						
Operating Margin %						
SGA Expense						
Net Income						
Operating Cash Flow						
Capital Expenditure						
EBITDA						
Return on Assets %						
Return on Equity %						
Debt to Equity						

CONTACT INFORMATION:

Phone: 919-677-8000   Fax: 919-677-4444
Toll-Free: 800-727-0025
Address: 100 SAS Campus Dr., Cary, NC 27513 United States

STOCK TICKER/OTHER:

Stock Ticker: Private   Exchange:
Employees: 14,051   Fiscal Year Ends: 12/31
Parent Company:

SALARIES/BONUSES:

Top Exec. Salary: $ Bonus: $
Second Exec. Salary: $ Bonus: $

OTHER THOUGHTS:

Estimated Female Officers or Directors: 1
Hot Spot for Advancement for Women/Minorities: Y

SC Johnson & Son Inc

NAIC Code: 325600

www.scjohnson.com

TYPES OF BUSINESS:

Household Products Manufacturing
Household Products
Cleaning Products
Auto Care Products
Insect Repellents

BRANDS/DIVISIONS/AFFILIATES:

Drano
Pledge
Shout
Windex
Off!
Raid
Exposis
Babyganics

CONTACTS: *Note: Officers with more than one job title may be intentionally listed here more than once.*

Fisk Johnson, CEO
Salman Amin, COO
Mark H. Eckhardt, Exec. VP
Fisk Johnson, Chmn.

GROWTH PLANS/SPECIAL FEATURES:

S.C. Johnson & Son, Inc. is one of the world's largest manufacturers of household chemical products, with many proprietary brand names. The firm was established in 1886 as a flooring company and has since been managed by the Johnson family for over five generations. The company produces home cleaning, home storage, pest control control, auto care and air care products. Its home cleaning products include the Drano home drain cleaner, Pledge dust and pet hair cleaner, Shout stain remover for clothes and fabrics, Fantastik surface cleaner, Scrubbing Bubbles bathroom cleaner, Windex glass and window cleaner and Duck bathroom cleaner. Other products include Saran plastic wrap and Ziploc plastic bags for home storage; Off!, Raid, Baygon, Autan and ALLOUT for insect repellent; Grand Prix waxes, protectants and cleaners for auto care; and Oust air fresheners and Glade candles and home fragrances for the air care market. The company's patented Greenlist process allows scientific and environmental organizations to review and rate ingredients for use in the firm's products. This system allows the company to improve and update its products by health and environmental standards. The firm has operations in more than 70 countries worldwide. S.C. Johnson & Son also operates an online mail order service, which allows customers to order a select number of company products, available for shipping anywhere in the USA. In July 2016, S.C. Johnson announced the acquisition of Babyganics, a brand of baby household and personal care products. Later that year, in December, the company acquired Exposis, a premium brand of insect repellent available in Brazil. In April 2017, the firm announced that it will be initiating a multi-million-dollar expansion of its Bay City, Michigan plant.

FINANCIAL DATA: *Note: Data for latest year may not have been available at press time.*

In U.S. $	2016	2015	2014	2013	2012	2011
Revenue	10,000,000,000	9,800,000,000	9,700,000,000	9,600,000,000	9,400,000,000	9,100,000,000
R&D Expense						
Operating Income						
Operating Margin %						
SGA Expense						
Net Income						
Operating Cash Flow						
Capital Expenditure						
EBITDA						
Return on Assets %						
Return on Equity %						
Debt to Equity						

CONTACT INFORMATION:

Phone: 262-260-2000   Fax: 262-260-6004
Toll-Free: 800-494-4855
Address: 1525 Howe St., Racine, WI 53403 United States

STOCK TICKER/OTHER:

Stock Ticker: Private
Employees: 13,000
Parent Company:

Exchange:
Fiscal Year Ends: 06/30

SALARIES/BONUSES:

Top Exec. Salary: $ Bonus: $
Second Exec. Salary: $ Bonus: $

OTHER THOUGHTS:

Estimated Female Officers or Directors:
Hot Spot for Advancement for Women/Minorities: Y

SCANA Corporation

www.scana.com

NAIC Code: 221112

TYPES OF BUSINESS:

Electricity & Natural Gas
Telecommunications Services
Ethernet Services & Data Center Facilities
Communications Towers Management
Management & Maintenance Services
Service Contracts
Risk Management Services

BRANDS/DIVISIONS/AFFILIATES:

South Carolina Electric and Gas Company
Public Service Company of North Carolina Inc
SCANA Energy Marketing Inc
SCANA Services Inc
South Carolina Generating Company Inc
South Carolina Fuel Company Inc

CONTACTS: Note: Officers with more than one job title may be intentionally listed here more than once.

Kevin Marsh, CEO
Jimmy Addison, CFO
J. Swan, Controller
Stephen Byrne, COO, Subsidiary
Don Harris, COO, Subsidiary
Ronald Lindsay, General Counsel
Jeffrey Archie, Other Executive Officer
William Kissam, President, Subsidiary
Sarena Burch, Senior VP, Subsidiary
Kenneth Jackson, Senior VP

GROWTH PLANS/SPECIAL FEATURES:

SCANA Corporation is an energy-based holding company that has brought power and fuel to homes in the Carolinas and Georgia for over 160 years. Through its subsidiaries, SCANA is engaged in regulated electric and natural gas utility operations and other non-regulated energy-related businesses. South Carolina Electric and Gas Company (SCE&G) is a regulated utility that generates, transmits, distributes and sells electricity to over 709,000 customers in 24 counties, and provides natural gas to approximately 358,000 customers. Public Service Company of North Carolina, Inc. (PSNC Energy) is a regulated public utility that purchases, sells and transports natural gas to approximately 550,000 residential, commercial and industrial customers. SCANA Energy Marketing, Inc. is a natural gas marketer that serves approximately 450,000 residential, commercial and industrial customers throughout Georgia. Other subsidiaries include SCANA Services, Inc., which provides administration, management and other services to SCANA subsidiaries; South Carolina Generating Company, Inc. (GENCO), which supplies electricity for SCE&G; and South Carolina Fuel Company, Inc., a fuel supplier for SCE&G.

The company offers its employees medical, dental and vision insurance; a retirement plan; and a 401(k) plan.

FINANCIAL DATA: Note: Data for latest year may not have been available at press time.

In U.S. $	2016	2015	2014	2013	2012	2011
Revenue	4,227,000,000	4,380,000,000	4,951,000,000	4,495,000,000	4,176,000,000	4,409,000,000
R&D Expense						
Operating Income	1,153,000,000	1,308,000,000	1,007,000,000	910,000,000	859,000,000	813,000,000
Operating Margin %	27.27%	29.86%	20.33%	20.24%	20.56%	18.43%
SGA Expense						
Net Income	595,000,000	746,000,000	538,000,000	471,000,000	420,000,000	387,000,000
Operating Cash Flow	1,092,000,000	1,059,000,000	730,000,000	1,050,000,000	839,000,000	811,000,000
Capital Expenditure	1,579,000,000	1,153,000,000	1,092,000,000	1,106,000,000	1,077,000,000	884,000,000
EBITDA	1,654,000,000	1,871,000,000	1,546,000,000	1,441,000,000	1,309,000,000	1,233,000,000
Return on Assets %	3.31%	4.38%	3.36%	3.16%	2.98%	2.92%
Return on Equity %	10.65%	14.30%	11.14%	10.68%	10.44%	10.19%
Debt to Equity	1.13	1.08	1.10	1.15	1.19	1.18

CONTACT INFORMATION:

Phone: 803 217-9000   Fax: 803 343-2389
Toll-Free: 800-251-7234
Address: 100 SCANA Pkwy., Cayce, SC 29033 United States

STOCK TICKER/OTHER:

Stock Ticker: SCG
Employees: 5,910
Parent Company:

Exchange: NYS
Fiscal Year Ends: 12/31

SALARIES/BONUSES:

Top Exec. Salary: $1,216,901   Bonus: $
Second Exec. Salary: $631,619   Bonus: $

OTHER THOUGHTS:

Estimated Female Officers or Directors: 4
Hot Spot for Advancement for Women/Minorities: Y

Science Applications International Corp (SAIC)

www.saic.com

NAIC Code: 541512

TYPES OF BUSINESS:

IT Consulting
IT Infrastructure Management
Research & Development
Software Development
Engineering

BRANDS/DIVISIONS/AFFILIATES:

CONTACTS: Note: Officers with more than one job title may be intentionally listed here more than once.

Anthony Moraco, CEO
Charles Mathis, CFO
Edward Sanderson, Chairman of the Board
Steven Mahon, Executive VP
Douglas Wagoner, President, Divisional
Nazzic Keene, President, Divisional

GROWTH PLANS/SPECIAL FEATURES:

Science Applications International Corporation (SAIC) provides technical, engineering and enterprise IT services to commercial operations and government agencies. The company's clients include all four branches of the U.S. military (Army, Air Force, Navy and Marines), the U.S. Defense Logistics Agency, the National Aeronautics and Space Administration, the U.S. Department of State and the U.S. Department of Homeland Security. In 2016, 95% of total revenues were derived from contracts with the U.S. government or from subcontracts with other contractors engaged in work for the U.S. government, all of which were entities located in the U.S. The firm offers services in five areas: technology solutions, which include big data and analytics, cybersecurity, IT managed services, cloud, software and mobility services and network & communications; mission, SETA & program support, which consists of systems engineering, advisory and business transformation services; simulation and training; logistics & supply chain, which includes wholesale and retail distribution, aftermarkets parts distribution, product support & sustainment and proprietary software; and crisis management and security, which consists of critical infrastructure, force protection, public safety communications and security & surveillance.

FINANCIAL DATA: Note: Data for latest year may not have been available at press time.

In U.S. $	2016	2015	2014	2013	2012	2011
Revenue	4,315,000,000	3,885,000,000	4,121,000,000	11,173,000,000	10,587,000,000	
R&D Expense						
Operating Income	227,000,000	240,000,000	183,000,000	734,000,000	311,000,000	
Operating Margin %	5.26%	6.17%	4.44%	6.56%	2.93%	
SGA Expense	158,000,000	95,000,000	92,000,000	592,000,000	670,000,000	
Net Income	117,000,000	141,000,000	113,000,000	526,000,000	56,000,000	
Operating Cash Flow	226,000,000	277,000,000	183,000,000	343,000,000	769,000,000	
Capital Expenditure	20,000,000	22,000,000	16,000,000	48,000,000	65,000,000	
EBITDA	289,000,000	261,000,000	196,000,000	865,000,000	435,000,000	
Return on Assets %	6.64%	9.91%	3.08%	8.38%	.83%	
Return on Equity %	32.27%	39.05%	7.60%	22.58%	2.71%	
Debt to Equity	2.66	1.32	1.29	0.49	0.63	

CONTACT INFORMATION:

Phone: 703 676-4300 Fax:
Toll-Free:
Address: 1710 SAIC Dr., McLean, VA 22102 United States

STOCK TICKER/OTHER:

Stock Ticker: SAIC Exchange: NYS
Employees: 15,500 Fiscal Year Ends: 01/31
Parent Company:

SALARIES/BONUSES:

Top Exec. Salary: $1,038,462 Bonus: $
Second Exec. Salary: $614,039 Bonus: $

OTHER THOUGHTS:

Estimated Female Officers or Directors: 5
Hot Spot for Advancement for Women/Minorities: Y

Select Comfort Corporation

www.ir.sleepnumber.com

NAIC Code: 337910

TYPES OF BUSINESS:

Mattress Manufacturing

BRANDS/DIVISIONS/AFFILIATES:

DualAir
Sleep Number
Classic Series
Performance Series
Innovation Series
Memory Foam Series
x12 Series
Select Comfort

CONTACTS: Note: Officers with more than one job title may be intentionally listed here more than once.

Shelly Ibach, CEO
Jean-Michel Valette, Chairman of the Board
Robert Poirier, Chief Accounting Officer
Joseph Saklad, Chief Information Officer
Kevin Brown, Chief Marketing Officer
Mark Kimball, Chief Risk Officer
Suresh Krishna, COO, Divisional
Andrew Carlin, Executive VP
Melissa Barra, Other Executive Officer
Patricia Dirks, Other Executive Officer
Andrea Bloomquist, Other Executive Officer
David Callen, Senior VP

GROWTH PLANS/SPECIAL FEATURES:

Select Comfort Corporation was founded as a Minnesota-based corporation in 1987, and its business is to develop, manufacture, market and distribute adjustable-firmness beds and other sleep-related accessory products. The DualAir technology of its proprietary Sleep Number bed allows adjustable firmness on each side of the mattress and provides a sleep surface. In addition, the company markets and sells accessories and other sleep related products which focus on providing personalized comfort to complement the Sleep Number bed. The company offers Sleep Number beds in five series to help consumers choose the bed that is best for them-The Sleep Number Bed Classic Series is the classic design with personal adjustability, and includes Sleep Number c2 and c4 models. The Sleep Number bed Performance Series features comfort and value, and includes the Sleep Number p5 and p6 models. The Sleep Number bed Innovation Series offers personalized comfort combined with leading innovations in sleep technology, and includes the Sleep Number i8 and i10 models. The Memory Foam Series is breathable and contouring, and includes the Sleep Number m6 and m7 models. The Sleep Number x12 Series bed features the integration of multiple technology options, including Select's FlexFit 3 adjustable base and its SleepIQ technology, which monitor each individual's sleep patterns. The SleepIQ Technology uses embedded sensors to track an individual's sleeping habits and produces the insights on its app. The company uses information technology systems to operate, analyze and manage its business, to reduce operating costs and to enhance its customers' experience. Sleep Number beds are only sold at Sleep Number stores. In June 2016, Select Comfort opened its first store in Alaska, and its first outside the lower 48 U.S. states, in the city of Anchorage.

FINANCIAL DATA: Note: Data for latest year may not have been available at press time.

In U.S. $	2016	2015	2014	2013	2012	2011
Revenue	1,311,291,000	1,213,699,000	1,156,757,000	1,156,757,000	934,978,000	743,203,000
R&D Expense	27,991,000	15,971,000	8,233,000	8,233,000	6,194,000	4,175,000
Operating Income	76,650,000	75,096,000	101,746,000	101,746,000	119,787,000	90,453,000
Operating Margin %	5.84%	6.18%	8.79%	8.79%	12.81%	12.17%
SGA Expense	705,519,000	649,684,000	596,871,000	596,871,000	470,417,000	375,608,000
Net Income	51,417,000	50,519,000	67,974,000	67,974,000	78,094,000	60,478,000
Operating Cash Flow	151,645,000	107,942,000	144,468,000	144,468,000	100,626,000	91,046,000
Capital Expenditure	57,852,000	85,586,000	76,594,000	76,594,000	51,593,000	23,527,000
EBITDA	133,916,000	122,726,000	141,970,000	141,970,000	140,498,000	104,151,000
Return on Assets %	10.59%	10.23%	14.33%	16.65%	25.82%	27.95%
Return on Equity %	26.87%	21.08%	26.45%	30.17%	48.34%	64.55%
Debt to Equity						

CONTACT INFORMATION:

Phone: 763 551-7000   Fax: 763 694-3300
Toll-Free:
Address: 9800 59th Avenue North, Minneapolis, MN 55442 United States

STOCK TICKER/OTHER:

Stock Ticker: SCSS
Employees: 3,768
Parent Company:

Exchange: NAS
Fiscal Year Ends: 12/31

SALARIES/BONUSES:

Top Exec. Salary: $814,615   Bonus: $
Second Exec. Salary: $285,000   Bonus: $144,127

OTHER THOUGHTS:

Estimated Female Officers or Directors:
Hot Spot for Advancement for Women/Minorities:

Select Medical Holdings Corporation   www.selectmedicalcorp.com

NAIC Code: 622310

TYPES OF BUSINESS:

Extended Care Hospitals
Long-Term Acute Care
Outpatient Rehabilitation Clinics
Contract Therapy Services
Medical Equipment Distribution
Billing Services
Recruiting

BRANDS/DIVISIONS/AFFILIATES:

Select Medical Corporation
Concentra Inc

CONTACTS: *Note: Officers with more than one job title may be intentionally listed here more than once.*

David Chernow, CEO
Martin Jackson, CFO
Robert Ortenzio, Chairman of the Board
Scott Romberger, Chief Accounting Officer
Rocco Ortenzio, Co-Founder
Michael Tarvin, Executive VP
John Saich, Executive VP
Robert Breighner, Other Corporate Officer

GROWTH PLANS/SPECIAL FEATURES:

Select Medical Holdings Corporation, through its subsidiary Select Medical Corporation, operates specialty acute care hospitals for long-term stay patients in the U.S. The firm operates 123 specialty hospitals in 27 states, and 1,611 outpatient rehabilitation clinics in 37 states and the District of Columbia. Select Medical's business is divided between specialty hospitals and outpatient rehabilitation. The company's hospitals treat patients with complex medical conditions, such as respiratory failure, neuromuscular disorders, cardiac disorders, renal disorders and cancer. The majority of Select Medical's specialty hospitals are located in leased space within a host general hospital. The firm's outpatient rehabilitation segment is designed to help patients minimize physical and cognitive impairments and maximize functional ability. Services at its clinics include physical, occupational and speech rehabilitation programs, work injury prevention and management, sports performance and athletic training services. Moreover, the company provides clinical program development, billing support, staff retention strategies, training and assistance with equipment. Subsidiary Concentra, Inc. provides occupational medicine, urgent care, physical therapy and wellness services from more than 300 medical centers in 38 U.S. states. In addition to these locations, Concentra serves employers by providing a broad range of health services, operating more than 150 worksite medical facilities.

Employee benefits include health, dental, vision and prescription coverage; life insurance; short- and long-term disability; tuition reimbursement; and a 401(k).

FINANCIAL DATA: *Note: Data for latest year may not have been available at press time.*

In U.S. $	2016	2015	2014	2013	2012	2011
Revenue	4,286,021,000	3,742,736,000	3,065,017,000	2,975,648,000	2,948,969,000	2,804,507,000
R&D Expense						
Operating Income	299,847,000	274,790,000	284,476,000	301,436,000	336,859,000	310,719,000
Operating Margin %	6.99%	7.34%	9.28%	10.13%	11.42%	11.07%
SGA Expense	106,927,000	92,052,000	85,247,000	76,921,000	66,194,000	62,354,000
Net Income	115,411,000	130,736,000	120,627,000	114,390,000	148,230,000	107,846,000
Operating Cash Flow	346,603,000	208,415,000	170,642,000	192,523,000	298,682,000	217,128,000
Capital Expenditure	161,633,000	182,642,000	95,246,000	73,660,000	68,185,000	46,016,000
EBITDA	496,126,000	426,229,000	357,597,000	349,557,000	401,811,000	354,463,000
Return on Assets %	2.38%	3.45%	4.08%	4.10%	5.35%	3.92%
Return on Equity %	13.36%	15.87%	15.37%	15.21%	19.25%	13.42%
Debt to Equity	3.29	2.54	2.08	1.81	2.03	1.68

CONTACT INFORMATION:

Phone: 717 972-1100   Fax:
Toll-Free: 888-735-6332
Address: 4714 Old Gettysburg Rd., Mechanicsburg, PA 17055 United States

STOCK TICKER/OTHER:

Stock Ticker: SEM
Employees: 31,200
Parent Company:

Exchange: NYS
Fiscal Year Ends: 12/31

SALARIES/BONUSES:

Top Exec. Salary: $995,000   Bonus: $
Second Exec. Salary: $950,000   Bonus: $

OTHER THOUGHTS:

Estimated Female Officers or Directors: 1
Hot Spot for Advancement for Women/Minorities:

Service Corporation International Inc

www.sci-corp.com

NAIC Code: 812210

TYPES OF BUSINESS:

Funeral Homes and Funeral Services

BRANDS/DIVISIONS/AFFILIATES:

Dignity Memorial
Dignity Planning
National Cremation Society
Advantage Funderal and Cremation Services
Funeraria del Angel
Making Everlasting Memories
Neptune Society
Trident Society

CONTACTS: *Note: Officers with more than one job title may be intentionally listed here more than once.*

Thomas Ryan, CEO
Tammy Moore, Chief Accounting Officer
Michael Webb, COO
Robert Waltrip, Founder
Gregory Sangalis, General Counsel
Sumner Waring, Senior VP, Divisional
Steven Tidwell, Senior VP, Divisional
Eric Tanzberger, Senior VP

GROWTH PLANS/SPECIAL FEATURES:

Service Corporation International, Inc. is a provider of deathcare products and services in North America. The company is geographically diversified across 45 U.S. states, eight Canadian provinces, the District of Columbia and Puerto Rico. Service Corporation's funeral service and cemetery operations consist of more than 1,500 funeral service locations and 470 cemeteries, as well as crematoria and related businesses. The firm provides all professional services relating to funerals and cremations, including the use of funeral facilities and motor vehicles and preparation and embalming services. Funeral related merchandise, including caskets, burial vaults, cremation receptacles, flowers and other ancillary products and services are sold at funeral service locations. Service Corporation's cemeteries provide cemetery property interment rights, including mausoleum spaces, lots and lawn crypts, and sell cemetery related merchandise and services, including stone and bronze memorials, burial vaults, casket and cremation memorialization products, merchandise installations and burial openings and closings. Service Corporation has branded the company's funeral operations in North America under the name Dignity Memorial. Other brands include Dignity Planning, National Cremation Society, Advantage Funeral and Cremation Services, Funeraria del Angel, Making Everlasting Memories, Neptune Society and Trident Society.

FINANCIAL DATA: *Note: Data for latest year may not have been available at press time.*

In U.S. $	2016	2015	2014	2013	2012	2011
Revenue	3,031,137,000	2,986,380,000	2,994,012,000	2,556,382,000	2,410,481,000	2,316,040,000
R&D Expense						
Operating Income	511,885,000	550,279,000	607,549,000	388,170,000	399,789,000	363,699,000
Operating Margin %	16.88%	18.42%	20.29%	15.18%	16.58%	15.70%
SGA Expense	137,730,000	128,188,000	184,877,000	155,136,000	123,905,000	103,860,000
Net Income	177,038,000	233,772,000	172,469,000	143,848,000	152,546,000	144,903,000
Operating Cash Flow	463,595,000	472,186,000	317,355,000	384,709,000	369,246,000	388,112,000
Capital Expenditure	193,446,000	150,986,000	144,499,000	113,084,000	115,628,000	118,375,000
EBITDA	733,685,000	778,570,000	817,252,000	580,884,000	569,807,000	543,102,000
Return on Assets %	1.49%	1.97%	1.38%	1.27%	1.60%	1.56%
Return on Equity %	15.54%	18.31%	12.39%	10.43%	11.15%	10.09%
Debt to Equity	2.92	2.59	2.16	2.23	1.42	1.33

CONTACT INFORMATION:

Phone: 713 522-5141   Fax: 713 525-5586
Toll-Free:
Address: 1929 Allen Parkway, Houston, TX 77019 United States

STOCK TICKER/OTHER:

Stock Ticker: SCI   Exchange: NYS
Employees: 23,463   Fiscal Year Ends: 12/31
Parent Company:

SALARIES/BONUSES:

Top Exec. Salary: $1,200,000   Bonus: $
Second Exec. Salary: $952,000   Bonus: $

OTHER THOUGHTS:

Estimated Female Officers or Directors:
Hot Spot for Advancement for Women/Minorities:

ServiceMaster Company LLC (The)

www.servicemaster.com

NAIC Code: 561730

TYPES OF BUSINESS:

Lawn Care Services
Landscaping Services
Termite & Pest Control
Home Warranty
Disaster Restoration & Cleaning
Furniture Repair
Home Inspection

BRANDS/DIVISIONS/AFFILIATES:

ServiceMaster Global Holdings Inc
Merry Maids
American Home Shield

CONTACTS: *Note: Officers with more than one job title may be intentionally listed here more than once.*

Robert Gillette, CEO
Alan Haughie, CFO
Mark Tomkins, Chairman of the Board
John Mullen, Chief Accounting Officer
Jamie Smith, Chief Information Officer
Martin Wick, COO, Divisional
James Lucke, General Counsel
William Derwin, President, Divisional
Timothy Haynes, President, Divisional
Mary Wegner, President, Subsidiary
Anthony DiLucente, Senior VP
Susan Hunsberger, Senior VP, Divisional
Mary Runyan, Senior VP, Divisional

GROWTH PLANS/SPECIAL FEATURES:

The ServiceMaster Company, LLC provides various cleaning, restoration and maintenance services to approximately 75,000 homes and businesses every day. Its operations are divided into nine groups. The cleaning group offers the Merry Maids brand of residential cleaning services, as well as carpet cleaning, floor cleaning, tile/grout cleaning, upholstery cleaning, green cleaning, commercial cleaning, janitorial and hoarding clean-up services. The disaster restoration group provides disaster recovery, post-loss recovery and specialty damage recovery services. The fire damage restoration group provides fire damage restoration, smoke damage removal and pack-out services. The furniture and cabinet restoration group provides cabinet re-facing, residential furniture and woodwork repair, and commercial furniture and wood restoration services. The home warranties group provides warranties that cover home appliances and home systems through ServiceMaster's American Home Shield brand. The inspections group provides property inspections for home or commercial properties, and provides specialty inspections and services such as radon, water, mold, septic, carbon monoxide, lead-based paint, pool/spa, wood-destroying insects, energy assessments, new home construction reviews, well testing, gas leak detection, irrigation system inspections and infrared technology. The mold remediation group offers mold inspections and mold remediation services. The pest control group offers termite, pest, mosquito, bed bug, wildlife, commercial pest and industry-specific control and treatment services. Last, the water damage restoration group offers water damage restoration, flood damage restoration, basement flooding restoration and carpet drying services and solutions. The ServiceMaster operates as a subsidiary of the publicly-traded ServiceMaster Global Holdings, Inc. (NYSE: SERV).

FINANCIAL DATA: *Note: Data for latest year may not have been available at press time.*

In U.S. $	2016	2015	2014	2013	2012	2011
Revenue	2,745,999,872	2,593,999,872	2,456,999,936	2,292,999,936	2,214,000,128	2,104,999,936
R&D Expense						
Operating Income						
Operating Margin %						
SGA Expense						
Net Income	155,000,000	160,000,000	-57,000,000	-507,000,000	-714,000,000	46,000,000
Operating Cash Flow						
Capital Expenditure						
EBITDA						
Return on Assets %						
Return on Equity %						
Debt to Equity						

CONTACT INFORMATION:

Phone: 866-348-7672   Fax:
Toll-Free: 888-937-3783
Address: 860 Ridge Lake Blvd., Memphis, TN 38120 United States

STOCK TICKER/OTHER:

Stock Ticker: Subsidiary   Exchange:
Employees: 13,000   Fiscal Year Ends: 12/31
Parent Company: ServiceMaster Global Holdings Inc

SALARIES/BONUSES:

Top Exec. Salary: $ Bonus: $
Second Exec. Salary: $ Bonus: $

OTHER THOUGHTS:

Estimated Female Officers or Directors: 2
Hot Spot for Advancement for Women/Minorities:

ServiceNow Inc

www.service-now.com

NAIC Code: 0

TYPES OF BUSINESS:
Cloud-Based Workflow Software

BRANDS/DIVISIONS/AFFILIATES:
BrightPoint Security Inc
ITapp Inc

CONTACTS: Note: Officers with more than one job title may be intentionally listed here more than once.
Michael Scarpelli, CFO
Frank Slootman, Director
John Donahoe, Director
Robert Specker, General Counsel
David Schneider, Other Executive Officer
Chirantan Desai, Other Executive Officer

GROWTH PLANS/SPECIAL FEATURES:
ServiceNow, Inc. is a provider of cloud-based services that automate enterprise IT operations. The company's service includes a suite of applications built on its proprietary platform that automates workflow and provides integration between related business processes. The firm focuses on transforming enterprise IT by automating and standardizing business processes and consolidating IT across the global enterprise. Organizations deploy its service to create a single system of record for enterprise IT, lower operational costs and enhance efficiency. Additionally, customers use its extensible platform to build custom applications for automating activities unique to their business requirements. ServiceNow helps transform IT organizations from reactive, manual and task-oriented, to pro-active, automated and service-oriented organizations. The company's on-demand service enables organizations to define their IT strategy, design the systems and infrastructure that will support that strategy, and implement, manage and automate that infrastructure throughout its lifecycle while leveraging its self-service capability. The firm provides a broad set of integrated functionality that is highly configurable and extensible and can be efficiently implemented and upgraded. Its multi-instance architecture has proven scalability for global enterprises as well as having advantages in security, reliability and deployment location. The company offers its service under a Software-as-a-Service (SaaS) business model. Customers can rapidly deploy its service in a modular fashion, allowing them to solve immediate business needs and access, configure and build new applications as their requirements evolve. The firm's service, which is accessed through an intuitive web-based interface, can be easily configured to adapt to customer workflow and processes. ServiceNow serves more than 3,600 enterprise customers. During 2016, the firm acquired BrightPoint Security, Inc. and ITapp, Inc.

FINANCIAL DATA: Note: Data for latest year may not have been available at press time.

In U.S. $	2016	2015	2014	2013	2012	2011
Revenue	1,390,513,000	1,005,480,000	682,563,000	424,650,000	243,712,000	73,375,000
R&D Expense	285,239,000	217,389,000	148,258,000	78,678,000	39,333,000	7,030,000
Operating Income	-422,808,000	-166,365,000	-151,835,000	-66,267,000	-37,584,000	-4,163,000
Operating Margin %	-30.40%	-16.54%	-22.24%	-15.60%	-15.42%	
SGA Expense	1,129,400,000	625,043,000	437,364,000	256,980,000	137,954,000	42,585,000
Net Income	-451,804,000	-198,426,000	-179,387,000	-73,708,000	-37,348,000	-6,684,000
Operating Cash Flow	159,921,000	315,091,000	138,900,000	81,746,000	48,766,000	13,220,000
Capital Expenditure	124,312,000	89,231,000	54,379,000	55,321,000	42,066,000	7,959,000
EBITDA	-333,691,000	-101,559,000	-109,776,000	-42,115,000	-24,078,000	-2,118,000
Return on Assets %	-23.52%	-12.27%	-13.83%	-8.95%	-7.81%	
Return on Equity %	-94.74%	-39.86%	-43.59%	-23.11%	-15.34%	
Debt to Equity	1.31					

CONTACT INFORMATION:
Phone: 408-501-8550 Fax:
Toll-Free:
Address: 2225 Lawson Lane, Santa Clara, CA 95054 United States

STOCK TICKER/OTHER:
Stock Ticker: NOW
Employees: 4,801
Parent Company:

Exchange: NYS
Fiscal Year Ends: 12/31

SALARIES/BONUSES:
Top Exec. Salary: $450,000 Bonus: $
Second Exec. Salary: $350,000 Bonus: $

OTHER THOUGHTS:
Estimated Female Officers or Directors:
Hot Spot for Advancement for Women/Minorities:

Sherwin-Williams Company (The)

www.sherwin-williams.com

NAIC Code: 325510

TYPES OF BUSINESS:

Paints & Coatings Manufacturing
Retail Paint Stores
Wall Coverings
Automotive Finishing Products
Design Consulting

BRANDS/DIVISIONS/AFFILIATES:

Sherwin-Williams
Sayerlack
Pratt & Lambert
Martin Senour
Dutch Boy
Thompson's
Minwax
Krylon

CONTACTS: *Note: Officers with more than one job title may be intentionally listed here more than once.*

John Morikis, CEO
Allen Mistysyn, CFO
Jane Cronin, Chief Accounting Officer
Catherine Kilbane, General Counsel
Joel Baxter, General Manager, Divisional
David Sewell, President, Divisional
Robert Davisson, President, Divisional
Thomas Gilligan, Senior VP, Divisional
Sean Hennessy, Senior VP, Divisional
Robert Wells, Senior VP, Divisional

GROWTH PLANS/SPECIAL FEATURES:

The Sherwin-Williams Company is one of the largest international manufacturers, distributors and retailers of paint and related products to professional, industrial, commercial and retail customers. The company operates in four segments: paint stores group, consumer group, global finishes group and Latin America coatings group. The paint stores group consists of 4,180 company-operated stores, which sell Sherwin-Williams brand architectural paint, coatings and other associated products and brands. Several subsidiaries operate under this division, including Duron, Inc., a Maryland paint producer. It has operations in the U.S., Canada, Puerto Rico, Jamaica, St. Maarten, Curacao, Trinidad and Tobago and the Virgin Islands. This division also sells industrial products, marine products and finishes for original equipment manufacturers (OEM). The consumer group produces and distributes paint, coatings and related products to third-party customers and to the paint stores group (which represented 64% of the consumer group's sales in 2016). The global finishes group, through 288 branches, manufactures, licenses, distributes and sells paints and coatings, industrial and marine products, automotive finishes, refinish products and OEM coatings throughout Europe, North and South American and Asia. The Latin America coatings group develops, licenses, manufactures and sells architectural paint and coatings, OEM product finishes and protective and marine products in North and South America. The segment maintains 339 company-operated stores. In all segments, the company's varnish, applicators, paint, finishes and coatings are marketed under various name brands, including several private labels such as Sherwin-Williams, Sayerlack, Pratt & Lambert, Martin Senour, Dutch Boy, Thompson's, Minwax and Krylon. In April 2017, Sherwin-Williams acquired rival Valspar Corp. for approximately $11.3 billion. Later that month, the company divested Valspar's industrial wood coatings business to Axalta Coating Systems for $420 million.

FINANCIAL DATA: *Note: Data for latest year may not have been available at press time.*

In U.S. $	2016	2015	2014	2013	2012	2011
Revenue	11,855,600,000	11,339,300,000	11,129,530,000	10,185,530,000	9,534,462,000	8,765,699,000
R&D Expense						
Operating Income	1,750,462,000	1,645,708,000	1,304,036,000	1,146,366,000	946,578,000	775,525,000
Operating Margin %	14.76%	14.51%	11.71%	11.25%	9.92%	8.84%
SGA Expense	4,171,803,000	3,913,518,000	3,822,966,000	3,467,681,000	3,259,648,000	2,963,545,000
Net Income	1,132,703,000	1,053,849,000	865,887,000	752,561,000	631,034,000	441,860,000
Operating Cash Flow	1,308,572,000	1,447,463,000	1,081,528,000	1,083,766,000	887,886,000	735,812,000
Capital Expenditure	239,026,000	234,340,000	200,545,000	166,680,000	157,112,000	153,801,000
EBITDA	1,947,032,000	1,809,319,000	1,521,376,000	1,336,466,000	1,129,299,000	964,949,000
Return on Assets %	18.05%	18.25%	14.32%	11.92%	11.00%	8.49%
Return on Equity %	82.48%	112.57%	63.42%	43.94%	41.41%	32.14%
Debt to Equity	0.64	2.21	1.12	0.64	0.96	0.47

CONTACT INFORMATION:

Phone: 216 566-2000   Fax:
Toll-Free: 800-474-3794
Address: 101 W. Prospect Ave., Cleveland, OH 44115 United States

STOCK TICKER/OTHER:

Stock Ticker: SHW   Exchange: NYS
Employees: 42,550   Fiscal Year Ends: 12/31
Parent Company:

SALARIES/BONUSES:

Top Exec. Salary: $1,221,987   Bonus: $
Second Exec. Salary: Bonus: $
$1,095,795

OTHER THOUGHTS:

Estimated Female Officers or Directors: 2
Hot Spot for Advancement for Women/Minorities: Y

Sodexo Inc

www.sodexousa.com

NAIC Code: 722310

TYPES OF BUSINESS:

Food Service Outsourcing
Facilities Management
Laundry Services
Sports Arena Management
Plant Management
Grounds Keeping
Asset Management
Outsourced Procurement Services

BRANDS/DIVISIONS/AFFILIATES:

Sodexho Group
Sodexo Foundation
Entegra Procurement Services

CONTACTS: *Note: Officers with more than one job title may be intentionally listed here more than once.*

Michel Landel, CEO
Sian Herbert-Jones, CFO
Elisabeth Carpentier, Group Chief Human Resources Officer
Michel Landel, Pres.
Debbie White, CEO-Sodexo U.K. & Ireland
Pierre Bellon, Chmn.

GROWTH PLANS/SPECIAL FEATURES:

Sodexo, Inc. is the North American subsidiary of French firm Sodexo Group, a global contract foodservice supplier. The company is one of the largest providers of contract food and facilities management services in the U.S., Mexico and Canada, with more than 9,000 sites. In total, it serves 15 million consumers each day. Sodexo offers a wide variety of outsourcing solutions in food service, facilities management, business strategy, wellness, motivation solutions and corporate citizenship. The company provides these services to corporations; health care, long-term care and retirement centers; conference centers; schools; college campuses; military bases; and government and remote sites. Services to college stadiums and arenas involve concession stands, catering, physical plant management and sports field management. The firm also has a contract to manage the food operations for the U.S. Marine Corps, which includes meal preparation, operation of clean dining facilities and bringing national brands to Navy bases, Army bases and international locations. In addition, the company sponsors the Sodexo Foundation, an independent charitable organization that supports initiatives addressing the problems of hunger in children and families. The Entegra Procurement Services unit provides food and supplies purchasing management for 10,000 clients in hospitality and other industries.

The firm offers employees a pension plan; a 401(k) savings plan; health and family care spending accounts; employee assistance plans; tuition reimbursement; and medical, life, disability, dental and vision insurance.

FINANCIAL DATA: *Note: Data for latest year may not have been available at press time.*

In U.S. $	2016	2015	2014	2013	2012	2011
Revenue	9,300,000,000	9,200,000,000	8,800,000,000	9,350,000,000	9,200,000,000	9,000,000,000
R&D Expense						
Operating Income						
Operating Margin %						
SGA Expense						
Net Income						
Operating Cash Flow						
Capital Expenditure						
EBITDA						
Return on Assets %						
Return on Equity %						
Debt to Equity						

CONTACT INFORMATION:

Phone: 301-987-4000   Fax: 301-987-4438
Toll-Free: 800-763-3946
Address: 9801 Washingtonian Blvd., Gaithersburg, MD 20878 United States

STOCK TICKER/OTHER:

Stock Ticker: Subsidiary
Employees: 132,600
Parent Company: Sodexo Group

Exchange:
Fiscal Year Ends: 08/31

SALARIES/BONUSES:

Top Exec. Salary: $ Bonus: $
Second Exec. Salary: $ Bonus: $

OTHER THOUGHTS:

Estimated Female Officers or Directors: 2
Hot Spot for Advancement for Women/Minorities: Y

Sonoco Products Company

NAIC Code: 322220

www.sonoco.com

TYPES OF BUSINESS:

Coated and Laminated Packaging Paper Manufacturing

GROWTH PLANS/SPECIAL FEATURES:

Sonoco Products Company manufactures industrial and consumer packaging products and provides various packaging services, with 318 locations in 33 countries. Its operations are divided into four segments: consumer packaging, paper and industrial converted products (PICP), display and packaging, and protective solutions. Consumer packaging, which accounts for 43% of sales revenue, consists of 78 plants located worldwide which produces packaging solutions such as round composite cans, shaped rigid paperboard containers, fiber caulk/adhesive tubes, as well as aluminum, steel and peelable membrane easy-open closures for composite and metal cans; plastic bottles, jars, jugs, cups and trays; and printed flexible packaging and rotogravure cylinder engraving. PICP accounts for 35% of sales revenue and consists of 177 plants which provides the primary raw material for the company's fiber-based packaging. Sonoco uses approximately 62% of the paper this division manufactures and the remainder is sold to third parties. This vertical integration is supported by 19 paper mills with 28 paper machines and 23 recycling facilities throughout the world. Display and packaging accounts for 11% of sales revenue and consists of 24 plants which produce point-of-purchase displays, custom packaging, retail packaging and printed backer cards. This division also provides thermoformed blisters and heat sealing equipment, as well as supply chain management and paperboard specialties. Protective solutions derives 11% of sales revenue and produces custom-engineered, paperboard-based and expanded foam protective packaging. This division also produces temperature-assured packaging for pharmaceutical and food products. In 2017, the firm acquired Peninsula Packaging Company, a manufacturer of thermoformed packaging for fresh fruit and vegetables; and agreed to acquire Clear Lam Packaging, Inc., a developer and manufacturer of flexible and forming plastic packaging films.

BRANDS/DIVISIONS/AFFILIATES:

Peninsula Packaging Company

CONTACTS: *Note: Officers with more than one job title may be intentionally listed here more than once.*

M. Sanders, CEO
Allan McLeland, Vice President, Divisional
Barry Saunders, CFO
Harris Deloach, Chairman of the Board
James Kirkland, Chief Accounting Officer
Robert Tiede, COO
John Florence, General Counsel
R. Coker, Senior VP, Divisional
Rodger Fuller, Senior VP, Divisional
Kevin Mahoney, Senior VP, Divisional
Vicki Arthur, Senior VP, Divisional
Robert Puechl, Vice President, Divisional
Roger Schrum, Vice President, Divisional
Marcy Thompson, Vice President, Divisional
Adam Wood, Vice President, Geographical
James Harrell, Vice President, Geographical

FINANCIAL DATA: *Note: Data for latest year may not have been available at press time.*

In U.S. $	2016	2015	2014	2013	2012	2011
Revenue	4,782,877,000	4,964,369,000	5,014,534,000	4,848,092,000	4,786,129,000	4,498,932,000
R&D Expense						
Operating Income	431,425,000	382,544,000	391,511,000	361,295,000	347,059,000	322,480,000
Operating Margin %	9.02%	7.70%	7.80%	7.45%	7.25%	7.16%
SGA Expense	506,001,000	496,241,000	506,996,000	487,171,000	463,715,000	397,477,000
Net Income	286,434,000	250,136,000	239,165,000	219,113,000	196,010,000	217,517,000
Operating Cash Flow	398,679,000	452,930,000	417,915,000	538,027,000	403,915,000	245,275,000
Capital Expenditure	186,741,000	192,295,000	177,076,000	172,442,000	214,862,000	173,372,000
EBITDA	700,629,000	598,080,000	592,978,000	562,153,000	551,591,000	506,109,000
Return on Assets %	7.21%	6.07%	5.84%	5.37%	4.80%	5.98%
Return on Equity %	18.81%	16.56%	14.86%	13.69%	13.51%	14.98%
Debt to Equity	0.66	0.67	0.79	0.55	0.73	0.87

CONTACT INFORMATION:

Phone: 843 383-7000   Fax: 843 383-7008
Toll-Free:
Address: 1 N. 2nd St., Hartsville, SC 29550 United States

STOCK TICKER/OTHER:

Stock Ticker: SON   Exchange: NYS
Employees: 20,000   Fiscal Year Ends: 12/31
Parent Company:

SALARIES/BONUSES:

Top Exec. Salary: $1,039,817   Bonus: $
Second Exec. Salary: Bonus: $
$567,741

OTHER THOUGHTS:

Estimated Female Officers or Directors:
Hot Spot for Advancement for Women/Minorities:

Southwest Airlines Co

www.southwest.com

NAIC Code: 481111

TYPES OF BUSINESS:

Airline
Air Freight

BRANDS/DIVISIONS/AFFILIATES:

EarlyBird Check-in

CONTACTS: *Note: Officers with more than one job title may be intentionally listed here more than once.*

Gary Kelly, CEO
Tammy Romo, CFO
Michael Van De Ven, COO
Gregory Wells, Executive VP, Divisional
Jeff Lamb, Executive VP, Divisional
Robert Jordan, Executive VP
Andrew Watterson, Other Executive Officer
Thomas Nealon, President
Mark Shaw, Secretary
Ron Ricks, Vice Chairman of the Board

GROWTH PLANS/SPECIAL FEATURES:

Southwest Airlines Co. is one of the largest U.S. domestic air travel providers, primarily engaged in short haul, high-frequency airline services. The firm operates an all-Boeing 737 fleet, 704 total, serving 97 cities in 40 states throughout the U.S., Washington, D.C., Puerto Rico, Mexico, Jamaica, the Bahamas, Aurba and the Dominican Republic. About 73% of the company's customers fly nonstop, with an average aircraft trip being 721 miles, with an average duration of approximately two hours. The busiest routes include those to Chicago, Las Vegas, Phoenix, Baltimore, Denver, Houston, Dallas, Los Angeles, Oakland and St. Louis. Southwest primarily flies to conveniently located, secondary or downtown airports such as Houston-Hobby, Dallas-Love Field and Chicago-Midway, which are typically less congested than other airlines' hub airports. Southwest employs a point-to-point route system, which allows for more direct nonstop routing, thereby minimizing connections, delays and total trip time. It also offers the EarlyBird Check-in service, which allows customers to reserve a boarding position prior to general check-in for a fee. In December 2016, Southwest announced flights to and from Havana, Cuba, which is its 100th city in the network. Additionally, new destinations added were Cincinnati and Grand Cayman starting mid-2017.

Southwest's employee benefits include free, discounted and guest passes on Southwest Airlines flights; medical, vision, dental, life and long-term disability insurance; an employee assistance program; 401(K) plan; a profit-sharing plan; and an employee stock purchase plan.

FINANCIAL DATA: *Note: Data for latest year may not have been available at press time.*

In U.S. $	2016	2015	2014	2013	2012	2011
Revenue	20,425,000,000	19,820,000,000	18,605,000,000	17,699,000,000	17,088,000,000	15,658,000,000
R&D Expense						
Operating Income	3,760,000,000	4,116,000,000	2,225,000,000	1,278,000,000	623,000,000	693,000,000
Operating Margin %	18.40%	20.76%	11.95%	7.22%	3.64%	4.42%
SGA Expense	6,798,000,000	6,383,000,000	5,434,000,000	5,035,000,000	4,749,000,000	4,371,000,000
Net Income	2,244,000,000	2,181,000,000	1,136,000,000	754,000,000	421,000,000	178,000,000
Operating Cash Flow	4,293,000,000	3,238,000,000	2,902,000,000	2,477,000,000	2,064,000,000	1,385,000,000
Capital Expenditure	2,147,000,000	2,143,000,000	1,828,000,000	1,447,000,000	1,348,000,000	968,000,000
EBITDA	4,843,000,000	4,584,000,000	2,861,000,000	2,183,000,000	1,655,000,000	1,220,000,000
Return on Assets %	10.06%	10.50%	5.74%	3.97%	2.29%	1.06%
Return on Equity %	28.40%	30.86%	16.10%	10.52%	6.07%	2.71%
Debt to Equity	0.33	0.36	0.35	0.33	0.46	0.45

CONTACT INFORMATION:

Phone: 214 792-4000   Fax: 214 792-5015
Toll-Free:
Address: 2702 Love Field Dr., Dallas, TX 75235 United States

STOCK TICKER/OTHER:

Stock Ticker: LUV   Exchange: NYS
Employees: 53,500   Fiscal Year Ends: 12/31
Parent Company:

SALARIES/BONUSES:

Top Exec. Salary: $675,000   Bonus: $228,015
Second Exec. Salary: $474,375   Bonus: $128,364

OTHER THOUGHTS:

Estimated Female Officers or Directors: 14
Hot Spot for Advancement for Women/Minorities: Y

Spectrum Brands Holdings Inc

www.spectrumbrands.com

NAIC Code: 335912

TYPES OF BUSINESS:

Primary Battery Manufacturing

BRANDS/DIVISIONS/AFFILIATES:

Rayovac
VARTA
Black & Decker
Kwikset
Pfister
Armor All
STP
PetMatrix LLC

CONTACTS: *Note: Officers with more than one job title may be intentionally listed here more than once.*

Andreas Rouve, CEO
Douglas Martin, CFO
David Maura, Chairman of the Board
Omar Asali, Director
Nathan Fagre, General Counsel
Stacey Neu, Senior VP, Divisional

GROWTH PLANS/SPECIAL FEATURES:

Spectrum Brands Holdings, Inc. is a diversified branded consumer products company. The firm manufactures, markets and/or distributes its products in 160 countries throughout North America, Europe, the Middle East, Africa, Latin America and Asia-Pacific. Its products are sold and distributed through retailers, wholesalers, distributors, original equipment manufacturers (OEMs), construction companies and hearing aid professionals. Spectrum's products are divided into five groups: global batteries & appliances, hardware & home improvement, global pet supplies, home & garden and global auto care. Products within global batteries & appliances include consumer batteries such as alkaline, zinc carbon and NiMH rechargeables; hearing aid and specialty battery products; portable lighting products; small kitchen and home appliances; and personal care items such as shaving and grooming and hair care appliances. Products within the hardware & home improvement group include residential and commercial locksets, door hardware, garage hardware, window hardware, floor protection, faucets and plumbing products. Products within the global pet supplies division include small animal food and treats, cleanup and training aid products, pet health and grooming products and aquarium and aquatic health supplies. Products within the home & garden group includes household insecticides, repellent products and weed control solutions. Products within the global auto care group include aftermarket appearance products, performance chemicals and additives, as well as do-it-yourself air conditioner recharge products. Brands of the firm include Rayovac, VARTA, Black & Decker, Kwikset, Pfister, Dingo, Nature's Miracle, Cutter, Armor All, STP and A/C Pro. In May 2017, the firm acquired PetMatrix, LLC, a rapidly growing manufacturer and distributor of rawhide-free dog chews.

FINANCIAL DATA: *Note: Data for latest year may not have been available at press time.*

In U.S. $	2016	2015	2014	2013	2012	2011
Revenue	5,039,700,000	4,690,400,000	4,429,109,000	4,085,581,000	3,252,435,000	3,186,916,000
R&D Expense	58,700,000	51,300,000	47,855,000	43,334,000	33,087,000	32,901,000
Operating Income	656,200,000	474,100,000	481,933,000	351,177,000	301,746,000	227,944,000
Operating Margin %	13.02%	10.10%	10.88%	8.59%	9.27%	7.15%
SGA Expense	1,148,900,000	1,059,500,000	999,797,000	923,328,000	740,023,000	778,166,000
Net Income	357,100,000	148,900,000	214,092,000	-55,246,000	48,572,000	-75,171,000
Operating Cash Flow	615,000,000	444,300,000	432,690,000	256,509,000	254,815,000	227,389,000
Capital Expenditure	95,200,000	89,100,000	73,347,000	81,976,000	46,809,000	36,160,000
EBITDA	830,600,000	635,200,000	633,277,000	487,564,000	405,484,000	330,213,000
Return on Assets %	4.97%	2.32%	3.84%	-1.17%	1.31%	-2.00%
Return on Equity %	21.23%	11.42%	22.06%	-5.85%	4.83%	-7.28%
Debt to Equity	1.92	2.51	2.77	3.47	1.67	1.50

CONTACT INFORMATION:

Phone: 608 275-3340   Fax:
Toll-Free:
Address: 3001 Deming Way, Middleton, WI 53562 United States

STOCK TICKER/OTHER:

Stock Ticker: SPB
Employees: 15,700
Parent Company:

Exchange: NYS
Fiscal Year Ends: 09/30

SALARIES/BONUSES:

Top Exec. Salary: $735,000   Bonus: $
Second Exec. Salary: $550,000   Bonus: $

OTHER THOUGHTS:

Estimated Female Officers or Directors:
Hot Spot for Advancement for Women/Minorities:

Spectrum Health

www.spectrumhealth.org

NAIC Code: 622110

TYPES OF BUSINESS:

General Medical and Surgical Hospitals
Trauma Center
Neonatal Center
Burn Center
Poison Center
HMO
Long-Term Care
Children's Hospital

BRANDS/DIVISIONS/AFFILIATES:

Priority Health

CONTACTS: *Note: Officers with more than one job title may be intentionally listed here more than once.*

Richard C. Breon, CEO
Tina Freese Decker, Exec.VP-COO

GROWTH PLANS/SPECIAL FEATURES:

Spectrum Health is one of the largest health systems in western Michigan. The firm's not-for-profit system of care is dedicated to improving the health of families and individuals. Spectrum's organization includes 12 hospitals, 180 ambulatory sites, 115 acute care hospitals, more than 35,800 providers, more than 1,600 independent physicians, 2,300 active volunteers and its nationally-recognized health plan, Priority Health. Spectrum Health provides inpatient and outpatient services throughout Michigan and facilities are located in in cities such as Grand Rapids, Holland, Zeeland, Belding, Reed City, Fremont, Kentwood, Rockford, Cutlerville, Greenville, Wyoming, Big Rapids, Canadian Lakes, East Grand Rapids, Allendale, Hastings, Lake Odessa, Grand Blanc, Grand Haven, Coopersville, Stanwood, Evart and many more. The organization is also West Michigan's largest provider of post-acute care including skilled nursing, long-term acute, home and residential care. Spectrum Health's services include insurance, wellness products, state-of-the-art technology and medical treatments. Major services offered by the firm include cancer, continuing care, diabetes, endocrinology, digestive disease, heart and vascular, neurosciences, orthopaedics, pediatrics, rehabilitation, transplant and women's health.

Employees of the company receive benefits including medical, dental, vision, life, disability and AD&D coverage; flexible spending accounts; retirement plans; employee assistance services; tuition assistance; and paid time off.

FINANCIAL DATA: *Note: Data for latest year may not have been available at press time.*

In U.S. $	2016	2015	2014	2013	2012	2011
Revenue	5,220,515,000	4,625,176,000	4,107,828,000	3,937,360,000	3,849,984,000	3,667,801,000
R&D Expense						
Operating Income						
Operating Margin %						
SGA Expense						
Net Income	212,044,000	367,311,000	147,747,000	212,257,000	144,114,000	73,816,000
Operating Cash Flow						
Capital Expenditure						
EBITDA						
Return on Assets %						
Return on Equity %						
Debt to Equity						

CONTACT INFORMATION:

Phone: 616-391-1774   Fax: 616-391-2780
Toll-Free: 866-989-7999
Address: 100 Michigan St. NE, Grand Rapids, MI 49503 United States

STOCK TICKER/OTHER:

Stock Ticker: Nonprofit   Exchange:
Employees: 23,000   Fiscal Year Ends: 06/30
Parent Company:

SALARIES/BONUSES:

Top Exec. Salary: $ Bonus: $
Second Exec. Salary: $ Bonus: $

OTHER THOUGHTS:

Estimated Female Officers or Directors:
Hot Spot for Advancement for Women/Minorities:

Spirit Aerosystems Holdings Inc

www.spiritaero.com

NAIC Code: 336413

TYPES OF BUSINESS:

Aircraft Fuselage Wing Tail and Similar Assemblies Manufacturing
Aerostructures
Fuselages
Wings & Flight Control Components
Engineering, Design & Materials Testing
Custom Tool Fabrication
Spare Parts & Maintenance Services
Supply Chain Management

BRANDS/DIVISIONS/AFFILIATES:

Onex Corp

CONTACTS: Note: Officers with more than one job title may be intentionally listed here more than once.

Sanjay Kapoor, CFO
Robert Johnson, Chairman of the Board
Mark Suchinski, Chief Accounting Officer
Samantha Marnick, Chief Administrative Officer
John Pilla, Chief Technology Officer
Thomas Gentile, Director
Duane Hawkins, General Manager, Divisional
Michelle Lohmeier, General Manager, Divisional
Michelle Lohmeie, General Manager, Divisional
Stacy Cozad, Secretary
Ronald Rabe, Senior VP, Divisional
Krisstie Kondrotis, Senior VP, Divisional

GROWTH PLANS/SPECIAL FEATURES:

Spirit Aerosystems Holdings, Inc. is an independent designer and manufacturer of aircraft parts and aerostructures for commercial and military aircraft. With its headquarters in Wichita, Kansas, the firm operates throughout the U.S., Europe and Asia. The firm operates through three principal segments: fuselages, propulsion systems and wing systems. The fuselages segment includes development, production and marketing of forward, mid and rear fuselage sections and systems, primarily to aircraft OEMs, as well as related spares and MRO. Additionally, it offers services that include numerical control programming, materials testing, onsite planning and global supply chain management. The propulsion systems segment offers production, development and marketing of struts, pylons, nacelles, thrust reversers and related engine structural components primarily to aircraft or engine OEMs, as well as related spares and MRO services. The wing systems segment produces wings, wing components and flight control surfaces. Spirit Aerosystems is also engaged in tooling, the fabrication of custom tools and the manufacturing of structural components for military aircraft. The firm's tooling capabilities include tool design, computer numerical control (CNC) programming, machining, composite, aluminum and invar tooling. The company offers spare parts and components for all items of which it is the original production supplier and provides maintenance, repair and overhaul work for nacelles, fuselage doors, structural components and modification kits. Spirit Aerosystems is the largest independent supplier of aerostructures to Boeing and one of the largest to Airbus. The company is majority-controlled by Onex Corp.

Employee benefits include a company profit sharing bonus; 401(k); relocation benefits; medical, vision and life insurance; health care spending accounts; disability coverage; and tuition assistance.

FINANCIAL DATA: Note: Data for latest year may not have been available at press time.

In U.S. $	2016	2015	2014	2013	2012	2011
Revenue	6,792,900,000	6,643,900,000	6,799,200,000	5,961,000,000	5,397,700,000	4,863,800,000
R&D Expense	23,800,000	27,800,000	29,300,000	34,700,000	34,100,000	35,700,000
Operating Income	725,100,000	863,000,000	354,000,000	-364,300,000	92,300,000	356,100,000
Operating Margin %	10.67%	12.98%	5.20%	-6.11%	1.71%	7.32%
SGA Expense	228,300,000	220,800,000	233,800,000	200,800,000	172,200,000	159,900,000
Net Income	469,700,000	788,700,000	358,800,000	-621,400,000	34,800,000	192,400,000
Operating Cash Flow	716,900,000	1,289,700,000	361,600,000	260,600,000	544,400,000	-47,300,000
Capital Expenditure	254,000,000	360,100,000	220,200,000	272,600,000	249,000,000	249,700,000
EBITDA	926,600,000	1,041,900,000	526,500,000	-199,400,000	250,500,000	491,900,000
Return on Assets %	8.39%	14.41%	6.98%	-11.81%	.66%	3.79%
Return on Equity %	23.19%	42.16%	23.13%	-35.74%	1.75%	10.19%
Debt to Equity	0.54	0.51	0.70	0.77	0.58	0.58

CONTACT INFORMATION:

Phone: 316 526-9000 Fax:
Toll-Free: 800-501-7597
Address: 3801 S. Oliver St., Wichita, KS 67210 United States

STOCK TICKER/OTHER:

Stock Ticker: SPR
Employees: 14,400
Parent Company: Onex Corp

Exchange: NYS
Fiscal Year Ends: 12/31

SALARIES/BONUSES:

Top Exec. Salary: $770,773 Bonus: $
Second Exec. Salary: $758,746 Bonus: $

OTHER THOUGHTS:

Estimated Female Officers or Directors: 2
Hot Spot for Advancement for Women/Minorities: Y

Spirit Airlines Inc

NAIC Code: 481111

TYPES OF BUSINESS:

Airline
Low-Fare Carrier

BRANDS/DIVISIONS/AFFILIATES:

Free Spirit
Big Front Seat
$9 Fare Club

CONTACTS: Note: Officers with more than one job title may be intentionally listed here more than once.

Edward Christie, CFO
H. Gardner, Chairman of the Board
Edmundo Miranda, Controller
Robert Fornaro, Director
Thomas Canfield, General Counsel
Matthew Klein, Other Executive Officer
Martha Villa, Other Executive Officer
Rocky Wiggins, Senior VP
John Bendoraitis, Senior VP
Scott Haralson, Vice President, Divisional

GROWTH PLANS/SPECIAL FEATURES:

Spirit Airlines, Inc. is a leading low-fare airline in the U.S. The company flies to 59 destinations including the U.S., Mexico, the Caribbean, the Bahamas and Central and Latin America and offers over 420 daily flight departures. Its all-Airbus fleet currently consists of A321s, A320s and A319s, with an average age of 5.1 years. Approximately 45 A320neo and 10 A321neo aircraft are on order, along with 19 A320s and 18 A321s (which are scheduled for delivery through 2018). The firm also offers personalized packages through both scheduled and charter flights to its destinations. Spirit Airlines reduces its costs by offering typically standard services, such as checked baggage, on an optional, pay-for-service basis. The airline operates a fully integrated Spanish-language customer service plan that includes a web site and dedicated reservation line. Some of the other benefits the company offers its customers include the Big Front Seat seating option, with more leg room and side room than the standard six inches, more side room than the standard and fewer adjacent seats. The company's frequent flyer program is called Free Spirit. In addition, the firm offers a $9 Fare Club program if customers pay a membership fee of $59.95 for the first year, and $69.95 per year afterward without written cancellation. Members receive offers on exclusive deals on flights before promotions are offered to the public, and have access to reduced bag fee options.

FINANCIAL DATA: Note: Data for latest year may not have been available at press time.

In U.S. $	2016	2015	2014	2013	2012	2011
Revenue	2,321,956,000	2,141,463,000	1,931,580,000	1,654,385,000	1,318,388,000	1,071,186,000
R&D Expense						
Operating Income	443,661,000	509,122,000	355,263,000	282,292,000	173,990,000	144,382,000
Operating Margin %						
SGA Expense	569,098,000	464,786,000	388,811,000	329,631,000	275,587,000	233,091,000
Net Income	264,879,000	317,220,000	225,464,000	176,918,000	108,460,000	76,448,000
Operating Cash Flow	473,678,000	472,985,000	260,512,000	195,376,000	113,631,000	171,198,000
Capital Expenditure	551,956,000	558,959,000	186,569,000	19,812,000	23,771,000	14,093,000
EBITDA	549,545,000	585,140,000	399,965,000	314,357,000	189,840,000	152,482,000
Return on Assets %	9.32%	15.34%	16.19%	16.84%	13.02%	12.51%
Return on Equity %	20.22%	28.47%	25.44%	26.17%	20.67%	42.27%
Debt to Equity	0.64	0.48	0.13			

CONTACT INFORMATION:

Phone: 954 447-7920   Fax: 248-727-2688
Toll-Free: 800-772-7117
Address: 2800 Executive Way, Miramar, FL 33025 United States

STOCK TICKER/OTHER:

Stock Ticker: SAVE   Exchange: NAS
Employees: 5,742   Fiscal Year Ends: 12/31
Parent Company:

SALARIES/BONUSES:

Top Exec. Salary: $548,236   Bonus: $30,000
Second Exec. Salary: $352,750   Bonus: $

OTHER THOUGHTS:

Estimated Female Officers or Directors: 1
Hot Spot for Advancement for Women/Minorities:

Stanley Black & Decker Inc

www.stanleyblackanddecker.com

NAIC Code: 333991

TYPES OF BUSINESS:

Power Tools & Accessories Manufacturer
Security Solutions
Household Appliances
Home Improvement Products
Fastening & Assembly Systems
Plumbing Products
Automotive Machinery

BRANDS/DIVISIONS/AFFILIATES:

Bostitch
Black & Decker
Stanley
FatMax
Porter-Cable
DeWALT
GripCo
Craftsman

CONTACTS: *Note: Officers with more than one job title may be intentionally listed here more than once.*

Kathryn Sherer, Assistant General Counsel
Craig Douglas, Treasurer
James Loree, CEO
Lee McChesney, CFO, Divisional
Donald Allan, CFO
Jocelyn Belisle, Chief Accounting Officer
Rhonda Gass, Chief Information Officer
George Buckley, Director
Jeffery Ansell, Executive VP, Divisional
Bruce Beatt, General Counsel
James Cannon, Other Corporate Officer
Ben Sihota, President, Divisional
William Taylor, President, Divisional
John Wyatt, President, Divisional
Jaime Ramirez, President, Divisional
Joseph Voelker, Senior VP, Divisional
Michael Bartone, Vice President, Divisional
Steven Stafstrom, Vice President, Divisional
Michael Bartone, Vice President, Divisional

GROWTH PLANS/SPECIAL FEATURES:

Stanley Black & Decker, Inc. is a global manufacturer and marketer of power tools and accessories, hardware and home improvement products, security solutions and technology-based fastening systems. The firm is also a worldwide supplier of engineered fastening and assembly systems. Stanley Black & Decker products and services are marketed in hardware and home improvement stores around the globe. The firm operates in three business tools & storage, security and industrial. The tools & storage segment includes professional and consumer power tools and accessories, lawn and garden tools, consumer mechanics tools, storage systems and pneumatic tools and fasteners. The security segment provides both mechanical and electric access and security systems primarily for retailers; educational, financial and health care institutions; and commercial, government and industrial customers. The industrial segment manufactures and markets professional industrial and automotive mechanics tools and storage systems; metal and plastic fasteners and engineered fastening systems; hydraulic tools and accessories; plumbing, heating and air conditioning tools; assembly tools and systems; and specialty tools. The company sells these products to industrial clients in the automotive, transportation, aerospace, electronics and machine tool industries primarily through third-party distributors. Brand names include DeWALT, Porter-Cable, Bostitch, FatMax, Powers, Oldham, Guaranteed Tough and Black & Decker as well as Mac Tools, GripCo, CRC, LaBounty, Dubuis and Sargent & Greenleaf. In October 2016, the firm acquired the tools business of Newell Brands, for $1.95 billion. In May 2017, the company completed the acquisition of the Craftsman brand from Sears Holdings Corporation, for approximately $900 million.

Employee benefits include medical, dental, life and disability insurance; and a 401(k).

FINANCIAL DATA: *Note: Data for latest year may not have been available at press time.*

In U.S. $	2016	2015	2014	2013	2012	2011
Revenue	11,406,900,000	11,171,800,000	11,338,600,000	11,001,200,000	10,190,500,000	10,376,400,000
R&D Expense						
Operating Income	1,643,300,000	1,585,600,000	1,506,800,000	734,200,000	707,200,000	920,100,000
Operating Margin %	14.40%	14.19%	13.28%	6.67%	6.93%	8.86%
SGA Expense	2,602,000,000	2,459,100,000	2,575,000,000	2,700,900,000	2,509,100,000	2,536,000,000
Net Income	965,300,000	883,700,000	760,900,000	490,300,000	883,800,000	674,600,000
Operating Cash Flow	1,485,200,000	1,182,300,000	1,295,900,000	868,000,000	966,200,000	998,900,000
Capital Expenditure	347,000,000	311,400,000	291,000,000	365,600,000	386,000,000	302,100,000
EBITDA	1,828,600,000	1,745,200,000	1,711,800,000	1,188,300,000	1,117,100,000	1,330,200,000
Return on Assets %	6.26%	5.69%	4.69%	3.02%	5.55%	4.33%
Return on Equity %	15.85%	14.43%	11.50%	7.28%	12.92%	9.62%
Debt to Equity	0.59	0.66	0.59	0.55	0.52	0.41

CONTACT INFORMATION:

Phone: 860 225-5111   Fax: 860 827-3895
Toll-Free:
Address: 1000 Stanley Dr., New Britain, CT 06053 United States

STOCK TICKER/OTHER:

Stock Ticker: SWK   Exchange: NYS
Employees: 54,023   Fiscal Year Ends: 12/31
Parent Company:

SALARIES/BONUSES:

Top Exec. Salary: $1,387,500   Bonus: $
Second Exec. Salary: Bonus: $
$992,500

OTHER THOUGHTS:

Estimated Female Officers or Directors: 5
Hot Spot for Advancement for Women/Minorities: Y

Starbucks Corporation

www.starbucks.com

NAIC Code: 722515

TYPES OF BUSINESS:

Coffee Houses & Coffee Stores
Coffee-Related Accessories & Equipment
Wholesale Coffee Distribution
Tea and Accessories

BRANDS/DIVISIONS/AFFILIATES:

Starbucks Coffee Korea Co Ltd
President Starbucks Coffee Corporation
Tata Starbucks Limited (India)
Starbucks Reserve Roastery & Tasting Room
Starbucks
Teavana
La Boulange
Ethos

CONTACTS: *Note: Officers with more than one job title may be intentionally listed here more than once.*

Howard Schultz, CEO
Scott Maw, CFO
Kevin Johnson, Director
Lucy Helm, Executive VP
Michael Conway, President, Divisional
John Culver, President, Divisional
Clifford Burrows, President, Divisional

GROWTH PLANS/SPECIAL FEATURES:

Starbucks Corporation is a roaster, marketer and retailer of specialty coffee, operating in 75 countries, with more than 25,700 retail stores. The firm purchases and roasts high-quality coffees that it sells, along with handcrafted coffee, tea and other beverages and a variety of fresh food items, through company-operated stores. Starbucks also licenses its trademarks through other channels such as grocery stores and national foodservice accounts. In addition to its flagship Starbucks brand, the company's portfolio includes goods and services offered under the following brands: Teavana, Tazo, Seattle's Best Coffee, Starbucks VIA, Evolution Fresh, La Boulange and Ethos. The firm has four operating segments: Americas (the U.S., Canada and Latin America), accounting for 69% of total 2016 net revenues; Europe, Middle East and Africa (EMEA), 5%; China/Asia Pacific (CAP), 14%; and channel development, 9%; with all other segments, 3%. The Americas, EMEA and CAP segments include both company-operated and licensed stores. The Americas and EMEA segments include certain food service accounts. Additionally, the Americas includes the company's La Boulange retail stores. Seattle's Best Coffee is reported in a minor other segment, with less than 1% of total net revenues. The company owns a 50% interest in each of the following companies: Starbucks Coffee Korea Co. Ltd., President Starbucks Coffee Corporation (Taiwan) and Tata Starbucks Limited (India). It also licenses the rights to produce and distribute Starbucks-branded products to its 50% joint venture with Pepsi-Cola Company, The North American Coffee Partnership, which develops and distributes bottled Starbucks beverages. Starbucks Reserve Roastery & Tasting Room is the company's specialty store concept, where rare and exotic coffees are roasted and served at premium prices. About 30 stores were planned as of 2017, and up to 1,000 smaller Reserve stores may eventually be opened.

Starbucks offers employee health benefits, 401(k) and various assistance programs.

FINANCIAL DATA: *Note: Data for latest year may not have been available at press time.*

In U.S. $	2016	2015	2014	2013	2012	2011
Revenue	21,315,900,000	19,162,700,000	16,447,800,000	14,892,200,000	13,299,500,000	11,700,400,000
R&D Expense						
Operating Income	4,171,900,000	3,601,000,000	3,081,100,000	-325,400,000	1,997,400,000	1,728,500,000
Operating Margin %	19.57%	18.79%	18.73%	-2.18%	15.01%	14.77%
SGA Expense	7,424,900,000	6,607,800,000	5,629,500,000	5,224,000,000	4,719,300,000	4,301,200,000
Net Income	2,817,700,000	2,757,400,000	2,068,100,000	8,300,000	1,383,800,000	1,245,700,000
Operating Cash Flow	4,575,100,000	3,749,100,000	607,800,000	2,908,300,000	1,750,300,000	1,612,400,000
Capital Expenditure	1,440,300,000	1,303,700,000	1,160,900,000	1,151,200,000	856,200,000	531,900,000
EBITDA	5,310,000,000	4,907,300,000	3,972,200,000	453,800,000	2,672,400,000	2,394,400,000
Return on Assets %	21.04%	23.77%	18.57%	.08%	17.76%	18.12%
Return on Equity %	48.15%	49.72%	42.41%	.17%	29.15%	30.91%
Debt to Equity	0.54	0.40	0.38	0.29	0.10	0.12

CONTACT INFORMATION:

Phone: 206 447-1575   Fax: 206 447-0828
Toll-Free: 800-782-7282
Address: 2401 Utah Ave. S., Seattle, WA 98134 United States

STOCK TICKER/OTHER:

Stock Ticker: SBUX   Exchange: NAS
Employees: 254,000   Fiscal Year Ends: 09/30
Parent Company:

SALARIES/BONUSES:

Top Exec. Salary: $1,000,000   Bonus: $500,000
Second Exec. Salary: $1,500,000   Bonus: $

OTHER THOUGHTS:

Estimated Female Officers or Directors: 5
Hot Spot for Advancement for Women/Minorities: Y

State Farm Insurance Companies

www.statefarm.com

NAIC Code: 524126

TYPES OF BUSINESS:

Insurance, Direct Property & Casualty
Accident Insurance
Health Insurance
Life Insurance
Annuities
Automobile Insurance
Banking/Savings Association
Mutual Funds

BRANDS/DIVISIONS/AFFILIATES:

State Farm Mutual Automobile Insurance Co
State Farm Life & Accident Assurance Company
State Farm Fire & Casualty Company
State Farm General Insurance Company
State Farm Guaranty Insurance Company
State Farm Bank FSB

CONTACTS: *Note: Officers with more than one job title may be intentionally listed here more than once.*

Michael L. Tipsord, CEO
Michael L. Tipsord, Chmn.

GROWTH PLANS/SPECIAL FEATURES:

State Farm Insurance Companies is a mutual company providing personal property and casualty insurance through over 18,000 agent offices, 55 operation centers and more than 300 claim offices across the U.S. and Canada. The company provides auto, homeowners, renters, life, health, disability, long-term care, business, boat, farm and ranch, flood, motorcycle, personal and volcano damage insurance. Over half of its 84 million policies are auto policies. The group's major insurance companies include State Farm Mutual Automobile Insurance Company, State Farm Life & Accident Assurance Company, State Farm Fire & Casualty Company, State Farm General Insurance Company, and State Farm Guaranty Insurance Company. Through State Farm Bank, F.S.B., the company provides bank account, credit card and loan services including individual retirement accounts (IRA), money market, checking, savings and health savings accounts; and home mortgage and home equity, vehicle and business loans. State Farm is also a leading insurer in Canada, serving households in Alberta, New Brunswick and Ontario. In recent years, the firm received FAA approval to test unmanned aircraft systems for commercial use, enabling the insurer to research this new technology and potentially deploy it in ways that could benefit customers. Its plans are to explore the use of drones to assess potential roof damage during the claims process and respond to natural disasters. In 2017, State Farm said it would discontinue the retail sales of investment products as a result of the U.S. Department of Labor Conflict of Interest Rule, which subjects the company and its agents to potential lawsuits.

Employee benefits include medical, dental and life coverage; a 401(k); a company retirement plan; and a wellness program.

FINANCIAL DATA: *Note: Data for latest year may not have been available at press time.*

In U.S. $	2016	2015	2014	2013	2012	2011
Revenue	76,100,000,000	75,700,000,000	71,200,000,000	68,291,000,000	65,285,700,000	64,305,100,000
R&D Expense						
Operating Income						
Operating Margin %						
SGA Expense						
Net Income	400,000,000	6,200,000,000	4,200,000,000	5,189,000,000	3,159,200,000	845,000,000
Operating Cash Flow						
Capital Expenditure						
EBITDA						
Return on Assets %						
Return on Equity %						
Debt to Equity						

CONTACT INFORMATION:

Phone: 309-766-2311   Fax: 309-766-3621
Toll-Free: 877-734-2265
Address: 1 State Farm Plaza, Bloomington, IL 61710 United States

STOCK TICKER/OTHER:

Stock Ticker: Mutual Company   Exchange:
Employees: 70,000   Fiscal Year Ends: 12/31
Parent Company:

SALARIES/BONUSES:

Top Exec. Salary: $ Bonus: $
Second Exec. Salary: $ Bonus: $

OTHER THOUGHTS:

Estimated Female Officers or Directors: 3
Hot Spot for Advancement for Women/Minorities: Y

Stericycle Inc

www.stericycle.com

NAIC Code: 562112

TYPES OF BUSINESS:

Medical Waste Treatment

BRANDS/DIVISIONS/AFFILIATES:

Bio-Systems
Ster-Safe
Shred-it

CONTACTS: *Note: Officers with more than one job title may be intentionally listed here more than once.*

Charles Alutto, CEO
Dan Ginnetti, CFO
Mark Miller, Director
Joseph Arnold, Executive VP
John Schetz, Executive VP
Brenda Frank, Executive VP
Ruth-Ellen Abdulmassih, Executive VP
Richard Hoffman, Senior VP

GROWTH PLANS/SPECIAL FEATURES:

Stericycle, Inc. is engaged in the business of medical waste disposal. Through its national networks of 252 processing facilities, 340 transfer sites and 102 other service facilities, the firm is able to serve the U.S. and 21 other countries, including Argentina, Brazil, Canada, Chile, Ireland, Japan, Mexico, Portugal, Romania, Korea, Spain, and the U.K. In order to dispose of medical waste, Stericycle utilizes various technologies, including autoclaving, an electro-thermal-deactivation system (ETD), chemical treatment and incineration. While Stericycle's customers are mainly hospitals, clinics, acute care facilities and dental offices, it also handles disposal of expired or surplus products from pharmacies and pharmaceutical manufacturers. The company generally provides its customers with its own waste containers, such as the plastic Bio Systems containers, to avoid needle sticks and leakages. After treatment, the residual ash is passed on to a third-party landfill and the containers are returned to customers. Stericycle utilizes its own branded methodologies, which include Steri-Safe, a compliance program designed to familiarize clients with regulatory policies, mail-back programs, product recalls, returns and onsite waste disposal services. The company serves more than 1 million customers worldwide, including large-quantity generators such as hospitals, blood banks and pharmaceutical manufacturers; and small-quantity generators such as outpatient clinics, medical and dental offices, long-term and sub-acute care facilities and retail pharmacies. In addition, Stericycle owns Shred-it, a global leader in secure information destruction. Documents are cross-cut shredded and then baled to be sold as office paper for recycling.

The company offers its employees medical, dental, vision, life, AD&D, long-term care, auto and home insurance; flexible spending accounts; an employee assistance program; tuition reimbursement; short- and long-term disability; a prepaid legal program; a 401(k) plan; an employee stock purchase plan; and paid vacation, holidays and funeral leave.

FINANCIAL DATA: *Note: Data for latest year may not have been available at press time.*

In U.S. $	2016	2015	2014	2013	2012	2011
Revenue	3,562,342,000	2,985,908,000	2,555,601,000	2,142,807,000	1,913,149,000	1,676,048,000
R&D Expense						
Operating Income	433,775,000	487,612,000	556,336,000	535,619,000	468,836,000	424,311,000
Operating Margin %	12.17%	16.33%	21.76%	24.99%	24.50%	25.31%
SGA Expense	904,179,000	712,803,000	489,937,000	390,610,000	356,817,000	311,522,000
Net Income	206,359,000	267,046,000	326,456,000	311,372,000	267,996,000	234,751,000
Operating Cash Flow	547,249,000	390,328,000	448,500,000	403,467,000	387,448,000	306,104,000
Capital Expenditure	136,160,000	114,761,000	86,496,000	73,109,000	65,236,000	53,301,000
EBITDA	678,478,000	615,817,000	658,326,000	621,397,000	545,154,000	487,801,000
Return on Assets %	2.53%	4.47%	7.88%	8.38%	7.97%	8.07%
Return on Equity %	6.43%	11.11%	17.91%	18.91%	19.56%	20.89%
Debt to Equity	1.02	1.11	0.80	0.73	0.82	1.07

CONTACT INFORMATION:

Phone: 847 367-5910   Fax: 847 367-9493
Toll-Free: 800-643-0240
Address: 28161 N. Keith Dr., Lake Forest, IL 60045 United States

STOCK TICKER/OTHER:

Stock Ticker: SRCL   Exchange: NAS
Employees: 25,000   Fiscal Year Ends: 12/31
Parent Company:

SALARIES/BONUSES:

Top Exec. Salary: $325,000   Bonus: $775,000
Second Exec. Salary: $585,000   Bonus: $

OTHER THOUGHTS:

Estimated Female Officers or Directors:
Hot Spot for Advancement for Women/Minorities:

Stifel Financial Corp

NAIC Code: 523110

www.stifel.com

TYPES OF BUSINESS:

Stock Brokerage/Investment Banking
Underwriting
Broker-Dealer
Investment Advisory Services
Research
Insurance
Annuities

BRANDS/DIVISIONS/AFFILIATES:

Stifel Nicolaus & Company Inc
Century Securities Associates Inc
Keefe Bruyette & Woods Inc
Miller Buckfire & Co LLC
Stifel Nicolaus Europe Limited
Stifel Bank & Trust
Stifel Trust Company Delaware NA
1919 Investment Counsel LLC

CONTACTS: *Note: Officers with more than one job title may be intentionally listed here more than once.*

Ronald Kruszewski, CEO
James Zemlyak, CFO
James Marischen, Chief Accounting Officer
Thomas Weisel, Co-Chairman
Richard Himelfarb, Executive VP, Subsidiary
Ben Plotkin, Executive VP, Subsidiary
Mark Fisher, General Counsel
Victor Nesi, Other Corporate Officer
Thomas Michaud, Senior VP
David Sliney, Senior VP

GROWTH PLANS/SPECIAL FEATURES:

Stifel Financial Corp. is a financial holding company headquartered in St. Louis, Missouri, USA. Its principal subsidiary is Stifel, Nicolaus & Company, Inc., a full service retail/institutional brokerage and investment banking firm. Other subsidiaries include Century Securities Associates, Inc., an independent broker-dealer; Keefe, Bruyette & Woods Inc., Miller Buckfire & Co. LLC and Sterne Agee Group Inc., which are all broker-dealers; Stifel Nicolaus Europe Limited, the company's European subsidiary; Stifel Bank & Trust, a retail and commercial bank; 1919 Investment Counsel & Trust Company NA and Stifel Trust Company Delaware NA, which are both trust companies; and 1919 Investment Counsel LLC and Zieglar Capital Management LLC, which are asset management firms. Stifel Financial's principal activities are: private client services, including securities transaction and financial planning services; institutional equity and fixed income sales, trading and research, as well as municipal finance; investment banking services, including mergers and acquisitions, public offerings and private placements; and retail and commercial banking, including personal and commercial lending programs. The company's global wealth management business division provides securities transaction, brokerage and investment services through a network of 2,172 financial advisors located in 329 branch offices in 45 states and the District of Columbia. The company's institutional business division includes research, equity and fixed income institutional sales and trading, investment banking, public finance and syndicate. This group serves more than 2,200 clients globally. In 2015, the firm acquired Sterne Agee Group, Inc. In 2016, it acquired Eaton Partners, LLC; and agreed to acquire City Financial Corporation, along with its wholly-owned subsidiary, City Securities Corporation.

The company offers its employees medical, dental, vision and prescription drug coverage; health care, dependent care and commuter flexible spending accounts; life insurance; short- and long-term disability; tuition assistance; business travel accident insurance; an employee assistance program; a 401(k) plan; and an employee stock ownership plan (ESOP).

FINANCIAL DATA: *Note: Data for latest year may not have been available at press time.*

In U.S. $	2016	2015	2014	2013	2012	2011
Revenue	2,575,496,000	2,331,594,000	2,208,424,000	1,973,446,000	1,612,650,000	1,396,831,000
R&D Expense						
Operating Income	142,582,000	141,567,000	290,794,000	185,229,000	225,872,000	118,877,000
Operating Margin %	5.53%	6.07%	13.16%	9.38%	14.00%	8.51%
SGA Expense	1,909,975,000	1,742,058,000	1,547,413,000	1,448,337,000	1,135,754,000	1,003,050,000
Net Income	81,520,000	92,336,000	176,067,000	162,013,000	138,573,000	84,134,000
Operating Cash Flow	-349,175,000	-379,509,000	250,269,000	702,219,000	-264,267,000	45,888,000
Capital Expenditure	28,211,000	69,822,000	26,632,000	32,278,000	18,837,000	59,730,000
EBITDA						
Return on Assets %	.47%	.80%	1.90%	2.02%	2.32%	1.83%
Return on Equity %	3.05%	3.83%	8.03%	9.11%	9.90%	6.58%
Debt to Equity	0.67	0.33	0.30	0.19	0.31	0.06

CONTACT INFORMATION:

Phone: 314 342-2000   Fax: 314 342-1159
Toll-Free: 800-679-5446
Address: 501 N. Broadway, St. Louis, MO 63102 United States

STOCK TICKER/OTHER:

Stock Ticker: SF   Exchange: NYS
Employees: 7,100   Fiscal Year Ends: 12/31
Parent Company:

SALARIES/BONUSES:

Top Exec. Salary: $200,000   Bonus: $3,021,000
Second Exec. Salary: Bonus: $1,992,750
$250,000

OTHER THOUGHTS:

Estimated Female Officers or Directors:
Hot Spot for Advancement for Women/Minorities:

Strategy&

www.strategyand.pwc.com

NAIC Code: 541610

TYPES OF BUSINESS:

Management Consulting

BRANDS/DIVISIONS/AFFILIATES:

PricewaterhouseCoopers (PWC)
Katzenbach Center

CONTACTS: Note: Officers with more than one job title may be intentionally listed here more than once.

Leslie Moeller, Global Managing Dir.
Mark Berlind, General Counsel
Jochim Rotering, Sr. Partner-Oper.
Peter B. Mensing, Managing Dir.-Europe
Mike Connolly, Sr. Partner-Health Svcs.
Leslie Moeller, Sr. Partner
Jay Davis, Global Dir.-Oper.
Ivan de Souza, Managing Dir.-Global Markets

GROWTH PLANS/SPECIAL FEATURES:

Strategy& is a management consulting firm which provides services to businesses and government institutions worldwide. Strategy& serves industries as diverse as aerospace and defense, automotive, chemicals, consumer products, energy and utilities, financial services, health, industrials, media and entertainment, oil and gas, private equity, public sector, retail, technology, telecommunications and transportation. The firm offers consulting services in the fields of corporate finance, deals, digital business and technology, enterprise strategy, marketing and sales, operations, organization/change/leadership, as well as product and service innovation. Strategy&'s capabilities-driven strategy focuses on evaluating pragmatic choices before implementing strategies in order to achieve the highest level of coherence, competitive sustainability outpace and reliability. The Katzenbach Center at Strategy& develops client-centered organizational models, applications and innovations focused on producing new thinking and higher performance through cultural change. The company has offices around the world, including Africa, Asia-Pacific, Europe, the Middle East, North America and South America. The firm's clients have included Deutsche Post World Net, Mediaset, Quest Diagnostics and Wolters Kluwer. Strategy& is owned by PricewaterhouseCoopers.

The firm offers employees a formal work-life balance program; substantial sick leave and family care leave; flexible work arrangements that may include job-sharing, flex time, sabbaticals and a compressed work week; and access to training at the PwC Open University.

FINANCIAL DATA: Note: Data for latest year may not have been available at press time.

In U.S. $	2016	2015	2014	2013	2012	2011
Revenue	1,194,027,000	1,147,000,000	1,300,000,000	1,050,000,000	1,000,000,000	
R&D Expense						
Operating Income						
Operating Margin %						
SGA Expense						
Net Income						
Operating Cash Flow						
Capital Expenditure						
EBITDA						
Return on Assets %						
Return on Equity %						
Debt to Equity						

CONTACT INFORMATION:

Phone: 212-697-1900   Fax: 212-551-6732
Toll-Free:
Address: 101 Park Ave., 18/Fl., New York, NY 10178 United States

STOCK TICKER/OTHER:

Stock Ticker: Subsidiary   Exchange:
Employees: 3,000   Fiscal Year Ends:
Parent Company: PricewaterhouseCoopers (PWC)

SALARIES/BONUSES:

Top Exec. Salary: $ Bonus: $
Second Exec. Salary: $ Bonus: $

OTHER THOUGHTS:

Estimated Female Officers or Directors: 1
Hot Spot for Advancement for Women/Minorities:

Stryker Corporation

www.stryker.com

NAIC Code: 339100

TYPES OF BUSINESS:

Equipment-Orthopedic Implants
Powered Surgical Instruments
Endoscopic Systems
Patient Care & Handling Equipment
Imaging Software
Small Bone Innovations

BRANDS/DIVISIONS/AFFILIATES:

Sage Products LLC
Physio-Control International Inc

CONTACTS: *Note: Officers with more than one job title may be intentionally listed here more than once.*

Kevin Lobo, CEO
Glenn Boehnlein, CFO
William Berry, Chief Accounting Officer
Bijoy Sagar, Chief Information Officer
Michael Hutchinson, General Counsel
M. Fink, Other Executive Officer
David Floyd, President, Divisional
Graham McLean, President, Divisional
Timothy Scannell, President, Divisional
Lonny Carpenter, President, Divisional
Katherine Owen, Vice President, Divisional
Yin Becker, Vice President, Divisional

GROWTH PLANS/SPECIAL FEATURES:

Stryker Corporation develops, manufactures and markets specialty surgical and medical products for the global market. Products include orthopedic implants, patient care and handling equipment, powered surgical instruments and endoscopic systems. The firm's products are produced by three segments: orthopaedics, MedSurg, and neurotechnology and spine. The orthopaedics segment's products consist primarily of implants for knee and hip joint replacements and trauma surgeries as well as products designed for upper and lower extremity small bone indications, with a focus on small joint replacement. The MedSurg segment includes surgical instruments and surgical navigation systems; endoscopic and communications systems; patient handling and emergency medical equipment; and reprocessed and remanufactured medical devices. The neurotechnology and spine segment's products primarily include neurosurgical and neurovascular devices, including products for traditional brain and open skull base procedures. This segment's offerings also include products used for minimally invasive endovascular techniques; orthobiologic and biosurgery products, including synthetic bone grafts and vertebral augmentation products; minimally invasive products for the treatment of acute ischemic and hemorrhagic stroke; and spinal implant products such as cervical, thoracolumbar and interbody systems. The company's products are sold in over 100 countries worldwide. During 2016, the firm acquired Sage Products, LLC, a developer, manufacturer and distributor of intensive care disposable products; Physio-Control International, Inc., which produces monitors/defibrillators and CPR-assisted devices; and Synergetic's neuro portfolio, including the Malis generator, Spetzler Mails disposable forceps, Sonopet tips and radio frequency generator.

Stryker offers its employees medical, vision, prescription, dental, long- and short-term disability and life insurance; an employee stock purchase plan; a 401(k); flexible spending; an employee assistance program; onsite fitness centers and cafeteria; wellness programs; maternity leave; adoption assistance; and tuition reimbursement.

FINANCIAL DATA: *Note: Data for latest year may not have been available at press time.*

In U.S. $	2016	2015	2014	2013	2012	2011
Revenue	11,325,000,000	9,946,000,000	9,675,000,000	9,021,000,000	8,657,000,000	8,307,000,000
R&D Expense	715,000,000	625,000,000	614,000,000	536,000,000	471,000,000	462,000,000
Operating Income	2,166,000,000	1,861,000,000	1,246,000,000	1,256,000,000	1,741,000,000	1,686,000,000
Operating Margin %	19.12%	18.71%	12.87%	13.92%	20.11%	20.29%
SGA Expense	4,137,000,000	3,610,000,000	4,336,000,000	4,066,000,000	3,466,000,000	3,150,000,000
Net Income	1,647,000,000	1,439,000,000	515,000,000	1,006,000,000	1,298,000,000	1,345,000,000
Operating Cash Flow	1,812,000,000	899,000,000	1,782,000,000	1,886,000,000	1,657,000,000	1,434,000,000
Capital Expenditure	490,000,000	270,000,000	233,000,000	195,000,000	210,000,000	226,000,000
EBITDA	2,712,000,000	2,258,000,000	1,624,000,000	1,563,000,000	2,018,000,000	2,201,000,000
Return on Assets %	8.97%	8.47%	3.07%	6.95%	10.13%	11.54%
Return on Equity %	18.23%	16.82%	5.83%	11.40%	15.94%	18.10%
Debt to Equity	0.70	0.38	0.37	0.30	0.20	0.22

CONTACT INFORMATION:

Phone: 269 385-2600　　　　Fax: 269 385-1062
Toll-Free:
Address: 2825 Airview Blvd., Kalamazoo, MI 49002 United States

STOCK TICKER/OTHER:

Stock Ticker: SYK　　　　　　　　　　Exchange: NYS
Employees: 33,000　　　　　　　　　Fiscal Year Ends: 12/31
Parent Company:

SALARIES/BONUSES:

Top Exec. Salary: $1,129,167　　Bonus: $
Second Exec. Salary: $554,000　　Bonus: $387,800

OTHER THOUGHTS:

Estimated Female Officers or Directors: 7
Hot Spot for Advancement for Women/Minorities: Y

Sutter Health Inc

www.sutterhealth.org

NAIC Code: 622110

TYPES OF BUSINESS:

General Medical and Surgical Hospitals
Neonatal Care
Pregnancy & Birth
Training Programs
Medical Research Facilities
Home Health Services
Hospice Networks
Long-Term Care

BRANDS/DIVISIONS/AFFILIATES:

Memorial
Sutter
Kahi Mohala
Alta Bates
Eden
Menlo Park Surgical
California Pacific
Sutter Health Plus

CONTACTS: *Note: Officers with more than one job title may be intentionally listed here more than once.*

Sarah Krevans, CEO

GROWTH PLANS/SPECIAL FEATURES:

Sutter Health, Inc. is one of the nation's largest nonprofit health care systems. Through its affiliates, the firm serves 100 Northern California communities via 5,500 physicians, which are members of the Sutter medical network. Sutter Health operates approximately 24 hospitals, 35 outpatient centers, six cardiac centers, nine cancer centers, five acute rehabilitation centers, seven behavioral health centers, five trauma centers and nine neonatal intensive care units (ICUs). The company's hospitals are branded under the Memorial, Sutter, Kahi Mohala, Alta Bates, Eden, Menlo Park Surgical, California Pacific and Novato Community names. Many of the hospitals operate charitable foundations. Sutter Health is a regional leader in labor and delivery, neonatology and pediatrics services, as well as orthopedics, bariatric, cosmetic, diabetes, heart and vascular, mental health, sleep disorders, transplant services and cancer care services. The company was one of the first health networks in its area to implement eICU (electronic ICU) centers, which allow enhanced comprehensive and consistent monitoring of ICU patients by feeding monitoring data to a central location. Sutter Health Plus is an HMO that offers affordably-priced health plans to individuals and employer groups.

FINANCIAL DATA: *Note: Data for latest year may not have been available at press time.*

In U.S. $	2016	2015	2014	2013	2012	2011
Revenue	11,873,000,000	10,998,000,000	10,161,000,000	9,600,000,000	9,560,000,000	9,079,000,000
R&D Expense						
Operating Income						
Operating Margin %						
SGA Expense						
Net Income	554,000,000	81,000,000	402,000,000	300,000,000	549,000,000	697,000,000
Operating Cash Flow						
Capital Expenditure						
EBITDA						
Return on Assets %						
Return on Equity %						
Debt to Equity						

CONTACT INFORMATION:

Phone: 916-733-8800   Fax:
Toll-Free:
Address: 2200 River Plaza Dr., Sacramento, CA 95833 United States

STOCK TICKER/OTHER:

Stock Ticker: Nonprofit
Employees: 55,000
Parent Company:

Exchange:
Fiscal Year Ends: 12/31

SALARIES/BONUSES:

Top Exec. Salary: $ Bonus: $
Second Exec. Salary: $ Bonus: $

OTHER THOUGHTS:

Estimated Female Officers or Directors: 3
Hot Spot for Advancement for Women/Minorities: Y

Sales, profits and employees may be estimates. Financial information, benefits and other data can change quickly and may vary from those stated here.

Symantec Corp
NAIC Code: 0

TYPES OF BUSINESS:
Computer Software, Security & Anti-Virus
Remote Management Products
Consulting-Cyber Security
Information Protection Products

BRANDS/DIVISIONS/AFFILIATES:
Norton
Blue Coat Inc

CONTACTS: *Note: Officers with more than one job title may be intentionally listed here more than once.*
Daniel Schulman, Chairman of the Board
Mark Garfield, Chief Accounting Officer
Gregory Clark, Director
Francis Rosch, Executive VP, Divisional
Nicholas Noviello, Executive VP
Scott Taylor, Executive VP
Michael Fey, President
Amy Cappellanti-Wolf, Senior VP

GROWTH PLANS/SPECIAL FEATURES:
Symantec Corp. provides a range of software, appliances and services designed to secure and manage information technology (IT) infrastructure. The company provides customers worldwide with software and services that protect, manage and control information risks related to security, data protection, storage, compliance and systems management. The firm has two operating segments: enterprise security and consumer security. The enterprise security segment protects organizations so they can securely conduct business while leveraging new platforms and data. This segment includes Symantec's threat protection products, information protection products, cyber security services, and website security offerings, previously named trust services. These products and services help secure information in transit and wherever it resides in the network path, from the user's device to the data's resting place. In addition, these products help to prevent the loss of confidential data by insiders, and help customers achieve and maintain compliance with laws and regulations. The consumer security focuses on making it simple for customers to be productive and protected at home and at work. The firm's Norton-branded services provide multi-layer security and identity protection on major desktop and mobile operating systems, to defend against increasingly complex online threats to individuals, families, and small businesses. Norton Security products help customers protect against increasingly complex threats and address the need for identity protection, while also managing the rapid increase in mobile and digital data, such as personal financial records, photos, music and videos. Symantec operates in over 35 countries. In January 2016, the firm completed its sale of Veritas to The Carlyle Group for $5.3 billion. In August of the same year, Symantec acquired Blue Coat, Inc., a provider of web security, for $4.65 billion. The following November, the firm agreed to acquire LifeLock, Inc. for $2.3 billion.

Symantec offers employees a 401(k) with company match, tuition reimbursement and adoption assistance.

FINANCIAL DATA: *Note: Data for latest year may not have been available at press time.*

In U.S. $	2016	2015	2014	2013	2012	2011
Revenue	3,600,000,000	6,508,000,000	6,676,000,000	6,906,000,000	6,730,000,000	
R&D Expense	748,000,000	1,144,000,000	1,038,000,000	1,012,000,000	969,000,000	
Operating Income	457,000,000	1,149,000,000	1,183,000,000	1,123,000,000	1,079,000,000	
Operating Margin %	12.69%	17.65%	17.72%	16.26%	16.03%	
SGA Expense	1,587,000,000	2,702,000,000	2,880,000,000	3,185,000,000	3,251,000,000	
Net Income	2,488,000,000	878,000,000	898,000,000	765,000,000	1,172,000,000	
Operating Cash Flow	796,000,000	1,312,000,000	1,281,000,000	1,593,000,000	1,901,000,000	
Capital Expenditure	272,000,000	381,000,000	260,000,000	336,000,000	286,000,000	
EBITDA	766,000,000	1,611,000,000	1,731,000,000	1,800,000,000	2,241,000,000	
Return on Assets %	19.90%	6.55%	6.43%	5.58%	9.10%	
Return on Equity %	51.77%	14.96%	16.00%	14.55%	24.36%	
Debt to Equity	0.60	0.29	0.36	0.38	0.40	

CONTACT INFORMATION:
Phone: 650 527-8000   Fax:
Toll-Free:
Address: 350 Ellis St., Mountain View, CA 94043 United States

STOCK TICKER/OTHER:
Stock Ticker: SYMC   Exchange: NAS
Employees: 13,000   Fiscal Year Ends: 03/31
Parent Company:

SALARIES/BONUSES:
Top Exec. Salary: $536,750   Bonus: $500,000
Second Exec. Salary: Bonus: $
$1,000,000

OTHER THOUGHTS:
Estimated Female Officers or Directors: 3
Hot Spot for Advancement for Women/Minorities: Y

SYNNEX Corporation

NAIC Code: 423430

TYPES OF BUSINESS:

IT Supply Chain Services
Distribution Services
Contract Assembly Services
Outsourcing Services

BRANDS/DIVISIONS/AFFILIATES:

SYNNEX Infotec Corporation
SYNNEX Canada Limited
SYNNEX US
Concentrix

CONTACTS: Note: Officers with more than one job title may be intentionally listed here more than once.

Kevin Murai, CEO
Marshall Witt, CFO
Matthew Miau, Chairman Emeritus
Dwight Steffensen, Chairman of the Board
Dennis Polk, COO
Christopher Caldwell, Executive VP
Simon Leung, General Counsel
Peter Larocque, President, Divisional

GROWTH PLANS/SPECIAL FEATURES:

SYNNEX Corporation is a leading business process services company, serving resellers, retailers and original equipment manufacturers (OEMs) around the world. The firm operates in two segments: technology solutions and Concentrix. The technology solutions segment distributes computer systems and complimentary products to a variety of customers, including value-added resellers, system integrators and retailers. This segment also provides assembly services to OEMs, including integrated supply chain management; build-to-order and configure-to-order system configurations; materials; and management and logistics. Subsidiary SYNNEX Infotec Corporation distributes IT equipment, electronic components and software in Japan. The Concentrix segment offers a range of services under the Concentrix trademark, including customer management, software development, web hosting, hosted software, domain name registration and back office processing. SYNNEX delivers these services through various methods, including voice, chat, web, email and digital print. The company purchases IT systems from OEM suppliers, such as Asus Tek Computer, Inc.; HP, Inc.; Hewlett Packard Enterprise Company; Intel Corporation; Lenovo Group Ltd.; Lenmark Interntional, Inc.; Microsoft Corporation; Panasonic Corporation; Samsung Electronics Co. Ltd.; Seagate Technologies, LLC; and Xerox Corporation. SYNNEX then sells them to its reseller and retail customers. The firm currently distributes over 30,000 technology products from over 300 IT, CE and OEM suppliers to more than 20,000 resellers, system integrators and retailers. The firm operates approximately 40 distribution and administration facilities in the U.S., Canada, Japan and Mexico. Other Subsidiaries of the firm include SYNNEX Canada Limited and SYNNEX U.S. In November 2016, the firm commenced operations at its new state-of-the-art facility in New Zealand, which will be home to more than 300 staff, impacting employment generation and economic growth in Australia and New Zealand.

SYNNEX employees receive medical, dental, vision, life and AD&D insurance; flexible spending accounts; 401(k); an employee assistance program; tuition reimbursement and more.

FINANCIAL DATA: Note: Data for latest year may not have been available at press time.

In U.S. $	2016	2015	2014	2013	2012	2011
Revenue	14,061,840,000	13,338,400,000	13,839,590,000	10,845,160,000	10,285,510,000	10,409,840,000
R&D Expense						
Operating Income	379,596,000	354,552,000	308,507,000	240,828,000	255,012,000	256,228,000
Operating Margin %	2.69%	2.65%	2.22%	2.22%	2.47%	2.46%
SGA Expense	903,369,000	837,239,000	790,497,000	414,142,000	401,725,000	374,270,000
Net Income	234,946,000	208,525,000	180,034,000	152,237,000	151,376,000	150,331,000
Operating Cash Flow	326,951,000	643,609,000	-234,772,000	35,707,000	242,793,000	219,153,000
Capital Expenditure	123,233,000	100,106,000	57,377,000	28,965,000	14,481,000	40,153,000
EBITDA	500,889,000	458,062,000	400,206,000	265,290,000	279,642,000	280,901,000
Return on Assets %	4.81%	4.50%	4.47%	4.84%	5.22%	5.63%
Return on Equity %	12.31%	11.93%	11.74%	11.15%	12.22%	13.97%
Debt to Equity	0.30	0.35	0.15	0.04	0.06	0.19

CONTACT INFORMATION:

Phone: 510 656-3333   Fax: 510 668-3777
Toll-Free: 800-756-9888
Address: 44201 Nobel Dr., Fremont, CA 94538 United States

STOCK TICKER/OTHER:

Stock Ticker: SNX   Exchange: NYS
Employees: 105,500   Fiscal Year Ends: 11/30
Parent Company:

SALARIES/BONUSES:

Top Exec. Salary: $633,794   Bonus: $
Second Exec. Salary: Bonus: $
$459,499

OTHER THOUGHTS:

Estimated Female Officers or Directors: 2
Hot Spot for Advancement for Women/Minorities:

Synopsys Inc
NAIC Code: 0

TYPES OF BUSINESS:
Computer Software-Electronic Design Automation
Consulting & Support Services

BRANDS/DIVISIONS/AFFILIATES:
DesignWare IP
Sentaurus
Proteus
CATS
Yield
WinterLogic
Simpleware Limited
Gold Standard Simulations Limited

CONTACTS: *Note: Officers with more than one job title may be intentionally listed here more than once.*
Trac Pham, CFO
Aart De Geus, Chairman of the Board
Sudhindra Kankanwadi, Chief Accounting Officer
Chi-Foon Chan, Co-CEO
Joseph Logan, Executive VP, Divisional
Brian Beattie, Executive VP, Divisional
John Runkel, General Counsel

GROWTH PLANS/SPECIAL FEATURES:
Synopsys, Inc. is a supplier of electronic design automation (EDA) software and related services for the design, creation and testing of integrated circuits (ICs). The company's products and services are divided into four groups: core EDA, intellectual property (IP), manufacturing solutions and professional services. Core EDA products and services include the company's digital and custom IC design software, its functional register transfer level verification products, and its field-programmable gate array design software. Designers use these core EDA products to automate the IC design process and to reduce errors. IP products and services include the company's DesignWare IP portfolio, system-level design products, as well as software quality and security testing solutions. Synopsys is a leading provider of high-quality, silicon-proven IP solutions for system-on-chips (SoCs), including wired and wireless interfaces, logic libraries, embedded memories, processor solutions, IP subsystems for audio/sensor/data fusion functionality and analog IP. Manufacturing solutions' software products and technologies enable semiconductor manufacturers to more quickly develop new fabrication processes that produce production-level yields. This group's solutions include Sentaurus technology computer-aided design device and process simulation products; Proteus mask synthesis tools; CATS mask data preparation software; and Yield Explorer Odyssey and Yield Manager management solutions. Last, professional services include consultation and design services that address all phases of the SoC development process. These services assist Synopsys customers with new tool and methodology adoption, chip architecture and specification development, functional and low-power design and verification, and physical implementation and signoff. This division also provides a range of training and workshops on the company's latest tools and methodologies. In 2016, the firm acquired WinterLogic, Simpleware Limited, Gold Standard Simulations Limited, Cigital and Cigital's spinoff company, Codiscope.

Employee benefits include medical, dental and vision coverage; life, AD&D and disability insurance; an employee assistance program; educational assistance; adoption benefits; and a wellness program.

FINANCIAL DATA: *Note: Data for latest year may not have been available at press time.*

In U.S. $	2016	2015	2014	2013	2012	2011
Revenue	2,422,532,000	2,242,211,000	2,057,472,000	1,962,214,000	1,756,017,000	1,535,643,000
R&D Expense	856,705,000	776,229,000	718,768,000	669,197,000	581,628,000	491,871,000
Operating Income	317,395,000	266,466,000	248,717,000	246,493,000	190,024,000	212,843,000
Operating Margin %	13.10%	11.88%	12.08%	12.56%	10.82%	13.86%
SGA Expense	668,330,000	639,504,000	608,294,000	569,773,000	573,088,000	475,878,000
Net Income	266,826,000	225,934,000	259,124,000	247,800,000	182,402,000	221,364,000
Operating Cash Flow	586,635,000	495,160,000	550,953,000	496,705,000	486,068,000	440,316,000
Capital Expenditure	71,040,000	90,647,000	106,913,000	69,068,000	57,493,000	60,230,000
EBITDA	540,351,000	496,245,000	466,863,000	464,766,000	359,966,000	341,393,000
Return on Assets %	5.18%	4.60%	5.67%	5.82%	4.85%	6.65%
Return on Equity %	8.43%	7.29%	8.86%	9.36%	7.92%	10.53%
Debt to Equity			0.01	0.02	0.04	

CONTACT INFORMATION:
Phone: 650 584-5000   Fax: 650 965-8637
Toll-Free: 800-541-7737
Address: 690 E. Middlefield Road, Mountain View, CA 94043 United States

STOCK TICKER/OTHER:
Stock Ticker: SNPS   Exchange: NAS
Employees: 10,669   Fiscal Year Ends: 10/31
Parent Company:

SALARIES/BONUSES:
Top Exec. Salary: $500,000   Bonus: $
Second Exec. Salary: $500,000   Bonus: $

OTHER THOUGHTS:
Estimated Female Officers or Directors: 3
Hot Spot for Advancement for Women/Minorities: Y

Syntel Inc

NAIC Code: 518210

www.syntelinc.com

TYPES OF BUSINESS:

Business Process Outsourcing
Outsourcing Services
e-Business Solutions
Application Development & Management

BRANDS/DIVISIONS/AFFILIATES:

CONTACTS: Note: Officers with more than one job title may be intentionally listed here more than once.

Sanjay Garg, CEO, Subsidiary
Anil Agrawal, CFO
Daniel Moore, Chief Administrative Officer
Bharat Desai, Co-Chairman of the Board
Prashant Ranade, Director
Anil Jain, Other Corporate Officer
Raja Ray, Other Corporate Officer
Sujay Puthran, Other Corporate Officer
Rakesh Khanna, President
Rahul Aggarwal, Senior VP, Divisional
V. S. Raj, Senior VP, Divisional
Gangidi Reddy, Senior VP, Divisional
Murlidhar Reddy, Senior VP, Divisional
Rajiv Tandon, Senior VP, Divisional
Avinash Salelkar, Vice President, Divisional
Ben Andradi, Vice President, Geographical

GROWTH PLANS/SPECIAL FEATURES:

Syntel, Inc. is a global provider of digital transformation, information technology (IT) and knowledge process outsourcing services to Global 2000 companies. The firm operates through five business segments which each help Syntel customers adapt to market change by providing an array of technology-based, industry-specific solutions. These segments include banking and financial services; healthcare and life sciences; insurance; manufacturing; and retail, logistics and telecom (RLT). Banking and financial services includes companies that provide banking, capital markets, cards, payments, investments and transaction processing services to third parties. The healthcare and life sciences segment includes healthcare payers and providers, as well as pharmaceutical and medical device providers, among others. This division focuses on addressing regulatory requirements and emerging industry trends such as integrated care, wider use of electronic health records and the increasing prevalence of healthcare banking. The insurance segment serves the needs of global property and casualty insurers, insurance brokers, as well as personal, commercial, life and retirement insurance service providers. The manufacturing segment provides technology services and business consulting in a range of sub-sectors, including industrial products, aerospace and automotive manufacturing, as well as to processors of raw materials, natural resources and chemicals. The RLT segment serves retailers and distributors, including supermarkets, specialty premium retailers, department stores and large mass-merchandise discounters who seek Syntel's assistance in becoming more efficient and cost-effective, as well as in helping to drive business transformation. This division also serves the entire travel and hospitality industry, including airlines, hotels, restaurants, as well as online and retail travel, global distribution systems, intermediaries and real estate companies.

FINANCIAL DATA: Note: Data for latest year may not have been available at press time.

In U.S. $	2016	2015	2014	2013	2012	2011
Revenue	966,550,000	968,612,000	911,429,000	824,765,000	723,903,000	642,404,000
R&D Expense						
Operating Income	262,297,000	283,745,000	268,350,000	267,602,000	211,940,000	138,228,000
Operating Margin %	27.13%	29.29%	29.44%	32.44%	29.27%	21.51%
SGA Expense	108,528,000	100,256,000	109,217,000	96,587,000	103,044,000	108,721,000
Net Income	-57,390,000	252,526,000	249,740,000	219,658,000	185,543,000	122,856,000
Operating Cash Flow	-11,650,000	223,521,000	233,400,000	199,966,000	188,688,000	109,052,000
Capital Expenditure	17,513,000	17,013,000	19,218,000	20,495,000	32,255,000	38,232,000
EBITDA	293,009,000	299,312,000	284,492,000	282,076,000	226,385,000	155,108,000
Return on Assets %	-6.11%	19.07%	22.48%	25.49%	28.04%	21.49%
Return on Equity %	-11.76%	23.97%	29.90%	34.10%	35.04%	26.01%
Debt to Equity			0.13	0.19		

CONTACT INFORMATION:

Phone: 248 619-2800   Fax: 248 619-2888
Toll-Free:
Address: 525 E. Big Beaver Rd., Ste. 300, Troy, MI 48083 United States

STOCK TICKER/OTHER:

Stock Ticker: SYNT   Exchange: NAS
Employees: 23,011   Fiscal Year Ends: 12/31
Parent Company:

SALARIES/BONUSES:

Top Exec. Salary: $473,340   Bonus: $36,819
Second Exec. Salary: $433,017   Bonus: $26,735

OTHER THOUGHTS:

Estimated Female Officers or Directors:
Hot Spot for Advancement for Women/Minorities:

SYSCO Corporation

NAIC Code: 424410

www.sysco.com

TYPES OF BUSINESS:
Food-Wholesale Distribution
Restaurant Supplies Distribution
Medical & Surgical Supplies Distribution
Cleaning Supplies Distribution

BRANDS/DIVISIONS/AFFILIATES:
SYGMA Network Inc

CONTACTS: *Note: Officers with more than one job title may be intentionally listed here more than once.*
William Delaney, CEO
Joel Grade, CFO
Jackie Ward, Chairman of the Board
Wayne Shurts, Chief Technology Officer
Paul Moskowitz, Executive VP, Divisional
R. Charlton, Executive VP, Divisional
William Day, Executive VP, Divisional
Russell Libby, Executive VP, Divisional
Thomas Bene, President

GROWTH PLANS/SPECIAL FEATURES:

SYSCO Corporation, through its subsidiaries, is one of the largest distributors of food and food-related products to the foodservice industry in North America. The firm provides products and services to more than 425,000 customers, including restaurants, healthcare companies, educational facilities and lodging establishments. Restaurants account for approximately 63% of the company's sales; healthcare, 9%; education and government, 8%; travel, leisure and retail, 8%; and other sources, 12%. SYSCO distributes a wide variety of frozen and imported foods; fresh meats and seafood; dairy items; fresh produce; and nonfood items, including tableware, restaurant/kitchen equipment, medical/surgical supplies and cleaning supplies. Subsidiary SYGMA Network, Inc. distributes a full line of food products, non-food products and customer-specific proprietary products to certain chain restaurant customer locations. The company operates 199 distribution facilities throughout the U.S., Bahamas, Canada and Ireland, with a fleet of approximately 10,200 delivery vehicles (consisting of tractor and trailer combinations, vans and panel trucks). In May 2017, the firm announced it would be expanding its Sysco Atlanta facility, including an addition of 100,000 square feet to the existing 562,000-square-foot building. The new section will feature freezer space, cold dock space and a vehicle maintenance facility. The project will add approximately 100 new jobs over the next few years.

The firm offers employees life, disability, medical, dental and vision insurance; annual performance incentives; an assistance program; tuition assistance; a stock purchase plan; matching charity gifts; a 401(k); direct deposit; and product discounts.

FINANCIAL DATA: *Note: Data for latest year may not have been available at press time.*

In U.S. $	2016	2015	2014	2013	2012	2011
Revenue	50,366,920,000	48,680,750,000	46,516,710,000	44,411,230,000	42,380,940,000	39,323,490,000
R&D Expense						
Operating Income	1,850,500,000	1,229,362,000	1,587,122,000	1,658,478,000	1,890,632,000	1,931,502,000
Operating Margin %	3.67%	2.52%	3.41%	3.73%	4.46%	4.91%
SGA Expense	7,189,972,000	7,322,154,000	6,593,913,000	6,209,113,000	5,785,945,000	5,389,646,000
Net Income	949,622,000	686,773,000	931,533,000	992,427,000	1,121,585,000	1,152,030,000
Operating Cash Flow	1,933,142,000	1,555,484,000	1,492,815,000	1,511,594,000	1,404,180,000	1,091,518,000
Capital Expenditure	527,346,000	542,830,000	523,206,000	511,862,000	784,501,000	636,442,000
EBITDA	2,401,863,000	1,815,975,000	2,155,427,000	2,188,498,000	2,314,341,000	2,348,309,000
Return on Assets %	5.47%	4.40%	7.21%	8.01%	9.55%	10.61%
Return on Equity %	21.73%	13.04%	17.81%	20.09%	23.88%	27.00%
Debt to Equity	2.10	0.43	0.45	0.50	0.58	0.48

CONTACT INFORMATION:
Phone: 281 584-1390 Fax: 281 584-2880
Toll-Free:
Address: 1390 Enclave Pkwy., Houston, TX 77077 United States

STOCK TICKER/OTHER:
Stock Ticker: SYY Exchange: NYS
Employees: 51,700 Fiscal Year Ends: 06/30
Parent Company:

SALARIES/BONUSES:
Top Exec. Salary: $1,245,833 Bonus: $
Second Exec. Salary: $770,833 Bonus: $281,250

OTHER THOUGHTS:
Estimated Female Officers or Directors: 8
Hot Spot for Advancement for Women/Minorities: Y

T Rowe Price Group Inc

www.troweprice.com

NAIC Code: 523920

TYPES OF BUSINESS:

Investment Management & Mutual Funds
Retirement Accounts
Advisory Services

BRANDS/DIVISIONS/AFFILIATES:

T Rowe Price Associates Inc
T Rowe Price International Ltd
T Rowe Price Hong Kong Limited
T Rowe Price Singapore Private Ltd
Emerging Markets Value Stock Fund

CONTACTS: *Note: Officers with more than one job title may be intentionally listed here more than once.*

Kenneth Moreland, CFO
Brian Rogers, Chairman of the Board
Jessica Hiebler, Chief Accounting Officer
William Stromberg, Director
Edward Bernard, Director
Robert Sharps, Other Corporate Officer
Christopher Alderson, Other Corporate Officer
David Oestreicher, Other Executive Officer
Edward Wiese, Vice President

GROWTH PLANS/SPECIAL FEATURES:

T. Rowe Price Group, Inc. is a financial services holding company. The firm derives revenue primarily from investment advisory services that it provides to individual and institutional investors. The firm manages approximately $763.1 billion in assets. T. Rowe Price operates its investment advisory business through subsidiaries T. Rowe Price Associates, Inc. and T. Rowe Price International, Ltd. In Hong Kong and Singapore, T. Rowe Price operates through T. Rowe Price Hong Kong Limited and T. Rowe Price Singapore Private Ltd., respectively. Products and services for the individual investor include mutual funds, retirement accounts, rollover IRAs, college savings plans, private asset management, high-net-worth services, banking services and advisory services. In addition to investment services, T. Rowe Price offers institutional clients retirement plan services, including small business and corporate retirement plans as well as public sector plans for religious institutions, schools and hospitals. The company introduces new mutual funds and other investment portfolios in an attempt to complement and expand its investment offerings and respond to competitive developments in the marketplace. The firm manages a broad range of domestic and international stock, bonds and mutual funds and other investment portfolios. T. Rowe Price also offers administrative services to its clients, including mutual fund transferring, accounting and shareholder services, record keeping and transfer agent services for defined contribution retirement plans, discount brokerages and trust services. In 2015, the firm launched the Emerging Markets Value Stock Fund, which invests in emerging markets companies that are out of favor and undervalued but possess identified catalysts that could drive their stock prices higher.

The firm offers its employees medical, dental, prescription, vision, retiree, travel, life, AD&D, short- and long-term disability insurance; a nurse hotline; Lasik vision discount; fitness club reimbursement; a 401(k); flexible spending accounts; adoption assistance; tuition reimbursement; and community support programs.

FINANCIAL DATA: *Note: Data for latest year may not have been available at press time.*

In U.S. $	2016	2015	2014	2013	2012	2011
Revenue	4,222,900,000	4,200,600,000	3,982,100,000	3,484,200,000	3,022,500,000	2,747,100,000
R&D Expense						
Operating Income	1,733,400,000	1,898,900,000	1,890,900,000	1,637,400,000	1,364,300,000	1,226,900,000
Operating Margin %	41.04%	45.20%	47.48%	46.99%	45.13%	44.66%
SGA Expense	1,573,900,000	1,523,300,000	1,405,600,000	1,498,600,000	1,137,400,000	1,060,600,000
Net Income	1,215,000,000	1,223,000,000	1,229,600,000	1,047,700,000	883,600,000	773,200,000
Operating Cash Flow	170,500,000	1,506,400,000	1,291,300,000	1,233,200,000	902,800,000	948,400,000
Capital Expenditure	148,300,000	151,300,000	126,200,000	105,800,000	76,900,000	82,300,000
EBITDA	1,866,800,000	2,025,200,000	2,002,600,000	1,728,400,000	1,445,600,000	1,299,300,000
Return on Assets %	20.99%	22.45%	22.76%	22.48%	22.16%	20.76%
Return on Equity %	24.34%	23.76%	23.80%	23.96%	24.31%	22.91%
Debt to Equity						

CONTACT INFORMATION:

Phone: 410 345-2000   Fax: 410 345-2394
Toll-Free: 800-638-7890
Address: 100 E. Pratt St., Baltimore, MD 21202 United States

STOCK TICKER/OTHER:

Stock Ticker: TROW   Exchange: NAS
Employees: 6,329   Fiscal Year Ends: 12/31
Parent Company:

SALARIES/BONUSES:

Top Exec. Salary: $350,000   Bonus: $
Second Exec. Salary: Bonus: $
$350,000

OTHER THOUGHTS:

Estimated Female Officers or Directors:
Hot Spot for Advancement for Women/Minorities:

Team Health Holdings Inc

www.teamhealth.com

NAIC Code: 621111

TYPES OF BUSINESS:

Physicians and Hospital Staff Services
Hospital Administrative Services
Pediatrics
Radiology & Teleradiology Services
Urgent Care

BRANDS/DIVISIONS/AFFILIATES:

Blackstone Group LP (The)
TEAMHealth

GROWTH PLANS/SPECIAL FEATURES:

Team Health Holdings, Inc. is a physician-led company offering outsourced integrated care services. This more than 19,000-clinician-strong healthcare provider offers outsources staffing, administrative support and management services across the full continuum of care under the TEAMHealth brand name. Practice areas include emergency medicine, anesthesiology, hospital medicine, hospital medicine subspecialties, ambulatory care, post-acute care and behavioral health. Team Health's staff include residents, physicians, medical directors and advanced practice clinicians. In February 2017, the firm was taken private by The Blackstone Group LP. That May, Team Health acquired the clinical operations of Synergy Emergency Physicians, Inc.

CONTACTS: Note: Officers with more than one job title may be intentionally listed here more than once.

Leif M. Murphy, CEO
Michael Wiechart, COO
H. Massingale, Chairman of the Board
David Jones, CFO
Oliver Rogers, Executive VP
Steven Clifton, Executive VP
Leif Murphy, President
Lynn Massingale, Chmn.

FINANCIAL DATA: Note: Data for latest year may not have been available at press time.

In U.S. $	2016	2015	2014	2013	2012	2011
Revenue	3,700,000,000	3,597,246,976	2,819,642,880	2,383,595,008	2,069,022,976	1,745,328,000
R&D Expense						
Operating Income						
Operating Margin %						
SGA Expense						
Net Income		82,711,000	97,738,000	87,409,000	63,772,000	65,521,000
Operating Cash Flow						
Capital Expenditure						
EBITDA						
Return on Assets %						
Return on Equity %						
Debt to Equity						

CONTACT INFORMATION:

Phone: 865 693-1000   Fax:
Toll-Free: 800-818-1498
Address: 265 Brookview Ctr. Way, Ste. 400, Knoxville, TN 37919 United States

STOCK TICKER/OTHER:

Stock Ticker: Private   Exchange:
Employees: 14,000   Fiscal Year Ends: 12/31
Parent Company: Blackstone Group LP (The)

SALARIES/BONUSES:

Top Exec. Salary: $ Bonus: $
Second Exec. Salary: $ Bonus: $

OTHER THOUGHTS:

Estimated Female Officers or Directors: 3
Hot Spot for Advancement for Women/Minorities: Y

Team Inc

NAIC Code: 237120

TYPES OF BUSINESS:

Piping System Maintenance & Construction Services

BRANDS/DIVISIONS/AFFILIATES:

TeamQualspec
TeamFurmanite
Quest Integrity

CONTACTS: *Note: Officers with more than one job title may be intentionally listed here more than once.*

Greg Boane, CFO
Andre Bouchard, Executive VP
Arthur Victorson, President, Divisional
Jeffrey Ott, President, Divisional
Declan Rushe, President, Divisional
Ted Owen, President

GROWTH PLANS/SPECIAL FEATURES:

Team, Inc. is an industrial services provider. These services include the inspection and assessment required in maintaining high temperature and high pressure piping systems and vessels utilized in the refining, petrochemical, power, pipeline and other heavy industries. Team operates through three segments: TeamQualspec, TeamFurmanite and Quest Integrity. TeamQualspec provides standard and advanced non-destructive testing (NDT) services, pipeline integrity management services, field heat treating services, as well as related engineering and assessment services. These services can be offered while facilities are running (on-stream), during facility turnarounds or during new construction or expansion. TeamFurmanite provides turnaround and on-stream services. This division's turnaround services are project related and include field machining, technical bolting, field valve repair, heat exchanger repair and isolation test plugging services. Its on-stream services include leak repair fugitive emissions control and hot tapping. Quest Integrity provides management solutions, which encompass two broadly-defined disciplines: highly-specialized in-line inspection services for unpiggable process piping and pipelines using proprietary in-line inspection tools and analytical software; and advanced condition assessment services. The company's services are offered globally through more than 220 locations in 20 countries.

FINANCIAL DATA: *Note: Data for latest year may not have been available at press time.*

In U.S. $	2016	2015	2014	2013	2012	2011
Revenue	1,196,696,000	842,047,000	749,527,000	714,311,000	623,740,000	
R&D Expense						
Operating Income	-3,118,000	68,465,000	53,421,000	55,602,000	56,497,000	
Operating Margin %	-.26%	8.13%	7.12%	7.78%	9.05%	
SGA Expense	323,973,000	189,528,000	171,455,000	158,355,000	139,737,000	
Net Income	-12,676,000	40,070,000	29,855,000	32,436,000	32,911,000	
Operating Cash Flow	79,564,000	43,471,000	52,861,000	58,643,000	36,652,000	
Capital Expenditure	45,812,000	28,769,000	33,016,000	26,068,000	23,933,000	
EBITDA	45,555,000	91,252,000	74,889,000	74,323,000	73,966,000	
Return on Assets %	-1.10%	7.94%	6.31%	7.50%	8.66%	
Return on Equity %	-2.36%	12.50%	9.98%	12.31%	14.81%	
Debt to Equity	0.64	0.23	0.23	0.25	0.35	

CONTACT INFORMATION:

Phone: 281-331-6154   Fax:
Toll-Free: 800-662-8326
Address: 13131 Dairy Ashford Rd., Sugar Land, TX 77478 United States

STOCK TICKER/OTHER:

Stock Ticker: TISI   Exchange: NYS
Employees: 7,400   Fiscal Year Ends: 05/31
Parent Company:

SALARIES/BONUSES:

Top Exec. Salary: $575,000   Bonus: $
Second Exec. Salary: Bonus: $
$450,000

OTHER THOUGHTS:

Estimated Female Officers or Directors:
Hot Spot for Advancement for Women/Minorities:

Tech Data Corp

www.techdata.com

NAIC Code: 423430

Computer & Software Products, Distribution
Training
Assembly Services

Tech Data Corp. is a worldwide distributor of information technology (IT) products, logistics management and other value-added services. The company serves more than 105,000 value-added resellers (VARs), direct marketers, retailers and corporate resellers in over 100 countries throughout Europe, Latin America and North America. It offers a variety of products from manufacturers and publishers, including Lenovo, Apple Computer, Autodesk, Toshiba, Xerox, Kodak and Panasonic. Products are typically purchased directly from manufacturers or software publishers on a non-exclusive basis and then shipped to customers from one of Tech Data's 32 regionally located logistics centers. The company's vendor agreements do not restrict it from selling similar products manufactured by competitors. The firm also provides resellers with extensive pre- and post-sale training, service and support as well as configuration and assembly services and e-commerce tools. Tech Data provides products and services to the online reseller channel and does business with thousands of resellers through its web site. The firm's entire electronic catalog is available online, and its electronic software distribution initiative allows resellers and vendors to easily access software titles directly from a secure location on the web site. In September 2016, the firm agreed to purchase Avnet Inc.'s technology solutions unit for approximately $2.6 billion.

Note: Officers with more than one job title may be intentionally listed here more than once.

Robert Dutkowsky, CEO
Alain Amsellem, CFO, Geographical
Joseph Trepani, CFO, Geographical
Charles Dannewitz, CFO
Steven Raymund, Chairman of the Board
John Tonnison, Chief Information Officer
Richard Hume, COO
David Vetter, Executive VP
Beth Simonetti, Other Corporate Officer
Patrick Zammit, President, Geographical
Joseph Quaglia, President, Geographical
Nestor Cano, President, Geographical
Jeffrey Taylor, Senior VP

Note: Data for latest year may not have been available at press time.

In U.S. $	2016	2015	2014	2013	2012	2011
Revenue	26,379,780,000	27,670,630,000	26,821,900,000	25,358,330,000	26,488,120,000	
R&D Expense						
Operating Income	401,428,000	267,635,000	227,513,000	263,720,000	327,858,000	
Operating Margin %	1.52%	.96%	.84%	1.04%	1.23%	
SGA Expense	990,934,000	1,114,234,000	1,116,553,000	1,009,872,000	1,037,839,000	
Net Income	265,736,000	175,172,000	179,932,000	176,255,000	206,396,000	
Operating Cash Flow	188,993,000	119,381,000	379,148,000	120,753,000	503,412,000	
Capital Expenditure	33,972,000	28,175,000	30,388,000	38,365,000	44,370,000	
EBITDA	454,159,000	334,478,000	303,894,000	317,945,000	383,997,000	
Return on Assets %	4.25%	2.63%	2.57%	2.79%	3.36%	
Return on Equity %	13.40%	8.63%	8.95%	9.05%	10.09%	
Debt to Equity	0.17	0.18	0.16	0.18	0.02	

Phone: 727 539-7429 Fax: 727 538-7808
Toll-Free: 800-237-8931
Address: 5350 Tech Data Dr., Clearwater, FL 33760 United States

Stock Ticker: TECD Exchange: NAS
Employees: 9,500 Fiscal Year Ends: 01/31
Parent Company:

Top Exec. Salary: $1,122,124 Bonus: $
Second Exec. Salary: $711,382 Bonus: $

Estimated Female Officers or Directors: 1
Hot Spot for Advancement for Women/Minorities:

Tenet Healthcare Corporation

www.tenethealth.com

NAIC Code: 622110

TYPES OF BUSINESS:
General Medical and Surgical Hospitals
Specialty Care Facilities
Outpatient Centers
Diagnostic Imaging Centers
Rural Health Care Clinics
HMOs

BRANDS/DIVISIONS/AFFILIATES:
Conifer Holdings Inc

CONTACTS: *Note: Officers with more than one job title may be intentionally listed here more than once.*
Trevor Fetter, CEO
Daniel Cancelmi, CFO
R. Ramsey, Chief Accounting Officer
Audrey Andrews, General Counsel
Paul Castanon, Other Corporate Officer
J. Evans, President, Divisional
Keith Pitts, Vice Chairman

GROWTH PLANS/SPECIAL FEATURES:
Tenet Healthcare Corporation specializes in the provision of healthcare services, primarily through the operation of general hospitals. The company operates 79 hospitals, 20 short-stay surgical hospitals, over 470 outpatient centers, nine facilities in the U.K. via subsidiaries, partnerships and joint ventures. Subsidiary Conifer Holdings, Inc. provides healthcare business process services in the areas of revenue cycle management, technology-enabled performance and health management to health systems, individual hospitals, physician practices, self-insured organizations and health plans. Each of the company's general hospitals offers acute care services, operating and recovery rooms, radiology services, respiratory therapy services, clinical laboratories and pharmacies. In addition, most offer intensive care, critical care or coronary care units, physical therapy, as well as orthopedic, oncology and outpatient services. Some of the hospitals also offer tertiary care services such as open-heart surgery, neonatal intensive care and neuroscience. Along with hospitals, Tenet's subsidiaries operate three academic medical centers, two children's hospitals, two specialty hospitals and one critical access hospital, for a combined total of 20,354 licensed beds, serving primarily urban and suburban communities in 12 states. In May 2017, the firm agreed to sell three Houston, Texas hospitals to HCA Holdings, Inc.

The company offers its employees medical, dental and vision insurance; life and AD&D insurance; a 401(k) plan; an employee stock purchase plan; and credit union membership.

FINANCIAL DATA: *Note: Data for latest year may not have been available at press time.*

In U.S. $	2016	2015	2014	2013	2012	2011
Revenue	19,621,000,000	18,634,000,000	16,615,000,000	11,102,000,000	9,119,000,000	8,854,000,000
R&D Expense						
Operating Income	1,219,000,000	1,056,000,000	925,000,000	663,000,000	749,000,000	650,000,000
Operating Margin %	6.21%	5.66%	5.56%	5.97%	8.21%	7.34%
SGA Expense						
Net Income	-192,000,000	-140,000,000	12,000,000	-134,000,000	152,000,000	82,000,000
Operating Cash Flow	558,000,000	1,026,000,000	687,000,000	589,000,000	593,000,000	497,000,000
Capital Expenditure	302,000,000	293,000,000	933,000,000	683,000,000	508,000,000	475,000,000
EBITDA	2,077,000,000	1,853,000,000	1,750,000,000	861,000,000	1,176,000,000	949,000,000
Return on Assets %	-.79%	-.66%	.06%	-1.06%	1.61%	.68%
Return on Equity %	-34.65%	-20.86%	1.70%	-14.12%	12.63%	4.60%
Debt to Equity	36.12	20.81	17.96	14.15	4.51	3.94

CONTACT INFORMATION:
Phone: 469-893-2200   Fax:
Toll-Free:
Address: 1445 Ross Ave., Ste. 1400, Dallas, TX 75202 United States

STOCK TICKER/OTHER:
Stock Ticker: THC   Exchange: NYS
Employees: 131,610   Fiscal Year Ends: 12/31
Parent Company:

SALARIES/BONUSES:
Top Exec. Salary: $1,275,000   Bonus: $
Second Exec. Salary: $925,000   Bonus: $

OTHER THOUGHTS:
Estimated Female Officers or Directors: 5
Hot Spot for Advancement for Women/Minorities: Y

Tenneco Inc

NAIC Code: 336300

www.tenneco.com

TYPES OF BUSINESS:

Automotive Parts Manufacturer
Advanced Suspension Technologies
Ride Control Products
Emissions Systems
Performance Mufflers
Noise Control Systems

BRANDS/DIVISIONS/AFFILIATES:

Monroe
Walker
Fonos
DynoMax
Rancho
Clevite
Axios
Fric-Rot

CONTACTS: *Note: Officers with more than one job title may be intentionally listed here more than once.*

Gregg Sherrill, CEO
Brian Kesseler, COO
Timothy Jackson, Executive VP, Divisional
Josep Fornos, Executive VP, Divisional
Henry Hummel, Executive VP, Divisional
Martin Hendricks, Executive VP, Divisional
Peng Guo, Executive VP, Geographical
Kenneth Trammell, Executive VP
James Harrington, General Counsel
Joseph Pomaranski, General Manager, Divisional
Gregg Bolt, Senior VP, Divisional
John Kunz, Vice President

GROWTH PLANS/SPECIAL FEATURES:

Tenneco, Inc. is a leading manufacturer of automotive emission control and ride control products and systems for both original equipment manufacturers (OEMs) and aftermarket retailers. The firm designs, manufactures and sells individual components for vehicles as well as groups of components that are combined as modules or systems within vehicles. The firm maintains 91 emission control manufacturing facilities and 15 engineering centers across six continents. Tenneco's primary brands are Monroe ride control products and Walker, Fonos and DynoMax emission control products. Other brands include Rancho, Clevite, Elastomers, Axios, Kinetic and Fric-Rot ride control products and Thrush emission control products. Tenneco sells to more than 70 OEMs worldwide. Its leading customers are General Motors Company, which accounts for 17% of net sales, and Ford Motor Company, 13%. In the aftermarket sector, Tenneco's customers serve more than 500 full-line and specialty warehouse distributors, retailers, jobbers, installer chains and car dealers such as National Auto Parts Association (NAPA), Advance Auto Parts, Uni-Select, O'Reilly Auto Parts, Aftermarket Auto Parts Alliance and AutoZone in North America; Temot Autoteile GmbH, Autodistribution International, Group Auto Union, Auto Teile Ring and AP United in Europe; and Rede Presidente in South America. The firm's products are sold primarily in North America (49% of sales) and Europe, South America, Asia and India (51%). In August 2016, the firm opened a new Clean Air manufacturing plant in Lansing, Michigan, to support General Motors (GM) and its crossover vehicle platform; and announced plans to open one in Spring Hill, Tennessee, to support programs for GM's Spring Hill assembly plant.

FINANCIAL DATA: *Note: Data for latest year may not have been available at press time.*

In U.S. $	2016	2015	2014	2013	2012	2011
Revenue	8,599,000,000	8,209,000,000	8,420,000,000	7,964,000,000	7,363,000,000	7,205,000,000
R&D Expense	154,000,000	146,000,000	169,000,000	144,000,000	126,000,000	133,000,000
Operating Income	533,000,000	524,000,000	499,000,000	428,000,000	435,000,000	389,000,000
Operating Margin %	6.19%	6.38%	5.92%	5.37%	5.90%	5.39%
SGA Expense	589,000,000	491,000,000	519,000,000	453,000,000	427,000,000	428,000,000
Net Income	363,000,000	247,000,000	226,000,000	183,000,000	275,000,000	157,000,000
Operating Cash Flow	489,000,000	517,000,000	341,000,000	503,000,000	365,000,000	245,000,000
Capital Expenditure	345,000,000	309,000,000	341,000,000	269,000,000	269,000,000	228,000,000
EBITDA	740,000,000	722,000,000	700,000,000	629,000,000	633,000,000	586,000,000
Return on Assets %	8.73%	6.19%	5.76%	4.92%	7.91%	4.82%
Return on Equity %	71.10%	53.11%	48.60%	53.90%	223.57%	
Debt to Equity	2.20	2.59	2.15	2.35	4.33	

CONTACT INFORMATION:

Phone: 847 482-5000   Fax: 847 482-5940
Toll-Free:
Address: 500 N. Field Drive, Lake Forest, IL 60045 United States

STOCK TICKER/OTHER:

Stock Ticker: TEN   Exchange: NYS
Employees: 31,000   Fiscal Year Ends: 12/31
Parent Company:

SALARIES/BONUSES:

Top Exec. Salary: $1,165,000   Bonus: $342,947
Second Exec. Salary: $895,000   Bonus: $210,773

OTHER THOUGHTS:

Estimated Female Officers or Directors: 4
Hot Spot for Advancement for Women/Minorities: Y

Tesla Inc

NAIC Code: 336111

www.teslamotors.com

TYPES OF BUSINESS:

Automobile Manufacturing, All-Electric
Battery Manufacturing
Lithium Ion Battery Storage Technologies
Energy Storage Systems

BRANDS/DIVISIONS/AFFILIATES:

Model S
70D
Model X
Model 3
Tesla Powerwall
Gigafactory
SolarCity
Solar Roof

CONTACTS: *Note: Officers with more than one job title may be intentionally listed here more than once.*

Elon Musk, CEO
Deepak Ahuja, CFO
Jason Wheeler, CFO
Jeffrey Straubel, Chief Technology Officer
Jon McNeill, President, Divisional
Douglas Field, Senior VP, Divisional

GROWTH PLANS/SPECIAL FEATURES:

Tesla, Inc. manufactures high-performance all-electric automobiles and energy storage products. Its sales have been impressive, despite the relatively high price of its initial models, and the company is widely admired for its innovation, design, engineering and marketing. The Model S features a lightweight aluminum body. The car can be ordered with either of two battery packs. The 70kWh battery version, called the 70D, offers all-wheel drive at a price of about $75,000. The 85 kWh model features 265-mile range and 0-60 acceleration of 5.4 seconds in the standard edition or 4.2 seconds in the performance model. Batteries come with an 8-year, 125,000-mile warranty. The Model X crossover, featuring gullwing doors, can cost more than $130,000 when fully equipped. Tesla also plans to launch a Model 3 sedan in 2017 with a base price of about $35,000, capable of traveling about 215 miles per charge. Battery-wise, each Tesla car has thousands of small, lithium-ion batteries linked together, similar to the batteries found in consumer electronics. The firm's network of convenient car charger stations, called Tesla Superchargers, can fully-charge a Tesla in 75 minutes and are located in North America, Europe and Asia. The Tesla Powerwall is an easy-to-install home-sized energy storage system intended to store local, solar-generated power for later use. The company's Gigafactory near Reno, Nevada, manufactures battery packs for the company's energy storage products and plans to do the same for its vehicles. The factory is expected to have an annual capacity equal to 35 gigawatt-hours' worth of batteries (the equivalent of generating one billion watts for a single hour). In November 2016, the firm acquired SolarCity, a solar energy provider. Later that month, the firm unveiled Solar Roof, a roofing option that is cheaper than a conventional roof per average square foot, while reducing a home's electricity bill.

FINANCIAL DATA: *Note: Data for latest year may not have been available at press time.*

In U.S. $	2016	2015	2014	2013	2012	2011
Revenue	7,000,132,000	4,046,025,000	3,198,356,000	2,013,496,000	413,256,000	204,242,000
R&D Expense	834,408,000	717,900,000	464,700,000	231,976,000	273,978,000	208,981,000
Operating Income	-667,340,000	-716,629,000	-186,689,000	-61,283,000	-394,283,000	-251,488,000
Operating Margin %	-9.53%	-17.71%	-5.83%	-3.04%	-95.40%	-123.13%
SGA Expense	1,432,189,000	922,232,000	603,660,000	285,569,000	150,372,000	104,102,000
Net Income	-674,914,000	-888,663,000	-294,040,000	-74,014,000	-396,213,000	-254,411,000
Operating Cash Flow	-123,829,000	-524,499,000	-57,337,000	257,994,000	-266,081,000	-114,364,000
Capital Expenditure	1,440,471,000	1,634,850,000	969,885,000	264,224,000	239,228,000	197,896,000
EBITDA	399,561,000	-334,183,000	48,181,000	67,591,000	-366,998,000	-236,960,000
Return on Assets %	-4.38%	-12.74%	-7.11%	-4.19%	-43.35%	-46.27%
Return on Equity %	-23.10%	-88.83%	-37.24%	-18.69%	-227.22%	-118.03%
Debt to Equity	1.25	1.91	2.05	0.89	3.29	1.21

CONTACT INFORMATION:

Phone: 650 681-5000   Fax:
Toll-Free:
Address: 3500 Deer Creek, Palo Alto, CA 94304 United States

STOCK TICKER/OTHER:

Stock Ticker: TSLA   Exchange: NAS
Employees: 17,782   Fiscal Year Ends: 12/31
Parent Company:

SALARIES/BONUSES:

Top Exec. Salary: $501,931   Bonus: $
Second Exec. Salary: Bonus: $
$501,923

OTHER THOUGHTS:

Estimated Female Officers or Directors: 1
Hot Spot for Advancement for Women/Minorities:

Texas Instruments Inc (TI)

www.ti.com

NAIC Code: 334413

TYPES OF BUSINESS:

Chips-Digital Signal Processors
Semiconductors
Calculators
Educational Software
Power Management Products
Broadband RF/IF & Digital Radio
MEMS
Microcontrollers (MCU)

BRANDS/DIVISIONS/AFFILIATES:

DLP

CONTACTS: *Note: Officers with more than one job title may be intentionally listed here more than once.*

Richard Templeton, CEO
Ellen Barker, Senior VP
Kevin March, Chief Accounting Officer
Brian Crutcher, Executive VP
Bing Xie, Senior VP
Teresa West, Senior VP
Kevin Ritchie, Senior VP
Darla Whitaker, Senior VP
Stephen Anderson, Senior VP
R. Delagi, Senior VP
Niels Anderskouv, Senior VP
Haviv Ilan, Senior VP
Rafael Lizardi, Senior VP
Cynthia Trochu, Senior VP

GROWTH PLANS/SPECIAL FEATURES:

Texas Instruments, Inc. (TI), founded in 1930, is a global designer and manufacturer of semiconductors with operations located in more than 35 countries and serves over 100,000 customers worlwide. It operates in three segments: analog, embedded processing and other. Analog semiconductors change real-world signals, such as sound, temperature, pressure or images, by conditioning them, amplifying them and often converting them to a stream of digital data that can be processed by other semiconductors, such as embedded processors. Analog semiconductors are also used to manage power in every electronic device, whether plugged into a wall or running off a battery. Product lines include High Volume Analog & Logic (HVAL), Power Management (Power), High Performance Analog (HPA) and Silicon Valley Analog (SVA). Embedded processors are designed to handle specific tasks and can be optimized for various combinations of performance, power and cost, depending on the application. The devices vary from simple, low-cost products used in electric toothbrushes to highly specialized, complex devices used in wireless base station communications infrastructure equipment. Products include processors, microcontrollers and connectivity. Lastly, the other division includes semiconductors such as the firm's proprietary DLP optical semiconductor products, which enable clear video and microprocessors that serve as the brains of everything from high-end computer servers to high definition televisions (HDTVs). This segment also includes educational products, such as handheld graphing calculators, business calculators and scientific calculators as well as a wide range of advanced classroom tools and professional development resources, including educational software. In March 2017, the firm released a new processor called the SimpleLink microcontroller platform, which is built on a foundation of drivers, libraries and frameworks that allows the code to be reused, which will expand and accelerate product development.

TI offers its employees medical, dental, vision and life insurance; an employee assistance program; professional financial services; and product discounts on cars, appliances and software.

FINANCIAL DATA: *Note: Data for latest year may not have been available at press time.*

In U.S. $	2016	2015	2014	2013	2012	2011
Revenue	13,370,000,000	13,000,000,000	13,045,000,000	12,205,000,000	12,825,000,000	13,735,000,000
R&D Expense	1,370,000,000	1,280,000,000	1,358,000,000	1,522,000,000	1,877,000,000	1,715,000,000
Operating Income	4,799,000,000	4,274,000,000	3,947,000,000	2,832,000,000	1,973,000,000	2,992,000,000
Operating Margin %	35.89%	32.87%	30.25%	23.20%	15.38%	21.78%
SGA Expense	1,767,000,000	1,748,000,000	1,843,000,000	1,858,000,000	1,804,000,000	1,638,000,000
Net Income	3,595,000,000	2,986,000,000	2,821,000,000	2,162,000,000	1,759,000,000	2,236,000,000
Operating Cash Flow	4,614,000,000	4,268,000,000	3,892,000,000	3,384,000,000	3,414,000,000	3,256,000,000
Capital Expenditure	531,000,000	551,000,000	385,000,000	412,000,000	495,000,000	816,000,000
EBITDA	5,968,000,000	5,439,000,000	5,198,000,000	4,146,000,000	3,319,000,000	4,012,000,000
Return on Assets %	22.01%	17.33%	15.15%	11.09%	8.68%	13.19%
Return on Equity %	35.21%	28.94%	26.20%	19.86%	16.05%	20.90%
Debt to Equity	0.28	0.31	0.35	0.38	0.38	0.38

CONTACT INFORMATION:

Phone: 972 995-3773   Fax: 972 995-4360
Toll-Free: 800-336-5236
Address: 12500 TI Blvd., Dallas, TX 75266-0199 United States

STOCK TICKER/OTHER:

Stock Ticker: TXN   Exchange: NAS
Employees: 29,865   Fiscal Year Ends: 12/31
Parent Company:

SALARIES/BONUSES:

Top Exec. Salary: $1,164,083   Bonus: $
Second Exec. Salary: $822,917   Bonus: $

OTHER THOUGHTS:

Estimated Female Officers or Directors: 3
Hot Spot for Advancement for Women/Minorities: Y

Sales, profits and employees may be estimates. Financial information, benefits and other data can change quickly and may vary from those stated here.

Textron Inc

NAIC Code: 336411

TYPES OF BUSINESS:

Helicopters & General Aviation Aircraft Manufacturing
Aerospace
Electrical Test & Measurement Equipment
Fiber Optic Equipment
Off-Road Vehicles
Financing

BRANDS/DIVISIONS/AFFILIATES:

Bell Helicopter
Textron Systems
Textron Aviation
Textron Financial Corporation
E-Z-GO
Jacobsen
Kautex
Greenlee

CONTACTS: *Note: Officers with more than one job title may be intentionally listed here more than once.*

Scott Donnelly, CEO
Frank Connor, CFO
Mark Bamford, Chief Accounting Officer
Cheryl Johnson, Executive VP, Divisional
Robert Lupone, Executive VP

GROWTH PLANS/SPECIAL FEATURES:

Textron, Inc. is a global multi-industry company active in the aircraft, defense, industrial and finance industries. The company divides its operations into five segments: Bell Helicopter, Textron Systems, Textron Aviation, industrial and finance. Bell Helicopter supplies helicopters, tilt rotor aircraft and helicopter-related spare parts and services for military and commercial applications. It also offers commercially-certified helicopters to corporate; offshore petroleum exploration; utility; charter; and police, fire, rescue and emergency medical helicopter operators. Textron Systems manufactures weapons systems and surveillance and intelligence products for the defense, aerospace, homeland security and general aviation markets. It sells most of its products to U.S. government customers, but also to customers outside the U.S. through foreign military sales sponsored by the U.S. government and directly through commercial sales channels. Textron Aviation is home to the Beechcraft, Cessna and Hawker brands, which account for more than half of all general aviation aircraft flying. Its product portfolio includes five business lines: business jets, general aviation and special mission turboprop aircraft, high performance piston aircraft, military trainer and defense aircraft and a customer service organization. The industrial segment includes the business of E-Z-GO, Jacobsen, Kautex and Greenlee. These companies design, manufacture and sell diverse products such as golf carts, off-road utility vehicles, turf maintenance equipment, blow-molded fuel systems, electrical test and measurement instruments and fiber optic connectors. The finance segment consists of Textron Financial Corporation and its subsidiaries, which primarily support the company's other segments.

Textron offers its employees medical, prescription, dental and vision coverage; flexible spending accounts; life, AD&D, business travel and disability insurance; adoption assistance; discounts on products and auto and home insurance; and educational assistance.

FINANCIAL DATA: *Note: Data for latest year may not have been available at press time.*

In U.S. $	2016	2015	2014	2013	2012	2011
Revenue	13,788,000,000	13,423,000,000	13,878,000,000	12,104,000,000	12,237,000,000	11,275,000,000
R&D Expense						
Operating Income	1,173,000,000	1,140,000,000	1,096,000,000	847,000,000	1,053,000,000	337,000,000
Operating Margin %	8.50%	8.49%	7.89%	6.99%	8.60%	2.98%
SGA Expense	1,304,000,000	1,304,000,000	1,361,000,000	1,126,000,000	1,168,000,000	1,183,000,000
Net Income	962,000,000	697,000,000	600,000,000	498,000,000	589,000,000	242,000,000
Operating Cash Flow	1,012,000,000	1,090,000,000	1,208,000,000	810,000,000	927,000,000	1,063,000,000
Capital Expenditure	446,000,000	420,000,000	429,000,000	444,000,000	480,000,000	423,000,000
EBITDA	1,499,000,000	1,601,000,000	1,503,000,000	1,236,000,000	1,436,000,000	986,000,000
Return on Assets %	6.39%	4.75%	4.35%	3.83%	4.42%	1.67%
Return on Equity %	18.25%	15.09%	13.86%	13.50%	20.53%	8.46%
Debt to Equity	0.59	0.67	0.90	0.72	1.15	1.56

CONTACT INFORMATION:

Phone: 401 421-2800   Fax: 401 421-2878
Toll-Free:
Address: 40 Westminster Street, Providence, RI 02903 United States

STOCK TICKER/OTHER:

Stock Ticker: TXT   Exchange: NYS
Employees: 36,000   Fiscal Year Ends: 12/31
Parent Company:

SALARIES/BONUSES:

Top Exec. Salary: $1,146,500   Bonus: $
Second Exec. Salary: Bonus: $
$940,385

OTHER THOUGHTS:

Estimated Female Officers or Directors: 10
Hot Spot for Advancement for Women/Minorities: Y

Thermo Fisher Scientific Inc

www.thermofisher.com

NAIC Code: 423450

TYPES OF BUSINESS:

Laboratory Equipment & Supplies Distribution
Contract Manufacturing
Equipment Calibration & Repair
Clinical Trial Services
Laboratory Workstations
Clinical Consumables
Diagnostic Reagents
Custom Chemical Synthesis

BRANDS/DIVISIONS/AFFILIATES:

Thermo Scientific
Applied Biosystems
Invitrogen
Fisher Scientific
Unity Lab Services
Affymetrix Inc
FEI Company
Finesse Solutions Inc

CONTACTS: *Note: Officers with more than one job title may be intentionally listed here more than once.*

Marc Casper, CEO
Jim Manzi, Chairman of the Board
Peter Wilver, Executive VP
Mark Stevenson, Executive VP
Thomas Loewald, Other Executive Officer
Patrick Durbin, President, Divisional
Stephen Williamson, Senior VP
Daniel Shine, Senior VP
Seth Hoogasian, Senior VP
Peter Hornstra, Vice President

GROWTH PLANS/SPECIAL FEATURES:

Thermo Fisher Scientific, Inc. is a distributor of products and services principally to the scientific-research and clinical laboratory markets. The firm serves over 400,000 customers including biotechnology and pharmaceutical companies; colleges and universities; medical-research institutions; hospitals; reference, quality control, process-control and research and development labs in various industries; and government agencies. It operates in four segments: life sciences solutions, analytical instruments, specialty diagnostics and laboratory products and services. Life sciences solutions provides a portfolio of reagents, instruments and consumables used in biological and medical research, discover and production of new drugs and vaccines. This division also provides diagnosis of disease. Analytical instruments provides a broad offering of instruments, consumables, software and services used for a range of applications in the laboratory, on the production line and in the field. These products are used by customers in pharmaceutical, biotechnology, academic, government, environmental, research, industrial markets, as well as clinical laboratories. Specialty diagnostics offers a range of diagnostic test kits, reagents, culture media, instruments and associated products in order to serve customers in healthcare, clinical, pharmaceutical, industrial and food safety laboratories. Laboratory products and services offers everything needed for the laboratory to enable customers to focus on core activities and become more efficient, productive and cost-effective. This segment's products are used primarily for drug discovery and development, as well as for life science research in order to advance the prevention and cure of diseases and enhance quality of life. The company's five primary brands include Thermo Scientific, Applied Biosystems, Invitrogen, Fisher Scientific and Unity Lab Services. During 2016, the firm acquired Affymetrix, Inc.; and FEI Company. By mid-2017, it acquired Finesse Solutions, Inc.; acquired Core Informatics; and agreed to acquire CDMO Patheon.

Employee benefits include tuition reimbursement, retirement plans and training & development opportunities. Benefits vary by country.

FINANCIAL DATA: *Note: Data for latest year may not have been available at press time.*

In U.S. $	2016	2015	2014	2013	2012	2011
Revenue	18,274,100,000	16,965,400,000	16,889,600,000	13,090,300,000	12,509,900,000	11,725,900,000
R&D Expense	754,800,000	692,300,000	691,100,000	395,500,000	376,400,000	340,600,000
Operating Income	2,449,200,000	2,336,200,000	2,503,000,000	1,609,600,000	1,482,100,000	1,245,200,000
Operating Margin %	13.40%	13.77%	14.81%	12.29%	11.84%	10.61%
SGA Expense	4,975,900,000	4,612,100,000	4,896,100,000	3,446,300,000	3,354,900,000	3,126,500,000
Net Income	2,021,800,000	1,975,400,000	1,894,400,000	1,273,300,000	1,177,900,000	1,329,900,000
Operating Cash Flow	3,156,300,000	2,816,900,000	2,619,600,000	2,010,700,000	2,039,500,000	1,691,000,000
Capital Expenditure	444,400,000	422,900,000	427,600,000	282,400,000	315,100,000	266,500,000
EBITDA	4,251,500,000	4,039,500,000	4,251,900,000	2,581,500,000	2,494,700,000	2,165,400,000
Return on Assets %	4.65%	4.71%	5.07%	4.29%	4.34%	5.52%
Return on Equity %	9.42%	9.42%	10.12%	7.87%	7.72%	8.74%
Debt to Equity	0.71	0.53	0.60	0.56	0.45	0.38

CONTACT INFORMATION:

Phone: 781 622-1000   Fax: 781 933-4476
Toll-Free: 800-678-5599
Address: 168 Third Ave., Waltham, MA 02451 United States

SALARIES/BONUSES:

Top Exec. Salary: $1,407,471   Bonus: $
Second Exec. Salary: $850,301   Bonus: $

STOCK TICKER/OTHER:

Stock Ticker: TMO
Employees: 55,000
Parent Company:

Exchange: NYS
Fiscal Year Ends: 12/31

OTHER THOUGHTS:

Estimated Female Officers or Directors: 1
Hot Spot for Advancement for Women/Minorities: Y

Sales, profits and employees may be estimates. Financial information, benefits and other data can change quickly and may vary from those stated here.

Thor Industries Inc

www.thorindustries.com

NAIC Code: 336214

TYPES OF BUSINESS:

Recreational Vehicle Manufacturing
Motor Homes
Automotive Parts & Accessories
Buses

BRANDS/DIVISIONS/AFFILIATES:

Airstream Inc
CrossRoads RV
Thor Motor Coach Inc
Keystone RV Company
Postle Operating LLC
Jayco Inc
Heartland Recreational Vehicles LLC
KZ Inc

CONTACTS: *Note: Officers with more than one job title may be intentionally listed here more than once.*

Robert Martin, CEO
Colleen Zuhl, CFO
Peter Orthwein, Chairman of the Board
W. Woelfer, General Counsel
Kenneth Julian, Vice President, Divisional

GROWTH PLANS/SPECIAL FEATURES:

Thor Industries, Inc. is a leading manufacturer of a wide range of recreational vehicles (RVs). The company's primary RV subsidiaries are Airstream, Inc.; CrossRoads RV; Thor Motor Coach, Inc.; Keystone RV Company; Heartland Recreational Vehicles LLC; K.Z., Inc.; Postle Operating, LLC; and Jayco Corp. Together they produce towable RVs, which account for 73% of annual net sales, as well as motorized RVs, which account for 24% of net sales (3% goes toward other/related sales). Towable RVs include conventional travel trailers, fifth wheels and park models; truck and folding campers; and equestrian and other specialty towable vehicles. Park models are recreational dwellings towed to a permanent site such as a lake, woods or park, with the maximum size of park models in the U.S. being 400 square feet. Motorized RVs include Class A, B and C motorhomes, which are self-powered vehicles built on a chassis and self-contained with their own lighting, heating, cooking, refrigeration, sewage holding and water storage facilities. Thor also manufactures and sells related parts and accessories. In July 2016, it acquired Jayco Corp. for $576 million, a manufacturer of recreation vehicles such as camping, travel and fifth-wheel trailers, as well as motorhomes.

FINANCIAL DATA: *Note: Data for latest year may not have been available at press time.*

In U.S. $	2016	2015	2014	2013	2012	2011
Revenue	4,582,112,000	4,006,819,000	3,525,456,000	3,241,795,000	3,084,660,000	2,755,508,000
R&D Expense						
Operating Income	392,094,000	290,639,000	248,764,000	217,429,000	176,487,000	138,549,000
Operating Margin %	8.55%	7.25%	7.05%	6.70%	5.72%	5.02%
SGA Expense	306,269,000	250,891,000	208,712,000	194,650,000	169,154,000	180,858,000
Net Income	256,519,000	199,385,000	179,002,000	152,862,000	121,739,000	106,273,000
Operating Cash Flow	341,209,000	247,860,000	149,261,000	145,066,000	118,841,000	114,802,000
Capital Expenditure	51,976,000	42,283,000	30,406,000	24,305,000	10,063,000	33,749,000
EBITDA	437,480,000	324,456,000	278,663,000	246,965,000	206,229,000	176,848,000
Return on Assets %						
Return on Equity %						
Debt to Equity	0.28					

CONTACT INFORMATION:

Phone: 574-970-7460   Fax:
Toll-Free:
Address: 601 E. Beardsley Ave., Elkhart, IN 46514-3305 United States

SALARIES/BONUSES:

Top Exec. Salary: $750,000   Bonus: $
Second Exec. Salary: $600,000   Bonus: $75,000

STOCK TICKER/OTHER:

Stock Ticker: THO   Exchange: NYS
Employees: 10,450   Fiscal Year Ends: 07/31
Parent Company:

OTHER THOUGHTS:

Estimated Female Officers or Directors:
Hot Spot for Advancement for Women/Minorities:

TIBCO Software Inc

www.tibco.com

NAIC Code: 0

TYPES OF BUSINESS:

Software-Business Process
Data Management Software
Consulting & Support Services

BRANDS/DIVISIONS/AFFILIATES:

Jaspersoft
Spotfire
StreamBase
BusinessEvents
Mashery

CONTACTS: *Note: Officers with more than one job title may be intentionally listed here more than once.*

Murray Rode, CEO
Tom Berquist, CFO
Thomas Been, CMO
Michele Haddad, Sr. VP-Global Human Resources
Matt Quinn, CTO
Thomas Laffey, Executive VP, Divisional
Ram Menon, Executive VP
William Hughes, Executive VP
R. Bradley, President
John Ederer, Vice President, Divisional

GROWTH PLANS/SPECIAL FEATURES:

TIBCO Software, Inc. is a provider of middleware and infrastructure software, focused on creating and marketing software for use in the integration of business information, processes and applications. The company offers a range of standards-based infrastructure software products that help customers streamline business process management by offering real-time access to information. TIBCO's software products are capable of instantly correlating information about an organization's operations and performance with information about expected behavior and business rules, allowing customers to anticipate and respond to business developments. TIBCO offers products in two main categories: interconnect everything and augment intelligence. The interconnect everything category comprises three groups: data and systems, which includes application integration, messaging and master data management; APIs (application program interfaces), which includes API management; and people and processes, which includes business process management. The augment intelligence category also comprises three groups: dashboard and reporting, which includes Jaspersoft branded software; data visualization, which includes Spotfire branded software; and streaming analytics, which includes the StreamBase and BusinessEvents brands of software. Industries served by the firm include airlines, banking, capital markets, government, healthcare, insurance, life sciences, logistics, manufacturing, oil and gas, rail, retail, telecommunications and utilities. In 2015, the firm acquired Mashery, an industry leader in application API management.

TIBCO offers its employees medical, dental, vision, disability, life and AD&D insurance; a 401(k) program; credit union membership; an employee assistance program; a discount stock purchase plan; and tuition reimbursement.

FINANCIAL DATA: *Note: Data for latest year may not have been available at press time.*

In U.S. $	2016	2015	2014	2013	2012	2011
Revenue	1,000,000,000	1,000,000,000	1,022,400,000	1,069,950,016	1,024,612,992	920,246,016
R&D Expense						
Operating Income						
Operating Margin %						
SGA Expense						
Net Income						
Operating Cash Flow						
Capital Expenditure						
EBITDA						
Return on Assets %						
Return on Equity %						
Debt to Equity						

CONTACT INFORMATION:

Phone: 650 846-1000   Fax: 650 846-1218
Toll-Free: 800-420-8450
Address: 3307 Hillview Ave., Palo Alto, CA 94304 United States

STOCK TICKER/OTHER:

Stock Ticker: Private   Exchange:
Employees: 2,965   Fiscal Year Ends: 11/30
Parent Company: Vista Equity Partners

SALARIES/BONUSES:

Top Exec. Salary: $ Bonus: $
Second Exec. Salary: $ Bonus: $

OTHER THOUGHTS:

Estimated Female Officers or Directors: 2
Hot Spot for Advancement for Women/Minorities:

TJX Companies Inc (The)

www.tjx.com

NAIC Code: 448140

TYPES OF BUSINESS:

Discount Apparel Stores
Domestics
Footwear
Jewelry
Home Furnishings
Accessories

BRANDS/DIVISIONS/AFFILIATES:

Marmaxx
HomeGoods
TJX Canada
T J Maxx
Marshalls
Winners
HomeSense
Trade Secret

CONTACTS: *Note: Officers with more than one job title may be intentionally listed here more than once.*

Scott Goldenberg, CFO
Carol Meyrowitz, Chairman of the Board
Richard Sherr, President, Divisional
Kenneth Canestrari, President, Geographical
Michael MacMillan, President, Geographical
Ernie Herrman, President

GROWTH PLANS/SPECIAL FEATURES:

The TJX Companies, Inc. is a low-price apparel and home fashion retailer, operating over 3,800 stores in the U.S. and worldwide. TJX's stores offer merchandise sold at 20% to 60% below department and specialty store regular prices. The firm operates through four major divisions: Marmaxx, made up of T.J. Maxx and Marshalls; HomeGoods, made up of the HomeGoods retail chain; TJX Canada, comprised of Winners, HomeSense and Marshalls; and TJX international, operating T.K. Maxx, HomeSense and Trade Secret. The Marmaxx group is the largest off-price retailer in the U.S., with 2,221 stores. T.J. Maxx and Marshalls stores offer brand-name family apparel, including footwear and accessories, and home fashions, including home basics, accent furniture and giftware. The chains are similar, although Marshalls features a full-line shoe department and larger men's and juniors' departments, while T.J. Maxx carries an extended line of jewelry and accessories. The HomeGoods segment offers discounted home fashions in 579 stores throughout the U.S. TJX Canada operates a total of 255 Winners, 101 HomeSense and 41 Marshalls locations throughout Canada. The TJX international segment operates 503 T.K. Maxx stores in the U.K., Ireland, Poland, Austria, the Netherlands and Germany; 44 HomeSense locations in the U.K.; and 35 Trade Secret stores in Australia. In addition, this segment operates Sierra Trading Post, an off-price internet retailer (sierratradingpost.com) of brand name and quality outdoor gear, family apparel and footwear, sporting goods and home fashions. Sierra Trading Post also operates eight retail stores in the U.S. The company purchases its inventory from over 18,000 vendors worldwide.

TJX offers its employees medical, dental, vision, disability and life insurance; 401(k) & profit sharing plans; auto/home insurance; savings & discount programs; paid vacation; and adoption assistance.

FINANCIAL DATA: *Note: Data for latest year may not have been available at press time.*

In U.S. $	2016	2015	2014	2013	2012	2011
Revenue	30,944,940,000	29,078,410,000	27,422,700,000	25,878,370,000	23,191,460,000	
R&D Expense						
Operating Income	3,704,700,000	3,606,501,000	3,350,570,000	3,106,526,000	2,411,414,000	
Operating Margin %	11.97%	12.40%	12.21%	12.00%	10.39%	
SGA Expense	5,205,715,000	4,695,384,000	4,467,089,000	4,250,446,000	3,890,144,000	
Net Income	2,277,658,000	2,215,128,000	2,137,396,000	1,906,687,000	1,496,090,000	
Operating Cash Flow	2,937,343,000	3,008,369,000	2,590,329,000	3,045,614,000	1,916,034,000	
Capital Expenditure	889,380,000	911,522,000	946,678,000	978,228,000	803,330,000	
EBITDA	4,335,265,000	4,194,239,000	3,914,403,000	3,627,112,000	2,943,798,000	
Return on Assets %	20.13%	20.77%	21.68%	21.43%	18.40%	
Return on Equity %	53.14%	52.15%	54.13%	55.46%	47.42%	
Debt to Equity	0.39	0.39	0.30	0.21	0.24	

CONTACT INFORMATION:

Phone: 508 390-1000   Fax: 508 390-2091
Toll-Free:
Address: 770 Cochituate Rd., Framingham, MA 01701 United States

STOCK TICKER/OTHER:

Stock Ticker: TJX   Exchange: NYS
Employees: 235,000   Fiscal Year Ends: 01/31
Parent Company:

SALARIES/BONUSES:

Top Exec. Salary: $1,525,001   Bonus: $
Second Exec. Salary: Bonus: $
$1,052,309

OTHER THOUGHTS:

Estimated Female Officers or Directors: 4
Hot Spot for Advancement for Women/Minorities: Y

T-Mobile US Inc

NAIC Code: 517210

TYPES OF BUSINESS:

Mobile Phone and Wireless Services
Wireless Internet Services

BRANDS/DIVISIONS/AFFILIATES:

Deutsche Telekom AG
T-Mobile International AG
T-Mobile USA
MetroPCS Communications Inc
T-Mobile Tuesdays
DIGITS

CONTACTS: Note: Officers with more than one job title may be intentionally listed here more than once.

J. Carter, CFO
Timotheus Hottges, Chairman of the Board
Neville Ray, Chief Technology Officer
G. Sievert, COO
John Legere, Director
Elizabeth Sullivan, Executive VP, Divisional
Peter Ewens, Executive VP, Divisional
David Carey, Executive VP, Divisional
David Miller, Executive VP
Thomas Keys, President, Divisional
Peter Osvaldik, Senior VP, Divisional

GROWTH PLANS/SPECIAL FEATURES:

T-Mobile US, Inc. (T-Mobile) is a national provider of wireless voice, messaging and data services, and is one of the largest cellular companies in America. The company represents the combined operations of T-Mobile USA and MetroPCS Communications, Inc. The firm offers wireless service under both the T-Mobile and MetroPCS brands. T-Mobile uses GSM (global system for mobile communications) technology and is a member of the North American GSM Alliance, a group of U.S. and Canadian digital wireless carriers that provide seamless GSM wireless communications for its members in North America and internationally. Along with GSM, the firm uses technology platforms based on HSPA+ (high speed packet access plus), CDMA (code division multiple access) and LTE (long-term evolution) to service over 73 million customers in the postpaid, prepaid and wholesale markets. The company's products include internet and e-mail; games and applications for mobile devices; messaging; voicemail; mobile device wallpapers; music and sounds; and handset protection services in case of loss, theft, malfunction or accidental damage to the product. T-Mobile US operates as a subsidiary of T-Mobile International AG, which itself is the mobile communications subsidiary of Deutsche Telekom AG. In June 2016, T-Mobile launched T-Mobile Tuesdays, a new app that features free prizes for its customers, such as a free pizza from Dominos or a complimentary Lyft ride. In December 2016, the company launched DIGITS, which allows customers to use and operate their T-Mobile number across all connected devices, including tablets, wearables and computers. In May 2017, T-Mobile announced plans for full nationwide 5G coverage by 2020.

FINANCIAL DATA: Note: Data for latest year may not have been available at press time.

In U.S. $	2016	2015	2014	2013	2012	2011
Revenue	37,242,000,000	32,053,000,000	29,564,000,000	24,420,000,000	5,101,278,000	
R&D Expense						
Operating Income	3,802,000,000	2,065,000,000	1,416,000,000	996,000,000	823,969,000	
Operating Margin %	10.20%	6.44%	4.78%	4.07%	16.15%	
SGA Expense	11,378,000,000	10,189,000,000	8,863,000,000	7,382,000,000	696,789,000	
Net Income	1,460,000,000	733,000,000	247,000,000	35,000,000	394,172,000	
Operating Cash Flow	6,135,000,000	5,414,000,000	4,146,000,000	3,545,000,000	1,181,451,000	
Capital Expenditure	8,670,000,000	6,659,000,000	7,217,000,000	4,406,000,000	840,323,000	
EBITDA	10,300,000,000	7,162,000,000	6,176,000,000	4,901,000,000	1,524,377,000	
Return on Assets %						
Return on Equity %						
Debt to Equity	1.50	1.57	1.55	1.18	1.40	

CONTACT INFORMATION:

Phone: 425-378-4000   Fax: 425-378-4040
Toll-Free: 800-318-9270
Address: 12920 SE 38th St., Bellevue, WA 98006-1350 United States

STOCK TICKER/OTHER:

Stock Ticker: TMUS   Exchange: NAS
Employees: 50,000   Fiscal Year Ends: 12/31
Parent Company: Deutsche Telekom AG

SALARIES/BONUSES:

Top Exec. Salary: $1,500,000   Bonus: $
Second Exec. Salary: Bonus: $
$800,000

OTHER THOUGHTS:

Estimated Female Officers or Directors:
Hot Spot for Advancement for Women/Minorities:

Toll Brothers Inc

NAIC Code: 236117

TYPES OF BUSINESS:

Construction, Home Building and Residential
Mortgages & Insurance
Property Management
Landscaping
Country Club Communities
Golf Courses
Security Monitoring
Lumber Distribution

BRANDS/DIVISIONS/AFFILIATES:

CONTACTS: Note: Officers with more than one job title may be intentionally listed here more than once.

Douglas Yearley, CEO
Martin Connor, CFO
Robert Toll, Chairman of the Board
Richard Hartman, COO
Joseph Sicree, Senior VP

GROWTH PLANS/SPECIAL FEATURES:

Toll Brothers, Inc. designs, builds, markets and arranges financing for single-family detached and attached homes in luxury residential communities. The firm is also involved, both directly and through joint ventures, in building or converting existing rental apartment buildings into high-, mid- and low-rise luxury homes. Toll Brothers markets its services to move-up, empty-nester, active-adult, age-qualified and second-home buyers through its operations in 19 U.S. states. The company is present in major suburban and urban residential areas including the Philadelphia, Pennsylvania metropolitan area; Virginia and Maryland suburbs of Washington, D.C.; central and northern New Jersey; Boston, Massachusetts; Westchester, Dutchess and Ulster Counties, New York; San Diego and Palm Springs, California; the San Francisco Bay area; Phoenix, Arizona; Las Vegas and Reno, Nevada; and Chicago, Illinois. The average base sales price of the company's homes is roughly $721,000. Toll Brothers operates its own land development, architectural, engineering, mortgage, title, landscaping, lumber distribution, house component assembly and manufacturing operations. In addition, the company owns and operates golf courses in conjunction with several of its master planned communities. The company operates a portfolio of 543 communities with 48,837 homes sites. In 2016, the firm acquired all the assets of Coleman Real Estate Holdings, LLC, one of the largest home building companies on the Boise market.

The firm offers employees discounts on homes, mortgages, titles, home appliances and kitchen cabinets; life, medical and dental insurance; long- and short-term disability coverage; a 401(k); and educational reimbursement. After two years of service, employees are able to use the company's furnished resort luxury guesthouses for their personal vacations.

FINANCIAL DATA: Note: Data for latest year may not have been available at press time.

In U.S. $	2016	2015	2014	2013	2012	2011
Revenue	5,169,508,000	4,171,248,000	3,911,602,000	2,674,299,000	1,882,781,000	1,475,881,000
R&D Expense						
Operating Income	490,061,000	446,870,000	397,249,000	201,067,000	63,429,000	-47,748,000
Operating Margin %						
SGA Expense	535,382,000	455,108,000	432,516,000	339,932,000	287,257,000	261,355,000
Net Income	382,095,000	363,167,000	340,032,000	170,606,000	487,146,000	39,795,000
Operating Cash Flow	148,771,000	60,182,000	313,200,000	-568,963,000	-168,962,000	52,850,000
Capital Expenditure	28,426,000	9,447,000	15,074,000	26,567,000	14,495,000	9,553,000
EBITDA	612,148,000	559,119,000	528,237,000	292,907,000	135,528,000	-4,720,000
Return on Assets %	4.03%	4.12%	4.46%	2.62%	8.67%	.77%
Return on Equity %	9.04%	8.99%	9.46%	5.28%	17.06%	1.54%
Debt to Equity	0.89	0.89	0.88	0.75	0.72	0.63

CONTACT INFORMATION:

Phone: 215 938-8000   Fax: 215 938-8023
Toll-Free:
Address: 250 Gibraltar Road, Horsham, PA 19044 United States

STOCK TICKER/OTHER:

Stock Ticker: TOL   Exchange: NYS
Employees: 3,500   Fiscal Year Ends: 10/31
Parent Company:

SALARIES/BONUSES:

Top Exec. Salary: $1,000,000   Bonus: $
Second Exec. Salary: Bonus: $
$1,000,000

OTHER THOUGHTS:

Estimated Female Officers or Directors:
Hot Spot for Advancement for Women/Minorities:

Total System Services Inc (TSYS)

www.tsys.com

NAIC Code: 522320

TYPES OF BUSINESS:

Credit Card Processing
Risk Management Tools
Fraud Detection
Debt Collection Services
Printing Services
Customer Relationship Management
Business Process Management

BRANDS/DIVISIONS/AFFILIATES:

China Unionpay Data Services Co Ltd
Columbus Productions Inc
Total System Services de Mexico SA de CV
TSYS Acquiring Solutions LLC
TransFirst

CONTACTS: *Note: Officers with more than one job title may be intentionally listed here more than once.*

M. Woods, CEO
Paul Todd, CFO
Dorenda Weaver, Chief Accounting Officer
Patricia Watson, Chief Information Officer
Pamela Joseph, Director
G. Griffith, Secretary
William Pruett, Senior Executive VP

GROWTH PLANS/SPECIAL FEATURES:

Total System Services, Inc. (TSYS) is one of the world's largest electronic payment processors of consumer credit, retail, debit, stored value, government services and commercial card accounts for financial and non-financial institutions. TSYS serves clients throughout the Americas, Africa, Europe, the Middle East and the Asia Pacific region. The company also offers value-added products and services, including risk management tools and techniques like fraud detection and prevention and behavior analysis tools as well as revenue enhancement tools, such as customer relationship management (CRM) and client advising. TSYS's operations are divided into four segments: North America services, accounting for approximately 47% of revenues; merchant services, accounting for 20%; international services, accounting for 12%; and NetSpend, accounting for 21%. Merchant services include processing services, acquiring applications, related systems and integrated support services. NetSpend provides general purpose reloadable prepaid debit and payroll cards to underbanked and other consumers in the U.S. The company also offers additional services, such as business process management, mail and correspondence processing, teleservicing, data documentation, offset printing, collections and account solicitation and client services. The firm's subsidiaries include Columbus Productions, Inc., which provides commercial printing and finishing solutions; and TSYS Acquiring Solutions, L.L.C., a supplier of transaction processing, related systems and integrated support services. The company also owns a 49% equity interest in a joint venture company called Total System Services de Mexico, S.A. de C.V. as well as a 44.5% interest in China Unionpay Data Services Co., Ltd. In April 2016, TSYS completed its acquisition of TransFirst, a U.S. merchant services provider.

The company offers U.S. employees life, AD&D, disability, medical, dental and vision insurance; flexible spending accounts; and adoption assistance.

FINANCIAL DATA: *Note: Data for latest year may not have been available at press time.*

In U.S. $	2016	2015	2014	2013	2012	2011
Revenue	4,170,077,000	2,779,541,000	2,446,877,000	2,132,353,000	1,870,972,000	1,808,966,000
R&D Expense						
Operating Income	573,382,000	534,107,000	431,640,000	386,247,000	357,652,000	322,456,000
Operating Margin %	13.74%	19.21%	17.64%	18.11%	19.11%	17.82%
SGA Expense	603,633,000	390,253,000	343,128,000	295,555,000	251,010,000	228,540,000
Net Income	319,638,000	364,044,000	322,872,000	244,750,000	244,280,000	220,559,000
Operating Cash Flow	717,909,000	600,194,000	560,201,000	452,398,000	455,753,000	436,319,000
Capital Expenditure	142,573,000	203,316,000	235,923,000	137,833,000	118,065,000	95,945,000
EBITDA	950,123,000	795,853,000	679,658,000	591,598,000	525,464,000	488,916,000
Return on Assets %	6.19%	9.44%	8.61%	8.57%	12.58%	11.57%
Return on Equity %	16.13%	20.41%	19.52%	16.28%	17.91%	17.35%
Debt to Equity	1.57	0.75	0.83	0.90	0.13	0.04

CONTACT INFORMATION:

Phone: 706 649-2310   Fax: 706 649-2456
Toll-Free:
Address: One TSYS Way, Columbus, GA 31901 United States

STOCK TICKER/OTHER:

Stock Ticker: TSS   Exchange: NYS
Employees: 11,500   Fiscal Year Ends: 12/31
Parent Company:

SALARIES/BONUSES:

Top Exec. Salary: $869,000   Bonus: $
Second Exec. Salary: Bonus: $300,000
$451,845

OTHER THOUGHTS:

Estimated Female Officers or Directors: 3
Hot Spot for Advancement for Women/Minorities: Y

Sales, profits and employees may be estimates. Financial information, benefits and other data can change quickly and may vary from those stated here.

Toyota Motor Sales USA Inc (TMS)   www.toyota.com/usa/operations

NAIC Code: 336111

TYPES OF BUSINESS:

Automobile Manufacturing

BRANDS/DIVISIONS/AFFILIATES:

Toyota Motor Corporation
Toyota Motor Manufacturing Alabama Inc
Toyota Motor Manufacturing Indiana Inc
Toyota Motor Manufacturing Kentucky Inc
Toyota Motor Manufacturing Mississippi Inc
Toyota Motor Manufacturing Texas Inc
Toyota Motor Manufacturing West Virginia Inc
Toyota Auto Body California Inc

CONTACTS: Note: Officers with more than one job title may be intentionally listed here more than once.

James Lentz, CEO
Michael Groff, Pres.

GROWTH PLANS/SPECIAL FEATURES:

Toyota Motor Sales, USA, Inc.'s operations include Toyota Motor Engineering & Manufacturing North America, Inc. (TEMA), which is responsible for the engineering design and development, R&D and manufacturing activities in the U.S., Mexico and Canada for Toyota. The firm operates through various subsidiaries that together operate 10 factories/plants in the U.S. and manufactures 13 different models. Toyota Motor Manufacturing, Alabama, Inc. is an engine plant that produces engines for the Tacoma, Tundra, Sequoia, Camry, RAV4, Venza and Highlander. Toyota Motor Manufacturing, Indiana, Inc. manufactures approximately 350,000 of the Sequoia, Highlander, Highlander Hybrid and Sienna each year. Toyota Motor Manufacturing, Kentucky, Inc. is the largest North American manufacturing facility and produces over 550,000 vehicles each year, including the Avalon, Avalon Hybrid, Camry, Camry Hybrid, Venza and Lexus ES. Toyota Motor Manufacturing, Mississippi, Inc. is TEMA's newest plant and assembles the Corolla model. Toyota Motor Manufacturing, Texas, Inc. manufactures the Tundra and Tacoma Pickups and is the first plant to integrate production facilities for many of its suppliers on the same grounds. Toyota Motor Manufacturing, West Virginia, Inc. produces engines and transmissions for vehicles such as the Camry, Lexus RX350, Matrix, Corolla and Highlander. Toyota Auto Body California, Inc., acting primarily as a supplier of parts for Tacoma trucks, was TEMA's first manufacturing facility in the U.S. Bodine Aluminum, Inc., with plants in St. Louis and Troy, Missouri and Jackson, Tennessee, produces engine and transmission components for use in all U.S. manufacturing facilities. Finally, in collaboration with Subaru's parent company, Fuji Heavy Industries, Ltd., Subaru of Indiana Automotive, Inc. assembles the Camry model. In total, Toyota produced about 1.38 million vehicles in the U.S. in 2016. In 2017, the firm moved its headquarters to Plano, Texas.

FINANCIAL DATA: Note: Data for latest year may not have been available at press time.

In U.S. $	2016	2015	2014	2013	2012	2011
Revenue	98,245,124,503	93,053,000,000	78,110,000,000	61,283,000,000	46,338,000,000	52,941,000,000
R&D Expense						
Operating Income						
Operating Margin %						
SGA Expense						
Net Income						
Operating Cash Flow						
Capital Expenditure						
EBITDA						
Return on Assets %						
Return on Equity %						
Debt to Equity						

CONTACT INFORMATION:

Phone: 888-255-3154   Fax:
Toll-Free:
Address: 1001 Preston Rd., Plano, TX 75093 United States

STOCK TICKER/OTHER:

Stock Ticker: Subsidiary   Exchange:
Employees: 44,256   Fiscal Year Ends: 03/31
Parent Company: Toyota Motor Corporation

SALARIES/BONUSES:

Top Exec. Salary: $ Bonus: $
Second Exec. Salary: $ Bonus: $

OTHER THOUGHTS:

Estimated Female Officers or Directors:
Hot Spot for Advancement for Women/Minorities:

Trader Joe's Company Inc

NAIC Code: 445110

www.traderjoes.com

TYPES OF BUSINESS:

Grocery Stores
Specialty Groceries
Vitamins & Dietary Supplements
Organic Foods

BRANDS/DIVISIONS/AFFILIATES:

ALDI Group

CONTACTS: *Note: Officers with more than one job title may be intentionally listed here more than once.*

Daniel T. Bane, CEO
Charles Pillitier, Sr. VP-Oper.
Brandt Sharrock, VP-Real Estate
Daniel T. Bane, Chmn.

GROWTH PLANS/SPECIAL FEATURES:

Trader Joe's Company, Inc. operates a chain of approximately 459 company-owned and -operated specialty grocery stores in over 40 states and Washington, D.C., with about half of its stores located in California, where the company was founded. Although the stores sell some brand-name products, the vast majority of the selection is comprised of more than 3,000 Trader Joe's private-label products, including specialty vegetarian, kosher, organic food and vitamin supplement products as well as regional fare, such as Thai and Mexican foods. Prices tend to be comparable to or lower than traditional groceries, as a result of Trader Joe's efforts to buy many items and ingredients directly from suppliers and the chain's focus on its private label lines. The company also keeps costs down by eliminating service departments and using spaces of 15,000 square feet or less for its stores. Selections and inventory tend to vary from state to state and store to store because of the company's commitment to experimentation, regional and seasonal products and bringing variety to its customers. The firm is owned by a trust created by Theo Albrecht, co-founder of German supermarket chain ALDI Group.

Trader Joe's offers employees medical, dental and vision insurance; a company-paid retirement plan; a 10% employee discount; and paid time off. Medical, dental and vision coverage is available to both full and part-time employees of the firm.

FINANCIAL DATA: *Note: Data for latest year may not have been available at press time.*

In U.S. $	2016	2015	2014	2013	2012	2011
Revenue	12,500,000,000	12,000,000,000	11,000,000,000	9,725,000,000	9,500,000,000	9,000,000,000
R&D Expense						
Operating Income						
Operating Margin %						
SGA Expense						
Net Income						
Operating Cash Flow						
Capital Expenditure						
EBITDA						
Return on Assets %						
Return on Equity %						
Debt to Equity						

CONTACT INFORMATION:

Phone: 626-599-3700   Fax: 626-301-4431
Toll-Free:
Address: 800 S. Shamrock Ave., Monrovia, CA 91016 United States

STOCK TICKER/OTHER:

Stock Ticker: Subsidiary   Exchange:
Employees: 41,000   Fiscal Year Ends: 06/30
Parent Company: ALDI Group

SALARIES/BONUSES:

Top Exec. Salary: $ Bonus: $
Second Exec. Salary: $ Bonus: $

OTHER THOUGHTS:

Estimated Female Officers or Directors: 2
Hot Spot for Advancement for Women/Minorities:

TransDigm Group Incorporated

NAIC Code: 336413

www.transdigm.com

TYPES OF BUSINESS:

Aircraft Control Surface Assemblies Manufacturing
Aftermarket Aircraft Parts

BRANDS/DIVISIONS/AFFILIATES:

SCHROTH Safety Products GmbH

CONTACTS: *Note: Officers with more than one job title may be intentionally listed here more than once.*

W. Howley, CEO
Terry Paradie, CFO
Kevin Stein, COO
Peter Palmer, Executive VP
John Leary, Executive VP
Jorge Valladares, Executive VP
Joel Reiss, Executive VP
Roger Jones, Executive VP
James Skulina, Executive VP
Bernt Iversen, Executive VP, Divisional
Robert Henderson, Vice Chairman

GROWTH PLANS/SPECIAL FEATURES:

TransDigm Group Incorporated designs, produces and supplies highly-engineered proprietary aerospace components and subsystems for use in both commercial and military aircraft. Its products are designed and manufactured through a network of 34 subsidiaries and sold almost entirely to global aerospace customers. Roughly 54% of revenues are generated from aftermarket sales, primarily to the commercial and military aftermarkets, and 90% of sales are estimated to be from proprietary products. Primary offerings include mechanical /electro-mechanical actuators and controls; ignition systems and components; gear pumps; engineered connectors; power conditioning devices; specialized fluorescent lighting; specialized AC/DC electric motors and components; engineered latching and locking devices; lavatory hardware and components; open cowlings; specialized cockpit displays; elastic polymers for use in various clamping and heating applications; and nickel-cadmium batteries and battery chargers. Each of these broad product categories typically consists of an assortment of individual products that are customized by TransDigm to meet the needs of a particular aircraft platform or customer. The firm's customers include distributors of aerospace components; worldwide commercial airlines, including national and regional airlines; large commercial transport and regional and business aircraft original equipment manufacturers (OEMs); various armed forces of both U.S. and foreign governments; defense OEMs; system suppliers; and various other industrial customers. In 2017, the firm acquired Takata Corporation's SCHROTH Safety Products GmbH, as well as certain aviation and defense assets and liability for approximately $90 million.

FINANCIAL DATA: *Note: Data for latest year may not have been available at press time.*

In U.S. $	2016	2015	2014	2013	2012	2011
Revenue	3,171,411,000	2,707,115,000	2,372,906,000	1,924,400,000	1,700,208,000	1,206,021,000
R&D Expense						
Operating Income	1,267,760,000	1,074,002,000	927,820,000	749,455,000	699,775,000	487,135,000
Operating Margin %	39.97%	39.67%	39.10%	38.94%	41.15%	40.39%
SGA Expense	382,858,000	321,624,000	276,446,000	254,468,000	201,709,000	133,711,000
Net Income	586,414,000	447,212,000	306,910,000	302,789,000	324,969,000	172,134,000
Operating Cash Flow	668,930,000	520,938,000	541,222,000	470,205,000	413,885,000	260,578,000
Capital Expenditure	43,982,000	54,871,000	34,146,000	35,535,000	25,246,000	18,026,000
EBITDA	1,389,430,000	1,167,665,000	1,024,205,000	822,970,000	768,002,000	475,141,000
Return on Assets %	6.09%	5.84%	2.79%	2.26%	6.45%	4.78%
Return on Equity %				29.81%	31.69%	24.52%
Debt to Equity					2.95	3.85

CONTACT INFORMATION:

Phone: 216 706-2960   Fax: 216 706-2937
Toll-Free:
Address: The Tower at Erieview, 1301 E. 9th St., Ste. 3000, Cleveland, OH 44114 United States

STOCK TICKER/OTHER:

Stock Ticker: TDG
Employees: 9,300
Parent Company:

Exchange: NYS
Fiscal Year Ends: 09/30

SALARIES/BONUSES:

Top Exec. Salary: $611,250   Bonus: $23,328
Second Exec. Salary: $498,750   Bonus: $14,834

OTHER THOUGHTS:

Estimated Female Officers or Directors:
Hot Spot for Advancement for Women/Minorities:

Sales, profits and employees may be estimates. Financial information, benefits and other data can change quickly and may vary from those stated here.

Travelers Companies Inc (The)

NAIC Code: 524126

www.travelers.com

TYPES OF BUSINESS:

Direct Property & Casualty Insurance
Reinsurance
Automobile & Homeowners' Insurance
General Liability & Commercial Multi-Peril Insurance
Marine Insurance
Risk Management Services

BRANDS/DIVISIONS/AFFILIATES:

National Property
Inland Marine
Ocean Marine
Boiler & Machinery
Simply Business

CONTACTS: Note: Officers with more than one job title may be intentionally listed here more than once.

Alan Schnitzer, CEO
William Heyman, Other Executive Officer
Jay Benet, CFO
Douglas Russell, Chief Accounting Officer
Andy Bessette, Chief Administrative Officer
Brian MacLean, COO
John Dasburg, Director
Maria Olivo, Executive VP, Divisional
Kenneth Spence, Executive VP
Michael Klein, Executive VP
John Clifford, Executive VP
Gregory Toczydlowski, Executive VP
Thomas Kunkel, Executive VP
Avrohom Kess, Other Executive Officer

GROWTH PLANS/SPECIAL FEATURES:

The Travelers Companies, Inc. is a holding company principally engaged in providing commercial and personal property and casualty (P&C) insurance products and services to businesses, government units, associations and individuals. The company operates in three segments: business & international insurance (BII), bond & specialty insurance (BSI) and personal insurance. BII offers an array of P&C insurance and insurance related services to its clients, primarily in the U.S., as well as in Canada, the U.K., Ireland and other select parts of the world. Domestically, this segment provides small-, mid- and large-sized businesses with P&C products, including multi-peril, commercial property, general liability, commercial auto and workers' compensation insurance. It provides traditional and customized property insurance programs to large- and mid-sized customers through National Property; builders' risk insurance through Inland Marine; international trade services through Ocean Marine; and comprehensive breakdown coverages for equipment through Boiler & Machinery. Internationally, the BII segment offers P&C insurance and risk management services to customers in the technology, public services, financial and professional services sectors. BSI provides surety, crime, management and professional liability coverages and risk management services to primarily domestic customers, utilizing various degrees of financially-based underwriting approaches. The personal insurance segment writes a broad range of P&C insurance covering individual's personal risks. The primary products within this segment include automobile and homeowner's insurance. In March 2017, the firm agreed to acquire Simply Business, a distributor of small business insurance policies in the U.K., from Aquiline Capital Partners LLC for an enterprise value of approximately $490 million.

FINANCIAL DATA: Note: Data for latest year may not have been available at press time.

In U.S. $	2016	2015	2014	2013	2012	2011
Revenue	27,625,000,000	26,800,000,000	27,162,000,000	26,191,000,000	25,740,000,000	25,446,000,000
R&D Expense						
Operating Income	4,053,000,000	4,740,000,000	5,089,000,000	4,945,000,000	3,166,000,000	1,352,000,000
Operating Margin %	14.67%	17.68%	18.73%	18.88%	12.29%	5.31%
SGA Expense	4,154,000,000	4,079,000,000	3,952,000,000	3,757,000,000	3,610,000,000	3,556,000,000
Net Income	3,014,000,000	3,439,000,000	3,692,000,000	3,673,000,000	2,473,000,000	1,426,000,000
Operating Cash Flow	4,202,000,000	3,434,000,000	3,693,000,000	3,816,000,000	3,230,000,000	2,169,000,000
Capital Expenditure						
EBITDA						
Return on Assets %	2.98%	3.35%	3.54%	3.49%	2.34%	1.34%
Return on Equity %	12.78%	14.09%	14.76%	14.52%	9.83%	5.66%
Debt to Equity	0.27	0.26	0.25	0.25	0.22	0.25

CONTACT INFORMATION:

Phone: 917 778-6000   Fax:
Toll-Free: 800-328-2189
Address: 485 Lexington Ave., New York, NY 10017 United States

STOCK TICKER/OTHER:

Stock Ticker: TRV   Exchange: NYS
Employees: 30,900   Fiscal Year Ends: 12/31
Parent Company:

SALARIES/BONUSES:

Top Exec. Salary: $553,831   Bonus: $3,825,000
Second Exec. Salary: Bonus: $
$1,000,000

OTHER THOUGHTS:

Estimated Female Officers or Directors: 7
Hot Spot for Advancement for Women/Minorities: Y

TreeHouse Foods Inc

www.treehousefoods.com

NAIC Code: 311421

TYPES OF BUSINESS:
Food Manufacturing & Distribution

BRANDS/DIVISIONS/AFFILIATES:
Bay Valley Foods LLC
Sturm Foods
S T Foods
Cains
Associated Brands Inc
Protenergy Natural Foods Inc
Flagstone foods
TreeHouse Private Brands

CONTACTS: *Note: Officers with more than one job title may be intentionally listed here more than once.*
Sam Reed, CEO
Matthew Foulston, CFO
Thomas ONeill, Chief Administrative Officer
David Vermylen, Director
Rachel Bishop, Other Executive Officer
Dennis Riordan, President
Erik Kahler, Senior VP, Divisional
Lori Roberts, Senior VP, Divisional

GROWTH PLANS/SPECIAL FEATURES:
TreeHouse Foods, Inc. is a food manufacturer servicing primarily the retail grocery and foodservice distribution industry. The firm operates through its U.S. subsidiaries Bay Valley Foods LLC; Sturm Foods; S.T. Foods; Cains; Associated Brands, Inc.; Protenergy Natural Foods, Inc.; Flagstone Foods; TreeHouse Private Brands, Inc.; American Italian Pasta Company; Nutcracker Brands, Inc.; Linette Quality Chocolates, Inc.; Ralcorp Frozen Bakery Products, Inc.; Cottage Bakery, Inc.; and The Carriage House Companies, Inc. Its Canadian subsidiaries include E.D. Smith Income Fund, ABI Canada and Protenergy Canada. The company's products include salad dressings and sauces, non-dairy powdered and liquid coffee creamer, Mexican sauces, pickles and jams and pie fillings. The firm manufactures these products under private labels for retailers such as mass merchandisers and supermarkets. TreeHouse Foods also markets its products to the foodservice industry, industrial customers who use the firm's products as ingredients in other products or repackage them in portion control packages and sells items under its own brands, primarily on a regional basis to retail customers. The company operates in three segments: North American retail grocery, food away from home and industrial & export. The North American retail grocery division sells branded and private label products to customers within the U.S. and Canada under brand names such as Bennett's, Hoffman House, Farman's and Peter Piper. The food away from home segment sells products such as pickles, salsas, non-dairy powdered creamers and aseptic and refrigerated products to the U.S. and Canadian food service industries under the labels Schwartz and Saucemaker. TreeHouse Foods' industrial & export group offers co-pack business and non-dairy powdered creamers for use in industrial applications. In May 2017, the firm completed the sale of its Soup and Infant Feeding business to Riverbend Foods, LLC, a newly formed portfolio company of Insight Equity.

FINANCIAL DATA: *Note: Data for latest year may not have been available at press time.*

In U.S. $	2016	2015	2014	2013	2012	2011
Revenue	6,175,088,000	3,206,405,000	2,946,102,000	2,293,927,000	2,182,125,000	2,049,985,000
R&D Expense						
Operating Income	-96,792,000	239,736,000	218,154,000	178,164,000	176,827,000	188,275,000
Operating Margin %	-1.56%	7.47%	7.40%	7.76%	8.10%	9.18%
SGA Expense	745,336,000	342,152,000	333,395,000	256,063,000	239,752,000	244,158,000
Net Income	-228,594,000	114,910,000	89,880,000	86,988,000	88,363,000	94,407,000
Operating Cash Flow	478,613,000	285,318,000	211,957,000	216,690,000	204,559,000	156,071,000
Capital Expenditure	187,075,000	86,096,000	99,218,000	81,183,000	79,520,000	77,796,000
EBITDA	212,030,000	338,805,000	294,521,000	282,856,000	274,033,000	275,839,000
Return on Assets %	-4.46%	3.02%	2.71%	3.31%	3.58%	3.93%
Return on Equity %	-10.49%	6.35%	5.92%	7.09%	7.84%	9.20%
Debt to Equity	1.08	0.65	0.82	0.73	0.76	0.84

CONTACT INFORMATION:
Phone: 708 483-1300   Fax:
Toll-Free:
Address: 2021 Spring Rd., Ste. 600, Oakbrook, IL 60523 United States

STOCK TICKER/OTHER:
Stock Ticker: THS
Employees: 16,027
Parent Company:

Exchange: NYS
Fiscal Year Ends: 12/31

SALARIES/BONUSES:
Top Exec. Salary: $1,056,250   Bonus: $
Second Exec. Salary: $578,468   Bonus: $

OTHER THOUGHTS:
Estimated Female Officers or Directors: 3
Hot Spot for Advancement for Women/Minorities: Y

Trimble Navigation Ltd

www.trimble.com

NAIC Code: 334511

TYPES OF BUSINESS:

GPS Technologies
Surveying & Mapping Equipment
Navigation Tools
Autopilot Systems
Data Collection Products
Fleet Management Systems
Outdoor Recreation Information Service
Telecommunications & Automotive Components

BRANDS/DIVISIONS/AFFILIATES:

Embedded Technologies
Applanix
Trimble Outdoors
Sefaira Ltd
AXIO-NET GmbH
Beena Vision Systems Inc
Savcor Oy
Silvadata

CONTACTS: Note: Officers with more than one job title may be intentionally listed here more than once.

Steven Berglund, CEO
Robert Painter, CFO
Julie Shepard, Chief Accounting Officer
Ulf Johansson, Director
Nickolas Vande Steeg, Director
Sachin Sankpal, Other Corporate Officer
Darryl Matthews, Senior VP, Divisional
Christopher Gibson, Senior VP, Divisional
Bryn Fosburgh, Senior VP, Divisional
James Kirkland, Senior VP
Jurgen Kliem, Vice President, Divisional
James Veneziano, Vice President, Divisional

GROWTH PLANS/SPECIAL FEATURES:

Trimble Navigation, Ltd. provides global positioning products to industrial, commercial, governmental and agricultural customers. With offices in 27 countries, the firm operates in four segments: engineering/construction, field solutions, mobile solutions and advanced devices. Engineering and construction products incorporate global positioning systems (GPS); optical, global navigation satellite systems (GNSS); and radio, laser and cellular technologies to facilitate precise surveying, site preparation and interior measurement by small crews. The field solutions segment offers handheld geographic information system (GIS) data collectors for fieldwork and manual and automated navigation systems for tractors and other agricultural equipment. The mobile solutions segment offers a fleet management tool for large enterprise clients, consisting of vehicle-mounted hardware together with a web-based subscription service. The combined businesses within the advanced devices segment are hardware centric, generally rely on original equipment manufacturer (OEM) distribution and have products that can be utilized in a number of different end-user markets. Products sold by this segment include the product lines from the company's Embedded Technologies, Applanix, Military and Advanced Systems (MAS) and Timing businesses. In 2016, the company made two acquisitions: Sefaira Ltd., a leading provider of software for high-performance building design; and AXIO-NET GmbH, a provider of GNSS corrections and professional data services. In 2017, Trimble acquired Beena Vision Systems, Inc., a manufacturer of vision-based automatic wayside inspection systems for the railroad industry; Savcor Oy, an international supplier of forestry solutions for enterprise management and performance optimization; and Silvadata, a provider of cloud-based data, workflow automation and collaboration services.

Employee benefits include medical, dental and vision coverage; life and AD&D insurance; 401(k); an employee stock purchase plan; profit sharing; health care and dependent care flexible spending accounts; short- and long-term disability; business travel accident insurance; and an employee assistance program.

FINANCIAL DATA: Note: Data for latest year may not have been available at press time.

In U.S. $	2016	2015	2014	2013	2012	2011
Revenue	2,362,200,000	2,290,400,000	2,395,546,000	2,288,124,000	2,040,113,000	1,644,065,000
R&D Expense	349,600,000	336,700,000	317,992,000	299,421,000	256,458,000	197,007,000
Operating Income	181,000,000	154,400,000	260,823,000	251,737,000	212,568,000	156,402,000
Operating Margin %	7.66%	6.74%	10.88%	11.00%	10.41%	9.51%
SGA Expense	633,600,000	629,900,000	634,689,000	564,982,000	509,494,000	425,179,000
Net Income	132,400,000	121,100,000	214,118,000	218,855,000	191,060,000	150,755,000
Operating Cash Flow	407,100,000	354,900,000	407,083,000	414,635,000	340,700,000	241,629,000
Capital Expenditure	26,300,000	44,000,000	54,945,000	70,877,000	55,241,000	24,944,000
EBITDA	368,800,000	376,500,000	452,464,000	441,314,000	395,179,000	281,764,000
Return on Assets %	3.60%	3.20%	5.65%	6.10%	6.24%	6.67%
Return on Equity %	5.85%	5.29%	9.35%	10.62%	11.02%	10.27%
Debt to Equity	0.21	0.27	0.28	0.29	0.46	0.31

CONTACT INFORMATION:

Phone: 408 481-8000   Fax: 408 481-2218
Toll-Free: 800-874-6253
Address: 935 Stewart Dr., Sunnyvale, CA 94085 United States

SALARIES/BONUSES:

Top Exec. Salary: $860,000   Bonus: $
Second Exec. Salary: Bonus: $
$433,287

STOCK TICKER/OTHER:

Stock Ticker: TRMB   Exchange: NAS
Employees: 8,388   Fiscal Year Ends: 12/31
Parent Company:

OTHER THOUGHTS:

Estimated Female Officers or Directors: 5
Hot Spot for Advancement for Women/Minorities: Y

Trinity Health

www.trinity-health.org

NAIC Code: 622110

TYPES OF BUSINESS:

General Medical and Surgical Hospitals
Assisted Living Facilities
Hospice Programs
Senior Housing Communities
Management & Consulting Services

BRANDS/DIVISIONS/AFFILIATES:

Senior Emergency Departments

CONTACTS: *Note: Officers with more than one job title may be intentionally listed here more than once.*

Richard J. Gilfillan, CEO
Michael A. Slubowski, Pres.
Benjamin R. Carter, Exec.VP
Edmund F. Hodge, Chief Human Resource Officer
P. Terrence O'Rourke, Exec. VP-Clinical Transformation
Benjamin R. Carter, Exec. VP-Finance
James Bosscher, Chief Investment Officer
Paul Conlon, Sr. VP-Clinical Quality & Patient Safety
Rebecca Havlisch, Chief Nursing Officer
Louis Fierens, Sr. VP-Supply Chain & Capital Projects Mgmt.

GROWTH PLANS/SPECIAL FEATURES:

Trinity Health is one of the nation's largest multi-institutional Catholic healthcare delivery systems, serving patients and communities in 22 states. Trinity Health operates 93 hospitals, 121 continuing care facilities, which include home care, hospice, PACE and senior living facilities that provide nearly 2 visits annually. The organization returns approximately $1 billion to its communities annually in the form of charity care and other community benefits programs. Trinity Health is known for its focus on the country's aging population, and is the innovator of Senior Emergency Departments, the largest non-profit provider of home healthcare services in the nation. Trinity Health is also the nation's leading provider of PACE (Program of All-inclusive Care for the Elderly) based on the number of available programs.

The firm offers employees health and dental coverage, short- and long-term disability, paid time-off, life insurance, flexible spending accounts, 403(b) and 401(k) plans, tuition reimbursement and professional education as well as adoption assistance.

FINANCIAL DATA: *Note: Data for latest year may not have been available at press time.*

In U.S. $	2016	2015	2014	2013	2012	2011
Revenue	15,900,000,000	14,388,150,000	13,600,000,000	8,978,385,000	8,469,453,000	
R&D Expense						
Operating Income						
Operating Margin %						
SGA Expense						
Net Income	700,000,000	671,630,000	951,405,000	666,439,000	367,053,000	
Operating Cash Flow						
Capital Expenditure						
EBITDA						
Return on Assets %						
Return on Equity %						
Debt to Equity						

CONTACT INFORMATION:

Phone: 734-343-1000   Fax:
Toll-Free:
Address: 20555 Victor Parkway, Livonia, MI 48152-7018 United States

STOCK TICKER/OTHER:

Stock Ticker: Nonprofit   Exchange:
Employees: 97,000   Fiscal Year Ends: 06/30
Parent Company:

SALARIES/BONUSES:

Top Exec. Salary: $ Bonus: $
Second Exec. Salary: $ Bonus: $

OTHER THOUGHTS:

Estimated Female Officers or Directors: 4
Hot Spot for Advancement for Women/Minorities: Y

Trustmark Companies

www.trustmarkins.com

NAIC Code: 524113

TYPES OF BUSINESS:

Life Insurance
Health Insurance
Employee Benefits Management

BRANDS/DIVISIONS/AFFILIATES:

CoreSource
Starmark
HealthFitness Corporation

CONTACTS: Note: Officers with more than one job title may be intentionally listed here more than once.

Joseph L. Pray, CEO
Phil Goss, CFO
Jim Coleman, CMO
Krsitin Zelkowitz, Chief Human Resources Officer
Dan Simpson, CIO

GROWTH PLANS/SPECIAL FEATURES:

Trustmark Companies offer health and life insurance and benefits administration services to employer groups through three major operating subsidiaries. These subsidiaries include CoreSource, Starmark and HealthFitness Corporation. CoreSource is one of the nation's largest employee benefit administrators, managing health care for over 1.1 million people across the U.S. It serves self-insured employers with claims administration, case management, provider network development, information management, fraud detection, COBRA administration and prescription-drug benefit administration. Starmark serves the health and life insurance needs of employers for smaller businesses with 2 to 99 employees. HealthFitness offers onsite and web-based workplace programs that help improve employee health and fitness. HealthFitness programs include medical screenings, risk assessment, corporate fitness, health management and coaching. In total, Trustmark Companies has over 2 million covered plan participants. In September 2016, HealthFitness announced a strategic partnership with WELLBEATS, a leading provider of virtual fitness programs, in which WELLBEATS programs will be available to employers.

FINANCIAL DATA: Note: Data for latest year may not have been available at press time.

In U.S. $	2016	2015	2014	2013	2012	2011
Revenue	915,002,500	882,683,041	917,505,556	947,327,068	932,700,000	963,300,000
R&D Expense						
Operating Income						
Operating Margin %						
SGA Expense						
Net Income	9,522,536	8,645,781	11,716,081	29,017,258		
Operating Cash Flow						
Capital Expenditure						
EBITDA						
Return on Assets %						
Return on Equity %						
Debt to Equity						

CONTACT INFORMATION:

Phone: 847-615-1500   Fax: 847-615-3910
Toll-Free:
Address: 400 Field Dr., Lake Forest, IL 60045 United States

STOCK TICKER/OTHER:

Stock Ticker: Mutual Company   Exchange:
Employees: 4,350   Fiscal Year Ends: 12/31
Parent Company:

SALARIES/BONUSES:

Top Exec. Salary: $ Bonus: $
Second Exec. Salary: $ Bonus: $

OTHER THOUGHTS:

Estimated Female Officers or Directors:
Hot Spot for Advancement for Women/Minorities: Y

Tutor Perini Corporation

www.tutorperini.com

NAIC Code: 237310

TYPES OF BUSINESS:

Construction Services
Hospitality & Casino Construction
Construction Management Services
Civic & Infrastructure Construction
Design Services

BRANDS/DIVISIONS/AFFILIATES:

CONTACTS:
Note: Officers with more than one job title may be intentionally listed here more than once.

Leonard Rejcek, CEO, Divisional
Ronald Tutor, CEO
Gary Smalley, CFO
Ryan Soroka, Chief Accounting Officer
James Frost, COO
Michael Klein, Director
John Barrett, Secretary

GROWTH PLANS/SPECIAL FEATURES:

Tutor Perini Corporation and its subsidiaries provide general contracting, construction management and design-build services worldwide. It operates in three segments: building, civil and specialty contractors. The building segment focuses on large, complex projects in the hospitality and gaming, transportation, health care, municipal offices, sports and entertainment, education, correctional facilities, biotech, pharmaceutical, industrial and high-tech markets. The civil segment focuses on public works construction, including the new construction, repair, replacement and reconstruction of public infrastructure such as highways, bridges, mass transit systems and wastewater treatment facilities. The company's customers primarily award contracts through the public competitive bid, in which price is the major determining factor; or through a request for proposals, where contracts are awarded based on a combination of technical capability and price. The specialty contractors segment engages in electrical, mechanical, HVAC (heating, ventilation and air conditioning), plumbing and pneumatically paced concrete for construction projects in the commercial, industrial, hospitality, transportation and gaming markets.

The firm offers employees medical, dental, vision and life insurance; a flexible spending account; an employee assistance program; educational assistance; and reimbursement on health club memberships.

FINANCIAL DATA:
Note: Data for latest year may not have been available at press time.

In U.S. $	2016	2015	2014	2013	2012	2011
Revenue	4,973,076,000	4,920,472,000	4,492,309,000	4,175,672,000	4,111,471,000	3,716,317,000
R&D Expense						
Operating Income	201,920,000	105,413,000	241,690,000	203,822,000	-221,811,000	168,376,000
Operating Margin %	4.06%	2.14%	5.38%	4.88%	-5.39%	4.53%
SGA Expense	255,270,000	250,840,000	263,752,000	263,082,000	260,369,000	226,965,000
Net Income	95,822,000	45,292,000	107,936,000	87,296,000	-265,400,000	86,148,000
Operating Cash Flow	113,336,000	14,072,000	-56,678,000	50,728,000	-67,863,000	-30,524,000
Capital Expenditure	15,743,000	35,912,000	75,013,000	42,360,000	41,352,000	66,747,000
EBITDA	276,199,000	161,595,000	288,126,000	244,657,000	-162,211,000	220,428,000
Return on Assets %	2.37%	1.15%	3.01%	2.60%	-7.68%	2.69%
Return on Equity %	6.44%	3.25%	8.26%	7.30%	-20.86%	6.35%
Debt to Equity	0.43	0.51	0.57	0.49	0.58	0.43

CONTACT INFORMATION:

Phone: 818 362-8391   Fax:
Toll-Free:
Address: 15901 Olden Street, Sylmar, CA 91342 United States

STOCK TICKER/OTHER:

Stock Ticker: TPC   Exchange: NYS
Employees: 11,603   Fiscal Year Ends: 12/31
Parent Company:

SALARIES/BONUSES:

Top Exec. Salary: $1,750,000   Bonus: $
Second Exec. Salary: Bonus: $250,000
$1,000,000

OTHER THOUGHTS:

Estimated Female Officers or Directors:
Hot Spot for Advancement for Women/Minorities:

Uber Inc

NAIC Code: 561599

TYPES OF BUSINESS:

Car Ride Dispatch Service, Mobile App-Based
Freight Truck Dispatch Service
Restaurant Meal Delivery Service
Transportation Marketplace Technologies
Self-Driving Truck Technologies
Self-Driving Car Technologies

BRANDS/DIVISIONS/AFFILIATES:

UberX
Uber
Uber Freight
Otto
UberEATS

CONTACTS: *Note: Officers with more than one job title may be intentionally listed here more than once.*

Travis Kalanick, CEO
Ryan Graves, Head-Global Oper.
Thuan Pham, CTO
Salle Yoo, General Counsel
Ryan Graves, Head-Global Oper.
Salle Yoo, General Counsel

GROWTH PLANS/SPECIAL FEATURES:

Uber, Inc. is a California-based creator of the Uber mobile app which connects drivers and ridesharing services with passengers. The application serves over 550 cities worldwide and is in cities in about 68 countries throughout the Americas, Europe, the Middle East, Africa and Asia Pacific. Upon receiving a ride request, Uber sends the closest driver to fulfill it. Riders can rate their experiences with drivers for other riders to view. The company retains a fee from each ride that it books and then passes the balance of the fare to the drivers. Uber has expanded very aggressively on a worldwide basis, although it merged its operations in China with local competitor Didi, after Uber incurred massive losses in China. This enabled the firm to concentrate its expansion efforts and cash in other markets, including the vast market in India. Uber is a major competitor in India, where it has been purchasing cars and leasing them out to local drivers who want to work with the firm. Uber is also expanding into delivery services of many types. UberEATS is a restaurant-prepared meal delivery service that is available in dozens of cities worldwide. Uber, through its cutting-edge technologies and industry-leading experience base, is in a position to potentially revolutionize the freight trucking dispatch industry. In 2016, the firm launched Uber Freight, which connects shippers with trucks. Also during 2016, it acquired the self-driving truck technology firm Otto. While the company remained privately held as of early 2016, it has attracted several billion dollars in investment capital and has been able to maintain a sufficient cash balance to enable it to fund its global expansion.

Uber refers to its contract drivers as Partners. A commercial drivers license is required. The average Uber Partner in the U.S. receives about $20 per hour of work. Among corporate employees, approximately 36% were women, as of 2017. About 9% were black and 6% Latino.

FINANCIAL DATA: *Note: Data for latest year may not have been available at press time.*

In U.S. $	2016	2015	2014	2013	2012	2011
Revenue	6,500,000,000	2,900,000,000	850,000,000	104,000,000	65,000,000	30,000,000
R&D Expense						
Operating Income						
Operating Margin %						
SGA Expense						
Net Income	-2,800,000,000	-2,200,000,000	-400,000,000	-56,000,000	-30,000,000	-9,000,000
Operating Cash Flow						
Capital Expenditure						
EBITDA						
Return on Assets %						
Return on Equity %						
Debt to Equity						

CONTACT INFORMATION:

Phone: 866-576-1039   Fax:
Toll-Free:
Address: 182 Howard St., Ste. 8, San Francisco, CA 94105 United States

STOCK TICKER/OTHER:

Stock Ticker: Private   Exchange:
Employees: 18,000   Fiscal Year Ends:
Parent Company:

SALARIES/BONUSES:

Top Exec. Salary: $ Bonus: $
Second Exec. Salary: $ Bonus: $

OTHER THOUGHTS:

Estimated Female Officers or Directors: 1
Hot Spot for Advancement for Women/Minorities:

Under Armour Inc

www.underarmour.com

NAIC Code: 424300

TYPES OF BUSINESS:

Apparel and Clothing Brands, Designers, Importers and Distributors
Outdoor and Sports Apparel
Shirts
Footwear
Gloves

BRANDS/DIVISIONS/AFFILIATES:

HEATGEAR
COLDGEAR
ALLSEASONGEAR
Endomondo
MyFitnessPal
UA Record
UA HealthBox
UA SpeedForm

CONTACTS: Note: Officers with more than one job title may be intentionally listed here more than once.

Kevin Plank, CEO
David Bergman, CFO
Andy Donkin, Chief Marketing Officer
Paul Fipps, Chief Technology Officer
John Stanton, General Counsel
Karl-Heinz Maurath, Other Executive Officer
Michael Lee, Other Executive Officer
Colin Browne, Other Executive Officer
Kerry Chandler, Other Executive Officer
Kevin Eskridge, Other Executive Officer
Kevin Haley, President, Divisional
Jason LaRose, President, Geographical
Patrik Frisk, President

GROWTH PLANS/SPECIAL FEATURES:

Under Armour, Inc. (UA) develops, markets and distributes branded performance apparel, footwear and accessories for men, women and youth. It offers several lines of apparel and accessories that utilize a variety of synthetic microfiber fabrications engineered to replace traditional cotton products in the world of athletics and fitness. UA's active wear and accessories are designed to wick perspiration away from the skin, help regulate body temperature, enhance comfort and mobility and improve performance regardless of weather conditions. Its products are designed and merchandised along three gear lines: HEATGEAR, for hot weather; COLDGEAR, for cold weather; and ALLSEASONGEAR, for weather between the extremes. Within each product line, UA's garments come in three fit types: compression (tight fitting), fitted (athletic cut) and loose (relaxed). Annually, apparel accounts for 67% of the firm's revenues, while footwear and accessories (such as gloves for baseball batting, golf and running) account for 21% and 8% respectively. Licensing arrangements for the sale of UA products represent the remaining 3% of revenue. UA's larger customer, Dick's Sporting Goods, accounted for 14.4% of annual revenue, with no other customer accounting for more than 10% of net revenue. Unaffiliated manufacturers operating in 14 countries manufacture virtually all of the company's products. International professional football, baseball, basketball, hockey, rugby and soccer players as well as athletes in major collegiate sports and junior athletes of all levels use the firm's products. The company is the official supplier of footwear to the NFL (National Football League). In January 2016, the company launched a new suite of connected fitness products including UA Record app, UA HealthBox, UA SpeedForm and UA Heart Rate. In June 2016, the firm partnered with the NBA (National Basketball Association) to launch the NBA FIT App, a social health and fitness experience integrated with tips and videos from basketball players.

Employees are referred to as Teammates; approximately 70% of them played high school sports. The headquarters includes a giant gym and basketball court.

FINANCIAL DATA: Note: Data for latest year may not have been available at press time.

In U.S. $	2016	2015	2014	2013	2012	2011
Revenue	4,825,335,000	3,963,313,000	3,084,370,000	2,332,051,000	1,834,921,000	1,472,684,000
R&D Expense						
Operating Income	417,471,000	408,547,000	353,955,000	265,098,000	208,695,000	162,767,000
Operating Margin %	8.65%	10.30%	11.47%	11.36%	11.37%	11.05%
SGA Expense	1,823,140,000	1,497,000,000	1,158,251,000	871,572,000	670,602,000	550,069,000
Net Income	256,979,000	232,573,000	208,042,000	162,330,000	128,778,000	96,919,000
Operating Cash Flow	304,487,000	-44,104,000	219,033,000	120,070,000	199,761,000	15,218,000
Capital Expenditure	386,746,000	298,928,000	140,528,000	87,830,000	50,650,000	79,392,000
EBITDA	562,241,000	502,253,000	426,048,000	315,647,000	251,777,000	197,004,000
Return on Assets %	6.07%	9.37%	11.32%	11.87%	12.40%	12.15%
Return on Equity %	10.70%	15.40%	17.31%	17.35%	17.72%	17.10%
Debt to Equity	0.38	0.37	0.18	0.04	0.06	0.11

CONTACT INFORMATION:

Phone: 410 454-6428   Fax: 410 367-2400
Toll-Free: 888-727-6687
Address: 1020 Hull St., Fl. 3, Baltimore, MD 21230 United States

SALARIES/BONUSES:

Top Exec. Salary: $475,000   Bonus: $500,000
Second Exec. Salary: $633,462   Bonus: $250,000

STOCK TICKER/OTHER:

Stock Ticker: UA   Exchange: NYS
Employees: 15,200   Fiscal Year Ends: 12/31
Parent Company:

OTHER THOUGHTS:

Estimated Female Officers or Directors:
Hot Spot for Advancement for Women/Minorities:

Sales, profits and employees may be estimates. Financial information, benefits and other data can change quickly and may vary from those stated here.

United Continental Holdings Inc newsroom.united.com/corporate-fact-sheet

NAIC Code: 481111

TYPES OF BUSINESS:

Airline
Air Freight
Regional Airlines

BRANDS/DIVISIONS/AFFILIATES:

United Airlines Inc

CONTACTS: *Note: Officers with more than one job title may be intentionally listed here more than once.*

Oscar Munoz, CEO
Andrew Levy, CFO
Chris Kenny, Chief Accounting Officer
Linda Jojo, Chief Information Officer
Gregory Hart, COO
Robert Milton, Director
Michael Bonds, Executive VP, Divisional
Brett Hart, Executive VP
J. Kirby, President

GROWTH PLANS/SPECIAL FEATURES:

United Continental Holdings, Inc. is the holding company for United Airlines, Inc. The airline operates approximately 4,523 flights per day to 339 airports across six continents, serving 212 domestic destinations and 127 international destinations. Hubs are located in major cities around the world, including Chicago, Denver, Houston, Los Angeles, Newark, San Francisco, Washington D.C. and Guam. United provided transportation to 143 million passengers in 2016. The company is a member of the Star Alliance, which offers more than 18,500 daily flights to 1,330 airports in 192 countries through its member airlines. The firm's fleet includes 1,220 international aircraft, regional jets and turbo props, consisting of Airbus, Boeing, Bombardier, Embraer and Canadair aviation brand lines. In 2016, United announced that it had ordered 25 new Boeing 737-700 aircraft, which are scheduled to be delivered at the end of 2017.

United offers its employees travel passes; medical, dental, vision, life, personal and business accident insurance; flexible spending accounts; a 401(k) plan and profit sharing plans; a perfect attendance program; and on-time bonuses.

FINANCIAL DATA: *Note: Data for latest year may not have been available at press time.*

In U.S. $	2016	2015	2014	2013	2012	2011
Revenue	36,556,000,000	37,864,000,000	38,901,000,000	38,279,000,000	37,152,000,000	37,110,000,000
R&D Expense						
Operating Income	4,338,000,000	5,166,000,000	2,373,000,000	1,249,000,000	39,000,000	1,822,000,000
Operating Margin %	11.86%	13.64%	6.10%	3.26%	.10%	4.90%
SGA Expense	11,578,000,000	11,809,000,000	11,191,000,000	10,951,000,000	9,297,000,000	9,087,000,000
Net Income	2,263,000,000	7,340,000,000	1,132,000,000	571,000,000	-723,000,000	840,000,000
Operating Cash Flow	5,542,000,000	5,992,000,000	2,634,000,000	1,444,000,000	935,000,000	2,408,000,000
Capital Expenditure	3,223,000,000	2,747,000,000	2,005,000,000	2,164,000,000	2,016,000,000	700,000,000
EBITDA	6,338,000,000	6,658,000,000	3,490,000,000	2,962,000,000	1,596,000,000	3,309,000,000
Return on Assets %	5.58%	18.76%	3.05%	1.53%	-1.91%	2.16%
Return on Equity %	25.67%	129.20%	42.08%	32.95%	-63.22%	47.55%
Debt to Equity	1.24	1.15	4.46	3.66	23.35	6.32

CONTACT INFORMATION:

Phone: 872-825-4000   Fax: 847 700-2214
Toll-Free:
Address: 233 South Wacker Drive, Chicago, IL 60606 United States

STOCK TICKER/OTHER:

Stock Ticker: UAL   Exchange: NYS
Employees: 87,000   Fiscal Year Ends: 12/31
Parent Company:

SALARIES/BONUSES:

Top Exec. Salary: $715,000   Bonus: $740,909
Second Exec. Salary: Bonus: $820,000
$500,000

OTHER THOUGHTS:

Estimated Female Officers or Directors: 2
Hot Spot for Advancement for Women/Minorities: Y

United Natural Foods Inc

www.unfi.com

NAIC Code: 424410

TYPES OF BUSINESS:

Food Distribution
Natural & Organic Foods Distribution
Nutritional Supplements Distribution
Personal Care Products Distribution
Retail Stores

BRANDS/DIVISIONS/AFFILIATES:

United Natural Trading Co
Woodstock Farms Manufacturing
Earth Origins Market
Drive Organics
Blue Marble Brands
Field Day

CONTACTS: *Note: Officers with more than one job title may be intentionally listed here more than once.*

Steven Spinner, CEO
Michael Zechmeister, CFO
Eric Dorne, Chief Administrative Officer
Sean Griffin, COO
Paul Green, President, Divisional
John Hummel, President, Divisional
Chirstopher Testa, President, Divisional
Craig Smith, Senior VP, Divisional
Danielle Benedict, Senior VP, Divisional
Joseph Traficanti, Senior VP

GROWTH PLANS/SPECIAL FEATURES:

United Natural Foods, Inc. (UNFI) is a national distributor of natural and organic foods and related products. The company, which is a Certified Organic Distributor, carries more than 100,000 natural and organic products. These are sold under regional brand, national brand, private and master distribution labels. The firm offers six types of products: grocery and general merchandise; personal care items; produce; nutritional supplements; sports nutrition perishables; and frozen foods and bulk and food service products. UNFI serves over 43,000 customers, including supernatural chains (large chains of natural foods supermarkets), independently owned natural products retailers and conventional supermarkets located across the U.S. The company also distributes through the food service, international and buying club channels. The company has been the primary distributor to one of the largest natural food chains in the U.S., Whole Foods Market, Inc. for more than 17 years, with its agreement to expire in 2020. The firm's operations consist of three principal divisions: wholesale, which includes the operations of its 21 distribution centers; retail, which consists of UNFI's 13 owned and managed retail store through its subsidiary which does business as Earth Origins Market, and one natural products retail store in British Columbia which does business as Drive Organics; and manufacturing & branded products, which is comprised of its subsidiary United Natural Trading Co. (which does business as Woodstock Farms Manufacturing). Woodstock Farms is an importer, processor, packager and wholesale distributor of natural and organic products, trail mixes, nuts, seeds, dried fruit and confections. The Blue Marble Brands portfolio is a collection of 15 organic, natural and specialty food brands representing more than 650 unique products. Field Day brand is primarily sold to customers in the independent natural products retailer channel.

UNFI offers employees medical, dental, life and disability insurance; an assistance program; and educational assistance.

FINANCIAL DATA: *Note: Data for latest year may not have been available at press time.*

In U.S. $	2016	2015	2014	2013	2012	2011
Revenue	8,470,286,000	8,184,978,000	6,794,447,000	6,064,355,000	5,236,021,000	4,530,015,000
R&D Expense						
Operating Income	224,109,000	241,957,000	210,788,000	185,494,000	155,158,000	129,681,000
Operating Margin %	2.64%	2.95%	3.10%	3.05%	2.96%	2.86%
SGA Expense	1,049,690,000	1,017,755,000	916,857,000	837,953,000	755,744,000	688,859,000
Net Income	125,766,000	138,734,000	125,482,000	107,854,000	91,342,000	76,673,000
Operating Cash Flow	296,609,000	48,864,000	62,419,000	44,331,000	66,244,000	49,844,000
Capital Expenditure	41,375,000	129,134,000	147,303,000	66,554,000	31,492,000	40,778,000
EBITDA	295,487,000	308,067,000	263,919,000	222,411,000	195,077,000	166,731,000
Return on Assets %	4.65%	5.72%	6.23%	6.69%	6.31%	5.78%
Return on Equity %	8.65%	10.55%	10.71%	10.38%	9.88%	10.22%
Debt to Equity	0.38	0.38	0.36	0.14	0.11	

CONTACT INFORMATION:

Phone: 401 528-8634   Fax:
Toll-Free:
Address: 313 Iron Horse Way, Providence, RI 02908 United States

STOCK TICKER/OTHER:

Stock Ticker: UNFI
Employees: 8,700
Parent Company:

Exchange: NAS
Fiscal Year Ends: 07/31

SALARIES/BONUSES:

Top Exec. Salary: $889,346   Bonus: $
Second Exec. Salary: $477,038   Bonus: $

OTHER THOUGHTS:

Estimated Female Officers or Directors: 3
Hot Spot for Advancement for Women/Minorities: Y

United Parcel Service Inc (UPS)

NAIC Code: 492110

www.ups.com

TYPES OF BUSINESS:

Couriers and Express Delivery Services
Logistics Services
Supply Chain Services
International Products & Services
Ground & Air Delivery Services
Visibility & Technology Services

BRANDS/DIVISIONS/AFFILIATES:

UPS Hundredweight Services
UPS Next Day Air
UPS Freight
Mail Boxes Etc
UPS Supply Chain Solutions
UPS Capital

CONTACTS: Note: Officers with more than one job title may be intentionally listed here more than once.

David Abney, CEO
Richard Peretz, CFO
Alan Gershenhorn, Other Executive Officer
Teri Mcclure, Other Executive Officer
Myron Gray, President, Divisional
James Barber, President, Divisional
Teresa Finley, Senior VP, Divisional
Kate Gutmann, Senior VP, Divisional
Mark Wallace, Senior VP, Divisional
Norman Brothers, Senior VP

GROWTH PLANS/SPECIAL FEATURES:

United Parcel Service, Inc. (UPS) is one of the world's largest package delivery companies and a global provider of supply chain management. It delivers packages each business day to 8.4 million receivers in over 220 countries. The firm delivers an average of 18.3 million pieces per day worldwide. It is also a major provider of less-than-truckload (LTL) transportation services. Offerings include domestic and international package products and services and supply chain and freight services. The U.S. domestic package products and services business delivers packages traveling by ground or air transportation. In addition to the standard ground delivery products, UPS Hundredweight Services offers guaranteed, time-definite service to customers sending multiple package shipments. UPS Next Day Air offers several service options guaranteeing next business day delivery by 8:00AM, 10:30AM, noon, 3-4:30PM or by the end of the day in the 48 contiguous U.S. states and limited areas of Alaska. International services include guaranteed early morning, morning and noon delivery to major cities around the world as well as scheduled day-definite air and ground services. The supply chain and freight segment consists of its forwarding and logistics operations, UPS Freight and other related businesses. The division's worldwide services include supply chain design and management, freight distribution, customs brokerage, mail and consulting services. UPS Freight offers a variety of LTL/truckload services to customers in North America. Other business units within this segment include Mail Boxes Etc.; UPS Supply Chain Solutions; and UPS Capital. In February 2017, the firm announced plans to invest $18 million in on-site solar energy as an owner/operator of solar assets, starting with at least eight of its U.S. facilities.

U.S. employees at UPS receive benefits including tuition assistance; medical, prescription, dental, life and vision coverage; and health care spending accounts.

FINANCIAL DATA: Note: Data for latest year may not have been available at press time.

In U.S. $	2016	2015	2014	2013	2012	2011
Revenue	60,906,000,000	58,363,000,000	58,232,000,000	55,438,000,000	54,127,000,000	53,105,000,000
R&D Expense						
Operating Income	5,467,000,000	7,668,000,000	4,968,000,000	7,034,000,000	1,343,000,000	6,080,000,000
Operating Margin %	8.97%	13.13%	8.53%	12.68%	2.48%	11.44%
SGA Expense	34,770,000,000	31,028,000,000	32,045,000,000	28,557,000,000	33,102,000,000	27,575,000,000
Net Income	3,431,000,000	4,844,000,000	3,032,000,000	4,372,000,000	807,000,000	3,804,000,000
Operating Cash Flow	6,473,000,000	7,430,000,000	5,726,000,000	7,304,000,000	7,216,000,000	7,073,000,000
Capital Expenditure	2,965,000,000	2,379,000,000	2,328,000,000	2,065,000,000	2,153,000,000	2,005,000,000
EBITDA	7,741,000,000	9,767,000,000	6,913,000,000	8,921,000,000	3,225,000,000	7,906,000,000
Return on Assets %	8.72%	13.13%	8.45%	11.64%	2.19%	11.13%
Return on Equity %	238.67%	210.10%	70.38%	78.58%	13.80%	50.67%
Debt to Equity	30.60	4.58	4.60	1.67	2.38	1.57

CONTACT INFORMATION:

Phone: 404 828-6000   Fax: 404 828-6562
Toll-Free: 800-874-5877
Address: 55 Glenlake Parkway, NE, Atlanta, GA 30328 United States

STOCK TICKER/OTHER:

Stock Ticker: UPS   Exchange: NYS
Employees: 434,000   Fiscal Year Ends: 12/31
Parent Company:

SALARIES/BONUSES:

Top Exec. Salary: $1,082,421   Bonus: $
Second Exec. Salary: $565,956   Bonus: $

OTHER THOUGHTS:

Estimated Female Officers or Directors: 4
Hot Spot for Advancement for Women/Minorities: Y

United States Cellular Corporation

www.uscellular.com

NAIC Code: 517210

TYPES OF BUSINESS:
Mobile Phone and Wireless Services

BRANDS/DIVISIONS/AFFILIATES:
Telephone and Data Systems Inc

CONTACTS: Note: Officers with more than one job title may be intentionally listed here more than once.

Kenneth Meyers, CEO
Steven Campbell, CFO
Leroy Carlson, Chairman of the Board
Douglas Shuma, Chief Accounting Officer
Michael Irizarry, Chief Technology Officer
Kristin MacCarthy, Controller
Leroy Carlson, Director Emeritus
Paul-Henri Denuit, Director Emeritus
Jay Ellison, Executive VP
Deirdre Drake, Other Executive Officer
Edward Perez, Senior VP, Divisional

GROWTH PLANS/SPECIAL FEATURES:

United States Cellular Corporation (U.S. Cellular) is a leading U.S. wireless telecommunications firm, providing wireless voice and data services to 5 million customers in 426 markets nationwide. The company maintains interests in consolidated and investment wireless licenses that cover portions of 23 states and a total population of 32 million people. U.S. Cellular offers a range of wireless devices such as handsets, modems, mobile hotspots, home phone and tablets for use by its customers. The firm has also installed service repair programs at certain facilities, which assist customers with over-the-counter exchanges, Smartphone advance exchanges, loaner phones, device recycling and device returns. U.S. Cellular sells wireless devices to agents and other third-party distributors for resale. The wireless services segment provides a variety of packaged voice and data pricing plans. The company offers post-pay plans and prepaid plans. Moreover, U.S. Cellular services include connected home, a self-installed home security and automation system for home monitoring purposes. U.S. Cellular also offers data-services and app-like experiences to non-smartphone devices via a technology known as binary runtime environment for wireless (BREW). These enhanced data services include downloading news, weather, sports information, games, ring tones and other services. In addition, U.S. Cellular has recently engaged in VoLTE (voice over long-term evolution) trials, with plans to upgrade equipment in select markets to allow the trial processes to continue following the services official launch. Telephone and Data Systems, Inc. owns approximately 83% of the company.

Employee benefits include medical, dental and vision coverage; life insurance and AD&D; short- and long-term disability; a 401(k) and Roth IRA; a pension plan; and tuition reimbursement.

FINANCIAL DATA: Note: Data for latest year may not have been available at press time.

In U.S. $	2016	2015	2014	2013	2012	2011
Revenue	3,939,000,000	3,996,853,000	3,892,747,000	3,918,836,000	4,452,084,000	4,343,346,000
R&D Expense						
Operating Income	-3,000,000	312,942,000	-143,390,000	146,865,000	156,656,000	280,780,000
Operating Margin %	- .07%	7.82%	-3.68%	3.74%	3.51%	6.46%
SGA Expense	1,480,000,000	1,493,730,000	1,591,914,000	1,677,395,000	1,764,933,000	1,779,203,000
Net Income	48,000,000	241,347,000	-42,812,000	140,038,000	111,006,000	175,041,000
Operating Cash Flow	501,000,000	555,114,000	172,342,000	290,897,000	899,291,000	987,862,000
Capital Expenditure	443,000,000	580,593,000	605,083,000	734,402,000	949,090,000	771,798,000
EBITDA	813,000,000	1,096,278,000	604,679,000	1,105,400,000	856,079,000	951,993,000
Return on Assets %	.67%	3.56%	- .66%	2.14%	1.71%	2.85%
Return on Equity %	1.33%	7.03%	-1.27%	3.93%	3.01%	4.93%
Debt to Equity	0.44	0.45	0.34	0.25	0.23	0.24

CONTACT INFORMATION:
Phone: 773 399-8900   Fax: 773 399-8936
Toll-Free: 888-944-9400
Address: 8410 W. Bryn Mawr Ave., Ste. 700, Chicago, IL 60631 United States

STOCK TICKER/OTHER:
Stock Ticker: USM   Exchange: NYS
Employees: 6,300   Fiscal Year Ends: 12/31
Parent Company: Telephone and Data Systems Inc

SALARIES/BONUSES:
Top Exec. Salary: $948,000   Bonus: $1,007,200
Second Exec. Salary: $623,917   Bonus: $194,569

OTHER THOUGHTS:
Estimated Female Officers or Directors: 6
Hot Spot for Advancement for Women/Minorities: Y

United Technologies Corporation

NAIC Code: 336412

TYPES OF BUSINESS:

Aircraft Engine and Engine Parts Manufacturing
Elevator & Escalator Systems
HVAC Systems
Aircraft Parts & Maintenance

BRANDS/DIVISIONS/AFFILIATES:

Otis
Pratt & Whitney

CONTACTS: Note: Officers with more than one job title may be intentionally listed here more than once.

Gregory Hayes, CEO
Akhil Johri, CFO
Robert Bailey, Chief Accounting Officer
Michael Dumais, Executive VP, Divisional
Charles Gill, Executive VP
Elizabeth Amato, Executive VP
David Gitlin, President, Divisional
Robert Leduc, President, Divisional
Robert Mcdonough, President, Divisional
Philippe Delpech, President, Divisional
David Whitehouse, Vice President

GROWTH PLANS/SPECIAL FEATURES:

United Technologies Corporation (UTC) provides high technology products and services to the building systems and aerospace industries worldwide. The company operates through four principle segments: Otis; UTC climate, controls & security; Pratt & Whitney; and UTC aerospace systems. Otis manufactures, sells, installs and services a wide range of passenger and freight elevators for low-, medium-, and high-speed applications, as well as a broad line of escalators and moving walkways. UTC climate, controls & security is the leading provider of HVAC (heating, ventilation and air conditioning) and refrigeration systems, including controls for residential, commercial, industrial and transportation applications. This segment is also a global provider of security and fire safety products and services such as alarms, access control systems and video surveillance systems. Pratt & Whitney supplies aircraft engines and maintenance services for the commercial, military, business jet and general aviation markets. Pratt & Whitney Canada (P&WC) is a world leader in the production of engines powering general and business aviation, as well as regional airline, utility and military airplanes and helicopters, and provides maintenance, repair and overhaul services, including the sale of spare parts. UTC Aerospace Systems supplies technologically advanced aerospace products and aftermarket solutions for aircraft manufacturers, airlines, regional, business and general aviation markets, military, space and undersea operations.

UTC offers employees benefits including medical and dental insurance, health care reimbursement accounts, long-term disability coverage, an Employee Scholar Program that features paid time off for academic pursuits as well as academic expense reimbursement, employee assistance programs, a retirement plan and select benefits for part time employees.

FINANCIAL DATA: Note: Data for latest year may not have been available at press time.

In U.S. $	2016	2015	2014	2013	2012	2011
Revenue	57,244,000,000	56,098,000,000	65,100,000,000	62,626,000,000	57,708,000,000	58,190,000,000
R&D Expense	2,337,000,000	2,279,000,000	2,635,000,000	2,529,000,000	2,371,000,000	2,058,000,000
Operating Income	8,172,000,000	7,291,000,000	9,769,000,000	9,209,000,000	7,684,000,000	8,099,000,000
Operating Margin %	14.27%	12.99%	15.00%	14.70%	13.31%	13.91%
SGA Expense	6,060,000,000	5,886,000,000	6,500,000,000	6,718,000,000	6,452,000,000	6,464,000,000
Net Income	5,055,000,000	7,608,000,000	6,220,000,000	5,721,000,000	5,130,000,000	4,979,000,000
Operating Cash Flow	3,880,000,000	6,326,000,000	7,336,000,000	7,505,000,000	6,646,000,000	6,590,000,000
Capital Expenditure	2,087,000,000	2,089,000,000	2,304,000,000	2,410,000,000	2,932,000,000	983,000,000
EBITDA	10,256,000,000	9,275,000,000	11,894,000,000	11,167,000,000	9,328,000,000	9,625,000,000
Return on Assets %	5.70%	8.51%	6.83%	6.35%	6.80%	8.30%
Return on Equity %	18.40%	25.97%	19.72%	19.80%	21.46%	23.01%
Debt to Equity	0.78	0.70	0.57	0.61	0.83	0.43

CONTACT INFORMATION:

Phone: 860 728-7000   Fax: 860 728-7028
Toll-Free:
Address: 10 Farm Springs Rd., Farmington, CT 06032 United States

STOCK TICKER/OTHER:

Stock Ticker: UTX   Exchange: NYS
Employees: 202,000   Fiscal Year Ends: 12/31
Parent Company:

SALARIES/BONUSES:

Top Exec. Salary: $1,450,000   Bonus: $3,000,000
Second Exec. Salary: Bonus: $1,100,000
$806,250

OTHER THOUGHTS:

Estimated Female Officers or Directors: 2
Hot Spot for Advancement for Women/Minorities: Y

UnitedHealth Group Inc

www.unitedhealthgroup.com

NAIC Code: 524114

TYPES OF BUSINESS:

Medical Insurance
Wellness Plans
Dental & Vision Insurance
Health Information Technology

BRANDS/DIVISIONS/AFFILIATES:

United Healthcare
OptumHealth
OptumInsight
OptumRX
United Healthcare Employer & Individual
UnitedHealthcare Medicare & Retirement
UnitedHealthcare Community & State

CONTACTS: *Note: Officers with more than one job title may be intentionally listed here more than once.*

Larry Renfro, CEO, Subsidiary
Stephen Hemsley, CEO
John Rex, CFO
Richard Burke, Chairman of the Board
Tom Roos, Chief Accounting Officer
D. Wilson, Executive VP, Divisional
Marianne Short, Executive VP
David Wichmann, President

GROWTH PLANS/SPECIAL FEATURES:

UnitedHealth Group, Inc. is a diversified health and insurance firm that serves over 75 million people worldwide. The company provides individuals with access to health care services and resources through approximately 1 million physicians and other care providers and 6,000 hospitals across the U.S. The company has four operating segments: UnitedHealthcare, which includes United Healthcare Employer & Individual, UnitedHealthcare Medicare & Retirement and UnitedHealthcare Community & State; OptumHealth; OptumInsight; and OptumRX. The United Healthcare segment provides consumer-oriented health benefit plans and services for large national employers, public sector employers, mid-sized employers, small businesses and individuals nationwide; health and well-being services for individuals age 50 and older; and network-based health services for beneficiaries of government-sponsored health care programs. The OptumHealth segment is engaged in care services, behavioral solutions, specialty benefits and financial services in fields such as dental, vision, disability, therapy and stop-loss coverage. The OptumInsight segment provides technology, operational and consulting services to participants in the health care industry. The OptumRX segment offers a comprehensive suite of integrated pharmacy benefit management (PBM) services to more than 66 million people through over 67,000 retail network pharmacies as well as mail order service facilities. In January 2017, UnitedHealth agreed to acquire Surgical Care Affiliates, Inc. for $2.3 billion.

The company offers its employees medical, vision, dental, life and disability insurance; flexible spending accounts; an employee assistance program; a 401(k); adoption assistance; and tuition reimbursement.

FINANCIAL DATA: *Note: Data for latest year may not have been available at press time.*

In U.S. $	2016	2015	2014	2013	2012	2011
Revenue	184,840,000,000	157,107,000,000	130,474,000,000	122,489,000,000	110,618,000,000	101,862,000,000
R&D Expense						
Operating Income	12,930,000,000	11,021,000,000	10,274,000,000	9,623,000,000	9,254,000,000	8,464,000,000
Operating Margin %	6.99%	7.01%	7.87%	7.85%	8.36%	8.30%
SGA Expense	28,401,000,000	24,312,000,000	21,681,000,000	19,362,000,000	17,306,000,000	15,557,000,000
Net Income	7,017,000,000	5,813,000,000	5,619,000,000	5,625,000,000	5,526,000,000	5,142,000,000
Operating Cash Flow	9,795,000,000	9,740,000,000	8,051,000,000	6,991,000,000	7,155,000,000	6,968,000,000
Capital Expenditure	1,705,000,000	1,556,000,000	1,525,000,000	1,307,000,000	1,070,000,000	1,067,000,000
EBITDA	14,985,000,000	12,714,000,000	11,752,000,000	10,998,000,000	10,563,000,000	9,588,000,000
Return on Assets %	5.99%	5.87%	6.67%	6.91%	7.42%	7.85%
Return on Equity %	19.46%	17.53%	17.39%	17.76%	18.58%	19.00%
Debt to Equity	0.67	0.75	0.49	0.46	0.45	0.46

CONTACT INFORMATION:

Phone: 952 936-1300   Fax: 952 936-0044
Toll-Free: 800-328-5979
Address: 9900 Bren Rd. E., Minnetonka, MN 55343 United States

STOCK TICKER/OTHER:

Stock Ticker: UNH   Exchange: NYS
Employees: 230,000   Fiscal Year Ends: 12/31
Parent Company:

SALARIES/BONUSES:

Top Exec. Salary: $1,300,000   Bonus: $
Second Exec. Salary: $1,100,000   Bonus: $

OTHER THOUGHTS:

Estimated Female Officers or Directors: 4
Hot Spot for Advancement for Women/Minorities: Y

Universal Health Services Inc

www.uhsinc.com

NAIC Code: 622110

TYPES OF BUSINESS:

General Medical and Surgical Hospitals
Radiation Oncology Centers
Behavioral Health Hospitals
Surgical Hospitals
Administrative Services
Physician Recruitment
Facilities Planning

BRANDS/DIVISIONS/AFFILIATES:

CONTACTS: Note: Officers with more than one job title may be intentionally listed here more than once.

Alan Miller, CEO
Steve Filton, CFO
Marc Miller, Director
Debra Osteen, Executive VP
Marvin Pember, Executive VP

GROWTH PLANS/SPECIAL FEATURES:

Universal Health Services, Inc. (UHS) owns and operates through its subsidiaries acute care hospitals, outpatient facilities and behavioral healthcare facilities. UHS owns and/or operates 319 impatient facilities and 33 outpatient and other facilities located in 37 U.S. states, Washington D.C., the U.K., Puerto Rico and the U.S. Virgin Islands. Among the acute care facilities in the U.S., 26 are impatient acute care hospitals, four are free-standing emergency departments, four are outpatient surgery/cancer care centers and one is a surgical hospital. Among the behavioral healthcare facilities: the U.S. comprises 189 impatient and 20 outpatient facilities; the U.K. comprises 100 impatient and two outpatient facilities; and Puerto Rico and U.S. Virgin Islands comprise four impatient and two outpatient facilities.

The company offers its employees medical, dental, vision, life, AD&D and disability insurance; coverage availability for blended families; family and caregiving support; wellness support; a savings plan; an employee stock purchase plan; and flexible spending accounts.

FINANCIAL DATA: Note: Data for latest year may not have been available at press time.

In U.S. $	2016	2015	2014	2013	2012	2011
Revenue	9,766,210,000	9,043,451,000	8,065,326,000	7,283,822,000	6,961,400,000	7,500,198,000
R&D Expense						
Operating Income	1,281,411,000	1,259,395,000	1,063,305,000	1,015,463,000	942,581,000	897,128,000
Operating Margin %	13.12%	13.92%	13.18%	13.94%	13.54%	11.96%
SGA Expense	4,682,854,000	4,307,360,000	3,975,625,000	3,702,378,000	3,570,688,000	91,765,000
Net Income	702,409,000	680,528,000	545,343,000	510,733,000	443,446,000	398,167,000
Operating Cash Flow	1,288,474,000	1,020,898,000	1,035,876,000	884,241,000	815,271,000	718,251,000
Capital Expenditure	519,939,000	379,321,000	391,150,000	358,493,000	363,192,000	323,931,000
EBITDA	1,681,473,000	1,560,558,000	1,424,066,000	1,336,790,000	1,224,249,000	1,192,989,000
Return on Assets %	7.03%	7.31%	6.30%	6.18%	5.58%	5.24%
Return on Equity %	15.98%	17.03%	15.60%	17.11%	17.68%	18.62%
Debt to Equity	0.88	0.79	0.85	0.98	1.37	1.59

CONTACT INFORMATION:

Phone: 610 768-3300   Fax: 610 768-3336
Toll-Free:
Address: 367 S. Gulph Rd., King Of Prussia, PA 19406 United States

STOCK TICKER/OTHER:

Stock Ticker: UHS   Exchange: NYS
Employees: 62,230   Fiscal Year Ends: 12/31
Parent Company:

SALARIES/BONUSES:

Top Exec. Salary: $1,600,061   Bonus: $
Second Exec. Salary: Bonus: $
$720,861

OTHER THOUGHTS:

Estimated Female Officers or Directors: 2
Hot Spot for Advancement for Women/Minorities: Y

Unum Group

www.unum.com

NAIC Code: 524114

TYPES OF BUSINESS:

Supplemental Insurance
Short- & Long-Term Disability Insurance
Long-Term Care Insurance
Income Protection Insurance
Life Insurance

BRANDS/DIVISIONS/AFFILIATES:

Unum Life Insurance Company of America
Provident Life and Accident Insurance Company
Paul Revere Life Insurance Company (The)
Colonial Life & Accident Insurance Company
Unum Limited

CONTACTS: Note: Officers with more than one job title may be intentionally listed here more than once.

Michael Simonds, CEO, Divisional
Timothy Arnold, CEO, Divisional
Peter ODonnell, CEO, Divisional
John McGarry, CFO
Kevin Kabat, Chairman of the Board
Vicki Corbett, Controller
Richard Mckenney, Director
Christopher Jerome, Executive VP, Divisional
Breege Farrell, Executive VP
Lisa Iglesias, General Counsel
Danny Waxenber, Senior VP

GROWTH PLANS/SPECIAL FEATURES:

Unum Group is a provider of group and individual income protection insurance products. The company also offers a portfolio of other insurance products, including long-term care insurance, life insurance, employer- and employee-paid group benefits and other related services. Unum operates in five segments: Unum U.S., Unum U.K., Colonial Life, closed block and corporate. The Unum U.S. segment includes group long-term and short-term disability insurance, group life and accidental death and dismemberment products and supplemental and voluntary lines of business. Subsidiaries in the U.S. include: Unum Life Insurance Company of America, Provident Life and Accident Insurance Company, The Paul Revere Life Insurance Company and Colonial Life & Accident Insurance Company. The Unum U.K. segment includes group long-term disability insurance, group life products and individual disability products. In the U.K., the firm operates through Unum Limited. The Colonial Life segment includes insurance for accident, sickness and disability products; life products; and cancer and critical illness products. Plans are marketed to employees at the workplace through an independent contractor agency sales force and brokers. The closed block segment consists of individual disability, group and individual long-term care as well as other insurance products that are no longer actively marketed. The firm's corporate segment is involved investment income assets not specifically allocated to the other business segments.

Unum offers its employees medical, dental, vision and prescription drug insurance; long- and short-term disability coverage; life insurance; a pension plan; a 401(k) plan; tuition reimbursement; an adoption assistance program; and an employee assistance program.

FINANCIAL DATA: Note: Data for latest year may not have been available at press time.

In U.S. $	2016	2015	2014	2013	2012	2011
Revenue	11,046,500,000	10,731,300,000	10,509,700,000	10,353,800,000	10,515,400,000	10,278,000,000
R&D Expense						
Operating Income	1,347,700,000	1,238,300,000	527,200,000	1,205,200,000	1,249,500,000	257,200,000
Operating Margin %	12.20%	11.53%	5.01%	11.64%	11.88%	2.50%
SGA Expense	1,858,800,000	1,831,400,000	1,756,200,000	1,699,900,000	1,704,000,000	1,687,200,000
Net Income	931,400,000	867,100,000	413,400,000	858,100,000	894,400,000	235,400,000
Operating Cash Flow	1,116,100,000	1,292,100,000	1,223,600,000	1,031,500,000	1,379,600,000	1,193,700,000
Capital Expenditure	85,000,000	100,200,000	114,500,000	105,500,000		
EBITDA						
Return on Assets %	1.52%	1.40%	.67%	1.41%	1.46%	.40%
Return on Equity %	10.56%	10.07%	4.80%	9.93%	10.40%	2.68%
Debt to Equity	0.33	0.28	0.30	0.30	0.31	0.29

CONTACT INFORMATION:

Phone: 423 294-1011   Fax:
Toll-Free: 800-887-2180
Address: 1 Fountain Sq., Chattanooga, TN 37402 United States

STOCK TICKER/OTHER:

Stock Ticker: UNM
Employees: 9,400
Parent Company:

Exchange: NYS
Fiscal Year Ends: 12/31

SALARIES/BONUSES:

Top Exec. Salary: $994,231   Bonus: $
Second Exec. Salary: $594,231   Bonus: $

OTHER THOUGHTS:

Estimated Female Officers or Directors:
Hot Spot for Advancement for Women/Minorities: Y

Sales, profits and employees may be estimates. Financial information, benefits and other data can change quickly and may vary from those stated here.

US Bancorp
NAIC Code: 522110

www.usbank.com/en/AboutHome.cfm

TYPES OF BUSINESS:
Banking
Lease Financing
Consumer Finance
Credit Cards
Discount Brokerage
Investment Advisory Services
Trust Services
Insurance

BRANDS/DIVISIONS/AFFILIATES:
US Bank NA

CONTACTS: Note: Officers with more than one job title may be intentionally listed here more than once.
Terrance Dolan, CFO
Jeffry von Gillern, Vice Chairman, Divisional
Richard Davis, Chairman of the Board
Craig Gifford, Chief Accounting Officer
Mark Runkel, Chief Credit Officer
P. Parker, Chief Risk Officer
Andrew Cecere, Director
Jennie Carlson, Executive VP, Divisional
James Chosy, Executive VP
Katherine Quinn, Executive VP
Leslie Godridge, Vice Chairman, Divisional
John Elmore, Vice Chairman, Divisional
Kent Stone, Vice Chairman, Divisional
James Kelligrew, Vice Chairman, Divisional

GROWTH PLANS/SPECIAL FEATURES:
U.S. Bancorp (USB) is a financial services holding company, with $450 billion in assets. USB operates more than 3,100 banking offices and 4,800 ATMs in the Midwest and Western regions of the U.S. Through U.S. Bank NA and other subsidiaries, the company is engaged in general banking, primarily in domestic markets, and serves individuals, businesses, institutional organizations, financial institutions and government entities. Lending services include traditional credit products, credit card services, financing, leasing, asset-backed lending and agricultural finance. Depository services include checking and savings accounts and time certificate contracts. Ancillary services include foreign exchange, treasury management and lock-box collection for corporate customers. A full range of asset management and fiduciary services are available for individuals, estates, business corporations, foundations and charitable organizations. USB's non-banking subsidiaries provide investment and insurance products as well as mutual fund processing services to a range of mutual funds. Mortgage services are available through the bank's offices, while consumer lending products are originated through banking offices, indirect correspondents and brokers.

The company offers employees benefits including medical, dental and vision insurance; flexible spending accounts; disability and life insurance; 401(k) and pension plans; an employee assistance plan; adoption benefits; and tuition reimbursement.

FINANCIAL DATA: Note: Data for latest year may not have been available at press time.

In U.S. $	2016	2015	2014	2013	2012	2011
Revenue	21,105,000,000	20,093,000,000	19,939,000,000	19,378,000,000	20,064,000,000	18,883,000,000
R&D Expense	955,000,000	887,000,000	863,000,000	848,000,000	821,000,000	758,000,000
Operating Income	8,105,000,000	8,030,000,000	7,995,000,000	7,764,000,000	7,726,000,000	6,629,000,000
Operating Margin %	38.40%	39.96%	40.09%	40.06%	38.50%	35.10%
SGA Expense	7,256,000,000	6,637,000,000	6,274,000,000	6,178,000,000	5,957,000,000	5,558,000,000
Net Income	5,888,000,000	5,879,000,000	5,851,000,000	5,836,000,000	5,647,000,000	4,872,000,000
Operating Cash Flow	5,336,000,000	8,782,000,000	5,332,000,000	11,446,000,000	7,958,000,000	9,820,000,000
Capital Expenditure						
EBITDA						
Return on Assets %	1.28%	1.36%	1.45%	1.54%	1.55%	1.45%
Return on Equity %	13.56%	14.13%	14.87%	15.73%	16.41%	16.01%
Debt to Equity	0.79	0.78	0.83	0.55	0.74	1.01

CONTACT INFORMATION:
Phone: 651 466-3000   Fax:
Toll-Free:
Address: 800 Nicollet Mall, Minneapolis, MN 55402 United States

STOCK TICKER/OTHER:
Stock Ticker: USB   Exchange: NYS
Employees: 71,191   Fiscal Year Ends: 12/31
Parent Company:

SALARIES/BONUSES:
Top Exec. Salary: $1,400,000   Bonus: $
Second Exec. Salary: Bonus: $
$800,000

OTHER THOUGHTS:
Estimated Female Officers or Directors: 5
Hot Spot for Advancement for Women/Minorities: Y

USAA

NAIC Code: 524126

TYPES OF BUSINESS:

Insurance, Direct Property & Casualty
Banking
Life Insurance
Real Estate Development
Discount Brokerage
Investment Management
Mutual Funds

BRANDS/DIVISIONS/AFFILIATES:

United Services Automobile Association
USAA Investment Management Company
USAA Alliance Services LLC
USAA Educational Foundation
USAA Casualty Insurance Company
USAA General Indemnity Company
USAA County Mutual Insurance Company
USAA Life Insurance Company

CONTACTS: *Note: Officers with more than one job title may be intentionally listed here more than once.*

Stuart Parker, CEO
Stuart Parker, Pres.
Shon Manasco, Chief Admin. Officer
Steven A. Bennett, General Counsel
Wendi E. Strong, Exec. VP-Enterprise Affairs
F. David Bohne, Pres., USAA Federal Savings Bank
Kevin J. Bergner, Pres., USAA Property & Casualty Insurance Group
Christopher W. Claus, Exec. VP-Enterprise Advice Group
Wayne Peacock, Pres., USAA Capital Corporation
Lester L. Lyles, Chmn.

GROWTH PLANS/SPECIAL FEATURES:

USAA (United Services Automobile Association) is a mutual insurance company that serves nearly 12 million members, comprised exclusively of U.S. military personnel and their families. It owns and manages over $137 billion in assets from offices in Texas, Colorado, Arizona, Virginia and Florida; and international offices in London and Frankfurt. USAA offers more than 150 financial services and products, primarily automobile, property and life insurance as well as automobile, mortgage and home equity loans. The company also manages checking accounts, savings accounts, credit cards and personal loans for its military customers. In addition, customers have access to mutual funds and brokerage services through USAA Investment Management Company. Members can access their accounts and conduct investing, banking and insurance business online. Additionally, subsidiary USAA Alliance Services, LLC has formed a series of partnerships to provide members with discounts on home security, travel services and insurance, floral services, car rentals and diamond and fine jewelry. The firm's USAA Educational Foundation division, a nonprofit entity, provides consumer education to the general public on topics including personal finance, safety and quality of life. Other subsidiaries include USAA Casualty Insurance Company, USAA General Indemnity Company, USAA County Mutual Insurance Company, USAA Life Insurance Company, USAA Federal Savings Bank and USAA Financial Advisors, Inc.

Employee benefits include medical and dental coverage, a 401(k), military leave, an employee assistance program, educational assistance and adoption assistance.

FINANCIAL DATA: *Note: Data for latest year may not have been available at press time.*

In U.S. $	2016	2015	2014	2013	2012	2011
Revenue	27,131,000,000	24,361,000,000	24,033,000,000	20,971,000,000	20,729,000,000	19,036,000,000
R&D Expense						
Operating Income						
Operating Margin %						
SGA Expense						
Net Income	1,779,000,000	2,266,000,000	3,317,000,000	2,726,000,000	2,832,000,000	2,128,000,000
Operating Cash Flow						
Capital Expenditure						
EBITDA						
Return on Assets %						
Return on Equity %						
Debt to Equity						

CONTACT INFORMATION:

Phone: 210-498-2211   Fax: 210-498-9940
Toll-Free: 800-531-8722
Address: 9800 Fredericksburg Rd., San Antonio, TX 78288 United States

STOCK TICKER/OTHER:

Stock Ticker: Mutual Company   Exchange:
Employees: 26,000   Fiscal Year Ends: 12/31
Parent Company:

SALARIES/BONUSES:

Top Exec. Salary: $ Bonus: $
Second Exec. Salary: $ Bonus: $

OTHER THOUGHTS:

Estimated Female Officers or Directors: 4
Hot Spot for Advancement for Women/Minorities: Y

UST Global Inc

NAIC Code: 541512

www.ust-global.com

TYPES OF BUSINESS:

IT Services & BPO
IT Services
Business Process Outsourcing (BPO)
Mortgage BPO
Consulting
Data Management
Enterprise Resource Planning
Business Intelligence

BRANDS/DIVISIONS/AFFILIATES:

Comcraft Group
Kanchi Technologies

CONTACTS: *Note: Officers with more than one job title may be intentionally listed here more than once.*

Sajan Pillai, CEO
Arun Narayanan, COO
Joe Nalkara, Pres.
Krishna Sudheendra, CFO
Murali Gopalan, Chief Commercial Officer
Manu Gopinath, Global Head-Human Resources
David Whitehouse, Chief Medical Officer
Sunil Kanchi, CIO
Alexander Varghese, Chief Admin. Officer
Catherine Gardner, Global Head-Legal, Risk & Compliance
Saurabh Ranjan, Managing Dir.-Global Oper.
Shaun Mitra, Chief Bus. Officer
Adam Krajchir, Chief Customer Officer
Gaurav Agarwal, VP
BG Moore, Chief of Staff
Krishna Prasad, Chief Solutions Officer
Bipin Thomas, Pres., Health Group
John Gustafson, Pres., Diversified Bus.
Paras Chandaria, Chmn.
Michael E. Hopewell, Managing Dir.-Europe

GROWTH PLANS/SPECIAL FEATURES:

UST Global, Inc., a division of Comcraft Group, provides information technology (IT) services and business process outsourcing (BPO) through its international facilities. The firm divides its services into ten divisions. Consulting services encompasses the firm's IT strategy, architecture, process management and change management service offerings. Technology build services builds custom applications or entire systems for clients. Application managed services provides end-to-end management for applications, helping clients to reduce total cost of ownership, improve service quality and enable business growth. Infrastructure managed services provides management for IT infrastructures. QA and testing services develop and execute quality assurance and testing strategies for optimal performance and results. Business process outsourcing (BPO) helps reduce costs while simultaneously driving innovation and delivering value to meet and exceed customer expectations and satisfaction. S+CC services (Smart plus connected communities) features energy management, asset management, enhanced safety/security, connected health care, connected transportation, connected sports, connected entertainment, connected education and connected maintenance. Mobility services help enterprises realize their mobile initiatives by performing assessments, building roadmaps, identifying and designing applications, and then testing, deploying and managing the apps. Smarter cities services build cities with tools to coordinate and analyze data for better decisions, anticipate problems and coordinate resources to operate efficiently. Engineering services is operated through Kanchi Technologies, and offers consultancy services, project management, business process improvement, integration of business technology, execution of global delivery strategies as well as auditing services.

FINANCIAL DATA: *Note: Data for latest year may not have been available at press time.*

In U.S. $	2016	2015	2014	2013	2012	2011
Revenue	445,200,000	455,000,000	450,000,000	435,000,000	420,000,000	
R&D Expense						
Operating Income						
Operating Margin %						
SGA Expense						
Net Income						
Operating Cash Flow						
Capital Expenditure						
EBITDA						
Return on Assets %						
Return on Equity %						
Debt to Equity						

CONTACT INFORMATION:

Phone: 949-716-8757   Fax: 949-716-8396
Toll-Free:
Address: 5 Polaris Way, Aliso Viejo, CA 92656 United States

STOCK TICKER/OTHER:

Stock Ticker: Private
Employees: 16,557
Parent Company: Comcraft Group

Exchange:
Fiscal Year Ends:

SALARIES/BONUSES:

Top Exec. Salary: $ Bonus: $
Second Exec. Salary: $ Bonus: $

OTHER THOUGHTS:

Estimated Female Officers or Directors: 2
Hot Spot for Advancement for Women/Minorities:

Valassis Communications Inc

www.valassis.com

NAIC Code: 541800

TYPES OF BUSINESS:

Coupon Marketing Products & Services
Direct Mail
Newspaper Advertising
Sampling
Software

BRANDS/DIVISIONS/AFFILIATES:

MacAndrews & Forbes Inc
Harland Clarke Holdings Corp
RedPlum
Intelligent Media Delivery

CONTACTS: *Note: Officers with more than one job title may be intentionally listed here more than once.*

Robert A. Mason, CEO
Ron Goolsby, COO
Robert L. Recchia, CFO
Suzie Brown, Exec. VP-Sales & Mktg.
Jim Parkinson, Chief Digital & Tech. Officer
Todd L. Wiseley, Exec. VP-Admin.
Todd L. Wiseley, General Counsel
Brian J. Husselbee, Pres.

GROWTH PLANS/SPECIAL FEATURES:

Valassis Communications, Inc. is a provider of media and marketing services, marketed under the RedPlum brand. The company provides its services to more than 58,000 national, regional and local advertisers. Industries Valassis supports includes consumer packaged goods, grocery, retail, food service, telecom and financial. Its offerings are divided into six segments: direct mail, in-store advertising, newspaper advertising, digital advertising, mobile marketing and marketing analysis. Direct mail distributes advertisements mid-week in order to engage consumers as they are planning weekend shopping trips. Direct mail ads include inserts, wraps and postcards; and this division also provides mailing lists and design templates. In-store advertising provides innovative, at-shelf solutions that garner attention, engage customers and drive action. In-store ads include coupon dispensers, floor graphics, shelf talkers and more. Newspaper advertising provides ads within newspapers such as coupons and product/brand advertisement. This division also provides coupon books, as well as newspaper inserts. Digital advertising includes display advertisements on computer and mobile screens, email marketing and digital couponing. Mobile marketing comprises internet-based applications such as campaigns, shopping apps and discounts, all targeted to drive awareness and branding on contextually relevant websites. Marketing analysis comprises Valassis' Intelligent Media Delivery platform in order for companies to engage and activate consumers wherever they plan, shop, share and/or buy. The data-driven intelligent solution targets responses, stimulates activity and predicts performance. Valassis is a wholly-owned subsidiary of Harland Clarke Holdings Corp., which itself is a subsidiary of MacAndrews & Forbes, Inc.

Valassis Communications offers its employees medical, dental, life, vision and AD&D insurance; an employee assistance plan; a retirement plan and 401(k); adoption assistance; and short- and long-term disability.

FINANCIAL DATA: *Note: Data for latest year may not have been available at press time.*

In U.S. $	2016	2015	2014	2013	2012	2011
Revenue	2,410,000,000	2,285,000,000	2,225,000,000	2,200,000,000	2,162,084,096	2,235,959,040
R&D Expense						
Operating Income						
Operating Margin %						
SGA Expense						
Net Income						
Operating Cash Flow						
Capital Expenditure						
EBITDA						
Return on Assets %						
Return on Equity %						
Debt to Equity						

CONTACT INFORMATION:

Phone: 734 591-3000   Fax:
Toll-Free: 800-437-0479
Address: 19975 Victor Pkwy., Livonia, MI 48152 United States

STOCK TICKER/OTHER:

Stock Ticker: Subsidiary   Exchange:
Employees: 7,000   Fiscal Year Ends: 12/31
Parent Company: MacAndrews & Forbes Inc

SALARIES/BONUSES:

Top Exec. Salary: $ Bonus: $
Second Exec. Salary: $ Bonus: $

OTHER THOUGHTS:

Estimated Female Officers or Directors: 4
Hot Spot for Advancement for Women/Minorities: Y

Vantiv Inc

www.vantiv.com

NAIC Code: 522320

TYPES OF BUSINESS:

Payment Processing-Intermediary
Online Payment Systems
Web-Enabled Payments

BRANDS/DIVISIONS/AFFILIATES:

Moneris Solutions Inc

CONTACTS: Note: Officers with more than one job title may be intentionally listed here more than once.

Charles Drucker, CEO
Stephanie Ferris, CFO
Jeffrey Stiefler, Chairman of the Board
Christopher Thompson, Chief Accounting Officer
Lawrence Drury, Chief Marketing Officer
Mark Heimbouch, COO
Kimberly Martin, Other Executive Officer
Nelson Greene, Other Executive Officer
Royal Cole, President, Divisional
Matthew Taylor, President, Divisional

GROWTH PLANS/SPECIAL FEATURES:

Vantiv Inc is an integrated payment processor differentiated by its single, proprietary technology platform. The company efficiently provides a suite of comprehensive services to merchants and financial institutions of all sizes to meet their payment processing needs. Its technology platform offers its clients a single point of service that is easy to connect to and use to access a broad range of payment services and solutions. Its single, proprietary technology platform is differentiated from its competitors' multiple platform architectures because of its single point of service and ability to collect, manage and analyze data across the payment processing value chain. The firm enables merchants to accept and process credit, debit and prepaid payments and provides them supporting services, such as information solutions, interchange management and fraud management, as well as vertical-specific solutions in sectors such as grocery, pharmacy, retail, petroleum and restaurants. The firm provides small and mid-sized clients with the comprehensive solutions that it has developed to meet the extensive requirements of its large merchant and financial institution clients. It then tailors these solutions to the unique needs of its small and mid-sized clients. In December 2016, Vantiv acquired Moneris Solutions, Inc. from Moneris Solutions Corporation for $425 million. In April 2017, the firm agreed to acquire Paymetric, a portfolio company of Francisco Partners. The following August, Vantiv and Worldpay Group PLC agreed to merge for $10.4 billion. The proposed merger, still awaiting a firm offer and regulatory approval, would allow Vantiv access to U.K. markets.

FINANCIAL DATA: Note: Data for latest year may not have been available at press time.

In U.S. $	2016	2015	2014	2013	2012	2011
Revenue	3,578,991,000	3,159,938,000	2,577,203,000	2,108,077,000	1,863,239,000	1,622,421,000
R&D Expense						
Operating Income	568,514,000	434,410,000	314,691,000	352,802,000	304,855,000	243,153,000
Operating Margin %	15.88%	13.74%	12.21%	16.73%	16.36%	14.98%
SGA Expense	771,958,000	686,318,000	570,339,000	433,751,000	398,875,000	323,787,000
Net Income	213,208,000	147,946,000	125,292,000	133,572,000	57,610,000	36,240,000
Operating Cash Flow	668,590,000	757,878,000	592,905,000	480,622,000	293,114,000	233,454,000
Capital Expenditure	141,821,000	84,730,000	103,179,000	61,578,000	64,648,000	66,620,000
EBITDA	838,568,000	711,352,000	589,760,000	538,255,000	372,721,000	383,980,000
Return on Assets %	3.15%	2.31%	2.38%	3.27%	1.54%	1.05%
Return on Equity %	18.79%	15.94%	14.99%	16.84%	7.99%	5.94%
Debt to Equity	2.35	3.11	3.64	2.25	1.07	2.80

CONTACT INFORMATION:

Phone: 513 900-5250   Fax:
Toll-Free:
Address: 8500 Governor's Hill Drive, Symmes Township, OH 45249 United States

STOCK TICKER/OTHER:

Stock Ticker: VNTV   Exchange: NYS
Employees: 3,526   Fiscal Year Ends: 12/31
Parent Company:

SALARIES/BONUSES:

Top Exec. Salary: $840,577   Bonus: $664,000
Second Exec. Salary: $614,712   Bonus: $100,000

OTHER THOUGHTS:

Estimated Female Officers or Directors:
Hot Spot for Advancement for Women/Minorities:

Varian Medical Systems Inc

www.varian.com

NAIC Code: 334510

TYPES OF BUSINESS:

Radiation Oncology Systems
X-Ray Equipment
Software Systems
Security & Inspection Products

BRANDS/DIVISIONS/AFFILIATES:

Varex Imaging Corporation

CONTACTS: Note: Officers with more than one job title may be intentionally listed here more than once.

Dow Wilson, CEO
Elisha Finney, CFO
R. Eckert, Chairman of the Board
Magnus Momsen, Chief Accounting Officer
Timothy Guertin, Director
John Kuo, General Counsel
Kolleen Kennedy, President, Divisional

GROWTH PLANS/SPECIAL FEATURES:

Varian Medical Systems, Inc. designs, manufactures, sells and services hardware and software products for treating cancer. These systems treat cancer with conventional radiotherapy as well as with advanced treatment such as fixed field intensity-modulated radiation therapy, image-guided radiation therapy, volumetric modulated arc therapy, stereotactic radiosurgery, stereotactic body radiotherapy and brachytherapy. Varian's software solutions also include informatics software for information management, clinical knowledge exchange, patient care management, practice management and decision-making support for comprehensive cancer clinics, radiotherapy centers and medical oncology practices. Its hardware products include linear accelerators, brachytherapy afterloaders, treatment simulation and verification equipment and accessories. Varian has 70 sales and support offices worldwide. In late-2016, the firm spun off its imaging components business into a stand-alone public company named Varex Imaging Corporation. In June 2017, it received FDA 510(k) clearance for its Halcyon cancer treatment system.

Varian offers employees medical, life, AD&D, disability, dental and vision plans; a 401(k); educational reimbursement; an employee assistance program; and a stock purchase plan.

FINANCIAL DATA: Note: Data for latest year may not have been available at press time.

In U.S. $	2016	2015	2014	2013	2012	2011
Revenue	3,217,800,000	3,099,111,000	3,049,800,000	2,942,897,000	2,807,015,000	2,596,666,000
R&D Expense	253,500,000	245,211,000	234,840,000	208,208,000	185,742,000	170,725,000
Operating Income	550,800,000	548,967,000	571,155,000	608,890,000	594,074,000	588,451,000
Operating Margin %	17.11%	17.71%	18.72%	20.69%	21.16%	22.66%
SGA Expense	557,000,000	488,514,000	495,680,000	432,589,000	416,520,000	376,713,000
Net Income	402,300,000	411,485,000	403,703,000	438,248,000	427,049,000	398,933,000
Operating Cash Flow	356,300,000	469,556,000	448,986,000	455,185,000	492,775,000	472,779,000
Capital Expenditure	80,400,000	91,384,000	89,649,000	76,277,000	61,103,000	70,928,000
EBITDA	648,000,000	631,117,000	644,126,000	679,071,000	660,325,000	643,900,000
Return on Assets %	10.84%	11.82%	11.82%	13.80%	15.88%	16.54%
Return on Equity %	23.30%	24.72%	24.24%	27.18%	31.01%	31.67%
Debt to Equity	0.16	0.19	0.23	0.26		

CONTACT INFORMATION:

Phone: 650 493-4000   Fax:
Toll-Free: 800-544-4636
Address: 3100 Hansen Way, Palo Alto, CA 94304 United States

SALARIES/BONUSES:

Top Exec. Salary: $1,152,438   Bonus: $
Second Exec. Salary: $718,131   Bonus: $

STOCK TICKER/OTHER:

Stock Ticker: VAR   Exchange: NYS
Employees: 7,800   Fiscal Year Ends: 09/30
Parent Company:

OTHER THOUGHTS:

Estimated Female Officers or Directors: 6
Hot Spot for Advancement for Women/Minorities: Y

VCA Inc

NAIC Code: 541940

www.vca.com

TYPES OF BUSINESS:

Animal Health Care Services
Veterinary Diagnostic Laboratories
Full-Service Animal Hospitals
Veterinary Equipment
Ultrasound Imaging

GROWTH PLANS/SPECIAL FEATURES:

VCA, Inc. is a leading animal healthcare company operating in the U.S. and Canada. The firm provides services and diagnostic testing to support veterinary care, and sells diagnostic equipment and other medical technology products to the veterinary market. VCA's hospitals offer a full range of general medical and surgical services for companion animals, as well as specialized treatments, including advanced diagnostic services, internal medicine, oncology, ophthalmology, dermatology and cardiology. In addition, the company provides pharmaceutical products and performs a variety of pet wellness programs such as health examinations, diagnostic testing, routine vaccinations, spaying, neutering and dental care. VCA's network of animal hospitals is supported by more than 5,000 veterinarians and sees more than 11.8 million patient visits annually. In January 2017, VCA agreed to be acquired by Mars, Inc. for $9.1 billion, including $1.4 billion in outstanding debt. VCA will operate as a distinct and separate business unit within the Mars Petcare segment, and the transaction was expected to close by year's end.

VCA offers its employees health, life, dental and vision insurance; tuition reimbursement; disability coverage; and veterinary care discounts.

BRANDS/DIVISIONS/AFFILIATES:

Mars Inc

CONTACTS: Note: Officers with more than one job title may be intentionally listed here more than once.

Robert Antin, CEO
Tomas Fuller, CFO
Tomas W. Fuller, CFO
Josh Drake, President, Subsidiary
Robert Antin, Chmn.

FINANCIAL DATA: Note: Data for latest year may not have been available at press time.

In U.S. $	2016	2015	2014	2013	2012	2011
Revenue	2,516,863,000	2,133,675,008	1,918,482,944	1,803,368,960	1,699,641,984	1,485,361,024
R&D Expense						
Operating Income						
Operating Margin %						
SGA Expense						
Net Income	209,196,000	211,048,992	135,438,000	137,511,008	45,551,000	95,405,000
Operating Cash Flow						
Capital Expenditure						
EBITDA						
Return on Assets %						
Return on Equity %						
Debt to Equity						

CONTACT INFORMATION:

Phone: 310 571-6500   Fax: 310 571-6700
Toll-Free: 800-966-1822
Address: 12401 W. Olympic Blvd., Los Angeles, CA 90064 United States

STOCK TICKER/OTHER:

Stock Ticker: WOOF   Exchange:
Employees: 11,500   Fiscal Year Ends: 12/31
Parent Company: Mars Inc

SALARIES/BONUSES:

Top Exec. Salary: $ Bonus: $
Second Exec. Salary: $ Bonus: $

OTHER THOUGHTS:

Estimated Female Officers or Directors:
Hot Spot for Advancement for Women/Minorities:

Verizon Communications Inc

www.verizon.com

NAIC Code: 517110

TYPES OF BUSINESS:

Mobile Phone and Wireless Services
Telecommunications Services
Wireless Services
Long-Distance Services
High-Speed Internet Access
Video-on-Demand Services
e-Commerce & Online Services

BRANDS/DIVISIONS/AFFILIATES:

Fleetmatics Group PLC

CONTACTS: *Note: Officers with more than one job title may be intentionally listed here more than once.*

Matthew Ellis, CFO
Lowell McAdam, Chairman of the Board
Anthony Skiadas, Chief Accounting Officer
Marc Reed, Chief Administrative Officer
Roger Gurnani, Chief Information Officer
Diego Scotti, Chief Marketing Officer
Craig Silliman, Executive VP, Divisional
Marni Walden, Executive VP
John Stratton, Executive VP

GROWTH PLANS/SPECIAL FEATURES:

Verizon Communications, Inc. is one of the world's largest providers of communications services. Its primary network technology platforms are 3G CDMA, based on spread-spectrum digital radio technology, and 4G LTE, which provides higher throughput performance and more improved efficiencies than 3G. It operates in two segments: wireless and wireline. The wireless segment's products and services include wireless voice, data products and other value added services and equipment sales across the U.S. The segment's network provides services to a customer base of nearly 114.2 million. Wireless' 4G LTE network is deployed in more than 500 markets, covering more than 309 million people. The wireline segment is comprised of four units: mass markets, global enterprise, global wholesale and other. The mass markets unit provides local exchange, long distance, broadband services and FiOS bundled services to residential and small business subscribers. Global enterprise offers voice, data and internet communications services to medium and large business customers, multi-national corporations and state and federal government customers. Global wholesale provides switched access and special access services to long distance and other carriers. The other division provides local exchange and long distance services for former MCI mass market customers, operator services, pay phone, card services and supply sales. In 2016, Verizon acquired Fleetmatics Group PLC for $2.4 billion, purchased assets of LQD WiFi LLC and agreed to acquire Yahoo!'s operating business for $4.83 billion. In 2017, the firm acquired the fiber-optics business of XO Communications for $1.8 billion; the drone operations management firm Skyward; and, after a bidding war with AT&T, Inc., Straight Path Communications, Inc., a wireless-spectrum holder, for $3.1 billion.

Employee benefits include 401(k); corporate discounts; health and dependent care spending accounts; life and AD&D insurance; commuter spending accounts; medical, dental and vision coverage; disability; adoption reimbursement; and tuition assistance.

FINANCIAL DATA: *Note: Data for latest year may not have been available at press time.*

In U.S. $	2016	2015	2014	2013	2012	2011
Revenue	125,980,000,000	131,620,000,000	127,079,000,000	120,550,000,000	115,846,000,000	110,875,000,000
R&D Expense						
Operating Income	27,059,000,000	33,060,000,000	19,599,000,000	31,968,000,000	13,160,000,000	12,880,000,000
Operating Margin %	21.47%	25.11%	15.42%	26.51%	11.35%	11.61%
SGA Expense	31,569,000,000	29,986,000,000	41,016,000,000	27,089,000,000	39,951,000,000	35,624,000,000
Net Income	13,127,000,000	17,879,000,000	9,625,000,000	11,497,000,000	875,000,000	2,404,000,000
Operating Cash Flow	22,715,000,000	38,930,000,000	30,631,000,000	38,818,000,000	31,486,000,000	29,780,000,000
Capital Expenditure	17,593,000,000	27,717,000,000	17,545,000,000	17,184,000,000	20,110,000,000	16,244,000,000
EBITDA	41,290,000,000	49,177,000,000	36,718,000,000	48,550,000,000	28,928,000,000	29,806,000,000
Return on Assets %	5.37%	7.49%	3.79%	4.60%	.38%	1.06%
Return on Equity %	67.40%	124.47%	37.64%	31.93%	2.53%	6.45%
Debt to Equity	4.68	6.31	8.98	2.30	1.43	1.39

CONTACT INFORMATION:

Phone: 212 395-1000   Fax:
Toll-Free: 800-837-4966
Address: 1095 Avenue of the Americas, New York, NY 10036 United States

STOCK TICKER/OTHER:

Stock Ticker: VZ   Exchange: NYS
Employees: 160,900   Fiscal Year Ends: 12/31
Parent Company:

SALARIES/BONUSES:

Top Exec. Salary: $1,600,000   Bonus: $
Second Exec. Salary: $921,154   Bonus: $

OTHER THOUGHTS:

Estimated Female Officers or Directors: 5
Hot Spot for Advancement for Women/Minorities: Y

Sales, profits and employees may be estimates. Financial information, benefits and other data can change quickly and may vary from those stated here.

VF Corporation

www.vfc.com

NAIC Code: 424300

TYPES OF BUSINESS:

Apparel and Clothing Brands, Designers, Importers and Distributors
Swimsuits
Outdoor Gear & Apparel
Image Wear
Outlet Stores
Footwear

BRANDS/DIVISIONS/AFFILIATES:

Vans
lucy
SmartWool
Wrangler
Timberland
North Face (The)
Nautica
Majestic

CONTACTS: *Note: Officers with more than one job title may be intentionally listed here more than once.*

Bryan McNeill, Chief Accounting Officer
Eric Wiseman, Director
Steven Rendle, Director
Laura Meagher, General Counsel
Martino Guerrini, President, Divisional
Kevin Bailey, President, Divisional
Curtis Holtz, President, Divisional
Karl Salzburger, President, Divisional
Scott Baxter, President, Divisional
Aidan O'Meara, President, Geographical
Scott Roe, Vice President

GROWTH PLANS/SPECIAL FEATURES:

VF Corporation, organized in 1899, is one of the world's largest brand-name apparel manufacturers and a leading producer of jeanswear, outerwear, footwear, sportswear and occupational apparel. VF products are sold globally throughout the U.S., Canada, Europe, Asia and Latin America. The company divides its brands into five business groups, called coalitions: outdoor & action sports, which includes outerwear, sportswear, footwear, equipment, backpacks, daypacks, luggage and accessories; jeanswear, which consists of jeans as well as shorts, casual pants, knit and woven tops and outerwear; imagewear, which includes occupational apparel, uniforms and owned and licensed sports and lifestyle apparel; sportswear, which includes outerwear, underwear, swimwear, sleepwear, luggage and accessories; and contemporary brands, which focuses on lifestyle brands. The outdoor & action sports coalition includes the firm's largest brand, The North Face, as well as Timberland, SmartWool, Vans, JanSport, Eastpak, Kipling, Napapijri, Reef and lucy. In jeanswear, Lee and Wrangler are its largest brand names. The image business includes the firm's uniforms and career occupational clothing. These brands include Red Kap work clothes; Bulwark flame resistant and protective clothing; and Horace Small apparel for law enforcement and public safety officials. The licensed business consists of VF's owned and licensed high profile apparel, marketed under the Majestic and Harley-Davidson brand names. Sportswear brands include Nautica and Kipling. In late-2016, the firm sold its contemporary coalition, which included the 7 For All Mankind, Splendid and Ella Moss brands.

FINANCIAL DATA: *Note: Data for latest year may not have been available at press time.*

In U.S. $	2016	2015	2014	2013	2012	2011
Revenue	12,019,000,000	12,376,740,000	12,282,160,000	11,419,650,000	10,879,850,000	9,459,232,000
R&D Expense						
Operating Income	1,499,226,000	1,660,996,000	1,437,724,000	1,647,147,000	1,465,267,000	1,244,791,000
Operating Margin %	12.47%	13.42%	11.70%	14.42%	13.46%	13.15%
SGA Expense	4,243,798,000	4,178,386,000	4,159,885,000	3,841,032,000	3,596,708,000	3,085,839,000
Net Income	1,074,106,000	1,231,593,000	1,047,505,000	1,210,119,000	1,085,999,000	888,089,000
Operating Cash Flow	1,477,919,000	1,146,510,000	1,697,629,000	1,506,041,000	1,275,000,000	1,081,371,000
Capital Expenditure	220,066,000	317,784,000	302,020,000	325,142,000	282,830,000	249,128,000
EBITDA	1,791,898,000	1,941,878,000	1,713,974,000	1,900,536,000	1,753,436,000	1,441,056,000
Return on Assets %	11.08%	12.55%	10.32%	12.13%	11.46%	11.26%
Return on Equity %	20.80%	22.36%	17.89%	21.60%	22.50%	21.17%
Debt to Equity	0.41	0.26	0.25	0.23	0.27	0.40

CONTACT INFORMATION:

Phone: 336 424-6000　　　　Fax:
Toll-Free:
Address: 105 Corporate Ctr. Blvd., Greensboro, NC 27408 United States

STOCK TICKER/OTHER:

Stock Ticker: VFC　　　　　　　　Exchange: NYS
Employees: 69,000　　　　　　　　Fiscal Year Ends: 12/31
Parent Company:

SALARIES/BONUSES:

Top Exec. Salary: $1,350,001　　Bonus: $
Second Exec. Salary:　　　　　　Bonus: $
$945,000

OTHER THOUGHTS:

Estimated Female Officers or Directors: 5
Hot Spot for Advancement for Women/Minorities: Y

Victoria's Secret

NAIC Code: 448120

TYPES OF BUSINESS:

Intimate Apparel-Women's, Retail
Cosmetics
Fragrances
Personal Care Products
Online Sales
Sports Apparel

BRANDS/DIVISIONS/AFFILIATES:

PINK
Victoria's Secret Beauty and Accessories
Very Sexy
Body by Victoria
Angels
Dream Angles
Victoria Sport
L Brands Inc

CONTACTS: *Note: Officers with more than one job title may be intentionally listed here more than once.*

Leslie H. Wexner, CEO
Brian VanOoyen, VP-Merch. Planning
Bridget Ryan-Berman, CEO-Victoria's Secret Direct
Sharen Jester Turney, CEO
Leslie H. Wexner, Chmn.

GROWTH PLANS/SPECIAL FEATURES:

Victoria's Secret, a wholly-owned subsidiary of L Brands, Inc., purchases, distributes and sells lingerie, personal care products and women's sports apparel through over 1,200 retail stores in the U.S., Canada, UK and Greater China and the internet. The stores offer branded merchandise such as IPEX, PINK, Very Sexy, Body by Victoria, VS Cotton, Dream Angels, Beauty Rush, Angels and Victoria Sport. The firm also owns a number standalone PINK stores in the U.S., Canada and the UK, which sell intimate apparel, denim, casual apparel and body products targeted to young women ages 13-25, and standalone Victoria's Secret Beauty and Accessories Stores, largely located in China. Victoria's Secret Beauty and Accessories stores offer a complete line of fragrance, cosmetics and body products for skin and hair. Additionally, Victoria's Secret and PINK have more than 410 stores in more than 70 other countries operating under franchise, license and wholesale arrangements. Once each year, Victoria's Secret conducts a televised fashion show featuring some of the world's top models and performances by acclaimed musicians such as Maroon 5 or Kanye West. In early 2016, parent L Brands reacquired the franchise rights to operate Victoria's Secret Beauty and Accessories stores in greater China, including 26 stores already open at the time of the acquisition.

The company offers employees medical, dental, vision and prescription drug coverage; a 401(k) plan; a discount stock purchase plan; life insurance; discounts on products; tuition reimbursement; a commuter discount program; and an employee assistance program.

FINANCIAL DATA: *Note: Data for latest year may not have been available at press time.*

In U.S. $	2016	2015	2014	2013	2012	2011
Revenue	7,781,000,000	7,672,000,000	7,207,600,000	6,884,200,000	6,574,000,000	6,121,000,000
R&D Expense						
Operating Income						
Operating Margin %						
SGA Expense						
Net Income	1,173,000,000	1,391,000,000	1,271,000,000	903,000,000	1,188,000,000	1,081,000,000
Operating Cash Flow						
Capital Expenditure						
EBITDA						
Return on Assets %						
Return on Equity %						
Debt to Equity						

CONTACT INFORMATION:

Phone: 614-577-7111   Fax:
Toll-Free: 800-411-5116
Address: 4 Limited Pkwy. E, Reynoldsburg, OH 43068 United States

STOCK TICKER/OTHER:

Stock Ticker: Subsidiary
Employees: 65,000
Parent Company: L Brands Inc

Exchange:
Fiscal Year Ends: 01/31

SALARIES/BONUSES:

Top Exec. Salary: $ Bonus: $
Second Exec. Salary: $ Bonus: $

OTHER THOUGHTS:

Estimated Female Officers or Directors: 3
Hot Spot for Advancement for Women/Minorities: Y

Visa Inc

NAIC Code: 522320

TYPES OF BUSINESS:

Credit Cards
Debit Cards
Prepaid Cards

BRANDS/DIVISIONS/AFFILIATES:

Visa Canada Corporaiton
CyberSource Corporation
Visa USA Inc
Visa International Service Association
Inovant LLC
Visa Europe Ltd
VisaNet
Visa Checkout

CONTACTS: Note: Officers with more than one job title may be intentionally listed here more than once.

Vasant Prabhu, CFO
Robert Matschullat, Chairman of the Board
James Hoffmeister, Chief Accounting Officer
Lynne Biggar, Chief Marketing Officer
Alfred Kelly, Director
Rajat Taneja, Executive VP, Divisional
William Sheedy, Executive VP, Divisional
Kelly Tullier, Executive VP
Ryan McInerney, President
Mary Richey, Vice Chairman, Divisional

GROWTH PLANS/SPECIAL FEATURES:

Visa, Inc. is a global payments technology company that connects consumers, businesses, financial institutions and governments in over 200 countries. The company's processing network, VisaNet, facilitates authorization, clearing and settlement of payment transactions worldwide. It also offers fraud protection for account holders and rapid payment for merchants. Visa is not a bank and does not issue cards, extend credit or set rates and fees for account holders in Visa-branded cards and payment products. In most cases, account holder and merchant relationships belong to, and are managed by, Visa's financial institution clients. Visa's tokenization replaces account numbers with digital tokens for online and mobile payments, benefiting merchants and issuers by removing sensitive account information and reducing fraud risk. Visa's chip payment technology addresses fraud at the physical point-of-sale by working with merchants and Visa financial institution clients in the U.S. Visa Checkout is a fast, simple and intuitive payment experience that allows consumers to pay for goods online, on any device, in just a few clicks. The company's core products and services can be condensed into three divisions: debit, providing debit solutions that support issuers' payment products that draw on demand deposit accounts; prepaid, providing prepaid payment solutions that support issuer's products that access a pre-funded amount; and credit, providing credit payment solutions that support issuers' deferred payment and customized financing products. Subsidiaries of the company include Visa Canada Corporation; CyberSource Corporation; Visa U.S.A., Inc.; Visa International Service Association; and Inovant, LLC. In 2016, the firm acquired Visa Europe Ltd., which previously operated as a separate company. In June 2017, Visa agreed to invest in Klarna, an online payment company in Europe, serving 60 million customers and 70,000 retailers.

FINANCIAL DATA: Note: Data for latest year may not have been available at press time.

In U.S. $	2016	2015	2014	2013	2012	2011
Revenue	15,082,000,000	13,880,000,000	12,702,000,000	11,778,000,000	10,421,000,000	9,188,000,000
R&D Expense						
Operating Income	7,883,000,000	9,063,999,000	7,697,000,000	7,239,000,000	2,139,000,000	5,456,000,000
Operating Margin %	52.26%	65.30%	60.59%	61.46%	20.52%	59.38%
SGA Expense	2,054,000,000	1,755,000,000	1,735,000,000	1,739,000,000	1,709,000,000	1,621,000,000
Net Income	5,991,000,000	6,328,000,000	5,438,000,000	4,980,000,000	2,144,000,000	3,650,000,000
Operating Cash Flow	5,574,000,000	6,584,000,000	7,205,000,000	3,022,000,000	5,009,000,000	3,872,000,000
Capital Expenditure	523,000,000	414,000,000	553,000,000	471,000,000	376,000,000	353,000,000
EBITDA	8,941,000,000	9,558,000,000	8,132,000,000	7,636,000,000	2,472,000,000	5,976,000,000
Return on Assets %	11.49%	16.05%	14.59%	13.11%	5.73%	10.70%
Return on Equity %	21.00%	22.10%	20.03%	18.27%	7.93%	14.18%
Debt to Equity	0.58					

CONTACT INFORMATION:

Phone: 650-432-3200   Fax:
Toll-Free: 800-847-2911
Address: P.O. Box 8999, San Francisco, CA 94128 United States

STOCK TICKER/OTHER:

Stock Ticker: V   Exchange: NYS
Employees: 11,300   Fiscal Year Ends: 09/30
Parent Company:

SALARIES/BONUSES:

Top Exec. Salary: $850,032   Bonus: $3,125,000
Second Exec. Salary: Bonus: $
$1,250,048

OTHER THOUGHTS:

Estimated Female Officers or Directors: 6
Hot Spot for Advancement for Women/Minorities: Y

VMware Inc

NAIC Code: 0

www.vmware.com

TYPES OF BUSINESS:

Computer Software, Network Management, System Testing & Storage
Virtual Infrastructure Automation
Virtual Infrastructure Management

BRANDS/DIVISIONS/AFFILIATES:

vSphere
Horizon
Fusion
Workstation
AirWatch
vCloud Hybrid Service
VMware vCloud Service Provider Program
vCHS Business Ventures

CONTACTS: Note: Officers with more than one job title may be intentionally listed here more than once.

Patrick Gelsinger, CEO
Zane Rowe, CFO
Michael Dell, Chairman of the Board
Kevan Krysler, Chief Accounting Officer
Rangarajan Raghuram, Co-COO, Divisional
Sanjay Poonen, COO, Divisional
Rajiv Ramaswami, COO, Divisional
Maurizio Carli, Executive VP, Divisional
S. Smith, Other Executive Officer

GROWTH PLANS/SPECIAL FEATURES:

VMware, Inc. is a leader in virtualization infrastructure software. It develops and markets its products through three areas: software-defined data center (SDDC), end-user computing and hybrid cloud computing. SDDC consists of four main product categories: compute, providing a hypervisor layer of software that enables compute virtualization through its flagship, vSphere; storage and availability, offering cost-effective holistic data storage and protection options to all applications running on vSphere; network and security, which abstracts physical networks and simplifies the provisioning and consumption of networking resources; and management and automation, which automates overarching IT processes involved in provisioning IT services and resources to users from initial deployment to retirement. The firm's end-user computing products enable IT organizations to deliver secure access to data, applications and devices to end-users. This segment's solutions include desktop applications through its Horizon, Fusion and Workstation brands, which control and deliver data, store images, provide cloud delivery and virtualization solutions for Macintosh and Windows; mobile solutions through AirWatch, which offer enterprise mobile management and security solutions; and social computing and other workspace services through Socialcast, an enterprise social platform, as well as through App Manager, a single sign-on identity service that delivers applications, desktops and data in a single portal of entry, called Workspace. VMware's hybrid cloud computing product enables customers to utilize off-premises vSphere-based hybrid cloud computing capacity through three programs: vCloud Hybrid Service, a service cloud that allows seamless extension from the customer's data center to the cloud; VMware vCloud Service Provider Program, a hosting and cloud computing vendor; and vCHS Business Ventures, which co-invests with large in-country telecommunications providers to enable user experience with the firm's vCloud Hybrid Service.

FINANCIAL DATA: Note: Data for latest year may not have been available at press time.

In U.S. $	2016	2015	2014	2013	2012	2011
Revenue	7,093,000,000	6,571,000,000	6,035,000,000	5,207,000,000	4,605,047,000	3,767,096,000
R&D Expense	1,503,000,000	1,300,000,000	1,239,000,000	1,082,000,000	999,214,000	775,051,000
Operating Income	1,439,000,000	1,197,000,000	1,027,000,000	1,093,000,000	871,943,000	735,171,000
Operating Margin %	20.28%	18.21%	17.01%	20.99%	18.93%	19.51%
SGA Expense	3,046,000,000	3,033,000,000	2,836,000,000	2,234,000,000	2,012,567,000	1,634,887,000
Net Income	1,186,000,000	997,000,000	886,000,000	1,014,000,000	745,702,000	723,936,000
Operating Cash Flow	2,381,000,000	1,899,000,000	2,180,000,000	2,535,000,000	1,897,524,000	2,025,633,000
Capital Expenditure	153,000,000	333,000,000	352,000,000	345,000,000	234,458,000	455,172,000
EBITDA	1,844,000,000	1,574,000,000	1,417,000,000	1,488,000,000	1,252,636,000	1,114,190,000
Return on Assets %	7.32%	6.44%	6.43%	8.84%	7.73%	9.35%
Return on Equity %	14.81%	12.86%	12.30%	16.15%	14.19%	16.87%
Debt to Equity	0.18	0.18	0.19	0.06	0.07	0.09

CONTACT INFORMATION:

Phone: 650 427-5000   Fax: 650 475-5005
Toll-Free: 877-486-9273
Address: 3401 Hillview Ave., Palo Alto, CA 94304 United States

STOCK TICKER/OTHER:

Stock Ticker: VMW   Exchange: NYS
Employees: 19,900   Fiscal Year Ends: 12/31
Parent Company:

SALARIES/BONUSES:

Top Exec. Salary: $504,168   Bonus: $1,597,248
Second Exec. Salary: Bonus: $
$1,000,000

OTHER THOUGHTS:

Estimated Female Officers or Directors: 3
Hot Spot for Advancement for Women/Minorities: Y

W R Berkley Corporation

www.wrberkley.com

NAIC Code: 524126

TYPES OF BUSINESS:

Insurance, Direct Property & Casualty
Reinsurance
Regional Insurance
Specialty Insurance
Risk Management
Liability Insurance

BRANDS/DIVISIONS/AFFILIATES:

GROWTH PLANS/SPECIAL FEATURES:

W.R. Berkley Corporation is one of the largest insurance holding companies in the U.S. The firm operates in two segments of the property and casualty insurance business insurance and reinsurance. The insurance segment derives 89.9% of annual net premiums written, and comprises Berkley's commercial insurance business, offering excess and surplus lines and admitted lines throughout the U.S. This division also includes the firm's insurance businesses located in the U.K., Europe, South America, Canada, Mexico, Scandinavia, Asia and Australia. The reinsurance segment (10.1%) offers reinsurance on a facultative and treaty basis, primarily in the U.S., U.K., Europe, Australia, the Asia-Pacific and South Africa.

CONTACTS: Note: Officers with more than one job title may be intentionally listed here more than once.

William Berkley, CEO
Richard Baio, CFO
William Berkley, Chairman of the Board
Eugene Ballard, Executive VP, Divisional
James Shiel, Executive VP, Divisional
Ira Lederman, Executive VP
Matthew Ricciardim, General Counsel

FINANCIAL DATA: Note: Data for latest year may not have been available at press time.

In U.S. $	2016	2015	2014	2013	2012	2011
Revenue	7,654,184,000	7,206,457,000	7,128,928,000	6,408,534,000	5,823,554,000	5,155,984,000
R&D Expense						
Operating Income	896,438,000	732,030,000	952,196,000	698,888,000	701,928,000	518,283,000
Operating Margin %	11.71%	10.15%	13.35%	10.90%	12.05%	10.05%
SGA Expense	138,908,000	127,365,000	2,157,456,000	2,000,684,000	1,799,623,000	1,621,329,000
Net Income	601,916,000	503,694,000	648,884,000	499,925,000	510,592,000	394,803,000
Operating Cash Flow	848,376,000	881,304,000	734,847,000	819,798,000	675,458,000	670,279,000
Capital Expenditure	50,829,000	63,562,000	41,958,000	63,150,000	40,556,000	45,320,000
EBITDA						
Return on Assets %	2.66%	2.31%	3.07%	2.45%	2.64%	2.19%
Return on Equity %	12.47%	10.96%	14.53%	11.56%	12.28%	10.23%
Debt to Equity	0.49	0.47	0.53	0.46	0.49	0.43

CONTACT INFORMATION:

Phone: 203 629-3000　　　Fax:
Toll-Free:
Address: 475 Steamboat Rd., Greenwich, CT 06830 United States

STOCK TICKER/OTHER:

Stock Ticker: WRB　　　　　　Exchange: NYS
Employees: 7,683　　　　　　　Fiscal Year Ends: 12/31
Parent Company:

SALARIES/BONUSES:

Top Exec. Salary: $1,000,000　　Bonus: $
Second Exec. Salary:　　　　　　Bonus: $
$993,769

OTHER THOUGHTS:

Estimated Female Officers or Directors: 16
Hot Spot for Advancement for Women/Minorities: Y

Wabco Holdings Inc

www.wabco-auto.com

NAIC Code: 336340

TYPES OF BUSINESS:

Brake Systems Manufacturing
Suspension Systems

BRANDS/DIVISIONS/AFFILIATES:

CONTACTS: *Note: Officers with more than one job title may be intentionally listed here more than once.*

Jacques Esculier, CEO
Prashanth Mahendra-Rajah, CFO
Mazen Mazraani, Other Executive Officer
Nicolas Bardot, Other Executive Officer
Lisa Brown, Other Executive Officer
Nick Rens, President, Divisional
Jorge Solis, President, Divisional
Sean Deason, Vice President

GROWTH PLANS/SPECIAL FEATURES:

Wabco Holdings, Inc. is a provider of electronic, mechanical and mechatronic products for commercial truck, trailer, bus and passenger car manufacturers. The firm manufactures and sells control systems, including advanced braking, stability, suspension, transmission control and air compressing and processing systems, that improve vehicle performance and safety and reduce overall vehicle operating costs. Its products are included in approximately two out of three commercial vehicles with advanced vehicle control systems and offered in sophisticated, niche applications in cars and sport utility vehicles. The company develops, manufactures and sells advanced braking, stability, suspension and transmission control systems mainly for commercial vehicles. The firm's highest selling products are pneumatic anti-lock braking systems, electronic braking systems, automated manual transmission systems, air disk brakes and a large variety of conventional mechanical products such as actuators, air compressors and air control valves for heavy- and medium-sized trucks, trailers and buses. The company also supplies advanced electronic suspension controls and vacuum pumps to the car and SUV markets in Europe, North America and Asia. Wabco sells replacement parts, diagnostic tools, training and other services to commercial vehicle aftermarket distributors, repair shops and fleet operators. Wabco primarily sells its products to four groups of customers worldwide: truck and bus; trailer original equipment manufacturers (OEMs); commercial vehicle aftermarket distributors for replacement parts and services; and major car manufacturers. The firm's main customers are Daimler and Volvo, with additional customers including Ashok Leyland, BMW, China National Heavy Truck Corporation, Cummins, Fiat, Hino, Hyundai, TATA Motors, ZF Friedrichshafen AG and several more.

FINANCIAL DATA: *Note: Data for latest year may not have been available at press time.*

In U.S. $	2016	2015	2014	2013	2012	2011
Revenue	2,810,000,000	2,627,500,000	2,851,000,000	2,720,500,000	2,477,400,000	2,794,100,000
R&D Expense	135,200,000	139,500,000	145,000,000	119,400,000	104,300,000	105,100,000
Operating Income	355,900,000	270,900,000	331,000,000	331,900,000	324,500,000	369,900,000
Operating Margin %	12.66%	10.31%	11.60%	12.20%	13.09%	13.23%
SGA Expense	377,700,000	368,400,000	386,800,000	352,800,000	308,200,000	327,200,000
Net Income	223,000,000	275,200,000	291,500,000	653,200,000	302,000,000	357,000,000
Operating Cash Flow	405,400,000	395,300,000	314,400,000	665,800,000	358,300,000	332,000,000
Capital Expenditure	114,000,000	100,600,000	135,900,000	121,500,000	100,500,000	105,200,000
EBITDA	453,900,000	367,600,000	432,600,000	417,100,000	416,000,000	448,100,000
Return on Assets %	7.89%	10.95%	12.08%	31.55%	17.92%	22.68%
Return on Equity %	29.97%	33.80%	29.23%	71.41%	47.79%	71.43%
Debt to Equity	1.36	0.63	0.36	0.04		0.08

CONTACT INFORMATION:

Phone: 732-369-7450   Fax:
Toll-Free:
Address: 2770 Research Dr., Rochester Hills, MI 48309-3511 United States

STOCK TICKER/OTHER:

Stock Ticker: WBC
Employees: 12,860
Parent Company:

Exchange: NYS
Fiscal Year Ends: 12/31

SALARIES/BONUSES:

Top Exec. Salary: $1,100,000   Bonus: $
Second Exec. Salary: $470,005   Bonus: $

OTHER THOUGHTS:

Estimated Female Officers or Directors: 2
Hot Spot for Advancement for Women/Minorities:

Walgreens Boots Alliance Inc

www.walgreens.com

NAIC Code: 446110

TYPES OF BUSINESS:

Drug Stores
Mail-Order Pharmacy Services
Pharmacy Benefit Management
Health Care Center Management
Online Pharmacy Services
Photo Printing Services
Specialty Pharmacy Services
Home Infusion Services

BRANDS/DIVISIONS/AFFILIATES:

boots.com
Walgreens.com
Alliance Healthcare
Walgreens
Duane Reade
Boots
No7
Soap & Glory

CONTACTS: *Note: Officers with more than one job title may be intentionally listed here more than once.*

Stefano Pessina, CEO
George Fairweather, CFO
James Skinner, Chairman of the Board
Kimberly Scardino, Chief Accounting Officer
Alexander Gourlay, Co-COO
Ornella Barra, Co-COO
Ken Murphy, Executive VP

GROWTH PLANS/SPECIAL FEATURES:

Walgreens Boots Alliance, Inc. is a global pharmacy-led health and wellbeing enterprise, with more than 13,100 stores worldwide. The company's global pharmaceutical wholesale and distribution network is comprised of more than 300 distribution centers delivering to over 230,000 pharmacies, doctors, health centers and hospitals on an annual basis. The firm operates through three business segments: retail pharmacy USA, retail pharmacy international and pharmaceutical wholesale. Retail pharmacy USA oversees pharmacy-led health and beauty retail businesses in 50 states, the District of Columbia, Puerto Rico and the U.S. Virgin Islands. It operates more than 8,100 retail stores, and fill approximately 740 million prescriptions (including immunizations) annually. The retail pharmacy international segment oversees pharmacy-led health & beauty retail businesses in eight countries. It operates more than 4,600 retail stores located in the U.K., Thailand, Norway, Ireland, The Netherlands, Mexico and Chile. Websites boots.com and Walgreens.com average 20 million and 58 million visits monthly. The pharmaceutical wholesale segment operates primarily under the Alliance Healthcare brand, and supplies medicines and other healthcare products to more than 110,000 pharmacies, doctors, health centers and hospitals from 288 distribution centers in 11 countries, primarily located in Europe. Walgreens' portfolio of retail and business global brands include Walgreens, Duane Reade, Boots and Alliance Healthcare, as well as global health & beauty product brands such as No7, Botanics, Liz Earl and Soap & Glory. In June 2017, the firm canceled its deal to buy Rite Aid after a long-term struggle with trying to obtain necessary regulatory approvals, and replaced it with a new deal: purchasing more than 2,100 stores, three distribution centers and related inventory.

The company offers employees medical, prescription and dental coverage; life and accident insurance; profit sharing and stock purchase plans; employee discounts; and a flexible spending account.

FINANCIAL DATA: *Note: Data for latest year may not have been available at press time.*

In U.S. $	2016	2015	2014	2013	2012	2011
Revenue	117,351,000,000	103,444,000,000	76,392,000,000	72,217,000,000	71,633,000,000	72,184,000,000
R&D Expense						
Operating Income	6,001,000,000	4,668,000,000	4,194,000,000	3,940,000,000	3,464,000,000	4,365,000,000
Operating Margin %	5.11%	4.51%	5.49%	5.45%	4.83%	6.04%
SGA Expense	23,910,000,000	22,571,000,000	17,992,000,000	17,543,000,000	16,878,000,000	16,561,000,000
Net Income	4,173,000,000	4,220,000,000	1,932,000,000	2,450,000,000	2,127,000,000	2,714,000,000
Operating Cash Flow	7,847,000,000	5,664,000,000	3,893,000,000	4,301,000,000	4,431,000,000	3,643,000,000
Capital Expenditure	1,325,000,000	1,251,000,000	1,106,000,000	1,212,000,000	1,550,000,000	1,213,000,000
EBITDA	7,719,000,000	6,410,000,000	5,029,000,000	5,223,000,000	4,630,000,000	5,451,000,000
Return on Assets %	5.89%	7.96%	5.31%	7.10%	6.98%	10.10%
Return on Equity %	13.74%	16.44%	9.68%	13.00%	12.85%	18.55%
Debt to Equity	0.62	0.43	0.18	0.23	0.22	0.16

CONTACT INFORMATION:

Phone: 847 315-2500   Fax: 847 914-2804
Toll-Free: 800-925-4733
Address: 108 Wilmot Rd., Deerfield, IL 60015 United States

STOCK TICKER/OTHER:

Stock Ticker: WBA   Exchange: NAS
Employees: 251,000   Fiscal Year Ends: 08/31
Parent Company:

SALARIES/BONUSES:

Top Exec. Salary: $977,118   Bonus: $
Second Exec. Salary: Bonus: $
$946,897

OTHER THOUGHTS:

Estimated Female Officers or Directors: 7
Hot Spot for Advancement for Women/Minorities: Y

Wal-Mart Stores Inc (Walmart)

www.walmartstores.com

NAIC Code: 452910

TYPES OF BUSINESS:

Discount Stores
Supermarkets
Warehouse Membership Clubs
Online Sales
Pharmacies
Vision Centers
Auto Repair Centers

BRANDS/DIVISIONS/AFFILIATES:

Walmart
Walmart Supercenter
Sam's Club
Neighborhood Market
walmart.com
Marketside
Moosejaw

CONTACTS: *Note: Officers with more than one job title may be intentionally listed here more than once.*

David Cheesewright, CEO, Divisional
Gregory Foran, CEO, Divisional
Marc Lore, CEO, Divisional
John Furner, CEO, Divisional
C. McMillon, CEO
Brett Biggs, CFO
David Chojnowski, Controller
Gregory Penner, Director
Daniel Bartlett, Executive VP, Divisional
Jacqueline Canney, Executive VP, Divisional
Jeffrey Gearhart, Executive VP, Divisional

GROWTH PLANS/SPECIAL FEATURES:

Wal-Mart Stores, Inc., one of the world's largest retailers, operates through a massive base of Walmart stores, Supercenters, Sam's Clubs, Marketside, Neighborhood Markets and walmart.com. The company operates in three business segments: Walmart U.S., Walmart international and Sam's Club. Walmart U.S. is a mass merchandiser of consumer products, groceries and drugs, operating under the Walmart brand, as well as walmart.com. This segment operates retail stores in the U.S., including all 50 states, Washington D.C. and Puerto Rico, with Supercenters in 49 states, Washington D.C. and Puerto Rico and Walmart discount stores in 41 states and Puerto Rico. Wal-Mart U.S. also operates a relatively small number Neighborhood Markets, which are about 40,000 square feet each. Its main line of business, the Walmart Supercenters, average 178,000 square feet each. Walmart International consists of operations in 27 countries outside the U.S., and includes numerous formats divided into three major categories: retail, wholesale and other. These categories consist of formats such as Supercenters, supermarkets, hypermarkets, warehouse clubs (including Sam's Clubs), cash & carry, home improvement, specialty electronics, restaurants, apparel stores, drug stores and convenience stores. Sam's Club operates membership-only warehouse clubs, as well as samsclub.com in the U.S. All memberships include a spouse/household card at no additional cost and Plus Members are eligible for cash rewards which provides $10 for every $500 in qualifying Sam's Club purchases up to a $500 cash reward annually. By mid-2017, the firm acquired Moosejaw, an online active outdoor retailer; and agreed to acquire internet apparel company, Bonobos, Inc.

FINANCIAL DATA: *Note: Data for latest year may not have been available at press time.*

In U.S. $	2016	2015	2014	2013	2012	2011
Revenue	482,130,000,000	485,651,000,000	476,294,000,000	469,162,000,000	446,950,000,000	
R&D Expense						
Operating Income	24,105,000,000	27,147,000,000	26,872,000,000	27,801,000,000	26,558,000,000	
Operating Margin %	4.99%	5.58%	5.64%	5.92%	5.94%	
SGA Expense	97,041,000,000	93,418,000,000	91,353,000,000	88,873,000,000	85,265,000,000	
Net Income	14,694,000,000	16,363,000,000	16,022,000,000	16,999,000,000	15,699,000,000	
Operating Cash Flow	27,389,000,000	28,564,000,000	23,257,000,000	25,591,000,000	24,255,000,000	
Capital Expenditure	11,477,000,000	12,174,000,000	13,115,000,000	12,898,000,000	13,510,000,000	
EBITDA	33,640,000,000	36,433,000,000	35,861,000,000	36,489,000,000	34,850,000,000	
Return on Assets %	7.28%	8.01%	7.85%	8.57%	8.39%	
Return on Equity %	18.14%	20.75%	20.99%	23.02%	22.45%	
Debt to Equity	0.54	0.53	0.58	0.54	0.66	

CONTACT INFORMATION:

Phone: 479 273-4000   Fax: 479 273-1986
Toll-Free: 800-925-6278
Address: 702 SW 8th St., Bentonville, AR 72716 United States

STOCK TICKER/OTHER:

Stock Ticker: WMT
Employees: 2,300,000
Parent Company:

Exchange: NYS
Fiscal Year Ends: 01/31

SALARIES/BONUSES:

Top Exec. Salary: $1,278,989   Bonus: $
Second Exec. Salary: Bonus: $
$1,071,743

OTHER THOUGHTS:

Estimated Female Officers or Directors: 13
Hot Spot for Advancement for Women/Minorities: Y

Walt Disney Company (The)

NAIC Code: 515210

corporate.disney.go.com

TYPES OF BUSINESS:

Cable TV Networks, Broadcasting & Entertainment
Filmed Entertainment
Merchandising
Television Networks
Music & Book Publishing
Online Entertainment Programs
Theme Parks, Resorts & Cruise Lines
Comic Book Publishing

BRANDS/DIVISIONS/AFFILIATES:

Walt Disney Studios (The)
ESPN Inc
Pixar Animation Studios
Marvel
Disneynature
LucasFilm Ltd
Disneyland Resort
Disney Cruise Line

CONTACTS: Note: Officers with more than one job title may be intentionally listed here more than once.

Robert Iger, CEO
Christine Mccarthy, CFO
Brent Woodford, Executive VP, Divisional
Mary Parker, Executive VP
Alan Braverman, General Counsel
Kevin Mayer, Other Executive Officer

GROWTH PLANS/SPECIAL FEATURES:

The Walt Disney Company is an international entertainment company operating in four primary business segments: media networks, studio entertainment, Disney consumer products and interactive media, and parks and resorts. The media networks segment is comprised of broadcast, cable, radio publishing and digital businesses through the Disney/ABC television and ESPN, Inc. divisions. Media networks within this segment include the Disney Channel, ABC, Freeform and ESPN. The studio entertainment segment is comprised of The Walt Disney Studios, which is the foundation on which the company was built more than 90 years ago. Today, this division brings quality movies, music and stage plays to consumers worldwide. Its studio entertainment brands and companies include: Walt Disney Studios Motion Pictures, Walt Disney Animation Studios, Pixar Animation Studios, Disney Music Group, Disney Theatrical Group, Disneytoon Studios, Marvel, Touchstone Pictures, Disneynature and LucasFilm Ltd. The Disney consumer products and interactive media segment develops and distributes physical products and digital experiences to consumers. These include toys, apps, apparel, books, games and more. Brands and companies within this division include Disney Consumer Products and Interactive Media, Disney Publishing Worldwide, Disney Store and Maker. The parks and resorts segment provides family travel and leisure experiences through its cruise line, theme parks and resorts. Brands and companies within this division include Disneyland Resort, Walt Disney World, Shanghai Disney Resort, Disneyland Paris, Tokyo Disney Resort, Hong Kong Disneyland, Disney Cruise Line, Disney Vacation Club, Aulani Disney Resort & Spa, Adventures by Disney and Walt Disney Imagineering. In 2016, Disney acquired a 15% stake in BAMTech, LLC, which holds Major League Baseball's streaming technology and content delivery businesses, for $450 million.

FINANCIAL DATA: Note: Data for latest year may not have been available at press time.

In U.S. $	2016	2015	2014	2013	2012	2011
Revenue	55,632,000,000	52,465,000,000	48,813,000,000	45,041,000,000	42,278,000,000	40,893,000,000
R&D Expense						
Operating Income	14,358,000,000	13,224,000,000	11,540,000,000			
Operating Margin %	25.80%	25.20%	23.64%			
SGA Expense	8,754,000,000	8,523,000,000	8,565,000,000			
Net Income	9,391,000,000	8,382,000,000	7,501,000,000	6,136,000,000	5,682,000,000	4,807,000,000
Operating Cash Flow	13,213,000,000	10,909,000,000	9,780,000,000	9,452,000,000	7,966,000,000	6,994,000,000
Capital Expenditure	4,773,000,000	4,265,000,000	3,311,000,000	2,796,000,000	3,784,000,000	3,559,000,000
EBITDA	17,749,000,000	16,487,000,000	14,828,000,000	12,161,000,000	11,719,000,000	10,319,000,000
Return on Assets %	10.42%	9.72%	9.06%	7.85%	7.72%	6.80%
Return on Equity %	21.39%	18.73%	16.59%	14.40%	14.73%	12.83%
Debt to Equity	0.38	0.28	0.28	0.28	0.27	0.29

CONTACT INFORMATION:

Phone: 818 5601000   Fax:
Toll-Free:
Address: 500 S. Buena Vista St., Burbank, CA 91521 United States

STOCK TICKER/OTHER:

Stock Ticker: DIS   Exchange: NYS
Employees: 195,000   Fiscal Year Ends: 09/30
Parent Company:

SALARIES/BONUSES:

Top Exec. Salary: $2,500,000   Bonus: $
Second Exec. Salary: Bonus: $
$2,045,231

OTHER THOUGHTS:

Estimated Female Officers or Directors: 7
Hot Spot for Advancement for Women/Minorities: Y

Waste Management Inc

www.wm.com

NAIC Code: 562000

TYPES OF BUSINESS:

Waste Disposal
Recycling Services
Landfill Operation
Hazardous Waste Management
Transfer Stations
Recycled Commodity Trading
Waste Methane Generation

BRANDS/DIVISIONS/AFFILIATES:

Think Green

CONTACTS: *Note: Officers with more than one job title may be intentionally listed here more than once.*

James Fish, CEO
Devina Rankin, CFO
Thomas Weidemeyer, Chairman of the Board
James Trevathan, COO
Bradbury Anderson, Director
Charles Boettcher, Other Executive Officer
Barry Caldwell, Other Executive Officer
Jeff Harris, Senior VP, Divisional
John Morris, Senior VP, Divisional
Darren Shade, Vice President

GROWTH PLANS/SPECIAL FEATURES:

Waste Management, Inc. provides comprehensive waste management services to municipal, commercial, industrial and residential customers throughout North America. Waste Management is the nation's largest collector of recyclables from businesses and households, collecting recyclable materials and depositing them at about a hundred local materials recovery facilities. The firm recycles several different materials including plastics, rubber, electronics and commodities. The company also has a pulp and paper trading group that reduces paper's overall long-term commodity price exposure. Waste Management owns or operates 248 landfill sites, as well as 310 transfer stations that consolidate, compact and transport waste. Its hazardous waste management services include geosynthetic manufacturing, radioactive waste services and landfill liner installation. Additionally, Waste Management promotes environmental initiatives such as Keep America Beautiful and Wildlife Habitat Council, as well as its own Think Green.

Waste Management offers its employees life, AD&D, medical, dental and vision insurance; prescription drug coverage; family assistance programs; flexible spending accounts; adoption assistance; education savings accounts; an employee stock purchase plan; and tuition reimbursement.

FINANCIAL DATA: *Note: Data for latest year may not have been available at press time.*

In U.S. $	2016	2015	2014	2013	2012	2011
Revenue	13,609,000,000	12,961,000,000	13,996,000,000	13,983,000,000	13,649,000,000	13,378,000,000
R&D Expense						
Operating Income	2,296,000,000	2,045,000,000	2,299,000,000	1,079,000,000	1,851,000,000	2,028,000,000
Operating Margin %	16.87%	15.77%	16.42%	7.71%	13.56%	15.15%
SGA Expense	1,410,000,000	1,343,000,000	1,481,000,000	1,468,000,000	1,472,000,000	1,551,000,000
Net Income	1,182,000,000	753,000,000	1,298,000,000	98,000,000	817,000,000	961,000,000
Operating Cash Flow	2,960,000,000	2,498,000,000	2,331,000,000	2,455,000,000	2,295,000,000	2,469,000,000
Capital Expenditure	1,339,000,000	1,233,000,000	1,151,000,000	1,271,000,000	1,510,000,000	1,324,000,000
EBITDA	3,597,000,000	3,290,000,000	3,591,000,000	2,308,000,000	3,088,000,000	3,230,000,000
Return on Assets %	5.72%	3.60%	5.89%	.42%	3.57%	4.36%
Return on Equity %	22.21%	13.43%	22.43%	1.62%	13.15%	15.58%
Debt to Equity	1.67	1.63	1.42	1.66	1.44	1.50

CONTACT INFORMATION:

Phone: 713 512-6200   Fax:
Toll-Free:
Address: 1001 Fannin St., Ste. 4000, Houston, TX 77002 United States

STOCK TICKER/OTHER:

Stock Ticker: WM   Exchange: NYS
Employees: 41,200   Fiscal Year Ends: 12/31
Parent Company:

SALARIES/BONUSES:

Top Exec. Salary: $1,091,772   Bonus: $
Second Exec. Salary: Bonus: $
$705,996

OTHER THOUGHTS:

Estimated Female Officers or Directors: 1
Hot Spot for Advancement for Women/Minorities: Y

Waters Corporation

www.waters.com

NAIC Code: 334516

TYPES OF BUSINESS:

Equipment-Liquid Chromatography Instruments
Mass Spectrometry Systems
Thermal Analyzers
Rheometry Equipment
Software Development
Food Safety Technology

BRANDS/DIVISIONS/AFFILIATES:

ACQUITY UPLC
ACQUITY Arc System
Rubotherm GmbH

CONTACTS: *Note: Officers with more than one job title may be intentionally listed here more than once.*

Christopher OConnell, CEO
Sherry Buck, CFO
Douglas Berthiaume, Chairman of the Board
Terrance Kelly, President, Divisional
Rohit Khanna, Senior VP, Divisional
Ian King, Senior VP, Divisional
David Terricciano, Senior VP, Divisional
Michael Harrington, Senior VP, Divisional
Elizabeth Rae, Senior VP, Divisional
Mark Beaudouin, Senior VP

GROWTH PLANS/SPECIAL FEATURES:

Waters Corporation is an analytical instrument manufacturer. The firm operates in two segments: waters division and TA division. The waters division offers high-performance liquid chromatography (HPLC) and ultra-performance LC (UPLC). HPLC is a standard technique used to identify and analyze the constituent components of a variety of chemicals and other materials and has the capabilities to separate and identify approximately 80% of all known chemicals and materials. HPLC is also used in a variety of other applications such as analyses of foods and beverages for nutritional labeling and compliance with safety regulations, the testing of water and air purity within the environmental testing industry as well as applications in other industries, such as chemical and consumer products. ACQUITY UPLC is a proprietary technology that utilizes a packing material with small, uniform diameter particles to accommodate the increased pressure and narrow chromatographic bands that are generated by these small particles. By using ACQUITY UPLC, researchers and analysts achieve chemical separations and faster analysis times in comparison with many analyses performed by HPLC. The TA division, which stands for thermal analysis, measures the physical characteristics of materials as a function of temperature. TA techniques are widely used in the development, production and characterization of materials in various industries such as plastics, chemicals, automobiles, pharmaceuticals and electronics. This division also includes rheometry instruments, which characterize the flow properties of materials and measures their viscosity, elasticity and deformation. Its ACQUITY Arc System is a quaternary liquid chromatograph (LC) that gives analytical laboratories running established LC methods a choice for replicating or improving their separations performance. In September 2016, the firm acquired Rubotherm GmbH, a manufacturer of gravimetric analysis systems.

Waters offers employees medical insurance, retirement planning programs, sickness/disability programs, life insurance and an employee assistance program.

FINANCIAL DATA: *Note: Data for latest year may not have been available at press time.*

In U.S. $	2016	2015	2014	2013	2012	2011
Revenue	2,167,423,000	2,042,332,000	1,989,344,000	1,904,218,000	1,843,641,000	1,851,184,000
R&D Expense	125,187,000	118,545,000	107,726,000	100,536,000	96,004,000	92,347,000
Operating Income	624,339,000	567,451,000	517,908,000	517,343,000	511,490,000	528,600,000
Operating Margin %	28.80%	27.78%	26.03%	27.16%	27.74%	28.55%
SGA Expense	513,031,000	495,747,000	512,707,000	492,965,000	477,270,000	490,011,000
Net Income	521,503,000	469,053,000	431,620,000	450,003,000	461,443,000	432,968,000
Operating Cash Flow	629,076,000	560,293,000	511,648,000	484,876,000	449,280,000	497,374,000
Capital Expenditure	94,967,000	103,012,000	106,248,000	118,450,000	104,749,000	85,436,000
EBITDA	741,474,000	668,149,000	619,162,000	599,850,000	584,529,000	597,610,000
Return on Assets %	11.67%	11.51%	11.57%	13.33%	15.66%	17.14%
Return on Equity %	23.91%	23.72%	23.59%	27.85%	34.25%	37.72%
Debt to Equity	0.73	0.72	0.65	0.67	0.71	0.57

CONTACT INFORMATION:

Phone: 508 478-2000   Fax: 508 872-1990
Toll-Free: 800-252-4752
Address: 34 Maple St., Milford, MA 01757 United States

SALARIES/BONUSES:

Top Exec. Salary: $849,750   Bonus: $
Second Exec. Salary: $405,563   Bonus: $

STOCK TICKER/OTHER:

Stock Ticker: WAT   Exchange: NYS
Employees: 6,899   Fiscal Year Ends: 12/31
Parent Company:

OTHER THOUGHTS:

Estimated Female Officers or Directors: 3
Hot Spot for Advancement for Women/Minorities: Y

Wayfair LLC

www.wayfair.com

NAIC Code: 454111

TYPES OF BUSINESS:

Online Furniture Store

BRANDS/DIVISIONS/AFFILIATES:

Wayfair.com
AllModern (AllModern.com)
Joss & Main (JossandMain.com)
Dwell Studio (DwellStudio.com)
Birch Lane (BirchLane.com)
Wayfair Media Solutions
advertising.wayfair.com

CONTACTS: *Note: Officers with more than one job title may be intentionally listed here more than once.*

Niraj Shah, CEO
Michael Fleisher, CFO
Nicholas Malone, Chief Accounting Officer
Edmond Macri, Chief Marketing Officer
Jeremy Delinsky, Chief Technology Officer
Steven Conine, Co-Chairman
James Savarese, COO
John Mulliken, Senior VP, Divisional
Steve Oblak, Senior VP

GROWTH PLANS/SPECIAL FEATURES:

Wayfair LLC is a private e-commerce home furnishings company. Based in Boston, Massachusetts, the firm also has offices and warehouses in New York, Kentucky and Utah, U.S., as well as in London, Berlin and Sydney. Its e-commerce business model comprises more than 7 million products from over 7,000 suppliers across five distinct brands: Wayfair.com, Joss & Main, AllModern, DwellStudio and Birch Lane. Wayfair.com is the firm's flagship mass market brand that focuses on offering the largest selection of home furnishings & decor, from low- to high-end and across all styles. Joss & Main is the company's online flash sales site that combines inspiring home design with significant savings. AllModern comprises original design for modern home enthusiasts. DwellStudio is an online design studio for modern, fashion-forward home furnishings. Birch Lane is for classic style and timeless home designs. In addition to Wayfair's five main brands, the company also generates net revenue through two other sources: retail partners and Wayfair Media Solutions. Wayfair's relationships with retail partners allow consumers to purchase Wayfair products through the retail partners' sites. Wayfair Media Solutions (located online at advertising.wayfair.com) provides opportunities for manufacturers, retailers and advertisers market to Wayfair's large consumer audience.

FINANCIAL DATA: *Note: Data for latest year may not have been available at press time.*

In U.S. $	2016	2015	2014	2013	2012	2011
Revenue	3,380,360,000	2,249,885,000	1,318,951,000	915,843,000	601,028,000	
R&D Expense						
Operating Income	-196,217,000	-81,350,000	-147,784,000	-16,019,000	-21,394,000	
Operating Margin %	-5.80%	-3.61%	-11.20%	-1.74%	-3.55%	
SGA Expense	1,004,028,000	621,183,000	457,902,000	239,721,000	166,331,000	
Net Income	-194,375,000	-77,443,000	-148,098,000	-15,526,000	-21,055,000	
Operating Cash Flow	62,814,000	135,121,000	4,125,000	34,413,000	3,945,000	
Capital Expenditure	128,086,000	62,184,000	45,985,000	15,779,000	14,980,000	
EBITDA	-140,645,000	-48,904,000	-125,781,000	-2,928,000	-12,059,000	
Return on Assets %	-26.69%	-12.38%	-39.94%	-22.73%	-20.30%	
Return on Equity %	-120.75%	-28.25%	-261.84%			
Debt to Equity	0.36	0.11				

CONTACT INFORMATION:

Phone: 866-263-8325   Fax:
Toll-Free: 877-929-3247
Address: 4 Copley Place, 7/Fl, Boston, MA 02116 United States

STOCK TICKER/OTHER:

Stock Ticker: W   Exchange: NYS
Employees: 5,637   Fiscal Year Ends:
Parent Company:

SALARIES/BONUSES:

Top Exec. Salary: $200,000   Bonus: $50,000
Second Exec. Salary: $200,000   Bonus: $50,000

OTHER THOUGHTS:

Estimated Female Officers or Directors: 5
Hot Spot for Advancement for Women/Minorities: Y

Web.com Group Inc

www.web.com

NAIC Code: 518210

TYPES OF BUSINESS:

Web Hosting Products & Services
Web Design Services

BRANDS/DIVISIONS/AFFILIATES:

Web.com
1ShoppingCart.com
SolidCactus.com
Renovationexperts.com
leads.com
Yodle Inc
DonWeb.com

CONTACTS: *Note: Officers with more than one job title may be intentionally listed here more than once.*

David Brown, CEO
Kevin Carney, CFO
Roseann Duran, Executive VP

GROWTH PLANS/SPECIAL FEATURES:

Web.com Group, Inc. is a provider of Do-It-For-Me and Do-It-Yourself (DIY) web site building, internet marketing, lead generation and technology solutions that enable small and mid-sized businesses to build and maintain an internet presence. The firm serves roughly 3.5 million customers. Its primary service offerings include web site design and publishing, internet marketing and advertising, search engine optimization, search engine submission, lead generation, logo design and web analytics. In addition to its primary service offerings, the firm provides a variety of services to customers who desire more advanced capabilities, such as e-commerce solutions and other sophisticated internet marketing services and online lead generation. Through its Web.com product, Web.com Group offers a variety of DIY web site building and marketing solutions for small and mid-sized businesses that are more technically savvy. It offers standardized, scalable managed hosting services that place numerous customers on a single shared server. Web.com Group also offers complete custom web site design services. Through 1ShoppingCart.com and SolidCactus.com, the company offers a set of sales and marketing tools for businesses selling products and services online. Renovationexperts.com provides lead generation service specific to contractors, homebuilders and remodeling professionals. In addition, leads.com offers leads in home services categories. Subsidiary Yodle, Inc. provides cloud-based local marketing solutions to small businesses, including an online, mobile and social presence. In January 2017, the firm acquired DonWeb.com, located in Argentina, a web-hosting and domain registration company catering to the Latin American market.

Employee benefits include medical, vision and dental coverage; life insurance; short- and long-term disability; an employee assistance program; tuition reimbursement; flexible spending accounts; and a 401(k) with company match.

FINANCIAL DATA: *Note: Data for latest year may not have been available at press time.*

In U.S. $	2016	2015	2014	2013	2012	2011
Revenue	710,505,000	543,461,000	543,937,000	492,315,000	407,646,000	199,205,000
R&D Expense	65,800,000	24,313,000	29,683,000	32,468,000	34,258,000	19,252,000
Operating Income	44,704,000	61,714,000	37,663,000	10,241,000	-36,010,000	-40,767,000
Operating Margin %	6.29%	11.35%	6.92%	2.08%	-8.83%	-20.46%
SGA Expense	285,213,000	212,085,000	207,828,000	196,358,000	167,618,000	96,907,000
Net Income	3,990,000	89,961,000	-12,458,000	-65,664,000	-122,217,000	-12,309,000
Operating Cash Flow	127,840,000	152,731,000	117,206,000	102,460,000	77,965,000	14,924,000
Capital Expenditure	22,140,000	14,747,000	15,166,000	14,713,000	22,298,000	4,270,000
EBITDA	122,752,000	118,059,000	112,442,000	69,807,000	6,150,000	-11,311,000
Return on Assets %	.29%	7.51%	-.99%	-5.04%	-8.96%	-1.44%
Return on Equity %	1.68%	43.64%	-7.24%	-39.59%	-56.40%	-6.55%
Debt to Equity	2.74	1.72	2.87	3.27	4.25	2.62

CONTACT INFORMATION:

Phone: 904 680-6600   Fax: 904 880-0350
Toll-Free:
Address: 12808 Gran Bay Pkwy. W., Jacksonville, FL 32258 United States

STOCK TICKER/OTHER:

Stock Ticker: WEB   Exchange: NAS
Employees: 3,600   Fiscal Year Ends: 12/31
Parent Company:

SALARIES/BONUSES:

Top Exec. Salary: $560,000   Bonus: $336,000
Second Exec. Salary: $350,000   Bonus: $100,000

OTHER THOUGHTS:

Estimated Female Officers or Directors: 3
Hot Spot for Advancement for Women/Minorities: Y

WellCare Health Plans Inc

www.wellcare.com

NAIC Code: 524114

TYPES OF BUSINESS:
Insurance-Medical & Health, HMOs & PPOs

BRANDS/DIVISIONS/AFFILIATES:
WellCare
Ohana
Easy Choice
Staywell
Care 1st
Harmony
Missouri Care
Universal American Corporation

CONTACTS: Note: Officers with more than one job title may be intentionally listed here more than once.
Kenneth Burdick, CEO
Andrew Asher, CFO
Christian Michalik, Director
Michael Polen, Executive VP, Divisional
Kelly Munson, Executive VP, Divisional
Michael Radu, Executive VP, Divisional
Anat Hakim, General Counsel
Michael Yount, Other Executive Officer
Timothy Trodden, Other Executive Officer
Darren Ghanayem, Other Executive Officer
Rhonda Mims, Other Executive Officer

GROWTH PLANS/SPECIAL FEATURES:
WellCare Health Plans, Inc. manages government-sponsored healthcare programs with a focus on Medicaid and Medicare programs. The firm offers a variety of managed care health plans for families, children and the aged, blind and disabled, as well as prescription drug plans. The company has served health plans and prescription drug plans for approximately 3.9 million members. WellCare's Medicare plans have been offered under the WellCare name, except for its Hawaii and California coordinated care plans (CCPs), which are under the names Ohana and Easy Choice, respectively. For Medicaid plans, the brands depend on the state and consist of: Staywell, Care 1st, Ohana, Harmony, Missouri Care and WellCare. In April 2017, the firm acquired Universal American Corporation, which offers an array of Medicare Advantage health plans and comprises a portfolio of approximately 119,000 Medicare Advantage members located in Texas, New York and Maine.

WellCare offers employees several family benefit plans, wellness plans, dental and vision, prescription drug coverage, life insurance, AD&D, disability, 401(k), flexible spending accounts, tuition reimbursement and an employee assistance plan.

FINANCIAL DATA: Note: Data for latest year may not have been available at press time.

In U.S. $	2016	2015	2014	2013	2012	2011
Revenue	14,237,100,000	13,890,200,000	12,959,900,000	9,527,900,000	7,409,032,000	6,106,868,000
R&D Expense						
Operating Income	529,500,000	336,100,000	148,300,000	281,100,000	296,439,000	407,667,000
Operating Margin %	3.71%	2.41%	1.14%	2.95%	4.00%	6.67%
SGA Expense	1,361,500,000	1,360,200,000	1,156,500,000	856,500,000	690,842,000	718,003,000
Net Income	242,100,000	118,600,000	63,700,000	175,300,000	184,728,000	264,246,000
Operating Cash Flow	748,300,000	712,600,000	299,300,000	178,900,000	-30,739,000	161,999,000
Capital Expenditure	105,300,000	137,000,000	74,800,000	62,000,000	61,268,000	49,576,000
EBITDA	676,200,000	462,900,000	277,100,000	334,300,000	332,092,000	451,438,000
Return on Assets %	4.26%	2.44%	1.60%	5.72%	7.15%	11.16%
Return on Equity %	12.98%	7.13%	4.09%	12.34%	15.14%	27.11%
Debt to Equity	0.49	0.52	0.56	0.39	0.09	0.12

CONTACT INFORMATION:
Phone: 813 290-6200   Fax:
Toll-Free: 800-795-3432
Address: 8725 Henderson Rd., Renaissance 1, Tampa, FL 33634 United States

STOCK TICKER/OTHER:
Stock Ticker: WCG   Exchange: NYS
Employees: 7,400   Fiscal Year Ends: 12/31
Parent Company:

SALARIES/BONUSES:
Top Exec. Salary: $1,000,000   Bonus: $
Second Exec. Salary: $590,385   Bonus: $

OTHER THOUGHTS:
Estimated Female Officers or Directors: 3
Hot Spot for Advancement for Women/Minorities: Y

Sales, profits and employees may be estimates. Financial information, benefits and other data can change quickly and may vary from those stated here.

Wells Fargo & Co

www.wellsfargo.com

NAIC Code: 522110

TYPES OF BUSINESS:

Banking
Credit & Debit Cards
Personal Trust Accounts Management
Mutual Fund Administration
Mortgages
Insurance Services
Investment Banking
Asset Management

BRANDS/DIVISIONS/AFFILIATES:

Wells Fargo Bank NA

CONTACTS: *Note: Officers with more than one job title may be intentionally listed here more than once.*

John Shrewsberry, CFO
Franklin Codel, Senior Executive VP, Divisional
Stephen Sanger, Chairman of the Board
Richard Levy, Chief Accounting Officer
Hope Hardison, Chief Administrative Officer
Kevin Rhein, Chief Information Officer
Michael Loughlin, Chief Risk Officer
Elizabeth Duke, Director
James Strother, General Counsel
Mary Mack, President, Subsidiary
Timothy Sloan, President
Anthony Augliera, Secretary
Avid Modjtabai, Senior Executive VP, Divisional
David Carroll, Senior Executive VP, Divisional
Avid Modjtabai, Senior Executive VP, Divisional

GROWTH PLANS/SPECIAL FEATURES:

Wells Fargo & Co. (WFC) is a holding company that provides diversified financial services. Headquartered in San Francisco, the company operates in all 50 U.S. states; Washington, D.C.; and 42 countries, including those in Europe, Africa, Central America and the Asia Pacific region. The firm operates primarily through Wells Fargo Bank, NA, with assets of $2 trillion. WFC operates in three business segments: community banking, wholesale banking and wealth and investment management. Through these segments WFC provides retail, commercial and corporate banking services through banking locations and offices, the internet and other distribution channels to individuals, businesses and institutions. Other financial services include wholesale banking, mortgage banking, consumer finance, equipment leasing, agricultural finance, commercial finance, securities brokerage, investment banking, insurance agency and brokerage services, computer and data processing services, trust services, investment advisory services, mortgage-backed securities servicing and venture capital investment. In June 2017, WFC agreed to sell Wells Fargo Insurance Services USA to USI Insurance Services.

Wells Fargo offers its employees a 401(k) plan, tuition reimbursement, adoption assistance, discounted checking and savings accounts and scholarships for dependent children.

FINANCIAL DATA: *Note: Data for latest year may not have been available at press time.*

In U.S. $	2016	2015	2014	2013	2012	2011
Revenue	88,267,000,000	86,057,000,000	84,347,000,000	83,780,000,000	86,086,000,000	80,948,000,000
R&D Expense						
Operating Income	32,120,000,000	33,641,000,000	33,915,000,000	32,629,000,000	28,471,000,000	23,656,000,000
Operating Margin %	36.38%	39.09%	40.20%	38.94%	33.07%	29.22%
SGA Expense	33,061,000,000	31,654,000,000	30,870,000,000	31,097,000,000	30,160,000,000	28,933,000,000
Net Income	21,938,000,000	22,894,000,000	23,057,000,000	21,878,000,000	18,897,000,000	15,869,000,000
Operating Cash Flow	169,000,000	14,772,000,000	17,529,000,000	57,641,000,000	58,540,000,000	13,665,000,000
Capital Expenditure		135,000,000	150,000,000			
EBITDA						
Return on Assets %	1.09%	1.23%	1.35%	1.41%	1.31%	1.16%
Return on Equity %	11.78%	12.78%	13.67%	13.99%	13.16%	12.18%
Debt to Equity	1.45	1.16	1.11	0.99	0.88	0.97

CONTACT INFORMATION:

Phone: 866 249-3302 Fax:
Toll-Free: 800-869-3557
Address: 420 Montgomery St., San Francisco, CA 94163 United States

STOCK TICKER/OTHER:

Stock Ticker: WFC Exchange: NYS
Employees: 264,900 Fiscal Year Ends: 12/31
Parent Company:

SALARIES/BONUSES:

Top Exec. Salary: $2,329,502 Bonus: $
Second Exec. Salary: Bonus: $
$2,070,498

OTHER THOUGHTS:

Estimated Female Officers or Directors: 8
Hot Spot for Advancement for Women/Minorities: Y

Westlake Chemical Corporation

www.westlake.com

NAIC Code: 325110

TYPES OF BUSINESS:

Plastics & Rubber, Manufacturing
PVC Piping
Vinyls
Olefins

BRANDS/DIVISIONS/AFFILIATES:

Westlake Chemical Partners LP
Suzhou Huasu Plastic Co Ltd
Westlake Chemical OpCo LP
Axiall Corporation
North American Pipe
Royal Building Products

CONTACTS: Note: Officers with more than one job title may be intentionally listed here more than once.

Albert Chao, CEO
M. Bender, CFO
James Chao, Chairman of the Board
George Mangieri, Chief Accounting Officer
L. Ederington, Chief Administrative Officer
Robert Buesinger, Senior VP, Divisional
Michael Mattina, Senior VP, Divisional
Lawrence Teel, Senior VP, Divisional
Simon Bates, Vice President, Divisional
Andrew Kenner, Vice President, Divisional

GROWTH PLANS/SPECIAL FEATURES:

Westlake Chemical Corporation manufactures and markets vinyls, basic chemicals and fabricated products for use in the packaging, automotive, construction and coatings industries. The company operates in two business segments: olefins and vinyls. The olefins business provides ethylene, polyethylene, styrene and co-products. These olefins are used to create a variety of petrochemical products including packaging film, coatings, injection molding and complex chemicals. Principal products for the vinyls business include polyvinyl chloride (PVC), vinyl chloride monomer (VCM), chlorine, caustic soda and ethylene. Westlake manufactures and markets specialty pipe and fittings, water, sewer, irrigation and conduit pipe products under the North American Pipe and Royal Building Products brand names. Westlake maintains more than 25 manufacturing facilities in North America, Europe and Asia, with a total production capacity of nearly 40 billion pounds. Additionally, subsidiary Westlake Chemical Partners LP operates, acquires and develops facilities for the processing of natural gas liquids and related assets; Suzhou Huasu Plastic Co. Ltd. operates a PVC fabrication facility in China; and Westlake Chemical OpCo LP operates an olefins facility in Lake Charles, Louisiana and an ethylene production facility in Calvert City, Kentucky. In 2016, the firm acquired Axiall Corporation, a manufacturer and international marketer of chemicals and building products, with manufacturing sites in North America.

Westlake offers employees life, AD&D, medical, dental, vision and long-term disability insurance; a 401(k); paid time off; and an assistance program.

FINANCIAL DATA: Note: Data for latest year may not have been available at press time.

In U.S. $	2016	2015	2014	2013	2012	2011
Revenue	5,075,456,000	4,463,336,000	4,415,350,000	3,759,484,000	3,571,041,000	3,619,848,000
R&D Expense						
Operating Income	581,454,000	959,827,000	1,123,991,000	953,464,000	615,351,000	446,796,000
Operating Margin %	11.45%	21.50%	25.45%	25.36%	17.23%	12.34%
SGA Expense	295,436,000	225,364,000	193,359,000	147,974,000	121,609,000	112,210,000
Net Income	398,859,000	646,010,000	678,523,000	610,425,000	385,555,000	258,966,000
Operating Cash Flow	833,852,000	1,078,836,000	1,032,376,000	752,729,000	624,054,000	362,296,000
Capital Expenditure	628,483,000	491,426,000	431,104,000	679,222,000	386,882,000	176,843,000
EBITDA	1,015,518,000	1,243,854,000	1,329,756,000	1,118,062,000	772,759,000	583,821,000
Return on Assets %	4.84%	11.92%	14.63%	16.33%	11.54%	8.32%
Return on Equity %	11.74%	20.82%	25.45%	28.45%	21.25%	15.88%
Debt to Equity	1.04	0.23	0.26	0.31	0.40	0.43

CONTACT INFORMATION:

Phone: 713 960-9111 Fax:
Toll-Free:
Address: 2801 Post Oak Blvd., Ste. 600, Houston, TX 77056 United States

STOCK TICKER/OTHER:

Stock Ticker: WLK
Employees: 8,870
Parent Company:

Exchange: NYS
Fiscal Year Ends: 12/31

SALARIES/BONUSES:

Top Exec. Salary: $979,667 Bonus: $
Second Exec. Salary: $783,667 Bonus: $

OTHER THOUGHTS:

Estimated Female Officers or Directors:
Hot Spot for Advancement for Women/Minorities:

William Morris Endeavor Entertainment LLC (WME-IMG)

www.wma.com
NAIC Code: 711410

TYPES OF BUSINESS:

Talent Agency
Literary Agency
Sports Marketing & Agents
Media Consulting
Book Publishing

BRANDS/DIVISIONS/AFFILIATES:

William Morris Agency Inc
Endeavor Agency (The)
Silver Lake Partners

CONTACTS: Note: Officers with more than one job title may be intentionally listed here more than once.

Ari Emanuel, Co-CEO
Patrick Whitesell, Co-CEO
David Wirtschafter, Pres.
David Wirtschafter, Co-CEO

GROWTH PLANS/SPECIAL FEATURES:

William Morris Endeavor Entertainment LLC, formed by the merger of the former William Morris Agency and the Endeavor Agency, is one of the largest talent and literary agencies in the world. The firm operates in departments including books, commercials, lectures, motion pictures, music, athletics, television, voice-overs and theater. The books department represents a multitude of fiction and non-fiction authors. The department works closely with the motion picture and television departments to bring books to both large and small screens. The commercials department creates special interest home videos, infomercials, home shopping and industrial programming as well as overseeing sponsorships and promotional events. The lectures division represents a roster of speakers across a broad spectrum of issues and topics. The motion pictures department represents both established and up-and-coming directors and actors. The music group represents clients across a range of musical genres. The athletics department represents athletes and sports properties and seeks to secure endorsements, sponsorships and other opportunities on behalf of its clients. The television group represents television programming and creative talent. The voice-over division represents a range of voice-over talent including Spanish language voice-over actors. The company also represents Broadway and theatrical tours; books agency clients into fairs and special events; and coordinates public, corporate and private speaking engagements. The firm's consulting segment offers entertainment marketing strategies to customers such as General Motors, Hasbro, Starbucks, Swarovski and Bluefly.com.

FINANCIAL DATA: Note: Data for latest year may not have been available at press time.

In U.S. $	2016	2015	2014	2013	2012	2011
Revenue	2,400,000,000	2,200,000,000	2,100,000,000			
R&D Expense						
Operating Income						
Operating Margin %						
SGA Expense						
Net Income						
Operating Cash Flow						
Capital Expenditure						
EBITDA						
Return on Assets %						
Return on Equity %						
Debt to Equity						

CONTACT INFORMATION:

Phone: 310-285-9000   Fax: 310-285-9010
Toll-Free:
Address: 1 William Morris Pl., Beverly Hills, CA 90212 United States

STOCK TICKER/OTHER:

Stock Ticker: Private   Exchange:
Employees: 4,500   Fiscal Year Ends: 12/31
Parent Company: Silver Lake Partners

SALARIES/BONUSES:

Top Exec. Salary: $ Bonus: $
Second Exec. Salary: $ Bonus: $

OTHER THOUGHTS:

Estimated Female Officers or Directors:
Hot Spot for Advancement for Women/Minorities:

WW Grainger Inc

www.grainger.com

NAIC Code: 423830

TYPES OF BUSINESS:

Industrial Equipment & Products-Wholesale
Maintenance & Repair Products
Online Sales
Safety Products
Logistics Services

BRANDS/DIVISIONS/AFFILIATES:

Grainger.com
Acklands-Grainger
Zoro
Zoro.com
Fabory Group (The)
MonotaRO
Grainger Mexico

CONTACTS: *Note: Officers with more than one job title may be intentionally listed here more than once.*

Donald Macpherson, CEO
Ronald Jadin, CFO
James Ryan, Chairman of the Board
Eric Tapia, Chief Accounting Officer
Michael Ali, Chief Information Officer
John Howard, General Counsel
Joseph High, Other Executive Officer
Laura Brown, Senior VP, Divisional
Paige Robbins, Senior VP, Divisional

GROWTH PLANS/SPECIAL FEATURES:

W. W. Grainger, Inc. (Grainger) offers facilities maintenance products and related services and information solutions to approximately 3 million businesses and institutions. The company is divided into two segments: U.S. and Canada. The U.S. segment markets over 1 million products, including material handling equipment, safety and security supplies, lighting and electrical products, power and hand tools, pumps and plumbing supplies, cleaning and maintenance supplies, forestry and agriculture equipment, building and home inspection supplies and vehicle and fleet components. The U.S. business operates through its website, Grainger.com, and in over 284 branches and 39 regional contact centers in all 50 states, as well as through a network of 18 distribution centers. The Canada segment, operating as Acklands-Grainger, is a leading broad-line distributor of industrial and safety supplies, including tools, fasteners, instruments and welding and shop equipment. This business operates through 151 branches and five distribution centers across Canada. Grainger has a single channel online business called Zoro, which is a distributor of MRO (maintenance, repair and operating) products serving U.S. businesses and consumers via Zoro.com. Other businesses, include The Fabory Group, a European distributor of fasteners, tools and industrial supplies; 51%-owned MonotaRO, a provider of small- and mid-sized Japanese businesses with products that help them operate and maintain their facilities; and Grainger Mexico, which provides local businesses with MRO supplies and other related products primarily from Mexico and the U.S.

Employee benefits include health, dental and prescription coverage; a profit sharing plan; an employee assistance program; adoption benefits; dependant care assistance; critical illness insurance; and a group legal plan.

FINANCIAL DATA: *Note: Data for latest year may not have been available at press time.*

In U.S. $	2016	2015	2014	2013	2012	2011
Revenue	10,137,200,000	9,973,384,000	9,964,953,000	9,437,758,000	8,950,045,000	8,078,185,000
R&D Expense						
Operating Income	1,119,497,000	1,300,320,000	1,347,117,000	1,296,854,000	1,131,125,000	1,052,429,000
Operating Margin %	11.04%	13.03%	13.51%	13.74%	12.63%	13.02%
SGA Expense	2,995,060,000	2,931,108,000	2,967,125,000	2,839,629,000	2,785,035,000	2,458,363,000
Net Income	605,928,000	768,996,000	801,729,000	797,036,000	689,881,000	658,423,000
Operating Cash Flow	1,002,976,000	989,904,000	959,814,000	986,498,000	816,195,000	746,108,000
Capital Expenditure	284,249,000	373,868,000	387,390,000	272,145,000	249,860,000	196,942,000
EBITDA	1,334,247,000	1,512,243,000	1,552,805,000	1,481,437,000	1,292,916,000	1,209,818,000
Return on Assets %	10.39%	13.66%	15.19%	15.50%	14.17%	15.27%
Return on Equity %	29.54%	27.80%	24.82%	25.40%	24.40%	27.24%
Debt to Equity	1.02	0.61	0.12	0.13	0.15	0.06

CONTACT INFORMATION:

Phone: 847 535-1000   Fax:
Toll-Free: 800-323-0620
Address: 100 Grainger Pkwy., Lake Forest, IL 60045 United States

STOCK TICKER/OTHER:

Stock Ticker: GWW   Exchange: NYS
Employees: 25,600   Fiscal Year Ends: 12/31
Parent Company:

SALARIES/BONUSES:

Top Exec. Salary: $1,183,263   Bonus: $
Second Exec. Salary: $875,000   Bonus: $

OTHER THOUGHTS:

Estimated Female Officers or Directors:
Hot Spot for Advancement for Women/Minorities: Y

Wyndham Worldwide Corporation   www.wyndhamworldwide.com

NAIC Code: 721110

TYPES OF BUSINESS:

Hotels, Motels & Resorts
Property Management
Hotel Development
Vacation Property Exchange and Rental
Timeshare Resorts
Franchising
Vacation Ownership

BRANDS/DIVISIONS/AFFILIATES:

Wyndham Hotel Group
Wyndham Destination Network
Wyndham Vacation Ownership
Wyndham Hotels and Resorts
Ramada
Days Inn
Club Wyndham
Shell Vacations Club

CONTACTS: Note: Officers with more than one job title may be intentionally listed here more than once.

Geoffrey Ballotti, CEO, Divisional
Gail Mandel, CEO, Divisional
Stephen Holmes, CEO
Thomas Conforti, CFO
Scott McLester, Executive VP
Mary Falvey, Executive VP
Thomas Anderson, Executive VP
Nicola Rossi, Senior VP

GROWTH PLANS/SPECIAL FEATURES:

Wyndham Worldwide Corporation (WW) is a hospitality company offering individual consumers and business customers an array of hospitality products and services, as well as various accommodation alternatives and price ranges through its portfolio of world-renowned brands. The company's brands include Wyndham Hotels and Resorts, Ramada, Days Inn, Super 8, Howard Johnson, Wingate by Wyndham, Microtel Inns & Suites by Wyndham, TRYP by Wyndham, Dolce Hotels and Resorts, RCI, Landal GreenParks, Novasol, Hoseasons, cottages.com, James Villa Holidays, Wyndham Vacation Rentals, Wyndham Vacation Resorts, Shell Vacations Club and WorldMark by Wyndham. Wyndham Hotel Group is a world-renowned hotel company with 8,035 hotels and more than 697,600 hotel rooms. The group franchises in the upscale, upper midscale, midscale, economy and extended stay segments with a concentration on economy brands. It also provides property management services for full-service and select limited-service hotels, which is predominantly a fee-for-service business. Wyndham Destination Network, a fee-for-service business, provides managed vacation accommodations, with a vacation exchange network comprising more than 3.8 million members. Overall, the network has more than 121,000 vacation properties worldwide, including cottages, villas, chalets, vacation ownership condominiums, fractional resorts, second homes, yachts, private residence clubs, traditional hotel rooms and city apartments. Wyndham Vacation Ownership (WVO) is a timeshare/vacation ownership business with 219 resorts and approximately 887,000 owners. WVO develops and markets vacation ownership interests (VOI) to individual consumers, provides consumer financing, as well as property management services at the resorts. WVO brands include Club Wyndham, WorldMark by Wyndham, Wyndham Vacation Resorts Asia Pacific and Shell Vacations Club.

The firm offers employees medical, dental, vision and life insurance; domestic partner benefits; flexible spending accounts; an educational assistance program; an employee assistance program; adoption reimbursement; and travel discounts on Wyndham properties and the firm's affiliated car rental partners.

FINANCIAL DATA: Note: Data for latest year may not have been available at press time.

In U.S. $	2016	2015	2014	2013	2012	2011
Revenue	5,599,000,000	5,536,000,000	5,281,000,000	5,009,000,000	4,534,000,000	4,254,000,000
R&D Expense						
Operating Income	1,057,000,000	1,015,000,000	941,000,000	910,000,000	852,000,000	767,000,000
Operating Margin %	18.87%	18.33%	17.81%	18.16%	18.79%	18.03%
SGA Expense	1,543,000,000	1,574,000,000	1,557,000,000	1,471,000,000	1,389,000,000	1,221,000,000
Net Income	611,000,000	612,000,000	529,000,000	432,000,000	400,000,000	417,000,000
Operating Cash Flow	973,000,000	991,000,000	984,000,000	1,008,000,000	1,004,000,000	1,003,000,000
Capital Expenditure	191,000,000	222,000,000	235,000,000	238,000,000	208,000,000	239,000,000
EBITDA	1,328,000,000	1,275,000,000	1,191,000,000	1,030,000,000	945,000,000	980,000,000
Return on Assets %	6.25%	6.31%	5.44%	4.49%	4.32%	4.52%
Return on Equity %	73.43%	55.51%	36.76%	24.31%	19.22%	16.19%
Debt to Equity	7.39	5.21	3.81	2.83	2.08	1.69

CONTACT INFORMATION:

Phone: 973 753-6000   Fax: 973 496-7658
Toll-Free:
Address: 22 Sylvan Way, Parsippany, NJ 07054 United States

STOCK TICKER/OTHER:

Stock Ticker: WYN   Exchange: NYS
Employees: 37,800   Fiscal Year Ends: 12/31
Parent Company:

SALARIES/BONUSES:

Top Exec. Salary: $1,571,150   Bonus: $
Second Exec. Salary: $795,395   Bonus: $

OTHER THOUGHTS:

Estimated Female Officers or Directors: 2
Hot Spot for Advancement for Women/Minorities: Y

Sales, profits and employees may be estimates. Financial information, benefits and other data can change quickly and may vary from those stated here.

Wynn Resorts Limited

www.wynnresorts.com

NAIC Code: 721120

TYPES OF BUSINESS:

Hotel Casinos
Online Poker

BRANDS/DIVISIONS/AFFILIATES:

Wynn Las Vegas Resort & Country Club
Encore at Wynn Las Vegas
Wynn Macau Resort
Encore Theater
Encore at Wynn Macau
Wynn Palace
Wynn Boston Harbor

CONTACTS: *Note: Officers with more than one job title may be intentionally listed here more than once.*

Stephen Wynn, CEO
Stephen Cootey, CFO
Craig Billings, CFO
John Strzemp, Chief Administrative Officer
Kim Sinatra, Executive VP
Matt Maddox, President

GROWTH PLANS/SPECIAL FEATURES:

Wynn Resorts Limited is a developer, owner and operator of destination casino resorts. It owns and operates two destination casino resorts: The Wynn Las Vegas Resort & Country Club in Las Vegas, Nevada, which includes Encore at Wynn Las Vegas; and the Wynn Macau Resort in the Macau Special Administrative Region of China. The firm's Las Vegas operations offer 4,748 rooms and suites. The 189,000-square-foot casino features 234 table games, a poker room, 1,907 slot machines and a race and sports book. The resort also features 33 food and beverage outlets; three nightclubs; two spas and salons; a Ferrari and Maserati automobile dealership; wedding chapels; an 18-hole golf course; 290,000 square feet of meeting space; and a 99,000 square foot retail promenade featuring boutiques from Alexander McQueen, Cartier, Chanel and Louis Vuitton. At the Encore Theater, the company offers headlining entertainment acts from personalities such as Beyonce. The company's Wynn Macau resort operations, including Encore at Wynn Macau, features 1,008 rooms and suites, approximately 284,000 square feet of casino gaming space with 957 slot machines and 303 table games, eight restaurants, two health clubs, spas and 57,000 square feet of retail space. Wynn Palace, in Macau, is a resort featuring 1,706 rooms and suites, an 8-acre performance lake, sky casinos, floral sculptures, gaming space, meeting facilities, spa, salon, retail spaces and fine dining. The Wynn Boston Harbor is a new development under construction in Everett, Massachusetts (adjacent to Boston), and is scheduled to open by mid-2019.

FINANCIAL DATA: *Note: Data for latest year may not have been available at press time.*

In U.S. $	2016	2015	2014	2013	2012	2011
Revenue	4,466,297,000	4,075,883,000	5,433,661,000	5,620,936,000	5,154,284,000	5,269,792,000
R&D Expense						
Operating Income	521,662,000	658,814,000	1,266,278,000	1,290,091,000	1,029,276,000	1,008,240,000
Operating Margin %	11.68%	16.16%	23.30%	22.95%	19.96%	19.13%
SGA Expense	757,680,000	552,951,000	533,047,000	469,095,000	482,143,000	519,702,000
Net Income	241,975,000	195,290,000	731,554,000	728,652,000	502,036,000	613,371,000
Operating Cash Flow	970,546,000	572,813,000	1,098,317,000	1,676,642,000	1,185,718,000	1,515,835,000
Capital Expenditure	1,240,928,000	1,925,152,000	1,345,940,000	506,786,000	240,985,000	184,146,000
EBITDA	1,004,692,000	912,782,000	1,588,043,000	1,656,596,000	1,394,956,000	1,433,524,000
Return on Assets %	2.15%	1.99%	8.38%	9.30%	7.08%	9.03%
Return on Equity %	1052.75%				54.86%	28.35%
Debt to Equity	64.10					1.34

CONTACT INFORMATION:

Phone: 702 770-7555   Fax: 702 733-4681
Toll-Free:
Address: 3131 Las Vegas Blvd. South, Las Vegas, NV 89109 United States

STOCK TICKER/OTHER:

Stock Ticker: WYNN   Exchange: NAS
Employees: 24,600   Fiscal Year Ends: 12/31
Parent Company:

SALARIES/BONUSES:

Top Exec. Salary: $2,500,000   Bonus: $
Second Exec. Salary: $1,500,000   Bonus: $

OTHER THOUGHTS:

Estimated Female Officers or Directors: 3
Hot Spot for Advancement for Women/Minorities: Y

XPO Logistics Inc

NAIC Code: 488510

TYPES OF BUSINESS:

Freight Transportation Arrangement

BRANDS/DIVISIONS/AFFILIATES:

CONTACTS: *Note: Officers with more than one job title may be intentionally listed here more than once.*

Troy Cooper, CEO, Subsidiary
Bradley Jacobs, CEO
John Hardig, CFO
Lance Robinson, Chief Accounting Officer
Mario Harik, Chief Information Officer
Scott Malat, Other Executive Officer

GROWTH PLANS/SPECIAL FEATURES:

XPO Logistics, Inc. is a global logistics provider of supply chain solutions to companies worldwide. The firm provides powerful load management information technology, and equipment capacity for temperature-controlled and other special types of handling. Expedite services includes more than 400 trucks exclusive to XPO, with access to another 13,000 carriers; and web-based managed transportation; air cargo capacity up to 200,000 pounds; immediate pickup and direct delivery; and hazardous/driver assist options. The firm's intermodal service comprises 10,000 53-foot XPO-controlled containers, with access to another 65,000; 50,000-unit small boxes, cross-border and transloading services; and approximately 2,200 contracted drayage trucks. Sectors served by the company include consumer, including freight movements between manufacturers, warehouses, distribution centers and retailers; industrial, including raw materials, parts and finished goods; last mile, including retail and e-commerce arrangements for the home delivery and installation of heavy goods; temperature sensitive, including pharmaceutical, medical and other sensitive freight; high value/high security; and government freight. Through its subsidiaries the firm runs its business in 34 countries at more than 1,400 locations, serving over 50,000 customers, shipping an average of 150,000 shipments and over five billion inventory units every day. In 2016, XPO Logistics joined the Fortune 500 for the first time; and announced plans to invest more than $400 million in IT that year in its cloud-based data for price prediction and last-mile customer experience management. That October, the firm sold its truckload business to TransForce, Inc. for approximately $558 million.

FINANCIAL DATA: *Note: Data for latest year may not have been available at press time.*

In U.S. $	2016	2015	2014	2013	2012	2011
Revenue	14,619,400,000	7,623,200,000	2,356,600,000	702,303,000	278,591,000	177,076,000
R&D Expense						
Operating Income	488,100,000	-28,600,000	-40,900,000	-52,325,000	-27,964,000	1,724,000
Operating Margin %	3.33%	-.37%	-1.73%	-7.45%	-10.03%	.97%
SGA Expense	1,651,200,000	912,900,000	335,900,000	155,205,000	50,894,000	27,008,000
Net Income	69,000,000	-191,100,000	-63,600,000	-48,530,000	-20,339,000	759,000
Operating Cash Flow	625,400,000	90,800,000	-21,300,000	-66,302,000	-24,300,000	6,611,000
Capital Expenditure	483,400,000	249,000,000	44,600,000	11,585,000	6,981,000	754,000
EBITDA	1,111,300,000	299,100,000	56,600,000	-32,008,000	-25,614,000	2,908,000
Return on Assets %	.51%	-3.19%	-6.06%	-8.63%	-8.62%	-48.37%
Return on Equity %	2.36%	-11.46%	-10.60%	-16.73%	-17.42%	-89.53%
Debt to Equity	1.77	1.97	0.36	0.43	0.53	

CONTACT INFORMATION:

Phone: 855-976-4636   Fax:
Toll-Free:
Address: Five Greenwich Office Park, Greenwich, CT 06831 United States

STOCK TICKER/OTHER:

Stock Ticker: XPO
Employees: 87,000
Parent Company:

Exchange: NYS
Fiscal Year Ends: 12/31

SALARIES/BONUSES:

Top Exec. Salary: $607,000   Bonus: $1,375,000
Second Exec. Salary: $511,539   Bonus: $1,075,000

OTHER THOUGHTS:

Estimated Female Officers or Directors: 2
Hot Spot for Advancement for Women/Minorities:

Yum! Brands Inc

www.yum.com

NAIC Code: 722513

TYPES OF BUSINESS:

Fast Food Restaurants

BRANDS/DIVISIONS/AFFILIATES:

KFC
Pizza Hut
Taco Bell

CONTACTS: *Note: Officers with more than one job title may be intentionally listed here more than once.*

Roger Eaton, CEO, Divisional
Brian Niccol, CEO, Divisional
Greg Creed, CEO
David Russell, Chief Accounting Officer
Marc Kesselman, General Counsel
Tracy Skeans, Other Executive Officer
David Gibbs, President

GROWTH PLANS/SPECIAL FEATURES:

Yum! Brands, Inc. is a restaurant company with over 43,500 restaurants in more than 135 countries and territories, marketed under the KFC, Pizza Hut and Taco Bell brand names. The firm develops, operates or franchises this worldwide system of fast-food and dine-in restaurants, which prepare and sell competitively-priced food items. Most restaurants in each concept offer the ability to dine in and/or carry out food. KFC and Taco Bell offer a drive-thru option in most of its stores. Pizza Hut offers the drive-thru option on a much more limited basis, but typically offers delivery service. KFC was founded in Corbin, Kentucky by Colonel Harland D. Sanders, who created a secret blend of 11 herbs and spices used for making Kentucky Fried Chicken (KFC). Today, KFC operates in 128 countries and territories worldwide, via more than 20,000 stores, 93% of which are franchised. Its menu items include fried and non-fried chicken products, as well as side items and beverages. Pizza Hut began in 1958 in Wichita, Kansas, and is the largest restaurant chain in the world specializing in the sale of ready-to-eat pizza products. The firm operates in 103 countries and territories worldwide via more than 16,400 stores, 97% of which are franchised. Last, Taco Bell began in 1962 in Downey, California, and operates in 22 countries and territories via more than 6,600 stores, 87% of which are franchised. Taco Bell specializes in Mexican-style food products, including tacos, burritos, quesadillas, salads, nachos and other related items. In November 2016, the firm spun off its Yum! China business, separating into two independent, publicly-traded companies. East Dawning (Yum!'s fusion of the KFC business model) and Little Sheep (specializing in hot pot restaurants, condiments and meat processing) were merged into Yum! China.

Yum! offers its employees receive health and retirement benefits.

FINANCIAL DATA: *Note: Data for latest year may not have been available at press time.*

In U.S. $	2016	2015	2014	2013	2012	2011
Revenue	6,366,000,000	13,105,000,000	13,279,000,000	13,084,000,000	13,633,000,000	12,626,000,000
R&D Expense						
Operating Income	1,625,000,000	1,921,000,000	1,557,000,000	1,798,000,000	2,294,000,000	1,815,000,000
Operating Margin %	25.52%	14.65%	11.72%	13.74%	16.82%	14.37%
SGA Expense	1,161,000,000	1,504,000,000	1,419,000,000	1,412,000,000	1,510,000,000	1,372,000,000
Net Income	1,619,000,000	1,293,000,000	1,051,000,000	1,091,000,000	1,597,000,000	1,319,000,000
Operating Cash Flow	1,204,000,000	2,139,000,000	2,049,000,000	2,139,000,000	2,294,000,000	2,170,000,000
Capital Expenditure	422,000,000	973,000,000	1,033,000,000	1,049,000,000	1,099,000,000	940,000,000
EBITDA	1,934,000,000	2,668,000,000	2,296,000,000	2,542,000,000	2,939,000,000	2,471,000,000
Return on Assets %	23.89%	15.74%	12.33%	12.32%	17.89%	15.38%
Return on Equity %		105.20%	56.61%	50.50%	80.31%	77.61%
Debt to Equity		3.35	1.98	1.34	1.36	1.64

CONTACT INFORMATION:

Phone: 502 874-8300   Fax:
Toll-Free:
Address: 1441 Gardiner Ln., Louisville, KY 40213 United States

STOCK TICKER/OTHER:

Stock Ticker: YUM
Employees: 90,000
Parent Company:

Exchange: NYS
Fiscal Year Ends: 12/31

SALARIES/BONUSES:

Top Exec. Salary: $1,188,942   Bonus: $
Second Exec. Salary: $530,769   Bonus: $500,000

OTHER THOUGHTS:

Estimated Female Officers or Directors: 3
Hot Spot for Advancement for Women/Minorities: Y

Zillow Inc
NAIC Code: 519130

TYPES OF BUSINESS:
Online Real Estate Information

BRANDS/DIVISIONS/AFFILIATES:
Zillow.com
Zestimates
Rent Zestimates
Zillow Mortgage Marketplace
Zillow Mobile
Trulia
Zillow Digs

CONTACTS: *Note: Officers with more than one job title may be intentionally listed here more than once.*
Spencer Rascoff, CEO
Kathleen Philips, CFO
Richard Barton, Chairman of the Board
David Beitel, Chief Technology Officer
Amy Bohutinsky, COO
Lloyd Frink, Director
Errol Samuelson, Other Executive Officer
Stanley Humphries, Other Executive Officer
Greg Schwartz, Other Executive Officer
Paul Levine, President, Subsidiary

GROWTH PLANS/SPECIAL FEATURES:
Zillow, Inc. operates a real estate information marketplace dedicated to providing information about homes, real estate listings and mortgages and enabling homeowners, buyers, sellers and renters to connect with real estate and mortgage professionals. The company maintains a database of over 110 million homes in the U.S. that are either for sale, for rent or not currently on the market. Individuals and businesses that use Zillow have updated information on more than 59 million homes and added more than 343 million home photos, creating exclusive home profiles that are available nowhere else. These profiles include detailed information about homes, such as property descriptions, listing information and purchase and sale histories. In conjuncture with the database, the firm offers its users its proprietary automated valuation models, Zestimates and Rent Zestimates, on more than 100 million homes. In addition to its primary web site, Zillow.com, the company also operates Zillow Mortgage Marketplace, connecting borrowers with lenders in order to find loans and good mortgage rates; Zillow Mobile, a real estate mobile platform; Zillow Rentals, a marketplace and suite of tools for rental professionals; Postlets, which allows postings and listings to appear on sites such as Zillow, Trulia, Yahoo! Homes and HotPads; and Diverse Solutions, a provider of easy-to-implement technology and web sites that help real estate professionals manage their brands and businesses. Additionally, the company operates Zillow Digs, a home improvement marketplace where consumers can find visual inspiration and local cost estimates.

FINANCIAL DATA: *Note: Data for latest year may not have been available at press time.*

In U.S. $	2016	2015	2014	2013	2012	2011
Revenue	846,589,000	644,677,000	325,893,000	197,545,000	116,850,000	66,053,000
R&D Expense	273,066,000	198,565,000	86,406,000	48,498,000	26,614,000	14,143,000
Operating Income	-192,854,000	-149,531,000	-44,695,000	-16,949,000	5,797,000	997,000
Operating Margin %	-22.78%	-23.19%	-13.71%	-8.57%	4.96%	1.50%
SGA Expense	694,614,000	477,534,000	233,228,000	147,186,000	70,396,000	40,338,000
Net Income	-220,438,000	-148,874,000	-43,610,000	-12,453,000	5,939,000	1,102,000
Operating Cash Flow	8,645,000	22,659,000	45,519,000	31,298,000	32,298,000	14,826,000
Capital Expenditure	71,722,000	68,108,000	44,242,000	25,972,000	16,750,000	8,821,000
EBITDA	-112,310,000	-72,644,000	-9,071,000	6,305,000	18,570,000	8,187,000
Return on Assets %	-7.01%	-7.86%	-6.93%	-2.73%	2.82%	1.56%
Return on Equity %	-8.45%	-9.11%	-7.54%	-2.93%	3.11%	1.85%
Debt to Equity	0.14	0.08				

CONTACT INFORMATION:
Phone: 206 470-7000   Fax:
Toll-Free:
Address: 1301 Second Ave., Fl. 31, Seattle, WA 98101 United States

STOCK TICKER/OTHER:
Stock Ticker: Z   Exchange: NAS
Employees: 2,776   Fiscal Year Ends: 12/31
Parent Company:

SALARIES/BONUSES:
Top Exec. Salary: $648,673   Bonus: $
Second Exec. Salary: Bonus: $40,000
$466,500

OTHER THOUGHTS:
Estimated Female Officers or Directors: 2
Hot Spot for Advancement for Women/Minorities: Y

Zimmer Biomet Holdings Inc

www.zimmerbiomet.com/

NAIC Code: 339100

TYPES OF BUSINESS:

Orthopedic Supplies
Human Bone Joint Replacement Systems
Orthopedic Support Devices
Operating Room Supplies
Powered Surgical Instruments
Dental Implants

BRANDS/DIVISIONS/AFFILIATES:

Persona
Zimmer
Transposal
JuggerKnot
3i T3
Timberline
LDR Holding Corporation
RespondWell

CONTACTS: Note: Officers with more than one job title may be intentionally listed here more than once.

David Dvorak, CEO
Larry Glasscock, Director
Daniel Williamson, President, Divisional
Adam Johnson, President, Divisional
David Nolan, President, Divisional
Stuart Kleopfer, President, Geographical
Robert Delp, President, Geographical
Katarzyna Mazur-Hofsaess, President, Geographical
Sang Yi, President, Geographical
Daniel Florin, Senior VP
Chad Phipps, Senior VP
Tony Collins, Vice President

GROWTH PLANS/SPECIAL FEATURES:

Zimmer Biomet Holdings, Inc. designs, manufactures and markets musculoskeletal products for the healthcare industry. These include orthopedic reconstructive products; sports medicine, biologics, extremities and trauma products; spine, bone healing, craniomaxillofacial and thoracic products; dental implants; and related surgical products. Zimmer Biomet collaborates with healthcare professionals worldwide to advance the pace of innovation. The company's products and solutions help treat patients suffering from disorders of, or injuries to bones, joints or supporting soft tissues. Knee products include the Persona, NexGen, Vanguard and Oxford branded systems. Hip products include the Zimmer, Taperloc, Arcos, Continuum and G7 branded systems. Surgical, sports medicine, biologics, foot and ankle, extremities and trauma products include the Transposal and Transposal Ultra fluid waste management systems, automatic tourniquet systems, JuggerKnot soft anchor system, Gel-One cross-linked hyaluronate, Trabecular Metal reverse shoulder system, Comprehensive shoulder system, Zimmer Natural Nail system and DVR plating system. Dental products include the Tapered Screw-Vent implant system, 3i T3 implant system and Puros allograft products. Spine and craniomaxillofacial and thoracic products include the Polaris spinal system, Timberline lateral fusion system, Mobi-C cervical disc, SternaLock closure and fixation systems brand lines. Other products include PALACOS bone cement and SinalPak fusion stimulator. In late-2016, the firm acquired LDR Holding Corporation, a global medical device company that designs and commercializes novel and proprietary surgical technologies for the treatment of patients suffering from spine disorders; and the RespondWell telerehabilitation platform designed to provide personalized, clinician-supervised post-surgical physical therapy in the comfort of a patient's home.

FINANCIAL DATA: Note: Data for latest year may not have been available at press time.

In U.S. $	2016	2015	2014	2013	2012	2011
Revenue	7,683,900,000	5,997,800,000	4,673,300,000	4,623,400,000	4,471,700,000	4,451,800,000
R&D Expense	365,600,000	268,800,000	188,300,000	204,200,000	225,600,000	238,600,000
Operating Income	825,900,000	467,300,000	1,034,700,000	1,035,600,000	1,047,400,000	1,024,100,000
Operating Margin %	10.74%	7.79%	22.14%	22.39%	23.42%	23.00%
SGA Expense	2,932,900,000	2,291,900,000	1,844,000,000	1,880,800,000	1,822,100,000	1,991,900,000
Net Income	305,900,000	147,000,000	720,100,000	761,000,000	755,000,000	760,800,000
Operating Cash Flow	1,632,200,000	816,700,000	1,052,800,000	963,100,000	1,151,900,000	1,176,900,000
Capital Expenditure	530,200,000	434,100,000	342,300,000	292,900,000	264,500,000	288,100,000
EBITDA	1,796,800,000	1,152,200,000	1,382,800,000	1,409,700,000	1,426,100,000	1,394,100,000
Return on Assets %	1.13%	.79%	7.49%	8.18%	8.61%	9.21%
Return on Equity %	3.12%	1.79%	11.23%	12.51%	13.28%	13.49%
Debt to Equity	1.10	1.16	0.21	0.26	0.29	0.28

CONTACT INFORMATION:

Phone: 574-267-6639   Fax: 574-267-8137
Toll-Free: 800-613-6131
Address: 345 East Main St., Warsaw, IN 46580 United States

STOCK TICKER/OTHER:

Stock Ticker: ZBH   Exchange: NYS
Employees: 18,500   Fiscal Year Ends: 05/31
Parent Company:

SALARIES/BONUSES:

Top Exec. Salary: $1,112,077   Bonus: $
Second Exec. Salary: Bonus: $
$612,644

OTHER THOUGHTS:

Estimated Female Officers or Directors: 3
Hot Spot for Advancement for Women/Minorities: Y

Sales, profits and employees may be estimates. Financial information, benefits and other data can change quickly and may vary from those stated here.

ADDITIONAL INDEXES

INDEX OF FIRMS NOTED AS HOT SPOTS FOR ADVANCEMENT FOR WOMEN & MINORITIES

3M Company
Abbott Laboratories
ABM Industries Inc
Accenture LLP
Acosta Inc
Adobe Systems Inc
Advance Auto Parts Inc
Adventist Health System
Aetna Inc
AFLAC Inc
Agero Inc
Airbnb Inc
Alaska Air Group Inc
Alliance Data Systems Corporation
Allscripts Healthcare Solutions Inc
Ally Financial Inc
Almost Family Inc
Amazon.com Inc
American Airlines Group Inc
American Express Co
American Financial Group Inc
Amerigroup Corporation
AmerisourceBergen Corp
Amgen Inc
AMSURG Corporation
Anixter International Inc
Anthem Inc
Aon Hewitt
Applied Materials Inc
Arrow Electronics Inc
Arthur J Gallagher & Co
Ascena Retail Group Inc
Ascension Health
AT&T Inc
Automatic Data Processing Inc (ADP)
Avnet Inc
Ball Corporation
Bank of America Corp
Bank of New York Mellon Corp
BB&T Corporation
Becton Dickinson & Co
Belden Inc
Best Buy Co Inc
Bio Rad Laboratories Inc
Biogen Inc
Black & Veatch Holding Company
BlackRock Inc
BMC Software Inc
Boeing Company (The)
Booz Allen Hamilton Holding Corp
Boston Consulting Group Inc (The, BCG)
Boston Scientific Corp
Brinker International Inc
Bristol-Myers Squibb Co
Brown & Brown Inc
Buffalo Wild Wings Inc
CACI International Inc
Capital One Financial Corp

Cardinal Health Inc
CarMax Inc
Carnival Corporation
Catholic Health Initiatives
CBS Corporation
CDW Corporation
Celanese Corporation
Celgene Corporation
Centene Corporation
CenturyLink Inc
Cerner Corporation
CH Robinson Worldwide Inc
Charles River Laboratories International Inc
Charles Schwab Corporation (The)
Chemed Corporation
Chevron Phillips Chemical Company LLC
Cigna Corporation
Cisco Systems Inc
Citigroup Inc
Cleveland Clinic Foundation (The)
Clorox Company (The)
Coca-Cola Bottling Co Consolidated
Comcast Corporation
Community Health Systems Inc
Container Store Inc (The)
Convergys Corporation
Cooper Companies Inc
Corning Inc
CoStar Group Inc
Costco Wholesale Corporation
Cox Communications Inc
Cox Enterprises Inc
CR Bard Inc
Crown Holdings Inc
Cullen-Frost Bankers Inc
CVS Health Corporation
Dana Incorporated
Darden Restaurants Inc
DaVita Healthcare Partners Inc
Dell Technologies Inc
Deloitte LLP
Delta Air Lines Inc
DIRECTV
Discovery Communications Inc
DTE Energy Company
Duke Energy Corporation
Edward D Jones & Co LP
Edwards Lifesciences Corporation
Eli Lilly and Company
EMCOR Group Inc
Enterprise Holdings Inc
Equity Lifestyle Properties Inc
Estee Lauder Companies Inc (The)
Exelon Corporation
EY LLP
F5 Networks Inc
Facebook Inc
FactSet Research Systems Inc
Fairview Health Services
FCA US LLC
FedEx Corporation
Fidelity National Information Services Inc
FirstEnergy Corporation
Fluor Corp

Ford Motor Co
Frito-Lay North America Inc
Frontier Communications Corporation
FTI Consulting Inc
Gartner Inc
General Electric Co (GE)
General Motors Company (GM)
Gilead Sciences Inc
GoDaddy Inc
Goldman Sachs Group Inc
Google (Alphabet Inc)
Group 1 Automotive Inc
Hanesbrands Inc
Harris Corporation
Hartford Financial Services Group Inc (The)
Health Care Service Corporation (HCSC)
HealthSouth Corporation
HEB Grocery Company LP
Henry Schein Inc
Hershey Co
Hibbett Sports Inc
Hillenbrand Inc
Hill-Rom Holdings Inc
Hilton Inc
Home Depot Inc (The)
Honeywell International Inc
Houston Methodist
Hub International Limited
Humana Inc
Hyatt Hotels Corporation
IAC/InterActiveCorp
IDEXX Laboratories Inc
ILG Inc
Illinois Tool Works Inc
INC Research/inVentiv Health
Ingram Micro Inc
Ingredion Inc
In-N-Out Burgers Inc
Intel Corporation
Interpublic Group of Companies Inc
Intuit Inc
Jabil Circuit Inc
Jack Henry & Associates Inc
JB Hunt Transport Services Inc
JetBlue Airways Corporation
Johnson & Johnson
Jones Lang LaSalle Inc
JP Morgan Chase & Co Inc
Juniper Networks Inc
Kaiser Permanente
Kelly Services Inc
Kimpton Hotel & Restaurant Group LLC
Kindred Healthcare Inc
Kohl's Corporation
Kroger Co (The)
Laboratory Corporation of America Holdings
Lam Research Corporation
Lennar Corporation
Level 3 Communications Inc
LHC Group Inc
Liberty Global plc
Liberty Mutual Group Inc
LifePoint Health Inc

Lincoln National Corporation
LinkedIn Corp
Loews Hotels Holding Corporation
Lowe's Companies Inc
Magellan Health Inc
Marcus Corporation (The)
Marriott International Inc
Marsh & McLennan Companies Inc
Mary Kay Inc
MasterCard Inc
MAXIMUS Inc
Mayo Clinic
McAfee Inc
McCormick & Company Inc
McDonald's Corp
McKesson Corporation
McKinsey & Company Inc
MedStar Health
Medtronic plc
Mercer LLC
Merck & Co Inc
Mercy
Microsoft Corporation
Modine Manufacturing Company
Molina Healthcare Inc
Moody's Corporation
Morgan Stanley
Mutual of Omaha Companies (The)
NBCUniversal LLC
NCR Corporation
NetSuite Inc
New York Life Insurance Company
Newell Brands Inc
Nielsen Holdings plc
Nike Inc
Nordstrom Inc
Northwestern Mutual Life Insurance
Company
Norwegian Cruise Line Holdings Ltd
(NCL)
Oliver Wyman Group
Omnicom Group Inc
Oracle Corporation
O'Reilly Automotive Inc
Oshkosh Corporation
Owens Corning Inc
PAREXEL International Corporation
Patterson Companies Inc
Paychex Inc
PerkinElmer Inc
PetSmart Inc
Pfizer Inc
PG&E Corporation
Phillips 66
Pinnacle Entertainment Inc
PPG Industries Inc
PRA Health Sciences Inc
Priceline Group Inc (The)
PriceSmart Inc
PricewaterhouseCoopers (PwC)
Principal Financial Group Inc
Progressive Corporation (The)
Providence St Joseph Health
Prudential Financial Inc
Publix Super Markets Inc

PulteGroup Inc
Qualcomm Inc
Quest Diagnostics Inc
Quintiles IMS Holdings Inc
Raymond James Financial Inc
Red Hat Inc
REI (Recreational Equipment Inc)
Resources Connection Inc
Revlon Inc
Rite Aid Corporation
Ross Stores Inc
Royal Caribbean Cruises Ltd
Ryder System Inc
Safeco Insurance Company of America
Safeway Inc
SalesForce.com Inc
Sam's Club
SAS Institute Inc
SC Johnson & Son Inc
SCANA Corporation
Science Applications International Corp
(SAIC)
Sherwin-Williams Company (The)
Sodexo Inc
Southwest Airlines Co
Spirit Aerosystems Holdings Inc
Stanley Black & Decker Inc
Starbucks Corporation
State Farm Insurance Companies
Stryker Corporation
Sutter Health Inc
Symantec Corp
Synopsys Inc
SYSCO Corporation
Team Health Holdings Inc
Tenet Healthcare Corporation
Tenneco Inc
Texas Instruments Inc (TI)
Textron Inc
Thermo Fisher Scientific Inc
TJX Companies Inc (The)
Total System Services Inc (TSYS)
Travelers Companies Inc (The)
TreeHouse Foods Inc
Trimble Navigation Ltd
Trinity Health
Trustmark Companies
United Continental Holdings Inc
United Natural Foods Inc
United Parcel Service Inc (UPS)
United States Cellular Corporation
United Technologies Corporation
UnitedHealth Group Inc
Universal Health Services Inc
Unum Group
US Bancorp
USAA
Valassis Communications Inc
Varian Medical Systems Inc
Verizon Communications Inc
VF Corporation
Victoria's Secret
Visa Inc
VMware Inc
W R Berkley Corporation

Walgreens Boots Alliance Inc
Wal-Mart Stores Inc (Walmart)
Walt Disney Company (The)
Waste Management Inc
Waters Corporation
Wayfair LLC
Web.com Group Inc
WellCare Health Plans Inc
Wells Fargo & Co
WW Grainger Inc
Wyndham Worldwide Corporation
Wynn Resorts Limited
Yum! Brands Inc
Zillow Inc
Zimmer Biomet Holdings Inc

INDEX OF SUBSIDIARIES, BRAND NAMES AND AFFILIATIONS

INDEX OF SUBSIDIARIES, BRAND NAMES AND AFFILIATIONS, CONT.

INDEX OF SUBSIDIARIES, BRAND NAMES AND AFFILIATIONS, CONT.

INDEX OF SUBSIDIARIES, BRAND NAMES AND AFFILIATIONS, CONT.

INDEX OF SUBSIDIARIES, BRAND NAMES AND AFFILIATIONS, CONT.

INDEX OF SUBSIDIARIES, BRAND NAMES AND AFFILIATIONS, CONT.

INDEX OF SUBSIDIARIES, BRAND NAMES AND AFFILIATIONS, CONT.

INDEX OF SUBSIDIARIES, BRAND NAMES AND AFFILIATIONS, CONT.

INDEX OF SUBSIDIARIES, BRAND NAMES AND AFFILIATIONS, CONT.

INDEX OF SUBSIDIARIES, BRAND NAMES AND AFFILIATIONS, CONT.

LabVIEW for LEGO MINDSTORMS; **National Instruments Corporation**
LabVIEW Real-Time; **National Instruments Corporation**
LabWindows/CVI and Measurement Studio; **National Instruments Corporation**
Lacerte; **Intuit Inc**
Lake Region Medical; **Integer Holdings Corporation**
Lancope Inc; **Cisco Systems Inc**
LandAndFarm; **CoStar Group Inc**
LandsofAmerica; **CoStar Group Inc**
Lane Bryant; **Ascena Retail Group Inc**
Larry H Miller Dealerships; **Larry H Miller Group**
Larry H Miller Megaplex Theaters; **Larry H Miller Group**
Larry H Miller Real Estate; **Larry H Miller Group**
LaSalle Investment Management; **Jones Lang LaSalle Inc**
Laserage Technology Corporation; **Ametek Inc**
LaserCyte Dx; **IDEXX Laboratories Inc**
Last Chance; **Nordstrom Inc**
Lattice Strategies LLC; **Hartford Financial Services Group Inc (The)**
L'Auberge Baton Rouge; **Pinnacle Entertainment Inc**
L'Auberge Casino Resort; **Pinnacle Entertainment Inc**
Lawry's; **McCormick & Company Inc**
Lay's; **Frito-Lay North America Inc**
LDR Holding Corporation; **Zimmer Biomet Holdings Inc**
leads.com; **Web.com Group Inc**
LEAF; **Corning Inc**
Legg Mason Funds; **Legg Mason Inc**
Leisure Group Inc; **Liberty Interactive Corporation**
Leisure Product Enterprises LLC; **Patrick Industries Inc**
Lennar; **Lennar Corporation**
Leonard Green & Partners LP; **Container Store Inc (The)**
Lerner College of Medicine; **Cleveland Clinic Foundation (The)**
Lerner Research Institute; **Cleveland Clinic Foundation (The)**
Letairis; **Gilead Sciences Inc**
Leucadia National Corporation; **Jefferies LLC**
Level 3 Communications Inc; **CenturyLink Inc**
LHC Group Inc; **LifePoint Health Inc**
Liberty Cablevision of Puerto Rico LLC; **Liberty Global plc**
Liberty International Underwriters; **Liberty Mutual Group Inc**

Liberty Mutual; **Liberty Mutual Group Inc**
Liberty Mutual Group Inc; **Safeco Insurance Company of America**
Liberty Mutual Surety; **Liberty Mutual Group Inc**
Liberty Northwest; **Safeco Insurance Company of America**
Liberty Specialty Markets; **Liberty Mutual Group Inc**
LifePoint Hospitals Inc; **LifePoint Health Inc**
LifeStent; **CR Bard Inc**
Lilyette; **Hanesbrands Inc**
Lincoln; **Ford Motor Co**
Lincoln Financial Group; **Lincoln National Corporation**
Lincoln Navigator SUV; **Ford Motor Co**
Linde AG; **Lincare Holdings Inc**
LinkedIn.com; **LinkedIn Corp**
Lippincott; **Oliver Wyman Group**
Lippincott; **Marsh & McLennan Companies Inc**
Liquid Robotics; **Boeing Company (The)**
Liquid-Plumr; **Clorox Company (The)**
LISS Systems Limited; **ExlService Holdings Inc**
Listerine; **Johnson & Johnson**
LithoVue; **Boston Scientific Corp**
Loews Corporation; **Loews Hotels Holding Corporation**
Loews Miami Beach Hotel; **Loews Hotels Holding Corporation**
Loews Portofino Bay Hotel at Universal Orlando; **Loews Hotels Holding Corporation**
Loews Royal Pacific Resort at Universal Orlando; **Loews Hotels Holding Corporation**
Loews Santa Monica Beach Hotel; **Loews Hotels Holding Corporation**
Loews Sapphire Falls Resort at Universal Orlando; **Loews Hotels Holding Corporation**
LOFT; **Ascena Retail Group Inc**
Lombardini; **Kohler Company**
LongHorn Steakhouse; **Darden Restaurants Inc**
Longs Drugs; **CVS Health Corporation**
LoopNet; **CoStar Group Inc**
Lourdes Hospital; **Ascension Health**
LoyaltyOne; **Alliance Data Systems Corporation**
Lubrizol Additives; **Lubrizol Corporation (The)**
Lubrizol Advanced Materials Inc; **Lubrizol Corporation (The)**
LucasFilm Ltd; **Walt Disney Company (The)**
Lucky Generals; **Omnicom Group Inc**
lucy; **VF Corporation**

Lucy; **Epic Systems Corporation**
Lupron; **AbbVie Inc**
Luvata Heat Transfer Solutions Inc; **Modine Manufacturing Company**
lynda.com; **LinkedIn Corp**
Lyrica; **Pfizer Inc**
M; **Juniper Networks Inc**
M&A Institute; **Deloitte LLP**
M&M World; **Mars Inc**
M&Ms; **Mars Inc**
MacAndrews & Forbes Inc; **Valassis Communications Inc**
Maestro; **MasterCard Inc**
Magellan Complete Care; **Magellan Health Inc**
Maggiano's Little Italy; **Brinker International Inc**
Maggiore; **Avis Budget Group Inc**
Maidenform; **Hanesbrands Inc**
Mail Boxes Etc; **United Parcel Service Inc (UPS)**
Main Plaza Corporation; **Cullen-Frost Bankers Inc**
MainStay Investments; **New York Life Insurance Company**
Maintenance Supply Headquarters; **Lowe's Companies Inc**
Majestic; **VF Corporation**
Making Everlasting Memories; **Service Corporation International Inc**
Mallory Alexander International Logistics LLC; **Old Dominion Freight Line Inc**
Managed IP PBX; **Cox Communications Inc**
Maple Grove Medical Center; **Fairview Health Services**
Marazzi; **Mohawk Industries Inc**
Marcus Theatres Corp; **Marcus Corporation (The)**
Marina Bay Sands Pte Ltd; **Las Vegas Sands Corp (The Venetian)**
Marine Concepts/Design Concepts; **Patrick Industries Inc**
Marine Electrical Products Inc; **Patrick Industries Inc**
Marketing Cloud; **SalesForce.com Inc**
Marketside; **Wal-Mart Stores Inc (Walmart)**
Marlex; **Chevron Phillips Chemical Company LLC**
Marmaxx; **TJX Companies Inc (The)**
Marriott Hotels; **Marriott International Inc**
Marriott International Inc; **Ritz-Carlton Hotel Company LLC (The)**
Mars Inc; **VCA Inc**
Marsellus; **Hillenbrand Inc**
Marsh; **Oliver Wyman Group**
Marsh & McLennan Companies Inc; **Mercer LLC**

INDEX OF SUBSIDIARIES, BRAND NAMES AND AFFILIATIONS, CONT.

INDEX OF SUBSIDIARIES, BRAND NAMES AND AFFILIATIONS, CONT.

INDEX OF SUBSIDIARIES, BRAND NAMES AND AFFILIATIONS, CONT.

INDEX OF SUBSIDIARIES, BRAND NAMES AND AFFILIATIONS, CONT.

INDEX OF SUBSIDIARIES, BRAND NAMES AND AFFILIATIONS, CONT.

INDEX OF SUBSIDIARIES, BRAND NAMES AND AFFILIATIONS, CONT.

INDEX OF SUBSIDIARIES, BRAND NAMES AND AFFILIATIONS, CONT.

INDEX OF SUBSIDIARIES, BRAND NAMES AND AFFILIATIONS, CONT.

INDEX OF SUBSIDIARIES, BRAND NAMES AND AFFILIATIONS, CONT.

CPSIA information can be obtained
at www.ICGtesting.com
Printed in the USA
LVOW06s0512310817
546939LV00003B/4/P